FROMMER'S
SCOTLAND AND WALES
ON $40 A DAY

by Darwin Porter

Assisted by Danforth Prince
and Margaret Foresman

1988–89 Edition

Published by Prentice Hall Press
A Division of Simon & Schuster, Inc.
Gulf + Western Building
One Gulf + Western Plaza
New York, New York 10023

ISBN 0-13-796574-5

Manufactured in the United States of America

CONTENTS

MAPS

A DISCLAIMER: Although every effort was made to ensure the accuracy of the prices and travel information appearing in this book, it should be kept in mind that prices do fluctuate in the course of time, and that information does change under the impact of the varied and volatile factors that affect the travel industry.

Readers should also note that the establishments described under Readers' Selections or Suggestions have not in many cases been inspected by the author and that the opinions expressed there are those of the individual reader(s) only. They do not in any way represent the opinions of the publisher or author of this guide.

Inflation Alert!!!

It is hardly a secret that a wave of inflation has battered the countries of northern Europe, and Britain has been hard hit. The author of this book has spent laborious hours researching to try and ensure the accuracy of prices appearing in this guide. As we go to press, I believe we have obtained the most reliable data possible. However, in a system that in one year alone saw one London hotelier raise his prices three times in one season, I cannot offer guarantees for the tariffs quoted. In the lifetime of this edition—particularly its second year (1989)—the wise traveler will add *at least* 20% to the prices quoted.

SCOTLAND AND WALES ON $40 A DAY

The Reason Why

THE ISLAND OF BRITAIN is made up of three separate entities, England, Scotland, and Wales, today joined under the same constitutional monarchy. For too long people coming to this island have aimed primarily at England and, even more restrictively, at London, the British capital.

Now travelers have awakened to the fact that Scotland, which occupies more than a third of the land mass of the island, is a country with mainly different ancestral stock, different traditions, and a different lifestyle from those of England. These differences have been perpetuated in the minds and hearts of North Americans of Scottish descent, many of whose ancestors emigrated following the fateful Battle of Culloden, when the hopes of the Stuart dynasty were forever dashed, or at the time of the Clearance, when crofters and small villagers were forced from their ancient homes and made their way to the New World. These people, of strong and stubborn stock, have made themselves a flourishing part of sections of the United States and Canada, and many of them return regularly to the land of their forefathers to reaffirm their Scottishness.

Wales, also an important part of the island which is Britain, is smaller—comprising less than one-twelfth of the land mass, and has been even later than Scotland to be recognized as a rewarding place for tourists to visit. Part of this may be attributable to the fact that although Welsh people also emigrated to the United States, there was never in this country the strong clan system, and with it the strong and lasting family-roots feeling that there is among the Scots. It is as if the Welsh who emigrated maintained themselves more as individuals, while the Scots tended to band together and to keep their communications lines intact even when they were stretched across oceans and endless land.

Today the Welsh have realized that they too have something travelers seek—a beautiful land, tranquility, and hospitable people—so that more and more people are going to Wales.

This, therefore, is a guidebook for only Scotland and Wales, with a chapter on a visit to Isle of Man, in the Irish Sea, included. I'll take you to places where you can wait to be served haggis, borne steaming into the room by a kilted Scot and the skirl of bagpipes, and to islands where you can sleep in the house of the laird, lulled by the sound of the surf and awakened by the shrill shrieks of sea birds circling the cliffs. Then I'll invite you to watch the most beautiful sunrise in the world from the window of a black-and-white Tudor farmhouse, the home of a happy Welsh family, and to see the sun set from high in the mountains of Snowdonia.

Such experiences as these have two characteristics in common: they represent the best way to live in Scotland and Wales—and they are inexpensive. For the inns, guest houses, and restaurants recommended in this book are, with a few exceptions, those designed for and primarily patronized by Britishers, whose average wage is far below the North American standard. Prices in this guide at the establishments recommended are therefore moderate, often low, in terms of the U.S. dollar.

You'll be taken to pubs dating back to the time of William the Conqueror and Henry VII, the Welshman who became King of England, that offer complete luncheons for £5 ($8) and less. You'll be guided deep into the Scottish Highlands to a stone hotel up Glencoe which was founded long before the Campbells massacred the MacDonalds in the bloody days of yore, where you can stay and have a substantial Scottish breakfast for £17 ($27.20) per night.

Details of these countries and Isle of Man start in just a few pages. First, I'll outline the order of discussion, then tell you a bit about the $40-a-day limit I've placed on basic expenditures.

THE ORGANIZATION OF THIS BOOK: Here's how *Scotland and Wales on $40 a Day* sets forth its information.

Chapter I, directly ahead, deals with an introduction to the rich history of Scotland and its people, and discusses the various modes of transportation of reaching this far-northern country. The chapter also takes in food and drink, ranging from haggis to scotch whisky, and discusses the best means of getting around Scotland once you're there, including plane, bus, rail, and rented car. The chapter also includes some vital data on the ABCs of life in Scotland.

Chapters II and III head north from England to the Borders, rich in castles in romantic ruins and Gothic skeletons of abbeys, with our final destination the capital city of Edinburgh, considered one of the most beautiful cities of Europe. After surveying the rich scene in Edinburgh, its sights, food, accommodations, shopping bargains, and nightlife, we'll explore the most exciting attractions in the environs of the Scottish capital.

Chapter IV is a visit to the country along the River Forth from Stirling to the history-rich lands along the south side of the Firth of Forth, where Mary Queen of Scots lived and loved.

Chapters V, VI, and VII explore the scenic highlights that are easily reached from Edinburgh, many of which can be visited on a day trip if you're rushed for time. These include the ancient "kingdom" of Fife, a name suggesting romantic episodes and pageantry during the reign of the early Stuart kings; the heatherclad hills of Tayside, one of the most beautiful regions of the country; and finally, the Trossachs, that wild Highland region of great beauty known as "The Lady of the Lake Country," and legendary Loch Lomond, the largest of Scotland's lochs, known around the world for its "bonnie banks" because of a song.

Chapter VIII heads to the great northeast, visiting Aberdeen, "the granite city," and Royal Deeside with its Balmoral Castle, summer home of the royal family, and its famed Highland games at Braemar.

Chapter IX cuts a path through the Malt Whiskey Trail, where you can visit the distilleries and have a wee dram at the end of your tour. This section also covers the most interesting stopovers in the Spey Valley, taking in the winter ski center at Aviemore.

Chapters X and XI head for the Highlands, whose capital is Inverness, visiting Loch Ness along the way for a monster-watch. After that, it goes to "The Far North," to the little-known provinces of Sunderland and Caithness, until it reaches the "end of the line" at John o' Groats.

Chapters XII, XIII, and XIV head down the western coastline of the Highlands, sampling some of the most rewarding towns, villages, and cities of Argyll, including Oban, before visiting the Kintyre peninsula and the islands of Arran, Gigha, Islay, and Jura where George Orwell wrote *1984*.

Chapters XV and XVI visit Glasgow, Scotland's largest city, and the holiday resorts of Bute and Dunoon before taking in some of the most rewarding targets, such as Culzean Castle, in the country of Robert Burns, the national bard.

Chapter XVII finds us in the Lowlands of Scotland, another border region, this one Dumfries and Galloway, a land also rich in associations with Burns.

Chapters XVIII and XIX take the "road to the isles," going to such famous islands of Scotland as Skye, where Flora MacDonald went with Bonnie Prince Charlie, then on to Mull and the ecclesiastical center of Iona. The remote but enticing Outer Hebrides, including Lewis and Harris (famed for its tweed), is also explored in this section. These are islands rich in their Celtic past. Finally, the section concludes with a visit to the remote Orkney and Shetland Islands, with their Norse character, including a stopover at remote **Fair Isle.**

Chapter XX introduces the country and the people of Wales, the little neighbor of England on the west, together with some of the history of how the Celtic ancestors of Cymru (Wales) battled for centuries before bowing to English rule.

Chapter XXI visits Southeast Wales, where the Romans preceded modern man, and **Chapter XXII** goes to Cardiff, the capital of the principality, a modern, bustling city.

Chapter XXIII heads through Southwest Wales, site of Norman strongholds, beautiful vales, deserted mines, industrial growth, and seacoast resorts, plus the pilgrimage Cathedral of St. David.

Chapter XXIV focuses on the heart of Wales, from the coast of Cardigan Bay on the west through mountains and rolling pastureland dotted with sheep and cattle, to the border, where the Saxon king of Mercia built the great Offa's Dyke in the eighth century, along which you can walk today.

Chapter XXV goes into the mountains of Snowdonia National Park, with its slate mines, swift-flowing rivers, heavy forests, pastureland, and sandy beaches, dotted here and there with isolated farms and little villages that look as though they were carved from the mountain's granite.

Chapter XXVI introduces you to parts of Wales that may have escaped your notice before—the Lleyn Peninsula and the island of Anglesey—in the northeast, where saints once lived and Druids practiced their rites. You'll also visit the site where the Prince of Wales receives his title, Caernarfon Castle.

Chapter XXVII is a journey through the northeast part of Wales, with resorts, castles, secluded vales, and some of the most beautiful scenery in the country, a section where little villages along the border and the estuary of the River Dee once sheltered their countrymen who were late in leaving the English town of Chester back when it had a law that any Welshman found within its walls after the gates were locked at night would be hanged.

For a final visit, Part III (specifically **Chapter XXVIII**) visits the Isle of Man, whose capital is Douglas. It is a land steeped in history, folklore, and legend, and—surprise—it's not a part of the United Kingdom, nor has it ever been.

$40 A DAY—WHAT IT MEANS: You can live in Scotland and Wales on a number of price levels. The unknowing can lavish huge sums on sterile holidays, but comfort and charm are not necessarily priced so high at all. I aim to establish that fact by showing you exactly what you can get for $40 a day.

The specific aim of this book—as it is in all its companion books—is to show you clearly how to keep *basic living costs* (room and three meals a day) down to $40 per person per day. There is nothing gimmicky about this goal, as readers of my other books have found. Since the cost of entertainment, shopping, and transportation is all in *addition* to that basic $40-a-day figure, I prescribe reasonable standards for the budget-minded.

Half of this book is devoted to recommendations for comfortable rooms and well-prepared meals—within the $40-a-day budget. You'll find well-furnished rooms in Edinburgh and in the country, usually with innerspring mattresses and almost always with hot and cold running water. The same holds true for Cardiff and the major tourist centers of Wales. None of the rooms in this price bracket, unless otherwise stated, has a private bath.

The $40-a-day budget roughly breaks down this way: $25 per person (based on double occupancy) for a room and breakfast, $5 for lunch, and $10 for dinner.

You'll note also that I do include in these pages recommendations below those allowances for those wishing to live a more spartan life on $30 a day or for those who wish to have a good old-fashioned splurge at $50 a day.

Many of the accommodations, especially in the more expensive category, were chosen because of a unique historical, cultural, or architectural feature that gives them special value. This is truer for the country than it is for either of the capitals of Edinburgh and Cardiff, where the $40-a-day hotels were selected more for their facilities, comfort, and conveniences than for any spectacular charm.

A TRAVELER'S ADVISORY: Having traveled the length and breadth of Scotland and Wales in compiling this edition, I am struck very forcibly by the fact that the best value for your money can be found outside the capitals and major cities of Edinburgh, Glasgow, and Cardiff.

While realizing that Scotland's capital city, Edinburgh, is the mecca for most visitors, "Auld Reekie" (as it's called) is also the most expensive city previewed in this guide. It is of course possible to show examples of inexpensive and good-value accommodation in Edinburgh. But the truth is, there just isn't enough to go around during the peak summer months and at Festival time. Many visitors may be disappointed with the price in relation to what they are offered.

The advice I give is to spend what time you need—perhaps two days in Edinburgh—then go out and explore the real Scotland: meet the people, spend a couple of days in Inverness, along the Whisky Trail, visit two or three of the islands, and allow yourself the opportunity to wander through the Highlands. Likewise, the countryside of lesser-known Wales is equally as enticing. Tourist centers are easily accessible by the inexpensive and good express coach (bus) system or by the intercity railways.

Pound the pavements of the towns, cities, and hamlets of Scotland and Wales: the shopping is good and the price of the accommodation fair. Many places haven't increased their prices by more than the current 6% inflation rate in more than two years, and many offer bargain-break reductions for two or more nights (but you won't be granted these in summer, of course).

SOME DISCLAIMERS: No restaurant, inn, shop, hotel, or guesthouse paid to be mentioned in this book. What you read are entirely personal recommendations—in many cases proprietors never knew that their establishments were being visited or investigated for inclusion in a travel guide.

A Word of Warning: Unfortunately, prices change, and they rarely go downward. Scotland and Wales have no governmental control of hotel prices. "Mine host" can charge a guest anything he or she "bloody well chooses." Competition is what keeps the rate down. Always, when checking into a hotel or guesthouse, inquire about the price and agree on it. This can save much embarrassment and disappointment when it comes time to settle the tab.

Hotel owners sometimes complain that $40-a-dayers have arrived at their establishments and demanded to be charged prices quoted exactly as they appear in the guide. That is not possible. Prices presented here are only for general guidelines. In a fluctuating economy and over a period of time, they will become outdated. That cozy little family dining room of a year ago can change colors, blossoming out with cut-velvet walls and dining tabs that include the decorator's fee and the owner's new Bentley.

Finally, even in a book revised frequently, it may develop that some of the people, animals, or settings I've described are no longer there. Imported Viennese chefs have nervous breakdowns, red-cheeked Scottish or Welsh maids elope with charming Italians, overstuffed sofas are junked in favor of streamlined modern ones, and 19-year-old dogs go to heaven—so any and all of these particulars could be different. But while people, dogs, and sofas come and go, many of the old inns and pubs of Scotland and Wales have weathered the centuries intact, and barring war, fire, or flood, should be standing proudly to greet you on your visit.

AN INVITATION TO READERS: Like all the books in this series, *Scotland and Wales on $40 a Day* hopes to maintain a continuing dialogue between its author and its readers. All of us share a common aim—to travel as wisely and as well as possible, at the lowest possible cost. In achieving that goal, your comments and suggestions can be of aid to other readers. Therefore if you come across a particularly appealing hotel, restaurant, shop, or bargain, please don't keep it to yourself. And this applies to any comments you may have about existing listings. The fact that a hotel or restaurant is recommended in this edition doesn't mean that it will necessarily appear in future editions if readers report that its service has slipped or that its prices have risen too drastically. You have my word that each and every letter will be read by me personally, although I find it well-nigh *impossible to answer* each and every one. Be assured, however, that I'm listening. Send your comments to Darwin Porter, c/o Prentice Hall Press, Gulf + Western Building, One Gulf + Western Plaza, New York, NY 10023.

TIME OUT FOR A COMMERCIAL: Let's face it: most visitors who explore Scotland and Wales will also visit England. Sometimes Scotland and Wales are treated like a footnote to a visit to England.

Even in a book as fat as this one, it is not possible to cover England too. To do justice to the treasures and lore of England, the "mother book" of this series is called *England on $40 a Day*. It can be purchased as a companion volume.

This older book, published in various revised editions since 1964, is written in the same theme as Scotland and Wales, describing hundreds of budget hotels and inns, B&B houses, restaurants, tea rooms, and pubs—often offbeat favorites that offer the most authentic and enriching travel experience.

In addition, budget-conscious travelers will find all the information needed on low-cost transportation, sightseeing, shopping bargains, and inexpensive nightlife throughout this fascinating country.

So if you plan to travel not only to Scotland and Wales, but wish to explore London and the countryside of England, take along our older sister. You'll need her help.

The $35-A-Day Travel Club—How to Save Money on All Your Travels

In this book we'll be looking at how to get your money's worth in Scotland and Wales, but there is a "device" for saving money and determining value on *all* your trips. It's the popular, international $35-A-Day Travel Club, now in its 26th successful year of operation. The Club was formed at the urging of numerous readers of the $-A-Day and Dollarwise Guides, who felt that such an organization could provide continuing travel information and a sense of community to value-minded travelers in all parts of the world. And so it does!

In keeping with the budget concept, the annual membership fee is low and is immediately exceeded by the value of your benefits. Upon receipt of $18 (U.S. residents), or $20 U.S. by check drawn on a U.S. bank or via international postal money order in U.S. funds (Canadian, Mexican, and other foreign residents) to cover one year's membership, we will send all new members the following items.

(1) Any *two* of the following books

Please designate in your letter which two you wish to receive:

Frommer's $-A-Day Guides
    Europe on $30 a Day
    Australia on $30 a Day
    Eastern Europe on $25 a Day
    England on $40 a Day
    Greece (including Istanbul and Turkey's Aegean Coast) on $30 a Day
    Hawaii on $50 a Day
    India on $25 a Day
    Ireland on $30 a Day
    Israel on $30 & $35 a Day
    Mexico (plus Belize and Guatemala) on $20 a Day
    New York on $50 a Day
    New Zealand on $40 a Day
    Scandinavia on $50 a Day
    Scotland and Wales on $40 a Day
    South America on $30 a Day
    Spain and Morocco (plus the Canary Is.) on $40 a Day
    Turkey on $25 a Day
    Washington, D.C., & Historic Virginia on $40 a Day

Frommer's Dollarwise Guides
    Dollarwise Guide to Austria and Hungary
    Dollarwise Guide to Belgium, Holland, & Luxembourg
    Dollarwise Guide to Bermuda and The Bahamas
    Dollarwise Guide to Canada
    Dollarwise Guide to the Caribbean
    Dollarwise Guide to Egypt

Dollarwise Guide to England and Scotland
Dollarwise Guide to France
Dollarwise Guide to Germany
Dollarwise Guide to Italy
Dollarwise Guide to Japan and Hong Kong
Dollarwise Guide to Portugal, Madeira, and the Azores
Dollarwise Guide to the South Pacific
Dollarwise Guide to Switzerland and Liechtenstein
Dollarwise Guide to Alaska
Dollarwise Guide to California and Las Vegas
Dollarwise Guide to Florida
Dollarwise Guide to the Mid-Atlantic States
Dollarwise Guide to New England
Dollarwise Guide to New York State
Dollarwise Guide to the Northwest
Dollarwise Guide to Skiing USA—East
Dollarwise Guide to Skiing USA—West
Dollarwise Guide to the Southeast and New Orleans
Dollarwise Guide to the Southwest
Dollarwise Guide to Texas
(Dollarwise Guides discuss accommodations and facilities in all price ranges, with emphasis on the medium-priced.)

Frommer's Touring Guides
Egypt
Florence
London
Paris
Venice
(These new, color illustrated guides include walking tours, cultural and historic sites, and other vital travel information.)

Serious Shopper's Guides
Italy
London
Los Angeles
Paris
(Practical and comprehensive, each of these handsomely illustrated guides lists hundreds of stores, selling everything from antiques to wine, conveniently organized alphabetically by category.)

Arthur Frommer's New World of Travel
(From America's #1 travel expert, a sourcebook with the hottest news and latest trends that's guaranteed to change the way you travel—and save you hundreds of dollars. Filled with hundreds of alternative new modes of travel that will lead you to vacations that cater to the mind, the spirit, and a sense of thrift.)

A Shopper's Guide to the Caribbean
(Two experienced Caribbean hands guide you through this shopper's paradise, offering witty insights and helpful tips on the wares and emporia of more than 25 islands.)

Beat the High Cost of Travel
(This practical guide details how to save money on absolutely all travel items—

accommodations, transportation, dining, sightseeing, shopping, taxes, and more. Includes special budget information for seniors, students, singles, and families.)

Bed & Breakfast—North America
(This guide contains a directory of over 150 organizations that offer bed & breakfast referrals and reservations throughout North America. The scenic attractions, and major schools and universities near the homes of each are also listed.)

Dollarwise Guide to Cruises
(This complete guide covers all the basics of cruising—ports of call, costs, fly-cruise package bargains, cabin selection booking, embarkation and debarkation and describes in detail over 60 or so ships cruising the waters of Alaska, the Caribbean, Mexico, Hawaii, Panama, Canada, and the United States.)

Dollarwise Guide to Skiing Europe
(Describes top ski resorts in Austria, France, Italy, and Switzerland. Illustrated with maps of each resort area plus full-color trail maps.)

Guide to Honeymoon Destinations
(A special guide for that most romantic trip of your life, with full details on planning and choosing the destination that will be just right in the U.S. [California, New England, Hawaii, Florida, New York, South Carolina, etc.], Canada, Mexico, and the Caribbean.)

Marilyn Wood's Wonderful Weekends
(This very selective guide covers the best mini-vacation destinations within a 175-mile radius of New York City. It describes special country inns and other accommodations, restaurants, picnic spots, sights, and activities—all the information needed for a two- or three-day stay.)

Motorist's Phrase Book
(A practical phrase book in French, German, and Spanish designed specifically for the English-speaking motorist touring abroad.)

Swap and Go—Home Exchanging Made Easy
(Two veteran home exchangers explain in detail all the money-saving benefits of a home exchange, and then describe precisely how to do it. Also includes information on home rentals and many tips on low-cost travel.)

The Candy Apple: New York for Kids
(A spirited guide to the wonders of the Big Apple by a savvy New York grandmother with a kid's-eye view to fun. Indispensable for visitors and residents alike.)

Travel Diary and Record Book
(A 96-page diary for personal travel notes plus a section for such vital data as passport and traveler's check numbers, itinerary, postcard list, special people and places to visit, and a reference section with temperature and conversion charts, and world maps with distance zones.)

Where to Stay USA
(By the Council on International Educational Exchange, this extraordinary

guide is the first to list accommodations in all 50 states that cost anywhere from $3 to $30 per night.)

(2) A one-year subscription to *The Wonderful World of Budget Travel*

This quarterly eight-page tabloid newspaper keeps you up to date on fast-breaking developments in low-cost travel in all parts of the world bringing you the latest money-saving information—the kind of information you'd have to pay $25 a year to obtain elsewhere. This consumer-conscious publication also features columns of special interest to readers: **Hospitality Exchange** (members all over the world who are willing to provide hospitality to other members as they pass through their home cities); **Share-a-Trip** (offers and requests from members for travel companions who can share costs and help avoid the burdensome single supplement); and **Readers Ask . . . Readers Reply** (travel questions from members to which other members reply with authentic firsthand information).

(3) A copy of *Arthur Frommer's Guide to New York*

This is a pocket-size guide to hotels, restaurants, nightspots, and sightseeing attractions in all price ranges throughout the New York area.

(4) Your personal membership card

Membership entitles you to purchase through the Club all Arthur Frommer publications for a third to a half off their regular retail prices during the term of your membership.

So why not join this hardy band of international budgeteers and participate in its exchange of travel information and hospitality? Simply send your name and address, together with your annual membership fee of $18 (U.S. residents) or $20 U.S. (Canadian, Mexican, and other foreign residents), by check drawn on a U.S. bank or via international postal money order in U.S. funds to: $35-A-Day Travel Club, Inc., Frommer Books, Gulf + Western Building, One Gulf + Western Plaza, New York, NY 10023. And please remember to specify which *two* of the books in section (1) above you wish to receive in your initial package of members' benefits. Or, if you prefer, use the last page of this book, simply checking off the two books you select and enclosing $18 or $20 in U.S. currency.

Once you are a member, there is no obligation to buy additional books. No books will be mailed to you without your specific order.

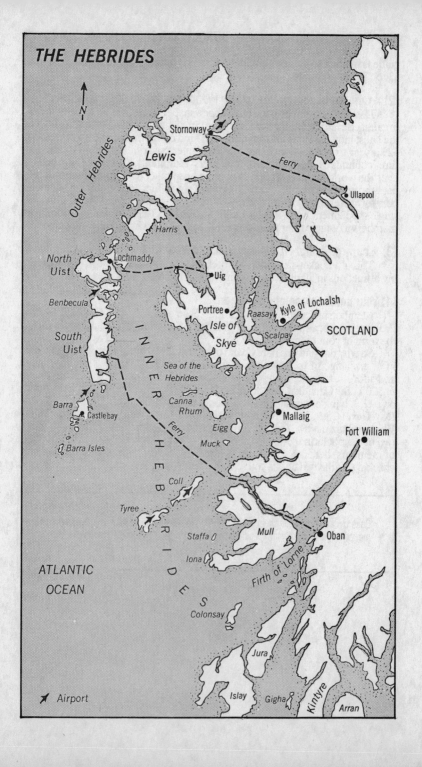

Part One

SCOTLAND

Chapter I

INTRODUCING SCOTLAND

1. The Country
2. Flying to Scotland
3. Getting Around Scotland
4. Golf and Fishing
5. The ABCs of Scotland

IN SCOTLAND, a land of bagpipes and clans, you'll find some of the most dramatic scenery in Europe. Stretching before you will be the Lowlands, but in the far distance the fabled Highlands loom.

If you traverse the country, you'll discover lochs and glens, heather-covered moors, twirling kilts and tam o'shanters, pastel-bathed houses and gray stone cottages, mountains, rivers, and streams filled with trout and salmon. Eagles soar and deer run free. Lush meadowlands are filled with sheep, and rocky coves and secret harbors wait to be discovered. You'll hear the sound of Gaelic, see a Shetland pony, be awed by the misty blue hills, and can attend a Highland gathering. You'll find quiet contemplation or you can enjoy an activity-filled calendar.

Many visitors think of Scotland as Edinburgh and search no further. Travel farther north and you'll find the real Scotland, along with overwhelming hospitality and a sense of exploration.

A small nation, Scotland is only 275 miles long and some 150 miles wide at its broadest point. No one lives more than 40 miles from salt water.

In spite of the smallness of its size, Scotland has extended its influence around the world, giving the world both dreamers and daredevils, along with warriors and preachers such as John Knox. Inventors came from Scotland, including Alexander Graham Bell, as well as such explorers as Mungo Park and David Livingstone. Scotland gave the world such philanthropists as Andrew Carnegie, along with such poets as Robert Burns and such towering novelists as Sir Walter Scott. But, curiously, its most famous resident is neither man nor woman. It's the Loch Ness monster!

Scotland has its own legal system and issues its own currency. However, English and Scottish banknotes have equal value and are accepted in both countries. The Church of Scotland is separate from that of England. The language of the Scot is said to be nearer to the original English than what is spoken these days. In fact, an English person often finds it hard to understand the speech of a true and gentle Highlander, who grew up in view of ancient sandstone and granite mountains.

If you go by road or rail, you will hardly be aware of crossing out of England into Scotland. The border is just a line on a map. But even though the two countries have been joined constitutionally since 1707, Scotland is very different from England. It is very much its own country.

You may come to Scotland on a sentimental journey to see where your forebears were born. Or you may be lured there by its majestic sights. Whatever, your reason, you'll find a land of paradox and romantic tradition.

You'll also find one of the biggest welcomes in Europe. But remember one thing. Scotch is a whisky and not the name of the proud people who inhabit the country. They are called Scots or Scottish. Even if you forget and call them Scotch, they'll forgive you. What they won't forgive is calling them English.

1. The Country

A BRIEF HISTORY: This northernmost country of the three that make up the island of Great Britain has for many centuries been the home of a spirited, independent people who were tough enough and brave enough to live in this mostly rugged land and to maintain their freedom from outside control all the way up to the time a Scotsman, King James VI, went to sit on the English throne as James I in 1603.

Scotland is the oldest geological formation of Great Britain, divided physically into three regions: the granite Highlands, including lochs, glens, and mountains, plus the hundreds of islands to the west and north; the central Lowlands, where three valleys and the estuaries (firths) of the Clyde, Forth, and Tay rivers make up a fertile belt from the Atlantic Ocean to the North Sea; and the southern Uplands, the smooth, rolling moorland broken with low crags and threaded with rivers and valleys, between the central plain and the English border.

After the last Ice Age, which made many changes in the terrain of the country, the first human beings may have moved in as long ago as 6000 B.C. to the area known as the Argyll peninsula. They were followed by Mesolithic people from Ireland and then by Neolithic Bronze Age and Iron Age tribes. Standing stones, brochs, cromlechs, cairns, and burial chambers attest to this early occupation of the land. Celtic invaders came from the continent of Europe to the islands to the west around 3,000 years before the Christian era, and while some may have come directly to this part of the world, it is thought likely that they came first to Ireland and then, for reasons lost in the distant mists of time, crossed the Irish Sea to Wales, with some coming on to what is now Scotland.

When the Romans arrived to take Britain into the fold of the Roman Empire, they didn't have very good luck with conquering the people of the Highlands and made no impression at all on the islands. The Romans called the land Caledonia. In A.D. 82 Agricola pushed into the southern Uplands and the central Lowlands, where marching stations and some permanent encampments were set up. The men from the Mediterranean and their cohorts were unsuccessful in subduing what they called Picts, who would storm fiercely from forests and glens, dressed in animal skins and, it is reported, painted blue with the juice from the woad plant. Some historians say that it was this habit of painting their bodies blue that caused the Romans to dub them *Picti,* or painted ones, although opinions differ as to the derivation of the name.

However, Celts they doubtless were, but not Irish Celts. They were Brythonic Celts, or Britons, or Celt-Iberians, more closely related to the Celts of Cornwall, Wales, and Brittany.

By about A.D. 90 the Romans had given up on trying to subdue these wild Caledonians, and the legionnaires were pulled back to the south. The building of Hadrian's Wall effectively marked the northern limits of Roman influence. By the year A.D. 500 these short, dark Picts had been again attacked, this time by a different breed of Celt, the Dalriad Irish, called Scots. These red- or sandy-haired fair-skinned Celts called the land they came to, specifically the Argyll peninsula, Scotia after the name of their section of Ireland.

These Scotians mixed with the Celt-Iberians in the way that conquering forces do, but mainly they forced them into the remote recesses of the country. In the Highlands, as among the Welsh, there are some people of nearly pure Celt-Iberian type still around. It is probable that the earliest Celts were exponents of Druidism.

The power of the Scotians in the land was cemented firmly when a man named Columba, having heard of the heathen Pictish tribes of the northern half of the country to which his fellow Dalriad Irish had migrated, came in 563 to bring Christianity to them. The little island of Iona, which may once have been a Druid stronghold, became the base of St. Columba's Christian mission. He and his followers succeeded in spreading the religion which had been introduced to the land by St. Ninian in Strathclyde and Galloway and St. Mungo in the Strathclyde area where Glasgow stands. It wasn't long before people from all over the country, even the kings and nobles, came to learn from Columba's ministry.

By the 9th century the name Caledonia had been dropped, and the name Scotland was in wide usage. Scots and Picts were united in 843, and by the 11th century they became joined with the British and Angles, who occupied the west and south, forming the kingdom of Scotland.

The history of Scotland was thus inextricably bound up with religion, which affected strongly the medieval period and the Stuart dynasty. Norsemen were brought into the Scottish kingdom in the 13th century when the Outer Hebrides were conquered, and in the 15th century the Orkneys and Shetlands, Norse to the core, were brought in through a marriage dowry of a Danish princess to the Scottish king.

Even before the coming of the Normans to take over in Great Britain, there was unrest in Scotland, with a breakdown in the power of the Roman Catholic organization, such as it was in this country. Border raids were the order of the day against the northern part of England, even after a strong anglicization set in during the 11th century. When it wasn't border raids, it was battles over succession to the Scottish throne that kept things stirring—the time of the Scots who "wi' Wallace bled" and whom Bruce (Robert the Bruce) often led, as extolled by Robert Burns.

Edward I, the Plantagenet king of England known as "Longshanks," who was crowned in 1272, had a burning ambition to rule over an undivided island nation of England, Scotland, and Wales. He did pretty well in Wales, with a network of 17 castles and other strongholds intended to suppress the rebellious Welsh, but he didn't succeed so well in Scotland. To the day of his death he tried to conquer the northern land, battling forces led first by Wallace and later by Bruce, who became King Robert I. He failed, but so great were his efforts considered that his tomb at Westminster bears the epitaph: "Here lies Edward the Hammer of the Scots."

It was during these years of bitter battles (like the Battle of Bannockburn when the English forces were wiped out) and brief peace that the Scots entered into an alliance with the French which was to have far-reaching effects. The line of Stuart kings originated, the family having become powerful as the stewards of

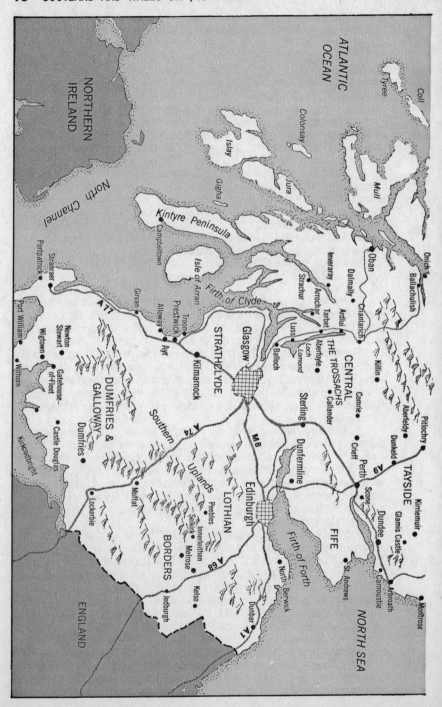

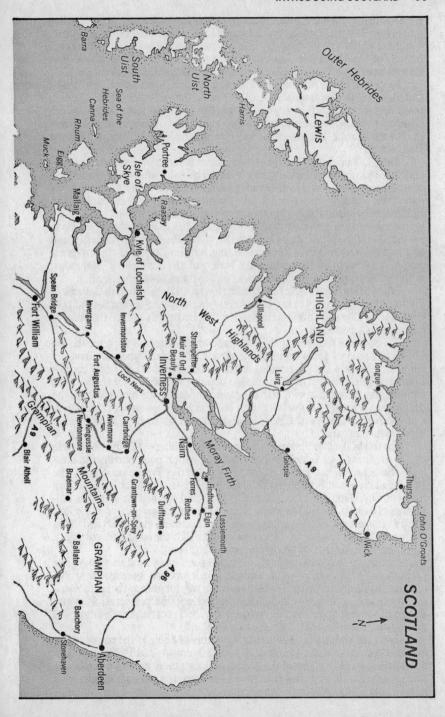

the English king, hence the name Stewart or Stuart. Most of them were less than great kings, but there was so much turmoil in the land that they hung in there. The great lords could never agree, and they passed a few centuries battling each other. The Douglases were especially strong in their efforts to take the Scottish throne, entering into alliances with the English but going down to defeat.

In spite of all the turmoil brought about by baronial ambition, weak kings, and foreign alliances, there was progress toward the end of the Middle Ages in trade, industry, the arts, and peace. And then came the Reformation, which changed, probably forever, religion in Scotland. It also resulted in the ending of the French alliance, because of the link between the French crown and Roman Catholicism.

The Catholic church had for a long time not been very popular in Scotland, and the admonitions of the Calvinistic John Knox—who admonished loudly and constantly—were heeded by many of the earls and other nobility. This may not have been a true religious belief with the great ones, but it certainly had a healthy political popularity. Protestantism is still the major belief in Scotland, with Presbyterianism at the top of the heap. The kirk that Knox and his followers founded is the established Church of Scotland (Presbyterian). There is also an unestablished Anglican communion, the Scottish Episcopal church (not a part of the Church of England), and a variety of "free churches," Methodist, Baptist, Congregational, and the like, as well as non-Christian minorities.

When Mary Stuart took the Scottish throne, she was a Roman Catholic of French upbringing and womanly passions trying to govern an unruly and restless land. Her life was ended in England by the headsman's axe, on the order of her cousin, Queen Elizabeth I.

The power of the great lords of Scotland was broken in 1603, when the son of Mary Queen of Scots assumed the throne of England upon the death of Elizabeth. He was already reigning in Scotland as James VI and now became James I of England, first of the Stuarts to occupy the throne. The Union of the Crowns may have put "paid" to the accounts of the Scottish claimants to the throne, but it wasn't long until religion became a prime source of discontent, with the papist leanings of James II and those who would have been his heirs bringing further turmoil.

The son of the Old Pretender, himself the son of James II, who was in exile on the continent, was Bonnie Prince Charlie, the focal point of risings in Scotland. Because of the power being shown by the Protestant forces, the Episcopalians of southern Scotland rallied for a time to the Jacobite cause. The battle of Culloden, when the Duke of Cumberland crushed the Jacobites (adherents of James), ended the whole thing. Many of the supporters of the Pretender's cause were killed in battle, some were executed, and others fled to the United States and other safe havens in the mid-18th century. The wearing of Highland dress (tartans and such) was made illegal until 1782.

All was not sweetness and light from that point on in Scottish history. The Clearances—1750 to 1850—when crofters (small farmers) were forced to give up their tiny farms (owned by the laird) to make way for grazing sheep, industrial growth and unrest, plus social changes and political pressures, wars and slumps of varying importance in the economy, and progress in education and the arts—all these have left their mark on Scotland.

Today the country is no longer in the status of being at the mercy of the manager for an absentee landlord, the English crown, and Parliament. The Scots have a voice in affairs of the nation, although there are still a number of zealous nationalists who would like to see this become a separate country with its own parliament. Although the government is administered from Westminster, Scotland has its own departments in management control and there is a Scottish secretary of state, as well as a substantial parliamentary delegation. There is no move afoot to renounce the British crown, but many people would like to see a limited self-government established in Edinburgh. This allegiance to the crown may be colored somewhat by the affection the Scottish people developed for Queen Victoria, who loved and often stayed at Balmoral Castle. Queen Elizabeth and her family have followed in Victoria's steps, and they are a popular part of the Scottish scene quite frequently.

As in Wales and England, counties, or shires, of Scotland were reorganized and consolidated by an act of Parliament in 1974. Today they are administered as the counties of Western Isles, Highland, Grampian, Strathclyde, Dumfries and Galloway, Central, Lothian, Tayside, and Fife.

THE PEOPLE: Scotland is a country of friendly and hospitable people, who are descended from an interesting mixture of bloodlines: Celt-Iberian (Pict), Roman, Norse, Saxon, Irish Celtic, Jute, Angle, Norman, and French, with perhaps a few more sources thrown in, what with the seafarers of many nations who have come here through the centuries.

At one time, in parts where the Celtic heritage was strongest, the language of the country was Gaelic, and even today in some remote parts that language is still remembered in a few words and phrases, as it is seen in place names. The later Gaelic was always much like Erse or Irish Gaelic, although there are similarities to the languages that were once the native tongues of Cornwall and Brittany and the one that is still widely spoken in Wales.

Scotland has a population today of some 5.2 million people, about 75% of whom live in the central Lowland area, the fertile strip across the country from the Firth of Forth to the Firth of Clyde, where most of the industry of the country is found.

The deepest tradition of Scotland appears to be based on the clan system of old, with tartans, bagpipes, and all that playing a large part in the thinking of people when they talk about the country. This is a romantic memory, however, and the fact is that many, many of the Scots—Lowlanders—have little or no connection with the clansmen of earlier times.

Many of the Scots were laden with a lasting guilt feeling by the preachings of John Knox and the forced adherence for a long time to teachings of the kirk and harsh Scottish Presbyterianism. Although the customs have changed in resort areas, brought about by the coming of many tourists to the country, there is still a strain of puritanism which can be seen in Sunday closings, with many of the people of the country observing the Sabbath as a day of rest.

Outside the big cities of Edinburgh and Glasgow, people live in small towns and on farms, some even in the tiny crofts clinging to steep hillsides in the western Highland county.

The strength and independence of spirit of the Scots has been carried by their people who have spread all over the world, making good in many fields— as writers and artists, doctors and inventors, and scientists. Many, however, have stayed home and made their mark in the world from the place where Bronze Age aborigines began the long journey into modern Scotland.

THE CULTURE: The major thrust of Scottish arts' contributions since the late 1800s has been in literature and painting, although there are some outstanding architectural works in the country. In many cases, Scotland-born artists, writers, and musicians have lived and worked in London and have come to be more broadly categorized as *British* rather than Scottish, so my review is bound to be incomplete in some points.

Literature

From the religious and philosophical writings in Latin of **John Duns Scotus** (1266–1308), a Franciscan priest born in the Berwickshire village of Duns, to the 20th century, it has been difficult to define the term *Scottish literature*. Besides Latin among ecclesiastics, there is writing in Gaelic, in Lowland Scots (or Lallan Scots), in standard English, and in varying mixes of English and Scots. Among Gaelic and Scots writers, there are varying degrees of merit, but I will deal mainly with well-known figures who composed their works in Scots vernacular and in English.

There are few examples of Scottish literature before the latter part of the 14th century. It was not until the 15th century that alliteration, satire, and fantasy were set down in poetry by such writers as **Robert Henryson, William Dunbar, Gavin Douglas,** and **Sir David Lyndsay,** even **King James I** *(The Kingis Suair)*. These poets have been called Scottish Chaucerians, or *makaris*, because of the ideals of poetic utterance and metrical forms from the English master. The poetry of Dunbar and Henryson in particular had fairly strong influence on modern Scottish renaissance poets.

First Blast of the Trumpet against the Monstrous Regiment of Women was the literary work of **John Knox** (1505–1572), minister, reformer, and historian *(History of the Reformation)* who engaged in a long religious struggle with Mary, Queen of Scots. Other than the writings of Knox, neither the 16th nor the 17th century saw spectacular literary output in Scotland, what there was being in English. Writers of note in the early 17th century were poet **William Drummond** and **Sir Thomas Urquhart,** best known as the translator of Rabelais.

The 18th century saw a spate of lucid and powerful prose by Scots writing in English—**Tobias Smollett** *(Roderick Random* and *Humphrey Clinker),* **Adam Smith** *(The Wealth of Nations),* **David Hume** *(Treatise on Human Nature),* and **James Boswell,** friend and biographer of Dr. Samuel Johnson. It was also in the 18th century that the great Scottish poet, **Robert Burns,** lived, wrote, and died, leaving a legacy of verse combining the humor and vigor of Scots speech, the lilt of songs, and poetic modes and themes. Burns, Scotland's national bard, known especially for love lyrics and satires, is revered throughout the world. A number of minor poets were also literary lights of the Burns era—**Allan Ramsay** (father of the painter), **James Thomson,** and **James Macpherson** among them.

Ushering in the 19th century was another great Scottish writer, **Sir Walter Scott,** novelist and poet. He is known for medieval romanticism and perceptive description of his locales *(The Lay of the Last Minstrel,* a long poem, *Ivanhoe,* and many other novels). A notable Scotland-born writer of essays in the 19th century was **Thomas Carlyle** *(Sartor Resartus).* An acclaimed poet was **James Hogg,** who also wrote an acclaimed prose work, *The Private Memoirs and Confessions of a Justified Sinner.* Few other verse writers of the early 19th century are remembered.

Smack in the middle of the 19th century, another lion of the literary world was born in Edinburgh. **Robert Louis Stevenson** (1850–1894) penned such classics as *Treasure Island, Kidnapped,* and *The Strange Case of Dr. Jekyll and Mr. Hyde,* as well as poems, especially for children.

It was at the end of the 19th century that a school of writing was formed in Scotland called the *Kailyard* (or *Kaleyard*), which is literally translated as "kitchen garden." The Kailyard writing was characterized by descriptions of Scottish life as homey and cozy and the use of Scots dialect. The sentimental viewpoint was sometimes good, although it could weaken an otherwise strong statement. Writers who disagreed with the Kailyard school often used their own writing to blast the idealization of village life, using themes of brutality and tragic melodrama. Stevenson was an early opponent of the "Kailyard treacle."

Notable men of letters who lived and worked in the late Victorian and mostly into the Edwardian eras—some even longer than that—are **Andrew Lang,** poet, essayist, and historian also known for his collections of fairy tales; **John Buchan** *(The Thirty-Nine Steps);* and **Douglas Brown** *(The House with the Green Shutters,* an anti-Kailyard novel). One of the top figures in this period was **Sir James M. Barrie,** Scotland's greatest dramatist *(Peter Pan* and *Dear Brutus),* most of whose life was spent in London. His novel, *A Window in Thrums,* was weakened by its sentimental (Kailyard) viewpoint.

Few people associate that quintessential Londoner, Sherlock Holmes, with Scotland, but the great detective's creator, **Sir Arthur Conan Doyle,** was born in Edinburgh and studied medicine at the university in that capital city.

Other fiction in Scotland has proceeded in the 20th century more or less in the tradition of Scott and Stevenson. After World War I, the so-called Scottish renaissance began to blossom, a move for national identity for Scotland with a use in literature of a synthetic language called Lallans, a name formerly applied to Lowland Scots but now consisting of a mix of dialects. The poet **Hugh MacDiarmid,** a "mad, persuasive Gael," was the chief proponent of this nationalistic move, but he failed to see his aims carried out fully and lastingly. This is not to say that Scots vernacular is not used by novelists and poets. It's just that English has become the language of literature in Scotland as in Wales, despite objectors.

Besides MacDiarmid, 20th-century writers of note are **Edwin Muir,** an anti-renaissance Orkney Islander known for his great metaphysical poetry and his translations of Kafka; **James Bridie,** playwright and co-founder of the Glasgow Citizens' Theatre; **Eric Linklater,** Orkney Island–born writer of satirical and comic novels; and **Lewis Grassic Gibbon,** novelist.

A writer who has won the hearts of readers (and television audiences) around the world, **James Herriot** *(All Creatures Great and Small),* was born and educated in Scotland, but he writes about the Yorkshire Dales where he has practiced veterinary medicine during his adult life.

Art

Painting was no big thing in early Scotland. Decorative painting became popular in houses and public buildings in the late 16th and early 17th centuries, probably stemming from a growing familiarity of the Scots with their trading partners on the continent, in Holland and Belgium as well as Scandinavia. Tempera painting on ceilings and paneling can still be seen in such places as Gladstone's Land in Edinburgh and Provost Skene's House in Aberdeen. Most of this painting was the work of local artisans, who used bright colors to produce such designs as fruit and flowers, scenes and quotations from the Bible, and other conventional patterns. The tempera technique eventually gave way to ornamental plasterwork.

The origins of Scottish art are traced to this decorative painting of panels and ceilings. The first-known portrait painter in Scotland, **George Jamesone,** worked as an apprentice to one of the craftsmen in Aberdeen who was active in decorative design and execution.

A school of portraitists developed in Scotland in the early 18th century, following a rich tradition in England. **Allan Ramsay** (1718–1784), son of the poet and wigmaker of the same name, was Scotland's first fine artist. His best work, a picture of his wife, hangs in the National Gallery in Edinburgh, and he is represented in many outstanding collections. Ramsay is believed to have been an influence on England's Sir Joshua Reynolds. Ramsay eventually moved to London, but his major successor in the field, **Sir Henry Raeburn** (1756–1823), son of a yarn boiler, did most of his work in Edinburgh. **Sir David Wilkie** (1785–1841), Scottish genre painter and portraitist, is well represented in the National Gallery of Scotland and in other galleries.

After the end of the 19th century, dominant in the Scottish art world until World War I were landscape painter **William MacTaggart** and the painters of the Glasgow school. Names important in art circles in Scotland since that time have been **S. J. Peploe, Leslie Hunter, F. C. B. Cadell, W. G. Gillies, MacLauchlan Milne,** and another **William MacTaggart,** this one grandson of the earlier artist.

Architecture

Examples of both ecclesiastical and secular architecture can be seen through the country, although the Vikings didn't leave much of the Celtic church structures. Anglo-Norman colonization saw most architectural efforts directed toward ecclesiastical edifices in the 11th and 12th centuries. Parish churches at Dalmeny and Leuchars and the church of David I in Dunfermlin are examples of Norman design.

A turn to Gothic style came with the monasteries from the early Middle Ages, and in the cathedrals, such as the ones in Glasgow, Elgin, and Dunblane, you can see the pointed arches and vaulting and the lancet windows. When the barons built churches other than cathedrals, they used a Scottish design with stepped buttresses, crenelated towers, and roofs of stone slab. On St. Giles in Edinburgh, you can see one of the few remaining crown spires used in late Gothic ecclesiastical construction.

Finely crafted sculpture in tomb covers and crosses can be seen in the west where Celtic traditions survived the longest. The tomb slabs have such carvings as galleys, claymores, and other martial depictions, and the crucifixion is seen on the crosses.

The ornamentation of churches was removed after the Reformation, but their structural function was retained. In Aberdeen, pre-Reformation woodwork is in existence at King's College and St. Machar's.

Brochs of stone from about the beginning of the Christian era were vertical defense forerunners of Scottish castles. The Norman motte and bailey fortifications came next, with early stone-built castles having stone curtain walls. In the early Middle Ages, curtain walls and towers were combined, and in many castles, the strong keeps were supplanted by gatehouses. By the 14th century, heavily fortified castles strengthened the power of feudal lords. At Linlithgow, Falkland, and Stirling, castles in the European Renaissance style show the trend royal builders followed.

Baronial mansions from the late 16th and early 17th centuries show Scottish architectural influence that came into use, with gables, garrets, turrets, towers, and facade adornment. **Sir William Bruce** (1630–1710) and **James Smith** (1644–1731) were early architects of note. The classical style used by Bruce can be seen at Kinross House and the courtyard at the Palace of Holyroodhouse. Smith's preference was Palladian. He was followed in use of this style by **William Adam,** father of famous architects **Robert Adam** (1728–1792) and **James Adam** (1730–1794).

Robert Adam's work can be seen in Syon House and at Kenwood in London, particularly in his interiors, as well as at Mellerstain in Scotland. Handsome examples of the later design of this fine artist can best be seen at Culzean Castle. Robert and his brother James designed the Adelphi buildings in London. The so-called "Adam style" of design is known for light, decorative re-working of Greek and Roman classical motifs.

A 19th-century revival of medieval architectural design can be seen at Abbotsford, while the baronial style was brought back in the construction of Balmoral Castle. By the end of that century, a more pleasing revival was carried out by **Charles Rennie Mackintosh** (1868–1928), who used the Scottish vernacular method, even including it in his art nouveau designs, a path followed by **Sir Robert Lorimer** in restoring old castles. The restoration idea has caught hold, so that many old houses, manors, and castles are now being given new leases on life instead of being demolished.

Of interest are the dovecots or pigeon houses seen in many places throughout the country. Their style varies from the tall beehive look to cylinders to rectangular, freestanding boxes, some with stepped roofs, sundials, and even moats and turrets.

Crafts

Hand-spun and woven or knitted goods can still be found in Scotland, produced somewhat in the old way, although such items as clan plaids and tweeds from Harris and Lewis are mostly made under industry control. Shawls knitted on Shetland come in the natural colors of undyed wool, from fawn to black.

Offered at craft centers and at many shops are ornaments of granite (miniature curling stones, for instance) and serpentine. Jewelry is also made of semiprecious stones, including Cairngorm and Tay pearls.

Orkney chairs with straw hoods are made by craftsmen, and you can find other items such as buttons and cutlery handles of horn, sheepskin rugs, and fine leather goods, including sporrans, a feature of the kilt outfits.

Music

Not much is known of music in Scotland before the early Middle Ages, but apparently it developed through the centuries in the Celtic church and then under Roman authority as well as feudal monarchy. Two traditions exist in the realm of Scottish folk songs—Lowlands and eastern (mostly English-speaking) areas and Gaelic music of the Highlands and Hebrides—and it is in the folk idiom that distinguishing characteristics of Scottish music can be found. Gaelic and Lowlands cultural interchange was almost nonexistent before the 18th century, but Robert Burns borrowed Gaelic tunes for some of his Lowland verses, and Gaelic roots are heard in certain Lowland words and names.

The first Lowland songs and ballads were written down in the Skene Manuscript (now in the National Library of Scotland) around 1615, and about 1650, numerous published editions of Lowland tunes began to appear. Gaelic songs were not written down until the 19th century, and because the Highlands tunes often differed from clan to clan, you may still hear a version never written or recorded.

A feature of what is generally accepted as Scottish music is the Scotch snap, a form of syncopation consisting of two notes, the second of which is three times as long as the first. The Scotch snap is found in some Scottish song tunes and in the pseudo-Scottish melodies of the 18th century, when it apparently originated.

The folk music of the Orkney and Shetland Islands derived from Scandinavian origins. The ancient Norn language was spoken in Orkney until the late 17th century and in Shetland until the mid-18th, but it was allowed to die out, and since folk tunes were sung in that language, they too have almost died out.

The three national musical instruments of Scotland are the harp, the bagpipe, and the fiddle. The most ancient of these is the harp, of Irish origin, which had a vogue in both the Highlands and the Lowlands for at least 1,000 years. It lost popularity by the 18th century, with the fiddle, flute, and lute taking precedence and some harp music even being passed to the bagpipes. Interest in the harp has revived in this century.

The fiddle (derived from the early *fedyl*) edged out two former competitors, the *rebec* and the *croud* (the Welsh *crwth*), for predominance in the bowed string instrument category. Today, especially in Strathspey and Shetland, you can hear it in both solo and concert form.

Along with the Loch Ness monster and the tartan, the bagpipe evokes the image of Scotland throughout the world. Therefore it may come as a surprise to many to learn that it originated in the Near East. It may have been introduced into Britain by the conquering Romans who found Scotland too tough to tame. The great Highland bagpipe has survived in Scotland against heavy political odds and for various reasons. This instrument of the great outdoors survived the defeat at Culloden when the playing of it was outlawed (along with the wearing of the kilt). Its survival was assured partly because it was prized as a military instrument, the dread sound of the piper often sending terror through enemy ranks. After Culloden, piping was encouraged in new Highland regiments, and the Scot became feared throughout the world for his prowess as a soldier and for the brave skirl of the pipes.

The *ceol mór* (great music) is the *pibroch,* a highly developed theme with variations. The art of pibroch is unique to the Highlands. Lighter types of bagpipe music, called *ceol beag* (small music), are marches, dances, and airs. The Lowland or Border bagpipe, bellows-blown, lost popularity in the 19th century. The great Highland bagpipe has two or more pipes sounded by mouth-blown reeds. Wind is fed to the pipes by arm pressure on a skin bag. It is estimated that it takes about seven years to learn to play the great Highland bagpipe well. Once a solo instrument, it is now known chiefly through its use by the pipe bands of Scottish regiments mentioned above.

Church, court, and concert music have largely developed similarly to that of other places in the British Isles, except for long gaps in progress caused by troubled times and repression by barons and British overlords. Before the Reformation, most towns of any size had active song schools, mainly under church direction. One major change brought on by Calvinist reformers was denigration of the organ as a "popish instrument" and subsequent destruction in the 17th and 18th centuries of organs everywhere, with little church music being composed until this century. None of this, however, interfered with the Gaelic "long psalms" of Celtic Scotland in which each line is intoned musically by the leader with the congregation then singing the line.

Choral and orchestral music are encouraged today, and universities have healthy music departments. There is a Scottish National Orchestra as well as the BBC Scottish Symphony Orchestra, plus various ensembles and guilds.

FESTIVALS: The best-known festival in Scotland is the **Edinburgh Festival,** held for three weeks in late summer (more about this in the chapter on Scotland's capital). Called an "arts bonanza," it draws major talent from around the world, artists who have distinguished themselves in music, drama, and other fields. More than a thousand shows are presented, and a million tickets are sold. Book, jazz, and film festivals are also staged at this time, but nothing tops the **Military Tattoo** against the backdrop of spotlit Edinburgh Castle.

The people of the **"Burns Country"** celebrate the life and works of Robert Burns each year in early summer, with a program of exhibitions, music, and poetry. Three large open-air events take place during the festival, including the Tam O'Shanter Ride, a reenactment of his famous poem.

The best known Gaelic festival is the **National Mod,** whose climax is the crowning of the Bard, honoring the finest original poem in Gaelic. The site of this festival varies from year to year.

Some of the Scottish festivals are of pagan origin, including the **Beltane Festival** in June in Peebles (the Border Country) and **Lanimer Day** at Lanark in June. Also in June, Dumfries stages the age-old **Guid Nychtburris.**

The most northerly town in Great Britain, Lerwick in the Shetland Islands, still clings to tradition by staging an ancient Norse fire festival on the last Tuesday in January. Known as **Up-Helly-Aa,** it has an aim to encourage the return of the sun after the pitch-dark days of winter. Its highlight is the burning of a Norse longboat replica.

HIGHLAND GAMES AND GATHERINGS: Highland gatherings or games

have their origins in the fairs organized by the tribes or clans for the exchange of goods. At these gatherings there were often trials of strength among the men, and the strongest were selected for the chief's army.

The earliest games were held more than a thousand years ago. The same tradition is maintained today: throwing hammers, putting rounded stones found in the rivers, tossing tree trunks, running in flat races and up steep hillsides. The playing of bagpipes and the performance of dances have always been part of the gatherings. The "Heavies," a breed of gigantic men, always draw the most attention with their prowess. Of all the events, the most popular—and the most spectacular—is the tossing of the caber (that is, the throwing of a great tree trunk!).

The most famous gathering nowadays is that at Braemar, held in early September of each year and patronized by the royal family. When that "chief of chiefs" takes the salute, Queen Elizabeth II is fulfilling a role assumed by an ancestor of hers in the 11th century.

Another British queen, Victoria, who had a deep love for Scotland, popularized the Highland games which for many decades had been suppressed after the failure of the 1745 rebellion. In 1848 the Queen and her consort, Prince Albert, attended the Braemar Gathering and saw her ghillie, Duncan, win the race up the "hill of Craig Choinnich," as she recorded in her journal.

Other major games are held at Ballater (Grampian), Aberdeen, Elgin, and Newtonmore.

TARTANS AND KILTS: Today the clans, the ancient families, and those who

enjoy common ancestry are identified mainly by their tartans, the word first recorded in 1471 to describe the previously named "chequered garment" or "mantle." The kilt has a much older history as a style of dress. It was recorded in Bronze Age frescoes in Crete and worn by soldiers such as the Romans.

After the 1745 rebellion led by Bonnie Prince Charlie, the checkered multicolored cloth was banned. However, when Sir Walter Scott invited King George IV to visit Scotland, the king arrived in a kilt wearing pink tights underneath. Thus the tartan came back into fashion, helped in no small measure by Prince Albert, consort to Queen Victoria.

There are some 300 clan designs today. Many kilt shops throughout Scotland will help you determine if you have your own family tartan.

Garb o' the Gods

Few people know that anywhere from seven to ten yards of wool tartan goes into the average kilt, and even fewer non-Scotsmen know what is actually worn beneath the voluminous folds strapped onto the muscular thighs of a parading Scotsman.

For a Highlander purist, the answer is nothing. That answer is true for any defender of the ancient tradition that only a Stewart can wear a Stewart tartan, that only a MacPherson can wear a MacPherson tartan, and that only a Scotsman looks good in a kilt. Of course any true Scotsman would wager his claymore (sword) that only a foreigner would stoop to wearing "unmentionables" (that's shorts to us) under his kilt.

Alas, commercialism has reared its ugly head with the introduction of undergarments to match the swirling folds of the bagpipe players. Nevertheless, salesmen in stores specializing in Highland garb still tell the story of a colonel, the 11th Earl of Airlie, who'd heard that the soldiers of his elite Highland Light Infantry were mollycoddling themselves with undershorts. The next day, his eyebrows bristling, he ordered the entire regiment to undress. To his horror, he found that half a dozen of his soldiers had disgraced the regiment by wearing "what only an Englishman would wear." He publicly ordered the offending garments removed. When he gave the orders to "drop your kilts" the next day, not a soldier in the regiment wore "trews" (shorts).

Naturally, years passed before a similar level of indiscretion manifested itself among the Highland infantry. Even with the general decline of standards today, the mark of a man in the Highlands is still whether he can stand drafts up against his legs and the feel of rough cloth against tender parts.

If you're not fortunate enough to be of Scottish extraction, or if you're distantly Scottish and can't trace which clan you specifically came from, there is still hope. Long ago Queen Victoria authorized two "Lowland" designs as suitable garb for Sassenachs (Saxons, Englishmen, and, more remotely, Americans). So if, during your jaunts in the Highlands, you decide to wear a kilt, and a true Scotsman sees you in a Sassenach tartan, he probably will assume that your unmentionables are appropriately covered with "unmentionables."

A TASTE OF SCOTLAND: Like the scenery, the cuisine of Scotland is varied and magnificent when it wants to be and when it sticks to the robust and satisfying food available on its doorstep. Many of its chefs, at least the more inexperienced ones, are less successful in imitating continental kitchens. Others, more skilled, have gone on to win acclaim in Europe.

For years the cuisine was the domain of the laird and the crofter—that is, oats and fish. Now Scotland has a well-stocked larder with imports from all over the world, but everything seems to taste better when it's made from local produce. Scottish delicacies such as Highland lamb, Angus beef, and salmon tempt the palates of the world.

From the hills come deer, from the moors red grouse, and from the lochs and rivers some of the best salmon and trout in the world. From its wide and varied coastline come an array of fish dishes, including shellfish, lobster, and crab, as well as the inevitable scampi. From lush pastures emerge some of the finest beef cattle in the world, and from the Highlands and other areas comes a lamb that is justly celebrated. Woodcock, snipe, and pheasant are there in season to lure the gourmet.

Scotland is also known for its baking, especially scones and shortbreads.

The Scots eat early. Dinner in some places, especially the more economical guesthouses, is served only between 7 and 8 p.m. as a rule (no exceptions for latecomers). In major hotels you can often order dinner until 9 p.m., but rarely later. Lunch is traditionally served from 12:30 to 2 p.m.

Some guest houses, B&Bs, or small hotels offer a "high tea" at around 6 or

6:30 p.m. This meal is found only in Scotland and northern England, and consists of bread, butter, jam, and cakes, as well as tea and a cooked dish, say, haddock and chips, a gammon steak (that's ham), or perhaps cottage pie. Some places also serve a normal dinner later, but I guarantee you won't have room for it if you made the most of your "tea."

Many Scots who dine out always head for the nearest hotel. Compared to most countries of Europe, Scotland appears to have fewer independent restaurants—that is, those operating outside hotels. Such large cities as Edinburgh and Glasgow are the exception to that rule, of course.

Many of these smaller, independently run restaurants found in villages and small towns offer a tea-roomy menu, catering mainly to summer tourists before settling down for a long winter hibernation. Cafés and coffee bars abound in the towns; many serve acceptable fare, especially in their baked goods. Others manage to get by by offering the typical and monotonous plate of fish and chips along with overcooked peas, invariably frozen.

Regardless of their world reputation, Scots do not survive on a basic diet of oatmeal. However, Dr. Johnson was not amused by the excessive amount of oats he was served in Scotland. He suggested that the grain in England was "given to horses." On the other hand the Scottish genius for superior breakfasts won his approval in spite of the oats, and he was a hard man to please. Scots still use oats and not just for the traditional morning porridge which many people find the best in the world. They do many things with oats, including rolling herring in it and frying it. Oatcake, a crunchy, biscuit-like roundel, has always been a great staple of life in Scotland, in all its many varieties.

In Pursuit of the Haggis and Other Fare

The national dish of Scotland is haggis, which is often accompanied by the national drink, malt whisky. Regardless of what you might be told facetiously, haggis is not a bird. Therefore you should turn down invitations—usually offered in pubs—to go on a midnight haggis hunt. Cooked in a sheep's paunch (nowadays more likely a plastic bag), it is made with bits and pieces of the lung, liver, and heart of a sheep mixed with suet and spices, along with onions and oatmeal. Haggis is most often served with neeps (turnips) and tatties (potatoes). It is sometimes served with "clapshot." That is a Scottish version of a dish known south of the border as "bubble and squeak." This again is another concoction of potatoes and turnips.

One of Scotland's best-known exports is pedigree Aberdeen Angus beef. In fact the famous "ye olde" roast beef of England often came from Scotland. To earn much-needed currency, the frugal Scots had to ship their beef to England, reserving the blood for themselves which they turned into black pudding. Game plays an important part in the Scottish diet, perhaps less so than in years gone by. Still, in the north and west is much game, including woodcock, red deer, grouse, and capercaillie. Rabbit and hare have always been well known in the crofter's kitchen.

Scottish lamb is known for its tender, tasty meat. A true connoisseur can taste the difference in lamb meat determined by its grazing grounds. These could range from the coarse pastureland and seaweed of the Shetlands to the heather-clad hills of the mainland. Many Scots seem to prefer lamb roasted simply without fancy sauces, but they also use the meat in a number of hot pots and casseroles, along with stews and mutton pies. These are elegant dishes. What probably sustained little MacDonald when he or she was growing up is "mince and tatties." That means mashed potatoes cooked with ground meat.

Chicken appears with frequency on the Scottish table. An old Scottish dish, a roasting chicken, is called stoved howtowdie. With rounds of spinach and poached eggs and bacon added as a garnish, it's called howtowdie wi' drappit eggs.

The beginning course—called a "starter" in Britain—for all these meat dishes is usually a bowl of soup, a welcome form of nourishment in a misty climate. The barley—Rabbie's "barley bree"—that doesn't make it to the whisky distillery may end up in Scotch broth, which is often flavored with the neck of mutton. The other national soup is cock-a-leekie, made with boiling fowl along with leeks. Traditionally prunes were added to sweeten the mixture, especially if the leeks were bitter. Scotland has a number of interesting variations on the typical stock in the soup kettle. For example, one soup is made with young nettles along with sausages, sour cream, and spinach. Another is called cullen skink, a fish soup made with finnan haddock, onion, milk, potato, and other ingredients. Sometimes a soup may be familiar—for example, crab soup—but in Scotland it will appear on the menu under the label of partan bree. One food critic wrote that some of the names are so obscure on certain Scottish menus that even Rabbie Burns himself would have confusion reading them.

From Loch, Sea, and River

Fish is one of the mainstays of the diet, and well it should be in this land of seas, rivers, and lochs (lakes). Many Scots eat fish for breakfast, including whitefish, haddock, herring, and the pink-fleshed brown trout. A popular dish is finnan haddie (haddock), which is said to have originated in Findon, south of Aberdeen. It is often poached lightly in milk or cream. The modest herring is transformed into the elegant kipper, sometimes called the Loch Fyne kipper, because the best kippers are said to come from there. Kippered herring is also served for breakfast. Another well-known dish is Arbroath smokies which are made from fresh haddock which is then smoked. A popular way of serving it is to cook it in an oven with milk, butter, and seasoning.

Salmon is the game fish of Scotland. When it is turned into smoked Scottish salmon, it is exported to grace the more elegant tables of the world. Scotland has such great salmon rivers as the Tay, Esk, Tweed, Islay, and Spey. But the salmon isn't as plentiful as it once was. For that reason, salmon and trout farming are practiced today to keep up with the increasing demand.

The Sweet Tooth

Dundee marmalade, made originally with oranges from Seville, is now a mandatory accompaniment with toast at many of the breakfast tables of Britain. Dundee, in fact, was the site of the world's first marmalade factory. The city is also known for its famed Dundee cake, a light fruit cake. Victorians considered it fashionable to serve Dundee cake at teatime.

Desserts, using local ingredients, often become imaginative concoctions such as plum and Drambuie mousse.

The Scots are among the good bakers of Europe. Many small tea rooms still prefer to bake their own scones, buttery shortbread, and fruity breads instead of ordering them from a baker. The Scot definitely has a sweet tooth, and many local areas have become known for a particular specialty, such as Orkney fudge. You can order boiled sweets such as "soor plooms," along with many variations known by local names: Jeddart snails, Hawick balls, Berwick cockles, Moffat toffees, and Edinburgh rock. The heather honey is justly celebrated, and jams make use of Scotland's abundant harvest of soft fruit. Raspberries, for example, are said to be among the finest in the world.

At least once you should order the cloutie dumpling, which takes its name from the cloth (or clout) in which the dumpling was boiled. It is said that no two dumplings ever taste the same. Mothers pass their own favorite recipes down to their daughters. One version recently sampled is made with black treacle, eggs, mixed peel, apples, carrots, chopped suet, and a medley of currants, raisins, and sultanas, along with "secret spices," most often cinnamon and ginger.

You will most definitely want to try some of the excellent cheeses produced in Scotland. The mild or mature cheddars are perhaps the best known. A famous hard cheese, Dunlop, comes from the Orkney Islands as well as Arran and Islay. One of the best-known cheeses from the Highlands is called Caboc, a creamy rich cheese—formed into cork shapes and rolled in pinhead oatmeal. Many varieties of cottage cheese are often flavored with herbs, including chives and garlic.

Quenching Your Thirst

"It is the only liquor fit for a gentleman to drink in the morning if he can have the good fortune to come by it . . . or after dinner either." Thus wrote Sir Walter Scott of the drink of his country—scotch whisky. Of course if you're there, or for that matter almost anywhere in the British Isles or on the continent of Europe, you don't have to identify it as *scotch* whisky when you order. That's what you'll get if you simply order whisky. In fact, in some parts of Scotland, England, and Wales, they look at you oddly if you order scotch on the rocks or scotch and water or soda as you probably do in the United States.

Perhaps they have a right to feel that the name whisky should be reserved for the drink made in Scotland, because it was the early inhabitants of this land who led the way in production of *aqua vitae* (waters of life), after the process of distillation was introduced by a Celtic monk in the 4th century. They tried to make it in Wales with small success. Ireland was more fortunate, using the process to make Irish whiskey (with an *e),* but it was the Dalriad Celts, called Scots, who moved from Ireland (Scotia) to Caledonia (today's Scotland) around the 5th century A.D. who began the production of *uisge beatha,* their name for the water of life.

Like Christianity and the kilt, also brought in by the Scotians, it caught on and has been of great importance in the country and eventually in the world ever since. It was the forerunner of bourbon whisky in the United States, the process being the same, only the barley used in Scotland being changed to corn (maize) in Kentucky.

For a long time the making of whisky was the work of the monasteries. Following the dissolution by Henry VIII, the people of Scotland soon found it necessary to begin their own distillation at home. After all, the liquid was supposed to have medicinal properties, and a few householders had already begun making their own brew, being far from the monastic sources. Use of the "medicine" increased rapidly, and by the time of the Reformation, Calvinists found public drunkenness a serious problem. The rich, inspired by the Auld Alliance with France, depended on French wines for their pleasure, and the working people drank ale.

By 1579 so popular had the drink made at home become that the Parliament of Scotland restricted the distillation of whisky because of a grain shortage, imposed heavy fines on anyone who visited a tavern on Sunday, and permitted only certain of the landowning upper gentry to make as much as they wished for family use. Commoners were prohibited from making their own, and hanging was the penalty for disobedience.

The law had little effect on the stubborn and independent Scots, and illegal production of whisky became one of the most widespread cottage industries in the land. Parliament tried again in 1644, this time subjecting whisky and other malt liquors to an excise tax, which only succeeded in introducing a highly successful smuggling business from stills to those who purveyed and imbibed the beverages.

During the late 17th and 18th centuries, consumption of whisky increased tremendously. Hosts were considered stingy if they didn't assure that each of their guests, male and female, was dead drunk at the end of a social event. A dram of the fiery brew was almost poured down the throat of any newcomer to any outlying farm, while upper-class families used it as a breakfast beverage. The lower classes, many of whom were paid their wages in whisky, used it as a release from the tedium of their lives and working conditions. The use of ale fell off drastically, mainly because people preferred the stronger drink.

By the time of the American Revolution, illegal stills and smuggling were at such a height that of the 408 stills producing whisky in Edinburgh, less than 2% were licensed and paid the excise tax. The product from the licensed distilleries suffered because the makers cut corners and produced an inferior product to pay the tax. To continue production of their illegal whisky, for which there was a good market, farmers tried many deceptive practices to obscure the telltale spiral of smoke from the peat fire required to dry the malted barley necessary to the distillation process. Smuggling was even aided by the clergy, who would sometimes store contraband under the pulpit or transport it in coffins.

Battles between the distillers and the whisky tax collectors were many, being especially bloody in the Highlands and the Western Islands, where it was considered that the plentiful imbibing of the product contributed to the blood feuds so common there. Excisemen were even known to accept payoffs for overlooking stills and loads of smuggled goods. One famous tax collector who was forgiven his transgressions in trying to levy the excise duty was Robert Burns, who became Scotland's most honored poet—and who was known to favor a wee dram himself.

In 1823 the authorities drastically reduced the excise tax on whisky, a move that encouraged illicit distillers to become legitimate businessmen. One of the first to realize that there was no great future in conducting his business illegally was George Smith of Glenlivet, who built a new and modern factory and produced a superior, legal whisky. His and other distillers' move to the right side of the law slowly—very slowly—put the illegal operators out of business.

Arguments abounded then as they do now as to the exact ingredients and process necessary to produce scotch whisky. Some purists claim that the water used must flow over granite. Others insist that it must flow through peat. The climate in which the potable is made affects the product, but the basic raw ingredients have always been and remain malted barley and ample fresh spring water. Water sources are guarded with great care. The malted barley, produced through a process of germination of the grain, is usually dried with smoke from a peat fire, which gives it a distinctive flavor. Several steps in the distillation must be followed to change the liquid from a distasteful "white lightning" to the beverage placed in oak casks for aging.

There are also differences of opinion as to the proper casks to use, barrels in which Spanish sherry had been shipped being among the favorites. However, barrels that have been soaked in madeira or even in American bourbon are also used. Aging in the casks is required, with a minimum of 3 years and a maximum of 12 years resulting in the optimum produce. Once a scotch whisky is bottled, the aging process stops.

The true difference in the scotch whiskies you may have become accustomed to seeing on bars or shelves of liquor stores in the United States is whether they are blends or single-malt whiskies. Many connoisseurs prefer single malts, whose tastes depend on their points of origin: Highlands, Lowlands, Islay, or Campbeltown on Kintyre. These are usually seen as "sipping whiskies," not to be mixed with water (well, maybe soda) and not to be served with ice. Many have come to be used as an after-dinner drink, served in a snifter like cognac.

The blended scotches came into being both because the single malts were for a long time too harsh for delicate palates and because they were expensive and time-consuming to produce. A shortcut came into being in which the clear and almost tasteless alcohol produced in the traditional way could be mixed with such ingredients as American corn, Finnish barley, Glasgow city tapwater, and caramel coloring, with a certain percentage of malt whiskies which flavors the entire bottle.

Whichever you prefer, both the single malts and the blends must be made within the borders of Scotland and then aged for at least three years before they can legally be called scotch whisky. Plus that, no one has ever been able to produce it like the Scots do, although many other distillers have tried, in places as far removed from each other as Japan and Norway.

Two other after-dinner drinks, in addition to single-malt scotch whisky, are scotch-based liqueurs—Drambuie and Glayva. The recipe for Drambuie, which is better known to Americans than Glayva, is supposed to have been given to its first producers, the Mackinnons of Strath on the Isle of Skye, by an impecunious guest, Bonnie Prince Charlie. The name of the drink is derived from the Gaelic *an dram buidheach,* meaning a dram that satisfies.

The making of Scottish beer—the ales drunk by the common folk in earlier days—almost died out when palates became more adapted to scotch whisky and when a malt tax was levied in the 18th century, to be followed in 1880 by beer duty, replacing the sugar and malt tax. Housewives made the drink for their households far back in the days before records were kept, but it was not until the monks in abbeys which sprang up all over the country began producing ale that the industry really grew. Brewing was first from barley or oats that had been subjected to open-air fermentation. It was sometime after the 14th century that hops were introduced from Bohemia via England, so that the beverage similar to today's beer was produced.

The brewing industry in Scotland has made a comeback in this last quarter of the 20th century, with Scottish beer, the dark "scotch ale," being produced. Real ale is beer made from malted barley, hop flowers, yeast, and water, with a "fining" process (use of an extract from the swim bladders of certain fish) to complete the brewing. Ales are fermented in casks in a series of steps, and a product is now being turned out by various breweries in Scotland which has been gaining in popularity.

Scottish ale is either dark or light, but it is malty and full of flavor.

2. Flying to Scotland

Although many North Americans think only in terms of going to Scotland via London, this is becoming more and more unnecessary if your travel goal is the northern section of the British Isles.

FLIGHTS FROM NORTH AMERICA: The only airport in Scotland capable of handling transatlantic flights is **Prestwick Airport,** 30 miles southwest of Glasgow. It's considered small when compared to such industry giants as London's Heathrow, but it is often preferred by visitors to Britain who wish to begin their journey in the north. They cite its human scale and efficient handling of people and luggage.

Consequently, many visitors to Scotland opt for a direct flight from some point in North America to Prestwick, avoiding complicated transfers through the congestion of either Heathrow or Gatwick in London.

The only U.S.-based airline that flies directly from the United States into Scotland is **Northwest Airlines.** It began in 1926 when it won a government contract for the mail routes between Minneapolis/St. Paul and Chicago. By 1928 it had expanded its routes to include passenger service over Canada, the Dakotas, and Montana. By 1927 service to both the East and West Coasts of the United States was firmly established, as well as breakthrough routings to the Far East.

It flies from more destinations in the U.S. to the Far East than any other airline, but its routes to Prestwick are among its most popular. Selected from a fleet of 747s, its planes fly across the Atlantic from Boston and New York to the green hills of Scotland as frequently as four times a week in peak season. Most of these flights are nonstop; others touch down briefly in Shannon, Ireland.

Connections through either of those East Coast cities are good for passengers originating in Chicago or the airline's home base in Minneapolis/St. Paul, as well as through any of the other North American cities (plus Edmonton and Winnipeg) serviced by Northwest.

The most economical passage is available in low season. This stretches between November 1 and December 11 and from Christmas Day until March 31. Even then, slightly lower fares are available for travel on weekdays (Monday through Thursday) rather than for weekends. At press time, the round-trip fare, a low-season APEX ticket, either from New York's JFK or Boston to Prestwick costs $398 on weekdays, rising to $448 on weekends.

Midwinter travel is fine, if you can schedule it. Most travelers, however, prefer to see Scotland in its verdant glory during the sunnier months. Shoulder-season fares apply during the entire months of April, May, and October, offering savings over high season. High season is from the beginning of June until the end of September. During that period, APEX fares from Boston to Prestwick cost $683 on weekdays, rising to $733 on weekends, plus a $3 departure tax.

APEX (which stands for Advance Purchase Excursion) tickets come with restrictions. To qualify, a passenger must book his or her seat and pay for the ticket at least 21 days prior to departure. Once in Scotland, a passenger must wait between seven days and six months before using the return half of the ticket.

Fares to Prestwick from cities other than New York and Boston can best be discussed with a travel agent or a Northwest phone representative. Their toll-free number, reachable from throughout the United States, is 800/225-2525.

Northwest also sells Executive-Class seating, which is only a barely discernible downgrading from first class (which exists only on that airline's flights to the Far East). Executive Class offers lots of space to stretch within your recliner seat and dozens of extra touches.

A recently organized Scotland-based airline, **Highland Express Airways,** offers service between Prestwick Airport and North America. The airline connects with Newark (N.J.) Airport in the U.S. and the Toronto airport in Canada on direct, scheduled flights complete with in-flight service and entertainment. Also in the works are flights between Prestwick and Birmingham, England, and between Prestwick and London's Stansted Airport. Highland Express has projected low-cost flights, using the Boeing 747 aircraft. The company was founded by a co-founder of Virgin Atlantic Airways.

FLIGHTS VIA LONDON: Most visitors fly to London, then take a flight to Scotland from there, usually arriving at either Glasgow or Edinburgh.

It is not within the realm of this guide to discuss flights to London, except to say that the choice of airlines is staggering. The premier airline of the United Kingdom, **British Airways** is the major carrier, offering more flights into England than any other airline. The most heavily used fare to London from North America is the APEX ticket, valid for a stay abroad of from seven days to six months. It must be purchased at least 21 days in advance.

The cheapest fares are offered in low season, stretching between November 1 and December 10 and from Christmas Day until the end of March. Shoulder season is slightly more expensive, lasting from April 1 until the end of May and for the entire month of October. High season is the most expensive (and also the most crowded), lasting from June 1 until the end of September. Travel just prior to Christmas (between December 13 and 24) is considered high season.

Serious economizers will want to investigate **Virgin Atlantic Airways,** which flies between Newark and Gatwick at competitive prices.

From London to either Edinburgh or Glasgow, you have a choice of options. You can also fly to Dundee, Aberdeen, and Inverness.

The most convenient is **British Airways,** which operates a shuttle service from Heathrow Airport in London to both Edinburgh and Glasgow. Flights last about an hour. Other lines competing on this run include **British Midland, Air UK, Air Ecosse,** and **Dan Air.**

Loganair, Scotland's airline, has main routes from the Midlands (such as Manchester), flying to both Glasgow and Edinburgh, as well as Inverness. They arrange connecting flights from Edinburgh to London's Heathrow via British Midland Airways.

Dan Air services both Aberdeen and Inverness from London's Gatwick Airport.

Several of these airlines offer a variety of off-peak reduced fares. Check with the airlines or a local travel agent.

CHARTER FLIGHTS: Strictly for reasons of economy, some travelers may wish to accept the numerous restrictions and possible uncertainties of a charter flight to Scotland. Charters require that passengers strictly specify departure and return dates, and full payment is required in advance. Any changes in flight dates are possible (but not always) upon payment of a large penalty. Any reputable travel agent can advise you about fares, cities of departure, and, most importantly, the reputation of the charter company.

AIRPORTS: The major international airport, as mentioned above, is **Prestwick International Airport,** some 30 miles from Glasgow. Many domestic and European flights land at **Abbotsinch Airport,** about eight miles to the west of the heart of Glasgow. **Edinburgh Airport** handles many arrivals from Europe and London. Even though a small country, Scotland has a network of airports so that you can fly to its major cities, such as Aberdeen and Inverness. There is also good air service to the Orkney and Shetland Islands.

3. Getting Around Scotland

From Newcastle upon Tyne, the A68 heading northwest takes you to where Scotland meets England, an area long known as "Carter Bar." At this point, all of Scotland lies before you, and an unforgettable land it is.

I'd recommend to many visitors that they approach the Border Country after a stopover in the York area of England. That way, they can start exploring Scotland in the east with Edinburgh as their goal, then go up through Royal Deeside and on to Inverness, crossing over and down the west side of Glasgow, emerging at Gretna Green, near Carlisle in England's Lake District.

The Border Country is a fit introduction to Scotland, as it contains many reminders of the country's historic and literary past. A highlight of the tour is a visit to Abbotsford, the house Sir Walter Scott built on the banks of the salmon river, the Tweed.

However, if you're approaching Scotland from the west of England, you'll travel through Ayrshire—the Land of Burns. This is the former home of Scotland's most famous novelist and her national poet, Robert Burns.

Burns knew so well the southwestern corner of Scotland, which is bounded by an indented coastline of charm which attracts many artists who prefer the quiet, secluded life that prevails there. Distances aren't long, but many motorists have taken two or three days to cover some 100 miles.

The southwestern Lowlands are often called Galloway, their ancient title, and they contain some of the most impressive scenery in all the country.

At Ayr, Troon, and Prestwick (with its international airport), you'll find sandy beaches and golf courses; and you'll also find that the fishing is good in southern Scotland, as is pony-trekking.

Below I'll survey the most popular means of transport for traveling within the country.

BY TRAIN: There is something magical about traveling on a train in Britain. You sit in comfortable compartments on upholstered seats, next to the reserved British. You're served your meal in the dining car like an aristocrat, and the entire experience can be a relaxing interlude.

You should, of course, be warned that your Eurailpass is not valid on trains in Great Britain. The cost of rail travel here can be quite low, particularly if you take advantage of certain cost-saving travel plans, some of which can only be purchased in North America, before leaving for Scotland.

BritRail Pass

This pass gives unlimited travel in Scotland and is valid on all British Rail routes, on Lake Windermere steamers, and on Sealink ferry services to the Isle of Wight. It is not valid on ships between Great Britain and the continent, the Channel Islands, or Ireland. A seven-day **economy-class pass** costs $115 for one person, rising to $155 in first class. A 14-day pass is $175 in economy, $230 in first class; a 21-day pass, $220 and $290; and a one-month ticket, $260 and $335.

Children up to 4 years of age travel free, and those from 5 to 15 may travel at reduced rates in economy class, but they must pay the full adult fare if they choose to go first class. The youth rates in economy class are $95 for 7 days, $150 for 14 days, $190 for 21 days, and $225 for a month. BritRail also offers a **Senior Citizen Pass** to persons 65 or older. This is a first-class pass, but passengers pay only the adult economy-class fare. Prices for BritRail passes are higher for Canadian travelers.

BritRail passes cannot be obtained in the British Isles but should be secured before leaving North America either through travel agents or by writing to or visiting **BritRail International** in the United States at 630 Third Ave., New York, NY 10017 (tel. 212/599-5400); 333 N. Michigan Ave., Chicago, IL 60601 (tel. 312/263-1910); 510 W. 6th St., Los Angeles, CA 90014 (tel. 213/626-0088); or Plaza of the Americas, North Tower, Suite 750, L.B. 356, Dallas, TX 75201 (tel. 214/748-0860). In Canada, write to or visit 94 Cumberland St., Suite 601, Toronto, ON M5R 1A3 (tel. 416/929-3333), or 409 Granville St., Vancouver, BC V6C 1T2 (tel. 604/683-6896).

BritRail passes do not have to be predated. Validate your pass at any British Rail station when you start your first rail journey.

A train, the *Flying Scotsman*, takes 4½ hours to make the 400-mile journey from London to Edinburgh. Because of either connecting trains or direct service, Scotland can be reached by rail from any train station in England or Wales. Sleeping cars operate between London, Bristol, and Plymouth to all major Scottish cities, including Edinburgh, Inverness, and Perth.

For information on rail travel in Scotland, call or write Director of Public Affairs, ScotRail, 58 Port Dundas Rd., Glasgow G4 OHG, Scotland (tel. 041/332-9811).

Travelpass for Scotland

BritRail passes are valid on all lines of the British Rail system in England, Scotland, and Wales. Many of the outlying hamlets of the northwestern section of Scotland, however, are not connected via railroad lines to any of that country's larger cities and towns. Therefore travel by ferryboat or bus is sometimes necessary to supplement access from some points of the rail system.

For the serious traveler in Scotland, a **Scottish Highlands and Islands Travelpass** is available for transportation on rail, ferries, and buses throughout the northwestern section of Scotland. This includes direct service between Scotland's major cities and the Orkney and Shetland Islands, as well as the Outer Hebrides and the Firth of Clyde. The pass is available at any BritRail travel office in the U.S. and Canada (see above).

The pass is valid for 7 days at a cost of $68; for 14 days at $113. It is good for travel only between March and October, since many of the ferryboats don't operate in winter. A slightly different variation of the pass is offered for purchase within Britain. If you purchase it there, it will be good for either an 8- or 12-day validity. The cost is prorated to be approximately equal to what it would be if purchased in North America. If you wait until you arrive in Scotland to purchase the pass, you can do so in Edinburgh at the BritRail office in Waverley Station or at the Travel Centre at the bus station in St. Andrew's Square. In Glasgow, passes are sold at the Central Station or at the Queen Street Station, and also at the Travel Centre in Buchanan Bus Station. In Inverness, passes are offered at the BritRail Enquiry Office.

Freedom of Scotland

At any rail station or travel agent in Scotland, you can inquire about the "Freedom of Scotland" ticket which allows you unlimited rail travel for either 7 or 14 days. The 7-day ticket goes for £32 ($51.20), the 14-day ticket for £47 ($75.20); children 5 to 15 pay half price.

It's also possible to take reasonably priced one-day tours by train (also bus and boat) from most major towns in Scotland. Before you leave home, you can obtain detailed information, including schedules and fares, by writing the Director of Public Affairs, British Rail—Scottish Region, ScotRail, 58 Port Dundas Rd., Glasgow G4 OHG, Scotland (tel. 041/332-9811).

InterCity Saver Tickets

Britain's government-sponsored InterCity rail network offers special discounts on train rides between major destinations in Britain. The aim is to have virtually all long-distance journeys within Britain included in the InterCity Saver network. Children under 5 travel free, and children 5 to 16 pay half fare. For the latest data, check with a travel agent or with BritRail upon your arrival, asking about the InterCity Saver ticket by name.

Roughly, here's how the plan works. Say you want to travel between London and Edinburgh, one of the most popular routes. From Kings Cross Station in London, passengers prebook their passage at least two hours before departure time. You can also book a passage with a travel agent, but in that case you must reserve before 4 p.m. on the day prior to taking your trip. If booking for travel on a Monday, you must reserve before 4 p.m. on Saturday.

You are limited to travel at certain times of the day. Departing London for Edinburgh, you can go by any train except those scheduled during rush hour (before 9:30 a.m. and those running between 3 and 6 p.m.). On weekends you can use any train departing from London. Passengers returning to London from Edinburgh are not restricted, and can take any train they please. The trip can be completed in as little as 4½ hours at speeds up to 125 miles per hour.

The cost from London's Kings Cross Station to Edinburgh is about £47 ($75.20) round trip if travel is on one of the designated trains between Sunday and Thursday and on Saturday in winter. It costs around £57 ($91.20) round trip for travel on Friday or on summer Saturdays. This is a considerable bargain when stacked against a regular unrestricted second-class rail fare from London to Edinburgh.

Similar arrangements exist for long-distance travel between major cities of England and major points of Scotland. For shorter distances, however, particularly for travel between points of Scotland, the options are more limited.

InterCity Nightrider

You can travel from London to either Glasgow or Edinburgh at a cost of £19 ($30.40) for a single one-way passage. If you wish to travel to Aberdeen, the same ticket sells for £20 ($32). The trains have first-class seating and leave London around 11 p.m., arriving in Scotland in time for breakfast. There are no sleepers, and you cannot pay a supplement to get one.

TRAVEL BY PRIVATE CAR: Many Scots will tell you that the "road money" is invariably spent in the south—meaning England. Regardless, Scotland has many excellent roads, often "dual carriageways," as well as fast trunk roads linking the Lowlands to the Highlands. In some of the remoter areas, especially the islands of western Scotland, single-lane roads exist. Here caution in driving is most important. Passing places are provided.

Sheep—found all over the country—have absolutely no car sense. They will suddenly break from grazing and dart across the highway (often a mother sheep with two little lambs tagging along). Many of the roads of Scotland are unfenced, and livestock can be a serious problem when you're driving either day or night. Drive slowly when you're passing through areas filled with sheep. One of the saddest sights in Scotland is seeing the needless slaughter of sheep by fast-lane drivers.

Driving Requirements

To drive a car in Scotland, your passport and your own driver's license must be presented along with your deposit. No special British or international license is needed. The prudent driver will secure a copy of the *Highway Code,* available from almost any stationer or news agent. It is now compulsory to wear a seatbelt if you're in the front seat of a car or minibus, either as driver or passenger.

Although not mandatory, a membership in one of the two major auto clubs in Britain can be helpful: the **Automobile Association,** the world's largest, and the **Royal Automobile Club.** The headquarters of the AA are at Fanum House, Basingstoke, Hampshire (tel. 0256/20123); the RAC offices are at 83 Pall Mall, London, SW1 5HW (tel. 01/839-7050). Membership in one of these clubs is usually handled by the agent from whom you rent your car. Upon joining, you'll be given a key to the many telephone boxes you see along the road, so that you can phone for help in an emergency.

Car Rentals

Once you get over the initial awkwardness of driving on the left-hand side, you'll quickly discover that the best way to see the real Britain is to have a car while you're there. It gives you the freedom that nothing else can provide—to visit that out-of-the-way antique shop that doesn't know about tourist prices or to escape the towns for a picnic lunch beside a quiet mill pond, whatever. And for two or more persons, economy can be a major factor in traveling by car.

All you need to rent a car from most companies in Scotland (or Wales) is to be older than 21 and in possession of a valid driver's license. You should also possess a major credit card or be prepared to make a cash deposit at the time of pickup. Underaged drivers will be happy to note that they can rent a car at age 18 from British branches of Hertz. But Hertz charges more for similar cars than does Budget Rent-a-Car, for example.

There are many car-rental services in Scotland and Wales, in addition to Budget and **Hertz.** These include **Avis** and a lesser-known company, **Kemwel.** There are hundreds of British-owned car-rental firms. **Europcar** is another popular one, affiliated with the U.S.-based National Car Rental. Most of these firms charge rates comparable to those of their American-affiliated competitors.

Some of the small firms offering "discount rates" can be tricky. For example, lured by its rates (which were lower than those of the better-known companies), I used a minor firm two years ago. Because they're small, they can't afford service depots in Britain. On the one hand you might save money temporarily but then again you might find yourself stranded in the Highlands, as I did. A phone call to the head office got me a recorded phone message that the offices were closed until Monday morning. It was Saturday afternoon. A kindly farmer came to my rescue and I was able to locate a mechanic in a neighboring village. But you might not be so lucky.

Among the major U.S.–based firms with branches in Britain, **Budget Rent-a-Car** is the most economical. My prerental research revealed them to be less expensive than Avis or Hertz. The quality of the vehicle I rented was top-notch, while only two days of advance reservation were needed to qualify for Budget's lower rates. Additionally, the insurance policies at Budget were more comprehensive than those at Hertz and Avis, making a motorist responsible for the first £350 ($560) worth of damage to his or her car. Standard policies at Budget's two largest competitors required a financial responsibility of at least £650 ($1,040). The cost of purchasing a waiver at all three firms was around £5 ($8) extra per day—a small cost considering the amount of financial responsibility which an accident would entail.

As of this writing, Budget's weekly rental of its cheapest car, a two-door Ford Fiesta with manual transmission, came to only $147 per week with unlimited mileage. Reservations can be made in the United States by calling toll-free 800/527-0700. All car-rental firms in Britain impose a 15% government tax. If you want a better car, Budget maintains sizable fleets of bigger and more luxurious cars at attractively competitive rates. If you encounter difficulties on the road, Budget maintains a 24-hour-a-day number within Britain which you can call for emergency assistance.

Accident Compensation

There is no automatic compensation. Some auto insurance companies operate a "knock for knock" cover. All other claims are settled by the courts. I would advise you to carry good personal accident and "third-party" insurance. If you consider it necessary in the United States or Canada, the same rules apply in Scotland.

Motor Fuel

The environs of Glasgow and Edinburgh contain plenty of gas stations (called "petrol"). However, in remote areas they are often few and far between, and many are completely closed on Sunday. If you're planning a lot of Sunday driving in some of these remote parts, always make sure your tank is full on Saturday.

BY BUS: No doubt about it, the cheapest means of transport for the budget traveler to Scotland is the bus or coach. It is not only the least expensive means to get from London to Scotland, it is also the least expensive means of travel within the country.

All major towns have a local bus service. Every tourist information center throughout the country will provide details about half-day or full-day bus excursions to scenic highlights.

If you want to explore a particular area, you can often avail yourself of an economical bus pass. For example, these economy bus tickets include the Waverley Wanderer for southeast Scotland or the Reiver Rover for the Borders area. If you're planning to travel extensively in Scotland, refer to the Travelpass already described under the train section.

Many adventurous travelers also like to explore the country on one of the postal buses, which carry not only mail but a limited number of passengers to certain rural areas. Ask at any local post office for details. A general timetable is also available at the head post office in Edinburgh.

The **Scottish Citylink Coaches** are a good bet. They link the major cities (Glasgow and Edinburgh) with the two most popular tourist centers, Inverness and Aviemore. The times are fast, the prices low. For example, it takes only three hours to reach Aviemore from Edinburgh. Inverness is just 3½ hours from Edinburgh. There is also a direct Scottish Citylink overnight coach making the run from London to Aviemore and Inverness at reasonable fares.

Many other popular runs are offered by the coaches, including links between Glasgow and Fort William, Inverness and Ullapool, and Glasgow and Oban.

For more detailed information, get in touch with Highland Scottish, Seafield Road, Inverness (tel. 0463/237575), or Scottish Citylink, Buchanan Bus Station, Glasgow (tel. 041/332-9191).

BY FERRY: You can use a variety of special excursion fares to reach Scotland's islands. They are available from Caledonian MacBrayne for the Clyde and the islands of the west or from P&O Ferries, serving Orkney and Shetland. Caledonian MacBrayne, operating about 30 ferries in all, sails to 23 Hebridean or Clyde islands. The fares, times of departure, and other requirements are so complicated that a special book is published by the Highlands and Islands Development Board. It details all the data you'll need for road, rail, sea, and air timetables to the Highlands and islands. Renewed annually, it is available throughout Scotland. The title is *Getting Around the Highlands and Islands*.

There are very reasonably priced fares for vehicles and passengers on certain multiroute journeys using Hebridean and Clyde ferry services. The most popular service is the short crossing between Kyle of Lochalsh and Kyleakin on the Island of Skye. Longer passages go to the Outer Hebrides, including Lewis and Harris. For some of the longer journeys you can rent two- or four-berth cabins. You can also avail yourself of a number of options, including Mini Cruises or Hebridean Drive-Away Tours (packaged tours for motorists).

Many bargain tickets are offered, including Excursion Return, Family, Island Hopscotch, Car-Rover, and Earlybird. Car Rover tickets, valid for 8 or 15 days for the Firth of Clyde and the Western Islands, are available from British Rail and Sealink offices. Short day cruises are available on the Firth of Clyde.

More details can be supplied by **Caledonian MacBrayne,** The Ferry Terminal, Gourock PA19 1QP, Renfrewshire (tel. 0475/33755).

As mentioned, **P&O Ferries** operates the services to the Orkney and Shetland Islands. Information is available from Orkney & Shetland Services, Jamieson's Quay, Aberdeen AB9 8DL (tel. 0224/572615).

BY HITCHHIKING: It is not illegal and is normally quite safe and practical. It is, however, illegal for pedestrians to be on motorways. The cleaner and tidier you look, the better your chance. Have a sign with your destination written on it. It helps, of course, not to be overloaded with backpacks and luggage. Try to avoid "In Cold Blood" maniacs, but how can you be sure?

WHERE TO GO: The French, the second partner in the "Auld Alliance," used to call it Le Grand Tour d'Ecosse, or the grand tour of Scotland. Johnson and Boswell made the tour, and visitors, most often North American, continue to follow in their footsteps to this day. But since many are faced with hundreds of miles of grand scenery, including mist-shrouded glens and mountains, heathered moorlands, and timeless islands, they must make tough decisions about what to see and what to save for another day.

Some prefer to plan their tours around the grand castles of Scotland, whose locations range from the Borders to the Highlands. Each of these unique and magnificent properties will be documented in the chapters ahead. They include Blair Castle, the home of the 10th Duke of Atholl (who still has a private army); Floors Castle, home of the Duke and Dutchess of Roxburghe; Glamis Castle, setting for Shakespeare's *Macbeth;* Dunrobin Castle, home of the Earls and Dukes of Sutherland for eight centuries; Scone Palace, home of the Earls of Mansfield for more than four centuries; and Hopetoun House, Scotland's greatest Adam mansion.

For those with a very limited time schedule, I'll outline some popular itineraries through Scotland. The first is for those motorists entering Scotland through the southeast, known as "the Borders." At Newcastle upon Tyne (in England), I suggest you take the A696 in the direction of Otterburn. It becomes the A68 and will lead you right into Jedburgh and then via the A6091 into Melrose, the heart of the Border Country with their ancient abbeys. From Melrose, take the A6091 west in the direction of Galashiels. The road runs into the A7 north. At Galashiels, turn west onto the A72 in the direction of Peebles. This will take you through the Tweed Valley, with all its associations with Sir Walter Scott, the novelist. From Peebles it is but a short drive along a secondary road, the A703, and then the main A702 leading into the capital of Scotland, Edinburgh, which many critics consider one of the most beautiful cities of Europe.

While based in Edinburgh, you can take many interesting excursions in every direction. Among these, you can cross the Forth Bridge, taking the southern coastal road along the Forth. You can head east, to the ancient Kingdom of Fife. You can visit the fishing villages of East Neuk, eventually reaching the capital of golf, St. Andrews, if you've continued to follow the coastal road. You will be at a point 49 miles from Edinburgh. There are several ways to return to Edinburgh. If you're rushed for time, you can take the A91 west. In the vicinity of Loch Leven and its historic castle, this becomes an express highway, heading back to Edinburgh across the Forth Bridge.

The second excursion requires stopovers of at least three nights. You can leave Edinburgh on the express highway, the M9, that goes to Stirling, 37 miles away, where you'll be within sight of the famous castle in about an hour. You can spend an hour or two walking around its old town with its castle, before heading for the Trossachs, one of the most beautiful scenic areas of Scotland. The A84 heads west in the right direction, but eventually you must cut onto the A821, a little northwest of Callander. The Trossachs have been called "Scotland in miniature." The Trossachs take in such delights as Loch Katrine and, the most famous of all, Loch Lomond. Sometimes this is called "Rob Roy Country" or "Lady of the Lake Country," because Sir Walter Scott used the area as a setting for his novels. You can either stay overnight in the Trossachs or continue west to Loch Lomond. I've devoted an entire chapter to these attractions alone, with many suggestions for hotels in the area.

The next day you can leave Loch Lomond and, along its western shore, connect with the A83 which will take you to Inveraray, a small holiday resort, seat of the Duke of Argyll at Inveraray Castle. From Inveraray, you can head north along the A819 to Dalmally, which lies along the A85. Continue east from Dalmally until you reach the junction with the A82. There you can head north, going through Glen Coe, site of the famous 1692 massacre. If you stay on the A82, you'll reach Fort William, which has the greatest concentrations of budget hotels in the area.

After a night in Fort William, continue north along the A82 until you reach the junction of Invergarry. There you can turn west along the A87, the road to the isles, which will take you to the Kyle of Lochalsh, where frequent ferries ply back and forth to Skye, the most visited of Scottish islands. Skye deserves at least a day and night, more if you can spare it.

If you have the time and can add another two days to your schedule, head back to Invergarry. Instead of turning south to Fort William, continue on the road north to Inverness. The distance from Invergarry to Inverness is 41 miles. The A82 will take you along the western bank of Loch Ness where, as you drive along, you can try to spot the monster rearing its head from the water.

If you take this motor jaunt, you will not by any means have seen Scotland. There's the granite city of Aberdeen and the great northeast, including Royal Deeside, site of Balmoral Castle where the Queen herself takes some of her holidays. There's Glasgow, the biggest city of Scotland and its cultural center, a place filled with art treasures and far better as a sightseeing attraction than its industrial grime reputation suggests. There's the Robert Burns country, centering around Ayr, followed by the southern Lowlands of Dumfries and Galloway, bordering England.

All of these attractions, including the Far North, taking in the remote counties of Sutherland and Caithness, have been documented in this guide. These itinerary suggestions are only for those in a hurry. Perhaps if your time is too limited, you'll return again at some future date and see the other parts as well, for each is rich in attraction, lore, and adventure.

TOURS: Many questions arise for persons planning their first trip to the British Isles as well as to other European destinations. Sometimes, a prospective traveler isn't really sure what he or she wants to do or see in, say, Scotland or perhaps Wales, aside, of course, from Edinburgh and its imposing castle. Troublesome thoughts that may arise are: How do I plan my trip to be sure of seeing the most outstanding sights of the area I want to cover? How much of a problem will I have in trying to get from place to place, complete with luggage? Am I too old to embark on such a journey, perhaps alone? Will I meet people who share my interests with whom to chat and compare notes?

My answer to all these questions—indeed, my advice to many people going to the British Isles for the first time—is simply: Go on a good tour. By this I don't mean just a tour of one city or of one building. I refer to a vacation tour where you and your needs will be looked after from your arrival at Heathrow or Gatwick in England to your departure en route back to the United States. Choose a tour suited to the time you have for your trip, the money you can spend, and the places you want to go.

One of the best operators of such trips I have observed is **Trafalgar Tours Limited,** 15 Grosvenor Place, London SWIX 7HH, England (tel. 01/235-7090), with offices in the U.S. and Canada. The New York office is at 21 East 26th St., New York, NY 10010 (tel. 212/689-8977). In the U.S., you can also call toll-free, 800/854-0103.

Trafalgar has an exceptional offering of tours of the British Isles, with eight well-planned schedules including visits in Scotland, ranging from just a trip to Edinburgh to others that take travelers to the Lowlands, Highlands, and islands. Six of the trips also include visits to points in Wales, from a dip into the principality just to see the beauty of Tintern Abbey's mighty ruins to more thorough journeys through this not-so-well-known but nonetheless interesting and hospitable little part of Britain. These tours are from four to 22 days in length, and prices are anywhere from around $250 to $1,350, not counting the air fare. The prices, of course, vary with the destinations and the length of time spent.

Because you may be traveling in territory with which you may not be really familiar, you will enjoy your trip more if you take along a copy of this guide, which gives the background of areas you'll see, where to shop, and other practical information. You may please your fellow tour members by taking them to a cozy pub you find recommended in these pages or pointing out an out-of-the-way but interesting sight to visit on one of your free afternoons.

The great advantage of such tours, particularly for persons who are hesitant about setting out alone or as a couple to foreign shores, is that everything is arranged for you—transportation in the British Isles, hotels, services, sightseeing trips, excursions, luggage handling, tips, taxes, and many of your meals. But you're not led around like a little lamb. Plenty of time is provided on most trips for shopping, recreation, or little side trips, perhaps to see the town where your grandmother was born. I see many travelers on such tours clutching a Frommer guide to keep track of what they're seeing or want to see.

Whether you have a few days or several weeks for your trip, don't put off your British Isles experience just because you're too timid or are afraid to travel alone. You're sure to meet some congenial people in your tour group, a number of whom may have had the very same mental reservations you've had about setting off on such a journey. You'll be glad you went.

4. Golf and Fishing

Scotland is a very sports-oriented country, and if it's an action-packed holiday you're seeking, you've come to the right place. In recent years Scotland has established itself as a winter sports center (refer to Aviemore in the Cairngorms), and sailing, pony-trekking, and waterskiing are among its other chief sports.

However, most visitors come here for the golf and fishing, considered among the best in the world.

GOLF: Scotland gave the world golf, but no one knows just when. As one brochure so colorfully puts it, "Its origins are lost in the mists of antiquity." By the early 1500s it was firmly entrenched. In fact Mary Queens of Scots is reputed to have played golf. If golfing has a capital, it is St. Andrews, often called "the home of golf." Not only does it have four courses of its own, nearly a dozen more are within easy reach of the center.

In all, there are some 400 golf courses in Scotland, with 30 courses in Edinburgh. These stretch from the estuary of the Solway Firth at the English border to the Shetland Isles, the northernmost land mass of Britain. Scotland is particularly noted for its link courses, including those at Troon and Turnberry. Links courses were created on ground that provides a link between the land and the sea.

Some of the most important courses include the Old Course at St. Andrews in the east, where a visitor is likely to see the Open Championship being played. For five centuries this golf course has confounded experts by its unpredictable changes and high winds. St. Andrews is also the home of the Royal and Ancient, established in 1754 and the headquarters of golf ever since. It dictates the rules and regulations of this now-worldwide sport. Around the corner from the Royal and Ancient, on Albany Place, is Tom Auchterlonie's famous shop, where the Auchterlonie family has produced golf clubs for generations.

Gleneagles Hotel is a mecca for golfers. The setting is the only five-star hotel in Scotland. Unlike the Old Course at St. Andrews, American golfers at Gleneagles find the turf of its greens more like those they are familiar with Stateside.

The Turnberry Hotel Golf Course, on the west coast of Scotland, exists in the shadow of the famed Edwardian Hotel, now splendidly restored. In addition to the Ailsa Course, the most famous, there are half a dozen championship links courses in the general vicinity. These include Royal Troon, which was laid out along the beachfront, and the Prestwick Golf Course, which has been the scene of 24 Opens. Turnberry, incidentally, was the creation of Mackenzie Ross, considered the greatest of Scottish golf architects. After the war, he created two magnificent golf courses from what had been an airfield.

Less visited by Americans, Royal Dornoch in remote Sutherland in the northwest of Scotland, some 60 miles beyond Inverness, has one of the greatest courses. One American golf magazine rated it as among the six finest golf courses in the world. Golf, according to records, was played on this course as early as 1616. It is known for its 14th hole, "Foxy," a 450-yard double "dog-leg."

Charges can vary widely in Scotland, ranging up to £20 ($32) per round at some of the more prestigious courses. Others charge an average of £7 ($11.20) to £12 ($19.20) per round. The larger courses have caddies who charge a fixed fee for their services. Tipping is left up to you. At the clubhouse on most courses you can rent equipment, or else you can do so at pro shops at hotels. Many clubs prohibit the use of caddy cars. Sometimes, especially in summer, the major clubs have catering facilities for food and drink.

FISHING: Many anglers consider Scotland a paradise for fishermen, citing its fast-flowing rivers, the availability of Atlantic salmon ("the king of all gamefish"), and some of the most beautiful scenery in Europe, along with the marvelous hospitality extended by its innkeepers.

The Tweed and the Tay are just two of the famous Scottish salmon rivers. In Perthshire, Tay is the broadest and longest river in the country. The Dee, with all its royal associations, is the famous salmon-fishing river of Aberdeenshire. The royal family fishes this river. The Queen herself has been seen casting from these banks.

Other anglers prefer to fish the Spey, staying at one of the inns along the Malt-Whisky Trail (see Chapter IX). Certain well-heeled fishermen travel every year to Scotland, preferring to fish in the lochs and rivers of the Outer Hebrides (see Chapter XVIII).

Fishing need not be just for the rich, although it would seem like it at times. Permits are needed (often arranged by your hotel). For one of the grandest beats on the River Tay, this permit for a week could run into hundreds of pounds. However, there are many lesser-known rivers where a club ticket costs only dollars a day.

In general the season for salmon fishing in Scotland runs from the latter part of February until sometime in late October. But these dates vary from region to region.

If you're dedicated, write to the Scottish Tourist Board, Ravelston Terrace Edinburgh 4 (tel. 031/332-2433) for more specific information.

5. The ABCs of Scotland

The aim of this "grab bag" section—dealing with the minutiae of your stay —is to make your adjustment to the Scottish way of life easier. It is maddening to have your trip marred by an incident that could have been avoided had you been tipped off earlier. To prevent that from happening, I'll try to anticipate the addresses, data, and information that might come in handy on all manner of occasions.

For more specific listings, refer to "Practical Facts" under the sections on Glasgow, Edinburgh, and Inverness.

ANCESTRAL ROOTS: If you have a name beginning with "Mac" (which simply means son), or if your name is Donaldson, or one of the dozens and dozens of other Scottish names, you may have been descended from a clan. This was a group of kinsmen ruled over by a chief and claiming a common ancestry. Mac-Donald is, in fact, one of the oldest clans, dating back to the 13th century. Clans and clan societies have their own museums throughout Scotland, and local tourist offices will have details about where to locate them. Some of the more prominent ones are previewed in this guide.

In bookstores throughout Scotland, you can also purchase clan histories and maps. In Edinburgh and Glasgow, genealogical firms specialize in tracing Highland family histories.

If you'd like to do it yourself (a lot cheaper), you may want to go to **New Register House,** 3 West Register St., Edinburgh EH1 3YT. You can write them for a full list of their search fees and a full extent of their records before going there yourself. Scottish ancestor hunters come here bitten by the genealogy bug, and seats get crowded in summer. The house has on record details of every birth, marriage, and death in Scotland since 1855. There are also old parish registers, dating from 1553, which list baptisms, marriage banns, and burials. These records, however, are far from complete, and the adequacy of recorded events varies. It also has census returns for every decade from 1841 to 1891. They also have such data as the recordings of foreign marriages of Scots, adopted children's registers, and war registers.

BABYSITTERS: They're most often called "childminders" in Britain. The fame of the Scottish "nanny" has traveled around the world, and if you're traveling with small children, your best bet is to ask your hotel to recommend someone as a babysitter, possibly a staff member. Expect to pay the cost of travel to and from your hotel.

Unlike most places in Scotland, Edinburgh is big enough to have an organized babysitting service. It's called **Guardians,** and it's at 28 Strathalmond (tel. 031/339-2288).

BANKS: Hours can vary widely from town to town. Most banks in Scotland are open Monday to Wednesday from 9:30 a.m. to 12:30 p.m. and 1:30 to 3:30 p.m. On Thursday some banks, especially those in the big cities, also open from 4:30 to 6 p.m. On Friday, hours are often from 9:30 a.m. to 1:30 p.m. One of the most reliable banks to do business with is the Bank of Scotland, with branches throughout the country.

BAR AND PUB HOURS: The hours in which you can enjoy an alcoholic drink are much more relaxed in Scotland than in England. Basically, you can get a drink from 11 a.m. to 11 p.m., but this can vary widely, depending on the discretion of the local innkeeper or tavern owner. Not all pubs are open on Sunday. Those that keep Sunday hours generally stay open from 12:30 to 2:30 p.m. and 6:30 to 11 p.m. Hotel residents can usually purchase alcoholic drinks outside the regular hours.

CIGARETTES: Most U.S. brands are available in major cities and towns. Expect to pay more than £1.50 ($2.40) per pack. *Warning:* Smoking is banned at an increasing number of places, including many bed-and-breakfast houses which accept only nonsmokers as guests. Make sure you enter a "smoker" on the train. Also, in most buses you can smoke only in a specially designated section. Some restaurants also restrict smoking, as do certain theaters and other public places. Check carefully before lighting up to avoid embarrassment.

CLIMATE: Temperatures can range from 30° to 110° Fahrenheit in Britain; so no Britisher will ever really advise you about the weather—it is far too uncertain. However, the Lowlands of Scotland usually have a moderate year-round temperature. In spring, the average temperature is 53°, rising to about 65° on the average in summer. By the time the crisp autumn has arrived, the temperatures have dropped to spring levels. In winter the average temperature is 43° F. Temperatures in the north of Scotland are colder, especially in winter, and you should dress accordingly. It rains a lot in Scotland, but perhaps not as much as age-old myths would have it. For example, the rainfall in Edinburgh is exactly the same as that in London. But you should always take your raincoat with you. See "Weather."

CLOTHING SIZES: Regardless of what the charts say, these can vary widely in Britain. If you're making serious purchases, it is always better, if possible, to try on a garment. Women will find the size of stockings in Britain the same as in America. Likewise, men will find suits and shirts the same size.

CRIME: This is not a serious problem for the average visitor going to Scotland. Most of the country is extremely safe, and its people are among the most honest and hardworking in Europe. However, caution should always be taken. Never leave your car unlocked, for example, and always protect your valuables. The area in and around Glasgow is one of the most dangerous parts, with dozens upon dozens of cases of muggings reported weekly.

CURRENCY EXCHANGE: As a general guideline, the price conversions in this book have been computed at the rate of £1 (one pound sterling, which comes both in paper bill and coin form) for each $1.60 (U.S.). Bear in mind, however, that international exchange rates are far from stable, and this ratio might be hopelessly outdated by the time you actually arrive in Scotland. Scotland issues its own pound notes, but the money of England and Scotland is interchangeable. A pound is made up of 100 pence, written "p."

CUSTOMS: Overseas visitors may import 400 cigarettes and one quart of liquor. But if you come from the Common Market (EEC) area, you're allowed 300 cigarettes and one quart of liquor, provided you bought them and paid tax in that EEC country. If you have obtained your allowance on a ship or plane, then you may only import 200 cigarettes and one liter of liquor. There is no limit on money, film, or other items that are for your own use. Obviously commercial goods, such as video films and nonpersonal items, will require payment of a bond and will take a number of hours to clear and deal with. Do not try to import live birds or animals. You may be subjected to heavy fines, and the pet will be destroyed.

Upon leaving Britain, citizens of the United States who have been outside the country for 48 hours or more are allowed to bring back to their home country $400 worth of merchandise duty free—that is, if they haven't claimed such an exemption within the past 30 days. Beyond that free allowance, you'll be charged a flat rate of 10% duty on the next $1,000 worth of purchases. If you make purchases in Britain, it is most important to keep your receipts. On gifts, the duty-free limit has been increased to $50.

DENTISTS: You can find one listed in the yellow pages of the telephone book or you can ask at your hotel. Appointments are usually necessary, but if you are in pain a dentist will generally fit you in.

DOCUMENTS FOR ENTRY: While every U.S. citizen needs a valid passport to enter Britain, no entry visa is required.

DOCTORS: Hotels have their own list of local practitioners, for whom you'll have to pay. If not, dial "0" (zero) and ask the operator for the local police, who will give you the name, address, and phone number of a doctor in your area. Emergency treatment is free, but if you're admitted to a hospital, referred to an outpatient clinic, or treated for an already-existing condition, you will be required to pay. You will also pay if you visit a doctor in his or her office or if the doctor makes a "house call" to your hotel. Be safe. Take out adequate medical/accident insurance or extend your existing insurance to cover you while you're abroad.

DRUGSTORES: In Britain they're called "chemist" shops. Every police station in the country has a list of emergency chemists. Dial "0" (zero) and ask the operator for the local police. Emergency drugs are normally available at most hospitals, but you'll be examined to see that the drugs you request are really necessary.

ELECTRICAL APPLIANCES: The electrical current is 240 volts, AC (50 Hz). Some international hotels are specially wired to allow North Americans to plug in their appliances, but you'll usually need a transformer plus an adapter for your electric razor, hairdryer, or soft contact lens sterilizer. Ask at the electrical department of a large hardware store for the size converter you'll need.

EMBASSY AND HIGH COMMISSION: They're in England. The **U.S. Embassy** is at 24 Grosvenor Square, London W.1 (tel. 01/499-9000), and the **Canadian High Commission** is at Canada House, Trafalgar Square, London, S.W.1 (tel. 01/629-9492).

EMERGENCY: For police, fire, or ambulance, dial 999. Give your name and address, plus your phone number, and state the nature of the emergency. Misuse of the 999 service will result in a heavy fine (cardiac arrest, yes; dented fender, no).

ETIQUETTE: In short, be normal and be quiet. The Scots do not like hearing other people's conversations. In pubs, you are not expected to buy a round of drinks unless someone has bought you a drink. Don't talk religion or politics in pubs.

FARMHOUSE HOLIDAYS: This is a unique way to see the rural life of Scotland. Farmers all over Scotland take in visitors year round. Jane Buchanan of Scottish Farmhouse Holidays, 10 Drumtenant, Ladybank, Fife KY7 7UG, Scotland (tel. 0337/30451), sets up these holidays which are available at 65 farmhouses throughout the country. The cost of B&B is £10 ($16) for adults, £6 ($9.60) for children 6 to 12, and £4 ($6.40) for youngsters under 5. Dinner, bed, and breakfast is priced at £14 ($22.40) for adults, £9 ($14.40) for children 6 to 12, and £5 ($8) for the under 5 group. There are no supplements for high-season or single-room occupancy. If you're interested, the quickest way to make a booking is to call the number given above.

FILM: All types are available, especially in Glasgow, Inverness, and Edinburgh. Processing takes about 24 hours, and many places will do it almost while you wait. There are few restrictions on the use of your camera, except when notices are posted as in churches, theaters, and certain museums. If in doubt, ask.

HAIRDRESSING: Ask at your hotel. You should tip the "hairwasher" 40p (64¢) and the stylist £1 ($1.60), more if you have a tint or permanent. Hairdressing services are available in most department stores, and for men, at the main railway stations in Edinburgh and Glasgow.

HOLIDAYS: Christmas Day, Boxing Day (December 26), New Year's Day, January 2, Good Friday and Easter Monday, May Day, spring bank holiday, and the first Monday in August. A major event on the Scottish calendar is Burns' Night, honoring the poet. Throughout the land at various suppers, the national bard's poems are recited and, of course, haggis is brought in, piping hot.

LIBRARIES: Every town has a public library, and as a visitor you can use the reference sections. The lending of volumes, however, is restricted to local citizens.

LOST PROPERTY: Don't give up hope if you leave your prize possessions on a bus or in a taxi—or elsewhere. Report the loss to the police first, and they will advise you where to apply for its return. Taxi drivers are required to hand lost property to the nearest police station.

For lost passports, credit cards, or money, report the loss and circumstances immediately to the nearest police station. For lost passports, you should then contact your embassy (see "Embassy and High Commission"). For lost credit cards, report to the appropriate organization; the same holds true for lost traveler's checks.

LUGGAGE STORAGE: You may want to make excursions throughout Britain, taking only your essentials along. Very few B&B hotels have space to store lots of luggage, and you might want to return to a different hotel. It's possible to store suitcases at most railway stations. At stations, you must be prepared to allow luggage to be searched for security reasons, but be warned: if you object, you could be viewed with suspicion.

MAIL DELIVERY: Have your mail addressed Poste Restante at any of the big towns, or give your hotel address. A letter generally takes about seven to ten days to arrive in the U.S. When claiming personal mail, always carry along identification.

MEASURES: For the measurement of distance, Britain uses miles and inches.

MEDICAL SERVICES: Medical treatment is free only for unforseen emergency conditions that arise during your stay in Scotland. You'll need to consult a physician privately for any other medical treatment you require. The larger hotels will get in touch with their house doctor should you need him or her. The same holds true for dental emergencies. However, you'll normally pay a small charge for any treatment.

OFFICE HOURS: Business hours are 9 a.m. to 5 p.m., Monday to Friday. The lunch break lasts an hour, but most places stay open all day.

PETS: See "Customs." It is illegal to bring in pets, except with veterinary documents, and even then they are subject to a quarantine of six months. Hotels have their own rules, but generally do not allow dogs in restaurants or public rooms and often not in the bedrooms either.

POLICE: The best source of help and advice in emergencies is the police (dial "0," zero, and ask for the police for non-life-threatening situations or 999 for emergencies). If the local police can't assist, they will have the address of a person who can. Losses, theft, and other crimes should be reported immediately to the police.

POLITICS: There are two main parties, Conservative and Labour. The Conservatives believe in free enterprise and freedom of the individual to make his or her own decisions, with some government support. Labour believes in state ownership and control, with the state providing maximum support for the individual. The Liberals and SDP have joined in an uneasy alliance to form the Social Democratic and Liberal Party, but have not yet made any noticeable impact. The Labour Party is very strong in Scotland, particularly around the central district, taking in Glasgow, where most of the people live.

POST OFFICE: Post offices and sub post offices are centrally situated and are open from 9 a.m. to 5 p.m. Monday to Friday; on Saturday, 9 a.m. to noon.

RELIGION: Times of services are posted outside the various places of worship. Scotland, which has its own church, known as the Church of Scotland, is in the main a Protestant nation. But at least in the larger cities all the major faiths are represented. Nearly all the churches in Scotland are friendly and hospitable to visitors.

REST ROOMS: These are usually found at signs saying "Public Toilets." Hotels can be used, but they discourage nonresidents. Garages (filling stations) sometimes have facilities for the use of customers, but not always. There's no need to tip, except in hotels where there is an attendant.

SENIOR DISCOUNTS: These are only available to holders of a British pension book.

SHOE REPAIRS: Many of the large department stores of Britain have "Shoe Bars" where repairs are done while you wait.

SHOPPING: Your best buys are in tartans, knitwear, tweeds, and whisky. There is a wide array of cashmere and lambswool knitwear, along with an excellent selection of Harris tweeds for both women and men. Collectors still go to Scotland for antiques, and it is also known for its silver and sports equipment. Edinburgh crystal is legendary. You might also take home a kilt and a set of bagpipes.

STORE HOURS: In general, stores are open from 9 a.m. to 5:30 or 6 p.m. Most stores close early one day each week. That is often on a Tuesday or Wednesday afternoon. The night for late shopping is Thursday, when stores remain open until 7 p.m. in Glasgow or until 8 p.m. in Edinburgh.

TAXES: There is no local sales tax. However, Great Britain imposes a standard Value Added Tax (called VAT for short) of 15%. Most Common Market countries already have a tax similar to VAT. In Britain, hotel rates and meals in restaurants are now taxed this 15%. The extra VAT charge will show up on your bill unless otherwise stated. It is in addition to the service charge. Should the service charge be 15%, you will, in effect, by paying 30% higher than the prices quoted. The service charges, if included as part of the bill, are also taxable!

As part of an energy-saving scheme, the British government has also added a special 25% tax on gasoline ("petrol").

TELEGRAMS: Inland telegrams have been replaced by telemessages at £4.50 ($7.20), plus VAT, for 50 words. If your message is sent Monday to Saturday before 8 p.m., the message will be delivered by the first mail delivery the next morning. Overseas cables can still be sent from main (not sub) post offices or by telephone. An overseas telegram costs £2.25 ($3.60) plus 42p (67¢) a word. You'll probably be advised at the post office that it will be less expensive to call home.

TELEPHONES: Phone numbers in Britain don't have much consistency of pattern. (It's what the British call a "real hotch-potch.") Next-door neighbors may have a six-figure number and an eight-figure number. You'll need all the figures, which can go all the way to ten. Consult Directory Enquiries to aid you. Dial 192, give the operator the town where you want the number, the subscriber's name, and then the address.

If you're calling from a pay phone, the machine will accept all British coins except 1p. Put your money in first, wait for it to register, then dial your number. Phone booths contain detailed instructions about how to make a call in the British Isles. Of course, if you're still confused, you can dial the operator for assistance. You'll see special phone booths used only by phone-card holders. These useful phone cards, which are sold at post offices and even at the tourist board, function somewhat like a credit card. They are sold in denominations of £1, £2, £4, £10, and £20. You put your card into the phone box and make your call. The card is valid until all of its units have been used.

TELEX: Telexes are more common in Europe than in the U.S., but are still mostly restricted to business premises and hotels. If your hotel has a Telex, they

SCOTLAND AND WALES / Road Mileage Chart

	Aberdeen	Aberystwyth	Ayr	Berwick-'on-Tweed	Braemar	Bristol	CARDIFF	Carlisle	Dover	Dundee	EDINBURGH	Fishguard	Fort William	Glasgow	Harwich	Holyhead	Inverness	John o' Groats	Kyle of Lochalsh	Liverpool	LONDON	Oban	Southampton	Stranraer	Swansea	York
Swansea	494	73	366	148	483	85	40	273	274	448	392	72	469	369	266	184	535	664	548	153	203	461	161	374		251
Stranraer	228	325	51	158	194	378	390	101	473	167	124	381	184	84	410	313	250	379	263	221	402	176	425		374	222
Southampton	547	201	417	388	512	77	121	324	143	477	421	215	520	420	153	272	579	706	599	221	77	512		425	161	245
Oban	178	412	125	180	141	465	477	188	560	117	123	468	49	92	524	400	134	244	147	308	489		512	176	461	309
LONDON	503	211	394	338	482	115	167	301	71	434	378	260	497	397	76	253	536	663	576	202		489	77	402	203	193
Kyle of Lochalsh	189	499	212	243	159	552	564	275	647	186	216	555	179	195	611	487	84	189		395	576	147	599	263	548	396
John o' Groats	232	615	328	342	202	668	680	391	734	259	285	671	195	295	672	603	129		189	511	663	244	706	379	664	479
Inverness	105	486	199	215	75	539	549	262	607	132	158	542	66	166	545	474		129	84	382	536	134	579	250	535	352
Holyhead	439	111	305	311	393	206	216	212	339	364	308	167	308	315	474		474	603	487	92	253	400	272	313	184	188
Glasgow	145	320	33	101	110	373	385	96	468	83	44	376	101		432	308	166	295	195	216	397	92	420	84	369	217
Fort William	165	430	133	190	125	473	485	196	568	127	144	486		101	532	408	66	195	179	316	497	49	520	184	469	317
Fishguard	491	56	373	393	461	154	112	280	331	432	376		486	376	337	167	542	671	555	160	260	468	215	381	72	261
EDINBURGH	125	320	73	57	91	373	385	96	449	56		376	144	44	413	308	158	285	216	216	378	123	421	124	392	194
Dundee	67	376	117	113	52	430	441	152	505		56	432	127	83	469	364	132	259	186	272	434	117	477	167	448	259
CARDIFF	490	105	382	368	470	45		289	238	441	385	112	485	385	246	216	549	680	564	169	167	477	121	390	40	244
Braemar	59	405	143	148		458	470	181	553	52	91	461	125	110	504	393	75	202	159	307	482	141	512	194	483	285
Ayr	177	317		134	143	370	382	93	465	117	73	373	133	33	439	305	199	328	212	213	394	125	417	51	366	214
Aberystwyth	445		317	311	405	125	105	224	282	376	320	56	430	320	281	111	486	615	499	104	211	412	201	325	73	205
Aberdeen		445	177	182	59	493	490	221	576	67	125	491	165	145	505	439	105	232	189	341	503	178	547	228	494	319

will send it for you. You may need to arrange the receipt of an expected message in advance.

TIME: Britain is based on Greenwich Mean Time with BST, British Summer Time (GMT=1 hour) being used roughly from April to October. When Edinburgh or Glasgow is noon, New York is 7 a.m., Chicago is 6 a.m., Denver is 5 a.m., and Los Angeles an early 4 a.m.

TIPPING: Many establishments add a service charge. If the service has been good, it is usual to add an additional 5% to that. If no service is added to the bill, give 10% for poor service; otherwise, 15%. If service is bad, tell them and don't tip! Scotland is still one of the few countries of Europe where I've had helpful personnel refuse tips. But they're learning.

TOURIST INFORMATION: There are more than 160 tourist information centers in Scotland. All are well signposted in their cities or towns, and some are closed in winter. For more specific listing, refer to Edinburgh or Glasgow. If you wish to write for information about Scotland, the address is the **Scottish Tourist Board,** 23 Ravelston Terrace, Edinburgh EH4 3EU.

WEATHER: This is of vital concern in Scotland. It can seriously affect your travel plans. For reports covering the whole of Scotland, call 031/246-8021 in Edinburgh or 041/246-8021 in Glasgow. For weather forecasts in the Edinburgh area, call 031/246-8091, and in Glasgow and the environs, 041/246-8091.

YOUTH HOSTELS: Scotland has youth hostels scattered all over the country, some in baronial castles. Anyone over 5 years of age can use the facilities if they comply with membership requirements. Visitors should apply for membership in the Youth Hostel Association in their home country. That membership will be recognized in Scotland. The national office of the Scottish Youth Hostels Association is at 7 Glebe Crescent, Stirling FK8 2JA, if you wish to write them for more specific information.

Chapter II

THE BORDERS

CASTLES IN ROMANTIC ruins and Gothic skeletons of abbeys stand as reminders, in this ballad-rich land of plunder and destruction, of interminable battles that raged between England and the proud Scots. For a long time the so-called Border Country was a no-man's land. And this is also the land of Sir Walter Scott, that master of romantic adventure in a panoramic setting, who died in 1832. Today he is remembered for such works as *Rob Roy, Kenilworth, Ivanhoe,* and *The Bride of Lammermoor.*

Southeast Scotland contains the remains of four great abbeys built by David I in the mid-12th century: Dryburgh (where Scott was buried), Melrose, Jedburgh, and Kelso. It is known for the famous "Common Ridings" gatherings celebrating major events in the past.

The Borders are also the home of the cashmere sweater and the tweed suit. Many mills can be visited in the Borders, and you can often find good shopping buys. Ask at the local tourist offices for nearby mills that will accept visitors at certain times of the year (hours likely to vary greatly).

Ask, if available, for a Borders Woollen Trail brochure, which will explain how you can visit the mills, the museums, and the mill shops. You can see the cloths being woven, following the process from start to finish.

One mill you can visit is **Murray Brothers,** Tower Mill, at Hawick (tel. 0450/73420), where you'll find a superb collection of Scottish knitwear in lambswool, Shetland, and super-soft cashmere for both women and men. They also sell a selection for women of matching kilts, skirts, and jackets in pure wool tweeds in a host of traditional tartans and fashion checks. It's still a privately owned family business.

1. Jedburgh

Designated a royal burgh by William the Lion in 1165, the little town of Jedburgh, which is divided by the River Jed, developed around Jedburgh Abbey on a Roman road called Dere Street. Today, the market town gives little hint of the turbulence of its early history, brought about by its position in the beleaguered border area.

Jedburgh lies 325 miles from London, 48 from Edinburgh.

BED AND BREAKFAST: The accommodations offered by **Mrs. A. Richardson, 124 Bongate** (tel. 0835/62480), are more like a private home than a guesthouse —in fact it's an apartment in a block of buildings. The Richardsons have two bedrooms, one with twin beds, the other with a double and single, classified as a family room. The house is centrally heated, the windows double-glazed, and the accommodations have hot and cold water basins. The cost is £9 ($14.40) per person nightly. Mrs. Richardson gives you a hot beverage and cookies before you go to bed, and in the morning, a big breakfast. She'll also cook an evening meal, if asked beforehand, which she serves at 6:30.

Normanie, The Friars (tel. 0835/63382), is the home of Elizabeth Tomkowicz, a friendly Scottish woman who met and married Kazik Tomkowicz, born in Poland and a volunteer pilot with the RAF during World War II. He worked in the garage business, moving around England, Scotland, and Canada before settling down with Elizabeth. They have two twins and one single room, costing from £8.50 ($13.60) per person nightly, including a good Scottish breakfast. Son Anton, who works "in the motor trade," still lives at home, perhaps held there by his mother's homemade shortbread and butter which is available to guests all day along with tea and coffee.

WHERE TO EAT: A pub with a downstairs dining room built of old abbey stones, **The Carters' Restaurant** (tel. 0835/3414), is in a building with a colorful history—a local grammar school from 1779, before finding its present role. This is the favorite gathering place of the people of Jedburgh who know that its owner, Michael Wares, serves good food and drink. Soups, bar snacks, and coffee are served daily in the lounge bar. The restaurant offers either British or continental dishes daily. Lunches are served all week from noon to 2 p.m. Dinners are more elaborate, served Monday to Thursday from 6 to 9 p.m. (till 10 p.m. on Friday and Saturday). The place is also open Sunday from Easter till October. The fixed-price menu of £8 ($12.80) allows for a choice of main course and includes coffee. There is also a full à la carte menu.

SIGHTS: This royal burgh and border town is famous for its ruined **Jedburgh Abbey,** founded by King David in 1147, and considered one of the finest abbeys in Scotland. Inside is a small museum, containing fragments of medieval works. The abbey is open April to September, Monday to Saturday from 9:30 a.m. to 7 p.m. or dusk (on Sunday from 2 to 7 p.m. or dusk). From October to March it keeps the same hours, except it is closed on Thursday afternoon and all day on Friday. Admission is £1 ($1.50) for adults and 50p (80¢) for children.

On Queen Street, you can visit the **Mary Queen of Scots House** (tel. 0835/63331), where she stayed and almost died after a tiring ride visiting her beloved Bothwell at Hermitage Castle in 1566. The house, containing articles dealing with her life (a watch, a communion service, her death mask), paintings, and engravings, is open from March to October only, from 10 a.m. to noon and 1 to 5 p.m. Monday to Saturday, 1 to 5 p.m. on Sunday. Admission is £1 ($1.60) for adults, 75p ($1.20) for children.

The **Castle Jail Museum,** Castlegate (tel. 0835/63254), stands today on the site of Jedburgh Castle. When it was opened in 1825 it was considered a "modern reform jail." Charging 50p (80¢) for adults, 35p (56¢) for children for admission, it is open from 10 a.m. to noon and 1 to 5 p.m. weekdays, from 2 to 5 p.m. on Sunday.

COUNTRY HOTELS ON THE OUTSKIRTS: In an idyllic setting, the **Jedforest Country House Hotel** (tel. 08354/274) stands in 50 acres of wooded valley. A winding driveway takes you past a thriving series of conifers leading to the solidly constructed 125-year-old house, with steep gables and high ceilings, along with detailed cove molding. At the wide staircase, you are likely to be greeted by one of the dogs belonging to the owners, Alan and Judy Ainley. The main house contains eight well-furnished and impeccably clean rooms, each fitted with old-fashioned accessories such as brass headboards and big windows. An annex contains four contemporary rooms, each of which has a private bath and color TV. With breakfast included, bathless rooms rent for £21 ($33.60) in a single and from £34 ($54.40) in a twin or double. With bath, the cost is £37 ($59.20) in a twin or double. You can congregate whenever you want near the coal-burning fireplace of the half-timbered pub (where bar meals are available) or around the pool table and dartboard of its adjacent games room. Elegant meals are served in the brown-and-white Victorian dining room for £11 ($17.60) per person. The historical house, four miles south of Jedburgh, has its own mile of private water for fishing, free to residents.

    Ferniehirst Mill Lodge (tel. 0835/63279). For experienced equestrians, this place offers a combination of trail riding, comfortable lodgings, and good food. It also attracts nonriders who enjoy the beauty of the surrounding hills. To reach it, you turn into an inconspicuous driveway which meanders down a narrow graveled path and over one of the River Jed's metal bridges. The core of the establishment was originally constructed as a mill. Today the ochre-colored building lies adjacent to the stables which house approximately 20 corn-fed horses owned by John and Beryl Tough (pronounced "Took"). Riding packages are offered for experienced riders. But the 11 small but comfortable pine-paneled rooms in a modern steep-roofed bungalow are offered to everyone. All but two contain a private bath. With breakfast included, the cost is £18 ($28.80) per person nightly. A fixed-price dinner is offered for £12 ($19.20). A day's horseback ride, which could be a welcome break from motor touring, goes for £30.50 ($48.80).

    If you follow the A698 northeast of Jedburgh, the road will lead to—

2. Kelso

    Another typical historic border town, Kelso lies at the point where the Teviot meets the Tweed. A settlement that grew up around a river ford, which was important as the first such crossing place west of Berwick, developed into a town around Kelso Abbey, established in 1128. In 1614, when Robert Ker was created first Earl of Roxburghe, the town became a "burgh of barony."

    In the town's marketplace, the "Old Pretender," James Stuart, was proclaimed king, designated James VIII.

    The Kelso of today is a flourishing market town, the center of an agricultural district boasting farming and stock raising.

FOOD AND LODGING: An inexpensive stopover in the Border Country is offered at **Bellevue Guest House,** Bowmont Street (tel. 0573/24588). Jean and Tom Hill, who own this simple guesthouse, ask £11.50 ($18.40) per person nightly for B&B. If you speak to Jean the morning before, she'll fix a tasty Scottish dinner for £5.50 ($8.80). Each of the rooms is nicely fixed up for guests and contains hot and cold water. Two double rooms come with private shower and toilet. Central heating is installed, and the Hills have a residential liquor license.

    Cross Keys Hotel, 36-37 The Square (tel. 0573/23303). The elegantly detailed facade of this green-and-white hotel can easily be recognized on the main square of town. As its name implies, an enlarged version of a gilded pair of crossed keys caps the central Italianate-style tower. Considered one of Scotland's older coaching inns, it has an interior that has been modernized. It now includes an elevator, and there are private baths and video machines in each of the contemporary bedrooms. Most of the 25 accommodations contain a private shower or bath, as well as color TV and a phone. A youth-oriented pub is on the lower level, and a more sedate cocktail bar upstairs is usually frequented by hotel residents. The Cross Keys sometimes closes in December and January. It charges £27 ($43.20) in a single, and £19 ($30.40) per person in a double. Breakfast is included in the prices. The hotel has a small health center with sunbeds, a sauna, and a gym.

SIGHTS: Once a great ecclesiastical center, **Kelso Abbey** has lain in ruins since late in the 16th century when it suffered its last and most devastating attack, was declared officially defunct, and the lands and remaining buildings were given to the Earl of Roxburghe. It was the oldest (1128) and probably the largest of the border abbeys, as well as one of the richest, under the Scottish clergy. In 1919, the Duke of Roxburghe gave the abbey to the nation.

Kelso is the home of the present Duke of Roxburghe, who lives at **Floors Castle,** built in 1721 by William Adam. Part of the castle, which is open to the public, contains superb French and English furniture, porcelain, tapestries, and paintings by such artists as Gainsborough, Reynolds, and Canaletto. There are a licensed restaurant, coffeeshop, and gift shop as well as a magnificent walled garden and garden center. The castle was a major location for the film *Greystoke*, concerning the Tarzan legend. The house is open in April, May, June, and September, Sunday to Thursday. In July and August it is open Sunday to Friday. Otherwise it is closed to individual groups except coach parties. The house is open at 10:30 a.m., the last guests shown through at 4:45 p.m. The grounds and gardens may be visited from 11 a.m. to 5:30 p.m. Admission is £2 ($3.20) for adults, £1.30 ($2.08) for children. For further information, phone 0573/23333.

A HISTORIC HOME ON THE OUTSKIRTS: The seat of the Earl of Haddington, **Mellerstain** (tel. 057381/225), lies in the Borders, and it is most often visited on a day trip from Edinburgh, 37 miles away. One of Scotland's famous Adam mansions, it lies near Gordon, nine miles northeast of Melrose and seven miles northwest of Kelso. It's open from May to September daily, except Saturday, from 12:30 to 4:30 p.m. and charges £2 ($3.20) for adults, 80p ($1.28) for children.

Mellerstain enjoys associations with Lady Grisel Baillie, the Scottish heroine, and Lord Haddington is her descendant. William Adam built two wings of the house in 1725. The main building was designed by his more famous son, Robert, some 40 years later.

You're shown through the interior, with its decorations and ceilings designed by Robert Adam, and are allowed to view the impressive library as well as paintings by old masters and antique furniture. Later, from the garden terrace you can look south to the lake, with the Cheviot Hills in the distance, a panoramic view. Afternoon tea is served, and souvenir gifts are on sale.

From Kelso, it is only a short drive on the A699 to—

DRYBURGH: Sir Walter Scott is buried at **Dryburgh Abbey.** These Gothic ruins are surrounded by gnarled yew trees and cedars of Lebanon, said to have been planted there by knights returning from the Holy Land during the years of the Crusades. Near Dryburgh is "Scott's View," over the Tweed to his beloved

Eildon Hills, considered one of the most beautiful views in the region. Admission is £1 ($1.60) for adults, 50p (80¢) for children. The abbey ruins are open from 9:30 a.m. to 6:30 p.m. weekdays, 2 to 6:30 p.m. on Sunday mid-March to mid-October. Off-season closing is at 4 p.m.

The adjoining town is St. Boswells. This old village, 40 miles from Edinburgh, stands on the Selkirk–Kelso road, near Dryburgh Abbey. It lies 4 miles from Melrose and 14 miles from Kelso.

Four miles from Dryburgh Abbey is—

3. Melrose

Lying 37 miles from Edinburgh, Melrose enjoys many associations with Scott, who was instrumental in getting repairs made to the ruins of Melrose Abbey in the early 19th century. In the shadow of the Eildon hills, the town developed, in the way towns had of doing in the Middle Ages, around the abbey.

In summer, visitors throng the attractive little town, finding it a good center for exploration of the border area.

ACCOMMODATIONS: In the heart of the town, the **King's Arms Hotel,** High Street (tel. 089682/2143), is a simple Georgian stone building with a white portico. It was constructed as a coaching inn 300 years ago. Today cars, not carriages, are parked in its adjoining car park. Bar snacks are offered at midday and in the evening, with the usual choices, including scampi, chicken, and light steaks. You get a good plateful for £3.50 ($5.60) and up. There are a number of vegetarian dishes in that price range, too. Rooms are comfortable, renting for £16 ($25.60) per person, including a full breakfast.

Burt's Hotel, Market Square (tel. 089682/2285). In the center of town, within walking distance of the abbey, this inn offers a taste of small-town Scottish flavor. It was built in 1722 between the main square and a pleasant garden, which today sends the aroma of summer greenery into the restaurant. The hotel offers 21 comfortable rooms, 18 of which contain private baths. There is an attractive bar with Windsor chairs and a coal-burning fireplace. Depending on the plumbing, accommodations with breakfast included cost £23 ($36.80) in a single, £42 ($67.20) to £46 ($73.60) in doubles. Inexpensive bar lunches and dinners are tasty. You can also take lunch in the hotel restaurant for £8 ($12.80) and up or an à la carte dinner, costing from £14 ($22.40), which might include dishes from duckling with cherries to medaillons of Hungarian-style pork.

Waverley Castle Hotel (tel. 089682/2244). The gray stone palace was built as late as 1869, even though it looks much older. The interior decor has been much modernized, but the dining room still retains its elegant old style. The River Tweed flows through part of the five acres of parkland surrounding the establishment. Rooms are comfortable and well kept. Summer rates, with a full Scottish breakfast and a three-course dinner included, range from £32 ($51.20) per person in a twin or double, going up to £36 ($57.60) in a single on the same arrangement. Children under 14 share their parents' room free, and discounts are granted for any stay that exceeds two nights. About a mile from Melrose Abbey on the outskirts of town, the hotel is on Skirmish Hill, where the last major clan battle in Scottish history, the Battle of Melrose, was fought.

SIGHTS: The beautiful ruins of **Melrose Abbey** (tel. 089682/2562) are all that's left of the ecclesiastical community established by Cistercian monks in 1136. The pure Gothic lines of the ruins were made famous by Sir Walter Scott, whose appreciation of the site led to repairs of the decayed remains and made them a popular goal for travelers. The heart of Robert the Bruce was supposed to have been interred in the abbey, although the location is unknown. Look for the beautiful carvings and the tombs of other famous Scotsmen buried in the chancel. In Scott's *The Lay of the Last Minstrel,* the abbey's east window received rhapsodic treatment, and in *The Abbot* and *The Monastery,* Melrose appears as "Kennaquhair."

The abbey is open April through September daily from 9:30 a.m. to 7 p.m. (on Sunday from 2 to 7 p.m.); October through March from 9:30 a.m. to 4 p.m. (on Sunday from 2 to 4 p.m.), charging an admission of £1 ($1.60) for adults, 50p (80¢) for children.

A short distance from the abbey you can visit the **Melrose Motor Museum,** Newstead Road (tel. 089682/2624), which has an excellent collection of vintage automobiles, mainly from the period "between the wars." It is open April to October daily from 10 a.m. to 6 p.m., charging an admission of £1 ($1.60) for adults, 30p (48¢) for children.

ABBOTSFORD: This was the home of Sir Walter Scott that he built and lived in from 1812 until he died. It contains many relics collected by the famous author, including one hall filled with spoils he collected from the battlefield at Waterloo. Other exhibits include clothes worn by Scott, as well as his death mask. Especially interesting is his study, with his writing desk and chair. In 1935 two secret drawers were found in the desk. One of them contained 57 letters, part of the correspondence between Sir Walter and his wife-to-be. The Scott home, still inhabited by his relatives, is open from March 23 to October 31, weekdays from 10 a.m. to 5 p.m. (on Sunday from 2 to 5 p.m.), charging £1.50 ($2.40) for adults, 75p ($1.20) for children. For more information, telephone 0896/2043. The house lies near Melrose, just off the A7, south of the junction with the A72, some 2½ miles southeast of Galashiels.

4. Selkirk

In the heart of Scott country, this royal burgh and county town can make an ideal center for exploring some of the historic homes in the Borders. It is also noted for its tweed industry, and many mills can be visited on day trips. In addition to its association with Scott, Selkirk was also the birthplace of the African explorer, Mungo Park. Both the explorer and the novelist are honored with statues.

FOOD AND LODGING: An imposingly proportioned stone and slate mansion, **Heatherlie House Hotel** (tel. 0750/21200), was built a century ago by a local mill owner. Today its steep gables and Victorian turrets are owned by Mitchell Speirs and his wife, Maureen. Maureen, whose father was a gamekeeper at Culzean Castle, is an avid gardener, working hard on her well-established grounds with their ancient trees. A coal-burning fireplace adds warmth to both the public bar and the high-ceilinged dining room, where meals are served daily from 10 a.m. to 10 p.m. All the bedrooms in this centrally heated hotel have private baths. The charge is £20 ($32) per person for B&B, £27.50 ($44) for half board.

A MANSION IN THE ENVIRONS: The biggest attraction in the area is **Bowhill,** the 18th- and 19th-century home of the Dukes of Buccleuch, containing a rare art collection, French furniture, porcelain, silverware, and mementos of Sir Walter Scott, Queen Victoria, and the Duke of Monmouth. Today, this Border home of the Scotts of Buccleuch contains paintings by Canaletto, Claude, Raeburn, Gainsborough, and Reynolds. See what is considered the finest collection of miniatures in the world. The house is open only from the first week in July to the third week in August (dates vary slightly from year to year) from 1 to 4:30 p.m., on Sunday from 2 to 6 p.m. Admission to the house and grounds is £2 ($3.20). There is an Adventure Woodland play area, a unique needlework exhibition, a Victorian kitchen, an audio-visual presentation, a gift shop, and a tea room/restaurant. Bowhill is three miles west of Selkirk on the A708 Moffat road. For information, including details of Sotheby's Works of Art courses, phone 0750/20732.

5. Hogg Country

James Hogg, the Ettrick Bard, lived from 1770 to 1835. He was a poor herb laddie from an upland parish, but he went on to become a major poet. He is best known today for his ballad poem, "The Queens Wake," the last line of which reads: "He taught the wandering winds to sing." He wrote many novels which met with success among the Edinburgh gentry (although he was often characterized as a drunken, foul-mouthed buffoon), but what he made from writing was dissipated in unsuccessful farming ventures. Among his friends were Scott and Wordsworth.

The lovely valleys of Ettrick and Yarrow, which converge just above the county town of Selkirk, make up the greater part of the old county of Selkirkshire. St. Mary's Loch (see below) has seen more writers and artists than almost any other Border beauty spot. Turner also came here to paint the area.

On the way from Moffat to St. Mary's Loch, visitors will see the "Grey Mare's Tail," an impressive 200-foot-high waterfall. Only the heartiest of walkers should follow the stream to its source in the small dark Loch Skeen.

The Southern Upland Way passes close to St. Mary's Loch: the longest long-distance route in Scotland, running from Portpatrick on the west coast to Cockburnspath on the east.

ST. MARY'S LOCH: This hamlet lies on the B708 Moffat to Selkirk road. It is at a point between two lochs, not only the more famous, St. Mary's, but the Loch of the Lowes. Here you will find a statue of James Hogg gazing out over the hills he loved so well. Under his eye there also stands the old inn once run by the redoubtable Tibbie Shiels. Tibbie was known to hundreds who came to view "long St. Mary's silent lake," to call uninvited on James Hogg, and to enjoy her hospitality.

Tibbie Shiels Inn, St. Mary's Loch (tel. 0750/42231), is steeped in Scottish lore. An excursion here involves a lonely motoring jaunt over grass-covered moors where your only companions are likely to be sheep grazing contentedly beside the road. Tibbie Shiels (1782–1878) was known in the region for her green grozet wine and her strict adherence to hard work and humor. In later years she housed Walter Scott and his friend, James Hogg. She sometimes berthed as many as 35 hunters, anglers, artists, and "literary gents" at one time. Visitors who came to her tiny "wren's nest" also included Robert Louis Stevenson, Thomas Carlyle, Wordsworth, and even Gladstone. Today this unpretentious establishment is owned by Shanks and Hildegard Fleming. After living in both Antigua and Bahrein, they abandoned Shank's profession as an architect to maintain their pub and a handful of bright old-fashioned bedrooms set aside for guests. These rent for £12 ($19.20) per person, including a Scottish breakfast. Since the house is midway along the footpaths of Scotland's Southern Upland Way, many of the overnight guests are hikers and backpackers intent on seeing rural Scotland at its best. À la carte dinners cost from £8 ($12.80), while bar lunches go for £4 ($6.40). Yarrow trout, fresh salmon, and Scottish steaks are specialties. The inn does not receive overnight guests from the beginning of November to the beginning of February.

YARROW: This hamlet is the site of a historic hotel (see below). The village is situated amid the rolling Border hills at the intersection of the A708 and B709 roads, lying only yards from the River Yarrow. Many find it an ideal place for an angling or walking holiday. Fishing can be enjoyed in the rivers Yarrow and Ettrick, and in nearby St. Mary's Loch, for which permits can be obtained at your hotel.

The Gordon Arms (tel. 0750/82222). This very isolated hotel benefits from its reputation as the meeting place of Sir Walter Scott and the Ettrick Bard, James Hogg. Roadside traffic is generally light, but occasionally the inn will host a bus-tour group, bringing crowds of people into its dining room. Fixed-price lunches cost from £5.50 ($8.80). Rooms are pleasantly comfortable, with B&B costing £11 ($17.60) to £13 ($20.80) per person. Half board is priced at £16 ($25.60) to £21 ($33.60) per person. In chilly weather, a blaze in a coal-burning fireplace keeps things cozy.

ETTRICKBRIDGE: The name comes from a bridge which was built by Sir Walter Scott of Harden in 1628. The bridge is no longer there, having been replaced by another one in 1780. However, the Scott coat-of-arms can still be seen on the upstream side of the parapet. The two alehouses that James Hogg knew have long vanished. As compensation, however, you can stay at one of the most charming places in the Borders (see below).

Ettrickshaws Country House Hotel, Ettrickbridge, by Selkirk (tel. 0750/52229). You'll cross a metal bridge above a gravel-bottomed river before pulling up to this elegant country hotel. The white stucco and red sandstone facade was built by a local mill owner in 1891. The row of lime trees he planted then are now more than 80 feet tall, partially shading the impeccably maintained house and the wooded acres surrounding it. Inside there are hundreds of personalized touches, ranging from the paneling to the coal-burning fireplaces capped with carved mantelpieces. This is one of my favorite retreats in the region, partly because of its allegiance to the architectural style of its day. The owners, Terry and Shirley Ashton, stress such traditional Scottish dishes as salmon, beef, venison, and game. With dinner and breakfast included, high season rates are £35 ($56) per person, dropping to £30 ($48) per person off-season.

6. Innerleithen

Most visitors know its chief sight, Traquair House, better than they do the town itself. Lying a few miles east of Peebles, Innerleithen is a modest little mill town. The unmarred beauty of the River Tweed valley as seen from the town's surrounding hillsides remains constant.

The Ballantyne cashmeres are manufactured here, and annual games and a Cleikum ceremony take place in July. Scott's novel, *St. Ronan's Well,* is identified with the town.

FOOD AND LODGING: A small border-town hostelry, **Traquair Arms Hotel** (tel. 0896/830229) was built as a coaching inn around 1780 and has later Victorian additions. It was an ideal resting place for nobility en route to Traquair House. Hugh and Marian Anderson offer a warm and friendly Scottish welcome to their hotel, where open fires await you in the bar lounge, and the dining room, decorated in subtle pastels, has fresh flowers daily to enhance the pleasant surroundings. You can relax to enjoy dinner from the à la carte or steakhouse menus. If you prefer less formal dining, choose from the extensive bar meal menu. Vegetarian and special diets can be arranged. All dishes are freshly prepared on the premises by the chef/proprietor and his staff. The Andersons also offer bedrooms with baths, tea/coffee-making facilities, and views over the valley. B&B costs £16 ($25.60) per person. The hotel is within a five-minute walk of the River Tweed, and salmon and trout fishing can be arranged for guests.

Tighnuilt House (tel. 0896/830491) is a large country house in the Tweed valley. Activities include hill rambles and forest walks, golf on local courses, river and still-water fishing, and pony trekking. Tighnuilt is a family-run guest-house with home-cooking and a friendly atmosphere offering facilities for 15 guests. All rooms contain wash basins and open onto beautiful views over the Tweed valley. Rooms include three large family units. B&B costs from £14 ($22.40) per person daily, and an evening meal costs from £9 ($14.40) per person. The house is surrounded by lovely gardens and woodland, and your hosts are Robin and Margaret Mayhew.

TRAQUAIR HOUSE: Traquair is considered the oldest inhabited and most romantic house in Scotland. Dating back to the tenth century, it is rich in associations with Mary Queen of Scots and the Jacobite risings. Its treasures include glass, embroideries, silver, manuscripts, and paintings. Of particular interest is a brewhouse equipped as it was two centuries ago and still used regularly. The great house is lived in by the Stuarts of Traquair. There are craft workshops to be seen in the grounds with working artisans creating pottery, woodwork, candlemaking, painting, and silkscreen printing. The house and grounds are open from the Monday before Easter until the third Sunday in October, daily from 1:30 to 5:30 p.m. During July, August, and the first two weeks in September, hours are 10:30 a.m. to 5:30 p.m., with last admittance at 5 p.m. Rates are £2.20 ($3.52) for adults, £1.10 ($1.76) for children. To make inquiries, telephone 0896/830323. Special events are held on most weekends from July to early September.

7. Peebles

This royal burgh and county town, 23 miles from Edinburgh, is a market center in the Valley of the Tweed. Scottish kings used to come here when they went to hunt in Ettrick Forest. The town is noted for its large woolen mills. Peebles is also known as a "writer's town." Sir John Buchan (Baron Tweedsmuir), the Scottish author and statesman who died in 1940 and is remembered chiefly for writing the Stevensonian adventure story *Prester John* in 1910, lived here. He was also the author of *The Thirty-Nine Steps* (1915), the first of a highly successful series of secret-service thrillers. In 1935 he was appointed Governor-general of Canada. Robert Louis Stevenson once lived at Peebles, and drew upon the surrounding countryside in *Kidnapped*, which was published in 1886.

FOOD AND LODGING: Built in 1693, the **Cross Keys Hotel,** Northgate (tel. 0721/20748), lays claim to being one of the oldest inns in Scotland. Originally it was erected as a town house for William Williamson of Cardrona (his initials can be seen in the roof tiles), and after its conversion it became an important link in the Edinburgh–London stagecoach route. It'll be known to lovers of the novels of Sir Walter Scott, who stayed here and wrote about it in his books. Much of the original character remains in the interior. There are two excellent bars, with trestle tables, Windsor chairs, and open fireplaces. The dining room has a rounded bay opening onto the garden. There are eight comfortable bedrooms with hot and cold water. B&B costs £19 ($30.40) in a double room, £11.50

($18.40) in a single, including service and VAT. Mrs. Meg Bone, the owner, cooks most of the food, even doing the baking. A dinner costs from £8 ($12.80), and bar lunches and snacks are available. A bistro wine bar, also on the premises, is called the Kings Orchard. Food is served from noon to 2 p.m. and 6 to 10 p.m.

The **Green Tree Hotel,** Eastgate (tel. 0721/20582), was originally a coaching inn, dating back to the early 19th century. It has enough room to provide a good stopover accommodation, adjacent to the public car park and the bus station. Its rear windows open onto a garden, with lawns, gravel paths, and flowering shrubbery. Completely refurbished in 1986, the hotel offers 14 bedrooms, 11 with private baths. For cooler months, there are electric blankets, although the hotel has central heating. The price for B&B is £17.50 ($28), VAT included. High tea is offered for £3.50 ($5.60) and dinner for £9.50 ($15.20). The fully licensed bar serves snacks all day.

Dilkusha Hotel and Restaurant, Chambers Terrace (tel. 0721/20590). Much of the paneling in this house came from India (the former owner was a timber baron who had forests there). The house itself is built of stone and has one of the most beautiful dining rooms in town. John and Isobel McDonald, the owners, rent five rooms to paying guests. Many of them look out over a valley to the imposing church in the center of town. Some of the furniture inside is art nouveau, and many of the sitting rooms contain blazing fireplaces crafted from red marble. Each of the accommodations contains a private bath. Singles rent for £23 ($36.80), while doubles cost £36 ($57.60), with breakfast included. Even if you're not living here, you may want to patronize the place for its food. In the refurbished Laurel Restaurant, with its wood paneling, lunches are served from 12:15 to 2:15 p.m. and dinners from 4:30 to 9 p.m. Prices range from £4.50 ($7.20) to £11.50 ($18.40). The name of this establishment, Dilkusha, means "home of contentment" in Hindi.

Winkston Farm House (tel. 0721/21264) lies two miles out of Peebles on the Peebles–Edinburgh road. It's ideal for those seeking a farmhouse vacation. Run by Mrs. Janice Haydock, it's a lovely old Georgian farmhouse with ten acres of land where chickens run free, sheep graze, and a friendly horse greets you. Mrs. Haydock has one family, one twin, and one double room to rent, and each contains hot and cold running water and shaver points. There is a shower and toilet down the hallway. Bed and a full Scottish breakfast is £9.25 ($14.80) per person nightly. A sitting room contains a color TV and a coal fire, and there is a separate dining room as well.

Horse Shoe Inn, at Eddleston (tel. 07213/225), lies 4½ miles north of Peebles and is one of the finest places for dining in the area. In a rustic setting, you can dine at two different price levels here. The least expensive is The Smiddy Bar, with its tavern atmosphere, which offers meals for £7 ($11.20). The bill of fare is likely to include such dishes as beef bourguignon, chicken curry, and smoked fish pie. If you're flush, you can stake out a table at the more elegant and expensive Restaurant Forge, where meals begin at £12 ($19.20). For that, you get exceptional value here. Good seasonal produce appears in attractively presented dishes which are likely to include prime Scottish steak, roast duck in cranberry sauce, and pheasant with apples and juniperberries in Calvados-flavored cream. Food is served daily from 11:30 a.m. to 2 p.m. and 5 to 10 p.m.; on Sunday from 12:30 to 2:15 p.m. and 6:30 to 10 p.m.

THE SIGHTS: On the north bank of the Tweed stands **Neidpath Castle** (tel. 0721/20333), one mile west of Peebles on the A72 road. This is an early 14th-century L-shape tower house, with a magnificent situation above the river. A rock-cut well and a pit prison are within the 11-foot thick walls. The castle was besieged by Cromwellian forces in 1650, and soon after the Civil War, it was upgraded for 17th-century living. However, by late in the 18th century, it had become more or less a ruin. It is open from the Thursday before Easter until late October from 10 a.m. to 1 p.m. and 2 to 6 p.m. weekdays, from 1 to 6 p.m. on Sunday. Admission is 75p ($1.20) for adults, 25p (40¢) for children.

Kailzie Gardens (tel. 0721/22054), 2½ miles southeast of Peebles on the B7062, is a 17-acre site with a walled garden from 1812. It was restored in modern times and now provides a stunning array of plants, including some 300 varieties of fuchsia. There is a collection of pheasants, waterfowl, and owls, along with a wild garden and a Burnside walk. It is open March to October daily from 11 a.m. to 5:30 p.m., charging an admission of £1 ($1.60) for adults and 35p (56¢) for children.

Dawyck Botanic Garden (tel. 07216/254), lying on the B712, 8 miles southwest of Peebles and about 28 miles from Edinburgh, was given to the nation in 1978. It is run by the Royal Botanic Garden in Edinburgh. The previous owners of the estate were interested in trees, and there is a large variety of mature specimens. Conifers, some of them exceeding 100 feet, provide an impressive backdrop for the many species of flowering shrubs. There is also a fine display of early spring bulbs, plus pleasant woodwalk walks rich in wildlife interest. It is open April to September from 10 a.m. to 5 p.m., charging an admission of 70p ($1.12) per car.

8. More Historic Homes

Within easy reach of most of the tourist destinations described above are two more historic houses which may make you want to extend your stay in the Borders.

THIRLESTANE CASTLE: One of the most imposing country houses of Scotland, Thirlestane Castle at Lauder (tel. 05782/630) overlooks Leader Water, about a half mile from town. If you're coming from Edinburgh, it is 29 miles to the south of the Scottish capital. The castle has been in the ownership of the Lauderdale family since 1218. A T-shaped building, the castle has a keep from around the end of the 16th century. The structure was much altered after Queen Victoria took the throne to begin her long reign. The castle is famed for its stair turrets and its corner towers. The interior rooms are known for their ornamental plaster ceilings, considered the finest in the country from the Restoration period. In the old nurseries, there's a Historic Toy Collection, and a Border Country Life Museum has been installed on the grounds, depicting life in the Borders from prehistoric times until the present. This family home and grounds are open on Easter Sunday and Monday, during May, June, and September on Wednesday, Thursday, and Sunday, and in July and August daily except Saturday. The grounds are open from noon to 6 p.m., the castle and museum from 2 to 5 p.m. Admission to the castle, toy collection, and museum is £2 ($3.20) for adults, £1.50 ($2.40) for children.

MANDERSTON: Some two miles east of Duns on the A6105 stands one of the finest Edwardian houses built in Britain in the classical style. Manderston (tel. 0361/83450) is today the home of Mr. and Mrs. Adrian Palmer. Called the "swan song of the great classical house," it is known for its spectacular silver staircase (the architect was told "to spare no expense"). Stables and a marble dairy surround the property, as well as formal gardens and lakeside walks. It is open from mid-May until the end of September on Thursday and Sunday from 2 to 5:30 p.m. Admission charges are likely to be around £2.20 ($3.52).

EDINBURGH

SCOTLAND HAS OFTEN BEEN COMPARED to a sandwich in that the central belt is considered the meatier part. Within a relatively small compass of land, you can not only visit the capital at Edinburgh but also enjoy such beauty as the Trossachs (the Scottish Lake District), the silver waters of Loch Lomond, or take in the cragginess of Stirling Castle. Central Scotland should be treated as far more than just a gateway to the Highlands.

Edinburgh is often called the fairest city in Europe. While based there, you can take many day trips, such as to the seaside and golfing resort of North Berwick. The Scots suggest you take a "look aboot ye."

From Edinburgh, on the opposite shore of the Firth of Forth, reached by a bridge, the Kingdom of Fife is rich in treasures, Falkland Palace, the hunting retreat of the Stuart kings, and the unspoiled fishing villages along the coast, collectively known as "East Neuk," among them.

But first, before branching out to explore all the major attractions in the environs, in this and the chapters immediately following, we will come up from the Lowlands to pay a call on the Queen herself.

1. Introducing Edinburgh

Scotland's capital city is Edinburgh, off the beaten path for those doing the mad whirlwind tour of Europe, as it lies 373 miles north of London.

The city is associated with John Knox, Mary Queen of Scots, Robert Louis Stevenson, Sir Arthur Conan Doyle (creator of Sherlock Holmes), David Hume, Alexander Graham Bell, Sir Walter Scott, and Bonnie Prince Charlie—to name-drop only a bit.

From the elegant Georgian crescents of the New Town to the dark medieval "wynds" of the Old Town, down the wide, magnificent Princes Street (Stevenson's "liveliest and brightest thoroughfare"), Edinburgh lives up to its reputation as one of the fairest cities in Europe. Of course it's not as sophisticated as Paris, nor as fast-paced as London. And it's banal to call it the Athens of the North, although the Greek Revival movement of the 19th century made many of the buildings look like pagan temples.

What Edinburgh has to offer is unique. It's Scottish (scotch is a drink—so play it safe and refer to the hearty, ruddy-faced people as Scots)—and that means it's different from English. It wasn't sameness that made these two countries fight many a bloody border skirmish.

Most travelers know that since World War II Edinburgh has been the scene of an ever-growing International Festival, with its action-packed list of cultural events. But that shouldn't be your only reason for visiting the ancient seat of Scottish royalty. Its treasures are available all year. In fact the pace the rest of the time, when the festival-hoppers have gone south, is more relaxed. The prices are lowered, and the people themselves, under less pressure as hosts, return to their traditional hospitable nature.

GETTING THERE: Edinburgh is two hours by bus or rail from the major international airport of Scotland, Prestwick, and it lies in the center of most of the rail and bus lines leading from Scotland to England. Edinburgh's airport, connected by frequent 30-minute bus rides to midtown, receives flights only from within the British Isles, Dublin, and Amsterdam.

Most foreign visitors head to Edinburgh from London. The fastest (but not the cheapest) method of transport is by plane. The standard economy fare between London and Edinburgh is £72 ($115.20). However, you can always opt for an APEX ticket, costing £74 ($118.40) round trip, a substantial savings if you plan to return to London after your visit to Scotland. Under the APEX ticket you are required to make payment and reserve at least two weeks in advance. The use of the return portion of the ticket must be within one year of the original departure. APEX tickets can be purchased only for specified flights, usually only those departing either city during non-rush hours.

Edinburgh is also well connected by rail and bus to other points in Britain. The standard second-class round-trip rail fare from London to Edinburgh is £85 ($136), but substantial amounts of money can be saved by booking a special Intercity Saver Ticket in advance. The round-trip fare from London to Edinburgh can be as low as £47 ($75.20) if certain conditions are met. For more information, refer to the "Getting Around Scotland" section in Chapter I.

The least expensive way to go is by bus from London, the trip to Edinburgh taking eight hours and costing £11 ($17.60) one way or £21 ($33.60) for a round-trip ticket.

AN ORIENTATION: Edinburgh is divided into an **Old Town** and a **New Town.** Chances are, you will find lodgings in the New Town and visit the Old Town only for dining, drinking, shopping, or sightseeing.

The New Town, characterized by the world-famous **Princes Street,** came about in the 18th century in what is now known as the "Golden Age of Edinburgh." Everybody from Robert Burns to James Boswell visited Edinburgh in that era. The first building went up in New Town in 1767, and by the end of the century classical squares, streets, and town houses had been added.

Princes Street runs for about a mile, following a straight pattern. It is known for its shopping and also its beauty, as it opens onto the Princes Street Gardens with stunning views of the Old Town.

North of Princes Street, and running parallel to it, is the second great street of New Town, **George Street.** It begins at Charlotte Square and runs east to St. Andrew Square. It was dedicated to George III. Directly north of George Street is another impressive thoroughfare of Edinburgh, **Queen Street,** opening onto Queen Street Gardens on its north side.

In Edinburgh, you also hear a lot about **Rose Street,** which lies directly north of Princes Street. It has more pubs per square block than any other place in Scotland, and is also filled with shops and restaurants.

Everyone, seemingly, has heard of **"The Royal Mile,"** which is the main street of the Old Town. Actually it is not one street, but four. Beginning at Edinburgh Castle, it runs all the way to Holyrood Palace. The mile consists of Castlehill, Lawnmarket, High Street, and Canongate. A famous street which lies to the south of the castle (you have to descend to it) is **Grassmarket,** where convicted criminals were once hung on the dreaded gallows that stood there.

Of course Edinburgh consists of a lot more squares, terraces, crescents, gardens, and streets than those mentioned. Discovering its hidden lanes and branching out to some of its interesting satellite communities will be one of the reasons for coming here.

GETTING AROUND: Edinburgh doesn't benefit from a modern underground (subway to Americans) system, so you'll find that **buses** will probably be your chief method of transport in the Scottish capital. The fare you pay is determined by the distance you ride. The minimum fare is 20p (32¢) for two stops or fewer, and the maximum fare is 60p (96¢) for 18 to 21 stops. Children up to 15 years of age pay reduced fares.

Lothian Region Transport, operators of Edinburgh buses, has devised several types of term bus passes for extended tourist visits to their city. The **Edinburgh Freedom Ticket** allows one day of unlimited travel on city buses at £1.25 ($2) for adults and 65p ($1.04) for children. Another form of extended ticket is a **Tourist Card,** allowing unlimited travel on all city buses for a specified number of days, and special discounts at certain restaurants and for tours of selected historical sites. A two-day TouristCard costs £6.95 ($11.12) for adults and £4.45 ($7.12) for children, and a 13-day TouristCard goes for £20.70 ($33.12) for adults and £11.60 ($18.56) for children.

Finally, for daily commuters or for diehard Scottish enthusiasts, a **RidaCard** season ticket allows unlimited travel on all buses at £5 ($8) for one week, £17.60 ($28.16) for four weeks. Travel must begin on a Sunday.

These tickets and further information may be obtained at the **Waverley Bridge Transport Office,** Waverly Bridge in Edinburgh, or the **Lothian Region Transport Office,** 14 Queen St., Edinburgh EH2 1JL (tel. 031/554-4494).

As a last resort, try hailing a cab or waiting at a taxi stand. Meters begin at 80p ($1.28).

PRACTICAL FACTS: The place to go for emergency problems, such as lost passports, is the **American Consulate** (031/556-8315).

If you've **lost property** (or had it stolen) go to the Police Headquarters at Fettes Avenue (tel. 031/331-3131). However, in an emergency, call the **police** at 999. Use that same number in calling for an **ambulance** or reporting a **fire.**

In a **medical emergency,** you can seek help from the Edinburgh Royal Infirmary, Lauriston Place (tel. 031/229-2477).

To get your **prescription** filled, go to Boots The Chemist, 48 Shandwick Pl. (tel. 031/225-6757). Hours are weekdays from 8:45 a.m. to 9 p.m. and on Sunday from 11 a.m. to 4:30 p.m.

For a **dental problem,** go to the Dental Surgery School, 31 Chambers St. (tel. 031/225-9511). Hours are 9 to 10:15 a.m. and 2 to 3:15 p.m.

Shopping hours for most Edinburgh shops include only a half day on Wednesday. The bigger stores along Princes Street are open all day Wednesday, however. Nearly all stores are closed on Sunday. Most shops are open from 9 a.m. to 5:30 p.m. Many shops remain open on Thursday night until 8 p.m.

Banking hours in Edinburgh are usually Monday through Wednesday from

9:30 a.m. to 12:30 p.m. and 1:30 to 3:30 p.m. On Thursday, hours are 9:30 a.m. to 12:30 p.m., and 1:30 to 3:30 p.m., and also 4:30 to 6 p.m. On Friday, hours are 9:30 a.m. to 3:30 p.m. There is a Bureau de Change of the Clydesdale Bank at 5 Waverley Bridge and at Waverley Market.

In Edinburgh, the head **post office** is at 2–4 Waterloo Pl., and it's open Monday to Friday from 9 a.m. to 5:30 p.m., on Saturday to 12:30 p.m.

Edinburgh is a city of **churches.** If you're Catholic, you can attend St. Mary's Metropolitan Cathedral, Broughton Street (tel. 031/556-3339). The Scottish Episcopal Church is represented at St. Mary's Cathedral, Palmerston Place (tel. 031/225-6293). Baptists can worship at Bristo Church, Buckingham Terrace (tel. 031/332-3682), and the Hebrew congregation meets at the Synagogue at 4 Salisbury Rd. (tel. 031/667-3144). There is also a Methodist church, Central Halls, at Tollcross (tel. 031/229-7937).

American Express has an office at 139 Princes St. (tel. 031/225-7881).

For **tourist information,** go to 5 Waverley Bridge (tel. 031/226-6591).

For a **launderette,** go to The Automatic, 38 Comely Bank Pl. (tel. 031/-332-6830).

2. Where to Stay

Searching for a suitable hotel isn't too difficult in Edinburgh, as the city offers a full range of accommodations at different price levels throughout the year. However, during the three-week period of the festival, the establishments fill up with international visitors, so it's prudent to reserve in advance. To take care of emergency lodging all year, the **Edinburgh Tourist Centre,** Waverley Market, 3 Princes St. (tel. 031/557-2727), compiles a well-investigated and lengthy list of small hotels and guesthouses that provide B&B for as little as £8.50 ($13.60) per person. Guesthouses in this latter category may have only one to three bedrooms per household to rent. The bureau's hours during the peak season, May 1 to September 30, are 8:30 a.m. to 8 p.m. Monday through Saturday, and from 11 a.m. to 8 p.m. on Sunday (open till 9 p.m. during July and August). A 75p ($1.20) booking fee is charged. There's also an information and accommodation desk at Edinburgh Airport, with a telephone link to the center. It's open according to the frequency of incoming flights.

You can write in advance, enclosing your requirements and the fee, but you should allow about four weeks' notice, especially during the summer and particularly during the festival weeks.

Assuming you arrive in Edinburgh when the hotels aren't fully booked or that you will reserve a room in advance, I've prepared a representative sampling of the leading candidates in our budget range.

EAST OF PRINCES STREET: A substantial Georgian house, **Greenside Hotel,** 9 Royal Terrace (tel. 031/557-0022), owned by Dorothy and David Simpson, is furnished with a number of antique pieces to give it the right spirit. There are singles (one with private bath), doubles (three with their own plumbing), twins, and a family room, 13 spacious units in all, each centrally heated and all with hot and cold water. They rent for £16 ($25.60) to £23 ($36.80) per person, including VAT. The Simpsons have provided a color TV set in their lounge, where they also serve coffee. Most guests approve of the full breakfast with enthusiasm. The terrace is quiet, and the hotel lies only a five-minute walk from the city center. The Simpsons are proud that their building has been described as being of "historical architectural interest." The beautiful circular staircase is the only way up to the third floor, so be prepared to carry your luggage. Overnight parking is available.

Angusbeag Guest House, 5 Windsor St. (tel. 031/556-1905). Elma Dickson

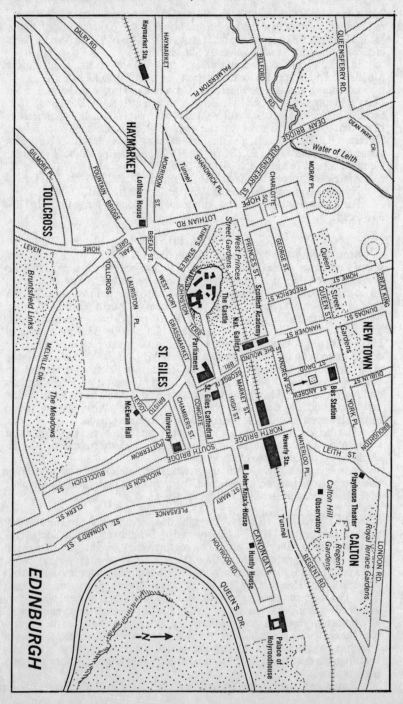

is the creative force behind this immaculately clean, terraced property. Translated from the Gaelic as "little Angus," the establishment is housed in a 160-year-old Georgian building whose hall ceilings are beautifully molded in shades of Wedgwood blue and green. Only three rooms are available for rental, and they are priced at £12 ($19.20) per person daily, including breakfast. Mrs. Dickson, who in her own words is "an ambassador for Scotland," prepares ample breakfasts for each of her guests which she serves in the TV room and lounge. From Princes Street, take bus 4, 44, or 15. As soon as the bus turns into London road, get off at the first stop.

Claymore Hotel, 6 Royal Terrace (tel. 031/556-2693), is owned by Fiona and Mike Pirie who welcome guests to their family-run hotel on one of the most beautiful terraces in Edinburgh. Their well-run B&B is a few minutes' walk from Princes Street, Waverley Station, and the bus station. The hotel has ten bedrooms, all with showers, color TV, and beverage facilities, with adequate baths and toilets separately located. The price for a bed and a full Scottish breakfast ranges from £14 ($22.40) per person. There is a residents' lounge and a comfortable lounge bar.

NEAR THE HAYMARKET: Pleasantly situated in a quiet crescent, the **Adam Hotel,** 19 Lansdowne Crescent (tel. 031/337-1148), is within a few minutes of Princes Street. Its Georgian style is intact, a gracious place for an Edinburgh stay. Mr. and Mrs. Morley own and manage it, and have provided many comforts, including central heating. All the nine bedrooms have color TV, radios, innerspring mattresses, and plentiful hot water, and they're nicely decorated. The room rate is £13.50 ($21.60) to £14 ($22.40) per person, the latter price for a room with shower. Good breakfasts cooked by Mrs. Morley and served to guests by Mr. Morley are included in the rates.

Grosvenor Guest House, 1 Grosvenor Gardens (tel. 031/337-4143), is a handsomely kept, well-taken-care-of Edwardian town house that is suitable for those who like to be within walking distance of most of the attractions in the heart of Edinburgh, including Princes Street. Despite its heartbeat location off Haymarket, the house is in a tranquil area. Only seven rooms are rented by John Gray, and they are comfortably furnished and beautifully maintained, costing from £15 ($24) in a single and from £25 ($40) to £30 ($48) in a double, the latter with private bath. Only two of these chambers contain private plumbing, and these are likely to be grabbed up first. There is also a trio of family rooms where children sharing with their parents are granted a reduction. On cool nights (and there are a lot of them in Edinburgh) electric blankets are provided. A full Scottish breakfast served in the communal dining room is included in the rate, and guests can also relax and read in a large lounge.

West End Hotel, 35 Palmerston Pl. (tel. 031/225-3656), is a privately owned and inviting B&B house, where Donald Parker welcomes you. He offers a relaxed and friendly atmosphere. The B&B rate is £16 ($25.60) per person inclusive, and lunches and dinners can be arranged. The bedrooms are comfortably furnished, and each unit has hot and cold running water, electric heater and kettle, radio, and TV.

Clifton Private Hotel, 1 Clifton Terrace (tel. 031/337-1002), lies near Haymarket Station, just opposite the Hearts Memorial on Clifton Terrace, a westward extension of Princes Street. But it isn't proximity to major sights that makes this such a top-notch hotel. It's the friendliness and home-cooking you'll be treated to here. The proprietors, Mr. and Mrs. J. Guthrie, accept B&B guests for £12 ($19.20). All rooms have hot and cold running water, and there are free baths or showers, plus plenty of towels daily. A vending machine is available for hot drinks. Biscuits are also on sale. In addition, there is an inexpensive evening meal at 5:30 p.m., a high tea for £4 ($6.40). That means a main meat course, followed by home baking—fruit-pie goodie and Scottish scones. You'll see how clean Scottish homes can be, if you stay here.

Lairg Private Hotel, 11 Coates Gardens (tel. 031/337-1050). Everything about this place evokes Victorian-era Scotland, except for its modern-minded owner, who happens to be from Italy. Rimini-born Umberto Salucci, the owner and chef, provides well-prepared dinners for his guests whenever they request it at a cost of £6 ($9.60) per meal. A few of his establishment's 11 rooms are very large, suitable for up to five persons. The stone house has ornate plaster ceilings, wide moldings, and a beautiful stairwell. Throughout the year it provides comfortable lodgings, except for brief periods when it's filled with visiting rugby players from Wales. Per-person rates, depending on the season, range from £13 ($20.80) to £16 ($25.60) with breakfast included.

Mrs. Margaret B. Bostock, 12 Clifton Terrace (tel. 031/337-5785), continues to be a favorite with readers. The landlady quickly becomes "Margaret" to her satisfied guests. The location of her Victorian house is across from the old Haymarket Station, about a five-minute walk west from Princes Street. For £12 ($19.20) per person nightly, she'll rent you an attractive bedroom, often with twin beds, and perhaps an Adam ceiling. A wee tap on the door and in pops Mrs. Bostock with a tray of coffee (or tea), along with teacakes served on her beautiful bone china. Each morning a Scottish breakfast, fit fortification for the day, is served on Royal Albert china in her charming dining room. You get friendly chatter and good touring advice. But most important of all, you get comfortable beds and a good night's sleep.

St. Valery Guest House, 36 Coates Gardens (tel. 031/337-1893), has long been a reader favorite in the past, managed by the Donaldsons who maintain high standards. Rooms are spread across two floors, and each is pleasantly furnished, containing hot and cold running water. The charge is £12.50 ($20) per person for B&B, and a full breakfast, included in the rates, is served in a cozy front room. If you wish, a hairdresser can come to your room, and there is a photographer available if you'd like your stay at the St. Valery recorded on film. The location is central.

NEAR ROYAL CIRCUS: In a quiet area of Edinburgh but convenient for Princes Street, **St. Bernard's Guesthouse,** 22 St. Bernard's Crescent (tel. 031/332-2339), is an immaculate and tastefully decorated Victorian house. The 11 bedrooms rented by Jake Sangster, the manager, all have hot and cold water basins and color TV. They rent for £11 ($17.60) to £13 ($20.80) per person for B&B. The morning meal, cooked by Mr. Sangster, is a big one. Buses 34 and 35 will take you downtown, but it is only about a 15-minute walk to the main shopping area.

SOUTH OF UNION CANAL: An elegant converted Victorian house, **Orwell Lodge Hotel,** 29 Polwarth Terrace (tel. 031/229-1044), stands in its own grounds and provides ample parking space. It is serviced by regular public transport with bus stops to and from the city at the entrance to the grounds. It is also conveniently situated for visits to places of historical interest in the city and is within easy reach of theaters, cinemas, sports grounds, and golf courses. The hotel is centrally heated and presents a choice of single, double, and twin-bedded rooms. Each unit has its own tea- and coffee-making facilities and is fitted with intercom, radio, and color TV. Showers are installed in twin and double rooms. Under the personal supervision of Moira Glendinning, the hotel provides a friendly family atmosphere, good traditional Scottish home cooking, and a well-trained and attentive staff. The charge of £13 ($20.80) per person per night includes a full Scottish breakfast. All other meals and snacks (morning coffee, lunch, afternoon tea, high tea, dinner, and packed meals) are available at reasonable prices. The hotel offers a small but select wine list. Service and VAT are included in the prices quoted.

Quinton Lodge, 24 Polwarth Terrace (tel. 031/229-4100). This stone-fronted Victorian house is set on three-fourths of an acre of walled-in gardens. The interior of the establishment has a scattering of antiques, an entrance hall set with stained glass, and ornately detailed gilded cornices. Bruno Diciacca has hot-beverage facilities and hot and cold water basins in each of his seven bedrooms. B&B costs from £13 ($20.80) per person. The lodge is about a ten-minute bus ride from Waverley Station (take bus no. 9, 10, or 27, and get off at Orville Lodge Hotel).

Lindsay Guest House, 108 Polwarth Terrace (tel. 031/337-1580). Longtime Edinburghers Carol and Jimmy King are the owners of this fine Victorian house. Each of the sandstone-fronted buildings on the street was constructed for 19th-century mill owners and merchants. Today the Lindsay House is one of the few that hasn't been subdivided into apartments. From the garden, guests can spot canoeists gliding down the Union Canal whose waters run beside the property. The house has been redecorated, and its ornate plaster ceilings highlighted in pastel colors to match the carpeting. Each of the bedrooms contains a color TV and tea-making equipment, and comes with breakfast included in the price. Per-person rates run £14 ($22.40) in a twin-bedded room and £26 ($41.60) in a single. To get there, take bus 9, 10, or 27 from Princes Street and get off at Ashley Terrace, a few steps from the hotel.

Robertson Guest House, 5 Hartington Gardens (tel. 031/229-3862), is a century-old Victorian guesthouse crafted from stone. It contains a front and back garden, plus seven comfortable rooms maintained in functional working order by Thomas and Doreen Sewall. Each has a TV and hot and cold running water. A few have a private shower as well. Depending on the plumbing, B&B rates range from £11 ($17.60) to £14 ($22.40) per person nightly.

Granville Guest House, 13 Granville Terrace (tel. 031/229-1676). Mrs. Bee Archibald has been the subject of many favorable readers' letters over the years. Her traditionally styled guesthouse has a stone facade, a front stoop flanked with iron railings, and an old-fashioned kind of Scottish warmth. There are many fireplaces scattered throughout her establishment, but there is central heating also. Each room has TV. A visit with Mrs. Archibald often provides memories of huge Scottish breakfasts and a vivid personality. Her seven rooms, each bathless, rent for £11 ($17.60) per person in a twin and £12 ($19.20) in a single. Towels are changed daily. The establishment is within walking distance for some of the heart of Edinburgh; others, however, will prefer to take bus 9, 10, or 27, getting off at Viewforth or Polwarth.

INVERLEITH: North of Princes Street near the Royal Botanic Garden stands a landmark building which accepts paying guests.

Eight Howard Place at the same address (tel. 031/556-4900), was the birthplace of Robert Louis Stevenson, who was born there in 1850. It is one of the special B&Bs of Edinburgh, but it has only two double rooms to rent. These cost from £16 ($25.60) per person nightly. One of the rooms has a private shower. Built in 1820 as a Georgian terrace house, it is open from April to October only. One of the rentable rooms on the ground floor was the chamber in which the famed author was born. The house has a scattering of Sheraton antiques, high ceilings, and moldings. It's owned by Mr. and Mrs. John Mirylees. His family has owned the house since 1927. The location is five blocks north of Princes Street.

ON THE MAIN A7 ROUTE SOUTH: Newington Road/Mayfield Gardens/ Minto Street form the continuation of the North Bridge from Princes Street, being the main A7 route to the south. If you find yourself on Dalkeith Road, running parallel to Minto Street, this is a secondary road, forming the A68 route to the south.

Suffolk Hall Hotel, 10 Craigmillar Park (tel. 031/667-9328), is an impressive yellow-brick Victorian mansion standing on a corner with a quiet garden. The owners, George and Mary Robertson, take a sincere interest in the comfort of their guests. They've decorated the entire house stylishly. There is a cocktail lounge as well as a living room lounge with color TV. In the dining room you can have breakfast, lunch, or dinner. All bedrooms have a radio, color TV, direct-dial phones, and hot-beverage-makers, and most have private baths. Rates are £22 ($35.20) in a bathless single, £28 ($44.80) in a single with bath. Doubles cost £30 ($48) to £40 ($64), depending on the plumbing. All tariffs include breakfast, service, and VAT. The hotel is centrally heated.

Kirtle House, 8 Minto St. (tel. 031/667-2813), is run by Mr. and Mrs. McGlashan, a friendly and pleasant couple, who welcome you to their address a short bus ride from Princes Street. Theirs is a Georgian-style, semi-detached terrace house built in 1819, with a total of seven bedrooms that are comfortable, have adequate heat, showers, and are clean. B&B ranges from £13 ($20.80) to £16 ($25.60) per person, depending on the plumbing. The McGlashans serve a breakfast that is abundant and satisfying.

A warm and comfortable guesthouse, **Hamilton House,** 12 Moston Terrace (tel. 031/667-2540), is in a quiet location, about 1½ miles from the city center. The house, operated by John and Gill Hamilton, offers pleasant rooms with hot and cold water basins and central heating. They rent for £10 ($16) to £15 ($24) per person for B&B. Evening meals are available on request, and you can arrange for light snacks at other times.

Kildonan Lodge Hotel, 27 Craigmillar Park (tel. 031/667-2793). Bill Ross, the owner of this century-old Victorian house, rents nine bathless rooms to visitors. The centrally heated establishment contains a residents' cocktail bar, plus a restaurant where a good dinner is served at a fixed price of £6 ($9.60). Rooms are comfortable and pleasantly furnished, costing £13.50 ($21.60) to £15.50 ($24.80) per person, with breakfast included.

Kingsley Guest House, 30 Craigmillar Park (tel. 031/667-8439). Wilma and Bill Hogg are the genial hosts of this pleasant seven-room guest house on the south side of town. The 100-year-old stone building is flanked by a small garden, a car park, a visitors' lounge, and a pine staircase. Scottish nights of exhibition music and dancing can be arranged for guests by Wilma ("we're the natives, although we don't wear kilts"). All bedrooms have hot and cold water basins and rent for £9.50 ($15.20) to £12 ($19.20) per person. For this, you get a comfortable bed, breakfast, and a "Scottish welcome." No meals other than breakfast are served. A color TV lounge is inviting.

NEWINGTON: The following guesthouse recommendations lie within the central belt of Edinburgh, and most of them are only 1½ miles from Princes Street. Newington is by far the most densely populated hotel and guesthouse area in the city, originally having been built as large detached residences some 145 years ago.

Ashdene Guest House, 23 Fountainhall Rd. (tel. 031/667-6026), is a Victorian house on three floors, in a quiet place, ten minutes by bus from the city center. All rooms are furnished to a high standard and have TV, hot and cold running water, central heating, and electric fires. Hot beverage facilities are provided in each room, along with electric shaver points. Ironing equipment is also available. All rooms have showers, and some have private toilets. The price, including a substantial Scottish breakfast, is £13 ($20.80) to £16 ($25.60) per person (the latter with private baths), and dinner can be arranged for guests making advance bookings. Mr. and Mrs. Daulby take pleasure in welcoming their visitors and will help plan trips to other parts of Scotland for anyone requesting assistance. Help with accommodations in other parts of Scotland can also be arranged.

Newington Guest House, 18 Newington Rd. (tel. 031/667-3356), takes you into the world of Mr. and Mrs. Bouchet. It's one of the special little B&B guesthouse establishments of Edinburgh, and deserves to be better known. Jeanne Bouchet, whose husband is French, has traveled far and wide, and their house reflects their interest. From Japan and the South Pacific, they returned with souvenirs and mementos of their journey. The house is warmed by their collection. Each of their eight bedrooms is attractively decorated, often using cane and wickerwork, along with flowery wallpaper and fabrics. Some rooms are big enough for families to rent. Rates are £15 ($24) in a single and from £11.50 ($18.40) to £13.50 ($21.60) per person in a double, depending on the plumbing and including a generous Scottish breakfast (and that means porridge).

International Guest House, 37 Mayfield Gardens (tel. 031/667-2511), in the Newington sector, is a Victorian guesthouse that is a "secret address" to many Scots themselves who live in those drafty manor houses and occasionally come into the capital for a visit. George and Rita Coleman have converted the town house into one of the most recommendable guesthouses in the city. Their living room, for example, is very much like that in a private home. You're invited to lounge and read there, or socialize with your fellow guests. Only seven bedrooms are offered, and each is comfortable and attractively furnished. Six of the accommodations contain full private facilities en suite (a seventh room has its own bath, but it's not connected to the unit). Mr. and Mrs. Coleman charge from £16 ($25.60) in a single and from £27 ($43.20) to £32 ($51.20) in a double, including a full Scottish breakfast. Tea or coffee along with crackers are provided before you retire.

Thrums Private Hotel, 14 Minto St. (tel. 031/667-5545), takes the fictional name of J.M. Barrie's designation of his hometown of Kirriemuir. The proprietors, Mr. and Mrs. Maloney, run an exceptionally friendly establishment with a helpful staff. The hotel has seven bedrooms, several of which have private facilities. All the rooms have hot and cold water, color TV, radios, hot-beverage facilities, and electric blankets. Prices start at £15 ($24) in a single, rising to £32 ($51.20) in a double with private bath. Family rooms are also available. The tariffs include a full Scottish breakfast, VAT, and service. The hotel operates an à la carte restaurant for lunches and dinners, prices for a three-course meal ranging from £4 ($6.40) to £12 ($19.20). Sandwiches and light snacks are also available, and residents can order drinks. Good fresh produce is used in preparation of meals. The Thrums is centrally heated and has a peaceful garden and private car park.

Sonas Guest House, 3 East Mayfield (tel. 031/667-2781). Translated from the Gaelic, the name of this establishment means "peaceful happiness." That is what Irene and Dennis Robins try to create in their high-ceilinged stone house on the south side of town. Built in 1876, the building has a small garden both in front and back. Eight comfortable rooms are rented, costing £11 ($17.60) to £13 ($20.80) per person nightly, with breakfast included. Partly because they have two daughters, they welcome children. To get there, take bus 3 or 31, getting off at Minto Street.

Gifford Guest House, 103 Dalkeith Rd. (tel. 031/667-4688). Sports lovers will appreciate the proximity of this pleasant guesthouse to the Olympic-size Commonwealth Pool and its related sports facilities. John and Helen McBride are the animal-loving owners of this place, and they offer a warm welcome to incoming guests. Three rooms have color TV and showers, and all have hot beverage equipment. Rooms rent for £10 ($16) to £12 ($19.20) per person, either single or double occupancy depending on the season. The guesthouse lies about a mile from Princes Street and can be reached by bus 14, 21, or 33. There's private parking.

Rosedene Guest House, 4 Queen's Crescent (tel. 031/667-5806), stands in a lovely southside neighborhood on a curved street where a central park is shared communally by the residents. This 1850 detached Victorian house contains beautifully molded ceilings and a scattering of antiques. There's even a small garden in front with flowerbeds. There are nine comfortable rooms, one of which has private bath facilities. Lena and Tony Gallo charge from £10 ($16) per person nightly, with a full breakfast included. From Princes Street (on the shop side), you can take bus 3 or 31, getting off outside the Don-Maree Hotel.

42 Mayfield Road (tel. 031/667-3117). One of the most memorable landladies in Edinburgh operates a fine rose-covered guesthouse in her three-story, semi-detached stone house. It was built in 1879, and has been well-maintained and even somewhat modernized since it was taken over by Mrs. Prue Morris and her Welsh husband, Jack. There is a scattering of antiques ("nothing fancy") in the public rooms, and a pot of tea which is ready for brewing practically at any hour of the day. Mrs. Morris serves a generous breakfast, and her friendliness has been the subject of many a reader's report. Her five bedrooms rent for £10.50 ($16.80) per person nightly, including breakfast and access to the front and rear gardens.

Rowan Guest House, 13 Glenorchy Terrace (tel. 031/668-2191). Alan and Angelia Vidler are the owners of this semi-detached Victorian stone house on the south side of town. The pleasantly furnished interior contains a scattering of Victorian and Edwardian furniture, and the nine comfortably furnished bedrooms rent for £13 ($20.80) per person, with breakfast included. There's a TV for the use of guests in a room where breakfast is served, as well as a front and back garden. Tea and coffee are available free 24 hours a day. To get there, take bus 3, 31, 7, 8, or 37 from Princes Street, getting off at Bright's Crescent.

Clarin Guest House, 4 East Mayfield (tel. 031/667-2433). Anna and Carmine Franzese, the owners of this friendly guesthouse were born in Italy, but their children now speak with a Scottish burr. Together they maintain this stone-fronted Victorian house with a small garden in front. Each of their comfortably furnished double rooms contains a color TV, tea-making equipment, and a simple decor. Depending on the season, the charge for B&B is £10 ($16) to £14 ($19.20) per person. There are no single rooms—only twins, doubles, and family accommodations. Some have private showers.

Rimswell House, 33-35 Mayfield Gardens (tel. 031/667-5851), is a well-decorated family house built a century ago. It is owned and run by Peter Fraser, who charges £10.50 ($16.80) to £14.50 ($23.20) per person, depending on the season. Prices include a full Scottish breakfast.

MURRAYFIELD: In the West End residential section, **Ross Private Hotel,** 2 Murrayfield Ave. (tel. 031/337-4060), is a large Victorian house with bay windows, gables, and chimneys, the domain of the cheerful and friendly owner, Jean Tulloch. Informality prevails here. Each of her nicely furnished bedrooms has hot and cold water, and there's a bathroom on each floor. All is centrally heated, and there are tea- and coffee-making facilities in each unit. Including breakfast, the daily rate ranges from £10 ($16) to £11 ($17.60) per person. Mrs.

Tullich's guests like to congregate in the TV lounge nightly. During the day they enjoy the open view south to the Pentland Hills. Car parking is available in front of the hotel.

    Clans Hotel, 4 Magdala Crescent (tel. 031/337-6301). The stone facade of this small hotel is on a quiet street, overlooking the lush gardens of the Donaldson School for the Deaf on a road to the Murrayfield Rugby Ground. Its interior is filled with old and comfortable furniture, not especially antique, but well used and pleasant. The seven rooms rent for £15 ($24) in a bathless single, £25 ($40) in a bathless double, and £30 ($48) in a double with bath, including breakfast.

NORTH OF HOLYROOD PARK: A good bet for a family is the **Alexander Hotel,** 21 Spring Gardens (tel. 031/661-1157), outside the center of Edinburgh, but still convenient to public transportation. The B&B house lies north of Holyrood Park, with its famous Arthur's Seat. Anne Goodlet and her husband, James, who was a pattern maker, own the hotel and have refurnished it from top to bottom. All of the seven accommodations contain color TV and are immaculately kept and comfortable, costing from £14 ($22.40) in a single and from £13.50 ($21.60) per person in a double. The Scottish breakfast is hearty fare that will fortify you for the day.

NEAR PRESTONFIELD: On the south side of the city in a quiet residential section near famous old Prestonfield House, the **Dorstan Private Hotel, 7** Priestfield Rd. (tel. 031/667-6721), is an unlicensed family-run hotel offering modern comfort and convenience behind a 19th-century facade. Iain and Mairae Campbell welcome you and your family, housing you in comfortable rooms, most with baths or showers, phones, TV, and hot-beverage facilities. They charge £13 ($20.80) to £17 ($27.20) per person. The hotel is centrally heated. It lies about ten minutes from the city center and is near Queens Park.

    Millfield Guest House, 12 Marchhall Rd. (tel. 031/667-4428). This large, semi-detached sandstone house is well situated on the residential south side of Edinburgh. The interior is filled with period furnishings, Victorian accents, and lots of cozy comfort, plus several sunny bay windows. The house is owned by Charles and Elizabeth Broomfield. Breakfasts are likely to include helpings of homemade brown bread, porridge, and fruit juice. Depending on the season, per-person rates range from £9.50 ($15.20) to £11 ($17.60). Water lovers will appreciate the proximity to the Royal Commonwealth Swimming Pool, a short distance away. To get to Millfield, take bus 21 or 33 from Princes Street and get off on Dalkeith Road.

    Ardenair, 29 Kilmaurs Rd. (tel. 031/668-2336). Part of the allure of this place comes from its array of well-seasoned furniture collected by Jill and Douglas McLennan as part of their antique business. The 80-year-old Victorian house is very much a family place, complete with birthday parties for the McLennan daughters, Susie and Jennifer. Some guests consider that the morning breakfast is one of the highlights of their stay in Edinburgh. Jill's mother, Mrs. Mann, prepares homemade scones to accompany the full Scottish repasts served with a smile. The back garden of this southside house borders the park of Holyrood Castle. Guests are invited to climb to the roof for a closer look at the castle, particularly during any special events staged there. The McLennans rent three doubles. With breakfast included, the cost ranges from £11 ($17.60) per person. Since the rooms are rented to students during term time, they are available to tourists from mid-March to mid-April and mid-December to mid-January. To get to Ardenair, take bus 33, 21, 14, or 49 from Waverley Station or from Princes Street.

PORTOBELLO: In East Edinburgh, Portobello opens onto the Firth of Forth and is linked by good bus connections to the center of the city. It is also known for its Portobello Golf Course (public). One of the best B&Bs in this section is **Hopebank,** 33 Hope Lane (tel. 031/657-1149). Mrs. Jane Williamson runs this stone-built Victorian villa, with both a front and rear garden. She offers a total of five comfortably furnished bedrooms, three of which have private showers. The rate is £12 ($19.20) per person in a room with a shower, £11 ($17.60) per person if bathless. Mrs. Williamson's well-decorated house and hospitality are in character with her personality. Breakfasts are expansive. You help yourself to Scottish oatcakes and marmalade and jams she makes herself, along with sausage and eggs. This establishment is about a 20-minute bus ride from the center (take bus 15, 26, or 86). Officially, it is open only from April to September, but Mrs. Williams might take you out of season if you phone in advance.

JOPPA: An attractive century-old stone house, the **Stra'ven Guest House,** 3 Brunstane Rd. North (tel. 031/669-5580), belongs to a charming and able couple, Mr. and Mrs. Grant. They pride themselves on their Scottish hospitality and enjoy receiving guests. Their centrally heated house lies only 15 minutes by bus from the center of the city (nos. 15, 26, and 89). If you catch the no. 86 bus on Princes Street, it will take you to Joppa Road, which connects with the blocklong Brunstane Road, a cul-de-sac leading to the water. In season, the B&B rate is £9 ($14.40) per person based on double occupancy, £10 ($16) in a single. All the bedrooms contain hot and cold running water and tea/coffee-making facilities, as well as color TV. They also have a small kitchen for the use of guests. One of their sons plays the bagpipes and is in demand not only to play for their guests but to photograph them with the pipes. The Grants are proud of the view from their windows: the neighboring stone-gabled houses, the cut-flower garden against a stone wall—and best of all, the nearby beach. They have been known to go on picnics with their guests or to take them for 18 holes of golf. But they can't stay away too long, as they do their own cooking, preparing those tasty dishes for which Scotland is so well known. Meals are not skimpy here, and second helpings are quickly provided.

    Seaview Guest House, 17 Seaview Terrace (tel. 031/669-8146), is run by Mary and Jim Bloss. She was once the head caterer to the High Court in Edinburgh. The meals she serves here in a dining room overlooking the Firth of Forth indicate her experienced culinary background. Congenial hosts, the Blosses accept B&B guests at £12 ($19.20) per person. A small guesthouse, Seaview has been redecorated, and its rooms are spacious and well appointed, the housekeeping spotless. The location is in a quiet residential area, yet it is convenient to the city center by public transportation. The Blosses have a wealth of information about Edinburgh, and on occasion may be able to pull a few strings and get certain guests in to watch the High Court in action.

3. Where to Dine

    The Scots are hearty eaters, and you'll like the sizes of their portions as well as the quality of their fare, with choices from river, sea, and loch. You can dine on a cock-a-leekie soup, fresh Tay salmon, haggis, neeps, tatties, Aberdeen Angus filet steak, potted hough, poacher's soup, and good old stovies and rumbledethumps. If none of the above tempts you, you'll find that the French cuisine has made an inroad, along with Italian, Indian, and Chinese.

    Country Kitchen, 4 South Charlotte St. (tel. 031/226-6150), is probably the best known self-service restaurant in Edinburgh. But it's strictly for daytime dining, as its hours are daily except Sunday from 8 a.m. to 7:30 p.m. Food is well above average, and judgment goes into the selection of fresh produce which is then carefully prepared. The place is very health conscious, as reflected by the calorie counts that appear after each selection. Desserts such as apple strudel, for example, are low in sugar content. Vegetarians will find comfort here, but there is also a selection of lean meat and fresh fish such as oat-coated haddock. Salads are imaginatively concocted. Meals cost from £5 ($8) at this whole-food eatery, and wine and lager are also served.

Handsel's Wine Bar, 22 Stafford St. (tel. 031/225-5521), is a popular, well-run wine bar, perhaps the finest in the city. It's part of an 1821 Georgian town house which also contains the more expensive Handsel's Restaurant. The white, pink, and black decor is inviting, with an open fireplace and a Victorian pine bar. The wine list is commendable in that it offers a selection of reasonably priced half bottles. Hot food is served daily except Sunday from noon to 2:30 p.m. and 7:30 to 10 p.m. Robust, honest flavors make up the chef's repertoire. The cookery is creative and nouvelle. Try, for example, the seafood soup with garlic bread, and, to follow, perhaps fresh fish or Borders lamb. Desserts are especially good, as exemplified by the chocolate roulade or Blairgowrie raspberries (in season).

Cosmo's Ristorante, 58A North Castle St. (tel. 031/226-6743), is one of the most heavily patronized Italian restaurants in the Scottish capital. Courtesy, efficiency, and good cookery are featured here. Cosmo Tamburro is your host. In season you can ask for fresh mussels in wine and garlic as an appetizer. Pastas and soups are homemade. If you order pasta as a main course, it's served in a double portion, and you're charged accordingly. I've found the veal dishes the best cooked, and good value at that. You may be attracted to the fritto misto (fried seafood). The cassata siciliana is well made. Count on spending from £10 ($16) for lunch or £14 ($22.40) for dinner. The restaurant serves lunch from 10:15 a.m. to 2:15 p.m. and dinner from 6:30 to 10:30 p.m. It's closed for Saturday lunch, as well as on Sunday and Monday.

Madogs, 38a George St. (tel. 031/225-3408), provides a flair to the Scottish capital with its American and Mexican cuisine. With its menu and movie posters, it suggests someplace in California. It offers an excellent selection of American canned beers, exotic cocktails, or if preferred, pitchers of draft beer or margaritas, plus a good selection of French and American wines. Sopa de frijoles negros (hot black bean soup) is served with sherry and sour cream. The hot and cold sandwiches at lunchtime prove to be very popular. Chili is another favorite. Eggs Benedict and eggs ranchero are also served. The dinner menu has a continental and Mexican range: teriyaki steak, tequila pepper steak, duck with mole sauce, paella, tostados, and enchiladas. The split-level restaurant is graced with hanging baskets and potted plants. The waitresses at lunchtime and the waiters in the evening prove to be efficient. Expect to spend from £12 ($19.20). Hours are daily from noon to 2:30 p.m. and 6:30 to 11 p.m. However, on Friday and Saturday, it stays open until 1:30 a.m. No lunch is served on Sunday except during the festival.

Circles Coffee House, 324 Lawnmarket (tel. 031/225-9505), lies along the Royal Mile, about 300 feet from Edinburgh Castle. A stone structure dating from the 18th century, it makes a good luncheon stop if you're sightseeing in the area. The atmosphere suggests a coffeehouse, and at the self-service counter, you make your selections of homemade soup, quiche, lasagne, and dollops of salads priced per portion. Follow this by freshly made trifle, fruit salad, cheesecake, shortbread, or scones, plus a selection of home-baked pastries. Meals begin at £4 ($6.40). Hours are 9:30 a.m. to 6 p.m. seven days a week. However, during the festival, it remains open until 11 p.m. It's licensed, so you can drop in for a drink as well as a coffee.

Henderson's Salad Table, 94 Hanover St. (tel. 031/225-2131), is a Shangri-La for health-food lovers, as well as those who want an array of rich, nutritious salads. It's self-service, and you can pick and choose, paying per mammoth dollop. The ingredients are combined ingeniously—eggs, carrots, grapes, nuts, yogurt, cheese, potatoes, cabbage, watercress, you name it. A Scottish chef reigns in the kitchen. Reflecting his background, many hot Scottish dishes are served on request. You can have a number of hot plates, such as peppers stuffed with rice and pimiento. Meals start at £5 ($8). Desserts are homemade, so rich and pure you'll strain trying to choose between them. You may settle for a fresh fruit salad or a cake with double whipped cream and chocolate sauce. Henderson's is open regularly from 8 a.m. to 10:45 p.m. The scene takes place in a semi-basement, and the furnishings are appropriate: pinewood tables (often shared) and crude box-stools. The Sherry Bar serves "tapas." The wine cellar provides a choice of 50 wines, some 20 of which may be had by the glass. Live classical music is played most evenings. The bar may be reached by the same entrance as the Salad Table. The restaurant is near the Tourist Information Centre, one long block from Princes Street. From The High, near St. Giles, you can walk down the seemingly endless steps leading in the direction of Princes Street.

Sunflower Country Kitchen, 4-8 S. Charlotte St. (tel. 031/226-6160), is around the corner from the pedestrian traffic of Princes Street. Many of its recipes are wholesome versions of traditional country dishes. Everything is cooked or baked on the premises at this cafeteria restaurant, specializing in whole-food cooking. The calorie count is clearly posted on the wall menu, so you know if you're cheating. Clients select their food from a tile buffet illuminated with hanging lamps fashioned from terracotta flowerpots. Magazines can be borrowed from the racks, allowing guests to spend peaceful moments reading or writing letters after a well-balanced meal. There's even a no-smoking section, and live piano music begins in the afternoon at 3:30. The low-fat recipes include a cheese-onion burger, several kinds of quiche, whole-wheat macaroni and cheese, an array of tempting salads, and hot food for cold weather, including lasagne and chicken risotto. There's even baked haddock breaded in ground oats and "nutty tatties" (mashed potatoes breaded in almonds and baked). Full meals cost from £5 ($8). The establishment is open from 8 a.m. to 7 p.m. weekdays and 8 a.m. to 6:30 p.m. on Saturday (closed Sunday).

Get Stuffed Restaurant, 192 Rose St. (tel. 031/225-2208). Behind a facade crafted from blackened cubes of chiseled stone, this tavern-style restaurant specializes in steaks. Part of its decor includes an array of wall-mounted, well-stuffed cloth cows. The menu includes such char-broiled temptations as T-bone steaks, double hamburgers (eight ounces), whole stuffed chicken, and T-bone veal, plus other steaks from 10 to 20 ounces and Scottish beef. Also offered are onion rings, baked potatoes, and a selection of desserts such as zabaglione and ice cream. Full meals, costing from £12 ($19.20), are served. Lunch is from noon to 2 p.m. and dinner from 6:30 to 11 p.m. weekdays, from 5 to 11 p.m. on Saturday. The place is open on Sunday from 6 to 10 p.m. mid-July to the end of August.

Restaurant Alp Horn, 167 Rose St. (tel. 031/225-4787). A meal here is like a vacation in Switzerland. The establishment is contained within a blackened stone building on a street famous for its variety of pubs. The carved wooden door opens to reveal an interior accented with red-checked gingham curtains, potted palms, and simple wooden tables and chairs. As you'd expect, the menu offers air-dried meats (Grisons style), a wide array of fondues, venison (in season), and a version of Rösti, the famous potato dish of Switzerland. All of this might be capped off with a slice of Black Forest cake. The establishment is open daily except Sunday and Monday. Lunch is served from noon to 2 p.m., dinner from 6:30 to 10 p.m. Full meals cost from £15 ($24).

Medio Metro, 31 Frederick St. (tel. 031/225-4579). Possibly the trendiest place in town, this glossy restaurant offers a dramatically spotlit environment evoking a photographer's stage setting. You enter a room ringed with plants and dark-green marble where a black-and-chrome bar dispenses all the usuals plus several interesting apéritifs. For food, you'll be ushered into the spacious and monochromatic rear, where bentwood chairs, high arches, and multi-tiered seating lure visitors with an innovative decor. Perhaps you'll sit in the warmth of the beehive-shaped hearth, whose stucco-covered chimney adds a modern touch to a traditional Scottish log fire. Full meals, costing from £12 ($19.20), might include kebab specialties, beef Stroganoff, chicken Kiev, steak pizzaiola, and pasta and pizza in almost infinite varieties. There's even a deli-style display case filled with tempting pastries to accompany your tea or coffee. The black-and-white outfits of the good-looking staff complement the almost colorless decor. The restaurant is open seven days a week from noon to 2:30 p.m. and 6 to 11 p.m.

Helios Fountain, 7 Grassmarket (tel. 031/229-7884), is considered one of the best vegetarian restaurants in Edinburgh. The food at this Old Town restaurant is prepared from organically or biodynamically grown produce, and the menu is carefully selected and produced daily. Wholesome fare is presented from 10 a.m. to 6 p.m. (until 8 p.m. at festival) except Sunday. Full tables testify to the quality of the place. While sitting on cushioned stools and benches, enjoying an herb tea, you can select one of the good-tasting soups (ever had parsnip?), later enjoying a nut roast or a quiche (perhaps pepper and broccoli) made with "free range" eggs. Casseroles are especially notable, including pimiento and chestnut. Meals cost from £6 ($9.60). It's all very Rudolf Steiner country.

Kalpna, 2 St. Patrick Square (tel. 031/667-9890), was once rated by a prestigious British food guide as among "the best in Britain," yet it is remarkably reasonable in price, considering the quality of its ingredients. It is a southern Indian vegetarian restaurant distinguished by the quality of its cookery. Its name is translated as "imagination," and that is reflected in the often subtle flavors. However, the food can also be sharply spiced and beautifully colored when it reaches your plate. Lassi (a yoghurt drink) is the preferred drink, perhaps Kingfisher beer. A set lunch is offered for only £3.50 ($5.60), a table d'hôte dinner for £6 ($9.60). Hours are noon to 2 p.m. and 5:30 to 11:30 p.m.

The Witchery by the Tower, Castlehill, Royal Mile (tel. 031/225-5613), bills itself as "the oldest most haunted" restaurant in town, reputedly visited by the ghosts of three witches once known here. The Witchery, at the entrance to Edinburgh Castle, is today intimate, friendly, and unique, steeped in eight centuries of history. The building was linked with witchcraft in the Old Town when, between 1470 and 1722, more than 1,000 persons were burned alive as witches or wizards on Castlehill. One of the ghosts allegedly unable to stay away from the Witchery is known as Old Mother Long Nose, an old lady who practiced herbal medicine in the 17th century and was nicknamed by the children because of her long, witchy-looking nose. She was burned on the hill, but a model of her sits at the center table in the dining room, sharing it with guests, not ghosts. In 1979, after the building housing the restaurant had sat empty and crumbling for some 100 years, James Thomson bought it, restored it, and opened the restaurant, utilizing tradition and his trade as a chef. Based on his research into the building's macabre history, Thomson had it decorated with witchcraft symbols on the walls, together with authentic artifacts of witchcraft.

In addition to the place's eerie fascination, Thomson sees to it that the cuisine is noteworthy, using his creative flair to make this a member of the "Taste of Scotland" program for good Scottish food and hospitality. Menus change according to the season, and might include Loch Fyne oysters, Skye prawns, mussels, Tay salmon, Dover sole, trout, lobster, venison, noisette of Scottish lamb, and prime Aberdeen Angus steaks. Vegetarian dishes are also offered, and the desserts are all homemade. Try the Edinburgh fog, treacle tart, or award-winning sorbets. Some 40 wines and 40 malt whiskies are available. The Witchery is open from noon to 11 p.m. seven days a week. Reservations for dinner are advised. Expect to pay around £5 ($8) for lunch, £12 ($19.20) to £15 ($24) for dinner.

The Pancake Place, 130 High St. (Royal Mile) (tel. 031/225-1972). Pancakes need not always be sweet, nor always eaten with breakfast either. Franchises of this restaurant have recently sprouted up like thistles throughout Scotland. The menu features pancakes of course, in all their varieties, and they also turn out a repertoire of stuffed baked potatoes and hamburgers. Both lunch and dinner pancakes come with a wide scope of fish, chicken, or meat fillings. Try a Rocky Mountain burger—two pancakes layered with two beefburgers and topped with a tangy cheese sauce. This, along with an appetizer of homemade soup and dessert (what else but pancakes again?), would come to £5 ($8). Hours are from 8 a.m. to 11 p.m. in summer, from 9:30 a.m. to 6 p.m. in winter.

Whigham's Wine Cellars, 13 Hope St. (tel. 031/225-8674), lie in the basement of a post office. Before the premises became a fashionable wine-cellar restaurant, actual wine was bottled here. Whigham's has been in business since the mid-18th century, and it used to ship wines by the cargo to the American colonies. Walk across its mellowed old stone floors until you find an intimate alcove. A range of continental wines are offered, and some come from as far away as California. The bartender will prepare several wine cocktails, often laced with rum or brandy. Each day you can make your selection from an assortment of appetizers and plats du jour. Their smoked fish (not just salmon) is exceptional, and meals come to £10 ($16). Hours are from noon to 2:30 p.m. and 6 to 9 p.m. Closed Friday for dinner and all day Sunday.

Café Cappuccino, 15 Salisbury Pl. (tel. 031/667-4265), offers, besides an aromatic cup of cappuccino, an à la carte menu of fish, grills, omelets, salads, and desserts, along with fancy ice-cream dishes. A filling meal would cost around £5 ($8). However, a more selective choice, such as a cheese omelet with a side order of grilled tomatoes, would cost only £2.50 ($3.13). The café is open daily except Sunday from 9 a.m. to 8:30 p.m.

Mr. Boni's Ice Cream Parlour, 4 Lochrin Buildings (tel. 031/229-5319), is well known as the maker of homemade ice cream in Edinburgh, but you can get more than that delectable dessert at this establishment. They have a good range of sandwiches, including a tasty sardine and tomato. Jumbo hot dogs are also served, as are quarter-pound beefburgers on a sesame-seed bun with french fries. They claim to make their beefburgers from a "secret and special" recipe. Light meals begin at £5 ($8). Of course you can also drop in just for dessert. Various versions of banana splits are featured, along with double-thick shakes and frappés. The choice in ice cream is vast: you're faced with everything from heather honey lemon to black currant and bilberry. Hours are Monday, Tuesday, and Wednesday from 10:30 a.m. to 10:30 p.m., on Thursday to 11:30 p.m., on Friday and Saturday to midnight, and on Sunday from 12:30 a.m. to 9:30 p.m. There's actually a Mr. Boni, incidentally.

Bar Italia, 100 Lothian Rd. (tel. 031/228-6379), stresses in its oversize menu that culture stems as much from the stomach as from the brain. If that's so, then the owners of this Italian restaurant could be included among the most civilized people in Edinburgh, as the variety and scope of their menu show. A filling bowl of pasta in a mushroom-and-cream sauce, along with a green salad, is a favorite order. You might be tempted to try one of their pizzas, such as the Napoletana (black olives, anchovies, mozzarella, tomatoes, and herbs). If your appetite justifies a more elaborate meal, the restaurant offers a repertoire of meat and chicken main courses. A three-course regalia of prosciutto and melon as an appetizer, followed by veal scaloppine with mushrooms in a cream sauce, then a dessert of pear Melba and coffee, will cost £12 ($19.20). Hours are noon to 3 a.m. daily.

Bar Roma, 39A Queensferry St. (tel. 031/226-2977), offers the same menu as its sister restaurant, Bar Italia (described above), in a different section of Edinburgh. More spacious than Bar Italia, it offers the same menu and culinary philosophy of its sister. Hours are noon to 2:30 a.m. daily.

Broons Restaurant, 63 Clerk St. (tel. 031/668-1895), is a cozy family-type restaurant where you get good food and friendly service, all for the low price of about £7 ($11.20) per person. The house specialty is steak Balmoral with asparagus and whisky sauce, or you might try their lemon sole or lamb, finished off with ice cream Melba or perhaps homemade apple pie. Meals cost from £7 ($11.20) to £12 ($19.20). Weekday hours are from noon to 2 p.m. and 5 to 10 p.m.; Saturday from noon to 10 p.m.; and Sunday from 1 to 9 p.m.

FOOD AND DRINK AT LEITH: In the northern regions of Edinburgh, Leith is the old port of Edinburgh, opening onto the Firth of Forth. Once it was a city in its own right until it was slowly absorbed into Edinburgh. After decades of decay, parts of it are gradually being restored into modernized "flats," along with a trendy collection of restaurants, wine bars, and pubs. Some of the best are previewed below.

Skipper's Bistro, 1A Dock Pl., Leith (tel. 031/554-1018). One of the foremost restaurants in Edinburgh's port area, this former pub was skillfully "gentrified" by Allan and Jen Corbett. Today the walls are covered with an alluring shade of red designed to show off the well-polished brass, the antique chairs, and the marble-topped bars. Fish is a specialty, served in fixed-price combinations of £12 ($19.20) for two courses, £14 ($22.40) for three courses. Coffee rounds off the flavor of the meals, which might include pâté with cognac, a Stilton and celery soup, a marinade of kipper, trout au gratin, scallops thermidor, and a mousseline of seafood, perhaps steak Diane. Lunches and dinners are both served from 12:30 to 2 p.m. and 7:30 to 10 p.m. Closed Sunday. This place lies off Commercial Street near a canal.

The **Waterfront Wine Bar,** 1C Dock Pl., Leith (tel. 031/557-7427), is a pleasant place whose brick and stone walls are adorned with old prints, maps, photographs, and other nautical memorabilia. There's a coal fireplace in a side room, plus a conservatory, with its own coal stove, overlooking the water. A large vine acts like a pergola, letting dappled sunlight play across the tables. During the summer, you can be seated at a table on a floating raft. Wine lovers enjoy vintage wine by the glass and a large selection by the bottle. Food is available, with an array of daily specials listed on the blackboard, perhaps including a prawn salad or lamb kebabs. In summer, barbecues are prepared outdoors. The establishment charges around £11 ($20.80) for a full meal, serving from 11 a.m. daily except Sunday. It closes at 11 p.m. Monday through Wednesday, at 1 a.m. on Thursday and Friday, and at midnight on Saturday. It lies off Commercial Street toward the water.

The **Shore Bar and Restaurant,** 3 The Shore, Leith (tel. 031/553-5080). Built on a canal, in a high-ceilinged room rich with exposed hardwood and nautical accessories, this has become one of the most alluring restaurants at this old port. The only indication that you've arrived here is a sign that says "Wine and Spirit Merchants" painted in gilt letters on the big-windowed facade. Val and Calum Buchanan, the owners, converted a rundown pub into this cozily intimate rendezvous point for Edinburghers wanting to get away from it all. The blue and white dining room has white napery and a blackboard menu which changes daily. Lunch and dinner are served every day except Sunday and might include Stilton and leek soup, shark steak, monkfish with green pepper sauce, beef with apricots, and meat loaf with sour cream. Full meals cost from £6 ($9.60) at lunch, £12 ($19.20) at dinner. Hours are noon to 2:30 p.m. and 6:30 to 10:30 p.m. daily except Sunday.

DINING AT CRAMOND: At least once you should get out into the countryside surrounding Edinburgh. One way to do this is to take bus 41 for about five miles from the West End to the little Scottish village of Cramond. Few visible traces remain today of its Roman occupation.

Quietly nestling on a sloping street is the **Cramond Inn,** on Cramond Glebe Road (tel. 031/336-2035), which has been serving food and drinks to wayfarers for 300 years (it was known to Robert Louis Stevenson). Picture upholstered booths, opera-red carpeting, some beer-barrel upholstered chairs, a collection of local watercolors, a low ceiling, large foot-square old beams, dark oak and creamy-colored walls, recessed windows, a small stone fireplace—and you'll begin to get the feel of the inn. The manager is Sam Proudfoot, who took over this task from his father. The restaurant can serve many diners, but you'd better call in advance, as it's most popular. The prices are quite reasonable, considering the quality of food—some of the finest of Scottish dishes. The steak-and-kidney pie is a taste treat, but I'm drawn to the haggis, the famed dish of Scotland, made with an assortment of chopped meats, oatmeal, and spices. For an appetizer, the Scotch broth is a favorite, although the game soup is the gourmet's choice. A specialty of the house is roast duck. Meals begin at £10 ($16). The inn serves lunch from noon to 2:30 p.m., dinner 6 to 10:30 p.m. The restaurant is closed Sunday. Bar lunches are served in the lounge bar seven days a week from noon to 2 p.m.

4. The Major Sights

Before leaving the Scottish capital, you'll want to take a look at both the Old Town and the New Town. Both have their different attractions—the Old Town's largely medieval; the New Town, Georgian.

Those on the most rushed of schedules may have time to see only the most important attractions. These include (1) Edinburgh Castle, (2) the Palace of Holyroodhouse, (3) a walk along the Royal Mile, (4) the National Gallery of Scotland, and (5) a look at the Gothic Scott Monument in the East Princes Street Gardens. The best way to get around to most of these attractions is to take my walking tour of Edinburgh (see below).

I'll begin the exploration on the Royal Mile of the Old Town, a collective term for Canongate, Lawnmarket, and the High.

At one end on Castle Rock sits—

EDINBURGH CASTLE: It is believed that the ancient city grew up on the seat of the dead volcano, Castle Rock. History is vague on possible settlements, although it is known that in the 11th century Malcolm III (Canmore), and his Saxon queen, Margaret, founded a castle on this spot. The good Margaret was later venerated as a saint. The only fragment left of their original castle, in fact the oldest structure in Edinburgh, was established by her. It is St. Margaret's Chapel, built in the Norman style, the present oblong structure dating principally from the 12th century. The five-ton Mons Meg, a 15th-century cannon, is in the French Prisons and on view to the public.

Inside the castle (tel. 031/225-9846), you can visit the State Apartments—particularly Queen Mary's Bedroom—where Mary Queen of Scots gave birth to James VI of Scotland (later James I of England). The Great Hall with its hammer-beam ceiling was built by James IV. It displays armaments and armor. Scottish Parliaments used to convene in this hall.

The highlight, however, is the Crown Chamber, which houses the Honours of Scotland, used at the coronation of James VI, along with the scepter and the sword of state of Scotland. The French Prisons were put to use in the 18th century, and these great storerooms housed hundreds of Napoleonic soldiers during the early 19th century. Many of them made wall carvings which you can see today. The castle may be visited from 9:30 a.m. to 5:05 p.m. (last ticket sold) Monday to Saturday and from 11 a.m. to 5:05 p.m. on Sunday April to the end of September; from 9:30 a.m. to 4:20 p.m. Monday to Saturday, and 12:30 to 3:35 p.m. on Sunday from October to the end of March. Admission is £2 ($3.20) for adults, £1 ($1.60) for children. Family tickets are sold for £4 ($6.40).

Your entrance ticket to the castle includes entry to the galleries of the **Scottish United Services Museum** (tel. 031/225-7534). These are situated on either side of Crown Square and in the North Hospital block. This is a national museum dealing with the history of the navy, army, and air force at all periods. It is considered unique and comprehensive, the longest established collections of British armed forces historical material in the United Kingdom. The exhibitions alone are the largest single part of the areas in the castle open to the public.

The Scottish regiments of the British Army figure strongly, and new displays in the North Hospital block deal with the story of the Scottish soldier in an exciting fashion. In other sections, uniforms, equipment, badges, and medals present more traditional displays. The history of the Royal Navy and Royal Air Force in their Scottish contexts are interpreted in smaller galleries adjacent to the Scottish Crown Jewels.

The **Camera Obscura,** Castlehill (tel. 031/226-3709), is right beside the castle at the head of the Royal Mile. It's at the top of the Outlook Tower and offers a magnificent view of the surrounding city. Trained guides point out the landmarks and talk about Edinburgh's fascinating history. In addition, there are several entertaining exhibitions, all with an optical theme, and a well-stocked shop selling books, crafts, and records. Hours are 10 a.m. to 5 p.m. daily November to March, 9:30 a.m. to 6 p.m. April to October. Admission is £1.60 ($2.56) for adults, 80p ($1.28) for children.

ALONG THE ROYAL MILE: Ideally, if you have the time, walk from the castle down the hill the full length of the Royal Mile, all the way to the Palace of Holyroodhouse at the opposite end. Along the way you'll see some of the most interesting old structures in Edinburgh, with their turrets, gables, and towering chimneys. Of all the buildings that may intrigue you, the most visited are John Knox's House and **St. Giles Cathedral.**

The cathedral is known as the High Kirk. Inside, one outstanding feature is its Thistle Chapel, designed by Sir Robert Lorimer and housing beautiful stalls and notable heraldic stained-glass windows. The chapel is open from 10 a.m. to 5 p.m. John Knox, the leader of the Reformation in Scotland, was minister of St. Giles from 1560 to 1572.

Lady Stair's House lies in a close of the same name off Lawnmarket. It was built in 1622 by a prominent merchant burgess. It takes its name from a former owner, Elizabeth, the Dowager-Countess of Stair. Today it is a treasurehouse of portraits, relics, and manuscripts relating to three of Scotland's greatest men of letters—Robert Burns, Sir Walter Scott, and Robert Louis Stevenson. It is open Monday to Saturday from 10 a.m. to 5 p.m. (until 6 p.m. from June to September). For information, telephone 031/225-2424, ext. 6593.

The **Museum of Childhood,** 42 High St. (tel. 031/225-2424; ext. 6645), stands just opposite John Knox's House on the Royal Mile. It was the first museum in the world to be devoted solely to the history of childhood. Three floors contain nearly every facet of the world of children, ranging from antique toys and games to exhibits on health, education, costumes, juvenile "arsenals," and many other items representing the childhood experience of members of different nationalities and periods. Because of the youthful clientele it naturally attracts, visitors are warned that it has been described as the "noisiest museum in the world." It is open weekdays from 10 a.m. to 6 p.m. June to September, to 5 p.m. the rest of the year, and from 2 to 5 p.m. on Sunday during the Edinburgh Festival. Admission is free.

Farther down the street at 45 High St. is **John Knox's House** (tel. 031/556-6961), whose history goes back to the late 15th century. Even if you're not interested in the reformer who founded the Scottish Presbyterian church, you may want to visit his house, as it is characteristic of the "lands" that used to flank the Royal Mile. All of them are gone now, except Knox's house, with its timbered gallery. Inside, you'll see the tempera ceiling in the Oak Room, along with exhibitions of Knox memorabilia. The house may be visited daily (except Sunday) from 10 a.m. to 5 p.m. for £1 ($1.60) for adults, 70p ($1.12) for children.

Continue along Canongate in the direction of the Palace of Holyroodhouse. At 163 Canongate stands one of the handsomest buildings along the Royal Mile. The **Canongate Tolbooth** was constructed in 1591 and was once the courthouse, prison, and center of municipal affairs for the burgh of Canongate.

Across the street is **Huntly House,** an example of a restored 16th-century mansion. Now it is Edinburgh's principal museum of local history. You can stroll through period rooms and reconstructions Monday to Saturday from 10 a.m. to 5 p.m. (until 6 p.m. from June to September). During the festival it is also open on Sunday from 2 to 5 p.m. For information, telephone 031/225-2424, ext. 6689.

THE PALACE OF HOLYROODHOUSE: At the eastern end of the Royal Mile, the palace (tel. 031/556-7371) was built adjacent to an Augustinian abbey established by David I in the 12th century. The nave, now in ruins, remains today. James IV founded the palace nearby in the early part of the 16th century, but of his palace only the north tower is left. Much of what you see today was ordered built by Charles II.

In the old wing occurred the most epic moments in the history of Holyroodhouse, when Mary Queen of Scots was in residence. Mary, who had been Queen of France and widowed while still a teenager, decided to return to her native Scotland. She eventually entered into an unsuccessful marriage with Lord Darnley but spent more time and settled affairs of state with her secretary, David Rizzio. Darnley plotted to kill the Italian, and he and his accomplices marched into Mary's supper room, grabbed Rizzio over her protests, then carried him to the Audience Chamber, where he was murdered by 56 stab wounds. A plaque marks the spot of his death on March 9, 1566.

Darnley was to live less than a year after, dying mysteriously in a gunpowder explosion. Mary, of course, was eventually executed on the order of her cousin, Elizabeth I. One of the most curious exhibits in Holyroodhouse is a piece of needlework by Mary, depicting a cat-and-mouse scene (Elizabeth's the cat!).

The State Apartments also contain some fine 17th-century Flemish tapestries, especially a whole series devoted to Diana, and a recently restored 17th-century state bed. In the Great Gallery are more than 100 portraits, depicting Scottish kings, including Macbeth, painted by a Dutchman, de Wet.

The palace suffered long periods of neglect, although it basked in glory at the ball in the mid-18th century thrown by Bonnie Prince Charlie. The present Queen and Prince Philip live at Holyroodhouse whenever they visit Edinburgh. When they're not in residence, you can visit the palace weekdays from 9:30 a.m. to 5:15 p.m. (on Sunday from 10:30 a.m. to 4:40 p.m.) in high season. Winter hours are 9:30 a.m. to 3:45 p.m., weekdays (closed on Sunday). The admission is £1.50 ($2.40) for adults and 70p ($1.12) for children. When the Historical Apartments only are open, admission is 80p ($1.28) for adults and 40p (64¢) for children.

THE NEW TOWN: At some point the Old Town became too small. The burghers decided to build a whole new town across the valley, so the marsh was drained and eventually turned into public gardens. Princes Street is the most striking boulevard. Architecturally, the most interesting district of the New Town is the north side of Charlotte Square, designed by Robert Adam. It was young architect James Craig, who shaped much of the Georgian style of the New Town, with its crescents and squares.

At 7 Charlotte Square, a part of the northern facade, is the restored building known simply as the **Georgian House** (tel. 031/225-2160). It is a prime example of Scottish architecture and interior design in the zenith of the New Town. Originally the home of John Lamont XVII, known as "the last of the patriarchs and the first of the moderns," the house has recently been refurbished and reopened to the public by Scotland's National Trust. The furniture in this Robert Adam house is mainly Hepplewhite, Chippendale, and Sheraton, all dating from the 18th century. In a ground-floor bedroom is a sturdy old four-poster with an original 18th-century canopy. The dining room table is set for a dinner on fine Wedgwood china, and the kitchen is stocked with gleaming copper pots and pans. It is open April to October from 10 a.m. to 5 p.m. (on Sunday from 2 to 5 p.m.), in November on Saturday from 10 a.m. to 4:30 p.m. and on Sunday from 2 to 4:30 p.m. Last visitors are admitted 30 minutes before closing time. Admission (including audio-visual) is £1.50 ($2.40) for adults, 75p ($1.20) for children.

Note: As an Old Town complement to the New Town Georgian House, the National Trust has opened in a 1620 tenement in the Royal Mile, **Gladstone's Land** (tel. 031/226-5856), an upstairs apartment of four rooms furnished as it might have been in the 17th century. On the ground floor, reconstructed shop booths display replicas of goods of the period. It is open April through October, Monday through Saturday from 10 a.m. to 5 p.m., on Sunday from 2 to 5 p.m. In November, hours are from 10 a.m. to 4:30 p.m. on Saturday, from 2 to 4:30 p.m. on Sunday. Last admission is 30 minutes before closing. The admission charge is £1.50 ($2.40) for adults, 75p ($1.20) for children.

The Gothic-inspired **Scott Monument** lies in the **East Princes Street Gardens.** It is the most famous landmark of Edinburgh, completed in the mid-19th century. Sir Walter Scott's heroes are honored by small figures in the monument. You can climb the tower weekdays in summer from 9 a.m. to 6 p.m. for 50p (80¢). Off-season, you must scale the monument before 3 p.m. **West Princes Street Gardens** has the first ever **Floral Clock,** which was constructed in 1904.

ART TREASURES: For the art lover, Edinburgh has a number of masterpieces, and many visitors come here just to look at the galleries. Of course, the principal museum is the **National Gallery of Scotland,** on The Mound (tel. 031/556-8921), in the center of Princes Street Gardens. The gallery is small as national galleries go, but the collection came about with great care and was expanded considerably by bequests, gifts, and loans. A short chronology of the collection's history and a display of catalogues is incorporated in *The Eye-Opener,* a lively introduction to the gallery, featuring an informative and entertaining slide-tape show. Watch out for the clever effects.

Recent major acquisitions include Giulio Romano's *Vièrge à la Legende.* Other Italian paintings are Verrocchio's *Ruskin Madonna,* Andrea del Sarto's *Portrait of a Man,* and Domenichino's *Adoration of the Shepherds.* However, the most acclaimed among them is Tiepolo's *Finding of Moses.*

A renowned feature of the gallery is the Duke of Sutherland loan of some 40 paintings which include two Raphaels, *Holy Family with a Palm Tree* and the *Bridgewater Madonna;* Titian's two Diana canvases, as well as his favorite subject, Venus, this time rising from the sea; and the *Seven Sacraments,* painted by the great 17th-century Frenchman Nicolas Poussin, for Fréart de Chantelou.

The Spanish masters are less well represented but shine forth in El Greco's *Savior* and the mysterious *Fabula* (on loan), Velázquez's *Old Woman Cooking Eggs,* an early work by that great master, and *Immaculate Conception* by Zurbarán, his friend and contemporary.

The northern schools are impressively represented by fine but not numerous examples. An early Netherlandish masterpiece, historically linked to Edinburgh, is Hugo van der Goes's Trinity Altarpiece, loaned by the Queen. The Flemish school emerges notably in Rubens's *The Feast of Herod* and *The Reconciliation of Jacob and Esau.* The Dutch excel with Rembrandt's *Woman in Bed,* superb landscapes by Cuyp, Ruisdael, and Hobbema, and in one of the gallery's most recent acquisitions, *Interior of St. Bavo's Church, Haarlem,* by Pieter Saenredam, his largest and arguably finest painting, bought in 1982.

The most valuable gift to the gallery since its foundation, the Maitland Collection, includes Cézanne's *Mont St-Victoire,* as well as works by Degas, Van Gogh, Renoir, Gauguin, and Seurat, among others. A rare early Monet, *Shipping Scene—Night Effects,* was bought in 1980. In the same year, for the first time in living memory, a stunning landscape, *Niagara Falls, from the American Side,* by the 19th-century American painter Frederic Church, went on show.

The greatest English painters are represented by excellent examples—Gainsborough's *The Hon. Mrs. Graham,* Constable's *Dedham Vale,* along with works by Turner, Reynolds, and Hogarth. Naturally, the work of Scottish painters decks the walls (in the new wing, opened in 1978), none finer than Henry Raeburn, at his best in the whimsical *The Rev. Robert Walker Skating on Duddingston Loch.*

The gallery is open from 10 a.m. to 5 p.m. weekdays (2 to 5 p.m. on Sunday). During the festival, hours are 10 a.m. to 6 p.m. weekdays and 11 a.m. to 6 p.m. on Sunday. Admission is free. This is one of the three National Galleries of Scotland.

Britain's only museum devoted to 20th-century art is the **Scottish National Gallery of Modern Art,** Belford Road (tel. 031/556-8921). In 1984 it moved into a former school building completed in 1828 and converted into an art gallery. It is set in 12 acres of grounds just 15 minutes' walk from the west end of Princes Street. The collection is truly international in scope and quality in spite of its modest size.

Major sculptures sited outside the building include pieces by Henry Moore, Hepworth, and Epstein. Inside, the collection ranges from a fauve Derain and cubist Braque and Picasso to recent works by Richard Long and Chia. There is naturally a strong representation of English and Scottish art.

Highlights of the collection include works by Matisse, Miró, Magritte, Léger, Jawlensky, Kirchner, Kokoschka, Dix, Ernst, Ben Nicholson, Nevelson, Pollock, Beuys, Balthus, Hanson, De Andrea, Lichtenstein, Kitaj, and Hockney.

Prints and drawings can be studied in the Print Room. The licensed café sells coffee and nonalcoholic drinks as well as light refreshments and salads. Hours are 10 a.m. to 5 p.m. on weekdays, 2 to 5 p.m. on Sunday. Admission is free. The only bus that passes the gallery is the infrequent no. 13. However, nos. 18, 20, and 41 pass along Queensferry Road, leaving only a five-minute walk up Queensferry Terrace and Belford Road to the gallery.

ROYAL OBSERVATORY: The Royal Observatory Visitor Centre, Blackford Hill (tel. 031/667-3321), shows the works of the Scottish National Observatory at home and abroad, featuring the finest images of astronomical objects, Scotland's largest telescope, and a display of antique instruments. There is also a spectacular panoramic view of the city from the balcony. The observatory is open from 10 a.m. to 4 p.m. Monday to Friday, from noon to 5 p.m. Saturday and Sunday. Admission is 65p ($1.04) for adults, 35p (56¢) for children.

ROYAL BOTANIC GARDEN: Gardeners and nature lovers in general will be attracted to the Royal Botanic Garden, Inverleith Row (tel. 031/552-7171, ext. 260). The main areas of interest within the garden are the Exhibition Plant Houses, Inverleith House, Exhibition Hall, the Alpine House, the Demonstration Garden, the annual and herbaceous borders (summer only), the copse, the Woodland Garden, the Wild Garden, the Arboretum, the Peat Garden, the Rock Garden, the Heath Garden, and the Pond.

The range of Exhibition Plant Houses includes displays of the fern forests of the southern hemisphere, the giant water lilies of Amazonia, and desert succulents of arid areas. It is open all year from 9 a.m. to one hour before sunset. The plant houses and Exhibition Hall are open from 10 a.m. to 5 p.m. Admission is free.

LAURISTON CASTLE: This fine country mansion standing in extensive grounds overlooking the Firth of Forth lies on the outskirts of Edinburgh about 3¼ miles northwest of Princes Street. If going by car, take the Queensferry Road (A90) as if heading for the Forth Road Bridge, but turn off to the right at the Quality Street junction (look for directional signs pointing to Lauriston Castle). Then proceed down Cramond Road South until you come to the entrance on the right to the castle. If using public transport, take the Lothian Region bus no. 41 from the Mound, Hanover Street, or George Street.

The house is associated with John Law (1671–1729), the founder of the first bank in France, and its collections are strong in English Georgian and French Louis styles of furniture. The house gives one a good picture of the leisure lifestyle of the upper classes prior to World War I. Look for the Derbyshire Blue John ornaments and the Crossley wool "mosaics." The house is open from 11 a.m. to 1 p.m. and 2 to 5 p.m. daily except Friday from April to October. From October to March, it is open on Saturday and Sunday only, from 2 to 4 p.m. Visits are by guided tour only, each tour lasting approximately 40 minutes and the last one beginning 40 minutes before closing time. Admission is 80p ($1.28) for adults, 40p (64¢) for children. For more information, telephone 031/336-2060.

ROYAL MUSEUM OF SCOTLAND: Two long-established museums were combined in 1985 to form a union with one administration, international collections in the arts and sciences, and a treasure trove of Scottish material. Displays range through the decorative arts, ethnography, natural history, geology, archeology, technology, and science. They were formerly the Royal Scottish Museum and the National Museum of Antiquities.

The Chambers Street building at the city center near the Royal Mile (tel. 031/225-7534), begun in 1861, is one of the finest examples of Victorian architecture in Edinburgh and houses international collections in the arts and sciences.

The Findlay Building, Queen Street, at the east end of the city center (tel. 031/557-3500), opened in 1890, contains collections of Scottish memorabilia from prehistoric times to the present. The collections were initiated more than 200 years ago by the Society of Antiquaries.

Hours for the two buildings of the Royal Museum are from 10 a.m. to 5 p.m. Monday to Saturday, from 2 to 5 p.m. on Sunday. Admission to both is free, except for some special temporary exhibitions. To reach the Chambers Street branch, centrally situated about a ten-minute walk southward from Waverley Station, one of some 23 Lothian Region buses can be used. The Queen Street branch is also about a ten-minute walk from Waverley Station, this time to the north and about five minutes from the bus station. You can take one of 11 Lothian Region buses to reach it.

SCOTTISH NATIONAL PORTRAIT GALLERY: Housed in a red stone Victorian Gothic building by Rowand Anderson, the portrait gallery, 1 Queen St. (tel. 031/556-8921), at the east end of Queen Street, gives you a chance to see what the famous people of Scottish history looked like. The portraits, several by Gainsborough and Reynolds, include everybody from Mary Queen of Scots to James VI and I, from Sir Walter Scott to Rabbie Burns, from Flora Macdonald to Ramsay Macdonald. Charging no admission, the gallery is open from 10 a.m. to 5 p.m. weekdays and from 2 to 5 p.m. on Sunday.

EDINBURGH ZOO: One of the leading zoos of Britain, the Edinburgh Zoo (tel. 031/334-9171), on the southern slope of Corstorphine Hill, takes in about 80 acres in a setting of natural beauty. Established shortly before World War I, it is entered from the A8 (the Corstorphine road), lying some four miles west of the heart of town. It has a varied and extensive collection of animal life, and has long been known for its large breeding colony of Antarctic penguins which stage a voluntary parade every day at feeding time. The zoo is open from 9 a.m. to 6 p.m. in summer (to 5 p.m. in winter), charging an admission of £2.50 ($4) for adults and £1.50 ($2.40) for children. To reach it, take bus 12, 26, 31, 85, 86, or C4 from Princes Street.

CRAIGMILLAR CASTLE: In the southeastern sector of Edinburgh, this castle is one of the city's most interesting sights, but perhaps because of its obscure location, it is one of the most overlooked. The location is out the A68, about 3½ miles south of the heart of the city. The 14th-century keep that once stood proudly here is now in ruins, but it is impressive, nevertheless. In the early 1400s this keep was enclosed by a "curtain wall" which saw much bloodshed. Inside, the apartments were built primarily in the 16th and 17th centuries.

Mary Queen of Scots often spent time here, and it is said that the murder of Darnley was also plotted here. The castle is open in summer Monday to Wednesday and on Saturday from 9:30 a.m. to 7 p.m. (to 1 p.m. on Thursday and from 2 to 7 p.m. on Sunday). Off-season, its hours are 9:30 a.m. to 4 p.m. Monday through Wednesday and Saturday, to 1 p.m. on Thursday (from 2 to 4 p.m. on Sunday). Admission is 50p (80¢) for adults and 25p (40¢) for children.

CALTON HILL: This hill is often credited with giving Edinburgh a look somewhat like that of Athens. It is a hill of monuments, and when some of them were created they were called "instant ruins" by critics of the day. The landmark Calton Hill lies off Regent Road at the eastern sector of Edinburgh. Rising 350 feet, the hill is visited not only by those wishing to see its monuments, but by those wanting to enjoy the panoramic views of the Firth of Forth and the city spread beneath it. The Parthenon was reproduced in part on this location in 1824. However, the city fathers ran out of money and the monument—often referred to as "Scotland's shame"—was never finished. The Nelson Monument, containing relics of the hero of Trafalgar, dates from 1815 and rises more than 100 feet over the hill. A time ball at the top falls at one o'clock every day. The monument is open in summer from 10 a.m. to 5 p.m. (otherwise from 10 a.m. to 3 p.m.), charging admission. Why all these monuments? The original intent—at least the intent of the builders of the "Parthenon"—was to honor the brave Scottish dead who were killed fighting in the Napoleonic Wars.

DEAN VILLAGE: Most visitors who want to see all the major sights of Edinburgh head here to view one of the most photographed and most characteristic sights in the city. Set in a valley, the village, filled with nostalgic charm, is about 100 feet below the level of the rest of Edinburgh. A few minutes from the West End, its location is at the end of Bell's Brae, off Queensferry Street, on the Water of Leith. The settlement dates from the 12th century, and the fame of Dean Village grew as a result of its being a grain milling center. One of the most celebrated views is enjoyed by looking downstream under the high arches of Dean Bridge, designed by Telford in 1833. It's customary to walk along the water in the direction of St. Bernard's Well.

THE FESTIVAL: The highlight of Edinburgh's year—some would say the only time when the real Edinburgh emerges—comes in the last weeks of August during the **Edinburgh International Festival.** Since 1947 the festival has brought to Edinburgh artists and companies of the highest international standard in all fields of the arts, including music, opera, dance, theater, exhibition, poetry and prose, and "Auld Reekie" takes on a cosmopolitan air.

During the period of the festival, one of the most exciting spectacles is the **Military Tattoo** on the floodlit esplanade in front of Edinburgh Castle, high on its rock above the city. Vast audiences thrill to the delicate maneuvers of the famous Scottish regiments, the precision marching of military units from all parts of the world, and of course the stirring skirl of the bagpipes and the swirl of the kilt.

Less predictable in quality but infinitely greater in quantity is the **Edinburgh Festival Fringe,** an opportunity for anybody—whether an individual, a group of friends, or a whole company of performers—to put on their own show wherever they can find an empty stage or street corner. Late-night reviews, outrageous and irreverent contemporary drama, university theater presentations, maybe even a full-length opera—Edinburgh gives them all free rein. As if that were not enough, Edinburgh has a **Film Festival,** a **Jazz Festival,** a **Television Festival,** and a **Book Festival** (every second year) at the same time.

Ticket prices vary from £1 ($1.60) up to about £15 ($24) a seat, but if you move fast enough, there are not many events that you cannot see for £2 ($3.20).

Information can be obtained at the following places: **Edinburgh Festival Society,** 21 Market St., Edinburgh EH1 1BW (tel. 031/226-4001); **Edinburgh Festival Fringe,** 170 High St., Edinburgh EH1 1BW (tel. 031/226-5257); **Edinburgh Military Tattoo,** The Tattoo Office, 22 Market St., Edinburgh EH1 1QB (tel. 031/225-1188); **Edinburgh Film Festival,** Department M, Edinburgh

International Film Festival, The Filmhouse, 88 Lothian Rd., Edinburgh EH3 9BX (tel. 031/228-6382); **Edinburgh Jazz Festival,** 116 Canongate, Edinburgh EH8 8DD (tel. 031/557-1642); **Edinburgh Television Festival,** 17 Great Poulteney St., London W1R 3DG (tel. 01/437-5100); **Edinburgh Book Festival,** 25a South West Thistle Street Lane, Edinburgh EH2 1EW (tel. 031/225-1915); and **Edinburgh Accommodation Bureau,** Tourist Accommodation Service, Waverley Market, Waverley Bridge, Edinburgh EH1 1BP (tel. 031/557-2727).

TOURS: If you want a quick introduction to the principal attractions in and around Edinburgh, then consider one or more of the tours offered by the **Lothian Region Transport,** whose offices are at 14 Queen St. You won't find a cheaper way to hit the highlights, and later you can go back on your own if you want a deeper experience. The coaches (buses to Americans) leave from Waverley Bridge, near the Scott Monument. The tours start in April and run through late October. A curtailed winter program is also offered. A half-day coach tour (which takes about four hours) leaves daily at 9:30 a.m. and 1:30 p.m. (on Sunday at 1:30 p.m. only), costing £7.10 ($11.36) and visiting the castle, the Palace of Holyroodhouse, and St. Giles Cathedral. Operating throughout the day are half a dozen smaller tours that show you some of the environs. For more information, telephone 031/554-4494). From June to September, day-and-a-half tours are offered to many parts of Scotland.

A WALKING TOUR OF EDINBURGH: Edinburgh, as any local will tell you, is best done on foot. So if you don't mind burning up some shoe leather, here is a walking tour of the major attractions.

Begin by walking up to Edinburgh Castle to visit St. Margaret's Chapel, said to have been built by Margaret in 1076. You can also see Mons Meg, a 15th-century artillery piece. The castle well is 110 feet deep and has been in use since 1313 at least. The Scottish National War Memorial is in the castle, which was designed by Sir Robert Lorimer. The Crown Room on the east side of Crown Square contains royal regalia, including the Honours of Scotland, the crown, scepter, and sword. Queen Mary's apartments are on view and the old Parliament Hall dates from the 15th century.

The Royal Mile starts from the Castle Esplanade at Castle Hill. The house at the top of Castle Wynd steps is known as Cannonball House because of the ball embedded in the gable on its west side. On the left in Outlook Tower is the Camera Obscura with its living color pictures of Edinburgh. At the church of Tolbooth St. John's, services are celebrated in Gaelic. The street now becomes Lawnmarket, once the center for linen sellers. Here you can be measured for a kilt or purchase woolens and cloth.

Farther on, see Gladstone's Land, a National Trust property dating from the 17th century, with an arcaded ground floor, some 16th-century windows and gables, plus an outside staircase. The original shop booths on the street have been restored.

Next you come to Brodie's Close, the 18th-century home of the notorious Deacon Brodie, a respectable councillor by day and a thief by night. He was hanged in 1788. The mechanism used for the "drop" had previously been improved by Brodie himself—for use on others! Brodie is said to have given Stevenson the idea for his story of Dr. Jekyll and Mr. Hyde.

Opposite is Lady Stair's House, dating from the 17th century and now a museum devoted to Scotland's three great literary figures: Burns, Scott, and Stevenson. Lawnmarket ends at the crossroads of Bank Street and George IV Bridge, and you can see the brass strips on the road in the southeast corner of the busy junction marking the site of the scaffold where public hangings were continued until 1864.

The Royal Mile continues as High Street, with Parliament Square on the right. The square is largely occupied by St. Giles Cathedral. John Knox is thought to have been buried within the square, and an arrangement of white stones on the ground marks the site of the old Tolbooth, built in 1466 and destroyed in 1817. The building was the chapter house for St. Giles, then a meeting place for Parliament and the law courts before becoming a prison from which many aristocrats emerged for execution. The old keys of the tolbooth and the door through which they emerged are kept at Abbotsford, home of Sir Walter Scott. Also in the square is Parliament House, built in 1632, along with Parliament Hall, a fine Gothic hall with an open timber roof. The building is now the Courts of Justice, and it is sometimes possible to attend sessions by using door 11.

Farther on is John Knox's House, dating from the late 15th century and with some early 17th-century additions. The house contains relics of John Knox, famous pastor and cleric, and some interesting pictures of old Edinburgh. Almost opposite is the Museum of Childhood, really intended more for adults than for children. The displays cover the many facets of childhood—what children ate, read, played with, and collected. Still farther on is Chessells Court, once an excise office, the robbing of which was Deacon Brodie's last crime.

Next comes the City Museum in Huntly House and, opposite it, the Canongate Tolbooth, now part of a museum and housing a collection of Highland dress and tartans. Acheson House, next door to Huntly, is a Scottish Craft Centre.

At the end of the road rises the Palace of Holyroodhouse, the official residence of the Queen whenever she is in Edinburgh. It was begun in 1500 by James IV and added to many times. To Holyrood came Mary Queen of Scots in 1561, and it was here that her famous interview with John Knox took place, also the murder of Rizzio and her marriage to Bothwell. After James VI left the palace to become King of England, it ceased to be a residence for any length of time. However, various monarchs have stayed here ever since, including Queen Victoria, who used to stop over on her way to Balmoral. Edward VII lived here while studying in Edinburgh. Most interesting to see are the picture gallery, the state apartments, and the historic apartments.

Afterward, walk back up Canongate and High Street to Canongate Church, then take Tolbooth Wynd to the footpath leading to Regent Road and Princes Street. When you reach Regent Road, turn left and continue along Waterloo Place with Calton Hill on the right. The hill is topped by the Nelson Monument, the City Observatory, and the unfinished Parthenon, intended to be a memorial to the dead of the Napoleonic Wars. In this street is the General Post Office and the Philatelic Bureau and, opposite, the Register House, where most of Scotland's historic and legal records since the 13th century are stored.

Walk on the Waverley Railway Station to the left and then, in the East Gardens, you will find the Scott Monument, a 200-foot spire forming a canopy over the statue of Sir Walter Scott and his dog. Next on the left is the National Gallery of Scotland and the Royal Scottish Academy.

Then you come to the West Gardens and the famous Floral Clock, believed to be the oldest in the world, built in 1903. A cuckoo announces each quarter hour and the flowers often portray some current local event. Also in the gardens is the American War Memorial, erected by Americans of Scottish descent and sympathies, and the Churches of St. John and St. Cuthbert, the former having a brass-rubbing center in its church hall.

5. Where to Shop

Whole books have been written about shopping in Edinburgh. But in the limited space I've been allowed, only a tantalizing preview of the shops and possible merchandise can be covered. There are big and beautiful stores along Princes Street, facing the gardens and opening onto the castle, but there is just as much opportunity for seeking out souvenirs along the Royal Mile or more substantial purchases such as kilts and woolen goods.

ALONG PRINCES STREET: Next to Waverley Station is **Waverley Market Shopping Center,** offering something for everyone, all under one roof in the center of Edinburgh. On three levels, you can browse through some 70 interesting shops. A Food Court has tempting snacks, and top-quality produce is for sale in the Food Hall. Unique, handmade items can be purchased in the craft center. The market is open seven days a week, from 9 a.m. to 6 p.m. Monday to Saturday (until 8 p.m. on Thursday), and 11 a.m. to 5 p.m. on Sunday.

At 48 Princes Street at the corner of South St. David's Street is **Jenners** (tel. 031/225-2442). Everyone in Edinburgh has probably been to Jenners at least once. Its neo-Gothic facade, opposite the Sir Walter Scott Monument, couldn't be more prominent. Its array of Scottish and international merchandise qualifies it as one of the best-stocked department stores in town.

Debenham's, 112 Princes St. (tel. 031/225-1320). This, along with Jenners, competes for the honor of the best department store in Edinburgh. Its modernized Victorian shell stocks a wide array of Scottish and international merchandise in a marble-covered department-store format.

Tartan Gift Shops, 96 Princes St. (tel. 031/225-5551). If you've ever suspected that you might be Scottish, this establishment will show you a chart indicating the place of origin (within Scotland) of your family name. You'll then be faced with a bewildering array of hunt and dress tartans for your personal use. The high-quality wool is sold by the yard as well as in the form of kilts for both men and women. There's also a line of lambswool and cashmere sweaters, and all the accessories to round out your perfect image as a Scot. The battery of staff here is helpful. The shop is on two levels of a Princes Street building, in a format which the staff calls "seven steps up, seven steps down."

Romanes and Patterson, 62 Princes St. (tel. 031/225-4966), sells only items made in the United Kingdom. Almost everything is pure wool, with the exception of one line of women's summer skirts, which are made of a combination of wool and polyester. Children's kilts are also available, as well as a wide array of clothing for women. The men's department is limited to sweaters and accessories, and a full line of cashmere sweaters from Pringle is available on the lower level. The establishment is open every day of the week during normal shopping hours, as well as every Sunday from 12:30 to 5 p.m. The company's biggest outlet is at the address given above, and there are three other outlets in Edinburgh: at 139 Princes St., at the corner of Lawnmarket and High Street along the Royal Mile, and at 51 High St.

Boots the Chemists, 101-103 Princes St. (tel. 031/225-8331). This three-story emporium is *the* chemist and pharmacist of Edinburgh. Its well-trained staff sells an array of prescription and over-the-counter drugs, as well as leisure goods, garden toys, sports equipment, toys and games, along with audio and photographic equipment.

Laura Ashley, 126 Princes St. (tel. 031/225-1218). Would it be possible to say more about Laura Ashley? In her life, she was credited more than anyone else with bringing homey English chintz back into style, as well as ruffled English blouses. This particular branch of her worldwide empire specializes in garments ranging from those for babies of six months through children's wear and teenage, bridal, and adult fashions in sizes 8 to 16 (United Kingdom sizing). In home furnishings, such as towels, sheets, wallpaper, and linens, you'll find the whole range of Laura Ashley products at the Edinburgh branch at 137 George St. (tel. 301/225-1121).

Clan Royal, 134c Princes St. (tel. 031/225-2319), is one of dozens of stores in Edinburgh selling kilts, fancy gift items (such as tartan-patterned bow ties), wool tartan blankets, scarves, breakfast and teatime jellies and preserves, and lots more.

ALONG THE ROYAL MILE: Founded as a charity nearly 40 years ago to encourage the highest standards of Scottish craft work, the **Scottish Craft Centre,** Acheson House, 140 Canongate (tel. 031/556-8136), has a constantly changing exhibition of crafts, and everything is for sale. It is open Monday to Saturday from 10 a.m. to 5:30 p.m. At your leisure, you can browse among all sorts of typical Scottish products—knitwear, pottery, glass, and jewelry. Everything is reasonably priced, and a mailing service is available.

John Morrison Ltd., 461 Lawnmarket (tel. 031/225-8149), is a marvelous place at which to shop for a tartan. Orders can be mailed throughout the world if you can't take delivery of your Highland dress. Women can order an authentic hand-tailored kilt or a semi-kilt or a kilt skirt. The store also provides evening sashes and stoles to match a skirt. The store specializes in kilts for men, a heavy hand-woven worsted in one's favorite tartan. To go with it, there are doublets and jackets. That's followed up with accessories, a jabot and cuffs along with kilt hose and a tie.

The Scottish Shop, 336-340 Lawnmarket (tel. 031/226-4272). Convenient to Edinburgh Castle, this Highland-inspired gift shop lies near the top of the Royal Mile. It sells a wide variety of woolen goods, walking sticks, jewelry, thistle-shaped wine glasses, and many other souvenir items.

The Shetland Connection, 491 Lawnmarket (tel. 031/225-3525). The owner of this shop, Moira-Anne Leask, is viewed as a boon to some of the knitting industries in the Scottish islands. A battalion of crofters knit the intricately stitched cablewear and Fair Isle designs especially for her shop, which sits on the Royal Mile not far from Edinburgh Castle. Many of the designs follow her own directives. These include sweaters, hats, gloves, and scarves, each made of 100% wool. The store is open seven days a week from 10 a.m. to 6 p.m. VAT refunds and mailing service are available.

Forsyth's of Edinburgh, 183 Canongate (tel. 031/556-6399) has an extensive selection of high-quality woolens at good prices for the value. The staff is helpful and polite, and the shop has clothes and knitwear "of Scottish character for ladies and gentlemen."

ALONG VICTORIA STREET: Victoria Street is called a terrace in the Old Town. In the shadow of the castle, you can enter it on the Royal Mile, walking down a steep hill until you reach Grassmarket. However, you can catch your breath along the way by dropping in at the following.

John Nelson, 22 Victoria St. (tel. 031/225-4413). This art lover's dream carries a well-indexed array of antique prints and maps, including many historical maps of Scotland, the Americas, and the West Indies. In addition, if you're looking for depictions of everything from ivy-covered ruins to antique portrayals of birds and flowers, this is the place. Most of the prints range from 1760 to 1880, while the maps cover the cartographer's skill between 1560 and 1880.

Hours are usually 10 a.m. to noon and 1:30 to 5 p.m. Monday to Friday, 10 a.m. to 1 p.m. and 2 to 5 p.m. on Saturday.

OTHER SHOPPING SUGGESTIONS: For choice items in brass, go to **Top Brass,** 77 Dundas St. (tel. 031/557-4293). Each of the one-of-a-kind items which come from this brilliantly stocked shop originated within a 100-mile radius of Edinburgh. Co-owners Nick Carter and Tom O'Donnell scour the Highlands and north England for the best brassware of the 19th and early 20th century, polishing it to a soft luster. This is not only the most desirable brass shop in Edinburgh, but one of the most comprehensive in Scotland. The owners offer an array of brass headboards, fire fenders, light fixtures, chandeliers, and antique hardware. Larger items can be packaged and shipped.

The best-kept secret for knitted goods is the **Castlecliff** workshops, 25 Johnstone Terrace (tel. 031/226-2623). This is a training school and offers hand-knit sweaters, scarves, socks, and hats. Sweaters cost only about £26 ($41.60) to £28 ($44.80) for adults, around £7 ($11.20) for children's sizes.

Robert Anthony, 108B Rose St. (tel. 031/226-4550), is one of the best jewelry shops in the city. It has a large selection of gold chains and antique and second-hand jewelry. If you're not interested in an expensive purchase, you might choose one of the souvenir nine-karat gold items of Edinburgh, including Highland dancers and Scottish bagpipes.

For the collector, **The Dolls Hospital,** 35a Dundas St., Newtown (tel. 031/556-4295), merits a stop. It presents both original and reproduction dolls in many shapes and sizes.

BRASS RUBBING: For beautiful wall hangings and other gifts, you can make your own brass rubbings or buy them ready-made at the **Scottish Stone & Brass Rubbing Centre,** Trinity Apse, Chalmers Close (near the Royal Mile), which is open Monday to Saturday from 10 a.m. to 5 p.m. (to 6 p.m. from June to September). You can visit the center's collection of replicas molded from ancient Pictish stones, rare Scottish brasses, and medieval church brasses. No experience is needed to make a rubbing. The center will show you how and supply materials. For information, phone 031/225-2424, ext. 6638.

SCOTLAND'S CLAN TARTAN CENTRE: Whether you have a clan to your name or would like to borrow one, the **James Pringle Woolen Mill,** 70-74 Bangor Rd., Leith (tel. 031/553-5161), is the place to find it. The mill produces a large variety of top-quality wool items, including a range of Scottish knitwear such as cashmere sweaters, tartan and tweed ties, travel rugs, tweed hats, tam-o'-shanters—what have you. In addition, the mill has the only Clan Tartan Centre in Scotland, where more than 2,500 sets and trade designs are accessible through their research facilities offered for your use. A free audio-visual presentation shows the history and development of the Tartan. The James Pringle Woollen Mill and its Clan Tartan Center are open from 9 a.m. to 5:30 p.m. Monday to Saturday; on Sunday, April to the end of December, from 10 a.m. to 5:30 p.m. You can visit free, as well as taking advantage of free taxi service to the mill from anywhere in Edinburgh (ask at your hotel).

VISIT TO A CRYSTAL FACTORY: Visitors are welcomed at **Edinburgh Crystal,** Eastfield, Penicuik (tel. 0968/75128), about ten miles south of Edinburgh, just off the A701 to Peebles, devoted entirely to handmade crystal glassware. Tours of the factory, during which you can watch the glassmakers at work, cost 75p ($1.20) for adults, 25p (40¢) for children. They are available from 9 a.m. to 3:30 p.m. Monday to Friday. In the factory shop, you can purchase crystal products slightly below the factory's export quality. The shop is open Monday to Saturday from 9 a.m. to 5 p.m., as well as on Sunday during July, August, and September. A spacious restaurant, Pentland View, serves "Taste of Scotland" fare. The crystal factory dates back to the 1860s.

6. Pubs and Nightlife

Unless you arrive in Edinburgh at festival time, the old city doesn't have a very advanced nightlife. Many Scots go to bed early. However, after touring during the day, you can still find some amusement.

FOLK MUSIC: The folk music center of Edinburgh, **Forrest Hill Bar,** 25 Forrest Rd. (tel. 031/225-2451), is also known as Sandy Bell's. Informal music and singing sessions happen there, and for anyone visiting Edinburgh it's a good place to start off and get the feel of the folk scene. It's best to go between 9 and 11 p.m.

Folk music is presented in many clubs and pubs in Edinburgh, but these strolling players tend to be somewhat erratic or irregular in appearances. It's best to read notices in pubs such as the Forrest Hill Bar and talk to the tourist office to see where the ceilidh will be on the night of your visit.

THE BEST OF THE PUBS: Established in 1806, **Deacon Brodie's Tavern,** 435 Lawnmarket (tel. 031/225-4402), is the neighborhood pub along the Royal Mile. It perpetuates the memory of Deacon Brodie, good citizen by day, robber by night. Mr. Brodie, it is believed, was the inspiration for Robert Louis Stevenson's *The Strange Case of Dr. Jekyll and Mr. Hyde.* Brodie ended up on the gallows on October 1, 1788. The tavern and wine cellars contain a cocktail and lounge bar. It offers a traditional pub setting and lots of atmosphere, making it popular with visitors and locals alike. The tavern is open from 11 a.m. to 11 p.m. daily except Sunday. Inexpensive snacks are served from 11 a.m. to 2:30 p.m., costing from £2.50 ($4), and including cottage pie, Scotch eggs, cheese, and the ploughman's special.

Ma Scott's, 202 Rose St. (tel. 031/225-7401), is a corner pub with tufted settles placed back to back. It still has its Victorian water fountains on the bar. After a revamp, the pub, formerly known as Scott's, was named after its hearty empress who once commanded authority over the rugby players drawn to its precincts. Today it is run by Douggie Wilson. In a totally unpretentious atmosphere, right off Princes Street, you can enjoy good drinks, bar snacks, and dinners. Meals cost from £6 ($9.60). In summer, it is always open at noon daily except Sunday, when it's closed. On Monday, Tuesday, and Wednesday, it shuts down at 11:30 p.m., on Thursday at midnight, and on Friday and Saturday at 2 a.m. In winter, hours are reduced across the board by about half an hour.

The **Guildford Arms,** West Register Street (tel. 031/556-1053), dates back to the "mauve era" of the 1890s. This Victorian-Italianesque corner pub, still harboring its oldtime memories, has one of the most intriguing decors of any pub in Edinburgh—or Scotland for that matter. Next door to the world-famed Café Royal, it lies near the King James Hotel. It still has seven arched windows with etched glass, plus an ornate ceiling, as well as a central bar and around-the-wall seating. It's large, bustling, and at times can be a bit rough, but it's got plenty of character. Hours are from 11 a.m. to 11 p.m. weekdays, from 12:30 to 2:30 p.m. and 6:30 to 11 p.m. on Sunday. Bar lunches, offered only from noon to 2 p.m., cost from £4 ($6.40).

Café Royal Circle Bar, West Register Street (tel. 031/556-1884), is the most famous pub of Edinburgh and a long-enduring favorite. One part of this pub is now occupied by the superb but rather expensive Oyster Bar of the Café Royal.

However, life in the Circle Bar continues at its old pace. The opulent trappings of the Victorian era are still to be seen here, perhaps a little the worse for wear after all these years. Look for the Doulton tile portraits of famous men, including one of Benjamin Franklin. Go up to the serving counter, which stands like an island in a sea of drinkers, and place your order, perhaps for real ale or else a lunchtime snack (or both). Light lunches, including chili con carne, cost from £2.50 ($4). Hours are 11 a.m. to 11 p.m. daily (on Sunday only from 7 to 10:30 p.m.).

Black Bull, 12 Grassmarket (tel. 031/225-6636). Because of this establishment's location on a shop-lined street below the Royal Mile, it is often overlooked by visitors. You can take a shortcut on foot from Edinburgh Castle by descending a steep flight of stone steps, but most pub crawlers enjoy window shopping along the city streets. The pub is decorated like a scarlet version of a Victorian railway car, with tasseled lampshades, a country Victorian mantelpiece, and an ascending series of platforms leading up to the carved bar. Of course, the head of a black bull is one of the pub's focal points. The place jumps at night to the recorded music of whatever group is hot at the time. During the day, lunches, and good ones at that, cost from £2 ($3.20). These might be accompanied by a glass of vintage port or a delightfully tart cider pulled from a tap. The pub is open from 11 a.m. to 11 p.m.

Abbotsford Restaurant and Bar, 3 Rose St. (tel. 031/225-5276). Since both the downstairs pub and the upper-level restaurant are among the most popular establishments of their kind in Edinburgh, no one will mind if you drop in just for a drink. Of course, you might be so entranced by the Victorian ambience that you'll decide to stay for dinner as well. The establishments are in a red sandstone corner building on one of the most popular nightlife streets of Edinburgh. The paneling of the lower section is full grained and well polished, in keeping with the ornately detailed plaster ceiling and the rectangular bar area in the center of the room. A fire burns in chilly weather. Upstairs, some of the most generous portions in the city are served at the hearty, reasonably priced meals. Waitresses are friendly and helpful, as they place the dishes on the immaculate napery-covered tables. Lunches begin at £6.50 ($10.40) for three courses and might include helpings from a cold table, roast lamb, roast beef, or a mixed grill. Dinners are more elaborate, costing £10 ($16) for three courses and including such specialties as roast duck in orange sauce, grilled steak, fried haddock, or haggis with mashed turnips, finished off with a Scottish trifle. You'll find this alluring establishment near the rear entrance to Jenners Department Store. The Abbotsford is open from 11 a.m. to 2:30 p.m. and 5 to 11 p.m. Closed Sunday.

Kenilworth, 152-154 Rose St. (no phone), is an intriguing bar named after the novel by Sir Walter Scott. Originally built as a private home, the locale was sold to a brewery in 1904 when it was lavishly decorated and turned into a very popular pub in the Edwardian style. In 1981 its owners initiated a piece-by-piece renovation of each detail of the elaborately crafted interior. Even the exquisite blue and white wall tiles were carefully and accurately reproduced by a ceramics factory in Glasgow. The tiles, coupled with the rows of stained-glass windows, a massive wooden bar, a coal-burning fireplace, and a jukebox make for a very alluring bar. The clientele is likely to include a cross section of most of the performing arts of Edinburgh. Ales cost from 90p ($1.44), and hours are 11 a.m. to 11 p.m.

Key West, 2B Jamaica St. (tel. 031/225-3422). The inbred world of Scottish gay life finds an outlet in this narrow building in a residential section of town. Don't come expecting Florida sunshine, even though many of the encircling paintings evoke the tropics. The lights are dim, the hot music plays on and on, and conversations occasionally bloom. You can go to Key West from 4 p.m. to midnight Monday to Thursday, to 1 a.m. on Friday and Saturday. Sunday hours are 6:30 to 11 p.m.

THEATERS: The resident company at the **Royal Lyceum Theatre,** Grindlay Street (box office tel. 031/229-9697), enjoys an enviable reputation for its presentations, which may range from Shakespeare to some exciting new playwright.

King's Theatre, 2 Leven St. (tel. 031/229-1201), is the premier theater of Edinburgh, offering a wide repertoire of classical entertainment, including ballet and opera. West End productions from London are also presented here.

Traverse Theatre, 112 West Bow, Grassmarket (tel. 031/226-2633), below Edinburgh Castle, is technically a private theater club, but you may be able to gain admission. The theater is famous throughout Great Britain for its experimental productions. Some have been quite controversial.

Playhouse Theatre, 18-22 Greenside Place (box office tel. 031/557-2590), is the biggest entertainment center in the city. Pop concerts featuring top stars in both England and America have appeared here. Musical productions are presented, along with visiting ballet and opera companies. Perhaps you'll be fortunate enough to see the Scottish Ballet performing *Swan Lake.*

MUSIC: At the setting for musical events, **Usher Hall,** Lothian Road (tel. 031/228-1155), you can see everything from Gilbert and Sullivan highlights to soloists from the D'Oyly Carte Opera Company.

Queen's Hall, 5 Hope Park Crescent (tel. 031/668-3456), is where you are likely to hear the Edinburgh Symphony Orchestra. You might also be treated to the Edinburgh "Pops" here.

FILMS: Chances are, language won't be a problem.

The leading cinema houses include **Filmhouse,** Lothian Road (tel. 031/228-2688).

You can also see films at **ABC,** also on Lothian Road (tel. 031/229-3030).

Another leading cinema is **Dominion,** Newbattle Terrace (tel. 031/447-2660).

If you don't like what's playing at any of the above, try the **Odeon Cinema,** Clerk Street (tel. 031/667-7331).

MAINLY DISCO: Containing the largest dance floor in Edinburgh, **Outer Limits,** Coasters Complex, 3 West Tollcross Rd. (tel. 031/228-3252), offers almost guaranteed action. The complex was originally built in the 1920s as a dance hall, but today its vast capacity witnesses disco fever. The main area, Outer Limits, charges admission of between £2 ($3.20) and £3 ($4.80) during its adult hours Friday, Saturday, and Sunday from 10:30 p.m. to 4 a.m. (On some week nights, the place is reserved for teenagers and is unlicensed at that time.) On the premises are separate rooms devoted to reggae, the blues, and country western. These are open only on Friday and Saturday from 10:30 p.m. to 4 a.m., charging an admission of £2 ($3.20) each. Throughout the complex, a pint of lager costs £1.25 ($2). Each area has a separate entrance from the street.

Buster Browns, 25 Market St. (tel. 031/226-4224). When this place opened its doors it was the first disco of its type in Edinburgh. It's still going strong, attracting a lively clientele. It is open seven days a week from 9:30 a.m. to 3 a.m. The entrance fee, depending on your sex and the time you enter, ranges from £2 ($3.20) to £3.50 ($5.60).

Chapter IV

ALONG THE RIVER AND FIRTH OF FORTH

1. Stirling
2. Dunblane
3. Doune
4. Linlithgow
5. North Berwick
6. Dirleton
7. Dunbar
8. Dalkeith
9. Haddington

SOME OF THE MOST interesting castles and mansions in Scotland lie within easy reach of Edinburgh, along the narrow midsection of the country marked by the River Forth and the land around the Scottish capital as it widens into the broad estuary known as the Firth of Forth.

Across this belt, much of the early history of Scotland was written, often in blood, as Highland clans and Lowland thanes vied for power from the time the country was known as Caledonia to very recent days, viewed in the sweep of history. Always, too, there was the rivalry with the kings of England who wanted to rule all of the British Isles and sent wave after wave of troops to try to subdue the stubborn Scots during the centuries.

This is the land of Mary Queen of Scots, whose associations with the castles, most now in ruins, from Stirling to the cold waters of the North Sea, enrich the lore of the Forth and its environs on the south side.

1. Stirling

Almost equidistant from Edinburgh and Glasgow, Stirling is dominated by its impressive castle, perched on a 250-foot basalt rock on the main east-west route across Scotland, formed by the River Forth and the River Clyde and the relatively small section of land between them. The ancient town of Stirling, which grew up around the castle, lies in the heart of an area so turbulent in Scottish history that it was called "the cockpit of Scotland," the scene of several battles. One of the most memorable of these was the Battle of Bannockburn in 1314, when Robert I Bruce defeated the army of Edward II of England.

Stirling can easily be reached by car or train from either Glasgow or Edinburgh. From Edinburgh, a bus takes about 1½ hours to travel the distance of 37 miles.

Stirling is the central crossroads of Scotland, giving easy access by rail and road to all its major towns and cities. If you use it as a base, it is also only a short drive to many tourist attractions, including Loch Lomond, the Trossachs, and the Highlands.

The town center boasts several excellent shopping facilities, including the Thistle Centre indoor shopping precinct.

WHERE TO STAY: In the heart of town, the **Golden Lion Hotel,** 8-10 King St. (tel. 0786/75351), is privately owned. For those seeking a traditional Scottish hotel, it might be an ideal choice, as it offers a total of 86 comfortably furnished rooms, the majority of which contain private baths or showers. Each unit also has a color TV, coffee equipment, a direct-dial phone, and a radio alarm. Depending on the plumbing (or lack of it), a single ranges from £25 ($40) to £37 ($59.20), a double from £41 ($65.60) to £54 ($86.40), which puts the place in the splurge category. Built in 1786 as a coaching inn, the hotel lies only a block from Holyrood Church, the most famous in Stirling, behind a buff gold facade. Its dining facilities are recommended separately.

King's Gate Hotel, 5 King St. (tel. 0786/73944), is a 19th-century hotel lying in the heart of Stirling, just a short walk from the modern shopping plaza, the Thistle Centre. You climb a flight of stairs to the second-floor reception area where the publican will step out of his nautically cozy pub to assist newcomers. Mr. and Mrs. Wallace offer a total of 15 bedrooms, five of which contain a private bath. These rooms are furnished practically, often with cove moldings. They were formed from a series of flats or apartments which were linked together in 1974. Depending on the plumbing, a single rents for £18 ($28.80) to £21 ($33.60), a double costing £26 ($41.60) to £29 ($46.40).

Terraces, 4 Melville Terrace (tel. 0786/72268), is a 14-bedroom Georgian town house standing on a raised terrace in the vicinity of the shopping center. In its relatively modest price range, it is perhaps the finest choice in Stirling for those seeking good food and lodging. Eleven of the bedrooms contain a private bath or shower, and each unit is comfortably and attractively furnished. The charge in a single is £21 ($33.60) to £25 ($40), in a double £16 ($25.60) to £20 ($32) per person. The hotel serves a fine Scottish cuisine, offering both set meals and table d'hôte menus. Dinners cost from £8.50 ($13.60).

Sunnedene, 10 Causewayhead Rd. (tel. 0786/62310), is an excellent B&B run by Marion and Hamish MacPhee, who have recently tastefully redecorated two of their three bedrooms and the bathroom. The hospitable MacPhees charge £10 ($16) per person for a night's stay. One reader reports that Sunnedene is "right out of *Better Homes & Gardens.*"

Dalglennan Guest House, 4 Allan Park (tel. 0786/3432), is a centrally heated B&B establishment owned by Mrs. J. Brodie. She charges £9 ($14.40) in a single room, £8.50 ($13.60) per person in a double or twin. Her rooms are clean; there is individual room heating, hot and cold water, and if you are in the mood, a lounge for watching TV. The guesthouse is in the residential section of Stirling, near tennis courts and swimming baths, and it's walkable from the bus and train stations.

WHERE TO EAT: On the banks of the River Forth, the **Riverway Restaurant,** Kildean, outside Stirling (tel. 0786/75734), is a fully licensed restaurant run by the Ball family, with a local reputation for good food at moderate tariffs. The restaurant is only half a mile from the center of Stirling, just off the M9 on the road to the Trossachs, with panoramic views of the Ochil Hills. The Riverway offers well-prepared food, such as grilled pork chops, rainbow trout meunière, and farmhouse grill. At lunchtime, you can order a real Scottish menu, including, say, lentil broth, Scotch haggis and turnip, and perhaps rhubarb crumble with custard sauce, a meal costing less than £4 ($6.40). The high tea menu, really a filling early supper, costs from £4.50 ($7.20) and has such rib-sticking fare as grilled hamburgers, fried haddock, honey-baked gammon with mixed salads, and sirloin steaks. Wine of the house is sold by the glass or the bottle. Hours are from noon until last orders are taken at 6:30 p.m. seven days a week. On Wednesday and Thursday, visitors often enjoy looking around the cattle market and rubbing elbows in the restaurant with the local farm folk.

The Golden Lion, 8-10 King St. (tel. 0786/75351), is a high-ceilinged, Edwardian-style dining room, serving a robust British cuisine. During the day (that is, from noon to 2:30 p.m.), bar lunches prevail. Costing from £4 ($6.40), the fare is likely to include lasagne, homemade steak pie, and the chef's roast of the day. However, at dinner from 7 to 10 p.m., a different cuisine prevails. Most diners gravitate to the carvery roast table where a chef will carve your selection of meat, perhaps a roast rib of Angus beef that is likely to be both tender and juicy. Other main dish selections feature a whole Dover sole or chicken suprême.

THE BEST PUB: Dating from 1733, **Settle Inn,** 91 St. Mary's Wynd (tel. 0786/74609), is said to be the oldest inn in this ancient town. Much rejuvenated, it has a fireplace built of stone. Sitting in front of it on a chilly day is about the best place to anchor in all of Stirling. The atmosphere is as you'd expect, one of time-blackened beams and old stone, with benches and chairs placed around for a medley of guests ranging from tourists to locals. You get good bar food here, not only Scottish pie but well-stuffed sandwiches along with hot dishes every day including cottage pie and perhaps a creamy pasta. Meals cost from £3.50 ($5.60). The inn is open from 11 a.m. to 11 p.m. daily.

SIGHTS: On the right bank of the Forth, **Stirling Castle,** Upper Castle Hill (tel. 0786/62517), dates from the Middle Ages, when its location on a dividing line between the Lowlands and the Highlands caused it to become known as "the key to the Highlands." There are traces of earlier (7th century) royal habitation of the Stirling area, but it became a firm part of written history when Scots bled with Wallace and were led by Bruce during the Wars of Independence (from England) in the 13th and 14th centuries. The castle became an important seat of Kings James IV and James V, both of whom added to the structures, the latter following classic Renaissance style, then relatively unknown in Britain. Here Mary Queen of Scots lived as an infant monarch for the first four years of her life.

After the final defeat of Bonnie Prince Charlie's army, stopped here in 1746, the castle became an army barracks and headquarters of the Argyll and Sutherland Highlanders, one of Britain's most celebrated regiments. The castle and visitors' audio-visual center is open from 9:30 a.m. to 6 p.m. Monday to Saturday and 10:30 a.m. to 5:30 p.m. on Sunday from April to the end of September; from 9:30 a.m. to 5:30 p.m. Monday to Saturday and 12:30 to 4:20 p.m. on Sunday from October to the end of March. Last tickets are sold 45 minutes before closing times. Admission is £1.50 ($2.40) for adults, 75p ($1.20) for children. A family ticket is available for £3 ($4.80).

Also at the castle, you can visit the **Museum of the Argyll and Sutherland**

Highlanders (tel. 0786/75165). It presents an excellent exhibition of colors, pipe banners, and regiment silver, along with medals (some of which go back to the Battle of Waterloo). Admission-free, it is open from April to September on Monday to Saturday from 10 a.m. to 5:30 p.m. (Sunday, 11 a.m. to 5 p.m.). Off-season hours are from 10 a.m. to 4 p.m.

The **Church of the Holy Rude** on St. John Street is said to be the only church in the country that is still in use which has witnessed a coronation. The date was 1567 when the 13-month-old James VI was crowned. John Knox preached the sermon. The church itself dates from the early 15th century, and in its day it attracted none other than Mary Queen of Scots. It is open daily from 10 a.m. to 5 p.m. May to September.

One of the most interesting excursions is to **Bannockburn,** a name that looms large in Scottish history. It was here that Robert the Bruce, his army of 6,000 outnumbered three to one, defeated the forces of Edward II in 1314. Before nightfall Robert the Bruce had won back the throne of Scotland. The battlefield lies off the M80, two miles south of Stirling.

At the **Bannockburn Heritage Centre** (tel. 0786/812664), an audio-visual presentation tells the story of these events. The Queen herself came here in 1964 to unveil an equestrian statue of the Scottish hero. The center is open daily from 10 a.m. to 6 p.m. April to October, charging an admission of 80p ($1.28) for adults and 40p (64¢) for children. At the Borestone, where Robert the Bruce commanded his forces, you can see Stirling Castle and the Forth Valley.

2. Dunblane

A small cathedral city on the banks of the Allan Water, Dunblane lies about seven miles north of Stirling, on the road to Perth. It takes its name from the Celtic Church of St. Blane, which once stood on the site now occupied by the fine 13th-century Gothic cathedral.

Sports enthusiasts are attracted to the area because of its golfing, fishing, and hunting possibilities.

FOOD AND LODGING: On the main highway between Perth and Dunblane, the **Red Comyn Inn,** Perth Road (tel. 0786/824343), lies only a short ride from the city center. This slate-roofed, stone-built two-story house rents out seven comfortably furnished bedrooms, none with private bath. The overnight charge is £9.50 ($15.20) per person in a double, £13 ($20.80) in a single, with breakfast costing extra. Actually, Margaret and Fred Cumming welcome more diners to their two-acre site than they do overnighters. Guests can enjoy real ale in the inn's beer garden, or, if the weather is bad, retreat to one of the lounge bars. Food is served from 8 a.m. to midnight daily. Bar meals cost from £3.50 ($5.60), with dinners going for £11 ($17.60). Dishes might include Red Comyn salmon, roast venison, or Perth trout.

DUNBLANE CATHEDRAL: An excellent example of 13th-century Gothic ecclesiastic architecture, Dunblane Cathedral was spared the ravages of attackers who destroyed other Scottish worship centers. Altered in the 15th century and restored several times in the 19th and 20th centuries, the cathedral may have suffered the most from neglect subsequent to the Reformation. A Jesse Tree window is in the west end of the building, and of interest are stalls, misericords, a pulpit with carved figures of early ecclesiastical figures, and other striking features, including the wooden, barrel-vaulted roof with colorful armorials. A Celtic stone from about A.D. 900 can be seen in the north aisle.

Bishop Robert Leighton, an outstanding leader of the 17th century who did much to resolve religious bickerings, is represented by his personal library, in a 1687 structure on the grounds of the old manse. It is of interest because of the bishop's material on the 17th century and the effects of the troubled times on Scotland. The **Cathedral Museum** is in the Dean's House and contains articles and papers pertaining to both the cathedral and the town. Admission-free, it is open June to September Monday to Saturday from 10:30 a.m. to 12:30 p.m. and 2:30 to 4:30 p.m. The story of Dunblane and its ancient cathedral is displayed here in this 1624 house, and you can also visit an enclosed garden with a restored old well.

3. Doune

Some 41 miles from Edinburgh, this small market town with its 15th-century castle is a good center for exploring the Trossachs. The Rivers Teith and Ardoch flow through Doune.

FOOD AND LODGING: A pleasant stone structure, **The Woodside,** Stirling Road (tel. 07861/841237), stands on the A84 main Stirling–Oban road. In the heart of Perthshire, it was originally a coaching inn and dates back to the 18th century. It contains 14 well-furnished bedrooms. With private baths, singles rent for £22 ($35.20), and doubles cost from £36 ($57.60), including a full breakfast. The lounge is brightened by red plush seating and is brimful with antiques. The lounge bar has an open fire and offers a selection of more than 100 malt whiskies. You can enjoy a selection of traditional salad dishes on the bar luncheon menu with soused herring and homemade pâté salads. Grilled Aberdeen Angus steaks are also served. The dining room overlooks the garden, and you sit in high-backed carved Edwardian chairs, enjoying such specialties as venison, salmon, and lobster in season. Dinner is likely to cost from £12 ($19.20). On Sunday dinner is served only to residents.

Your best bet for dinner is **Broughtons,** Burnbank Cottages, Blair Drummond (tel. 0786/841897), which lies less than three miles south on the A873. A continental cuisine is served and done so with a certain flair. Whenever possible, only fresh ingredients are used (not abused) in the kitchen. À la carte dinners cost £13.75 ($22) and up. Hours are from 6 to 9 p.m. The restaurant is closed Sunday and Monday.

SIGHTS: On the banks of the River Teith, **Doune Castle** (tel. 0786/84203) stands four miles west of Dunblane. Once it was a royal palace. Now owned by the Earl of Moray, it was restored in 1883, making it one of the best preserved of the medieval castles of Scotland. The castle is open in summer from 9:30 a.m. to 7 p.m. Monday to Saturday, from 2 to 7 p.m. on Sunday. In winter, closing is at 4 p.m. as well as on Friday and on alternate Saturdays, Christmas holidays, and New Year's. Admission is £1 ($1.60) for adults, 50p (80¢) for children.

After visiting the castle, guests can drive 1½ miles to the **Doune Motor Museum** (tel. 0786/841203), which charges £1.60 ($2.56) for adults, 80p ($1.28) for children. The motor museum contains about 40 vintage and postvintage motor cars, including the second-oldest Rolls-Royce in the world. It is open daily from April 1 to October 31. In April and May the last admissions are at 4:30 p.m. From June to August the hours are 10 a.m. to 5:30 p.m., and in September and October, the last admissions are again at 4:30 p.m.

South of Doune is the **Blair Drummond Safari and Leisure Park** (tel. 0786/841456). You meet the typical cast of animal safari characters here, and the park also offers a jungle cruise, a giant astraglide, and an amusement arcade, as well as a pets corner and an aquatic mammals show. Open from the first week in April to the first week in September, the park can be visited from 10 a.m. daily, with last admission at 4:30 p.m. Adults pay £3 ($4.80); children 3 to 14 are charged £2 ($3.20); and children under 3 get in free. A safari bus is available for visitors with three-wheeler or soft-top cars, costing £3.30 ($5.28) for adults, £2.30 ($3.68) for children. You can have refreshments at the Jambo Bar or in the Ranch Kitchen (tel. 0786/841430), or use one of the picnic areas. To reach the park, take exit 10 off the M9 onto the A84 near Stirling.

4. Linlithgow

In this royal burgh, a county town in West Lothian, 18 miles west of Edinburgh, Mary Queen of Scots was born. The roofless **Palace of Linlithgow,** site of her birth in 1542, can still be viewed here today, even if it is but a shell of its former self.

FOOD AND LODGING: In accommodations, **Woodcockdale Farm,** Lanark Road (tel. 0506/842088), is a farmhouse with guest accommodations on the A706, 1½ miles from Linlithgow. Mrs. W. Erskine has rooms to rent which fit many needs. She offers three double rooms, one family room with a double and twin beds, and another two rooms with double and bunk beds. The bathroom adjoins the first-floor rooms, a toilet and shower adjoins the ground-floor rooms. The daily rate is £9 ($14.40) per person for a bed and a full "Taste of Scotland" traditional breakfast. Children are welcome at reduced rates. Included are tea, cookies, or cake at 10 p.m. before you retire. The living room has color TV. The house is centrally heated.

If you prefer a more central location, **The Cedars Guest House,** High Street (tel. 0506/845952), has five bedrooms, served by one public bath with shower. The guesthouse is comfortably and pleasantly simple, with singles costing £11 ($17.60) to £16 ($25.60) and doubles going for £10 ($16) to £12 ($19.20) per person, including a Scottish breakfast. Guests are received throughout the year.

For dining, **Champany** (tel. 050683/4532), lies two miles to the northeast (off the A904). This was once a farmhouse built of stone, but it has been handsomely converted into a chop and ale house, one of the finest places for dining in the area. The dining room is circular, with a steep hexagonal ceiling. Victorian mahogany furniture adds a sedate touch. They specialize in grills, and you'll find some of the best steaks in Scotland here. The owner has a butchery, and you can choose your own cut and watch it being grilled. On a recent visit I had a rib loin, accompanied by chili sauce with tomatoes, a fresh, crisp salad to follow, finishing with a pineapple shortcake made with fresh fruit. Lunch or dinner costs from £16 ($25.60), worth the price considering the quality of the food. Lunch is served from noon to 2 p.m. and dinner from 6:30 to 10 p.m. The restaurant is open daily except Sunday night. The Champany also has a charming Country Life Bar, specializing in real ale.

SIGHTS: The birthplace of Mary Queen of Scots, as mentioned above, **Linlithgow Palace,** once a favorite residence of Scottish kings, was built square-shaped. In the center are the remains of a royal fountain erected by James V. The suite occupied by the queen was in the north quarter, but this was rebuilt for the homecoming of James VI (James I of Great Britain) in 1620. The palace was burned in 1746, destroying one of the gems in the Scottish architectural crown. The Great Hall is on the first floor, and a small display shows some of the more interesting relics of architecture. The castle is open from 9:30 a.m. to 7 p.m. Monday to Saturday, from 2 to 7 p.m. on Sunday April to September, in all cases closing at 4 p.m. in winter. Admission is £1 ($1.60) for adults, 50p (80¢) for children. For information, phone 031/2262570.

South of the palace stands the medieval kirk of **St. Michael the Archangel.** It is considered one of the best examples of a medieval parish church remaining in the country. The golden crown is of late vintage, having taken the place of one from the Middle Ages which fell in 1820. It is open from June to September daily from 10 a.m. to noon and 2 to 4 p.m., charging no admission. Off-season hours are the same, but it is open only Monday to Friday. For information, phone 0506/842195.

From Linlithgow, it is but a 3½-mile drive east on the Queensferry road (A904) to the **House of the Binns** (tel. 050683/4255), the historic home of the Dalyells. The mansion, with its fine Jacobean plaster ceilings, portraits, and panoramic vistas, receives visitors Easter weekend and then from May 1 to September 30 daily except Friday from 2 to 5 p.m. The parkland is open from 10 a.m. to 7 p.m. Admission is £1.80 ($2.88) for adults, 90p ($1.44) for children.

HOPETOUN HOUSE: This is Scotland's greatest Adam mansion, and a fine example of 18th-century architecture. It is the seat of the Marquess of Linlithgow, whose grandfather and father were respectively the Governor-general of Australia and the Viceroy of India. Set in the midst of beautifully landscaped grounds laid out along the lines of Versailles, the mansion (tel. 031/331-2451) lies near the Forth Road Bridge at South Queensferry, off the A904. On a tour you're shown through splendid reception rooms filled with 18th-century furniture, paintings, statuary, and other works of art. From a rooftop viewing platform, you look out over a panoramic view of the Firth of Forth. Even more enjoyable, perhaps, is to take the nature trail, explore the deer parks, investigate the Stables Museum, or stroll through the formal gardens, all in the grounds. Near the Ballroom Suite, refreshments are available. Hopetoun is open Easter weekend and from April to mid-September daily from 11 a.m. to 5:30 p.m. Last entry to the house is at 5 p.m. For £2 ($3.20) for adults and £1 ($1.60) for children, visitors can view the house (including the museum and rooftop viewing platform), the deer parks, nature trail, and Stables Museum. The drive is ten miles from Edinburgh.

5. North Berwick

This royal burgh, created in the 14th century, was once an important Scottish port. In East Lothian, 24 miles east from Edinburgh, it is today a holiday resort popular with the Scots and an increasing horde of foreigners just discovering the place. Visitors are drawn to its golf courses, beach sands, and harbor life on the Firth of Forth. You can climb the rocky shoreline or else enjoy the heated outdoor swimming pool in July and August.

WHERE TO STAY: Opening onto East Bay, on the waterfront, **Cragside Guest House,** 16 Marine Parade (tel. 0620/2879), is one of the best B&B accommodations in this popular summer spot. Six comfortable and pleasantly decorated rooms are rented, all with hot and cold water basins and hot beverage facilities. The charge is from £11 ($17.60) per person nightly, with a full Scottish breakfast included. You can take half board for £15 ($24) per person. The golf course is two minutes away.

Blenheim House Hotel (tel. 0620/2385) is one of the best hotels in town for those willing to pay more. It receives guests year round. It's small, offering only 11 rooms, each pleasantly furnished. Six contain their own private baths. Rates are £20 ($32) per person in a bathless room, £22 ($35.20) per person with bath, and a Scottish breakfast is included. Good dinners are also offered, with generous portions. Service is until 9 p.m. The hotel is popular in summer, so reservations are important.

Point Garry Hotel, West Bay Road (tel. 0620/2380), overlooks the West Golf Course and the sea, and is adjacent to the first tee and 18th green of the golf course. On a quiet residential street with dahlias growing in its garden, this is an imposing Victorian house, one of the best small hotels in North Berwick. Mr. and Mrs. E.W. Stewart welcome visitors in one of their 15 bedrooms, eight of which contain private baths. The charge for half board ranges from £27 ($43.20) to £29 ($46.40) per person nightly. Good Scottish food is served in a dining room overlooking the water, and the establishment is fully licensed.

Another good bargain is the **Brentwood Private Hotel,** Clifford Road (tel. 0620/2783). It too is small, offering only ten rooms, but each is pleasantly furnished and comfortably appointed. The three baths are shared. The cost is from £10 ($16) per person, with a full Scottish breakfast included. It's also possible to have half board, costing from £14 ($22.40) per person. Open all year.

WHERE TO EAT: An inviting trattoria, **Vagabondo,** 35 High St. (tel. 0620/ 3434), serves some of the best cuisine in town, with meals costing from £11 ($17.60). A cheerful, popular place, run by a friendly staff, it serves lunch from noon to 2 p.m. and dinner from 6 to 10 p.m. (closed Monday only in winter). Lunch is not served on Sunday. Carefully chosen ingredients are cooked with expertise. You might opt for the mussels in onion sauce, the spaghetti and veal, or pepper steak. For dessert, the most spectacular finish is the crêpes Suzette.

SIGHTS IN THE ENVIRONS: At the Information Centre, Quality Street (tel. 0620/2197), you can pick up data on how to take boat trips to the offshore islands, including **Bass Rock,** a breeding ground inhabited by about 10,000 gannets and one or two crusty lighthouse keepers. The volcanic island is one mile in circumference. It's possible to see the rock from the harbor. The viewing is even better at **Berwick Law,** a volcanic lookout point surmounted by the jawbones of a whale.

Some two miles east of the resort on the A198 stand the dramatic ruins of the 14th-century diked and rose-colored **Tantallon Castle,** rising magnificently on cliffs. This was the ancient stronghold of the Douglases from the time of its construction in the 14th century until its defeat by Cromwell's forces in 1651. Overlooking the Firth of Forth, the castle ruins still are formidable, with a square, five-story central tower and an interesting dovecote, plus the shell of its east tower, a D-shaped structure with a wall from the central tower. Tantallon Castle can be visited weekdays from 9:30 a.m. to 7 p.m. and on Sunday from 2 to 7 p.m. from late March to the end of September, with closing at 4 p.m. from October to the end of March. It is also closed on Tuesday and Wednesday. Admission is £1 ($1.60) for adults, 50p (80¢) for children.

6. Dirleton

Another popular excursion from Edinburgh is to this little town that vies for the title of "prettiest village in Scotland." The town plan, drafted in the early 16th century, is essentially unchanged today. Dirleton has two greens shaped like triangles, with a pub opposite Dirleton Castle (see below), placed at right angles to a group of cottages. Dirleton is a preservation village and as such is subject to careful control of any development. It's on the Edinburgh–North Berwick road (the A198).

WHERE TO STAY: Unspoiled by certain obligatory modernizations, the **Castle Inn** (tel. 062085/221) is a most satisfactory village inn for the individual traveler or family who wants an accommodation with a personal touch. It's directly opposite the village green and the castle, a long, low building in the center, with ten dormer windows and a pair of entrances. The proprietor, Douglas Stewart, has four bedrooms with private baths, and another four in an annex, each pleasantly furnished and containing hot and cold water. The charge here for B&B (including all the famed Scottish dishes) is £14 ($22.40) and an evening meal is from £7 ($11.20). During the day it's possible to obtain light snacks. Guests have a lounge with a free-standing stone fireplace, decorated with copper pots. Against rugged stone walls are settles and trestle tables. Behind the bar the decoration is Victorian mahogany.

DIRLETON CASTLE: A rose-tinted 13th-century castle with surrounding gardens, Dirleton Castle, started in the 13th century by the wealthy Anglo-Norman de Vaux family, looks like a fairytale fortification, with its towers, arched entries, and an oak ramp similar to the drawbridge that once protected it. Well preserved, the castle was built with prison, bakehouse, and storehouses carved from the bedrock. Ruins of the great hall and kitchen can be seen, as well as what's left of the lord's chamber where the de Vaux family lived. You can see the windows and window seats, a wall with a toilet and drains, and other household features. The 16th-century main gate has a hole through which boiling tar or water could be poured to discourage unwanted visitors.

The castle's country garden and a bowling green are still in use, with masses of flowering plants rioting in the gardens and bowlers sometimes seen on the green. A 17th-century dovecot with 1,100 nests stands at the east end of the garden. A small gate at the west end leads onto one of the village greens.

The castle can be visited from April to September, weekdays from 9:30 a.m. to 7 p.m. (on Sunday from 2 to 7 p.m.); October to March, weekdays from 9:30 a.m. to 4 p.m. (on Sunday from 2 to 4 p.m.). Admission to the castle and gardens is £1 ($1.60) for adults and 50p (80¢) for children.

7. Dunbar

In East Lothian, southeast of North Berwick, Dunbar, another royal burgh, is a popular seaside resort at the foot of the Lammermuir Hills. The River Tyne reaches the North Sea nearby, and it was here that Cromwell landed his invasion forces, heading for Edinburgh.

WHERE TO STAY: A mile outside Dunbar, the **Battleblent Hotel,** West Barns (tel. 0368/62234), lies on the road to Edinburgh, 26 miles away. Jim and Faye Ferguson own the castle-like home set on a hill surrounded by three acres of their own land overlooking Balhaven Bay on the Firth of Forth. The bedrooms are large, high-ceilinged, and comfortable, with private baths, color TV, direct-dial phones, hot-beverage facilities, and radio-alarms. B&B prices per person in this centrally heated hotel are £18.50 ($29.60) with a continental breakfast, £21.50 ($34.40) with a full Scottish morning meal. Assisted by their sons, Martin and Kevin, the Fergusons offer good food in the dining room and popular bar meals. Locals and tourists socialize in the Tudor Lounge Bar or dance and dine in the Country Club Bar. Get Mr. Ferguson to show you his collection of international coins in the downstairs bar.

Springfield Guest House, Belhaven Road (tel. 0368/62502), is one of the best guesthouses in Dunbar, attracting a lot of summer visitors to this East Lothian royal burgh. In the western part of town, it stands on the main road. In all, it rents out only seven bedrooms, and there are three public baths which are shared. The house is pleasantly decorated, the rooms comfortable, and guests can enjoy a garden out back. The charge in a single is from £13.50 ($21.60), rising to £23 ($36.80) in a double. A light evening meal can be served, and the hotel receives guests only from March through October.

SIGHTS: On a rock above the harbor are the remains of **Dunbar Castle,** built on the site of an earlier castle that dated from 856. Mary Queen of Scots fled there with Darnley in 1566, immediately after the murder of her secretary, Rizzio. Today the kittiwakes live where once the "Black Agnes of Dunbar," the Countess of March, held off the English. The Battle of Dunbar was fought in 1650 between Cromwell's army and the Scots led by David Leslie. The Scots, fighting valiantly, lost and nearly 3,000 were killed in one day.

About 6½ miles west of Dunbar sits **Hailes Castle,** just off the A1 road and also reached by a little road running from East Linton to Haddington. On the bank of the River Tyne, the castle was not a fortress for military action but rather a fortified mansion home and is considered one of the outstanding examples of 13th-century masonry construction. Mary Queen of Scots slept here in 1545 when she was being escorted to Dunbar from Edinburgh by the Earl of Bothwell during a period in which the English were trying to force her to marry the boy who was to become King Edward VI. If you want a good shudder, you can climb by ladder down into the pit prisons at the base of the castle's towers. No ladders were provided for the descent of prisoners into the dark, damp pits— they were simply dropped through the hatches. At Hailes, you can see a vaulted bakehouse in the cellar of a 15th-century structure, plus a chapel. You can go through a little gate in the north wall of the castle and stroll along a grassy promenade along the Tyne. The castle is open weekdays from 9:30 a.m. to 7 p.m., on Sunday from 2 to 7 p.m. from late March to the end of September, until 4 p.m. from October to the end of March except Tuesday and Wednesday. Admission is £1 ($1.60) for adults, 50p (80¢) for children.

If you take a walk up the hill from the main gate of Hailes Castle, on the south wall, you'll come to **Traprain Law,** where an ancient hill-fort stood in the Iron Age, although there's not much to see there now except the view of the castle below. It is believed that this was once occupied by the Votadini, a tribe allied to the Romans.

8. Dalkeith

A small town in Midlothian, Dalkeith was a baronial burgh when the Douglas clan held sway. Today, the town center is modern, but there are also several historic buildings. On the A68 road, near the busy A7, Dalkeith lies between the South Esk and North Esk rivers, seven miles southeast of Edinburgh.

WHERE TO STAY: A 20-room hostelry, the **County Hotel and Restaurant,** 152 High St. (tel. 031/663-3495), is run by Philip Coppola and sons. All rooms have private bath facilities, color TV, radios, hot-drinks equipment, and direct-dial phones. The charge is £23 ($36.80) in a single, £32 ($51.20) for double occupancy, the tariffs including VAT and a full Scottish breakfast. The restaurant serves meals all day, and the hotel also has a bar and an elevator to all floors.

Less expensive is the **Birchlea Guest House,** 127 High St. (tel. 031/663-4280), which has only eight bedrooms to rent, all with TV and hot beverage facilities. The hotel is comfortable, the management most accommodating. A single is rented for £9 ($14.40) nightly, while a double goes for £18 ($28.80), these tariffs including a full Scottish breakfast. The guesthouse is open all year.

WHERE TO EAT: With the longest name of any restaurant or dining spot in town, **George's Pizza and Spaghetti House and Cavaliere Restaurant,** 124-126 High St. (tel. 031/663-4492), also serves the best food. Not only that, but you can "wine and dine," as their advertisement proclaims, until 1:30 a.m., and in "sleepy" Dalkeith too. Many people drop in just to enjoy pizza, which comes in several varieties, along with a bottle of wine. The pastas, including the creamy lasagne, are generally excellent, and you can also order more substantial fare, including some of the best of Scottish beef, served in the classic grilled T-bone way, or given a continental flair and served with a perfectly balanced brandy sauce. Fresh fish, including mussels, are served in savory sauces, with meals costing from £8 ($12.80) up. The atmosphere is that of a typical Italian trattoria, and hours are Monday through Thursday from 5 p.m. to 1 a.m., on Friday to 1:30 a.m., on Saturday from noon to 1:30 a.m. (the busiest day), and even on Sunday from 4 p.m. to 1:30 a.m. It's quite a town rendezvous point.

SIGHTS: This is the site of **Dalkeith Palace,** rebuilt and redesigned by Sir John Vanbrugh, circa 1700. Such monarchs as George IV, Victoria, and Edward VII have stayed here during visits to Edinburgh.

Visitors flock here for **Dalkeith Park,** Buccleuch Estates (tel. 031/663-5684), to explore the woodland and riverside walks in and around the extensive grounds of the palace. Luring guests are natural trails and an adventure woodland play area, a tunnel walk, and an Adam bridge. The park is open daily from 11 a.m. to 6 p.m. from the first of April until the end of October. During November the park is open only on Saturday and Sunday from 11 a.m. to dusk. To reach the park, go seven miles south of Edinburgh on the A68. The price of admission is 65p ($1.04).

9. Haddington

Created as a royal burgh by David I, this small town of East Lothian lies on the Tyne River, about 17 miles east of Edinburgh. In the 15th century it was Scotland's largest town, but its fortunes declined thereafter.

FOOD AND LODGING: The finest inn in town is the **George,** 91 High St. (tel. 062082/3372). If you want a room, it offers 13 comfortably appointed ones, five of which contain private baths. The cost is from £25 ($40) in a single, rising to £37 ($59.20) in a double, including a full Scottish breakfast. You can also stay here on the half-board arrangement, the least expensive way, at a rate of £32 ($51.20) in a single £27.50 ($44) per person in a double. Guests are received throughout the year except in December and January. The food is a medley of Scottish and continental dishes, and service is polite and friendly and also efficient. Lunch costs from £2.15 ($3.44) up, while a dinner goes for £9 ($14.40) and up.

Browns Hotel, 1 West Rd. (tel. 062082/2254), is the domain of Colin Brown, who is the most accomplished chef in the area. In this Georgian hotel, he welcomes guests for dinner only Monday to Saturday from 7:30 to 9 p.m., offering a table d'hôte at £14.50 ($23.20). The menu changes based on seasonal produce and the inspiration of Mr. Brown who is ably assisted by his mother, Margaret. The cookery shows both British and French influences, and the place is full of character. This is a small, special restaurant, and you should reserve a table. On the village green, the hotel also rents out six attractively furnished bedrooms, four of which contain a private bath or shower. Charges for B&B range from £21 ($33.60) to £23 ($36.80) per person.

SIGHTS: On the right bank of the river, in the industrial suburb of Giffordgate, the Scottish reformer John Knox was believed to have been born in 1505. Much to the chagrin of the Catholic Mary Queen of Scots, he rose from these dire origins to found the Scottish Presbyterian church.

St. Mary's Church, built in the 14th century, in red and gray sandstone, contains the tomb of Jane Welsh, who was born in the town. She married the historian Thomas Carlyle.

The **Jane Welsh Carlyle Museum,** Lodge Street (tel. 062082/3738), is the former home of this woman who was an influential thinker in her own right. Her home, with its drawing room, garden rooms, and Regency gardens, is open April to September from 2 to 5 p.m. Wednesday to Saturday, costing 50p (80¢) for adults, with accompanied children admitted free.

You can visit **St. Mary's Pleasance,** Sidegate, which are the gardens of Haddington House. They have been brought back to life in the style of the 1600s. In season you can wander among the sunken gardens, enjoying the roses and herbs.

Chapter V

THE KINGDOM OF FIFE

1. Dunfermline
2. Falkland
3. The East Neuk
4. St. Andrews

NORTH OF FORTH from Edinburgh, the county of Fife still likes to call itself a "kingdom." Its name, even today, suggests the romantic episodes and pageantry during the reign of the early Stuart kings. Fourteen of Scotland's 66 royal burghs lay within this shire. Many of the former royal palaces and castles, either restored or in colorful ruins, can be visited today, and I've previewed the most important ones coming up.

As Edinburgh is so near, the temptation is to set up headquarters in one of that city's many elegant hotels or B&B houses and explore Fife from that base. However, serious golfers may want to stay at one of the hotels in St. Andrews.

1. Dunfermline

This ancient town was once the capital of Scotland. It is easily reached by the Forth Road Bridge which was opened by Queen Elizabeth II in 1964. Dunfermline lies five miles northwest of the Forth Bridge, a distance of 14 miles northwest of Edinburgh.

FOOD AND LODGING: One of the best all-around budget hostelries in town is **The City Hotel,** 18 Bridge St. (tel. 0383/722538). You don't get fancy frills here, but you are offered good, substantial, and well-maintained bedrooms right in the heart of town. Often attracting commercial travelers, the hotel offers a total of 17 bedrooms, ten of which contain a private bath or shower. The B&B rate ranges from £21 ($33.60) to £26 ($41.60) in a single, £17 ($27.20) to £19 ($30.40) per person in a double. Dinner is also served, costing from £9.50 ($15.20), a good buy.

Want something cheaper? Try the well-recommended **Garvock Guest House,** 82 Halbeath Rd. (tel. 0383/729039), which lies about a mile from the heart of Dunfermline. If you're driving, you'll find this 19th-century home within easy access of the M90. It is also on a regularly scheduled bus route. Five comfortably furnished bedrooms, none with private bath, are rented to visitors, costing £11 ($17.60) in a single, £10 ($16) per person in a double. The owners are hospitable.

Outside of the hotels, one of the best all-around dining rooms for those on a budget is **New Victoria,** 2 Bruce St. (tel. 0383/724175). However, to reach it, you must walk up two landings, and you can do so any time daily (except Sunday) from 9:30 a.m. to 6:30 p.m., until 10 p.m. on Saturday. Overlooking the abbey, the dated dining room serves a substantial cuisine, a kind of good old-fashioned cookery based on healthy ingredients. There's also plenty of it. You might begin with a robust soup at lunch and then follow with steak and kidney pie, perhaps sautéed fish or roast beef. It's also a good choice if you're in the neighborhood seeking a high tea.

SIGHTS: On the site of a Celtic church, **Dunfermline Abbey** occupies the location of an 11th-century house of worship dedicated to the Holy Trinity, under the auspices of Queen Margaret, wife of Malcolm Canmore, who later became St. Margaret. Culdee Church dated back to the 5th and 6th centuries until it was rebuilt in 1072. Traces of both buildings are visible beneath gratings in the floor of the old nave. In 1150 it was replaced with a large abbey, the nave of which remains, an example of Norman architecture. Later St. Margaret's shrine, the northwest baptismal porch, the spire on the northwest tower, and the flying buttresses were added. When Dunfermline was the capital of Scotland, 22 royal persons were buried within the abbey. Except for Queen Margaret and King Robert the Bruce, no visible memorial or burial place is known. Robert the Bruce's tomb lies beneath the pulpit. The abbey church is open daily from 9:30 a.m. to 5 p.m. from April to September (on Sunday from 2 to 5 p.m.). From October to March it closes at 4 p.m.

The **Royal Palace** witnessed the birth of Kings Charles I and James I. Only the southwest wall remains of this once-gargantuan edifice. The last king to reside here was Charles II in 1651.

Andrew Carnegie, the American industrialist and philanthropist, was born here in 1835. The **Andrew Carnegie Birthplace Museum,** Moodie Street (tel. 0383/724302), lies at the corner of Moodie Street and Priory Lane and comprises the 18th-century weaver's cottage in which he was born and a memorial hall provided by his wife. It was completely refurbished in 1984. Displays tell the story of the weaver's son from Dunfermline who emigrated to America to become one of the richest men in the world and one of the most generous private benefactors of his era. Admission is free, and the museum is open on weekdays, April to October, from 11 a.m. to 5 p.m., on Sunday from 2 to 5 p.m. From November to March it is open daily from 2 to 4 p.m.

From the fortune he made in steel, Mr. Carnegie became a great benefactor, giving away more than $400 million before his death in 1919. Dunfermline, as his birthplace, received the first of the 2,811 free libraries he provided throughout Britain and the United States. It also received public baths and **Pittencrieff Park and Glen,** so rich in history and natural charm. A statue in the park honors the hometown boy who made good, who once worked as a bobbin boy in a cotton factory.

From Dunfermline, you can take an excursion six miles west to—

CULROSS: This old royal burgh has been renovated by the Scottish National Trust, and is one of the most beautiful in the country. As you walk its cobbled streets, admiring its charming whitewashed houses, you'll feel you're taking a stroll back into the 17th century. Many of the cottages have crow-stepped gables and red pantiled roofs.

Set in tranquil walled gardens, **Culross Palace** was built in the village between 1597 and 1611, containing a most beautiful series of paintings on its wooden walls and ceilings. It has been restored and may be visited, April to September, daily from 9:30 a.m. to 7 p.m. (on Sunday from 2 to 7 p.m.). From October to March it's open daily from 9:30 a.m. to 4 p.m. (on Sunday from 2 to 4 p.m.). Admission is £1 ($1.60) for adults, 50p (80¢) for children.

The other important attraction is **Culross Abbey,** a Cistercian monastery whose founding father was Malcolm, Earl of Fife in 1217. Parts of the nave are still intact, and the choir serves as the Culross parish church. There is also a central tower. Hours are mid-March to mid-October weekdays from 9:30 a.m. to 6:30 p.m. (Sunday 2 to 6:30 p.m.). Off-season visits are possible weekdays from 9:30 a.m. to 4 p.m. (Sunday 2 to 4 p.m.).

2. Falkland

Now owned by the National Trust of Scotland, **Falkland Palace and Garden** (tel. 03375/397) was once the hunting palace of the Stuart kings. This royal burgh of cobblestone streets and crooked houses lies at the northern base of the hill of East Lomond, 21 miles north of Edinburgh.

FOOD AND LODGING: Since the early 18th century, the **Covenanter Hotel** (tel. 0337/5224) has been a popular inn. With modest modernization, it offers a good standard of accommodation. It's built ruggedly of local stone, with high chimneys, wooden shutters, and a modest Georgian entry. The location is on a tiny square opposite the church and palace. You enter a gleaming white entry hall with a circular staircase leading to the lounges and bedrooms. The dining room is strictly "old style" and for the before-dinner drinks there is an intimate pub, the Covenanter Cocktail Bar. The inn is owned by George Menzies, who charges from £26 ($41.60) in a single and from £32 ($51.20) in a double, including a full breakfast and VAT. All the bedrooms have private baths, phones, and central heating. Lunches are served from noon to 2 p.m., three courses costing £5.50 ($8.80). Dinner is both table d'hôte at £9.50 ($15.20) and à la carte at around £13 ($20.80).

Kind Kyttock's Kitchen, Cross Wynd (tel. 0337/57477), stands right near the palace and welcomes you most of the year with a stone fireplace where logs burn brightly. The "kitchen" is also an art gallery, displaying local crafts and paintings. A specialty is four homemade oatcakes with cheese. The bread is always homemade, very fresh tasting, as you'll discover if you order an open sandwich. For a tea, I suggest the homemade pancake with fruit and fresh cream. Even better, however, are the homemade tarts with fresh cream. Salads are fresh and good tasting. A cup of Scotch broth, served with a slice of home-baked whole-meal bread, is a favorite. Light meals cost from £5 ($8). Liz and Bert Dalrymple, who run the place, serve from 10:30 a.m. to 5:30 p.m. Off-season, it is open only on weekends. Closed in January.

SIGHTS: Since the 14th century Falkland has been connected with Scottish kings. Originally a castle stood on the site of today's palace, but it was replaced in the 16th century. Falkland then became a favorite seat of the Scottish court. A grief-stricken James V died here. Mary Queen of Scots used to come to Falkland for "hunting and hawking." It was also here that Francis Stuart, fifth Earl of Bothwell, came with his men and tried to seize his cousin, James VI, son of Mary Queen of Scots. Bullet marks may be seen on the front of the towers of the gatehouse (1592). Cromwell's forces occupied Falkland in 1654.

The royal chapel and apartments are open April 1 to the end of September weekdays from 10 a.m. to 6 p.m. and on Sunday from 2 to 6 p.m., weekends only in October. Last entry at 5:30 p.m. The gardens, incidentally, have been laid out to the original royal plans. At Falkland is the only royal tennis court left in Scotland. For a ticket to both the palace and gardens, adults pay £1.80 ($2.88); children 90p ($1.44). Or you can be admitted to the gardens at only £1.20 ($1.92) for adults and 60p (96¢) for children.

Back at Dunfermline you can connect with the coastal road, heading east to—

LARGO: Alexander Selkirk, the original Robinson Crusoe, was born here in 1676. This Scottish sailor, son of a shoemaker and tanner, was once charged with "indecent behavior in church," but he never had to pay the penalty, whatever it was, as he was away at sea. He disappeared in the South Seas, but was discovered in 1709. He returned to Largo in 1712. A statue in the village honors this hometown boy, who was clearly the inspiration for the Daniel Defoe classic. A house Selkirk purchased for his father is still standing.

3. The East Neuk

Within a half hour's drive of St. Andrews are some of the most beautiful and unspoiled fishing villages of eastern Scotland.

PITTENWEEM: If you're here in the morning, try to get caught up in the action at the fish auction held under a large shed (except Sunday). The actual time depends on the tides. Afterward you can go for a walk through the village, taking in the sturdy stone homes, some of which have been preserved by Scotland's National Trust.

At the **Anchor Inn** (tel. 0333/311326) you can enjoy locally caught seafood which is featured on all menus. The inn specializes in bar lunches at £5 ($8) and bar suppers at £6 ($9.60). These menus most often feature not only fresh local fish but prawns and scampi. Children, incidentally, are welcome at lunchtime. In addition, set lunches go for around £5.50 ($8.80) and à la carte dinners, often with local lobster, for about £13 ($20.80), including wine. Lunch is served Monday to Saturday from noon to 2 p.m.; Sunday, 12:30 to 2 p.m. Dinner is daily including Sunday from 6 to 10 p.m. High teas are offered from 4 to 6 p.m. The Anchor, circa 1828, is an architecturally elegant building with a black-and-white Georgian facade and a cozy atmosphere inside. The inn doesn't offer any accommodations, however.

ANSTRUTHER: This was once an important herring-fishing port and is now a summer resort, with the **Scottish Fisheries Museum** (tel. 0333/310628), down by the harbor. Tracing the history of the fishing industry in Scotland, it charges £1 ($1.60) admission for adults, 50p (80¢) for children. The museum is open April to October from 10 a.m. to 5:30 p.m. (on Sunday from 2 to 5 p.m.) and November to March from 2 to 5 p.m. daily except Tuesday.

You can also go aboard a floating museum in the harbor. The **North Carr Lightship**, stationed off Fife Ness, has a re-created interior.

The **Isle of May**, a nature reserve, lies in the Firth of Forth, and is accessible by boat from Anstruther. It is a bird observatory and a field station, and contains the ruins of a chapel from the 12th century as well as an early 19th-century lighthouse.

From the museum you can walk to the tiny hamlet of **Cellardyke**, adjoining Anstruther. It has many charming stone houses and its own ancient harbor, where in the year that Victoria took the throne 140 vessels used to put out to sea.

Food and Lodging

Smuggler's Inn, High Street (tel. 0333/310506), stands in the heart of town, a warmly inviting inn that evokes memories of smuggling days around here. The original inn that stood on this spot dates back to 1300. In Queen Anne's day it was a well-known tavern. The ceilings are low, the floors uneven, and, of course, the stairways are winding. Overlooking the harbor, rooms are rented for £18.50 ($29.60) per person with bath. The half-board rate is £23 ($36.80) to £24 ($38.40) per person. Mr. and Mrs. McSharry offer à la carte dinners for £11 ($17.60) and bar suppers, both served from 7 to 10:30 p.m. Bar lunches or suppers cost from £2.50 ($4) to £5 ($8). If featured, ask for the local Pittenweem prawns.

The Haven, at Cellardyke Harbour (tel. 0333/310574), is an old-style licensed restaurant and lounge bar serving good food. Noted for comfort and service, it offers simple but well-prepared lunches that might include steak pie, local crab salad, and Aberdeen Angus steaks. A soup of the day is homemade, and roast chicken is often featured. At supper the menu is more elaborate and is likely to include smoked salmon or lobster bisque. Main dishes offered are fried filet of haddock, very popular in this region, although you can also order duck à l'orange. Owned and run by Graham Guthrie and David Barnett, the Haven serves à la carte lunches and dinners. For three courses, either at noon or in the evening, count on spending from £5 ($8) to £10 ($16). Bar snacks are offered for both lunch and dinner as well, including a choice of about eight fish, meat, and poultry dishes, plus cold meats and salads. There is also a flower-filled garden bar where on a good day you can sip and sup while enjoying the view. In summer, meals are served from 12:15 to 4 p.m.; in winter, from 12:15 to 2:15 p.m. Only in summer are formal dinners offered, from 7:30 to 9:30 p.m. However, you can obtain bar suppers year round from 4 to 10:30 p.m.

The Cellar, 22-24 East Green (tel. 0333/310378), serves good, old-fashioned Scottish food, including smoked salmon, local fish, and laird's pie. The restaurant was installed in the cellar of two old stone houses which lie near the harbor. Service is friendly and polite, and hours of business are from 12:30 to 2 p.m. and 7:30 to 9:30 p.m. The Cellar shuts down on Sunday and Monday. Expect to spend around £7 ($11.20) for lunch, from £14 ($22.40) for dinner.

ELIE: With its step-gabled houses and little harbor, this is my favorite village along the coast. Elie and its close neighbor, **Earlsferry,** overlook a crescent of golden sand beach, with more swimming possibilities to be found among sheltered coves. The name Elie is believed to be derived from the "ailie," or island, of Ardross which now forms part of the harbor and is joined to the mainland by a road. A large stone building, a former granary, at the harbor is a reminder of the days when Elie was a busy trading port.

Earlsferry, to the west, got its name from an ancient ferry crossing, which Macduff, the Thane of Fife, is supposed to have used on his escape from Macbeth.

Food and Lodging

Even if you're not stopping over in Elie, I suggest you drop in at the **Ship Inn** (tel. 0333/330246) on the Toft, there to enjoy a pint of lager, real ale, or whisky from a large selection. In summer, you can sit out in fair weather, looking over the water. In colder months, a fireplace burns brightly. The pub has a nautical atmosphere and doesn't do much in the way of food, but the friendly owner who runs it, J. R. N. Hendry, will prepare soup and a sandwich if you're hungry. Food items begin at 60p (96¢). The Hendrys welcome Americans, Mrs. Hendry having strong connections with the U.S. She's descended from Priscilla Mullins and John Alden of the *Mayflower* set. Her parents went back to England in 1908, and her father, Sir Stephen Pigott, is known for having built the

Queen Mary and the *Queen Elizabeth*. Her sister, who stayed Stateside, was married to Sen. Estes Kefauver, now deceased. Hours at the Ship are 11 a.m. to midnight Monday to Saturday, 12:30 to 2:30 and 6:30 to 11 p.m. on Sunday. The building occupied by the pub dates from 1778, and a bar has been in business here since 1830.

The Elms Guest House, Park Place (tel. 0333/330404), is the finest in town. Run by Mrs. G.M. Boak, this 1880 building is set on the wide main street behind a conservative stone facade, with a crescent-shaped rose garden in front. Seven bedrooms are comfortably furnished and are centrally heated and contain hot and cold running water. Two rooms are suitable for families, and there is also a chalet suite on the grounds with its one shower and toilet along with one double bed and bunk beds. It's best to take half-board terms here, costing from £17 ($27.20). Home cooking with local produce, including fresh Elie lobster and crab caught by your host, is a feature in the spacious, often sun-filled dining room. The guesthouse is licensed.

Sights

To the east of the harbor at Elie stands a stone structure known as the **Lady's Tower,** used by Lady Janet Anstruther, a noted 18th-century beauty, as a bathing cabana.

Another member of the Anstruther family, Sir John, added the interesting **Bell Tower** to the parish church that stands in the center of the village.

Beyond the lighthouse, on a point of land to the east of the harbor, lies **Ruby Bay,** so named because garnets can be found there. Farther along the coast is **Fossil Bay,** where a variety of fossils can be found.

CRAIL: Considered the pearl of the East Neuk of Fife, Crail is an artists' colony, and many painters live in cottages around this little harbor. Natural bathing facilities are found at Roome Bay, and there are many beaches nearby. The Balcomie Golf Course, in good condition, is one of the oldest in the world.

Croma Hotel (tel. 0333/50239) is a guesthouse near the harbor with ten bedrooms. It's the home base of all-American ball player Jack Healy and his attractive wife, Rosemarie, originally from Ireland. Brooklyn-born Jack is a strapping, handsome former Pan Am executive. From Samoa he brought handcrafts and trinkets, and has hung them against the wall-size geographic maps from Pan Am. This, the Chart Room, is fully licensed, and it's Jack's domain. Rosemarie has decorated the dining room in green and white and used Windsor chairs set in front of the bay window. Many of the artists who live in this little fishing village come here for drinks and evening meals. The Healys charge £12 ($19.20) per person for B&B. They serve a table d'hôte lunch for £5 ($8) and an evening meal for £8 ($12.80). You can also have a bar meal in the Chart Room.

4. St. Andrews

On a bay of the North Sea, St. Andrews is sometimes known as the "Oxford of Scotland." Founded in 1411, the **University of St. Andrews** is the oldest in Scotland and the third oldest in Britain. At term time you can see the students in their characteristic red gowns.

The university's most interesting buildings include the tower and church of St. Salvator's College and the courtyard of St. Mary's College, dating from 1538. An ancient thorn tree, said to have been planted by Mary Queen of Scots, stands near the college's chapel. The church of St. Leonard's College is also from medieval days. The Scottish Parliament in 1645 met in what was once the University Library and is now a students' reading room. A modern University

Library, containing more than three-quarters of a million books and many rare and ancient volumes, was opened in 1976.

The historic sea town in northeast Fife is also known as the home of golf in Britain. The world's leading golf club, the **Royal & Ancient,** was founded here in 1754. All of St. Andrews's four golf courses—the Old, the New, the Jubilee, and the Eden—are open to the public. Of course, the hallowed turf of the Old Course is the sentimental favorite.

The old gray royal burgh of St. Andrews is filled with many monastic ruins and ancient houses; regrettably, they represent but a few mere skeletons of medieval St. Andrews.

WHERE TO STAY: Perhaps the finest budget accommodation in St. Andrews, **Kinburn "Castle" Hotel,** Double Dykes Road (tel. 0334/73620), was built in the 19th century in the baronial Scottish architectural style. Today this family-run hotel, operated by Moira and Ronnie Murdock, welcomes guests from around the world. They rent out 22 well-furnished bedrooms, 17 with private bath. Most of the rooms are spacious and all are well equipped. Depending on the room assignment and plumbing, singles cost from £18.50 ($29.60) to £26 ($41.60), two persons paying from £36 ($57.60) to £48 ($76.80). Units contain TV, phone, and beverage-making equipment. Guests register at a converted church pulpit. Meals served in the Turret Restaurant include seafood, roasts, and Scottish game.

The **Russell Hotel,** The Scores (tel. 0334/73447), has one of the most ideal locations for a moderately priced hotel in St. Andrews, overlooking St. Andrews Bay, just a two-minute walk from the first tee of the Old Course. A Victorian structure, it is so well maintained and run by Angus and Jennifer Mitchell that you may want to pay the slightly higher rates to stay here. Depending on the plumbing, singles range from £36 ($57.60) to £40 ($64), doubles from £19 ($30.40) to £21 ($33.60) per person, including breakfast. The hotel offers only seven bedrooms, five with private baths, but each with hot and cold running water, color TV, beverage-making equipment, and shaver points. Many locals from nearby come here for the excellent bar lunches or the fine food served in the restaurant at night. Try a lager in the cozy Victorian pub.

A substantial and renovated accommodation, **Argyle House Hotel,** 127 North St. (tel. 0334/73387), is in the center of town. While it has the rates of a simple guesthouse, it offers many of the amenities of a larger hotel. There are two bars and lounges. In one, you can have coffee (fresh-perked) or a before-dinner drink, and the other one has a pool table, or you can play chess, bridge, scrabble, and Trivial Pursuit. Owners Tom and Joan Dowie and their courteous staff make this an excellent place to stay. There are 21 bedrooms, 13 of which have private showers, the others with hot and cold water basins. All the units have color TV and facilities for making hot beverages. Charges are £11.50 ($18.40) to £16 ($25.60) per person for B&B. Evening meals are offered for £7 ($11.20).

Number Ten, 10 Hope St. (tel. 0334/74601), in a classic Georgian building only a two-minute walk from the first tee of the Old Course, is run by Maureen and Ken Featherstone. They are constantly improving the standards and quality of their guesthouse, which is centrally heated and has an elegant lounge with color TV. Most of the rooms have complete private baths, and others have hot and cold water basins. All have facilities for making hot beverages. The charge for B&B in a room without bath is £11 ($17.60) per person, rising to £15 ($24) per person with bath. Children under 12 share their parents' room for half price. A good evening meal is offered for £5.50 ($8.80). Prices include VAT and service.

Peover House, Murray Park (tel. 0334/75787), belongs to Ellen Bessant, who has a few pleasant rooms to rent in her centrally heated house, all with upgraded fittings, furniture, and carpeting. She charges £11 ($17.60) to £15 ($24) per person for a bed and a full Scottish breakfast. All rooms have hot-beverage facilities, and one has a private bath and TV. The rooms are comfortable, each bed with an electric blanket, and there's plenty of hot water. Mrs. Bessant will cater to your wishes, and will get you started on a tour of historic St. Andrews. You are welcomed in the lounge which has a color TV. Her house is only a few minutes' walk from the sea, golf courses, good local restaurants, and a shopping center.

Right across the street is **Suncrest,** 23 Murray Park (tel. 0334/75310), an excellent B&B owned and operated by Jim and Pat Ledder, who go out of their way to make guests comfortable. Bed and a good breakfast are priced at £9.50 ($15.20) to £17 ($27.20) per person, the higher rate being for a room with private bath. Half-board prices are from £13.75 ($22) to £22.50 ($36) per person. Shorecrest is a five- to ten-minute walk from the Old Course Clubhouse, and Jim Ledder can arrange for you to play golf at the New Course as well as making other sightseeing excursions.

Cleveden House, 3 Murray Pl. (tel. 0334/74212), belongs to Tom and Maggie Wilson, who love sharing their knowledge of St. Andrews. They'll guide you to reasonable restaurants, give you a map for a walk throughout the town, and fix a good Scottish breakfast. They'll also provide homemade shortbread with your tea or coffee in the residents' lounge. For B&B, they charge £11.50 ($18.40) to £13.50 ($21.60) per person, the price depending on the plumbing. All units have hot and cold water basins.

Ashleigh House, 37 St. Mary St. (tel. 0334/75429), is an impressive stone guesthouse in its own grounds, in a quiet part of St. Andrews, only a few minutes from the golf courses, shops, harbor, and other attractions. Mrs. Gunn offers a warm welcome to her centrally heated accommodations. Depending on the room and the number of occupants, she charges £9.50 ($15.20) to £13 ($20.80) per person for B&B.

WHERE TO EAT: Enjoying an air of informality, **The Merchant's House,** 49 South St. (tel. 0334/72595), is operated by Angus and Jennifer Mitchell. Originally a 16th-century private house, its most formal front room features old ceiling frescoes. It is building a reputation for its quality cuisine and reasonable prices, with meals costing from £7 ($11.20). Dishes are likely to include filet steak fondue, spinach and mushroom lasagne, and beef bourguignon. It is open seven days a week from 10 a.m. to 10 p.m. Incidentally, this is considered an eating house and coffeeshop which means the customer can have as much or as little as he or she chooses.

Victoria Café, 1 St. Mary's Place (tel. 0334/76964), corner of Bell Street, is both a pub and a restaurant. You climb a wide flight of stairs past a ceramic bust of Mercury to reach the upstairs bar and dining room. There you enter a setting of green walls, brass lamps, bentwood chairs, and potted plants. The food is straightforward, honest, and of good quality. Most dishes are simply prepared, including club steak, pasta, and quiche. Meals cost from £5 ($8). You can also order freshly baked potatoes, roast chicken, and salads. Hot meals are served from noon to 9 p.m., but drinks are offered from 11 a.m. to midnight.

Pepita's Restaurant, 11 Crail's Lane (tel. 0334/74084), tucked away in a narrow alleyway, is one of the best eating places in St. Andrews. Owned by John Hodgson and managed by his son, Peter, the restaurant has high standards of both cuisine and service, drawing patrons from locals and tourists alike. The chefs have developed a luncheon menu consisting of such dishes as lasagne, chicken and mushroom casserole, and chili con carne, all served with a baked potato and a salad of your selection. An international cuisine is offered for dinner, the menu changing frequently. You might choose Loch Fyne herring, Greek salad, or haggis Drambuie from among the appetizers, following with a main dish with chef's vegetables or mixed salad and a jacket potato complementing the meat, fish, or vegetarian entries. Lunch costs from £3.50 ($5.60), dinner going for £5 ($8) to £9 ($14.40). Hours are from 9:30 a.m. to 1 a.m. (last orders around 11 p.m.) Monday to Saturday. On Sunday, the establishment is open from 11:30 a.m. to midnight from February to the end of November. The Sunday specialty is traditional roast beef and Yorkshire pudding. Pepita's has an extensive wine list, including a French house wine.

The Pancake Place, 177-179 South St. (tel. 0334/75671), offers a rustic atmosphere, and good, inexpensively priced, rib-sticking food. Don't go here if you're on a diet. Pancakes, naturally, are featured in this franchise restaurant, and they often come in unusual combinations—that is, smoked haddock in a mornay sauce or chicken curry. To begin, you might order a bowl of homemade soup. If you don't want a pancake, try one of their crisp salads, made with ham, chicken, or cheddar cheese. A wide selection of sweet pancakes is offered for dessert, ranging from Alaska to Florida, and they also serve scones in the morning here. Meals cost from £5 ($8). The Pancake Place is open seven days a week from 10 a.m. to 5:30 p.m. In summer, from June to September, they are likely to be open in the evening, but telephone first to make sure.

SIGHTS: In the area of the Celtic settlement of St. Mary of the Rock, other ecclesiastical centers culminated in **St. Andrews Cathedral and Priory** (tel. 0334/72563). The early cathedral Church of St. Rule Regulus may have been built in the late 11th century and modified in the mid-12th century. In the 1160s the larger cathedral was founded. Built in both the Romanesque and Gothic styles, it was the largest church in Scotland, establishing St. Andrews as the ecclesiastical capital of the country. Today the ruins can only suggest the former beauty and importance of the cathedral. The east and west gables and a part of the south wall of the nave remain, and standing also is "the Pends," part of the old entrance gateway to the cathedral precinct. There is a collection of early Christian and medieval monuments, as well as artifacts discovered on the cathedral site. It is open April to September daily from 9:30 a.m. to 7 p.m. (on Sunday from 2 to 7 p.m.). From October to March hours are daily from 9:30 a.m. to 4 p.m. (on Sunday from 2 to 4 p.m.). Admission is 50p (80¢) for adults and 25p (40¢) for children.

The **Holy Trinity Church** ("the Town Kirk"), a beautifully restored medieval church, stood originally in the grounds of the now-ruined cathedral, near the 12th-century St. Regulus Tower with its 108-foot accessible stairway to the top and a fine view of the city. It was removed to the present site in 1410 and considerably altered after the Reformation of 1560. It was restored to its present condition in the early 20th century, with much fine stained glass and carvings.

Also of great interest is the ruined 13th-century **Castle of St. Andrews,** with its bottle dungeon and secret passages. Founded in the early part of the 13th century, it was reconstructed at several periods in its history. Cardinal Beaton's murder in 1546 set off the first round of the Reformation struggle. It is open from 9:30 a.m. to 6:30 p.m. weekdays, from 2 to 6:30 p.m. on Sunday mid-March to mid-October. Off-season, closing is at 4 p.m.

Chapter VI

EXPLORING TAYSIDE

THE TROUBLE WITH exploring Tayside is you may find it so fascinating in scenery that you'll never make it on to the Highlands. Carved out of the old counties of Perth and Angus, Tayside is named for its major river, the 119-mile-long Tay. Its tributaries and dozens of lochs and highland streams are some of the best salmon and trout waters in Europe. One of the loveliest regions of Scotland, Tayside is filled with heather-clad Highland hills, long blue lochs under tree-clad banks, and miles and miles of walking trails.

It is a region dear to the Scots, a symbol of their desire for independence, as exemplified by the Declaration of Arbroath and the ancient coronation ritual of the "Stone of Destiny" at Scone. In cities, Perth and Dundee are among the six leading centers of Scotland.

Tayside also provided the backdrop for many novels by Sir Walter Scott, including *The Fair Maid of Perth, Waverley,* and *The Abbot.*

Its golf courses are world famous, ranging from the trio of 18-hole courses at Gleneagles to the open championships links at Carnoustie.

We'll begin our trip in an offshoot southern pocket of the county at Loch Leven, then take in Perth and its environs, heading east to Dundee, and later along the fishing villages of the North Sea, cutting west again to visit Glamis Castle, and, finally, ending our journey of exploration even farther west in the lochs and glens of the Perthshire Highlands.

1. Loch Leven

Lying about 12 miles north of Dunfermline (head toward Kinross on the M90), the loch has seven islands. Loch Leven Castle, of course, is in ruins. So is the **Priory of Loch Leven,** built on the site of one of the oldest Culdee establishments in Scotland, and lying on St. Serf's, the largest of the islands in the loch.

In Kinross, 25 miles north of Edinburgh, you can make arrangements to visit Loch Leven Castle by boat, the only means of access.

LODGINGS IN KINROSS: Dating back some 200 years, **Kirklands Hotel,** High Street (tel. 0577/63313), was originally a coaching inn. This glistening white building is right in the center of the small historical town, and after a period of some 30 years, it is again privately owned. Bob Boath and his family have refurbished the hotel, placing color TV and hot-beverage facilities in all the rooms, which also have hot and cold water basins. Charges for B&B are £19 ($30.40) in a single, from £30 ($48) in a double.

LOCH LEVEN CASTLE: "Those never got luck who came to Loch Leven." This proverbial saying sums up the history of the Douglas fortress, **Loch Leven Castle,** on Castle Island, dating from the late 14th century. Among its more ill-fated prisoners, none was more notable than Mary Queen of Scots. Within its forbidding walls she signed her abdication on July 24, 1567. However, she effected her escape from Loch Leven on May 2, 1568. Thomas Percy, seventh Earl of Northumberland, supported her cause. For his efforts, he too was imprisoned and lodged in the castle for three years until he was handed over to the English, who beheaded him at York. The castle is open from 9:30 a.m. to 7 p.m. weekdays, from 2 to 7 p.m. on Sunday April to September. Closed in winter. Admission to the castle is free, but the charge for the ferry is 50p (80¢) for adults, 25p (40¢) for children.

2. Perth

From its majestic position on the Tay, the ancient city of Perth was the capital of Scotland until the middle of the 15th century. Here the Highland meets the Lowland. Sir Walter Scott immortalized the royal burgh in *The Fair Maid of Perth.*

WHERE TO STAY: Offering modern accommodation, the **Two-O-Eight Hotel,** 208 Crieff Rd. (tel. 0738/28936), was built by its present owners, Norman and Dorothy Doris, in the mid-'70s. It's on the main road in a suburban setting on the west boundary of the city, yet just a 20-minute walk to the center of Perth. A regular bus service stops at the hotel every 20 minutes. There are 16 bedrooms, each with hot and cold running water and innerspring mattresses. There is a fully licensed bar where you can order drinks and watch TV. The per-person rate nightly for B&B is £11 ($17.60), plus VAT. Mrs. Doris serves a high tea between 5 and 6 p.m. for £4 ($6.40). With such dishes as ham salad and fried haddock and chips, it's like a light supper, particularly if you turn in early.

Pitcullen Guest House, 17 Pitcullen Crescent, on the A94 road (tel. 0738/

26506), stands in a residential district, a short walk from the city center. It's a turn-of-the-century stone building, with dormers and a crescent-shaped bay window. The owner, Mrs. Grainger, keeps her B&B rate at a minimum, asking £10 ($16) to £13.50 ($21.60) per person nightly. Most of her guests also ask for an evening meal for £5 ($8). There's central heating, hot and cold water, and tea- and coffee-making facilities in the rooms, and if you are in the mood, a color TV in the residents' lounge.

Corinna Hotel, 44 Atholl St. (tel. 0738/24623), is owned and managed by the Davies family. Bed and a continental breakfast served in your room is priced at £10 ($16) per person, the tariff rising to £12 ($19.20) if you prefer a full breakfast. The bedrooms are centrally heated and have hot and cold water basins, color TV, and hot-beverage facilities. An à la carte supper menu is available from 6:30 to 8:30 p.m. daily, with home-cooking by Mrs. Davies and a choice of eight to ten main courses. Meals cost from £5 ($8).

WHERE TO EAT: One of the biggest buffet spreads in the city is served at the **Bush Mill,** Stakis City Mills Hotel, West Mill Street (tel. 0738/28281). From noon to 2:30 p.m. you help yourself from a table of hot and cold dishes. You can order homemade soups and a choice of home-cooked meats. There is a serve-yourself salad bar where you pay according to your selection. Meals begin at £5 ($8). You can also order a four-course table d'hôte dinner for £9.50 ($15.20) in the Laird's Table from 7 to 9 p.m. nightly. Good Angus beef is offered in The Steakhouse, which is open from 12:30 to 2:30 p.m. and 5 to 10 p.m. Full dinners cost from £12 ($19.20). The hotel takes its name from a millstream that flows under the structure. You can view the running water through panels of glass.

The **Pizza Gallery,** 32 Scott St. (tel. 0738/37778), is the best place to go for pizzas. It is a spacious restaurant, modern and on one level. Pizzas range in price from £1.95 ($3.12) to £4.40 ($7.04), and include all the usual concoctions, plus some with more artistic flair (for example, anchovies, olives, and green peppers). For about £6.50 ($10.40), you can order a meal, including a chef's salad and a large plate of pasta, plus a dessert. The restaurant is licensed to sell wine by the glass or carafe. Hours are daily from 10 a.m. to 10:45 p.m.

SIGHTS: The main sightseeing attraction of "the fair city" is the **Kirk of St. John the Baptist,** of which the original foundation, it is believed, dates from Pictish times. However, the present choir dates from 1440 and the nave from 1490. In 1559 John Knox preached his famous sermon here attacking idolatry, and it caused a turbulent wave of iconoclasm to sweep across the land. The church was restored as a World War I memorial in the mid-1920s. In the church is the tombstone of James I, who was murdered by Sir Robert Graham.

The **Black Watch Regimental Museum,** Balhousie Castle, Hay Street (tel. 0738/21281), contains the memorabilia of the 42nd and 73rd Highland Regiments. You get to see 2½ centuries of British military history, including paintings, silver, and uniforms. Admission is free but it's appreciated if you make a donation to the museum fund. It is open Monday to Friday from 10 a.m. to 4:30 p.m. April until the end of September. On Sunday it is open from 2 to 5 p.m. Off-season hours are Monday to Friday from 10 a.m. to 3:30 p.m.

John Dewar & Sons, the famous whisky distillers, at Inveralmond, has organized tours during which time you can see the blending and bottling of scotch, including cooperage and dispatch. Telephone 0738/21231 before heading there, however.

The Fair Maid's House, North Port (tel. 0738/25976), was the old Glover's Hall that Sir Walter Scott chose as the home of his heroine in *The Fair Maid of*

Perth. Now a craft shop, it sells high-quality Scottish crafts, including woolen goods, silver, glass, and pottery. The shop is open Monday to Saturday from 10 a.m. to 5 p.m. Upstairs is a gallery which presents changing exhibitions of contemporary art. The gallery hours are 11 a.m. to 4 p.m. Monday to Saturday.

Branklyn Garden, on the Dundee Road (A85), has been called the finest two acres of private garden in Scotland. It was bequeathed to the National Trust for Scotland, having been established in 1922 by Mr. and Mrs. John Renton. It has a superb collection of rhododendrons, alpines, and herbaceous and peat-garden plants from all over the world. Open daily from March to October, it can be visited from 10 a.m. to sunset for an admission of £1 ($1.60) for adults and 50p (80¢) for children. For information, phone 0738/25535.

You can watch glassmakers at work at the **Caithness Glass factory,** at Inveralmond (tel. 0738/37373), where there is also a visitor center. Of special interest is the intricate art of paperweight making. Glassmaking can be observed from 9 a.m. to 4:30 p.m. Monday to Friday. The factory shop and restaurant are open from 9 a.m. to 5 p.m. Monday to Saturday, from 1 to 5 p.m. on Sunday.

A LODGE IN THE ENVIRONS: On the road to Inverness, **Hunters Lodge,** at Bankfoot (tel. 0738/87325), lies six miles north of Perth (turn off the A9 at Bankfoot services). Bruce and Jeudi Hunter, the owners, are winners of the BBC "best pub grub in Scotland" award. Naturally, they specialize in bar snacks. The Hunters are noted for their Scottish specialties. For an appetizer, your selection might be their own special pâté or one of their homemade broths (guests often ask for the recipes). The best fish dish is Scottish salmon, which they poach to perfection and serve in a white wine sauce. For dessert, why not the Drambuie cheesecake? Expect to spend from £10 ($16) for all that, plus the cost of your drink. For children, a "Toytown Special" menu is offered. The restaurant hours are 11 a.m. to 2:30 p.m. and 5 to 9 p.m. Derivations of the dining room cuisine are served in the bar in generous portions for less expensive rates. Hunters Lodge also offers a traditional Scottish high tea at £4.50 ($7.20), big enough for a good supper. It's served daily from 5 to 7 p.m. Self-catering cabins and lodges are situated on the grounds. B&B in the lodge costs £13.50 ($21.60) per person with a continental breakfast, £15 ($24) per person with a cooked breakfast, based on double occupancy. Singles are charged £18.50 ($29.60) to £20 ($32), depending on the breakfast choice. All bedrooms in the lodges have private baths, color TV, radio alarms, and hot-beverage facilities.

3. Scone

On the River Tay, Old Scone was the ancient capital of the Picts. On a lump of granite, the "Stone of Destiny," the monarchs of the Dark Ages were enthroned. The British sovereign to this day is still crowned on the stone, but in Westminster Abbey. Edward I removed the stone there in 1296. Charles II was the last king crowned at Scone; the year: 1651.

Scone Palace (tel. 0783/52300), the seat of the Earl of Mansfield, was largely rebuilt in 1803, incorporating parts of the palace erected in 1580. Inside is an impressive collection of French antiques, furniture, china, ivories, and 16th-century needlework, including some bed hangings executed by Mary Queen of Scots. A fine collection of rare conifers is found on the grounds in the Pinetum. This is the birthplace of David Douglas and his fir trees. Rhododendrons and azaleas grow profusely in the gardens and woodlands around the palace. To reach the palace, head north of Perth on the A93. It lies two miles from the city center. The site is open from Good Friday until the second Monday in October on weekdays from 9:30 a.m. to 5 p.m. (on Sunday from 1:30 to 5 p.m.), charging an admission of £2.20 ($3.52) for adults, £1.80 ($2.88) for children, including entrance to both the house and grounds. The palace has a coffeeshop and restaurant, and state room dinners are sometimes held.

4. Gleneagles

This is a famous golfing center on a moor between Strath Earn and Streth Allan. The center gets its name from the Gaelic Glenn-an-Eaglias, "glen of the church." The golf courses here are said to be unrivaled anywhere in the world. Well-heeled golfers flock to the famed Gleneagles Hotel, one of the showcases of Scotland, which has entertained everybody from the Duke of Edinburgh to Richard Burton. Opened in 1924, this is a self-contained resort, with four championship golf courses. Regrettably, it is far beyond the budget of this guide. However, in the neighboring village of Auchterarder you can find reasonably priced rooms and meals, and can visit Gleneagles as if it were a sightseeing expedition. (It's also possible to drive north of Gleneagles and stay at Crieff—see below.)

FOOD AND LODGING AT AUCHTERARDER: The most centrally located accommodation in the area is the **Coll Earn House Hotel,** High Street (tel. 07646/3553). It is also the most desirable moderately priced place to stay in the entire area, and it comes highly recommended by the Scottish Tourist Board. A family-run place, it is a well-kept country home with eight large, comfortably furnished bedrooms. From its heyday as a private home are such luxurious amenities as wall paneling and stained-glass windows, the elegant trappings of another day. It receives guests throughout the year, charging them £22 ($35.20) to £27 ($43.20) in a well-furnished single, the price going up to £52 ($83.20) to £72 ($115.20) in a double, each with private bath.

One of the best bargains in this high-priced area is **Oakwood Guest House,** Castle Wynd (tel. 07646/2401), which has only a handful of rooms, each well kept. The reception and service are friendly, and arrangements can be made for evening meals. It's cheapest to take the half-board arrangement, costing £18.50 ($29.60) per person daily. Otherwise, expect to pay £12.50 ($20) in a single, £24 ($38.40) in a double.

5. Crieff

At the edge of the Perthshire Highlands, Crieff makes a pleasant stopover, what with its possibilities for fishing and golf. This small burgh, 18 miles from Perth, was the seat of the court of the Earls of Strathearn until 1747. Once gallows in its marketplace were used to execute Highland cattle rustlers.

You can take a "day trail" into Strathearn, the valley of the River Earn, the very center of Scotland. Highland mountains meet gentle Lowland slopes, and moorland mingles with rich green pastures. North of Crieff the road to Aberfeldy passes through the narrow pass of the Sma' Glen with hills rising on either side to 2,000 feet. The Glen is a famous beauty spot.

In addition you can explore a distillery, glassworks, a pottery center, and an aircraft museum.

FOOD AND LODGING: In many respects, the best all-around choice for a moderately priced accommodation in the area is **Cultoquhey House Hotel,** Gilmerton (tel. 0764/3253). However, because it lies about two miles from the heart of town (on the A85 road), it is best suited for motorists. It was built in the Scottish baronial architectural style, standing on some six acres of beautiful grounds, a quiet, tranquil oasis. The rooms open onto vistas over Strathearn to the Ochil Hills. The owners, who personally supervise the operation of the hotel, offer a total of 12 rooms, three of which are suitable for families. Each of these also has a private bath or shower. The B&B rates range from £28 ($44.80) to £31 ($49.60) in a single, £26 ($41.60) to £29 ($46.40) per person in a double, a worthy splurge choice. Rooms, for the most part, are spacious, and each unit is comfortable, sometimes with four-poster beds. It's also possible to stay here on half-board arrangements, costing from £34 ($54.40) to £37 ($59.20), per person, enjoying the good Scottish fire. On chilly nights, log fires are kept burning. In all, it's a relaxing, informal atmosphere which you can enjoy from April to February.

Now a century old, **Gwydyr,** Comrie Road (tel. 0764/3277), is a fine house about a five-minute walk from the center of the burgh. Ian and Christine Gillies, along with their warm and hospitable staff, welcome you to this gracious hotel. The B&B charge is £11.25 ($18) in a single, £23.50 ($37.60) in a double, and all of their accommodations contain hot and cold running water and color TV. The beds are comfortable, and as an added convenience you're given facilities for making tea or coffee. The dining room serves well-prepared food, using local ingredients whenever possible. They offer a selection of dishes, all reasonably priced. The dining room is open from 7 to 8 p.m. A four-course dinner goes for £7.35 ($11.76), including coffee. If you're at the place for lunch, you can take it in the bar, enjoying soups, pâté, fried haddock, or ham steaks. The cellar is well stocked with wines, beers, and liquors. In the residents' lounge, guests gather around a color television. Gwydyr stands on its own grounds, a large garden overlooking MacRosty Park. You'll have an uninterrupted view of Ben Vorlich and Glen Artney to the south.

The **Crieff Hotel,** East High Street (tel. 0764/2632), is one of the best little hotels in town, lying in the center. Owners Allan and Catherine Hendry not only have some good rooms to rent, but they have one of the best restaurants in Crieff. They give you a real Scottish welcome, sheltering you in one of their pleasant and comfortable units at a cost of £13.50 ($21.60) in a bathless single, £18.50 ($29.60) in a single with private bath, color TV, radio, and hot-beverage facilities. Doubles cost from £26 ($41.60) to £36 ($57.60), the price depending on the plumbing and other amenities. All tariffs include a full Scottish breakfast, and prices include VAT. Also available to residents at reduced rates are the sauna, Jacuzzi, sunbed-exercise room, and hairdressing salon.

Lunch is served daily from noon to 2 p.m. with specials at £2.75 ($4.40). Traditional Scottish high tea is served from 4:30 to 6:30 p.m., and an à la carte menu is presented from 7 to 9:30 p.m. Dinner costs from £8.50 ($13.60) and is likely to include such specialties as salmon from the Tay, grouse, and pheasant. There is a well-stocked bar and a lounge bar. Golf, fishing, hill walking, and shooting are available in the vicinity.

For food outside the hotels already recommended, try the **Highlandman Restaurant,** East High Street (tel. 0764/4866). Gerald and Anne Withers have taken over what used to be a garage and new-car showroom on the eastern edge of town. Few reminders of the grease-and-oil age remain, however, in this well-scrubbed and friendly place, where glowing parquet floors and immaculate napery are the setting. Open only from Easter until late September, the establishment serves seven days a week from 10 a.m. to 9 p.m. They are well known for their steak pie and their changing array of fresh fish ("We sell hundreds of stones worth of fish every week.") Full meals cost from £5 ($8) and up. Children's specials and sandwiches are also available, and the restaurant is fully licensed.

SIGHTS: Scotland's oldest distillery, **Glenturret Distillery Ltd.** (tel. 0764/2424), was established in 1775. On the banks of the River Turret, it is reached from Crieff by taking the A85 toward Comrie. At a point three-quarters of a mile from Crieff, turn right at the crossroads; the distillery is a quarter mile up the road. It is all signposted. Visitors can see the milling of malt, mashing, fermentation, distillation, and cask filling, followed by a free "wee dram" dispensed at the end of the tour. Visitors are welcome from 9:30 a.m. to 5:30 p.m. Monday to Friday March to December and on Saturday from 10 a.m. to 5 p.m. April to October. Tours leave every ten minutes. The Glenturret Heritage Centre incorporates a 100-seat audio-visual theater and an Exhibition Display Museum. The distillery shop has the full range of the Glenturret Pure Single Highland Malt scotch whisky and the Glenturret malt liqueur, together with an extensive range of souvenirs. At the Smugglers Restaurant and Whisky Tasting Bar you can taste older Glenturret whiskies, such as 10 year old, high proof, 12 and 15 year old, and the Glenturret malt liqueur. Guided tours, taking about 25 minutes, cost £1.25 ($2) for adults and 60p (96¢) for persons 12 to 17 years old. Children under 12 are admitted free. Admission to the Heritage Centre is 50p (80¢), the presentation lasting about 20 minutes.

Stuart Strathearn, Muthill Road (tel. 0764/4004), is a factory welcoming visitors who want to see how handmade crystal is produced. Factory hours are from 9 a.m. to 5 p.m. Monday to Saturday, from 10 a.m. to 5 p.m. on Sunday. From June to September, the closing hour is 7 p.m. You can see the traditional craftsman's skill in the Stuart Crystal film and demonstrated by factory glassworkers. The shop on the premises has a large selection of Stuart Crystal seconds and its own engraved crystal giftware. In the grounds of the factory is a picnic area, plus a children's playground.

Crieff Visitors Centre, also on Muthill Road (tel. 0764/4014), which opened in 1985, was built by Buchan's Thistle Potteries and Perthshire Paperweight, two medium-size craft factories, to enable visitors to see their skills in manufacturing pottery and glass. Buchans established the Thistle Potteries more than a century ago and is the last survivor of the famous Portobello potteries. Visitors can go on an escorted tour through the factory on weekdays, seeing all the elements of the process for free. Sometimes tours can be taken on Sunday afternoon in high season. Perthshire Paperweights has recently been designed to allow visitors to watch the processes. It is also open during working hours, but Friday afternoon is the least interesting time, because the staff is only preparing the next week's glass. The center has a large showroom displaying the products of both factories, including both firsts and seconds in the pottery, although all paperweight seconds are destroyed. There is a modern restaurant. Hours are from 9 a.m. to 5 p.m. seven days a week, although factory tours are only possible during normal production hours.

The **Strathallan Aircraft Museum** is at Strathallan Airfield (tel. 0764/2545), four miles northwest of Auchterarder, from which you follow the B8062 for Crieff and then the signs for the museum. If you're coming from Crieff, take the A822 to Muthill and follow the signs. The collection is open daily, April 1 to October 31, from 10 a.m. to 5 p.m. (later in July and August). Aircraft on display include a Lancaster bomber, a Hurricane fighter, and a Westland Lysander. There are also displays of aero engines and many other items of a nostalgic nature. Wet weather need not deter a visitor, as most exhibits are indoors. Flying weekends are held every summer. Admission is £1.50 ($2.40) for adults, £1 ($1.60) for children.

Three miles south of Crieff, you can visit the gardens of **Drummond Castle** (tel. 076481/257), a mile north of Muthill, which was the seat of the late Earl of Ancaster. The second Earl of Perth laid out these ten-acre gardens in 1662 along continental lines. The grounds are open from May to the end of August from 2 to 6 p.m. seven days a week. Admission is £1 ($1.60) for adults, 50p (80¢) for children.

6. Comrie

An attractive little village in Strathearn, 25 miles from Perth, Comrie stands at the confluence of the Earn, Ruchill, and Lednock rivers. The A85 runs through the village to Lochearnhead, Crianlarich, and on to Oban on the western seaboard. It's convenient as an overnight stop for travelers crossing Scotland. Waterskiing, boating, and sailing are available on Loch Earn.

WHERE TO STAY: Dating back to 1765, the **Royal Hotel,** Melville Square (tel. 0764/70200), was awarded the "royal" after a visit by Her Majesty, Queen Victoria. It's an L-shaped stone inn with white trim and six dormer accommodations among its bedrooms. Its drinking lounge, with walls and chairs in Gordon tartan, has an intriguing collection of photos, sketches, and prints of famous people who have stayed here, everybody from Madame Sarah Bernhardt to Lloyd George. The dining room, where there's a log fireplace, has recently been redecorated. All the bedrooms are most comfortable, with private baths, direct-dial phones, radios, color TV, hot-beverage facilities, and electric blankets, although the hotel is centrally heated. The charge for B&B is £21 ($33.60) per person. Half board is priced at £31 ($49.60) per person.

A PLACE FOR TARTANS: On the A85 road, the **Scottish Tartans Museum,** Davidson House, Drummond Street (tel. 0764/70779), contains the world's largest collection of tartans and Highland dress portrayed in pictures, models, and prints: It is open from April to October on weekdays from 10 a.m. to 5 p.m. and on Sunday from 2 to 4 p.m. In winter, hours are Monday to Friday from 2 to 3:30 p.m. and on Saturday from 10 a.m. to 1 p.m. There is a reconstruction of a weaver's cottage with occasional demonstrations of hand-spinning and dying of cloth, as well as a dye garden featuring plants, shrubs, and trees used in past times to dye tartan. The Scottish Tartans Society undertakes research inquiries on a fee basis and has a register of all known tartans. Admission to the museum is 80p ($1.28) for adults, 50p (80¢) for children.

7. Dundee

This royal burgh and old seaport is an industrial city, one of the largest in Scotland, lying on the north shore of the Firth of Tay. When steamers took over the whaling industry from sailing vessels, Dundee took the lead as home port for the ships from the 1860s until World War I. Long known for its jute and flax operations, the fame of Dundee today is linked with the production of the rich Dundee fruitcakes and Dundee marmalades and jams.

This was the home of the man who invented stick-on postage stamps, James Chalmers.

Spanning the Firth of Tay is the **Tay Railway Bridge,** opened in 1888. Spanning the tidal estuary, the bridge is some two miles long, one of the longest in Europe. There is also a road bridge a 1¼ miles long, with four lanes and a walkway in the center.

Although many travelers pass through the city en route to Glamis Castle, 12 miles north, there are good places to stay in Dundee and some interesting sights.

FOOD AND LODGING: A 19th-century building beside the road, **Carlton House**

Hotel, 2 Dalgleish Rd. (tel. 0382/43456), has a mansard rood and adjoining modern wing, all in colors of beige, nut brown, white, and curtains of tangerine. Every room has color TV, a radio, a room call system, and a private shower. B&B in a single is £14 ($22.40) and for two, £22 ($35.20), including VAT. You can have dinners in the pleasantly decorated Tudor dining room or a drink in the bar lounge. A three-course evening meal ranges in price from £5.50 ($8.80).

Craigtay Hotel, 101 Broughty Ferry Rd. (tel. 0382/451142), is run by Mr. and Mrs. L.G. Hawes, who also operate the just-recommended Carlton House Hotel. It too is small, friendly, and family run, but charges slightly higher prices. A single costs from £18 ($28.80) per night, and a double, from £25 ($40), including VAT. All rooms are pleasantly furnished with color TV, radios, phones, and private toilets with a bath or shower. Good Scottish food is served in the Latin-style dining room and bar. Both hotels are well situated, lying on main bus routes three minutes from the center.

For a dining choice, try the house of authentic Indian meals, **Gunga-Din Restaurant,** 99c-101 Perth Rd. (tel. 0382/65672), which lies to the west of the city in the university sector. Nearly everything is prepared to order, so don't come here seeking fast food if you're rushed. The university students and others who patronize Gunga-Din know that the meats and vegetables are seasonally fresh, and care is taken to follow original Indian recipes. You could begin a savory meal with the prawn soup, followed by a wide variety of meat or fish dishes (don't hesitate to ask the waiter for assistance). Among these, try chicken biriyani cooked with pilaf nuts, raisins, herbs, pepper, and tomatoes in clarified butter. Dessert might be an Indian ice cream. All this would cost about £7 ($11.20). You can dine for much less if you stick to the vegetable curries. The restaurant, owned by Mr. Farid Ahmed, is open from noon to 2 p.m. and 6 to 11:30 p.m. Monday through Saturday. On weekends you should reserve a table for dinner by calling in the morning.

The **Pizza Gallery,** 2 Panmure (tel. 0382/29629), is a two-level modern establishment off a shoppers' street. It is open daily from 10 a.m. to 11 p.m., offering a choice of some 16 pizzas at a price of £2.75 ($4.40) to £4.10 ($6.56). For reasons known only to themselves, the pizzas are named after famous artists. The Picasso is uncharacteristically basic (cheese and tomato), but the Goya is more inspired with anchovies, green pepper, and olives. For eaters wanting a more complete meal, soup followed by a large chef's salad, a heaping plate of spaghetti, and finally a strawberry cheesecake would cost £6 ($9.60). The restaurant is licensed to sell wine by the glass or the carafe, and it enjoys much popularity among the denizens of Dundee.

SIGHTS: At Victoria Dock, the frigate *Unicorn* (tel. 0382/21555), a 46-gun ship of war commissioned in 1824 by the Royal Navy, has been in large part restored, and visitors can see the main gundeck, where the men assigned to duty with the 18-pound cannons lived and worked, the quarterdeck with 32-pound carronades, the captain's quarters, and the officers' quarters where an exhibition on the Royal Navy can be studied. The frigate can be visited daily except Tuesday from early April to early October from 11 a.m. to 1 p.m. and 2 to 5 p.m. on weekdays, from 2 to 5 p.m. on Sunday. Admission is 50p (80¢) for adults, 25p (40¢) for children.

For a spectacular view of Dundee, the Tay bridges across to Fife, and mountains to the north, go to **Dundee Law,** a 572-foot hill a mile north of the city. The hill is an ancient volcanic plug.

About five miles east of the city center on the sea front, at **Broughty Ferry,** a little fishing hamlet, later the terminus for the ferry that crossed the Firth of Tay until the bridges were built, is **Broughty Castle Museum,** St. Vincent Street (tel. 0382/23141), which has exhibits on military history, local lore, and a fine section on whaling, including ship models, paintings based on the whaling industry, and whaling equipment, as well as displays on the ferry and lifeboat services. The museum is open weekdays except Friday from 10 a.m. to 1 p.m. and 2 to 5 p.m., on Sunday from 2 to 5 p.m. in July, August, and September. Admission is free. The museum is in a reconstructed estuary fort, Broughty Castle, originally built in 1498.

8. Carnoustie

This seaside resort, 61 miles northeast of Edinburgh, is celebrated for its championship golf course. Lying between Dundee and Arbroath (eight miles away), Carnoustie opens onto the North Sea. In summer its five miles of sand give plenty of beach space to its visitors.

FOOD AND LODGING: A good place to stay, **Glencoe Hotel,** Links Parade (tel. 0241/53273), also serves some of the best and most reasonably priced food in town. Nonresidents are welcome to drop in. This privately owned hotel, the domain of David and Carolyn Peters, is fully licensed, standing in a spot overlooking the Tay estuary. Only 11 bedrooms, each with color TV and direct-dial phone, are offered in this centrally heated hotel. All of the doubles come with private bath or shower. The charge is £18 ($28.80) per person. A full Scottish breakfast is included in that tariff, along with VAT and service. The Glencoe is the hotel nearest the championship golf course: it's directly opposite the first tee and the last green and adjacent to the Burnside Course. There is a resident lounge with TV, plus contemporary sun parlors with unobstructed views of the golf course. In the modern cocktail lounge you can order your favorite scotch malt whisky. A fixed-price dinner menu in the dining room goes for £8 ($12.80) and includes four courses of well-prepared food. First, you get the appetizer, followed by soup, then a main course such as roast leg of lamb with mint sauce, followed by an apple tart with fresh Scottish cream. Some of the specialties, such as Scottish salmon, cost more when chosen from the table d'hôte. Dinner is served daily from 7:30 to 9 p.m. A slightly cheaper and simplified version of the dinner menu is offered at lunch from noon to 2 p.m. daily.

Villa Rosa Hotel, 13 Philip St. (tel. 0241/52182), is an 1812 house which seemingly at one time was a large family home, with gardens and interesting architectural features. It's in the center of town, just off the High Street, a few minutes' walk from the seafront, the beach, and the first tee of the championship golf course. The interior, with its classic hallway and open staircase, has a reception lounge, a cocktail bar, another lounge with color TV, and a dining room with a bay window. Owners Mr. and Mrs. Tom McGovern, charge £9.50 ($15.20) nightly per person for B&B, including VAT. The dinner costs £5 ($8) for four courses.

Earlston Hotel, 24 Church St. (tel. 0241/52352), lies about half a mile from the Carnoustie Open Championship Golf Course. It stands in a row of attached brick buildings, with a pair of bays and dormers. The interior is harmoniously decorated, the dining room spacious yet cozy. Of the 17 well-furnished bedrooms, seven have private showers or toilets. Depending on the season, the single rate ranges from £17.50 ($28) to £21 ($33.60), and doubles cost £29 ($46.40) to £36 ($57.60). The hotel is fully licensed, and its restaurant provides both table d'hôte and à la carte meals.

Dalhousie Hotel, 47 High St. (tel. 0241/52907), often attracts golfers. A family-run hotel, it extends gracious Scottish hospitality to its visitors, feeding them well and bedding them down in comfort in one of the rooms they have for rent. The charge is only £9.50 ($15.20) to £11.50 ($18.40) per person, including a hearty Scottish breakfast. No one goes away from the table hungry. Dinner costs from £4 ($6.40). The hotel lies about a three-minute walk from a beach, and children are catered to, having their own paddling pool and play area.

Braemore Guest House, 24 Dundee St. (tel. 0241/52076), provides budget accommodations under the care and hospitality of its owner, Margaret Warhurst. She charges only £8.50 ($13.60) per person for an overnight stay and will cook one of her well-prepared dinners for £5 ($8). Her home is centrally located, within a few minutes' walk of the golf courses, putting greens, the shops, and public transport. She has become the favorite guesthouse for many Americans. The bedrooms have basic necessities and are neat, with hot and cold running water.

9. Arbroath

Samuel Johnson wasn't that much impressed with Scotland on his jaunt there, but he did say that the view of Arbroath repaid him for some of the hardships suffered in his journey. Arbroath is a popular coastal resort with a colorful fishing harbor and rugged, red sandstone cliffs weathered into grotesque shapes. Smugglers once used the sandstone caves along the coast. Arbroath "smokies" (smoked haddock) are one of the fish delicacies along the east coast of Scotland.

The "Fairport" of Sir Walter Scott's *The Antiquary,* the royal burgh of Arbroath lies 17 miles northeast of Dundee.

FOOD AND LODGING: A friendly oasis, the **Sandhutton Guest House,** 16 Addison Pl. (tel. 0241/72007), is also economical. Mary and Peter Pert make it all personal, and their little courtesies and assistance can make all the difference. All their bedrooms have color TV and hot-beverage facilities. The Perts ask £9 ($14.40) per person for B&B, and they serve a full cooked meal—eggs and bacon as you like them. There is a separate dining room, where for £4 ($6.40) you can have a tasty evening meal, but not in July and August—they're too busy then. However, they'll recommend budget restaurants nearby. There's a lounge with color TV for their guests. All their bedrooms are decorated in a home-like manner and have wash basins with hot and cold water, and electric blankets. As Mary says, "Cleanliness and comfort we can guarantee." They have no singles, but if possible they'll offer a lone guest a double if they are not crowded and can spare the room.

Inverpark House Hotel, Bank Street (tel. 0241/73378), is owned by a colorful and gracious host, Denis Mackintosh, who offers excellent bedrooms which he rents nightly for £12.50 ($20) per person, including a substantial breakfast. The units are comfortably furnished and well maintained. Many people in Abroath come here just to sample the food. During both lunch and dinner, good meals are available in the bar. You might try, as I did, a bowl of soup, a plate of roast meat with a vegetable, then a dessert, all for only £3.50 ($5.60). If you don't want beef, pork, or lamb, try the fresh haddock in a cream sauce. Everything is freshly cooked on the premises. Denis has no passion for the frozen foods of today. "I like my meat, fish, and vegetables fresh every day," he says. "Why shouldn't my customers want the same?"

Oronsay, 18 Addison Pl. (tel. 0241/73986), is a homey, friendly place run by Mr. and Mrs. David Brown. They have three attractive, large, clean bedrooms with hot and cold water basins. A full Scottish breakfast is included in the cost of £9 ($14.40) per person. The dining room and TV lounge are tastefully decorated.

SIGHTS: Associated with the Declaration of Arbroath of 1320, when the Scottish Parliament met here and drew up a famous letter to send to the pope asserting Scotland's independence from England, **Arbroath Abbey,** on the High Street, was founded as a priory in 1178 by William the Lion to honor his late friend, Thomas à Becket, murdered in Canterbury eight years earlier. The red sandstone abbey, a rich and influential ecclesiastical center, became dilapidated after the beginning of the 17th century, but it was once again in the news in 1951, when the Stone of Scone, stolen from Westminster Abbey, turned up on the altar here. A historical pageant is presented in the abbey annually. For more information, phone 031/226-2570. Hours are the same as for the museum described below.

The **Abbot's House,** within the precincts of Arbroath Abbey (tel. 0241/78756), has been restored as a museum, with a collection of relics and stone sculpture. April to the end of September hours are 9:30 a.m. to 7 p.m. Monday to Saturday, from 2 p.m. to 7 p.m. on Sunday. The remainder of the year, the hours are the same, except for a 4 p.m. closing. Admission charges are 50p (80¢) for adults, 25p (40¢) for children.

A collection of Pictish sculptured stones and medieval stonework from the original village church of Arbroath can be seen at **St. Vigeans,** half a mile north of the town center. It's open Monday to Saturday. Admission is free. Phone 031/226-2570 for information.

10. Montrose

Instead of heading immediately for Glamis Castle, I suggest you continue along the coastal road from Arbroath toward Montrose. Along the way you'll pass stretches of rugged beauty. Sandstone cliffs rise sharply out of the water, and little slate-roofed cottages house the families who make their living from the often turbulent sea.

Montrose stands on a bottleneck of Montrose Basin, a broad estuary inhabited by hundreds of wild birds, notably pink-footed geese. This harbor town, with its well-known golf links, is a North Sea coastal resort for holiday-makers. Its spired church and town hall date from the 18th century. David I granted Montrose its charter, and in 1352 it became one of Scotland's many royal burghs. Montrose lies 30 miles northeast of Dundee by road.

FOOD AND LODGING: One of the Welcome Inn chain, the **Central Hotel,** High Street (tel. 0674/72152), is a well-run hostelry. It's in the heart of town, where you can get all the necessities and still sleep in peace. A bathless single with breakfast is £15 ($24), and a double or twin runs £26 ($41.60) nightly. If you want a private bath, the tariff rises to £19.50 ($31.20) in a single, £31 ($49.60) in a double. In the restaurant, lunch starts at £5 ($8), high tea costs from £2.75 ($4.40), and dinner from £8 ($12.80). In the bar, you can have a simple lunch at a low tab. All prices include VAT.

Corner House Hotel, High Street (tel. 0674/73126), is a licensed hostelry, privately owned and situated in the town center. It is known for good food and serves bar meals all day. An extensive menu is offered in the dining room. Lunch costs £3.50 ($5.60), high tea from £4 ($6.40), and à la carte dinners from £9 ($14.40). Joyce and Graham Reid rent comfortable rooms costing £20 ($32) in a single for B&B, £47 ($75.20) in a double, prices including VAT.

Park Hotel, John Street (tel. 0674/73467), is one of the best hotels in town.

Rated three stars, it has been refurbished and extended. It stands on the midlinks between the heart of town and the beach. Rooms are comfortably appointed and well kept, a single (bathless) renting for £25 ($40) per night. Most rooms have private bath, in which case a single goes for £35 ($56), a similar double or twin for £46 ($73.60). Rooms have color TV and phone, and there are 59 in all, so you have a good chance of getting a room even in high season. Food is served either at a luncheon buffet table or in a large restaurant. Meals cost from £7.50 ($12).

11. Kirriemuir

A little town of red sandstone houses and narrow, crooked streets, Kirriemuir is in the heart of the raspberry country of Scotland, on a rise looking out on Strathmore. The town's main claim to fame is as the birth and burial place of Sir James M. Barrie, creator of the immortal *Peter Pan*. Kirriemuir is the "Thrums" of Barrie's novels.

WHERE TO STAY: If you'd like to stop over in Kirriemuir, **Thrums Hotel** (tel. 0575/72758) is almost next door to the birthplace of J.M. Barrie. Grahame McKinney, who owns the hotel, guarantees a warm and friendly welcome. The bedrooms have recently been upgraded, and all have color TV and hot and cold water basins. The tariff is £13.50 ($21.60) per person for B&B, VAT included. The hotel also has a reputation for good bar lunches, high teas, and dinners, with Tay salmon and Aberdeen Angus steaks always available.

A BARRIE PILGRIMAGE: The author and dramatist, Sir James M. Barrie, was born in 1860, son of a father who was employed as a hand-loom weaver of linen. **Barrie's Birthplace,** 9 Brechin Rd. (tel. 0575/72646), a property of the National Trust for Scotland, contains manuscripts and mementos of the writer. A little wash house outside the four-room cottage was used by the young Barrie as his first theater. Besides his creation of *Peter Pan*, Barrie also wrote such stage successes as *The Admirable Crichton* and *Dear Brutus*. The house is open from 11 a.m. to 5:30 p.m. weekdays, from 2 to 5:30 p.m. Sunday Easter week and May to the end of September. Admission is 80p ($1.28) for adults, 40p (64¢) for children.

To reach **Barrie's grave** in Kirriemuir Cemetery, you turn left off Rrechin Road and follow Cemetery Road upward. The path is clearly marked to take you to the grave pavilion.

A **camera obscura** in the Barrie Pavilion on Kirriemuir Hill gives views over Strathmore to Dundee and northward to the Highlands.

12. Glamis Castle

After Balmoral Castle, most visitors to Scotland want to see Glamis Castle at Glamis (pronounced Glaams), for its architecture and its link with the crown. For ten centuries it has been connected to British royalty. Her Majesty, Queen Elizabeth, the Queen Mother, was brought up here; her daughter, now Queen Elizabeth II, spent a good deal of her childhood here; and Princess Margaret, the Queen's sister, was born here, becoming the first royal princess born in Scotland in three centuries.

The little village of Glamis grew up around the castle. The Scottish Transport Festival is held here each July.

WHERE TO EAT: In the vicinity of the castle, try the **Strathmore Arms** (tel. 030784/248), for one of the best lunches in the area. It has a cold buffet, with a tempting array of goodies, including cold roasts, fish, crisp salads, and quiches. You might begin with a cup of Scottish broth, then go on to sample the tasty homemade steak-and-kidney pie. Lunch, costing from £5 ($8), is served from noon to 2 p.m. You might also want to patronize the place for afternoon tea at £1.75 ($2.80). À la carte dinners, served from 7:30 to 9:30 p.m., can be ordered from an extensive menu featuring French and Scottish cuisine. Expect to pay from £11 ($17.60).

THE CASTLE AND A MUSEUM: As it exists today, **Glamis Castle** dates in part from the middle of the 15th century, but there are records of a castle's having been in existence in the 11th century, at which time it was one of the hunting lodges of the Kings of Scotland. King Malcolm II was carried there mortally wounded in 1034 after having been attacked by his enemies while hunting in a nearby forest.

Glamis Castle has been in the possession of the Lyon family since 1372, when it formed part of the dowry of Princess Joanna, daughter of King Robert II, when she married John Lyon, secretary to the king. The castle was altered in the 16th century and restored and enlarged in the 17th, 18th, and 19th centuries. It contains some fine plaster ceilings, furniture, and paintings. The present owner, the Queen's cousin, is the 17th Earl of Strathmore and Kinghorne. He lives at the castle with his wife and three children. He is the direct descendant of the first earl.

The castle is open to the public, who have access to the Royal Apartments and many other rooms, and also to the fine gardens, May to September, Sunday through Friday, at £2 ($3.20) for adults, £1 ($1.60) for children. If you wish to visit only the grounds, laid out by a gardener working under the influence of Capability Brown, you pay only half price. For further details on the castle's hours, get in touch with the Administrator, Estates Office (tel. 030784/242).

Also in Glamis, you may want to visit the **Angus Folk Museum,** Kirkwynd Cottages, run by the National Trust of Scotland. From the former county of Angus, rich in folklore, were collected domestic utensils, agricultural implements, furniture, and clothing. The museum is open May 1 to September 30 from noon to 5 p.m. (last entry at 4:30 p.m.), charging adults £1 ($1.60); children pay 50p (80¢).

13. Dunkeld

A cathedral town, Dunkeld lies in a thickly wooded valley of the Tay River, at the edge of the Perthshire Highlands. Once a major ecclesiastical center, it is one of the seats of ancient Scottish history. It was an important center of the Celtic church, for example.

FOOD AND LODGING: A prim white corner hostelry, the Atholl Arms Hotel, Tayside Terrace (tel. 03502/219), stands in the center of the village. Inside it has the aura and furnishings of a gracious country home. The lounge is all in white, with a fireplace, brightly covered armchairs, and a row of antique platters. There are 20 bedrooms, each having its own heating and hot and cold water. Four contain private baths or showers. In the morning a cup of hot coffee can be brought to your bedside. The terms, including VAT, are £16 ($25.60) nightly per person, with a country-style breakfast. An evening meal is priced at £10 ($16) VAT included. Snack lunches and afternoon tea are also available.

The **Taybank Hotel** (tel. 03502/340), just off the main road, is almost on the Tay River—very quiet for a good night's rest. The hotel is a Victorian former private home. Owned by Mr. and Mrs. Reid, the hotel has an atmosphere that is intimate and comfortable. From the first of March until early October, guests are received and charged £14 ($22.40) per person for B&B. No formal dinners are served; instead you can order bar suppers, costing £5 ($8).

SIGHTS: Founded in A.D. 815, the **Cathedral of Dunkeld** was converted from a church to a cathedral in 1127 by David I. The 14th and 15th centuries witnessed subsequent additions. The cathedral was first restored in 1815, and at that time traces of the 12th-century structure clearly remained, as they do to this day. It can be visited from Easter to Remembrance Sunday in early November daily from 9:30 a.m. to 7 p.m. Admission is free.

The National Trust for Scotland has been effective in restoring many of the old houses and shops around the marketplace and cathedral that had fallen into decay. The trust owns 20 houses in High Street and Cathedral Street as well. Many of these houses were constructed in the closing years of the 17th century after the rebuilding of the town following the Battle of Dunkeld. The trust has opened the **Ell Shop,** open from the first of April until the end of May and from the first of September until Christmas, Monday to Saturday from 10 a.m. to 1 p.m. and 2 to 4:30 p.m. In summer it is open daily except Sunday from 10 a.m. to 6 p.m.

The **Scottish Horse Museum,** The Cross, has exhibits tracing the history of the Scottish Horse Yeomanry in the museum in one of the "Little Houses of Dunkeld," the area between the cathedral and the town's main street in which Jacobean cottages are preserved and maintained by the National Trust for Scotland. From the time of the raising of the cavalry force in Scotland and South Africa in 1900 to its amalgamation with the Fife & Forfar Yeomanry in 1956, the Scottish Horse mounted yeomanry regiment was the only such fighting body besides the Lovat Scouts. The museum is open from 10:30 a.m. to 5 p.m. Monday to Saturday and from 11 a.m. to 5 p.m. on Sunday (closed for 1½ hours at lunchtime) Easter to the end of September. Admission is 30p (48¢) for adults, free for children.

Shakespeare fans may want to seek out the oak and sycamore in front of the destroyed **Birnam House,** a mile to the south. This was believed to be a remnant of the Birnam Wood to which the Bard gave everlasting literary fame in *Macbeth.* In Shakespeare's drama, you may recall, the "woods of Birnam came to Dunsinane."

The **Hermitage** was called a "folly" when it was constructed in 1758, lying off the A9 about two miles west of Dunkeld. Today it makes for one of the most scenic woodland walks in the area. The folly was built above the wooded gorge of the River Braan and restored in 1984.

14. Pitlochry

After leaving Edinburgh, many motorists stop here for the night before continuing on the Highland road to Inverness. However, once they discover the charms of Pitlochry, they want to linger. This popular holiday resort center is a touring headquarters for the Valley of the Tummel.

Pitlochry doesn't just entertain tourists, although it would appear that way in summer. It also produces scotch whisky and tweeds.

WHERE TO STAY: Comfortable accommodations are provided at **Acarsaid,** 8 Atholl Rd. (tel. 0796/2389), a combination of the old and very new. A stone Edwardian house with three decorative gables is sandwiched between two modern extensions made of stone, natural wood, and glass. Delft-blue trim bonds it together harmoniously. The hotel has 19 bedrooms, each with private bath or shower; all have hot and cold water and electric stoves. The half-board rate is £27.50 ($44) per person nightly. B&B costs £18.50 ($29.60) per person. Prices include VAT but not service. The owners will tell you about the most scenic spots in the Perthshire area.

Airdaniar Hotel, 160 Atholl Rd. (tel. 0796/2266), was a private home when built originally at the turn of the century. It has distinction, and its stone walls in all shades of beige and brown, its extended sunroom, its three acres of tidy and well-planted garden, make it instantly likable. Andrew and Sue Mathieson enjoy an excellent reputation for food and are members of the "Taste of Scotland" program. The well-kept bedchambers are furnished with color TV, hot-beverage facilities, and radio/intercoms. Many have private baths. For a bed and a full Scottish breakfast, the charge is £17.50 ($28) per person. This tariff goes up to £24.50 ($39.20) per person for half board. Family rooms are available with reductions for children on request. The hotel has been completely refurbished, and central heating has been installed throughout. Guests are invited to dine in the Grouse and Claret restaurant and bar where they can order good food and drink.

Balrobin Hotel, Higher Oakfield (tel. 0796/2901), is a traditional Scottish country house, standing on its own grounds only a few minutes from the town center, commanding views of the Tummel Valley. The owner, H. H. D. Hohman, was a manager for ten years of three- and four-star hotels, and he maintains a high standard, providing an enjoyable stay for clients. His hotel is centrally heated. All 12 of the bedrooms have color TV, hot-beverage facilities, and electric blankets, and ten have private baths. The charge is from £18 ($28.80) per person for dinner, bed, and breakfast. The hotel has a residential license, and home cooking with a daily choice of menu is a specialty.

The **Green Park Hotel** (tel. 0796/2537) is not only one of the finest hotels in the area, but it offers some of the best food, good-tasting, reasonably priced fare. On the grounds of Loch Faskally, this country-house hotel lies at the northwest end of Pitlochry, about a five-minute walk from the center. Anne and Graham Brown are well spoken of locally for the care and attention they devote to their restaurant. A rather large choice of food items is available at the bar lunch, noon to 2 p.m., including golden pea soup with ham and grilled rainbow trout amandine, followed by a steamed marmalade sponge and custard sauce, costing £4.50 ($7.20). A fixed-price dinner goes for £11 ($17.60). For dessert, perhaps you'll be there on the night the chef does a specialty, "Dream of Rob Roy." You help yourself to the coffee in the lounge. The dining room is open March through October daily from 6:30 to 8 p.m.

Killiecrankie Hotel (tel. 0796/3220) enjoys a lovely rural setting. A hotel since the 1930s, it is family owned and run by Duncan and Jennifer Hattersley-Smith, who receive guests from Easter until the middle of October. They have only a dozen rooms, each of which is pleasantly and attractively decorated, using natural pine furnishings constructed locally. Upholstered furnishings are in Laura Ashley fabrics. Of the 12 rooms, a total of eight have private baths or showers en suite. Two chambers are set aside for families. The B&B rate is only £23 ($36.80) per person nightly, but most guests prefer the half-board tariff of £38 ($60.80) per person, because the food is so excellently prepared. In addition to the "Taste of Scotland" fare in the traditionally furnished dining room, a high standard of less expensive bar food is also served. Fresh fish and game in season are combined with the best of local meats, everything served by a kilted young staff.

Moulin Inn, 11-13 Kirkmichael Rd., Moulin by Pitlochry (tel. 0796/2196), lies about a mile from the heart of town on the A924. It forms two sides of the village square of Moulin, having been developed around a coaching inn from the 1600s at the foot of Ben-y-Vrackie. It is owned by the Laird of Balnakeilly. It offers 18 well-furnished bedrooms, 12 of which contain private baths. In spite of the age of the inn, many of the accommodations were recently built, with modern amenities, such as central heating, installed. They offer a half-board rate of £24.50 ($39.20) to £28.50 ($45.60) per person. Otherwise, a single with breakfast included can be rented for £17.50 ($28) to £21 ($33.60); a double goes for £29 ($46.40) to £36.50 ($58.40). A fine cuisine, including many Scottish specialties such as fresh salmon, is served in the pleasant restaurant, opening onto views of the surrounding hills. Your hosts can also arrange trout-fishing permits.

Tigh-Na-Cloich Hotel (tel. 0796/2216) is on a hillside overlooking the town, valley, river, and hills. It is a century-old house converted into a hotel, with a flower garden and path extending almost to the main street. The public room is large, pleasant, and connected to an attractive sun parlor. The bedrooms are clean, comfortable, and the owners, George and Gleniss Ross, see to it that guests have big towels which are warmed on the towel bar. Electric blankets, TV, and hot-beverage facilities are part of the amenities. The rates are £14 ($22.40) per person for a room without bath, £13 ($20.80) per person for a room with private bath or shower and toilet. Dinner, costing £8 ($12.80), can be selected from four appetizers, main dishes, and good desserts.

The **Viewmore Guest House,** 27 Atholl Rd. (tel. 0796/2065), is a comfortable accommodation run by Mrs. Sally McAdam. She charges £9 ($14.40) per person for B&B. The house has a pleasant lounge, a new annex, and plenty of parking.

WHERE TO EAT: In a 200-year-old building, the **Luggie Restaurant,** Rie-Achen Road (tel. 0796/2085), retains much of the character built up over the decades. The American owners, Sandy and Joy Charleson, offer morning coffee from 9:30 to 11:30 a.m., with an assortment of freshly baked scones, cakes, and cookies from their own bakery. Lunch, from 11:30 a.m. to 2:30 p.m., features local salmon, trout, 17 different salads, and up to ten desserts. A selection of hot dishes is available daily. Expect to spend from £3 ($4.80) to £6 ($9.60) for a good midday meal. Afternoon tea is served after lunch until 5 p.m. From 6:30 to 9 p.m. mid-April to October, dinner is served, highlighting traditional Scottish cuisine. A table d'hôte meal is offered, priced at £5.95 ($9.52), and a broad à la carte selection costs from £7 ($11.20). There is an extensive wine list. Reservations are recommended.

SIGHTS AND ACTIVITIES: The town is particularly renowned for its **Pitlochry Festival Theatre,** Scotland's "theatre in the hills." Telephone 079681/2680 for information. Founded in 1951, the festival theater draws people from all over the world to its repertoire of plays, Sunday concerts, and changing art exhibitions, presented from sometime in May until the end of September. A theater opened in 1981 on the banks of the River Tummel near the dam and fish ladder, with a car park, a restaurant serving coffee, lunch, and dinner, and other facilities for visitors.

The **Pitlochry Dam** was created because a power station was needed, but in effect the engineers created a new loch. The famous "Salmon Ladder" was built to help the struggling salmon upstream. An underwater portion of the ladder—a salmon observation chamber—has been enclosed in glass to give fascinated sightseers a look. An exhibition (tel. 0796/3152) is open here from Easter to late October daily from 9:45 a.m. to 5:30 p.m., charging adults 30p (48¢) and children 15p (24¢).

EXCURSIONS FROM PITLOCHRY: From the town you can take excursions in almost any direction. Heading northwest for three miles along the A9, you come to the **Pass of Killiecrankie,** where "Bonnie Dundee" and his Jacobites won their famous victory over the armies of General Mackay fighting for King William in 1689. This is one of the scenic highlights of the area. A **Visitors Centre** (tel. 0796/3233) stands near the site of the famous battle. It presents an interesting exhibition and is also a center for rangers and naturalists. Dedicated Scots will answer questions on walks, whatever, which are possible in the area. The center is open from 9:30 a.m. to 6 p.m. in June, July, and August, from 10 a.m. to 5 p.m. April, May, September, and October, charging an admission of 10p (16¢).

If time remains, try to see another attraction, **Queen's View,** where Victoria herself picnicked, in 1844. At the eastern end, Victoria looked down the length of the loch toward Schiehallion. The view is reached by taking the B8019 for 2½ miles northwest of Pitlochry. An obelisk commemorates the visit of the Queen. The beauty spot, the Linn of Tummel, along with 50 acres, came to the National Trust for Scotland during World War II. It is filled with magnificent woodland walks, in which you can enjoy the Douglas fir, spruce, larch, oak, and sycamore.

15. Blair Atholl

Eight miles to the northwest of Pitlochry stands the gleaming white **Blair Castle** (tel. 079681/207), the home of the Duke of Atholl, just off the A9. Built in the Scottish baronial style and dating from 1269, the castle allows you to view more than 30 rooms. Inside is an impressive collection of paintings, furniture, china, lace, arms and armor, and Masonic regalia, along with many family portraits. It is open Easter week, then Sunday and Monday in April, and again daily from the third Sunday in April until the second Sunday in October. Hours are weekdays from 10 a.m. to 6 p.m. (from 2 to 6 p.m. on Sunday). Last entrance is at 5 p.m. Admission is £2 ($3.20) for adults, £1.20 ($1.92) for children. The Duke of Atholl has the only official private army in Great Britain, known as the "Atholl Highlanders."

FOOD AND LODGING: Once lords and ladies who couldn't find room at Blair Castle stayed at the **Atholl Arms Hotel** (tel. 079681/205), where some of the grand balls of old Perthshire were held. Now the Atholl Arms is a stately stone-gabled roadside inn, attracting motorists en route to Inverness. A cocktail lounge has been created, and there's a public bar to attract locals. The grandiose ballroom has been turned into a dinner and dance restaurant, complete with a minstrels' gallery. There's also a more intimate dining room with a collection of antique mahogany chairs. The menu offers substantial choices. The bedrooms are individually styled and well fitted; each one I inspected had a completely different character. Each has hot and cold water and central heating. The rate is £20 ($32) in a single and from £31 ($49.60) in a twin or double, each including private bath or shower, VAT, service, and a full breakfast. It's also possible to take the half-board rate of £25 ($40) per person daily. Bar snacks are served at lunch, and a four-course table d'hôte dinner, costing £10.50 ($16.80), is offered in the evening.

Bruar Falls Hotel (tel. 079683/243) is a two-level cottage-style building, with a roadside stone wall and surrounding gardens. It was built around 1700 and used as a billet by some of the Highlanders in the 1745 Rebellion. It has the charm of an oldtime inn, but with contemporary necessities. Three miles from the nearest village, it is a ten-minute walk from the Falls of Bruar, where 200 feet of water falls in three levels. These falls were immortalized by Robert Burns in verse when he visited them in 1778. On summer evenings it's still light enough for nearby walks, to be climaxed by dinner in the old farmhouse restaurant. You are welcomed by Allan and Ann Grant. There are eight comfortably furnished rooms, none with private bath, costing £12 ($19.20) per person nightly. Food is served continuously either as bar snacks or more formal meals from 7:30 a.m. to 10:30 p.m. Specialties, costing from £8 ($12.80) for a full meal, include fresh salmon, haggis, and T-bone steak.

16. Aberfeldy

The "Birks o' Aberfeldy" are among the beauty spots made famous by Robert Burns. Once a Pictish center, this small town makes a fine base for touring Perthshire's glens and lochs. Loch Tay lies six miles to the west; Glen Lyon, 15 miles west; and Kinloch Rannoch, 18 miles northwest.

In Aberfeldy, General Wade in 1733 built the bridge spanning the Tay. In the town's shops are good buys in tweeds and tartans, plus other items of Highland dress.

FOOD AND LODGING: A long, low hostelry, **Crown Hotel,** Bank Street (tel. 0887/20448), has many years of innkeeping behind it. It stands directly on the roadway, with a rear garden. It's an all-purpose hotel, equipped with good-size public rooms, a cocktail as well as a public bar, a resident's TV lounge, a sitting room with comfortable chairs drawn around a fireplace, and a dining room. Each bedroom has a hot and cold running water basin, and there are adequate corridor bathrooms. B&B is economical here, costing £12 ($19.20) per person. I also recommend the dinner. Half board costs from £17.50 ($28) to £19.50 ($31.20). It's a lively inn, and during the summer season there's entertainment.

Nessbank House, Crieff Road (tel. 0887/20214), is small and homey, a stone house built more than a century ago. At the edge of Aberfeldy, it has a large, attractive garden running alongside the "Birks." From the garden a private gate leads into the Den of Moness, a deep wooded glen along the course of a mountain stream. The hotel is run by Laura and Bill Houston, who accept guests who enjoy their breakfasts and evening meals. Their daily terms including these two meals range from £18 ($28.80) per person. The food is freshly cooked, and whenever possible, fruit and vegetables from their own kitchen garden are used. Bedrooms have views and are equipped with tea- and coffee-making facilities, along with electric blankets, water basins, and razor points. The house has been refurbished, and there is a welcoming log fire in the lounge. The hotel also has a restricted liquor license and maintains a modest cellar.

Crossroads Guest House, Kenmore Street (tel. 0887/20293), is owned by a considerate couple, Mr. and Mrs. Kidd, who do much to aid their house guests. Not only is their establishment well maintained and attractive, it's also economical. The daily rate here of £9 ($14.40) per person includes a big Scottish breakfast with oatmeal. Tea and cookies are served before you retire.

The **Weem Hotel** (tel. 0887/20381) is a pleasant country inn with two floors of comfortable bedrooms, many with private bathrooms. This 17th-century inn, owned by Terry Wise and Mrs. Judith Hardaker, stands one mile from Aberfeldy on the B846 Loch Rannoch road and has a sweeping view of the Tay Valley. The inn has its own attractive gardens. The old wood-paneled bar with its open log fire is welcoming. The B&B rate is £15 ($24) per person. Half board costs £25 ($40) per person per night. The hotel owns nearly two miles on the left bank of the River Tay, and fishing is free to guests. There are 22 golf courses within 35 miles of the hotel, including the Taymouth Castle 18-hole course some three miles away.

The **Cruachan Hotel,** Kenmore Street (tel. 0887/20545), stands at the edge of town in about three acres of flowery gardens and greenery. The hotel is small and immaculately kept, renting out only three singles, six doubles, and one family room, each containing hot and cold running water. The single rate is £13.50

($21.60), from £33 ($52.80) in a double, including breakfast and VAT. Two rooms have private plumbing facilities and cost an additional £2 ($3.20) per person nightly. Dinner is an optional £9.50 ($15.20) and is served to residents only. On the grounds is a nine-hole putting green for the use of guests.

17. Killin

Just over the border from Tayside, Killin is a village on the Dochart at the lower end of Loch Tay, in the geographical center of Scotland. Lying 45 miles west of Perth by road, Killin is both a summer holiday resort and a winter sports center. The **Falls of Dochart** are world famous, but the town is noted for beauty spots, and there are sights of historical interest as well.

WHERE TO STAY: A 19th-century stone house overlooking the River Lochay, the **Dall Lodge Hotel** (tel. 05672/217) is on the outskirts of the village. Mr. and Mrs. Ian Mackay, the owners, rent out six rooms with private baths and three without. All units have hot and cold water basins, hot-beverage facilities, electric blankets, and beautiful views. For B&B, the charge is £13.50 ($21.60) per person. Guests are invited to enjoy TV in the comfortable lounge, where coffee and drinks are also served. The restaurant, the Poachers Table, serves dinners costing £9 ($14.40), consisting of mainly Scottish cuisine on the four-course menu. Salmon, trout, venison, haggis, Aberdeen Angus beef, Scottish hill lamb, and cloutie dumpling are among the menu items. The restaurant has a good selection of wines and scotch malt whiskies. Dinner is served until 10 p.m.

Falls of Dochart Hotel (tel. 05672/237), under the guidance of Steve and Linda Bergin, offers real value. In a dining room of character, a Scottish-continental cuisine is served. Some rooms have shower units at no extra charge, and all of them have hot and cold running water. The daily rate for half board is from £17.50 ($28) per person, rising another £2 ($3.20) for those desiring a private bath. You can have a premeal drink in the cocktail lounge. Tariffs include service and VAT, and children are granted a 30% reduction if they share a room with their parents.

Fishers Hotel, Main Street (tel. 05672/285), is a small country hotel set in the heart of the highlands, handy for many points of interest. The owners, Kevin and Pat O'Reilly, pride themselves on the homey atmosphere and good food. Guests can enjoy a drink and meet the locals in the cozy Finlarig Bar. The dining room is inviting, and you can order a four-course meal for around £5.50 ($8.80). The B&B rate is from £9.50 ($15.20) per person, plus £2 ($3.20) per person for a room with private plumbing facilities. The O'Reillys have a fishing boat with outboard motor and ghillie for salmon and trout fishing on Loch Tay.

WHERE TO EAT: An inviting little establishment, the **Mustard Pot,** Station Road (tel. 05672/503), is aptly named. Its owners, Hetty and Muriel, are actually named Mustard. There is a tea room, although they have a selection of carefully chosen Scottish gifts and crafts items for sale. They close down in late autumn, reopening around Easter for the summer trade. They are open daily from 10 a.m. to 5:30 p.m., except on Sunday when they open at 2:30 p.m., serving mainly afternoon tea. Their teas come with freshly baked goods along with fresh salads, homemade soups, and well-stuffed toasted sandwiches. Vegetarians are understood and appreciated here. Meals cost from £4 ($6.40). If you like to smoke or drink alcohol, you should go elsewhere.

The **Clachaig Hotel** (tel. 05672/270), a Victorian house built of stone, has one of the best pubs in Killin. Opening onto the famous falls of Dochart, it serves far more than pub grub. Such "Taste of Scotland" dishes are offered as Tayside salmon and haggis, and you can also enjoy fruit crumbles and the famous clootie dumplings, made with spices, raisins, currants, and treacle, among other ingredients. John and Maureen Mallinson, your hosts, will charge from £6 ($9.60) for a good and satisfying meal. Lunch is from noon to 5 p.m., dinner from 5:30 to 9:30 p.m. Service is seven days a week. The hotel also has pleasant and comfortable rooms, costing from £13 ($20.80) in a single, rising to £24 ($38.40) in a double.

SIGHTS: Besides the Falls of Dochart mentioned above, **Killin Church,** with a font more than 1,000 years old, is also worth seeing. Less than a quarter of a mile from the church stands an upright stone said to mark the grave of Fingal. An island in the Dochart was the ancient burial place of the MacNab Clan.

The ruins of **Finlarig Castle** contain a beheading pit near the castle gate which was written about in Scott's *The Fair Maid of Perth*. Perched a thousand feet above the loch, the castle was the seat of "Black Duncan of the Cowl," a notoriously ruthless chieftain of the Campbell Clan.

Chapter VII

THE TROSSACHS AND LOCH LOMOND

THE TROSSACHS is the collective name given that wild Highland area lying east and northeast of Loch Lomond. Both the Trossachs and Loch Lomond are said to contain Scotland's finest scenery in moor, mountain, and loch. The area is famed in history and romance ever since Sir Walter Scott included vivid descriptive passages in *The Lady of the Lake* and *Rob Roy.*

In Gaelic, the Trossachs means "the bristled country," an allusion to its luxuriant vegetation. The thickly wooded valley contains three lochs—Venachar, Achray, and Katrine. The best centers for exploring are the village of The Trossachs and the "gateways" of Callander and Aberfoyle.

Legendary Loch Lomond, the largest and most beautiful of Scottish lakes, is famed for its "bonnie banks." Lying within easy reach of Glasgow, the loch is about 24 miles long. At its widest point, it stretches for five miles. At Balloch in the south the lake is a Lowland loch of gentle hills and islands. But as it moves north, the loch changes to a narrow lake of Highland character, with moody cloud formations and rugged steep hillsides.

1. Callander

For many, this small burgh, 16 miles northwest of Stirling by road, makes the best base for exploring the Trossachs and Loch Katrine, Loch Achray, and Loch Venachar. For years, motorists—and before them passengers traveling by bumpy coach—stopped here to rest up on the once-difficult journey between Edinburgh and Oban.

Callander stands at the entrance to the **Pass of Leny** in the shadow of the Callander Crags. The Rivers Teith and Leny meet to the west of the town.

WHERE TO STAY: Full of charm and character, **Highland House Hotel,** South Church Street (tel. 0877/30269), is a Georgian-style stone building, in a quiet street lined with trees, half a block from the river. You will be warmly welcomed by Keith and Pat Cooper, resident proprietors. All bedrooms have a high standard of furnishing, together with hot-beverage facilities, and hot and cold water basins. Some units have private baths with showers. The B&B rate ranges from £12.50 ($20) to £14.25 ($22.80) per person, the latter being the price for private plumbing. Typically Scottish menus are offered in the dining room. Prepared fresh daily using only the freshest produce, dinner costs around £12 ($19.20). The choice of menus is complemented by a fine wine list. In the evening, guests relax in the residents' lounge where there is color TV or sit in the intimate bar beside a log fire, perhaps tasting the wide selection of malt whiskies.

Dalgair House Hotel, 113-115 Main St. (tel. 0877/30283), is a family-run hotel that offers modern comfortable surroundings, personal service, and excellent food. The bedrooms all have private showers and toilets, continental quilts, shaver points, and heating. The B&B charge is £20 ($32) per person. Food is served at the Dalgair's restaurant, adjacent to the guesthouse. Fresh Scottish produce is used whenever available, and there is a good wine list. Typical dishes include cock-a-leekie soup, trout Rob Roy, and pork oaties. Mr. and Mrs. Ian M. Brown, who run both the guesthouse and restaurant, will serve you tea and hot homemade scones at 10 p.m. Mr. Brown has involved his three sons in the operation, teaching them all phases of the business. The cocktail lounge is one of the most attractive in Perthshire, serving both as a restaurant and coffee lounge, offering food, drink, and the piano music of your host, Mr. Brown.

White Shutters Guest House, South Church Street (tel. 0877/30442), is spotless and charming. To reach it, head down the main artery of Callander, turning into South Church Street. Run as a B&B, the house is some two centuries old. The owners, Isabel and Jack Dickinson, make you feel you are their treasured personal guest. In this congenial atmosphere you have a country-house feeling. For a single room, their rate is £8.50 ($13.60), rising to £17 ($27.20) in a double, including a full Scottish breakfast and a 10 p.m. supper of scones, cake, biscuits, and tea. A walk down the road will bring you to a foot-bridge over the River Teith, taking you into open countryside and scenic walks. The guesthouse is open only from April to the end of October.

WHERE TO EAT: In Callander, I like to take meals at **Pips Coffee House and Gallery,** 23 Ancaster Square (tel. 0877/30470), which is visually striking from both inside and out. Janet and John Holt are your friendly hosts. Behind the canopies and brasswork of the facade is an interior decor made inviting by white wooden furniture and tartan carpeting. Many of the pictures and prints on the walls are for sale, and there is also a display of Limoges porcelain. Fresh, crisp salads, home-baking, sandwiches, and homemade soups are the specialties of the house. Naturally, you can order well-brewed coffee along with freshly whipped Scottish cream. Pips offers an à la carte menu, including, for example, a smoked Scottish salmon and cucumber salad. Three-course meals average £5 ($8). In the evening in summer one or two hot main dishes are always available in addition to the regular menu, which has an outstanding selection of desserts and pastries. The restaurant is not licensed, but clients are welcome to bring their own wine. Pips is open daily from 10 a.m. to 8 p.m. (on Sunday from 11 a.m. to 6 p.m.) from May until September. After that, they are open at 10 a.m., closing at 5 p.m. daily (on Sunday, 11 a.m. to 5 p.m.).

Motorists seeking "A Taste of Scotland" may want to drive out to the **Lade Inn,** which lies outside Callander on the Trossachs road at Kilmahog (tel. 0877/30152). Here you get real Scottish hospitality and good, hearty food in a small country inn that has much character. In season local trout and salmon are prepared in the kitchen, and the homemade soups are always rich in flavor, as is the locally made pâté, which often uses game. The licensed hotel is open from 11 a.m. to 11 p.m. throughout the summer. It is open year round, but winter hours are curtailed. Lunches, costing from £5.50 ($8.80), are normally served from noon to 2 p.m.; dinner, from £10 ($16), is offered from 6 to 9:30 p.m.

STAYING IN THE LENY AREA:
A short distance west of Callander in the extensive lands once the property of the Buchanans, Lairds of Leny, is **Leny House** (tel. 0877/31078), a spacious country house, whose oldest part dates from 1513 when it was a small fortress. Enlarged by 1845 to its present form, the house was used for clandestine meetings and arms storage in the Jacobite Rebellion. The house, now owned by Alan and Frances Roebuck, is a comfortable B&B today, with six rooms for rent. The charge for accommodation and an excellent breakfast is £13 ($20.80) to £15 ($24) per person. Two of the units have private baths. The house and furnishings retain the character expected in a Scottish ancestral home. A residents' lounge with TV is among the amenities. Leny House stands in 16 acres of park and farmland, with grazing cattle, sheep, horses, and a goat herd. The wild Leny Glen, Leny Falls, and the River Leny are nearby. The gallows hill used by the ruling Buchanans in the 15th century, known as the "Knoll of Justice," is visible in the grounds of Leny House.

Lubnaig Hotel, Leny Fues (tel. 0877/30376), occupies a Victorian stone structure in its own acre of garden. Phyllis and Michael Ingham, the owners, receive guests in their ten-bedroom hostelry that has plenty of character, with its many gables and bay windows. The hotel has two lounges in which guests can enjoy drinks and/or watch color TV. A cocktail lounge overlooks the garden. The pleasant bedchambers have private showers, hot-beverage facilities, and central heating. The charge in a single is £17.50 ($28), with doubles costing £31 ($49.60) to £37 ($59.20). Good food, prepared under the supervision of Mrs. Ingham, is served in the dining room, or hotel guests can order bar snacks if they wish. Expect to pay from £9 ($14.40) for a meal that offers Scottish cuisine, enjoyed as you look at heraldic emblems and swords used to decorate the walls. Breakfast is fully Scottish, with traditional dishes. With the hotel not far from the confluence of the River Leny and the River Teith, fishing for salmon and trout and canoeing are possible, as is pony trekking.

FOOD AND LODGING ON LOCH VOIL:
If you take my advice (see below) and visit Rob Roy's Grave at Balquhidder, you may find this remote area of Scotland so enchanting you'll want to continue to drive west, exploring the Braes o'Balquhidder and the banks of Loch Voil.

This was an area known to Rob Roy MacGregor, who died in 1734 but lives on in legend as the Robin Hood of Scotland. Your best anchor is at the **Ledcreich Hotel and Restaurant,** Balquhidder (tel. 08774/230), where Senga Bedford and John Gilhooly will welcome you to their secluded and tranquil country house, about two miles outside the village. Set on 20 acres, the house dates in part from the 1700s. There are eight bedrooms, and cozy ones at that, rented for £28 ($44.80) in a single and £50 ($80) in a double. All the units have showers or baths and are individually furnished to a high standard of comfort and decor. Antiques are used in some. The food served here is excellent, with a choice of international and Scottish cuisine, so you may want to book in on the half-board plan, costing £40 ($64) per person.

SIGHTS IN THE CALLANDER ENVIRONS: In the scenic Leny Hills to the west of Callander, beyond the Pass of Leny, lie **Leny Park** and **Leny Falls.** At one time, all the lands in Leny Park were part of the Leny estate, home of the Buchanan clan for more than 1,000 years. In the wild Leny Glen, a naturalist's paradise, deer can be seen safely grazing as visitors go by on recreational walks. Leny Falls is an impressive sight, near the confluence of the River Leny and the River Teith.

Four miles beyond the Pass of Leny, with its beautiful falls, lies **Loch Lubnaig** ("the crooked lake"), divided into two reaches by a rock and considered fine fishing waters. Nearby is **Little Leny,** the ancestral burial ground of the Buchanans.

More falls are found at **Bracklinn,** 1½ miles northeast of Callander. In a gorge above the town, Bracklinn is considered one of the most scenic of the local beauty spots. Other places of interest include the **Roman Camp,** the **Caledonian Fort,** and the **Foundations of St. Bride's Chapel.** The tourist office will give you a map pinpointing the above-recommended sights. While there, you can also get directions for one of the most interesting excursions from Callander, to **Balquhidder Church,** 13 miles to the northwest, the burial place of Rob Roy. Off the A84, the church also has the St. Angus Stone from the 8th century, plus a 17th-century bell. It possesses some Gaelic Bibles.

2. Aberfoyle

Looking like an alpine village in the heart of Rob Roy country, this small holiday resort is the gateway to the Trossachs, lying near Loch Ard. A large crafts center contains a wealth of gift items related to the Highlands.

FOOD AND LODGING: Erected during Edwardian days, **Inverard Hotel,** Loch Ard Road (tel. 08772/229), is an old stone Scottish country home. It stands on its own grounds and has a sunroom overlooking country scenery. The additions done in an alpine fashion add warmth. The dining room, with its pine trestle tables, Windsor chairs, rugged stone walls, and the lounge with its tartan carpeting, stone and wood paneling, make for intimacy and charm. Scottish dishes are featured, and there's a cocktail lounge for premeal drinks. All this is the concept of its enterprising owners, Mr. and Mrs. R. Williamson. They offer riding lessons, pony trekking, and deer stalking. Trout and salmon fishing are available, and packed lunches for £3 ($4.80) are quickly prepared for picnics and excursions. While guests usually stay at least a week, there are daily terms for B&B: £15 ($24) per person. In a room with private bath the charge is £16 ($28.80) per person nightly. Meals, ordered separately, cost £8.50 ($13.60) at dinner.

On the B829 about five miles directly west of Aberfoyle, on a quiet country road leading to Loch Lomond and Loch Katrine, Graham and Fiona Hewitt operate their little stone cottage, **Gartnerichnich** (tel. 08777/214), as a B&B. Their six-acre smallholding is practically a working farm, with livestock and gardens which supply most of the produce for their table. They charge £9.50 ($15.20) per person for a clean, modern, comfortable bedroom with its own bath. An antique spring bed and mattress is made cozier with an electric blanket. You can dine here for £13.50 ($21.60) to £15.50 ($24.80) on meals for which largely whole-foods are used, including whole-meal flour for bread, oatcakes, scones, and cakes.

IN THE ENVIRONS: About four miles to the east of Aberfoyle along the A81, the **Inchmahome** Priory stands on an island in Lake Menteith. From the Port of Menteith, you can sail to the island if the weather's right. Once there, you'll find the ruins of a 13th-century Augustinian house where Mary Queen of Scots was sent as a baby in 1547. The ferry charges £1 ($1.60) for adults, 50p (80¢) for children if it's running. Everything depends on the weather. For information, phone 0786/62421.

A visitor center is installed in the **David Marshall Lodge,** off the A821, lying one mile to the north of Aberfoyle. It is open from the middle of March until the middle of October, daily from 11 a.m. to 7 p.m. From the lodge you'll enjoy good views of Ben Lomond, the Menteith Hills, and the Campsie Fells. It is a good starting point for walks into **Queen Elizabeth Forest Park,** one of the most beautiful parts of Scotland, lying between the eastern shore of Loch Lomond and the Trossachs. Some 45,000 acres of moor, woodland, and mountain have been set aside for walking and exploring. It is a nature lover's delight.

3. The Trossachs

The Duke's Road (A821) north from Aberfoyle climbs through the Achray Forest, past the David Marshall Lodge information center, operated by the Forestry Commission, where you can stop for snacks and a breathtaking view of the Forth Valley. The road runs to the Trossachs—the "bristly country"—between Lochs Achray and Katrine.

Loch Katrine, at the head of which Rob Roy was born, owes its fame to Sir Walter Scott who set his poem *The Lady of the Lake* there. The loch is the principal reservoir of the city of Glasgow. A small steamer, S.S. *Sir Walter Scott,* plies the waters of the loch which has submerged the Silver Strand of the romantic poet.

Sailings are between early May and late September, between Trossachs Pier and Stronachlachar at a round-trip fare of £2 ($3.20) for adults, £1.20 ($1.92) for children. Complete information as to the sailing schedules is available from the Strathclyde Water Department, Lower Clyde Division, 419 Balmore Rd., Glasgow, Scotland G22 6NU (tel. 041/336-5333). Light refreshments are available at Trossachs Pier.

On Loch Achray, lying between Lochs Venachar and Katrine, stands the **Loch Achray Hotel,** Trossachs (tel. 08776/229), a pleasant place from which to tour the Trossachs between Loch Achray and Loch Katrine. Achray Burn flows through the hotel garden. Simple bedrooms rent for £12 ($19.20) per person, including a full Scottish breakfast. Add £2 ($3.20) per person if you want a private bath. Food is served from 11 a.m. to 9 p.m., with such standard fare offered as eggs mayonnaise and fresh fish dishes. You can drop in here for a good meal, paying from £8.50 ($13.60) for the privilege. A nice, friendly atmosphere exists, and near the hotel is some of the most spectacular scenery in the country.

LOCH LOMOND

This largest of Scotland's lochs was the center of the ancient district of Lennox, in the possession of the branch of the Stewart family from which sprang Lord Darnley, second husband of Mary Queen of Scots and father of James VI of Scotland, who was also James I of England. The ruins of Lennox Castle are on Inchmurrin, one of the 30 islands of the loch—one having ecclesiastical ruins, one noted for its yew trees planted by King Robert the Bruce to ensure a suitable supply of wood for the bows of his archers. The loch is fed by at least ten rivers from west, east, and north. On the eastern side is Ben Lomond, rising to a height of 3,192 feet.

The song "Loch Lomond" is supposed to have been composed by one of Bonnie Prince Charlie's captured followers on the eve of his execution in Carlisle Jail. The "low road" of the song is the path through the underworld which his spirit will follow to his native land after death, more quickly than his friends can travel to Scotland by the ordinary high road.

The road from Dumbarton to Crianlarich runs along the western shore of the loch. However, the easiest way to see the loch is not by car but by the *Countess Fiona*, which sails daily from the first of April until the end of September. Built in 1936 for the Caledonian Steam Packet Company, she now departs from Balloch Pier. Tickets are sold directly on the boat, and no advance reservations are necessary. In July and August the boat leaves twice a day, once in the morning, once in the afternoon. In shoulder season (spring and autumn), the boat leaves Balloch Pier daily at 10:15 a.m. There are no sailings in winter. A full cruise round-trip ticket costs £7 ($11.20) per person. For information on sailing times and space availability, call 041/248-2699 for a recorded message.

Nearly all visitors to Loch Lomond seem to locate at one of the villages along the western shore.

4. Balloch

At the southern end of Loch Lomond, Balloch is the most touristy of the towns and villages around the lake. It lies only a half-hour drive from the heart of Glasgow, and there is regular train service from Glasgow to Balloch Station. The town grew up on the River Leven, as it leaves Loch Lomond, flowing south to the Clyde. Today it is visited chiefly by those wanting to take boat trips on the *Countess Fiona*, which leaves in season from Balloch Pier. The most popular time to visit is during the Highland Games held here every year.

FOOD AND LODGING: When it was built, the **Balloch Hotel,** Balloch Road (tel. 0389/52579), a white-walled establishment, sat isolated at a point where the river flowed into Loch Lomond. In 1860 the Empress Eugénie, wife of Napoleon III, slept in Room 9 during her tour of Scotland. Today the warmly decorated pub and adjoining restaurant are filled with engravings of scenes from Scottish history. Well-prepared and plentiful food makes this one of the most alluring stopovers in the area. Fixed-price meals in the restaurant begin at £5 ($8), and pub lunches are cheaper. If you'd like to make Balloch your base for exploring Loch Lomond, comfortable bedrooms cost from £21.50 ($34.40) in a bathless single to £25.50 ($40.80) in a single with bath. Twins or doubles go for £32.25 ($51.60) to £38.25 ($61.20), depending on the plumbing. There is no charge for children under 12 staying in their parents' room. All units contain color TV and hot-beverage facilities.

A COUNTRY PARK: Set on 200 acres, **Balloch Castle Country Park** is on the "bonnie, bonnie banks of Loch Lomond." The present Balloch Castle (tel.

0389/58216), replacing one that dated from 1238, was constructed in 1808 for John Buchanan of Ardoch. Built in the "castle-Gothic" style, it has a Visitor Centre that explains the history of the property. The site has a walled garden, and the trees and shrubs, especially the rhododendrons and azaleas, reach the zenith of their beauty in late May and early June. You can also visit a "Fairy Glen." The location is about three-quarters of a mile from the center of Balloch, and it is open all year daily from 8 a.m. to dusk, charging no admission.

Dumbarton District's Countryside Ranger Service is based at Balloch Castle, conducting guided walks at various locations around Loch Lomond throughout the summer.

5. Inverbeg

This hamlet on the western shore of Loch Lomond stands in a beauty spot of Scotland, and can be reached in about 40 minutes from Glasgow. The location is about three miles north of Luss. The hamlet is known for its oldtime ferry inn (see below), the second-oldest youth hostel in Scotland, and several well-known art galleries. A small fleet of Loch Lomond cruisers can usually be seen in the harbor of Inverbeg Bay, and a ferry to Rowardennan and Ben Lomond plies three times daily in summer.

WHERE TO STAY: The site on which the **Inverbeg Inn** (tel. 043686/678) stands has always been important as the ferryboat landing that serviced the western end of Loch Lomond. The sprawling roadside building that the visitor sees today was constructed in 1814. Earlier inns probably stood on this same site. Today, directed by the Bisset family, the establishment serves savory pub lunches as well as more formal restaurant meals throughout the year. The first thing a cold-weather visitor might see is a blazing fireplace heating the reception room near the entrance. About half the comfortably furnished bedrooms look out over a garden in the rear. Depending on the plumbing and the season, singles cost £18 ($28.80) to £23 ($36.80), with doubles going for £28 ($44.80) to £45 ($72). Seven of the 14 rooms contain a private bath. Fixed-price evening meals cost from £9.50 ($15.20), with pub lunches going for half that or less. You might want to stop in only for a meal.

6. Tarbet

On the western shores of Loch Lomond, Tarbet is not to be confused with the larger center of Tarbert, headquarters of the Loch Fyne herring industry. Loch Lomond's Tarbet is merely a village and a summer holiday base with limited accommodations.

In the distance you can stare at the majesty of Ben Lomond. King Haakon of Norway came this way in the 13th century, laying waste to the countryside. To the north, now the site of the Inveruglas power station, the Clan MacFarlane had their rallying point.

Boats can be launched from the pier, and Tarbet is one of the stops on the route of the steamship *Countess Fiona*.

FOOD AND LODGING: A blend of the old and the new is found at the **Tarbet Hotel** (tel. 03012/228). Local historians say that some form of hotel has stood on this spot for the past 400 years. A coaching inn was built on the site in 1760, and in the Victorian era a baronial facade and military crenellations were added. The exterior suggests that the interior would be as antiquely grand as the stone facade. However, the present owners, the Galbraith family, have modernized the inner part. A cozy cocktail lounge looks past a row of yew trees onto the lake. Good food is served in the spacious dining rooms, and there are some 91 simple but comfortable rooms to rent. A bathless single goes for £18 ($28.80), increasing to £36 ($57.60) in a similar double. Rooms with bath cost £26 ($41.60), in a single, rising to £46 ($73.60) in a double. Half board is available for an additional £10.25 ($16.40) per person daily. The hotel is closed in January.

7. Arrochar

At the head of the sea-arm of Loch Long, 1½ miles west of Loch Lomond, this village is easily reached by road and rail from Glasgow. It is a center for climbers. William and Dorothy Wordsworth found inspiration here in 1803, drawn to the beauty and tranquility of the place, resting below "The Cobbler" at 3,000 feet. There are several idyllic spots along the loch, with my favorites following.

FOOD AND LODGING: A choice place to stay in Arrochar is **Rossmay Guest House** (tel. 03012/250). This white-walled cottage was built beside Loch Long in 1897 as compensation by the railroad company for a Mrs. Gillespie, whose former house had been demolished by a falling boulder during the construction of a nearby line. Today the flower-ringed house is one of my favorite places along the loch, thanks to the discreet charm of its owners, John and Peggy Rose. Peggy is a certified teacher of Scottish country dancing, and she considers her homemaking talents as part of her work as an "ambassador for Scotland." She usually posts the menu for that night's dinner on a blackboard. A three-course, temptingly fresh Scottish dinner costs from £5 ($8) per person. In chilly weather, the art deco–style fireplace blazes merrily throughout the day. Many of the freshly decorated rooms benefit from a panoramic view of the loch. Doubles pay from £9 ($14.40) per person, with singles costing £10 ($16), including a Scottish breakfast. Many international guests who stay here pass their days in one of John Rose's rented motorboats, which hold up to three persons.

8. Ardlui

This peaceful hamlet lies at the far northern end of Loch Lomond. If you're returning south for the night, it could make a good luncheon stopover during your day tour of Loch Lomond. If you're arriving late, it also makes for a good accommodation stopover as well.

FOOD AND LODGING: The slate-roof building housing the **Ardlui Hotel** (tel. 03014/243) was constructed beside Loch Lomond as a hunting lodge in the 19th century. Its present owners have done much to preserve the outdoorsy feeling of the original structure. The stone walls of the Elizabethan-style pub are ringed with stuffed birds, a blazing fireplace, and a well-polished wooden bar. In summer the terrace beside the parking lot becomes an outdoor café, servicing the needs of the adjoining caravan park. One of the pleasantly furnished bedrooms rents for £18 ($28.80) in a single and £30 ($48) to £36 ($57.60) in a double, with breakfast included. The high-ceilinged dining room serves à la carte lunches and dinners, and bar meals (less expensive) are available in the pub.

9. Crianlarich

This popular Highland touring center, 78 miles from Edinburgh, lies at the junction of the roads from Loch Tay, Loch Lomond, Oban, and Fort William. As such, it is the center of much traffic, especially during the summer months. Climbers, walkers, and fishermen have long been attracted to the wild mountainous country surrounding Crianlarich. If you're seeking a tranquil oasis in the area, head northwest along the A82 in the direction of Tyndrum. In a few minutes you'll come to the hamlet of Inverherive.

FOOD AND LODGING: Standing on a knoll, **Inverherive House** (tel. 08383/220), near Crianlarich, is a clearly visible, attractive, stucco and half-timbered building. Joyce and Andrew Russell, the hosts, have upgraded and refurbished the house and grounds, opening the old fireplaces and making them workable.

Everything is well furnished and beautifully maintained, and their three family rooms and two double bedrooms are most comfortable. The charge for B&B is £9 ($14.40) per person, but it's better to take the half-board rate of £14 ($22.40) as their cookery is excellent. Each bedroom has hot and cold running water, and there is a separate shower room. All the bedrooms are heated, and guests gather in the evening to watch television in the lounge. Tea and cookies are served in front of the fireplace. From the windows, you can look out onto a commanding view of some Highland scenery.

Crianlarich marks the end of our trail. You can either head east to Killin, or else return on the same road south to Ardlui, following along the western shore of Loch Lomond. South of Arrochar, you can take the A83 west to visit Strone Gardens and eventually Inveraray.

At the summit of the pass from Glen Croe to Loch Fyne stands a rough stone seat inscribed "Rest and Be Thankful." The road is on the military route from Dumbarton to Inveraray, completed in 1748.

Chapter VIII

ABERDEEN AND ROYAL DEESIDE

1. Braemar
2. Ballater
3. Banchory
4. Stonehaven
5. Aberdeen

TRAVELING NORTH from the lochs, heading toward Royal Deeside, you pass through Glen Shee and Glen Clunie, a most spectacular route which will give you your first taste of Highland scenery.

As you journey across uncrowded roads into Scotland's northeast, you'll pass heather-covered moorland and peaty lochs, wood glens and salmon-filled rivers, granite-stone villages and fishing harbors, as well as North Sea beach resorts.

This is the Grampian region, with such centers as Aberdeen and Braemar, and such sights as Balmoral Castle. Even the Queen herself comes here for holidays.

GETTING THERE: The northeast of Scotland is not as inaccessible as it sounds. Aberdeen is served by a number of carriers, including British Airways and Air Ecosse. For flights to and from Aberdeen, phone 0224/722331. From Aberdeen Airport, you can take a good bus service to the heart of town, about six miles away. Aberdeen is also served by an air link from Prestwick, Scotland's transatlantic airport, if you're flying directly from North America to Scotland.

Aberdeen has direct rail links to the major cities of Britain. Special fares are offered on most routes, both to holders of Rail-Cards and to those with "Inter-City Saver" and "Nightrider," along with weekend return tickets.

The least expensive way to come is by coach. Several coach companies have express routes serving Aberdeen, and many offer special round-trip fares and low-cost "standby" tickets on long-distance routes. Coach and bus travel in the northeast is provided by Northern Scottish, whose headquarters in Aberdeen is at the Bus Station, Guild Street (tel. 0224/596265).

It's also easy to drive to the northeast. From the south, drive via Edinburgh, the Forth and Tay road bridges, and take the coastal road. From the north and west, approach the area from the much-improved A9, linking Perth, Inverness, and Wick.

1. Braemar

This little Deeside resort is the site of the **Royal Highland Gathering,** which takes place annually, either in late August or early September. It is usually attended by Queen Elizabeth. The royal "link" dates from the 1840s when Queen Victoria first attended the games.

The capital of the Deeside Highlands, Braemar is overrun with foreign visitors, as well as the British themselves, during the gathering. Anyone thinking of attending would be wise to make application for accommodation anywhere within a 20-mile radius of Braemar not later than early April.

The gathering in Braemar is the most famous of the many Highland games. The spectacular occasion is held in the **Princess Royal and Duke of Fife Memorial Park.** Competitions include tossing the caber, throwing the hammer, sprinting, vaulting, a tug-o'-war, the long leap, Highland dancing, putting a 16-pound ball, sword dancing, relay races, and, naturally, a bagpiping contest. At a vast refreshment tent, Scottish lassies serve tea, coffee, buns, and other refreshments.

FOOD AND LODGING: An old hunting lodge in two acres of grounds is now the **Braemar Lodge Hotel,** Glenshee Road (tel. 03383/627), a friendly hotel with a bar, lounge, and reading room for guests. George and Vi Milne rent eight warm bedrooms, all with TV and hot-beverage facilities, and most with showers and toilets. B&B costs from £18 ($28.80) per person. Dinner, served in the restaurant from 7 p.m., includes "Taste of Scotland" dishes on the à la carte menu, with meals costing from £6 ($9.60). Lunch is also available. The food is excellent, served by attractive young women. Guests should indicate their intention of dining at the hotel in advance, so that a table can be reserved and menus planned. The staff is happy to help with information on local sights. The hotel is on the road to the Glenshee ski slopes. Close to the hotel is the cottage where Robert Louis Stevenson wrote *Treasure Island.*

Callater, Glenshee Road (tel. 03383/275), has rural charm, off the side of the road in its own garden. A stone building with bay and dormer windows, it is used a great deal by sportsmen. Owners Mr. and Mrs. William Rose can accommodate 18 guests, charging £20 ($32) per person for dinner and B&B. Mrs. Rose will help prepare a picnic lunch for you for £2 ($3.20), and afternoon tea, served in the residents' lounge, for £2 also. Their beds are comfortable, and in cold months hot-water bottles are provided. All rooms have hot and cold water basins, hot-beverage facilities, and an electric heater.

Moorfield House Hotel, Chapel Brae (tel. 03383/244), occupies an imposing position overlooking the famed Braemar Royal Games Park. It has two bedrooms with showers, costing £15 ($24) per person for B&B and three bathless accommodations priced at £12.50 ($20) per person. All bedrooms have hot and cold water basins. The hotel is centrally heated, and the food is very good. A bar meal either at midday or in the evening costs £3 ($4.80) to £5 ($8), and dinner goes for £8 ($12.80). All prices include VAT.

Cranford Guest House, Glenshee Road (tel. 03383/244), is a modest hostelry set up from the roadway, with its own garden. Mrs. McKellar keeps her small house tidy, and her bedrooms are homey and snug. During the colder months she provides electric blankets, and all the rooms are centrally heated and contain hot and cold running water. She has also built an extension, housing two more double bedrooms with their own private facilities. She charges £10 ($16) per person for B&B, plus £2 ($3.20) additional for a room with private bath. If you request dinner in the evening, you're treated to a home-cooked repast at a cost of £6 ($9.60). There is a residents' lounge, plus a sun lounge, each with central heating. In the winter months Mrs. McKellar also caters to skiers, as the Glenshee ski slopes are only eight miles away on the main Perth–Aberdeen road. There is bus service every day to the slopes. Also there's an 18-hole golf course open to visitors for £4.50 ($7.20) to £5 ($8) per day.

Bellevue, Chapel Brae (tel. 03383/633), is a B&B accommodation run by Mrs. G. J. Beech, whose rooms and visitors' lounge are all furnished in excellent taste. Most of the rooms look out at the mountains. The cost per person is £8.50 ($13.60) nightly. You can get directions to Bellevue from the local tourist office. Mrs. Beech will prepare one of the finest meals in town for £7 ($11.20), by prior arrangement. She enjoys getting fresh ingredients, preparing them, cooking them, and serving the meal herself. She has very high standards.

SIGHTS: The romantic 17th-century **Braemar Castle** (tel. 03383/219) lies half a mile northeast of Braemar on the A93. A fully furnished private residence of architectural grace, scenic charm, and historical interest, it is the seat of Capt. A. A. Farquharson of Invercauld. Opening onto the Dee River, it was built in 1628 by the Earl of Mar. John Farquharson of Inverey, the "Black Colonel," attacked and burned it in 1689. The castle is built in the shape of an L, with a spiral stairway and a circular main tower. Fully furnished, it has barrel-vaulted ceilings and an underground prison and is known for its remarkable star-shaped defensive curtain wall. It can be visited from May 1 until the first Monday in October daily except Friday from 10 a.m. to 6 p.m., costing £1.20 ($1.92) for adults, 60p (96¢) for children. The castle has a gift shop, a free car park, and a piper in attendance.

Balmoral Castle (see below), one of the sightseeing attractions most visited in the northeast, is off-limits when the royal family is in residence. However, if you're a royal family watcher, you might be able to see them at **Crathie Church,** nine miles east on the A93. They attend Sunday services here when they are in residence at Balmoral. Services are at 11:30 a.m. Otherwise the church is open to view weekdays from 9:30 a.m. to 5:30 p.m. April to October (on Sunday from 2 to 5:30 p.m.).

Nature lovers may want to drive to the **Linn of Dee,** a narrow chasm on the River Dee which is considered a local beauty spot. The location is six miles west of Braemar.

Other beauty spots include **Glen Muick, Loch Muick,** and **Lochnagar.** This Highland glen, off the South Deeside road, contains a Scottish Wildlife Trust Visitor Centre reached by a minor road. An access road joins the B976 16 miles east of Braemar.

Corgarff Castle was built in 1537 as a tower house but was converted into a Redcoat Garrison, now restored. In 1748 it was enclosed within a loopholed wall shaped like a star. It was the scene of the burning of Margaret Forbes and her family by the Gordons in 1571. April to September it can be visited weekdays from 9:30 a.m. to 7 p.m. (on Sunday from 2 to 7 p.m.) It is closed in winter. Admission is 50p (80¢) for adults and 25p (40¢) for children. The location is off the A939, 15 miles northwest of Ballater

2. Ballater

On the Dee River, with the Grampian mountains in the background, Ballater is a holiday resort center where visitors flock to attend one of Scotland's most popular sightseeing attractions, Balmoral Castle (see below).

The town still centers around its **Station Square,** where the royal family used to be photographed as they arrived to spend holidays. The railway has since been closed.

From Ballater you can drive west to view the magnificent scenery of **Glen Muick and Lochnagar,** where you'll see herds of deer.

WHERE TO STAY: The former manse of the Free Church of Scotland, **Moorside,** Braemar Road (tel. 0338/55492), a stone building with twin bay windows flanking the main entry, is a century old. It stands only 200 yards from the center of the village on the main road leading out of Ballater toward Braemar on the A93. The proprietor, I. Hewitt, keeps the establishment open from March to October, charging £13 ($20.80) per person for B&B. Half board is £20 ($32) per person. There are eight bedrooms, all with private baths. One unit is on the ground floor. All rooms are centrally heated and have electric blankets, hot and cold water, and tea/coffee-making facilities. There is an attractive dining room and lounge with color TV. Ample parking is available.

Westbank Hotel, Albert Road (tel. 0338/55305), is a substantial granite village house, neatly kept and immaculate. It's just one block from the Dee River and the shops, and it overlooks the Ballater golf course. Run by owners Ron and Joy Webster, the hotel has seven bedrooms costing £10 ($16) per person for B&B, VAT included. Traditional Scottish fare is served in the dining room, and there are log fires throughout the house. With a restricted license and private car park, the Websters also offer organized pony trekking and hill walking, as well as help in planning other excursions.

The **Invercauld Arms Hotel,** 5 Bridge Square (tel. 0338/55417), looks like an ancient Victorian mansion nestling beside the River Dee in the heart of Royal Deeside. The proprietors, Mr. and Mrs. James Anderson, welcome you to accommodations that contain modern amenities. The 27 rooms all have private baths. Antiques crafted by Queen Victoria's cabinetmaker are in some of the more traditionally furnished units. Many of the rooms have views of the river and the adjacent Dee Bridge. Depending on the season, B&B prices range from £22 ($35.20) to £26 ($41.60) per person, with half board costing £32 ($51.20) to £36 ($57.60) per person. In a single, a £5 ($8) daily supplement is assessed. All tariffs include VAT and service in addition to a full Scottish breakfast. The fully licensed hotel has a spacious restaurant, serving country-house fare. Diners can enjoy the views and the period furnishings while they order from a varied menu and wine list. The roasts are especially good here. Expect to pay from £12 ($19.20) for dinner, which is served from 7:30 to 9:30 p.m. Lunch, offered in the bar from a cold buffet table from noon to 2:30 p.m., will cost from £2.75 ($4.40). The hotel is open all year.

Aspen Hotel, Braemar Road (tel. 0338/55486), is one of the most traditional and architecturally interesting hotels in the area. Mr. and Mrs. W. P. Murdock welcome guests into their well-run hotel, housing and feeding them well. As owners of the local bakery, they not only supply the hotel's baked goods, but had the honor of making the wedding cake for Princess Anne. Their rooms are pleasantly and attractively furnished, and some have private bath or shower. The B&B rate runs from £11 ($17.60) per person nightly, or you can take half board (most recommended) at £18 ($28.80) per person. The hotel, open from the first of April until mid-November, has a large car park, a garden, and a spacious residents' lounge.

Dee Valley, 26 Viewfield Rd. (tel. 0338/55408), may charm you, mainly because of its owner, Evelyn Gray, who never fails to be helpful and friendly. Her very simple place was once a private nursing home, used by the Duke of Kent and his brother. She has four double or twin rooms, each with hot and cold water, radios, and hot-beverage facilities. A single rents for £11 ($17.60), a double going for £20 ($32), including a full breakfast. Dinner is another £5 ($8) per person. Showers are included, as are VAT and service charges. On the ground floor is the neat dining and sitting room. Mrs. Gray will tell you of the special Scottish events that you can enjoy, including the Ballater donkey derby.

Glen Lui, Invercauld Road (tel. 0338/55402), stands on two acres of private grounds overlooking the golf course at Ballater (access from the grounds). An ideal center for a holiday in Royal Deeside, Glen Lui is run by Mr. and Mrs. R. Kerr. Their hotel is small, with only one single and nine double rooms, all with shower and toilet and such touches as razor points. The B&B rate is £18 ($28.80) per person. For half board, the charge is £28 ($44.80) per person. What sets Glen Lui above the standard small hotels along the Deeside is the cuisine, reinforced by a good wine cellar. It's important to reserve, as Glen Lui, owing to its size, can fill up quickly. The hotel is open from March to November.

Morvada Guest House, Braemar Road (tel. 0338/55501), is run by John and Freda Nimmo, who offer seven bedrooms, three of which have private shower, toilet, and wash basin. The rooms are comfortable and well furnished, and have tea/coffee-making facilities. They offer a full breakfast and a varied menu for the evening meal which is served at 7 p.m. Charges are £10 ($16) for B&B and £16 ($25.60) for half board.

DINING CHOICES: In the heart of town, the **Green Inn,** 9 Victoria Rd. (tel. 0338/55701), was once a temperance hotel (that's a non-alcohol hostelry). That condition has now been rectified, and the pink-granite Green Inn, built in 1840, is one of the finest dining rooms in town, especially if you're seeking traditional Scottish dishes. In fair weather, tables are eagerly sought out on the garden patio. The chef places his emphasis on local produce, including home-grown vegetables when available. In season venison is served in delectable ways, and you can always count on fresh salmon and the best of Angus beef. Snack lunches are served from noon to 2 p.m., costing £2.50 ($4) to £6 ($9.60). Dinner, costing from £10 ($16), is from 7 to 9 p.m., and reservations are advised. Three double bedrooms are rented here, all with private bath/shower and TV. Colin Hamilton, the proprietor, charges £15 ($24) per person for B&B. The establishment is open from March through October.

Oaks Restaurant, Craigendarroch Hotel and Country Club, Braemar Road (tel. 0338/55217), serves traditional fare in the atmosphere of a country house. You get the best of Scottish beef and lamb along with game and fish. There's usually a well-stocked larder. The service is friendly and polite, and the price of £18.75 ($30) per meal is well worth it because of the quality of ingredients used. Open all year, it serves dinner from 7:30 to 10 p.m., when reservations are necessary. The hotel also rents out 29 rooms, mostly doubles, each with private bath, costing from £65 ($104) nightly.

BALMORAL CASTLE: "This dear paradise" is how Queen Victoria described this castle, rebuilt in the Scottish baronial style by her beloved Albert. It was completed in 1855. Today Balmoral, eight miles west of Ballater, is still a private residence of the British sovereign. Albert, the prince consort, leased the property in 1848 and bought it in 1852. As the castle left by the Farquharsons proved too small, the present edifice was built in its place. Its principal feature is a 100-foot tower. On the grounds are many memorials to the royal family. The grounds can be visited daily, except Sunday, in May, June, and July from 10 a.m. to 5 p.m. Only the castle ballroom is open to the public, housing an exhibition of pictures, porcelain, and works of art. In addition to the gardens there are country walks, pony trekking, souvenir shops, and a refreshment room. Admission is £1.20 ($1.92) for adults. Children are admitted free. For information, telephone 03384/334).

3. Banchory

On lower Deeside, this pleasant resort is rich in woodland and river scenery. From this base, you can take excursions to two of the most popular castles in the Grampian region, Crathes and Craigievar.

FOOD AND LODGING: A large country inn, the **Burnett Arms Hotel,** 25 High St. (tel. 03302/2545), in the heart of Banchory, was once a coaching stop dating back before 1840. There are 17 bedrooms, each nicely appointed and furnished. Eleven contain private bath. All have hot and cold water, central heating, electric blankets, a radio, baby-listening service, and if you ask for it, color TV. B&B costs £19 ($30.40) per person daily, including VAT. The dining room is fully licensed, as are the lounge bar and cocktail bar.

Douglas Arms Hotel, High Street (tel. 03302/2547), is a village inn right in the heart of everything. It's very casual, and the warmth of its staff and its good meals make it worthwhile. There is a lounge with an open log fire, furnished and decorated in an original but comfortable style, where you can get an excellent malt whisky. The traditional public bar is thought to be the oldest in the area. The bedrooms are pleasingly furnished and fitted with all the necessary amenities to make your stay as restful as possible. The cost in a single for B&B is £24.50 ($39.20), and a double goes for £34.50 ($55.20). Traditional afternoon cream teas are served, as well as high teas with home-baked goods offered. During the peak summer months, Scottish music nights are arranged for your entertainment, and other live music nights are presented throughout the year. There's something in the entertainment line for all ages here, and outside activities can be arranged.

SIGHTS: Some two miles east of Banchory lie **Crathes Castle and Gardens** (tel. 033044/525), within a well-wooded 600-acre estate. Just north of the A93 on the north bank of the Dee, this late 16th-century, baronial castle contains remarkable painted and paneled ceilings. It is also celebrated for its 3¾ acres of walled gardens with sculptured yews planted in 1702. The castle is open Easter weekend until the end of September daily from 11 a.m. to 6 p.m. and also on the first four weekends in October at the same hours. The grounds and gardens are open all year from 9:30 a.m. to dusk. A combined ticket to both the castle and gardens is £2.50 ($4) for adults, £1.25 ($2) for children. To visit just the gardens costs adults £1.80 ($2.88), children 90p ($1.44). Additional facilities included in the charges are a Visitor Centre with exhibitions, a shop, a licensed restaurant, an adventure playground, and well-marked trails ranging from a half mile to seven miles in length.

Structurally unchanged since its completion in 1626, **Craigievar Castle,** at Alford (tel. 033983/635), is an exceptional tower house where Scottish baronial architecture reached its pinnacle of achievement. It has magnificent contemporary plaster ceilings in nearly all its rooms. It had been continuously lived in by the descendants of the builder, William Forbes, until it came under the care of the National Trust for Scotland in 1963. The family collection of furnishings is complete. It is open May 1 to September 30 daily from 2 to 6 p.m. except Friday, with last entrance at 5:15 p.m. Admission is £1.80 ($2.88) for adults, 90p ($1.44) for children. The grounds are open throughout the year from 9:30 a.m. to sunset. Cragievar is 26 miles west of Aberdeen, five miles north of Lumphanan.

A mile from the castle is **Macbeth's Cairn,** where, according to legend, Macduff put an end to Macbeth.

4. Stonehaven

South of Aberdeen, this is a flourishing seaside resort with a big Leisure Centre, offering a multitude of sports to visitors. Besides these modern additions, however, much of historic interest has been retained since Stonehaven was a thriving fishing port. Cowie village, at the north of the bay on which Stonehaven lies, and the old fishermen's quarter are still here. The old town was founded in the 17th century, centered around the harbor. A Mercat Cross stands in the High Street. The new town began as an 18th-century settlement across the River Carron to the north.

FOOD AND LODGING: In the West End of Stonehaven, **The Heugh Hotel,** Westfield Road (tel. 0569/62379) is built in the Scottish baronial style, standing on its own private grounds. A railroad magnate built it in 1892 as a private home, and in 1933 it was converted into a small hotel. Today it offers six well-furnished bedrooms, each with private bath. Joy and Wilhelm Hermanns are the considerate hosts, welcoming guests and charging £28 ($44.80) in a single, £38 ($60.80) in a double, including a full Scottish breakfast. Each bedroom has a color TV and beverage-making facilities. The hotel has oak paneling and an inglenook fireplace. Non-residents can visit for bar snacks from noon to 2 p.m., including spaghetti carbonara, farmer's chicken, or chili, costing from £7 ($11.20) for meals. Dinner from £12 ($19.20) is served from 6 to 9:45 p.m., including such dishes as chicken Kiev, vol-au-vent Royal, and filet of pork Mozart with mushrooms and hollandaise.

George A. Robertson, 68 Allardice St. (tel. 0569/62734), is a tea room that does its own baking. Here you can try many of the cakes, pastries, and shortbreads for which Scotland is known. You can also order soups, sandwiches, and potatoes cooked in their jackets. Simple meals cost from £2.50 ($4), and service is from 7 a.m. to around 5 p.m. except on Sunday.

SIGHTS: In Stonehaven's oldest building, a tolbooth, constructed in the late 16th century to house stores for Dunnottar Castle (see below), the **Tolbooth Museum,** the Harbour, contains displays of local history, particularly on the subjects of fishing and barrel-making. It is open from 10 a.m. to noon and 2 to 4 p.m. Monday, Thursday, Friday, and Saturday and from 2 to 5 p.m. Wednesday and Sunday June to the end of September. Admission is free. For information, phone 0779/77778.

In the new town, the inventor of the pneumatic tire, Robert William Thomson, is honored by a plaque at 9 Market Square. His 1845 invention was called the "aerial wheel" at the time.

Set on a promontory with three sides protected by cliffs, **Dunnottar Castle** (tel. 0569/62173), about two miles south of Stonehaven (half a mile off the Montrose–Stonehaven road, the A92), was erected, beginning in the 14th century, as the home and fortress of the Keiths, the Earls Marischal, and Wardens of the Regalia for the Scottish kings. According to legend, an early Christian settlement on the site, more than 150 feet above the sea, was founded by St. Ninian in the 5th century. A short-lived stone house of worship erected in the 13th century caused the excommunication of Sir William Keith a century later because he started his castle keep on what were still consecrated grounds. The partially restored castle can be visited from 9 a.m. to 6 p.m. on weekdays, from 2 to 5 p.m. on Sunday. Admission is 80p ($1.28) for adults, 40p (64¢) for children.

Dunnottar Castle was the last fortress to hold out against Cromwell in the Civil War. During this conflict, the Royal Regalia of Scotland, under the protection of the Earl Marischal, was smuggled out of the castle and taken to **Kineff Old Church,** a mile closer to Stonehaven, where it was hidden under the floor from 1652 until the Restoration in 1660. The church of that day was replaced by the present structure. It is reached by taking the B967 off the A92 and following a little country road.

5. Aberdeen

The harbor in this seaport in the northeast of Scotland is one of the largest fishing ports in the country, literally infested with kipper and deep-sea trawlers. **The Fish Market** is well worth a visit, as it's the liveliest in Britain.

Bordered by fine sandy beaches (delightful if you're a polar bear), Scotland's third city is often called "the granite city," as its buildings are constructed largely of granite, in pink or gray, hewn from the Rubislaw quarries.

Aberdeen is the capital of the oil workers who help harvest the riches from six North Sea oilfields. Their numbers have dwindled in recent years, however. The city lies on the banks of the salmon- and trout-filled Don and Dee Rivers. Spanning the Don is the **Brig o'Balgownie,** a steep Gothic arch, begun in 1285.

WHERE TO STAY: Because of the increasing numbers of tourists and business visitors to the Granite City, now established as Europe's offshore oil capital, hotels are likely to be heavily booked any time of year, so that you may find yourself in the position of Dr. Johnson and Boswell in 1773, who "found the inn so full that we had some difficulty in obtaining admission." In that case, it's best to go to the **Information Centre,** St. Nicholas House, Broad Street (tel. 0224/632727). There's a wide range of accommodation, whether you prefer to stay in a family-run B&B or a guesthouse or a hotel, with a warm, friendly welcome assured. The information center staff can usually find just the kind of lodging you prefer.

Cedars Private Hotel, 339 Great Western Rd. (tel. 0224/583225), is one of the finest little B&Bs in the whole city. Privately owned and run in a personal way, it is a detached structure that has been modernized and freshened up to welcome visitors. They book into one of the 13 comfortably furnished bedrooms, each of which has a private bath or shower. Three of these units are set aside for families. The B&B rate in a single is £19 ($30.40), dropping to £16 ($25.60) per person in a double. Parking space is usually available, and the hotel remains open all year.

Albert & Victoria Guest House, 1-2 Albert Terrace (tel. 0224/641717), are two adjoining Victorian-style houses (almost cottages) in a quiet residential part of the town. Yet they are only minutes away from the west end of Union Street. The owners, Mr. and Mrs. Canale, will prepare filling three-course breakfasts, and their rooms are centrally heated. As a bonus, there's a color TV in every room. The daily price for a single is £13.50 ($21.60) for B&B, and for a double £19.50 ($31.20). As a typical nicety Mrs. Canale will provide hot drinks 24 hours a day (well, almost). There's street parking for your car.

Craig Rossie Guest House, 293 Great Western Rd. (tel. 0224/581548), may well be the most desirable guesthouse in the area. It's set back from the roadway, with a well-kept garden. It's the end home of a row of fine stone houses, this one having a bay tower. The hostess is Mrs. E. Meechan, who lives there with her husband and two children. A night here is like being in a true Scottish home, where manners and hospitality are important. The bedrooms are centrally heated, and you'll have hot and cold water and color TV in your room. The inclusive charge is £9 ($14.40) per person nightly for double occupancy, £12 ($19.20) for one person, and that includes an excellent, filling breakfast. Buses 17, 18, and 19 stop nearby.

Klibreck, 410 Great Western Rd. (tel. 0224/316115), belongs to Dorothy Ramsay, who is known for her friendly good nature. Her two-story guesthouse is built of granite, part of a flank of "row houses," with front bay windows and a third-floor dormer. Klibreck is in a quiet residential area in the west end of the city, and the center is just ten minutes away by bus. Every room is centrally heated; there's color TV in the guests' lounge, and each room has hot and cold running water. B&B costs £12 ($19.20) per person nightly in a single, £21 ($33.60) in a double. If you ask early enough, you can have a homemade dinner for £5.50 ($8.80) per person.

Jays Guest House, 422 King St. (tel. 0224/638295), is one of the nicer guesthouses in Aberdeen, mainly because of the high standards and friendliness of its owner, Mrs. Alice Jennings. She keeps everything running smoothly, and her rooms, seven in all, are bright and airy. The cost is £12 ($19.20) in a single, a double going for £10 ($16) per person nightly, including a good breakfast from a varied menu. Each room can accommodate up to two guests, and one unit has its own shower. All the accommodations contain color TV, hot and cold water basins, hot-beverage facilities, and central heating. The location is just a short bus ride to downtown Aberdeen, and stands in the vicinity of the university and the Offshore Survival Centre.

Morrison's Guest House, 444 King St. (tel. 0224/637809), lies on the same street as Jays. A well-kept and maintained guesthouse, it rents out seven double bedrooms at a cost of £22 ($35.20) nightly. Rooms have many amenities, such as hot and cold running water, tea-making facilities, and TV sets. Breakfasts are good fare, and the welcome is friendly.

Strathboyne Guest House, 26 Abergeldie Terrace (tel. 0224/593400), has a good location near Duthie Park, which is recommended as a sightseeing attraction. Mrs. C.J. Gillanders is a warm hostess, offering pleasant bedrooms with a number of amenities, including hot-beverage facilities. For B&B, her rates are among the most reasonable in high-priced Aberdeen: from £10.50 ($16.80) per person nightly. Dinner can be arranged if you want it, but you should request it by that morning. Half board costs from £15 ($24) per person. The granite house offers street parking, and will serve you late tea.

Four Ways Guest House, 435 Great Western Rd. (tel. 0224/310218), is a granite structure, once a manse, lying in the west end of Aberdeen, convenient for exploring Royal Deeside. Hazel and Albert McDonald are proud that several of the original architectural features of this once-private home have been maintained. However, the house and its private bedrooms have been brought up-to-date, with many modern amenities, including central heating. The rate in a single, including a Scottish breakfast, is £13.50 ($21.60), rising to £22 ($35.20) in a double.

Mannofield Hotel, 447 Great Western Rd. (tel. 0224/315888), is like a Victorian architectural fantasy, with step gables, turrets, spires, and bay windows. One of the best of the reasonably priced hotels in town, it offers ten well-furnished bedrooms, three of which have a private shower. The charge is £22 ($35.20) in a single, rising to £36 ($57.60) for the best doubles, including a full Scottish breakfast. Personal attention is given by the owners, and everything is well kept and maintained. The food is good, using fresh produce whenever available. You may want to stay here on half-board terms of £29 ($46.40) per person nightly.

DINING IN ABERDEEN: The best Italian restaurant in the granite city is **Trattoria Luigi's,** 4 Bridge St. (tel. 0224/590001), which is also the most centrally located. Right off Union Street, it allows you to pop in for a freshly baked pizza or linger over a longer meal in this bustling trattoria. Careful preparation of good quality ingredients produces dishes that are authentic and full of "south of the border" flavor. Of course, everything tastes better with the garlic bread served here. Some of the best pasta in town is offered, perhaps spaghetti carbonara or baked lasagne. If you want something more exotic, try the deep-fried octopus rings. Slices of tender veal are served in a white wine sauce. Lunches cost from £6.50 ($10.40), dinners £15 ($24) although you can come out much cheaper, of course. It is open Monday through Saturday from noon to 2:30 p.m. and 6 to 11 p.m. On Friday and Saturday, last orders (but not closings) are 30 minutes later. There is no lunch on Sunday when only dinner is served.

Shish Mahal, 468 Union St. (tel. 0224/643339), on the "main drag," is a spacious, second-floor (British first floor) restaurant that offers one of the best values in town. The excellent Indian cuisine at very reasonable prices makes it a special favorite of young people. Ask the friendly, obliging staff for help with the menu if you need it. The menu includes splendid tandoori meats and breads, biryanis, and curries. There is also a good choice of vegetarian dishes for those who shun meat. Lunches cost from £2.50 ($4) to £5.50 ($8.80), dinners from £5.50 ($8.80) to £11 ($17.60). It is open for lunch from noon to 2 p.m. and dinner from 2 to 11:30 p.m. You can order a full, hot meal throughout the day, which is unusual for Aberdeen.

Oliver's Bar and Diner, Caledonian Thistle Hotel, Union Terrace (tel. 0224/640233), is one of an increasing number of restaurants in Scotland featuring American themes. Ollie's Diner turns toward the movies, with a striking decor of black and white, just like those vintage silent-screen reels. Among popular food items named for the early film comics are the cheesy Stan Burger and Ollies Burger, each served with baked potato or crisp french fries. These and other charcoal-grilled hamburgers come with a variety of toppings, ranging from peppers and onions to mozzarella cheese to chili sauce, or you can have them plain. They also offer Texan chili "for those who like it hot" and clam fries with crisp french fries. You can also enjoy salads, soups, and desserts. Meals cost from £7.50 ($12). Wines, including some good California selections, are also served. You can even order an American beer. The bar is open from 11 a.m. to 2:30 p.m. and 5 to 11 p.m. (to midnight Thursday to Saturday). On Sunday hours are only from 6:30 to 11 p.m. The diner is open from noon to 2:30 p.m. and 6 to 11:30 p.m. (on Sunday from 6:30 to 11 p.m.).

Stakis Steak House, Holburn Street (tel. 0224/596442), is a standard steak house belonging to a Scottish hotel group. It is well run with competitive prices, offering a good meal for £10 ($16). You get a choice not only of steaks, but such other main dishes as chicken and fresh fish (often haddock). The price of a main course covers the cost of an appetizer, bread, butter, and dessert from the trolley. The steak house is open Monday to Saturday from noon to 2:30 p.m. and 5 to 10 p.m. and on Sunday from 12:30 to 3 p.m. and 5 to 10 p.m.

Victoria Restaurant, 140 Union St. (tel. 0224/639639), is the largest independent restaurant in town, originally having opened its doors in 1948. It is also the most popular budget restaurant in the city, and as such draws a lively family trade. However, it is open only from 9 a.m. to 7:30 p.m. Against a backdrop of a streamlined modern decor, it offers a selection of pizzas and hamburgers, along with other flavorful concoctions, including chili con carne, moussaka, or cannelloni. For lunch you might want to sample one of their omelets. Meals cost from £5 ($8).

Ferryhill House Hotel, Bon Accord Street (tel. 0224/590867), is one of the best pubs or "free houses" in Aberdeen. It is also a small hotel, but most patrons go there for food and drink, as it's known for having the finest and largest selection of malt whiskies and real ales in the area. Bow windows open onto the well-kept grounds, and the place is attractively decorated, making for a warm, inviting ambience. There's a choice of drinking areas. Many guests like to pop in here for the good pub grub served at lunch, including cold table selections and freshly made sandwiches. In summer, the action overflows outside on the grounds. Meals cost from £5 ($8), and the establishment is open daily from 11 a.m. to 11 p.m. except on Sunday afternoon when it closes.

SIGHTS: In Castlegate is the **Mercat Cross,** a hexagonally shaped structure, built in 1686, and considered the most handsome of the old crosses in Scotland.

Aberdeen University is a fusion of two separate colleges. King's College is older, dating from 1483, and it contains the oldest school of medicine in Great Britain. The chapel of King's College is crowned by a stately tower from 1505. Marischal College, founded in 1593, is recognized as one of the finest granite buildings in the world.

The university is in Old Aberdeen, as is the **Cathedral of St. Machar,** founded in 1131. The present structure dates from the 15th century. Its splendid heraldic ceiling contains three rows of shields representing the kings and princes of Europe along with the Scottish ecclesiastical and aristocratic hierarchy. The modern stained-glass windows are magnificent, the work of Douglas Strachan. The cathedral is open daily from 9 a.m. to 5 p.m. Its telephone number is 0224/485988, and that of the manse is 0024/483688.

Provost Skene's House, 45 Guestrow (tel. 0224/50086), is named for a rich merchant who was Lord Provost of Aberdeen during 1676–1685. Off Broad Street, it is now a museum with period rooms and artifacts of domestic life. Admission is free, and the house can be visited Monday to Saturday from 10 a.m. to 5 p.m.

The **Aberdeen Maritime Museum,** Shiprow (tel. 0224/585788), is housed in Provost Ross's House, the oldest surviving building in the city. Built in 1593, the museum building is open Monday to Saturday from 10 a.m. to 5 p.m., charging no admission. Its exhibitions begin with the development of Aberdeen harbor and extend through the Arctic whaling trade right up to the present North Sea oil adventure. In whatever way, the point is made repeatedly of a people who had to earn a living from a turbulent sea.

Aberdeen Art Gallery, Schoolhill (tel. 0224/646333), built in 1884 in a neo-classical design by A. Marshall MacKenzie, houses one of the most important provincial art collections in Great Britain. It contains 18th-century portraits by Raeburn, Hogarth, Ramsay, and Reynolds and acclaimed 20th-century art-works by Paul Nash, Ben Nicholson, and Francis Bacon. The exhibits also include excellent works by Impressionists such as Monet, Pissaro, Sisley, and Bonnard, and there is also a collection of Scottish domestic silver and examples of other decorative arts. Special exhibitions and events are frequently offered. Hours are 10 a.m. to 5 p.m. Monday to Saturday (on Sunday from 2 to 5 p.m.). Admission is free.

At 61 Schoolhill, **James Dun's House** (tel. 0224/646333) is a museum offering displays relating to families. An 18th-century house, it was once the residence of James Dun, who was the master of the Aberdeen Grammar School. Admission-free, it can be visited from 10 a.m. to 5 p.m. Monday to Saturday.

Gordon Highlanders Regimental Museum, Regimental Headquarters, Viewfield Road (tel. 0224/318174), offers exhibitions of the many battle campaigns of the regiment, including colors and banners, medals, and uniforms. Hours are Sunday and Wednesday from 2 to 5 p.m., and no admission is charged.

Aberdeen also has several beautiful gardens, including the **Cruickshank Botanic Gardens** at Chanonry (tel. 0224/40241), under the auspices of the University of Aberdeen. It has alpines, shrubs, and many herbaceous plants, along with rock and water gardens. It is open all year from 9 a.m. to 4:30 p.m. Monday to Friday. In summer it is also open on Saturday and Sunday from 2 to 5 p.m. No admission is charged.

Duthie Park Winter Gardens on Polmuir Road contain many exotic flowers and plants, along with an aviary and fish. It's known for its "hill of roses." It is open all year from 10 a.m. to dusk, charging no admission.

A MUSEUM AT ALFORD:

About 25 miles west of Aberdeen on the A944 at Alford is the **Grampian Transport Museum** (tel. 0336/2292), where exhibits and displays trace the development of transport in northeast Scotland. Some 100 vehicles of all types—bicycles, motorcycles, veteran and classic cars, steam vehicles, fire engines, agricultural vehicles, trucks, horse-drawn carriages, trams, and sledges—can be seen, several dating from before 1900. There are also photograph displays and reconstructions of a village wheelwright's shop and a 1930s garage workshop. An added, nonvehicular attraction is the Mortier dance organ, the largest in Scotland, built in 1923, whose music enhances the atmosphere of days gone by.

The museum is open daily from 10:30 a.m. to 5 p.m. from the end of March to the end of September, as well as the first two weekends in October. Admission is £1.20 ($1.92) for adults, 50p (80¢) for children. The ticket also admits visitors to the **Alford Valley Railway Museum,** housed in the reconstructed Alford village station of the Great North of Scotland Railway. On Sunday in season, trips are offered on the Alford Valley lines passenger trains, running on two-foot-gauge tracks.

EXCURSIONS IN "CASTLE COUNTRY":

Aberdeen is the center of "castle country," as 40 inhabited castles lie within a 40-mile radius. Some of the most popular castle excursions are previewed below.

Drum Castle: The handsome mansion (tel. 03308/204) was added in 1619, but the great square tower dates from the late 13th century, making it one of the three oldest tower houses in the country. Historic Drum lies ten miles west of Aberdeen, off the A93. It is open May 1 to September 30 from 2 to 6 p.m. The grounds are open daily from 9:30 a.m. to dusk. Admission to the house is £2 ($3.20) for adults, £1 ($1.60) for children. The grounds can be visited free.

Considered one of the most impressive of the fortress-like castles of Mar, **Castle Fraser** (tel. 03303/463) stands in a 25-acre parkland and woodsy setting. The sixth laird, Michael Fraser, launched the structure in 1575, and it was completed by his son in 1636. The castle is filled with treasures, including Jamie Fleeman's chest. Its Great Hall is spectacular, and you can wander around the grounds, including a walled garden. It is open daily from 2 to 6 p.m. from the first of May until the end of September, charging an admission of £1.80 ($2.88) for adults and 90p ($1.44) for children. The location is off the B993, three miles south of Kemnay and 16 miles west of Aberdeen.

Near the village of Fyvie, on the Aberdeen–Banff road, **Fyvie Castle** (tel. 06516/266) has been opened (1987) to the public by the National Trust for Scotland. The oldest part of the castle, dating from the 13th century, has been called the grandest existing example of Scottish baronial architecture. There are five towers, one each attributed to Fyvie's five families—the Prestons, Melddrums, Setons, Gordons, and Leiths—who lived there over five centuries. Originally built in a royal hunting forest, Fyvie means "deer hill" in Gaelic. The interior, reflecting the opulence of the Edwardian era, was created by the first Lord Leith of Fyvie, a steel magnate. His collections contain arms and armor, 16th-century tapestries, and important artworks by Raeburn, Gainsborough, Ramsay, and Batoni. The castle, rich in ghosts, curses, and legends, is open daily from 2 to 6 p.m. May to September. Admission is £1.80 ($2.88) for adults, 60p (96¢) for children. Fyvie Castle stands eight miles southeast of Turriff off the A947.

Haddo House (tel. 06515/440) was the creation of William Adam in 1731, having taken the place of the Place of Kellie. This Palladian house has been the home of the Gordons of Haddo for more than five centuries. The castle is inhabited by the Marchioness of Aberdeen and Temair, who has turned it into the headquarters of the Haddo House Choral and Operatic Society. It is impressive in its way, and also looks home-like enough for people actually to live there. The country park of some 180 acres surrounding the house is maintained by the Grampian Regional Council. It is open from the first of May until the end of September daily from 2 to 6 p.m. (last entrance at 5:15 p.m.). The country park is open daily all year from 9:30 a.m. to dusk, and the garden hours are daily from 9:30 a.m. to 8 p.m. Admission is £1.80 ($2.88) for adults, 90p ($1.44) for children. The house is off the B999 some four miles north of Pitmedden, 19 miles north of Aberdeen.

Not a castle, but a reconstructed 17th-century garden, **Pitmedden Garden** (tel. 06513/2352) was originally laid out according to plans of Sir Alexander Seton in 1675. It is today the centerpiece of 100 acres of woodland and farmland. Guests can visit the Visitor Centre and explore a herb garden as well as a museum of farm life. Rare breeds of livestock are found in the fields, and one can take a woodland walk, later enjoying a picnic if you brought a basket. Admission to the garden and museum is £1.50 ($2.40) for adults and 75p ($1.20) for children. The museum is open from the first of May until the end of September daily from 11 a.m. to 6 p.m. The garden and grounds are open all year daily from 9:30 a.m. to dusk. Guided tours must be prearranged. The location is on the A920, a mile west of Pitmedden village and 14 miles to the north of Aberdeen.

Muchalls Castle (tel. 0569/30217) was constructed by the Burnetts of Leys in the early part of the 17th century. Overlooking the sea, it is now owned by Mr. and Mrs. Maurice A. Simpson, who allow public visits May to September on Tuesday and Sunday from 3 to 5 p.m., charging an admission of 30p (48¢) for adults and 10p (16¢) for children. The castle has intricate plaster ceilings and fireplaces, along with a secret staircase. The location is at the village of Muchalls, five miles north of Stonehaven and nine miles south of Aberdeen.

AVIEMORE, SPEYSIDE, AND THE MALT WHISKY TRAIL

AVIEMORE AND THE SPEY VALLEY is one of the richest parts of Scotland for the visitor. From salmon fishing to whisky distilleries, there is much to see and do.

Aviemore is also the winter sports capital of Britain, enjoying mass popularity in summer as well. Aviemore Centre, previewed in this chapter, is endowed with a multitude of outdoor pursuits, like golfing, angling, skiing, and ice skating.

Those seeking a more traditional Scottish ambience will gravitate to one of the many Speyside villages, each with its own attractions and atmosphere. Ranking next to Aviemore, Grantown-on-Spey is another major center.

From Fort William, head north to Spean Bridge, where you can connect with the A86 going east toward Newtonmore. You will eventually reach the A9 going on to Aviemore. The more popular route is from Edinburgh. Take the Forth Bridge north, heading for Perth. After passing through Perth, follow the A9 north to Aviemore. However, to see the most interesting part of the Spey Valley, you should turn east at Carrbridge, north of Aviemore, heading for the old resort of Grantown-on-Spey. You can follow the A95 east for some of the most interesting stopovers along the Malt Whisky Trail.

If you're taking the A9 north from Perth, your first stopover might be at Dalwhinnie, which has the highest whisky distillery in the world at 1,888 feet. Near trout-stocked Loch Ericht, it offers magnificent views of lochs and forests. On the other hand, if you're driving up from Fort William via Spean Bridge, you'll pass Loch Laggan, which Queen Victoria originally selected as her "home in the Highlands" before she was lured to Balmoral. Queen Victoria didn't stick around, but today's "ferrox" trout fishermen certainly do.

Much of the section covered in this chapter falls within the Moray District, lying on the southern shore of Moray Firth, a great inlet cutting into the north-eastern coast of Scotland. Triangular in shape, Moray stretches south from the coast to the wild heart of the Cairngorm mountains near Aviemore. It is a land steeped in history, as its many castles, battle sites, and ancient monuments testify. It is also very sports oriented, attracting not only fishermen but golfers. Golfers can purchase a five-day ticket from Tourist Information Centres, allowing them to play at more than 11 courses in the area.

The major tourist attraction of the Moray District is the Malt Whisky Trail, running through the glens of Speyside. Here distilleries, many of which can be visited, are known for their production of *uisge beatha* or "water of life." Whisky is its more familiar name. Half of all the malt distilleries in the country lie along the Spey River valley and its tributaries. Here peat smoke and Highland water are used to turn out a unique brew. Several of the distilleries in Moray have opened their doors to visitors. If you're lucky, they'll give you a free sample. The Malt Whisky Trail is 70 miles long. There are five malt whisky distilleries in the area, including Glenlivet, Glenfiddich, Glenfarclas, Strathisla, and Tamdhu. Allow about an hour to visit each of them.

1. Newtonmore

This Highland resort on Speyside is a good center for the Grampian and Monadhliath mountains, and it offers excellent fishing, golf, pony trekking, and hill walking.

A track from the village climbs past the Calder River to Loch Dubh and the massive Carn Ban (3,087) feet, where eagles fly. Castle Cluny, ancient seat of the MacPherson chiefs, is six miles west of Newtonmore.

FOOD AND LODGING: A good place to stay is the **Pines Hotel,** Station Road (tel. 05403/271), on a hill overlooking the Spey Valley, with the Cairngorms, the Grampians, and the Monadhliath mountains all in view. The resident proprietors, John and Fran Raw, offer six comfortable bedrooms, all with baths/showers, toilets, hot and cold water basins, shaver points, hot-beverage facilities, heaters, and electric blankets. The tariff is £14.50 ($23.20) per person for B&B. Half board is recommended at £21.50 ($34.40) per person. The menu of home-cooked foods may list trout, salmon, chicken, beef, lamb, or venison, all freshly supplied locally and complemented by an extensive wine list. Fine malt whisky and liqueurs can be sampled at the Pine Bar in front of an open log fire in the TV lounge. The Pines is open from Easter to mid-October. Bookings of less than three days cannot be accepted in advance of more than one day before the date you request. As its name implies, the hotel is in the middle of its own pine-wooded grounds of more than 1½ acres.

Ard-Na-Coille (tel. 05403/214). Today the antiques that fill the interior of this elegant house evoke its earlier days as a hunting lodge. It was built in 1920 by the director of a Scottish oil company, who used it as a hunting lodge only six weeks a year. Nowadays a partially completed jigsaw puzzle on an oak table in the plushly comfortable salon encourages guests to get involved with the cozy spirit of the house. Amid racks of antique porcelain, spaciously high-ceilinged bathrooms which haven't been altered since they were built, carefully refinished antiques, and old English engravings, the owners rent ten rooms to paying guests. About half the units contain private baths or showers. Each room is tastefully furnished, most often with old furniture and English-style chintz. Depending on the plumbing, rates for B&B are £18 ($28.80) to £28.50 ($45.60) per person. For a freshly prepared dinner, the charge is £10 ($16). The establishment is closed in November and December. Ard-Na-Coille translates from the Gaelic as "high in the woods."

Craig Mhor Hotel (tel. 05403/210). This charmingly embellished stone-walled Victorian hotel contains the kind of front porch where, in summer, wicker chairs provide a peaceful lookout over the formal rose garden. An elaborate iron balcony runs across the front, highlighting the slate-covered gables and turrets. Inside, the 39 pleasant bedrooms rent for £12.50 ($20) in a single and £24 ($38.40) in a double, with breakfast included. For half board, the charge is an additional £7 ($11.20) per person. Mrs. S.M. Berry serves a good dinner on immaculate napery in a sunny dining room. The establishment was originally built as a private house in a spacious garden (which still remains) on the main street of town. Today the genteel clientele and the polite staff help evoke a gracious aspect of a century-old past.

Alvey House, Golf Course Road (tel. 05403/260), is an impressive stone house, where Erica and Andrew McLay accept paying guests at their well-run family hotel. Standing on its own grounds, the house is surrounded by the Grampian mountains with vistas onto the Spey valley. Their rooms are well furnished and comfortable, and some units have private plumbing. The B&B rate is £12 ($19.20) to £14 ($22.40) per person nightly. Half board ranges from £19 ($30.40) to £21 ($33.60) per person, the latter with private bath. The food is excellent, featuring "Taste of Scotland" specialties on the menu. The hotel lies about 50 yards from the first tee of the 18-hole golf course at Newtonmore. Plenty of sports are available, including fishing and sailing, but, to me, nothing beats walking along the many nature trails in the area. Birdwatchers are drawn to the region.

A CLAN MUSEUM: Most motorists zip through it on the way to Aviemore, but sightseers may want to stop off and visit the **Clan MacPherson House & Museum,** Main Street (tel. 05403/332), at the south end of the village. Displayed are clan relics and memorials, including the Black Chanter and Green Banner as well as a "charmed sword," and the broken fiddle of the freebooter, James MacPherson—a Scottish Robin Hood. Sentenced to death in 1700, he is said to have played the dirge "MacPherson's Rant" on his fiddle as he stood on the gallows at Banff. He then offered the instrument to anyone who would think well of him. There were no takers, so he smashed it. Relics associated with Bonnie Prince Charlie are also here. Hours are from 10 a.m. to 5:30 p.m. Monday to Saturday, from 2:30 to 5:30 p.m. on Sunday. Admission is free.

2. Kingussie

Your next stop along the Spey might be at this little summer holiday resort and winter ski center (it's pronounced King-youcie), just off the A9, the so-called capital of Badenoch, a district known as "the drowned land" because the Spey can flood the valley when the snows of a severe winter melt in the spring. There you can visit the six-acre **Highland Folk Museum,** on Duke Street (tel. 05402/307), just off High Street, with its comprehensive collection of artifacts, including weaponry, bagpipes, and fiddles illustrating more than two centuries of Highland customs, plus the work of craftspeople. Naturally, there are tartans. A furnished cottage with a mill and a farming shed stand on the museum grounds. There is a reproduction of an 18th-century cruck-framed house with turf walls from Badenoch. Hours are April to October on weekdays, 10 a.m. to 6 p.m. (on Sunday from 2 to 6 p.m.). November to March the museum is open from 10 a.m. to 3 p.m. weekdays. It is owned and maintained by the Highland Regional Council. Admission is £1.25 ($2) for adults and 65p ($1.04) for children.

WHERE TO STAY: If you'd like to stop here instead of at Aviemore, I recommend the following establishments.

The **Osprey Hotel,** Ruthven Road (tel. 05402/510), is a convenient place to stay, with nine comfortable bedrooms, all with hot and cold running water, central heating, electric blankets, electric fires, and heated towel rounds. Four units have private toilets and either baths or showers or both. The proprietors, Duncan and Pauline Reeves, charge £15 ($24) to £25 ($40) per person for B&B, depending on the time of year. All food served is fresh 100% whole, and homemade, from the whole-meal bread on. A dinner costs from £13 ($20.80). Fresh vegetables are used exclusively (in summer a large number are compost-grown). The Reeves are noted for their prime Scottish meats, including local venison, beef, lamb, pork, and "free-range" chickens. In summer they also offer fish from local rivers, including the Spey. The salmon and trout offered, either fresh or peat-smoked, is superb. Breakfast often features oak-smoked haddock and kippers and local "heather honey." More than 200 wines in their list cover the majority of the wine-producing areas of Europe. The coffee is outstanding, and in every way this small, homey hotel is a good experience. Comfort is its watchword, not pseudo-luxury. A licensed bar, residents' lounge, and TV lounge are housed in the hotel, and babysitter/listening service is provided. The Reeves will offer information and assistance in arranging for pony trekking or horseback riding. Laundry and ironing facilities are available. It's closed mid-April to mid-May.

Mairi MacWilliam accommodates guests at **Arden House,** Newtonmore Road (tel. 05402/369), at a charge of £9.50 ($15.20) per person for B&B, including VAT and service. She has rooms with hot and cold running water. The stone-fronted Edwardian house is centrally heated, and guests can relax in the residents' lounge, or in summer, in the garden. You'll be greeted in a pleasant reception area. Ample parking is available, and the house is open all year.

You might also try **Dunmore House,** 67 High St. (tel. 05402/529), where Mrs. Leask takes guests for £8 ($12.80) per person for B&B. She has a cozy residents' lounge and a pleasant dining room. However, her house is closed November through March.

WHERE TO DINE: If you're not dining at a hotel, try the **Wood'n Spoon,** 3 High St. (tel. 05402/251), run by Michael and Mary Eley. All the food is homemade and prepared fresh to order, including soups, pies, quiches, and salads. You can enjoy some of the best fish caught in the Spey, most often done in butter with its natural flavors preserved, not smothered in sauces. Try the traditional stovie potatoes (diced potatoes with onions and minced meat) and the Spey Valley trout. Venison burgers and homemade smoked fish pâté are also on the menu. The chef's specialty is steaks, and his lasagne is well known locally. Luncheon is served from noon to 2:30 p.m. and dinner 5:30 to 9:30 or 10 p.m. Expect to pay about £9 ($14.40) for a complete meal. Adjoining the Wood'n Spoon is the Creel Pub, with a unique bar made from a real turn-of-the-century fishing boat. The pub's decor is in the same period. You can enjoy real ales here.

For a more elegant dining experience, try **The Cross,** High Street (tel. 05402/762). In France no one would be particularly surprised to find this chic *restaurant avec chambres* serving superlative food in an out-of-the-way setting. But in a remote village in the Highlands it comes as a bit of a surprise. The establishment is in a stone-rimmed building fronted with Victorian-era plate-glass windows. In the 1800s it was a grocery store. The focal point of the bar in the entrance area is a stone fireplace which, when I was last there, blazed merrily with alderwood fire. A visit to this unusual restaurant involves as much theater as it does fine food. Tony Hadley, the owner, personally explains the composition of each menu item in a carefully rehearsed, tastefully seductive tone.

Diners enjoy delicate specialties prepared by Tony's wife, Ruth. Her specialties vary with the season, depending on the availability of produce in the local markets. They might include a liver-and-walnut terrine, onion-and-cider soup, orange-flavored local pigeon, salmon eclairs, calves' liver with pear, spring herb soup, Dufftown filet, a smoked sturgeon parfait, quail stuffed with blue cheese, or a mousseline of pike, followed by kiwi and hazelnut ice cream for dessert. There are more than 300 different wines to round out any menu. Between courses a choice of 27 different sorbets is likely to be served. A favorite test is to allow guests to guess the flavoring. On my last visit the flavor came from the delicate mountain ash (rowan). You might get a mixture of geranium leaf with rose petal. This fare is offered on Sunday and Tuesday through Friday for dinner, a complete meal costing from £12 ($19.20). On Saturday, a £15 ($24) gastronomic menu is presented, with an array of savory courses served to diners who were smart enough to reserve ahead. Dinner is the only meal offered at The Cross, served from 6:30 to 9:30 p.m. Closed Monday. If you'd like to spend the night, the Hadleys offer a handful of bedrooms, costing from £12.50 ($20) per person.

A FOLK MUSEUM: Kingussie is the home of the **Highland Folk Museum,** Duke Street (tel. 05402/307), the first folk museum established in Scotland (1934). Collections are based on the life of the Highlanders. You'll see domestic, agricultural, and industrial items. Open-air exhibits are a turf-built kailyard (kitchen garden), a Lewis "black house," and old vehicles and carts. It's open from 10 a.m. to 6 p.m. Monday to Saturday and 2 to 6 p.m. on Sunday April to the end of October; from 10 a.m. to 3 p.m. Monday to Friday in winter. Admission is £1 ($1.60) for adults, 50p (80¢) for children. Traditional events such as spinning, music-making, and showing of handcrafts are held throughout the summer.

3. Kincraig

This village, visited chiefly for its Highland Wildlife Park (see below), enjoys a scenic spot at the northern end of Loch Insh, overlooking the Spey Valley to the west and the Cairngorm mountains to the east. The location is only six miles from the sports at Aviemore, so you may want to stay here instead.

FOOD AND LODGING: A good place to stay is **Invereshie House** (tel. 05404/ 332). The severe facade of this comfortable hotel was built in the 18th century, incorporating the original core of a hunting lodge from 1695. Set into 25 acres of forested hills, Invereshie provides cozy comfort in a country-house setting. Patricia and Andrew Hamilton, the hosts, give guests a warm Highland welcome in delightful surroundings. B&B costs from £20 ($32) per person in the main house, with five traditional cottages sleeping four to six persons and going for £60 ($96) to £200 ($320), depending on the season. If you choose to stay here on the half-board arrangement, expect to pay from £30 ($48) per person. The hotel restaurant features the use of good local produce, game, and fish, plus fresh vegetables. If you stay here, you can enjoy a drink in the elegantly rustic pub installed in the oldest part of the house.

ANIMALS IN THE ENVIRONS: In the vicinity of Kincraig the most notable sight is the **Highland Wildlife Park** (tel. 05404/270), a natural area of parkland with a collection of the wildlife of the Highlands, some now extinct elsewhere in Scotland. Herds of European bison, red deer, shaggy Highland cattle, wild horses, St. Kilda Soay sheep, and wild goats (ibex) range the park. In cages are wolves, polecats, wildcats, beavers, badgers, and pine martens. Protected birds to be seen are golden eagles and grouse. Of special interest is the capercaillie (meaning "horse of the woods"), a large Eurasian grouse that is a native of Scotland's pine forests. There is a children's park, along with a souvenir shop, a café, and a picnic site. The park is open daily from 10 a.m. to 6 p.m. March to the end of October. Admission is £6 ($9.60) per car.

4. Aviemore

This year-round holiday complex on the Spey was opened in 1966 in the heart of the Highlands, at the foot of the historic rock of Craigellachie. This rock was the rallying place for Clan Grant.

WHERE TO STAY: Best for the budget is the **Aviemore Chalets Motel,** Aviemore Centre (tel. 0479/810624), offering comfortable, centrally heated chalet accommodation. Each chalet, named after a Highland clan, has a double bed and a set of bunk beds, with continental quilts, individual reading lamps, built-in clothes storage, a hot and cold water basin, a shower, and a heated drying cupboard. Based on four persons per room, the rate is £25 ($40) per chalet per night midweek and £30 ($48) per chalet on Friday, Saturday, and Sunday. Self-catering suites sleeping up to six persons, ideal for families, cost from £45 ($72) per chalet. In the complex, there are various eating places, including the Stakis Steak Inn, with a children's menu, and the Stakis Badenoch Hotel with a daily table d'hôte menu at dinner and a full Highland breakfast. The Aviemore Chalets Motel is open all year.

Craiglea Guest House (tel. 0479/810210). Mr. and Mrs. Hugh Nunn are the motivating personalities behind this Edwardian guesthouse which was built in 1905 near the rail station. Occupants of the ten well-furnished rooms congregate around the color TV in the visitors' lounge, where comfortable chairs are warmed by the heat from an iron stove. There's also a sauna on the premises. Per-person rates in a bathless room, with breakfast included, run from £10.50 ($16.80) daily. Hugh Nunn is a skiing enthusiast and has much local advice.

Cairngorm Hotel (tel. 0479/810233). One of the best-known hotels in town is across from the railway station in a Victorian building crafted from local stone. The modernized interior has a pub, lounge bar, and restaurant. Of the 23 comfortably furnished bedrooms, 18 contain private baths. B&B costs £23

($36.80) in a single, £21 ($33.60) per person in a double. Half board can be arranged on stays of more than two days for £30 ($48) per person daily.

Ravenscraig Guest House (tel. 0479/810278) is on the main highway near the edge of town after you pass Aviemore Centre going toward Inverness. Robert and Christine Thompson have 12 rooms, ranging from singles to family units, all with showers. There's a comfortable residents' lounge with color TV and tea- and coffee-making facilities, plus a garden where guests may relax in warm weather. The guesthouse has central heating and clothes-drying facilities. The tariff is £11 ($17.60) to £12 ($19.20) for B&B. It's open all year, and you can arrange for skiing through the Thompsons.

Mrs. F. McKenzie rents rooms at **Balavoulin** (tel. 0479/810672), in the same vicinity as Ravenscraig. The hotel has been completely refurbished, and all five of the bedrooms have private plumbing facilities, hot-beverage equipment, and color TV. B&B costs from £16 ($25.60) per person, and dinner in the hotel's restaurant goes for £8 ($12.80). The Balavoulin has a lounge bar with free entertainment.

Carrick Lodge Hotel, Carrick Road (tel. 0292/262846), is one of the best little hotels in the area. Privately owned and personally supervised by its owners, it is a Victorian home in a tranquil residential section. Built of stone, the hotel rents out ten well-furnished bedrooms, three of which are set aside for families. Of these, six contain a private bath or shower. The B&B rate ranges from £21 ($33.60) in a single, £20 ($32) per person in a double or twin. Open all year, the hotel also provides an evening meal on request.

Lynwilg Hotel, Loch Alvie (tel. 0479/810207). This sprawling peach-color hotel lies in an isolated position beside the highway about two miles south of Aviemore. Its interior contains a rough-and-ready pub where locals enter through a separate entrance. There is also a tastefully decorated restaurant called the Stag and Trout. There, amid polished paneling, antique fishing equipment, and hunting trophies, you can enjoy the best of Scottish lamb and beef, locally caught trout, as well as salmon, plus pheasant, venison, and other game in season. If you prefer, there is also an intimate cocktail bar on the premises. The restaurant is open only for dinner, from 7:30 to 9 p.m., but bar lunches and bar suppers are served from 12:30 to 2 p.m. and 6:30 to 8 p.m. Expect to pay around £5 ($8) for a good lunch, from £11 ($17.60) for dinner, unless you choose to stay here on the half-board arrangement, costing from £25.50 ($40.80) per person in a bathless room, from £27.50 ($44) per person in a room with bath and toilet. Otherwise, bathless rooms rent for £15.50 ($24.80) per person for B&B, units with bath costing £17.50 ($28) per person. The owners, John and Linda Statham, can arrange shooting for pheasant, grouse, roe, and hind, as well as deer stalking and fishing on the nearby rivers and boating on Loch Alvie.

WHERE TO EAT: The biggest news in Aviemore a few years back was the opening of the **Dalfaber Country Club** (tel. 0479/811244), part of a time-share project. At the edge of the resort, the country club opens its restaurants to nonmembers. The restaurants are set behind the indoor swimming pool of the main clubhouse. For dinner, the choice is the Louisiana Barbecue Pit, capped with a soaring ceiling of pine, the kind of rustic woodsiness you'd expect to find in Aspen. The restaurant's centerpiece is an open barbecue pit, the smoke from which is funneled upward through a gently tapering copper and iron chimney. The bar area's comfortable wicker chairs offer a spot for a relaxing sojourn, often to the tune of a live pianist who appears three times a week or Highland singers who show up on weekends. On Sunday, a three-course roast menu is offered at £5.50 ($8.80) per person. The rest of the week, barbecued steaks are a specialty, as well as duckling baked in hay and black cherry sauce, salmon in puff pastry, Châteaubriand, and roast pheasant. For an à la carte dinner, you'll spend about £11 ($17.60). This menu changes weekly but always offers the barbecued steak. Dinner is served from 7 to 10 p.m.

If you show up for lunch, the adjacent room, the Café Martinique, will serve you a homemade Scotch broth, followed by such dishes as cold poached salmon, or perhaps an open-faced sandwich on brown bread. The decor is a medley of knotty pine, big windows, and live plants. Desserts are a specialty, consisting of homemade ice creams in fanciful combinations with such flavorings as Kahlúa or rose hips. Lunch is served daily from noon to 2:30 p.m. Dinner is served simultaneously with the Barbecue Pit.

The Winking Owl (tel. 0479/810646). This all-purpose drinking and dining facility contains a variety of rendezvous points beneath one contemporary roofline. Set on the main street of town, it becomes especially popular in winter, when skiers flock into pine-paneled rooms that might as easily be found at any ski resort in Switzerland. The upper-level Nest Bar offers a full array of single-malt whiskies, keg beer, and wine by the glass. The ground-floor cocktail bar invites with a more sedate ambience, intimately lit for a quiet before-dinner drink. On the ground floor, the dining room is decorated with plaid designs accented by naturally finished pine. Bar lunches, priced from £5 ($8), are served daily from noon to 2 p.m. Dinner is from 6:15 to 9 p.m. and less expensive bar suppers are available every night. The restaurant offers table d'hôte menus for £8 ($12.80). On the à la carte menu such specialties are offered as smoked salmon, snails in garlic butter, Gaelic steak with whisky and cream sauce, and Highland game soup, along with freshly cooked vegetables. Perhaps your main course will be a pheasant.

Happy Haggis, Grampian Road (tel. 0479/810430), is a pasta emporium run by Hungarians. It offers one of the best food values in town if you're economizing. At lunch it serves take-away beefburgers from noon to 2 p.m., and take-away is also available from 4 to 11 p.m. The best features, however, are the pasta dinners served seven days a week in both summer and winter from 5 to 11 p.m. Surrounded by glowing sheathing of varnished pine, you can eat all the pasta you want for only £2.75 ($4.40) per person. You can select from five different kinds of pasta, including verde and whole wheat, and ten different sauces which will be applied in any combination you want. A side salad is also available, and wine is sold by the carafe.

SIGHTS AND ACTIVITIES: In winter, ski runs are available for both beginners and experts (four chair lifts and seven T-bar tows). Après-ski activities include swimming in a heated indoor pool 82 feet long, folk singing, table tennis, or just relaxing and drinking in one of the many bars in the complex.

The ice rink is the second-largest indoor ice rink in Britain, with seven curling lanes and ice skating on a separate 4,000-square-foot pad. At night younger people are attracted to the pubs, while others seek out one of the Scottish nights, country dancing, supper dances, or dancing in the large Osprey Ballroom with a sprung maple floor. In summer, sailing, canoeing, pony trekking, hill walking, and mountain climbing, as well as golf and fishing, are just some of the many activities.

In the heart of the resort, **Aviemore Center** (tel. 0479/810624) is an all-purpose cultural, sports, and entertainment complex. Built nearly a quarter of a century ago, within a loop road, it contains four hotels and their grounds. The center's activities are suitable for everyone and include ice skating, swimming, saunas, solarium, squash, table tennis, snooker, discos, putting, go-karting, and much more. Most sports facilities are open daily from 8 a.m. to 1 p.m. and 2 to 5 p.m. and also from 6 to 9 p.m. Admission to the pool is £1 ($1.60) for adults, 60p

(96¢) for children. The Speyside Theatre, seating 720, changes its film programs three times a week, and often is host to live shows and concerts. Also on the grounds is the Highland Craft Centre, a small shopping emporium.

In the village of Inverdruie, 1½ miles east of Aviemore, on the ski road to Cairngorm, is the **Inverdruie Visitor Centre.** There, you'll find the **Cairngorm Whisky Centre & Museum** (tel. 0479/810574), open Monday to Saturday from 10 a.m. to 6 p.m. (later in high season), on Sunday from 12:30 to 2:30 p.m. April to September. In the museum are relics of whisky distilling in times past together with models of their modern equivalents. An audio-visual presentation is given on the history of whisky (scotch, of course) and the industry. Despite the museum aspects, this is primarily a retail shop, stocking malt whiskies from 105 distilleries. In a tasting room, admission £2 ($3.20) per person, you can taste minute quantities of up to four different brands, then purchase your favorite in the shop if you wish.

Also at the Inverdruie center is the **Rothiemurchus Farm Visitor Centre,** with an audio-visual presentation. From here, guided walks and farm tours are organized by the ranger service. You can see red deer and Highland cattle as you tour.

Another opportunity at the Inverdruie center is to visit the **Old School Craft Shop** (tel. 0479/810005), where pottery, rugs, handknit articles, woodwork, and other fine traditional craftwork can be seen and purchased, as well as books and maps. You may want to visit the **Mostly Pine Tearoom,** with lots of antiques, and the **Ski-Road Skis Gift Shop,** featuring sports and fashion wear.

IN THE ENVIRONS: The area surrounding Aviemore is rich in attractions. You can journey to the sky on the **Cairngorm Chairlift,** whose lowest section lies ten miles east of Aviemore. A round-trip passage on this longest chair lift in Scotland costs £2.80 ($4.48) per person during working hours, 9 a.m. to 4 p.m. daily in winter and summer. In winter, the uppermost reaches are closed during periods of high wind. The highest section is 4,084 feet above sea level. A midway stop is the **Ptarmigan Restaurant,** the loftiest (altitude-wise) eating spot in Britain at 3,600 feet. Hours are 9 a.m. to 4 p.m. The decor is rustic and woodsy, modern yet unpretentious, with meals costing £10 ($16). In summer, on a clear day you can see Ben Nevis in the west, and the vista of Strathspey from here is spectacular, from Loch Morlich set in the Rothiemurchus Forest to the Spey Valley.

Skiers are attracted to the area anytime after October, when snow can be expected. Ski equipment and clothing can be rented at the Day Lodge at the main Cairngorm car park. Weather patterns can change quickly in the Cairngorm massif, so for information about this and other aspects of the chairlift, phone 047986/261. To reach the area, take the A951 branching off from the A9 at Aviemore, then head for the car park near Loch Morlich.

North of Aviemore, the **Strathspey Railway** is billed as providing "a trip into nostalgia." The railway follows the valley of the River Spey between Boat of Garten and Aviemore, a distance of around six miles. The train is drawn by a coal-burning steam locomotive. The newest locomotive used was made some 35 years ago, the oldest being of 1935 vintage. Plans are in process to restore and use a locomotive made in 1899. The round trip requires 17 minutes in each direction. Only two service designations—first class and third class, in conformity with railroad tradition—are offered. Round-trip passage costs £3.60 ($5.76) first class, £2.40 ($3.84) third class. Schedules change frequently, but in July and August, trains make five round-trip journeys daily except Friday. In spring and fall, the trains run only on weekends, making four round-trip journeys each on Saturday and Sunday. The trains do not run in winter.

The backers of this railway, which takes you through scenes unchanged in a century, set out to re-create the total experience of travel on a Scottish steam railway that once carried wealthy Victorians toward their hunting lodges in "North Britain." The rail station at Boat of Garten where you can board the train has also been restored. To complete the experience, you can wine and dine aboard on Saturday, when a single-seating dinner is served, costing £14.50 ($23.20), and at a single-seating lunch on Sunday, when the price is £9.50 ($15.20). Reservations for the meals must be made in advance. The dining car is a replica of a Pullman parlor car, the *Amethyst*. For reservations and hours of departure, call 047983/258.

5. Carrbridge

You can follow the A9 north from Aviemore to Carrbridge, where you'll find the **Landmark Visitor Centre** (tel. 047984/613), which provides a vivid screen history of the Highlands, as well as a giant woodland maze, an adventure playground, a sculpture park, a plant center, a nature trail, and a balancing trail. There's even a tree-top trail. This was the first visitor center of its kind in Europe. It also has a good restaurant. Open all year, it charges a combined admission of £1.95 ($3.12) for adults and £1.15 ($1.84) for children.

As an alternative to Aviemore, Carrbridge might also be the headquarters of your Speyside visit.

FOOD AND LODGING: For comfortable accommodations, I recommend the **Struan House Hotel** (tel. 047984/242). This gabled black-and-white Victorian house is flanked with potted flowers that grow in tubs in summer near the roadside. Inside, elegant moldings, thick doors, fireplaces, brass accessories, and a convivial dining room covered with knotty-pine paneling are just some of the embellishments. This was formerly the hunting lodge of a baronial estate. A Gothic-inspired fireplace burns beside a wooden bar which is faintly reminiscent of something you might have found in the Old West. Rates in the 17 well-furnished bedrooms run from £13 ($20.80) per person, with breakfast included. Depending on the accommodation and the season, half board ranges from £21 ($33.60) to £23 ($36.80) per person.

6. Grantown-on-Spey

This holiday resort, with its gray granite buildings, stands in a wooded valley and commands splendid views of the Cairngorm mountains. It is a key center of winter sports in Scotland. Fishermen are also attracted to its setting, because the Spey is renowned for its salmon. Lying 34 miles southeast of Inverness by road, it was one of Scotland's many 18th-century planned towns, founded on a heather-covered moor in 1765 by Sir James Grant of Grant, becoming the seat of that ancient family. Grantown became famous in the 19th century as a Highland tourist center, enticing visitors with its planned concept, the beauty of surrounding pine forests, the Spey River, and the mountains around it.

From a base here you can explore the valleys of the Don and Dee, the already-mentioned Cairngorms, and Culloden Moor, scene of the historic battle in 1746.

FOOD AND LODGING: Set on the narrowest edge of the historic square of the town, the elegant, comfortable **Garth Hotel,** The Square, Castle Road (tel. 0479/2836), was built as a private house in the 17th century. There is still something prosperous and wholesome about it, a feeling enhanced by the well-polished brass hardware and the four-acre garden which, crisscrossed by a series of footpaths, extends toward the back. Guests enjoy the use of a spacious upstairs lounge, whose thick walls, high ceilings, woodburning stove, and vine-covered veranda make it the perfect place for morning coffee or afternoon tea. There's an expansive bay window illuminating the plaid carpeting of the popular cocktail lounge. An array of sun parasols on the side lawn take advantage of the area's warm weather breezes. Gordon McLaughlan, the owner of this attractive hotel, rents out 14 comfortable and handsomely furnished bedrooms. Depending on the plumbing, the per-person rate for B&B ranges from £16 ($25.60) to £18 ($28.80) daily, plus another £9 ($14.40) per person for dinner served in a pleasantly attractive room.

Rosehall Hotel (tel. 0479/2721). Devotees of late Victorian architecture might fall in love with this perfectly symmetrical stone-walled establishment which is one of the prettiest guesthouses along the main street. It was built around 1890 by a local doctor who took advantage of its position on the main square of town by adding enormous fan-shaped windows across each of the gables of the third story. Today the immaculately clean guesthouse is the property of a former furniture maker, Vivian McLennan who, with his charming wife, Margaret, retired to his native Scotland. At night you are likely to meet him behind the bar of the cozy in-house pub, whose half-timbered walls evoke "merrie olde Scotland" at its most sociable. A pleasantly high-ceilinged dining room that juts out the back is the only modern addition this lovely house has seen. Many of the 14 well-furnished bedrooms contain private baths. Rooms 7 and 9 are favorites, possibly because of their big-windowed views over the historic town square. B&B costs from £14 ($22.40) per person, and another £2.50 ($4) per person if a private bath is included. A fixed-price dinner is another £8 ($12.80).

The **Strathspey Hotel,** High Street (tel. 0479/2002), is a listed building, erected in 1803, the second-oldest licensed premises in Grantown, open most of the year. The resident owners, Evelyn and Sandy Pirie, assure guests of a warm welcome to their seven-bedroom hostelry. All units have been completely refurbished to a high standard, as have all the bathrooms. Four of the accommodations have complete plumbing facilities, two have showers, and one is just across the hall from its private bath. The hotel is centrally heated, and all bedrooms have color TV and hot-beverage facilities. The cost of B&B is £12.50 ($20), and a dinner is priced at £6.50 ($10.40). The hotel has a lounge bar, public bar, and parking area at the rear of the building.

Riversdale Guest House, Grant Road (tel. 0479/2648), is a lovely old residence owned by Helen and Jim Shedden, who accept paying guests. Its many dormers and gables, its bay windows, its surrounding stone wall and flower garden make it an attractive place for your stay. Their area attracts nature lovers, those who like to swim, skate, go sailing, pony trekking, or canoeing, and it's ideal for birdwatchers, who try to spot ospreys, crested tits, and less exotic birds. All bedrooms have much comfort, central heating, and hot and cold water. The rate per person is £9 ($14.40). If you want an evening meal, it's best to let the owners know when reserving your room. You're given a hearty, filling meal, perhaps roast beef and Yorkshire pudding, followed by dessert and coffee, at a cost of £5.50 ($8.80). All prices are inclusive of VAT, and there is no service charge.

Umaria Guest House, Woodlands Terrace (tel. 0479/2104), is a former private home now turned into an attractive guesthouse, owned by Brenda and Brian Brodie. It's built of rugged stone, with twin gables and bay windows facing the street. It's pleasantly situated on the edge of this country town, only a few minutes' walk from the riverside and center. The owners are keen on Scottish cooking, and you'll get traditional dishes for breakfast and dinner. The B&B rate per person is £8.50 ($13.60); with dinner, £14 ($22.40). Children get a reduction. Each bedroom has personalized decorating, individual tea-making equipment, and electric blankets on the beds.

Dar-Il-Hena, Grant Road (tel. 0479/2929), is run by Jack and Ann Bairstow. Reader Donald E. Bishop of Tacoma, Washington, writes, "This guesthouse has to be the all-time favorite as well as the 'best value' in all of Great Britain." Quite a recommendation. Its rooms are very spacious, the woodwork attractive, and the food and service outstanding. It is a good place at which to center during your tour of "The Whisky Trail." The cost for B&B is from £9.50 ($15.20) per person, plus another £5.50 ($8.80) for an excellent evening meal.

Craggan Mill, Grantown-on-Spey (tel. 0479/2288), is a licensed restaurant and lounge bar run by Bruno and Ann Belleni. Look for a white stucco country-style building, with a warmly rustic interior. Assuming that you and a companion differ in your preference for a British or Italian cuisine, the owners offer both cuisines at attractive prices. Therefore your appetizer might be smoked trout in deference to Scotland, or ravioli, inspired by sunny Italy. For a main course the selection might be breast of chicken with cream or chicken cacciatore, followed by a dessert of either rum-raisin ice cream or peach Melba. A choice of one of the courses just mentioned would cost about £7.95 ($12.72). Hours are noon to 2 p.m. and 6 to 10 p.m. A good selection of Italian wines is also offered.

7. The Glenlivet

To reach your first distillery, you leave Grantown-on-Spey, heading east along the A95 until you come to the junction with the B9008. Continue south along this route, and you can't miss it. The **Glenlivet Reception Centre** is ten miles north of the nearest town, Tomintoul. For information, call 08073/427. Near the River Livet, this is one of the most famous distilleries in Scotland, and it's open to visitors from early April until the end of October from 10 a.m. to 4 p.m. Monday to Saturday. It's also possible, if you wish, to find accommodations in the area.

In the heart of the Grampians, this hamlet attracts not just those wanting to visit the distillery, but others seeking to participate in such Highland sports as birdwatching, walking, fishing, golfing, and pony trekking, along with shooting and skiiing in winter. For hill walking, the range of the Ladder Hills and the Cairngorms are within easy reach of The Glenlivet.

FOOD AND LODGING: Standing on seven acres of private grounds, the **Minmore House Hotel** (tel. 08073/378), in the hamlet of The Glenlivet, is an impressive country house. Guests are welcomed to one of the 11 well-furnished bedrooms, all with private baths or showers. B&B costs £16 ($25.60) to £20.50 ($32.80) per person. Children 5 to 14 can share their parents' rooms for half price. Before being converted into a hotel, the Minmore was the home of The Glenlivet Distillery owners. The hotel operators have furnished their drawing room in an elegant style, and it opens onto views of the Ladder Hills and an outdoor heated swimming pool. Guests enjoy drinks in the oak-paneled lounge bar, with an open log fire on chilly nights. The Scottish food is excellent, and it's served in a dining room in the Regency style, with mahogany tables and matching chairs with brass inlay.

GLENFARCLAS DISTILLERY: Back on the A95 you can visit the Glenfarclas Distillery at Ballindalloch (tel. 08072/257), one of the few malt-whisky distilleries that is still independent of the giants. Glenfarclas is now owned and managed by the fifth generation of the Grant family. Founded in 1836, it is open all year Monday to Friday and also on Saturday during July, August, and September. Hours are 9:30 a.m. to 4:30 p.m. An exhibition center displays not only mementoes of the scotch whisky industry but also a genuine illicit still. There is a small craft shop, and each adult visitor is offered a dram of Glenfarclas Malt Whisky. There is no admission charge.

8. Dufftown

James Duff, the fourth Earl of Fife, founded this town in 1817. The four main streets of town converge at the battlemented clock tower which is also the Tourist Information Centre.

FOOD AND LODGING: Immediately opposite the clock tower, the **Fife Arms Hotel,** The Square (tel. 0340/20220), stands in a simple stone building on the main square of town. This cozy establishment is owned by the most charming bartender in town. Ian Murray and his wife, Sheila, welcome guests into their pub and into a trio of rooms they rent to paying guests. B&B costs from £12 ($19.20) per person nightly. A dinner in the paneled pub costs £4 ($6.40) to £8 ($12.80), depending on what you order. If you're in Dufftown only for the day, you can drop in for a pub snack.

For dining, there is no better choice than **Taste of Speyside,** Balvenie Street (tel. 0340/20860). A brother and sister team, Anne McLean and Joe Thompson, avidly promote a Speyside cuisine. They also feature Speyside malt whiskies, and in the bar they sell the product of each of Speyside's 46 distilleries. A £3.50 ($5.60) platter is offered at noon, including a slice of smoked salmon, a slice of smoked trout, pâté flavored with malt whisky, locally made cheese (cow or goat), salads, and homemade oatcakes. This same arrangement goes for £4 ($6.40) at night. Many guests are happy with a bowl of nourishing soup made fresh daily and served with homemade bread. There's also a choice of meat pies, including venison with red wine and herbs. A small but limited selection of hot dishes is also offered, including freshly caught wild salmon or rack of Highland lamb. For dessert, try Scotch Mist, containing fresh cream, malt whisky, and crumbled meringue. It would be difficult to spend more than £9 ($14.40) for a full meal, and many guests get by with about half that much. Contained within the ground floor of a terraced house in the center of town, near the main square, it is open in spring, summer, and autumn from 11 a.m. to 10 p.m. daily except Sunday. In winter, it is open Thursday, Friday, and Saturday from 6 to 10 p.m. and Sunday for lunch only, 11 a.m. to 3 p.m.

SIGHTS: Dufftown is a center of the whisky-distilling industry. It is surrounded by seven malt distilleries. The major one most visitors want to see is **Grant's Glenfiddich Distillery in Dufftown** (tel. 0340/20373), open Monday through Friday from 9:30 a.m. to 4:30 p.m. Visitors are shown around the plant, and the process of distilling is explained by charming young women in tartans. A film of the history of distilling is also shown. At the finish of the tour, you're given a free dram of malt whiskey, and the whole tour is free. There is a souvenir shop where you can buy glasses, tankards, and hip flasks, plus other tokens of your visit to what is one of the few malt distilleries left in Scotland that is still owned by the founding family and not by a combine. The first whisky was produced on Christmas Day back in 1887.

Other sights include **Balvenie Castle,** the ruins of a moated stronghold from the 14th century. During her northern campaign against the Earl of Huntly, Mary Queen of Scots spent two nights here. From 1459 to the 17th century the

Earls of Atholl retained Balvenie. It is open April to the end of September from 9:30 a.m. to 7 p.m. Monday to Saturday, 2 to 7 p.m. on Sunday. It's closed in winter. Admission is 50p (80¢) for adults, 25p (40¢) for children.

Mortlach Parish Church is one of the oldest places of Christian worship in the country. It is reputed to have been founded in 566 by St. Moluag. A Pictish cross stands in the graveyard. The present church was reconstructed in 1931, incorporating portions of an older building.

Auchindoun Castle in Glen Fiddich is a massive ruin on a steep hillside above the River Fiddich about 1½ miles southeast of Dufftown. The three-story keep is enclosed by Pictish earthworks. The castle was constructed by Robert Cockran, a favorite of King James III, who was hanged by the Scottish barons in 1482. Because the building is unsafe, it can only be viewed from the outside.

9. Keith

Keith grew up because of its strategic location, where the main road and rail routes between Inverness and Aberdeen cross the River Isla. It has a long and ancient history, but owes its present look to the "town planning" of the late 18th and early 19th centuries.

Today it is a major stopover along the Malt Whisky Trail.

FOOD AND LODGING: Good accommodations are found at the **Royal Hotel,** Church Road (tel. 05422/2528). In addition to being a cozy and comfortable hotel, this establishment also serves as a social center of Keith. On any given day a hotel resident might encounter meetings of the Rotary Club, the Ladies' Circle, a Farmers' Discussion Group, Weight Watchers, or the Round Table. In summer everyone in Keith seems to show up for the twice-monthly ceilidh in one of the lounges. This stone hotel, built on the roadside in 1883, has a dozen pleasant rooms renting for £16 ($25.60) for a bathless single, £17.50 ($28) for a single with bath. Bathless doubles cost £26 ($41.60), doubles with private baths going for £28 ($44.80). Fixed-price meals are served in the upstairs dining room, costing £5 ($8) for lunch, £9 ($14.40) and up for dinner.

SIGHTS: The oldest operating distillery in the Scottish Highlands, the **Strathisla Distillery** on Seafield Avenue (tel. 05422/7471) was established in 1786. It offers guided tours Monday to Friday from 9 a.m. to 4:30 p.m. June to early September.

There is also a fine woolen mill in the town, **G. & G. Kynoch,** Isla Bank Mills, Station Road (tel. 05422/2648), which has been in business since 1788 producing high-quality tweeds and woolens. The mill shop is open daily from 8:30 a.m. to 4:15 p.m., and mill tours are conducted on Tuesday and Thursday at 2:30 p.m.

10. Rothes

A Speyside town with five distilleries, Rothes is just to the south of the lovely Glen of Rothes. Founded in 1766, the town lies between Ben Aigan and Conerock Hill. A little settlement, the basis of the town today, grew up around Rothes Castle, ancient stronghold of the Leslie family, who lived there until 1622. Only a single massive wall of the castle remains.

FOOD AND LODGING: In 1902, the railroad began service on its line into Rothes, and the impressively proportioned stone **Station Hotel,** 51 New St. (tel. 03403/240), opened with great fanfare to greet the train's arrival. In 1965, the railway line was discontinued, but the hotel still exists, maintaining both its name and its tradition for hospitality. The ten bedrooms are accessible via a darkly paneled grand staircase. The rate for B&B is from £13 ($20.80) per person nightly. All rooms are bathless. Much of the hotel's business comes from its pub, cocktail bar, and restaurant.

A DISTILLERY VISIT: Among the several distilleries bearing the name of, or having been launched by, the Grant family is the **Glen Grant Distillery** opened in the mid-19th century. It can be visited to this day anytime from Easter to September, Monday to Friday from 10 a.m. to 4 p.m. A Visitor Reception Centre offers guided tours. Call 03403/494 for information.

11. Fochabers

This village on the Inverness–Aberdeen road dates from 1776 and was created as one of the early planned towns by John Baxter for the fourth Duke of Gordon. Most of the buildings along High Street are protected and have not been changed much in 200 years. On the Spey, Fochabers is distinguished by its **Market Cross** and **Tower of Gordon Castle.**

FOOD AND LODGING: If you're stopping over, try the **Grant Arms Hotel,** High Street (tel. 0343/820202), which has one single room, three doubles, three twin-bedded, and one family room. The B&B costs £12.50 ($20) in a single, £21 ($33.60) in a room with a matrimonial bed, and £23 ($36.80) in a twin-bedded accommodation. There's a residents' lounge with color TV and a cocktail bar, where you can get a good bar lunch if you're just passing through. Bar snacks include homemade soup and a hot dish of the day. High teas, served between 5 and 6:30 p.m., begin at £3 ($4.80). The proprietors, Mr. and Mrs. Sutherland, provide central heating, and there's ample parking. The hotel is open all year.

SIGHTS: Baxters is a famous name in Britain, known for its specialty foods. The **Baxters Visitor Centre** (tel. 0343/820393) tells the story of how it all began more than a century ago, with an audio-visual show. The Old Baxter Shop is a replica of the original George Baxter & Sons. You can take guided tours of the factory where royal game soup and other delicacies are produced. It is open April to October, Monday to Friday from 10 a.m. to 4:30 p.m., charging no admission. In summer, it is also open from noon to 4:30 p.m. on Sunday. The location is half a mile west of Fochabers.

Fochabers Folk Museum, Pringle Antiques, High Street, housed in a former church, has 16 carts and gigs displayed on the top floor, with many items of other days in Fochabers to be seen on the ground floor. The surrounding area includes a complete village shop. The museum is open from 9:30 a.m. to 5:30 p.m. Monday to Friday. Admission is 40p (64¢) for adults, 20p (32¢) for children.

12. Elgin

The center of local government in the Moray District, an ancient royal burgh, this cathedral city lies on the Lossie River, 38 miles from Inverness by road. The city's medieval plan has been retained, with wynds and pends connecting the main artery with other streets. The castle, as was customary in medieval town layouts, stood at one end of the main thoroughfare, with the cathedral at the other. Nothing remains of the castle.

WHERE TO STAY: Ringed with stately trees, the **Braelossie Hotel,** Sheriffmill Road (tel. 0343/7181), is nothing less than a Victorian palace. You'll enter a baronial reception hall, where a sweeping staircase leads to the upstairs bedrooms.

Its grandeur doesn't prevent the place from being one of the most popular drinking and dining establishments in town. In what used to be one of the parlors, a busy lunchtime crowd enjoys pub meals along with beer and malt whisky. The owners rent out ten bedrooms, all with private baths and comfortably furnished, costing from £20 ($32) in a single, from £32 ($51.20) in a double. Breakfast is included in the tariffs.

You may prefer the **Royal Hotel,** corner of Station Road and Moss Street (tel. 0343/2320), a pleasant, privately owned hotel standing on its own grounds about four minutes from the center of Elgin. It lies in the vicinity of the railway station and in proximity to golf and tennis courts. A pleasant, privately owned hotel, it offers B&B for £14 ($22.40) per person. Bar lunches and the evening meal range from £4 ($6.40), and steak dinners go for £9 ($14.40). You may relax in traditional style in the cocktail bar with a peat fire burning on cooler days. A separate games room is available for children, and there is a comfortable TV lounge for children's use. This grand old house with its double staircase with wrought-iron banisters and a mahogany rail boasts many other features of architectural interest. It was built in 1865 by James Grant, the founder of the Glen Grant Distillery, who also built all the railways in northwest Scotland north to Wick. The hotel is open all year.

South Bank Guest House, 36 Academy St. (tel. 0343/7132), has 11 bedrooms for which the charge is £9 ($14.40) per night per person for B&B. Two of the rooms are small singles. There are no private baths, but the public facilities are conveniently placed. Electric heaters are in all the rooms. Bob and Maureen Murphy, the proprietors, serve an evening meal for £5 ($8). Guests can enjoy TV in an attractive lounge, and the Murphys have a residents' license to serve alcohol.

Mrs. Isobel McGowan, 63 Moss St. (tel. 0343/41993), runs a non-smoker's haven, with good beds and an excellent breakfast. The house, built before 1838, has central heating. B&B costs from £9 ($14.40) per person. Parking is available, and the house is within easy walking distance of the city center and the railway station.

WHERE TO DINE: When Dr. Samuel Johnson and James Boswell came this way on their Highland tour in 1773, they reported having a "vile dinner" at the Red Lion Inn. Today, you shouldn't have that complaint in Elgin.

For lunch or dinner, stop at the **Abbey Court Restaurant,** 15 Greyfriars St. (tel. 0343/2849). It is an excellent and sophisticated dining choice. The owner, Barrie Chown, along with his wife, Helen, ripped out walls and added lots of stone- and earth-colored quarry tile, along with an artificial pergola, a separate bistro corner, and a more formal dining area in the rear with lots of plants. The effect is vaguely like a Mediterranean garden terrace. Pasta is homemade fresh, and fresh fish is delivered daily. It would be difficult to spend more than £12 ($19.20) for a full meal, and most meals cost from £8 ($12.80). Specialties include smoked salmon, scallops, snails, lemon or dover sole, trout, and prime Angus beef in many varieties. Game, such as pheasant or venison, is also a feature. Hours are daily except Sunday from noon to 2 p.m. and 6:30 to 10 p.m. Because Mr. Chown is a local wine importer, he stocks more than 120 varieties of vino.

The Oakwood, Forres Road (tel. 0343/2688). The facade you'll see beside the road was built in 1932 in a mosaic of randomly angled logs. The building itself is considered the oldest roadside inn in Britain. The location is about a five-minute drive from the heart of Elgin. Today you pass by a wishing well in the forecourt and through a high-ceilinged entrance whose plank-covered walls are highlighted with stained-glass windows. You'll be able to dine well and inexpensively on an array of pub lunches or more elaborate evening meals. Bar lunches cost £4 ($6.40), and dinners go for £12 ($19.20). At night you can select from such specialties as cream of pheasant soup, Oakwood pâté, chicken livers with whisky sauce, grilled Lossie sole, and an array of grilled meats, including sirloin and Aberdeen Angus. Salmon, prepared in a variety of ways, is also a specialty. Bar lunches are on from noon to 2 p.m., high teas from 4:30 to 6 p.m., and à la carte dinners from 7 to 9 p.m.

SIGHTS: Once called the "lantern of the north," the **Cathedral of Moray** (tel. 0343/7171) is now in ruins. It was founded in 1224 but almost destroyed in 1390 by the "wolf of Badenoch," the natural son of Robert II. After its destruction, the citizens of Elgin rebuilt their beloved cathedral, turning it into one of the most attractive and graceful buildings in Scotland. The architect's plan was that of a Jerusalem cross. However, when the central tower fell in 1711, the cathedral was allowed to fall into decay. A faithful cobbler who still respected its grandeur became its caretaker some years later. At his death in 1841, he had removed most of the debris that had fallen. Today tourists wander among its ruins, snapping pictures. Best preserved is the 15th-century chapter house. The location is on King Street. It is open April to September, Monday to Saturday from 9:30 a.m. to 7 p.m. (on Sunday from 2 to 7 p.m.). Off-season, its hours are 9:30 a.m. to 4 p.m. Monday to Saturday (on Sunday from 2 to 4 p.m.).

    Elgin Museum, 1 High St. (tel. 0343/3675), has collections of archeology including Pictish stones. Exhibits on the natural and social history of the area are here, plus an important collection of fossils in which are displayed Elgin reptiles. The museum is open from 10 a.m. to 4 p.m. Monday to Friday April to September, from 10 a.m. to noon on Saturday all year. Admission is 25p (40¢) for adults, 10p (16¢) for children.

    Lady Hill stands on High Street, opposite the post office. This is the hilltop location of what was once the royal castle of Elgin. Edward I of England stayed here in 1296 during the Wars of Independence. Only a fragment of the mighty castle now remains. A column, put up in 1839 in memory of the last Duke of Gordon, surmounts the hill.

    Scottish woolens and cashmeres are available in great variety at the **Mill Shop,** Newmill (tel. 0343/7821), which also has lots of souvenirs on sale. You may be lucky enough to catch a tour of the mill.

    If you have a car, you can see some interesting sights in the environs, including the impressive ruins of the palace of the bishops of Moray. Called **Spynie Palace,** the location is 2½ miles north of Elgin, off the A941 highway to Lossiemouth (coming up). Since the structure is considered unsafe, it is not open to visitors. However, it can be seen from the Spynie Canal Bridge on the Elgin–Lossiemouth road.

    Birnie Kirk, at Birnie, three miles south of Elgin and west of the A941 highway to Rothes, was for a time the seat of a bishopric. It dates from about 1140 when it was constructed on the site of a much earlier church that was founded by St. Brendan. It is one of the few Norman churches in Scotland still in regular use, and it is open daily.

13. Lossiemouth

    Almost due north of Elgin on the North Sea coast, this popular holiday resort at the mouth of the Lossie River, with long stretches of sandy beaches, is also a busy fishing port. Golfing, sea and river fishing, sailing, and surfing are enjoyed.

FOOD AND LODGING: On a bluff above the beach, **Skerry Brae,** Stotfield

Road (tel. 034381/2040), is an ivy-covered stone building erected at the turn of the century. Its original inhabitant commissioned art deco–style murals which still cover the walls of what is now the cocktail lounge. He also installed an indoor swimming pool in what is now the summer disco. He also planted an enormous bed of crocus shaped like a map of India, which later became a parking lot. He even installed a periscope so that he could survey his neighbors' rooftops while seated in his cellar. The establishment's six bedrooms, each comfortably furnished, rent for £14.50 ($23.20) per person if bathless, the price rising about £2 ($3.20) per person with a private bath. A full Scottish breakfast is included in the tariff. A fixed-price evening meal served in a comfortable dining room goes for £8.50 ($13.60). You can select from such dishes as several kinds of steak (T-bone, sirloin, rump, minute), along with curries.

The 1629, 20 Clifton Rd. (tel. 034381/3848), was installed in one of the oldest buildings in this port. Right in the heart of the action, it overlooks the Moray Firth. Decorated in a traditional antique style, it offers the finest dinners in Lossiemouth, an array of continental dishes and seafood. These might include beef Wellington, duckling with orange sauce, spaghetti with mussels, avocado pâté, smoked Scottish salmon, and lobster when available. Specialties include "the three ambassadors" (tender filets of veal, beef, and pork in a creamy mushroom sauce with fruit), baked halibut with lobster and a cream sauce, and paupiettes of sole mornay. A four-course table d'hôte seafood menu is served from £10 ($16). Dinner is served from 6:45 to 9 p.m. Bar lunches, costing under £5 ($8), are served in the downstairs dining room from noon to 2 p.m. Sunday lunch is traditional and lavish. The establishment is open seven days a week, and it's wise to make a reservation for dinner.

SIGHTS: Of interest is the **Lossiemouth Fishery and Community Museum,** Pitgaveny Street (tel. 034381/3772). It has exhibits showing the fishing industry of the port, along with scale models of fishing vessels. A special feature is a reconstruction of the study of James Ramsay MacDonald, with his original furnishings. MacDonald was born in 1866 and spent his childhood in Lossiemouth. He went on to become Britain's first Labour prime minister. The museum is open April to the end of September from 11 a.m. to 1 p.m. and 2 to 5 p.m. Monday to Saturday. Admission is 50p (80¢) for adults, 25p (40¢) for children.

On the outskirts, **Duffus Castle,** off the B9012 four miles northwest of Elgin, stands today in massive ruins. At a point two miles south of the village of Duffus, this was the original seat of the Duffus family. It is a fine example of a Norman motte-and-bailey castle, and is unique in being enclosed by an outer ditch. Admission is free. A 14th-century tower crowns the Norman motte.

AT BURGHEAD: West of Lossiemouth at the eastern headland overlooking Burghead Bay, the little town of Burghead is worth visiting to go to the **Burghead Museum,** 16-18 Grant St., where the famous Burghead Bulls are on display. These carved Pictish stones found in the area are accompanied with exhibits on geology, archeology, and the history of Burghead. The museum is open on Tuesday from 1:30 to 5 p.m., on Thursday from 5 to 8:30 p.m., and on Saturday from 10 a.m. to noon all year. For information, call the Falconer Museum in Forres (tel. 0309/73701).

If you don't want to drive on to Inverness for the night, you might stop over in the following town.

14. Forres

This ancient burgh, mainly residential in character, stands on the Aberdeen–Inverness road, between Elgin and Nairn (ten miles to the east).

Near the mouth of the Findhorn, it is one of Scotland's oldest towns. Once a castle associated with Duncan and Macbeth stood here.

FOOD AND LODGING: The best hotels include the **Ramnee,** Victoria Road (tel. 0309/72410), a charming house set back from the road and entered through well-kept gardens. The Dinnes family personally supervises the day-to-day running of the place, keeping it spotless. There are two lounges plus a pleasant dining room with wood panels and napery where meals are served. A full breakfast is included in the overnight cost, and dinner consists of a four-course table d'hôte menu featuring grilled steak, fish, or poultry. There is a bar for the use of residents. The bedrooms are large, and where bathrooms have been added, the workmanship has been professional—you don't feel that your toilet has been carved out of a corner of your room. The charge is from £19 ($30.40) per person for a room with bath or shower. A set dinner costs £10 ($16), and à la carte meals are also available. VAT is included in the tariffs.

Nearby, the **Park Hotel,** Victoria Road (tel. 0309/72328), is very much the same sort of house. Set on spacious, well-kept grounds, it overlooks Findhorn Bay and the Moray Firth. The bedrooms are comfortable and well appointed, containing hot and cold running water. Two of the 12 units have private baths. The owners welcome guests, charging them £15 ($24) to £17.50 ($28) for B&B. Bar lunches are served, and an evening meal goes for £8 ($12.80) and up. In season, fresh fruit and vegetables come from the garden, the produce being used in the hotel's kitchen. The hotel also has a cocktail bar, drawing room, and television lounge.

Royal Hotel, Tytler Street (tel. 0309/72617). The elaborate Victorian facade of this hotel is about a hundred yards from the rail and bus stations. Each of the rooms contains color TV, coffee-making equipment, and an intercom. Rooms are comfortably furnished and well maintained, costing from £19 ($30.40) to £21 ($33.60) in a single and from £33 ($52.80) to £38 ($60.80) in a double. On the premises are a rustically outfitted pub, with a peat-burning fireplace, and a redecorated lounge bar.

SIGHTS: In and around Forres are some interesting things to see. **Falconer Museum,** Tolbooth Street (tel. 0309/73701), in the town center, has exhibits on local and natural history of Forres and its environs. The work of Hugh Falconer, paleontologist, is shown, and local birds and animals are among permanent displays. The museum is open from 9:30 a.m. to 5:30 p.m. Monday to Saturday in May, June, and September; from 9:30 a.m. to 6:30 p.m. Monday to Saturday and 2 to 6:30 p.m. on Sunday in July and August; and from 10 a.m. to 4:30 p.m. Monday to Friday October to the end of April. Admission is free.

An intriguing sight is **Sueno's Stone** on Burghead Road. The stone stands 23 feet high and has on one side a wheel cross and on the other a series of warlike scenes. It may be around 1,000 years old, and perhaps commemorated a victory over the Vikings.

Another stone, the **Witch's Stone,** on Victoria Road, is believed to date from Pictish times. It perhaps was an altar to the sun god. It gets its name because it marks the resting place of one of three barrels in which three so-called witches were rolled down Cluny Hill, and it is also where the three witches are reputed to have met with Macbeth.

You can also visit **Darnaway Farm Visitor Centre,** off the A96 three miles west of Forres. At Tearie Farm (tel. 03094/469), you can see the workings of a large modern estate, including a viewing platform where you can watch as cows are milked. There is also an audio-visual program. There are nature trails and woodland walks. It is open from the first of June until mid-September from 11 a.m. to 5 p.m. daily. Admission is £1 ($1.60).

Tours, costing £2 ($3.20) per person, depart from the Visitor Centre for **Darnaway Castle,** the seat of the Earl of Moray. The oldest section dates from the 15th century. In Randolph's Hall you can see a portrait of the murdered "Bonnie Earl." The splendid oak ceiling is one of only two such ceilings in Scotland. The castle can be visited from 11 a.m. to 5 p.m. on Sunday and Wednesday from the first of June until the end of August.

A much greater sight, however, is **Brodie Castle** at Brodie (tel. 03094/371), the home of the Brodie family since 1160 or before. It lies 3½ miles west of Forres, to the north of the A96 to Inverness. It has seen many additions over the years, but the present structure is mainly from the mid-17th century. The house has a splendid collection of furniture and paintings, and the gardens are noted for their daffodils in spring, with some 426 varieties having been raised here. It is open during the Easter holidays and from the first of May until the end of September, Monday to Saturday from 11 a.m. to 5:15 p.m. and on Sunday from 2 to 5:15 p.m. The grounds are open all year—daily from 9:30 a.m. to dusk. Admission is £1.80 ($2.88) for adults and 90p ($1.44) for children.

15. Findhorn

As you travel westward from Elgin to Forres, a turn to the right and then to the left will bring you to Findhorn, a tiny village that used to be a busy commercial fishing port. These days, the unique tidal bay at the mouth of the River Findhorn makes the village an ideal center for yacht racing, sailing, and windsurfing. Across the bay from Findhorn is the Culbin Sands, under which lies a buried village.

FOOD AND LODGING: In Findhorn, a good place to stay is the **Culbin Sands Hotel** (tel. 0309/30252), which has panoramic views of Moray Firth, Findhorn Bay, and Culbin Forest, and is within two minutes' walk of sandy beaches that stretch for eight miles. In their family-run hotel, Eric and Meg Scales rent 14 bedrooms, all with hot and cold water basins, costing £13.50 ($21.60) in a single, £26 ($41.60) in a double, for B&B, VAT included. Extra cots can be supplied in rooms, and half price is charged for children under 12. The hotel boasts three well-stocked bars, a pleasant dining room, and a color TV lounge. Bar lunches are served in both the cocktail and public bars seven days a week. In the restaurant, you can have a table d'hôte dinner for £5.50 ($8.80) or else order à la carte. Throughout the season there is both disco action along with live entertainment, and fishing, pony trekking, and waterskiing are within easy reach of the place. Ample parking facilities are offered. It's best to reserve well in advance if you plan to visit Findhorn in the high season.

The **Crown & Anchor Inn** (tel. 03093/30243) dates from 1739 when it was built to cater to travelers making the run between Edinburgh and Inverness. The hospitable inn is run as a "free house," renting out six comfortably furnished bedrooms, including a family room with a double bed and two bunk beds. Each accommodation has its own shower and toilet. Including a full Scottish breakfast, the charge is £15 ($24) person nightly. Bar snacks and meals are served all day seven days a week. Locals drop in to enjoy the real ales and malt whiskies served in the bar.

SIGHTS: Just before you enter Findhorn village, you'll see the home of the **Findhorn Foundation,** The Park (tel. 0309/30311). It is an international education community based on spiritual principles and founded in 1962. It owns and runs the Findhorn Bay Caravan Park (tel. 0309/30203) and the Phoenix Shop, where you can purchase whole-foods, books, and crafts. Tours of the foundation complex are given every afternoon from April to September. If you're interested in residential courses, write or call 0309/73655.

Not far away is the RAF airfield of Kinloss. **Kinloss Abbey** here has long been in ruins. It was founded in 1150 by David I. After the Reformation, it fell into disrepair.

Chapter X

INVERNESS, NAIRN, AND LOCH NESS

1. Inverness
2. Nairn
3. Drumnadrochit
4. Invermoriston
5. Fort Augustus
6. Whitebridge

FROM ITS ROMANTIC GLENS and its rugged mountainous landscapes, the Highlands suggest a timeless antiquity. Off the coast, mysterious islands, such as Skye with its jagged peaks, rise from the sea, inviting further exploration coming up in the chapters ahead.

You can see deer grazing only yards from the highway in some remote parts, and you can stop by a secluded loch for a picnic. Fishermen find the lochs and rivers filled with trout and salmon, and many hotels offer fishing privileges on nearby lochs. After a ride across bleak moorlands, you come to a cottage overgrown with golden gorse and purple foxglove.

The beauty of the Highlands has been praised by such authorities as Robert Burns, Dr. Johnson, and Daniel Defoe. The shadow of Macbeth still stalks the land, and locals will tell you that this 11th-century king of Scotland was much maligned by Shakespeare. Throughout the region the legend of Bonnie Prince Charlie is still strong. Scots still talk of how he rallied the clans only to face defeat at Culloden.

The area's most famous resident is said to live in mysterious Loch Ness. The Loch Ness monster reputedly was first sighted by Saint Columba, the Irish holy man who tangled with it before going on to convert the pagan King Brude and his warlike Picts to Christianity.

Most of the main arteries are good, but other roads in the Highlands are single track, slowing you down considerably. Remember that the sheep have the right of way.

Centuries of invasions, rebellions, and clan feuds are but distant memories now, and the Highlands are among the most peaceful and tranquil parts of

Great Britain. They're not as remote as they once were, when Londoners seriously believed that the men of the Highlands had tails.

By road, rail, and bus, getting there is relatively easy today. From the south, you can take fast roads through either Edinburgh or Glasgow, heading for your ultimate destination. If you don't want to drive, there are Motorrail terminals at Edinburgh, Stirling, and Inverness. Direct rail service operates from London to Inverness. You can also go by coach or plane.

1. Inverness

The capital of the Highlands, Inverness is a royal burgh and seaport, at the north end of Great Glen, lying on both sides of the Ness River. It is considered the best base for touring the north. At the Highland Games, with their festive balls, the season in Inverness reaches its social peak.

Inverness is one of the oldest inhabited localities in Scotland.

On **Craig Phadrig** are the remains of a vitrified fort, believed to date from the fourth century B.C., where the Pictish King Brude is said to have been visited by St. Columba in A.D. 565. The old castle of Inverness stood to the east of the present Castlehill, the site still retaining the name **Auld Castlehill.** Because of the somewhat shaky geography of Shakespeare in dramatizing the crime of Macbeth by murdering King Duncan, some scholars claim that the deed was done in the old castle of Inverness while others say it happened at Cawdor Castle, 4½ miles to the south where Macbeth held forth as Thane of Cawdor. However, a spokesman for Cawdor Castle says that historically King Duncan was killed in combat by his cousin Macbeth on August 14, 1040, at Pitgaveny near Elgin, which is about 40 miles from the castle.

King David built the first stone castle in Inverness around 1141. The **Clock Tower** is all that remains of a fort erected by Cromwell's army between 1652 and 1657. The 16th-century **Abertarff House** is now the headquarters of An Comunn Gaidhealach, the Highland association that preserves the Gaelic language and culture.

Inverness today has a castle, but it's a "modern" one—that is, dating from 1835. Crowning a low cliff of the east bank of the Ness, the **Castle of Inverness** occupies the site of an ancient fortress blown up by the Jacobites in 1746. Today the castle houses county offices and law courts. Mary Queen of Scots was denied admission to the castle in 1562, and she subsequently occupied a house on Bridge Street. From the window of this house, she witnessed the execution of her cousin, Sir John Gordon. For not gaining admission to the castle, she took reprisals, taking the fortress and hanging the governor.

Opposite the town hall is the **Old Mercat Cross,** with its **Stone of the Tubs,** an Inverness landmark said to be where women rested their washtubs as they ascended from the river. Known as "Clachnacudainn," the lozenge-shaped stone was the spot where the early kings were crowned.

West of the river rises the wooded hill of **Tomnahurich,** known as "the hill of the fairies." It is now a cemetery, and from here the views are magnificent.

In the Ness are wooded islands, linked to Inverness by suspension bridges and turned into parks.

PRACTICAL FACTS: The office of the **Inverness, Loch Ness, and Nairn Tourist Board** is at 23 Church St. (tel. 0463/234353).

In an **emergency,** dial 999 for fire, police, or an ambulance.

For **banking,** the Bank of Scotland is at 9 High St. (tel. 0463/230907). It is open Monday, Tuesday, and Wednesday from 9:30 a.m. to 12:30 p.m. and 1:30 to 3:30 p.m. On Thursday it is open from 9:30 a.m. to 12:30 p.m., 1:30 to 3:30 p.m., and 4:30 to 6 p.m. On Friday it is open from 9:30 a.m. to 3:30 p.m.

The head **post office** is at Queensgate (tel. 0463/234111). It is open Monday to Friday from 9 a.m. to 5:30 p.m. and on Saturday from 9 a.m. to 12:30 p.m.

If you'd like to **park your car** and tour downtown Inverness, there is a multistory park on Rose Street, charging very reasonable rates.

The **bus station** is at Farraline Park, off Academy Street (tel. 0463/233371), and the **railway station** is on Academy Street (tel. 0463/238924).

Taxis are also found on Academy Street by the Station Square (tel. 0463/222700).

If you're interested in **bus tours** of the Highlands and **pleasure cruises,** particularly of Loch Ness, go to Highland Omnibuses, Farraline Park (tel. 0463/233371). In summer, cruises go along the Caledonian Canal from Inverness into Loch Ness.

Need your clothes washed? The **Hilton Laundromat** is at the Old Town Shopping Centre, Hilton (tel. 0463/232659).

WHERE TO STAY: In a peaceful spot above the River Ness, the **Redcliffe Hotel, 1** Gordon Terrace (tel. 0463/232767), is a small hostelry set in its own grounds, within a three-minute walk of the main shopping area of the city. The hotel is run by Ian and Dorothy MacLellan and family, who take pleasure in extending a traditional Scottish Highland welcome. They rent out six bedrooms, three with their own private bathrooms and all with color TV and hot-beverage facilities. B&B costs £13.50 ($21.60) to £15.50 ($24.80) per person, depending on the plumbing. There is a comfortable licensed lounge bar where bar meals are provided, or you may prefer the dining room. There traditional high tea is served from 5 p.m., followed by an à la carte dinner. On the menu there are usually such items as salmon, venison, trout, and several Scottish dishes, including haggis. Bar meals start at £2 ($3.20), high tea at £3.50 ($5.60), and dinner at about £7 ($11.20).

On the east side of the River Ness, which flows from Loch Ness to the sea, a short street hugging the riverside, Ness Bank, has a number of guesthouses and private hotels in varying price ranges but all with a delightful view of the river and the Eden Court Theatre on the other side.

Riverside House Hotel, 8 Ness Bank (tel. 0463/231052), is an immaculate place run by Valerie Somerville and Muriel Young. Occupying perhaps the most scenic spot on the river, it stands opposite St. Andrews Cathedral and Eden Court Theatre, only three minutes walk from the city center. All year, they rent out ten bedrooms in their refurbished and centrally heated hotel. All units have color TV, hot-beverage facilities, electric blankets, and hot and cold water basins, while some have private bathrooms. Tariffs for B&B are £12 ($19.20) per person in a bathless double, £15 ($24) per person in a double with bath. Singles cost £14 ($22.40). The residents' lounge, which is open all day, is tastefully decorated. Good home-cooking with a choice of menu is featured in the dining room, and a liquor license makes libations available for guests.

Cuchullin Lodge Hotel, 43 Culduthel Rd. (tel. 0463/231945), was built in the 1870s as a private home of one of the chairmen of the Highland Railways. Later it was sold to a whisky distiller. Today its family owners maintain it as a hotel. Its stone walls and slate roof contain 13 comfortable bedrooms, 11 of which offer private bath and a scattering of antiques. Singles rent for £17 ($27.20) nightly, and doubles go for £16 ($25.60) per person. It's economical to take the half-board rate of £25.50 ($40.80) per person nightly. You get well-prepared dinners.

Millburn Hotel, 2 Millburn Rd. (tel. 0463/232241). The mid-Victorian core of this pleasant hotel was built as the country residence of Lord Palmerston. Between his terms as prime minister, he hosted such celebrities as Lady

Caroline Lamb. Fifty years ago the grand old house was converted into a hotel, and much later a small-windowed modern addition was added onto the ground-floor facade. The hotel offers an array of comfortably furnished bedrooms, a popular pub, and well-prepared dinners and bar lunches. The owners charge £18.50 ($29.60) to £23 ($36.80) per person for B&B, depending on the accommodation.

Moray Park Hotel, Island Bank Road (tel. 0463/233528). Set across from a flowering garden, this Victorian hotel has trails of ivy growing across its stone facade. The seven bedrooms include tea-making equipment, clean linens, and lots of sunlight in fair weather. The rate for B&B is £11 ($17.60) to £15 ($24) per person. It's best to book in here on the half-board plan, costing £18.50 ($29.60) to £22.50 ($36) per person. As there are only a few bedrooms, it is important to call ahead to see if there is space. Well-prepared meals are served in a pleasant dining room, and there is also a cocktail bar.

Loch Ness House Hotel, Glenurquhart Road (tel. 0463/231248). Many guests appreciate this hotel's location in a flowering garden on the A82, the road into Inverness, about two miles south of town. The stone facade opens into a pink and burgundy Victorian interior, where comfortable rooms and good food are supplied in a tasteful setting. The Copper Kettle bar is warmed by a log fire, and you can also order drinks in the lounge bar. Most of the 26 bedrooms contain private baths, color TV, direct-dial phones, and tea-making equipment. A full Scottish breakfast is included in the price: from £21 ($33.60) in a bathless single to £29 ($46.40) in a single with bath, from £20 ($32) per person in a bathless double or twin to £25 ($40) per person in a double or twin with bath. Alastair and Marjorie MacPherson are your hosts.

Cummings Hotel, Church Street (tel. 0463/232531). The sandstone facade of this comfortable hotel dates from around 1870, and the interior has been pleasantly modernized. It's set directly in the center of town, not far from the tourist office. The 40 bedrooms, the reception area, the lounge bar, and the dining room have all been redesigned along pleasingly contemporary lines. However, the polite staff still evokes a certain old-world charm. Bathless rooms go for £21 ($33.60) in a single or from £20 ($32) per person in a double, with breakfast included. Rooms with private bath cost £26.50 ($42.40) in a single and from £23 ($36.80) per person in a double. Full dinners in the restaurant cost from £7 ($11.20). The hotel is best known in Inverness as the site of a popular nightlife spectacle.

Queensgate Hotel, Queensgate (tel. 0463/237211). It sits on one of the busiest streets of downtown Inverness, so it's difficult to miss its beige stone facade. The interior has been modernized in a conservatively international style well suited to a number of "commercial gents" who find it a convenient stopover point in the city. Each of the 60 bedrooms contains a private bath with shower, radio, phone, color TV, and hot-beverage facilities. A single room costs from £25 ($40) a night, while a double goes for £40 ($64), with breakfast included.

Ardroag House, 4 Old Edinburgh Rd. (tel. 0463/231545). One of the best and most reasonably priced guesthouses in Inverness is this stone-pointed house on a residential hillside a few blocks from the commercial center of town. It was built a century ago by a Frenchman for his soon-to-be-married daughter. When the marriage never took place, the house was sold and has since had a changing series of owners. Anne C. Houston is now the proprietor of the house named after a peninsula where she lived for several years outside the village of Dunvegan on the Isle of Skye. None of the five well-furnished bedrooms has a private bath, but there are adequate shared facilities. With breakfast included, singles rent for £12 ($19.20) and doubles for £10 ($16) per person. Guests breakfast at a large table near the bay window of the ground-floor residents' lounge.

Brae Ness, Ness Bank (tel. 0463/231732), is run by four resident owners, Margaret and John Hill and Jean and Tony Gatcombe. These two friendly couples are eager to help visitors enjoy Inverness. Brae Ness is a Georgian house built in 1830 that has been upgraded to incorporate modern comforts while still retaining much of its original character. Most of the 14 bedrooms have private plumbing, and all have electric blankets and hot-beverage facilities. For B&B, expect to pay £11.50 ($18.40) per person, plus another £2.50 ($4) for a room with a bath. In the dining room home-cooking and baking are served, and traditional Scottish fare such as salmon, venison, and other local produce in season is offered, a dinner costing from £7 ($11.20). The hotel isn't licensed, but you are invited to bring in your own wine. Brae Ness has a TV lounge, plus a separate drawing room with a log fire, and all units are centrally heated.

Elsewhere in the city, Mrs. Margaret Charlesworth takes in guests at **Amapola,** 12 Bishops Rd. (tel. 0463/234028), charging £9 ($14.40) per night for B&B to lodgers in her two doubles and two family rooms. TV and tea/coffee-making facilities, plus heaters, are in all bedrooms, as well as hot and cold running water. There is a clean and convenient bathroom and another room with shower and toilet. Central heating has been installed in the house.

Moraine, 5 Porterfield Rd. (tel. 0463/240436), is the domain of Mr. and Mrs. Telford. Margaret Telford is a most hospitable hostess, often meeting late arrivals with hot tea and cookies. Their home is beautifully kept and most comfortable, and the Scottish breakfast is hearty, yet the charge is only from £9 ($14.40) per person nightly.

The Firs, Dores Road (tel. 0463/225197), is a remodeled stone manor house lying on the bank of the River Ness in the city. Mrs. Susan M. Moodie's B&B has fine furnishings, large rooms, and plenty of parking. To stay here costs from £12 ($19.20) to £15 ($24) per person for a bed and a filling breakfast.

About a ten-minute walk from the railway station, **Mr. and Mrs. F. R. Boynton,** 12 Annfield Rd. (tel. 0463/233188), operate a warm, friendly B&B. The rooms are cozy and comfortable, and Foster and Nell Boynton supply their guests with electric blankets, just in case. They charge £8.50 ($13.60) per person for a bed and a tasty and filling breakfast.

Kincraig, 11 Lovat Rd. (tel. 0463/238300), is a recently opened B&B, where hospitable, helpful John and Margaret McCaffery go out of their way to make guests feel at home. The house is a ten-minute walk from the railway station. The bedrooms are well appointed, costing £9.50 ($15.20) per person for B&B.

WHERE TO EAT: The restaurant at the Eden Court Theatre complex is called the **Bishops Table,** Bishops Road (tel. 0463/221723), after Bishop Eden who was in charge of the adjacent cathedral in the 19th century and lived in the Bishops Palace, now used as offices and dressing rooms for the theater. The restaurant offers a superb value buffet with freshly prepared hot and cold food, at prices starting at less than £4 ($6.40) at lunchtime. Full evening meals commence at around £6 ($9.60). The restaurant offers expertly prepared salmon and venison in season, the best Scottish beefsteaks, and of course, haggis is regularly on the menu. Morning coffee is served from 10:30 a.m. to noon, lunch from noon to 2 p.m., afternoon tea from 2:30 to 5:30 p.m. Dinner is served, except on nonperformance Monday, from 5:45 to 7:45 p.m. all year.

Dickens International Restaurant, 77-79 Church St. (tel. 0463/224450). The decor of this establishment looks almost like an English colonial bar in Singapore. Ionic columns combine with rattan furniture and potted palms to create an atmosphere that would have pleased W. Somerset Maugham. On a downtown street near the tourist office, this restaurant offers a wide selection of European,

Chinese, and international dishes, including many vegetarian specialties. There are eight kinds of beef and steak dishes. On the menu are Dickens' own steak, Peking duck, fresh local salmon, roast loin of local venison or cutlets, and Châteaubriand, along with a wide range of appetizers and a good selection of seafood (several dishes are made with prawns). The widest choice of side dishes in Inverness is found here. Full meals average £12 ($19.20). Sunday lunch is also available, costing from £4 ($6.40). Meals are served from 11 a.m. to 11 p.m.

Whinpark Hotel, 17 Ardross St. (tel. 0463/232549), is where two of Scotland's foremost chefs have joined to provide a *restaurant avec chambres,* considered one of the best dining-out places in the country. Using the finest of fresh local produce, George Mackay and Stevie Mackenzie, the chef/proprietors of this establishment, work well together to form a constantly changing menu that is a blend of classical and nouvelle cuisine. Prime Aberdeen Angus steak, freshly caught lobster, and River Ness salmon are imaginatively presented, attested to by repeat diners. Lunch is served Monday to Friday from noon to 2 p.m. and dinner daily from 6:30 to 9 p.m. An evening meal costs from £13 ($20.80) per person. If you're staying elsewhere, you can visit just for meals, but reservations are essential. Whinpark is also a good lodging choice, with rooms costing £18 ($28.80) in a single, £30 ($48) in a double, the prices including a hearty Scottish breakfast.

Stakis Steakhouse, Bank Street (tel. 0463/236577), a member of a chain, is one of the most attractive restaurants in the center, lying on the banks of the river in a green, brown, and white garden-style decor of big windows and padded banquettes. There's plenty of space for everyone, and the steaks and grilled meats are among the best in town. In the amber glow of polished brass lamps, guests enjoy bar lunches every day except Sunday from noon to 2:30 p.m. Hot meals begin at £2.25 ($3.60). There's an amply stocked self-service salad bar. A full à la carte dinner will cost about £12 ($19.20). Specialties include the Stakis prime Angus steak, chicken Kiev, roast chicken, and a full assortment of juicy steaks, some weighing in at your choice of 8 or 16 ounces. Dinner is served every night of the week from 5 to 10:30 p.m. (on Sunday from 6 to 10:30 p.m.).

Brookes Wine Bar, 75 Castle St. (tel. 0463/225662). Owner David MacKenzie set up this establishment in what used to be a pram shop. You'll find it on the street that runs beside the castle behind a Victorian plate-glass facade. Inside the decor is slightly French, an atmosphere enhanced by the posters of vineyards. The environment combines the elements of a Los Angeles bistro and a French garden at the same time. In many ways this is the most avant-garde place in town, certainly one of the most alluring. This was the first wine bar to open in the Scottish Highlands. Wine is sold by the bottle or by the glass, and you can also order a giant bottle of beer imported from Germany, costing £1.95 ($3.12). There are 20 wines to choose from by the glass, priced at £1.35 ($2.16) and up, plus 100 or more by the bottle, costing from £4.75 ($7.60).

As for food, you can choose what you want from a selection in a glass-fronted, refrigerated food case, offering cold meats, fish, chicken, pâtés, mousse, a selection of salads, cheeses, and puddings. Hot dishes are also available, ordered from a menu written daily on the blackboard at the counter. The entire operation works on a counter-service basis, and hot dishes are brought to your table. You might order hot mushrooms gratinée, chicken Kiev, baked potato, or pan-fried filets of chicken breast with orange and ginger sauce served with buttered tagliatelle. For dessert, try the cream-filled ginger meringues or fresh red frangipani tart with cream. A full three-course meal costs from £6.90 ($11.04). The wine bar is open Monday to Friday from 11:30 a.m. to 3 p.m. and 5 to 11 p.m. On Saturday, it is open from 11:30 a.m. to 11:45 p.m. It's best to call about Sunday opening times, as they fluctuate. The establishment is closed on holiday Mondays from September to April (usually the first Monday of the month).

Pancake Place, 25 Church St. (tel. 0463/226156), can be convenient if you want something good, filling, cheap, and centrally located. Right in the heart of Inverness, this is a member of a chain. A large modern establishment, it has tile floors and an exposed stone wall. Its selection of "savoury-filled pancakes" includes everything from a Rocky Mountain burger to haddock mornay. Cool crisp salads, such as cheddar cheese and cold ham, are always featured, as is a large selection of sweet pancakes. With a warning that the selection could destroy your diet, you're presented with a list that ranges from California to Tahiti, from Valencia to Hawaii for inspiration. A satisfying meal here will cost from £5 ($8). It is open Monday to Saturday from 9 a.m. to 10 p.m. and on Sunday from 10 a.m. to 10 p.m.

Crawfords Restaurant, 19 Queensgate (tel. 0463/233198), is an all-purpose restaurant and cafeteria, with at least three distinct serving areas. Its versatility allows it to be used for a simple snack or for a complete meal, depending on where you choose to sit. The basement level contains a simple collection of tables and chairs, where a waitress will serve grilled burgers and salads, American-style pancakes, omelets, and an array of grilled meats. You can even order breakfast at any hour of the day. Full meals in the basement cost from £5 ($8) apiece. On the ground level is a cafeteria where wine and lager are sold by the glass, and quiches and salads complement the cafeteria food. Finally, there's a take-out bakery behind deli-style cases set up near the front door, if you want to sate your sweet tooth and run. The restaurant and cafeteria are open Monday to Saturday. Restaurant hours are 10 a.m. to 7 p.m., and cafeteria hours are 8 a.m. to 5:30 p.m.

Pizzaland, 7-9 Lombard St. (tel. 0463/234328). Pizza in Inverness? It's enough to stir up a Highland uprising. Actually, the modern Scots don't survive entirely on haggis and neeps. Increasingly continental in their tastes, shoppers along this mall come here for pizzas in many combinations, 19 varieties in all with whole-meal pies. If you don't want pizza, you can order homemade lasagne and help yourself from the salad bar, which has a wide selection. Some of the pizza combinations are unusual. I suggest you skip the ham and pineapple and turn to more traditional selections, such as pepperoni and onion. Meals cost from £2.50 ($4). The pizzeria serves daily from 10 a.m. to 11 p.m.

St. Andrews Cathedral, adjacent to the Eden Court Theatre complex, operates a **Tea Garden** from around Easter until the first week of September. Indoors when wet or cold, the Tea Garden offers homemade broth, filled rolls, home-baking, tea, coffee, and soft drinks. To sample something of everything costs less than £1.75 ($2.80). The women of the cathedral give their services voluntarily and do all the baking themselves, the proceeds going to cathedral funds. Hours are 10:30 a.m. to 4 p.m. Flasks will be filled, and rolls and cakes may be taken away.

Eating and Shopping on the Outskirts

Culloden Pottery Restaurant and Gift Shop, The Old Smiddy, Gollanfield (tel. 0667/62340). A meal in this establishment's pleasant restaurant is usually combined with a browse through an adjacent gift shop and pottery studio. The pottery specializes in earthenware and stoneware. Visitors can watch potters at work. Their products and other Scottish handcrafted items are sold in the gift shop. The restaurant is suitable for whole food and vegetarian light meals. Meals are served seven days a week from 9:30 a.m. to 5:30 p.m. (in July, August, and September, the place accepts orders until 7:15 p.m.). A full meal costs from £5 ($8) and might include a parsnip bake, an array of quiches, salads, and a changing array of casseroles. You'll find this establishment in a rambling collection of buildings about midway between Inverness and Nairn on the A96. Bob and Denise Park are your hosts. The restaurant is open daily from Easter to Christmas.

SIGHTS: The city has a luxurious theater complex on the bank of the River Ness, the **Eden Court Theatre,** Bishops Road (tel. 0463/221718), which has a superb restaurant, bars, and an art gallery. Included in the repertoire are variety shows, drama, ballet, pop music, movies, opera, rock and folk concerts, and a summer-season traditional Scottish show with top stars. The theater, which opened in 1976, was constructed with an ingenious use of hexagonal shapes and has a horseshoe-shaped auditorium. Programs are advertised in most hotels and guesthouses. The box office is open from 10:30 a.m. to 8 p.m. Monday through Saturday.

St. Andrews Cathedral, adjacent to the theater complex, is open to visitors from 9 a.m. to 9 p.m., and this northernmost diocese of the Episcopal Church of Scotland boasts a fine example of this form of architecture. The icons given to Bishop Eden by the Tsar of Russia should be viewed. For information, get in touch with the Provost, 15 Ardross St. (tel. 0463/233535).

Inverness Museum and Art Gallery, Castle Wynd (tel. 0463/237114), has on display collections representing the social and natural history, archeology, art, and culture of the Scottish Highlands, with special emphasis on the Inverness district. There is an important collection of Highland silver, with a reconstructed silversmith's workshop; displays on the "Life of the Clans"; a reconstruction of a local taxidermist's workshop; a reconstructed Inverness kitchen of the 1920s; displays of Highland weapons; and an art gallery. There is also a permanent exhibition on the story of the Inverness district, from local geology and archeology to the present day. This includes extensive natural history displays. Other facilities include a public cloakroom and toilets, a souvenir shop, a coffeeshop for meals and refreshments, a regular program of temporary exhibitions and events, and an information service. The museum is open all year Monday to Saturday from 9 a.m. to 5 p.m. (closed on Sunday). Admission is free.

AFTER DARK: For an evening of fun, try **Scottish Showtime,** in the Cummings Hotel, Church Street (tel. 0463/232531). It has become a Highland tradition that the best of the region's entertainers appear at least once at this hotel in the center of Inverness. A bekilted and bagpiped evening here combines Scottish songs with music, dancing, and Highland humor into an enthusiastic ceilidh that many guests remember for a long time. Showtime is Monday through Saturday at 8:30 p.m., beginning in early June and running into the autumn. Tickets cost £4 ($6.40) for adults and £1.75 ($2.80) for children. They can be purchased at the door just before showtime, at the hotel reception desk, or at Record Rendezvous, 14a Church St., just opposite the tourist office. On weekends it's a good idea to phone ahead for a reservation.

SIGHTS IN THE ENVIRONS: From Inverness, you can visit **Culloden Battlefield,** five miles to the east. This is the spot where Bonnie Prince Charlie and the Jacobite army were finally crushed at the battle on April 16, 1746. A cairn marks the site on Drummossie Moor where the battle raged. **Leanach Cottage,** around which the battle took place, still stands and was inhabited until 1912. The cottage, now restored, is a battle museum. A path leads from the museum through the Field of the English, where 76 men of the Duke of Cumberland's forces who died during the battle are said to be buried. Features of interest include the

Graves of the Clans, communal burial places with simple stones bearing individual clan names alongside the main road and through the woodland; the great memorial cairn, erected in 1881; the **Well of the Dead,** a single stone with the inscription "The English Were Buried Here"; and the huge **Cumberland Stone,** from which the victorious "Butcher" Cumberland is said to have reviewed the scene. The battle lasted only 40 minutes; the prince's army lost some 1,200 men out of 5,000, and the king's army 310.

A Visitor Centre (tel. 0463/790607) is open from 9:30 a.m. to 5:30 p.m. April to the end of May and in October, from 9 a.m. to 7:30 p.m. daily June to the end of September. Admission of £1.20 ($1.92) for adults, 60p (96¢) for children includes a visit to an audio-visual presentation of the background and history of the famous battle of 1746.

Between Inverness and Nairn, about six miles to the east of Inverness, are the **Stones of Clava,** one of the most important prehistoric monuments in the north. These cairns and standing stones are from the Bronze Age.

On the Moray Firth by the village of Ardersier, 11 miles northeast of Inverness, **Fort George** (tel. 0463/224380) was called "the most considerable fortress and best situated in Great Britain" in 1748 by Lt. Col. James Wolfe, who went on to fame as Wolfe of Québec. Built following the Battle of Culloden, the fort was occupied by the Hanoverian army of King George II and is still an active army barracks. The rampart, almost a mile around, encloses some 42 acres. Dr. Samuel Johnson and James Boswell visited here in 1773 on their Highland trek.

The fort contains the **Queen's Own Highlanders Regimental Museum,** with exhibits of regimental gear from 1778 to today, representing such military units as the 77th and 78th Highlanders, Seaforth Highlanders, 79th and Queen's own Cameron Highlanders, Lovat Scouts, militia, volunteers, and territorial army, as well as the Queen's Own Highlanders. The public can visit some parts of the fort as well as the museum from 9:30 a.m. to 7 p.m. Monday to Saturday and from 2 to 7 p.m. on Sunday April to the end of September, with closing time being 4 p.m. October to the end of March. Admission to the fort is £1 ($1.60) for adults, 50p (80¢) for children. Once inside, you can visit the museum free.

2. Nairn

A favorite family seaside resort on the sheltered Moray Firth, Nairn is a royal burgh lying at the mouth of the Nairn River. Its fishing harbor was constructed in 1820, and golf has been played here since 1672, as it still is today. A large uncrowded beach, tennis, and angling draw a horde of vacationers in summer.

FOOD AND LODGING: If you're staying in Nairn, I recommend the **Windsor Hotel,** Albert Street (tel. 0667/53108), a fine sandstone building which has been renovated and refurbished to good effect. The resident proprietors, Mr. and Mrs. Charles Woolley, see to it that the hotel provides a comfortable family atmosphere and first-class cuisine. The 60-bedroom establishment is centrally heated, and 55 of the units have bathrooms/showers. All contain color TV, phones, video, and hot-beverage facilities. The single rate for bed and a full Scottish breakfast is £22 ($35.20) to £26.50 ($42.40) in a single with private plumbing, doubles going for £30 ($48) to £45 ($72). The color TV lounge, residents' lounge, and fully licensed lounge and cocktail bars add to the enjoyment of guests. The hotel is close to centers of transportation and sports facilities, and is open all year.

Greenlawns Private Hotel, Seafield Street (tel. 0667/52738), a good center for touring northern Scotland, is within easy reach of beaches, bowling greens, golf courses, tennis courts, an indoor swimming pool, and a shopping center. Guests relax in a pleasant sun lounge. Parking is available on the grounds. All bedrooms have hot and cold running water, electric blankets, heating, TV, and coffee- and tea-making facilities. Bill and Isabel Caldwell do much to see that their guests have a comfortable stay, charging them from £12 ($19.20) per person for B&B. The hotel has a restricted license to serve alcoholic beverages.

Sunny Brae, Marine Road (tel. 0667/52309). This modern guesthouse was built in a spacious garden in 1970 and is now lovingly run by Peter and Carole Cruickshank. The front yard slopes down toward a view of a sandy beach, the sea, and the far-away mountains of Sutherland. None of the ten comfortable bedrooms contains a private bath, but the establishment offers plenty of well-equipped shared facilities. A full array of sports activities, including tennis courts, golf courses, a children's play area, bowling and putting greens, and an indoor heated swimming pool, are within easy reach. Depending on the season, the per-person rate for B&B ranges from £14 ($22.40) to £15.50 ($24.80) nightly. Half board is another £6.50 ($10.40) per person.

Ross House Hotel, Seabank Road (tel. 0667/53731), was originally built in the 19th century as a hunting lodge for the Earl of Cawdor. It occupies a half-acre garden on the western end of town in a well-heeled neighborhood. Mr. and Mrs. Gordon Asher charge £14.50 ($23.20) per person in a bathless room, £16.50 ($26.40) per person in a unit with bath. These prices include a generous Scottish breakfast. There are a total of 16 comfortably furnished bedrooms, only two of which have a private bath. Bar lunches are served daily, and à la carte dinners are offered nightly from 7 to 9 p.m., costing from £9 ($14.40), including flavorful combinations of local Nairn salmon and prime Aberdeen beefsteak.

Invernairne Hotel, Thurlow Road (tel. 0667/52039), is set among a row of private houses in a residential part of town. Its Italianate 19th-century design has been enlarged and expanded over the years. It sits in two acres of wooded garden right beside the beach and attracts history and family research buffs. The building was acquired by John and Jean Lawson, who have upgraded it, adding baths and showers. Singles rent for £20 ($32), with doubles going for £38 ($60.80). The Lawsons grow their own vegetables and raise chickens for eggs, offering traditional, well-prepared food. The hotel has an attractive and friendly bar area, offering real ale, regular jazz, and an array of wines by the glass. Closed in December and January.

Carnach House Hotel, Inverness Road, Delnies (tel. 0667/52094), just two miles out of Nairn near the A96 road, stands in eight acres of lawns and woodlands overlooking the Moray Firth. The Wilkinson family, proprietors of this fine country house, offers a warm welcome. They rent out eight spacious bedrooms with private plumbing, color TV, direct-dial phones, and hot-beverage facilities, charging £40 ($64) for a double for B&B. Singles cost £23 ($36.80). The food is good and dinner, using much local fish and game, costs around £10 ($16).

The Taste Bud Bar & Restaurant, 44 Harbour St. (tel. 0667/52743), lies in the old fishing quarter of town, with its original stone kitchen range and beams intact. Mr. Rafferty, a gracious host, has wisely employed a friendly and helpful staff. Most people come here for the traditional fare, including locally smoked seafood (that means salmon) along with the home-prepared haggis and the best of Angus beef. In season the kitchen is likely to offer venison. Whenever possible, freshly grown vegetables are served to accompany the main courses. Children are welcome, and it's very much a family place. Fully licensed, the restaurant serves from 11 a.m. to 2:30 p.m. and 5 to 10 p.m. weekdays, from 12:30 to 2 p.m. and 6:30 to 10 p.m. on Sunday. Meals cost around £10 ($16).

CAWDOR CASTLE: To the south of Nairn, you encounter 600 years of Highland history at **Cawdor Castle,** Cawdor (tel. 06677/615). Since the early 14th century it's been the home of the Thanes of Cawdor. The castle has all the architectural ingredients you associate with the medieval: a drawbridge, an ancient tower (this one built around a tree), and fortified walls. The severity is softened by the handsome gardens, flowers, trees, and rolling lawns. As I mentioned earlier, even the Scots can't agree as to where Macbeth, who actually was made Thane of Cawdor by King Duncan, committed his foul deed of murdering the king—at Cawdor or in the castle that once stood on Auld Castlehill in Inverness, if at all. In fact, recent historic discoveries indicate that the king was indeed killed by his cousin, Macbeth, but that the slaying was in combat at Pitgaveny near Elgin. The castle is open to the public from 10 a.m. to 5:30 p.m. every day from May 1 to early October. Admission is £2.20 ($3.52) for adults, £1.20 ($1.92) for children. Last admission is at 5 p.m.

LOCH NESS

Sir Peter Scott's *Nessitera rhombopteryx* continues to elude her pursuers. "Nessie," as she's more familiarly known, has captured the imagination of the world, drawing thousands of visitors yearly to the bonnie banks of Loch Ness, south of Inverness. Midget yellow submarines and all types of high-tech underwater contraptions have gone in after the Loch Ness monster, but no one can find her in spite of the photographs that have appeared.

Some people in Inverness aren't sure if they ever want the monster captured. The Brahan Seer, Coinneach Odhar, who forecast the Battle of Culloden and other events, including his own death, predicted a violent end for Inverness if the monster were ever captured. He claimed that Inverness would be consumed by fire and flood.

The Loch Ness monster has been described as the world's greatest mystery. Half a century ago the A82 was built alongside the banks of the loch's western shores. Since that time many more sightings have been claimed.

Dr. Robert Rines and his associates at the Academy of Applied Science in Massachusetts maintain an all-year watch with sonar-triggered cameras and strobe lights suspended from a raft in Urquhart Bay.

The loch is 24 miles long, one mile wide, and some 754 feet deep. If you'd like to stay along the loch and monster-watch, instead of seeking lodgings at Inverness, you can do so at the centers previewed below. Even if the monster doesn't put in an appearance, you can enjoy the splendid scenery.

In summer, from both Fort Augustus and Inverness, you can take several boat cruises across Loch Ness.

3. Drumnadrochit

This pleasant redundant hamlet lies about a mile from Loch Ness at the entrance to Glen Urquhart. It's the nearest village to the part of the loch in which the sighting of the monster has been reported most frequently.

FOOD AND LODGING ON THE OUTSKIRTS: One of my favorite hotels in the region is the **Polmally House Hotel** (tel. 04562/343). It graciously re-creates the pleasures of manorial country-house living, offering a contemporary kind of style which reflects the sophistication of its owner. According to a packet of letters discovered by Nick and Alison Parsons, the house was probably built in 1776, a year familiar to Americans. The 18-acre estate lies two miles west of Drumnadrochit on the A831. You'll drive between the confines of a beechwood hedge, past magnificent trees, a pond, and an assortment of tamed geese and ducklings before pulling up at the entrance. Inside, a series of plushly furnished rooms, each tastefully filled with well-polished antiques and vases of freshly plucked flowers, create a personalized kind of comfort. Nick worked as a foreign correspondent for Reuters in both Italy and Central America, which explains the tasteful positioning of foreign art with 18th-century Scottish furnishings.

Nine spacious and elegant bedrooms contain high ceilings, leaded-glass windows, flowered wallpaper, and a personalized kind of antique charm. Seven rooms have private bath. Rates, with a Scottish breakfast included, are £25 ($40) in a bathless single and £28 ($44.80) per person in a double or twin with bath. The hotel has a tennis court, a swimming pool, and a croquet lawn flanked with garden statuary. The blue and white restaurant attracts members of the local community as well as hotel residents. Most dishes are prepared by Alison herself, using home-grown eggs and the best of strictly fresh local ingredients. Specialties include pork and chicken liver pâté layered with filets of venison; flaked Arbroath smokie baked with cream and cheese; dill-cured wild salmon with locally smoked wild salmon; fresh salmon steak baked with sherry, cream, and anchovies; and noisettes of spring lamb with fresh herbs and butter. Full à la carte meals cost from £14 ($22.40) per person.

In the vicinity stands the **Lewiston Arms,** Lewiston, near Drumnadrochit (tel. 04562/225), an old whitewashed coaching inn lying just off the principal road in the village of Lewiston. Many motorists prefer to stop off here instead of going on to Inverness. The inn offers only one single and seven doubles, none with private bath. The tariffs are £13 ($20.80) in a single, £24 ($38.40) in a double. You might ask for the half-board rate of £20 ($32) per person nightly, which is very good value. Bedrooms are simply but adequately furnished. Outside is an attractive garden. In all, it's a good center for exploring the Loch Ness area. The place is owned and run by Nicholas and Helen Quinn, a team with a spotless little inn off the fast A82, right beside the castle.

SIGHTS: The village of Drumnadrochit has a big attraction, the **Loch Ness Monster Exhibition** (tel. 04562/573), which opened in 1980 and has been packing them in ever since. You can follow the story from A.D. 565 to the present in pictures, audio, and video, as well as climbing aboard the sonar research vessel, *John Murray*. The Exhibition Centre is now the most visited place in the Highlands of Scotland, with more than 200,000 visitors annually. It is open from 9 a.m. to 9:30 p.m. mid-June to the end of August, from 9:30 a.m. to 8:15 p.m. in spring and fall. However, because of fluctuating hours, telephone in advance if you're planning a winter visit. Admission is £1.65 ($2.64) for adults, 75p ($1.20) for children.

The ruined **Urquhart Castle,** one of Scotland's largest castles, is 1½ miles southeast of Drumnadrochit on a promontory overlooking Loch Ness. The chief of Clan Grant owned the castle in 1509, and most of the existing building dates from that period. In 1692 the castle was blown up by the Grants to prevent its becoming a Jacobite stronghold. It is here at Urquhart Castle that sightings of the Loch Ness monster are most often reported. It is open April to September on weekdays from 9:30 a.m. to 7 p.m. (on Sunday from 2 to 7 p.m.). Off-season its hours are 9:30 a.m. to 4 p.m. on weekdays (from 2 to 4 p.m. on Sunday). Admission charges are £1 ($1.60) for adults and 50p (80¢) for children.

4. Invermoriston

If you stop at this hamlet, you'll be in one of the beauty spots along Loch Ness. Glenmoriston is one of the loveliest glens in the Highlands. You can take walks along the riverbanks, with views of Loch Ness. The location is at the junction of Loch Ness Highway (A82) and the road to the Isle of Skye (A887).

Roderick MacKenzie, a Jacobite officer who sacrificed his life by acting as a decoy for Bonnie Prince Charlie, is commemorated by a roadside cairn at Glenmoriston.

You can see a memorial cairn erected as a tribute to John Cobb, the world-famous racing motorist who died in 1952 while attempting to break the water speed record on the loch.

FOOD AND LODGING: A good place to stay is the **Glenmoriston Arms Hotel** (tel. 0320/51206). Two centuries ago the owners of the local estate built this roadside inn. Today the 17th generation of the original builders is still in charge, the day-to-day management directed by Judith and Robert Shepherd. A drink beside the stone fireplace of the establishment's lounge bar is almost like a huntsman's fantasy. It's a lot like a woodsy, intimate hunting lodge, lined with antique weapons, old trophies, well-polished paneling, and more than 160 varieties of single-malt whiskies. Much of the pleasure of this place comes from the Shepherds, who offer eight attractive bedrooms, six of which contain a private bath and color TV. B&B with private bath costs £40 ($64) in a double, £27 ($43.20) in a single. Without bath, the rate is £20 ($32) in a single, £36 ($57.60) in a double. Its in-house restaurant is highly recommended, specializing in locally caught fish and venison, garnished in season with freshly plucked vegetables. A fixed-price dinner costs from £10 ($16). You'll find the hotel at the junction of the A82 and the A887.

If you're touring along the lake, one of the best places to stop for a meal is **Tigh-na-Bruach** at Glenmoriston (tel. 0320/51208). A former Victorian hunting lodge, it opens directly on the shores of Loch Ness and is set in six acres of landscaped grounds. Mr. and Mrs. Graham Duncan serve meals from noon to 2 p.m. and 5:30 to 9 p.m. seven days a week, costing from £7 ($11.20). You can enjoy such dishes as cannelloni, chicken breast with lobster and prawn sauce, or a 10-ounce sirloin with whisky sauce. All that remained of the lodge after a disastrous fire in 1984 were these rustically decorated stables where a fireplace welcomes you on nippy nights.

5. Fort Augustus

This Highland touring center stands at the head (the southernmost end) of Loch Ness. The town took its name from a fort named for the Duke of Cumberland. Built after the 1715 Rising, the present Benedictine Abbey stands on its site.

FOOD AND LODGING: The sprawling white-painted **Caledonian Hotel** (tel. 0320/6256) is owned by Mrs. Maureen MacLellan and her daughter, Penelope. Initially constructed in 1903, it has been modernized into both a comfortably unpretentious stopover for visitors and a rendezvous point for locals. The Corbie Bar, named after a variety of local blackbird, is a pleasant spot for a drink. This might be followed by a fixed-price meal, costing from £7.50 ($12), in the dining room. There, everything is homemade, from the pâté to the Loch Lochy trout served with a mousseline sauce of butter and herbs, finished off with a chocolate and whisky mousse. B&B costs £12.50 ($20) per person in a bathless room, rising to £14.50 ($23.20) per person with bath. History buffs might be interested in an accommodation in the stone-walled annex (actually a former cottage) which is said to have housed Bonnie Prince Charlie "only a stone's throw from the fort."

The **Lovat Arms** (tel. 0320/6206) stands across the street from the Caledonian Hotel. It is a most desirable accommodation which appears nondescript when approached from the main road through Fort Augustus. However, the view improves considerably when you go around to the front of the building. It is a well-proportioned slate and stone building with plenty of charm. The modernized interior contains a popular lounge bar. Family run, the hotel charges from £17 ($27.20) to £22 ($35.20) in a single ranging up to £32 ($51.20) to £43 ($68.80) in a double. Rooms are most comfortable and pleasantly furnished, and you get a hearty Scottish breakfast. The hotel is known for its good, fresh food, and it also has a well-stocked cellar. Consider the half-board arrangement, a real bargain at only £26 ($41.60) to £31 ($49.60) per person daily.

The **Brae Hotel** (tel. 0320/6289), set on two acres of ground, has a view of Fort Augustus and the Caledonian Canal from its perch on a hill. The resident proprietor, Dileas Leslie, rents eight bedrooms, two with private bathroom and two with shower. Tariffs for B&B are £11.50 ($18.40) per person in a bathless room, £15 ($24) with bath. The hotel is centrally heated, and there is a cocktail bar and an attractive dining room. The lounge and the sun porch afford panoramic views. You can enjoy bar snacks from £1.25 ($2); lunch, either eaten at the hotel or packed to take on excursions, costs from £2.50 ($4); and dinner is £7.50 ($12). You can board a bus to Inverness or to the center of Drumnadrochit right at the foot of the hill.

SIGHTS: Bisecting the village is the **Caledonian Canal,** and the lochs are a popular attraction when boats are passing through. Running across the loftiest sections of Scotland, the canal was constructed between 1803 and 1822. Almost in a straight line, it makes its way from Inverness in the north to Corpach in the vicinity of Fort William. The canal is 60 miles long, 22 of which were made by man. The other part goes through natural lochs. In summer you can take several pleasure craft along this canal, leaving from Fort Augustus.

The **Great Glen Heritage Exhibition,** Canal Side (tel. 0320/6341), is beside the canal's swing bridge in the center of Fort Augustus. This is an open-plan museum dealing with the history of the Scot from Pict to modern Highlander. The center is open daily from 9:30 a.m. to 5 p.m. April to October. Admission is free.

6. Whitebridge

So far, all the properties we've considered lie along the western bank of Loch Ness, the most tourist-trodden section. For escapists who want to venture over to the eastern bank, I have the following tranquil oasis. The location is in the valley of Stratherrick, standing at 600 feet to the south of Loch Ness. Excellent brown trout fishing is available in the area, and outings for salmon and sea trout can be arranged. Birdwatchers are also attracted to the area, especially those interested in birds of prey. The location, about 25 miles south of Inverness, is in the foothills of the Monadhliath mountains.

Whitebridge Hotel at Whitebridge (tel. 04563/226) is a pleasant Victorian house in a tranquil location on the eastern side of Loch Ness. The view from the front porch takes in not only a well-maintained lawn, but the rocky summit of Beinn Sg'urrach, whose correct pronunciation will gladly be given by the resident owners, Douglas and Evelyn Bailey. They rent out a dozen well-furnished bedrooms, each of which has a color TV and coffee-making facilities. Several of their accommodations also have a private bath. The per-person rate, with a big breakfast included, is £16 ($25.60) in a bathless room, rising to £19 ($30.40) with bath. There are two bars and a restaurant to provide good food and drink.

THE FAR NORTH

THIS SECTION OF THE HIGHLANDS is not for everyone. It is the loneliest part of Scotland. But for some, that is part of its undeniable charm. Crumbling watchtowers no longer stand guard except over the sheep-cropped wilderness. Moss-green glens give way to inland lochs and sea fjords.

It is good country for touring if the weather is right. Many relics of Scotland's turbulent past dot the landscape. Castles are left in ruins. Today many potteries, craft centers, and factories in the area encourage visitors. These include silversmithing, stone polishing, glassmaking, and most definitely weaving.

But mostly the visitor comes here for the scenery, which is always intriguing, both along the coastline and inland. In summer the deep-blue lochs and towering cliffs, as well as the gentle glens, are to be enjoyed in the sun.

Most tours of "The Far North" start from Inverness. You can cross the new Kessock Bridge over the Beauly Firth heading for Black Isle, which is my favorite part of the entire northwest.

You can then follow the A9 up the east coast to the cathedral town of Dornoch, which is one of the most interesting centers for overnighting. The next day you can drive through Sutherland heading for Wick and John o' Groats, which is the end of the line for the mainland of Great Britain. Heading west, you pass through Thurso, and from nearby Scrabster you can catch the ferry to the Orkney Islands.

You can continue around the coast to Cape Wrath and Durness, a wild and secluded part of Scotland. Eventually you reach Ullapool, the final destination of this chapter. From Ullapool, you can explore the Outer Hebrides (see Chapter XVIII).

Several of the destinations of this chapter fall within the counties of Sutherland and Caithness, which are just becoming known in international tourism. However, our first stopovers will be in Easter Ross, just a short drive west from Inverness.

1. The Black Isle

This is, in my opinion, one of the most enchanting peninsulas of Scotland, a land rich in history, beauty, and mystery. Part of Ross & Cromarty, it lies north of Inverness, and a car tour of it is about 37 miles. But allow plenty of time for stopovers along the way.

There is much confusion about its name, because it is neither black nor an island. In summer the land is actually green and fertile, and tropical plants flourish here. It's filled with forests, fields of broom and whin, and scattered coastal villages. No one seems to agree on how it got its name, so I'll avoid all the various controversies.

What is known is that the "isle" or peninsula has been inhabited for 7,000 years, as 60-odd prehistoric sites testify to this day. Pictish kings, whose thrones passed down through the female line, once ruled this land. The Vikings held sway, and the evidence of many Gallows Hills testify that justice was harsh.

WHERE TO STAY AND EAT: There are choices available around the peninsula. I'll begin—

At Fortrose

Royal Hotel, Union Street (tel. 0381/20236), overlooks the ancient monument of Fortrose Cathedral. Despite the traditional exterior, the establishment has been tastefully redecorated inside, with two bars, a dining room, a residents' lounge, and 11 bedrooms. Double or twin accommodations rent from £14.50 ($23.20) per person, with singles going for £17.50 ($28), all tariffs including breakfast. Family rooms are also available. One of the resident proprietors of this hotel, run by the Stephens family, is the chef who produces high-quality meals for residents and nonresidents alike.

At Rosemarkie

Marine Hotel (tel. 0381/20253). This palatial building was constructed of red sandstone around 1830 by a local landowner. Since then it has been enlarged and adapted into an old-world kind of hotel, rich with Victorian proportions and awash with sea breezes and sunlight from its panoramic windows. The approximately 50 bedrooms can be booked between April and September. Guests relax in one of the large lounges set aside for their use, or else they gravitate to the darkly furnished pub, with its iron stove and antique weapons. Rates at the Marine depend on the season and the plumbing, set at £15 ($24) to £19 ($30.40) per person for B&B. With dinner included, prices are £23 ($36.80) to £30 ($48) per person. Children under 12 receive discounts of up to 50%. Bathing, sailing, tennis, and golf can all be arranged through the reception desk.

The Plough Inn, High Street (tel. 0381/20164), is one of the most prominently positioned buildings in this hamlet. It was originally constructed as a private house, but today its tall and narrow facade contains a comfortably modernized restaurant and lounge bar, plus a pub catering mainly to the local trade. Meals are served in the lounge bar at both lunch and dinner, costing from

£5 ($8). The MacMillans serve "Taste of Scotland" food, making use of produce from their own garden and of meats of local origin, together with other home-grown ingredients. In season, you can sample the fresh salmon caught off the beach at Rosemarkie. There is a garden eating area and a playground behind the pub by a stream. The pub is open from 11 a.m. to 11 p.m., and hot food is served from noon to 2 p.m. and 6:30 to 9 p.m.

At Cromarty

The **Royal Hotel** (tel. 03817/217). The only hotel in town sits on an embank-ment near one of the deepest estuaries in Europe. Around 1940 the British navy combined a series of waterfront buildings, including a bonding warehouse and several private houses, into living quarters for sailors. Today the hotel is a com-fortably cozy enclave alive with woodburning stoves and open fireplaces. It is directed by Stewart and Betty Morrison. There's a comfortable lounge bar, plus a public bar and a panoramic dining room that spills onto a glassed-in extension opening onto the harbor. Rooms, all with baths, rent for £15.50 ($24.80) per person. A fixed-price evening meal is another £10 ($16). You can also enjoy a good bar menu, with a tempting list of burgers, crêpes, and salads; light meals cost from £2.50 ($4).

Le Chardon, Church Street (tel. 03817/471), celebrates the "Auld Alli-ance" between France and Scotland—French flair and quality Scottish produce are perfectly blended into a successful French nouvelle cuisine, which is surpris-ing to encounter in such a sleepy hamlet. Mena and Robyn Aitchison, the own-ers, operate their attractive little bistro—outlined in a mulberry color—within an easy walk of Hugh Miller's Cottage. There they turn out such delectable dishes as a ragoût of beef with pecans, sauté liver marsala, sole with tartar sauce, and for dessert, crème de menthe cheesecake. These dishes only suggest their vast repertoire, as the menu changes daily. Dinners, served Tuesday through Sunday from 7:30 to 10 p.m., cost from £14 ($22.40). Reservations are neces-sary. Lunch is served only on Sunday from noon to 2 p.m., costing £8.50 ($13.60).

SIGHTS: If you're touring the island, your first goal might be **Fortrose.** Along the way you'll pass a celebrated wishing well or "clootie well," which is fes-tooned with rags. Dedicated to St. Boniface, the well has a long tradition, dating back to pagan times. It is said that anyone removing a rag will inherit the misfor-tunes of the person who placed it there.

In the sleepy village of Fortrose stand the ruins of **Fortrose Cathedral,** which can be visited free on weekdays April to September from 9:30 a.m. to 7 p.m. (on Sunday from 2 to 7 p.m.). Off-season it is open from 9:30 a.m. to 4 p.m. weekdays and on Sunday from 2 to 4 p.m. Founded in the 13th century, it was dedicated to St. Peter and St. Boniface. There is still some fine detailing from the 14th century, left I might add, after Cromwell's men removed many of its stones to help build a fort at Inverness. The famous Brahan Seer was sen-tenced to death here. Lady Seaforth had him dipped head first into a spiked barrel of boiling tar after he'd revealed her husband's indiscretions with the prostitutes of Paris.

Fortrose adjoins **Rosemarkie,** up the road. The site of Rosemarkie has been inhabited since the Bronze Age, and it once was far more important than it is today. A center of Pictish culture, it saw the arrival of the first Christian mis-sionaries. It is reported that St. Moluag founded a monastery here in the sixth century. Rosemarkie became a royal burgh in 1216. The twin hamlets share a golf course today, and they are the site of the Chanonry Sailing Club, whose annual regatta brings entries from all over Scotland.

Right beyond Rosemarkie is the mysterious **Fairy Glen,** said to have been the home of "the black witch."

Cromarty stands at the tip of the peninsula where the North and South Sutars guard the entrance to the Cromarty Firth, the second-deepest inland waterway estuary in Europe, always considered of strategic importance to the Royal Navy. Once a flourishing port and a former royal burgh, the town gave the world a famous son: Hugh Miller. **Hugh Miller's Cottage,** on Church Street (tel. 03817/245), is on view to the public today, containing many of his personal belongings and collections of geological specimens. It is open from the third week of April until the end of September from 10 a.m. to noon and 1 to 5 p.m. June to September it is also open on Sunday from 2 to 5 p.m. Admission is 80p ($1.28) for adults and 40p (64¢) for children. Born here in 1802, Miller was a stonemason as a young man. But in time he became a recognized expert in the field of geology, as well as a powerful man of letters in Scotland. His thatched cottage was built in 1711.

2. Muir of Ord

This small town to the west of Inverness, in the vicinity of Beauly, makes a good touring center for a history-rich part of Scotland. If you stay at the recommendation below, you can branch out on day excursions in many directions, taking in not only Loch Ness, Sutherland, Inverness, and the Black Isle, but branching farther afield if that is your desire. Sportsmen are attracted to the region as it offers good fishing, roe and red deer stalking, golfing, and shooting.

FOOD AND LODGING: I like to stay at the **Ord House Hotel** (tel. 0463/870492), an undeniably charming country hotel. Several generations ago the ancestors of the present owners, the Calders, left northern Scotland for India. They returned to Muir of Ord when the British withdrew, setting up a hotel in a house built in 1602 by a local laird of the MacKenzie family. The gracefully proportioned house sits in the midst of a 30-acre parkland, awash with flowering shrubs and duck ponds. The Calders have entertained everybody from an archbishop to the head of an Apache Indian tribe. Drinks are served nightly beside an open fireplace in a paneled salon whose thick walls are set with bull's-eye glass. You'll find vases of flowers, labyrinthine hallways, and antique rifles. The decor was done with both charm and humor. Eight of the well-furnished bedrooms contain a private bath. The half-board rate is £28 ($44.80) per person in a bathless room, going up to £32 ($51.20) per person with private bath. Reservations are important here, and the hotel is open only between April and October.

3. Beauly

The French monks who settled here in the 13th century named it literally "beautiful place," and it still is. The ruins of **Beauly Priory** which the monks built can still be visited. Beauly lies some 12 miles west of Inverness on the A862. You'll see the Highland Craftpoint on your left as you come from Inverness. In summer, they have an interesting exhibition of Scottish handcrafts.

FOOD AND LODGING: A red sandstone building, the **Priory Hotel,** The Square (tel. 0463/782309), is directly on the historic main square of town, a short walk from the ruins of the priory. The century-old building was originally constructed as a grocery store. Today its attractively modernized interior houses live musical bands every Friday, Saturday, and Sunday night (also Sunday afternoon). The restaurant and bar are good choices for savory meals in a plush contemporary setting. You'll find an array of grills and steaks, with full meals costing from £8 ($12.80). All of the 12 comfortably furnished bedrooms contain private baths, phones, and TV. Rates run £23.50 ($37.60) in a single and £20 ($32) per person in a double, with breakfast included. The staff, directed by Stuart and Eveline Hutton, do everything they can to make you feel at home.

Chrialdon (tel. 0463/782336) is a charming country guesthouse near Beauly, run by John and Valerie Hodgson. In a restored Victorian house, they rent impeccably clean rooms at a price of £9.50 ($15.20) per person, including a satisfying breakfast. If you're lucky—and tired of bacon and eggs—Mrs. Hodgson might even make you French toast. A good dinner is served for £6.50 ($10.40).

SIGHTS AND SHOPPING: Dating from 1230, the **Beauly Priory** is the only remaining one of three priories constructed for the Valliscaulian order, an austere body deriving its main components from the Cistercians and the Carthusians. Some notable windows and window arcading can still be seen in the ruins. Hugh Fraser of Lovat erected the Chapel of the Holy Cross on the nave's north side in the early 15th century. The ruins are open from 9:30 a.m. to 7 p.m. April to September. In the off-season, hours are from 9:30 a.m. to 4 p.m. weekdays, 2 to 4 p.m. on Sunday (closed all day Monday and Tuesday morning). Admission is 50p (80¢) for adults, 25p (40¢) for children.

On the south bank of the River Beauly southwest of the town is **Beaufort Castle,** a 19th-century baronial mansion which is the seat of the Frasers of Lovat, whose ancestor was the "Lovat of the Forty-five." The original seat of the Lovats was Castle Dounie, built about 1400, but it was destroyed by "Butcher" Cumberland after his victory at Culloden.

If you're interested in tweeds, don't miss **Campbell & Company's Highland House of Tweed** (tel. 0463/782239), operated by the same family since 1856. An excellent selection of fine tweeds and tartans is offered, and you can have your material faultlessly tailored if you wish. Blankets, travel rugs, tweed hats (deerstalkers and fishing hats), and kilts are sold here, as well as sweaters in cashmere and lambswool. Shetland knits can be found here also. The establishment is open from 9 a.m. to 1 p.m. and 2 to 5:30 p.m. Monday to Saturday (closing at 1 p.m. on Thursday).

4. Strathpeffer

This is a resort that has known greater days. One reader once wrote, "Deathly quiet, with an older clientele, it is somewhat hard to believe that it isn't 1920." At a location six miles west of Dingwall, Strathpeffer is coming more and more back in the news, with the revived interest in the Victorian era.

It makes a good center for touring Easter Ross, where the countryside is dominated by the 3,433-foot summit of **Ben Wyvis.**

One of the few spas of Scotland, Strathpeffer reached the pinnacle of its vogue in the 19th century. The English gentry came north for the healing properties they found in the sulfur and chalybeate springs. In time they were followed by the aristocrats of Europe and, later still, the industrial barons of an emerging America.

When the enthusiasm for "taking the waters" waned, Strathpeffer went into a long slumber. But because of that slumber, it emerges as an interesting period relic today.

FOOD AND LODGING: The most imposing hostelry in town, the **Highland Hotel** (tel. 0997/21457), is a turn-of-the-century giant sitting on a hillside overlooking the town square. It's characterized by pagoda-like towers and a long, colonnaded balcony. It could easily be confused with similar hotels in the Swiss

Alps because of its gables and elaborate roofline. But inside, you'll find the ambience distinctly Scottish. The owners spent thousands of pounds to refinish the acres of paneling that cover the pub and the enormous reception hall. There, guests congregate after dinner, sometimes heading in groups of twos and threes to the settees scattered over the sweeping front veranda. Much of the establishment's clientele is elderly, many of whom arrive as part of motorcoach tours from other parts of Britain. If you decide to stay here in one of the 127 bedrooms, your recently refurbished accommodation will offer straightforward and simple comforts, lots of space, and several amenities. Rooms with private baths cost £24 ($38.40) to £35 ($56) in a single, £19 ($30.40) to £30 ($48) per person in a double, depending on the accommodation and the season.

    Timaru House Hotel (tel. 0997/21251). The facade of this blue-and-white Victorian house looks like a Westerner's fantasy of a Russian dacha. The railings are composed of delicately cast iron, and the eaves are partially concealed by an elaborate array of architectural gingerbread. It was built in 1870 by a New Zealander of Scottish descent, who named it after a sheep-herding region of New Zealand where he had made his fortune. The building was established as one of Strathpeffer's first guesthouses in 1910. Today its ten bathless rooms are maintained by Ian and Helen Robb, who have modernized parts of the interior into a contemporary collection of parlors, sitting rooms, and an airy dining room. B&B is priced at £12 ($19.20) per person, and half board costs £20 ($32) per person. The licensed hotel offers special rates for children, and is open all year. Gardeners will appreciate the elaborate care the Robbs take with their flower garden in the sloping front lawn.

A DOLL MUSEUM: Mrs. Angela Kellie invites visitors to her **Museum of Dolls,** Spa Cottage, The Square (tel. 0997/21549), which contains a permanent display of dolls and teddy bears. In summer, Mrs. Kellie demonstrates spinning in the entrance hall. She also runs a dolls' hospital at her home.

SUTHERLAND

    It's been called the "gem of Scotland." It's got more sheep than people (20 to 1), and is probably the least-written-about area of Scotland, but its devotees (and not just the local residents) maintain that it is the most beautiful county in Scotland. Adding to the scenic sweep of haunting beauty are lochs and rivers, heather-covered moors and mountains—in all 2,000 square miles of territory. The Duke of Sutherland used to own most of it.

    It is a country of quiet pleasures, as it offers few amusements in the conventional sense, except such sporting activities as golf and fishing. It is an ancient unspoiled landscape that has witnessed a turbulent history.

    To the northwest of Inverness, Sutherland has three coastlines—to the north and west, the Atlantic; to the east, the North Sea. Most villages you'll pass through have populations of only a hundred or so hearty souls, a refreshing change of pace in an overpopulated world. Sutherland was the scene of the notorious Highland clearances that left the county virtually to the sheep, as many of its residents made their way to the New World where many thousands went on to greater prosperity. The sheep, known as "the white plague," took over after their departure. One critic called the dislocation of the people of Sutherland in the 19th century "an orgy of ruthless social engineering." In many a deserted glen you can still see traces of former crofting villages.

    Bonarbridge is the gateway to Sutherland (see Ardgay, below). The ubiquitous Thomas Telford was the first to bridge the Kyle of Sutherland in 1812, but his construction was washed away in 1892. The present bridge is said to retain some of the style of the original Telford design.

The most interesting stopover in Sutherland is the ancient cathedral city of Dornoch, and the major man-made sightseeing attraction is Dunrobin Castle, which can easily be reached while headquartering at Dornoch. The turf of the Royal Dornoch Golf Club has been called "sacred" by aficionados. Golf was first played there in 1616!

If you're seeking an inland stopover, I'd suggest Lairg, which every summer witnesses the biggest one-day lamb sale in the country.

North from Lairg along the A836 you cross high moors and brooding peaks until you come to Tongue.

For the nature lover there is much here, ranging from the mighty cliffs of Clo Mor, near Cape Wrath (known for its large colonies of puffins), to waterfalls such as Eas-Coul-Aulin (the highest in Britain) and the Falls of Shin, where you can see salmon leap. Masses of land suddenly rise from a barren landscape, including Ben Loyal, known as the "queen of Scottish mountains."

5. Ardgay

This might be your first stopover if you're heading northwest from Inverness into the relatively unexplored (at least by Americans) northwest corner of Scotland.

Across from Bonarbridge, Ardgay opens onto Dornoch Firth. Apart from the road on the west coast, all roads in the north lead to and from Ardgay, which stands 35 miles to the north of Inverness.

The place is for the more adventurous tourist, and this includes geologists, archeologists, ornithologists, fishermen, and golfers. These people seem to appreciate the rivers, lochs, hills, glens, and rugged mountains that can be explored from Ardgay. A nine-hole golf course is at Bonarbridge, and there is a championship course at Royal Dornoch, 12 miles away.

FOOD AND LODGING: Built to withstand the elements, the **Croit Mairi Guest House** (tel. 08632/504) is simple and functional on the outside. Inside, it is made warm and inviting by the hospitality of Ian and Win Brinklow, who offer six bedrooms for rent. To protect against the cold, their home is centrally heated, the windows double glazed. The building was constructed on the site of an old Highland croft, which has been incorporated into the modern guesthouse. Bedrooms are comfortably furnished and contain shaver points and hot and cold running water. There are two bathrooms with showers for guests. Rates for B&B are £9 ($14.40) per person, rising to £14 ($22.40) per person for half board. All units are twin or double, except for one family accommodation with three beds. The Brinklows are noted for their good home-cooked food and wine (ever had a bottle of Scottish wine?). Their breakfasts are hearty fare, enough to fortify you for a day's touring. The location is about a mile from the Ardgay train station, and half a mile off the A9. A pot of tea will be served shortly after you arrive, and you can slowly take in the view of the Dornoch Firth and the Kyle of Sutherland.

6. Dornoch

Village-like Dornoch is the major town of Sutherland, and has long been known for its **Royal Dornoch Golf Club,** the most northerly first-class course in the world. It is also a good base for exploring Dunrobin Castle (see below), the major attraction in the area. On the sheltered shores of Dornoch Firth, the cathedral town also attracts tourists in summer to its beaches.

Built in the 13th century, **Dornoch Cathedral** was sacked during the Reformation. Its founder was Gilbert, Archdeacon of Moray and Bishop of Caithness. It has seen many restorations, including one in 1924, but its fine

13th-century stonework can still be seen. The cathedral houses the marble tomb of the first Duke of Sutherland, who died in 1833. It is open daily from 9 a.m. to dusk.

FOOD AND LODGING: One of the most unusual hotels in northern Scotland, the **Dornoch Castle Hotel** (tel. 0862/810216), is contained within the massive walls of what used to be the residence of the bishops of Caithness. It was built of local stone in the center of town in the late 15th or early 16th century. Today its winding stairs, labyrinthine corridors, and impenetrable cellars have been converted into a well-directed hotel and restaurant. My favorite place is the high-ceilinged stone-walled pub, whose windows filter the music from the Saturday-night bagpipe concerts held in summer on the town square. Long before the hotel was taken over by a Scotsman, Michael Ketchin, and his Netherlands-born wife, Patricia, the room served as a courtroom for ecclesiastical trials. Nowadays hunting trophies instead of crucifixes adorn the massive stone walls.

Because some of the 22 bedrooms were recently added, the architectural style differs from room to room. Most of the accommodations contain a private bath, and many rooms benefit from views of a statue of Peter Pan that a former owner placed as a centerpiece in the rear garden. Prices vary with the season and the plumbing. Doubles or twins begin at a low of £40 ($64), going up to £60 ($96). Singles are priced from £19 ($30.40) to £26 ($41.60). You can enjoy a fixed-price dinner for £11 ($17.60) up in the stone-walled dining room. Menu specialties include such items as roast Angus beef with Yorkshire pudding, and several kinds of steak, including filet of Angus beef Balmoral style (in a red wine and whisky sauce with asparagus). You might also enjoy Sutherland lobster Hebridean style in a cheese and Drambuie sauce. Table reservations are suggested, and the hotel is open from April to October.

Burghfield House Hotel (tel. 0862/810212). The English steelmaker who built this house for his bride in 1895 asked that it contain only three enormous bedrooms. Later, Lord Rothermere, owner of London's *Daily Mail*, adapted it to his own use in the 1920s before selling it to the Currie family in 1946. Today the establishment contains 46 bedrooms, most of them in a new wing and an annex stretching along the flowerbeds of a five-acre park. Depending on the season, tulips and other seasonal flowers bloom inside the iron pots near the entrance. About half the bedrooms contain private bath, and all the units are comfortable and well furnished. The half-board rate is £28 ($44.80) to £38 ($60.80) per person, and guests are accepted from April to mid-October. Inside you are likely to find a fire blazing. You can relax in the lounge bar, then wander through the gardens filled with rhododendrons and beech hedges. The original Victorian core of the building has a slate roof capped with iron thistles and Celtic crosses.

For food or shopping, try the **Dornoch Craft Centre** (tel. 0862/810555), next to the Dornoch Castle Hotel in the center of town. The present-day center occupies the floors of what was the town jail dating from 1844. You can wander through the selection of Scottish crafts, jewelry, and pottery, then visit the Textile Hall and browse through the range of knitwear, tartans, mohair goods, and tweeds. On the top floor is a small coffeeshop selling sandwiches and drinks, with light snacks costing from £1.25 ($2). The center is open weekdays from 9 a.m. to 5 p.m., and stays open on Sunday July to the end of September.

7. Golspie

Today a family resort with a golf course, Golspie was once part of the vast holdings of the Earls and Dukes of Sutherland. The town, lying on the A9 road, looks out across the water to the Dornoch Firth. A crescent of sandy beach is an attraction to visitors.

FOOD AND LODGING: In a row of residential houses overlooking the sandy beaches, the **Golf Links Hotel** (tel. 04083/3408) is the last building. Constructed of stone, the house contains ten well-furnished bedrooms with private baths. Depending on the season, B&B costs £17.50 ($28) to £19.50 ($31.20) per person. A first-class chef prepares the varied Scottish and continental menu served in a dining room opening onto a view of Ben Bhraggie. A fixed-price dinner goes for £9 ($14.40), or you can order à la carte. The contemporary lounge bar looks through big plate-glass windows onto Dornoch Firth. Bar lunches are served daily around noon. Much of the establishment's clientele is made up of golfers drawn to the nearby Golspie course, on which they receive a 25% reduction in greens fees. A handful of self-service units is in the annex, which also has a hairdressing salon.

DUNROBIN CASTLE: Golspie is visited chiefly because of a towering attraction half a mile northeast on the A9 road, **Dunrobin Castle** (tel. 04083/3177), home of the Earls and Dukes of Sutherland. It is the most northerly of the great houses of Scotland, and also the biggest in the northern Highlands. In her *Highland Journal* (1872), Queen Victoria described it as "a mixture of an old Scotch [sic] castle and French château." Dating in part from the early 15th century, it is an impressive sight, whose formal gardens are laid out in the manner of Versailles. On the grounds is a museum overlooking these gardens, containing many relics from the Sutherland family. Trophies and regimental colors of the 93rd Sutherland Highlanders are on view. They formed the celebrated "thin red line" at the 1854 Battle of Balaclava. Of the castle's 180 rooms, only 18 are open to the public. Others form the apartments of the Countess of Sutherland and her son, Lord Alistair Strathnaver, while many rooms are empty. Among the sections to be seen are an ornately furnished dining room, a billiard room-cum-family museum, and the room and gilded four-poster bed occupied by Queen Victoria when she visited in 1872.

The castle is open mid-June to mid-September from 10:30 a.m. to 5:30 p.m. Monday to Saturday. Admission is £2 ($3.20) for adults, £1 ($1.60) for children.

8. Lairg

Lairg is the most central village from which to tour the far north of Scotland. It lies 22 miles west of Dornoch along the A839. An angling center on Loch Shin, it has important hydro schemes. From here you can explore not only the coastal attractions, but the wide, open spaces of central Sutherland. You can also visit such local beauty spots as the Falls of Shin, on the River Shin between Lairg and Invershin. They are well known as a salmon leap.

FOOD AND LODGING: The most elegant place to stay in central Sutherland, at surprisingly affordable prices, is **Achany House** (tel. 0549/2433), a castle with two towers that lies outside Lairg. This 18th-century mansion, at the edge of the Shin forest, is still very much a family home, as reflected by its sometimes lavish interior, with fireplaces, well-upholstered sofas, library shelves, antiques, gilt-framed mirrors, and ancestral portraits. It attracts lovers of the tranquil life as well as sportsmen interested in such active pursuits as riding, fishing, and shooting. During the day you can easily drive far afield for golfing and beaching. The six bedrooms, four with private baths or showers, are well furnished and attractively maintained, costing from £19 ($30.40) to £23 ($36.80) per person for

B&B. It's best to stay here on the half-board arrangement, priced at £29.50 ($47.20) to £33.50 ($53.60) per person. The food is reason enough to stop over, combining the best of the "tastes" of Scotland and England, including the best beef and salmon, as well as venison in season. The gracious hospitality extended here can make for a memorable stay.

Aultnagar Lodge Hotel (tel. 054982/245) translates in English as "The Laughing Burn." Originally it was a hunting lodge built by the millionaire and philanthropist, Andrew Carnegie. A half-timbered structure, it rises 300 yards from the main A836 Bonar Bridge–Lairg road. Standing on about two dozen acres of woodland, it opens onto the Kyle of Sutherland, set against a backdrop of mountains. Run casually and informally, it is modestly furnished. Life here is relaxed and tranquil—that is, unless it's Scottish night and a local pipe band comes in to play. Guests can relax in the residents' lounge or enjoy a malt whisky in the cocktail bar. Original tapestry covers the lounge walls, and a log fire is a cozy gathering place. Most of the major bedrooms have their own bath, some opening onto views. The hosts charge £16.50 ($26.40) to £23 ($36.80) per person for B&B. The food is good, whenever possible using local produce. You might book in here on half-board terms, paying £27 ($43.20) to £34 ($54.40) per person per night. Guests are received from April to October.

9. Tongue

If you head north from Lairg along the A836, you will eventually reach the curiously named port town of Tongue, which is one of the best centers for those wanting a base to explore this dramatic and rocky coastline of Sutherland. On the way there, you'll cross lofty moors guarded over by the often misty peaks of Ben Hope and Ben Loyal.

Tongue opens onto the Kyle of Tongue, which has sandy beaches and good fishing.

West of Tongue on a promontory stand the ruins of **Castle Varrich,** said to have been built by the Vikings. Possibly dating from the 14th century, this castle was the Mackay stronghold. In fact many Mackays from North America visit Tongue annually seeking some legend and lore about their ancestral roots.

Tongue House, from 1678, was also a home base for the chief of the Mackays, but it is now owned by the estate of the Duke of Sutherland. On the shores of the Kyle on Tongue, it has a walled garden and is open to the public only on a Sunday in August.

FOOD AND LODGING: The best place to stop over in town has been the **Tongue Hotel** (tel. 084755/206) ever since Victoria's day. Opening onto the Kyle of Tongue, the hotel still possesses some of its initial character and antiques. The Robertson family are gracious Highland hosts, and are usually eager to tell you of nearby attractions, including fishing the local lochs and rivers. In fact, at the entrance is a pair of scales on which you can weigh your catch of the day. Comfortable bedrooms, most of which have private baths, rent for £15.50 ($24.80) to £18.50 ($29.60) per person for B&B. For a room with private bath, add another £5 ($8) per person. The hotel has a cocktail bar and good food, including Scottish salmon and lamb, along with a fine wine list. Dinners cost from £10.50 ($16.80). Guests are accepted from April to October.

Ben Loyal Hotel (tel. 084755/216) is another good choice, everything under the careful attention of Ian Pattinson, who receives guests throughout the year except in December and January when Tongue gets very quiet indeed. He rents a total of 13 pleasantly furnished bedrooms at rates ranging from £15 ($24) to £19 ($30.40) per person for B&B. The half-board tariff is £20 ($32) to £25 ($40) per person nightly. Six of the bedrooms in the centrally heated hotel have private baths. An attractive bungalow annex, containing another six units, is open from May to September. All the accommodations have hot and cold water basins, electric blankets, and shaver points. The lounge, dining room, and Castle Varrich wing have views of Ben Loyal (the mountain for which the hotel was named) and out to the Kyle of Tongue. Good home cooking is served, with emphasis on the best local meat and fish, plus the hotel's own garden produce in season. A fine wine list complements meals. The Ben Bar is a convivial spot to relax and try the malt or blended Scotch whisky. The Ben Loyal Hotel structures incorporate 19th-century stables, a former post office, a shop, and a village bakery.

CAITHNESS

It doesn't look like the Highlands at all, but Caithness is the most northerly county of mainland Scotland. You won't find rugged mountains here; rather, the landscape is filled with gentle, rolling land. At many points vistas open onto the Pentland Firth.

Caithness is ancient—in fact, within its 700 square miles you'll find signs of the Stone Age. The Grey Cairns of Camster, still enigmatic, are an example of archeology from 4000 B.C. The county is filled with not only cairns, but mysterious stone rows and circles, along with standing stones. It has many churches from the Middle Ages, as well as towering castles on cliff tops. The Queen Mother's home, Castle of Mey, dating from 1570, lies between John o' Groats and Thurso.

The Vikings once occupied this place, with its rock stacks, old harbors, craggy cliffs, and quiet coves, and many place names are in Old Norse. Rich in bird and animal life, Caithness is unspoiled country. Sportsmen are drawn to the area, finding the wild brown trout in some 100 lochs, along with salmon in such rivers as the Thurso and the Wick.

Most people head for Caithness, with John o' Groats as their final destination. John o' Groats, with its many souvenir shops, is popularly called the extreme northern tip of the British mainland. Actually, Dunnet Head is farther north by a few miles.

Others drive all the way to Scrabster where there is a ferry harbor. This is the main car-and-passenger service which operates all year to the Orkney Islands. There are day trips on Monday and Thursday in summer.

10. Wick

This famous old herring port opens onto the eastern coastline of Caithness. It is a popular stopping-over point for those heading north to explore what is often called the John o' Groats Peninsula. Wick has some claim as a holiday resort as well.

Robert Louis Stevenson spent part of his boyhood in Wick when his father worked here on a project. Today a sleepy nostalgia hangs over the town.

FOOD AND LODGING: Lying only 200 yards from the harbor, the **Harbour Guest House,** 6 Rose St. (tel. 0955/3276), is one of the finest in town. That is, if you can get in, as it offers only ten rooms which fill up quickly in the summer season. A traditional stone cottage, it has been successfully converted to receive paying guests, who share the two public bathrooms. Open all year, the guesthouse charges a modest £9.50 ($15.20) per person for B&B.

Breadalbane Guest House, Breadalbane Crescent (tel. 0955/3312), stands on a residential street a few hundred yards above the center of town. This elegant Victorian building retains many 19th-century accents. You register in a tall-ceilinged hallway with dark wood paneling. Later you are shown to one of the five bedrooms (one set aside for families) which share the one public bath. Guests are received all year, paying from £9 ($14.40) per person for B&B.

If you'd like more modern and more expensive accommodations, head for the **Ladbroke Mercury Motor Inn,** Riverside (tel. 0955/3344). The motor inn provides the most up-to-date accommodation in the area, and you can use it as a base for exploring John o' Groats in the north. It rents out nearly 50 accommodations, each well furnished with many amenities, at a rate of £50 ($80) in a double and £35 ($56) in a single. Each centrally heated bedroom has its own color TV, coffee-making facilities, and well-maintained private bath. Some family rooms with bunk beds are rented as well. In this far-northern outpost, you can make a selection of malt whiskies in the lounge bar, later enjoying a good dinner in the inn's restaurant, where both continental and Scottish fare are served. The inn is open all year.

SIGHTS: Most visitors will want to seek out **Caithness Glass,** Harrowhill (tel. 0955/2286), the factory where you can watch the blowing of glass, touring the glasshouse. Glassmaking is from 9 a.m. to 4:30 p.m. Monday to Friday. The shop and cafeteria are open from 9 a.m. to 5 p.m. Monday to Friday, from 9 a.m. to 1 p.m. on Saturday (to 4 p.m. on Saturday June to September).

The **Wick Heritage Centre,** 20 Bank Row (tel. 0955/4179), can also be visited. It has many exhibitions pertaining to the herring-fishing industry in Wick in days of yore. You can also see farm implements from Caithness. It is open June to September from 10:30 a.m. to 12:30 p.m. and 2 to 5 p.m. Monday to Saturday. Admission is £1 ($1.60) for adults, 50p (80¢) for children.

In the environs you can visit the **Grey Cairns of Camster,** mentioned in the introduction. These two megalithic cairns lie six miles north of Lybster on the Watten Road, off the A9.

The ruins of the **Castle of Old Wick** are also worth exploring. The location is off the A9, a mile and a half south of Wick. Once known as Castle Olipant, the ruined structure dates back to the 14th century.

If you like castle ruins, you may also want to seek out the **Castles Sinclair and Girnigoe,** three miles north of Wick. Follow the airport road in the direction of the Noss Head Lighthouse. These adjacent castles were built on the edge of a cliff overlooking the Bay of Sinclair. At one time they were the strongholds of the Sinclairs, the Earls of Caithness. The older structure, Girnigoe, dates from the latter 1400s; Sinclair was constructed in the early years of the 17th century. By 1679 both castles had been deserted and were allowed to fall into ruins.

11. John o' Groats

For those who wanted to go to Land's End at the tip of the Cornish peninsula in England, John o' Groats is the northern equivalent. Tourists are fond of having their pictures taken at the "Last House," standing at the end of the A9. From John o' Groats there are views north to the Orkney Islands and the Pentland Firth. Once you get there, there isn't much. But that doesn't stop intrepid visitors from making the trip, if only to say they've been there.

John o' Groats is named after a Dutch ferryman, Jan de Groot. His tombstone can still be seen at Cabisbay Church. Many visitors like to walk along the coast, going to Duncansby Head and along to the great Stacks. The town abounds in souvenir shops, some selling Groatie buckies, or small Arctic cowrie shells once used as decoration by the first settlers on Caithness.

In the summer months you can take a seven-day passenger-only ferry service to Orkney. Bus tours of the island are included. The Orkney Islands are just a 45-minute sail from John o' Groats across the Pentland Firth.

FOOD AND LODGING: The famous and much-photographed **John o' Groats House Hotel** (tel. 095581/203) is the most northerly such establishment on the British mainland. Its oldest part dates from 1850. Like the town, the hotel overlooks the Pentland Firth and the Orkney Islands. You can make this family-run place your base for touring Caithness. The hotel has 17 comfortably furnished rooms, only three of which have private baths. The rate for B&B is £16 ($25.60) to £21 ($33.60) per person.

    Seaview Hotel (tel. 095581/220) is an alternate choice. A small nine-room hotel, it lies outside the town center. You get a friendly welcome as you're shown to your comfortable room, which is reasonably priced at £13 ($20.80) to £15 ($24) per person for B&B. All accommodations have tea-making equipment, hot and cold running water, and electric blankets. Some contain private showers are well. Good food is served, with home-baking and farm produce. The hotel is open year round.

12. Thurso

Motorists pass through this northern port heading for adjacent Scrabster where they can board ferries year round for the Orkney Islands. There isn't much to do in Thurso itself except visit the ruins of **St. Peter's Church,** near the harbor. The church was from the Middle Ages, but what you see today is mainly from the 17th century. The ruins are to be found in the old restored district of Thurso.

    There is a golf course nearby, and to the north the cliffs of Holborn Head and Dunnet Head, which boasts a lighthouse. A nuclear energy establishment was installed to the west at Dounreay.

FOOD AND LODGING: A modern and well-kept hostelry in town is the **Pentland Hotel,** Princes Street (tel. 0847/63202), run by Uisdean and Flora Maclean, who take some of the chill off the weather not only by their friendly welcome but also with their central heating as well. This fully licensed hotel, which is open all year, has 56 well-furnished bedrooms, 34 of which contain private bath. Depending on the plumbing, singles range from £15 ($24) to £23 ($36.80), with doubles going for £25 ($40) to £36 ($57.60) nightly. The atmosphere is casual and relaxing. You are served good food nightly until 8:30 p.m., with fresh fish, lamb, and beef featured.

    Motorists may want to drive out to the **Banniskirk House,** at Banniskirk on the A895 (tel. 084783/609), a Victorian mansion standing on 20 acres of forested land. A tranquil spot, it is about seven miles from Thurso and the ferries to the Orkney Islands. From March to October, rooms are rented costing from £11 ($17.60) per person for B&B. An evening dinner is offered for £7.50 ($12). Fishing on the loch or river can be arranged.

13. Ullapool

If you continue along the northern coastline of Scotland, you will leave Caithness and reenter Sutherland, passing by Tongue and other ports. For most motorists, their ultimate destination is Ullapool, 60 miles northwest of Inverness.

    However, most visitors come from Inverness. The road from Inverness to Ullapool takes you through the wild Northwest Highlands, and once you reach Ullapool a car-ferry from there will deposit you at Stornaway on Lewis, one of the islands of the Outer Hebrides. On an arm of the sea called Loch Broom, Ullapool has long been an embarkation point for travelers crossing the Minch, a section of the North Atlantic separating Scotland from the Outer Hebrides.

Ullapool is an interesting village, the largest in Wester Ross. It was built by the British Fishery Society in 1788 as a port for herring fishermen, and it is still a busy harbor. The original town plan has not been changed, and many of the original buildings stand much as they were at the time of their construction, although mellower and more weatherbeaten.

A short drive south to Gairloch takes you into the heart of Wester Ross, with its splendid scenery, mountains, and Atlantic seascape.

FOOD AND LODGING: One of the most charming little 15-room inns in this part of Scotland, **Ceilidh Place,** West Argyle Street (tel. 0854/2103), grew from a coffeeshop in a boat shed. You get warmth, hospitality, and a certain sophistication from the owners, Robert and Jean Urquhart, who receive guests from the middle of March until the end of October. Family accommodations are provided in the clubhouse, and these rentals are cheaper, of course. Otherwise, you can opt for a handsomely furnished double or twin with a private bath. Depending on your selection, rates range from a low £8.50 ($13.60) (clubhouse bed only) to a high of £26 ($41.60). You'll welcome the fresh, tasty salads in this part of the world, and in the afternoon you'll want to take a proper tea, enjoying the shortbread, scones, and tea bread. By all means, stick around for perhaps the best table d'hôte dinner in Ullapool, a four-course meal, including coffee, costing from £11.50 ($18.40). The Urquharts will arrange loch fishing, pony trekking, and sea angling for their guests. Regular concerts, presenting classical, jazz, and folk music, as well as poetry, are presented in a separate building.

Actually the best hotel in town, for those willing to spend the extra pounds, is the **Royal Hotel,** Garve Road (tel. 0854/2181). It sits on a knoll on the "Inverness side" of town, overlooking the harborfront. Graced with curved walls and large sheets of glass, it was rebuilt in 1961 from an older building, with an east wing added in the 1970s. A Best Western hotel, it offers a total of 57 well-furnished bedrooms, 51 of which contain a private bath. The rate in a single ranges from £29 ($46.40) to £38 ($60.80), in a double from £22 ($35.20) to £32 ($51.20) per person. Twenty-one of these units have balconies opening onto views over Lock Broom. Live entertainment in season is offered, and home-cooked bar meals are a feature. In the evening, the chef presents an array of varied dishes on a well-chosen menu, with dinners costing from £12 ($19.20). Later guests sit around a log fire in the well-appointed lounge. The hotel is a special favorite with families, offering bunk beds where required, a baby-sitting and listening service, and other amenities.

Altanaharrie Inn (tel. 085483/230) is one of those places you feel you should not tell anyone about, for fear they won't have room for you when you get there. There are only four bedrooms—doubles and twins—each with a private bath or shower. But it is one of those places that calls for inclusion because of its uniqueness and total integration into the life of the region. The Altanaharrie was once a drover's inn on the banks of Loch Broom. There is no access by road, so guests are brought over the loch by private launch. Once you've landed, Fred Brown and his Norwegian wife, Gunn Eriksen, greet you with a warm log fire in a lounge to have a dram before dinner, which is likely to consist of locally caught seafood. Much meat, local venison, and fish such as trout and lobster are obtained nearby. They make their own bread, and they like to know beforehand if you're "eating in" so that they can cater accordingly. Overnight will cost you from £58 ($92.80) per person nightly, including dinner, VAT, your room, and breakfast.

Essex Cottage, West Terrace (tel. 0854/2663), is a small guesthouse sitting on a bluff overlooking Loch Broom. Bedrooms have hot and cold water basins, some with windows overlooking the loch, where you can watch glorious sunsets in summer. David McFadden, the owner, charges £14.50 ($23.20) for half board. He is a good cook as well as a pleasant host, serving excellent breakfasts and dinners.

Brae Guest House, Shore Street (tel. 0854/2421), is one of the better guesthouses in town. A whitewashed stone cottage, it is set along the harborfront at the edge of the commercial district. From May to September, guests are received in one of 12 comfortably furnished bedrooms, none of which has a private bath. The rate for B&B is from £12.50 ($20) nightly. This was once a private house, built in the 1780s, and today it is owned and operated by George and Rosanne Ross. They also serve food on the premises from 5 to 8:30 p.m., a full meal costing from £5 ($8). You can order such dishes as wild Atlantic salmon or steak with onion gravy.

Outside of the hotels and guesthouses already recommended, one of the best places for meals is **The Frigate,** Shore Street (tel. 0854/2488), which is open from March to October from 6:30 p.m. until "very late" depending on business. Don't confuse the street-level café with the upstairs restaurant. Meals costing from £12 ($19.20) are likely to feature freshly caught fish and seafood such as salmon, prawns, and scallops. Sometimes local lobster appears on the menu. Vegetarian dishes are also an item, and you can always order a steak. The location is along the harborfront in the center of town.

EXCURSIONS IN THE ENVIRONS: There are a number of excursions that can be made from Ullapool, including a trip 12 miles southeast of town to the **Corrieshalloch Gorge,** a national nature reserve along the A835 at Braemore. From this point, the Falls of Measach plunge 150 feet into a mile-long wooded gorge. Guests use a suspension bridge, constructed by Sir John Fowler, as their grandstand perch to view the spectacular sight.

Another interesting excursion is to the **Inverewe Gardens** (tel. 044586/200), reached along the A832, six miles northeast of Gairloch. Open all year, these gardens can be visited for £1.80 ($2.88) for adults and 90p ($1.44) for children. They are open from 10 a.m. to 6:30 p.m. Monday to Saturday and on Sunday from noon to 6:30 p.m. (in the off-season watch for 5 p.m. closings). A century and a quarter ago these gardens were created by Osgood MacKenzie, who planted species from many countries. An exotic mixture flourishes so that the gardens have color year round. Many plants from the South Pacific, the Himalayas, and South America flourish here.

From either Ullapool or Achiltibuie, it's possible to take excursions in season to the **Summer Isles,** a beautiful group of islands which are uninhabited, lying off the coast. The islands get their names because sheep are transported to the islands in summer for grazing. The largest of the islands is Tanera More, which had a small settlement of hearty souls until after World War II. The islands are a mecca for birdwatchers.

Dundonnell, 29 miles south of Ullapool, at the head of Little Lochbroom, is an interesting excursion if you're traveling by car. It is reached from Braemore junction along the "destitution road," so called because it was built to help relieve the distress and poverty among Scots of the parish during the potato famine of 1846. After Braemore junction, the road goes toward **Loch-a-Bhraoin,** a four-mile-long freshwater lake, near which are the graves of a group of Lochaber men who had been cattle rustling in the strath. A Lochbroom man disguised as a beggar followed them, and when they were asleep, he killed them all except the one they had left on guard. He was allowed to live to tell the tale.

FORT WILLIAM AND LOCHABER

FORT WILLIAM, the capital of Lochaber, is the major touring center for the western Highlands. Wildly beautiful Lochaber, the area around Fort William, has been called "the land of bens, glens, and heroes."

Dominating the area is **Ben Nevis**, Britain's highest mountain, rising 4,418 feet. In summer when it's clear of snow, there's a safe path to the summit. Fort William stands on the site of a fort built by General Monk in 1655, which was pulled down to make way for the railroad. This district is the western end of what is known as Glen Mor—the Great Glen, geologically a fissure that divides the northwest of Scotland from the southeast and contains Loch Lochy, Loch Oich, and Loch Ness. The Caledonian Canal, opened in 1847, linked these lochs, the River Ness, and Moray Firth. It provided sailing boats a safe alternative to the stormy route around the north of Scotland. Larger steamships made the canal out of date commercially, but fishing boats and pleasure steamers still use it. Good roads run the length of the Great Glen, partly following the line of General Wade's military road. From Fort William you can take steamer trips to Staffa and Iona.

The ruins of **Old Inverlochy Castle,** scene of the famous battle in 1645, can be reached by driving on the A82 two miles north of Fort William. At a point just one mile north of Fort William is **Glen Nevis,** one of the most beautiful in Scotland.

About 18 miles west of Fort William, on the A830 toward Mallaig, at Glenfinnan at the head of Loch Shiel is the **Glenfinnan Monument,** which marks the spot where Bonnie Prince Charlie unfurled his proud red-and-white silk banner on August 19, 1745, in the ill-fated attempt to restore the Stuarts to the British throne. The monument is topped by the figure of a kilted Highlander. At a Visitors' Centre you can learn of the prince's campaign from Glenfinnan to Derby and back to the final defeat at Culloden.

If you're still following our trail, we head back to Inverness and then south along the western bank of Loch Ness. After leaving Loch Ness, our first stop-over on the route to Fort William is—

1. Invergarry

A Highland center for fishing and deer stalking, Invergarry is noted for its fine scenery. It too is a good center for exploring Glen Mor and Loch Ness. At Invergarry is the beginning of the road through the West Highland glens and mountains, forming one of the famous "Road to the Isles" that terminates at Kyle of Lochalsh.

Near Invergarry, you can visit the **Well of the Heads,** on the west side of Loch Oich near its southern tip, erected in 1812 by MacDonnell of Glengarry to commemorate the decapitation by the family bard of seven brothers who had murdered the two sons of a 17th-century chief of Clan Keppoch, a branch of the MacDonnell Clan. The seven heads were washed in the well before being presented to the chief of the MacDonnells at Glengarry.

On the grounds of the Glengarry Castle Hotel (see below) are the ruins of the **Invergarry Castle,** the stronghold of the MacDonnells of Glengarry. The situation of the castle on Raven's Rock, overlooking Loch Oich in the Great Glen, was a strategic one in the days of clan feuds and Jacobite risings. Because the castle ruins are not considered safe, you should view them only from the outside.

FOOD AND LODGING: Sitting in a pleasant garden, the **Lundie View Guest House,** Aberchalder (tel. 08093/291), accommodates guests for £9 ($14.40) per person for B&B. The house has a residents' lounge and is centrally heated, with babysitter/listening service provided. Open all year, the guesthouse lies 3½ miles northeast of Invergarry on the A82. Surrounded by beautiful scenery, the house stands in the Great Glen. Pony trekking, fishing, walking, and touring are convenient, and just four miles away you can take your chance at spotting the Loch Ness monster.

Glengarry Castle Hotel (tel. 08093/254) is a mansion built between 1866 and 1869 on extensive grounds that contain the ruins of Invergarry Castle. With its gables and chimneys, it is an impressive sight, lying on the River Garry, which runs into Loch Oich. The mansion is privately owned and run by Mr. and Mrs. MacCallum, who have modernized it. They now rent 28 bedrooms, 25 of which contain private bath and toilet. Several of their rooms are spacious and most often used by families. Glengarry makes a pleasant base for a holiday, combining fishing, tennis, walking, and rowing. There are two spacious lounges where drinks are served to residents, and the dining room has a most friendly staff, offering good home-cooked meals made from local produce. Considering the amenities, and especially the 60 acres of grounds, the hotel is quite a bargain: singles range from £20 ($32) to £29 ($46.40), and doubles go from £17 ($27.20) to £26 ($41.60) per person, including a good country breakfast. Lunches cost from £5.80 ($9.28), with dinners going for £10.50 ($16.80). The hotel is open only from April to October.

Craigard House (tel. 08093/258) is a comfortable guesthouse where Brian and Joan Hirst rent out comfortable, immaculate bedrooms. The price is £10 ($16) per person. The Hirsts serve superb food, and they are friendly and informative, making guests feel at home. You can relax and chat in front of roaring fires in the house's fireplaces.

2. Spean Bridge

This village is a busy intersection of the Fort William–Perth and Fort William–Inverness roads, as well as having daily train service to Fort William, Glasgow, and London, and bus service to Inverness and Fort William. Two miles outside the town, in Glen Spean, is the striking **Commando Memorial** by Scott Sutherland which the Queen Mother unveiled in 1952. In this area many commandos were trained during World War II. Numerous war movies have been filmed here.

FOOD AND LODGING: On the outskirts of the village on the A86 going toward Newtonmore and Perth is **Coire Glas** (tel. 039781/272), a motel-style guesthouse with 15 bedrooms. Mr. and Mrs. MacFarlane have added onto the back of their one-story home, to come up with an attractive and convenient place for visitors to stay overnight or for long periods. All the rooms are equipped with hot beverage facilities and hot and cold running water, and ample bathroom facilities are provided. The MacFarlanes charge £10 ($16) per person per night for B&B. If you book a room with private toilet and shower, a supplement of £2 ($3.20) per person nightly is assessed. Dinner is £7.50 ($12). A lunch will be packed for you upon request. Spean Bridge is a central area for touring the loch country, and from Coire Glas, looking across a wide, grassy lawn, you can see Ben Gurry, which is a part of the Ben Nevis range.

Letterfinlay Lodge (tel. 039781/622) is the "Forsyth Family" hotel, a comfortable, well-appointed establishment on the A82 near Spean Bridge, about halfway between Fort Augustus and Fort William. Between the highway and Loch Lochy, against a backdrop of rugged scenery, it operates all year, and is known both for its personal service and level of cuisine, mostly plain Highland dishes that use high-quality ingredients, such as fresh salmon and sea trout, Aberdeen Angus beef, and Scottish hill lamb. Your bedroom window is likely to look out upon Loch Lochy. All units, including some family rooms, are tastefully furnished, with hot and cold running water. In the corridors are ample toilets and baths. Some units contain private bath or shower as well. Depending on the plumbing, charges are from £14 ($22.40) to £20 ($32) per person, these tariffs including a full Scottish breakfast. Dinner, including coffee, is about £10.50 ($16.80). The hotel also offers a sun lounge and a cocktail bar. Trout fishing is available at the doorstep.

Spean Bridge Hotel (tel. 039781/250). This sprawling roadside house has a tradition of hospitality stretching back to 1780, when it was a coaching inn. It contains 26 well-furnished rooms, most of which have private bath. Rates, depending on the season and the accommodation, range from £14 ($22.40) to £22 ($35.20) per person, with breakfast included. The hotel has a pair of lounges, one of which has an open fireplace. Bar snacks are served at lunchtime in the cocktail bar. There's also a friendly pub attached to the hotel, attracting the locals. Home-cooking is a feature of the dining room, where dinner costs from £10 ($16). The hotel also rents out 14 chalets and a modern annex on the grounds.

3. Fort William

This town, on the shores of Loch Linnhe, is a good center for exploring the western Highlands. A fort was built here in the 17th century to help crush any rebellion Highlanders might be plotting. After several reconstructions, it was finally torn down in 1864 and little remains of it today. During the notorious Highland Clearances, many starving and evicted people were shipped from here to America, dozens stricken by cholera on their long ship crossing.

Today Fort William is a bustling town, thriving very well on the summer tourist trade. It is filled with shops, many selling tartans and tweeds, as well as hotels and cafés.

WHERE TO STAY: There is no shortage of B&B accommodations in Fort William, most with a good view of Loch Linnhe. The Tourist Information Office (tel. 0397/3781) at the train-bus station can supply you with a list. My recommendations are:

Ben View Guest House (tel. 0397/2966), in the midst of the cluster of hotels and guesthouses fronting on the loch in the heart of the city, is a two-story red stone building with central heating and comfortable rooms. Tariffs in high season are £11.50 ($18.40) per person for B&B. The Ben View has two single rooms, 11 doubles, and two family rooms. Guests can relax in a pleasant residents' lounge or dine overlooking the loch, a dinner costing £7 ($11.20). The house is closed December through February.

Innseagan House, Achintore Road (tel. 0397/2452), is about 1½ miles south of Fort William on the A82. The original building is more than 100 years old, but extensive modernization has created a pleasant combination of old and new. The house is licensed and offers rooms with private bath. The tariff for half board is from £16 ($25.60) per person. Ample parking space is available, as the house sits in its own extensive grounds. It is open April to October.

The Moorings Hotel (tel. 03977/550) lies three miles from Fort William at Banavie, and it is definitely worth the pilgrimage. A family-run place, it is owned by two gracious hosts, Mary and James Sinclair. Standing on its own grounds, it lies beside the Caledonian Canal at Neptune's Staircase. The hotel opens onto views of Ben Nevis and has a pleasant garden. Rooms are comfortably furnished and immaculately maintained. Several of the 18 accommodations contain private bath. Depending on the plumbing, B&B ranges from £18.50 ($29.60) to £30 ($48) per person. Half board is an excellent deal, costing from £33 ($52.80) to £35 ($56) per person. Mrs. Sinclair is clearly the best cook in the area. She is known for her "Taste of Scotland" specialties, including Orkney chicken, smoked Highland mackerel mousse, cullen skink, and Achiltibuie mussels. Meals, served in a Jacobean-style restaurant, cost £10 ($16) and up. The traditional Highlander cuisine is backed up by a good wine list and a wide selection of malt whiskies.

Lochview Guest House, Heathercroft, Argyll Road (tel. 0397/3149), is a comfortable, modernized guesthouse that grew out of a former crofter's house. On a hillside above Fort William, it has good views over the Ardgour foothills and Loch Linnhe. It rents out six well-furnished rooms, some with private baths and all with hot-beverage facilities. B&B costs from £9 ($14.40) to £12 ($19.20) per person. For half board, the charge is £15 ($24) to £18 ($28.80).

Nevis Bank Hotel, Belford Road (tel. 0397/2595), is a popular choice, especially if you're arriving in Fort William by train. It is a modern and up-to-date building, lying in the eastern part of town, about a 12-minute stroll to the center. It stands at the intersection with the access road to Ben Nevis, so it's also convenient for touring. The hotel, which is in private hands, offers a total of 30 comfortably appointed bedrooms, all with private baths. Singles cost from £22.50 ($36), doubles or twins going for £22 ($35.20) per person. It's also possible to stay at this Best Western hotel on half-board terms, from £30.50 ($48.80) per person nightly. The home features traditional Scottish fare, using fresh ingredients. On weekends the hotel is host to a Highland cabaret in the Ceilidh bar, and in summer it's possible to book motor launches for cruises on Loch Linnhe.

Crolinnhe Guest House, Grange Road (tel. 0397/2709), is a completely refurbished 200-year-old, elegantly furnished, two-story house overlooking Loch

Linnhe. Kenneth and Flora MacKenzie receive B&B guests in their charming house for £9.50 ($15.20) per person in their four bedrooms, one with private bath. Kenneth owns a kilt business, and he and Flora are gracious and entertaining hosts.

Stronchreggan View Guest House, Achintore Road (tel. 0397/4644), is a pleasant house operated by Mrs. Patricia McQueen, a friendly, hospitable woman. She rents rooms for £15 ($24) per person for dinner, bed, and breakfast. The residents' lounge is filled with comfortable furniture and looks on a view of the loch and the mountains across the road.

WHERE TO DINE: Like its counterpart in Oban, **McTavish's Kitchens** and its coffeeshop are under the same management on the High Street (tel. 0397/2406), and are dedicated to preserving the hearty Scottish cuisine. McTavish's has a self-service cafeteria on the ground floor and a large licensed restaurant upstairs. The cafeteria is open from mid-May to the end of October, with light meals served throughout the open hours. Homemade soup of the day is offered with a range of chef's specials that change from day to day. Main courses include haggis and salmon mayonnaise. The cafeteria is licensed, and you can enjoy dinner with a glass of wine for as little as £6.50 ($10.40) per person. If you prefer waitress service, go to the restaurant upstairs, where you can have a before-dinner drink in the adjoining Laird's Bar, surrounded by photographs of the old Scottish laird. The restaurant's specialties include venison, smoked salmon, fresh local prawns from Loch Linnhe, lobster when available, and Scotland's national dish, haggis. A budget special includes homemade soup, a main course served with vegetables, and a dessert of deep-dish apple pie with cream, costing £7.50 ($12). If you choose a "Taste of Scotland" menu, expect to pay £12 ($19.20) and up.

The restaurant features a Scottish evening from mid-May until the end of September from 8:30 to 10:30 p.m., with singers, a piper, a Highland dancer, a fiddler, and a small dance band. Admission for the entertainment is £2 ($3.20) for adults and £1 ($1.60) for children.

Oscar's, 66 High St. (tel. 0397/2654), run by Stanley Eagan, is modernized and comfortable, serving one of the more reasonably priced menus in town. It has a welcoming pub and an informal dining area on the street level. Upstairs a gray and red dining room serves more formal meals. Food in both places is served continuously from noon to 10:30 p.m., although dinner is specifically from 5 to 10:30 p.m. Full meals cost from £9 ($14.40) per person, and include trout, venison, filet or sirloin steak, prawn mornay, and various versions of chicken. It's also possible to drop in just for a snack.

Ben Nevis, High Street (tel. 0397/2295), is named after Britain's highest mountain. On the main street of town, this multipurpose establishment contains a popular pub on the ground floor and a more formal restaurant upstairs. The pub has a pool table, half timbering, and stone trim, along with recorded rock music and long rows of wooden tables. A good selection of bar snacks is offered. Lunch downstairs lasts from noon to 2 p.m. Upstairs, a fixed-price lunch goes for the bargain price of £2.50 ($4) for three courses. High teas are served between 5 and 7 p.m. Dinners last from 5 to 9:30 p.m. A full evening meal will cost from £8.50 ($13.60) and might include a savory array of steaks, especially prime Scottish beef, along with deep-dish apple pie and several kinds of specialty coffees.

SIGHTS: You can visit the **West Highland Museum,** on Cameron Square (tel. 0397/2169), containing all aspects of local history, including a large Jacobite and tartan section. A special exhibition is devoted to Prince Charles Edward and the

'45 Rising. The museum is open from 10 a.m. to 1 p.m. and 2 to 5 p.m. Monday to Saturday October to the end of May, from 9:30 a.m. to 5:30 p.m. in June and September, and from 9:30 a.m. to 9 p.m. in July and August. Admission is 50p (80¢) for adults, 25p (40¢) for children.

Neptune's Staircase is a series of eight lochs which were constructed at the same time as the Caledonian Canal, raising Telford's canal 64 feet. The location of the "staircase" is three miles northwest of Fort William off the A830 at Banavie.

AFTER DARK: The most popular nightlife choice in town is **Gregory's Wine Bar and Bistro,** 141 High St. (tel. 0397/4232). Alastair McGregor is the voluble and articulate creator of this multipurpose entertainment center. During the course of a working day, which begins at 9 a.m., it changes from a morning tea room to a luncheon pub, and then is transformed into a bistro-style restaurant serving "high tea," before completing its act as a disco. There are three bars within the establishment, any of which serves a wide variety of malt whisky, as well as ale from a keg, along with German beer and about 30 kinds of wine. Live music is sometimes heard, often on Sunday night. At those times, a cover charge of £1 ($1.60) to £2 ($3.20) is collected. A menu of simple but well-prepared food items is available all day until 1:45 a.m.

4. Mallaig

This small fishing village is a good touring center for the western Highlands and the islands. Steamers call here for the Kyle of Lochalsh, the Isle of Skye, the Outer Hebrides, and the sea lochs of the northwest coast. At the tip of a peninsula, Mallaig is surrounded by moody lochs and hills. The distance between Morat and Mallaig is just three miles.

FOOD AND LODGING: The most comfortable hotel in the port is the **Marine Hotel,** 10 Station Rd. (tel. 0687/2217). Behind a simple modern facade, it is a family-owned business which lies in the vicinity of the train station. The owners offer a total of 21 pleasantly furnished bedrooms, six of which contain a private bath or shower. B&B rates range from £12 ($19.20) to £14 ($22.40) per person nightly. All rooms are heated and contain beverage-making facilities. Guests gather in the cocktail bar or TV lounge after enjoying a home-cooked meal, usually locally caught seafood. The Marine stays open all year, welcoming visitors on the "road to the isles."

One of the best of the modest accommodations is the **Gleann-Fideach Guest House,** Gilles Park (tel. 0687/2454), containing a total of eight comfortably furnished bedrooms. Open year round, it charges from £21 ($33.60) in a double for bed and a Scottish breakfast.

Another choice is **Hillside Guest House** (tel. 0687/2253), which has seven rooms, mainly doubles, each pleasantly comfortable enough. The charge is from £16 ($25.60) in a double, including breakfast, one of the best rates in the village. Guests are accepted only from April to October.

5. Onich

On the shores of Loch Linnhe, this charming little village lies to the north of Ballachulish Bridge. It's a good center if you're taking the western route to Inverness, or going to Skye and Fort William.

Onich Hotel (tel. 08553/214) is handsomely perched on the shores of Loch Linnhe, commanding views of the Ardgour and Glencoe mountains and the Firth of Lorne. Its gardens slope down to the water. Under family management, the hotel reflects a personal touch, both in its welcome of real Highland hospitality and in the appointments of its bedrooms and lounges. The hotel is owned by Ian and Ronald Young, brothers who have run the inn since 1964. They have a loyal band of guests who return yearly. Ian looks after the administration, and Ronald does the cooking, for which he has built up a reputation for high quality. The cuisine is backed up by a fine wine list. Dinners cost from £9.50 ($15.20). The 25 bright, airy bedrooms have been modernized, although none has private baths. They rent for £22.50 ($36) per person nightly for B&B. Guests gather in either the Clan cocktail bar or the Deerstalker lounge bar. The hotel attracts the athletic-minded, as it's a center for walking, climbing, loch bathing, golf putting, fishing, sailing, and pony trekking.

Glenmorven House (tel. 08553/247). Andrew and Jean Coke welcome guests into their private hotel on a large property at the edge of Loch Linnhe. Their rooms are comfortably furnished and well kept, and some have private baths. The rate for half board is £22 ($35.20) per person nightly. Rooms open onto views of the loch or the mountains in the background. You get good Scottish food and plenty of it at this licensed hostelry. There's a garden, and the Cokes will tell you about the sightseeing or the sports facilities available, including free boats for fishing.

6. Ballachulish

This small village enjoys a splendid scenic position on the shores of Loch Leven at the entrance to Glencoe. The Ballachulish Bridge links North and South Ballachulish. A good center for touring the western Highlands, the village has the following recommendations:

Ballachulish Hotel (tel. 08552/666) stands right on the shores of Loch Leven, at the point where hills split Leven from Loch Linnhe. Built in the style of a Scottish manor house and recently extensively remodeled, it offers hospitality, warmth, relaxation—just what you're seeking in a Highland hotel. The new decor blends new colors with old-style elegance. The bedrooms have a high standard of comfort and convenience, but vary considerably in style and plumbing. All have color TV, direct-dial phones, and hot-beverage facilities. Bathless singles rent for £15 ($24) to £18.50 ($29.60), depending on the season. Singles with bath cost £23 ($36.80) to £26.50 ($42.40). Doubles without bath cost the same price per person as bathless singles, but doubles with bath go for £18 ($28.80) to £32 ($51.20) per person, the latter being the charge for a suite with a four-poster bed and spa bath. All prices include a Scottish breakfast, VAT, and service. Open year round, the hotel serves good food, handsomely presented, made with fresh ingredients. A table d'hôte dinner is priced at £11 ($17.60). There are very good bar snacks too. The fare ranges from sandwiches to pizzas, from fish to fresh chips to hot and cold meat dishes. Residents from nearby gather in the hotel's bars, mingling with foreign visitors (and by that I mean the English). From the windows of the hotel you can look out onto views of hill and loch. The staff will arrange boat trips on the lochs or fishing expeditions.

If you're searching for a bargain, knock on the door of the **Craigellachie Guest House** (tel. 08552/531), an eight-room guesthouse where visitors are treated cordially and housed comfortably in clean, inviting surroundings. The cost is £8 ($12.80) to £9 ($14.40) per person, these tariffs including a full Scottish breakfast. Guest share a public bathroom. An evening meal can be ordered. It's more economical to stay here on half-board terms of £14.50 ($23.20) per person.

7. Glencoe

On the shores of Loch Leven, near where it joins Loch Linnhe, the Ballachulish Bridge now links the villages of North and South Ballachulish, at the entrance to Glencoe. The bridge saves a long drive to the head of the loch if you are coming from the north, but many visitors enjoy the scenic drive to Kinlochleven to come upon the wild and celebrated Glencoe from the east.

Glencoe runs from Rannoch Moor to Loch Leven between some magnificent mountains, including 3,766-foot Bidean nam Bian. Known as the "Glen of Weeping," Glencoe is where, on February 13, 1692, Campbells massacred MacDonalds—men, women, and children—who had been their hosts for 12 days. Although massacres were not uncommon in those times, this one shocked even the Highlanders because of the breach of hospitality. When the killing was done, the crime of "murder under trust" was regarded by law as an aggravated form of murder, and carried the same penalties as treason.

The glen, much of which now belongs to the Scottish National Trust, is full of history and legend. A tiny lochan is known as "the pool of blood" because by its side some men are said to have quarreled over a piece of cheese, and all were killed.

This is an area of massive splendor, with towering peaks and mysterious glens where you can well imagine the fierce battle among the kilted Highlanders to the skirl of the pipes and the beat of the drums.

FOOD AND LODGING: Choices are available both in the glen and in the village.

In the Glen

Almost where Glen Etive joins Glencoe, under the jagged peak of Buachaille Etive Mor dominating the road (A82), lies the **King's House Hotel** (tel. 08556/259), five miles north of the village of Glencoe. A building has stood here since the time of the Jacobite Rising of 1745, when it was required to accommodate troops on their way south from Fort William. It is now a center for skiing and attracts thousands from far and near. Believed to be one of the oldest licensed inns in Scotland, King's House Hotel has been enlarged and modernized. Warm, well-furnished rooms, many with private bath, are provided, and of course views of the majestic scenery. The lounge too has views, and the dining room relies on a lot of good fresh produce for its appetizing meals. There is a fine wine cellar, plus a bar. Such pleasant amenities as a drying room are provided for those who want to walk, fish, or go climbing. The rate per person per night for B&B is £17 ($27.20). Some double rooms contain private bath, and these cost an extra £3.50 ($5.60) per person nightly. A set dinner is featured for £11 ($17.60).

A ski lift is almost opposite the hotel. The Buachaille Etive Mor guards Glencoe's eastern end. This mountain provides a challenge for climbers and was the training ground for Sir John Hunt and the party he took to the top of Everest in Coronation year.

Besides access from the Glasgow–Inverness highway, guests at the King's House Hotel can be met at the Bridge of Orchy railway station by arrangement. Glen Orchy, to the south, is well worth a visit too, with the wild river and mountain scenery being beautiful and photogenic. It was the birthplace of the Gaelic bard Duncan Ban MacIntyre, whose song, "In Praise of Ben Doran," is considered a masterpiece.

Clachaig Inn (tel. 08552/252). After the bleakness of Glencoe, the trees ringing this place make it seem like an oasis. The white stone and black trim of the house are visible only via a winding gravel-covered road off the main highway. The owners direct the activity in the dining room where Oriental rugs cover the floor. They rent a handful of contemporary chalets in the back garden, plus a scattering of bedrooms in the main house. Their charge in a bathless single is £14 ($22.40) nightly. The rate in a double or twin, depending on the plumbing, is £12 ($19.20) to £14 ($22.40) per person. A full Scottish breakfast is included in the price.

In Glencoe Village

As you turn away from Loch Leven to enter the historic glen, you will find accommodations available in the village of Glencoe.

Glencoe Hotel (tel. 08552/245) is a spruce and stucco building with a slate mansard roof, dominating its area. A few double- and twin-bedded rooms have private baths, while other single, double, twin, and family rooms have hot and cold running water and tea-making equipment. The hotel is fully heated and has a restaurant and three bars. The charge is from £12 ($19.20) to £17 ($27.20) per person for B&B. Dinner costs from £8 ($12.80), and bar meals and snacks are served all day. The hotel is open all year.

Chapter XIII

THE ARGYLL PENINSULA

1. Port Appin
2. Oban
3. Seil and Isle of Luing
4. Kilmartin
5. The Crinan Canal
6. Lochgilphead
7. Loch Awe
8. Dalmally
9. Inveraray
10. Cairndow
11. Strachur

THE BOUNDARIES OF ARGYLL have shifted and changed over the years. Part of it was once an independent kingdom known as Dalriada. It has always been an important area of Scotland. Not all of the sections of Argyll are in this chapter. For more about Argyll, refer to the upcoming chapter.

In Gaelic, Argyll is known as Earraghaidheal which means "coastland of the Gael." Argyll takes up a lot of the land of the deeply dissected western Highlands, its rivers flowing into the Atlantic. Its summers along the coast are usually cool and damp, and its winters are relatively mild but wet, with little snow.

In the southeast the **Argyll Forest Park,** lying west and northwest from Loch Long, stretching almost to Loch Fyne, is actually three forests, made up of Benmore, Ardgartan, and Glenbranter, covering an area of 60,000 acres. It contains some of the most magnificent scenery in Scotland, and there are dozens of forest walks for trail blazers. Sometimes these walks lead through forests to lofty peaks, and as such, they are strenuous except for the most skilled and hearty of folk. Others, however, are tamer, including paths from the Younger Botanic Garden by Loch Eck leading to Puck's Glen.

The major center for this district is Oban, meaning "small bay." It is a great port for the Western Isles and a center of Gaelic culture. It is the gateway to Mull, largest of the Inner Hebrides; to the island of Iona, the cradle of Scottish Christianity; and to Staffa, where Fingal's Cave inspired Mendelssohn to write the Hebrides Overture. The ferries to the offshore islands run only twice a day until summer; then there are cruises to Iona from early June to late September. For information about island ferry services to Mull, Iona, and the Outer Hebrides, get in touch with **MacBrayne Steamers** at their office in Oban (tel. 0631/62285).

A number of colorful sites are near the port town, including Port Appin and Inveraray, where visitors can soak up the atmosphere of the district away from the major towns.

After leaving Fort William, just previewed in Chapter XII, our trail around the entire length of the Scottish mainland picks up again after crossing the Ballachulish Bridge. If you've already seen Glencoe (reached along the A82), you can hug the coastal road (the A828) which will eventually take you into Oban. But along the way you can enjoy the following stopovers.

1. Port Appin

To the north of Oban lies a beautiful lochside district, including Lismore Island. Port Appin makes a good stopover if you're exploring this part of Argyll. It's a hamlet of stone cottages.

According to myth, there's a subterranean undersea passage at Port Appin where a piper supposedly entered with his dog. Only his dog returned, and he was hairless.

FOOD AND LODGING: For a super-splurge in Port Appin, the **Airds Hotel** (tel. 0631/73236) is one of the most outstanding hotels of Scotland. For food, comfort, and service, it's a gem. Eric and Betty Allen make it so. Theirs is an old ferry inn in one of the most beautiful spots in the historic district of Appin. Many of the rooms look out onto the island of Lismore, the mountains of Morvern, and Loch Linnhe. Everything is immaculately maintained, handsomely decorated, and the setting is tranquil, good as a headquarters for either boat excursions or walking tours. There is also an annex in the hotel garden which is furnished in the same high standard of the parent building, consisting of one double-bedded room, one twin-bedded room, a bath, and a toilet. The Airds takes in guests from April until the end of November, charging them £52 ($83.20) to £68 ($108.80) per person for half board. Rates are always cheaper in the annex, of course.

It is the food that makes the Airds such an outstanding place to visit. Mrs. Allen is one of the great cooks of Scotland, and a meal here will cost from £20 ($32), plus the cost of your drink. (Snacks are available at lunch if you're just dropping in.) In her repertoire of fine Scottish cuisine, home-baking is a specialty, and fresh produce is used in making up the menus. Specialties include Loch Fyne kippers, smoked mackerel salad, and an exceptional kidney soup. Sole is often served stuffed with crab mousse, or perhaps you'll sample the roast haunch of venison with rowan jelly if featured. Desserts are mouthwatering concoctions, including the likes of walnut fudge tart. Reservations for dinner are absolutely necessary. It's served only at 8 p.m.

CASTLE STALKER: On an islet near Port Appin is a famous landmark, Castle Stalker, the ancient seat of the Stewarts of Appin, built in the 15th century by Duncan Stewart, son of the first chief of Appin. Dugald, the ninth chief, was forced to sell the estate in 1765, and the castle slowly fell into ruin. It was recently restored and is once again inhabited. It is open March to September by appointment (tel. 0631/73234). The cost is £2.50 ($4) for adults, £1.50 ($2.40) for children, including the boat trip.

2. Oban

One of Scotland's leading coastal resorts, the bustling port town of Oban is set in a sheltered bay that is almost landlocked by the island of Kerrera. About 85 miles north of Glasgow, this yachting center and small burgh lies about 50 miles south of Fort William. A busy fishing port in the 18th century, Oban is now heavily dependent on tourism for its economic base.

In Oban, Gaelic is taught in schools as a "leaving certificate subject."

In September the Oban Highland Games are held, with massed pipe bands marching through the streets. The Oban Pipe Band plays regularly throughout the summer, parading up and down main street.

WHERE TO STAY: As a holiday resort, Oban has a number of good hotels and guesthouses within easy reach of the seafront and the piers from which cruises to the offshore islands can be booked.

Queens Hotel, Esplanade (tel. 0631/62505), is close to the town center, commanding a magnificent view of Oban Bay, Kerrera, Lismore, Mull, and Marvern, as well as the scenic views in Oban and down the Firth of Lorn. The hotel, completely modernized, is fully licensed, with a number of inviting public rooms. Open from April 1 to the end of October, the hotel charges from £13 ($20.80) to £20 ($32) per person for B&B. The half-board rate is £17.50 ($28) to £26 ($41.60) per person. All 45 bedrooms have private baths. Ample car parking is available.

Lancaster, Esplanade (tel. 0631/62587), is distinguished by its attractive pseudo-Tudor facade. On the crescent of the bay, it commands views from its public rooms of the islands of Lismore and Kerrera, including the more distant peaks of Mull. Open all year, the hotel is managed by its resident owners who welcome you to one of their well-furnished bedrooms, charging £19 ($30.40) to £21 ($33.60) per person, including breakfast. A number of rooms offer central heating, and 17 have private bath or shower. Dinner is from £8 ($12.80). The Lancaster is the only hotel in Oban featuring a heated indoor swimming pool, a sauna bath, a spa bath, and a solarium.

Royal Highland Hotel, Breadalbane Street (tel. 0631/64520). Set on a hill just a few minutes' walk from the harborfront, this painted stone Victorian building was enlarged with a sprawling modern extension set off to the side. The accommodations vary widely in age and design, and each is simply and comfortably furnished. The charge for B&B is £10 ($16) to £16 ($25.60) per person, or you can stay here on a half-board arrangement at a cost of £15.50 ($24.80). A hearty dinner is served in a pleasant dining room. The hotel is closed in October.

Roseneath Guest House, Dalriach Road (tel. 0631/62929). Irene and David Robertson and their young children are the guiding forces behind this guesthouse, set a few blocks from the commercial center of town. The establishment is housed in a granite and red sandstone Victorian house where a polished brass fist invites you to pull the old-fashioned doorbell. Inside, there's an environment of gleaming paneling, thick pine doors, and stained-glass windows. The rate charged for one of the ten comfortably furnished bedrooms, some with private baths, is £9 ($14.40) to £14 ($22.40) per person, depending on the season, with breakfast included. The town's bowling green, swimming pool, tennis and squash courts are a short distance away.

Balmoral Hotel, Craigard Road (tel. 0631/62731). The granite walls of this centrally located hotel date from 1896. From the side, the solidly symmetrical building looks almost like an 18th-century farmhouse in Pennsylvania. Once you're inside, the flavor is unmistakably Scottish. You'll reach both the reception desk and the second-floor restaurant by climbing a corkscrew-style "hanging staircase," one of the most unusual in Oban. The hotel offers 10 comfortably furnished bedrooms, five of which contain private baths. The owners charge £15.50 ($24.80) to £19.50 ($31.20) per person for B&B. The hotel and its restaurant are closed between October and April. For more information about the in-house restaurant, refer to the "Where to Dine" section.

The **Columba Hotel,** Esplanada (tel. 0631/62183), is one of the most impressive Victorian buildings in Oban. It was built in 1870 by Mr. McCaig, a philanthropist who also ordered the construction of the hilltop extravaganza known as McCaig's Tower (see below). The hotel's main core is of massive blocks and local granite, plus a substantial extension of red sandstone stretching out toward the North Pier. The location is among the best in town. You'll enter by passing through a pair of carved granite columns and climbing up a short distance into the reception hall. A modernized and big-windowed dining room offers views of the port. The hotel's Poop Deck is perhaps the most popular nighttime rendezvous in Oban. Year round, the Columba rents 51 well-furnished bedrooms for £30 ($48) to £35 ($56) per person for B&B, a worthwhile splurge considering the fine amenities of this central accommodation.

Ardblair Guest House, Dalriach Road (tel. 0631/62668). As its publicity says, "There are two sides of Ardblair." Neither side of what its critics call an architectural hodgepodge is plush, yet both offer homey comfort and a genuine welcome to visitors. Bill Reid expanded his family's 19th-century home with the addition of a bunker-like annex. The resulting guesthouse is one of the largest in Oban, filled with a comfortable clutter of objects from many different eras, ranging from well-grained antiques to leatherette in vogue at the time of the Queen's coronation. The warm-hearted charm of the place, however, comes mainly from Mr. Reid himself, and he is assisted by a kindly staff of helpers. Residents can read their morning newspapers on the glassed-in sunporch, offering a panoramic view of the port and many of the other houses of Oban. None of the 22 simply furnished bedrooms contains private bath, but there are adequate public facilities. This is also one of the most reasonably priced of Oban's B&Bs: from £8 ($12.80) to £9 ($14.40) per person per night. A five-course evening meal is another £5.50 ($8.80) per person, and it's served with a smile and lots of flavor.

Heatherfield Hotel, Albert Road (tel. 0631/62681). You'll find blue iris and climbing roses growing next to the gray granite walls of this Victorian guesthouse owned by Anne Mossman. Its modernized and spacious interior contains a comfortable mix of upholstered and leatherette chairs. Rates in the ten well-furnished rooms, none of which contains private bath, range from £11 ($17.60) per person for B&B, the charge going up to £16.50 ($26.40) per person for those desiring half board. The hotel is on a winding, tree-lined street filled with fluttering birds. Albert Road is a steep street above the port.

Wellpark Hotel (tel. 0631/62948) is a substantial stone house with a gabled bay window, positioned on the seafront and commanding views of the bay and the islands of Kerrera, Mull, and Lismore. It's also one of the best bargains in Oban. Mr. and Mrs. R.B. Dickison welcome you, charging £15.25 ($24.40) per person for B&B. All rooms have private showers and toilets, phones, radios, color TV, and hot-beverage facilities. They are centrally heated and pleasantly comfortable. The hotel is quiet at night. Open from April to October, it has parking in the grounds.

The **Kelvin Guest House and Restaurant,** Shore Street (tel. 0631/62150), is across the street from the railway station and near the dock where the ferry leaves for Mull and Iona. It's an enjoyable place to stay, only two or three blocks from the heart of town where the street is quiet. For £10.50 ($16.80) per person, you can have a bed and a breakfast including kippers and Scottish porridge. The house has a bar, and you will be looked after in the dining room by a well-trained staff.

The house of **Jeanne and Allan Adcroft,** Connel, Shore Road (tel. 0631/71212), is in a position with views of the nearby lake outside Oban. The Adcrofts charge £9 ($14.40) for B&B, with an additional £6 ($9.60) if you'd like to partake of a good dinner. The hosts are hospitable and interesting conversationalists.

Braehead, Albert Road (tel. 0631/63341), is a comfortable guesthouse owned by Mrs. Catherine Hunter, who welcomes guests as if they were part of her family. She rents rooms with hot and cold water basins, charging £9.50 ($15.20) per person for a bed and a full Scottish breakfast. For half board, the charge is £15 ($24) per person, and Mrs. Hunter serves excellent food, especially her soups.

WHERE TO DINE: I always like to go to **McTavish's Kitchens,** 34 George St. (tel. 0631/63064), which, like its cousin in Fort William, is dedicated to preserving the local cuisine. Downstairs is a self-service restaurant which is open in summer from 9 a.m. till 9 p.m., serving breakfast, main meals, haggis, shortbread, scones, strawberries, cakes, teas, and coffees. The two bars are the upstairs Lairds Bar and, around the corner from the self-service, the Mantrap Bar with a "real mantrap." The licensed second-floor restaurant has a more ambitious Scottish and continental menu with higher prices, but there are also budget lunches for around £2.99 ($4.78) for two courses and high teas for £3.95 ($6.32). The table d'hôte menu includes an appetizer, a main course that might be fresh salmon, and a dessert such as strawberries or raspberries in season. The price is £6.45 ($10.32). The à la carte menu offers haggis, Loch Fyne kippers (oak-smoked herring), prime Scottish steaks, smoked salmon, salmon steak, venison, local mussels, scallops cooked in wine sauce, lobster thermidor, and lobster salad among other dishes.

A feature of the restaurant is the entertainment, with music by local artists, Scottish dance music, singing, piping, fiddling, and Highland dancing, from 8:30 to 10:30 p.m. daily mid-May to the end of September. Admission is £2 ($3.20) for adults, £1 ($1.60) for children. It's half price for persons who dine here. The bagpipes provide haunting melodies, new and old.

Studio Family Restaurant, Craigard Road (tel. 0631/62030), lies on a hill on a narrow street in the heart of town. Fully licensed, it has a bright, modern decor and is run by Robert and Fiona Silverman. A dormered stone building, the restaurant is known for steaks and local seafood. The chef offers such daily specials as grilled filet of trout, and you can rely on the prime filet steak. There is also a selection of burgers. A fixed-price dinner is served for £6.50 ($10.40) from 5 to 7 p.m. After that and until 10 p.m., the menu is à la carte, a meal beginning at £8 ($12.80). Lunch is daily except Sunday from noon to 2:30 p.m.

The **Box Tree,** 108 George St. (tel. 0631/64409), in the heart of town, is one of the most charming and reasonably priced little restaurants in Oban. Licensed, it offers a cozy and inviting atmosphere, with a polite, friendly staff maintaining a high standard of service. The meals, which are among the most inexpensive in town, range from around £3 ($4.80) for a two-course lunch. They specialize in Scottish fare, with some continental dishes also. The restaurant, on one of the main streets of Oban, set back from the water, is open weekdays from 9 a.m. to 10 p.m. in summer, from 10 a.m. to 5 p.m. in winter.

Balmoral Hotel, Craigard Road (tel. 0631/62731). The restaurant contained within this previously recommended hotel is one of the best in the area for "Taste of Scotland" fare. Filled with a 19th-century kind of charm, it contains Windsor chairs and reproduction Georgian-style tables which the owners, Susana and David Garland, have crafted from darkly stained wood. The walls are covered with framed dining menus from the 1930s, few of which offer the variety of savory fare encountered today. Specialties include sliced châteaubriand with mushrooms, Isle of Mull rainbow trout, grilled salmon steak, rollmop herring, smoked Tobermory trout, Scottish haggis with cream and whisky, and deep-fried clams, along with venison casserole, roast pheasant with burgundy sauce, and six kinds of steak. Full meals cost from £12 ($19.20) apiece, but bar meals are cheaper, going for around £5 ($8). The hotel that contains this restaurant is open all year, but the dining room serves only from April to October. Lunch is from noon to 2 p.m. and dinner from 6:30 to 9:30 p.m. Reservations are necessary.

Jay's Restaurant, George Street (tel. 0631/65357). Even though it's in the middle of Oban, this slate-roofed tea house looks somewhat like a roadside diner. It's near many of the town's low-cost B&Bs, so it can be a handy choice. Just above the port, the restaurant has a crew of uniformed waitresses offering a wide array of many kinds of dishes throughout the day. In summer it's open from 9 a.m. to 11 p.m. Morning coffee includes freshly baked pastries and scones, or you can order a full breakfast. You can also order snacks, lunches, afternoon teas, high teas, and full dinners. It's even licensed for alcohol. Lunch costs from £3.50 ($5.60), while dinners run from £5.50 ($8.80). Steak fondue is a house specialty, as well as "carpetbag steak." Other food items include beef burgers, braised venison in red wine sauce, and Gaelic coffee.

SIGHTS IN AND AROUND OBAN:

From Pulpit Hill in Oban there is a fine view across the Firth of Lorn and the Sound of Mull. Overlooking the town is an unfinished replica of the Colosseum of Rome, **McCaig's Tower,** built by a banker, John Stuart McCaig, in 1897–1900 as a memorial to his family and to try to curb local unemployment during a slump. Its walls are two feet thick and from 37 to 40 feet high. The courtyard within is landscaped and the tower is floodlit at night. Outsiders have been heard to refer to the tower as "McCaig's Folly," but Obanites deplore this term, as they are proud of the structure.

On the island of Kerrera stands **Gylen Castle,** home of the MacDougalls, dating back to 1587.

Near the little granite **Cathedral of the Isles,** one mile north of the end of the bay, is the ruin of the 13th-century **Dunollie Castle,** seat of the Lords of Lorn who once owned a third of Scotland.

You can visit **Dunstaffnage Castle,** 3½ miles to the north, which was believed to have been the royal seat of the Dalriadic monarchy in the eighth century. The present castle was probably built in 1263. It is believed to have been the location of the Scots Court until the unification under Kenneth McAlpine and the transfer to Scone of the seat of Scottish government. The castle is open April to September from 9:30 a.m. to 7 p.m. (on Sunday from 2 to 7 p.m.); October to March, from 9:30 a.m. to 4 p.m. (on Sunday from 2 to 4 p.m.). It is closed on Thursday and Friday. Admission is 50p (80¢) for adults, 25p (40¢) for children.

Oban Glassworks, Lochavullin Estates (tel. 0631/63386), is a branch of Caithness Glass, where you can watch the intricate art of paperweight making from 9 a.m. to 5 p.m. Monday to Friday. The factory shop, with some good bargains, is open from 9 a.m. to 1 p.m. May to September and 9 a.m. to 5 p.m. the rest of the year.

3. Seil and Isle of Luing

Those seeking a hidden oasis in the district south of Oban can leave town on the 816, turning west at Kilninver on the 844 until Clachan Bridge is reached. The locals claim, somewhat whimsically, that this is "the only bridge across the Atlantic Ocean." Easdale is an attractive, tiny slate village, nestling under the cliffs of Seil Island, with a view of Mull. Here you have complete serenity.

You can also continue in this same direction until you see the ferry connections to the Isle of Luing, where you'll find one of the finest dining recommendations in Scotland at Cullipool.

FOOD AND LODGING AT EASDALE: A symmetrical stone building, the **Easdale Inn** (tel. 08523/256), sits at the back of a curved lawn whose borders are ringed with a stone wall. It was built as the residence for a local quarrymaster, who insisted that his dwelling be constructed from a combination of local granite and the imported sandstone that arrived as ship's ballast. Built in 1850, the house is the property of Mike and Sue Atkinson, who maintain seven well-furnished bedrooms, four of which contain private baths and one a four-poster bed. The establishment charges £15 ($24) to £20 ($32) per person, with breakfast included, depending on the season and the accommodation. Most guests enjoy a drink in the cozy pub before heading toward the dining room. During the day this room is illuminated by its very tall windows. A fresh fixed-price dinner costs another £9 ($14.40). In the surrounding gardens you can see palm trees which flourish in Seil's soft climate. The hotel is open from March until the end of October.

DINING ON THE ISLE OF LUING: You can drive from the Scottish mainland across Seil until you reach the Cuan ferry. There, in just a minute and a half, you'll be delivered to the charming little offshore island of Luing. You'll find the **Longhouse Buttery and Gallery,** Cullipool (tel. 08524/209), a worthy target. This restaurant was once awarded the Sunday *Times* "Taste of Scotland" award for its excellence in traditional fare, including such items as local venison, home-cooked desserts, venison pâté, fresh Luing prawns, whole-meal breads, pickled salmon, and fresh vegetables, often from their own garden. This is the domain of Edna Whyte and Audrey Stone. The location is in a low whitewashed croft that is immaculately maintained. Inside it is most inviting, with an effective use of pine. Edna Whyte's etchings of local scenes add to the cozy ambience. The restaurant is open from 11 a.m. to 5 p.m. Monday to Saturday mid-May to early October. A set lunch costs from £7.50 ($12). Vegetarian meals can also be arranged. No dinner is served, and the establishment is closed on Sunday.

4. Kilmartin

This is only a roadside hamlet along the A816, 7½ miles north of Lochgilphead, but it is visited for two main reasons: it offers some of the best food in the area, and it's known for its **Kilmartin sculptured stones.** You're allowed to wander around a church of the West Highlands where a number of grave slabs are on view, along with fragments of two crosses. For safekeeping, some of the stones have been taken inside the church. After an inspection, you might consider at least stopping over for a meal or perhaps the night before continuing on your journey.

FOOD AND LODGING: A good place to stay is the **Kilmartin Hotel** (tel. 05465/244), a gabled stone building originally constructed some 150 years ago as a coaching inn. Today, visitors enjoy an attractive mixture of urban sophistication and small-time charm, both complemented by an eclectic medley of British antiques. Ms. Jean Blandford, the owner, who worked in advertising in London before settling here, rents out five simply furnished bathless bedrooms, costing from £13 ($20.80) per person for B&B. In the stone-accented pub, visitors can enjoy drinks and bar meals in the warmth of a beechwood fire in a fireplace whose lintel is an old millstone. The proprietor of the hotel works hard to make her cuisine the best in the neighborhood. A four-course candlelit dinner in the antique-filled dining room costs from £10 ($16). The culinary specialties are prepared by chef Jackie Simons. She turns out such delectable items as pears with prawns (served with an herb mayonnaise), grapes filled with stilton pâté, sorrel mousse, roast venison with cherry sauce, rump steak cooked with red wine, turkey filet in a mushroom sauce, trout poached in rosé, lamb chops with a rosemary cream sauce, and pork chops with apple cider. Food is served from 11:30 a.m. to 2 p.m. and 6 to 9 p.m. Monday to Saturday, from 12:30 a.m. to 2 p.m. and 6:30 to 9 p.m. on Sunday.

Cairn (tel. 0546/5254) is a sophisticated bistro in this sleepy hamlet. A former draper's cottage, it was built in the mid-19th century when coaches passed through Kilmartin, heading for Oban. You can dine either "Downstairs" (less expensive) or "Upstairs," which is a restaurant with an à la carte menu. In the Upstairs main restaurant, dinner is served from 7:30 to 10 p.m. The Downstairs is open Monday to Sunday from 10 a.m. to 10 p.m. The food has flair and style, including both Scottish and continental dishes, ranging from beef goulash, prawn créole, smoked trout, soused herring, and roast chicken. Depending on your dining choice, meals range from £5 ($8) to £12 ($19.20).

5. The Crinan Canal

The nine-mile-long canal, constructed during 1793–1801, was designed to provide water communication between the Firth of Clyde, Argyll, the western Highlands, and the islands. It runs roughly north from Ardrishaig and curves gradually to the west before reaching Loch Crinan on the Sound of Jura. Four miles north of **Cairnbaan** which is on the canal is the ruined hill-fort of **Dunadd,** once capital of Dalriada, kingdom of the Scots. There are numerous Bronze Age stone circles in the vicinity.

Carnasserie Castle, also to the north of the canal, built in the late 16th century, was the home of John Carswell, the first post-Reformation bishop of the isles, whose translation of John Knox's liturgy into Gaelic was the first book to be published in that language.

Crinan, a yachtsman's haven on the Sound of Jura, is overlooked by the early 11th-century **Duntrune Castle,** one of the oldest castles in Scotland, and still inhabited by the descendants of the original owners, the Clan Malcolm. Crinan is a charming little village.

FOOD AND LODGING: Off the B841, the **Crinan Hotel** (tel. 054683/235), seven miles northwest of Lochgilphead, is a splurge inn with a bright, attractive decor and modern comforts and conveniences. Because of its location on a canal and yacht basin, it is naturally a favorite with yachtsmen, who book its 22 rooms with private bath in July and August, the peak sailing months. If you're reserving (and I highly recommend that you do), ask for one of the rooms with private balconies opening onto mountains and lochside sunsets. The hotel is managed by Nicolas Ryan, who once worked as a bellboy on the old *Queen Mary,* later rising rapidly within the Cunard organization. Bedrooms rent for £35 ($56) in a single, from £60 ($96) in a double, including a breakfast that often features oat-cakes and hot croissants. Open from mid-March to mid-October, the hotel serves good food—dishes such as fresh salmon, Crinan clams mornay, roast duckling in black cherry sauce, and Scottish sirloin. Meals are served from 12:30 to 2 p.m. and 7 to 9 p.m. A table d'hôte dinner costs £20 ($32). Luncheon in fair weather is served al fresco. The hotel is one of the best-run in the area.

6. Lochgilphead

In the lovely heart of Argyll, Lochgilphead lies along the western shores of Loch Fyne. It makes a good stopover point "halfway" between for those intent on exploring the Oban district and the Kintyre peninsula (previewed in Chapter XIV). Actually, Lochgilphead sits at the head of its own little loch, Gilp, which flows into Loch Fyne. The town dates from the early 19th century when it was built "from scratch" by an entrepreneur hoping to attract settlers and factories. Industry didn't come, and the sleepy market town is all the lovelier for that reason today.

FOOD AND LODGING: On the main street of town, the **Argyll Hotel** (0546/2221) is a black-and-white, low-lying hostelry. Its simple exterior belies the plushness of parts of the refurbished interior, where thick carpeting, an array of old furniture, and a panorama of framed depictions of clipper ships complete a tasteful decor. There's an attractive modern-style restaurant, serving good food, especially fresh fish, and a bar/lounge that is so inviting you may be tempted to linger, especially if some entertainment is being featured, as it often is (ranging from cabaret to a local ceilidh). Rooms are comfortably furnished and well maintained, with B&B costing from £16 ($25.60) per person. Five of the 12 rooms contain private baths or showers.

7. Loch Awe

Twenty-two miles long and in most places only about a mile wide, Loch Awe for years acted as a natural moat protecting the Campbells of Inveraray from their enemies to the north. Along its banks and on its islands are many reminders of its fortified past.

In this area the Forestry Commission has vast forests, and a new road now makes it possible to travel around Loch Awe, so that it is more than ever a popular angling center. Sharp-eyed James Bond fans may even recognize some scenes that appeared in one of the films.

FOOD AND LODGING: At the foot of Ben Cruachan, the **CarraigThura Hotel,** Loch Awe by Dalmally (tel. 08383/210), sits at the top of a curving driveway leading up from a tree-flanked road. The granite walls were originally constructed as part of a private home. Today, some of the baronial ostentation remains in the oak-paneled salons, where log fires illuminate old weapons and hunting trophies. A modern extension contains a busy pub. The Whiteford family runs the hotel with a friendly, personal atmosphere. They rent rooms with bath in the main hotel for £20 ($32) to £25 ($40) per person, depending on the exposure, with breakfast included. Singles are an extra £3 ($4.80). Bargain seekers will ask for a room in the annex. There, depending on the plumbing and based on double occupancy, the rate ranges from £12 ($19.20) to £16 ($25.60) per person. The hotel offers separate smoking and no-smoking bedrooms, and there's no lighting-up in the handsome dining room. The menu features Scottish specialties. In the hotel's adjacent cocktail bar, you can order light snacks, hot meals, and salads. There is also a lounge for drinks in the hotel. The Carraig-Thura's location is excellent, with breathtaking views of the loch and the mountain.

SIGHTS AROUND LOCH AWE: Among the reminders of the days when the Campbells of Inveraray held supreme power in the Loch Awe region, there is a ruined castle at Fincharn, at the southern end of the loch, and another on the island of Fraoch Eilean. The **Isle of Inishail** has an ancient chapel and burial ground, and at the northern end of the loch are the ruins of **Kilchurn Castle,** built by Sir Colin Campbell in 1440. The bulk of Ben Cruachan, 3,689 feet, dominates Loch Awe at its northern end and attracts climbers. On the ben is the world's second-largest hydroelectric power station, which pumps water from Loch Awe to a reservoir high up the mountain. Below the mountain are the **Falls of Cruachan** and the wild **Pass of Brander,** where Robert the Bruce routed the Clan MacDougall in 1308.

The Pass of Brander where Loch Awe narrows was the scene of many a fierce battle in bygone times, and something of that bloody past seems to brood over the narrow defile. Through it the waters of the Awe flow on their way to Loch Etive. This winding sea loch is 19 miles long, stretching from Dun Dunstaffnage Bay at Oban to Glen Etive, reaching into the Moor of Rannoch at the foot of the 3,000-foot Buachaille Etive (the Shepherd of Etive), into which Glencoe also reaches.

8. Dalmally

To the east of the top of Loch Awe, Dalmally is small but because of its strategic position it has witnessed a lot of Scottish history passing through, including Robert Bruce, who came this way. Its church, built in an octagonal shape, is from the 18th century. A more interesting sight, however, is the ruins of **Kilchurn Castle,** at the northern tip of Loch Awe, west of Dalmally. It can be viewed from the outside only. Once it was one of the strongholds of the Campbells of Glen Orchy. Its keep dates from 1440. It was occupied by the Bredalbanes until the mid-18th century, when Hanoverian troops overran it.

FOOD AND LODGING: Built some 200 years ago, **Craig Lodge** (tel. 08382/216) was originally a private shooting lodge owned by the Marquis of Breadalbane. The elegant salon was added in the 1930s. Today the seven surrounding acres of land include two acres of lushly cultivated gardens, a rocky cliff (craig) which gave the property its name, and four miles of a salmon-filled river, as well as a private lake. The domain is the property and artistic statement of Mary-Anne and Calum McFarlane-Barrow, who until they returned to Scotland lived in both Cyprus and Tunisia. The lodge is their private home, laden with lovely furniture, woodburning stoves, and open fireplaces. An antique, ornately carved billiard table sits amid comfortable sofas and a grandfather clock in a room where a guest can enjoy a drink or a cup of tea, depending on the time of day.

The establishment contains six spacious and elegant bedrooms, each with private bath, plus two self-contained cottages. Depending on the season, the half-board rate is £27 ($43.20) to £32 ($51.20) per person. Children under 12 pay 50% of the adult price. Tariffs include a full Scottish breakfast with fresh eggs from a neighboring farm. Open from Easter to October, the lodge offers good food, much of it grown on the premises. It is often personally prepared by Mrs. McFarlane-Barrow. Guests can rent fishing equipment or go hunting (in season) in the surrounding forests. For a per-diem charge, salmon fishing can also be arranged.

9. Inveraray

This small resort and royal burgh occupies a splendid setting on the upper shores of Loch Fyne. It is particularly attractive when you approach from the east on the A83 road. Across a little inlet of the loch, you can see the town lying peacefully on a bit of land fronting on the loch.

FOOD AND LODGING: A white-walled hostelry, the **Fernpoint Hotel** (tel. 0499/ 2170), is near the pier in the center of town. It was completed in 1751 as the private residence for the first mayor (provost) of Inveraray. The resident owner, Robert McArthur, will point out the mound where the region's hanging tree stood in 1685, when 17 Campbells were executed. Robert and his wife, Beryl, help to organize McArthur clan reunions from time to time, when McArthurs from around the world return home to meet their kinfolk. The hotel is flanked by a table-dotted lawn, a rounded tower, and a big-windowed popular meeting place called the Jacobean bar. There, in a stone-rimmed milieu of hewn timbers and high ceilings, local residents mingle with visitors over a nip of malt whisky. The rates for the six pleasantly modernized accommodations vary with the season and the exposure. Per-person charges (service not included) range from £14 ($22.40) to £20 ($32), with a full Scottish breakfast. The only room in the hotel that doesn't contain a private bath is £3 ($4.80) cheaper. Fixed-price evening meals go for £10 ($16), plus service. Visitors eager to sample a "Taste of Scotland" menu can do so here, sampling such specialties as local trout, grilled steak stuffed with haggis (and served with a Drambuie sauce), or venison casserole. For your bottle of wine, you might ask for elderberry, followed later by a liqueur distilled from a silver birch tree.

The **Argyll Arms Hotel** (tel. 0499/2466). The front windows of what used to be known in the region as the Great Inn open onto a view of Loch Fyne and Loch Shira. The three-story core of the building was first constructed in 1755. The pleasantly modernized Victorian-style interior is overseen by Niall Iain and Inez MacLean, who manage it in partnership with the trustees of the Duke of Argyll. The hotel lies near the entrance to the castle. The bar is one of the town's most popular lunch spots, where meals are served either on the glassed-in veranda or within a high-ceilinged lounge. In the evening, more formal meals are offered in the dining room. You can also drop in for afternoon tea. Rooms are pleasantly and comfortably furnished, a few containing private baths or showers. The charges range from £16 ($25.60) to £25 ($40) per person, with breakfast included. Units opening onto views of the loch are more expensive, of course. A fixed-priced evening meal costs from £10 ($16), and well-prepared pub lunches go for £5 ($8).

The **George,** Main Street (tel. 0499/2111), is a small inn, open year round. The rates range from £11 ($17.60) to £12.50 ($20) per person for B&B, depending on the season. There are two rooms with private baths or showers. The rooms are simply furnished, with a minimum of plumbing, decidedly old-fashioned. The dining room, however, is attractively modern with bright furnishings. Downstairs there's a public bar with stone walls and a flagstone floor, a part of which was connected with the stables when the George was a stagecoach inn. Here you can order snacks at lunch, costing from £3 ($4.80), along with your lager. A three-course dinner goes for £10 ($16).

The **Old Rectory,** Newton Street (tel. 0499/2280), opens directly onto the loch with a beautiful view. Charles and Catherine MacLaren remodeled it, and it is now a comfortable and cheerful guesthouse. The charge is £9 ($14.40) per person for bed and a good Scottish breakfast. Evening tea is served in the sitting room.

SIGHTS: The hereditary seat of the Dukes of Argyll, **Inveraray Castle** (tel. 0499/2203) has been headquarters of the Clan Campbell since the early 15th century. In 1644 the original village was burned by the Royalist Marquess of Montrose. The third Duke of Argyll built a new town and castle between 1744 and 1788. The castle was badly damaged by fire in 1975, but it has been restored. The present laird, the 12th Duke of Argyll and 26th MacCailein Mor, chief of the Clan Campbell, has opened the castle to the public, with a special welcome for anyone who is related to Clan Campbell. The castle is among the earliest examples of Gothic revival in Britain, and offers a fine collection of pictures and 18th-century French furniture, old English and continental porcelain, and a magnificent Armoury Hall, which alone contains 1,300 pieces. There is a castle shop for souvenirs and a tea room where homemade cakes and scones are served.

In the grounds of Inveraray Castle is a **Combined Operations Museum,** the only one of its kind in the United Kingdom. It displays the role played by No. 1 Combined Training Centre at Inveraray from 1940 to 1945. On exhibit are scale models, newspaper reports of the time, campaign maps, photographs, wartime posters and cartoons, training scenes, and other mementoes of training operations in which Allied military personnel participated.

The castle and museum are open daily from the first Saturday in April until the second Sunday in October, charging £2 ($3.20) for adults and £1 ($1.60) for children to enter the castle, 75p ($1.20) for adults and 50p (80¢) for children to see the museum exhibits. They are closed on Friday except in July and August.

At one end of the main street of the town is a Celtic burial cross from Iona. The parish church is divided by a wall enabling services to be held in Gaelic and English at the same time.

Vacationing fishing enthusiasts may want to visit the **Castle Fisheries** (tel. 0499/2233), two miles north past the castle on the Oban road. Primarily a farm providing trout for the table, facilities are set up so that visitors can try their luck in one of the trout ponds, while the children play in the playground area or enjoy snacks from the refreshment stand. Admission is £1 ($1.60) for adults and 50p (80¢) for children, with an additional charge to those who go fishing. It is open from 10 a.m. to 6 p.m. April to October (fishing all year). If you want to fish, you must pay £8 ($12.80) for a day's license. The first four fish you catch are free. After that you pay a small surcharge.

The **Bell Tower** of All Saints' Episcopal Church, set in pleasant grounds, contains Scotland's finest bells, the third-heaviest ring of ten in the world. An easy staircase leads to a safe pedestrian walkway on top of the tower to see the bells and fine views over the loch and glen. The tower is open from 10 a.m. to 1 p.m. and 2 to 5 p.m. weekdays, from 3 to 6 p.m. on Sunday May to the end of September. It costs adults 50p (80¢) and children 25p (40¢) to ascend the tower, but the ground-floor exhibition is free. For more information, telephone 0499/2433.

The **Argyll Wildlife Park** (tel. 0499/2264) contains more than 100 species of wildfowl from around the world, including a spectacular collection of owls. You can trek along forest walk, spying on wild goats, roe deer, and wallabies. There is a woodland picnic area beside Loch Fyne, plus a gift shop. The park is open daily from 9 a.m. to 7 p.m. Admission is £1.80 ($2.88) for adults and 90p ($1.44) for children.

The **Auchindrain Museum of Country Life** (tel. 04995/235), six miles southwest of Inveraray, is an open-air museum of traditional Highland farming life. It is a unique survival of the past, whose origins are so far back as to be a subject for archeology. The farming township stands more or less as it was in the 1800s, but studies reveal at least four centuries before that. At present, Auchindrain consists of 20-odd acres of the "infield," about which stand 21 houses and barns of the 18th and 19th centuries. Some are furnished to their appropriate period, and others contain displays. There is also a display center and a museum shop. Open daily during the summer, it charges adults £1.50 ($2.40); children pay 75p ($1.20). There is no charge for children 7 years old and under. The museum is closed Saturday during April, May, and September. Auchindrain and mid-Argyll are in an area crammed with things and places of interest for historians, antiquarians, and archeologists.

If you head south along Loch Fyne, you will come to the **Crarae Glen Garden** (tel. 0546/86633) along the A83, ten miles southwest of Inveraray. Considered one of the most beautiful gardens of Scotland, it is open to the public from 9 a.m. to 6 p.m., charging adults an admission of £1 ($1.60); children are admitted free. In 50 acres are rich plantings, including azaleas, conifers, and rhododendrons, along with waterfalls and splendid vistas onto the loch.

10. Cairndow

Barely visible from the main highway (the A83), the hamlet nestles between a hill and Loch Fyne, on the loch's eastern shore. It is a peaceful haven with a view of the loch and the high mountains. **Strone Woodland Garden** (tel. 04996/284) is open from April to October, containing unusual tree shrubs and the tallest tree in the United Kingdom. The location is along the A815, 12 miles east of Inveraray. It is open daily from 9 a.m. to 9 p.m., charging adults an admission of £1 ($1.60).

FOOD AND LODGING: One of the oldest coaching inns in the Highlands, the **Cairndow Stagecoach Inn & Stables Restaurant** (tel. 03012/286), has entertained illustrious guests through the years, including Dorothy Wordsworth in 1803. Even Queen Victoria had her horses changed here in 1875. Nowadays, Douglas and Catherine Fraser welcome you in the best tradition of Scottish hospitality. Their inn lies just off the A83 on the upper reaches of Loch Fyne. In a relaxed country atmosphere, comfortably furnished rooms are rented, including two family rooms, at a rate of £13 ($20.80) per person for B&B, half price for children 3 to 12. All units have hot and cold running water, and half a dozen have baths. Many of the units open onto a view of the loch. In the public bar and lounge you can sample many malt whiskies while chatting with the locals. In summer there is occasional entertainment at the inn, and once a month, a barn dance. The stables from coaching days have been converted into the Stables Restaurant, with a beamed ceiling, candlelight, and views over the loch. A table d'hôte dinner is offered for £8.50 ($13.60), and you can also order à la carte, enjoying such local dishes as sauté haunch of venison in red wine sauce and Loch Fyne salmon steaks. Children's meals are also served, and "pub grub" is available in the bar during the day. The inn makes a good center for touring, or you can relax in the lochside garden.

11. Strachur

On the eastern banks of Loch Fyne, on the periphery of the Argyll Forest Park, stands one of the most famous inns in the western Highlands (see below). Five miles south along the loch will take you to the old **Castle Lachlan** at Strathiachian, the 13th-century castle of the MacLachlan clan. Now in romantic ruins, it was bombarded by the English in 1745. The MacLachlans were fervent Jacobites and played a major role in the uprising.

FOOD AND LODGING: A favorite of mine is the **Creggans Inn** (tel. 036986/ 279). Mary Queen of Scots is said to have landed at Creggans in 1563 on her way through the Highlands. Today a sprawling white-walled inn commemorates the approximate spot where she is said to have disembarked from her ship. The fully modernized hotel sits at the edge of Loch Fyne, surrounded by a wildlife refuge and gardens. Sir Fitzroy and Lady Veronica MacLean are the proprietors. When Lady MacLean isn't occupying herself with her gardens, she might be compiling one of her bestselling cookbooks, which are on sale at the inn. The establishment contains one of the few real charcoal grills in Scotland, which produces succulent versions of Aberdeen Angus steaks and lamb kebabs. You can also enjoy fresh jumbo prawns, local lamb cutlets, venison, and the MacLean's own version of smoked salmon. All baking is done on the premises, and Sunday brunch is an event here, as are occasional ceilidhs. An à la carte dinner costs from £15 ($24), and lunches are much cheaper but also very tasty.

Guests are free to use the upstairs sitting room, the garden-style lounge, and one of the two in-house bars. One of these features pub lunches beside an open fire. Twenty of the bedrooms contain their own private bath or shower, and each one is attractively furnished and comfortably appointed. B&B costs from £37 ($59.20) in a single and from £28 ($44.80) per person based on double occupancy. Lunch is served from 12:30 to 2 p.m. and dinner from 7:30 to 9:30 p.m. Always make a reservation if you're contemplating dining here in the evening.

Chapter XIV

ARRAN, KINTYRE, AND ISLAY

FOR MANY FOREIGN VISITORS the Atlantic seaboard of the old county of Argyll will represent a journey into the unknown. For those who want to sample a bygone era, this is one of the most rewarding trips off the coastline of western Scotland. My recommendations, both for accommodations and sight-seeing, lie on islands, easily reached by ferries, except the Kintyre Peninsula which is a virtual island in itself. You'll soon discover that the Gaelic traditions of the islands endure. Peace and tranquility prevail.

From the surf-washed Atlantic seaboard of the Isle of Islay to the Mull of Kintyre—celebrated in the song by Paul McCartney—there is much beauty here. Because of the mildness of the climate, subtropical gardens are possible. The land is rich and lush, especially at Arran, but when it gives way to the peat deposits of Islay that natural resource is used too. It lends its flavor to the making of fine malt whiskies—names such as Lagavulin, Bruichladdick, and Laphroaig.

Yachtsmen are drawn to the coastline of Argyll, finding many a sheltered harbor. This is active sports-oriented country, taking in golfing, walking, sea angling, and fishing. The best golf is at Machrie and Machrihanish.

Between distillery visits and birdwatching forays, you will find a diversity of scenic beauty, across hills and glens and past fast-rushing streams and little roads that eventually lead to coastal villages, nearly all of which have out their B&B signs in summer.

This chapter also takes in the unspoiled and remote island of Jura (easily reached from Islay), where George Orwell, the novelist, found the time and inspiration to write his prophecy of the future, *1984*. He found an idyllic home on an island known for its red deer and eagles.

And the best news for last: These islands as well as Kintyre, Scotland's longest peninsula, are among the most economical places to visit in Great Britain.

1. Isle of Arran

At the mouth of the Firth of Clyde, this island is often described as Scotland in miniature, because of its wild and varied scenery, containing an assortment of glens, moors, lochs, sandy bays, and rocky coasts that have made the country famous. Ferry services making the 50-minute crossing operate from Ardrossan to Brodick, the major village of Arran, lying on the eastern shore. In summer a small ferry runs between Lochranza in the north of Arran across to Claonaig in Argyll, providing a gateway to the Highlands and a visit to Kintyre. Sailing time is only 30 minutes.

Once on Arran, you'll find buses take you to the various villages, each with its own character. A coast road, 60 miles long, runs the length of the island.

Arran contains some splendid mountain scenery, notably the conical peak of **Goatfell** in the north, reaching a height of 2,866 feet. It's called "the mountain of the winds."

Students of geology flock to Arran to study igneous rocks of the Tertiary Age. Cairns and standing stones at **Tormore** intrigue archeologists as well.

Arran is also filled with beautiful glens, especially **Glen Sannox** in the northeast and **Glen Rosa**, directly north of Brodick. In one day you can see a lot, as the island is only 25 miles long, ten miles wide.

After the ferry docks at Brodick, you may want to head for Arran's major sight—**Brodick Castle** (tel. 0770/2202), 1½ miles north of the Brodick pierhead. The historic home of the Dukes of Hamilton, the castle dates from the 13th century and contains antiques, portraits, and objets d'art. It is open on Easter weekend, then on Monday, Wednesday, and Saturday from 1 to 5 p.m. until May. From May 1 to September 30, hours are daily from 1 to 5 p.m. (last entry at 4:40 p.m.). The gardens are open all year, daily from 10 a.m. to 5 p.m. Admission to both the castle and gardens is £2 ($3.20) for adults, £1 ($1.60) for children.

South from Brodick lies the village and holiday resort of Lamlash, opening onto Lamlash Bay. From here a ferry takes visitors over to **Holy Island** with its 1,000-foot peak. A disciple of St. Columba founded a church on this island.

In the north, Lochranza is a village with a unique appeal. It opens onto a bay of pebbles and sand, and in the background lie the ruins of a castle that reputedly was the hunting seat of Robert the Bruce.

BRODICK: Less than half a mile from the village center, the **Altanna Hotel** (tel. 0770/2232) provides a sweeping view of the valley and high hills of Arran. There's an 18-hole golf course across from the hotel, and the beach is only 300 yards away. Within half a mile there is tennis as well as boating, fishing, and pony trekking. The owners welcome guests, usually for at least a week, but when possible one can stay by the day. The rate is from £17.50 ($28) per person daily for half board. This includes VAT, and children are accepted at half the rate.

Hotel Ormidale (tel. 0770/2293), across from the Brodick golf course, stands in seven acres of its own garden and woodlands. It's just a five-minute walk to the beach and shops, and 15 minutes from the ferry. Golfers will find that the hotel is literally yards from the first tee. The hotel is fully licensed, offering 30 malt whiskies in the Tartan Lounge. There's a sun lounge and fisherman's bar for local color. The hotel is centrally heated, and the bedrooms have hot and cold water. B&B is £12.50 ($20) per person. The hotel offers an extensive bar meal menu. Local seafood is a specialty, and a three-course meal starts at £5.50 ($8.80). Prices are reduced for children under 12.

Kilmichael House Hotel (tel. 0770/2219), is a mansion house surrounded by its own gardens just one mile from the village, as well as golf, tennis, and the beach. If you wish, a picnic lunch can be prepared. In the evening before guests go to bed, tea and cookies are served in the living room (or something stronger, as the house is licensed). Each bedroom has a hot and cold water basin and electric blankets. For bed, breakfast, and dinner, the price is £15 ($24) per person, less for children.

Ennismore Hotel (tel. 0770/2265), is a solidly constructed Edwardian-style villa sitting directly opposite the waterfront on a quiet road lined with other hotels. The rambling front porch contains a comfortable bench from which guests can enjoy a view of the garden. Inside the cozy ground-floor lounge bar an electrified brick fireplace throws off a reddish glow. Many of the comfortable bedrooms contain private baths as well as central heating and electric blankets. B&B costs from £11 ($17.60) per person, with a fixed-price evening meal going for £7 ($11.20). A well-flavored cuisine is served.

LAMLASH: With a view across the bay to the Holy Isle, the **Glenisle Hotel** (tel. 07706/258), a whitewashed country place whose well-kept gardens, including a putting course, have flower beds and tall old trees. The public rooms are brightly treated, with a reception lounge, water-view dining room, plus a TV lounge. Each bedroom has its hot and cold water, a radio, electric blankets, tea and coffee makers, and room call. Daily cost for B&B is £9.50 ($15.20) per person, increasing to £13.50 ($21.60) per person in a unit with a private bath or shower. Dinner is an extra £6.50 ($10.40) per person. It's open from April to October.

The **Bay Hotel** (tel. 07706/224), opposite the yacht club, was once a fine country home, standing in its own garden, 100 yards back from the main road. Now converted into a hotel, it attracts guests who enjoy its home-cooking and comfortable bedrooms. Each chamber has innerspring mattresses, hot-beverage facilities, electric blankets, and hot and cold water basin. Mrs. Isobel Shaw, the wife of the owner, sets the pace of friendliness and consideration. For half board, her terms are £15 ($24) per person nightly, only £12 ($19.20) for B&B. It's open in mid-May, closing in September.

Carraig Mhor (tel. 07706/453) serves some of the finest food on the island, and its dinners are imaginatively prepared and beautifully served (but you should always call ahead for a reservation). This modernized cottage overlooking the water in the center of the village is the domain of David F. Martin. If you're passing through in the morning, you may want to drop in for coffee and freshly baked goods such as scones. Light lunches then follow, including quiches, omelets, soups, fresh salads, and always a hot dish of the day, perhaps a curry. At dinner you get a more varied menu and some smoothly elegant dishes. Light lunches cost from £5 ($8), and a three- or four-course dinner costs from £10.50 ($16.80) to £12.50 ($20). The restaurant/coffeeshop is open Tuesday to Saturday from 10:30 to 11:45 a.m. for coffee, from 12:15 to 1:45 p.m. for lunch, and from 7 to 9 p.m. for dinner.

WHITING BAY: Opposite a safe, sandy beach, **Burlington Private Hotel** (tel. 07707/255) is a small, family-run accommodation with a friendly atmosphere and pleasant surroundings. All bedrooms have continental quilts, electric blankets, heating, and hot and cold water basins. The charge for B&B is £11.50 ($18.40) per person or £15.50 ($24.80) per person for half board. The food is good, home-style cooking, freshly prepared daily. The hotel is within walking distance of the village and various sports facilities. The proprietors have been accepting guests for quite a while, and many clients are repeat customers. Burlington stands on a stretch of sandy shore, convenient for golf, fishing, bathing, bowling, and dancing. The family-style lounge has color TV.

Stanford Guest House (tel. 07707/313), owned by Mr. and Mrs. J. Ritchie, is a small family-run guesthouse directly on the seafront. It's convenient for various sports. Kate Ritchie prepares good breakfasts, and I advise arranging for an evening meal as well. The B&B rate is from £10 ($16) per person, including VAT. With dinner, the tab rises to £15 ($24). You can have a picnic lunch packed, too. For evening there's a TV set in the guest lounge and always an enjoyable view from the bay windows. Children are welcomed at reduced rates. It's a friendly, congenial home. Bikes can be rented, as well as a 14-foot boat with engine, plus fishing rods.

Invermay Hotel (tel. 07707/431) is a neat, three-story house right on the roadway, with a half-stone facade and bay windows. It faces the seafront across from a bathing beach, with scenic views. Run by Jill and Bobby Shand, who are considerate hosts, the guest home is well kept. Rooms contain hot and cold running water and razor sockets, and all beds have electric blankets. The charge is £11 ($17.60) per person nightly for B&B. However, I recommend the half-board rate of £15 ($24) per person. The Shands specialize in Scottish home-cookery such as porridge, haggis, cock-a-leekie soup, and other dishes. However, for those not desiring such dishes, there are other selections. Activities nearby include golf, fishing, climbing, pony trekking, and, of course, walking.

Royal Hotel (tel. 07707/286). This pleasingly proportioned stone house was built in 1899 as a temperance hotel. Today it's still unlicensed for alcohol, but full meals, and good ones at that, are served in the dining room. Guests enjoy a vista over the bay and its tidal flats from some of the bedrooms. Six of the nine accommodations contain private shower, with toilet facilities in the hallway. Owner Roy Budd charges from £10 ($16) per person for B&B, with another £5 ($8) added for a full dinner for in-house guests. You'll recognize the place by its garden out front where palm trees survive in the mild climate.

KILDONAN: A largish place, the **Kildonan Hotel** (tel. 077082/207) has 22 rooms, two of which are set aside for families. Only two have private baths. The hotel lies right on the sea: a minute's walk and your feet will touch the sand and the water. It's on the southerly tip of the island, and it offers diversions such as putting, boating, fishing, table tennis, and scuba-diving, or you can just sit in the sun lounge and watch the sea birds plummet from 100 feet into the water to catch fish. Opposite the hotel is Pladda Island, with a lighthouse and gray seals basking on the rocks. Rooms are suitably furnished and provide comfort. It's best to take the half-board rate, ranging in price from £18.50 ($29.60) to £23.50 ($37.60) per person nightly.

KILMORY: Good accommodations are offered at the **Lagg Hotel** (tel. 077087/255). There has been some kind of inn in this sheltered hollow since 1791. The pleasantly embellished building you see today was last enlarged in 1964. The resident proprietors maintain the gardens that stretch beside the rocky stream adjoining the ten-acre property. If the weather is sunny, you might enjoy tea on the lawn under the shade of palm trees which seem to thrive in this mild climate. In cooler weather, visitors are likely to be greeted by a log fire blazing in one of the establishment's two brick fireplaces around which exists an array of cozy nooks for a before-dinner cocktail. A fixed-price evening meal in the carvery-style restaurant costs £12 ($19.20). Guests select from an array of roast joints, and you can also be served salmon and trout from the nearby river. The Sunday buffet lunch, priced at £6.50 ($10.40) per person, is one of the most popular events on the island. The 17 well-furnished bedrooms, half of which have private baths, cost from £20 ($32) per person nightly for B&B. Half board is from £30 ($48) per person.

BLACKWATERFOOT: A friendly oasis, the **Rock Hotel** (tel. 077086/225) is named after a boulder rising above the gravel-covered shore a few yards from the 12-hole golf course and the area's sandy beach. In fact the cozy pub is so popular with golfers that it's nicknamed "the 13th hole" by the owners. The establishment offers eight pleasantly furnished bedrooms. None has a private bath; however, all but three of them open onto the sea and the distant Kintyre peninsula. Open all year, the hotel charges from £13 ($20.80) per person for B&B. For half board, you pay £21 ($33.60) per person.

    Kinloch Hotel (tel. 077086/444). This establishment's 49 bedrooms are contained within both its stucco-covered Victorian core and a contemporary wing jutting out along the coast. Through its functionally furnished public rooms trek an array of summer guests, mostly from the mainland of western Scotland. On the premises are a sauna, a heated indoor swimming pool, and a large dining room. The comfortable bedrooms contain large-windowed views of the sea, as well as private bath, radio, intercom, baby alarm, color TV, and tea-making equipment. The per-person rate for B&B runs from £22 ($35.20) daily, but it's better to take the half-board tariff of £30 ($48).

LOCHRANZA: I especially like the **Kincardine Lodge Hotel** (tel. 077083/267). The most striking thing about this place is its well-maintained garden, whose fish pond glistens just below the branches of a copper-colored beech. The staff sets out lawn furniture in summer beside the holly trees and rhododendrons. There, guests are invited to contemplate the view of the water and the village's ruined castle. The half-timbered lodge hotel was built in 1909, and today rents out seven pleasantly furnished rooms to paying guests. None of the units contains private bath. The charge for B&B ranges from £9 ($14.40) to £10 ($16) per person nightly, depending on the season. Half board, again depending on the time of year, ranges from £12.50 ($20) to £15 ($24) per person. In good weather tea is served on the lawn, followed by a good-tasting dinner using fresh produce.

    Castlekirk House (tel. 077083/210) is an unusual restaurant set in the red and graystone church that was built long ago across the tidal flat from the ruined castle. Bathed in the light filtering through the leaded glass of the enormous windows, you can enjoy the sumptuous Sunday lunch costing £5 ($8) for three courses, served from noon to 2 p.m. À la carte dinners, for £10 ($16) and up for a full meal, are served daily from 7 to 9 p.m. Typical dishes might include lentil créole soup, a casserole of pork with prunes, poached trout with cucumber sauce, or ragoût of venison. Your dessert might be a candy and date surprise pudding with fresh cream. The licensed restaurant has a range of drinks.

CORRIE: A good place to eat is the **Garden Room Bistro,** Ingledene Hotel (tel. 077081/225). Several years ago Calum Macalister Hall and his attractive wife, Susan, escaped from urban life to establish this charming garden-style restaurant beside the sea. In a setting of green and white latticework and light-hearted Victorian accessories, you can enjoy a before-dinner drink in the lounge before heading to your dinner table. In winter the warmth comes from an iron stove.

The windows encompass a view of the front garden and the gravel flats beside the sea. Full dinners cost from £10 ($16) apiece. Susan usually cooks, preparing such specialties as homemade Highlander's pâté, freshly made garlic bread, sole meunière, Caribbean chicken (served tropical style in a coconut shell), rainbow trout with an orange sauce, smoked oyster salad, salmon from the bay, and lamb cutlets with port and almonds. Each day's menu offers two kinds each of steak, chicken, or lamb. Between October and April the restaurant is closed. During the rest of the year it's open every day except Monday from noon to 10 p.m.

Ingledene Hotel (tel. 077081/225). The owners of the previously recommended Garden Room Bistro also maintain five apartment accommodations on the grounds. Golfers appreciate the nearby course, and vacationers enjoy the chance to be away from civilization in one of the island's smallest hamlets. Each apartment contains a full kitchen and a lot of extra touches. Depending on the season, an apartment for two persons costs £85 ($136) to £105 ($168) per week. An apartment suitable for four to five persons rents for £120 ($192) to £150 ($240) per week.

2. The Kintyre Peninsula

The longest peninsula in Scotland, Kintyre is more than 60 miles in length, containing much beautiful scenery, pleasant villages, and miles of sandy beaches. It is one of the most unspoiled areas of Scotland, owing perhaps to its isolation. Former Beatle Paul McCartney keeps a home here, drawn to Kintyre by its bucolic charm and individuality.

If you drive all the way to the tip of Kintyre, you'll be only 12 miles from Ireland. Kintyre is ancient Dalriada, the first kingdom of the Scots.

Kintyre is joined to the mainland of Scotland by a narrow neck of land near the old port of Tarbert. The largest town on the peninsula is the old port of Campbeltown, on the southeastern coast.

In the evening in some of the peninsula's village halls and hotels you might hear the music of the ceilidhs.

The land mass has many attractions for the intrepid visitor willing to spend the time to seek them out. One beauty spot is the **Carradale House Gardens** (tel. 05833/234), lying off the B842, 12½ miles northeast of Campbeltown. From April to September daily from 10 a.m. to 5:30 p.m., you can visit this walled garden from 1870. Because of its outstanding azaleas and rhododendrons, it is best seen in late April, May, and June. You can also see the remains of a fort built on an island, which you can reach by foot except at high tide. Admission is 20p (32¢) for adults.

One of the major attractions of the peninsula is the remains of **Skipness Castle and Chapel,** lying at Skipness, along the B8001, ten miles south of Tarbert, opening onto Loch Fyne. The hamlet was once an old Norse village. The ruins of the ancient chapel and big 13th-century castle look out onto the Sound of Kilbrannan and the Sound of Bute. In its heyday it could control shipping along Loch Fyne. A five-story tower remains.

TARBERT: A sheltered harbor protects this fishing port and yachting center lying on a narrow neck of land at the northern tip of the Kintyre peninsula, between West Loch Tarbert and the head of herring-filled Loch Fyne.

Tarbert means drawboat in Norse. It referred to a place where Vikings dragged their boats across land on rollers from one sea to another. It is said that in 1093 King Malcolm of Scotland and King Magnus Barelegs of Norway reached an agreement. The Western Isles were to belong to Norway, the mainland to Scotland. An island was defined as anything a Viking ship could sail around. King Magnus proclaimed Kintyre an island by having his dragon ship dragged across the mile of dry land from West Loch Tarbert on the Atlantic to East Loch Tarbert on Loch Fyne. After the Vikings gave way, Kintyre came under the control of the Macdonald Lordship of the Isles.

Called the gateway to Kintyre, Tarbert has several inexpensive hotels and pubs. The ancient **castle at Tarbert** dates from the 13th century, and was later extended by Robert the Bruce. James IV stayed here in the 15th century, and may have held a parliament. In Tarbert the castle ruins are called "Bruce Castle." They're found on a hillock above the village on the south side of the bay. The oldest part still standing is a keep dating from the 13th century.

Food and Lodging

Tarbert Hotel, Harbour Street (tel. 08802/264), is the most charming hotel in the center of town. It sits on the waterfront, within view of the anchored sailing vessels, behind an 18th-century Georgian facade that was elaborately embellished by the Victorians. A coal- and log-burning fireplace usually blazes in the parlor-style residents' lounge, whose red- and white-flocked wallpaper evokes the aura of a century ago. The restaurant is more modern in style, yet still cozy and alluring. The hotel serves bar meals, high teas, and à la carte dinners. Of the 20 comfortably furnished bedrooms, ten have private baths or showers, and each unit has a color TV. B&B costs £14 ($22.40) to £19 ($30.40) per person, the price depending on the plumbing.

On the outskirts, **West Loch Hotel** (tel. 08802/283) is a family-run establishment built 200 years ago as a staging post for coaches heading for Campbeltown and for farmers driving their cattle to the markets at Stirling. Today the comfortably outfitted black-and-white hotel is one of the most alluring in the region, with two bars, with either an open fireplace or a woodburning stove. The hotel has had a checkered history, serving over its past life as both a collection of apartments and then as a private house. It is now owned by Janet and Alastair Thom. One of the establishment's strong points is its cuisine, served in an intimate dining room lined with wine racks. Tempting pub meals can be consumed anywhere in the hotel. But if you want a full meal, the specialties include panfried local cod roe with tartar sauce, lemon sole filets poached in white wine (and served with grapes and cream), locally smoked trout with horseradish sauce, pheasant casserole with calvados cream, and apples, along with fresh local lobster (served cold with a salad or grilled with garlic butter), as well as smoked trout quiche and a casserole of beef cooked with Guinness and oranges.

Accommodations in one of the attractively furnished bedrooms, six in all, each without bath, cost from £15 ($24) per person in a double and from £22 ($35.20) in a single, with breakfast included. Full dinners cost from £14 ($22.40), but an excellent bar lunch goes for only £5 ($8). Both the hotel and restaurant are closed in November.

The **Anchorage Coffeeshop/Restaurant** (tel. 08802/881) is a little establishment run by Fiona Evamy, assisted by her husband, David. They serve good snacks throughout the day along with more substantial fare, such as seafood. Homemade goods are served with cream teas. For £5 ($8), you can get a satisfying meal here. Open seven days a week from 10 a.m. to 7 p.m., with later hours during the summer. You'll spot the coffeeshop next to the Islay Frigate Hotel, near the castle and adjacent to the Quayside.

CARRADALE: On the lusher eastern coast of Kintyre, north of Campbeltown, Carradale is a small town opening onto the shores of Kilbrannan Sound. People come here to walk and relax, but they can also go pony trekking or windsurfing, or have a picnic in several scenic areas, where log tables and benches have been provided.

Carradale Beach is equipped with facilities for certain water sports and for swimming, if you don't mind the chilly waters. The fishing fleet is anchored in the harbor. The herring boats set out from here each night.

Those interested in historic sites can seek out the ruins of **Saddell Abbey** along the B842 nine miles northwest of Campbeltown. This Cistercian abbey was built in the 12th century by one of the Lords of the Isles, either Somerled or his son, Reginald. The walls of the original building remain, and there are several sculptured grave slabs.

Food and Lodging

Carradale Hotel (tel. 05833/223) is a white-walled establishment built around 1800 as the first hotel to open on the eastern side of the peninsula. It's been owned by the same families, the Martins and the McDougalls, for about 80 years. Set in a garden in the center of this tiny hamlet, the hotel offers a comfortably high-ceilinged dining room, a lounge bar serving pub meals, an adjacent collection of squash courts, and a nine-hole golf course. Rooms are simply but pleasantly furnished, and the food is good (and you get plenty of it). B&B ranges from £15.50 ($24.80) to £22 ($35.20) per person, depending on the plumbing.

CAMPBELTOWN: This is a fishing port and a resort with a shingle beach at the southern tip of the Kintyre peninsula. Popularly known as the "wee toon," Campbeltown has long been linked with fishermen.

Campbeltown Loch contains **Davaar Island,** which is accessible at low tide by those willing to cross the Dhorlin, a half-mile run of shingle-paved causeway. It's also possible to take boat trips. Once on the island, you can visit a crucifixion cave painting, the work of Archibald MacKinnon, a local resident. He painted it in 1887. It takes about an hour and a half to walk around this tidal island, with its natural rock gardens.

On the quayside in the heart of town is the **Campbeltown Cross,** which dates from the 14th century. This Celtic cross is considered the finest piece of carving from the Middle Ages left in Kintyre.

Food and Lodging

Argyll Arms Hotel, Main Street (tel. 0586/53431). This stone building was formerly owned by the Duke of Argyll, who maintained a suite on the second floor even after he sold it as a hotel. Today the duke's suite is used as a conference room, and the clientele is more likely to include waves of tourists than the visiting friends of aristocracy. The decor is a barely modernized Victorian evocation, with red-flocked wallpaper and very dark, almost blackened, paneling. John (Reggie) McManus and his wife, Enid, are the friendly managers. The Farmer's Bar is a garrulous cubbyhole near the entrance where you are likely to meet nearly anyone in town. The Cabin Bar, in back, is more sedately formal. The in-house restaurant serves lunch and dinner every day of the week. A three-course shopper's lunch goes for £3.60 ($5.76). A fixed-price evening meal, served from 7 to 8 p.m., costs £8 ($12.80). Six of the 12 bedrooms have private baths. Depending on the plumbing, B&B costs £14.50 ($23.20) to £16.50 ($26.40) per person.

The White Hart, Main Street (tel. 0586/52440), is an 18-bedroom hotel with a corner tower, slate roof, and white walls on a street corner in the center of town. It was built in the 19th century as an upper-crust hotel, but after the end of the Edwardian era it went into decline. Today bedrooms have been renovated, and a well-recommended restaurant adds to the attraction. There is a residents' bar on the second floor, as well as a Coach House for bar meals and drinks, along with a pub popular with locals. Depending on the plumbing, singles range from £16.50 ($26.40) to £20 ($32), while doubles cost £14.50 ($23.20) to £17.50 ($28) per person, all with a full breakfast included. Full meals in the restaurant go for £12 ($19.20) and up.

Ballegreggan House (tel. 0586/52062) is a favorite little guesthouse, a Victorian stone villa managed by Morag and Bruce Urquhart and Morag's parents. The house offers six rooms without private baths. The charge for dinner, bed, and breakfast is from £14 ($22.40) per person. From the house, you have splendid views across the open countryside to Campbeltown Loch.

Seafield Private Hotel, Kilkerran Road (tel. 0586/52741), is a homey and comfortable guesthouse about half a mile from the center of town. The view from its front windows is over the waters of Campbeltown Loch. Each of the simple, cozy bedrooms has hot-beverage equipment, and nearly half contain private baths. The charge is from £16 ($25.60) in a single and from £15 ($24) per person in a double, with breakfast included. You can stay here on half-board terms of £23 ($36.80) to £28 ($44.80) per person. There's a cocktail bar on the premises, as well as a television lounge.

SOUTHEND: Some ten miles to the south of Campbeltown, the village of Southend stands across from the Mull of Kintyre. It has sandy beaches, a golf course, and views across the sea to the Island of Sanda and Ireland itself. Legend has it that footprints on a rock here marked the spot where St. Columba is said to have first set foot on Scottish soil. The footsteps can be seen imprinted in a flat-topped rock. The location is near the ruin of an old chapel. Other historians suggest that the footprints mark the spot where ancient kings were crowned.

Visitors can also go to **Dunaverty Rock,** called "Blood Rock" by the locals. This was once a MacDonald stronghold, then known as Dunaverty Castle. It was the scene in 1647 of a great massacre, as some 300 citizens lost their lives. Led by General Leslie, the Covenanters slaughtered the garrison. "Why all the interest in Glencoe?" asked one local resident. "We had far more people slaughtered at 'Blood Rock.'"

Visitors also drive down from Campbeltown, a distance of 11 miles, to see the **Mull of Kintyre.** From Southend you can take a narrow road until you reach the "gap." From there on, you should walk down to the lighthouse. This is one of the wildest and most remote parts of the peninsula, and it is its very desolation that appeals to visitors.

MACHRIHANISH: To the west of Campbeltown, opening onto the harsher west coast, Machrihanish contains one of the finest golf courses in the country. It was laid out by Tom Morris more than a century ago. Golfers play while enjoying views of the Isles of Gigha, Jura, and Islay. There are about a dozen blind spots over various horizons. When the tide comes in, players have to "drive across the Atlantic." The village also has one of the best surfing beaches in the country.

Food and Lodging

Ardell House (tel. 058681/235) is a large Victorian house converted into a private hotel, standing away from the road on a sweep of lawn. The bow windows have views across the bay to the islands of Jura. David and Jill Baxter and their two children offer a warm welcome and personal attention to paying guests in their private home. The 11 bedrooms all have hot and cold water basins, TV, and hot-beverage facilities, and most have private showers. They cost from £16 ($25.60) for B&B, from £24 ($38.40) for half board. Dinner features such delicacies as Tobermory sea trout and other freshly caught fish. The hotel has a color TV lounge and a self-service bar. Many of the guests are golfers, some returning year after year.

3. Isle of Gigha

One of the southern Hebrides, the six-mile-long Isle of Gigha is often called "sacred" and "legendary." Little changed over the centuries, it lies off the Kintyre peninsula's west coast. From Tayinloan you can board a ferry for Gigha. Weather permitting, sailings, which leave daily in season, take about 20 minutes to reach the island, depositing you at **Ardminish,** the main hamlet on the island. For ferry times, phone 05835/254.

Gigha is visited mainly by those wishing to explore its famous gardens, arguably the finest in Scotland. **Achamore House Gardens** (tel. 05835/254) lie a mile from the ferry dock at Ardminish. These extensive gardens contain roses, hydrangeas, rhododendrons, camellias, and azaleas, among other flowering plants. They are open year round from 9 a.m. to dusk, charging adults an admission of £2 ($3.20). Occupying a 50-acre site, these gardens were the creation of the late Sir James Horlick, who was considered one of the great gardeners of the world. The house is not open to the public. If time remains, try to explore some more of the island, which has had a rich Viking past. Cairns and ruins still remain. The Vikings used to store their loot here after plundering the west coast of Scotland. High on a ridge overlooking the village of Ardminish you can see the ruins of the Church of Kilchattan, dating back to the 13th century. From Norway came King Haakan some 700 years ago. He called the island "Gud" or good. Eventually that was corrupted to Gigha (pronounced "Ghee-a") by the Gaels. Creag Bhan is the highest hill, rising more than 330 feet. From the top you can look out onto the islands of Islay and Jura (coming up) as well as Kintyre. On a clear day you can also see Ireland, from whence came so many of the Celtic missionaries to convert the Hebridean islanders to Christianity. Ogham Stone is always sought out by those interested in antiquity. It is one of only two standing stones in the Hebrides that bears Ogham inscription, a form of script used back in the days of the Scottish kingdom of Dalriada. Gigha is the innermost island of the Hebrides, lying three miles off the Kintyre peninsula.

FOOD AND LODGING: Owned and restored by Mr. and Mrs. Landale, the **Gigha Hotel** (tel. 05835/254) is a small hostelry whose hospitable public bar is the major rendezvous on the island. It feeds the visitors who come over to see the Achamore Gardens for the day and return to the mainland, but it also shelters tranquility seekers who want to spend some time on Gigha. Managed on the Landales' behalf by Mr. and Mrs. Roebuck, the hotel offers nine handsomely furnished and attractively maintained twin-bedded rooms, accepting guests from April to October. The charge is from £23 ($36.80) per person for B&B, from £33 ($52.80) per person for half board. Even if you're visiting only for the day, you'll want to partake of the food served here. First, you might enjoy a drink in one of the cozy lounges, which have open fires. Later you can sample the traditional Scottish fare along with home-baked goods. Locally caught seafood such as lobster is served, and produce comes from the dairy farms on the island. Game is featured in season. You might begin your meal with a well-flavored bowl of soup, ideal on a chilly day. Lunches cost from £7 ($11.20); dinners, from £12 ($19.20). Meals are offered from noon to 2 p.m. and 7 to 8:30 p.m.

4. Isle of Islay

The southernmost island of the Inner Hebrides, Islay lies 16 miles west of the Kintyre peninsula and less than a mile southwest of Jura, from which it is separated only by a narrow sound. At its maximum breadth, Islay is only 20 miles wide (25 miles long).

Called "the Queen of the Hebrides," it is a peaceful unspoiled island of moors, salmon-filled lochs, sandy bays, and wild rocky cliffs. Islay was the ancient seat of the Lords of the Isles, and today you'll see the ruins of two castles and several Celtic crosses.

Near Port Charlotte are the graves of the U.S. seamen and army troops who lost their lives in 1918 when their carriers, the *Tuscania* and *Otranto,* were torpedoed off the shores of Islay. There's a memorial tower on the Mull of Oa, eight miles from Port Ellen.

The island is noted for its distilleries producing single-malt Highland whiskies by the antiquated pot-still method. Of these, **Laphroaig** at Port Ellen (tel. 0496/2418) allows guided tours on Tuesday and Thursday at 11 a.m. and 3 p.m. You should call first for an appointment.

MacBrayne Steamers operate daily service to Islay—you leave West Tarbert on the Kintyre peninsula, arriving in Port Askaig on Islay in about two hours. There is also service to Port Ellen.

The island's capital is Bowmore, on the coast across from Port Askaig. There you can see a fascinating Round Church—no corners for the devil to hide in. But the most important town is Port Ellen, on the south coast, a holiday and golfing resort as well as Islay's principal port. The 18-hole Machrie golf course is three miles from Port Ellen.

Islay (pronounced "eye-lay") is an island of great beauty, but there are also specific attractions worth seeking out, as any Ileach will tell you (the locals are called Ileachs).

The **Kildalton Crosses,** dripping with antiquity, lie to the northeast of Port Ellen about 7½ miles. In the Kildalton churchyard, they are considered two of the finest Celtic crosses in Scotland.

The ruins of the 14th-century fortress, **Dunyvaig Castle,** lie just south of Kildalton.

In the southwestern part of Islay, Port Charlotte has the **Museum of Islay Life** (tel. 049685/385), which has a wide collection of island exhibitions, ranging from unrecorded times to the present day. The museum is open all year. From April to September its hours are 10 a.m. to 5 p.m. Monday to Friday (on Saturday and Sunday from 2 to 5 p.m.). Off-season it is open Monday to Friday from 10 a.m. to 4:30 p.m. Admission is 60p (96¢) for adults, 30p (48¢) for children.

Loch Gruinart cuts into the northern part of Islay. For decades it has attracted birdwatchers, as the area has long been famous for hosting wintering geese. In 1984 the RAPB purchased 3,000 acres of moors and farmland around the loch, turning it into the **Loch Gruinart Nature Reserve.** Visitors can now enjoy seeing these geese undisturbed.

At Bridgend, you can visit the **Islay Woollen Mill** (tel. 049681/563), which has been in business for more than a century. Sheila and Gordon Covell carry on a tradition of weaving dating back to the 18th century. They make a wide range of country tweeds and accessories. Their mill shop is open from 10 a.m. to 5:30 p.m. six days a week. They sell tastefully designed Shetland wool ties, wool mufflers, Jacob mufflers and ties, flat caps, travel rugs, and wool scarves, among many other items.

FOOD AND LODGING: Fine choices for meals and accommodations are found throughout the island.

Port Askaig

Port Askaig Hotel (tel. 049684/245) is a genuine old island inn, dating from the 18th century but built on the site of an even older inn. It stands on the Sound of Islay overlooking the pier where a MacBrayne steamer berths daily. The hotel is quite charming, offering island hospitality and Scottish fare, including broiled trout, cock-a-leekie soup, roast pheasant, smoked Scottish salmon, and, of course, haggis. The hotel is a major destination for anglers on Islay, and the bar at the inn is popular with local fishermen. All year the friendly staff welcomes you to one of its well-appointed bedrooms, all with color TV, radios, and hot-beverage facilities, as well as central heating. For a five-course dinner, bed, and a full Scottish breakfast, the charge is from £30 ($48) in a bathless single, from £32 ($51.20) in a single with bath. Doubles cost from £28 ($44.80) per person in a bathless room, from £30 ($48) per person with bath. VAT and service are included in the rates. Your hosts are Mr. and Mrs. F.T. Spears.

Bridgend

Bridgend Hotel (tel. 049681/212). Victorian spires cap the slate-covered roofs, and climbing roses creep up the stone and stucco walls. The hotel forms part of a complex of buildings that includes a roadside barn and one of the most beautiful flower and vegetable gardens in Islay. The manager will identify the plants in the garden, which is sheltered by a combination of hillsides, stone walls, and windbreakers. This is one of the oldest hotels on Islay, with somber charm and country-style pleasures. Guests enjoy drinks beside open fireplaces in both the Victorian cocktail lounge and the rustic pub, where locals gather after a day in the surrounding fields. A table d'hôte dinner in the high-ceilinged room costs from £12 ($19.20). Rooms are comfortably and attractively furnished, and only one out of ten contains a private bath. The charge is from £19.50 ($31.20) per person, with breakfast included. The hotel is open all year.

Bowmore

Lochside Hotel, Shore Street (tel. 049681/244), in the center of town, is a simple white-walled hotel with a pleasantly paneled bar, a big windowed lounge bar, and a dining room with a view of the water. It is one of the most popular gathering places in town. Norman, Elaine, and Roderick Osborne welcome you, charging from £21 ($33.60) in a single with shower, and £44 ($70.40) in a double or twin with full private bath. Each well-furnished room contains a radio, color TV, phone, and coffee-making equipment. The food is personally prepared by the owners, and is considered among the best on the island, whenever possible using the freshest of ingredients, including locally caught seafood.

Port Ellen

Machrie Hotel & Golf Course (tel. 0496/2310) lies on the outskirts of Port Ellen. This strikingly isolated resort sits in the center of a 1,000-acre tract of treeless and windswept moor. The central core of the establishment is a 19th-century farmhouse, to which Murdo and Kathleen Macpherson have added a series of extensions, including the plushly appointed Kiln Bar and the Byre Restaurant. The Kiln Bar offers more than 70 varieties of malt whisky served in contemporary comfort. Guests dine at the Byre, whose banquettes curve tastefully around the alcoves of what used to be a cowshed. In addition to the handful of bedrooms within the main building, the resort offers 15 angular cottages, each of which contains two bedrooms, a living/dining room, a kitchen, color TV, central heating, plus a radio link to the main building. Regular rooms come with or without private bath. Singles begin at a low of £15 ($24), going up to £32 ($51.20), and doubles cost from £13 ($20.80) to £24 ($38.40) per person for B&B. The food is excellent, with set dinners going for £10.50 ($16.80).

Many of the hotel guests are avid golfers who play the par 71 championship links, free to residents. The Machrie course is one of the finest examples of a true Scottish links. It was laid out by Willie Campbell in 1890 between what is now the hotel and Laggan Bay, and has since been modernized.

White Hart Hotel (tel. 0496/2311) is for those who want a cheaper and more central location. Right in the center of the port, it enjoys a seaside location against a backdrop of grass-covered hills. It was built in an old-fashioned style that mandated a sweeping stairwell, high coffered ceilings, and an array of peat-burning fireplaces. There is so much space in this cavernous building that residents can enjoy the use of a large second-floor lounge, where enormous windows take in views of the misty Atlantic. The ground-floor pub is one of Port Ellen's most alive gathering places, adjoining a disco that is open several nights a week in summer. Bill and Linda Johnstone took over this place in 1984; they charge £8.50 ($13.60) for a fixed-price dinner. With breakfast included, bathless rooms cost £15.50 ($24.80) in a single, £30 ($48) in a double. Rooms with bath go for £20 ($32) in a single, £38 ($60.80) in a double.

Kildalton

Dower House Hotel (tel. 0496/2425). The Victorian castle that ruled the surrounding estate is now in ruins, but one of its outbuildings is still thriving as a hotel. Rorie and Yvonne Blunt-MacKenzie are the owners, who after leaving South Africa decided to escape to Islay. Their hotel was originally built as a row of stone-walled workers' cottages. Later it became the Dower House of the nearby estate, where the family matriarch lived after her grownup son took over the main house. Today, the traditional stone building is comfortably furnished. The rustic bar with its peat-burning open-hearth fireplace makes the ideal setting for sampling local malt whiskies. The views from the eight bedrooms, all with baths, encompass the sandy beach at the bottom of the garden as well as surrounding forest and hills. The tariff is from £19 ($30.40) to £21 ($33.60) per person for B&B, with dinners going for another £10 ($16). The cuisine makes maximum use of local fish, game, meats, and vegetables. Packed lunches can be arranged for those who want to go fishing, boating, or hiking. The hotel, closed from mid-October to Easter, lies about five miles north of Port Ellen.

Port Charlotte

Bruichladdich Hotel (tel. 049685/305) was built in 1897 by a local doctor, who used it as both his clinic and his living quarters. The ornate iron fence ringing the flower garden was one of the few to escape being melted down for armaments in World War II. Today the waterside house is the property of Mrs. Elspeth Pearce, who personally contributes to the daily preparation of the fresh cuisine that is proudly served from the mahogany sideboard of the intimate dining room. The clientele includes a scattering of urban refugees who relax with a drink every evening beside the peat-burning fireplace of the high-ceilinged bar/lounge. None of the seven bedrooms contains a private bath, but each is beautifully furnished and impeccably clean. On their way to the cozy upstairs residents' lounge, guests pass a stained-glass depiction, art nouveau style, of the Four Seasons. In Mrs. Pearce's own words, her hotel is a peaceful and elegant spot without a lot of razzmatazz.

On a clear day you can see the Irish coastline from the front windows. At anytime you can't miss the calling of flocks of birds as they fly over. Accommodations, which include freshly baked pastries as part of the full Scottish breakfast and dinner, cost from £25 ($40) per person daily. Children are welcome.

Port Charlotte Hotel (tel. 049685/321) is a favorite with divers, many of whom use it as a base while they seek treasure from the wrecks off the coastline. Derek and Bette Bell are the owners of this nautically minded hotel whose view overlooks the site of dozens of wrecked vessels. The social center of the establishment is the ground-floor pub where a peat-burning fireplace illuminates the framed documents and salvaged ships' artifacts that attest to the wealth of underwater riches in the area. Bar lunches and suppers are served, along with full meals, using fresh produce in a cozy dining room. Lunch is from 12:30 to 1:45 p.m. and dinner from 6:30 to 8:30 p.m. The 11 simple, comfortably furnished rooms cost £16 ($25.60) per person. With private bath, guests pay another £4 ($6.40) per person. Breakfast is included in the prices.

5. Isle of Jura

This is the fourth-largest island in the Inner Hebrides. It perhaps takes its name from the Norse "Jura," meaning "deer island." The red deer on Jura outnumber the people by about 20 to 1. At four feet high, the deer are the largest wild animals roaming Scotland. The hearty islanders number only about 250 brave souls, and most of them live along the east coast. The west coast is virtually uninhabited.

The capital, **Craighouse,** is hardly more than a hamlet. From Islay, you can journey to Jura by taking a five-minute ferry ride from Port Askaig, docking at the Feolin Ferry berth.

The breadth of Jura varies from two to eight miles, and at its maximum length it is 27 miles long. The island's landscape is dominated by the **Paps of Jura,** reaching a peak of 2,571 feet at Beinn-an-Oir. An arm of the sea, **Loch Tarbert** nearly divides the island, cutting into it for nearly six miles.

As islands go, Jura is relatively little known or explored. That's unfortunate, as its mountains, soaring cliffs, snug coves, and moors make it an inviting place to be—nowhere is there overcrowding. The island has actually suffered a drastic loss of population.

The square tower of **Claig Castle,** now in ruins, was the stronghold of the MacDonalds until they were subdued by the Campbells in the 17th century.

Literary historians know that George Orwell lived on Jura in the bitter postwar winters of 1946 and 1947. Even then a sick and dying man, he wrote his masterpiece, *1984,* a satire on modern politics. He almost lost his life on Jura when he and his adopted son ventured too close to the whirlpool in the Gulf of Corryvreckan. They were saved by local fishermen, and he went on to finish his masterwork, only to die in London of tuberculosis in 1950. His life span hardly matched that of Gillouir MacCrain, said to have been 180 when he died on Jura in the days of Charles I.

FOOD AND LODGING: The only hotel on the island, the **Jura,** Craighouse (tel. 049682/243), has so much lore connected to it that many guests return year after year, sometimes requesting the same table in the red-carpeted dining room that offers panoramic views of the scattering of nearby islands, most of which are deserted. Jura-bred venison is the establishment's specialty. You'll find it in succulent forms, ranging from filet steaks to venison burgers served beside an open fireplace in the cozy paneled bar. A fixed-price dinner goes for £10 ($16). Only four of the 18 bedrooms have private baths, rates for B&B going from £17.50 ($28) to £20.50 ($32.80), depending on the plumbing. For its clientele, which includes many yachtsmen and birdwatchers, the hotel stays open all year.

The Jura Hotel stands near a distillery in a sprawling, gray-walled building near the center of the hamlet. Sections of the building date from the 1600s, but what you see today was built along solidly conservative lines in 1956. Englishman Gordon Wright, his Kenya-born daughter, Fiona, and her husband, Steve Walton, are the managing directors of the place. They personally conduct special excursions via Land Rover and motorboat to such island curiosities as the Corryvreckan Whirlpool. For visitors arriving without cars, arrangements can be made to have you picked up at the ferryboat jetty at Feolin, across from Port Askaig on Islay.

Chapter XV

GLASGOW AND THE CLYDE

1. Glasgow
2. Dunoon
3. Rothesay and Isle of Bute

GLASGOW LIES ONLY 40 miles to the west of Edinburgh, but forms an amazing contrast. The attractions of Scotland's two leading cities are remarkably different. Just as Edinburgh can be used as the base for branching out in many directions, Glasgow too is at the center of some of Scotland's leading sights. In 40 minutes, for example, you can be touring the "bonnie banks" of Loch Lomond.

On Glasgow's doorstep is the scenic estuary of the Firth of Clyde which you can cruise down on paddle-streamer. The Firth of Clyde is one of the loveliest waterways in the world, with its long sea lochs, islands, and hills.

The good news is that Glasgow is no longer the smoking industrial city of yore, which used to be blighted in parts by the Gorbals, some of the worst slums in Europe. Urban-development schemes have brought about a great change in the major city of Scotland, but, tourist officials concede, reputations are long in dying.

Glasgow today is rich in sightseeing attractions of its own, including some of the greatest art in Britain. It also is a showcase for some of the greatest Victorian architecture in the country, a style appreciated far more in the 1980s than in previous decades.

And, as mentioned, it is also a good center for touring not only Loch Lomond, but Lock Katrine, as well as the resorts along the Ayrshire coast, an hour away by frequent train service. From Glasgow you can also explore the heart of the Burns Country, the Stirling area, Culzean Castle, and the Trossachs.

Greenock is an important industrial and shipbuilding town on the Clyde Estuary a few miles west of the center of Glasgow. It was the birthplace in 1736 of James Watt, inventor of the steam engine. A huge Cross of Lorraine on Lyle Hill above the town commemorates Free French sailors who died in the Battle of the Atlantic during World War II.

Past Greenock, sea lochs strike into the Strathclyde hills—Gareloch, Loch Long, and Loch Goil—with Holy Loch pointing more to the west. This was once a holiday region, but that was changed by World War II. Holy Loch has its Polaris base, and British atomic subs are stationed in these waters. There are new seaports on Loch Long and the Gareloch. Loch Long is long, but its name derives from the Gaelic word meaning "a ship," and the name really means the "loch of the ships." Long before the Clyde was world famous for shipbuilding, the galleys of the old chieftains sheltered in these waters. Vikings hauled their boats overland from Loch Long to raid the country around Loch Lomond.

Gourock, three miles west of Greenock, is a resort and yachting center. On the cliff side of Gourock is **"Granny Kempock,"** a six-foot-high stone of gray schist which was probably significant in prehistoric times. In past centuries it was used by fishermen in rites to ensure fair weather. Couples planning marriage used to circle Granny to get her blessing and to ensure fertility in their marriage.

From Gourock, car-ferries take travelers to **Dunoon** on the Cowal peninsula. You can also visit **Rothesay** and the **Isle of Bute,** where the Glaswegians themselves go for fun in the sun.

All of these attractions, including several destinations just visited and others coming up, are all part of Strathclyde, which means the valley of the River Clyde. But Strathclyde has gone far beyond its literal meaning. Today it is Scotland's biggest unit of local government, taking in some 5,348 square miles. The name itself is ancient, Irish chroniclers having written of the kingdom of Stratha Cluatha some 1,500 years ago.

Long before that, Strathclyde was known to the Romans, who called its people Damnonii. The old capital was Dumbarton, not Glasgow. Dumbarton was selected because its high rock provides a natural fortress. There were a lot of tribes the local people had to defend themselves against back in those days. Picts and Scots from the north attacked with frequency. Northumbrian Anglo-Saxons came up from the south to do damage, and Vikings descended from the far-northern climes. The region finally fell to the Scots of Dalriada in the 10th century.

The fortunes of Strathclyde changed dramatically in the 18th century. The Clyde estuary became the gateway to the New World. Glasgow merchants grew rich on tobacco and then cotton. It was the fastest growing region in Britain in the days of the Industrial Revolution. Factories turned out textiles, then heavy engineering, shipbuilding, and chemicals. Glasgow's fame grew and grew until it became known as "the Second City of the Empire."

The Clyde begins at its source in the high uplands of Lanarkshire. It runs along for 50 miles before flowing through Glasgow.

In what was once an industrial wasteland between Hamilton and Motherwell, the Strathclyde Regional Council has created the 1,600-acre **Strathclyde Regional Park,** with a two-mile loch, the site of many water sports including competition sailing. There is also a bird sanctuary and a nature reserve, along with the Hamilton Mausoleum.

1. Glasgow

Scotland's largest city stands on the banks of the River Clyde, which was the birthplace of the *Queen Mary* and *Queen Elizabeth,* plus many other ocean-going liners. Here is housed half of Scotland's population.

The commercial capital of Scotland, and Britain's third-largest city, Glasgow is very ancient, making Edinburgh, for all its wealth of history, seem comparatively young. The village that became the city grew up beside a ford 20 miles from the mouth of the River Clyde, long famous for its shipbuilding, iron and steelworks. Glasgow was a medieval ecclesiastical center and seat of learning. The ancient city is buried beneath 19th-century Glasgow, which is now undergoing vast urban renewal. Glasgow was founded by St. Kentigern, also called St. Mungo, who selected the site 1,400 years ago for his church.

In 1136 a cathedral was erected over his remains; in 1451 the university was started, the second established in Scotland. Commercial prosperity began in the 17th century when its merchants set out to dominate the trade of the western seas. The Clyde was widened and deepened, and the city's expansion engulfed the smaller towns of Ardrie, Renfrew, Rutherglen, and Paisley, whose roots are deep in the Middle Ages.

In Glasgow, local officials are speaking of a "renaissance," with predictions that it is gaining momentum. More and more it is emerging as a tourist city and a major sightseeing destination in Great Britain, a move aided in part by the decision to locate the Scottish Exhibition and Conference Centre here.

Buildings are being sandblasted of their industrial grime which took decades to build, obsolete housing has been replaced in section after section, overcrowding in the city center has been reduced, and the air has been cleaned up. The immediate result has been more open space and less traffic congestion.

Now that it can be seen again, the Victorian splendor of the city has re-emerged. John Betjeman and other critics have hailed Glasgow as "the greatest surviving example of a Victorian city." The planners of the 19th century thought on a grand scale, as they designed the terraces and villas to the west and south of the center.

ORIENTATION: Monumental Glasgow—that is "Victorian City" and "Merchant City," along with the Central Station—lie on the north bank of the River Clyde which runs through the metropolis. The ancient center of Glasgow has as its core the great Glasgow Cathedral, a perfect example of pre-Reformation Gothic architecture which, in part, dates back to the 12th century. Behind it lies the Necropolis, burial ground of many Victorian merchants. Across the square is Provand's Lordship, the oldest house in the city (built in 1471). Down High Street can be found the Tolbooth Steeple (1626) at Glasgow Cross, while nearer the River Clyde is Glasgow Green, Britain's first public park (1662).

From Ingram Street, South Frederick Street will take you to George Square, with its many statues, including one dedicated to Sir Walter Scott. This is the center of modern Glasgow.

Over the centuries the city headed west, first to Merchant City, a compact area of imposing buildings and enclosed vistas. This is the location of the National Trust for Scotland's shop and visitor center at Hutcheson's Hall. The broad pedestrian thoroughfares of Buchanan Street, Argyle Street, and Sauchiehall Street are the heart of the shopping district.

Glasgow's West End is just a short taxi journey from the city center. It is easily accessible from any part of the city, and the area lies close to the M8 motorway (inner ring road) and the Clydeside Expressway. An extensive network of local bus routes serve or pass through the West End, and the Glasgow underground operates a circular service and by boarding at any station on the system passengers can reach the four stations serving the district. These are Kelvinbridge, Hillhead (the most central), Kelvin Hall, and Patrick.

The West End is the finest example in Britain of a great Victorian city. The terraces of the Park Conversation Area rise to afford excellent views of the West End. Across Kelvingrove Park is the Art Gallery and Museum. Nearby, the tower of Glasgow University dominates Gilmorehill. Beyond is the Hunterian Art Gallery, home to a famous collection of Whistlers. Just a few strides away lies Byres Road, a street of friendly bars and shops, along with excellent restaurants. To the north is the Botanic Gardens.

Great Western Road through Kelvinside to Kelvinbridge reveals some fine terraces and churches en route back to central Glasgow.

A little more than three miles southwest of the city center lies the Pollok Country Park and the Pollok Estate. An extensive network of bus services passes close by the park area, which is also served by two suburban rail stations. An electric bus service is in operation from the Country Park Gates on Pollokshaws Road to Pollok House and the Burrell Collection Gallery. The Burrell Collection is housed in the heavily wooded Pollok Country Park. This is Scotland's top tourist attraction and the focal point of any visit to the South Side. Nearby is the 18th-century Pollok House.

Extensive parklands and greenery characterize the southern environs of the city. In addition to the Pollok Country Park and Estate, there is Haggs Castle Golf Club, home of the Glasgow Open, and Bellahouston Park, scene of the historic papal visit in 1983. En route to the Burrell Collection, you cross by the 148-acre Queens Park, honoring Mary Queen of Scots, where panoramic views of the city are possible from the hilltop. Close to Maxwell Park is the Haggs Castle Museum in a 400-year-old building.

TRANSPORTATION AND PRACTICAL FACTS: West of the city, the **Glasgow Airport** is at Abbotsinch (tel. 041/887-1111). You can use the regular city link bus service to go into the city center. If you want to go by bus to Glasgow from Prestwick Airport, there is infrequent service. For more information, phone 041/332-7133. There is, however, regular bus service to Glasgow from the Prestwick Bus Station, and there is also frequent train service from Prestwick to the Glasgow Central Station.

In Glasgow, you may want to reconfirm your homeward flight. If it's aboard **Northwest Airlines,** they have offices at Caledonian House, 38 Renfield St. (tel. 041/226-4175).

In Glasgow, **taxis** can be called to your address. The minimum fare is 80p ($1.28), and the average fare is £2.50 ($4). A surcharge of one-third the meter fare is added if the taxi is hired to travel outside the city limits of Glasgow.

Glasgow also has a good **bus network,** the average fare costing around 75p ($1.20). The Travel Centre for city transport is at St. Enoch Square (tel. 041/226-4826). If you're planning to tour the environs by bus, you might need to contact the Buchanan Bus Station, Buchanan Street (tel. 041/332-7133).

Glasgow also has a limited **underground system,** an average fare going for 30p (48¢). For more information, get in touch with the Travel Centre, St. Enoch Square (tel. 041/226-4826).

For **British Rail,** the headquarters in Glasgow is at the Central Station and the Queen Street Station (for questions, phone 041/204-2844).

For **tourist information,** go to the Greater Glasgow Tourist Board, 35–39 St. Vincent Pl. (tel. 041/227-4880). This is the most helpful office in the country.

WHERE TO STAY: One place giving a fine bargain for weekend stays is the **Newlands Hotel,** 290 Kilmarnock Rd. (tel. 041/632-9171). All the bedrooms have private baths and color TV, and breakfast and VAT are included in the unit price. The maximum charges are £30 ($48) in a single, £50 ($80) in a twin-bedded room. The Newlands has J.J. Booth's, a quiet little bar for diners and residents. Bloomsbury Square Restaurant offers both table d'hôte and à la carte menus, with lunch costing from £8 ($12.80) and dinner from £12 ($19.20). Bar lunches are also available, as well as afternoon teas. If you come to Glasgow from either Prestwick or Glasgow Airport, the Newlands makes a convenient stopover before you get into the bustle of the heart of the city. It's also adjacent to a commuter station with regular fast trains down town.

The **Dalmeny Hotel,** 62 St. Andrew's Dr. (tel. 041/427-1106), stands in the center of a huge Victorian estate of stone villas and mansions, all built when Britain was at the peak of empire. Five minutes from the center of the city, the structure is more than 100 years old, built of light-colored sandstone with thick

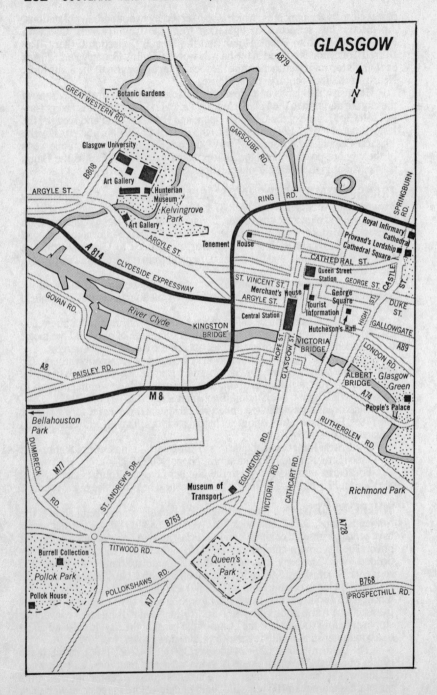

GLASGOW

A879

Botanic Gardens

GREAT WESTERN RD.

GARSCUBE RD.

Glasgow University

B808

Art Gallery

ARGYLE ST.

Hunterian Museum

Kelvingrove Park

Art Gallery

SPRINGBURN RD.

RING RD.

Royal Infirmary

Cathedral

Provand's Lordship

Cathedral Square

CATHEDRAL ST.

CASTLE ST.

Tenement House

A814

CLYDESIDE EXPRESSWAY

ARGYLE ST.

St. VINCENT ST.

Queen Street Station

GEORGE ST.

GOVAN RD.

River Clyde

Merchant's House

ARGYLE ST.

George Square

DUKE ST.

HIGH ST.

GALLOWGATE

KINGSTON BRIDGE

Central Station

Tourist Information

Hutcheson's Hall

A89

A8

PAISLEY RD.

HOPE ST.

GLASGOW ST.

VICTORIA BRIDGE

LONDON RD.

M 8

ALBERT BRIDGE

Glasgow Green

A74

People's Palace

Bellahouston Park

DUMBRECK RD.

M77

ST. ANDREW'S DR.

Museum of Transport

EGLINTON RD.

VICTORIA RD.

CATHCART RD.

RUTHERGLEN RD.

Richmond Park

A728

Burrell Collection

TITWOOD RD.

B763

Queen's Park

Pollok Park

POLLOKSHAWS RD.

B768

Pollok House

A77

PROSPECTHILL RD.

walls. The licensed hotel is in the Pollokshields section, south of the River Clyde. Pollokshields is a Victorian conservation area and highly residential. Your hosts are Bill and Betty Burns, who take pride in the running of their establishment. They conceive of their bedrooms as an "alternative home" for their clientele, charging from £21 ($33.60) in a single, from £34 ($54.40) in a double, and from £41 ($65.60) in a twin. All units have color TV, and some contain private bath or shower. Rates quoted include VAT and a full Scottish breakfast. Parents traveling with children can ask about the family room.

Kelvin Hotel, 15 Buckingham Terrace (tel. 041/339-7143), stands at the west end of Glasgow, off Great Western Road on the road to Loch Lomond, about a ten-minute drive from the heart of Glasgow. Near the university, it is also convenient to the Botanic Gardens and the BBC. The rooms are comfortable, although simply furnished—14 in all, ranging in price from £13 ($20.80) to £14 ($22.40) in a single, from £22 ($35.20) to £23 ($36.80) in a double, including breakfast. No room has a private bath. It stands on a street of restored Victorian terrace houses. There is locked parking in the rear.

Albion Hotel, 405 North Woodside Rd. (tel. 041/339-8620), is a recently refurbished 1860s structure set on a Victorian crescent opposite a park. West of the city center, it is reached by taking the underground to Kelvin Bridge. Graham and Irene Gordon rent out 16 well-furnished bedrooms, all with private shower, toilet, and sink, along with radio and TV as well as beverage-making facilities. Singles rent for £26 ($41.60), doubles for £36 ($57.60).

Burnbank Hotel, 67-85 West Princes St. (tel. 041/332-4877), set across from an inner city park, is an offbeat selection. Four family houses were joined together in the early 1970s, the builders retaining much of the original character of the houses. The Lind family rents out 38 comfortably furnished bedrooms, some with private bath or shower. The rate ranges from £17 ($27.20) to £22 ($35.20) in a single, from £16 ($25.60) to £18 ($28.80) per person in a double. What makes the house unusual is that it contains a wealth of antiques and artifacts, including racks of Staffordshire figures. The decor in the dining room is quite stunning, and in Nessie's Nest you have a choice of some 30 whiskies. The hotel lies northwest of the center, about a 15-minute walk from George Square (connected to buses 18 and 61).

Apsley Hotel, 903 Sauchiehall St. (tel. 041/339-4999), unlike some of its neighbors, is a *real* hotel, with a nice lobby and pleasantly and comfortably furnished bedrooms. Bathless singles rent for £17.50 ($28), singles with bath going for £19.50 ($31.20). Double or twin units cost from £25.95 ($41.52) to £29.95 ($47.92), depending on the plumbing. The higher-priced rooms have TV. Breakfast and VAT are included in the rates. The hotel restaurant has an excellent choice of food, with both restaurant and bar lunches being served from noon to 2:30 p.m. High tea is offered from 5:30 to 7:30 p.m. and dinner from 7 to 8 p.m., daily except Sunday. The Apsley is fully licensed, the lounge bar being open from noon to 2:30 p.m. and 5:30 to 11 p.m. Monday to Friday, from 5 to 11 p.m. on Saturday, and from 7 to 11 p.m. on Sunday. The hotel staff is cooperative. In the hallways is a scattering of antiques.

Kirklee Hotel, 11 Kensington Gate (tel. 041/334-5555), is unusual for a small hotel in that each of its bedrooms contains a full private bath. This stone-walled guesthouse lies on a quiet terrace in Glasgow's West End. Mr. and Mrs. Steven opted to eliminate their dining room and bar facilities in favor of lower prices for hotel residents. They charge £26 ($41.60) in a single and from £36 ($57.60) in a double, including a full breakfast served in each resident's room. The establishment is close to the university, the Botanic Gardens, and the city's major art galleries.

Marie Stuart Hotel, 46-48 Queen Mary Ave. (tel. 041/424-3939). Each of the 35 rooms of this family-run hotel is named after a Scotsman associated with Mary Queen of Scots. Whichever room you're assigned might provoke a fast review of Scottish history. If you run into problems, you can always consult the vividly personable owners, Margo and Bill Tennent. The establishment was originally built as a private home with stained-glass windows in the stairwell which are still intact. Singles cost from £16 ($25.60), while twins or doubles, depending on the plumbing, range from £30 ($48) to £38 ($60.80). The hotel stands in a flower-dotted residential neighborhood of substantial stone houses. Buses 10, 44, 59, and 183 go from the center of town, while the Blue trains stop at Cross Hill or Queen's Park Station. Guests are welcomed into the basement-level pub for a sampling of a wide array of malt whisky.

Kirkland House, 42 St. Vincent Crescent (tel. 041/248-3458), on a lovely, quiet street, offers pleasant rooms, one with its own shower. For a bed and a continental breakfast served in your room, the price is £14 ($22.40) per person. Each room has color TV, hot and cold water basins, and hot-beverage facilities. Kirkland House is about a ten-minute walk from the art museum.

The **Adamson Hotel,** 4 Crookston Dr. (tel. 041/882-3047), is a good, low-cost, homey choice if you don't mind being away from the center. Margaret Kay, the owner, a friendly, hospitable person, rents out a total of seven comfortably furnished bedrooms (none with private bath). The B&B rate is only £10 ($16) per person nightly, including a good breakfast which she prepares herself. Buses 52 and 54 run by her house. The house is well built, dating from the early 1800s, and it's extremely personal, guests meeting each other and introducing themselves in her little TV lounge. She'll also prepare a fixed-price dinner for £5 ($8).

The Big Splurge

The White House, 11-13 Cleveden Crescent (tel. 041/339-9375). From the outside this elegant hotel looks similar to the other Adam-style town houses flanking it on either side. The Ferguson family are the creative force behind the renovations that combined four of the houses into one unit. High Corinthian columns and ornate cove moldings in the reception area set the tone for the other houses, whose space flows into one another in a labyrinthine arrangement of hallways and corridors. These halls lead to 32 recently renovated accommodations. Each unit has a kitchenette, remote control color TV and in-house video, direct-dial phones, and often a surprisingly efficient arrangement of interior space. In some, sleeping lofts have been added as a trendy touch, while in others the plumbing and kitchenette facilities are concealed behind well-crafted antique doors. Naturally, the carpeting unifying the whole is a blue and green Ferguson tartan. The hotel charges weekday rates of £46 ($73.60) to £56 ($89.60) in a single and £57.50 ($92) to £70 ($112) in a double, with suites costing more, of course. Guests who arrive on a weekend, and plan to spend at least two nights, usually get discounts of up to 25%. The hotel has a room service snack menu and a restaurant offering a table d'hôte menu prepared by an expert chef. A courtesy bus transports hotel guests to and from one of my favorite restaurants in Glasgow, the Buttery, as well as Rogano and the Colonial. The White House stands in a well-tended residential section of the city.

Stakis Pond Hotel, 2-4 Shelley Rd. (tel. 041/334-8161). A good bet for a comfortable room in a pleasant setting is this 138-room modern hotel at the edge of town. It's set in a green area beside a duck-filled pond. Part of the benefits include the use of the glass-walled indoor pool, exercise machines, and saunas. Each of the functional and sunny bedrooms has a private bath and a video TV. Singles cost from £56 ($89.60) and doubles go for £67 ($107.20) nightly, these prices including a full breakfast. The hotel's pine-paneled steakhouse offers generous portions of well-prepared meals served in a salad bar/carvery system. One of the hotel's bars is set in a glassed-in balcony above the swimming pool.

Wickets Hotel, 52-54 Fortrose St. (tel. 041/334-9334), is an undiscovered gem. Lying in the West End, opposite The West of Scotland Cricket Ground, it is privately owned by Brian Kirke. The hotel is better known for its dining and drinking facilities than for its bedrooms. However, it offers seven attractively furnished rooms, mostly with private bath along with phones, color TV, and beverage-making equipment. Accommodations are bright, fresh, and modernized. Depending on the plumbing, singles cost £33 ($52.80) to £36 ($57.60), doubles £43 ($68.80) to £46 ($73.60). Food is served daily from 11 a.m. to 11 p.m., and the hotel has the only open-air beer garden in Glasgow. Randall's Wine Bar sells wine by the glass in an art deco setting, with Erté prints. The bar food is excellent, including such items as smoked chicken salad, with lunches costing from £4 ($6.40). Lord's Restaurant is half-timbered with old photos of famous British cricketeers. It offers a fixed-price dinner for only £10 ($16), including such dishes as deep-fried Camembert, bouillabaisse, and an entrecôte with cognac and cream.

Hospitality Inn, 36 Cambridge St. (tel. 041/332-3311). This downtown high-rise hotel is among the best in the moderately priced category. Its soaring reception area has the kind of tropical-style waterfall you'd expect to encounter in the Caribbean. However, the flavor of its bar and restaurant is satisfyingly Scottish. Each of the conservatively styled bedrooms has a TV, phone, radio, wake-up alarm, and full bath. Accommodations, which are suitable for one to two persons, cost £51.50 ($82.40) in a studio and £65 ($104) in a deluxe room. Some of the more expensive units hold up to four persons. The price of this hotel can go down on weekends to around £30 ($48) in a studio and £42 ($67.20) in a deluxe accommodation. The Palm Springs lounge is a red brick and exposed-wood Victorian medley of brass chandeliers and low-slung French-style armchairs. The Prince of Wales dining room is a pleasing study in soft greens and airy spaciousness. The garden-like coffeeshop offers one of the best food bargains in Glasgow; a set lunch costing £6.25 ($10). It offers a self-service array of tempting salads, each laid out on a bed of ice. The bar remains open every night for residents until 1 a.m., and room service is available all night long. There's even a basement-level car park, plus lots of in-house services such as a resident hairdresser.

The **Dalmeny Park Hotel and Restaurant,** Lochlibo Road, in Barrhead (tel. 041/881-9211). Ivy covers the stone walls of this Victorian hotel whose central core was originally constructed as a private home. It's surrounded by a small park whose graveled walks are suitable for after-dinner strolls. The elegant woodwork of the oldest section has been supplemented by a modern extension. A polite staff can be seen polishing brass in the sitting rooms. Accommodations vary according to the location and plumbing in the rooms. Many Americans prefer the older part; rooms in the newer section, however, contain private showers. Furnishings are a medley of modern and traditional. Singles range from £21 ($33.60) to £36 ($57.60) nightly, and doubles or twins cost £32 ($51.20) to £48 ($76.80). The food is good and served in bountiful portions. The hotel is on the A736 between Glasgow and Irvine, about 25 minutes from the heart of Glasgow, some 15 minutes from the Glasgow Airport.

WHERE TO DINE: The oldest existing restaurant in Glasgow, **Sloan's,** Argyll Arcade, 30 Buchanan St. (tel. 041/221-8917), dates from 1797, but it was all gussied up in late Victorian days. The decor is stridently red and elaborately done in the style known as Gay '90s. Climbing to the top of the staircase, which evokes those in fancy bordellos as shown in motion pictures, is part of the fun of coming here. The ballroom on the top floor used to host some of the most elaborate functions in town, and it is closed to the general public except for receptions. However, you can still enjoy a pint of ale in the mahogany-lined pub or join the crowd of lunching Glaswegians for full meals costing from £3 ($4.80). In the reflected light of etched- or stained-glass windows you can feast on such specialties as roast chicken and bacon, homemade steak pies, lasagne, beef curry, and mixed grills. Lunches are served from noon to 2:30 p.m. and high teas from 4 to 6 p.m.

Fraser's Restaurant, 45 Buchanan St. (tel. 041/221-3880), the shopper's choice, is an unlicensed, self-service restaurant. It's a city-center department-store selection, and connected to the main restaurant is a coffeeshop which is also self-service. Many Scottish fish dishes, including the smoked variety, are presented. A three-course lunch goes for £5 ($8), a high tea—virtually a light supper—for only £2.50 ($4). Hours are daily except Sunday from 9 a.m. to 4:45 p.m.

Ma Brown's Restaurant, 283 Sauchiehall St. (tel. 041/332-3661), is a cellar restaurant known for its fine food and real Scottish hospitality. The house is owned by a group of bakers who have been in business since 1858. A special two-course lunch costs only £2.25 ($3.60), including, for example, a homemade lentil soup and Loch Fyne herring fried in oatmeal. The chef's special is a roast Ayrshire chicken with bacon and a choice of vegetables. Service is from 9 a.m. to 7:30 p.m.

One of the best places for tea, light lunches, and snacks is the famed **Willow Tea Room,** 217 Sauchiehall St. (tel. 041/332-0521), on the major shopping artery of the city. The Willow Tea Room was all the sensation when it opened in 1904. Now it has been restored to its original design by Charles Rennie Mackintosh. On the ground floor is a well-known jeweler, M. M. Henderson Ltd. The "room de luxe" is found in the heart of the architecturally interesting old building, and it's elegantly furnished with tables and chairs made to the Mackintosh design. Light meals cost from £3.50 ($5.60), and they are served Monday to Saturday from 9:30 a.m. to 4:30 p.m. It's fashionable to drop in here for afternoon tea any time of day.

Kensington's Restaurant, 164 Darnley St. (tel. 041/424-3662), in the Stockwell China Bazaar, is a licensed table-service restaurant. Small and intimate, it is handsomely decorated. The location may be a bit hard to find, as it's tucked away in a quiet backwater on the south side of Glasgow. The chef offers seafood plucked from the west coast, along with home-killed venison. A specialty is the selection of Scottish desserts. Expect to spend around £8.50 ($13.60) for lunch, perhaps £15 ($24) or so for dinner. It is closed all day Sunday and serves no lunch on Saturday. Otherwise, its hours are noon to 2:30 p.m. and 7 to 10 p.m. Monday to Friday.

Potter's Wheel Restaurant, 67-77 Glassford St. (tel. 041/552-0523), is a tiny restaurant in a store specializing in crystal and china. It's unlicensed and self-service, presenting a standard repertoire of typically Scottish dishes, including haggis, neeps, and tatties, along with herring in oatmeal. There is a salad bar, and fresh vegetables are also regularly featured. Go here for midday meals only, anytime between 11:30 a.m. and 4:30 p.m. Expect to spend from £4 ($6.40) for a three-course lunch.

More Expensive Choices

Ubiquitous Chip, 12 Ashton Lane (tel. 041/334-5007), is a little white-washed restaurant with a courtyard paved with cobblestones. It lies in a mews-style lane off Byres Road. Original batiks and murals, along with much greenery, make this restaurant an inviting little choice. It is licensed and offers table service any day except Sunday. The menu has a tempting selection of Scottish lamb and beef, along with fish and (in season) game. The chef is a devotee of up-to-date British cookery, including such dishes as Ayrshire guinea fowl or marinated haunch of venison from Inverness served with rowan jelly. There is a praiseworthy concentration on fresh ingredients. Much of the food is wholefood vegetarian, and soups such as leek and lemon are imaginative. Flans are exceptional here, especially one made with almonds and prunes and flavored with cognac. The main restaurant is on the ground floor, and upstairs is the lunch bar where you can enjoy snacks for £3 ($4.80), served from noon to 2:30 p.m. A dinner in the main restaurant, from 5:30 to 11 p.m., will cost from £14 ($22.40). The wine list is considered one of the most reasonably priced and extensive in the United Kingdom. There are more than 100 malt whiskies.

The Buttery, 652 Argyll St. (tel. 041/221-8188), is the perfect huntsman's restaurant, filled with oak panels, impeccably clean napery, racks of wine bottles, and an aristocratic air of baronial splendor. The bar in the anteroom used to be the pulpit of a church. The waitresses wear high-necked costumes of which Queen Victoria would have approved. Everywhere you look you see 19th-century accessories. The Oyster Bar in the outer precincts serves weekday lunches for around £7 ($11.20). Menus include smoked salmon, rare roast beef, a terrine of Scottish seafood, and, of course, oysters. The more formal inner room serves an elegant menu, with full meals costing a splurgy £18 ($28.80). In the formal restaurant, hours are noon to 2:30 p.m. (no lunch on Saturday) and 7 to 9:30 p.m. The bar, however, stays open until 11 p.m. Reservations in the main dining room are suggested.

The Belfry, 652 Argyle St. (tel. 041/221-0630). Each element of the decor of this place, on the basement level of the just-previewed Buttery, came from a church in northern England, especially the pews and pulpits. Lots of illuminated stained glass creates a cozy ambience. It's probably the only pub in Glasgow that affords a contemplation of Christ in Majesty while its patrons enjoy a pint of ale. The cramped and partially exposed kitchen produces daily specials such as poached salmon in a lemon mayonnaise, smoked mackerel pâté, and chicken and broccoli pie. The establishment keeps the Sabbath holy, but is open every weekday for lunch and dinner (on Saturday it's open for dinner only). Full meals cost from £9 ($14.40), and can be accompanied by a vintage from the wine list. Hours are from noon to 2:30 p.m. and 6 to 10 p.m.

La Mirage Café-Bar, in the Copthorne Hotel, George Square (tel. 041/332-6711). The café's ground-floor location contains richly textured architectural elements culled from throughout Italy: from a bank in Venice, with marble floors, 19th-century settees, and a comfortably wooden bar; a Florentine gazebo crafted from mahogany and stained glass; and a quartet of illuminated Venetian lions from what used to be the legs of an antique couch. There's even neon humor above the bar, as well as plenty of palms to suggest Edwardian splendor. This restaurant, bar, and café is in the same building where a historic meeting took place between Sir Winston Churchill and Harry Hopkins, the emissary of FDR. The café serves an array of tasty hot and cold bar food, a choice of sandwiches, a wide array of international beers, and a steaming cup of Italian cappuccino. If you want a more substantial meal, you can dine on a raised dais in another part of the café. Meals, costing from £6 ($9.60), include chili beef, steak and mushroom pie, and lasagne bolognaise. Hot food is served Monday through Saturday from 11 a.m. to 7 p.m., but the place stays open for drinks until midnight. On Sunday, hot meals are served from 12:30 to 2 p.m. and 6:30 p.m. to midnight, with Sunday dinner being most popular.

Charlie Parker's, 21 Royal Exchange Square (tel. 041/248-3040), is an attractively trendy restaurant and nightspot. On the ground floor, its black and silver decor might best be described as a mixture of hi-tech and art deco. This room serves as the perfect foil for the dramatic illumination. In front is Charlie Parker's Cocktail Bar, open from noon to midnight Monday to Saturday, and in the rear is Charlie's Diner, a sort of New York diner with a range of steaks, burgers, and such specialties as chicken tortillas or fettuccine. Meals cost from £8 ($12.80). One of the most fashionable places in Glasgow is Charlie's Basement Restaurant, open from noon to 3 p.m. and 6 to 10:30 p.m. Meals cost from £12 ($19.20) and include such dishes as chicken suprême, Aylesbury duck, and lamb cutlets.

Lautrec's, 14 Woodlands Terrace (tel. 041/332-7013), is ensconced on the basement floor of a gray stone building in the city's residential West End. This popular gathering place has one of Glasgow's richest repositories of warmly textured Victoriana. Once you enter, you can wander toward the back for the best ambience, although the pub in front draws a lively crowd of beer and wine lovers. Ten kinds of wine are sold by the glass. However, if you order a bottle, you'll have a choice of more than 170 vintages. In back, at the top of a flight of stairs in what used to be someone's private library, is a skylit brasserie whose burnished paneling frames a changing exhibition of original artwork. Bar food is served below, but the true eating center is here, below hanging plants and brass lamps. A full meal will cost from £14 ($22.40) and might include chicken suprême, poached sole, several kinds of steak, lamb kebabs, hamburgers, snails in garlic butter, and pan-fried boneless breast of duckling. The establishment is open from 11 a.m. to 11 p.m. every day of the week except Sunday, when it opens at 6:30 p.m.

Rogano, 11 Exchange Pl. (tel. 041/248-4055), is considered one of the most perfectly preserved art deco interiors in Scotland. Its decor dates from 1934, when Messrs. Rogers and Anderson combined their talents and their names to create an ambience that has hosted virtually every star of the British film industry since the invention of the talkies. The doorman and bartender have been employed for decades. In an ambience filled with birchwood veneers, lapis lazuli clocks, etched mirrors, spinning ceiling fans, cozy semicircular banquettes, and dozens of potted palms, you can enjoy full meals ranging from £18 ($28.80) per person. There is a less expensive menu offered downstairs, where meals cost from £8.50 ($13.60). The restaurant, appropriately, is called Downstairs. The array of menu items, which changes every two or three months, is likely to include both Scottish and international specialties, with an emphasis on seafood. Perhaps you'll begin with crayfish bisque with brandy or cream of venison soup with toasted oatmeal. A seafood torte is served with a parsley and watercress sauce, and you might also prefer the suprême of brill wrapped in chicory and served with a cream sauce. There are at least six varieties of temptingly rich desserts, including Kahlúa Bavarois with a roasted coffee-bean sauce. Reservations are suggested. The main restaurant is open Monday to Saturday from noon to 2:30 p.m. and 7 to 10:30 p.m. Downstairs is open Monday to Thursday from noon to 11 p.m. and on Friday and Saturday until midnight.

Le Café Noir Brasserie and Bistro, 151 Queen St. (tel. 041/248-3525). If you look carefully up through the simulated grape arbors of this wine bar, you can still see its ornately detailed plaster ceiling. Many of the café's clients prefer to stand, either near one of the tiny tables or at the bar. If you want a table, you can gravitate to a spot under the skylight of the upper balcony. Scottish food is smoothly blended with French wines, and meals are served in generous portions every day, attracting office workers in the neighborhood. You should place your order for one of the day's blackboard specials at the bar. Food includes several kinds of quiche, game pie, smoked trout, as well as selections from the salad bar, along with many vintages of wine by the glass. Meals cost from £5 ($8). The brasserie upstairs is open from 8:30 a.m. to midnight Monday to Friday and 8:30 a.m. to 11:45 p.m. on Saturday (Sunday from noon to 11 p.m.). The bistro downstairs serves a table d'hôte lunch from noon to 2:30 p.m., costing £4 ($6.40). Afternoon tea, with sandwiches and scones, is offered from 2:30 to 5 p.m. Dinner, with à la carte meals costing from £12 ($19.20), is from 5 to 11 p.m. (Saturday noon to 11 p.m.). The decor is art deco, with wall murals and stained glass. The chef prepares an array of pasta dishes, steaks, and seafood. The bistro is closed Sunday.

Ad-Lib, 111 Hope St. (tel. 041/248-7102), is an American-style diner, with movie posters and a stainless-steel floor, standing opposite Glasgow's Central Station. It's one of the more popular dining spots in Glasgow, especially among young people. Ad-Lib is operated by Romano Wines. Service is Monday to Saturday from noon to 2 a.m. (yes, that late), and on Sunday from 6 p.m. to 1 a.m. Finding a place in Scotland that serves food on Sunday until 1 a.m. is still a bit of a rarity. The menu includes a wide range of all-beef hamburgers which are served with a choice of fries or baked potato, along with a selection of relishes. If you aren't into burgers, try one of the main kebab courses or perhaps a vegetarian crêpe. They also cook a pretty fair southern fried chicken and Angus beefsteaks. Desserts include pancakes with fudge sauce and apple pie à la mode. There is also a good range of salads, plus full bar service. Meals cost from £7 ($11.20).

Ho Wong Restaurant, 82 York St. (tel. 041/221-3550), lying two blocks from the Central Station, is one of the finest Chinese restaurants in the city. Jimmy Ho and David Wong were inspired by the Hong Kong kitchen, and have opened this "remote outpost" of their Oriental cuisine in faraway Glasgow. The cookery is consistently enjoyable, the service obliging. You can pause for a drink in the front, perusing the menu, before you are shown to your table in the rear. Hours are weekdays from noon to 2 p.m. and 5:30 p.m. to midnight (on Sunday, only from 6 p.m. to midnight). Set menus range in price from £13 ($20.80) to £18 ($28.80) per person, but you can dine for much less by ordering à la carte. If so, expect a check of £12 ($19.20), or less, depending on your appetite. Sweet and sour dishes, such as king prawns, lead the popularity charts. As a novelty, some dishes are labeled "bird's nest dishes," others "sizzling" dishes. There are at least eight duck dishes on the menu, along with four types of fresh lobster.

Diva, The Beacons Hotel, 7 Park Terrace (tel. 041/332-3520), is one of the most fashionable rendezvous points in the city, yet it charges reasonable prices for its fare. Inspired by Italian design, this "prima donna" is found in the basement of a popular West End hotel built in 1856. The restaurant is dominated by a bar in the center, which serves both sides of a large eating area. The menu is likely to appeal to almost anyone, ranging from succulent appetizers (such as steamed mussels in white wine, garlic, and cream) to freshly made salads such as niçoise. A good choice of Diva house wines might complement what is called "the main chance"—courses ranging from a stack of barbecued ribs to beef Stroganoff. Sunday lunch goes for £5.50 ($8.80), a table d'hôte meal offered for £6.50 ($10.40), with à la carte averaging £8.50 ($13.60). Hours are Monday to Saturday 11 a.m. to 11 p.m. (on Sunday from 12:30 to 4:30 p.m. and 6 to 11 p.m.).

SIGHTS: In Glasgow, the center of the city is **George Square,** dominated by the City Chambers which Queen Victoria opened in 1888. Of the statues in the square, the most imposing is that of Sir Walter Scott on an 80-foot column. Naturally, you'll find Victoria along with her beloved Albert, plus Robert Burns. The Banqueting Hall, lavishly decorated, is open to the public on most weekdays.

The **Cathedral of St. Kentigern,** first built in 1136, was burned down in 1192. It was rebuilt soon after, and the Laigh Kirk (Lower Church), the vaulted crypt said to be the finest in Europe, remains to this day. Visit the tomb of St. Mungo in the crypt where a light always burns. The edifice is mainland Scotland's only complete medieval cathedral, dating from the 12th and 13th centuries. Formerly a place of pilgrimage, 16th-century zeal purged it of all "monuments of idolatry." For the best view of the cathedral, cross the Bridge of Sighs into the necropolis, the graveyard containing almost every type of architecture in the world. The graveyard is built on a rocky hill and dominated by a statue of John Knox. It was first opened in 1832, and the first person to be buried there was a Jew, typical of the mixing of all races in this cosmopolitan city where tolerance reigns until the rival local football teams meet. The necropolis is full of monuments to Glasgow merchants, among them William Miller (1810–1872) who wrote the children's poem "Wee Willie Winkie."

The **Glasgow Art Gallery and Museum,** Kelvingrove (tel. 041/357-3929), is the finest municipal gallery in Britain. The art gallery contains a fine collection of Dutch and Italian old masters and French 19th-century paintings. Displayed are works by Giorgione *(The Adulteress Brought Before Christ),* Rembrandt *(The Man in Armour),* Millet *(Going to Work),* and Derain *(Blackfriars).* Salvador Dali's *Christ of St. John of the Cross* is on display. Scottish painting is of course well represented in the four galleries of British painting from the 17th century to the present day. The museum has an outstanding collection of European arms and armor, displays from the ethnography collections featuring the Eskimo and North American Indians, Africa, and Oceania, as well as a large section devoted to natural history. There are major new exhibits on the natural history of Scotland, featuring plant life, animal life, and geology. There are also small, regularly changing displays from the decorative art collections of silver (especially Scottish), ceramics, glass, and jewelry, plus furniture and other decorative art items by Charles Rennie Mackintosh and his contemporaries. The museum is open weekdays from 10 a.m. to 5 p.m., on Sunday from 2 to 5 p.m. Teas and light lunches are available in the museum. Admission is free.

The **Burrell Collection,** Pollok Country Park, 2060 Pollokshaws Rd. (tel. 041/649-7151), is housed in a building opened in 1983 to display the rich treasures left to Glasgow by Sir William Burrell, a wealthy shipowner who had a life-long passion for art collecting. A vast aggregation of furniture, textiles, ceramics, stained glass, silver, art objects, and pictures—especially 19th-century French art—can be seen in rooms reconstructed from Sir William's home, Hutton Castle at Berwick-upon-Tweed. They are the dining room, hall, and drawing room arranged around the courtyard. Included are artifacts from the ancient world, Oriental art, and European decorative arts and paintings. The collection may be visited from 10 a.m. to 5 p.m. Monday to Saturday and from 2 to 5 p.m. on Sunday. It's closed on Christmas and New Year's Day. Admission is free. There's a restaurant, and you can roam through the surrounding lawns and trees of the park.

Haggs Castle, 100 St. Andrews Dr. (tel. 041/427-2725), is a branch of the Glasgow Museums and Art Galleries designed especially for children. It explores the changing lifestyles of the 400 years of the castle's existence. In the castle is a reconstructed kitchen from 1585, a room that shows how an inhabitant lived in the 17th century, and a Victorian nursery. An 18th-century cottage in the grounds is used as an activities workshop, and children who visit can take part in sessions that include weaving, archery, buttermaking, and sampler sewing. The castle is open weekdays from 10 a.m. to 5 p.m., on Sunday from 2 to 5 p.m. Admission is free.

Pollok House, Pollok Country Park, 2060 Pollokshaws Rd. (tel. 041/632-0274), the ancestral home of the Maxwells, was built circa 1750 and has additions from 1890 to 1908 designed by Robert Anderson. The house and its 360 acres of parkland were given to the City of Glasgow in 1966. Today a branch of the Glasgow Museums and Art Galleries, it contains one of the finest collections of Spanish paintings in Britain, with works by El Greco, Goya, and Murillo, among others. There are displays of silver, ceramics, and glass from the Maxwell family's and the city's collections. Hours are from 10 a.m. to 5 p.m. Monday to Saturday, from 2 to 5 p.m. on Sunday. Admission is free.

Provand's Lordship, Castle and McLeod Streets (tel. 041/334-1134), is the oldest house in Glasgow, standing just opposite the cathedral, across Cathedral Square. It was built around 1471 by Bishop Andrew Muirhead. Mary Queen of Scots is believed to have lived here when she visited Glasgow in 1566 to see Lord Darnley, and some of the "Casket Letters" were probably written here. The house contains 17th- and 18th-century furniture and domestic utensils. It is in the care of Glasgow Museums and Art Galleries. The house is open Monday through Saturday from 10 a.m. to 5 p.m., on Sunday from 2 to 5 p.m. Admission is free.

People's Palace, Glasgow Green (tel. Glasgow 041/554-0223), a branch of the Glasgow Museums and Art Galleries, provides a visual record of the rise of Glasgow. The palace was built originally as a cultural center for the people of the East End of Glasgow, and it was constructed between 1895 and 1897. Exhibitions trace the foundation of the city in 1175–1178. Such turbulent interludes as the reign of Mary Queen of Scots are represented by the personal relics of the queen herself. The bulk of the collections are from the 19th century, representing Victorian Glasgow, including posters, programs, and props from the music hall era. Also displayed are items relating to trades and industries, the Glasgow potteries and stained-glass studios, trade unions, newspapers, and similar matters. Paintings of Glasgow by John Knox and others may be seen, plus portraits of Glaswegians from St. Mungo to Billy Connelly. The city museum may be visited weekdays from 10 a.m. to 5 p.m., on Sunday from 2 to 5 p.m. Admission is free. There is a tea room in the Winter Gardens.

The park in which the palace is situated, **Glasgow Green,** is the oldest public park in the city. Once a common pasture for the early town, it has witnessed much history. Seek out, in particular, Nelson's monument, the first of its kind in Britain; the Saracen Fountain, opposite the palace; and Templeton's Carpet Factory, modeled on the Doge's Palace in Venice.

Miss Toward's Tenement House, 145 Buccleuch St. (tel. 041/333-0183), has been called a "Glasgow flat that time passed by." Until her death, Agnes Toward was called an "inveterate hoarder of domestic trivia." She lived in an 1892 building at Garnethill, not far from the main shopping street, Sauchiehall. For 54 years she lived in this flat that is stuffed with the artifacts of her era, everything from a porcelain "jawbox" sink to such household aids as Monkey Brand soap. Upon her death, the property eventually came into the care of the National Trust for Scotland, which realized that it was a virtual museum of a vanished era. Approached through a "wally close," the museum is open from the first of April until the end of October daily from 2 to 5 p.m. Admission is £1 ($1.60) for adults, 50p (80¢) for children.

The **Royal Highland Fusiliers Museum,** 518 Sauchiehall St. (tel. 041/332-5639), displays mementoes of 300 years of the infantry of Glasgow and Ayrshire. Relics, such as weapons, medals, pictures, and uniforms trace the saga of the regiment's history from 1678. The regiment served under 15 monarchs on five continents. The museum is open from 9 a.m. to 4:30 p.m. Monday to Thursday and from 9 a.m. to 4 p.m. on Friday, charging no admission.

The **Hunterian Art Gallery,** University of Glasgow, 82 Hillhead St. (tel. 041/339-8855, ext. 5431), has some outstanding works by James McNeill Whistler and by Charles Rennie Mackintosh, including the Mackintosh House, a reconstruction of the architect's home on three levels, with his own furniture and decorated in the original style. The main gallery exhibits 18th-century British portraits and 19th- and 20th-century Scottish painting, with works by McTaggart, the Glasgow Boys, Scottish Colourists, Gillies, Philipson, and others. Hours are from 9:30 a.m. to 5 p.m. Monday to Friday and 9:30 a.m. to 1 p.m. on Saturday. The Mackintosh House closes from 12:30 to 1:30 p.m. weekdays. Closed on Sunday and public holidays. Admission is free except for the Mackintosh House which costs 50p (80¢) on weekday afternoons and Saturday.

The **Hunterian Museum** (tel. 041/339-8855, ext. 4221) has the same hours as the art gallery, and admission is free. It is in the main Glasgow University buildings on Gilmorehill, two miles west of the heart of the city. The best approach is from University Avenue. If you're going by bus, get off at University Avenue. This is Glasgow's oldest museum, having opened its door in 1807. The museum is named after William Hunter, its early benefactor who donated his private collections to get the collection going. The collection is wide-ranging, including fossils of dinosaurs, as well as coins. There are relics of the Roman occupation, and many rich clues from the past of Scotland, including plunder by the Vikings. The story of Captain Cook's voyages is pieced together in ethnographic material from the South Seas.

Although it has much industry and stark commercial areas, Glasgow contains many gardens and open spaces.

Chief among these is **Bellahouston Park,** Paisley Road West, 171 acres of beauty with a sunken wall and rock gardens as well as wildlife. It's open all year daily from 8 a.m. to dusk. Here you'll find the **Bellahouston Sports Centre** (tel. 041/427-5454), which is a base for a variety of indicated trails that make up runners' training courses.

Glasgow's **Botanic Gardens,** Great Western Road (tel. 041/334-2422), covers 40 acres—an extensive collection of tropical plants and herb gardens. It too is open all year, daily, including Sunday, from 7 a.m. to dusk. Admission is free.

Linn Park, on Clarkston Road, is 212 acres of pine and woodland, with many lovely walks along the river. Here you'll find a nature trail, pony rides for children, an old snuff mill, and a children's zoo. The park is open all year, daily from 8 a.m. to dusk.

Paisley

The largest town in the district, Paisley, seven miles west of Glasgow, became a famous name in the days of the Industrial Revolution with the arrival of the weaving trade. The Paisley shawl was born here. Actually the inspiration for the pattern came from India, but no matter—it is forever associated with this industrial town.

Before that, the town was best known for **Paisley Abbey,** one of the great attractions of Strathclyde. The church grew out of a Cluniac abbey founded in Paisley in 1163, which was nearly demolished on orders of Edward I of England in 1307. It was subsequently reconstructed. In the mid-16th century a tower fell in, causing great damage to the transept. But for 3½ centuries it was not rebuilt. Just the nave served as the parish church. But new work began around the turn of this century, and by 1928 Paisley Abbey was restored, containing a superb stone-vaulted roof. It also shelters the tomb of King Robert III. The town was founded by a monk, Saint Mirin, and a chapel is dedicated to him. You can also see an 11-foot-high Celtic cross from the 10th century. The abbey is open from 10 a.m. to 3 p.m. Monday to Saturday.

The **Paisley Museum and Art Galleries,** High Street (tel. 041/889-3151), is visited mainly because of its famous collection of Paisley shawls. It is open from 10 a.m. to 5 p.m. Monday to Saturday, charging no admission. This teardrop or tadpole-shaped pattern dominated the world of fashion for some 70-odd years, and today the shawls are extremely valuable as collector's items. The museum has collected these colorful textiles since 1905, and now has more than 700 examples of them. The museum also has a collection relating to the history of Strathclyde, along with some fine art and natural history displays.

Dumbarton

Only the most dedicated history buffs take the time to visit Dumbarton, on the north bank of the Clyde. Nearly all of its illustrious past has been swept away except for **Dumbarton Castle,** which guarded the narrowing of the river. It stood on a towering rock and has seen much of the history of the Strathclyde region. Along with Edinburgh Castle this was one of the last strongholds of Mary Queen of Scots in 1570. When Dumbarton fell in 1571, Queen Mary's fate was sealed. Nowadays mainly a barracks, it still has a 12th-century gateway and a dungeon. A sundial presented by Mary Queen of Scots is still there. The location on Dumbarton Rock is off the A814. It can be visited from 9:30 a.m. to 6:30 p.m. Monday to Saturday and 2 to 6:30 p.m. on Sunday mid-March to mid-October, closing time changing to 4 p.m. off-season. Admission is 50p (80¢) for adults, 30p (48¢) for children.

Kilbarchan

In the 18th and 19th centuries Kilbarchan, eight miles southwest of Glasgow off the A737, was known for its long rows of weavers cottages. The village has long been known for its Lillias Day festivities in early June, including a pageant that seems to have stepped intact out of the Middle Ages. Now the National Trust has opened a **Weaver's Cottage** (tel. 05057/5588) that dates from 1723. To show visitors how it was, it operates as a museum of weaving. The loom is more than two centuries old. Later you can wander through the garden of the cottage. It is open from the first of April until the end of May and from the first of September until the end of October on Tuesday, Thursday, Saturday, and Sunday from 2 to 5 p.m. In summer it is open daily from 2 to 5 p.m. Admission is 80p ($1.28) for adults and 40p (64¢) for children. To reach it, take the Clydeside Scottish bus service (no. 36) from the Buchanan Street Bus Station in Glasgow which leaves every 15 minutes.

WHERE TO SHOP: The principal shopping district is **Sauchiehall Street,** Glasgow's fashion center, containing many shops and department stores where you'll often find quite good bargains, particularly in woolen goods. The major shopping area, about three blocks long, has been made into a pedestrian mall.

The Barras, the weekend market of Glasgow, takes place about a quarter of a mile east of Glasgow Cross. Admission free, it is held all year from 9 a.m. to 5 p.m. on Saturday and Sunday. Rich in stalls and shops, this century-old market has some 800 traders selling their wares. You can not only browse for that special treasure, but can become a part of Glasgow life and be amused by the buskers.

The **Highland House of Lawrie,** 110 Buchanan St. (tel. 041/221-0217).

There's possibly no more prestigious store in Scotland than this elegant haberdashery where even Prince Philip goes to buy his kilts. Despite its aristocratic clientele, prices are more reasonable than you'd expect, and the welcome offered by the experienced sales staff is genuinely warmhearted. Don't be fooled by the array of crystal and gift items offered for sale on the street level, because the real heart and soul of the establishment lies on the lower level. There, an array of carefully constructed tweed jackets, tartan-patterned accessories, waistcoats, and sweaters are sold to both men and women. Each is impeccably crafted by kilt-making experts. Most of the merchandise is, of course, crafted from top-quality wool and suitable even in the dampest of Highland weather. Men's kilts contain as much as eight yards of material skillfully pleated to match the pattern. Women's hand-stitched kilts are also sold, as are those for children. Don't overlook the tweed blazers for men, which are reasonable in price. The establishment was founded in 1881, and is today the oldest established kilt makers in Scotland. The shop is open from 9 a.m. to 5:30 p.m. Monday to Saturday.

Fraser's Department Store, Buchanan Street (tel. 041/221-3880), is Glasgow's version of Harrods Department Store. The Glasgow store contains a soaring Victorian-era glass arcade rising four stories. Inside you'll find everything ranging from clothing to Oriental rugs, from crystal to handmade local artifacts of all kinds. Even a quick visit to see the Victorian embellishments might be worth a stopover, but you will surely see something you want to purchase.

William Porteous & Co. Ltd., 9 Royal Exchange Place (tel. 041/221-8623), is a long-established bookstore specializing in travel guides and maps for Scotland and the rest of the United Kingdom and Europe. They also have Scottish souvenir books and prints. They're open Monday to Saturday from 8:30 a.m. to 5 p.m.

Henry Burton & Co., 111 Buchanan St. (tel. 041/221-7380). One of the city's most prestigious men's outfitters is in a slightly cramped two-story building laden with well-crafted clothes. Established in 1847, the store has a most helpful staff who will be able to offer their competent advice. Most of the garments are for men, but a limited selection of knitwear for women is also sold.

Bag and Baggage, 11 Royal Exchange Square (tel. 041/221-8005). If the other purchases you couldn't resist place you in the market for a new suitcase, this store has a wide selection of reasonably priced but high-quality merchandise. Most of the valises and briefcases were designed for women, as well as many of the store's shoes.

The last two recommendations are not specific shops, but areas where you can find dozens of shops.

The **Argyll Arcade** stands at 30 Buchanan St. Even if the year of its construction (1827) were not set in mosaic tiles above the entrance, you'd still know that this is a very old collection of shops. Most of the establishments set beneath its glass canopy sell watches and jewelry, both antique and modern. In fact, the arcade contains what is said to be the largest single concentration of retail jewelers in Europe, surpassing even those of Amsterdam. The rents charged here are higher than comparable stores elsewhere in Glasgow, even exceeding the exorbitant rents charged along London's fashionable Bond Street.

The fame of the arcade has traveled far beyond Glasgow. It seems to be a Scottish tradition that a wedding ring becomes lucky when purchased within the arcade's narrow confines.

Since the arcade is officially classified as a historic building, a portion of its rents go toward maintaining it in mint condition. Over the years the arcade has given rise to many legends, including that of a pair of ghosts said to inhabit

Sloan's, previously recommended. Today, beneath the curved glass ceiling and the milling pedestrian traffic, the arcade maintains an impressive security system, designed to protect the area's two dozen shops and multi-million-pound inventories.

Victorian Village, 57 West Regent St. (tel. 041/332-0703). Antique lovers will want to browse through this warren of tiny shops in this slightly claustrophobic cluster. Much of the merchandise isn't particularly noteworthy, but there are many exceptional pieces. Several of the owners stock reasonably priced articles of 19th-century appeal. Other shops sell old jewelry and clothing, a helter-skelter of artifacts.

GLASGOW AFTER DARK: Glasgow, not Edinburgh, is the cultural center of Scotland, and the city is alive with nightclubs. Still, for many a Glaswegian, the best evening ever is to be spent drinking in his or her favorite pub (my selection coming up).

Cultural Glasgow

The Theatre Royal, at Hope Street and Cowcaddens Road (tel. 041/331-1234), is the home of the Scottish Opera, which long ago attracted attention on the world scene. The building, designed by C. J. Phipps, opened in 1895 and was completely refurbished as a home for the Scottish Opera, reopening in 1975. It offers 1547 comfortable seats, including spacious bars and buffets on all four levels. It has been called "the most beautiful opera theatre in the kingdom," by the *Daily Telegraph,* which noted its splendid Victorian Italian Renaissance plasterwork and glittering chandeliers. But it is not the decor that attracts operagoers; rather, the ambitious repertoire. The box office is open from 10 a.m. to 6 p.m. Monday to Saturday (from 10 a.m. to 7:30 p.m. on performance days). The Theatre Royal is also home to the Scottish Ballet, a national company with an international reputation, and it also hosts visiting theater and dance companies from around the world.

The **Glasgow Citizens Theatre,** at Gorbals Street and Ballater Street (tel. 041/429-0022), was founded 40 years ago by James Bridie, a famous Glaswegian whose plays are still produced. It is home to a repertory theater.

The **Pavilion Theatre,** Renfield Street (tel. 041/332-1846), is still alive and well, specializing in modern versions of vaudeville which, as they will assure you around here, isn't dead.

The **Kings Theatre,** at Bath Street and Elmbank Street (tel. 041/552-5961), has a wide range of productions, including straight plays, musicals, and amateur shows. During the winter season it is noted for its spectacular pantomime.

The **Mitchell Theatre,** Granville Street (tel. 041/221-3198), has earned a reputation for small-scale entertainment, ranging from dark drama to dance. A modern little theater, it adjoins the well-known Mitchell Library.

The **Tron Theatre Club,** Tron Theatre, 63 Trongate (tel. 041/552-4267), has done a fine job of rescuing the old Tron Church on Argyle Street and turning it into a theater. It presents contemporary drama and reinterpretations of the classics as well as cabaret in its spacious atmospheric bar.

Glasgow Arts Centre, 12 Washington St. (tel. 041/221-4526), directed by Graeme McKinnon, always seems to be doing or presenting something interesting, including productions aimed at children. Their activities range from presenting theatrical productions to folk concerts. They are open Monday to Saturday from 9:30 a.m. to 5 p.m. and 6:30 to 10 p.m. (on Sunday from 1:30 to 5 p.m.). In summer they are closed in the evening. Tickets to their presentations can be purchased over the phone.

The Leading Disco

Pzazz Disco, 23 Royal Exchange Square (tel. 041/221-5323). One of the most imaginative discos in Glasgow is incongruously located on the second floor of a building surrounded with 19th-century neoclassical monuments. Some visitors combine an evening at Pzazz with dinner at Charlie Parker's (see my restaurant recommendations) on the ground floor. The lighting inside the disco often prompts fashion photographers to use this locale as the site of their layouts. The decor is electronic, heavily infused with shades of electric blues and golds, with lots of mirrors to catch the reflections from the smallish dance floor. The disco is open only on Friday and Saturday from 10 p.m. to 3:30 a.m. The entrance fee is £3.50 ($5.60) per person, with drinks beginning at £1 ($1.60) apiece.

Favorite Pubs

Archie's Bar, 27 Waterloo St. (tel. 041/221-3210), is an exuberant modern bar, with a self-service area, offering cold meats and salads, along with four or five hot dishes, including steak pie, ham, fruit pies, and a trifle. Expect to spend from £2.50 ($4). Archie's is open from noon to 10 p.m. daily but closed on Sunday.

The **Potstill,** 154 Hope St. (tel. 041/333-0980), is the best place to go in Glasgow to sample malt whisky. A selection of more than 100 single-malt (unblended) whiskies, many at a variety of different strengths, can be tasted (perhaps not on the same night). You can also order malt whiskies at a variety of maturities—that is, years spent in casks. Many prefer the malt whisky that has been aged in a sherry cask. On one shelf is displayed a Dalmore and a Springbank whisky, each bottled more than half a century ago. They are to be looked at—never sampled. The "Still" runs from 11 a.m. to midnight daily except Sunday. You can also enjoy good bar food at lunch, including cold meat salads or sandwiches. Light meals cost from £3 ($4.80).

Bon Accord, 153 North St. (tel. 041/248-4427), is a real ale drinker's local. The brand names of what emerges on handpump may be unfamiliar to North Americans, but the tastes will probably delight. Of course, the pub is likely to satisfy your taste in malt whisky as well, perhaps introduce you to a new bottle. The place is clean and tidy, pleasantly decorated, a safe haven. Hours are 11 a.m. to 11 p.m., and you may want to come here for lunch, enjoying its good pub grub. You can order everything from a hamburger to Scotch pie. Count on spending from £1.50 ($2.40). Or else you can enjoy a cold table in the wine bar, costing £2.50 ($4) or a dinner for £8 ($12.80).

Tom Sawyer's, 242 Woodlands Rd. (tel. 041/332-5687), is a favorite of students from Glasgow University. It is open daily from noon to 10 p.m. (on Sunday from noon to 2:30 p.m. and 6:30 to 10 p.m.). This is a pub but others have likened it to a Stateside diner. Burgers and kebabs appear on the menu, along with fish and curry dishes. Cold meats and salads along with a few hot dishes are served at lunch. Meals cost from £5 ($8).

2. Dunoon

Dunoon on the Cowal Peninsula is where Glaswegians go in summer to stroll along its four-mile waterside promenade, taking in amusement arcades, gardens, views, piers, and dozens upon dozens of hotels. The area grew in prosperity when wealthy Glasgow merchants, their coffers enriched by cotton and tobacco, built summer retreats along the Clyde. Many of those former grand private homes have now been turned into hotels for the fun-in-the-sun crowd, who gravitate to the band concerts, flower shows, Highland games, and tournaments staged in the area during the season. The location is near Holy Loch, which has a U.S. submarine base.

The Cowal Peninsula itself has some of the most beautiful scenery in Scotland. To the north is the Argyll Forest Park, which is riddled with forest walks.

To reach Dunoon, you can loop around the "High Road" by Loch Lomond, arriving in about two hours from Glasgow. Or you can take one of the ferry hops in about 20 minutes. Ferries depart from Gourock.

Loch Eck is known for its fishing, and the sands of Kilbride Bay have fine sailing opportunities.

Dunoon, incidentally, is considered one of the major gateways to the western Highlands.

WHERE TO STAY: A few minutes' walk from the town center, the **Esplanade Hotel,** West Bay (tel. 0369/4070), presents a generous expanse of red-trimmed facade to a pedestrian walkway. Much of the illumination streaming into the bedrooms comes from expansive bay windows looking out over the front flower garden and the seafront promenade. Each well-furnished room has a TV, radio, and tea-making equipment, and a few of the accommodations come complete with private bath. Singles cost from £14 ($22.40), and doubles rent for £25 ($40). Half board is available at a rate of £20 ($32) per person. This family-run establishment offers drinks to residents on the putting green if they so desire. A sauna and sunbed are available for guests. The hotel remains open from April to October.

Cowal House Hotel, Kilbride Road, West Bay (tel. 0369/4103), was built as the palatial home of a wealthy Glaswegian merchant in the 1800s. Over the years it has been expanded to include a steep-roofed modern wing that more or less blends with the original bay-fronted core. The views from many of the 56 pleasantly furnished bedrooms encompass a sweep of the firth, as well as the flat, well-maintained lawn. Live entertainment is offered in season, and there's a bar on the premises. Depending on the plumbing, B&B costs £13.50 ($21.60) to £17 ($27.20) per person. It's best to take the half-board plan, costing £20.50 ($32.80) to £23 ($36.80).

Abbeyhill Hotel, Dhailing Road (tel. 0369/2204), is an Italianate Victorian-era building overlooking the Firth of Clyde whose palm trees on the front lawn add an extra dose of southern flavoring. Despite its design texture, the interior is undeniably Scottish. Each of the 14 comfortably furnished bedrooms contains a private bath as well as a color TV, along with tea-making equipment and radio / intercom. Many of the accommodations benefit from views of the sea, as seen through an array of arched and bay-fronted windows. Singles rent for £23 ($36.80) to £26 ($41.60), while doubles cost £37 ($59.20) to £41 ($65.60), including breakfast. Half board is priced at £32 ($51.20) to £35 ($56) per person.

Rosscairn Hotel, 51 Hunter St., Kirn (tel. 0369/4344). The ornate iron columns and balustrades accenting the facade of this stone house would incite envy in even the most kind-hearted homeowner. The establishment's ten comfortably furnished accommodations remain open throughout the year. Each contains a private bath and coffee-making equipment—in all, offering a cozy kind of home-style comfort. Doubles or twins go for £13 ($20.80) per person, with half board costing from £17.50 ($28) per person, based on double occupancy. Golfers will appreciate the fact that the grounds of the hotel adjoin the nearby Cowal Golf Course.

Abbot's Brae Hotel, Bullwood, West Bay (tel. 0369/5021). The imposing vertical lines of this gabled guesthouse jut above the forest surrounding it. Access is via a curved driveway, whose entrance lies a short distance from the town center. Many of the modernized bedrooms benefit from views of the sea. Each of the seven comfortably appointed rooms contains a color TV, clock radio, tea-making equipment, and central heating, along with private bath or shower. B&B costs from £14.50 ($23.20) per person. The half-board rate is £20.50 ($32.80) per person. The establishment is closed in December.

WHERE TO EAT: If you're looking for traditional Scottish fare, your best bet is **Beverley's Restaurant,** Ardfillayne Hotel, West Bay, 53 Bullwood Rd. (tel. 0369/2267). A Victorian candlelit restaurant, it serves good-tasting dinners from 7 to 10 p.m. (closed Monday) in a room inspired by the Scottish architect Charles Rennie Mackintosh. In this comfortable and welcoming environment, you get the best of Scottish meat and seafood, including local venison, tender steaks, salmon, and "the catch of the day" from Loch Fyne. Desserts, including whisky syllabub, are often based on old Scottish recipes. Most meals cost from £13 ($20.80), and reservations are advised. The owners of the restaurant, Bill and Beverley McCaffrey, owned and ran their own establishment in Spain before purchasing the Ardfillayne Hotel. Before that, Bill spent many years in the West End of London as chef and restaurant manager, and Beverley, who comes from Alberta, Canada, was in the hotel and restaurant business there and in Spain, as well as in Scotland.

During the day you'll do quite well at **Black's Tea Room,** 144 Argyll St. (tel. 0369/2311), which opens for morning coffee and freshly baked scones at 9 a.m. Through the day this no-frills place serves good plain fare, including properly made sandwiches, crisp salads at noon, and a selection of rich cakes and desserts. Light meals cost from £3.50 ($5.60). After high tea, the place closes at 5 p.m. and is shut all day Sunday.

A BOTANIC GARDEN NEAR DUNOON: One of the major attractions in the area is the **Younger Botanic Garden** at Benmore (tel. 0369/6261), seven miles north of Dunoon off the A815. The garden is open from 10 a.m. to 6 p.m. from April to October, charging an admission of 30p (48¢) for adults and 15p (24¢) for children. A property of Scotland since 1928, this garden is an important annex of the Royal Botanic Garden in Edinburgh. It is renowned for its collection of flowering trees and shrubs, along with its extensive plantings of many species of garden conifers. Between January and September there are 250 species of rhododendrons that burst into flower. They are best seen from the end of April until the beginning of June. The climate at Benmore is suitable for growing a variety of conifers, and the collections include some of the largest trees in Britain.

3. Rothesay and Isle of Bute

This island in the Clyde grew to prominence during the heyday of 19th-century prosperity in Glasgow. Glaswegians back then had no cheap charter flights to Ibiza, and for their holidays in the sun they turned to pleasures close at hand. Bute, whose capital is Rothesay, along with just-previewed Dunoon, became the playground for the industrial heartland of Scotland.

Times and fashion change, and Rothesay went very much out of style. But nowadays there are signs of a revival of interest.

Of course, as a holiday retreat, Bute far, far predated the Victorian era. Set on a horseshoe-shaped bay, against a backdrop of "great black hills," Rothesay was used by the kings of Scotland as a holiday retreat.

Getting there is fairly easy, as Bute lies only a quarter of a mile from the mainland. From Wemyss Bay on the mainland, you can take one of the roll-on, roll-off ferries operated by Caledonian MacBrayne. There are frequent sailings throughout the day, and a boat trip takes about half an hour. The Kyles of Bute are the narrow straits separating the island from Argyll.

FOOD AND LODGING: When it was built, the **Grand Marine Hotel,** Argyle Street (tel. 0700/3145), was the grandest hotel on the island. An ornate iron fence separates it from the street, while an even bigger one runs in a decorative band across the top of its mansard roof. Today its red sandstone facade has been painted white, at least in sections, but the property still retains an exterior sense of the Victorian era. The Grand Marine sits on a promenade in the center of the resort. All but four of its 32 bedrooms are bathless, each equipped with electric heaters, electric blankets, tea-making equipment, and hot and cold running water. An array of summer sports activities can be arranged by the family who manages the place. Open only from April to October, the hotel charges from £13.50 ($21.60) per person for B&B. Half board costs £18 ($28.80) per person nightly.

    Regent Hotel, 23 Battery Pl., Craigmore (tel. 0700/2411), a pleasantly big-windowed hotel on the seaside Promenade at the edge of town, a few minutes' walk from the center. It was designed as a solidly conservative three-story house until the owners added a series of panoramic extensions, one of which supports a parasol-dotted sun terrace overlooking Rothesay Bay. Ken and Maggie Brown, the owners, personally prepare the well-flavored food served in the modernized dining room. The comfortable bedrooms, each of which has a color TV, rent for £13 ($20.80) in a single and £12.50 ($20) per person in a double. Half board is £16.50 ($26.40) in a single and £16 ($25.60) per person in a double.

    The **Royal Hotel,** Albert Place (tel. 0700/3044). The Schooner Lounge, overlooking the village marina, is one of the island's best spots for a before-dinner drink. It's contained within the white- and cream-colored walls of this severely elegant hotel on the waterfront in the center of town. There are no fewer than three bars on the premises, one of which offers a cabaret show in summer. The 20 bedrooms have been updated in contemporary style. Seven units contain private baths or showers. The establishment, however, remains satisfyingly Scottish. B&B costs from £13.50 ($21.60) per person, and half board is from £18 ($28.80) per person.

    St. Ebba Private Hotel, 37 Mount Stuart Rd. (tel. 0700/2683), faces Loch Striven and the Kyles of Bute. The three-story building is a short distance from the center of town, standing behind a wide driveway and a flowering garden. Each of the pleasantly furnished bedrooms has private plumbing and hot-beverage facilities, some having color TV. The owners, Dave and Mary Baldry, charge from £15 ($24) per person for B&B, from £19 ($30.40) for half board. Bar lunches are served on request, and fishing trips, pony treks, and golfing can be arranged.

    Ardyne Private Hotel, 38 Mount Stuart Rd., Craigmore Promenade (tel. 0700/2052). The Baillie family are the proud owners of this rambling building whose solid walls are constructed of reddish sandstone with white trim. It sits behind well-tended shrubbery on the seafront. Many of the dozen tastefully decorated bedrooms look out over the water. Each contains hot and cold running water, electric blankets, and electric heaters. Between May and September, when it is open, the hotel charges from £16 ($25.60) per person daily for half board. Some rooms have private baths, costing £1 ($1.60) extra per day.

    Ardmory House Hotel, Ardmory Road at Ardbeg (tel. 0700/2346), occupies an imposing house whose white walls look vaguely Tudor in style except they aren't half-timbered. The lack of wooden beams on the exterior is compensated for by the pub, whose surfaces are crossed with heavy timbers in a style that would have won the approval of Anne Hathaway. The hotel also contains a sunwashed dining room whose open spaces are interrupted only by a mass of hanging plants. There's a trout pond on the surrounding grounds, lying just on the outskirts of Ardbeg. The five bedrooms, each comfortably furnished, contain private bath and color TV. They cost from £17 ($27.20) per person for B&B.

SIGHTS: In summer the best way to explore is aboard the *Waverley,* the last sea-going paddle steamer in the world. It leaves from Rothesay Pier, heading for the resorts and places of beauty in the Firth of Clyde. Information about departures can be obtained from the Rothesay and Isle of Bute Tourist Board, The Pier, in Rothesay (tel. 0700/2151).

Your arrival will be at the often-busy harbor of Rothesay, where you'll meet your first locals. They're called Brandanes around here, and they are proud of the ancient traditions of their town. A charter bestowed on it in 1401 gives it the honor of a royal burgh. Prince Charles, incidentally, holds as his premier Scottish title "Duke of Rothesay." Since King Robert III in 1398 bestowed the title on his eldest son, it has since passed onto the head of the eldest son of the reigning monarch.

A short walk from the harbor, **Rothesay Castle** has loomed large in Scottish history. One of the most important medieval castles in Scotland, it was built by the Viking king, Magnus Barelegs, in 1140. An even earlier fortress had stood there. In 1240 Norsemen stormed the castle, and damage they inflicted then is still evident. Much of the castle as you see it today dates from the 1500s, including a moat and high curtain walls considered unique in the country. Cromwell's men successfully held the castle in the 1650s. The castle fell in 1685 to a brother of the Earl of Argyll. It is open from 9:30 a.m. to 7 p.m. Monday to Saturday and 2 to 7 p.m. on Sunday in summer. Winter hours are the same, except that closing is at 4 p.m. It is also closed Thursday morning and Friday in winter and for Christmas and New Year holidays. Admission is 50p (80¢) for adults, 25p (40¢) for children.

If you're interested in local history, the **Bute Museum,** Stuart Street (tel. 0700/3380), has much lore. It provides not only a social history of Bute, but samples of its flora, fauna, and past history. It is open April to September, Monday to Saturday from 10:30 a.m. to 12:30 p.m. and 2:30 to 4:30 p.m. In summer it is also open on Sunday from 2:30 to 4:30 p.m. Off-season it is open Tuesday to Saturday from 2:30 to 4:30 p.m. Admission is 50p (80¢) for adults and 20p (32¢) for children.

At the top of the High Street, you can visit the ruins of **St. Mary's Chapel,** dating from the 14th century. It's about half a mile south of Rothesay along the A845. It has two notable canopied tombs, including one depicting a knight in full armor. Another tomb is dedicated to Stephanie Hortense Bonaparte, a niece of Napoleon who came to Bute seeking the quiet life.

Ardencraig Gardens at Ardencraig (tel. 0700/4225) were acquired by Rothesay in 1968 and can be visited free from the first of May until the end of September, Monday to Friday from 9 a.m. to 4:30 p.m. and on Saturday and Sunday from 1 to 4:30 p.m. The house, constructed in 1863, is still in private hands. Aviaries contain foreign bird species, and there are exotic fish ponds along with extensive greenhouses.

In addition, there are many other activities to occupy your days in Bute, including three golf courses and a pavilion, featuring Scottish shows throughout the summer.

Chapter XVI

AYR, PRESTWICK, AND BURNS COUNTRY

1. Ayr
2. Alloway
3. Culzean Castle
4. Prestwick
5. Troon
6. Kilmarnock

AS SIR WALTER SCOTT dominates the Borders, so does Robert Burns the country around Ayr and Prestwick. There are, in addition, a string of famous seaside resorts stretching from Girvan to Largs. Some of the greatest golf courses in Britain, including Turnberry, are found here; and Prestwick, of course, is the site of one of the major airports of Europe.

1. Ayr

Ayr is the most popular resort on Scotland's west coast. A busy market town, it offers 2½ miles of sands and makes a good center for touring the Burns Country. This royal burgh is also noted for its manufacture of fabrics and carpets, so you may want to allow time to browse through its shops. With its steamer cruises, fishing, golf, and racing, it faces the Isle of Arran and the Firth of Clyde.

For centuries Ayr has been associated with horse racing, and it now has the top racecourse in Scotland. One of the main streets of the town is named Racecourse Road for a stretch near the town center.

Ayr was the birthplace of the road builder John L. MacAdam, whose name was immortalized in the road surfacing called macadam.

WHERE TO STAY: A sandstone structure with two Doric columns at the entrance, the **Meteor Hotel,** 5 Racecourse Rd. (tel. 0292/263891), has parking space in the courtyard. The hotel offers good value in an area of more expensive lodgings—£12 ($19.20) per person for B&B, VAT included. There are rooms on the ground floor suitable for disabled persons. The Meteor has 22 bedrooms, most of them doubles. Of these, 12 have private baths, and all units have hot and cold water basins, and many have showers. The hotel is centrally heated, with radios and hot-beverage facilities in all the units. Proprietors Miss Logan and Mr. and Mrs. Logan invite their guests to enjoy the pleasant residents' lounge and bar. The hotel, a long block from the waters of the Firth of Clyde, is central for shops and entertainment. It is open all year.

Elms Court Hotel, Miller Road (tel. 0292/264191), is an inviting, modernized hotel within a few minutes' walk of the city center. There are 19 bedrooms, all of which have private bath or shower. Color TV has been installed in all units. There are a comfortable lounge and a well-appointed bar lounge. The dining room was recently redecorated, and the food served here is good. The charge is £18.50 ($29.60) per person for B&B or £24.50 ($39.20) per person with dinner included. You can recognize the Elms Court by the two stone lions couchant that guard the entrance. There is ample parking. The fully licensed hotel is open all year.

At **Chalmers Court Hotel,** Charlotte Street (tel. 0292/265458), a two-minute walk from the Esplanade which skirts the Firth, and a five-minute walk from the seafront, Miss Hood receives paying guests in her immaculate hostelry, charging them £10.50 ($16.80) per person per night for B&B. All bedrooms have water basins and electric fires. Guests relax in the spacious lounge with a view of the Firth of Clyde. Ample parking is available, and the hotel is open all year.

Aftongrange Hotel, 37 Carrick Rd. (tel. 0292/265679), is a stone house lying about two minutes from the heart of Ayr and the train station. The house was built for a local doctor about a century ago, and it still has architectural features of that era, including stained-glass windows set into the stairwell and a French cupola in the upper hallway. The owners, Bill and Rosina Farrell, rent eight of their high-ceilinged rooms. With breakfast included, the cost is £18 ($28.80) in a single, rising to £29 ($46.40) in a double. With private bath, the cost goes up another £4 ($6.40) per night. Each accommodation has a TV, tea-making equipment, a built-in radio, and a modest but comfortable series of appointments. A busy pub on the ground floor means that guests are only a few steps from drink and companionship. In lieu of dinner, the Farrells serve a Scottish high tea prepared by a farmer's daughter from a nearby hamlet, costing £4 ($6.40) per person.

Arran Doon, 21 Carrick Rd. (tel. 0292/266481), is a 100-year-old house owned by Mrs. Murdoch. Although none of her rooms have private baths, they all have color TV and hot-beverage facilities. Doubles rent for £20 ($32), with a Scottish breakfast included. Everything is comfortable and pleasantly furnished, the impeccable interior capped with detailed molding and ceiling medallions. There's a small garden in front.

Clifton Hotel, 19 Miller Rd. (tel. 0292/264521), is often conceded as one of the best guesthouses in the Ayr area. Reasonable in tariff and personally supervised by the owners, it is convenient to the center of town and to the promenade. This detached sandstone house is made even more alluring with its gardens in back. Lying in a tranquil residential area, it offers 11 well-furnished bedrooms, five of which contain a private bath or shower. The B&B rate ranges from £14 ($22.40) to £17 ($27.20) per person, with half board costing from £20 ($32) to £22.50 ($36) per person nightly. The little hotel is open all year.

Coila Guest House, 10 Holmston Rd. (tel. 0292/262642), is a large cheerful house near the center of town, operated by Mrs. M. Mitchell. Rooms are equipped with TV, hot and cold water basins, and hot-beverage facilities. The charge for B&B is £9.50 ($15.20) per person.

Mrs. Mitchell also operates **Langley Bank Guest House,** 39 Carrick Rd.

(tel. 0292/264246), where the same facilities are offered as at the Coila accommodation. Here the tariff is also £9.50 ($15.20) for B&B.

For a change of pace, why not try a stay at a farmhouse on a Strathclyde farm? **Trees Farm,** four miles east of Ayr on an unclassified road between the A70 on the north and the A713 on the south (tel. 0292/570270), is a 120-acre farm, where Mrs. Helen Stevenson has three bedrooms which she rents to visitors. The rate is £9 ($14.40) per person for a bed and a full Scottish breakfast. An evening dinner at £5 ($8) is optional. You can enjoy a cuisine using fresh farm produce. Mrs. Stevenson has color TV in the guest lounge, where she shares conversation with you. The farm receives guests from Easter until the end of September.

WHERE TO EAT: A good family-style eating place, the **Tudor Restaurant,** 8 Beresford Terrace (tel. 0292/261404), doesn't offer alcoholic drinks but serves one of the best table d'hôte menus in town daily from noon to 2 p.m. For only £3 ($4.80), you are given a meal that might include Scotch broth, beefsteak pie with turnips, peas, and potatoes, and fruit trifle with fresh cream. The traditional Scottish high tea, served from 3:15 to 8 p.m., is inclusive of tea, bread, scones, jam, and a cake. There is also an à la carte menu for high tea, on which are listed sandwiches, fish courses, meat, chicken, and desserts. The charge for filet of haddock with peas and french fries is £3.20 ($5.12). There is also a snacks box suitable for smaller appetites.

Raffles, 56 Smith St. (tel. 0292/66076), is one of the city's most popular luncheon pubs. It contains a warmly textured decor of stained-pine beams and copper-topped tables. A specialty here is stuffed baked potatoes, and you can also order beefburgers, lasagne, or deep-fried haddock. Meals cost from £3 ($4.80) and are served beginning at noon weekdays. Closing is at 9 p.m. Monday, Tuesday, and Wednesday, at 8 p.m. on Thursday and Friday, and at 7 p.m. on Saturday. Closed Sunday.

The Local Pub

Rabbie's Bar, Burns Statue Square (tel. 0292/69200). This famous pub might be considered a mixture of Scottish poetry with electronic music. The exposed stone of the walls are highlighted with snippets of pithy verses by one of the establishment's earlier clients, Robert Burns, who used to drop in for a pint of ale and conversation with his friends. Today there's a portrait of Rabbie painted directly onto the wall as a nostalgic reminder of another era. In spite of the establishment's history, don't come here expecting poetry readings in a quiet corner. The crowd, while not particularly literary, is talkative and fun. There's a large selection of imported beers, a busy stand-up bar, long rows of crowded banquettes and copper-topped tables, and an extra-large TV screen showing videos of whatever musical group is hot in the English-speaking world. Open 11 a.m. to 11 p.m.

SIGHTS: Ayr is full of Burns associations. The 13th-century **Auld Brig o' Ayr,** the poet's "poor narrow footpath of a street,/Where two wheelbarrows tremble when they meet," was renovated in 1910.

A Burns museum is housed in the thatched **Tam o' Shanter Inn** in Ayr High Street (tel. 0292/269794), an alehouse in Rabbie's day. It is open April to September, Monday to Saturday from 9:30 a.m. to 5:30 p.m. In summer it is also open on Sunday from 2:30 to 5 p.m. Off-season it is open Monday to Saturday from noon to 4 p.m. Admission is 35p (56¢) for adults and 20p (32¢) for children. Douglas Graham of Shanter, who furnished malted grain to this brewhouse, was immortalized by Rabbie in *Tam o'Shanter*.

The **Auld Kirk** of Ayr dates from 1654 when it replaced the 12th-century Church of St. John. Burns was baptized in the kirk.

Wallace Tower, High Street, is another attraction of Ayr, rising some 112 feet. Constructed in 1828, it has a statue of Sir William Wallace.

Another architectural curiosity is **Loudoun Hall,** Boat Vennal, off Cross in the heart of town. A wealthy merchant had this town house constructed in the late 1400s. It is considered one of the oldest examples of "burgh architecture" left in the country. Once it was occupied by the Campbells and later the Earls of Loudoun. It is open mid-July until the end of August from 11 a.m. to 6 p.m. Monday to Saturday.

On the outskirts, the **Maclaurin Gallery and Rozelle House** are installed in what had been stables and quarters for servants attached to a manor house. A Henry Moore bronze sculpture is on display, as well as changing exhibitions of sculpture, paintings, and crafts. Many residents of Ayr go here for an "outing," and there is also a nature trail through woodland. The location is about a mile and a half south of Ayr off the road to Burns Cottage at Alloway. Open year round, it can be visited Monday to Saturday from 11 a.m. to 5 p.m. April to October, it is also open from 2 to 5 p.m. on Sunday. No admission is charged. For information, call 0292/43708.

In the Environs

In Tarbolton village, 7½ miles northeast of Ayr off the A758, is the **Bachelors' Club,** Sandgate, a 17th-century house where in 1780 Burns and his friends founded a literary and debating society, now a property of the National Trust for Scotland. In 1779 Burns attended dancing lessons there, against the wishes of his father. There also, in 1781, he was initiated as a Freemason in the Lodge St. David. Eleven months later he became a member of Lodge St. James, which continues today in the village. Samuel Hay, 7 Croft St. (tel. 029254/1424), says the Bachelors' Club is open for visitors noon to 5 p.m. April until the end of October, and he will arrange to show it at other times if you telephone. Admission is 80p ($1.28) for adults, 40p (64¢) for children. Tarbolton is six miles from Prestwick Airport.

AFTER DARK: The most popular nightlife spot in Ayr is **Hoolahan's Bar & Diner,** 231 High St. (tel. 0292/262578). It has a catch-all ambience that includes everything from good-natured Scottish drinking to video panels. Amid a decor of painted signs and flickering video screens (as many as 20 might be going at one time), you can order club steaks and salads or full meals costing from £8 ($12.80) per person. Most guests, however, visit just for the entertainment and the changing array of activities. Depending on the night of the week, you can listen to a Heidelberg-style German band, or listen to rock and roll during a golden oldies night. A pint of beer costs £1 ($1.60). There's a disco in the rear which is open nightly from 8 to midnight, with no cover charge. Don't overlook this as a luncheon stopover either. Hours are Monday to Saturday from 11 a.m. to midnight and Sunday from 7:30 to 11 p.m. Food specialties include "bangers and mash," roast rib of beef, and chili con carne, along with seafood platter.

2. Alloway

Some 2 miles south of Ayr is where Robert Burns, Scotland's national poet, was born on January 25, 1759, in the gardener's cottage—the "auld clay biggin"—his father, William Burns, built in 1757.

WHERE TO STAY: A nearly 200-year-old inn, the **Burns Monument Hotel** (tel. 0292/42466), looks out onto the Doon River and the bridge, Brig o' Doon, immortalized in *Tam o'Shanter*. The inn is an attractive, historical place, with riverside gardens and a whitewashed bar. The rooms are pleasantly and attractively decorated, bright and cheerful, opening onto river views. All bedrooms have private bath. B&B costs £20 ($32) to £25 ($40) in a single, £32 ($51.20) to £40 ($64) in a double. Add another £10 ($16) for dinner.

The **Balgarth Hotel,** Dunure Road, at Doonfoot (tel. 0292/42441), lies two miles south of Ayr on the A719, a coastal road at the estuary of the Doon River, about half a mile from the village of Alloway. The hotel stands on its own grounds of pleasant gardens and woods, opening onto views of the Firth of Clyde and the Carrick Hills. Many motorists stop here en route to Ireland from the ferry station at Stranraer. Rooms are comfortably and pleasantly furnished —15 in all, most of which contain private bath. Singles rent for £18 ($28.80), going up to £22 ($35.20) with bath; doubles, £30 ($48) to £36 ($57.60). These tariffs include a full Scottish breakfast. Residents can order dinner for another £8.50 ($13.60). The hotel is open all year.

SIGHTS: Alloway is dominated by the **Burns Monument and Gardens** (tel. 0292/41321). The monument is a Grecian-style building erected in 1823, containing relics, books, and manuscripts associated with Robert Burns, dating back to the 1820s. It is open from 9 a.m. to 7 p.m. daily April to October and from 10 a.m. to 5 p.m. November to March. Admission, which includes entrance to Burns' Cottage and Museum, is £1 ($1.60) for adults, 50p (80¢) for children. The monument is two miles south of Ayr on the B7024.

More than 100,000 people visit **Burns' Cottage and Museum** (tel. 0292/41215) annually, and it still retains some of its original furniture, including the bed in which the poet was born. Chairs displayed here were said to have been used by Tam o'Shanter and Souter Johnnie. Beside the cottage in which the poet lived is a museum, open April to September on weekdays from 9 a.m. to 7 p.m., on Sunday from 2 to 7 p.m. November to March the hours are weekdays from 10 a.m. to dusk; closed Sunday. Admission to the cottage and the Burns Monument is £1 ($1.60) for adults, 50p (80¢) for children.

The Auld Brig over the Ayr, mentioned in *Tam o'Shanter,* still spans the river, and Alloway Auld Kirk, also mentioned in the poem, stands roofless and "haunted" not far away. The poet's father is buried in the graveyard of the kirk.

The **Land o' Burns Centre,** Murdoch's Lane (tel. 0292/43700) is a good place to stop. You can watch a multiscreen presentation of highlights of Burns's life, his friends, and his poetry. Information is available from the personnel, and a well-stocked gift shop is there, plus a tea room. The Russians are particularly fond of Burns and his poetry, and many come annually to visit the cottage and pore over his original manuscripts. Admission to the theater is 40p (64¢) for adults, 20p (32¢) for children. Hours are from 10 a.m. to 6 p.m. in July and August, 10 a.m. to 5:30 p.m. in June and September, and 10 a.m. to 5 p.m. October and May.

3. Culzean Castle

Built by the famous Scottish architect Robert Adam at the end of the 18th century, this magnificent clifftop creation is a fine example of his castellated style. Essentially a dwelling place, Culzean (pronounced "Cullane") Castle replaced an earlier Scots tower house as the family seat of the powerful Kennedy clan. In 1945 the castle and grounds were given to the National Trust for Scotland by the fifth Marquis of Ailsa and quickly became its most popular property.

The castle (tel. 06556/274) lies 12 miles south-southwest of Ayr. With a view of Ailsa Craig to the south and overlooking the Firth of Clyde, the castle is well worth a visit and is of special interest to Americans because of General

Eisenhower's connection with its National Guest Flat. In 1946 the guest apartment was given to the general for his lifetime in gratitude for his services as Supreme Commander of Allied Forces in World War II. An exhibition of Eisenhower memorabilia, sponsored by the Scottish Heritage U.S.A. Inc. and Mobil Oil, is incorporated in the tour of the castle. Mementos of Eisenhower include his North African campaign desk and a replica of the Steuben glass bowl given him by his cabinet when he retired from the presidency. Culzean stands near the famous golf courses of Turnberry and Troon, a fact that particularly pleased golf-loving Eisenhower. The tour also includes the celebrated round drawing room, delicately painted ceilings, and Adam's outstanding oval staircase.

The castle is open daily May to the end of September from 10 a.m. to 6 p.m. In April and October, hours are noon to 5 p.m. except on weekends and Easter week when hours are 10 a.m. to 6 p.m. Last admission is half an hour before closing. The charge is £1.80 ($2.88) for adults, 90p ($1.44) for children.

In the castle grounds is **Culzean Country Park,** which in 1969 became the first such park in Scotland. It has an exhibition center in farm buildings by Adam. The 565-acre grounds include a walled garden, an aviary, a swan park, a camellia house, and an orangery, as well as a deer park, miles of woodland paths, and beaches. It has gained an international reputation for its Visitor Centre (Adam's home farm) and related visitor and educational services. Up to 300,000 people visit the country park annually. The park is open from 10 a.m. to 6 p.m. April to the end of September, from 10 a.m. to 4 p.m. in October, and 9 a.m. to dusk from November to the end of March. Cars are charged £3 ($4.80) to enter the park in high season. It is open free except on Sunday in March during the winter. For information, phone 06556/269.

SIGHTS IN THE ENVIRONS: On the Firth of Clyde, the little town of **Turnberry,** south of the castle, was originally part of the Culzean Estate owned by the Marquis of Ailsa. It began to flourish after the marquis consented early in this century to allow the Glasgow and South Western Railway to develop golfing facilities, resulting in railway service, a recognized golfing center, and a first-class hotel. From the original two 13-hole golf courses, the complex has developed into the two 18-hole courses, Ailsa and Arran, known worldwide. The Ailsa, one of the most exacting courses yet devised, has been the scene of numerous championship tournaments and PGA events.

The two courses are named for the Isle of Arran and Ailsa Craig, which can be seen across the waters of the firth. **Ailsa Craig** is a 1,100-foot-high rounded rock ten miles offshore, a nesting ground and sanctuary for seabirds. Granite from this rock used to be taken to make the stones used in the Scottish game of curling.

There was once a **Turnberry Castle** about six miles south of this golfing locale. Only scant remains exist to mark the place many historians say was the birthplace of Robert the Bruce in 1274.

Just to the east of Turnberry, you might want to take a short drive to see **Souter Johnnie's Cottage** in Kirkoswald (tel. 06556/603), four miles west of Maybole on the A77. This was the home of the village cobbler, John Davidson (Souter Johnnie), at the end of the 18th century. Davidson and his friend, Douglas Graham, of Shanter Farm were immortalized by Burns in his poem *Tam o' Shanter.* The cottage contains Burnsiana and contemporary cobblers' tools. In the churchyard are the graves of Tam o' Shanter and Souter Johnnie, two of his best-known characters. The cottage is open April 1 to September 30 daily except Friday from noon to 5 p.m. It can be visited at other times by appointment. Admission is 80p ($1.28) for adults, 40p (64¢) for children.

Only about a mile from Souter Johnnie's Cottage is the 16th-century **Kilochan Castle,** stronghold of the Cathcarts of Carleton in the valley of the Water of Girvan.

A final sight is **Carleton Castle,** lying along the A77 some 14 miles south of Culzean Castle, six miles along the coast from the little seaside town of Girvan. In its heyday it was one of the Kennedy watchtowers built to guard the coastline against invaders. Now you see only what's left of it. A famous ballad grew out of a legend surrounding this castle. It was said to be the headquarters of a baron who married eight times. When he got tired of a wife, he pushed her over the cliff and found himself another spouse. However, he proved no match for his eighth wife, May Cullean. She got rid of him!

4. Prestwick

Prestwick is the oldest recorded baronial burgh in Scotland. But most visitors today aren't concerned with that ancient fact—rather, they fly in, landing at Prestwick's International Airport, which is in itself a popular sightseeing attraction, as spectators gather to watch planes take off and land from all over the world.

Behind St. Ninian's Episcopal Church is **Bruce's Well,** the water from which is reputed to have cured Robert the Bruce of leprosy. The **Mercat Cross** still stands outside what used to be the Registry Office and marks the center of the oldest part of Prestwick, whose existence goes back to at least 983. Prestwick is a popular holiday town, and is considered one of Scotland's most attractive resorts, with its splendid sands and golf courses. Prestwick opens onto views of Ayr Bay and the Isle of Arran.

WHERE TO STAY: A comfortable and spotless hostelry, **St. Nicholas Hotel,** 41 Ayr Rd. (tel. 0292/79568), has ample parking space at the side and tennis courts at the back. Margaret Preston is a congenial host who goes out of her way to make guests feel welcome. The bedrooms, most of which have private shower and toilet, are immaculate, as are all the public rooms. Mrs. Preston says she's a tyrant about cleanliness. The white walls and pale-blue ceilings in the hallways are set off by the plaid carpeting throughout. The charge is £16 ($25.60) per person per night for B&B in a room with toilet and shower, service and VAT included. The residents' lounge has color TV. In the dining room, good food and friendly service prevail, and you can have lunch, high tea, and dinner there. There are two cocktail lounges. All the windows of the St. Nicholas are double-glazed.

You also won't go wrong staying at **Kincraig,** next door at 39 Ayr Rd. (tel. 0292/79480), an attractive Victorian-Georgian house where Sylvia Vannin rents large, comfortable bedrooms for £10 ($16) per person per night for B&B. She also serves dinner for £6.50 ($10.40). The solidly built house has wide carpeted stairs with a beautiful carved balustrade. In the residents' lounge Mrs. Vannin uses cream naugahyde-covered furniture, which makes a comfortable and attractive room. Oak woodwork is used throughout the house, and an old-fashioned antique sideboard graces the dining room. The house has a restricted license.

St. Catherine, 28 Seabank Rd. (tel. 0292/78217), is a well-maintained guesthouse directed by Mrs. Jessie Manson. Lying in a quietly prosperous neighborhood, it's a well-maintained house with a garden in front, and it contains fine and spacious rooms. The ground-floor parlor has Wedgwood-blue cove moldings with Grecian figures, as well as a marble and brass fireplace. There's also a TV lounge. The comfortable bedrooms are furnished like those in a private home. Doubles cost from £19 ($30.40) nightly.

Parkstone Hotel, Esplanade (tel. 0292/77286), is a white-walled Victorian building with cookie-cutter gingerbread set under its steep eaves. Its modernized interior contains a pleasant pub in back, whose view of the sea attracts a busy lunchtime crowd. The hotel is the property of Stewart and Sandra Clarkson, who maintain their 30-room establishment in good working order. About half the rooms in this century-old establishment have private bath, and each contains color TV. In cold weather a coal fire burns in an oak-paneled room near the reception desk. For B&B, bathless singles rent for £21 ($33.60), with similar doubles going for £36 ($57.60). Singles with bath cost £25 ($40), doubles with bath being priced at £42 ($67.20).

Auchencoyle Hotel (tel. 0292/78316). This establishment's ground-floor pub is one of the most colorful rendezvous points in town. It's not hard to strike up a conversation with one of the clients. The big windows of the white facade look out over the local golf course, and the beach isn't far away. The half dozen modestly appointed rooms rent for £12 ($19.20) per person in a bathless single, going up to £14 ($22.40) per person in a double with shower and toilet. Children sharing a room with their parents pay half the adult price. Evening meals are served for £6.50 ($10.40) and up.

5. Troon

This holiday resort looks out across the Firth of Clyde to the Isle of Arran. It offers several golf links, including the "Old Troon" course. Bathers in summer find plenty of room on its two miles of sandy beaches, stretching from both sides of its harbor. The broad sands and shallow waters make it a safe haven also. From here you can take steamer trips to Arran and the Kyles of Bute.

Troon is mostly a 20th-century town, its earlier history having gone unrecorded. It takes its name from the curiously shaped promontory that juts out into the Clyde estuary on which the old town and the harbor stand. The promontory was called "Trwyn," the Cymric word for nose, and later this became the Trone and then Troon.

Fullarton Estate, on the edge of Troon beyond the municipal golf course, is the ancestral seat of the Dukes of Portland.

A massive statue of **Britannia** stands on the seafront as a memorial to the dead of the two World Wars. On her breastplate is the lion of Scotland emerging from the sea.

WHERE TO STAY: A good splurge choice is the **Piersland House Hotel,** Craigend Road (tel. 0292/314747). Critics considered this an unlikely spot for a large house when it was built a century ago by Sir Alexander Walker of the Johnnie Walker whisky family. Its four acres of gardens required the importation of 17,000 tons of topsoil to transform its marshy surface into the lushness which visitors see on a summer day. At lunchtime and in the evening, pub lovers around Troon flock here for a drink or buffet lunch near one of the hand-carved fireplaces. On sunny days, the staff sets tables up at the edge of the formal garden, turning it into an outdoor version of a neighborhood pub. Frankly, this establishment is better known as a social center than as a hotel. However, it offers 15 comfortably furnished bedrooms, each with a private bath. The rate is from £50 ($80) to £58 ($92.80) in a double or twin, from £32 ($51.20) to £36 ($57.60) in a single, with breakfast included. The food is considered among the best in the area, a set dinner costing from £12.50 ($20) and including such dishes as locally caught scallops and chicken in a white wine sauce.

Craiglea Hotel, South Beach (tel. 0292/311366). One of my favorite hotels in town has a white-painted stone facade, a steep roof, 24 well-furnished rooms, and a history of hospitality stretching back more than 100 years. There's an upstairs lounge looking over a view of the sea, a spacious dining room, a cocktail bar, and a thoughtful management directed by members of the Calderwood family. In cold weather a red-brick fireplace burns a coal fire in the downstairs parlor. The cozy rooms have high ceilings, thick pine doors, and in some, art nouveau furniture—lots of character. Bathless singles cost from £24 ($38.40), from £36 ($57.60) in a double. With bath, a single costs from £25 ($40) and a double goes for £40 ($64). All these tariffs include breakfast and VAT.

Glenside Guest House, 2 Darley Pl. off Bentinck Drive (tel. 0292/313677), is where Mrs. I. M. Chalmers makes guests feel welcome. Her corner house has heating and hot and cold water in all the bedrooms, a dining room with separate tables, a private car park, and a lounge with color TV. She charges £9.50 ($15.20) per person for B&B. The house is opposite the Episcopal church on Bentinck Drive, but be sure to go around the corner to Darley Place to find Glenside.

WHERE TO EAT: A harborside establishment, **The Lookout,** Troon Marina, Harbor Road (tel. 0292/311523), reminds you of the architecture found in similar waterfront structures at leading marinas back home. You'll climb a flight of steps to reach the second-floor bar with its adjoining restaurant. There, congregated within sight of the dozens of yachts in the marina, are the sports lovers of the area. In summer you can enjoy a lager on the terrace overlooking the yacht-clogged harbor. The sun parasols are emblazoned with Drambuie signs, and an occasional friendly Labrador might join his master on the terrace. You can eat in either the pub or in the adjoining restaurant which is known as Scoffs. Dress is casual, and the music is recorded. Menu items include "Scoffburgers," chili, lasagne, homemade soup, and fried chicken. Full meals cost £5 ($8) and up. Hours are 11 a.m. to 11 p.m. (it remains open until midnight on Friday and Saturday). In winter its hours are from 11 a.m. to 2:30 p.m. and 5 to 11 p.m.

Campbell's Kitchen, 3 South Beach (tel. 0292/314421), is a Troon bistro serving some of the most imaginative food in town. Decorated with plants and basket lamps, it serves meals daily except Monday. Lunch is from noon to 2:30 p.m. and dinner from 7 to 9:30 p.m. Evening reservations are imperative. Set back a block from the water, this establishment has a menu based on changing market conditions. The dinner offerings change monthly. Only fresh seasonal produce is used, with emphasis on local shellfish and seafood. There is a full selection of hors d'oeuvres as well as desserts, perhaps a fresh fruit sorbet. Meals cost £12 ($19.20) and up.

The Marine Hotel (tel. 0292/314444) is a landmark hotel standing on the Ayrshire coastline, overlooking the Royal Troon Golf Course. It is ideal for dining in a choice of rooms. Crosbie's Brasserie is the more informal and fun of the two. A lively all-day restaurant, the day begins with morning coffee, croissants, and pastries continuing on to a selection from the cold continental table at lunch and a superb selection of crêpes, steaks, pastas, and brochettes. Crosbie's is filled with shades of gray, pink, and blue. Waitresses are dressed "Blue Angel" style in black pants with pink or blue shirts. Hours are daily from 11 a.m. to midnight, at least for drinks. Main meals, with a full à la carte meal costing from £13 ($20.80), are served from noon to 3 p.m. and 6 to 11 p.m. The other more formal restaurant, Fairways, provides the proper setting for panoramic views of the Isle of Arran. Here you can enjoy traditional Scottish and French cuisine in an attractive setting at either lunch or dinner. A set lunch costs around £6 ($9.60), a table d'hôte dinner going for £15 ($24). Lunch is from noon to 2 p.m., dinner 7 to 10 p.m. daily.

6. Kilmarnock

This inland town is the site of the largest whisky-bottling concern in the world. Johnnie Walker, a grocer on King Street, started to blend whisky in Kilmarnock in 1820, and the product is known all over the world today.

The town also has associations with Rabbie Burns. The first edition of his poems was printed here in 1786. Burns published the poems to raise money to emigrate to Jamaica, but they were so successful he decided to remain in Scotland.

In Kay Park, the **Burns Monument** was erected. It is a red sandstone temple surmounted by a tower.

FOOD AND LODGING: A suitable choice if you're overnighting in the area is the **Burnside Hotel,** 18 London Rd. (tel. 0563/22952). It offers a total of 12 rooms, equally divided among singles, doubles, and family units. All occupants share the two public baths. Rooms are comfortably furnished and reasonable in price, costing from £13 ($20.80) per person for B&B. You can also stay here on half-board terms, priced from £16 ($25.60) per person nightly.

Caesar's, 112 John Finnie St. (tel. 0563/25706), is the best place in town for food. Most visitors pass through just for the day, and if you are, you can enjoy a midday carvery-style repast. You can then order a drink and settle down with your selection of a roast joint. Prices range from £5 ($8) to £8 ($12.80), depending on what you order The à la carte dinner menu is more elaborate and more expensive, costing from £13 ($20.80) for a selection from a continental menu, including such dishes as chicken Kiev and steak Diane. The 55-seat restaurant is both contemporary and traditional, with a black-and-red color scheme, the decor dramatized by the white tile floor. Service is friendly and polite. Lunch is served daily except Sunday from noon to 2 p.m., dinner from 6:30 to 9 p.m., perhaps later on Friday and Saturday. On Sunday hours are from 5 to 9 p.m. The place is closed on Monday.

SIGHTS IN THE ENVIRONS: Some 4½ miles southwest of Kilmarnock, **Dundonald Castle** is a notable landmark high on an isolated hill. Off the A759, it is not open to the public but may be viewed from the outside. It was built by Robert II, the first Stuart king, who died there in 1390, as did Robert III, his son, in 1406.

East along the River Irvine are the three lace-making towns of Galston, Newmilns, and Darvel, where Dutch and Huguenot immigrants settled in the 17th century.

DUMFRIES AND GALLOWAY

SOUTHWESTERN SCOTLAND, part of the famous "Lowlands," is often overlooked by motorists rushing north from the Lake District of England. But this country of Burns is filled with many rewarding targets, a land of unspoiled countryside, fishing harbors, artists' colonies of color-washed houses, and romantically ruined abbeys and castles dating from the days of the border wars.

It's a fine country for touring, and most of its hotels are small, of the Scottish provincial variety, but that usually means a friendly reception from a smiling staff and good and traditional Scottish cookery, using local produce.

I've documented the most important centers below, but have also included many offbeat places for those seeking a more esoteric trip.

1. Lockerbie

A border market town, Lockerbie lies in the valley of Annandale, offering much fishing and golf. It's a good center for exploring some sightseeing attractions in its environs.

Lockerbie was the scene in 1593 of a battle that ended one of the last great

Border family feuds. The Johnstones routed the Maxwells, killing Lord Maxwell and 700 of his men. Many of the victims had their ears cut off with a cleaver —a method of mutilation that became known throughout the Border Country as the "Lockerbie Nick."

FOOD AND LODGING: You'll find excellent accommodations at **Somerton House Hotel,** Carlisle Road (tel. 05762/2583), a fully licensed hostelry where your amiable hosts will be Sam and Pat Ferguson. On the south side of the town, standing in its acre of ground, the hotel has a beautiful garden and parking for scores of cars. The six bedrooms and public rooms are comfortable, and the staff and townspeople who come to the public lounge are friendly and hospitable. The late Victorian structure has elegant arch and oak woodwork and plaster rosette friezes. One of the bathrooms has facilities that would have pleased Queen Victoria. Bathless rooms rent for £17.50 ($28) per person, the price going up to £19 ($30.40) per person with bath. Meals in the high-ceilinged dining room include dinner, from £9.50 ($15.20). The cuisine is excellent, using local farm produce. Bar lunches are served from noon to 2:30 p.m. and dinner from 7 to 9 p.m.

SIGHTS IN THE ENVIRONS: Of interest are the remains of **Lochmaben Castle,** 3½ miles west of Lockerbie, said to have been the boyhood home (some historians say the birthplace) of Robert the Bruce. This castle, on the south shore of Castle Loch, was captured and recaptured 12 times and also withstood six attacks and sieges. James IV was a frequent visitor, and Mary Queen of Scots was here in 1565. The ruin of the early 14th-century castle is on the site of a castle of the de Brus family, ancestors of Robert the Bruce. However, the charming little hamlet of Lochmaben, with its five lochs, is reason enough to visit, regardless of who was or was not born there.

If you're heading north to Lockerbie on the A74, I'd suggest a stop in the village of Ecclefechan. There you can visit **Carlyle's Birthplace** (tel. 05763/666), five miles southeast of Lockerbie on the Lockerbie–Carlisle road. Even though the historian, critic, and essayist Thomas Carlyle isn't much read these days, the "arched house" in which he was born in 1795 is interesting, containing mementos and manuscripts of the author. It's open from Easter to October 31 daily, except Sunday, from 10 a.m. to 6 p.m., charging adults 80p ($1.28) and children 40p (64¢).

In the vicinity, you can also look out over **Burnswark,** which the Romans used as a hill fort and artillery range. This is a large earthworks area, with excavated ditches and ramparts. Admission-free, it is open throughout the day. You'll see a sign directing you to the site about 1½ miles north of the B725, the Ecclefechan–Middlebrie highway.

2. Moffat

An Annandale town, Moffat thrives as a center of a sheep-farming area, symbolized by a statue of a ram in the wide High Street, and has been a holiday resort since the mid-17th century, because of the curative properties of its water. It was here that Robert Burns composed the drinking song "O Willie Brew'd a Peck o' Maut." Today people visit this border town on the banks of the Annan River for its good fishing and golf.

North of Moffat is spectacular hill scenery. Five miles northwest is a huge, sheer-sided 500-foot-deep hollow in the hills called the **Devil's Beef Tub,** where border cattle thieves, called reivers, hid cattle lifted in their raids.

Northeast along Moffat Water, past White Coomb, which stands 2,696 feet high, is the **Grey Mare's Tail,** a 200-foot hanging waterfall formed by the Tail Burn dropping from Loch Skene. It is under the National Trust for Scotland.

WHERE TO STAY: Right in the center of town, the **Star Hotel** (tel. 0683/20156) is a comfortable family-run accommodation on the High Street. Doug and Monica House and Tim and Allison Leighfield, the proprietors, extend a welcome to guests who choose this tall (four-story), narrow, interesting-looking place for their stay in Moffat. The hotel has eight bedrooms, which rent for £17 ($27.20) per person in a double, £18 ($28.80) in a single, all with breakfast and VAT included. All the units are maintained at a high standard, and most contain private plumbing, TV, and hot-beverage facilities. There is a residents' lounge with TV and a pleasant cocktail bar, as well as a public bar where hotel guests can mingle with the local residents. The dining room has high-quality food and service.

Away from the heart of town on Hartfell Crescent is **Hartfell House** (tel. 0683/20153), an early Victorian house built in the days when Moffat was a thriving spa town attracting health-seekers from Edinburgh and Glasgow. The two-story building has a delightful garden facing the house, with a nine-hole putting green, and its inside attractions include crystal chandeliers, armoires, a window seat with the original parquet, and a bow window. The charge for comfortable, immaculate bedrooms is £11 ($17.60) per person for B&B. Dinner costs from £7 ($11.20). There is ample parking across the street. The house is open from March until the end of December. To find Hartfell Crescent, turn off High Street at the Clock Tower, then go straight up the hill. Hartfell Crescent is on the right off Old Well Road.

Balmoral Hotel, High Street (tel. 0683/20288), is an attractively furnished and decorated hotel that was once Ye Olde Spur Inn and Coaching House. The present lounge bar was originally in the room where Robert Burns met his crony, Clark, the Moffat schoolmaster. Brian Stokes and family, the resident proprietors, will give you a warm welcome and direct you to where to go for fishing, riding, walking, golfing, or just enjoying the views. They charge from £15 ($24) to £19 ($30.40) in one of their single rooms, from £27 ($43.20) to £31 ($49.60) in a double, with a Scottish breakfast included. Several of the accommodations are quite spacious.

Buchan House, Beechgrove (tel. 0683/20378), is another dependable choice. You are welcomed by Mrs. Janet McClelland, who shares her home with you, providing comfortable bedrooms and good food. Some of her rooms contain private shower. The rate for B&B runs from £8.50 ($13.60) to £9 ($14.40) per person nightly. It is Mrs. McClelland's custom to serve cookies and tea in the evening in her TV lounge. Guests meet each other and can enjoy pleasant conversation before retiring. She also does an excellent five-course dinner for only £5.50 ($8.80).

Cabana Guest House, Ballplay Road (tel. 0683/20400), is a well-maintained chalet bungalow in a quiet residential district within walking distance of the town center. Rooms are designer decorated with coordinated furnishings and bed linen. All have hot-beverage facilities, hot and cold water basins, and electric blankets, although the house is centrally heated. The owner, Mrs. Vera G. Waugh, charges £10 ($16) per person, and dinner is available for another £6 ($9.60). The pleasant dining room has separate tables. Mrs. Waugh adds a personal touch to make your stay enjoyable, including after-dinner mints with your coffee. There are plenty of ice cubes to be had, and ample private parking is offered. The house backs onto the meadow and hills.

Springbank, Beechgrove (tel. 0683/20070), is a tastefully decorated guesthouse run by Mrs. J. C. Walker. With full central heating, the comfortable rooms cost £8.50 ($13.60) per person, which includes breakfast and late evening tea with home-baked goods. The bedrooms all have hot-beverage facilities and electric blankets. The house has views to the hills.

WHERE TO EAT: The best all-around place for food in the heart of town is the **Moffat House Hotel,** High Street (tel. 0683/20039). Set on 2½ acres of its own grounds, this hotel was once an old manor, dating from 1751 when it was built by John Adam, one of the famous Adam brothers. Today it offers excellent food and wine at reasonable prices. Guests flock in here from noon to 2 p.m. to enjoy a fresh and well-prepared salad bar for £3.50 ($5.60). At night bar suppers, costing from £6 ($9.60), are served Monday to Thursday from 6 to 9 p.m. and Friday, Saturday, and Sunday from 5 to 9:30 p.m. Or else guests can dine in the more formal restaurant for £12 ($19.20) and up. Service is from 7 to 8:45 p.m., and the chefs prepare such elegant fare as haunch of venison, mallard duck in cherry sauce, tournedos rossini, and pheasant in an orange and pepper sauce.

3. Dumfries

A county town and royal burgh, this Scottish Lowland center enjoys associations with Robert Burns and James Barrie. In a sense it rivals Ayr as a mecca for admirers of Burns. He lived in Dumfries from 1791 until his death in 1796, and it was here that he wrote some of his best known songs, including "Auld Lang Syne" and "Ye Banks and Braes of Bonnie Doon." A statue of Burns stands on the High Street.

At the **Academy,** Barrie was a pupil, and he later wrote that he got the idea for *Peter Pan* from his games in the nearby garden.

At the Whitesands four bridges span the Nith. The earliest of these was built by Devorgilla Balliol, widow of John Balliol, father of a Scottish king. The bridge originally had nine arches, but now has six and is still in constant use as a footbridge.

The **Tourist Information Office,** Whitesands (tel. 0387/53862), is near the bridge. The wide esplanade was once the scene of horse and hiring fairs and now is a fine place to park your car and explore the town. Tour buses park here.

WHERE TO STAY: A good place to stay is **Newall House,** 22 Newall Terrace (tel. 0387/52676), run by Sheila and Charlie Cowie. Together they keep a friendly establishment and do so cheerfully and well. Their rooms are clean and comfortable and include tea- and coffee-making facilities, costing £9.50 ($15.20) for a single and £9 ($14.40) per person based on double occupancy. These tariffs include a well-cooked breakfast. Mrs. Cowie will also prepare an appetizing dinner, if given fair warning, for £5.50 ($8.80).

Fulwood Private Hotel, 30 Lovers Walk (tel. 0387/52262), is run by congenial, friendly hosts, Mr. and Mrs. J. B. Rowland, who believe in giving wayfarers pleasure, cleanliness, and comfort in their tiny home, containing only five bedrooms (the bath must be shared). They have a wealth of information about touring in the area. Their rate is £11.50 ($18.40) per person, including a full breakfast.

Aberdour Hotel, Newall Terrace (tel. 0387/54825), is competently operated by Mr. and Mrs. F. Bogie, who rent 12 comfortable rooms, charging £9 ($14.40) per person per night for B&B, £13 ($20.80) per person for half board. The fully licensed hotel has an attractive cocktail bar with black banquettes and a bright plaid rug, a comfortable lounge for guests, with low couches, convenient tables, and color TV. The whole place is clean and bright. It's open all year.

Huntingdon Hotel, 32 Lovers Walk (tel. 0387/54001), opposite the railway station, is more than handily placed. It's a good choice for budget-minded guests. Mrs. Dirom formerly had a two-star hotel in the Dumfries area, and is experienced at receiving foreign guests. She offers good service with a full English breakfast, charging £9.50 ($15.20) per person nightly. Electric blankets are provided when needed, and there is a license to serve drinks. The hotel is in an old, well-preserved building with a stone staircase and wrought-iron banisters.

Saughtree Guest House, 79 Annan Rd. (tel. 0387/52358), owned by Peter and Marjory Bruce, has good beds in the comfortable bedrooms, with radiators to take the chill off the rooms. For B&B, they charge £9 ($14.40) per person per night, or £13 ($20.80) per person for half board. At 10 p.m. Mrs. Bruce serves tea in the lounge and encourages her guests to get acquainted. Saughtree is open all year.

At the **Ben Guest House,** 29 Newall Terrace (tel. 0387/62950), the friendliness and wealth of information that the hosts, Mr. and Mrs. Kerr, impart are of primary importance. Their house dates from 1910 and stands in a quiet part of the Dumfries town center. The charge is £15 ($24) per person per night for B&B and a three-course dinner in the small ground-floor dining room overlooking the back garden. At the end of the garden is an ancient cemetery surrounding St. Mary's Presbyterian Church. Tea is served in the residents' lounge at 10 p.m., while guests are enjoying TV or chatting. In fact, you can have tea at any time. As Mr. Kerr says, "The kettle is always on the stove." The proprietor is a taxidermist, and many examples of his work decorate the house. You'll learn a lot of Dumfries and Scottish history here. Mr. Kerr and his sons sometimes take guests on what he calls "hysterical" tours, acquainting them with the fact and fiction connected with historic spots. In addition, he will also drive visitors on country tours for a modest charge. Nearly all the beauty spots and historic sites of Dumfries and Galloway are within a two-hour drive of the hotel. The Kerrs are also pleased to help visitors trace their Scottish ancestors, as the principal public reference library is close to their house.

WHERE TO EAT: It may seem ironic to recommend an Italian restaurant in the heart of Rabbie Burns territory, but **Bruno's,** 5 Balmoral Rd. (tel. 0387/55757), serves some of the best food in town. It is most unassuming, but that is part of its charm. Its minestrone is first rate, and its pastas such as lasagne are homemade. The chef doesn't serve the most imaginative Italian dishes ever sampled—in fact, the repertoire is most familiar, such as saltimbocca alla romana and pollo alla diavolo, but it's done with flair. The veal is particularly tender, and the tomato sauce well spiced and blended. Steak au poivre is also excellent. The waiters are friendly and skillful and offer good advice. Bruno's serves only dinner, from 6:30 to 10 p.m., nightly except Tuesday, and it will cost you from £10 ($16) per person, and it's worth it. Very popular with customers is a special menu for £9 ($14.40) which consists of three courses. There is also a £3.50 ($5.60) pasta menu.

Opus Salad Bar, 95 Queensberry St. (tel. 0387/55752). Don't let the obscure location of this attractive and informal licensed restaurant prevent you from visiting it (it's upstairs over a shop selling fabrics in the heart of Dumfries). It is open Monday through Saturday from 9 a.m. to 5 p.m., with an early closing on Thursday at 2:30 p.m. The cheerful owners, the Hallidays, serve hot meals at lunch, including, for example, lasagne, quiche, and pizza. A large selection of salads is also offered. Meals cost from £5 ($8). Tea is convenient to take here, as a selection of cakes, tarts, and scones is always available.

If you're looking for a place to have lunch or tea, go to **The Restaurant,** Barbour's Department Store, Buccleuch Street (tel. 0387/54343), where you can get tasty dishes in the dining room on the second floor. A cold-table lunch in summer goes for £4.50 ($7.20). In winter you can fortify yourself with a three-course table d'hôte, served hot, for £4 ($6.40). The dining room is licensed, and there's an elevator to take you up. It's open only during store hours, 9 a.m. to 5 p.m. weekdays.

"The Dining Room," in the Station Hotel, Lovers Walk (tel. 0387/54316), in what was built as *the* grand hotel of Dumfries and still lives up to high standards, today evokes the Edwardian age. It's a big-windowed dining room from which the Victorian gingerbread of the train station is on view. The decor of the restaurant is attractively high-ceilinged. The table d'hôte menu at £10.75 ($17.20) per person includes a satisfying array of such specialties as local salmon, haggis, cock-a-leekie soup, chicken "whisky sour," and local trout in a sauce of smoked salmon and mushrooms. A polite member of the uniformed staff might help turn the meal into a grand occasion. Reservations are suggested. Hours are 7 to 9:30 p.m. A drink in the hotel's popular bar, Somewhere Else, beforehand will give you an idea of the social life of this closely knit town.

Burns's Favorite "Howff"

The **Globe Inn,** 56 High St. (tel. 0387/52335), was a favorite haunt of Burns, who used an old Scottish expression, *howff,* to describe his local. He not only imbibed here, but had a child with the barmaid, Anna Park. The pub, in business since 1610, is reached down a narrow flagstone-paved passageway off the High Street. It has a separate restaurant. You can go here for meals, drinks, or to play a nightly game of dominoes. A little museum is devoted to Burns, and on window panes upstairs you can see verses he scratched with a diamond. In this convivial atmosphere, as overseen by Keith Brown, you can order cooked bar lunches, offered daily except Sunday, beginning at £2.75 ($4.40). The menu includes such items as kipper's pâté, haggis, mealed herring, and Globe steak pie. Meals are served from 11 a.m. to 5 p.m. weekdays, from 12:30 to 2:30 p.m. and 6:30 to 11 p.m. on Sunday. The pub closes at 11 p.m. daily.

SIGHTS: In **St. Michael's Churchyard,** a burial place for at least 900 years, stands the **Burns Mausoleum.** The poet was buried there along with his wife, Jean Armour, as well as five of their children. Burns died in 1796, but his remains weren't removed to the tomb until 1815. In the 18th-century Church of St. Michael you can still see the pew used by the Burns family.

St. Michael's is the original parish church of Dumfries and its founding is of great antiquity. The site was probably sacred before the advent of Christianity. It appears that a Christian church has stood there for more than 1,300 years. The earliest written records date from the reign of William the Lion (1165–1214). The church and the churchyard are interesting to visit because of all its connections with Scottish history, continuing through World War II.

Dumfries Museum (tel. 0387/53375), the largest museum in southwest Scotland, is in a converted 18th-century windmill on top of Corbelly Hill. The **Camera Obscura,** which can be found on the upper floor of the museum, provides panoramic views of the town and surrounding countryside. The museum is free and open from 10 a.m. to 1 p.m. and 2 to 5 p.m. Monday to Saturday, 2 to 5 p.m. on Sunday (closed Sunday and Monday October to the end of March). A charge of 50p (80¢) for adults and 25p (40¢) for children is made for the Camera Obscura, which is open from April to September during museum hours.

Scotland's national poet died in what is now called **Burns House** (tel. 0387/55297). The simple, unpretentious stone structure is on Burns Street and contains personal relics and mementos of the poet. Its hours are the same as the Dumfries Museum, and admission is 50p (80¢) for adults, 25p (40¢) for children.

A short walk from the town center across the 15th-century sandstone Devorgilla Bridge to Mill Road is the **Old Bridge House.** Built in 1660, the house now contains various period rooms. Admission is free, and it can be visited from 10 a.m. to 1 p.m. and 2 to 5 p.m. Monday to Saturday April to September, from 2 to 5 p.m. on Sunday.

A little farther along Mill Road on the banks of the River Nith is the **Robert Burns Centre** (tel. 0387/64808), in a converted 18th-century watermill. Facilities include an exhibition on the poet, a café, and an audio-visual theater showing films about Burns and the town of Dumfries. The center is open from 10 a.m. to 8 p.m. Monday to Saturday, from 2 to 5 p.m. Sunday April to the end of September, from 10 a.m. to 1 p.m. and 2 to 5 p.m. Tuesday to Saturday October to March. Admission is free, but a charge of 50p (80¢) for adults, and 25p (40¢) for children is made for access to the audio-visual theater.

A composite ticket costing £1 ($1.60) admits visitors to the audio-visual theater at the Robert Burns Centre, Burns, House, and the Camera Obscura, and may be purchased at any of these places.

The **Mid Steeple** in the High Street was built in 1707 as municipal buildings, courthouse, and prison. The old Scots "ell" measure of 37 inches is carved on the front of the building. A table of distances on the building includes the mileage to Huntingdon, England, which in the 18th century was the destination for Scottish cattle drovers driving their beasts south for the markets of London.

EXCURSIONS FROM DUMFRIES: Based in Dumfries, you can set out on treks in all directions to some of the most intriguing sightseeing goals in the Scottish lowlands.

South on the 710 leads to the village of New Abbey, dominated by the red sandstone ruins of **Sweetheart Abbey,** the Cistercian abbey founded in 1273 by Devorgilla, mother of John Balliol, the "vassal King." When her husband, John Balliol the Elder, died, she became one of the richest women in Europe. Most of Galloway, with estates and castles in England and land in Normandy, belonged to her. Devorgilla founded Balliol College, Oxford, in her husband's memory. She kept his embalmed heart in a silver and ivory casket by her side for 21 years until her death in 1289 at the age of 80, when she and the casket were buried beside Balliol in front of the abbey altar. So the abbey gained the name of "Dulce Cor," Latin for "sweet heart," which has since become a part of the English language.

Built into a wall of a cottage in the village is a rough piece of sculpture showing three women rowing a boat—an allusion to the bringing of sandstone across the Nith to build the abbey.

Also at New Abbey, the **Shambellie House Museum of Costume** on the A710 (tel. 038785/375) is in a Victorian country home that was designed by David Bryce. Now housing a branch extension of the **National Museum of Scotland,** it has a collection of fashionable dress made by Charles Stewart. Open May to the end of September, and charging no admission, it may be visited Thursday through Saturday and on Monday from 10 a.m. to 5:30 p.m. (on Sunday from noon to 5:30 p.m.).

Directly south from New Abbey on the A710 to Southerness are the **Arbigland Gardens and Cottage** at Kirkbean (tel. 038788/213), 15 miles southwest of Dumfries. This is where John Paul Jones, one of the founders of the American navy, was born. You can visit the woodland with its water gardens arranged around a secluded bay, walking in the pathways where the great admiral once walked as a boy. The gardens are open, May to September, on Tuesday, Thursday, and Sunday from 2 to 6 p.m., charging adults £1 ($1.60); children, 50p (80¢). There's a tea room.

Or, alternatively, you can head south from Dumfries on the B725 to **Caerlaverock Castle,** near the mouth of the River Nith, two miles south from

Glencaple. Once the seat of the Maxwell family, this impressive ruined fortress dates back to the 1270s. In 1300 Edward I laid siege to it. In 1640 it yielded to Covenanters after a 13-week siege. The castle is triangular with round towers. The interior was reconstructed in the 17th century as a Renaissance mansion, with fine carving. The castle is open April to September from 9:30 a.m. to 7 p.m. (on Sunday from 2 to 7 p.m.); October to March, from 9:30 a.m. to 4 p.m. (on Sunday from 2 to 4 p.m.). Admission is 50p (80¢) for adults, 25p (40¢) for children.

Near the castle is the **Caerlaverock National Nature Reserve** between the River Nith and Lochar Water. It is a noted winter haunt of wildfowl, including barnacle geese.

After leaving the castle, continue east along the A725 to the village of **Ruthwell**, about ten miles southeast of Dumfries. There, at the early 19th-century Ruthwell Church, you'll see one of the most outstanding crosses of the Dark Ages. Standing 18 feet high, the cross is believed to date from the 8th century. Engraved with carvings, it bears the earliest-known specimen of written English (a Christian poem in Runic characters).

North from Dumfries via the A76 is **Ellisland Farm** (tel. 038774/426), where Robert Burns made his last attempt at farming, renting the spread from 1788 to 1791. The present occupants of the house will show you through the Burns Room. It was at this farm that Burns wrote *Tam o' Shanter*. Admission is free, but visitors are asked to call for an appointment.

Continuing north, still on the A76, you reach **Thornhill**, a country resort—familiar to Burns—overlooking the River Nith. From here it's possible to branch out for excursions in many directions.

The main target is **Drumlanrig Castle** (tel. 0848/30248), the seat of the Duke of Buccleuch and Queensberry, built between 1679 and 1689. It lies three miles north of Thornhill, off the A76. This exquisite pink castle contains some celebrated paintings, including a famous Rembrandt, a Leonardo da Vinci, and a Holbein. In addition, it is further enriched by Louis XIV antiques, silver, porcelain, and relics related to Bonnie Prince Charlie. The castle stands in a parkland ringed by wild hills, and there's even an "Adventure Woodland Playground." The gardens are gradually being restored to their 1720 magnificence. There is a working crafts center in the old stable yard, with independent craft workers in a variety of skills. Teas are served in the old kitchen hung with gleaming copper. Opening dates vary slightly from year to year. It's normally open from Easter to late August, the dates depending on the movements of the duke and his family. Usually on weekdays in May and June it's open from 1:30 to 5 p.m. and in July and August from 11 a.m. to 5 p.m. (on Sunday from 2 to 6 p.m. throughout). Last entry is 45 minutes before closing. Admission is £2.20 ($3.52) for adults, £1.20 ($1.92) for children.

Of almost equal interest, **Maxwelton House** lies three miles south of Moniaive and 13 miles north of Dumfries on the B729. It was the stronghold of the Earls of Glencairn in the 14th and 15th centuries. But it is more remembered today as the birthplace (1682) of Annie Laurie of the famous Scottish ballad. From Maxwelton you can see that the braes are just as bonnie as ever. The braes, of course, refer to the neighboring hills. The house and museum are open from 2 to 5 p.m. Monday to Thursday in July and August. The garden and chapel are open from April to September at those same hours. The house can be visited at other times by appointment only. Admission for house, garden, and museum is £1.50 ($2.40) for adults, 50p (80¢) for children; to the garden only, 50p (80¢) for adults and 25p (40¢) for children. Phone 08482/385 for further information.

Back on the A76, you can branch northwest on the B797, heading in the direction of Mennock Pass. There, at **Wanlockhead,** you'll be in the highest village in Scotland. Once this village was a gold-mining center and known as "God's Treasure House." Gold was mined here for the Scottish crown jewels.

Other points of sightseeing interest include the following:

Drumcoltran Tower, off the A711, eight miles southwest of Dumfries and five miles northeast of Dalbeattie, is a fine example of a Scottish tower house still remaining. Set in the midst of farmland, it was built in an austere style around the mid-1500s. The tower can be visited from 9:30 a.m. to 6:30 p.m. weekdays and 2 to 6:30 p.m. on Sunday mid-March to mid-October, closing at 4 p.m. off-season. Admission is free.

Dating from the 15th century, **Lincluden College,** a Provost House and Collegiate Church, shelters the tomb of Princess Margaret, daughter of Robert III. The house has heraldic adornment that is notable, and on the grounds is a motte. The location is off the A76, about a mile north of Dumfries. It is open from 9:30 a.m. to 7 p.m. Monday to Saturday and 2 to 7 p.m. on Sunday in summer; from 9:30 a.m. to 4 p.m. weekdays and 2 to 4 p.m. on Sunday in winter, except for Thursday afternoon, Friday, and Christmas and New Year holidays. Admission is 50p (80¢) for adults, 25p (40¢) for children.

Old Bridge House, Mill Road, at Devorgilla's Bridge in Dumfries, dates from 1662, and it has been restored and furnished in a style typical of its era. It may be visited, admission free, April to September, Monday to Saturday from 10 a.m. to 1 p.m. (on Sunday from 2 to 5 p.m.). Devorgilla's Bridge itself was constructed in the 13th century.

Art lovers will want to seek out **Glenkiln,** lying on an unclassified road about ten miles west and northwest of Dumfries (a sign directs you). It is open at all times, charging no admission. In beautiful but lonely Lowlands country, at the Glenkiln Reservoir, you can see *King and Queen* sculptures by the late Henry Moore, along with works by such other great artists as Epstein and Rodin.

4. Castle Douglas

A cattle and sheep market town, Castle Douglas makes a good touring center for Galloway. It lies about 16 miles southwest of Dumfries at the northern tip of Carlingwark Loch. On one of the islets in the loch is an ancient lake dwelling known as a "crannog."

FOOD AND LODGING: A comfortable place to stay, the **Merrick Hotel,** King Street (tel. 0556/2173), is popular with Britain's community of birdwatchers who check in late autumn for views of migratory geese. The rest of the year, owners Arthur and Jean Webb welcome other visitors into their gray corner building. The seven simple but comfortable rooms contain electric blankets and hot and cold water basins. B&B costs £10 ($16) to £11 ($17.60) per person. Accommodation with half board goes for £14 ($22.40) to £15 ($24) per person. The hotel was built as a private home in 1840. The second-floor dining room offers good food and a prosperous sense of well-being to diners who drop in for meals in summer. In winter, meals are served only to residents.

Imperial Hotel, King Street (tel. 0556/2086). Messrs. David Fulton, father and son, are the amiable owners of this 19th-century coaching inn on the main street of town. Visitors get an idea of what the hotel looked like a century ago from an old photograph hanging behind the reception desk. There's a cocktail bar on the ground floor and an attractive Victorian dining room with patterned carpeting and a high ceiling. The 14 rooms are pleasantly furnished, impeccably clean, all with color TV and hot-beverage facilities, and sometimes they look out onto an inner courtyard where guests can park free. Rooms with bath cost from £20 ($32) in a single and from £35 ($56) in a double, with breakfast included. Bathless rooms rent for £16 ($25.60) in a single and from £30 ($48) in a double. Bar lunches are served daily from noon to 2 p.m. and high teas between 5:30 and 7 p.m.

On the Outskirts

Culgruff House Hotel, at Crossmichael, near Castle Douglas (tel. 055667/230), is one of the finest places to stay in the area. It is an elegant Victorian mansion covered in part with vines. Now a two-star hotel, it was the former mansion of the Duchess of Grafton. The setting, on 20 acres of private grounds, overlooks Loch Ken. Including breakfast and VAT and depending on the plumbing, rates are £16 ($25.60) to £30 ($48) nightly in a double, dropping to £8.50 ($13.60) to £15 ($24) in a single. Many of the rooms are quite spacious, and they're attractively and comfortably furnished. Since the cookery is good, you may want to take the half-board rate of £17.20 ($27.52) per person daily. Guests are received year round. This hotel is such outstanding value it should be better known.

SIGHTS: The favorite excursion is to **Threave Castle,** 1½ miles west on an islet in the River Dee west of town, the ruined 14th-century stronghold of the Black Douglases. The four-story tower was built between 1639 and 1690 by Archibald the Grim, Lord of Galloway. In 1455 Threave Castle was the last Douglas stronghold to surrender to James II, who employed "Mons Meg" (the famous cannon now in Edinburgh Castle) in its subjection. Over the doorway projects the "gallows knob" from which the Douglases hanged their enemies. The castle was captured by the Covenanters in 1640 and dismantled. Owned by the National Trust, the site must be reached by a *lengthy* walk through farmlands and then by small boat across the Dee. A ferry charge of 50p (80¢) for adults and 25p (40¢) for children is the only alternative to that very long walk. Last sailing to the castle is at 6:30 p.m. There is no charge for visiting Threave Castle, which is open from 10 a.m. to 7 p.m. weekdays, 2 to 7 p.m. Sunday April to the end of September and 10 a.m. to 4 p.m. weekdays October to March. For information, phone 055666/371.

Threave Garden (tel. 0556/2575) lies a mile southeast of the castle. The gardens are built around Threave House, a Scottish baronial mansion half a mile west of Castle Douglas, off the A75. It is under the protection of the National Trust for Scotland which uses it as a school for gardening and a wildfowl refuge. In April more than 300 varieties of daffodils burst into bloom. There is also a walled garden. The gardens are open daily from 9 a.m. to dusk, charging adults an admission of £1.80 ($2.88); children pay 90p ($1.44).

In and around Castle Douglas are several other attractions of interest, including **Orchardton Tower,** off the A711 5½ miles southeast of Castle Douglas. Unique in the country, this is an example of a round tower house. It was constructed in the mid-1400s by John Cairns, and if you ask the custodian who lives at the cottage nearby, you can see inside.

The **North Glen Gallery,** Palnackie, five miles southeast of Castle Douglas, is an interesting studio where you can see how glass is blown, sculpture assembled, and other techniques of welding. It is open daily from 10 a.m. to 6 p.m., charging an admission of 50p (80¢) for adults and 15p (24¢) for children. For information, phone 05560/200.

The **Mote of Urr,** off the B794 five miles northeast of Castle Douglas, is a circular mound enclosed by a deep trench. Students of history will know that this is an example of the motte-and-bailey type defense so popular in Norman days.

5. Kirkcudbright

Stewartry's most ancient burgh, Kirkcudbright (pronounced "Kir-coo-bree") lies at the head of Kirkcudbright Bay on the Dee Estuary. This intriguing old town contains color-washed houses inhabited, in part, by artists. In fact, Kirkcudbright has been called the "St. Ives (Cornwall) of Scotland." There is a lively group of weavers, potters, and painters who work in the 18th-century streets and lanes.

WHERE TO STAY: In accommodations, I'd suggest the **Selkirk Arms,** Old High Street (tel. 0557/30402), where Robert Burns stayed when he composed the celebrated "Selkirk Grace." (The grace was actually given on St. Mary's isle, the seat of the Douglases, Earls of Selkirk, and, in part, it went as follows: "But we ha'e meat, and we can eat, And sae the Lord be thankit.") The hotel is fairly small, 26 bedrooms, ten of which contain private baths or showers. You have a choice of rooms in the main building or in the annex. B&B costs from £18.50 ($29.60) to £21.50 ($34.40) per person, and half board is £25.50 ($40.80) to £31 ($49.60) per person. The hotel, open all year, has a TV lounge and a cocktail bar, and there is ample sheltered parking. Some rooms are in an annex across the street. The dining room places attention on the "Taste of Scotland" program, with regional dishes, but for a change of fare, will also provide Indonesian and Chinese specialties.

The font of Dundrennan Abbey (with a date on it of 1492) stands in the garden of the hotel. The Selkirk Arms also has a photostat of John Paul Jones's original commission as captain in the American navy. The neighborhood evokes memories of Jones, and there are little art galleries displaying the works of local painters.

Gordon House, 116 High St. (tel. 0557/30670), is a small hotel in a Georgian building listed as of historical and architectural interest. The 13 bedrooms are light and fresh, and have hot and cold water basins. Your hosts are David and Christine Wylde, who have musical evenings every Wednesday and Saturday. Rooms cost £19.50 ($31.20) for half board, £12.95 ($20.72) for B&B per person, including VAT and service. There is a comfortable lounge for hotel guests, complete with color TV, and a pleasant dining room. Bar lunches are available in the pub from 12:30 to 2 p.m., if you're just dropping by. Both dinner and supper are served from 6:30 to 10 p.m.

If you'd like a smaller, quiet place to stay, looking out on the River Dee and the bridge, **Beaconsfield,** Bridge Street (tel. 0557/30488), is ideal. Mrs. Fisher rents rooms for £18 ($28.80) per night based on double occupancy, for B&B. She serves dinner if you request it, except in July and August. Guests can enjoy color TV in the lounge. Mrs. Fisher has a wealth of antique objets d'art. Beaconsfield is open all year.

The **Park House** (tel. 0557/3077) lies just out of town on the A711. It is a century-old mansion with large stately rooms off a huge hallway. Dr. and Mrs. Boyd, the proprietors, welcome guests to rooms that rent for £9 ($14.40) per person for B&B. Besides an excellent breakfast, Mrs. Boyd offers evening tea in an upstairs room that has a view of Dr. Boyd's extensive garden.

WHERE TO EAT: Opposite the castle stands a Scots / French family-run eating place, the **Auld Alliance Restaurant,** 5 Castle St. (tel. 0557/30569). Savor the quality Scottish cuisine prepared and presented by the chef-proprietor using traditional and creative recipes. A local specialty is Kirkcudbright Bay scallops fried in garlic butter, garnished with smoked Ayrshire bacon, and finished in

Galloway cream and fresh herbs from the garden. Meals cost from £8 ($12.80). The restaurant is open seven days a week from Easter until Halloween for morning coffee, lunch from 11:30 a.m. to 2 p.m., Galloway teas until 5 p.m., and dinner from 6:30 to 8:30 p.m.

Ingle, St. Mary Street (tel. 0557/30606), brings continental flair to Kirkcudbright. The restaurant, housed in a stone building near the center of town, is a popular rendezvous point locally. Many come here just for the pizza, at least six different varieties, but such a limited selection does not do justice to the chef's repertoire. You can order steaks cooked on a traditional wood fire, or else barbecued (he also does barbecued chicken). His pasta dishes are of fine quality, including lasagne, or you might prefer the risotto. There is also a selection of fried fish. Dinner is served daily from 6 to 9:30 p.m. (closed Monday). A set menu is offered for £7.50 ($12), but you are more likely to spend £12 ($19.20) and up for an à la carte dinner.

SIGHTS: In the old town graveyard are memorials to Covenanters and to Billy Marshall, the tinker king who died in 1792 at the age of 120, reportedly having fathered four children after the age of 100.

Maclellan's Castle, built in 1582 for the town's provost, Sir Thomas Maclellan, easily dominates the center of town. This castellated mansion has been a ruin since 1752. Lying off the High Street, it is open April to September, Monday to Saturday from 9:30 a.m. to 7 p.m. (on Sunday from 2 to 7 p.m.). Off-season it is open from 9:30 a.m. to 4 p.m. (on Sunday from 2 to 4 p.m.). Admission is 50p (80¢) for adults and 25p (40¢) for children.

The **Tolbooth,** a large building, dates back to the 16th and 17th centuries, and in front of it is a **Mercat Cross** of 1610. The Tolbooth is a memorial to John Paul Jones (1747–1792), the gardener's son from Kirkbean who became a slave trader, a privateer, and in due course one of the founders of the American navy. For a time, before his emigration, he was imprisoned for murder in the Tolbooth.

Art exhibitions are regularly sponsored at **Broughton House** (tel. 0557/30437), a 17th-century mansion that once belonged to E. A. Hornel, the artist. The house contains a large reference library with a valuable Burns collection, along with pictures by Hornel and other artists, plus antiques and other works of art. You can stroll through its beautiful garden. Broughton House is open from 11 a.m. to 1 p.m. and 2 to 5 p.m. Tuesday to Saturday and 2 to 5 p.m. on Sunday mid-March to mid-October. In winter, it is open by prior arrangement only. Admission is 50p (80¢) for adults, 30p (48¢) for children.

In addition, the **Stewartry Museum in Kirkcudbright,** St. Mary Street (tel. 0557/30797), contains a fascinating collection of antiquities, depicting the history and culture of Galloway. It is open daily, except Sunday from 11 a.m. to 1 p.m. and 2 to 4 p.m. Easter to October, from 11 a.m. to 5 p.m. in July and August. Admission is 50p (80¢) for adults and 25p (40¢) for children.

IN THE ENVIRONS: North of town is the ruined **Tongland Abbey,** one of whose abbots, John Damian, once tried to fly from the battlements of Stirling Castle wearing wings of bird feathers, in the presence of James IV. He landed in a manure pile.

Dundrennan Abbey, seven miles southeast of Kirkcudbright, the ruins of a rich Cistercian house founded in 1142, includes much late Norman and Transitional work. Dundrennan is a daughter abbey of Rievaulx Abbey in Yorkshire and the mother abbey of Glenluce and Sweetheart Abbeys. The small village is partly built of stones "quarried" from the abbey. Mary Queen of Scots, after escaping from Loch Leven and being defeated at the Battle of Langside, spent her last night in Scotland at the abbey in May 1568. She went to England to seek help from Elizabeth who imprisoned her instead. The transept and choir, a unique example of the Early Pointed style, remain. The abbey is open April to September, Monday to Saturday from 9:30 a.m. to 7 p.m. (on Sunday from 2 to 7 p.m.). October to March it is open from 9:30 a.m. to 4 p.m. Monday to Saturday (on Sunday from 2 to 4 p.m.). Admission is 50p (80¢) for adults, 25p (40¢) for children.

6. Gatehouse-of-Fleet

This sleepy former cotton town, on the Water of Fleet, was the Kippletringan in Sir Walter Scott's *Guy Mannering*, and Burns composed "Scots Wha Hae wi' Wallace Bled" on the moors nearby and wrote it down in the Murray Arms Hotel there.

The town's name probably dates from 1642 when the English government opened the first military road through Galloway to assist the passage of troops to Ireland. In 1661 Richard Murray of Cally was authorized by Parliament to widen the bridge and to erect beside it an inn which was to serve as a tollhouse, with the innkeeper responsible for the maintenance of a 12-mile stretch of road. This is believed to have been the original house on the "gait," or road, which later became known as the "gait house of Fleet," and by 1790 it was being written in its present form and spelling. This ancient "gait house" is now part of the Murray Arms Hotel, used as a coffeeroom, and is therefore probably the oldest building still in existence in the town.

FOOD AND LODGING: In a listed historic building toward the bottom of the High Street, the **Angel Hotel** (tel. 05574/204), offers comfortable accommodation, good food, and friendly personal service. All bedrooms have hot and cold water basins, hot-beverage facilities, and electric blankets, and most contain TV. For a room with a full breakfast, the price is £12.50 ($20) per person. The hotel has a residents' lounge with reading material, a lounge bar with an open log fire, and a traditional dining room. Reasonably priced bar meals and snacks as well as à la carte dinners are offered by the resident proprietors, Matt and Mary Welsh. There is an open parking lot for use by guests.

The **Bank of Fleet Hotel,** 47 High St. (tel. 05574/302), is housed, as its name implies, in an old bank building. The charge is £12.50 ($20) per person for B&B. The bedrooms are cheerfully decorated with bright colors. A small residents' lounge has color TV. Comfortable brown banquette seats make the lounge bar inviting, and bar lunches are a specialty at noon. In a stone building, the hotel has a chimney at either end, with six chimney pots each. It's open all year.

SIGHTS IN THE ENVIRONS: West of Gatehouse, on the road to Creetown, is the well-preserved 15th-century tower of the McCullochs, with its sinister "murder hole" over the entrance passage. Through this trapdoor, boiling pitch was poured onto attackers.

Cardoness Castle was originally the seat of the McCulloch family, one of whom, Sir Godfrey McCulloch, was the last person in Scotland to be executed, at Edinburgh in 1697, by the "Maiden," the Scots version of the guillotine. The location is off the A75, a mile southwest of Gatehouse-of-Fleet. It is open from 9:30 a.m. to 7 p.m. Monday to Saturday, 2 to 7 p.m. on Sunday April to the end of September; the remainder of the year, closing time is 4 p.m. Admission is 50p (80¢) for adults, 25p (40¢) for children.

7. Creetown

This granite village lies in the heart of Sir Walter Scott's *Guy Mannering* country. It stands on a narrow coastal strip between the Galloway Hills and Wigtown Bay. It attracts sports-minded visitors, who are drawn to the availability of loch and river fishing, swimming, tennis, birdwatching, walking, and pony riding and trekking. There are 12 golf courses in Galloway, including one about a 15-minute drive from Creetown. Those interested in antiquities will find more mottes, forts, castles, and rock carvings per square mile in Galloway than anywhere else in Scotland.

FOOD AND LODGING: On a site occupied by a coaching inn since 1750 stands the **Ellangowan Hotel** (tel. 067182/201). The elaborate Victorian facade you'll see today was built in 1898, at which time the establishment was said to have been the second hotel in Scotland to have hot and cold running water in each of the bedrooms. Its walls are built from locally mined granite, whose solidity contrasts attractively with the elaborate gingerbread of the front porch. Mrs. Murray is the busy owner, and she's used to her international medley of guests, who have included the stars of *The Wicker Man* which was filmed here in the 1970s. The allure of the place is ruggedly genteel and slightly faded, with an assortment of locals enjoying the in-house pub. You'll be housed comfortably for the night, paying a B&B charge of £15 ($24) per person. A set dinner costs from £9 ($14.40). Children under the age of 7 pay half the adult rate.

A ROCK MUSEUM: This is nothing to do with music. The largest private collection of rocks, minerals, and gems on display to the public in either England or Scotland is at the **Creetown Gem Rock Museum and Gallery** (tel. 067182/357), approached on the A75 to Creetown. Many huge specimens from around the world can be seen. You can visit the workshop, in which cutting, shaping, and polishing take place. There is also a fluorescent display, an art gallery, a gift shop, and a good tea room. In summer, hours are from 9:30 a.m. to 6 p.m. daily; off-season from 9:30 a.m. to sunset. Admission is 70p ($1.12) for adults, 30p (48¢) for children. The museum draws some 50,000 visitors annually, and the collection keeps growing.

8. Newton Stewart

Sometimes called "the gateway to Galloway" and the "heart of Galloway," this small town on the River Cree was made a burgh or barony in 1677 after a son of the second Earl of Galloway built some houses beside the ford across the river and gave the hamlet its present name. When the estate was later purchased by William Douglas, he changed the name to Newton Douglas, but it didn't stick. The town has a livestock market and woolen mills. Cree Bridge, built of granite in 1813 to replace one swept away by a flood, links the town with **Minnigaff** where there is an old church with interesting carved stones and some ancient memorials.

FOOD AND LODGING: Opposite the Auction Mart, the **Crown Hotel,** on Queen Street (tel. 0671/2727), is a handsome old gray stone building with dormers and massive chimneys topped by many chimney pots. The manager rents clean, comfortable rooms. The cost in a single ranges from £14.50 ($23.20) to £20.50 ($32.80) nightly, with doubles or twins going for £14.50 ($23.20) to £16.50 ($26.40) per person, including VAT and a full breakfast. The more expensive accommodations include a private bath and toilet. Some units contain color TV sets. Probably one of the most attractive residents' lounges in Scotland is on the second floor—large and well furnished, with a parquet floor and an expanse of windows overlooking the garden. Octagonal rugs in rose and brown and a grand piano add to the beauty of the room. There's an adjoining TV lounge with a cocktail bar at the end. On the first floor are the public bar and the Log Cabin cocktail bar, both open to nonresidents. A spacious dining room has plaid carpeting and a piano. There a lunch goes for £4.80 ($7.68), and a dinner begins at £9 ($14.40).

Creebridge House Hotel (tel. 0671/2121). This stone manor house built in 1760 sits gracefully in a hollow, surrounded by formal gardens and fronted with a croquet lawn. It was once owned by the Earls of Galloway. Today it is a well-run hotel, restaurant, and pub. A fire is likely to be blazing for your arrival. Depending on space available, your meal might be served either in the dining room or in the pub. Known for its "Taste of Scotland" food, the establishment serves Loch Fyne pickled herring, Galloway sirloin prepared in a variety of ways (including with a brandied cream sauce), a traditional roast of beef on Sunday, fresh haddock, local ham, and a pork oatie with apples and cranberries. Most of the hotel's 18 well-furnished bedrooms contain private baths. B&B costs £23.50 ($37.60) per person, and half board is offered for £35 ($56) per person.

The **Galloway Arms Hotel,** on Victoria Street in the heart of town (tel. 0671/2282), displays the armorial bearings of the Earls of Galloway, original owners of the buildings that make up the hotel. The modern hotel has spacious and comfortable public rooms with large log fires. Bedrooms are centrally heated and most have private bathrooms. Rates in a single range from £20 ($32) to £24 ($38.40), rising to anywhere from £39 ($62.40) to £42 ($67.20) in a double. Tariffs depend on the location and the private facilities, and include a full breakfast as well as VAT and service. In the dining room you can select from a varied à la carte menu which lives up to the best traditions of Scottish cooking and makes use of the local produce, a complete dinner averaging £11 ($17.60). The main building dates from the 13th century. The Galloway Arms will enfold you all year.

EXPLORING THE ENVIRONS: Newton Stewart is associated with Scott, Stevenson, and Burns. Today it is chiefly a center for touring, especially north for nine miles to the beauty spot of **Loch Troolin** in the Glen Trool Forest Park, 200 square miles of magnificently preserved splendor. On the way to Loch Trool, you go through the village of Glentrool where you'll find the first car park for those wanting to take the Stroan Bridge walk, a distance of 3½ miles. The hearty Scots, of course, walk the entire loch, all 4½ miles of it.

You can use Newton Stewart as a base for exploring **Galloway Forest Park** to the north of the town. Covering some 150,000 acres, it lies off the A714 about ten miles northwest of Newton Stewart. It is filled with trails, forests, hills, and lochs, including Doon.

The **Galloway Deer Museum,** converted from a homestead, is on the A712 by Clattergshaws Loch, about six miles west of New Galloway. It can be visited April to September daily from 10 a.m. to 5 p.m., charging no admission. It has a live trout exhibit in addition to its many exhibitions of deer and other Galloway wildlife. A short walk away on Moss Raploch will take you to Bruce's Stone, on the east side of Clatteringshaws Loch. This memorial stone commemorates a victory by Bruce over the English forces.

In this same vicinity you can take **Raider's Road** (from the A712 near Clatteringshaws Dam). This is a ten-mile-long forest drive that takes in some of the most spectacular scenery in the national park.

9. Wigtown

This former county town of the district is still a center for fishing and wild-fowling even if its harbor is silted up. Two market crosses, an 18th-century one topped by a sundial and another that was erected in 1816, stand in the town's central square. In 1685 two women, Margaret Maclauchlan and Margaret Wilson, Covenanters who were accused of attending meetings of their sect, were tied to stakes at the mouth of the River Bladnoch and drowned by the rising tide after refusing to give up their beliefs. An obelisk marks the traditional site of their martyrdom. A monument to all Covenanters stands on Windy Hill back of the town.

FOOD AND LODGING: The best accommodation in the area, the **Craigmount Guest House** (tel. 09884/2291) receives visitors all year. The owner rents out five comfortably furnished and pleasantly decorated rooms, charging from £10 ($16) for B&B. Guests share bathroom facilities. If arrangements are made in advance, an evening meal can be provided. The driveway leading to this box-shaped painted old stone house rises steeply from the road at the edge of town. The painted panels of the comfortably conservative interior lend a cozy feeling to the establishment.

SIGHTS: Three miles northwest of Wigtown, near Torhouskie Farm, are the **Bronze Age Stones of Torhouse,** 19 standing stones in a circle with three in the center.

The remains of **Baldoon Castle** are a mile from Wigtown. This was the setting for Sir Walter Scott's *The Bride of Lammermoor.* It was the home of David Dunbar and his wife, supposed to be the principal characters of the *Bride.* The castle was captured by Wallace in 1297.

The area in and around Wigtown is rich in many sightseeing attractions. **Chapel Finian** is a small oratory which dates way back to the 10th century. It is in an enclosure some 45 feet wide. Off the A747, 12½ miles west and southwest of Wigtown, it is open during the day, charging no admission.

A Norman house of worship, **Cruggleton Church,** is found off the B7063, nine miles south and southeast of Wigtown. Mr. Fisher, a nearby farmer, will give you the keys if you wish to go inside. You can see the chancel arch windows and doors from the 12th century. Near the shore is an arch, the only remains of Cruggleton Castle.

Galloway House Gardens, at Garlieston (tel. 09886/225), some eight miles south of Wigtown, are open daily throughout the year, charging 70p ($1.12) for admission. The sixth Earl of Galloway had the mansion house constructed in 1740, and it is still in private ownership and not open to the public. The gardens contain some beech trees that are more than 250 years old. In spring, the place is ablaze with rhododendrons, daffodils, and azaleas, and there is a large walled garden with greenhouses and exotic plants. The garden leads down to a private beach that is suitable for picnics.

10. Whithorn

Ten miles south of Wigtown you come upon Whithorn, a modern town with a museum containing ancient crosses and tombstones, including the fifth-century **Latinus Stone,** the earliest Christian memorial in Scotland.

FOOD AND LODGING: An excellent place to stay just outside Whithorn is the **Castlewigg Hotel** (tel. 09885/213), a small licensed country hotel under the personal supervision of its owners, Stephen Summerson-Wright and Rhonda Howe. Castlewigg is two miles north of Whithorn on the A746, with views to the north toward Newton Stewart and to the east to Fleet Bay. More than 200 years old, the hotel building was the dower house of Castle Wigg, which lies in ruins, not open to the public, a mile or so off the road. The hotel charges £15 ($24) per person for B&B. Guests may enjoy the residents' lounge with color TV, the spacious dining room, and the lounge bar. Dinners cost around £10 ($16). From the à la carte menu you can order such fare as prawn cocktail, venison in red wine and port, and rainbow trout. The hotel specializes in hunting and fishing holidays. The Castlewigg sits in seven acres of grounds, about 150 yards off the main road, so there's ample parking. It's open all year.

ON ST. NINIAN'S TRAIL: A monastery was founded at Whithorn in A.D. 397 by St. Ninian, the son of a local chieftain. He built what was probably the first Christian church in Scotland, "Candida Casa" or "White House." In the 12th century Fergus, Lord of Galloway, built a priory. The church and monastery were destroyed in the 16th century. Excavations in the ruins have revealed fragments of wall covered in pale plaster believed to be from Ninian's Candida Casa. The ruins are entered through the Pend, a 17th-century arch on which are carved the Royal Arms of Scotland.

A moorland walk to the west coast 2½ miles away leads to **St. Ninian's Cave** in Port Castle Bay, used by the missionary as a retreat.

The **Isle of Whithorn,** three miles southeast of the town, is where St. Ninian landed about A.D. 395 on his return from studying in Rome, to bring Christianity to Scotland. The ruins of a plain 13th-century chapel are here but no signs of any earlier church. On the point of the promontory are the remains of an Iron Age fort and a late-17th-century tower.

11. Port William

On Luce Bay, this little holiday resort is a center for tennis, golf, and swimming.

By taking the 714 west, you'll reach **Drumtrodden Stones,** a cluster of ring and cup markings from the Bronze Age on a rock face. Just 400 yards to the south is an alignment of three adjacent surviving stones. It's hardly Stonehenge, but interesting nevertheless.

While still on an antiquity search, you can drive directly south of Port William a short distance to **Barsalloch Fort,** the remains of a fort dating from the Iron Age.

WHERE TO STAY: In the pleasant village, you can stay at the **Monreith Arms Hotel** (tel. 09887/206), a big stone building at the roundabout where you will find immaculate bedrooms, comfortable public rooms, and a pleasant dining room serving good food. Mr. and Mrs. T. Fox, in their fully licensed hostelry, offer B&B for £15 ($24) per person, and dinner from the à la carte menu for £8 ($12.80) and up. All bedrooms have private baths, TV, phones, and hot-beverage facilities. The hotel can arrange sea fishing trips in Luce Bay which is renowned for its tope fishing.

12. Glenluce

Lying on the Water of Luce near its estuary in Luce Bay, Glenluce is another attractive village, settled by early-day fishermen. It had close links with nearby Glenluce Abbey.

Castle of Park, a 16th-century mansion, overlooks the village from the brow of a hill across the river.

FOOD AND LODGING: A convenient and pleasant place to stay in Glenluce is the **Judge's Keep,** in the center of town (tel. 05813/203), where the Howle family receive guests in the fully licensed hotel for £11.50 ($18.40) per person for B&B. Dinner, prepared under Mr. Howle's close supervision in the immaculate kitchen on the ground floor, costs from £7 ($11.20), and it's well worth it. Bar meals are also available throughout the day. There is a TV lounge for guests, as well as public and lounge bars and ample car parking. The hotel offers salmon and trout fishing and can arrange for you to play golf at the local club.

GLENLUCE ABBEY: Some two miles northwest of the village of Glenluce, Glenluce Abbey, now in ruins, was a Cistercian house founded about 1190. It has a preserved 15th-century vaulted chapter house of architectural interest, as well as earthenware drainpipes remaining from the abbey's heyday. The border "wizard," Michael Scott, is said to have lured the plague to the abbey in the 13th century and shut it in a vault. The grave of Lochinvar, of ballad fame, is supposed to be on the abbey church's north side. Visitors can see the abbey from 9:30 a.m. to 6:30 p.m. weekdays and 2 to 6:30 p.m. on Sunday mid-March to mid-October, closing at 4 p.m. off-season. Admission is 50p (80¢) for adults, 25p (40¢) for children.

13. Portpatrick

Until 1849 steamers sailed the 21 miles from Donaghdee in Northern Ireland to Portpatrick, which became a "Gretna Green" for the Irish. Couples would land on Saturday, have the banns called on Sunday, and marry on Monday. When the harbor became silted up, Portpatrick was replaced by Stranraer as a port.

Commanding a clifftop to the south are the ruins of **Dunskey Castle,** a grim keep built in 1510 by John Adair.

WHERE TO STAY: Built of gray stone in 1872, the **Fernhill Hotel,** Heugh Road (tel. 077681/220), overlooks the Irish Sea. The building has been modernized, and dozens of trees have joined the massive yews of the garden. After heading up the long gravel driveway, guests often treat themselves first to a drink in the high-ceilinged modern pub, which was converted from a Victorian parlor. Afterward they can enjoy dinner in the ground-floor dining room, where they get a "Taste of Scotland," including locally caught and cured salmon, Galloway beef, and fish and lobster from local waters. The restaurant is open only between March and October. B&B costs from £21 ($33.60) per person.

The **South Cliff House Hotel** (tel. 077681/411) lies on an unnamed street just off South Crescent. It is far enough up on a cliff to afford a panoramic view of the Mull of Galloway, which can be seen from the large living room as well as from some of the bedrooms. The charge is £18 ($28.80) to £20 ($32) for half board. Dinners are well-prepared, with a good selection of dishes. Two of the six bedrooms have private baths or showers.

WHERE TO EAT: A sprawling, comfortable, and white-walled building, the **Old Mill House** (tel. 077681/358), is set into a garden beside a running stream at the edge of town. The restaurant offers good food and a big-windowed view of a forested ravine. Most guests gravitate toward the cozy pub, where a woodburning fire illuminates a collection of Georgian-style furniture. The charming staff, directed by Margaret and Derek Collier, charge from £5 ($8) for a three-course lunch. Meals are served without a break seven days a week from noon to 9 p.m. Specialties include fresh salmon, sirloin steak, and sole meunière. There's a terraced swimming pool in the garden, plus a craft shop in one of the outbuildings.

SIGHTS IN THE VICINITY: Ten miles south of Portpatrick is the quiet little hamlet of **Port Logan.** In the vicinity is **Logan House** (not open to the public), the seat of the McDouall family, which could trace their ancestry so far back that it was claimed they were as "old as the sun itself." This family laid out the gardens at Logan which are visited by people from all over the world. **Logan Botanic Garden,** an annex of the Royal Botanic Garden, Edinburgh, contains a wide range of plants from the warm temperate regions of the world. Cordylines, palms, tree ferns, and tender flowering shrubs grow well in the mild climate of southwest Scotland. The garden is open from 10 a.m. to 5 p.m. April to September. Admission is 70p ($1.12) per car. There is a pleasant refreshment room at the entrance. The site is 14 miles south of Stranraer off the B7065 road. For information, telephone 077686/231.

The ancient church site of **Kirkmadrine** lies in the parish of Stoneykirk, south of Portpatrick. The site now has a modern church but there is an old graveyard and early inscribed stones and crosses, including three of the earliest Christian monuments in Britain, showing the chi-rho symbol and inscriptions dating from the 5th or early 6th century.

14. Stranraer

The largest town in Wigtownshire, Stranraer is the terminal of the 35-mile ferry crossing from Larne, Northern Ireland. An early chapel, built by a member of the Adair family near the 16th-century **Castle of St. John** in the heart of town, gave the settlement its original name of Chapel, later changed to Chapel of Stranrawer and then shortened to Stranraer. The name is supposed to have referred to the row or "raw" of original houses on the "strand" or burn, now largely buried beneath the town's streets. The Castle of St. John became the town jail and in the late 17th century held Covenanters during Graham of Claverhouse's campaigns of religious persecution.

FOOD AND LODGING: For accommodations, try the **North West Castle,** Royal Crescent (tel. 0776/4413), overlooking Loch Ryan and the departure quay for Northern Ireland. The oldest part of the house was built in 1820 by Capt. Sir John Ross, R.N., the Arctic explorer. Of course, to honor the brave man your bedroom window should face northwest, an allusion to his search for the "North West Passage." The hotel owners will give you a brochure that relates the exploits and disappointments of the explorer. The original building has been altered and extended to meet the hotel's increasing popularity. At last count, a total of 74 rooms was offered, all of which contain private bath. Singles go from £25 ($40); doubles, from £21 ($33.60) per person per day for B&B. The lounges are cozy and pleasantly furnished, and the dining room is impressive, serving mainly continental fare with Scottish overtones. Fresh local ingredients are used. The bars downstairs are well stocked—I prefer the Explorers' Lounge with its views of the harbor. Further amenities include a garden, a sauna, and a solarium, plus a curling rink, games room, indoor swimming pool, and dancing to a live band on Saturday night.

Craignelder Hotel (tel. 0776/3281). One of the former owners of this house was a sea captain whose boat, the *Princess Victoria,* sank offshore in 1953. The establishment was built before World War I near the wharves that service the ferryboat to Ireland. The interior is functionally but attractively decorated with modern pieces, with the exception of an heirloom grandfather clock that ticks away in the dining room. Each of the 12 bedrooms contains hot and cold water basins, phones, and hot-beverage facilities. Singles, depending on the plumbing, range from £17 ($27.20) to £23 ($36.80), while doubles go for £30 ($48) to £36 ($57.60) for B&B. Alex and Betty Aird, the enterprising and friendly owners, will prepare à la carte dinners costing from £7 ($11.20).

L'Apértif Lounge, London Road (tel. 0776/2991), has some of the best and most reasonably priced food at the port. Operated by Italians, it has two lounges, one containing a pub popular with the locals. In the evening you also have the choice of ordering continental meals on an à la carte menu upstairs. Homemade soups, fresh salads, sandwiches, and hot dishes such as fried fish are offered at lunch, lasting from noon to 2 p.m. You can also get pizza here. A number of specialties are presented at night in the upstairs restaurant, where meals cost from £12 ($19.20). In the evening food is served from 5:30 to 9:30 p.m. The restaurant is closed on Sunday.

WHERE KENNEDYS ONCE LIVED: To the east of Stranraer are the **Castle Kennedy Gardens** and **Lochinch Castle** (tel. 0776/2024), a late-19th-century Scots baronial mansion. In the grounds are White and Black Lochs and the ruins of Castle Kennedy, built during the reign of James IV, but burned down in 1716. Restored in the middle of the 19th century, the gardens contain the finest pinetum in Scotland. Go in the right season and you can wander among rhododendrons, azaleas, and magnolias. The castle is not open to the public, but the gardens are, anytime daily from 10 a.m. to 5 p.m. Admission is £1 ($1.60) for adults and 25p (40¢) for children.

Chapter XVIII

THE HEBRIDEAN ISLANDS

GEOLOGISTS WANDERING through bog and bracken used to mingle with painters and birdwatchers, and stumble across an occasional sea-angler or mountain climber. But that was some time ago. These special-interest groups still frequent the islands of the Hebrides, but so do more and more general tourists.

Most everybody's heard of Mull and Iona, but what about Rhum, Eigg, and Muck? Sounds like a goblin Christmas recipe. Visitors can meet crofters (small farmers), fisher folk, and join in a real island ceilidh (singing party).

(Arran, Islay, that most southerly of the Hebridean islands, and the Isle of Jura are covered in other sections.)

Mull, featured in R. L. Stevenson's *Kidnapped,* has wild scenery, golf courses, and a treasure-trove tradition. Iona played a major part in the spread of Christianity in Britain, and a trip there usually includes a visit to Staffa, a tiny uninhabited volcanic island where Fingal's Cave inspired Mendelssohn.

These places are on the regular tourist circuit. However, more adventurous readers will also seek out Coll and Tyree, as well as the Isle of Colonsay, along with Rhum, Eigg, and Muck, even Canna. I'll even tell you where you can stay on the tiny island of Raasay, off the Isle of Skye.

The chain of Inner Hebridean islands lies just off the west coast of the Scottish mainland. To visit them, you'll be following a worthy tradition in the footsteps of Samuel Johnson and his faithful Boswell.

What about the Outer Hebrides? One of the lesser known parts of Western Europe, the Outer Hebrides are a splintered sweep of islands that stretch for some 130 miles. They go from the Butt of Lewis in the north all the way to Barra Head at the southernmost tip. They include such islands as Lewis and Harris (actually the same island), North Uist, Benbecula, South Uist, and Barra, along with several minor islands such as Bernera and Berneray.

With rugged cliffs, clean beaches, archeological treasures such as the Standing Stones of Callanish, and tiny bays, the Outer Hebrides are just beginning to awaken to their touristic possibilities.

Caledonian MacBrayne, from the ferry terminal, Gourock, near Glasgow (tel. 0475/33755), sails to 23 Scottish islands in the Firth of Clyde and the Western Isles, including Skye and Mull, as well as the Outer Hebrides. The company also offers inclusive tours for people and cars to "island-hop," using their services between islands. This is an ideal opportunity to visit places well away from the beaten track. The information office at Gourock is most helpful, and someone there will assist you in planning a trip if you wish to make up your own journey.

If you're driving from the mainland, say, from Fort William or Inverness, you can take the "Road to the Isles," heading for the Kyle of Lochalsh if your destination is Skye (if you're going to Mull and Iona, Oban is your port). On this "Road to the Isles," I'll have some recommended stopovers along the way.

1. Dornie

This small crofting village on the road to the Isle of Skye is the meeting place of three lochs—Duich, Long, and Alsh. On a rocky islet stands Eilean Donan Castle at Dornie, eight miles east of Kyle of Lochalsh on the A87.

FOOD AND LODGING: Just outside Dornie, across Loch Long and at the end of Loch Duich, is the **Loch Duich Hotel,** Ardelve, near Kyle of Lochalsh (tel. 059985/213). A long white house, it is set back from the road overlooking fields and then down Loch Duich to Eilean Donan Castle, surely one of the most attractive vistas in the country. In the other direction you'll see the Cuillins on Skye. The hosts will greet you warmly and show you to your pretty, simply furnished room. Some of the accommodations are tiny and under the eaves. Many have views of the already-mentioned castle. The hotel is owned by Rod and Geraldine Stenson, who have brought energy and enthusiasm to the place. They lived for two years on the island of Rhum, running a castle and a guesthouse, and there they learned to be self-sufficient. Geraldine cooks—really cooks! She turns out bread, oatcakes, pâtés, broth, scones, and shortbread, and even makes yogurt from their own goats' milk and cream cheese from the same herd. She offers breakfast, lunch, tea, and dinner daily. For her good honest fare, a three-course meal with coffee will cost £12 ($19.20). B&B is another £17 ($27.20) per person, with a proper porridge in the morning. At lunch light snacks are available, served in the bar or on the patio. They also have a boat, and you can rent it for fishing. Geraldine will cook your catch for supper.

SIGHTS: The romantic **Eilean Donan Castle** (tel. 059985/202) was built in 1220 as a defense against the Danes. In 1719 it was shelled by the British frigate *Worcester*. In ruins for 200 years, it was restored by Colonel MacRae of Clan

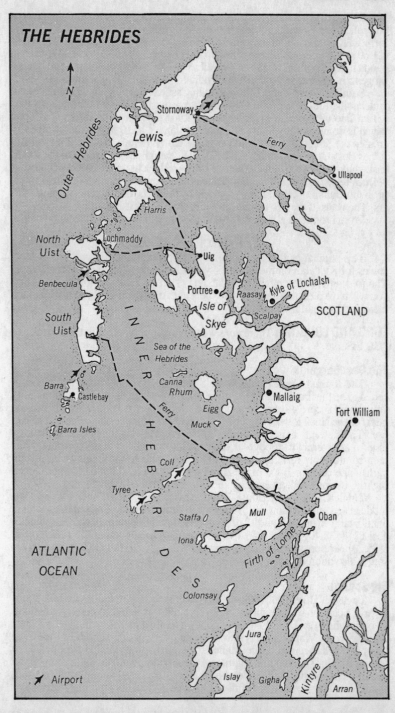

THE HEBRIDES

Outer Hebrides

Lewis

Stornoway

Ferry

Ullapool

Harris

North Uist

Lochmaddy

Uig

Benecula

Portree

Raasay

Kyle of Lochalsh

Isle of Skye

Scalpay

SCOTLAND

South Uist

Sea of the Hebrides

INNER

Canna
Rhum

Barra

Castle bay

Eigg

Mallaig

Muck

Fort William

Barra Isles

HEBRIDES

Ferry

Coll

Tyree

Staffa

Iona

Mull

Oban

ATLANTIC
OCEAN

Firth of Lorne

Colonsay

Jura

Gigha

Kintyre

Islay

Arran

✈ Airport

MacRae in 1932 and is now a clan war memorial and museum, containing Jacobite relics, mostly with clan connections. It is open April to September 30 daily, including Sunday, from 10 a.m. to 12:30 p.m. and 2 to 6 p.m., charging £1 ($1.60) for admission. There is a shop attached which sells good-quality tartan goods in kilts and kilted skirts, as well as woolens and souvenirs. You can arrange to have your selections mailed home.

South of Dornie and Eilean Donan Castle is Shiel Bridge. From here, an "unclassified road" leads to **Glenelg**, after a twisting climb over Ratagan Pass with a fine view of the mountain range known as the **Five Sisters of Kintail**, which is dominated by Sgurr Fhuaran, 3,505 feet high. In summer a car-ferry crosses the Sound of Sleat to Skye. It was from Glenelg that Dr. Johnson and James Boswell crossed to Skye in 1773. In Gleann Beag, two miles to the southeast, stand two of the best-preserved Iron Age brochs on the Scottish mainland —**Dun Telve** and **Dun Troddan.** Brochs are stone towers with double walls, probably built more than 2,000 years ago by the Picts for protection against raiders. The walls of the two brochs are more than 30 feet high.

From Dornie, it is a short drive to the—

2. Kyle of Lochalsh

This popular center is a good jumping-off point to the islands. A car-ferry leaves for Kyleakin on the Isle of Skye. There is no need to book in advance. The journey is only ten minutes. The ferry shuttles back and forth all day, and you will have plenty of time to drive the length of Skye in a day, returning to the mainland by night if you want to.

FOOD AND LODGING: There are several bargain choices available, as well as a "Big Splurge."

The Best Bargains

The **Retreat Guest House,** Main Street (tel. 0599/4308), is generally conceded to be the finest guesthouse in the area. However, because of its popularity you should secure advance reservations in summer. A hospitable place in the heart of the small town, it is personally run by the family who owns it. You can use "The Retreat" as a base for touring this most fascinating part of Scotland or else for an overnight stopover if you're going on to Skye in the morning. Thirteen comfortably furnished rooms are rented year round (none has a private bath). The cost for B&B ranges from £9 ($14.40) to £11 ($17.60) per person nightly. If requested, an evening meal can be provided at 6:45 p.m.

Tingle Creek Guest House, Erbusaig (tel. 0599/4430), open all year, is a modern accommodation with 14 rooms to rent to guests. Each of the rooms is comfortably furnished, and 12 of them contain private baths or showers. Singles cost £24 ($38.40) to £29 ($46.40), and doubles are priced at £15 ($24) to £22 ($35.20) per person. Half board, priced at £23 ($36.80) to £31 ($49.60) per person, is also offered.

Big Splurge

Lochalsh Hotel (tel. 0599/4202). There's no way a visitor can talk about Kyle of Lochalsh without mentioning this landmark hotel. It was built as a luxury oasis when the British Railway finally extended its tracks in this direction. During World War II it served as the headquarters of a branch of the Royal Navy which had mined the coastline. Today, in memory of that period, a large (defused) mine sits near the flagpole on the seaside lawn. The south shore of the Isle of Skye and the rock-studded inlet are visible through beautifully crafted, small-paned windows, whose full-grain hardwood and brass fittings are similar to those on an oceangoing yacht. The 40 bedrooms have been stylishly over-hauled, and all but two have private baths. B&B costs £27 ($43.20) to £47 ($75.20) per person. The ground-floor bar stocks a variety of malt whisky, and the dining room, which has a panoramic view, serves the best food in town. Evening meals cost £14 ($22.40) to £19 ($30.40) per person and include the best of Scottish cuisine and ingredients.

On a hillside above the hotel, the **Ferry Inn** is one of the most popular pubs in the area, attracting locals as well as visitors.

A Guest House at Plockton

At the top of the main street of Plockton, near Kyle of Lochalsh, sits the lovely guesthouse of Mrs. Byrne, **2 Railway Cottage** (tel. 059984/333). The owner extends typical Scottish warmth and hospitality. She charges £9 ($14.40) per person for a bed and a big, tasty breakfast. The entire house is clean, comfortable, and quiet, with a view of the village of Plockton, Loch Carron, and the surrounding hills. In the evening, guests are invited into the living room to watch TV, sip tea, and converse.

Food and Lodging at Balmacara

Balmacara Hotel (tel. 059986/283) lies three miles from the Kyle of Lochalsh. Both the contemporary design of the bedrooms and the panoramic waterside view of Loch Alsh are similar to what a visitor might find in an isolated section of Scandinavia. Parts of the interior are covered with full-grained horizontal planks of varnished pine, into which the square windows present a sweeping view, not only of water but of forests and the island of Skye. Owner Clive Williams is happy to talk about the many attractions of Wester Ross. Most guests congregate in the contemporary TV lounge or cocktail bar just before being served a good-tasting dinner. Each of the 30 comfortable bedrooms has a private bath. Singles cost from £24 ($38.40), with doubles or twins going for £39 ($62.40) to £43 ($68.80) per night, including a full Scottish breakfast. A fixed-price evening meal goes for £12 ($19.20), while a lighter lunch usually averages £5 ($8). The hotel is open all year.

3. Isle of Skye

From the Kyle of Lochalsh you can take a ferry to the mystical Isle of Skye, off the northwest coast of Scotland. The island has inspired many of the best-loved and best-known of Scottish ballads such as "Over the Sea to Skye" and "Will Ye Not Come Back Again." On the island you can explore castle ruins, duns, and brochs, enjoying a Highland welcome. For the Scots, the island will forever evoke images of Flora MacDonald, who conducted Bonnie Prince Charlie to Skye. She disguised him as Betty Burke after the Culloden defeat.

Once on Skye, you'll find ferry service back to Kyle or to Mallaig from Armadale. The Armadale ferry transports cars, but the service is less frequent than the one to Kyle. If you're planning to take your car, reservations are recommended.

Skye is the largest of the Inner Hebrides, 48 miles long and between three and 25 miles wide. It is separated from the mainland by the Sound of Sleat (pronounced "Slate"). At Kyleakin, on the eastern end, the channel is only a quarter of a mile wide and thus the ferry docks there.

Dominating the land of summer seas, streams, woodland glens, mountain passes, cliffs, and waterfalls are the Cuillin Hills, a range of jagged black mountains. The Peninsula of Sleat, the island's southernmost arm, is known as "The Garden of Skye." There are many stories as to the origin of the name Skye.

Some believe it is from the Norse "ski," meaning a cloud, while others say it is from the Gaelic word for winged. There are Norse names on the island, however, as the Norsemen held sway for four centries before 1263. Overlooking the Kyle is the ruined Castle Moal, once the home of a Norwegian princess.

For those who want to overnight or spend a longer holiday on the Isle of Skye itself, I offer the following suggestions, scattered in the island's various hamlets. However, in summer be sure to reserve in advance, as accommodations are limited.

KYLEAKIN: The ferry from Kyle of Lochalsh docks at this tiny waterfront village. For those seeking a quiet, well-kept place to stay, I recommend the following:

The **Dunringell Hotel** (tel. 0599/4180) sits in 4½ acres of extensive lawns in which rhododendrons, azaleas, and other flowering shrubs provide a riot of color from March to July. Dunringell is a spacious structure, built in 1912, with large bedrooms and public rooms. The cost of B&B is £13 ($20.80) per person nightly, plus another £7.50 ($12) for dinner. For a private bath, the charge is an additional £2.50 ($4) per person. VAT is included. Both a smoking and nonsmoking lounge are maintained for guests. For those who wish to participate, the proprietors, Mr. and Mrs. MacPherson, hold a short worship service in one of the lounges each evening.

The **White Heather Hotel** (tel. 0599/4577) consists of three interconnected buildings. Personally run by its owners, this is a licensed hotel with up-to-date amenities. From its lounges you can enjoy a view of Castle Moal, once lived in by a Norse princess. The hotel sits close to the edge of the road, in a position near the ferryboat and bus terminals. From March to November, 25 comfortably furnished rooms are rented, costing from £14 ($22.40) in a single and from £21.50 ($34.40) in a double. Half-board terms are available, costing from £19 ($30.40) per person daily.

PORTREE: Skye's capital, Portree, is the port for steamers making trips around the island and linking Skye with the 15-mile-long island of Raasay. Sligachan, nine miles south, and Glenbrittle, seven miles farther southwest, are centers for climbing the Cuillin (Coolin) Hills.

The **Isles Hotel**, on the town square just across from the Bank of Scotland (tel. 0478/2129), is, appropriately, owned and managed by John and Meg Isles, who live on the premises. The white stone building has a slate roof and three dormers overlooking the square. Seven of the 12 bedrooms have private baths / showers, and all units have color TV, hot and cold water basins, and hot-beverage facilities. With private plumbing, they rent for £17.50 ($28) to £18.50 ($29.60) per person, depending on the season. Two bathless singles cost from £15 ($24) to £16 ($25.60). The hotel has a restricted license and a residents' lounge. Dinner with a good choice of dishes is à la carte, and the hotel is open only from April to October.

The **Rosedale Hotel**, Beaumont Crescent (tel. 0478/2531), lying in a secluded part of Portree, has been owned and managed by the Andrew family since 1950. They have an enviable reputation for their good rooms, Scottish hospitality, and tasty cuisine. The bedrooms are modern, 20 in all, opening onto views of the harbor and Portree Bay. The units have private baths as well. Guests are received from May to October at a cost of £21 ($33.60) to £25 ($40) in a single, from £19 ($30.40) to £23 ($36.80) per person in a double, including a Scottish breakfast. In addition to two modern lounges, a cocktail bar carries a wide range of Highland malt whiskies. The hotel is in the midst of fishermen's cottages that flank a rock-strewn path along the water, near the steamer pier.

Viewfield House (tel. 0478/2217) is unique on the island. Several years ago a lovely California visitor was so enchanted by the environment and its bekilted, handsome manager, that she stayed for several weeks, eventually marrying him. The establishment amid 20 acres of landscaped gardens is awash with rhododendrons and copper beeches. It was constructed of reddish sandstone in two stages, the first in 1790 and the second a century later. It was the home of the factor (manager) of the vast MacDonald estates. Very little has changed architecturally in the house since the turn of the century, including the toilets in the upper halls which are known as "thunderbuckets." The first view most visitors get is of a trophy-filled entrance hall, where the stuffed carcasses of dozens of African beasts stare down from positions high on the paneled walls. Each of them was bagged during expeditions that followed Livingstone. One of the MacDonald ancestors spent 2½ years in the jungles, gathering these trophies.

The reigning matriarch of the establishment's dining room is Mrs. Evelyn MacDonald, who regales dinner guests with her octogenarian anecdotes and wry humor. Hugh MacDonald, her grandson, and his wife, Linda, manage the place. They accept paying guests in their 14 rooms between May and September. In spite of the electric heaters, the MacDonalds lay fires in the baronial salon and the paneled dining room every evening, creating a type of never-ending house party for their well-mannered guests. B&B costs £17 ($27.20) per person nightly, with half board going for £25 ($40) per person.

King's Haven Hotel and Restaurant (tel. 0478/2290). This Georgian family house was built on a hill above the harbor in 1820. It served as a school, a shop, and a bank until its England-born owners, Tony and Judith Vaughn-Sharp, took it over in 1974, transforming it into one of the most charming hotels and restaurants on Skye. Before that, they worked as a team hauling cargoes by truck around the island. That experience led them to this house, which was practically in ruins. They put on a new slate roof and overhauled the foundation, and the resulting coziness is well worth the effort. Five of the seven attractively furnished bedrooms contain private baths, and room 8 is a special favorite of mine. The cost, with breakfast included, ranges from £18.50 ($29.60) per person nightly.

Guests enjoy before-dinner drinks beside a fireplace in the warmly welcoming cocktail lounge before heading into the intimate dining room. There, beside an iron stove and a stone fireplace, diners are served local produce and meats personally prepared by Judith. The specialties change with the availability of ingredients in the local market. Some sample items might include Isle of Skye scampi in white wine, cheese, and mushroom sauce, or beef in red wine with tomatoes and garlic (flavored with three kinds of fresh herbs), or perhaps grilled Angus sirloin with a fresh garden salad. Dessert might be a blackcurrant fool with a homemade shortbread, followed by Gaelic coffee. A full dinner costs from £11.50 ($18.40). Meals are served daily exactly at 7:30 p.m. from Easter to October. Reservations are suggested.

SKEABOST BRIDGE: Eastward from Dunvegan is Skeabost Bridge, with an island cemetery of great antiquity. The graves of four Crusaders are here.

Nearby is the **Skeabost House Hotel** (tel. 047032/202), one of the most comfortable, refreshing, and inviting country homes of Skye, receiving paying guests from mid-April to mid-October. Thoroughly modernized, it is interesting architecturally with its dormers, chimneys, tower, and gables. Inside the taste level is high, with wood paneling and carpets. Once a private estate, it has been converted into a lochside hotel, standing on beautiful grounds that in summer are studded with flowering bushes. The location is 35 miles from Kyle of Lochalsh and five miles from Portree. Sports people are attracted to the hotel, gathering in the firelit lounge for a mellow scotch whisky. The atmosphere is of hardy tweeds with the distinctive aroma of a good cigar. The loch outside is well stocked with salmon and trout, and a short par-three golf course has been constructed. Of the 26 handsomely furnished rooms, 15 contain private bath. Singles are accepted at a rate of £22 ($35.20) to £27 ($43.20), depending on the plumbing, and doubles on a similar basis cost £25 ($40) to £27 ($43.20) per person. All tariffs include a full Scottish breakfast. The Scottish fare, featuring smoked salmon, is served on fine china with elegant silver. A bar buffet lunch goes for £5.50 ($8.80), a four-course dinner for £10.80 ($17.28).

UIG: This village is on Trotternish, the largest Skye peninsula, and ferry port for Harris and Uist in the Outer Hebrides. It is 15 miles north of Portree and 49 miles from Kyle of Lochalsh. **Monkstadt House,** a mile and a half north, is where Flora MacDonald brought Prince Charles, in the guise of a girl named Betty Burke, after their escape flight from Benbecula. In **Kilmuir** churchyard, five miles north, Flora was buried, wrapped in a sheet used by the prince. Her grave is marked by a Celtic cross.

The **Ferry Inn** (tel. 047042/242). John and Betty Campbell are the kindly owners of this unpretentious hotel, whose social center lies within the paneled ground-floor pub where bar meals are available at noon. In the evening you can order a more formal dinner in the dining room. You'll recognize this establishment by its roadside design of late Victorian gables. There's a modern TV lounge on the premises, a popular gathering spot. Rooms are comfortably and pleasantly furnished. Some contain private bath, the B&B rates ranging from £13 ($20.80) to £16 ($25.60) per person nightly.

DUNVEGAN: The village of Dunvegan grew up around **Dunvegan Castle** (tel. 047022/206), the principal man-made sight on the Isle of Skye, seat of the chiefs of Clan MacLeod who have lived there for 750 years. The castle, which stands on a rocky promontory, was once accessible only by boat, but now the moat is bridged and the castle open to the public. It holds many fascinating relics, including a "fairy flag." It is reputed to be the oldest inhabited castle in Britain. It is open in April and May (and through October) from 2 to 5 p.m. From May through September it is open from 10:30 a.m. to 5 p.m. daily except Sunday. Admission to the castle and grounds is £2 ($3.20) for adults, £1 ($1.60) for children. For the gardens only, the charge is 50p (80¢) for adults, 25p (40¢) for children, and they are open all day.

Boats leave the castle jetty at frequent intervals every day except Sunday from May to the end of September going to the **Seal Colony.** The seals in Loch Dunvegan, both brown and gray varieties, aren't bothered by the approach of people in boats and can be studied at close range. The 20-minute round trip costs £1.50 ($2.40) for adults, 75p ($1.20) for children.

Food and Lodging

Atholl House Hotel (tel. 047022/219) stands right in the village of Dunvegan, close to Dunvegan Castle. It is owned and managed by John and Mary Laing, who offer B&B costing from £15 ($24) per person in a bathless room, from £17.50 ($28) per person in a room with bath. Units contain facilities for making hot beverages. In the dining room, the Laings place emphasis on friendly service and well-prepared local produce, including lamb, venison, salmon, and shellfish in season. Atholl House is a member of the "Taste of Scotland" program, with high standards of accommodation, Scottish hospitality, and Scottish cuisine. It has a residents' license. From the hotel, you have magnificent views over mountain moorland and Loch Dunvegan.

Dunvegan Hotel (tel. 047022/202) sits on a hillside above the loch, with a facade pierced with a long, glassed-in front porch. Each of the six pleasant bedrooms contains a private shower and color TV. Toilets are in cubicles off the hallways. B&B costs from £15 ($24) to £17 ($27.20) per person. Pub and lounge facilities here are busy six nights a week. A cozy fire blazes in the ground-floor pub, and there's a "Hunting Lodge" in the basement. Hot bar meals, lunches, and afternoon teas are served. A pub meal costs around £5 ($8), with more substantial dinners offered in the restaurant for £8 ($12.80) and up.

Three Chimneys Restaurant, Colbost, near Dunvegan (tel. 047081/258), is installed in an old-fashioned Skye croft house on the shores of Loch Dunvegan. Its atmosphere is definitely "olde worlde," with stone walls, beamed ceilings, and open fires. The owners, Mr. and Mrs. Spear, prepare not only a "modern" cuisine, but a traditional Scottish one as well. Local salmon, shellfish, and trout appear regularly on the menu. Home-baked whole-meal bread, salads, and fresh fruit desserts are specialties. Lunch is from noon to 3 p.m., costing from £4 ($6.40), and dinner is from 7 to 10:30 p.m., when your tab is likely to run about £12.50 ($20). The restaurant is open for a set-menu dinner only on Sunday.

IN THE ENVIRONS: Some four miles from Dunvegan, the **Skye Water Mill and Black House Folk Museum,** on the Glendale Road (tel. 047081/291), contains implements and furniture of bygone days and has a peat fire burning throughout the day. A replica of an illicit whisky still can be seen behind the museum. The museum is open from Easter to the end of September from 10 a.m. to 7 p.m., charging 50p (80¢) for adults and 25p (40¢) for children. Still in working order, the watermill is two miles down the road, costing 25p (40¢) for adults and 10p (16¢) for children.

There's also a pottery and silversmith in Glendale, along with a watermill and an art gallery specializing in local views. **Skye Venture Cottage Industry,** 18 Holmisdal, Glendale-by-Dunvegan (tel. 047081/316), is where William and Julia MacKenzie, from Lewis, sell sweaters cottage-knit by women throughout the island. The MacKenzies weave goods and tweeds from undyed wool from their own sheep. They offer a wide range of garments in the style of Aran, Fair Isle, and Iceland, produced mainly on Skye. The store is open Monday to Saturday from 10 a.m. to 6 p.m.

At **Trumpan,** nine miles north of Dunvegan, are the remains of a church that was set afire in 1597 by MacDonald raiders while the congregation, all MacLeods, were inside at worship. Only one woman survived. The MacLeods of Dunvegan rushed to the defense, and only two MacDonalds escaped death.

THE SLEAT PENINSULA: A lot of Skye can look melancholy and forlorn, especially in misty weather. But for a change of landscape pace, head for the Peninsula of Sleat, the southeastern section of the island. It's long been known as the "Garden of Skye," because of the lushness of some of its vegetation. The reason for this is that its shores are washed by the warmer waters of the Gulf Stream. Sleat also possesses several sightseeing attractions.

A ruined stronghold of the MacDonalds, **Knock Castle** lies off the A851 12 miles south of Broadford. It can be visited, admission-free, throughout the day.

Another MacDonald stronghold, **Dunsgiath Castle** has some well-preserved ruins open to view. They are found at Tokavaig on an unclassified road (a sign directs you) at a point 20 miles south and southwest of Broadford.

Food and Lodging

A charming place to stay on the peninsula is **Fiordhem,** Ord (tel. 04715/226), where Bridget and Tony La Trobe welcome guests. The La Trobes have rebuilt a small fisherman's cottage 20 feet from the edge of Loch Eishort, with striking views of the Cuillin Mountains and the islands of Canna and Rhum. They offer five bedrooms, all with hot and cold water basins and hot-beverage facilities, charging £10.50 ($16.80) for B&B. Bridget is a good cook, and the dinners, costing £8 ($12.80), are creations of home-cooking and baking, with such items as fresh fish and seafood. The dining room is pleasantly furnished with antiques. In the sitting room there are comfortable armchairs, gleaming copper and brass, and an open fireplace for peat and log fires.

Clan Donald Centre

At Armadale (tel. 04714/227), even visitors whose last name isn't Mac-Donald may want to visit this center, with its museum, lovely gardens, pleasant restaurant, bookshop, and well-stocked gift shop. You'll reach it by traveling along a winding seaside road, eventually pulling into the impeccably maintained grounds surrounding the sculptured ruins of Armadale Castle and the recently restored baronial stables. Part of the castle houses an excellent multimedia exhibition introducing you to the almost lost culture of the ancient Gaelic world under the MacDonalds as Lords of the Isles. There are miles of trails, and the Countryside Ranger Service offers guided walks and talks to help you get to know the history and workings of a Highland estate.

Admission is £1.20 ($1.92) for adults and 80p ($1.28) for children. The center is open daily from April to the end of October from 10 a.m. to 5 p.m. Monday to Saturday, noon to 5 p.m. on Sunday. The Stables is a licensed restaurant offering home-baking and good food from teas and coffees through a light snack or a full meal with a "Taste of Scotland" menu. The driving distance from the ferryboat at Kyleakin takes about 30 minutes, and the center is also quite near the Armadale–Mallaig ferry.

ISLE ORNSAY: Dating from 1920, **Duisdale Hotel** (tel. 04713/202) is a solidly constructed granite lodge at the top of a hill on which has been planted a lovely flowering garden. Guests enjoy the isolation between Armadale (seven miles) and Kylerhea (14 miles), yet the country home is only 12 miles from where the ferry comes in at Kyleakin. You get 25 acres of garden and woodland overlooking the sea. An ex-officer in the British military services is in charge, and he sees that the high standards of this house's past are maintained. Guests can read quietly in one of the big-windowed lounges or seek more sports-oriented activities. The rooms are handsomely furnished and well maintained. Depending on the plumbing, the B&B rate ranges from £19.50 ($31.20) to £22.50 ($36) per person daily. Guests, often members of the yachting set, meet in the nautically decorated bar before going into dinner. There the food is traditionally Scottish, making use of local produce such as freshly caught seafood as well as homegrown vegetables whenever possible. Nonresidents are welcome, and meals cost from £12 ($19.20).

ARDVASAR: A 250-year-old coaching inn, the **Ardvasar Hotel** (tel. 04714/223) has as its oldest part a stone-trimmed pub in what was originally a stable. Today, every off-duty resident in the area heads here for a mug of lager. Bill and Gretta Fowler, the Scottish hosts, came from the mainland several years ago to set up what has become a well-reputed restaurant and hotel. The dozen bedrooms, eight of which contain private baths, rent for £18 ($28.80) in a bathless single, for £30 ($48) to £36 ($57.60) in a double, the latter rate for rooms with bath. Tariffs include a full Scottish breakfast and VAT. Among the sections of the hotel offering restful and relaxing accommodations is the residents' lounge with an open fire and a separate lounge with a giant TV. Bill, the chef, offers fixed-price dinners from £12.50 ($20). A meal might include smoked trout with lemon, homemade pâté with tomato vinaigrette, filet of chicken with pâté and garlic butter, fresh halibut with hollandaise, roast shoulder of lamb with haggis stuffing, or Scottish sirloin steak with local prawns and Drambuie. Dessert might consist of a chocolate rum pot with cream. Bar meals cost from £4.50 ($7.20).

4. Isle of Raasay

For an offbeat adventure, I'd suggest a side trip to this 14-mile-long island, which has a great panoramic view over the Isle of Skye.

A car-ferry, leaving from Sconsar on Skye, is in service about three times a day. From June 26 to around mid-August, the service is increased to four times a day. Check on times and details with the ferrymaster, who lives on Raasay, Alistair Nicolson (tel. 047862/226).

On a recent visit, I didn't find the gaiety and laughter Johnson and Boswell did on their 18th-century visit to the islands, but things are looking up on Raasay, with more young people staying here. For a while, young islanders were leaving to work elsewhere, especially in Glasgow, but the population in the last couple of years has increased from about 100 to 160, and the local school roll is no longer dwindling.

The very remoteness attracts many to Raasay. Visitors enjoy the quiet of the country lanes, the uncrowded feeling, and the beautiful scenery, plus the birdlife of the island.

On the island, the ruins of **Brochel Castle** knew a greater day when it was the ancient seat of the MacLeods of Raasay. The island also has some Pictish symbol stones.

WHERE TO STAY: A good place to stay on the island, the **Isle of Raasay Hotel** (tel. 047862/222), is run by Mrs. Isobel Nicholson, whose husband, Captain Alistair Nicholson, runs the ferryboat that brings you to Raasay from Skye. The hotel has 15 bedrooms, 12 with private baths and all with radios, phones, color TV, and hot-beverage facilities. The cost is £30 ($48) per person per day for a room plus breakfast and dinner. Menus in the dining room are good and varied, featuring fresh local fish, crab, game in season, and home-baked goods. The hotel is a renovated old stone mansion with added wings and central heating. It provides views across the glittering Narrows of Raasay to Skye.

5. Rhum

This enticingly named island lies about nine miles southwest of the previously explored Isle of Skye. There are those who will tell you not to go. "If you like a barren desert, where it rains all the time, you'll love Rhum," a skipper in Mallaig recently told me.

It's stark all right. And very wet. In fact, with more than 90 inches of rainfall recorded annually, it is said to be the "wettest" island of the Inner Hebrides.

Since the mid-'50s Rhum has been owned by the Nature Conservancy Council, an ecological conservation group, and they have wisely selected a considerate, conscientious warden, Laughton Johnston, to preside over the little "kingdom," which is only about eight miles wide and eight miles long. Obviously, conservation is of paramount importance on the island, and attempts are being made to bring back the sea-eagle, which used to live on the island in Victoria's day.

On this storm-tossed outpost, mountain climbers appear in summer to meet challenging peaks, and anglers are also attracted to the oceanic island by reports (which are accurate) of its good trout fishing. Bird-lovers seek out the Manx shearwaters which live on the island in great numbers. Red deer and ponies add color, along with the wildflowers of summer, to an otherwise bleak landscape.

To reach Rhum, you can take a passenger ferry from Mallaig, on the western coast of Scotland. It leaves about four times a week, and no cars are carried. A round-trip passenger fare from Mallaig to Rhum is £6.60 ($10.56).

FOOD AND LODGING: Quite astonishingly, in such a forbidding place, you come upon a hotel, **Kinloch Castle** (tel. 0687/2037), which has been called "Britain's most intact example of an Edwardian Country House." Perhaps it was its very inaccessibility that kept this mansion of imposing stature and grandeur unchanged over the years since its completion in 1901 for Sir George Bulloch, a wealthy British industrialist, and its decoration under the direction of his wife, Monica. Sir George wanted a retreat from the world, and in this monument to the opulence of the Edwardian era, he found it at the top of a loch on the eastern coast of Rhum. You can still see the ballroom, with its gold curtains and upholstery, a massive inglenook, and Adams-style fireplaces, with the monumental paintings and stuffed animals that were *de rigueur* in such mansions when Kinloch Castle was in its heyday.

From April to October, guests are accommodated at the castle, paying about £42 ($67.20) per person per day for a room and all meals, served on a dining table rescued from a yacht. The food is quite good, and in season you are likely to be served Scottish salmon and venison. None of the nine bedrooms has a private bath, as the original plans have not been altered (and who would want to?), but the shared bathrooms are spacious and elaborate lavatories still flush as well as they did when they were installed nearly 80 years ago.

CANNA: Some three miles northwest of Rhum, Canna is another of the so-called Small Isles and is one of the hardest to reach. It isn't really in the tourist business, and only the most persistent may want to seek it out. Ferry service from Mallaig is infrequent and unreliable, but sometimes, if a boat sails on a Saturday, it will stay long enough to give sightseers about four hours on Canna, enough time for a good look before they catch the return ferry. A wooden bridge connects Canna to Sanday, a tidal island, which makes a good exploration trip. You can seek out a Celtic cross and the outline of a Viking burial ship.

The laird of the island is concerned with the raising of Cheviot sheep and Highland cattle. In 1981, Canna was willed to the National Trust for Scotland. There are no hotels or other accommodations on the island.

6. Eigg and Muck

Two of the tiny islands lying in the Sea of the Hebrides, which separates the Inner from the Outer Hebrides, bear the interesting names, Eigg and Muck. They are connected to the mainland of Scotland and to the other islands only by ferry (except, of course, for personally owned fishing boats and government vessels). It's best for tourists to check with Caledonian MacBrayne for information on trips to these islands (tel. 0475/33755).

EIGG: The tiny island, about 4½ miles by three, lies some four miles southeast of the just-explored Rhum. The laird of the island purchased Eigg in 1975 at a reported cost of half a million dollars.

Visitors are welcome here to see the Sgurr of Eigg, a tall column of lava, said to be the biggest such pitchstone mass in the United Kingdom. Climbers on its north side try to reach its impressive height of 1,300 feet.

After your arrival at Galmisdale, the principal hamlet and pier, you can take an antique omnibus to Cleadale. Once there, you walk across moors to Camas Sgiotaig, with its well-known beach of the Singing Sands (its black-and-white quartz grains are decidedly off-key).

MUCK: Directly to the southwest of Eigg, Muck, unlike Rhum, has such an unappetizing name that visitors may turn away and not want to explore it. This little 2½ square miles is misnamed. Muck is not used in the sense we know it, but is based on a Gaelic word, *muic,* meaning the island of the sow. That, too, doesn't make it appealing, but it is much more attractive than its name, and many seabirds find it a suitable place for nesting.

Often storm-tossed by the ocean, Muck is actually a farm run by its resident laird. There are hardly more than two dozen people on Muck, and all of them are concerned in some way with the running of the island farm. It is reached by ferry service from Mallaig.

Food and Lodging

The laird of Muck runs the one hotel, **Port Mhor House** (tel. 0687/2365), a traditionally styled building for up to 17 guests, with warm pine-paneled walls and fittings. The kitchen uses produce from the farm and the hotel's own garden, and the fare here is excellent and hearty. Nonresidents can call ahead for dining reservations. Expect to pay from £9.50 ($15.20) for a meal. Later you can enjoy a malt whisky around an open log fire. A double bedroom rents for about £16 ($25.60) nightly. For reservations, write to the laird at Gallanach, Isle of Muck, Inverness-shire.

Naturalists come here looking for everything from rare butterflies to otters. The large colonies of nesting seabirds in May and June should not be missed. Visitors are allowed to visit the farm.

7. Coll and Tyree

If you like your scenery stark and tranquil, try Coll and Tyree, tiny islands that attract those visitors seeking remoteness. On Tyree (also Tiree), the shell-sand machair increases the arable area, differentiating it from the inner isles.

A lot of British pensioners live on Coll and Tyree, and they seem to like to keep the place pretty much to themselves.

The arrival of a car-ferry from Oban that carries passengers here allows the outside world to intrude, although sometimes gales cause cancellations of the voyage. The ferry sails from Oban to Mull and then, if conditions are right, goes on to Coll and Tyree. If you travel at the wrong time of the year (and nobody knows when the wrong time is), you could easily be stranded on an island for a while, waiting for the next departure. Details and bookings, essential for cars, are available from **Caledonian MacBrayne,** Ferry Terminal (tel. 0631/62285) at Oban.

Loganair also flies directly to Tyree from Glasgow, with about six scheduled flights weekly (none on Sunday).

Coll and Tyree are very much sister islands exposed to the open Atlantic. West of Mull, they are said to have the highest sunshine records in Britain (however, this has not been my experience!). They are the outermost of the Inner Hebrides.

Trees are rare on either island, but that doesn't mean they are bleak. Both are rich in flora, with some 500 species, along with a fascinating bird life. It is estimated that some 150 species are found here, including Arctic skuas and razorbills. Both common and gray seals have breeding colonies on the islands.

If that sun does come out in midsummer, you'll find silver beaches. Boat rentals and sea angling can be arranged on both Coll and Tyree. Many visitors bicycle around the island, and there are a few cars for rent. Tyree has the least expensive method of transport: a post bus serves most of the island.

Both islands have accommodations, but there are no officially designated campsites. Campers must ask a local farmer for permission, and it's usually granted.

COLL: Lying in the seemingly timeless world of the Celtic west, the little island of Coll, with a population of some 130 hearty souls, is rich in history, even prehistory.

Coll has a restored castle, **Breacachadh,** from the Middle Ages. On some occasions it is open to the public. In the 15th century this was a stronghold of the Macleans. This is a private residence but also a center for Project Trust, which prepares young people for voluntary service overseas.

The so-called "New" Castle, ordered built for Hector Maclean in 1750, provided shelter for Samuel Johnson and James Boswell within its walls when they were stranded on the island for ten days because of storms at sea. The purity of the castle was altered considerably by the Stewart family, who in the mid-19th century added many embellishments, including pepperpot turrets and parapets.

In the western part of the island at Totronald are two standing stones called **Na Sgeulachan** ("the teller of tales"). Once these stones were believed to have been erected by the Druids, but historians dismiss that suggestion. The stones predate the Druids and are thought to have been the site of a temple. Another idea is that they may have been an astronomical laboratory, recording the movements of the sun and moon.

The highest point on Coll is Ben Hogh, which many hearty visitors climb (340 feet) for a panoramic view of several Hebridean islands. The boulder on the hill, supported by smaller stones, is believed to have been left that way from the Ice Age.

Distances from one place to another are short on Coll, as the island averages about three miles in breadth. At its longest point, it stretches for some 13 miles.

On the road to Sorisdale, at **Killunaig,** stand the ruins of a church from the late Middle Ages and a burial ground. Going on to **Sorisdale,** you'll see the ruins of several houses which crofters once occupied earlier in this century. Hundreds of families once lived here, but many were chased away in the wake of the potato famine. Many crofters were also forced out in Land Clearance programs. Many, enduring great hardships at sea, including disease, went to Canada, Australia, and New Zealand.

Food and Lodging

The place to stay on Coll is the **Isle of Coll Hotel,** Arinagour (tel. 08793/334), where you will be welcomed by the director, Kevin J. Oliphant. This is a family-run country hotel on its own grounds. All its rooms are equipped with hot and cold running water, and such amenities are provided as a refreshment cabinet, electric razor points, electric blankets, and tea/coffee-making equipment. A single costs from £17.50 ($28) for B&B and a double goes for £30 ($48), these tariffs including a full Scottish breakfast. A good dinner will be provided for another £9.25 ($14.80) per person nightly. If you're planning to go exploring a packed lunch will be provided; otherwise, if you're staying on the grounds a good lunch or bar snacks are available. Other facilities include a sauna, a solarium, a lounge, two bars, and a games room. You can rent a bicycle here.

TYREE (ALSO TIREE): A fertile island, one of the richest in the Hebrides, flat Tyree earned the Gaelic nickname "the land below the wave-tops." Filled with farming communities, Tyree has a population of some 800 residents who enjoy its gentle landscape, sandy beaches, and rolling hills. At Vaul is a nine-hole golf course open to visitors.

As you travel about the island, you'll see many Hebridean crofters' houses with thatched roofs. Many of these were constructed in the early 1800s. The Duke of Argyll in 1886 caused a scandal when he sent in marines and police to clear the crofters off the land. Many were sent destitute to Canada. But crofters once again occupy the land.

Most of the population is centered around **Scarinish,** with its little stone harbor where lobster boats put in. Fishing isn't what it used to be, when the appearance of fast and dangerous squalls and storms were said to scatter the fishing fleet as far as the shores of North America.

Birdwatchers are drawn to the shores of Loch Bhasapoll, a favorite gathering place of wild geese and ducks. The Reef was an important air base for the Royal Air Force in World War II, and is still in use.

Ancient duns and forts are scattered around Tyree. The best of these is a broch at **Vaul Bay,** which has walls more than 12 feet thick. It is 30 feet in diameter.

At **Balephetrish,** on the northern rim of the island, stands a huge granite boulder. Locals call it "The Ringing Stone," because when it is struck it gives off a metallic sound.

In the western part of the island, at **Kilkenneth,** are found the ruins of the Chapel of St. Kenneth. The saint was a comrade of St. Columba. A sightseeing target for birdwatchers is a cave on the coast at Kenavara, where many seabirds can be observed.

Food and Lodging

Balephetrish Hotel (tel. 08792/549) is a severely designed white house within the confines of a thick wall. It's the personal domain of its owner, Jack Carter. He maintains a handful of simple bedrooms, five in all, each of which is carefully maintained. There are two public bathrooms. Your fellow guest at evening dinner is likely to be a geologist or a pensioner from the mainland. Rates are most reasonable: from £18 ($28.80) per person for half board. You get home-style cookery and home-grown vegetables in summer (no chemicals).

Tiree Lodge Hotel (tel. 08792/368) was a simple island home until someone added a sprawling white-walled wing of well-maintained accommodations, half of which contain private baths. Its big plate-glass windows benefit from the views of the emerald-green fields surrounding it. The hotel, run by Kenneth McDonald Hutchinson, is comfortable, clean, and unpretentious. Hearty breakfasts and good-tasting, traditionally generous Scottish dinners are served. B&B costs £15 ($24) to £18 ($28.80) per person, either single or double occupancy, and half board goes for £22.50 ($36) to £25.50 ($40.80) per person daily.

8. Mull

The largest island in the Inner Hebrides, with a coastline 300 miles long, Mull is rich in legend and folklore, a land of ghosts, monsters, and the wee folk. Over open fires that burn on cold winter evenings, the talk is of myths and ancient times. The island is wild and mountainous, characterized by sea lochs and sandy bays.

Unlike some of the islands of the Inner Hebrides, already considered, getting to Mull is easy. It's best reached on a car-ferry service from Oban, the trip taking 45 minutes. For times of departure, contact **Caledonian MacBrayne,** The Ferry Terminal (tel. 0631/62285), Oban. It's a roll-on/roll-off type operation for your car.

Many visitors come over just for the day, but that is not doing Mull justice, as there is much to see once you arrive, as any Muilleach would tell you (that's the name for the local inhabitants).

Accommodations have greatly increased in number in recent years, but you should always arrive with a reservation to protect yourself. That is doubly true at the time of the Mull Highland Games, held annually in July and filled with all the traditional events such as bagpipes, caber-tossing, and dancing. Another most popular time to visit is for the Tour of Mull Rally, held in early October of every year. First run in 1969, it has been an attraction ever since. Motorsports lovers thrill to the idea of 120 miles of island roads, and twisting, tortuous ones they are at that.

If you come over, be sure to wear a raincoat as Mull is considered the wettest island in the Hebrides, a fact that upset Dr. Johnson, an early visitor. Actually Johnson's visit in 1773 could be considered late, as Mull has an ancient history. It was known to the classical Greeks. Its prehistoric past is recalled in forts, duns, and stone circles.

Many visitors consider Mull more beautiful than Skye, and I, of course, don't want to get involved in that controversy, as both islands are different, each with its many attractions. But to make Mull even more enticing, it can be used as a launching pad to explore the famed islands of Iona and Staffa, coming up in the next section.

VILLAGES AROUND THE ISLAND: Now let's move around the island a bit, checking out food and lodging choices and local sights.

Craignure

Pennygate Lodge (tel. 06802/333) is a former Georgian manse now run as a family guesthouse. The property, which overlooks the Sound of Mull, is centrally heated and offers a total of nine rooms, including two family apartments. All are spacious and well furnished. Prices, which include a full Scottish breakfast, range from £12 ($19.20) for single occupancy to £19 ($30.40) for doubles, with reductions for children. Pennygate Lodge is open all year.

Salen

Glenforsa Hotel (tel. 06803/377) is largely single story and of Norwegian pine log construction, in secluded grounds by the Sound of Mull and the River Forsa, known in late summer for its sea trout and salmon. Of its 16 twin/double rooms, most have private plumbing. Ably directed by Mr. and Mrs. Robert Scott Howitt, assisted by their son Tim and his wife, Frances, the hotel specializes in half-board rentals, charging from £26 ($41.60) to £29 ($46.40) per person for bed, dinner, and breakfast. The establishment's herb garden is visible through the plate-glass windows of the dining room. The bar serves an array of tempting pub food, with venison, trout, and salmon offered in season for guests and nonresidents alike. The hotel has a grass airstrip adjacent to which Dakotas and other private and charter planes can land from dawn to dusk. A car park is alongside.

Craig Hotel (tel. 06803/347) is a three-story house built beside a craig (rock) on which St. Columba is said to have stood when he preached to the people of Mull. For half board, Jim and Lorna McIntyre charge from £24 ($38.40) in a single and from £42 ($67.20) in a double or twin for one of their well-kept, simply furnished bedrooms, seven in all. Visitors usually discover a log fire burning in the bar/lounge. The pleasantly appointed dining room serves country-style meals on wooden tables, whenever possible using fresh produce.

After exploring the ruins of Aros Castle, a good luncheon stop is **The Puffer Aground Restaurant** (tel. 06803/389). The design of the restaurant is based on the old steamships that used to ply the River Clyde. Exhibitions of marine paintings are presented in summer. This is a licensed table-service restaurant. It is open Tuesday to Saturday from Easter to mid-May serving from noon to 2:30 p.m. and 6:30 to 9 p.m., then Monday to Saturday from May to mid-October with the same hours. It provides home-style typically Scottish cookery, and whenever possible fresh Mull produce is used. You get seafood-stuffed crêpes, fish casseroles, salads, and homemade pies. To begin your meal, try the local shellfish soup laced with brandy and cream, and for dessert, the traditional "baked sponge." You can get a lunch for £5 ($8) to £6 ($9.60) and dinner for £7 ($11.20) to £11 ($17.60). Next to the restaurant is a craft shop. Both the restaurant and shop are located in a row of country cottages along the roadside.

Tobermory

The capital of Mull, Tobermory (or Tobar Mhoire, "well of Mary," in Gaelic) is the best equipped in accommodations.

The **Mull Museum** has local exhibitions relating to the island. They're displayed in an old bakery building on Main Street, open June to September, Monday to Friday from 11 a.m. to 5 p.m., charging 50p (80¢) for adults and 15p (24¢) for children.

Harbour House, 59 Main St. (tel. 0688/2209), has as its motto the Gaelic for "sit, rest, and take a break in your journey." Derek and Kathy McAdam, delightful people, run this clean, friendly little hotel, charging £24 ($38.40) per person for half board. The rooms all have hot and cold water basins, and the meals are well prepared and filling. The establishment, right off the harbor, faces mountains covered with all shades of rhododendron in spring. Trout fishing, sea angling, and pony trekking are available locally.

The **Tobermory Hotel,** 53 Main St. (tel. 0688/2091). Michael Ratcliffe and his charming wife, Christine, lived in various parts of the world when he worked as an aviator and helicopter pilot. Both of them graduated from a hotel management course before investing in what is now my favorite little hotel in Tobermory. It's on the edge of the colorful port in a relatively plain-faced building. Inside, however, a series of often sun-washed sitting rooms are alive with fresh flowers (shipped in frequently from Glasgow), plush sofas, and Indonesian batiks. Each of the 15 bedrooms has been overhauled into a stylish refuge. Only a few units have private bath, and there are adequate public facilities scattered among the labyrinthine upper hallways. B&B costs from £17 ($27.20) per person, with half board going for £23 ($36.80) per person daily. With a private bath, the daily charge goes up £3 ($4.80) per person daily. The Ratcliffes engage three very good chefs, who prepare an excellent three-course dinner for £8 ($12.80) per person, with coffee and after-dinner mints included. Nonresidents visiting Tobermory for the day might also want to stop in to enjoy a bountiful lunchtime buffet at noon.

The Ratcliffes have an added attraction they call the alter ego to the hotel: a sailing yacht, *Sea Topaz,* a hotel afloat. Daily at 5:30 p.m. visitors are welcomed aboard to cruise the waters of the Sound of Mull. Later, dinner is served aboard when the boat is anchored. Comfortable cabins permit passengers to sleep aboard, have breakfast the next morning, and then return to Tobermory. The Tobermory Hotel is in operation from early April to the end of October.

Ulva House (tel. 0688/2044). David and Joy Woodhouse are the owners of this black-and-white Victorian house set on a hill above a sweeping expanse of terraced lawn. Its two stories and jutting bay windows shelter a handful of comfortable bedrooms, none of which has private bath. Each, however, is stylishly furnished. Residents appreciate the fires that burn in the neo-Victorian sitting rooms, as well as the well-prepared food served in the panoramic dining room. The Woodhouses delight in their unusual cuisine, including a wide array of both Scottish and continental specialties. Half board costs from £26 ($41.60) per person, with B&B going at £18 ($28.80) per person. Children under 12 sharing a room with their parents pay half the adult rate. Some of the bedrooms open onto wide-angled views of a forest-ringed loch. Land-Rover expeditions are offered to see the eagles, otters, and red deer that make the island their home. You can rent binoculars for £2 ($3.20) per day.

Staffa Cottages and Guest House (tel. 0688/2464). The rambling stone facade of this family-run guesthouse is accented with Victorian-style gables. It lies a short walk from the harborfront, within a sheltered garden alive with flowering plants. The owners offer five guest bedrooms, none with private bath, along with a comfortably stone-trimmed reading and TV lounge. The home-style meals include generous pieces of salmon as well as local venison and game on occasion. B&B is from £11.50 ($18.40) per person a night, and half board costs from £19 ($30.40) per person. Guests are accepted all year.

Gannet's Restaurant, 25 Main St. (tel. 0688/2203), enjoys a quayside setting and is one of the best of the independent restaurants operating in this colorful port. Mike and Jan Fisher, your hosts, serve lunch and dinner seven days a week from noon to 2:30 p.m. and 6 to 10 p.m. You get the freshest of seafood, much of it caught locally, along with fresh salads, tender and juicy steaks, and some fine vegetable dishes, finished off by creamy desserts. During the day you might stop in for sandwiches and fresh coffee. Meals cost from £10 ($16) at night.

Dervaig

Considered the most charming village of Mull, Dervaig or "The Little Grove" lies an eight-mile drive west from Tobermory. A Maclean built the town in the closing year of the 18th century.

Today it is known for its **Mull Little Theatre** (tel. 06884/267). Founded in 1966, it seats 40 viewers which, according to the *Guinness Book of World Records,* makes it the smallest professional theater in Great Britain. The little theater group tours during the winter but comes home in summer for the season. See local posters for details of its latest productions. The theater was installed in what had been an old barn.

From Dervaig, you can take cruises to the lonely **Treshnish Isles,** a sanctuary for seabirds and seals. These islands form a group unto themselves, including Fladda (is flatter) and Lunga (is longer), along with the well-named Dutchman's Cap or Bac Mor.

FOOD AND LODGING: Small and exclusive, the **Druimnacroish Country House Hotel** (tel. 06884/274) is well worth the splurge. In Bellart Glen, this stone house owes its personality and charm to Wendy and Donald Maclean. It is the only hotel built, owned, and run by a Maclean on the island. Handsomely furnished and well appointed, the hotel now occupies what had once been listed as a "ruin" on an ordnance survey map. They attract an international coterie of guests to their seven beautifully furnished rooms which are available from April to October. Each has its private bath. As you enter your private room, you'll find a welcoming bottle of Tobermory whisky (a miniature, but a thoughtful gesture nevertheless). Guests book in here on the half-board plan, costing from £48 ($76.80) per person. Wendy is a superb cook, and you get not only produce from their three-acre garden, but some of the finest lamb, Angus steak, venison, and salmon that Scotland has to offer. One reader wrote, "I could cover a page about the gourmet quality of the food so graciously served by Donald. Also this is the only hotel where I could walk barefoot on clean carpets."

Bellachroy (tel. 06884/225) is a small hotel, consisting of eight double rooms. It remains open all year, welcoming visitors and charging them £19.50 ($31.20) per person nightly for a comfortable bed, a hearty Scottish breakfast the next morning, and a big dinner that evening. The Ballachroy is run by Andrew and Anne Arnold and is situated in one of the most beautiful parts of the Western Isles. Salmon and trout loch and river fishing are available nearby. Calgary Sands is five miles away and a golf course is eight miles distant at Tobermory.

Bunessan

In the center of the Ross of Mull, the southwestern section, you'll come across this hamlet on the way to the Iona ferry.

Argyll Arms Hotel (tel. 06817/240). This 200-year-old inn sits on the main road immediately opposite the harborfront. Anda and Helen Campbell are the island-born owners who have embarked on a campaign of tasteful renovations. In many ways the Argyll Arms is the social center of the village. Anda plays the accordion in the Scottish band that appears three times a week in summer in the hotel's lounge. There's also a pub on the premises, where a coal-burning fireplace takes the chill off. A steep staircase with a corkscrew-style iron balustrade leads up to a dozen comfortably furnished bedrooms, each without private bath. B&B costs £13 ($20.80) per person, and an à la carte menu is served for dinner, going for around £7 ($11.20).

Fionnphort

Lying at the western tip of the Ross of Mull, Fionnphort is a tiny port that sees a lot of traffic. This is where the road ends and regular ferry passage is available across the mile-long Sound of Iona to the Isle of Iona, one of the most visited attractions in Scotland (see the next section). Iona is clearly visible from Fionnphort. Less than two miles to the south is the tidal island of Erraid, where David Balfour had adventures in Stevenson's *Kidnapped*.

Acheban House (tel. 06817/205). This Georgian-style pink house could easily be located in Bermuda, except for the 5,000-year-old standing stone at the edge of the driveway. The house was built in 1820 for the vicar of a local church. He moved away when the church he served was deconsecrated and converted into a barn. Today a visitor is likely to be greeted with an open fire burning in the residents' lounge. The view from many of the windows is of a freshwater loch. The charge is from £18 ($28.80) per person daily for half board. B&B costs from £11 ($17.60) per person. They have five comfortable rooms—none with bath—to rent to guests between December and October. Acheban House lies about half a mile from the landing dock for the ferry to Iona. Translated from the Gaelic, the name of the establishment means "white fields."

Keel Row (tel. 06817/458). This home-style restaurant is within walking distance of the ferryboat terminal. The view from the restaurant's large windows encompasses the abbey, whose stone walls are almost camouflaged by the rocky shore of nearby Iona. Norman and Joyce Salkeld are the friendly owners of this simple establishment. There's a tiny bar near the entrance, along with a display case of home-baked pastries, including (usually) a temptingly delicious deluxe apple crumble. You select a seat at a series of modern thick wooden tables. Local salmon steak, served with lemon and salad, is offered every day, along with a kettle of homemade soup, omelets, steak casserole, rainbow trout, scallops in white wine, and other seafood. Full meals cost from £6 ($9.60). The restaurant is open from noon to 11 p.m. daily in season.

The **Pier House** (tel. 06817/279) is at the water's edge, with an excellent view of Iona. Mrs. Jean McLellan is a charming proprietor and makes guests feel like part of the family. She shares her living room with TV with guests staying here. The price for B&B is £8.50 ($13.60) per person, or you can take half board for £13 ($20.80) per person nightly. The evening meal is well prepared and tasty. The ferries for Iona and Staffa are just across the road from the house.

SIGHTS AND ACTIVITIES: Mull has a varied scenery, with many waterfalls. Its highest peak is **Ben More** at 3,169 feet, but it also has many flat areas as well. It is rich in wildlife, including roe deer, golden eagles, polecats, seabirds, and feral goats.

Guarding the bay (you'll see it as you cross on the ferry) is **Duart Castle,** restored right before World War I and once the seat of the fiery Macleans, who shed much blood in and around the castle during their battles with the Lords of the Isles. In the bay—somewhere—lies the *Florencia,* a Spanish galleon that went down laden with treasure. Many attempts have been made to bring it up, but so far all of them have failed.

To the southeast, near Salen, are the ruins of **Aros Castle,** once the stronghold of the Lords of the Isles, the MacDonalds. Its ruins date from the 14th century, and it was last occupied in the 17th century.

On the far south coast at Lochbuie, **Moy Castle** has a water-filled dungeon. The wild countryside of Mull was the scene of many of David Balfour's adventures in *Kidnapped* by Robert Louis Stevenson.

If you're driving along any of the single-track roads of Mull, remember to take your time and let the sheep and cattle cross.

Mull attracts sports lovers, many of whom can be seen in summer at one of its sandy beaches, including one at Calgary whose name was later used for a famous Canadian city.

There are two nine-hole **golf courses.** The Western Isles Golf Course at Tobermory dates from the 1930s, and is said to have possibly the best views of any golf course in the world. A newer course, flat and tight, opened in 1980 at Craignure.

Sea fishing and river **fishing** are also popular on Mull where anglers seek out salmon and three kinds of trout: rainbow, sea, and brown. The trout is found in the fast-flowing rivers and hill lochs of the island. Some sportsmen take to sea in pursuit of sharks and monster skate. Stalking, hiking, and hill walking are other pursuits for the fit.

The Major Sights

Torosay Castle at Craignure (tel. 06802/421) is a Victorian mansion constructed in the mid-19th century by David Bryce, a famous Scottish architect. In his early years Churchill was a frequent visitor. It is set in gardens designed at the turn of the century by Sir Robert Lorimer. One writer said that a visit here is like returning to "the Edwardian age of leisure," and so it is. To the surprise of hundreds of visitors, the armchairs are labeled "Please sit down" instead of "Please keep off." This is very much a family place, home to four generations. It is the only castle and garden in private occupation open daily to the public in the western Highlands. The castle has family portraits by such famous artists as Sargent, along with wildlife pictures. It has numerous exhibits to intrigue its visitors, including evidence for the Loch Ness monster. It's like browsing through a scrapbook of 100 years of family history. Later you can wander through 11 acres of Italian-style terraced gardens, including a water garden with shrubs that grow in the Gulf Stream climate, along with a Japanese garden and life-size figures by Antonio Bonazza. You can enjoy extensive views of the Appin coastline from Ben Nevis to Ben Cruachen. It is open daily from 10:30 a.m. to 5:30 p.m. from the first of May until the end of September. Admission is £1.50 ($2.40) for adults and 90p ($1.44) for children.

Duart Castle (tel. 06802/309), off the A849 on the eastern point of Mull, dates from the 13th century and was the home of the Maclean Clan. An imposing and majestic structure, it was sacked in 1691 by the Dukes of Argyll in retaliation for the Macleans' having supported the Stuarts in 1715 and 1745. It was allowed to fall into ruins. However, Sir Fitzroy Maclean, the 26th chief of the clan and the grandfather of the present occupant, began restoration in 1911, spending a considerable fortune. It was his ambition since he was a boy to see his ancestral home restored. At the age of 76 he began restoration. He lived until he was 102 so he could enjoy it. Many relics of clan history are found inside. Visitors can wander about, taking in such rooms as the Banqueting Hall which is in the keep, the great tower that is the heart of the castle. The castle is open May to September from 10:30 a.m. to 6 p.m., charging £1.80 ($2.88) for adults and £1 ($1.60) for children under 14.

The **Old Byre Heritage Centre,** near Dervaig, houses one of the most charming museums you could hope to find. A series of tableaux with life-size figures recapture the atmosphere of life on Mull during the second half of the 19th century. The scenes become alive with an audio dramatization featuring the voices of local people, many of whom helped in the original construction of the tableaux. The performance, which takes half an hour, tells the story of the harsh existence of the crofters evicted from their land in the Land Clearances. The museum is open daily from 10:20 a.m. to 5 p.m. from Easter to October. Admission is £1 ($1.60) for adults, 50p (80¢) for children. There is a gift shop and a tea room on the premises does light lunches, home-baked bread, and cakes. For more information, telephone 06884/229.

On the Ross of Mull, as you proceed to the southwestern corner of the island in the direction of the ferry to Iona, you will see a sign pointing south to the little village of Carsaig. The most adventurous may want to go on a three-mile hike from here to the **Carsaig Arches,** a group of tunnels formed by the sea in the basaltic rock. Along the way you'll pass **Nuns' Cave,** with strange carvings. It is said that sisters chased out of Iona at the time of the Reformation found refuge in this cave.

Another attraction lies opposite the Ross of Mull on the northern rim of Loch Scridain. Called **"The Burg,"** it is only for the stout of foot and heart. However, if you're insistent on following the trail of Dr. Johnson and Boswell, then you'll go. The Burg lies five miles west on a track road from the B8035. The trail to it is extremely rough and requires boots. At the extremity of this Ardmeanach peninsula—an area appropriately called "The Wilderness"—stands a fossil tree, **MacCulloch's Tree,** said to be 50 million years old. Standing 40 feet tall and about five feet broad, it was trapped in the flow of lava. The tree is named after the geologist who discovered it in 1819. The tree is visited only at half tide on a falling tide. To do so otherwise is to find yourself cut off for hours at a time along a turbulent shore.

Other athletes seek out **MacKinnon's Cave,** Dr. Johnson's "greatest natural marvel," which lies north along the coast. You can leave your car at Balmeanach Farm, then you must walk about a mile to the mouth of the cave across wet slippery boulders in part and through some murky mud. The cave is deeper than the more famed Fingal's Cave at Staffa. It is another setting for the old tale of the Piper and the hairless dog. The cave can only be entered when the tide is right, and torches are used to penetrate the blackness.

Mull Railway

Even passengers who arrive on Mull with their car might want to take an excursion on the only passenger railway in the Hebrides. It was inaugurated in 1983, and its puffing engine and narrow-gauge tracks give the impression of a frontier-style excursion into the past. The tracks begin at the Old Pier in Craignure, running 1½ miles to Torosay Castle and its famous gardens. Some of the engines are powered by steam, others by diesel. Regardless of the mode of power, the view remains one of unspoiled mountains, glens, and seaside. Otters, eagles, and deer can sometimes be seen in the course of the 20-minute journey.

Trains operate between early April and late September. The most frequent service occurs between June and mid-September when service begins weekdays at 10:40 a.m. and on weekends at 11:20 a.m. Most visitors use the train as an opportunity to spend a few hours to explore Torosay Castle before returning to the ferryboat at Craignure. One-way fares are 90p ($1.44) for adults and 70p ($1.12) for children. A special round-trip ticket is available for families of two parents and two children, costing £2.25 ($3.60).

For more information, call the **West Highland Railway Co.** in Craignure (tel. 06802/494; 06803/389-472 off-season).

9. Iona and Staffa

A remote, low-lying, and treeless island, Iona lies off the southwestern coast of Mull across the Sound of Iona. It is only 1 mile by 3½ miles in size. It is accessible only by passenger ferry from the Island of Mull (cars must remain on Mull). The ferry to Iona is run by local fishermen, and service is very informal, depending in large part on the weather.

Staffa, with its famous musical cave, is a 75-acre island in the Inner Hebrides, lying to the west of Mull. For transportation to Staffa, see below.

IONA: Someone once said, "When Edinburgh was but a barren rock and Oxford but a swamp, Iona was famous." It has been known as a place of spiritual power and pilgrimage for centuries. It was the site of the first Christian settlement in Scotland.

Since 1695 the island was owned by the Dukes of Argyll, but the 12th duke was forced to sell to pay $1 million in real estate taxes owed since 1949. The island was purchased by Sir Hugh Fraser, the former owner of Harrods and other stores. He secured Iona's future and made it possible for money raised by the National Trust for Scotland to be turned over to the trustees of the restored abbey.

Food and Lodging

Most of the islanders live by crofting and fishing. In addition, they supplement their income by taking in paying guests in season, usually charging very low or at least fair prices. You can, of course, check into the hotels recommended below, but a stay here in a private home may be an altogether rewarding travel adventure. If you don't stay on Iona, you must catch one of the ferries back to Mull, and they rarely leave after 5 p.m.

Accommodations are extremely limited, although there is the **St. Columba Hotel** (tel. 06817/304), which stands right outside the village, in the vicinity of the cathedral. It offers a total of 20 simply furnished rooms, two of which have private bath. The half-board rate ranges from £24 ($38.40) to £28 ($44.80) per person. The food is good, especially the fish dishes, but remember that dinner is served promptly at 7 p.m. People turn in early on Iona. Try to get a room overlooking the sea, but know that it's virtually impossible to secure an accommodation here in August without a reservation made well in advance. Guests are received from the first of April to mid-October.

The **Argyll Hotel** (tel. 06817/334) is a pleasant and friendly hotel well run by Mrs. Fiona Menzies, who welcomes modern-day pilgrims and houses them well. Her 19-bedroom hotel stands in the village overlooking the Sound of Iona and Mull in the distance. Her rooms are pleasantly and attractively furnished, and eight contain private baths. Depending on the plumbing, the rate in a single is £26 ($41.60) to £31 ($49.60), a double going for £24 ($38.40) to £30 ($48) per person for dinner, bed, and breakfast. VAT is included. You get good home-cooking and baking, and vegetarian meals are available. In summer, vegetables are home-grown, and there is a nice selection of wines. The hotel is licensed to serve alcoholic drinks to residents.

Seaview Cottage (tel. 06817/373) is the third house you approach from the Iona jetty. With a white facade, it has very thick stone walls, at least 100 years old. Today, modernized and cozy, it offers one comfortably furnished twin and one double room, neither of which has a private bath. Mrs. Norah Kirkpatrick charges from £10 ($16) per person for B&B. No evening meal is served, but the kindly Mrs. Kirkpatrick will direct visitors to either of the hotel restaurants or a nearby coffeeshop for meals. Guests are accepted only from Easter to October. Her husband, David, usually runs daily boat excursions to Fingal's Cave.

Staying at Iona Abbey

Some visitors consider a visit to Iona the highlight of their trip to Scotland. Aside from viewing it as an unusual historical and archeological site, many persons come back with a renewed interest in both their faith and the power of religion. The Iona Community is an ecumenical religious group who maintain seminars and a communal lifestyle near the ancient abbey. They offer full board and accommodation to visitors who want to share in the community's daily lifestyle. The only ordained members of the group are its two "wardens," each of whom is a member of the Church of Scotland.

During the peak summer months between June and September the community leads a series of discussion seminars, each of which lasts a week, stretching from Saturday to Saturday. The cost of a week's full board during one of these seminars is £96.60 ($154.56) per person. During one of the off-season months, except at Easter, guests can share in the daily life of the community if they stay for a minimum of three nights. Full board costs from £16 ($25.60) per person. Guests are expected to contribute a small portion of their day, about 30 minutes, to the execution of some kind of household chore. The daily schedule involves a wakeup call at 7:30 a.m., communal breakfast at 8 a.m., a morning religious service, and plenty of unscheduled time for conversation, study, and contemplation. Up to 50 guests can be accommodated at one time in bathless, bunk-bedded twin rooms. For further details, phone 06817/404.

For day visitors, the community leads tours through the rebuilt Benedictine abbey, maintains a gift and book shop, and runs a coffeeshop. Each is open daily from 10 a.m. to 4:30 p.m. (the coffeeshop is closed on Sunday). The community is closed for two weeks at the end of October, for two weeks around New Year's, and at Easter (possibly in January and February).

The Sights

Iona is known for its **"Graves of the Kings."** A total of 48 Scottish kings, including Macbeth and his victim, Duncan, were buried on Iona, as were four Irish kings and eight Norwegian kings.

Today the island attracts nearly 1,000 visitors a week in high season. Most of them come here mainly to see the **Abbey of Iona,** part of which dates back to the 13th century. But they also visit relics of the settlement founded there by St. Columba in 563, from which Celtic Christianity spread through Scotland. The abbey has been restored by an ecumenical group called the Iona Community, which conducts workshops on Christianity, sponsors a youth camp, offers tours of the abbey, and leads a seven-mile hike to the various holy and historic spots on the island each Wednesday. It is possible to stay at the abbey.

There are many visitors to the abbey, but the atmosphere on the island remains very rare, peaceful, and spiritual. It's possible to walk off among the sheep that wander freely everywhere to the top of Dun-I, a small mountain, and contemplate the ocean and the landscape as if you were the only person on earth.

One reader, Capt. Robert Haggart, Laguna, California, described his experience this way: "I was enchanted by the place. It really has a mystic atmosphere—one *feels* something ancient here, something spiritual, sacred, long struggles, and wonderment about the strength of religion."

The best way to get around Iona is to walk. If that's not for you, you can take horse-drawn carriage tours (for information about these, phone 06814/230).

STAFFA: The attraction of this island is **Fingal's Cave,** a lure to visitors for more than 200 years and the inspiration for music, poetry, paintings, and prose. Its Gaelic name, An Uamh Ehinn, means "musical cave." The place is unique in that it is the only known such formation in the world with basalt columns. Over the centuries, the sea has carved a huge cavern in the basalt, leaving massive hexagonal columns to create what Queen Victoria described, after a visit in the 19th century: "The effect is splendid, like a great entrance into a vaulted hall. The sea is immensely deep in the cave. The rocks under water were all colors— pink, blue and green." The sound of the crashing waves and swirling waters caused Mendelssohn to write the "Fingal's Cave Overture." Turner painted the cave on canvas, and Keats, Wordsworth, and Tennyson all praised it in their poetry.

The island of Staff has not been inhabited for more than 160 years. Visitors can still explore the cave. Boat trips go there. If you're on Mull or if you've crossed to Iona, you can take boat trips costing £4.50 ($7.20) for adults and £3 ($4.80) for children. You're taken to the rocky shores of Staffa. After docking, visitors are led along the basalt path and into Fingal's Cave. Inside, the noise of the pounding surf is deafening. Chances are you'll be taken over by an experienced Hebridean entrepreneur, seaman David R. Kirkpatrick. Weather permitting, he operates an open boat built in 1982 with canvas protection from the salt spray. The boat runs from Iona every day at 9:45 a.m., stopping at Fionnphort, Mull, just across the channel, at 10 a.m., then proceeding to Staffa for explorations of Fingal's Cave. Mr. Kirkpatrick leads passengers on foot to the cave. Time on Staffa is usually one hour and 15 minutes. Reservations are important: phone Mrs. Norah Kirkpatrick at tel. 06817/373. Rubber-soled shoes and warm clothing are recommended for this excursion.

Another cave, **Clamshell Cave,** can also be visited, but only at low tide, and one appropriately named **Boat Cave** is accessible only by water.

10. Isle of Colonsay

The most remote of the islands of Argyll, Colonsay is separated by 15 miles of sea from Mull. It lies 25 miles off the mainland of Argyll. With its sister, a tidal neighbor, Oransay, Colonsay shares some of the same characteristics of Iona, Tyree, and Coll. To the west it faces nothing but the open Atlantic. Only a lighthouse stands between Colonsay and Canada.

A ferry, operated by Caledonian MacBrayne, sails between Oban and Colonsay three times a week. The 37-mile crossing takes 2½ hours. The island is more tranquil than such touristy islands as Mull and Skye because it does not attract "day trippers" owing to its transportation situation.

FOOD AND LODGING: Dating from the 18th century, the **Isle of Colonsay Hotel** (tel. 09512/316) is considered the most isolated hotel in Great Britain. Kevin and Christa Byrne are the creative forces who direct the activities here. Sitting above the harbor, close to the ferryboat landing, it is the true social center of Colonsay. Its solidly constructed gables and chimneys rise above its surrounding herb and vegetable gardens at a point within five miles of practically everything on the island. Many guests check in here for close-up views of the island's abundant flora and fauna. The Byrnes will provide bicycles free to guests or drop them by courtesy car to go on rambles. All but three of the hotel's well-furnished bedrooms contains a private bath. Depending on the season, the hotel charges £23 ($36.80) to £33 ($52.80) per person for half board. Guests looking for self-contained cottages will find several lying away from the main building. Each has a combined living room and kitchen, a veranda, a double bedroom, an upper level with three single beds, and maid service. The cottages are suitable for up to six persons. Electricity (which is metered at cost) is not included in the weekly high-season rate, without meals, of £200 ($320) to £288 ($460.80).

A meal in the hotel's dining room is considered an event for the local residents, who appreciate the ambience of the cocktail lounge and the public bar. The Hebridean inn is licensed, serving food from noon to 1:30 p.m. and dinner at 7:30 p.m. A meal is likely to include a homemade soup, fresh mussels, trout, scallops, and prawns, with vegetables from the garden. Set dinners cost from £11.75 ($18.80).

SIGHTS: The island encompasses 20 square miles, its lands enjoying an equable climate because of the warming waters of the Gulf Stream. Plants do well here. It is estimated that there are some 500 species of flora. These plants are best seen if you wander through the **gardens of Colonsay House.** These gardens are filled with rare rhododendrons, magnolias, and eucalyptus, even palm trees. Colonsay House, seat of the laird, Lord Strathcona, is not open to the public, however. It dates from 1722.

Plants aren't the only attraction. Wildlife abounds, including golden eagles, falcons, gray seals, otters, and wild goats with elegant horns and long shaggy hair.

Prehistoric forts, stone circles, and single standing stones attest to the antiquity of Colonsay, which has been occupied since the Stone Age.

All parts of the island can be explored along its single-track roads. Many visitors prefer to rent a bicycle, and it's also possible to bring your car over on the ferry from Oban. And if you want to leave Colonsay, you can also rent sailing dinghies and rowboats. If you sail around the island, you'll be following a grand tradition. The Vikings did the same thing. They also had several ship burials on the island. Some of the sites have been excavated, but, regrettably, the ships had decayed. Back on the island, you can enjoy a game of golf at an 18-hole course.

The little island of Oransay was named for Oran, a disciple of St. Columba. It is joined at low tide by the Strand. Visitors wade across the sands during a two-hour period. The ancient monastic ruins seen here date from the 6th century, and tradition has it that they were founded by St. Columba. You can see some splendid tombstones of carved stone. The most notable is the Great Cross of Prior Colin, from the early 16th century.

Back at your hotel, if you're lucky you might join in a ceilidh on a summer-time evening.

THE OUTER HEBRIDES

You may at first feel you've come to a lunar landscape where there is a sense of infinite time. The Outer Hebrides are a fascinating arc of islands, with much to see and do there, ranging from visiting Barra, "the garden of the Hebrides" with 1,000 varieties of flowers, to exploring North Uist with its fish-filled lochs.

The character of these sparsely populated islands is unique, quite different from the chain of the Inner Hebrides that we have just visited. The string of the Outer Hebridean islands lie some 30 to 40 miles off the northwest coast of Scotland. The main islands to visit are Lewis and Harris (part of the same island in spite of their different names), North Uist, Benbecula, South Uist, and Barra. The archipelago also takes in three very minor offshore islands: Vatersay (Barra), Eriskay (South Uist), and Berneray (North Uist).

From the Butt of Lewis in the north to Barra Head in the south, the chain stretches for some 130 miles. Many golfers come here just to play golf on these far-northern courses, including one at Stornoway (Lewis) and at Askernish (South Uist). Anglers also come here to fish for salmon, brown trout, and sea trout among the fishing lochs found throughout the island chain.

Birdwatchers "flock" to the islands to see the habitats along cliffs, in peat bog, and farmland of the red-necked phalarope, the corncrake, the golden eagle, the Arctic skua, and the grayleg goose.

Deep in the heart of Gaeldom, the sound of Gaelic will be heard in the air. The gentle cadence of Gaelic is said to have been the language spoken in the Garden of Eden. Presbyterianism is still very strong here (so on Sunday, dress in black and behave yourself. In one B&B house, for example, TV-watching on Sunday is forbidden.) Before you go, you might read Compton Mackenzie's novel *Whisky Galore*.

The islands today, which knew two centuries of Viking invasions, are the retreat of many a disenchanted artist from the mainland. They come here, take over old crofters' cottages, and devote their lonely days to such pursuits as pottery making and weaving.

Much of the dim past can be seen on these islands, including a version of Stonehenge. But there can be joyful occasions as well. A good time to visit is in June and July when adults' and children's choirs compete for honors. You can attend these festivals celebrating Gaelic music and poetry along with piping.

Each of the main islands is equipped with accommodations for tourists (and reservations are important). Most of these places are small family-run guesthouses and hotels, and many are crofters' cottages that take in B&B guests, mainly in summer.

11. Lewis

The most northerly of the islands of the Outer Hebrides, and also the largest, Lewis is easily reached by ferryboat from Ullapool (see Chapter XI). The island was once known as "Lews," or more poetically, "the island of heather." The sweetness of the lamb grown here is said to come from their diet of heather.

The ferry comes into **Stornoway,** the capital of Lewis with a population of some 5,000 souls, making it the only real town in the Outer Hebrides. It is on the eastern side of the island. It is a land-locked harbor in which you can see gray seals along with fishing boats setting out. An airport, which also doubles as an RAF base, lies about 3½ miles from the center of Stornoway.

Lewis and Harris, as mentioned, form part of the same island, stretching for a combined length of some 95 miles. Lewis alone is about 60 miles long and from 18 to 28 miles across. Even though the whole world has heard of "Harris tweed," it might as well be called "Lewis tweed," as Stornoway has taken over the industry. There are some 600 weavers on the island, and one of the attractions of this rather bleak port is to visit a mill shop or a weaver's home, the latter probably a crofter's cottage.

Filled with marshy peat bogs, the landscape is relatively treeless, thanks in part to the Norse raider, Magnus Barelegs. Although Lewis used to have trees, Barelegs and his tree-burning Viking warriors left much of Lewis as bare as his shanks. Efforts at reforestation have been unsuccessful.

FOOD AND LODGING: The best hotel on Lewis—and a definite super splurge —is the **Caberfeidh Hotel,** Manor Park (tel. 0851/2604). Near the ferryboat terminal, it shelters guests from the chilly winds behind unadorned white walls that were designed like large building blocks in a contemporary arrangement of cubes. The location is convenient either if you arrive by ferryboat from Ullapool or fly into the Stornoway airport. The hotel is also the most expensive in the Outer Hebrides, but is considered well worth the cost.

Directed by Mr. Martin, it was built by a Mackenzie, who named it after the battle cry of that fighting clan. In Gaelic the name means "stag antlers." The decor includes an array of Mackenzie tartans and a collection of stags' heads. The lounge bar reverts to the Dark Ages for its decor. The bar itself is shaped like a Viking longship. The cocktail lounge, in a reversal, is furnished with a surprise touch of bamboo. Each of the comfortable bedrooms contains its own private shower or bath, radio, phone, TV, trouser press, and hairdryer. Singles rent for £50 ($80) with doubles costing from £63.25 ($101.20), with breakfast included. Half-board packages, which include all ferry charges, range from £120 ($192) for two nights. The dining room offers the best of local produce, fresh fish, especially trout and salmon, local beef and lamb, and scallops. Meals are savory and well prepared. The hotel is the site of summer musical fests called *ceilidhs,* drawing visitors to the entire town.

Seaforth Hotel, James Street (tel. 0851/2740) is one of the most modern hotels in the Outer Hebrides, contained within the unadorned cement and glass walls of this white-walled hotel. The 58 accommodations cost more than most of its nearby competitors, but many visitors to Lewis are willing to spend the extra money for better amenities in this far-northern clime. Each of the comfortable bedrooms contains a private bath or shower as well as a radio (a TV can also be provided). The public rooms have several full-size snooker tables, as well as a comfortable bar/lounge. There's even an in-house cinema whose films help to while away a cold winter night. Open throughout the year the hotel charges from £35 ($56) in a single and from £50 ($80) in a double. It's also possible to take the half-board arrangement at £39 ($62.40) to £43 ($68.80) per person daily. The dinner menu presents a satisfying array of choices, including heather-fed Lewis lamb, fresh salmon, scallops, and pheasant in season.

Caledonian Hotel, 6 South Beach (tel. 0851/2411), is a modern hotel that has undergone extensive renovation and refurbishing. The ten well-maintained bedrooms are centrally heated, and all have TV, radios, hot-beverage facilities, and hairdryers. Singles pay £18 ($28.80), and doubles cost £16 ($25.60) per person for B&B, with VAT included in the rates. Viking-style decor is used in the hotel, with battleaxes and swords offsetting the stonework, plaster, and varnished pine. The public bar and the more elite lounge are relaxing places to have a drink, and bar meals are served until 11 p.m. Entertainment is provided on weekends in season. The restaurant, overlooking the Stornaway Harbor, is open in summer, specializing in fish dishes.

Royal Hotel, Cromwell Street (tel. 0851/2109), a friendly and inviting little place, lies close to the street, near the waterfront and the heart of town. You'll find its three whitewashed stories across from Lews Castle. Windows are set with leaded panes of glass. On weekends you are likely to hear a ceilidh presented here. The rest of the time the public bar attracts local residents, including fishermen. There are tables for billiards, and pub lunches are offered at noon. In addition to functioning as one of the town's social centers, this hotel offers some of the most reasonably priced accommodations. Its 19 clean and comfortable bedrooms, each bathless, cost from £15.50 ($24.80) in a single and from £29 ($46.40) in a double, including breakfast.

County Hotel, Francis Street (tel. 0851/3250). Some of the details about this hotel's pub—the copper-plated foot railing, the cubbyhole beside the fireplace, the exposed wood—might be remembered after you leave. Since it's next door to the offices of a local newspaper, some of the editorial staff might be seen raising a mug next to yours. Many guests consider the hotel's locally patronized pub the heart and soul of the place, while others gravitate to the well-decorated reception area with open fires and oak paneling in the lounge bar. You'll find this hotel beneath a mansard roof on a street corner in the center of town. It contains only 11 rooms, each bathless, but there are adequate baths in the corridors. Rooms are comfortably furnished, ranging in price from £18.50 ($29.60) in a single and from £26 ($41.60) in a double, including breakfast.

Hebridean Guest House, Bayhead (tel. 0851/2268). Architecturally, this three-story house doesn't win any awards, but the quality of its Hebridean hospitality is among the best in town. Occupants of the four singles and the seven twins or doubles share three bathrooms with showers. For B&B, the rate is £10.50 ($16.80) to £11.50 ($18.40) per person nightly.

Park Guest House, 30 James St. (tel. 0851/2485). The entrance to the pleasantly enclosed front garden lies beneath an arch emblazoned in metal letters with the name of the hotel. Inside, the relatively ornate stone gables contain seven bedrooms, renting for £10 ($16) and up per person for B&B. Catherine and Roddy Afrin, the owners, offer an evening meal seven days a week using local produce wherever possible. Roddy is a trained chef. Meals cost £7.50 ($12), and they're excellent. The house has a TV lounge and a modernized kind of Edwardian nostalgia.

Tower Guest House, 32 James St. (tel. 0851/3150), occupies a street corner in a residential section of town. The design is Victorian, with an array of pseudo-feudal towers and crenellations. Only six of the bedrooms are rented to guests. Many visitors chose the half-board rate of £17 ($27.20) per person. B&B, available for latecomers, is £10.50 ($16.80) in a single and from £19 ($30.40) in a double.

Where to Eat in Stornoway

Restaurants are limited in number. Most guests dine at their hotels.

Asher Munzel, 42 Newton St. (tel. 0851/2145), is one of the leading independent restaurants. It is, in fact, the only Indian restaurant in the Western Isles. It also serves continental specialties. Licensed, it serves meals daily from 5 to 10 p.m. You can order tandoori dishes well spiced and tasty. The spices, well blended in all the dishes I've sampled, include garlic and cardamom. It's a good place for a quiet Indian meal, and you get polite service. The charge is from £10 ($16) for dinner.

During the day, if you want an inexpensive breakfast, lunch, snack, or high tea, head for **The Coffee Pot,** 5 Kenneth St. (tel. 0851/3270). It is an especially welcome haven when gales whip the sea spray through the streets of Stornoway, and nothing tastes better than a good cup of strong black coffee. You get home-baked goods, sandwiches, soups, and some hot dishes. Meals cost from £5 ($8), and service is from 7:30 a.m. to 7 p.m.

SIGHTS: After you've settled into your hotel, you may be ready to explore this unusual terrain. The major attraction lies to the west of Stornoway. There stands the Neolithic temple of Callanish, called the **Standing Stones of Callanish.** This unique cruciform setting of megaliths, at Callanish off the A858 16 miles west of Stornoway, is outranked in prehistoric archeological splendor only by Stonehenge on the lonely Salisbury Plain in England. From a circle of 13 stones, a road of 19 monoliths leads north. Branching off to the south, east, and west are rows of more stones. A tiny chambered tomb is inside the circle.

In the more immediate vicinity, you can visit **Lews Castle** (the old spelling), lying west of the harbor at Stornoway. Actually you can visit only the grounds since the castle, built in 1818 in Lady Lever Park, is not open to the public, as it is a technical college. Lord Leverhulme of Sunlight soap left the grounds to the public. You can wander among a stunning collection of rhododendrons—at their best in May—which were planted by Lady Matheson.

At Amol, 15 miles northwest of Stornoway, you can visit the **Lewis Black House,** a clachan or row of thatched houses that have been preserved to show visitors what a typical Hebridean dwelling looked like. The last inhabitants left in 1960. It's called Black House because it was believed that the smoke from the open peat fires was good for the thatched roof. Therefore the Leodhasach, as the islanders are called, built their houses with no chimneys so the smoke could go through the thatch. The house, with many of its original furnishings intact, was constructed without mortar. It is open from 9:30 a.m. to 7 p.m. Monday to Saturday in summer, closing at 4 p.m. in winter. Closed Sunday. Admission is 50p (80¢) for adults, 25p (40¢) for children.

More of the old way of life can be seen at the **Shawbost Folk Museum** which has Hebridean artifacts. You can also see a Viking watermill that has been re-stored. The museum is admission free, but a donation would be appreciated. It is found along the A858, 19 miles northwest of Stornoway. It is open April to November, Monday to Saturday from 10 a.m. to 6 p.m.

For the serious student of history, more ancient monuments can be seen on Lewis. The **Steinacleit Cairn and Stone Circle** are the ruined fragments of what was once a rather substantial house built in the mists of prehistory. The house was found beneath huge layers of peat. It lies at the southern end of Loch an Duin, Shader, 12 miles north of Stornoway. It can be visited throughout the day for no fee.

The **Clach an Trushal** at Balanthrushal, Barvas, is the largest single mono-lith in northern Scotland. It is 19 feet high and six feet wide. Near this same site was the battlefield of the last battle fought between the Macaulays of Uig and the Morrisons of Ness.

Dun Carloway Broch is a broch tower, about 30 feet high, left over from the Iron Age. It stands along the A858, 15 miles west and northwest of Stornoway. It can be visited throughout the day for no fee.

At Arnish, near Stornoway, is the **Bonnie Prince Charlie monument,** mark-ing the site of another one of his hiding places.

At Dun Borranish, near the village of Ardroil, the famous Lewis Chess-men were discovered in 1831 when they were dug up outside Uig Sands. Made of walrus tusks, they now form an outstanding exhibit in the British Museum in London (also in Edinburgh). If you're a chessplayer, you may want to purchase a reproduction set in Lewis.

Ui Church, at Aignish, off the A866 two miles east of Stornoway, is now in ruins. Pronounced "eye," it was the burial grounds of the Macleods of Lewis. You can see carved tombs. The ruins are on the Eye Peninsula, also known as "The Point."

At Ness, in the direction of that northerly outpost, the Butt of Lewis, is **St. Moluag's Church,** which is under the auspices of the Scottish Episcopal church. You can attend a service here every second Sunday of the month at 3 p.m. The chapel, known in Gaelic as Teampull Mhor or "big temple," is circa 12th century. It was founded by Olav the Black during the Norse occupation of the island. The original church is said to have been founded in the 6th century by a companion of St. Columba.

12. Harris

Harris, to the south of Lewis, might share the same island with Lewis, but it is different in geography. For example, if Lewis struck you as an enormous peat bog, you'll find Harris more ruggedly dramatic in scenery. North Harris, for example, is full of mountains, dominated by the Clisham, which at 2,600 feet is the highest mountain peak in the Outer Hebrides. Harris may not have as many ancient relics as Lewis, but, most visitors agree, the mountains, beaches, and scenic vistas make up for that lack. Explorers can seek out the beaches in the west, either for swimming or camping, or go to the bays in the east which are ideal for fishing and sailing.

The local people, some 3,000 in all, are called Hearach, and they too are different from the people of Lewis, even speaking with a different accent. If you've arrived in Lewis, you can drive to Harris, as the two "islands" are connected by a small single-track road, going from pass to pass. As you go along the rugged terrain, you might see a fell walker. Occasionally, you'll meet up with another car. If you do, "passing places" have been provided. In any case, you should drive slowly, because sheep might suddenly scamper in front of your wheels. The distance from Stornoway, the capital of Lewis, to Tarbert, the capital of Harris, is 38 miles.

Most visitors, however, prefer not to come overland. From the mainland of Scotland, they journey first to the Isle of Skye. From the little port of Uig on Skye, a ferryboat heads for Harris daily except Sunday. Even in the busiest season Harris is not overrun with visitors, as is Skye or Mull in the Inner Hebrides. From Harris you can also make connections to Lochmaddy on North Uist. This is the link the islanders of Harris have with their sister Outer Hebridean islands to the south.

Harris has long been known for its hand-weaving and tweed. However, as mentioned in the section on Lewis, that industry has now more or less passed to Stornoway. It is still possible to buy Harris tweed jackets in Harris. In summer you'll see them displayed on the walls of corrugated iron sheds along the road. You get very good prices here.

The main village of Harris is **Tarbert,** a one-street town. The island is bisected by two long sea lochs that meet at Tarbert, which is surrounded by rocky hills. Whatever you need in the way of supplies, you should pick them up here. Otherwise you'll be out of luck. If you're touring by private car, also fill up with "petrol" (gas) at Tarbert.

Ask at the information center about bus tours which are conducted in summer around Harris, and for an adventure, take the car-ferry that runs regularly across the sound to the little fishing community of Scalpay, an offshore island.

FOOD AND LODGING: You'll find accommodations in the capital of Tarbert, as well as in Scarista and Rodel.

At Tarbert

Harris Hotel, Ferry Terminal (tel. 0859/2154), has been a local landmark since it first accepted customers in 1904. Today it's one of the most popular and best-established places for eating, drinking, and sleeping in the Outer Hebrides. It's a lot like one of those inns that Johnson and Boswell might have sought if it had been there during their visit. It was built in the mid-1800s as a private house. Now its 20 comfortable bedrooms include 14 units with private bath. Each accommodation has hot and cold running water, lots of old-fashioned comfort, and a few modern amenities. Some family rooms are available, many looking out over the garden, one of the largest in Harris. Singles go for £17.25 ($27.60) and doubles for £15.65 ($25.04) to £18.65 ($29.84). Dinner is offered for £9.50 ($15.20) to £10.50 ($16.80), and the food is good and plentiful. This hotel contains the only pub in Tarbert, the social center of town, attracting many locals, including some "ghillies" who show guests who are here for fishing holidays how it's done. You can order pub grub at midday at the long, slender public bar. Customers receive personalized attention from the hotel's owners, Helen and John Murdo Morrison.

At Scarista

Scarista House (tel. 085985/238) is a lovely hotel on the A859, about 15 miles from Tarbert on the west coast of Harris. It was constructed long ago as a Georgian-style vicarage. Today its elegantly symmetrical facade is ringed with a stone wall and a sweeping vista of green turf and slate-gray water. A few of the summer guests enjoy an occasional bracing dip in the 55° water of nearby Scarista Beach. Others prefer to enjoy the well-stocked library.

Andrew and Alison Johnson are the creative forces behind the transformation of this building into a country-house hotel. Amid a setting of contemplative grace and frequently polished antiques, they serve the best breakfast in the Outer Hebrides. You'll enjoy freshly squeezed orange juice and a compote of fresh and dried fruits, along with porridge with cream and kippers from Lewis. This is only the beginning. These dishes are followed by Stornoway black pudding, bacon, sausage, and fresh eggs. This is accompanied by fresh herring rolled in oat flour and fried, as well as white pudding, made with suet, onions, spices, and oats. There's also fruit pudding, along with homemade whole-wheat bread and whole-wheat scones. If you plan to burn off this morning feast, a packed lunch will be provided. Most guests return to a spot near the fireplace of the hotel's beautifully appointed drawing room for a before-dinner drink. Alison supervises most of the cookery herself, turning out dinners of six courses. These rely on locally caught shellfish and heather-fed lamb among other ingredients. A full dinner costs from £16 ($25.60). Meals are served at 8 p.m. Half board costs £42 ($67.20) to £52 ($83.20) per person daily. Each of the seven handsomely decorated bedrooms has a private bath and central heating. The hotel is open from April to mid-October.

Staying at a Lighthouse

If you want the escapist's dream of the Outer Hebrides, you might find it at the **Eilean Glas Lighthouse** (tel. 085984/345) at Scalpay. Here Robert and Brenda Ford-Sagers, the managers, rent self-catering units in former lighthouse keepers' houses. They are stone, but modernized and fully equipped and furnished. These self-catering cottages are popular with groups of two to eight guests. Two date from 1824, one from around the turn of the century. Each has a modern kitchen and is a thick-walled refuge from the wild winds around it. All three sit 60 feet above the sea at the foot of a hill supporting the lighthouse. Rates depend on the season, ranging from £150 ($240) to £235 ($376) per week. It's also possible to stay here on a B&B arrangement. The cost is £15.50 ($24.80) per person in a bathless room, £18.50 ($29.60) per person with bath. A lighthouse was built here in 1789 to guide mariners in the Minch. The lightkeepers had a remote life, and so will you if you stay here, keeping company with the fisherfolk along with some seals, gannets, otters, cormorants, and a lot of birdlife.

If you don't want to stay here, you can enjoy a meal, costing from £8.50 ($13.60), in the restaurant overlooking the sea. Food is served whenever guests arrive. They can do so by taking the car ferry from Uig on Skye to Tarbert on Harris. They drive five miles to another ferryboat which takes you to Scalpay on Harris. This requires two waterborne excursions and lots of time. The Ford-Sagers will direct and guide you by phone in advance. Guests are received from March to October.

SIGHTS: Because of the lack of roads, you can't make a circular tour of Harris. However, using Tarbert as your base, you can set out in two major directions. One is northwest along the coastline of West Loch Tarbert, with the Forest of Harris to your north. The other is south from Tarbert, hugging the western coastal road along the Sound of Taransay, with Rodel as your final destination.

Taking the northwesterly route first, you come to an **Old Whaling Station** at Bunavoneadar. Norwegians set up a whaling station here in the early 20th century, but because of dwindling profits it was abandoned in 1930. Slipways and a chimney can still be seen.

Continuing north from here, along the B887, you will arrive at the **Amhuinnsuidhe Estate,** a Scottish baronial castle that was constructed by the Earl of Dunmore in 1868. Sir James Barrie stayed here while working on his novel *Mary Rose,* about a mysterious maid who disappeared into the mists. The river to the left has one of the most beautiful salmon leaps in Scotland.

The road beyond the castle continues to Hushinish Point. In addition to machair, the area around here in springtime becomes a bed of wildflowers. At Hushinish you can see the offshore little island of **Scarp,** which was once inhabited. Unlike most parts of the world, where towns are being created out of wildernesses, the reverse is the case in many parts of the Outer Hebrides. The population of Scarp, an island in point, has all gone. Sheep, however, graze here in summer.

In 1934 a German scientist attempted to send a packet of mail across the channel to Scarp by rocket. The rocket blew up on landing and the mail was damaged. But to this day a philatelist highly regards one of the "Scarp Rocket mail letters."

Returning to Tarbert, you can take the road south, the A859 (you can't miss it!). Some of the coastline of South Harris will remind you of the coastlines of Norway, with its sea lochs and "fjord fingers." The main road to Rodel is mostly two lane and well surfaced; however, if you take the east-coast road, you'll find it not only single track, but tortuous and winding.

Along the way you'll pass the Clach Mhicleoid, or standing stone. The locals call it **MacLeod's Stone.** This single monolith, placed above the Nisabost Sands, stands as a lonely sentinel at night, a silent witness to what it has seen over the centuries.

From here you can look out across the Sound of Taransay to the **island of**

Taransay which was named after St. Tarran. The island has several ancient sites, including the remains of St. Tarran's Chapel. Like Scarp, it was once populated, but now its grazing fields are turned over to sheep.

Continuing on the coastal road along the wild Atlantic—actually the Sound of Taransay—you'll see another ancient stone, the **Scarista Standing Stone.** But before reaching it you'll pass **Borve Lodge,** the former home of Lord Leverhulme, the soap tycoon who came here after his rejection by the people at Stornoway.

The road south passes the little promontory of Toe Head jutting out into the Atlantic. An ancient chapel, **Rudh'an Teampull,** stands here about three-quarters of a mile west of Northton and reached by a sand track. Many prehistoric sites were uncovered and excavated on the machair-studded tiny peninsula of Toe Head. Bone tools and Neolithic pottery were found, the earliest recorded habitations of the Western Isles.

The next hamlet you come to is **Leverburgh,** named after the soap magnate, Lord Leverhulme. He is credited with trying to bring the people of the area into the 20th century. That was back in 1923, but his efforts to rejuvenate the economy largely failed. From here you can take a small passenger ferry to North Uist and Berneray. You can also visit the An Clachan Centre at Leverburgh, where you can purchase many items of local craftware.

Finally, you drive east until you reach Rodel, where **St. Clement's Church** stands high in the village. Overlooking Loch Rodel, this church is one of the most important monuments in the Western Isles. Cruciform in plan, it has a western tower, a nave, and two cross aisles. Some of the masonry work in freestone is similar to that used at Iona Abbey. The church is believed to have been built around the closing years of the 15th century or the very early years of the 16th century. There are three tombs inside, including one that is considered among the finest in the islands. The tomb contains part of the MacLeod coat-of-arms.

In the Sound of Harris, separating Harris from North Uist, lie the islands of Ensay, Killegray, and Pabbay. Once they were populated, but now they have been turned over to grazing sheep.

13. North Uist

Standing stones and chambered cairns tell of a history-rich past on this old island—a real bogland—where hardy crofters try to wrestle a living from both a turbulent sea and an often disappointing land. North Uist is one of the least-frequented islands in the Outer Hebrides. That's a pity, because there is much beauty here, as you wander (usually alone) inspecting antiquity, as reflected by its brochs, duns, wheelhouses, and stark monoliths, all left by the island's prehistoric inhabitants.

The population of North Uist is about 2,000 persons, and the island is about 12½ miles wide by 35 miles at its longest point. North Uist is served by a circular road, most often the single-track variety with passing places, and there are several feeder routes branching east and west. Road surfaces are usually good.

The main village—you could hardly call it a town—is **Lochmaddy,** on the eastern shoreline. Whatever you need (if it's available in North Uist at all), you are likely to find it here. That could include everything from a post office to a petrol station.

Lochmaddy is the site of the terminal for the ferry from Uig on the Isle of Skye as well as from Tarbert on Harris, just previewed. Most visitors from the Scottish mainland use the connection through Skye. A small private ferry also runs from Newton Ferry, north of Lochmaddy, to Leverburgh on Harris. The latter is not a car-ferry, but allows passengers to board with small motorcycles or bicycles. A small vehicular ferry will also take you from Newton Ferry to the little offshore island of Berneray, referred to in the introduction to the Outer Hebrides. In keeping with the strict religious tradition of these islands, the ferry doesn't operate on Sunday, and neither, seemingly, does anything else. Talk about quiet! For information about car-ferry services, consult **Caledonian MacBrayne** at Lochmaddy (tel. 08763/337). British Airways flies daily except Sunday to and from Benbecula Airport (the nearest connection for North Uist) and Glasgow.

Causeways and bridges link Benbecula and South Uist to North Uist. Therefore you can go by car from North Uist to either of these islands without having to board a car-ferry. Both these southern Hebridean islands will be previewed later for those who want to continue their journey southward.

FOOD AND LODGING: You may want to stop over or to take a meal on North Uist. Some suggestions are:

At Lochmaddy

Lochmaddy Hotel (tel. 08763/331). You'll notice the peaked gables of this white-walled hotel a few steps from the ferryboat terminal. Its 15 bedrooms, two with private baths, frequently host the collection of fishermen who come from throughout Britain to capture the area's brown trout and salmon. George and Irene Pert, the managers, offer the use of the hotel's set of scales to anyone wishing to weigh his or her catch of the day. The establishment contains an accommodating pub, whose walls are lined with various kinds of trophies, along with a cocktail bar and a dining room. Breakfasts, included in the price of accommodation, might include peat-smoked kippers. At dinner you are likely to be offered heather-fed North Uist lamb. Bar meals are served at lunch as well as in the evening, and the bar also offers about the best collection of single-malt whiskies in the Outer Hebrides. Singles cost from £19 ($30.40) and doubles for £17 ($27.20) per person for B&B. Half board is from £29 ($46.40) per person daily.

At Locheport

Langass Lodge (tel. 08764/285) is a spacious house with multiple chimneys, originally built as part of a private hunting lodge. Today it serves as a comfortable family-run hotel, where Gordon and Kate Ann Fowlis are the pleasant owners. It lies amid trees and low shrubs about six miles from Lochmaddy on a site overlooking a loch. The surrounding countryside offers the kind of diversions, along with ample amounts of peace and quiet, that appeal to urbanites on a holiday. Most guests check in for stays of several days, with half board included, costing from £24.50 ($39.20) to £26.50 ($42.40) per person daily. B&B ranges from £16 ($25.60) to £18 ($28.80) per person, depending on the accommodation. "Taste of Scotland" meals are served, featuring local shellfish.

SIGHTS: For such a small island, the scenery of North Uist is extremely varied. Many visitors gravitate to the eastern shores which have a kind of untamed beauty. The coastline is literally dotted with lochs filled with trout, and everything is set against a backdrop of darkened, rolling, heather-clad hills. Nights come fast in winter, but sunsets linger long in summer. The western side of North Uist is less severe, a land of rich meadows filled with wildflowers in places. Here you find long white beaches, but the water temperature is definitely not like that of the Caribbean. Atlantic rollers come in here, attracting the heartiest of surfers.

In July, the big event—some residents look forward to it all year—is the Highland Games and cattle show at Hosta.

Rich in reminders of the past, North Uist has so many monuments you'd have to be a dedicated archeologist to see all of them. I'll cite only some of the most important ones to give you a taste of the Neolithic.

Heading northwest from Lochmaddy for 2½ miles you come to Blashaval. There you will find the **Three Standing Stones of the False Men.** Local tradition has it that this trio of stones, known in Gaelic as Na Fir Bhreige, were actually men, wife deserters from Skye turned into stone by a witch.

Continuing along the road a distance of four miles from Lochmaddy, you approach an island on the west side of Loch an Duin. However, access is possible on foot only at periods of low water level, and caution should be exercised. **Dun Torcuill,** a fortification found there, is considered one of the finest examples of a broch which provided defense for the villagers when attacked by raiders.

At the crossroads up ahead you can turn north along the B893 heading for the attractions of the northeast corner. If you follow this road to Newton Ferry, you can take a ferry in summer to Leverburgh in Harris, the journey lasting an hour. But it takes just 15 minutes to cross over to the little offshore island of **Berneray,** which has a few ancient sites, including the Borve Standing Stone. There is a privately run hostel here as well. The 140 or so people who live on the island are mainly engaged in crofting and fishing, and some of them may regard *you* as a sightseeing attraction. Regardless of what you look like, any stranger in these parts attracts attention.

After you return to Newton Ferry, you can head south again on the same road, stopping to look at some sights in the immediate area. A left-hand fork takes you to Trumisgarry. There you will see the ruins of an old chapel, for it was here that an early Christian settlement was founded. **St. Columba's Well** (Tobar Chaluim Chille, in Gaelic) is named after the saint.

Returning to the main road, we head west toward Sollas instead of returning east to Lochmaddy. The area on both sides of the road is filled with cairns and standing stones, too numerous to mention here. Many are from 2000 B.C., and some are hard to reach, including those on uninhabited islands.

We pass through Hosta, site of the Highland Games, heading for the **Balranald Nature Reserve,** along with some dedicated British birdwatchers, some of whom may be in pursuit of the white-tailed sea eagle. The location of this nature reserve is three miles northwest of Bayhead. There is a reception cottage at Goular near Hougharry where you can learn more about the birds inhabiting the Outer Hebrides. It is open daily, charging no admission, between April and September.

Back on the main road again, we pass through Bayhead heading to the southeast. Again the area is filled with an astonishing number of ancient monuments, many of which have disappeared since the 1920s, having been reclaimed by the Atlantic.

Since you can't visit them all, you might as well make a choice. When you come to the junction and see the A867 heading back to Lochmaddy, take it for a few miles. You'll see a sign pointing to **Barpa Langass,** a chambered cairn believed to be at least 3,000 years old. It's one of the best preserved on the island. Some historians believe a warrior chieftain was buried here, but others suggest that it was a communal burial ground. It lies on the slopes of Ben Langass. Bones and pottery fragments removed from excavations here were sent to the National Museum.

Returning to the main road again, retracing our trail, we head south again for **Carinish,** a hamlet known for its archeological sites, including the Carinish Stone Circle and the Barpa Carinish. But mainly it is visited because it is the site of the major attraction on the island, **Trinity Temple** (Teampull na Trionad, in Gaelic). The temple lies off the A865 some eight miles southwest of Lochmaddy. Admission-free, it is open at all times. The monastery is said to have been founded by Beathag in the 13th century. She was the first prioress of Iona and the daughter of Somerland, the Irish mercenary and founding father of the MacDonalds. In the Middle Ages this was the site of a great college. The scholar Duns Scotus was said to have attended. The Franciscan (1265–1308) became a leading divine and one of the greatest of medieval philosophers.

Nearby is **Teampull Clann A'Phiocair,** which was the chapel of the MacVicars. You can see a number of ancient "cup and ring" markings. The site of a clan battle is also nearby. Appropriately called the "Field of Blood," it is where the MacLeods of Harris and the MacDonalds of Uist met in 1601.

You can continue southeast to the island of **Grimsay,** which is connected by a causeway. It is known for its lobster ponds. You'll also find the remains of Michael's Chapel and the ruins of Dun Bay Grimsay, an ancient fortification.

After Grimsay, the road south heads to our next island attraction, Benbecula.

14. Benbecula

Many visitors treat Benbecula as a mere causeway linking North Uist with South Uist. But it is not devoid of attractions. Others touch down only briefly at its airport in the northwest, then rush off to other destinations.

Benbecula is small, only about six miles in diameter. Nearly all the population lives in the west. Most of the eastern part, real bogland, is without roads except for a narrow single-track "path" along the southeastern part.

If you're planning to spend time on the island, **Creagorry** might be your center, as you'll find facilities there, including accommodations, shops, and a post office. But the main center of the island is **Balivanich,** which is near the airport and a Royal Artillery base.

In the southwestern part of the island you can see the ruins of **Borve Castle,** the seat of the cadet chiefs of the MacDonalds of Clan Ranald of Benbecula. It was occupied in the 17th century. Near the shore, close to the castle, you can see the ruins of a small chapel, Teampull Bhuirgh.

Continuing north along the road to the airport, you'll come to the ruins of an ancient chapel at Nunton. A nunnery was here, but at the time of the Reformation the sisters were massacred. A large house nearby was the 18th-century residence of the Clan Ranald chieftains.

STAYING AT CREAGORRY: The place I suggest is the **Creagorry Hotel** (tel. 0870/2024). The front of this hotel has been concealed with a blank-fronted facade, but the original inn opened for business in the 1870s. You're likely to meet a handful of local fishermen in the spacious, somewhat spartan public bar. The lounge bar is more intimate, and often patronized by commercial travelers visiting Benbecula. The hotel owns the fishing rights to some of the nearby lochs, so sportsmen are also attracted. Bonnie Prince Charlie, disguised as a woman, hid out around here, waiting to cross over to Skye with Flora MacDonald. It's said that when the time for the passage finally came, it was slowed down because he kept losing his shoes in the bogland of Benbecula (never his favorite place). He sent hapless servants to retrieve them from the mud. The hotel has 20 bedrooms, whose occupants share three bathrooms. B&B is from £13.50 ($21.60) per person, and half-board tariffs run from £18.50 ($29.60) per person daily. The hotel is open all year.

STAYING AT LINICLATE: In a rambling modern building, the **Dark Island Hotel** (tel. 0870/2414) is capped by a series of skylights and reddish tiles. It is one of the most up-to-date and best-appointed hostelries of the Outer Hebrides, with a friendly, accommodating manager, S. Peteranna. Some 40 well-furnished bedrooms are offered, singles costing £28 ($44.80) and doubles going for £50 ($80). A few VIP units are more expensive. The hotel has two dining rooms, catering to all its guests, even those requiring special foods. Especially good are the fresh fish and lamb. There is also a pub, where you can order snacks along with your drinks. The staff will be happy to arrange golf and fishing for their guests, many of whom take advantage of the hotel's isolation to explore several almost-deserted nearby beaches if the weather's behaving.

15. South Uist

A rich treasure trove of antiquity can be found on South Uist, which has a surprising number of ecclesiastical remains scattered along its shores. Reached by causeway from our last stopover in Benbecula, South Uist deserves your time. The Clan Ranald, who ruled the island, left many ruins and fortresses known as "duns." Ornithologists and anglers are also attracted here.

Part bogland, the island is 20 miles long and six miles wide at its broadest point. A main road, the A865, bisects the island, with feeder roads, single-track lanes with passing places, branching off east and west. Some of the most interesting sights, all ruins, lie off on these little roads.

FOOD AND LODGING: If you choose to seek a place to stay or to take nourishment on South Uist, there are several recommendations.

At Lochboisdale

Lochboisdale Hotel, Ferry Terminal (tel. 08784/332), was originally built of two types of local stone. Today it contains the most popular pub in the area. It also serves as a simple but comfortable retreat for visiting anglers and yachtsmen, who congregate in the evening beside the bar near the darts board. Because the royal family favors South Uist on its summer cruises, someone in the bar might be able to relate a respectful anecdote to a foreign visitor. From the oversize plate glass of the hotel's modern extensions you're likely to see sheep grazing in the garden. This hotel was once owned by "The Great Mackenzie," whose personality made him one of South Uist's most unforgettable characters. Today the owners rent boats to fishermen or seaworthy guests. Scottish crafts are sold in the hotel's tiny shop. The comfortable but simply decorated bedrooms rent for £21.50 ($34.40) in a single and from £20.50 ($32.80) per person in a double or twin. Half-board costs from £31.50 ($50.40) per person. Of the 20 rooms, 14 have private baths or showers.

At Daliburgh

Borrodale Hotel (tel. 08784/444) has a modernized front porch and clean angles. A row of gables runs across the second story. The residents' lounge is most inviting, with stone walls and carpeting. The family that runs it extends a warm Hebridean welcome and will assist in arranging fishing and golf expeditions. The surrounding hills encourage midafternoon rambles through gorse and heather, after which guests return for well-prepared meals in the dining room. The hotel is centrally heated, and the 14 bedrooms, most with private baths or showers, all have hot and cold water basins. Charles Peteranna, the manager, charges £20 ($32) for B&B in a single, £40 ($64) in a double. Half board costs £29 ($46.40) per person. A full Scottish breakfast is served. A fully licensed cocktail bar and a public bar are on the premises.

At Garryhallie

Grianaig Guest House (tel. 08784/406). The solid walls of this family-run guesthouse sit on isolated terrain outside Garryhallie. The winds from the Atlantic can howl around the place, but it's much cozier inside. The Peteranna family, James and Muirne, have furnished it tastefully with patterned carpets and comfortable armchairs. Peat-burning fires add intimacy to the residents' lounge. Seven rooms are rented, some with private shower, and each is furnished in a simple but comfortable style that seems to suit the marine mentalities of the boating crowd attracted to South Uist. B&B, with private shower, costs £13 ($20.80) per person, and a good dinner is offered for £5.50 ($8.80).

SIGHTS AROUND THE ISLAND: The biggest village in South Uist is **Lochboisdale,** lying at the head of a deep sea loch in the southeastern part of the island. It was settled mainly in the 19th century by crofters who had been forced off their land in the notorious Land Clearances of those troubled years. However, the ruins of a small medieval castle can be seen at the head of the loch on the island of Calvay, one of the many places where Bonnie Prince Charlie hid out.

Lochboisdale is the site of the ferry terminal, which provides a link between South Uist and the mainland at Oban. The by-now-familiar line of **Caledonian MacBrayne** delivers cars and passengers to the island. There is a connection via Castlebay on Barra, which is not linked by a causeway to its sister island to the north.

Leaving Lochboisdale, the A865 goes west for three miles to Daliburgh where there is a hotel (see the review of the Borrodale coming up). From Daliburgh you can take the B888 south to **Pollachar** on the southern shore, a distance of six miles. The hamlet is named for the Pollachar Standing Stone, which you can see.

If you wish at this time, you can continue east along a minor road for 2½ miles to the Ludag Jetty. There you can take a private ferry to both the minor offshore island of Eriskay and to Barra. The attractions of both Eriskay and Barra will be previewed later.

Retracing your footsteps, you can head north again in the direction of Daliburgh. However, there are some attractions along the way.

Your first stop is to visit a contemporary church, **Our Lady of Sorrows,** at Garrynamonie, a short drive north of Pollachar, consecrated in 1964. A mosaic depicts "Our Lady," and the church can be visited until 7 p.m.

The next stop is farther north. The **Kilpheder Wheelhouse** lies at Kilpheder, two miles west of the A865. It is the meager ruins of a circular building from A.D. 200. It was split into "stalls" like the spokes of a wheel.

Back on the main road again, you can head for **Askernish,** the site of a nine-hole golf course. After a game of golf, continue along the route until you reach Mingarry. There, on a little road to the east, are the remains of a big chambered cairn.

At Airidh Mhuilinn, three miles north from Daliburgh, is a **memorial to Flora MacDonald.** Her birthplace is west of the A865, about 200 yards up a farm track half a mile north of Milton. This heroic woman (a reluctant heroine, that is) led Bonnie Prince Charlie across the water to Skye. She was born here in 1722. A cairn on the top of a little hill marks the spot of the birthplace of this woman so revered in legend.

From Flora MacDonald's birthplace you can see some of the most interesting sights of South Uist by staying on the minor roads around here. You'll also be able to take a look at the dramatic machair-fringed shoreline. You will pass through the hamlets of Bornish, Ormiclete, and Stoneybridge, before rejoining the main road at Howbeg, which, incidentally, was the birthplace of Neil MacDonald, who is considered the *real* hero—not Flora MacDonald—in helping Bonnie Prince Charlie escape from the redcoats.

At Ormiclete you come upon the ruins of **Ormiclete Castle,** which was constructed by the rulers of the island, the Clan Ranald chieftains, in the early 18th century. Fire swept the castle in 1715 on the eve of the Battle of Sherriffmuir in which the clan chieftain was killed. North of the area are a standing stone and a dun.

Passing through Howmore, you see several of the old thatched crofters' cottages which once were far more numerous in the area. The part of the island directly north of Howbeg, in both an easterly and a westerly direction, is rich in archeological remains. Several medieval chapels, now in ruins, are all that is left of what was a major ecclesiastical center of South Uist. An ancient graveyard near here was the burial ground of the Clan Ranald chieftains. On a hill to the west stands a present-day Church of Scotland (it has a central communion pew, one of the two left in the country).

Back on the A865 north, the road passes the **Loch Druidibeg National Nature Reserve,** considered the most significant breeding ground for the native grayleg goose in the country. Attracting the dedicated birdwatcher, it is a setting of machair and brackish lochs.

At Drimsdale lie the ruins of a big dun, a fortification in a loch where the villagers retreated when under attack. It continued as a stronghold for the Clan Ranald until the early 1500s.

The road continues past the Royal Artillery Rocket Range (heed those warning signs). On the flank of a Reuval Hill stands **"Our Lady of the Isles,"** a 30-foot statue of the Virgin and Child. The hill is called "the mountain of miracles." Erected in 1957, the statue was the creation of artist Hew Lorimer, and Catholic contributions from around the world financed the project. It is the largest religious statue in Britain.

Loch Bee, inhabited by mute swans, is a spacious body of water that nearly bisects the northern part of South Uist.

ERISKAY: This small island lying at the southern tip of South Uist is reached by car-ferry from Ludag. Departure times depend on the tides and the weather. If you want to see a staunchly independent Scottish island filled with hardworking, industrious people, some 200 in all, then go to Eriskay. You may learn more about Hebridean life here than elsewhere.

The major settlement was founded in the hard days of the notorious Land Clearances. Eriskay was given to crofters because the land was bad (the sheep were given the best grazing pastures). Many or most of today's residents are descended from those evicted crofters who were cleared of their lands along the coasts of Barra and South Uist. The crofters turned to fishing, and it is an occupation followed by the residents today.

Father Alan MacDonald is said to have built the island's church, St. Michael's, from the profits of a single night's fishing back in 1903. At the island's cooperative store, you can buy hand-knitted sweaters of excellent quality. Once their design patterns were commonplace, but now they are made only on Eriskay.

The island has a herd of ponies, a rare breed that has been barely saved from extinction by a preservation society. Usually measuring only 12 hands, this small pony is found only on Eriskay, and unless more people take an interest in it, it may disappear altogether.

It was on Eriskay that Bonnie Prince Charlie first landed in his attempt to win the crown from the Hanoverians. Apparently he got the cold shoulder from the natives and was forced to fish for his supper, spending the night in a hovel before leaving for more hospitable islands. However, to commemorate his memory to this day, a wildflower, a sea bindweed called the Prince's flower, was named after him.

Between Eriskay and South Uist, in the sound, lies the wreck of the S.S. *Politician.* It sank in 1941, carrying 24,000 cases of whisky. This event formed the core of the plot of Compton MacKenzie's novel *Whisky Galore.*

Eriskay, whose two peaks are Ben Stack at 400 feet and Ben Scrien at 600 feet, makes for a rare travel experience, but you must return to South Uist to find accommodation.

16. Barra

Called "the garden of the Hebrides," Barra lies at the southern end of the Outer Hebrides. Locals claim there are some 1,000 varieties of wildflowers. Once occupied by Vikings, the island is one of the most beautiful in the Hebridean chain, with heather-clad meadows, beaches, sandy grasslands, peaks, rocky bays, and lofty headlands. Since the days of the conquering Norsemen it has been associated with the Clan MacNeil (more about them later).

A circular road of ten miles will take you around Barra, which is about four miles by eight miles. At the northern end of Barra is **Cockle Strand,** the airport, a long and wide beach of white sand. Loganair, the Scottish airline, lands craft here from Glasgow, or from Benbecula and Stornoway on Lewis. It is said to be the only runway in Britain washed twice daily by sea tides.

From the mainland, it's also possible to reach Barra by taking one of the car-ferries operated by Caledonian MacBrayne. The ferry docks at **Castlebay,** a 19th-century herring port which is the capital of Barra. If you're at our last stopover in South Uist, you can also take a car-ferry from Lochboisdale to Castlebay. It's also possible to take a privately operated ferry from Eoligarry, north of the Cockle Strand airport, to Ludag on South Uist. The ferry does not operate on Sunday.

Most of the 1,200 inhabitants of Barra are centered at Castlebay, which is the best place to stock up on supplies. In the background of the port is **Ben Heaval,** at 1,250 feet the highest mountain on Barra. On its slopes you'll see a Virgin and Child carved of Carrara marble.

FOOD AND LODGING: There are accommodations and dining choices in Castlebay, Tangusdale, and Northbay.

Staying at Castlebay

Castlebay Hotel (tel. 08714/223). The gables of this hotel's stone facade look out over the bay which was once the home of a herring fleet. At the commercial heart of the island, a short distance from the ferryboat terminal, the hotel often attracts business travelers. It also gets a fair share of summer tourists. The 13 bedrooms are comfortable, albeit simply and functionally furnished. Four units contain private baths. B&B costs from £15.50 ($24.80) to £18.50 ($29.60) per person. Dinner is served in the dining room from 6:30 to 8 p.m., a meal costing from £8.50 ($13.60). You'll welcome the open fire in the spacious pub on a chilly day. This is the most popular rendezvous on the island. The hotel is open all year.

Craigard Hotel (tel. 08714/200) was swept by a fire in the late 1960s but it has long ago been fully restored. Standing a few steps from a Catholic chapel, the hotel offers seven clean, efficient, and functional rooms. The half-board rate ranges from £21 ($33.60) to £25 ($40) per person nightly. The pub on the premises offers one of the best views of local life on the island, since many of the neighborhood's sailors and fisherfolk gravitate here for diversion and conversation. The contemporary lounge bar offers a place for a more subdued libation without the peppery characters and salty dialogue. The white-walled gables of this hotel command a handsome view of the bay and Kismul Castle.

An Calla Guest House, at Kentangaval (tel. 08714/270), has a white-trimmed stone facade ringed with a wrap-around wall, which shelters its front garden from the blustery winds. This is one of the best bargains on the island, offering clean, homey, and comfortable accommodations. It also serves good and wholesome food in generous portions. In all, it's a winning choice for Hebridean hospitality. Open between April and October, the establishment charges from £10 ($16) in a single and from £18 ($28.80) in a double or twin. Half board is available at a rate of £16 ($25.60) per person daily.

At Tangusdale

Isle of Barra Hotel (tel. 08714/383). The low-slung rooflines of this seashore hotel are part of a design by an architect who won an award in the late 1970s for this hotel. For the Outer Hebrides, it is a luxury selection. It was erected as a project of the Highlands and Islands Development Board, which adorned its brick walls with nautical paraphernalia and contemporary tapestries. The hotel is in a tranquil position, commanding a view of the less-populated western shore of the island. Its pub, the most westerly in Scotland, is widely touted as "the last dram before America." From the dining room and from many of the bedrooms, you can see everything that's coming and going at sea. The location greatly appealed to the Shah of Iran when he was still in shaky power, with a revolution knocking at his door. The nanny to his children told him about her native Scotland and Barra, and his security agents checked it out. They found it an ideal place in which to conceal his children during those troubled times. The shah and his retinue are long gone today, but the hotel remains a favorite with the yachting crowd.

This unusual hotel charges from £22.50 ($36) for B&B. Half board is available for £28.50 ($45.60) per person. Some of the best food on Barra is served here, including ample quantities of fresh fish and heather-fed lamb, along with —when it's available—fresh island-grown produce. The hotel is open between April and October. Bicycles and fishing equipment can be supplied here.

At Northbay

Northbay Guest House (tel. 08715/255). A few of the steep roofs of this baronial-style hotel are capped with church-like belfries. You'll find it between Castlebay and the Cockle Strand airport, near an old windmill and the remains of a dun on the northeastern side of the island. Many of the hotel's guests come here for fishing holidays, since charter boats are available for rental. It's a comfortable choice, with wholesome food served as part of the half-board rates. Dinner begins promptly at 6 p.m. Guests appreciate the five comfortable but simple bedrooms. Prices here are definitely a bargain: from £9 ($14.40) per person for B&B. The half-board tariff begins at £13.50 ($21.60) per person daily. The house takes guests from April to October.

SIGHTS: The most important sightseeing attraction of Barra stands in the bay. **Kismul Castle** was built for strategic purposes on a small islet. It was the longtime stronghold of the notorious Macneils of Barra, a clan known for their piracy and lawlessness. Their 35th chieftain, Ruari the Turbulent, was so bold as to seize a ship of Elizabeth I. The oldest part of the castle is a tower from 1120, and the structure was mainly from the 15th and 16th centuries when an accidental fire swept through it in 1795. When the direct male line died out in 1863, leadership of the clan reverted to the Canadian branch. The 45th chieftain of the clan, the late Robert Lister Macneil of Barra, a U.S. architect, began restoration work on his ancestral home in 1938. After several interruptions, including World War II, the job was completed in 1970. The present chief is Ian Roderick Macneil of Barra, who allows visits from May to September only on Wednesday and Saturday afternoons. For about £1.50 ($2.40), a boatman will take you over and back at 2 and 3:30 p.m.

If you want to drive around the island for a look, you can head west from Castlebay until you reach Kinloch. There, on the left, is Loch St. Clair, reached by a tiny track road. In the loch on an islet stand the ruins of St. Clair Castle, called **MacLeod's Fort.** In the vicinity you can also see **St. Columba's Well,** named for the saint.

Continuing north to Borve, you will see the **Borve Standing Stones** on your left. At Borve, a fork in the road leads north where you can view on a hillside a chambered cairn. You can also visit the hamlet of **Craigston,** which has a church dedicated to St. Brendan, the Irish navigator many cite as the discoverer of America. In the area are two interesting ruins, including **Dun Bharpa,** a collection of stones encircled by standing stones. Probably used for burial purposes, it has a chambered cairn. In the north is Tigh Talamhanta, a ruined wheelhouse.

On the main road, continue north to Allasdale. At a former fort there to the northwest, **Dun Cuier,** you can view one of the few excavated Hebridean Iron Age forts. It is better preserved than most. From here you will also have a sweeping view of the open Atlantic. Opposite Allasdale, Seal Bay is one of the beauty spots of the island. The seals here do as much inspection of you as you do of them.

At **Northbay** at Loch an Duin, where a dam provides the island's water needs, you can see the remains of an old dun protruding from the water. Nearby are the ruins of an old watermill, one of the Norse-inspired mills where people of the islands used to take their grain to be ground.

Instead of returning immediately to Castlebay, which would make a full circular island tour, you can head north instead along a secondary road in the direction of Cockle Strand, the Barra airport mentioned earlier. The landing of planes on the beach here is in itself a sightseeing attraction.

You can continue north to **Eoligarry,** also mentioned earlier as the site of a small ferry terminal taking passengers twice a day to Ludag on South Uist. Departures are daily in summer if the weather's right, and only passengers and cyclists—no cars—are transported over.

Eoligarry's proud possession is **St. Barr's Church,** named after St. Findbarr of Cork (A.D. 550–623), who is said to have converted the islanders to Christianity after finding many of them practicing cannibalism when he arrived. Unlike his predecessor, the saint escaped the stewpot. The original 12th-century chapel was restored by Father Callum MacNeil. The Celtic stones in the churchyard are called "Crusader stones." This was the old burial ground of the MacNeil chieftains. The novelist Compton MacKenzie, author of *Whisky Galore,* is also buried here. He had a Hebridean home around these parts.

When Kismul Castle burned in 1795, the chieftain of Barra moved to **Eoligarry House,** on the bend of the road, whose ruins can be seen outlined in the walls of outhouses. Because the structure was considered dangerous, it was torn down in 1976.

Near Eoligarry, on the summit of a small hill, is **Dun Scurrival,** another ruined fort, this one measuring 39 by 52 feet.

VATERSAY: Across the bay from Barra stands the little island of Vatersay. A ferry goes there on a regular schedule from Castlebay, running once a day except Sunday. Since there are no accommodations, lonely, isolated Vatersay is visited mostly on a sunny day by those wanting to find a spot on one of its beautiful beaches. They always do—it's never crowded here.

The island is less than four miles long and wide, with a broad isthmus of shell sand, and the points on the island are connected by a little single-lane roadway, stretching for about five miles.

It's inhabited by about 100 tranquil souls who like to live near their cattle, as Vatersay is known for its excellent grazing. The local inhabitants are descendants, in part, from the "Vatersay Raiders." Crofters, mainly from Barra, took over the island, rebelling against their landlady, Lady Cathcart Gordon. They established homesteads, faced a legal challenge, and won the right to stay on the land.

Food can be purchased at the island's community center, and the rest of the day, if the weather is right, can be spent on one of the beaches. A monument on West Beach was raised in memory of *Annie Jane,* an emigrant ship wrecked off the coastline in 1853. The island also has some duns or remains of fortifications, the most significant of which is Dun a'Chaolais, in the western part of the island. Built on a rocky knoll about 100 feet high, this is a circular broch with an internal diameter of about 30 feet.

Chapter XIX

THE ORKNEY AND SHETLAND ISLANDS

1. The Orkney Islands
2. Fair Isle
3. The Shetland Islands

NORTHERN OUTPOSTS of civilization, the Orkney and Shetland archipelagos consist of about 200 islands, about 40 of which are inhabited. "Go to Shetland for scenery, Orkney for antiquities," or so the saying goes. That doesn't mean to imply that Orkney doesn't have scenery too. It does . . . in great abundance.

The distances are long. For example, from the southern tip of Orkney to the far reaches of northern Shetland is as far as from London to the cathedral city of York in northeastern England. That's a lot of land to cover, but it's more water than anything else. Getting there, however, remains relatively easy (more about that under the individual island headings).

These far-flung and scattered islands to the north of Scotland are rich in a great Viking heritage. Until ceded to Scotland by Norway as part of the dowry of Princess Margaret in 1472 (she'd married a Scottish king), the islands were part of the great Norse earldoms. They were a gathering place for Norse fleets, and celebrated in the *Orkneyinga Saga* which detailed the exploits of the Viking warriors of those days.

The Vikings did not settle the islands. Tribes of people dating from the Stone Age occupied both Shetland and Orkney. The Picts came later, and ruins of their round forts can still be seen dotting the coastlines. The handcraft of prehistoric man still stands in stark contrast to the rich rolling hills and landscape. The islands are also rich in flora and fauna, everything from gray seals with heads bobbing up from the sea to tiny ponies seen grazing Shetland's hills.

The island chains are not part of the Highlands, and totally differ from both the Inner and Outer Hebrides which we've just explored. Clans, Gaelic, and kilts were unfamiliar to the Orcadians and the Shetlanders—that is, until the Scots arrived. At first these merchants and newly acquired landlords were bitterly resented by the locals. Even today the islanders are fiercely independent. They speak of themselves as Orcadians and Shetlanders instead of as Scots. Not only are Orkney and Shetland different from the Highlands, they are different from each other, as we will soon see.

Change, as was inevitable, has come to Orkney and Shetland in the way of oil and modern conveniences. But tradition is still strong. It has a lot to do with climate and a lot to do with ancestry.

1. The Orkney Islands

It is said that a visit to the Orkney Islands is like going back to take a look at a thousand years of history. Orkney is an archipelago of islands extending for about 50 miles north and northeast. Covering a land area of 376 square miles, they lie some six miles off the Scottish mainland. The terrain has a lot of rich and fertile farmland, but also some dramatic scenery, such as Britain's highest perpendicular cliffs, rising to 1,140 feet.

The population of the entire chain is under 20,000 persons, spread sparsely across about 29 inhabited islands. The people are a little suspicious of strangers, and if you meet an Orcadian in a local pub, you will have to break the ice. After that, you are likely to engage in an interesting, enlightened conversation. These are an amazing people with a heritage very different from that of the rest of Scotland.

The climate is far milder than the location of the Orkney Islands in the far-northern reaches of Scotland would suggest. That is because of the warming currents of the Gulf Stream. There are few extremes in temperature. From May to July you get some astonishing sunsets, with the midsummer sun over the horizon for 18¼ hours a day. The Orcadians call their midsummer sky "Grimlins" from the old Norse word *grimla,* which means to twinkle or glimmer. There's enough light for golfers to play at midnight.

Who comes here other than golfers? The archeologist, the artist, the walker, the climber, and the birdwatcher are likely to share your breakfast table. Many students of history come here. They've read the *Orkneyinga Saga,* that product of the "golden age" of Orkney in which the pomp and heraldry of the archipelago were recorded. Orkney is a virtual archeological garden, as some 100 of the 500 known brochs—often called "the castles of the Picts"—are found here. Ordered built by Orkney chiefs, these brochs were fortified structures where nearly 100 islanders could find refuge from invaders. Wells were inside the structure to provide water.

Divers are attracted to Orkney, some drawn here to seek out such 25,000-ton battleships as the *Markgraf.* The warships of the German Imperial Navy were scuttled on June 21, 1919, on orders of Rear Admiral Ludwig von Reuter. Most of the vessels, including five battle cruisers, have been salvaged, but there are still plenty lying down there in the deep.

Fishermen come in droves. Unlike other parts of Scotland, fishing is free in Orkney, because of old Norse law and ancient Udal tradition. The wild brown trout here is said to be the best in Britain. The season runs from mid-March until the first week in October.

Some visitors come for the festivals. The last week in May at Stromness sees the convening of musicians, many from Scandinavia, for the Orkney Traditional Folk Festival. Some tunes played here haven't changed in a thousand years! There is also the St. Magnus Festival in summer. When an opera was once presented here, it was billed as a "world première at the edge of the world."

The flora and fauna have always lured visitors. A large number of the world's gray seal population visits Orkney to breed and molt. The islanders call the seal a "selkie." A large number of wildfowl migrate from Iceland and northern Europe in winter, and that includes the goldeneye. Others include the red-throated diver, known locally as the "rain goose," and the short-eared owl or "cattieface," as he is called, and such breeding seabirds as kittiwakes and guillemats. The resident bird of prey on the island is the hen harrier. Orkney is host to millions of birds, and some 300 species have been identified in the islands. These include the puffin, the most beloved seabird in Britain. In Orkney they are called "tammie-norries."

Orkney is also known for its flora, including the Scottish primrose, which is no more than two inches in height and is believed to have survived the Ice Age by growing in small ice-free areas. The amethyst, with a pale yellow eye, is found only in Orkney and parts of northern Scotland.

Many people enjoy the food of the islands, especially when it's local and fresh. That could include lobster, a local crab known as partans, prawn tails, oysters, and clams, along with such meat as Orkney lamb, regional cheeses, and home-baking.

If you want to know what events are taking place at the time of your visit, you will have to consult *The Orcadian,* a weekly published since 1854.

Otherwise, you can go to the **Tourist Information Centres** at both Kirkwall, on Broad Street (tel. 0856/2856), and Stromness, the two prinicpal "towns" of Orkney. In winter the office in Stromness (tel. 0856850/716) stays open for only two hours a day to meet the ferry coming from Scrabster on the mainland (the information booth is in the Ferry Terminal building). Stromness and Kirkwall are both on the same island, which, believe it or not, is called "the Mainland." Stromness is in the west, Kirkwall in the east.

Accommodations are few in the Orkneys, and could be too few at certain busy times during the summer. Hotel building isn't a major priority, as Orkney hasn't fully awakened to its touristic possibilities. Always reserve a room way, way in advance to keep from getting stranded in these far-northern climes.

GETTING THERE: If you're driving over, head for Scrabster, near Thurso, in the northern province of Caithness. There, P&O's *St. Ola* operates a roll-on/roll-off ferry service with two-hour sailings to Stromness on Mainland Orkney. This is the most scenic route, because you go by the dramatic cliffs of Hoy. Sailings are two or three times a day in summer. A round-trip fare is about £80 ($128), including a car. A single fare (passenger only) is £8 ($12.80) per person. If you don't have a car, it's faster and cheaper to go from "end-of-the-line" John o' Groats to Burwick. The time is only 45 minutes and the fare is £6 ($9.60), but you'll miss a lot of the stunning scenery. This ferry operates only in summer. The ferry, its bright blue the color of the Mediterranean sea, operates daily except Sunday. Departures from Scrabster are usually at noon, whereas departures from John o' Groats are at 10:30 a.m. and 4:15 p.m. in July, August, and September. For more information, phone **P&O Ferries** in Stromness at 0856/850655. **Thomas & Bews,** the operator of the John o' Groats connection, can be reached by phoning 095581/353.

Numerous flights also go to Orkney. Both **British Airways** and **Loganair,** the Scottish airways, operate daily scheduled services to Kirkwall Airport on Mainland Orkney. British Airways flies from Glasgow, Inverness, and Aberdeen, with connections from London, Birmingham, and Manchester. Loganair operates from Glasgow, Edinburgh, Inverness, and Wick.

GETTING AROUND: Island hopping is common in the north of Scotland. In fact, more northern Scots take to the air than anywhere else in Britain. **Loganair** operates scheduled flights from Kirkwall Airport on Mainland to the isles of Sanday, Stronsay, Westray, Eday, North Ronaldsay, and Papa Westray. To reach them, call 0856/2494 at the Kirkwall Airport.

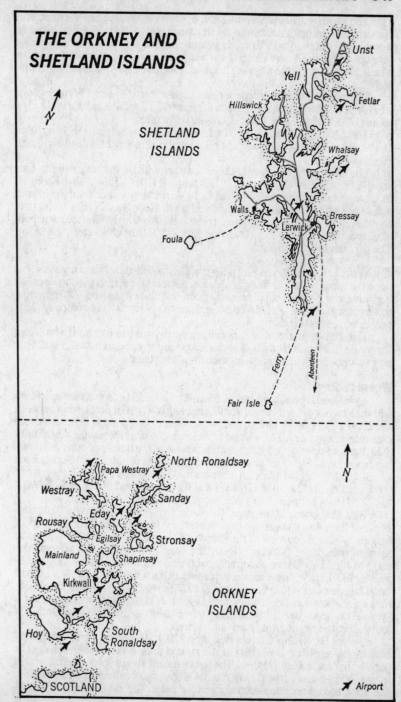

THE ORKNEY AND SHETLAND ISLANDS

N

SHETLAND ISLANDS

Unst

Yell

Hillswick

Fetlar

Whalsay

Walls

Lerwick

Bressay

Foula

Ferry

Aberdeen

Fair Isle

N

Papa Westray

North Ronaldsay

Westray

Sanday

Eday

Rousay

Egilsay

Stronsay

Mainland

Shapinsay

Kirkwall

ORKNEY ISLANDS

Hoy

South Ronaldsay

SCOTLAND

✈ Airport

The **Orkney Islands Shipping Co.** operates scheduled sea services from Kirkwall to Orkney's north and south islands: Eday, Papa Westray, Sanday, Stronsay, Westray, North Ronaldsay, and Shapinsay. From Houton there are services to the south isles: Flotta, Graemsay, and Hoy at Longhope and Lyness. The headquarters of the shipping line is at 4 Ayre Rd. (tel. 0856/2044) in Kirkwall.

There are also many private services to take you to Rousay, Wyre, Egilsay, or Hoy and others, departing from Stromness, Tingwall, and Kirkwall. The tourist office will have the latest details on departures.

The Churchill Barriers, erected to impede enemy shipping in World War II, have been turned into a road link between the islands of Mainland and South Ronaldsay.

Bus tours operate throughout the summer, visiting the major sights. One reliable operator is **"Go Orkney,"** 6 Old Scapa Rd. (tel. 0856/4260) in Kirkwall. You can go aboard naturalist David Lea's warm luxury coach, taking in such attractions as prehistoric monuments and seals. He knows Orkney better than anybody, and knows how to present the island interestingly. The tours are popular, and it's wise to book seats with the **Kirkwall Tourist Office** (tel. 0856/2856). The trips begin at 10:15 a.m.

KIRKWALL: On the bay of Firth, Kirkwall, established by Norse invaders, has been the capital of the Orkney Islands for at least 900 years. It used to be called Kirkjuvagr or "church bay," named after a church built around 1040 honoring the memory of King Olaf Harraldsson, later the patron saint of Norway. That church no longer stands.

The old Norse streets of Kirkwall are very narrow to protect the buildings from gale-like winds. But don't get the idea they're pedestrian walkways. That myth is dispelled when a car comes roaring down the street.

Where to Stay

Ayre Hotel, Ayre Road (tel. 0856/2197). Some 30 bedrooms are contained within the white-walled sprawl of this rambling waterfront hotel, lying between the copper spire of the church and the harbor. A hotel sauna takes the damp chill from a foggy day. There's also an enjoyable restaurant serving dinner until 8:30 p.m.; otherwise, pub lunches are available in the hotel's popular bar, costing from £3 ($4.80). Full dinners go for £12 ($19.20). Half-board costs from £25.50 ($40.80) to £41 ($65.60) per person. Guests on the B&B arrangement pay from £20.30 ($32.48) to £26.80 ($42.88) in a single and from £18.50 ($29.60) to £22.50 ($36) per person in a double, depending on the plumbing.

West End Hotel, Main Street (tel. 0856/2368), is a simple but solidly constructed three-story house which was once the town house of the Balfours of Shapinsay (see my preview of the island of Shapinsay if you'd like to stay at the former castle of the Balfours). Today the West End Hotel is the personal domain of Mrs. Eva Currie and family, who extend a warm Orkney welcome to guests. Most bedrooms contain private bath facilities and color TV. Good breakfasts are included in the rate of £11 ($17.60) to £14.50 ($23.20) per person. Meals are also available, costing from £5 ($8). A lounge bar on the premises is licensed to serve drinks to visitors and residents. Amenities include a TV lounge, central heating, and a private car park.

Queens Hotel, Shore Street (tel. 0856/2200), sits behind a buff-colored facade in the center of town. Part of the ground floor is occupied by the hotel's popular bar and cocktail lounge. The management also devotes much attention to the food served in the dining room. All but two of the seven comfortably furnished accommodations contain private bath. The B&B rate is from £13

($20.80) per person. Half board costs from £16 ($25.60) per person. The hotel is centrally heated and contains a TV lounge.

Lynnfield House, Holm Road (tel. 0856/2505), is a hip-roofed building rising above low shrubbery and grassy lawns. Its half dozen simply but comfortably furnished bedrooms rent for £17 ($27.20) to £23 ($36.80) per person for B&B. There's a bar on the premises, and the hotel is centrally heated.

Kirkwall Hotel, Harbour Street (tel. 0856/2232). Its four-story brick facade is one of the most visible structures in town. Its well-crafted design includes windows trimmed in yellow beige stone, along with a comfortably modernized interior. Of the 44 bedrooms, 38 contain private baths and/or showers, and all have color TV getting satellite stations from Europe and the United States, direct-dial phones, and hot-beverage facilities. With half board included, the rates are from £34 ($54.40) to £36 ($57.60) per person, while B&B costs £22 ($35.20) to $27 ($43.20) per person nightly, the higher prices for rooms overlooking the harbor. Guests congregate before dinner in the hotel's cocktail lounge.

Royal Hotel, Victoria Street (tel. 0856/3477), occupies a pair of centrally located houses, one of which opens onto the main street, another fronting a nearby courtyard. The lintel over the main entrance is dated 1670. The interior has been modernized into a contemporary format. Its 30-odd rooms accept guests throughout the year, charging them from £21 ($33.60) to £23 ($36.80) per person for B&B. About half of these accommodations have private bath, costing a few additional pounds. It's also possible to take half-board rates, from £31 ($49.60) per person daily.

Leckmelm, Annfield Crescent (tel. 0856/3917), is a comfortable guesthouse run by Mrs. Margaret Scott, who formerly had a popular similar house at Skaill on Westray. For B&B, she charges £8 ($12.80), the price going up to £12 ($19.20) for dinner, bed, and breakfast. Home-baking is a specialty.

Where to Dine

Old Ship Inn Steak and Salad House, Bridge Street (tel. 0856/3537). Sir Walter Scott is reported to have dined in a restaurant on this spot in 1814. He was visiting Kirkwall, which he featured in his novel *The Pirate*. He had some uncomplimentary verses to write about the town. Perhaps he was angered because he had to pick up his own check for dinner. The town fathers were said to have "long pockets and short arms."

Today the stone house that contains the restaurant has ten tables, and is often quite busy. But it lay empty for many years until it was reopened. Eric and Alison Martin are the managers, welcoming local residents, business people to Orkney, and mainly summer tourists. Their decor includes a nautically inspired theme of fishermen's netting, dotted with blown-glass lobsterpot buoys hanging from the light-grained paneling of the walls and ceiling. The restaurant is fully licensed, offering a selection of island-distilled malt whiskies along with a modest assortment of wines. In spite of the restaurant's name, the specialty is seafood, but steaks and salads are popular as well. Full meals cost from a low of £6 ($9.60) to a high of £22 ($35.20), depending on how elaborate you want to make them. The restaurant is open daily except Sunday from noon to midnight.

Foveran Hotel, St. Ola (tel. 0856/2389), outside of town, looks like a modern hotel of Scandinavian design. It offers the best cuisine in the area, lying in a treeless landscape, overlooking the Scapa Flow, site of the sinking of the German Imperial Fleet in 1919. Fully licensed, the hotel is visited mainly for its restaurant, but it also rents rooms. It employs a helpful and ingratiating staff who emphasize its "Taste of Scotland" menus. (Actually, the food might better be called "Taste of Orkney.") You get good-tasting homemade soups, along with pâtés and a rich array of seafood. The catch of the day might turn out to be lobster, grilled salmon, deep-fried squid, giant crab claws (known locally as "partan toes"), scallops, prawns, or brown trout. Vegetarian meals are also offered, as well as succulent portions of Orkney Island beef. Lamb from the nearby meadows is often served with a nut-and-mint stuffing. Farm-made cheeses are regularly featured, and the cooks are known for unusual creations making use of fresh raw materials. Dinner, served nightly from 7 to 9:30 p.m., is offered except on Sunday and Monday at a cost beginning at £12 ($19.20). The hotel also rents out eight pleasantly furnished bedrooms, all with private baths. The price for B&B in a single is £21 ($33.60), with doubles costing £17.50 ($28) per person. The hotel and its restaurant are closed from mid-October to mid-November.

Sights

For the best view of Kirkwall and the North Isles, head up **Wideford Hill,** about two miles west of town. There you will enjoy a panoramic sweep. On the western slope of this hill, 2½ miles west of Kirkwall, is the **Wideford Hill Cairn,** a trio of concentric walls built around a passage and a megalithic chamber.

Returning to Kirkwall, which was granted a royal charter from James III in 1486, you can visit "the pride of Orkney," **St. Magnus Cathedral.** It was the burial place of the martyred St. Magnus, the patron saint of the island chain. The cathedral, which bears a certain resemblance to the Cathedral of Durham in England, was founded in 1137 by Jarl Rognvald in honor of his uncle, the martyred saint to whom the cathedral is dedicated. The remains of both the saint and Jarl Rognvald were interred between the two large central piers. It is a "Norman" building, constructed of a gray and pinkish rose sandstone. Work continued for centuries, and additions were made in the transitional and very early Gothic styles. It is still in regular use as a church, and can be visited Monday to Saturday from 9 a.m. to 1 p.m. and 2 to 5 p.m. It is closed on Sunday except for services.

Across from the cathedral are the ruins of a 12th-century **Bishop's Palace,** with a round tower dating from the 16th century. King Haakon came here to die in 1263, following the battle of Largs. The Norse king had attempted to invade Scotland. The ruins can be inspected from 10:30 a.m. to 1 p.m. Monday through Saturday from April through September (on Sunday from 2 to 7 p.m.). The palace was originally constructed for William the Old, a bishop who died in 1168.

An easy walk from there will take you to the impressive ruins of **Earl Patrick's Palace.** Built in 1607, it has been called "the most mature and accomplished piece of Renaissance architecture left in Scotland." Earl Patrick Stewart was the illegitimate son of the brother of Mary Queen of Scots. One writer described his memory as "infamous." The palace figured in the novel by Sir Walter Scott, *The Pirate.* It keeps the same hours as the Bishop's Palace, charging an admission of 50p (80¢) for adults and 25p (40¢) for children.

Nearby is **Tankerness House,** on Broad Street, dating from 1574. This is an example of a merchant-laird's mansion, complete with courtyard and gardens. A museum here depicts life in Orkney over the past 5,000 years. The house, once called one of the finest town houses in the country, has crow-stepped gables. Exhibitions range from the bones of the earliest prehistoric inhabitants to Neolithic pottery up to farming and domestic utensils. You'll see, among other items, a Pictish stone symbol, bronze jewelry, and temporary exhibitions as well. It is open all year from 10:30 a.m. to 1 p.m. and 2 to 5 p.m. Monday to Saturday. From May to September, it is also open on Sunday from 2 to 5 p.m. Admission is £1 ($1.60) for adults, free for children.

In the environs, you can visit the **Grain Earth Houses** at Hatson, near Kirkwall. This is an Iron Age souterrain, with stairs leading to an underground chamber.

Another Iron Age souterrain, **Rennibister Earth House,** lies about 4½ miles west and northwest of Kirkwall. This excavation also has an underground chamber which has supporting roof-pillars.

At Holm, on the road south to the island of South Ronaldsay (refer to the section at the end of Mainland) you can visit Graemeshall House. There you are likely to be stunned at its collection of **Norwood Antiques,** which has many rare and unusual pieces of furniture. The collection was started by Norris Wood, described as a "working man," in the days after World War II when many valuable pieces of Orkney Islands furniture were available for "very little" money. Over the years he added to his treasures, buying island and European antiques, until today his, the only such collection in the Orkneys, contains porcelain and clocks from Dresden, Staffordshire pieces, French and Orkney Island timepieces including grandfather clocks, musical clocks, and German, Dutch, and Orkney Islands furniture, some from the 17th century. Norwood (the trade name made from Mr. Wood's name) Antiques is today directed by his daughter-in-law, Mrs. Cilla Wood, who advises allowing at least an hour to view the entire collection. It is open from 2 to 5 p.m. and 6 to 8 p.m. Tuesday, Wednesday, and Sunday. Admission is £1 ($1.60) for adults, 50p (80¢) for children. For information, phone 085678/217.

Shopping in Kirkwall

You may not think of the Orkney Islands as a place to shop, but there are many interesting purchases to be made here.

The Longship, opposite St. Magnus Cathedral, is the retail outlet of Ola Gorie, the Orkney jeweler found at 7 Broad St. (tel. 0856/3251) in Kirkwall. Now in its third decade, it has a wide range of high-quality jewelry, including some based on stone carvings found at archeological digs. Other sections of its jewelry were inspired by the rich bird and mammal population of the islands, along with plant forms. A collection based on designs by Charles Rennie Mackintosh has proved popular, as have some art nouveau pieces.

Scott's Fish Shop, 3 Bridge St. (tel. 0856/3170), is known throughout the world for its special cure of oak-smoked salmon. Local farm cheese is also sold when it's available.

The Orkney chair is a famous design, having been created by a crofter and fisherman. Made from prime oak, it is fumed and finished with a raw linseed oil. To see these traditional Orkney chairs and stools, you can visit **D. M. Kirkness,** 14 Palace Rd. (tel. 0856/3307), an establishment listed in the Scottish Tourist Board's "1001 Things to See" in Scotland. Now run by Elizabeth and John Davidson, the company was established in 1878, receiving its first royal order in 1896 in the last years of Queen Victoria. My favorite among the many designs is the hooded chair with drawers underneath the seat. Visits are welcomed during regular work hours.

For traditional tall-backed straw-weave chairs, go to **Robert Tower's Workshop,** at Rosegarth, St. Ola (tel. 0856/3521), outside Kirkwall.

EXPLORING MAINLAND: Heading south from Kirkwall along the southern coastal road in the direction of Stromness, we come first to the hamlet of Orphir. **Orphir Church,** along the A964, lies six miles southwest of Kirkwall. The ruins here are of the country's only circular medieval church. It was constructed in the first part of the 1100s and dedicated to St. Nicholas. In the vicinity is the site of **Earl's Bu,** a great banqueting hall of the Earls of Orkney.

At Orphir, you can see vast tracts of land set aside for birdwatching. If you're an angler, the fishing is free on Kirbister Loch.

Ferries leave the **Houton Terminal** for Hoy and Flotta five or six times a day.

Only a mile from the Houton Terminal, you can take time out for a luncheon break at the **Scorrabrae Inn** (tel. 085681/262), operated by a friendly couple, Alex and Elma Mair. In a spot sheltered from the often gale-like winds that hit this southern coastline, they selected a place that will give you a sweeping view of Scapa Flow where the German Imperial Navy was sunk in 1919. You can get good and tasty lunches, and also bar suppers if you're around in the evening, costing from £5 ($8). Hours are noon to 2 p.m. and 6 to 9 p.m.

In the area, you can also visit the **Cuween Hill Cairn,** along the A965, half a mile south of Finstown and six miles west and northwest of Kirkwall. The owner of a nearby farmhouse has the key that will open a door to reveal a low mound over a megalithic passage tomb, probably dating from the third millennium B.C. The ancient bones of men, along with their oxen and dogs, were excavated here.

Bypassing Stromness for the moment, a visitor can continue with a circular tour of the island. In the vicinity of Stromness, lying off the A965, is **Maes Howe,** ten miles west of Kirkwall. Dating from 2700 B.C., this is a superb achievement of prehistoric architecture. There is a passageway through which the sun shines only at the winter solstice. Constructed with precise masonry, it was built from single slabs more than 18 feet long and some four feet wide. It also contains the largest in suti collection of Viking runes in the world, the inscriptions the work of marauding Norsemen who broke into the chambered cairn in search of buried treasure.

The **Ring of Brodgar,** between Loch of Stenness and Loch of Harray, is found five miles to the northwest of Stromness. A stone circle of some 36 stones is surrounded by a deep ditch carved out of solid bedrock. The best stone circle in Scotland, it was placed with amazing precision in 1560 B.C. It has been suggested that it was a lunar observatory. Like Stonehenge, its exact purpose remains a mystery.

In the vicinity, explorers can seek out the **Stenness Standing Stones,** a quartet of four upright stones, all that's left from a stone circle from 3000 B.C.

The **Unstan Chambered Tomb** lies two miles northeast of Stromness along the A965, ten miles west of Kirkwall. This is a big (115 feet in diameter) burial mound dating from 2500 B.C. For its type, it is unsurpassed in Western Europe. There is a chambered tomb more than six feet high. It is open throughout the day. Admission is free. The key can be picked up at Diamond Cottage, near the cairn. For information, telephone 0856/850570. Unstan Ware is a name given to pottery discovered in the tomb.

Skara Brae, 7½ miles north of Stromness, was a collection of Neolithic village houses joined by covered passages. Last occupied about 2500 B.C., it was believed to have sheltered farmers and herders. The housing colony remained buried in the sands for 4,500 years, until a storm in 1850 revealed the ruins. You can see the remains of six houses and a workshop. Once there were ten dwellings. The homes were made from flagstone rock, the roofs of skins laid on wooden or whalebone rafters. A fireplace was in the center. Beds were placed against the side walls. The bed "linen" was bracken or heather, and the "quilts" were animal skins. This prehistoric village is considered the best preserved of its type in Europe. It is open from 9:30 a.m. to 7 p.m. Monday to Saturday and 2 to 7 p.m. on Sunday April to the end of September. From October to the end of March, closing time is 4 p.m. Admission is £1 ($1.60) for adults, 50p (80¢) for children.

The **Brough of Birsay,** at Birsay, at the northern end of Mainland about 11 miles north of Stromness, is the ruin of a Norse settlement and Romanesque church on an islet that can only be reached at low tide. You can see a replica of a Pictish sculptured stone (the original was removed for safekeeping to a museum). It is open daily in season, charging an admission of 50p (80¢) for adults and 25p (40¢) for children.

Nearby are the ruins of **Earl's Palace at Birsay,** a mansion constructed in the 16th century for the Earls of Orkney.

Click Mill, off the B9057, two miles northeast of Dounby, is the only still-functioning example of an old horizontal watermill on the island.

Food and Lodging at Birsay

Barony Hotel (tel. 085672/327). If you squint, this hilltop building would look almost more like a civic building than a private hotel. Nonetheless, guests discover nine simple but comfortable bedrooms inside its walls. None has a private bath, but there are several amenities for a pleasant Orkney stay, including a dining room, cocktail lounge, TV lounge, and the possibilities for such sporting diversions as fishing and golf nearby. With breakfast included, the cost ranges from £16.50 ($26.40) per person, with half board tallying up at £23.50 ($37.60). The hotel is open May to the end of September.

Links House (tel. 085672/221). The strong vertical lines and rough textured stone of this hotel's exterior hint at its Victorian origins. Inside, the premises have been modernized to include seven simple but comfortable bedrooms, none of which has a private bath. Paying guests are accepted between April and October, and charged from £9.50 ($15.20) per person nightly for B&B, making it one of the bargains of the island. Half board is available for £16.50 ($26.40) per person daily.

STROMNESS: Set against a hill, Brinkie's Brae, Stromness was once known as

Hamnavoe or "haven bay" in old Norse. With its sheltered anchorage, it is the main port of Orkney. Its stone-flagged main street is said to "uncoil like a sailor's rope." It's really about three-quarters of a mile of narrow street and not much else. The ferryboat *St. Ola* comes in here from the mainland, having left from Scrabster. Fishing boats find shelter here from storms in the north Atlantic.

With its waterfront gables, *nousts* (slipways), and jetties, Stromness on the west coast of Mainland strikes many visitors as more interesting than Kirkwall. In the old days you could see whaling ships in port, along with vessels belonging to the Hudson Bay Company. Some of the young men of Orkney often left with them to man lonely fur stations in the far outposts of Canada. For many transatlantic vessels, Stromness was the last port of call before the New World. At Login's Well, many ships were outfitted for Arctic expeditions.

Food and Lodging

Braes Hotel, Hellihole Road (tel. 0856/850495). Even nonresidents of this hotel sometimes congregate near the sweeping glass windows of its modern extension. The original core of the hotel is a solidly constructed stone building with jutting bay windows. Today it contains a pub, a sun terrace, a dining room, central heating, and a TV lounge, and provides easy access to golf, riding, sailing, fishing, and hunting. All five bedrooms have showers, TV, and hot-beverage facilities. Owners D. and M. Tait charge £17.75 ($28.40) in a single (no toilet) and from £29.35 ($46.96) to £30.60 ($48.96) in a double or twin, the latter price for rooms with toilets. All prices include breakfast and VAT.

Ferry Inn, John Street (tel. 0856/850280), as its name implies, is convenient to the nearby ferryboat. Guests stroll off the boat and check into this centrally located hotel. Its three-story white walls were originally constructed with a collection of working chimneys. Today its format has been modernized and central heating added. The 13 bedrooms are simply but adequately set out along utilitarian designs. B&B costs £13 ($20.80) per person, and half board goes for £18 ($28.80) per person. There's a pub on the premises where typical Scottish fare is served, including haggis, smoked salmon, steak pie. To finish, try a cloutie dumpling with cream. Meals cost from £6 ($9.60), and hours are from 11:45 a.m. to 2:30 p.m. and 6 to 10 p.m. The friendly management will help arrange one of the area's several sporting diversions for guests.

Stromness Hotel, Victoria Street (tel. 0856/850298), is the largest hotel in the Orkneys. It rises imposingly near the center of town in an elaborately Victorian format of symmetrical bay windows rising along three of the building's four floors. A cocktail lounge is on the premises, and there are many amenities, including central heating and a TV lounge. The 40 rooms are simply furnished and comfortable, and each contains a private bath. Singles cost from £18.25 ($29.20), with doubles priced from £30 ($48). Lunch is served daily from noon to 2 p.m., dinner 6:30 to 8:30 p.m. Meals are à la carte, featuring steak and fish (no food is served on winter Sundays).

Sights of Stromness

The major attraction within the town is **The Pier Arts Centre** on Victoria Street (tel. 0856/850209). Open all year except on Monday, it charges no admission. This complex opened on a restored pier, and has dazzled Orcadians with its "St. Ives school" of art, including works displayed by Barbara Hepworth and Ben Nicholson. Temporary exhibitions are also presented here. It is open Tuesday to Saturday from 10:30 a.m. to 12:30 p.m. and 1:30 to 5 p.m. On Sunday June through August only it is open from 2 to 5 p.m.

At the **Stromness Museum,** 52 Alfred St. (tel. 0856/850025), you can see a collection of artifacts relating to the history of Orkney, especially a gallery devoted to maritime subjects, such as the Hudson's Bay Company and the story of the sinking of the German Imperial Fleet at Scapa Flow in 1919. The museum was founded in the same year Victoria became queen (1837) and has been much changed and altered over the years. There is also a natural history section, with excellent collections of local birds and their eggs, fossils, shells, butterflies, and moths. Admission is 20p (32¢) for adults, 5p (8¢) for children under 14.

A small but well-planned bookshop, **Stromness Books and Prints,** 1 Graham Place (tel. 0856/850565), specializes in books about Orkney and has in stock copies of the *Orkneyinga Saga.*

BURRAY AND SOUTH RONALDSAY: These are two of the most visited of the southeastern isles, lying within an easy drive of Kirkwall on Mainland. Both Burray and South Ronaldsay are connected to the mainland by the "Churchill Barriers," which now form a causeway linking the islands of Glims Holm, Burray, and South Ronaldsay, which has the most sights.

In the autumn of 1939 a Nazi submarine penetrated British defenses and sneaked in to sink the H.M.S. *Royal Oak,* drowning some 800 men of the Royal Navy. To protect the ships in Scapa Flow, Britain blockaded these sounds. Originally sunken ships were used, and then Italian prisoners of war, captured in North Africa, built a causeway.

While on the island, these more than 500 Italians turned a Nissen hut into a beautiful chapel, using mainly scrap metal and other materials. It can be seen today at Lamb Holm—the locals pronounce it "home," It's in Holm parish, but they call the parish "Holm" "ham." You figure it out!

Where to Stay on Burray

The Sands Motel, Burray Village (tel. 085673/298). The three-story format of this stone-fronted building was originally built as a fish-curing station around the turn of the century. Today, all fishy relics and smells are gone, thanks to the friendly management of Mrs. Veronica Banks. She offers four self-catering apartments, each of which contains three bedrooms, a kitchen/lounge, and a private bath. Most visitors, however, rent a bedroom separately, avoiding contact with the other guests in the same unit. Each bedroom has a hallway leading to an exterior door. It's most likely that anyone renting just a bedroom might have the entire apartment, especially in low season. B&B costs £10.50 ($16.80) per person in a double, £12 ($19.20) in a single.

St. Margaret's Hope

Also joined by the barrier, the island of South Ronaldsay is unspoiled fertile countryside. St. Margaret's Hope, a tiny hamlet, was named after a young Norwegian princess, Margaret. Called the "Maid of Norway," she was Edward II's child bride. Had she lived, she was slated to become queen of both England and Scotland.

Here at St. Margaret's Hope, 11 miles south of Kirkwall, you can visit the **Orkney Wireless Museum,** open from the end of April until the end of September daily from 10 a.m. to 8 p.m. Admission is 60p (96¢) for adults and 35p (56¢) for children. This is a museum of wartime communications used at Scapa Flow, which was a major naval anchorage in both World War I and World War II. It witnessed the surrender of the German fleet at the end of World War I. Today this sea area, enclosed by Mainland and several other islands, has developed as a pipeline landfall and tanker terminal for North Sea oil. In the Wireless Museum, you can see many instruments used by service men and women who were assigned to protect the Home Fleet. You'll also view several wireless sets of the 1930s.

While at St. Margaret's Hope, consider a visit to **The Workshop** (tel. 0856/83201), the headquarters of a group of workers who knit woolen goods, especially sweaters, in their homes throughout the Orkneys for sale here. The center is in an old stone building, formerly a bakery, just behind the post office in the heart of town. Pottery is made in a studio on the premises, outstanding among the ceramicists being Elli Pearson. For information, phone the number given above. You'll get the central phone exchange and ask to be connected with The Workshop.

A good place to stop for a meal is the **Creel Restaurant,** Front Road (tel. 085683/311), a small, cozy eating place overlooking the bay. Dishes are concocted from fresh local produce, with a large selection of fresh seafood offered, as well as Orkney beef, chicken, pork, and lamb. This restaurant was the 1986 Scottish winner of the "Taste of Britain" award. The average cost of a full three-course dinner is £8 ($12.80) to £12 ($19.20). Reservations are preferred. Hours are 6 to 9 p.m.

HOY: If you crossed the Pentland Firth from Scrabster, you have already seen the most famous sightseeing attraction of this island, the second largest in the Orkney archipelago, stretching for some 13 miles. It's the **"Old Man of Hoy."** Lying off the cliffs of the northwestern part of the island, this high isolated pillar, climbed for the first time in 1966, is 450 feet high, the same as St. Paul's Cathedral in London. Rock climbers everywhere view it as one of their biggest challenges.

Hoy has some of the most dramatic coastlines in Scotland. When the sun hits it right, its cliffs of red sandstone seem to burst into flame.

Hoy—or "high island," as it was named by the old Norse—also claims the highest hill in Orkney. It's **Ward Hill**, rising to some 1,570 feet. One of the highest vertical cliffs in Britain, **St. John's Head** rises some 1,140 feet. A panoramic vista unfolds from here, and huge colonies of seabirds can be seen.

Hoy too has its prehistoric monuments. The red-sandstone **Dwarfie Stane,** unique for its type in Britain, was a burial chamber dating from the third millennium B.C. The location is near Rackwich. This vast megalithic monument consists of two cells. Entrance was by a passageway. Many legends, including one of a giant said to have inhabited this place, grew up around this monument.

The **Martello Towers** at Hackness can be seen only from the exterior. The towers were originally constructed as a deterrent to the U.S. Navy should it threaten British shipping to the Baltic in the War of 1812. They were used again in World War I.

You can sail to Hoy from Stromness on Tuesday, Wednesday, and Saturday. There are also departures from Scapa, near Kirkwall, on Monday and Friday. For more information, see the **Orkney Islands Shipping Co.,** 4 Ayre Rd. (tel. 0856/2044), or 22 John St. (tel. 850/381) in Stromness.

Food and Lodging

Burnmouth, at Burnmouth (tel. 085679/297), an old stone building owned by Mr. and Mrs. Wyeman, near Moaness Pier, is set among wild grasses near the spire of the village church. It offers only three simply furnished rooms, and the format is that of a private home. It accepts guests throughout the year, charging reasonable rates of £8.50 ($13.60) per person for B&B, plus £4.50 ($7.20) for an evening meal. The centrally heated establishment is not licensed to serve drinks, but it has a communal lounge.

SHAPINSAY: Even if you don't have time to inspect many of the islands of Orkney, you might go over to Shapinsay to get an idea of what one is like. Getting there is fairly easy if you're based on Kirkwall. The **Orkney Islands Shipping Co.,** 4 Ayre Rd. in Wyre (tel. 0856/2044), goes there twice a day except on Sunday. The crossing takes less than half an hour.

The island was the seat of the Balfours of Trenabie. John Balfour was a nabob, making his fortune in India before becoming M.P. for Orkney and Shetland in 1790. He launched the Scottish baronial castle, Balfour, which now accepts a limited number of guests. There is no more stunning place to stay in all of the Orkney islands.

The father of Washington Irving was born on Shapinsay, later going to America. There are several Neolithic sites on the island, but most of them remain unexcavated.

Visitors not heading for Balfour Castle come here mainly for Shapinsay's secluded beaches, its many walking trails, and its wildlife, including seals, which can be seen often.

Food and Lodging

Balfour Castle (tel. 085671/282). The region's most important benefactors were the worldwide shipping magnates, the Balfour family. John Balfour began work on this castle, but it was completed by his heir in 1847. In the southwest corner of Shapinsay, it dominates the approach to the island. In the 1950s the last member of the branch of Balfours, David, died without an heir. Into the drama then entered the late Tadeusz Zawadski and his Scottish wife, Catherine. Mr. Tadeusz many years before had escaped from the ravages of a war-torn Poland. He was one of two Polish army officers to escape from a Russian-instigated massacre of Polish army officers at Katyn Forest. He fled to France where he met his future wife while he was in a Polish resettlement camp. They moved to the Orkney Islands where a series of events led them to purchase the castle, with many of its original furnishings, along with 800 acres of farmland, following the death of the Balfour heir.

Today the castle accepts no more than six guests at a time. The widow Catherine, along with her children, runs the place, and guests are treated to conversation and entertainment provided by the family. Full board, before-dinner drinks, as well as wine with lunch and dinner, are offered for £68 ($108.80) per person daily (children under 15 pay half price). Overnight guests are accepted, but the family prefers visitors to stay a minimum of three days. After all, you've come this far, you might as well. The cuisine is temptingly concocted from such ingredients as local wild duck and such fruits of the sea as freshly caught scallops, crabmeat, and lobsters. If they're patient enough, guests can also catch their own dinner, which will be cheerfully prepared for them. The estate shelters what is considered the only forest in the Orkney Islands. Composed chiefly of sycamores, it was planted in the 19th century by the Balfours. In its center, a 12-foot stone wall surrounds the kitchen gardens. There, greenhouses produce peaches, figs, and grapes, each of which is served fresh to the wide-eyed disbelief of guests. Strawberries, cabbages, and salad greens grow well within the shelter of the wall, providing a constant summertime supply of fresh produce.

The estate is still a working farm, and the charmingly articulate Christopher is involved with the running of the beef cattle, sheep, and grain production. He still takes the time to tour the property with guests, and will also arrange fishing trips or birdwatching tours—between May and July the ornithological life here is unbelievably profuse. He'll also take guests to the family's privately owned 100-acre uninhabited island where members of a friendly colony of gray seals like to say hello to visitors.

WYRE: Within easy reach of the island of Mainland, Wyre is sandwiched between Gairsay (once the stronghold of a great Viking pirate) and Rousay to its northwest. The Old Norse word for the island was *vigr,* meaning an arrowhead (some have likened the shape of Wyre to an arrowhead). Because of its lack of suitable accommodations, Wyre is most often visited on a day trip from Mainland.

To reach the island, you can take a "roll-on, roll-off" service provided by the **Orkney Islands Shipping Co.,** 4 Ayre Rd. in Wyre (tel. 0856/2044). Call them for details about departure times. Boats begin in Tingwall at Evie on the northern coast of the Mainland, heading for Rousay (see below) and Wyre before returning to Tingwall. Should this connection prove inconvenient, you can call Mr. Flaws at Helziegatha on Wyre (tel. 085682/203), who provides a supplemental service.

Day-trippers, mainly British, are primarily interested in viewing the ruins of **Cobbie Row's Castle,** said to be the earliest stone castle that can be authenticated in Scotland. Mentioned in the *Orkneyinga Saga,* it was the home of Kolbein Hruga, who built it in the 12th century. It has a rectangular tower encircled by a trench. After slaughtering Jarl John, last of the Viking earls, in 1232, Snaekill Gunnason found refuge here.

Nearby you can see the ruins of the late-12th-century **St. Mary's Chapel,** with a nave and chancel along with walls of local whinstone. The Viking warrior

Kolbein is believed to have constructed this chapel in the Romanesque style for his son. It has been partically restored.

One of the most famous poets of the Orkney Islands, Edwin Muir, was a native of Wyre and wrote about life on the island in his memoirs.

ROUSAY: Called the "Egypt of the North," the island of Rousay lies off the northwest coast of Mainland. Almost moon-shaped, and measuring about six miles across, it is known for its trout lochs, which draw anglers from all over Europe who consider it some of the best fishing in the Orkney Islands.

Much of the land is taken over by heather-covered moors. Part of the island is also given to hills, including Ward Hill, which many people walk up for a panoramic sweep of Orcadian seascape. In the northwestern part of the island is **Hellia Spur,** considered one of the most important seabird colonies in Europe. Here you can see the much-photographed puffin, which likes to hang out around these cliffs.

But where does the Egypt come in? Rousay has nearly 200 prehistoric monuments, including one of the most significant, **Midhowe Broch and Tombs,** in the west of the island. Excavated in the 1930s at the expense of W. G. Grant, the whisky distiller, it dates from the Iron Age. The walled enclosure on a promontory is cut off by a deep rock-cut ditch. The cairn is more than 75 feet long and was split among a dozen stalls or compartments. The graves of some two dozen settlers, along with their cattle, were found inside. One writer called the cairn "the great ship of death."

The other major sight, the **Blackhammer Cairn,** lies north of the B9064 on the southern coast. This megalithic burial chamber is believed to date from the third millennium B.C. It was separated into about half a dozen different compartments for the dead.

Excavation began in 1978 on a Viking site at Westness. The place figured in a story in the *Orkneyinga Saga.* A farmer digging a hole to bury a dead cow came across an old Norse gravesite. Three silver brooches, shipped to the National Museum of Antiquities at Edinburgh, were discovered among the ruins. The earliest one dated from the ninth century.

To reach the island, refer to the services described under Wyre (see above).

Food and Lodging

For an Orcadian stopover, **Hanover House** (tel. 085682/346) provides shelter from the storm in three unpretentious but comfortable accommodations in an isolated house surrounded by a treeless landscape. The house has a cocktail lounge and a dining room serving good food, including fresh fish caught in local waters. The half-board tariff begins at £17 ($27.20) per person daily, and guests are received between March and October.

EGILSAY: Lying only a mile east of Rousay, and often visited on a boat trip from there, this little three-mile-long island, shaped like an arrowhead, is forever linked to the legend of St. Magnus, the martyr who became the patron saint of the Orkney Islands. Visitors come here to see the ruins of **St. Magnus Church,** dating from the 12th century. Its round tower was of the type built by monks in Ireland. Still standing, it reaches a height of some 50 feet, and once was even taller. An ecclesiastical center may have existed here long before the arrival of the Norse invaders. The chancel with barrel vaulting is more than a dozen feet long. Magnus fell into a trap, and was killed here around Easter in 1116 with a fatal axe blow to his skull.

Many varieties of seabirds and marsh fowl live on the island, which mainly attracts visitors on day trips because of its lack of adequate accommodations. A weekly steamer service, operated by the **Orkney Islands Shipping Co.,** 4 Ayre Rd. (tel. 0856/2044) in Kirkwall, goes to Egilsay. More frequent service is provided from the Tingwall Jetty in Evie on the northern coast of Mainland. For information about crossings, call Mr. Flaws at Helziegatha on Wyre (tel. 085682/203).

STRONSAY: One of the North Isles, Stronsay lies to the northeast of Mainland. Sanday is to its north and Eday to its northwest (see below). This island is not as rich in attractions as some of those previously visited. Mostly flat land with gentle bays, it has a number of lovely sand beaches and is known for its farming.

From the 1600s until around 1920 it was also known for its fishing. The herring catch here was the greatest in Orkney. Whaling, especially in the 19th century, was an important source of revenue. In the 1830s records report the capture of some four dozen whales in one day. Of course, this "catch" was not sustained or there would be fewer whales today than there are.

The main village on Stronsay is **Whitehall,** which is in the northeast of the island near a small promontory jutting out into the sea. In the "great day of the herring," as it is referred to, this was a boomtown. Now it's peaceful, overlooking the little offshore island of **Papa Stronsay,** which was an ecclesiastical center in Viking days, as recounted in the *Orkneyinga Saga.*

Birdwatchers also "flock" to the island, going to such cliffs as Odin Ness in the north. The puffin, everybody's favorite seabird, is also fond of visiting the island. Along some of the shores you can see the remains of kelp kilns which began in 1722 as a controversial industry introduced by James Fea of Whitehall. The industry fell on bad days in 1832.

The little island of **Auskerry** lies directly south of Stronsay. It has a lighthouse—now automatic—and sheep are sent to pasture here in warm weather. The island was once inhabited, as a standing stone, a prehistoric cairn, and a chapel ruin reveal. Some of the islanders still engage in weaving, especially on long winter nights.

Because of the scarcity of accommodations, Stronsay is best visited on a day trip. You can fly there from Kirkwall two or three times a day except on Sunday. **Loganair,** the Scottish airline, operates the service (tel. 0856/2494 in Kirkwall for flight data). **Orkney Islands Shipping Co.,** 4 Ayre Rd. (tel. 0856/2044) in Kirkwall, also crosses there by sea three times a week, departing from Kirkwall.

EDAY: Called the "Isthmus Isle of the Norsemen," Eday is the center of a hardworking and traditional crofting community. Life has not been easy for these people, as most of this north isle is rather barren in part, with heather-clad and hilly moorlands. These, however, often lead to sheer cliffs or give way to sand dunes with long sweeping beaches. Chambered cairns and standing stones speak of the ancient settlements. In the 18th and 19th centuries the island, which is today experiencing depopulation, was a major supplier of peat.

People come to this almost forgotten oasis today for birdwatching, beachcombing, and sea angling. Others prefer the peaceful walks in any direction, where they are drawn eventually to the Red Head cliffs, likely to be filled with guillemots and kittiwakes. The cliffs rise to a height of 200 feet, and on a clear day you can see Fair Isle.

On its eastern coastline, Eday opens onto Eday Sound where John Gow, the pirate, was captured. After a trial in London, he was hanged in 1725, his exploits detailed in *The Pirate* by Robert Louis Stevenson.

Gow, following his capture, was held prisoner at Carrick House, in the northern part of the island. Carrick House was built in 1633 by James Stewart, the second son of Earl Robert Stewart. He had been named Earl of Carrick.

Eday, as mentioned, also has its share of chambered cairns, and is in fact outranked only by Rousay in archeological sites.

Again, because of limited accommodations, Eday is most often visited on a day trip. **Loganair** (tel. 0856/2492) in Kirkwall on Mainland flies in twice a day, except on Sunday and Wednesday. **Orkney Islands Shipping Co.**, 4 Ayre Rd. (tel. 0856/2044) in Kirkwall, also crosses to Eday three times a week.

Food and Lodging

If you'd like to find lodgings on the island, you can get in touch with the **Eday Tourist Information Centre** (tel. 08572/248), which will supply you with details about farmhouses, meals, and B&B cottages offering meals. You can also visit the studios of working artists, and can travel about by bicycle or car, even boat, and can also hire a pony.

Furrowend Guest House (tel. 08572/221). Small family-run establishments like this one are more or less dependent on the personality of their owners. In this case Mrs. Rugman is the guiding light, offering an Eday welcome to visitors who select her low-slung water-view house. The trio of comfortable rooms found here rent for £9.50 ($15.20) per person nightly, with breakfast included. The half-board rate goes for £13 ($20.80) per person. She prepares good-tasting dinners for her guests. The house has several extra services, including the use of a TV lounge, the availability of in-house drinks, central heating, and several nearby hunting and fishing facilities.

The best place to eat on the island is **Fersness Farm** (tel. 08572/262). This crofter's cottage, which opens onto beautiful vistas, offers dinner from 7 to 9 p.m., costing from £8 ($12.80). Food is served family style, including such dishes as lobsters, scallops, and Orcadian oysters. Vegetarians are catered to—in fact, the owners often grow their own vegetables in this far northern clime. You also get fine Orcadian lamb, pork, and poultry, along with tender beef. The policy is to cater for a different party every night, so call in advance and make arrangements.

SANDAY: This island, meaning "sand island," is aptly named. The sand banks seem to keep growing, because a detailed and accurate map from the mid-18th century showed the island as much smaller than it is today. Among the North Isles, it is part of the eastern archipelago. Its long white sandy beaches are nearly always deserted, even on the sunniest day in summer.

One of the largest of the North Isles, some 16 miles in length, Sanday has one of the most spectacular chambered cairns found in the Orkney Island chain. It is the **Quoyness Chambered Tomb,** and it's found on the tidal island of Elsness. The tomb and its principal chamber date from around 2900 B.C., reaching a height of some 13 feet. Other ancient monuments, including Viking burial grounds and broch sites, have been found on Sanday.

Rare migrant birds and terns can be seen at the **Start Point Lighthouse.** The lighthouse is one of the oldest in the country, built at the beginning of the 19th century. Since the early 1960s it's been on "automatic pilot." Sanday desperately needed a lighthouse, as the number of ships wrecked off its shore is topped only by North Ronaldsay. The wreck of a German destroyer can be seen on the Sand of Langamay.

While on the island you may want to visit the **Isle of Sanday Knitters,** which has a large selection of high-quality knitwear in both classic and modern design.

A display and a sales room is found in the Wool Hall at Lady Village. For information, you can call 08575/367. This cooperative, the largest of its kind in the North Isles, employs more than 100 women.

Accommodations are extremely limited so arrive with a reservation if you're planning to stay over. **Loganair** from the Kirkwall Airport (tel. 0856/2494) flies in at least two times a day except on Sunday. Also, **Orkney Islands Shipping Co.**, 4 Ayre Rd. (tel. 0856/2044) in Kirkwall, crosses to the island about three times a week.

Food and Lodging

Belsair Guest House (tel. 08575/206) is a simple stone house whose two-story facade is unadorned except for a wooden extension jutting out the front. It contains a trio of simple bathless bedrooms. You'll be able to get a drink on the premises as well as a hot cooked meal. With breakfast included, the per-person rate is £8.50 ($13.60) daily, going up to £13 ($20.80) for half board. The guest-house is open all year.

NORTH RONALDSAY: Across the North Ronaldsay Firth, the far-northeastern island of North Ronaldsay, the most remote in the archipelago, is known for the countless ships wrecked off its coastline. A Swedish East India Company merchantman, *Svecia of Gothenburg,* went down off the coast in 1740 with a fortune in cargo. The first lighthouse in the Orkney Islands opened here in 1789. Sailors, warned of the treacherous reefs and skerries around North Ronaldsay, came to depend on its flashing beam.

More than 100 settlers still occupy the island, speaking a local dialect inherited from the Old Norse language. This is a closely knit community, the families having only half a dozen or so surnames.

The island is surrounded by a drystone dike more than five feet high. The sheep are kept outside this dike where they are forced to eat seaweed, which apparently accounts for the dark color and rich taste of their meat. The sheep on the island are owned cooperatively, each family alloted its share.

North Ronaldsay is also rich in ancient sites, and it was written about in the *Orkneyinga Saga.* Occupation of the island, however, predates the arrival of the conquering Norsemen. Standing stones and a broch have been found on the island.

Many visitors come here just to see the wildlife, including seals with their pups. There is a thriving colony of seabirds.

Because of the lack of accommodations, North Ronaldsay is usually visited on a day trip. **Loganair** (tel. 0856/2494) flies in from Kirkwall Airport twice daily on Monday, Wednesday, and Friday (only once on Saturday). **Orkney Islands Shipping Co.**, 4 Ayre Rd. (tel. 0856/2044) in Kirkwall, also sails here once a week.

WESTRAY: One of the biggest of the North Isles, Westray is a fertile island filled with friendly people—a real closely knit community, many of whom are said to have Spanish blood, owing to the wreck of an armada off its stormy shores. The western shoreline is the steepest, rising in parts to some 200 feet, from which panoramic vistas can be enjoyed. Seabirds such as guillemots can be seen around Noup Head, with its red sandstone cliffs.

Below these cliffs is the so-called Gentleman's Cave. A Balfour of Trenabie is said to have found refuge in this cave, along with his comrades. He'd fled here following the defeat at Culloden outside Inverness in 1746. As winter winds howled outside, these "traitors" drank to the welfare of the "king over the water," a reference to Bonnie Prince Charlie.

The island contains many sandy beaches along with some lochs. It is also a birdwatchers' paradise.

At **Pierowall,** the major hamlet, you can see Pierowall Church, a ruin with a chancel and a nave. There are also some finely lettered grave slabs.

The most famous attraction on the island is **Noltland Castle,** a former fortress overlooking Pierowall. A governor of the island, Thomas de Tulloch, had this castle built in 1420. Eventually it was occupied by Gilbert Balfour of Westray, and its present ruins date from around the mid-1500s. It was destroyed in part by a fire in 1746. One can still see a kitchen, a stately hall, and a winding staircase. Gilbert Balfour had it designed as a fortress (something his troubled life made him in dire need of) and it was constructed in a "three-stepped" or "Z" plan, which provided complete all-round visibility against attack. It was never finished. Leading a colorful life of intrigue—one of John Knox's "men without God"—Gilbert Balfour was involved in many intrigues spinning around Mary Queen of Scots. He was perhaps implicated in the murder of Darnley. Eventually he fled to Sweden, but his involvement there in more intrigues led to his hanging in 1576.

From Kirkwall, **Loganair** flies in twice a day except Sunday. For information about flights, phone 0856/2494 in Kirkwall on Mainland. The **Orkney Islands Shipping Co.,** 4 Ayre Rd. (tel. 0856/2044) in Kirkwall, goes there by sea three times a week.

Since accommodations are very limited on the island, always go there armed with a reservation.

Where to Stay

Mrs. Costie, Seafield (no phone) takes in guests who arrive mainly in the summer, although she stays open all year. Her place is simple but snug, containing one double room and one family room with three shared public baths. The cost for B&B is from £9 ($14.40) per person nightly. An evening meal can be arranged at 6 p.m. upon request.

PAPA WESTRAY: Some people fly to this small island, which is only about four miles long and a mile in width. If you do too, you will be taking what the *Guinness Book of World Records* claims is the shortest scheduled flight on earth —that is, the air route between Westray and Papa Westray. It takes only two minutes, sometimes less, to fly the distance of 1½ miles. Air connections are made from Kirkwall on Mainland, stopping over at Westray, before continuing on to Papa Westray. Flights are twice daily on Tuesday, Thursday, and Saturday. For information, call **Loganair** at the Kirkwall Airport (tel. 0856/2494). The **Orkney Islands Shipping Co.,** 4 Ayre Rd. (tel. 0856/2044) in Kirkwall, also sails to Papa Westray three times a week from Kirkwall.

Both the birdwatcher and the student of history are drawn to Papa Westray, which was believed to have been settled at least by 3500 B.C. One of the most northerly isles in the Orkney archipelago, it is rich in archeological sites.

In the fertile farmland around Holland, the **Knap of Howar** was discovered. This is the earliest standing dwelling house in northwestern Europe, dating before 3000 B.C. There are two adjacent houses. On the **Holm of Papa Westray,** which is uninhabited, a long chambered cairn of the Maes Howe type (on the island of Mainland) was discovered here. Fourteen compartments were built into this burial mound. Sometimes boat trips go over here in summer, but the waters of the sound are considered dangerous.

On the eastern shore of Loch Treadwell, visits are possible to **St. Treadwell's Chapel,** which is believed to have marked the arrival of Christianity in the Orkney Islands. The chapel, now in ruins, was dedicated to Triduana, a Celtic saint. When a Pictish king, Nechtan, admired her lovely eyes, she is said to have plucked them out and sent them by messenger to the king. She reportedly had hoped that that would teach him a lesson: that it was foolish to admire her physical beauty. After that she went to a nunnery. For many decades the chapel was a place of pilgrimage for those suffering from eye problems.

St. Boniface Church is also a Celtic site. Stone Celtic crosses were found here on a location north of the airfield. Grave slabs were carved of red sandstone. This is believed to have been a Christian Viking burial ground.

A major attraction is **Holland House,** formerly the home of the Traills of Holland. Dating from the 17th century, the house is a fine example of a circular "Horse Engine House," which was driven by 11 horses and a dovecote. At one time the Traills owned most of Papa Westray.

The northern end of the island has been turned into a nature reserve. Along with colonies of guillemots and kittiwakes, **North Hill** is a site for one of the largest breeding colonies of the Arctic tern. Once the great auk flew over this island, but the last male was shot in 1813. If you'd like to see what one looked like, you'll find him stuffed in the British Museum in London.

Food and Lodging

Beltane House (tel. 08574/267) is owned and operated by a local cooperative. A row of farm servants' cottages have been renovated to form a complex of island shops, youth hostel, and guesthouse. Facilities include a self-service drinks cabinet, a dining room, central heating, a communal TV room, and four bedrooms, each with a toilet and shower. The tariff is £19 ($30.40) per person for dinner, bed, and breakfast. Beltane House is open all year, but Keith Browne, the manager, says June and July are the busiest months, so you should make any arrangements to stay there far in advance.

2. Fair Isle

Called the "most isolated inhabited part of Britain," Fair Isle lies on the same latitude as Bergen, Norway. Measuring only about 1 mile by 3½ miles, it sits in the lonely sea, about midway between Orkney and Shetland, the latter administering it. Relentless seas pound its 20-mile coastline in winter, and powerful westerly winds fling Atlantic spray from one side of the island to the other.

It is home to fewer than 100 hearty, rugged, and self-reliant souls who have much more entertainment now than their dances every other week. Color TV has arrived.

An important staging point for migrating birds, Fair Isle is even better known for the patterned pullovers produced here. These pullovers came into fashion again in the 1970s, and they greatly aid the island's economy. Originally the fame of this intricate pattern was spread in the 1920s by the then Prince of Wales.

Fair Isle knitting is even a part of the curriculum at all primary schools, and many jobless men have turned to knitting as well.

The knitting pattern of Fair Isle is of mysterious origin. Some suggest that it was derived from Celtic sources; others maintain that it came from the island's Viking heritage. A more daring theory maintains that the themes were Moorish. A theory widely expounded is that some 300 Spanish sailors were shipwrecked off Fair Isle from the Armada in 1588. Those men who weren't pushed over the cliffs to keep them from devouring the winter food supply may have stuck around to teach the women these designs, among other things.

In the chic boutiques of London, Milan, New York, and Paris, you'll see these garments retailing at boutiques at expensive prices. But the home-grown product is sold on Fair Isle at half the price. You eliminate the middle person by buying the knitware locally.

In 1954 the island was acquired by the National Trust for Scotland. The bird observatory installed here is considered the most remarkable in the country. Since work began in 1948, some 200 different species have been ringed. Fair Isle is an important breeding ground for everything from the puffin to the Arctic skua, from the razorbill to the storm petrel.

GETTING THERE: In his book *Hebridean Connection,* Derek Cooper writes that Fair Isle "is as far away from London as Genoa or Prague and much more difficult to reach."

To reach Fair Isle, you can go by air on British Airways to the Sumburgh Airport on the island of Mainland in Shetland. There you can transfer to Tingwall for a **Loganair** flight to Fair Isle, 24 miles away. Loganair (tel. 059584/ 246) operates several flights a week in and out of Fair Isle, and a day trip is possible. Charter flights from Shetland, usually six-seaters, can also be arranged for parties.

There are twice-weekly mailboat sailings from Shetland in summer. The mailboat *Good Shepherd III* plies between Grutness on Shetland and Fair Isle. To reserve a passage, call 03512/222.

FOOD AND LODGING: Even if you're not a birdwatcher, you might stay at the **Fair Isle Bird Observatory** (tel. 03512/258). This isolated building sits in the shelter of treeless hillsides, near the sea at the northern end of the island. It was reconstructed in the 1960s in a low-slung, big-windowed format whose earth tones blend softly into the surrounding landscape. This establishment was the dream of a well-respected ornithologist, George Waterson, who concocted the plan after being captured by the Nazis and held as a prisoner of war. He bought Fair Isle in 1948, creating the observatory, before it eventually was acquired by the National Trust. Adjacent accommodations were constructed to provide housing for visitors, which is available from March to October. The establishment is most popular during spring and autumn bird migrations. It's always wise to reserve well in advance, since it almost always overflows with birdwatchers, especially during those seasons. On the premises you'll find a superb collection of reference books on birds. Sometimes the wardens will take guests on beforebreakfast tours of bird traps which, for tagging purposes, are placed in strategic points along the stone dikes surrounding the island.

The name of the place is sometimes abbreviated as FIBO. It's centrally heated, offers drinks and meals, and contains about 24 beds. Singles cost from £23 ($36.80), and twins run from £20 ($32) per person, and dormitory accommodations from £15 ($24) per person, with all meals included.

3. The Shetland Islands

The most northerly part of the British Isles, the rugged Shetland Islands, with their spectacular coastline, takes up some 500 square miles of islands, 100 in all, many merely islets or rocks, but 17 of which are inhabited. The major island is called Mainland, as it is in Orkney. This island on which the capital, Lerwick, is located, is about 55 miles long and 20 miles wide. It's been turned into what some critics have called "a gargantuan oil terminal," but that's not true, as it contains much scenic beauty. Still, Shetland handles about half of Britain's oil.

Nature in the way of fjord-like "voes" or sheer rock cliffs makes Shetland beautiful in both seascape and landscape. But it is a stark beauty, a wild sort of rugged look as you wander across windswept moors. Because there are few trees, the landscape looks barren. But after a while it begins to take on a fascinating interest, especially when you come upon a typical Shetlander, in his sturdy Wellington boots and thick woolen sweater, cutting peat along a bog as his ancestors did before him. The Shetlander is proud, warm, and hospitable, and often eager to share the treasures of his island chain with you. At no point in Shetland are you more than three miles from the sea, as the coastline stretches for some 3,000 miles.

The islands have been called that "long string of peat and gneiss that stands precariously where three seas—the Atlantic Ocean, the North Sea, and the Arctic Ocean—meet." The major airport is at Sumburgh on the southern tip of the southernmost island of Mainland, but even it is on a level with Leningrad.

After leaving Shetland, your next stop might be the Arctic Circle, as nothing lies between this island chain and that northern wilderness. Distances in this far-northern region often surprise visitors. For example, Lerwick, the capital, is a longer haul from the capital of Scotland, Edinburgh, than "Auld Reekie" is from London.

The far-northern outpost of Shetland, Muckle Flugga Lighthouse, is a stunning achievement of engineering. Standing poised on near-vertical rock, it is called "the last window on the world" through which Great Britain looks out to the north.

It's not as cold up here as you might think, as the Shetland archipelago benefits from the warming influence of the Gulf Stream. But even in summer the weather tends to be chilly, so dress the way you would in early spring in some northern clime such as New York. It does not rain *all* the time in Shetland, as many arriving visitors think. Actually, it has less than half the annual rainfall recorded in the Western Highlands.

In summer there is almost continuous daylight. The Shetlanders call it "Simmer Dim." Conversely in midwinter there are no more than five hours of daylight.

The history of Shetland is old, dating back some 5,000 years. Through these islands paraded Neolithic man, followed by Iron Age and Bronze Age man, who gave way to the Picts and the Celts. But the most enduring influence of all came from the Vikings, who ruled Shetland until some 500 years ago. The Norsemen came to this island and established their influence which was not only to last for centuries but is still evident today in language, culture, and customs.

Shetland was inhabited more than 2,000 years before the Romans, who called it Ultima Thule, tried unsuccessfully to colonize it.

The Vikings ruled from A.D. 800. But the islands were given to Scotland in 1469 as part of the wedding dowry of Princess Margaret when she married King James III. Scotland's takeover of Shetland marked a sad period in the life of the islanders, who found themselves ruled by often cruel and unreasonable feudal barons. Earl Patrick Stewart was assigned the dubious task of imposing Scottish rule on the islanders, who up to then had known only Viking law. He became one of the most hated of rulers. His son, as far as tyrannical rule was concerned, was called "a chip off the old block." Eventually both earls were executed in Edinburgh for their crimes.

Shetlanders in part still think of themselves as separate from Scots. After all, the nearest railway is at Bergen, Norway, which is closer than Aberdeen.

Today the fisherman who lives on his croft is likely to be seen on Commercial Street in Lerwick, picking up supplies and rubbing shoulders with North Sea oilmen. And, horror of horrors in this traditionally strait-laced community, flocks of hookers have winged their way into Shetland to help some of those oilmen part with their cash.

Because of all these riggers wanting rooms, it is imperative to have advance reservations if you're contemplating a visit. The overcrowding is not as bad as it was at the height of the oil boom, but it can get tight, especially in midsummer when most of the visitors arrive.

Away from all this oil activity, life in the Shetland islands goes on much as it always did, except for the profusion of modern conveniences and foodstuff. A lot of that foodstuff is shipped in, but the food on Shetland always tastes better when it's from Shetland. You don't have to stick just to fish, even though that wouldn't be a bad idea. Other local delicacies are served, including Reestit mutton (this is salted and smoked mutton with a distinctive flavor).

The islands are famous for their short ponies and their wool. In fact, many British visitors come here on shopping expeditions, as the island craftspeople are noted for their creativity, reflected in their handcrafts, jewelry, and knitware. In some places you can watch these items being made in the workshops of the artists. Hand-knitted sweaters are still produced in great numbers on the island, and anyone contemplating a visit might want to return with at least one.

The Shetland pony can roam freely among the hills and common grazing lands in the island chain. Some, however, are schooled for children to ride, and others are shipped to the south of England where they are highly regarded as pets. Once the pony was a "workhorse," enduring inhumane conditions. They were bred to work in British coalmines. The intention was to make them have as "much strength as possible" and to be "as near the ground as it can be got." Now this beautiful pony has an easier life.

Shetland also has 10% of all the seabirds in the British Isles, and several of the smaller islands or islets have nature reserves. Birdwatchers are drawn to the islands in great numbers, as there are 300 species recorded.

Seals are protected and welcomed here. You can see them drifting among the waves, sliding down in pursuit of a fish dinner, or lounging about on the rocks and beaches, enjoying a sunny day. You'll recognize most of them as the Atlantic gray seal, with its big angular head. The common seal, with a dog-shaped head, is most often found on the islet of Mousa, for which it has a special fondness.

If you want to see the otter, you have a better chance in Shetland than anywhere else in Britain. One fisherman took one as a pet when its mother rejected it and the otter learned to play with the family dog and cat.

Fishermen find some 200 freshwater lochs in Shetland, and deep-sea angling also makes for a memorable sport. Many world fishing records have been set in Shetland. "Ton-up" fish are common.

Count yourself lucky if you get to arrive in Shetland in time for one of its festivals. The Shetland Folk Festival takes place around the end of April and the beginning of May, just when the sap of the young fiddlers on the island is beginning to rise after a long winter's sleep. International artists fly in for four days of concerts, musical workshops, and informal jam sessions, climaxed by what they call their "Final Foy."

Hundreds of visitors from Britain brave the January chill to fly to Shetland, or sail there, for the spectacle *Up Helly Aa,* a Viking tradition left over from pagan days but celebrated here with great relish. The festival celebrates the return of the sun after a long winter's absence. Blazing torches light up the dark winter sky, as a replica of a Viking longship is paraded through the streets of Lerwick, then ceremonially burned.

GETTING THERE: At the crossroads of the North Atlantic, Shetland is more accessible than ever. For example, it is only a 2½-hour flight from London. Either by air or sea, Aberdeen is the major departure point from Scotland. **British**

Airways flies four times per day to Shetland from Aberdeen between 9:30 a.m. and 5 p.m., with reduced service on weekends. The flight takes less than an hour. **Loganair,** the Scottish airline, also operates a direct service from Edinburgh to Tingwall, which lies only five miles from Lerwick. This flight takes about two hours. If booking on British Airways, ask about their "Saver" fares, but this has to be done in advance. You might also ask about BA's "Airpass."

You can also visit Shetland by sea from Aberdeen and Orkney. Roll-on/ roll-off car ferries operate to Shetland from Aberdeen five times a week, carrying up to 600 passengers and 240 automobiles. On-board facilities include restaurants, cafeterias, bars, lounges, and gift shops. Departure time from Aberdeen is usually 6 p.m. Monday through Friday. The trip takes about 14 hours. For more information, get in touch with **P&O Ferries,** P.O. Box 5, Jamieson's Quay, in Aberdeen (tel. 0224/572615).

P&O offers ferry service once a week, departing Sunday at noon from Stromness, Orkney, heading for Lerwick in the Shetlands. Service is in both summer and winter. For information in Stromness, call 0856/850655.

A modern 1,000-passenger car-ferry, the *Noronna,* operates from the end of May until the beginning of September, carrying passengers on a weekly schedule, calling at Lerwick en route from Norway, Denmark, Iceland, and Faroe. Information can be obtained, along with a Smyril line brochure, from P&O.

GETTING AROUND: It's easier than you think, as there are some 500 miles of good roads—no traffic jams, no traffic lights. Many of the islands are connected by road bridges, and for those that aren't, car-ferries provide frequent service. Renting a car might be the best solution if you want to cover a lot of ground in the shortest possible time. You can either bring a car you've rented on the mainland, or pick one up in Shetland. In summer, bus tours operate to all the major places of interest.

Most of the inhabited islands are reached from the Shetland "Mainland," and passenger fares are nominal. For example, from Yell to Fetlar takes less than half an hour and costs only 25p (40¢) per passenger. Service is 13 to 16 times a day to the islands of Unst, Yell, Whalsay, Fetlar, and Bressay. Passenger/ cargo vessels service the islands of Fair Isle, Foula, the Skerries, and Papa Stour. Scheduled services to the little-visited places only operate once or twice a week, however. Boat trips to the islands of Mousa and Noss can be arranged in summer.

It's also possible to fly. A daily inter-island air service operates from Tingwall Airport on Mainland to the islands of Whalsay, Fetlar, and Unst. **Loganair** makes the run in craft usually seating eight passengers. There are weekly flights to Foula and Out Skerries in summer.

No major international car-rental firm as yet maintains an office in the Shetlands. However, Avis and Europcar have, as their on-island agents, **Bolts Car Hire** in Lerwick (tel. 0595/2855). A competitor is **John Leask & Co.** (tel. 0595/3162).

If you have a problem about transportation either to or around the islands, you can also check with the **Tourist Office** in Lerwick (tel. 0595/3434) and the **Shetland Islands Council,** Grantfield, Lerwick (tel. 0595/2024).

LERWICK: The capital of Shetland since the 17th century, Lerwick, on the eastern coast of Mainland, is sheltered by the little offshore island of Bressay, which can be visited. In the 19th century it was the herring capital of northern Europe, and before that, a haven for smugglers. The fishing fleet of the Netherlands put in here after combing the North Sea. Even before Victoria came to the throne in 1837, Lerwick had a bustling, cosmopolitan atmosphere. That is even truer today, with the influx of foreign visitors, including riggers from America and whatever from Russia.

Believe it or not, Lerwick is sometimes the sunniest place in Britain, experiencing some 12 hours of sunshine a day in the early summer.

Commercial Street is the town's principal artery, and it is said that beneath the steep and narrow lanes of Lerwick runs a network of passages used by smugglers. Lerwick today is the main port and shopping center of Shetland.

Where to Stay

The **Shetland Hotel,** Holmsgarth Road (tel. 0595/5515), is a modern brick, stone, and concrete hotel rising four floors with square windows. It presents a weatherproof facade to the street outside. It's one of the most modern hotels in Shetland, having opened in 1984. You'll find it close to the center of town, with a good view of the harbor. The hotel offers 64 contemporary units, each with a private bath and color TV. It's expensive for our limited budget, but many guests seem to prefer all the amenities in this far-northern clime, including a choice of three different cocktail bars, a heated indoor swimming pool, a sauna, a solarium, an exercise room, and a first-class restaurant. They have a sprinkling of family rooms along with some units for disabled guests. Singles range from £49 ($78.40), while doubles cost £28 ($44.80) per person.

The **Grand Hotel,** Commercial Street (tel. 0595/2836). As its name implies, a grander hotel would be hard to find anywhere in Shetland. With its pointed turrets, weathervanes, crow's-step gables, and solid stone walls, it's one of the most ornate buildings in Lerwick. Mr. and Mrs. Wilkins, the hotel's directors, have installed a four-poster room with views of Bressay. All the bedrooms have private plumbing, direct-dial phones, and hot-beverage facilities. Singles pay £30 ($48) for B&B, doubles and twins going for £40 ($64). The extensively modernized hotel has a hairdressing salon, beauty parlor, coffeeshop, two lounge bars, a dining room, and Shetland's only nightclub.

The **Queens Hotel,** Commercial Street (tel. 0595/2826). On blustery nights, the guests of this hotel get a close-up view of the waves from the shelter of their cozy bedrooms. That's because the water comes right up to the stone foundations of this establishment, sometimes sending mists of fine spray onto the windowpanes. The hotel is in the center of town in a cluster of stone-walled buildings whose multiple chimneys are usually smoking from their log- or peat-burning fireplaces. Inexpensive bar lunches are served in the cocktail lounge, and more formal dinners are served every night in the dining room between 6:30 and 8:30 p.m. Members of the Wilkins family, the directors, charge £24 ($38.40) to £32 ($51.20) in a single and £20 ($32) to £24 ($38.40) per person in a double or twin, with breakfast included. Half board ranges in price from £25 ($40) to £36 ($57.60) per person. The establishment has some 30 comfortably furnished bedrooms, many with private bath.

The **Lerwick Hotel,** South Road (tel. 0595/2166), is one of the biggest and most up-to-date hotels in Shetland. Its sprawling design somewhat resembles a series of individual modules linked together beside a gravel- and kelp-covered beach. Many of its comfortably streamlined bedrooms offer views of the offshore island of Bressay. Each contains a private bath and several additional comforts, including a TV set and a radio. Many of the hotel's clients are visiting businessmen, who congregate in one of the trio of in-house cocktail lounges. Dinner dances are held frequently in summer. There is a sauna, along with an exercise room and a solarium. The decor of some of the public rooms, including one of the bars, is in a modernized kind of marine style, with plenty of plants and thick carpets. Bar meals provide an inexpensive alternative to the full-service restaurant. The 40 well-furnished bedrooms rent for £48 ($76.80) in a single and from £22 ($35.20) per person in a double or twin, including breakfast. Half board ranges from £39 ($62.40) per person, depending on the room assigned.

Solheim Guest House, 34 King Harald St. (tel. 0595/3613), is set among a row of interconnected stone houses. The interior of this establishment is partially illuminated by a pair of jutting bay windows, into which Mrs. Wilson has placed lace curtains and several potted plants. Per-person rates in a double range from £10 ($16) to £11 ($17.60). Singles cost from £12 ($19.20) to £14 ($22.40). The guesthouse offers central heating and the use of a TV lounge.

Glen Orchy Guest House, 20 Knab Rd. (tel. 0595/2031). A trio of medium-sized gables and a single larger one accent the stone facade of this Victorian guesthouse. Mrs. Mary Stevenson is the owner, renting six simply furnished bedrooms to paying guests throughout the year. Singles cost from £13 ($20.80), with doubles going for £10.50 ($16.80) to £12 ($19.20) per person, with breakfast and central heating included.

Kumalang Guest House, 89 St. Olaf St. (tel. 0595/5731). This semidetached stone house is in the center of town. Only three simply furnished bedrooms are available to overnight guests, who pay £10 ($16) to £11.50 ($18.40) per person, with breakfast included. Half board is available at a cost of £14 ($22.40) to £15 ($24) per person daily. Facilities include a TV lounge and central heating.

Where to Eat

The Noost, 86 Commercial St. (tel. 0595/3377), right in the heart of town, is one of the most central places to eat, and one of the most reasonably priced in Lerwick. Attracting a wide range of people, including families, it is a good choice for a light snack, a simple bar lunch, an afternoon tea, or a full dinner, often featuring fresh fish. Meals cost from £5 ($8), going up. This is a friendly café, often attracting young people. Morning coffee is from 9 a.m. to 11:45 a.m., lunch 11:45 a.m. to 2 p.m., afternoon tea 2 to 4 p.m., and dinner 6:30 to 9 p.m.

Golden Coach, 17 Hillhead (tel. 0595/3848), is the only Chinese restaurant in the Shetlands. This friendly and intimate place is softly lit and contemporary in decor. Meals cost £8 ($12.80) and up. It is open Monday to Friday from noon to 2 p.m. and 5:30 to 11 p.m. On Saturday it is open from noon to 11 p.m. and on Sunday from 1 to 11 p.m.

The Ferry Inn, in the Shetland Hotel, Holmsgarth Road (tel. 0595/5515), is a popular and unpretentious place on the ground floor of what many regard as the finest hotel in Shetland, reached by a separate entrance. A self-service buffet, costing from £4.75 ($7.60), offers a selection of both hot and cold dishes. American and continental beers and wines are available all day. Prices include VAT, and the place is open from 11 a.m. to 11 p.m. In the hotel, and accessible only from inside the hotel, is the more sedate Oasis Food & Wine bar, offering morning coffee, lunch, afternoon tea, and dinner during the same hours as the Ferry Inn.

The **Queens Hotel,** Commercial Street (tel. 0595/2826), offers some of the best food in Lerwick. It caters to families, and food is served both in its bars and in its dining room. From 12:30 to 2 p.m. you get a wide selection of inexpensively priced dishes at lunch, including roast sirloin of beef with Yorkshire pudding, steak-and-kidney pie, braised lamb cutlets, and chicken curry, all for around £5 ($8). For dessert you might settle for a sherry trifle or apple pie and ice cream. Bar snacks, costing from £3 ($4.80), are served from 6:30 to 8:30 p.m. in both bars. However, you can dine more elegantly in an attractively decorated dining room, where a table d'hôte menu, served from 6 to 9 p.m., goes for £10 ($16) per person.

Sights

Your first stop might be at the **Shetland Tourist Organisation,** Market Cross in Lerwick (tel. 0595/3434), directed by Maurice S. Mullay. It's one of the most helpful such offices in Scotland. The staff there does many things—arranging rooms, and providing information about ferries, boat trips, car rentals, what to see and do, and local events. You can even rent fishing tackle there. They're used to unusual requests: sometimes visitors from Canada or America drop in here wanting their ancestors traced.

Your first question to the tourist office might be to find out details about a 40-foot replica of a **Viking longboat** anchored in the harbor of Lerwick. It's available for a tour of the harbor in the "morning light" or Dim Riv in summer. The boat was constructed by Lerwick craftsmen in 1980, and has been a popular tourist attraction ever since.

The **Shetland Library and Museum,** Lower Hillhead (tel. 0595/3868), has, in addition to a superb reading room, four galleries devoted to such themes as art and textiles, shipping, archeological digs, and oil exploration. Admission-free, it is open on Monday, Wednesday, and Friday from 10 a.m. to 7 p.m. and on Tuesday, Thursday, and Saturday from 10 a.m. to 5 p.m.

Fort Charlotte, built in 1665, is pentagonal in shape, containing high walls with gun points pointing, naturally, at the sea. Eight years after it was constructed, it was burned by the Dutch. Restoration came in 1781. It is open daily, charging no admission, and entrance is via Market Street.

At the north end of Hillhead stands the 1882 **Town Hall,** from whose clock tower a panoramic vista unfolds. The stained-glass windows depict a host of Vikings, and a rose window, if seen in the right light, becomes a blaze of colors. Some of the coats-of-arms are from such old cities as Christiana, now renamed Oslo.

Clickhimin Broch, about a quarter of a mile southwest of Lerwick, was fortified at the beginning of the Iron Age. Excavated in the 1950s, the site revealed 1,000 years of history. It was at one time turned into a broch, rising 17 feet and built inside the fort.

The **Shetland Workshop Gallery,** 4 Burns Lane (tel. 0595/3343), is two old dwellings joined on one of the oldest lanes in town. Nowadays it's a gallery for local artists and craftspeople, and you can visit and inspect their collection of silver and stone jewelry, sweaters, and Shetland shawls. They are open daily except Wednesday from 9:30 a.m. to 1 p.m. and 2:15 to 5 p.m.

Shopping

Shopping is so interesting in Lerwick that it might be termed a sightseeing attraction. Of the many shops, you may want to drop in to **John Tulloch Knitwear Shop** (tel. 0595/2946), which has one of the best collections of Shetland knitwear in town, all for sale at reasonable prices.

You might also visit **L. & M. Anderson,** 56 Commercial St. (tel. 0595/3007), which has a good assortment of Icelandic woolens, knitwear, silvercraft, local handcrafts, and Shetland souvenirs.

J.G. Rae, Ltd., 92 Commercial St. (tel. 0595/3686), has one of the best assortments of silvercraft in all the islands. Both silver and gold jewelry are produced entirely in Shetland. Designs are often based on Viking motifs.

After Dark

Seemingly everyone heads for the **Lounge Bar** on Mounthooly Street (tel. 0595/2231). The liveliest pub in Lerwick, this place is known for its impromptu performances. You might get lucky and see a toe-tapping Shetland reel. Fiddlers like to show up here for a session on Saturday around noon. At this jam-session headquarters of the islands, every local and visiting musician will perform, just for fun and free, on a spontaneous basis. No food is served, and a pint of beer costs £1 ($1.60). It's open from 11 a.m. to 2 p.m. and 5 to 11 p.m. daily.

SCALLOWAY: On the western coast, six miles west of Lerwick, Scalloway was once the capital of Shetland. This town in more recent years was the base for rescue operations in Norway during the darkest days of World War II. Still an important fishing port, Scalloway has been altered because of the oil boom.

Food and Lodging

Scalloway Hotel, Main Street (tel. 059588/444). It's easy to spot this white-walled hotel on the major artery of town. Many of its bedrooms overlook the sea, whose salt mists are somehow always a part of the atmosphere of this sea-side town. Eight of its 12 simply but cozily furnished bedrooms contain private baths, and each unit has a color TV and radio. There's a popular bar on the premises, and you can also patronize the well-directed restaurant contained in a modern extension, serving flavorful food to village residents as well as to visitors from the outside world. With breakfast included, singles range in price from £15.50 ($24.80) to £18 ($28.80), and doubles cost £14.50 ($23.20) to £17 ($27.20) per person. Half board runs from £20 ($32) to £23 ($36.80) per person daily.

Sights

Dominating the town is **Scalloway Castle,** which was commissioned by the dreaded Earl Patrick at the beginning of the 17th century. Now in ruins, the castle was built by islanders who were forced into slave labor by the wicked earl. The castle was allowed to deteriorate after the earl was executed in Edinburgh (no one in Scalloway wanted to perpetuate his memory). If the gate isn't open, you can knock on the door of the cottage across the way and obtain the key. The castle was built in the corbel-turreted medieval style.

The **Scalloway Woollen Company** (tel. 059588/243) is open to visitors Monday to Friday from 9 a.m. to 1 p.m. and 2 to 5 p.m. You can see the processing and finishing of Shetland knitware. Later you can visit the showroom where a selection of garments made locally is sold, along with Icelandic knitwear.

North of Scalloway, and five miles northwest of Lerwick, the **Tingwall Agricultural Museum** can be visited in the hamlet of Veensgarth, off the A971. The past of the Shetland crofter vividly comes alive here in a former granary dating from the mid-1700s. You can see a collection of tools and equipment used by the crofter, along with tools used by the wheelwright and blacksmith. You'll also see tushkars and flaachterspades used for the cutting of peat. The museum is open May to September on Tuesday, Thursday, and Saturday from 10 a.m. to 1 p.m. and 2 to 5 p.m., on Wednesday from 10 a.m. to 1 p.m., and on Sunday from 2 to 5 p.m. Admission is 50p (80¢) for adults, 20p (32¢) for children.

Shetland folklore evenings are held at the Tingwall Agricultural Museum during the summer months, followed by food and entertainment at the Tingwall Public Hall. Visitors can see something of Shetland history, taste traditional island food, and be entertained by local musicians and storytellers. There are usually two folklore evenings in June, two in July, and two in August. Dates vary, but information and tickets can be picked up at the Tourist Office in Lerwick.

EXPLORING WEST MAINLAND: It is said that you can see more of Shetland from the Scord of Weisdale than from any other vantage point in the archipelago. But West Mainland has many more attractions than panoramic vistas. For example, you can often see the craftspeople of Shetland at their work.

At Whiteness

Shetland's only stone-polishing business operates at **Hjaltasteyn,** nine miles west of Lerwick. Here gemstones are turned out from raw materials in fetching hand-wrought silver settings. The workshop is open Monday to Friday from 11 a.m. to 12:30 p.m. and 2:30 to 4 p.m. The admission-free showroom is open Monday to Friday from 9:30 a.m. to 1 p.m. and 2 to 5 p.m.

In summer, **Da Brig-Stanes Tearoom** (tel. 059584/351) will give you a good "cuppa" along with some Shetland hospitality. The scones and cakes are homemade, and you can also order homemade soup, well-stuffed sandwiches, and a typical ploughman's lunch, costing from £3.50 ($5.60). It is open Monday to Saturday from 10:30 a.m. to 4:30 p.m. and on Sunday from 2:30 to 5 p.m.

Continuing north at Weisdale, you can watch high-quality jewelry being made at **Shetland Silvercraft,** where the artisans base many of their designs on ancient Celtic and Viking patterns. Visitors may go through the workrooms, and later stop in for an inspection of the stocks available in the showroom. It is open Monday to Friday from 9 a.m. to 1 p.m. and 2 to 5 p.m.

For food and lodging in the area, head to **Westings Hotel** at Wormadale (tel. 059584/242). The architects of this contemporary hotel chose a treeless hillside near the pointed finger of a saltwater estuary. The design of the building is based on the style of an old building common in the region. It has a Scandinavian look to it with its asymmetrical roofs and low-slung horizontal lines. The hotel offers six reasonably priced accommodations, each with a TV, radio, tea-making equipment, and private bath. The hotel does not contain a public bar, but drinks are served to residents before dinner. Excellent food is offered in the dining room, including a wide array of well-prepared fish. The owners charge from £18 ($28.80) per person in a double or twin and from £24 ($38.40) in a single. Half board ranges from £26 ($41.60) to £28 ($44.80) per person. The owners will also organize pony treks on the backs of Shetland ponies or indicate which of the nearby spots to seek out for the best sea fishing or hill walks.

A good restaurant in the area is **The Norseman's Inn,** Voehead, near Weisdale (tel. 059572/304). It lies at the head of Weisdale Voe, which is considered the geographical heart of the archipelago. Its facilities are open daily except Monday and Tuesday, so it's handy and convenient for touring in the area. An open-burning fireplace is a welcome sight on a chilly day. If you drop in between noon and 2 p.m. you can enjoy bar lunches. Bar suppers in the evening are served from 7 to 11 p.m. If you arrive early, have a wee little dram in one of two bars, the Viking Public Bar, which attracts a local trade, and the more elegantly decorated Longship Lounge. The restaurant serves excellent food, and it's open from 7 to 10 p.m. Depending on the time of day and your choice of room, meals cost from £5 ($8) to £12 ($19.20).

Around Walls

You can continue your tour of West Mainland by heading west along the A971 in the direction of Walls. You come first to **Staneydale Temple,** 2¾ miles outside Walls. This early Bronze Age hall—perhaps Neolithic—once had a timbered roof. It is called a temple because it bears a remarkable resemblance to such sites in Malta. This lends support to the theory that the early settlers of Shetland came from the Mediterranean.

Continuing past several lochs and sea inlets, you come to **Walls,** a hamlet built on the periphery of two voes. Its natural habor is sheltered by the off-shore islet of Vaila.

For food and lodging, head for **Burrastow House,** at Burrastow (tel. 059571/307), lying about three miles southwest of Walls. Once it was a summer place for sheep farmers, but now this 18th-century building has been turned into a remarkable little hotel by Stella and Harry Tuckey. The food they serve here is among the best on the island, and many residents and visitors come just for dinner, the only meal served. Reservations are necessary, and food is offered from 7:30 to 10 p.m., with a set dinner costing from £14 ($22.40). It is closed on Thursday and from January through February. Apéritifs are enjoyed in a cocktail bar, and then guests retreat to an oak-paneled restaurant where the daily menu is likely to include fresh vegetables from the house's own garden, along with freshly baked bread and an array of freshly caught lobster, crab, and mussels. Tender juicy steaks are also served, and you might get a stuffed leg of lamb.

The house is set on the widest section of a rocky peninsula, extending toward uninhabited islands. Guests enjoy the country-house living in an isolated but friendly establishment, lying only a 40-minute drive from Lerwick. Only three bedrooms are offered, each well furnished and containing a private bath or shower. Double rooms go for £27 ($43.20) per person, but most guests prefer to stay here on the half-board plan of £36 ($57.60) per person daily.

EXPLORING NORTH MAINLAND: The most rugged and spectacular scenery Shetland has to offer is found in the northern part of the island. Some writers have found the area similar to Norway, and I concur. That is especially true in the tiny village of Voe, with its little wooden houses.

The most "touristic" thing to do in North Mainland is to pause at **Mavis Grind.** There, take a couple of stones. One you throw to your right into the North Sea and the other to your left into the Atlantic Ocean. You can drive north along the A970 until you reach the secondary road heading west to Esha Ness. I suggest you take this exciting detour, for at Esha Ness you will come upon what many consider to be the most beautiful and dramatic cliff scenery not only in Shetland, but in all of Britain.

Vidlin

But first, before reaching these sights you may want to take an earlier detour, going along the A970 until you reach the eastern junction of the B9071. This road to the eastern part of North Mainland will take you to Vidlin, where **Lunna Kirk** is one of the oldest churches in the archipelago, which is still used by its congregation. Construction began in 1753. The church has a "leper hole," in which the poor victims could listen to the sermon without being seen to shock the other healthy worshippers.

If you'd like to seek accommodations here, **Mrs. B. Ford,** Skeo Green, Lunning (tel. 08067/302), takes in guests. However, she has only one double room to rent, charging from £7.50 ($12) per person nightly for this home-like accommodation. If arrangements are made, she'll also prepare an evening meal for you.

Brae and Busta

Heading west back to the A970, continue north toward the sightseeing attraction of Mavis Grind, already mentioned. In the area, in the vicinity of the hamlets of Brae and Busta, you'll find some of the best food and hotels in Shetland.

The **Brae Hotel,** at Brae (tel. 080622/456), a favorite of the commercial traveler, is an earth-tone building next to the road. Its comfortable interior is paneled in full-grain wood, with spotlights to accentuate different conversation areas. Each of its 25 bedrooms offers a private bath, color TV, and phone. There's a cocktail bar, along with a billiard room, a unisex hairstyling salon, and a bank all located on the premises. The hotel is upmarket, and more expensive than most of those we've considered so far. But its extra amenities can command a good price. Of course its location, an easy drive from Sullom Voe, the site of the largest oil terminal in Europe, helps its business. Singles rent for £26 ($41.60) to £46 ($73.60), and doubles go for £50 ($80).

Busta House, at Busta (tel. 080622/506). "Busta" means homestead in Norwegian. This former laird's house is said to be the oldest continuously inhabited house in Shetland. The oldest section dates from 1580; the newest (the garden wing and more bedrooms), from 1984. It has been attractively restored and accented with many pieces of antique furniture. Robin Black and Gordon Stork are the pleasant owners of this place. Long ago Queen Elizabeth II visited the house, but today your fellow guests are likely to be oil executives, visiting sportsmen, and vacationing birdwatchers. Each of its 21 bedrooms is well furnished with private bath or shower, TV, trouser press, hairdryer, and phone. The charge is £30 ($48) in a single and £22 ($35.20) per person in a double or twin. A cocktail lounge serves drinks, and there's a quiet library for nonsmoking readers. In the nonsmoker's dining room you are served local produce such as game in well-prepared combinations. The cuisine is a combination of international and traditional Scottish. You get a choice of good wines with your meal, and the bar carries 115 malt whiskies. Later you can wander in the wooded gardens. The house is open all year. They can arrange for sailing, fishing, scuba diving, and car rental.

Hillswick

On the way to the spectacular scenery at Esha Ness, already mentioned, you come to the little fishing hamlet of Hillswick, opening onto the bay in Ura Firth. The village's most notable building is the **St. Magnus Bay Hotel** (tel. 080623/372), which used to be the Shetland terminal of the old North of Scotland Shipping Co. This family-run hotel was built of solid pine in Norway around the turn of the century, then shipped to Hillswick and reassembled. It occupies a panoramic position near the cliffs of St. Magnus Bay. It is a splendid piece of Edwardian style, with steep rooflines and ornament-capped gables. Some of its art nouveau pieces capture the World War I era.

This is possibly the best place on Mainland for a "Taste of Shetland" menu. The in-house restaurant contains a carvery and a bar licensed to sell drinks. Meal service is from 12:30 to 2 p.m. and 7:30 to 9 p.m. Specialties in the cozy dining room include fresh lobster in season, fresh haddock, sea trout, and a distinctively flavored Shetland lamb, along with Aberdeen Angus beef, freshly caught local salmon, and a Scottish specialty, cullen skink. A sauna takes the nip off a foggy evening. B&B costs £19 ($30.40) per person in a room with bath, half board going for £26 ($41.60) to £30 ($48) per person.

EXPLORING SOUTH MAINLAND: This part of Shetland, reached by heading south along the A970, is both ancient and modern. On the one hand there is the gleaming Sumburgh Airport, but nearby you stumble on the ruins of Jarlshof, which may have been inhabited for some 3,000 years.

As you go down the "long leg" of Shetland, as it is called, heading due south, passing a peaty moorland and fresh meadows, the first attraction is not on Mainland at all but on an offshore island called **Mousa.** The ferry point for reaching Mousa is in the hamlet of Sandwick, seven miles south of Lerwick.

If you don't have a car, there is daily bus service between Lerwick and Sandwick.

Mousa is an island off the southeastern coast of Mainland. A local boatman will often take you across at a price to be negotiated. When the tide is out, you can leave the boat and scamper across the rocks. Sheep can be seen grazing in the shadow of stone farmhouses, now abandoned and decaying. Often seals can be seen playing offshore, and seabirds swoop down over your head, particularly if they feel your intention is to disturb their young.

People come here not just for the natural beauty of the area, although I think that would be reason enough, but to see the famous **Broch of Mousa,** a Pictish broch that was a defense tower guarding the little islet for some 2,000 years. It reached the then-incredible height of some 40 feet and was constructed of local stones, with two circular walls, one within the other. They enclose a staircase that led to sleeping quarters. You're allowed to climb to the parapet, following in the footsteps of the ancient Pictish architects. It is considered the best-preserved example of an Iron Age broch in Britain. It takes about 15 minutes to cross from Mainland to Mousa.

South of Sandwick you reach the parish of Dunrossness. At Boddam is the **Shetland Croft House Museum** (tel. 0595/5057) east of the A970 on an unmarked road lying 25 miles south of Lerwick. Rural Shetland life comes alive here in this thatched croft house from the mid-1800s. The house is authentically furnished, including such items as box beds and butter churns. The museum also has some outbuildings and a functioning watermill. It is open from the first of May until the end of September Tuesday to Sunday from 10 a.m. to 1 p.m. and 2 to 5 p.m. Adults pay an admission of 50p (80¢); children, 20p (32¢).

Continuing south, you reach the outstanding man-made attraction in Shetland, **Jarlshof,** in the vicinity of the Sumburgh Airport. It has been called "the most remarkable archeological discovery in Britain." At the southern tip of Mainland, the site wasn't called Jarlshof. That was an invention of Sir Walter Scott, who visited this former laird's home in 1814. He wrote about it in his novel *The Pirate.*

A violent storm in 1905 performed the first archeological dig. Washing away sections of the large mound, it revealed huge stone walls. Excavations that followed turned up an astonishing array of seven distinct civilizations. The earliest was from the Iron Age, but habitation continued at the site through the 1500s. Everybody over the centuries lived here from wheelhouse people to Vikings, from broch builders to medieval settlers. A castle was built here in the 16th century by the treacherous earls, Robert and Patrick Stewart, referred to earlier, but it was sacked in 1609. It is open daily April to September from 9:30 a.m. to 7:30 p.m. and October to March from 9:30 a.m. to 4 p.m. On Sunday its hours are 2 to 4 p.m., and it is closed on Tuesday and again on Wednesday in the afternoon. Admission is 50p (80¢) for adults and 25p (40¢) for children.

In the vicinity you can see the **Sumburgh Lighthouse,** one of the many Scottish lighthouses that was constructed by the grandfather of the novelist Robert Louis Stevenson. Built in 1821, it can be visited by the public, but you must phone 0950/60374 for an appointment. The terminal at Sumburgh Airport opened in 1979 and has played a major role in the North Sea oilfields development. It services many of the offshore rigs today.

Nearby is the **Sumburgh Hotel,** Sumburgh, Virkie (tel. 0950/60201). The Victorian turrets of this century-old building—once the seat of the local lairds—rise impressively above a bleak but hilly landscape near the airport. It is near many of Mainland's major attractions, including Jarlshof and Sumburgh Head. You'll find two bars within the premises, as well as a well-run restaurant, the Voe Room, serving good food and drink. Each of the 23 comfortably furnished bedrooms contains a private shower, a toilet, and usually a TV set. B&B costs from £13.50 ($21.60) to £26 ($41.60) per person, half board going for £22 ($35.20) to £26 ($41.60) per person daily.

On the coast at the tip of Scatness, about a mile southwest of Jarlshof at the end of the mainland, you come upon the **Ness of Burgi,** which was a defensive Iron Age structure related to a broch.

Heading back north in the direction of Lerwick, you can veer to the west for a trip to **St. Ninian's Island,** which is really an "islet" in the southwestern corner of Shetland. It is reached by going along the B9122. The island is approached by what is called a tombolo—that is, a wide range of white Atlantic sand. Others call it a bridging sandbar. An early monastery once stood on this island, but it was not uncovered until 1958. Puffins with their orange beaks often favor the islet, which has a pure white sandy beach on each side.

The island became famous in 1958 when a group of students from Aberdeen came upon a spectacular cache of Celtic artifacts, mainly silverware, including brooches and other valuable pieces. Monks are believed to have hidden the treasure trove, perhaps fearing a Viking attack. The St. Ninian treasure was carted off to the National Museum of Antiquities, much to the regret of Shetlanders, who got "merely the mock" in the county museum in Lerwick, where reproductions are displayed.

BRESSAY: Lying about three-quarters of a mile across the sound from Lerwick, the Isle of Bressay is reached by frequent car-ferries, the crossing taking only seven minutes. Many visitors pass through here to visit the Isle of Noss with its bird sanctuary, lying off the eastern shore of Bressay.

But Bressay has interest of its own. In the 15th century it was the headquarters of the Dutch fishing fleet. Most of its settlers today, some 300 in all, live mainly in the west. Toward the south, the conically shaped Ward of Bressay at 743 feet offers a panoramic vista of Mainland. The Ord Lighthouse was designed by the Stevenson family in 1858, and it welcomes visitors between 2 and 6 p.m. (but call first: 09582/282). The inspector of ruins will find a trio of churches on Bressay, including St. Olaf's at Gunnista, St. John's at Kirkabister, and St. Mary's at Cullingsburgh.

ISLE OF NOSS: This island, lying off the eastern shore of Bressay, is home to some 150,000 breeding seabirds, more than 10,000 of which are gannets nesting on the face of Noss Head, a 600-foot cliff. Others in this vast colony include great and Arctic skuas, kittiwakes, and puffins (the latter is locally called a "tammie norie"). One of the eight bird sanctuaries in Shetland, the **Noss Nature Reserve** lies five miles east of Lerwick. Access is by the warden's boat, weather permitting. A notice board in Lerwick should contain the details, or you can check with the tourist office in Lerwick. It's usually possible to take an inflatable dinghy to the isle daily except Monday and Thursday.

WHALSAY: Lying three miles off the eastern coast of Mainland, the island of Whalsay, along with its some 1,000 people, is concerned mainly with fishing, including excellent wild trout fishing. Fishermen in the 19th century dubbed it "The Bonnie Isle," and the name has stuck. Once it was an important trading post for the Hanseatic League, the Baltic traders coming here to exchange such items as muslin and brandy for salted and dried fish. Their decaying storage warehouse, the Bremen Böd, can still be seen close to the pier at Symbister.

The island is also known for its homemade knitware, most often "paneled erseys." Some British visitors get locals to knit these on commission. They come in a wide range of colors and designs.

The island is reached by car-ferry from Laxo, north of Lerwick. Take the A970, then turn east along the B9071. The crossing takes less than an hour. Call 08066/376 to reserve space. **Loganair** (tel. 059584/246) also flies into Whalsay's small airfield.

The most important building on the island, **Symbister House,** is now a school. In 1830 Robert Bruce constructed this Victorian extravaganza, and it remained the home of his family until 1940.

The island has a historic ruin, believed to have been a temple, dating from 2000 B.C. The priests at the temple may have lived in the dwelling some 100 yards away.

Sometimes, if the weather is right, boat trips from Whalsay leave for the **Out Skerries.** These are the most easterly inhabited outcrop of rocks in the North Isles. They are occupied by some 100 hearty souls who somehow manage to eke out a living in such a bleak place. The settlers live on only two islands, Bruray and Housay, which are connected by a causeway. Many ships used to wreck on the treacherous rocks here, a situation greatly relieved in 1852 when a lighthouse was built. Birdwatchers come here in spring and autumn to enjoy the flocks of rare and exotic migratory birds.

A ferry goes to the islands from Lerwick, and in summer Loganair (tel. 059584/246) also flies in.

The island has an 18-hole golf course.

Accommodations on Whalsay are very limited, but you might try **Lingaveg Guest House** (tel. 08066/489), an extensively restored former manse, built in 1903. Timber-lined and with full central heating, the house has an open peat fire in the dining room. Mrs. Tatham welcomes guests all year, charging £11 ($17.60) per person for B&B, £15 ($24) per person for half board. The house's conservatory offers a panoramic view over Voer and other islands.

YELL: The largest of the North Isles, Yell seems to live in some distant past. A peaty land with a few farms, it is dotted with brochs and other historical sites. Some 1,200 people here live here, but there is talk of a coming depopulation problem. Its people have known many hard times.

Lying between Mainland and Unst, Yell has many heather-clad moors rich in archeological ruins. A dozen or so broch sites—often only grassy mounds—are recorded, along with the ruins of an equivalent number of chapels. The Kirk of Ness at Breakon is believed to have been a complex inhabited for 1,000 years. The oldest building, the Old Haa of Burravoe, dates from 1637. In early spring you can see otters at play or sunning themselves.

The largest settlement is at Mid Yell. Yell was part of the herring boom of the 19th century, but those days are over now.

Car-ferries to Yell operate from Toft on Mainland and from Belmont on Unst. They run throughout the year about every 30 minutes. For reservations, phone 095782/259. The crossing takes about half an hour.

For food and lodging, check with **Pinewood Guest House,** Upper Toft, Aywick, in East Yell (tel. 0957/2077). The angular extensions of this two-story modern house jut out toward the grasslands leading down to the seaside. Its owner, Mrs. Tulloch, accepts paying guests throughout the year, charging them from £13 ($20.80) per person in one of her trio of double rooms. Half board is available for another £18 ($28.80) per person.

FETLAR: The Vikings were said to have made Fetlar, 2½ miles east of Yell, their first colony in Shetland. The islanders, like the Norwegians, still believe in the mysterious troll, as Fetlar is steeped in folklore and legend. For example, at

Hjaltadance, a ring of stones is said to have been a group of dancing "trows" or wee folk who were petrified when caught by the morning sun.

The island is part of a **National Nature Reserve,** with protected species. It has Britain's highest density of breeding waders. Birdwatchers come here to see the red-necked phalarope and the whimbrel. If they're very lucky, they might get a glimpse of the rare snowy owl. That species started to breed here in 1967. The father chased out the sons, however, and he died in 1975. Now there are only females left.

If you're interested in looking at the birds, call the warden at Bealance (tel. 095783/246). He'll advise you where to go, if he doesn't take you there himself, and will point out areas to avoid so you won't disturb nesting sites.

The gray seal can be seen along the coast, especially in October and November, and otters are also on view. Fetlar, which in Norse means "flat land," is five miles wide by five miles long. Cattle and ponies are raised on the island, which seems little disturbed by time. It has a long history. Christian monks are believed to have established a base at Papil Water by the year A.D. 900. There is a beach around this area as well.

To reach Fetlar, a ferry runs three or four times a day from Gutcher on Yell, the crossing taking about 40 minutes. To secure passage for a car, phone 095782/259. Loganair (tel. 059584/246) also wings in.

For food and lodging, try **St. Rognvalds Guest House** (tel. 095783/240), a generously proportioned and isolated house whose white walls appear all the more conspicuous because of the treeless landscape around it. Only three simply furnished bedrooms are rented to guests, each maintained in shipshape by Mrs. Jane Ritchie. Singles cost from £12 ($19.20), and doubles are priced at £11 ($17.60) per person. Half board goes for £14.50 ($23.20) per person. Guests are offered use of a TV lounge.

UNST: The northernmost point of Britain, Unst is remote and beautiful but still easy to reach. After crossing over to Yell, you can drive along the A968 to the little harbor at Gutcher in the northeast of Yell. The ferry to Unst crosses from there about every hour. If you want to bring your car over, phone 095782/259 for a reservation. Loganair (tel. 059584/246) also flies to Unst on Wednesday.

Robert Louis Stevenson stayed here for a time right before he wrote *Treasure Island*. Alan Stevenson was designing and building the Muckle Flugga lighthouse on an outermost skerry, which is even farther north than Labrador.

Like Fetlar, Unst is steeped in folklore and legend, the old folks believing in the Scandinavian "troll." An Old Norse longhouse, believed to date from the ninth century, was excavated at Underhoull. The best beach is at Skaw, set against the backdrop of **Saxa Vord,** legendary home of the giant Saxi. A drive to the top will reward you with a view of the Burra Firth.

The roll-on/roll-off car ferry from Yell will come into Belmont. In the vicinity is **Muness Castle,** constructed in 1598 by Laurence Bruce, a relative of the notorious Earl Patrick Stewart who ruled Shetland harshly and was eventually executed in Edinburgh. Bruce was a bad guy too, and tyranny apparently ran in the family. Adam Crawford, who designed Scalloway Castle for the ruling earls on Mainland, also drew up the plans for Muness. Built with rubble and known for its fine architectural detail, the castle was inhabited for less than a century. French privateers or one of Bruce's enemies may have torched it. Normally it is open April to September from 9:30 a.m. to 7 p.m. If it is closed, ask for the key at the cottage across the way. For information, phone 095785/215.

The ruins of the **Kirk of Lund,** dating from the Middle Ages, can also be seen on Unst. Like Lunna Kirk, a church in Vidlin, it too had a "leper hole" through which victims could hear the service.

Visitors go to **Haroldswick** to post their cards and letters, as it is the most northerly post office in the British Isles.

Unst is also the home of the **Hermaness Bird Reserve,** considered one of the most important ornithological sites in Britain, its 600-foot cliffs filled with such species as kittiwakes, razorbills, guillemots, and the inevitable puffins.

For food and lodging, seek out the **Baltasound Hotel** at Baltasound (tel. 095781/334), which offers an odd combination of a tall-ceilinged hip-roofed Victorian core with a sprawling contemporary extension sweeping out across the treeless landscape. It contains a warm and spacious pub. The management also welcomes children, and there's a large garden area for them to play in while their adult companions enjoy single-malt whiskies in one of the bars. The hotel is a good choice for lunch or dinner. Many local specialties, made from fish and meats, are featured on the menu. Two of the hotel's well-furnished bedrooms contain private bath. B&B costs from £15 ($24) to £18 ($28.80) per person. Half board is available at £20 ($32) to £30 ($48) per person daily.

PAPA STOUR: The "great island of priests," in the shape of a large starfish, lies off the west coast of Mainland. Legend has it that its profusion of wildflowers had such a strong scent that old haaf fishermen could use the perfume—borne far out on the wind—to fix their positions. Papa Stour is very isolated, and once it was feared that the island might be depopulated, but about 40 settlers live there now. In the darkest days of winter, bad weather can cut it off for days. But if you see it on a sunny day, it has much beauty, including those wildflowers, which still grow in abundance.

Encircled by pillars of rock and reefs, it is known for its sea caves, considered among the most impressive in Britain. They were sculpted by turbulent winds and raging seas. The largest of these is **Kirstan's Hole,** extending some 80 yards.

Papa Stour, as its name indicates, was an early base for monks. Two centuries ago there was a leper colony here on the little offshore islet of Brei Holm.

Many stories and legends—best told over a whisky before a peat fire on a cold winter's night—are spun around Papa Stour. One concerns the ruins of a stone cottage at the entrance to Housa Voe on the top of Frau Stack. Lord Thorvald Thoressen, or so it is said, kept his daughter a prisoner here to preserve her virginity. Fortunately, as the tale goes, the girl was rescued by a dashing and daring young man.

Boats go to Papa Stour about three times a week from West Burrafirth on Mainland. Call Mr. Scott at 059586/335 for information about these constantly changing details.

For food and lodging, **Mrs. S. Holt-Brook,** at Longhouse (tel. 059573/238), rents one family room, simply but comfortably furnished, for which she charges from £12 ($19.20) for half board. Guests are received from April to October.

FOULA: This remote but very tiny island with five high peaks is an "Edge of the World" type place. It is like Fair Isle, the remotest inhabited place in Britain. But adventurous travelers go there for that reason, and experience some difficulty in doing so. Even in summer the seas are likely to be turbulent, and in winter Foula has been known to be cut off from the rest of Britain for some six weeks.

Called the "Island West of the Sun," Foula may have been the legendary Thule that the Romans saw but did not visit. In local dialect, Foula means "bird island," and the name fits. Uncountable numbers of birds haunt the isle and its towering sea cliffs, including the second-highest cliff face in Britain, the Kame at 1,220 feet. About 3,000 pairs of the world's great skuas live here. They're known as a "bonxie." The highest peak, however, is the Sneug, at 1,370 feet. On the island you'll hear many stories about the rock-climbing prowess of locals who go in search of gulls' eggs, facing dangerous falls.

The island lies 27 miles west of Scalloway on the west coast of Mainland. Until the beginning of the 19th century, old Norse was the language spoken here. Its people remain very traditional, and count yourself lucky if you get to see them dance the Foula reel, considered a classic dance in Shetland.

If the weather's right, a weekly mailboat sails to Foula from Walls on Mainland. Loganair also operates a summer service.

Because of the interest by visitors in recent years, some islanders have taken to doing B&B. These include **Mrs. I. Holbourn,** at Freyers (tel. 03933/3233), who accepts guests, even in January, into her pleasant home, which has a single, a double, and a family unit, each using a public bath. Her half-board rate is from £13 ($20.80) nightly.

Mrs. M. Taylor, at Leraback (tel. 03933/3226), does B&B too, offering only one double room all year. You get a warm welcome in an often-cold climate, all for the cost of £13 ($20.80) daily for half board.

Part Two

WALES

Chapter XX

INTRODUCING CYMRU (WALES)

1. The Country
2. Getting To and Around Wales
3. The ABCs of Wales

WALES IS A LAND of melody and magic, cromlechs and castles, seashore and mountains. For too long this historic and scenic part of the British Isles has been largely ignored by North American visitors to England and Scotland. However, those who visit here quickly realize that this is not just a small, somewhat primitive, sister of England. Wales is a distinctive state in the United Kingdom, and its people are friendly and hospitable hosts to a growing number of visitors from far places as well as to English people on holiday.

This small country extends less than 170 miles from its southernmost point to the northernmost coastal outcrop, and you might stretch your measurement to about 70 miles across at the widest part. Its western extremities reach toward Ireland across St. George's Channel and the Irish Sea. On clear days, from coastal promontories and mountain heights, you can see the Wicklow Mountains of the Emerald Isle.

In its small area—8,016 square miles—you can see many of the features found in England and Scotland: splendid ruins of ancient and medieval castles, walls, and fortresses; churches and cathedrals from the Middle Ages; little coastal fishing villages, typical seaside resorts, and old market towns; green valleys and sheep-dotted rolling hills; rugged mountains and a lakes region; industrial centers; and relics of prehistoric people.

Wales has maintained its native individuality and charm and willingly shares them with visitors, extending an especially warm welcome to North Americans.

In Welsh, its name is Cymru (pronounced "Cumry"). (Note: Spelling of *Cymru* and other words in Welsh may change depending on their usage in a sentence.)

1. The Country

Prehistoric mankind left traces of habitation in what is now Wales from Old Stone Age (Paleolithic) times (ranging from 500,000 to 10,000 B.C.) through the Bronze Age (1900 to 450 B.C.) and the Iron Age (450 B.C. to A.D. 43). Great chambered tombs have been found which date from 5,000 to 6,000 years ago. Celtic invaders made their way to the British Isles from the continent of Europe (with which there had once been a land link) in Iron Age times, and it is from them that the Welsh people of today claim descent.

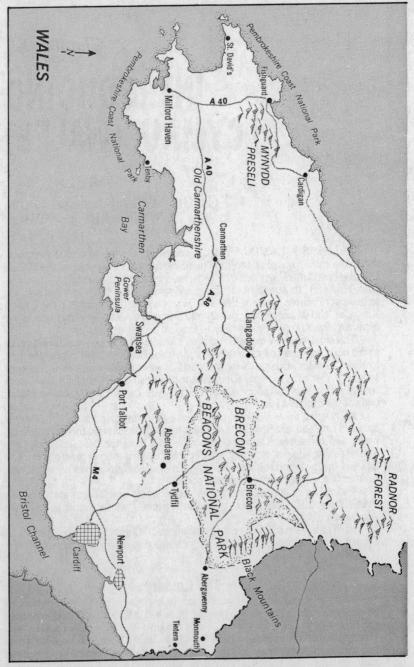

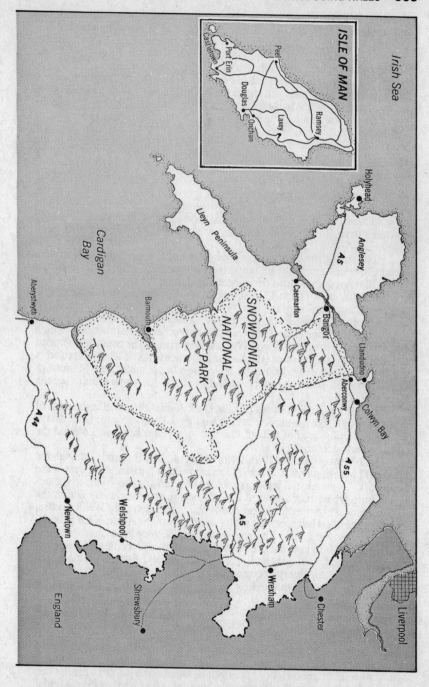

A BRIEF HISTORY: Around the dawn of the Christian era—although it had not yet dawned in Rome—the Roman legions came to make the island of Britannia a part of their empire, defeating a Celtic tribe, the Silures led by Caradoc, in the southeast corner of Wales along the Bristol Channel. By A.D. 90 Rome was in control there, establishing towns and military fortresses. The legions built a fort on the River Usk, called Isca, site of the town of Carleon today. A stone Roman ampitheater still stands there. Other legion military stations were set up at Monmouth, Abergavenny, Cardiff, and Neath. The Romans also set up military garrisons along the north coastline commanding the Conwy estuary and serving as protection for the Roman Chester in what is now England. Traces of a Roman market town and other relics of that era still exist in the southeast, although not to any great extent in any one place.

The Romans built roads to outlying fortresses at Carmarthen, Llandovery, and other sites, but mainly they stuck to the lowlands and did not apparently set out to subdue the natives of this then-wild country who took to the hills and mountains. Some of the hill-forts established by the Iron Age Celts were still the homes of their descendants, and some of these were very short distances from Roman forts. Remains of many of the hill-forts may be seen today.

Finds among the Roman ruins have given rise to the belief that there were secret Christians among the legionnaires or settlers from other places imported by the Romans to establish a permanent population.

From the end of some 400 years of Roman domination, the Celtic people hung onto their section of the island of Britannia, with internecine bloodshed and endless conflict with Picts, Vikings, and Saxons from nearby strongholds. In the 8th century, King Offa of Mercia to the east ordered construction of a high earthen bank between the Rivers Wye and Dee to mark the boundary between the part of England he ruled (the Midlands of today) and Wales, where such a border was not already defined by heavy woodlands and rivers. Sections of Offa's Dyke still exist and may be walked by sturdy souls who want to see the historic area.

The history of the Welsh during the Dark Ages is shrouded in the mists of legend and time, but it is known that the Vikings did not ignore the land, having settlements in the area of today's Llandudno and at other points around the coast, including Swansea.

The Normans came in 1066, laying claim to all of England, although the only part of Wales mentioned in the Domesday Book is a small area west of the River Usk. However, the invaders succeeded in driving the Welsh to the uplands, from where they launched assaults on the newcomers. By late in the 11th century a chain of forts had been established along the Welsh border, and the south coast had become a most remote part of the Anglo-Norman kingdom. Normans were made "marcher lords," establishing little kingdoms along the Welsh border to hold back the Celtic marauders, with castles at Chepstow, Usk, Monmouth, Abergavenny, Cardiff, Neath, and Swansea, among the many. In fact, when Henry I became king and took his older brother, Robert, prisoner, that unfortunate was kept incarcerated at Cardiff for the rest of his life.

The restless Welsh joined the Scots in invading England, and by the time the Plantagenet dynasty arose (1154), the ancient Welsh kingdom of Gwynedd (composed mainly of the northwest section of the country) had a powerful force under Owen ap Gwynedd. Rulers of the three other Welsh kingdoms allowed themselves to become subjects of King Henry II and were made barons. Owen agreed to do homage to Henry but only if he was made a prince, a title he was not given by the king. Subsequent to this, however, Llewelyn the Great, as ruler of Gwynedd and with the consent of King Henry III, claimed the title of Prince of Wales in 1267.

King Edward I, desiring to rule over an undivided nation, built the ring of castles that are most familiar to today's visitors and sent troops to subdue Wales, an endeavor occupying them from 1277 to 1282. In that year the last native Prince of Wales, Llewelyn II, was killed in a minor skirmish near Builth Wells (the site of his fatal encounter and his burial place can be visited). In 1301 Edward proclaimed his oldest son, later to become King Edward II, as Prince of Wales, a title held ever since by all male heirs to the British throne. Edward I was not so successful in subduing the Scots in order to achieve dominance over all the British Isles.

Wales simmered. The cause of national independence was not forgotten after the death of Llewelyn the Last. Social unrest grew under the yoke of English tyranny, and the Welsh bards kept past greatness and centuries of prophecy alive in the minds of the people. The families of Glyndwr (Glendower), Tudor, Mostyn, and Pengwern were considered leaders of the people.

"A scrambling and unquiet time," Shakespeare called the reign of King Henry IV (1399–1413), and so it was, with the Welsh doing their part to make it so. Owain Glyndwr, connected by blood to many of the royal lines of Wales and declared Prince of Wales by members of his own family, embarked on a campaign of pillage and devastation against English-held towns and castles. His banner was a red dragon on a white background, prototype of the Welsh flag of today, a red dragon on a green and white ground.

It was a fiery, bloody epoch in history, and Glyndwr succeeded in laying waste much of his country and gaining control of most of it. Some strong English nobles, notably Mortimer and Percy, joined his cause, and by the end of 1403, Glyndwr held the country except for Pembroke Castle, an English and Flemish stronghold, and the largest castles in the north. Parliaments were held at Machynlleth and at Harlech, which Glyndwr had designated as his capital. France sent military aid, and the Welsh leader even planned the future of England and Wales under the aegis of himself, marcher Earl Mortimer, and Percy, Earl of Northumberland.

From 1405, however, Glyndwr's forces lost ground, and soon thereafter the power was regained by the English king. Although a new king, Henry V, offered him and his followers in the rising a pardon in 1413, Glyndwr refused it and vanished from the stage of history. By a twist of fate, in 1485 a Welshman, Henry Tudor, became King Henry VII, sovereign of the British Isles.

There have, of course, been periods of travail in Wales since that time. Oliver Cromwell brought troops here during the Civil War, and there were sometimes internal struggles. The Chartist movement (1838–1848), aimed at social and political reforms, brought some violence, and labor struggles have also resulted in bloodshed, even as recently as during the coal-mine strike in 1984–1985.

An interesting historical footnote concerns the Rebecca Riots of 1843, when men dressed as women rode around destroying toll booths and tollgates in South Wales. The riots were quelled, but they were successful in having the road toll system stopped.

Wales was the landing place of a foreign invasion "force" in 1797, called the last invasion of Britain. Some 1,200 French troops, mostly released prisoners, landed near Fishguard from two frigates, only to be seized by a much smaller local militia. Legend has it that the local troops were augmented by a group of Welshwomen whose red shawls made them appear to the invaders as supplementary soldiers, helping frighten them into submission.

Today Wales and England are administered as a unit by Parliament sitting in London. The counties, or shires, as designated by official decree in 1974, are South Glamorgan, Mid Glamorgan, West Glamorgan, Gwent, Dyfed, Powys, Clwyd, and Gwynedd.

THE PEOPLE: Wales has a population of about 2,800,000 persons, some 275,000 living in the capital, Cardiff. English is the official language, but the old Celtic Welsh, the oldest surviving language in Europe, is a required course in school. However, only about 25% of the people speak both Welsh and English. Some 32,000 persons, living in remote areas, speak only Welsh. You will find many people, particularly in northern, western, and middle Wales, who will tell you that Welsh is their first language. Signs are mostly printed in both English and Welsh, and handbooks giving the meaning and pronunciation of words frequently seen are available at bookshops, tourist offices, and the like. Don't hesitate to ask how and try to pronounce Welsh words. I find the people here extremely kind and patient with North Americans—a characteristic they do not always exhibit toward the English, whom they feel have had ample opportunity to learn that *Llandudno* is not pronounced *Landudno*.

Many treatises I have seen about Welsh pronunciation say that the *ll* should be pronounced as *thl*. I differ, at least if I was taught correctly and if my ear does not deceive me as I listen to the people of the country. To me, it is sounded as *chl*, the *ch* having the sound used by the Scots in the word *loch* or the Germans in the word *ach*. Try it. Even if you only achieve a *kl* sound, the polite Welsh-speaking people will understand you, and they may even compliment you.

Many Welsh can still trace their descent from the early Celtic people, not surprising when you think that they and their ancestors have all remained for centuries within a small area. Their ancient forebears may have been builders of a hill-fort a stone's throw from where the family of a descendant still lives in the 20th century.

Of course, other bloodlines intermingled with the Celtic over the centuries, especially in coastal and border areas. The Romans, Vikings, Saxons, Picts, Irish, English—whatever—all their legacies of blood and culture have been successfully assimilated, and the people of this land are today proudly Welsh.

THE ECONOMY: Much of Wales is agricultural, with sheep, wool, cattle, and dairy products being the main output. A number of woolen mills are still in operation, where you can watch the carding, spinning, and dyeing processes on through to the weaving of handsome, warm blankets and woolen fabrics. The uplands, moors, and rolling green hills are suitable to the raising of sheep, and Welsh farmers long ago found the planting of crops not only not economic but also more demanding on a day-to-day basis than raising sheep. In the east part of Wales, sheep are in the uplands, while lower down you find cattle, pigs, oats, barley, and potatoes on the farms. In West Wales sheep graze on the bare mountains and cattle in the sheltered vales, with beef, barley, oats, and sugarbeets being produced. In Mid Wales, cattle markets are still held, with many animals being purchased and transported to the Midlands of England. Milk and butter are also produced here on a commercial basis.

Commercial fishing in the coastal waters is a time-honored pursuit, with port activity in oil tankers and refineries found in the Milford Haven area. Other water-oriented employment is in the shipping industry and on the docks and canals, although this has fallen off markedly in this last quarter of the 20th century.

Mining in Wales dates from prehistoric times, as coal, copper, gold, silver, lead, tin, slate, and iron ore have been brought from the ground. Many of the early mines are played out now, but it was mainly coal production that enriched the pockets and made ugly the valleys of South Wales. Efforts are being made successfully to reforest the ravished hills, purify the once-clear streams, and bring back some of the living green to the valleys. Some mining still goes on, but it's only a breath of that of the 19th century and the early years of the 20th. Some slate quarrying is still carried on in North Wales, but the major activity at the slate mines is tourist oriented today. Tinplating is still a flourishing industry in the southwest, as is steel production there and in Gwent.

The milling of grain was an important Welsh industry in the 17th century, as the fast-flowing streams were used to drive the mill wheels, and also the woolen mills. Several working grain (corn) mills still operate in West Wales, while others have been restored so that visitors can see the process. At the Welsh National Folk Museum at St. Fagans, you can watch one in operation, as well as at other locations throughout the country.

While the impact of the Industrial Revolution is most visible in South Wales, so are the results of its decline, affecting employment and living standards. However, here as well as elsewhere in the country, the government and many organizations and individuals have embarked on a major reclamation program aimed at turning what were blighted areas into attractive sites and making the rich historic treasures easily accessible to visitors. Industrial archeologists have focused on discovering and preparing sites all over Wales where the public can view and learn something of the history of all sorts of industry—abandoned metal mines, old ironworks, ports, tramroads, railroads, and canals.

The building of roads, bridges, tramways, railroads, and canals accompanied the growth of industry, and today they contribute to the enjoyment of visits to the country. The Romans were great roadbuilders, and some of their efforts can still be seen as overgrown trails while others have formed the base of modern roads or are even still in use. Thomas Telford, who built the Menai suspension bridge at Bangor, the handsome span at Conwy, and the aqueduct taking the Llangollen Canal over the River Dee, was also a roadbuilder. The London–Holyhead road, now the A5, was one of his major achievements. Robert Stephenson and Isambard Kingdom Brunel were responsible for the major railroad bridges of the country.

The need for suitable transport for mine products and workers led to the building of narrow-gauge railways ranging from gravity-horsepower-operated trams to steam-engine trains. See "The Great Little Trains of Wales" in this chapter for descriptions and information on these.

Canals were also an important part of the early industrial transport system. Tramroads brought products from often remote ironworks, coal mines, and slate quarries routing them to industrial sites and the major ports of Cardiff, Swansea, and Newport. Steam railroads made the use of many canals obsolete, but today some of them have been brought back into use for vacationers. See "Canal Boat Holidays" in this chapter.

All this reclamation of the landscape and the transition of such facilities as the little trains and the canals from industrial use to tourist attractions has been a shot in the arm to the country's economy, serving as a potent lure for visitors. These and the broad sandy beaches, castles, remote villages, busy market towns, resorts, scenic walks and drives, plus reminders of a prehistoric heritage all combine to make Wales worth visiting.

RELIGION: From the prehistoric time of bards and Druids, when Iron Age Celtic people worshipped in pagan fashion, the Welsh have been a religious people. Belief in spirits and magic spells died slowly over the centuries of Christian teaching—if indeed it's really dead. Throughout the country, standing stones, some predating Stonehenge, and relics of ancient altars bear mute testimony to the faith of other millennia. Even Stonehenge has a link to Wales. The center or altar stone and some 33 other huge blocks forming the inner ring of this once-sacred spot on the Salisbury Plain in England were quarried in Pembrokeshire and transported to their final resting place.

The Romans brought in their various deities, but they never caught on enough to survive or even gain many converts among the Celtic natives. Finds among the Roman ruins, however, indicate that either some legionnaires or some of the settlers imported to establish a permanent civilian population were secret Christians.

During the Dark Ages—the early and middle centuries of the first millennium A.D.—Christianity was brought to Wales by Irish Celts whose fierce evangelism stirred an answering fervor in the local people. Many stone monuments, including Celtic crosses, from the early Christian era survive. There are also holy wells, some still in use for their healing properties, such as St. Winifrede's at Holywell in the northeast corner of the country.

Not many Welsh today are Roman Catholic, although the ruins of abbeys and priories are numerous. Tintern Abbey is a prime example. All that's left of some Cistercian monasteries may be seen, these farming brothers having fitted well into early Welsh agricultural areas but losing their lands and homes in the dissolution ordered by King Henry VIII.

Don't make the mistake of thinking you'll find a strong Church of England in Wales. The counterpart is the Church in (not of) Wales, where you will note similarities of worship. Immense cathedrals still in use, such as St. David's, were originally Roman Catholic but are now Protestant. There appears to have been little difficulty in changing the path of righteousness.

Perhaps indicative of the independent spirit of the Welsh people is the fact that the majority of the population is nonconformist in its religion. Chapels abound, ranging from Baptist to Unitarian to Presbyterian to Methodist. In Mid Wales the Quakers established meeting houses.

The splendid a capella singing of the Welsh has its origins in the chapels, and most of their fine choral work heard at home and abroad is the singing of Welsh hymns in their own language.

Proof positive that the Welsh have long been a religious people can be found in the fact that so many place names begin with *llan,* the Welsh word for church.

THE CULTURE: Separating the cultural aspects of Wales (as of Scotland) from those of England presents problems so far as modern times are concerned. It's only natural that many hopeful artists, writers, musicians, and others of the cultural world tended to turn toward London, the British capital, for recognition. Of those who eschewed this trend, many chose to practice their art in the Welsh language rather than in English. In cases such as literature where this is true, I will deal mainly with the work of Wales-born, Anglo-Welsh writers, since only about 25% of the people living in this country today are familiar with the Welsh tongue.

Literature

Taliesin, the first great Welsh poet, lived in the 6th century in the part of Britain from Powys in northeast Wales to the Rheged (Strathclyde and Galloway in Scotland), establishing a tradition of Welsh literature that has persisted to this day. In the same period, the earliest Welsh chronicle recorder, **Gildas,** wrote of the invasion and defeat of Wales by the Saxons in a work later attributed to King Arthur. Another Wales-born writer of chronicles, **Geoffrey of Monmouth** (1090–1155), drew on Gildas and other predecessors in his *History*

small pony is found only on Eriskay, and unless more people take an

of the Kings of Britain, which presents "the matter of Britain" and King Arthur. The accuracy of Geoffrey's chronicle is questionable but it is still an interesting work.

An important figure in Welsh literature in the early Middle Ages was **Geraldus Cambrensis** (Gerald the Welshman), whose most famous work is *The Itinerary through Wales,* telling of an expedition made in 1188 with the Archbishop of Canterbury. The greatest medieval poet of Wales was Dafydd ap Gwilym (1325–1380), once elected Bard of the lordship of Glamorgan. Not original writing, but one of the greatest pieces of literature turned out in the Welsh language, was the translation of the Bible made in the 16th century by **Bishop Willian Morgan.** Literary figures who made their mark in Wales between the late Middle Ages and modern times include such names as **Henry Vaughan, Richard Savage, John Dyer,** and **Goronwy Owen.**

Like Welsh language writers, Anglo-Welsh poets, novelists, and short-story writers have been interested in interpreting Welsh life, especially those associated with the period from 1920 through World War II. The year 1920 more or less marks a revival of interest in Wales and its people, fostered by the decay of industry and rural life in South Wales and the Wales-England border counties.

In the early part of this century, several Wales-born persons were outstanding in literature. Among them are **Caradoc Evans,** prose writer and dramatist whose satirical work was not pleasing to his compatriots; **W. H. Davies** who wrote both poetry and prose; and poets **Edward Thomas** and **Huw Menai.** The 1920–1945 period produced some notable writers. Names easily recognized by American readers are **Richard Llewellyn** *(How Green Was My Valley);* **Richard Hughes** *(A High Wind in Jamaica);* **Emlyn Williams,** actor-dramatist *(Night Must Fall* and *The Corn Is Green);* and **T. E. Lawrence** *(Seven Pillars of Wisdom).*

Perhaps the top literary figure of this era was the poet **Dylan Thomas** (1914–1953), who was born in Swansea but did much of his writing in Laugharne, where he is buried. Another fine poet, **Alun Lewis,** writer of war verse and short stories, had a promising career cut short by death on active duty in Burma in World War II.

For a venture into old Welsh tales translated into English, I suggest *The Mabinogion.* The tales include mythology, folklore, heroism, pseudo-history—whatever the Welsh people liked to hear their bards expounded on in verse.

Art and Architecture

Augustus John, born in 1878 in Tenby, was the greatest Wales-born artist to be recognized by the world. He is known for use of vivid colors *(Spanish Flower Girl, Mother and Child),* and portraits of many notables, including Dylan Thomas and David Lloyd George. **Gwen John,** sister of Augustus, was also known for her artwork.

Of architecture, there are few traces from ancient times, although in the southeast, Roman ruins have been found, especially at Caerleon and Caerwent. Examples of outstanding medieval ecclesiastical construction are **Tintern Abbey,** now in ruins, and **St. David's Cathedral** near the west coast of Wales. **Cardiff Castle** is an Anglo-Norman edifice of the 12th century, although it has been heavily remodeled over the centuries. **Caerphilly Castle,** a rectangular structure with big, low towers, is a good example of military architecture of the Middle Ages. Other fortified royal residences of note are **Caernarfon Castle** built by Edward I at the end of the 13th century and **Harlech Castle,** also built by Edward I, on a high crag which at the time looked down on the sea. **Powis Castle** in Montgomeryshire was built in the 13th century but has been altered several times. It is occupied today by its owner, and there are no traces of wars and devastation to be seen.

Landed gentry and rich industrialists tended to fashion their houses with ornate grandeur, while simple cottages were good enough for the workers. Noteworthy are the many Tudor houses on farms and in towns near the English border, called "magpie" houses because of their black and white, half-timbered facades.

Welsh folk art includes such articles as ceramic Welsh dragons, lovespoons, and beautifully carved Welsh dressers. At various places in the country, you can watch artisans at work on these and other products and even make purchases.

Music

Throughout Wales—whether in rural areas or urban centers—among people of all walks of life, you find a love of both literature and music in the Welsh language stemming from old traditions. This is particularly true with regard to what has become the folk music of the country—Welsh hymns, a form of singing that has a unique importance in Welsh life. They are sung in the chapels, schools, mine valleys, political gatherings, at football games, in pubs, wherever the people of the country gather together. With their roots in folk songs of ancient times, the Welsh hymns have come to be a focus for national hopes and aims as well as for religion.

Music among the prehistoric forebears of today's Welsh people followed the course of other Celtic tribes, with ritual dancing, singing, and use of instruments developing from the "ringing rocks" of the Presceli Mountains to rattles, trumpets, lyres, and other string music-producers. Bards, probably accompanying their sung and chanted verse on lyres, were long known in Wales, earning their keep as historians and minstrels. They served the many little hereditary, pre-Saxon kingdoms that developed in the first few centuries of the Christian era, when the Welsh had become separated from their Celtic kinsmen who lived in the Gododdin (Strathclyde) section of Scotland and in today's Cornwall.

Church music was a part of Welsh life under the Celtic Church, with choruses and pilgrim chanting, while "mirthful and lulling" song was heard among warriors, and itinerant minstrels took secular music throughout the land. By the end of the Dark Ages, the harp had made an appearance in Wales, and other principal instruments were the *crwth,* a stringed instrument shaped like a lyre and played with a bow (widely known and surviving in Wales even after being replaced by the violin in other countries), and the bagpipes. Laws were recorded for bards, and lessons were given by the chief musicians.

It took a long time for Roman authority to replace the Celtic Church, which flourished in Wales from about the 5th century and did not die out until the 11th century. Ecclesiastical music lived through the change although in modified form, as prescribed by Rome. Monasteries, mainly Cistercian in this rural land, paid bards to serve as historians and entertainers both for church and secular patrons.

The coming to the throne of the Tudors saw an assimilation of Welsh nobility and musicians into London court life, with resultant weakening of Welsh language use and the bardic tradition. Development of street and market singing groups began in Wales, the crwth was replaced by the violin, and the triple harp became the principal instrument in the country. It was used by professional musicians as well as itinerant minstrels. Church music was of little importance in Tudor times and almost vanished with the dissolution of the monasteries.

As in changing from Celtic Church authority to that of Rome, so the Welsh were slow in transition from Roman Catholicism after the Reformation. However, the Welsh-speaking inhabitants of this British territory were quick in their acceptance of Puritanism and then of nonconformist organizations, even though these at first frowned on traditional music and abhorred dancing. Soon, however, such preachers as **John Wesley** introduced congregational singing into the churches, and the Welsh hymns were born. Hymn-singing festivals came into being, and singers included oratorio choruses (those of Handel and Mendelssohn as well as of Welsh composers) in their repertoires.

Many Welsh composers who showed promise (after the Middle Ages) went to England for training, remaining there to work, but with the industrial development of Wales and growth of urban population in the 19th century, many returned home. **Joseph Parry,** late 19th-century composer of hymn tunes and choral works, studied at the Royal Academy of Music and spent some years in the U.S. before coming home. **Grace Williams** composed for orchestras and piano and is known for Welsh folk-song arrangements. An opera, *Menna,* based on a Welsh legend, was written by **Arwel Hughes,** who became conductor of the BBC Welsh Orchestra in 1950. **Daniel Jones,** a Welsh symphony composer, wrote the music to the dramatic poem, "Under Milk Wood" written by his friend Dylan Thomas.

Choral and chamber music are very much features of Welsh life today. The repertoires of numerous choirs have been expanded by the *eisteddfods,* which have grown from small local affairs to big annual events. The *eisteddfod* came into being even before Wales was annexed by England, as a result of changes in the status of bards in the Middle Ages. The "meetings" were to discuss rules and rights of bards as performers and teachers and to hold events in which expertise was rewarded in playing the harp, playing and singing with a stringed instrument, and poetry. Today, a **National Eisteddfod** is held every year. Welsh musicians, vocalists, and choirs perform and prizes are given to the best in their categories. An art music with Welsh features has developed from the National Eisteddfods of this century. The **International Eisteddfod,** held annually in Llangollen, brings in music and dance from many countries.

FESTIVALS: A number of festive occasions are on the calendar in various parts of Wales. An outstanding event is the **Cardiff Searchlight Tattoo,** held at Cardiff Castle in the odd years (see Chapter XXII). There are also a **Margam Festival** at Margam Country Park held in July, an **Aberystwyth Summer Festival** of cultural and sporting events in late July and early August, and musical events, such as the **North Wales Music Festival** held at St. Asaph, Clwyd, the **Cardiff Festival of Music,** the **Swansea Festival of Music and Arts,** the **Fishguard Music Festival,** the **Beaumaris Festival** (music, art, and entertainment), and the **Welsh Proms,** with orchestra concerts, at St. David's Hall in Cardiff.

Throughout the country the **Noson Lawen,** an evening of Welsh entertainment, and the **Twmpath Dawns,** with country folk dancing, are frequently held, but the main Welsh cultural festival is the **Eisteddfod.**

So great is the interest in Welsh music, literature, and the arts that the Eisteddfodau have grown annually. Now there is a **National Eisteddfod** held every year in August, alternating sites between North and South Wales. At this event, contests have gradually been added until now there is competition in arts and crafts as well as literature and music, even including brass-band contests, choral and orchestral events, and in composing poetry and prose, acting and writing dramas, even ambulance work. The entire National Eisteddfod is conducted in Welsh.

The one with which you are perhaps more familiar is the **International Eisteddfod,** held annually at Llangollen the second week in July. More than 30 countries are represented at this event, competing in folk dancing, choral presentations, and folk singing. The artists wear their colorful native costumes.

For information on the Eisteddfodau and other special festival events that might be held during your trip to Wales, or even help you decide on the dates, get in touch with the **Wales Tourist Board,** P.O. Box 1, Cardiff, CF1 2XN, or the **British Tourist Authority,** 64 St. James's St., London S.W.1 (tel. 01/499-9325). For a free copy of the *Wales Events Diary,* published annually, write to either of these organizations.

FOOD AND DRINK: The food you'll be served in Wales is often indistinguishable from that you would have in England or Scotland, but there are a number of specialties you should try that you won't find elsewhere. "A Taste of Wales" restaurant program has been established whereby travelers can enjoy traditional Welsh cuisine. A symbol is displayed (which may look to you, as it does to me, like a Christmas tree bauble) bearing the words "Blas ar Gymru—A Taste of Wales." The symbol is an iron bakestone or griddle, and indicates that a restaurant, pub, café, hotel, guesthouse, or farmhouse offers traditional and contemporary Welsh food, as well as other choices.

The leek is one of the national emblems of Wales, and it is used in a number of dishes. The other national emblem is the daffodil, which doesn't appear in the culinary world except to decorate a table. The cause of selection of the leek for this national honor is lost in the dim past, although it is associated with St. David, patron saint of Wales. Legend says that he fed upon the leeks he gathered in the fields. As long ago as A.D. 633 the Welsh troops wore leeks as they fought against Saxons, and in medieval times they were again worn by Welshmen in the battle of Crécy. The Tudors were given leeks as gifts from the Welsh, and the colors of Henry VII—green and white—are reflected in the color of leeks. Today the leek is worn on St. David's Day, March 1, a national holiday.

Interestingly, the daffodil is known in Welsh as *cenhinen pedr,* meaning Peter's leek or *cenhinen fawrth,* March leek—so it's still the leek, edible or not, that is the national emblem.

Among dishes in which the leek is used is cawl mamgu, a rich soup or stew. The most commonly used recipe I found calls for lamb or mutton, turnips (the Welsh call them swedes), carrots, potatoes, parsnips, onions, and leeks. At home the broth is often served first with bread, the meat and vegetables being used as a main course. In some sections of the country, home-cured bacon is the meat used, brewed up with finely chopped vegetables. The leek pastie, usually made in the shape of a little leek, is a popular appetizer or side dish.

Potatoes were not a part of the staple diet in Wales until the early 18th century, when other crops failed. Since then the humble potato has become such a popular comestible that at many restaurants it's served at least two ways at lunch or dinner. They're not stingy with vegetables here, and you are expected to indulge in at least two if not three, such as carrots and brussels sprouts, plus the two or three potato dishes.

In the time since the potato became a dietary staple, many cooks of the country have become expert at presenting it in different forms. One which I especially like is Anglesey eggs, in which the leek is also used, as well as cheese. Punchnep is a combination of potatoes and turnips served with heavy cream. Teisen nionod, or onion cake, is a tasty, slow-baked potato-and-onion dish that I enjoy.

Most people are familiar with Welsh rarebit (or rabbit, if you prefer), but another cheese dish you should try that is not found elsewhere is Glamorgan sausage, a meatless concoction of onion, cheese, breadcrumbs, and seasonings, shaped like sausages, dipped in breadcrumbs, and fried. Another good dish is the skirrettes, served at the Skirrid Inn near Abergavenny (previewed in a later chapter). This is a sort of mashed-potato pancake with a difference. The difference is supplied by grated walnuts, prawns, hard-boiled eggs, onion, cheddar cheese, and spices. It's all given a breadcrumb coating and baked or deep-fried.

Faggots used to be made of meat fragments left over after pig slaughter, wrapped in membrane that covers the pig's abdominal organs, and shaped like sausages. Today it's all a little more palatable sounding, being made of liver, bacon, onions, breadcrumbs, and sage, cooked and served cold.

Bacon and gammon (ham) are basic menu items: the former is a basic ingredient in much Welsh cuisine, while bacon fat is used widely in cooking. A Welsh breakfast is almost indistinguishable from an English or Scottish morning repast, consisting of cereal or oatmeal porridge, some style of egg, ham and/or bacon, grilled tomato, and toast, plus juice, tea, or coffee.

Rabbit, chicken, turkey, duckling, game, even pheasant, appear on the menus, a rabbit casserole being offered in some restaurants as "A Taste of Wales," so popular is the meat. Special dishes include a poacher's pie (containing beef, rabbit, chicken, and game), and Welsh salt duck, which rivals any offered on Oriental menus.

Predominant on the list of what to eat while in Wales are the freshwater fish and the seafood. Trout and salmon prevail among the products of rivers and lakes, tumbling practically right from the fisherman's creel to your plate, with a little detour through the kitchen. Perhaps you'll get to taste a rare salmon, the gwyniad, which is found only in Bala Lake. Baked trout with bacon is a favorite.

From the ocean and coastal waters come crabs, lobsters, sewin (sea trout), crayfish, mackerel, herring, pollack, bass, hake, ling, whiting, and flat fish, as well as cockles, limpets, scallops, and mussels. The Romans were great cockle eaters, as revealed by huge mounds of the shells found in excavating the sites occupied by the long-ago conquerors. You might enjoy the cockle-and-bacon pie offered on some menus, or Gower scallops and bacon. Mussel stew and mussel and queenie (scallop) cawl, which is like a bouillabaisse, are popular dishes.

Now to the bread and cakes of Wales. The Welsh word for bread is *bara*. At least once, you should try laverbread (bara lawr), which has probably been part of the Welsh diet since prehistoric times. It's made of laver weed, a parchment-like seaweed, which is boiled and mixed with oatmeal, shaped into laverbread cakes, and fried like pancakes. It's full of vitamins and minerals. You'll find it on all "Taste of Wales" menus, so take a nibble at least. Bara ceirch, a flat oatcake, is rolled very thin and cooked on a griddle. A rich currant bread, bara brith, is found all over the country although the ingredients may vary. It's baked in a loaf, and some cooks use raisins and candied citrus peel along with the currants.

Perhaps you'll get a chance to sample Welsh cakes made with currants. They're available all over, but you may want to buy some at Dylan Thomas's boathouse at Laugharne and munch them with your tea as you look across the wide estuary where the poet had much the same view as his Iron Age predecessors. Oat biscuits are another treat, much like the oatmeal cookies you may have had back home. Desserts ("puddings" they're called here, whatever their form) seem to be mainly fruit crumbles—blackberry, apple, what have you—topped with custard and/or thick cream. Fresh fruits are popular in season.

No question about it, the Welsh eat a lot of good food. Pubs tend to be crowded at lunchtime and during the dinner hour, and servings are large. There are stops for tea in the late morning and late afternoon in offices, shops, homes, on construction sites, everywhere. You're rather expected to eat a hearty breakfast, have a biscuit or two with your tea, consume a hefty lunch, and then have an appetite for a substantial dinner whether at a restaurant, at a pub, or in a home. Don't worry. You'll get lots of exercise sightseeing, so you should burn off lots of calories.

Of course, you can find any kind of food you wish, from continental cuisine to Oriental, from Tex-Mex food to vegetarian concoctions just as you can back home. If you don't like laverbread, have a croissant.

Potables

Drinks in Wales, other than the ubiquitous tea (usually with cream and sugar), coffee, milk, and sodas, are the same ones found all over the British Isles: real ale and all the other hops brews, blended and single-malt scotch whiskies, even bourbon, Canadian, and Jack Daniel's sour-mash libations from North America.

Buckley's Brewery, in Llanelli, Dyfed, interestingly enough, is closely linked to the Methodist movement in Wales. The country's oldest manufacturer of the hops and yeast potables was founded by Henry Child, who was host to John Wesley on his visits to Wales. On Child's death, his son-in-law, the Rev. James Buckley, a disciple of Wesley, became manager of the prosperous brewery.

Beer, produced from barley, hops, yeast, and water, is found in abundance from real ale to bitter, the name of the most common kind of brew found in pubs. According to your taste, you may choose special bitter, best bitter, ordinary bitter, pale ale, mild ale, brown ale, stout, or extra stout.

I have tried both Swn y Don (Sound of the Waves) and Swn y Mor (Sound of the Sea) bourbons and found them interesting if not habit forming. Swn y Mor is available in Wales at some free house pubs and off-license places, as well as at some department stores. The maker is Brecon Brewery Ltd., Camden Arms, Brecon.

There are also a couple of Welsh Liqueurs, can y delyn and Merlin, and a few wines are available from leading wine shops in the country. However, there is no widespread commercial wine production.

2. Getting To and Around Wales

By air, coach, rail, private car, and ferry services, getting to Wales is relatively easy. I'll survey the most popular means of transport in reaching the little country before outlining popular methods of traveling around Wales once you're there. But first—

FLYING TO LONDON: There are no direct flights to Wales from North America, so London is usually used as the gateway to Cardiff and the busy industrial coastline of South Wales. Visitors heading directly to the rugged scenery of North Wales often arrange a flight into the expanded airport facilities of Manchester in the English Midlands. From England, it's more convenient to get to Wales by ground transportation.

Which Airline?

Selecting an airline to fly you to London isn't easy, as so many make that run. One good idea is to select the airline most frequently chosen by the British: **British Airways,** considered the premier airline of the U.K. Its wide-bodied jets meet every safety and comfort standard of the airline industry, at prices comparable to its competitors. BA flies to London from such U.S. gateways as New York, Boston, Washington (D.C.), Miami, Chicago, Detroit, Seattle, Philadelphia, Los Angeles, San Francisco, Anchorage, Orlando, and Pittsburgh. From Canada, the airline serves Toronto, Vancouver, and Montréal. Some flights connect with British Airways' terminal in JFK Airport in New York for continuing flights to London. About half of the cities mentioned above are served by

BA to London without an intermediate stop. In 1986, the airline added a service which is increasingly used by visitors planning on beginning their tour to North Wales, a nonstop flight between New York and Manchester four times a week.

Supersonic transport, limited to British Airways and its co-developer, Air France, is available on BA's fleet of Concordes, which soar with their passengers into London at twice the speed of sound. A BA flight takes you from North America to Heathrow, one of the world's most up-to-date air terminals.

Least Expensive "Regular" Fares

Currently, your cheapest options with regular airlines fall into two categories: **Super APEX** and **Standby.** The Super APEX is the most heavily used fare to London from North America. On most airlines, BA included, APEX tickets are valid for a stay abroad of from seven days to six months and must be purchased at least 21 days in advance. Travel dates in both directions must be reserved at the time of purchase, with a $75 penalty assessed for alterations or cancellations. For the purpose of APEX travelers (but not for users of certain other types of tickets), British Airways divides its year into three tariff schedules. The cheapest fares are offered in low season, November 1 to December 11 and from Christmas Day to the end of March. Shoulder season is slightly more expensive and is from April 1 to the end of May and during October. High season, the most expensive as well as the most crowded, is from June 1 to the end of September. Pre-Christmas travel, December 12 to 24, is considered high season.

Standby fares are offered by many airlines flying to London, sold at the airport on the day of departure and subject to availability. You risk waiting hours at the airport to find out whether you're confirmed, as well as risking being stranded at the airport for one to several days on either leg of your trip if no seats become available. Experienced standby passengers usually phone their chosen airline before leaving for the airport to learn how they stand. At British Airways, a standby fare, subject to change, costs $249 each way from New York to either London or Manchester. This type of fare is offered only during a period that corresponds roughly with high season, when flights tend to be heavily booked. Standby hopefuls are served on a first-come, first-flown basis, depending on the availability of space just before takeoff.

Economy, Business (or Executive), First Class, and **Supersonic** fares vary widely. Anyone flying with a standby or APEX ticket will be seated in the coach section of the aircraft. Passengers unable to meet the restriction imposed by BA or APEX tickets yet still want to save money can select the regular economy fare. This costs more than APEX, but it imposes no restrictions as to advance purchase or the duration of stay.

First-class seating is considerably upgraded from that of coach class. Seats are roomier and more comfortable, and there's more leg room. These seats expand into sleeperettes. Business class offers an option midway between coach and first class and is the preferred choice of frequent travelers.

Finally, for the ultimate splurge, British Airways offers the Concorde. For a hefty surcharge over a regular first-class passage, this supersonic bird will fly you to London in record-breaking time and in a style, as well as at a price, that the Pilgrims would never have dreamed of. Total in-flight time for the crossing from New York is three hours and 40 minutes.

The Competition

Passengers from North America to Britain have a wide choice of airlines.

American Airlines offers daily service to Gatwick airport from Dallas, a city not served by British Airways, as well as daily service from Chicago's

O'Hare Airport to Manchester. American also offers nonstop service from L.A. to Gatwick.

Pan American makes nonstop runs from New York three times a day to Heathrow. Pan Am also offers daily nonstop flights to Heathrow from Detroit, Miami, Los Angeles, and San Francisco, plus nonstop service from Seattle three times a week.

Northwest Airlines flies nonstop from both Minneapolis and Boston to Gatwick Airport. Flights leave daily from both cities in summer, with slightly reduced service in winter.

Canadians, for the most part, choose **Air Canada,** whose aircraft depart for London on nonstop flights from Vancouver, Calgary, Edmonton, Toronto, Montréal, and Halifax, after connecting with more than 31 Canadian cities.

No-Frills Flights

If you insist on a bare-bones flight, know that this may or may not be cheaper than the fare charged by the airline industry's giants. The situation has changed drastically from the days when you could get a $99 one-way special to London. At press time, **Virgin Atlantic Airways,** which is owned by the same people (Virgin Atlantic Records) who gave the world Boy George, charged from £289 ($462.40) to £309 ($494.40) for a one-way flight between New Jersey's Newark Airport and London's Gatwick. In some cases, this was actually more than the fare for an APEX ticket sold by British Airways. There are several restrictions placed on purchasers of tickets on Virgin Atlantic. For more information, check with your travel agent or call 212/242-1330 in the New York area. For other parts of the U.S. call toll-free, 800/862-8621.

Charter Flights

Strictly for reasons of economy, some travelers may wish to accept the numerous restrictions and possible uncertainties of a charter flight to England. Charters require that passengers strictly specify departure and return dates, and full payment must be made in advance. Any changes in flight dates are possible (if at all) upon payment of a large penalty. Any reputable travel agent can advise you about fares, cities of departure, and, most important, the reputation of the charter company.

FLYING TO WALES: After you've arrived in London, finding a convenient flight from London into Cardiff sometimes requires more than a bit of research. Few Welsh avail themselves of the air routes between Wales and London, preferring ground transportation. If you insist on flying, the Cardiff-Wales Airport, near the outlying district of Rhoose, offers direct service between Cardiff and Belfast, Brussels, Cork (Ireland), Dublin, the Channel Islands, and Leeds in England. At present, the only flight from London into Cardiff requires a transfer of flights on the Channel Island of Jersey and an inconvenient delay before the next leg of the flight.

At press time, there was a confusing collection of local airlines that flew in, including Dan Air Services and Jersey European Airways. For information about flights to and from Cardiff, call **Rhoose Airport** (tel. 0446/711211), **Dan Air** (tel. 0446/710053), or **Jersey European Airways** (tel. 0222/20877).

TRAVELING BY RAIL: Sleek "Inter City 125s" run from London (Paddington Station) to Cardiff at least every hour. These air-conditioned trains—the fastest diesels in the world—reach speeds of 125 miles per hour, covering the 145 miles to Cardiff in as little as one hour and 45 minutes.

Air travelers from all parts of the world can join up with the London–

Cardiff "Inter-City" at Reading, easily reached from either Gatwick or Heathrow Airports. Frequent "Railair" coaches, leaving every half hour, link all three terminals at London's Heathrow Airport with Reading Station, and hourly direct trains run between London's Gatwick Airport and Reading.

"Inter City" also runs twice per day from Newcastle or York to Cardiff via Sheffield, Derby, and Birmingham. Cardiff can also be reached by through train from many other centers in Britain, including Glasgow, Manchester, Edinburgh, Leeds, Hull, Brighton, and Portsmouth. In 1985 a direct North Wales–Cardiff line was launched.

If you're planning to travel not only in Wales, but in England and Scotland by rail, you may want to purchase a **BritRail Pass,** giving you unlimited travel on all British Rail routes. This pass, however, is not valid on the Sealink between Wales and Ireland. For details about this pass, refer to "Getting Around Scotland" in Chapter I.

If you decide not to purchase the BritRail Pass, you will still find a number of rail bargains offered. These include Runabout Season Tickets, giving you unlimited travel in a particular area after 9 a.m. Monday to Friday and at any time on weekends, along with Evening Rover Tickets, available for a tour along the coast and back. Ask at any British Rail station about what special discounts might be offered at the time of your visit.

The rail service in Wales is connected to all the British Rail network through Great Britain and consists of five main routes. They are the **North Wales Coastline,** an intercity route to Holyhead with connections to Blaenau, Ffestiniog, and Llandudno; **Mid Wales Line,** a service to Aberystwyth with connections to Pwllheli and Devil's Bridge (via the Great Little Train Vale of Rheidol Railway); **Borders of Wales,** from Chester through Shrewsbury, Hereford, to Newport with connections to Wrexham and Hawarden; **Heart of Wales,** connected to the Border of Wales line and the South Wales line, running from Swansea to Shrewsbury; and **South and West Wales** line, an intercity route from Newport to Fishguard with connections to Milford Haven, Pembroke, Barry Island, Penarth, Merthyr, Tydfil, and Treherbert.

TRAVELING BY COACH: Cardiff is linked to the rest of the United Kingdom by an extensive National Express coach service network. For information, call 0222/44751 or consult the National Express agent nearest you.

National Welsh, based in Cardiff, with ten regional centers in the operating area, is the largest bus and coach company in Wales. During the summer it runs a full-day tour program from Cardiff. For information, ask for details at the Cardiff Central Bus Station (tel. 0222/371331). National Welsh operates throughout Gwent, Mid and South Glamorgan.

Two other major coach companies operate local services in Wales. They are the **South Wales Transport,** operating throughout West Glamorgan and South Dyfed (tel. 0792/475511 in Swansea), and **Crosville Motors,** operating in North Dyfed, North Powys, Gwynedd, and Clwyd (tel. 0970/617951 in Aberystwyth).

You can ask about a number of discount tickets likely to be offered at the time of your visit. For example, this might include a Rover ticket, which is jointly offered by National Welsh and South Wales Transport. It enables a person to travel all over South Wales on an all-day bus ticket, and special vouchers for a number of attractions are also included. Rover bus weekly tickets and Rover Bus Plus tickets used on the fast motorway service Expresswest are also available.

Day Wanderers is a ticket offered by Crossville, allowing you unlimited travel for a day on any local bus service in North Wales. The Crossville Wanderer, offering seven consecutive days of travel on all Crossville bus routes, is also available.

TRAVELING BY CAR: Because so much of Wales is mountainous and undeveloped, the only practical way to see much of the countryside is by private car. There may be some initial awkwardness in driving on the left and coping with the ubiquitous traffic circles. You might be bothered by the unnerving habit the Welsh have of filling almost an entire lane of a narrow street with parked cars. Once you adjust to the differences, however, you'll benefit from your freedom to explore isolated country churches, secluded mountain vales, and that out-of-the-way village that might have produced your ancestors.

Car Rentals

The fine points of car rentals in Britain have been reviewed already in the "Getting Around Scotland" section of this book, Chapter I. Most visitors to Wales rent a car at one of the London airports, and then drive for three to four hours to reach the principality. My pre-rental research revealed **Budget Rent-a-Car** to be less expensive in most categories than **Avis, Godfrey Davis,** or **Hertz.** I've always found Budget's vehicles to be well-maintained, clean, and worth the rental cost. As of this writing, Budget's weekly rental of one of its most popular cars, a peppy Ford Fiesta (or a similar vehicle) with manual transmission, to be around £90 ($144) per week, with unlimited mileage. An even cheaper car available is the Mini, for about £10 ($16) less per week but less suited to the comfort of large-boned visitors. If you want a better car, Budget maintains sizable fleets of bigger and more luxurious vehicles at attractively competitive prices.

If you want to guarantee a dollar price for a rental at Budget to protect yourself against fluctuating exchange rates, you can prepay the estimated rental by phone with a credit card before you go. Reservations can be made in the United States by calling toll-free at 800/527-0700. All car-rental firms in the U.K. impose a 15% government tax. If you encounter difficulties on the road, Budget maintains a 24-hour-a-day phone number in Britain where you can call for emergency assistance.

Driving in Wales

You must have a valid driver's license from your home state. An international license is not necessary. Traffic in Wales, as in all of Britain, keeps to the *left.* At traffic islands or roundabouts, the vehicle on the right has the right-of-way. Always pass on the right. On narrow, single-track country lanes, use the nearest passing place and give priority to vehicles going uphill.

Distances and speed limits on road signs are given in miles. The maximum speed limit on motorways and dual carriageways (four-lane highways) is 70 miles per hour, 60 miles per hour on other roads, except winding country routes. In built-up areas, towns, and villages, lower limits are posted. In Wales, place names on road signs, particularly on main roads, may appear in both English and Welsh, the English name appearing above the Welsh.

Itineraries

You can spend several weeks touring Wales, but most visitors will not have that much time. Therefore, for those on the most limited of time schedules, I have proposed a one-week tour that covers just some of the highlights. It might be called "Wales in a Nutshell." This tour calls for overnights spent in Llandudno, Dolgellau, Llandrindod Wells, Tenby, and Cardiff.

The first day, you can go from Colwyn Bay for a visit to the Welsh Mountain Zoo and Flagstaff Gardens, allowing half an hour. Then travel along the

A55 to Conwy for lunch, after which you can visit Conwy Castle and Aberconwy House. For dinner, as well as a good night's sleep, return to Llandudno. By the end of the day you will have gone only a total of 19 miles, but it will seem like much longer.

On the second day, take the A55/A487 to Caernarfon for a stopover at Caernarfon Castle where you will see an audio-visual presentation. Then get on the A4085 heading for Beddgelert for lunch. Later you can go over the Nant Gwynant Pass to Betws-y-Coed to view Swallow Falls before going back to Llandudno. The day's journey adds up to a total of 59 miles.

On the third day, go through Conwy Valley to Blaenau Ffestiniog. Visit either Llechwedd Slate Caverns or Gloddfa Ganol before heading to Porthmadog. Have lunch there, then pay a visit to Snowdon Mill at Porthmadog before going on to Dolgellau for dinner and an overnight's stopover. The trip is a total of 79 miles.

On the fourth day, visit the Corris Craft Centre and the Centre for Alternative Technology before lunching in Aberystwyth. After a meal there, take a drive through the Elan Valley before going to Llandrindod Wells. There you can spend a Victorian evening, after having completed a day trip of 84 miles.

On the fifth day, pay a visit to Rock Park Spa in Llandrindod Wells before taking the A483 to Llandeilo. Have lunch there, and then continue through Carmarthen for dinner and an overnight stop at Tenby. This day trip takes in a total of 90 miles.

On the sixth day, explore Tenby in the morning before going to Swansea on the A40/A48 for lunch. Visit Margam Country Park before continuing on the M4 to Cardiff for dinner and an overnight stopover.

For the seventh and final day, take a tour of Cardiff Castle and see Llandaff Cathedral. Continue to St. Fagans for lunch. Walk around the Welsh Folk Museum and return to the city to shop for Welsh crafts. It will have been a busy day, but you will have traveled only eight miles total. For your final stay in Wales, cap it with a medieval banquet at Cardiff Castle.

CAR FERRIES BETWEEN WALES AND IRELAND: Sealink ferry services offer up to four sailings a day across the Irish Sea between Holyhead in Wales and Dun Laoghaire, just south of Dublin in Ireland, and between Fishguard, Wales, and Rosslare, on Ireland's southeastern point. You can go by car, as a through bus passenger, or by transferring from a train in either country. The Sealink fleet is composed of up-to-date, comfortable ships, with lounges, bars, restaurants, and duty-free shops.

For a car and up to four adults, a round trip costs from £99 ($158.40) to £199 ($318.40), depending on the time of year, time of the week, and type of ticket purchased. Cabins and berths are available at an extra charge. The ferries operate all year.

For information and reservations, contact any Sealink Travel Centre. In Cardiff, phone 0222/44751. Write for information or reservations to **Sealink UK Ltd.** at Turkey Shore Road, Holyhead, Gwynedd LL65 2DD, Wales; Fishguard Harbour, Goodwick, Dyfed SA64 OBU; or P.O. Box 29, London SW1V 1JX (tel. 01/834-8122).

THE GREAT LITTLE TRAINS OF WALES: Narrow-gauge railways were once important economic arteries of Wales in their duty of carrying the products of mines and associated industries to the bigger train lines and to the sea for ships to transport them throughout the world. Running from mountain-girdled estuaries through peaceful farm valleys, along lake shores, and to the summit of Snowdon—the little trains scurried and rattled and panted along for many years carrying slate, coal, lead, and iron from the source to the shipping points and to larger carriers. Some started as gravity-horsepower-operated trams. It wasn't long before they were also carrying workers and their families back up the mountains and into the wild areas on return trips, so they became in a sense passenger trains.

The width (gauge) of the tracks ranges from 15 inches to 23½ inches, with 31½ inches being the widest. They no longer carry goods, but today ten of the little trains are in operation, providing a special way to see some of the fine Welsh scenery. All have in common the charm of oldtime trains with polished paintwork and brass. They are drawn by small steam engines mainly, and their leisurely pace gives time for enjoyment. Elsewhere tramways and standard gauges operate.

You can get a **Narrow Gauge Tourist Ticket** which entitles you to seven days' unlimited travel on all the Great Little Trains, except the Snowdon Mountain Railway. Some of the lines listed below don't actually come under the "little trains" classification. Among them are the standard-gauge Gwili Valley Railway, the standard-gauge line at Llangollen, and the Great Orme, Aberystwyth, and Llechwedd tramways.

The seven-day ticket provides passage on the Ffestiniog Railway, Welsh Highland Railway, Llanberis Lake Railway, Talyllyn Railway, Bala Lake Railway, Welshpool & Llanfair Railway, Vale of Rheidol Railway, Fairbourne Railway, and Brecon Mountain Railway.

Details are available at all booking offices or from the **Narrow Gauge Railways of Wales,** Joint Marketing Panel, c/o Wharf Station, Tywyn, Gwynedd (tel. 0654/710472).

Ffestiniog Railway (tel. 0766/2340) runs between Porthmadog and Blaenau Ffestiniog from the end of March to November and over Christmas. Otherwise, there's limited weekend service.

Welsh Highland Railway (tel. 0766/3402) runs between Porthmadog and Pem-y-Mount—June to mid-July and September to October weekends only; daily from mid-July to the end of August; and on bank holidays.

Llanberis Lake Railway (tel. 028682/549) runs between Llanberis (Padarn) and Penllyn around the lake—Easter Friday to the first Sunday in October.

Talyllyn Railway (tel. 0654/710472) runs from Tywyn to Nant Gwernol—Easter to the end of August daily; weekends only in September.

Bala Lake Railway (tel. 0678/226 or 06784/666) runs between Llanuwchllyn and Bala (Lake Tegid)—Easter week and then mid-April to October.

Welshpool & Llanfair Railway (tel. 0938/810441) runs from Llanfair Caereinion and Welshpool—Easter to spring bank holiday; early June to September; weekends only from September to early October.

Vale of Rheidol Railway (tel. 0970/612377) runs between Aberystwyth and Devil's Bridge—Easter to spring bank holiday, then early June to early October.

Fairbourne Railway (tel. 0341/362), the smallest "little train," runs from Fairbourne to Barmouth Ferry—Easter week; Sunday only from April to mid-May; daily to mid-October.

Brecon Mountain Railway (tel. 0685/4854) runs from Pant to Ponsticill—Easter to the end of October except on certain specified dates.

The **Great Orme Tramway** at Llandudno (tel. 0492/76749) is a funicular, cable-operated tram taking passengers to the summit of the Great Orme, a massive headland thrusting out into the Irish Sea.

Snowdon Mountain Railway (tel. 0286/870223) runs from Llanberis to within a few yards of the top of Snowdon peak—the week before Easter to early October.

Llangollen Station (tel. 035284/500) runs standard-gauge trains on special occasions in summer.

The **Gwili Railway,** standard gauge (tel. 0639/2191), runs from Bronwydd Arms on the A484 road about three miles north of Carmarthen for a mile northward and back again—on weekends during the summer and in midweek late July to early August.

Aberystwyth Cliff Railway (tel. 0970/617642) has trams carrying passengers to the summit of Constitution Hill from the Aberystwyth Promenade—Easter to October.

Llechwedd Slate Caverns Tramway (tel. 0766/830306) takes passengers by battery-powered electric trains underground into the workings of the slate mines from a point on the A470 road north of Blaenau Ffestiniog, connecting with the Ffestiniog Railway. It operates from March to October daily.

CANAL BOAT HOLIDAYS: Most of the canals built in the late 18th century to meet transport needs of the growing industry in Wales were made obsolete by steam railroads. As long ago as 1884 the Llangollen Canal in North Wales began to be used by passenger boats. In the south, since 1970 the Brecknock & Abergavenny Canal has been restored for use of passenger boats and privately rented craft, taking people through part of the Brecon Beacons National Park. Other waterways made navigable again include a section of the Montgomery Canal near Welshpool. No other canals have yet been brought back to use by canalboats, although canoeing is possible on some. Pleasant walks are provided along old canal paths where the horses plodded along, towing the boats in the early days. This is true of portions of the Neath, Tennant, Swansea, Monmouthshire, and Glamorganshire Canals.

Today the 33-mile-stretch of canal between Brecon in Powys and Pontymoile in Gwent has been restored and is open to navigation and much used by vacationers. Modern canal cruise boats can be rented on a weekly basis from several boat firms along the canal, and there are also day boats and passenger boats available. There are such tourist facilities along the Mon & Brec, as it is called, as general stores, pubs, public phones, moorings, freshwater sources, trash-disposal points, and fishing possibilities. A "canal bus" service is operated in the Brecon Beacons National Park by **B & M Charters,** Wilsbrook, Raglan, Gwent (tel. 0291/690201). Trips are made from May to October, costing £2.50 ($4) for adults, £1.25 ($2) for children. There is boat access for the disabled, and refreshments and toilet facilities are available on board. The cruises start five miles south of Abergavenny, 300 yards off the Abergavenny–Newport road. Prior reservations are required.

If you're not traveling in your own rented canal boat, you can take a cruise in a passenger boat, which holds 50 persons for a 2½-hour trip over Pontcysyllte Aqueduct over the Dee. The **Old Wharf Canal Cruises** operate from April to September for a charge of £4 ($6.40) per person, with a basket meal included. For information, get in touch with Ric and Jennie Downey, Trevor Wharf, Trevor, Llangollen, Clwyd LL20 7TP (tel. 0978/823215).

Entering Wales at Llanymynech and running through Welshpool and Newtown, the Montgomery Canal, once used to transport coal and lime, now has a seven-mile stretch open for cruising, with a picnic site along the way. The towpath forms part of the Offa's Dyke path.

For information on the navigable canals and services, get in touch with the **British Waterways Board,** Canal Shop and Information Centre, Melbury House, Melbury Terrace, London NW1 6JX (tel. 01/262-6711). Previews of canal-connected museums and walks will be found in descriptions of the pertinent areas in this book.

3. The ABCs of Wales

Questions will arise, both before you go to Wales and while you are there, about things to do with the country to which you may not be able to find answers easily and quickly. I have tried to help, at least partially, with problems that may come up by listing the following facts.

Because both Scotland and Wales are part of the United Kingdom located on the same main British Isle, some of the data is given in Chapter I under "The ABCs of Scotland," as pertaining to both countries. In that section, you will find information on the following topics: car rentals, cigarettes, Customs, documents for entry, drugstores, electrical appliances, gasoline, hitchhiking, pets, taxes, telegrams, telephones, Telex, time, and tipping.

BABYSITTERS: You will find this no problem in hospitable Wales. Hotels and guesthouses are usually happy to secure a trustworthy and competent sitter for your children for an evening or even sometimes for a full day. In many cases, in smaller accommodations the hostess will handle the job.

BANKS: All main branches of British banks in Wales, including Barclays, Lloyds, and others, exchange foreign currency. You can also change your money at Thomas Cook Ltd. agencies and at other exchange bureaus in the country. Hours are usually from 9:30 a.m. to 3:30 p.m., although some offices keep later hours and are even open on Saturday, at least until noon.

CLIMATE: Wales enjoys a temperate climate, but there are variations in the time the seasons change from north to south, from seashore to mountains. For instance, spring comes a week or two earlier, to Anglesey in the far northwest than in Snowdonia to its east. In winter, mild sea breezes blow around the southern and western coastal areas. Winter can be hard in the mountains, and the peaks may be snow-capped until spring. It rains a lot in the hills and mountains, but then Wales has lots of bright, sunny days. It's best, in whatever section you plan to visit, to take a light wrap or sweater even in summer, unless you're a hardy northerner from the United States or Canada.

CRAFTS: Artisans in Wales work at many crafts in many parts of the principality, and welcome visitors to see and buy products in the making. Workshops belonging to the Wales Craft Council and their products are identified by the council's daffodil symbol. For information on such shops, a *Visit a Craftsman in Wales* guide is available, and crafts products are also offered at the **Wales Craft Council,** 20 Severn St., Welshpool, Powys, SY21 7AD, U.K. (tel. 0938/5313).

CURRENCY: Wales uses only British currency. As a general guideline, the prices in this book have been computed at the rate of £1 (one pound sterling) for each $1.60 U.S. Bear in mind, however, as warned in Chapter I, that international exchange rates are rather unstable, and the ratio used in this book may be outdated by the time you arrive in Wales.

DOCTORS/DENTISTS: A full list of doctors may be consulted at all major post offices. Visitors staying at hotels should refer to their receptionists.

EMBASSIES OR CONSULATES: Unfortunately there is no American consulate in Wales. If you lose your passport, you must get in touch with the U.S. Embassy in London, 24 Grosvenor Square, London W.1 (tel. 01/499-9000), for information as to how to proceed in securing a replacement.

EMERGENCIES: For ambulance, coast guards, fire, and police, dial 999. Give your name and address, plus your telephone number, and state the nature of the emergency. Misuse of the 999 service will result in a heavy fine.

HELP FOR THE DISABLED: Information for the physically handicapped is available from the **Wales Council for the Disabled,** Caerbragdy Industrial Estate, Bedwas Road, Caerphilly, Mid Glamorgan CF8 3SL (tel. 0222/887325). They can tell you about facilities suitable in touring, accommodations, restaurants, cafés, pubs, public rest rooms, attractions, and other phases of hospitality to make a trip pleasurable.

HOLIDAYS: Christmas Day, Boxing Day (December 26), New Year's Day, St. David's Day (March 1), Good Friday and Easter Monday, May Day, and bank holidays.

PUB HOURS: Normal pub hours, set by law, are from 11:30 a.m. to 3:30 p.m. and 5:30 to 10:30 p.m. Monday to Thursday. On Friday and Saturday, closing time is 11 p.m. Sunday hours are noon to 2 p.m. and 7 to 10 p.m.

POST OFFICE: Post offices and branches are open Monday to Friday from 9 a.m. to 5:30 p.m. and on Saturday from 9 a.m. to 1 p.m. (to 12:30 p.m. in a number of towns). The main post office in Cardiff, on Hill Street, Churchill Way, has a last posting time of 7:30 p.m. Monday to Friday, at 2:30 p.m. on Saturday.

REST ROOMS: Public toilets are plentiful in Wales, in all town centers and at frequent intervals along the roads. You can't miss them. The signs say it in English and in Welsh, but the message is clear: *Toilet* in English, *Toiled* in Welsh. You will usually find the facilities clean. In hotels, a more complicated Welsh word is sometimes used, but graphics will suffice to explain. You don't find rest rooms at filling stations in Britain.

SPORTS: A wide variety of outdoor activities can be enjoyed in Wales. You'll find golfing, tennis, squash, badminton, fishing, shooting, pony trekking, riding, hiking, rock climbing, and nature walks throughout the country. The array of water sports includes swimming in pools (outdoor or indoor), ocean swimming, surfing, windsurfing, waterskiing, sailing, powerboating, canoeing, snorkeling, and diving, depending on where you are. On the Gower peninsula, hang-gliding has become a popular sport. Leisure centers offer many sports facilities.

Spectator sports include some cricket, some soccer, but the most popular of all is rugby. Cardiff is one of the strongholds of this sport. For information on the sporting life of Wales, get in touch with the **Wales Tourist Board** (listed below under "Tourist Information"), or with the **Sports Council for Wales,** Sophia Gardens, Cardiff CF1 9SW (tel. 0222/397571).

STORE HOURS: In general, stores are open from 9 a.m. to 5:30 p.m. Every town has an early-closing day, usually Tuesday or Wednesday, which varies from place to place. If there's something you really need, don't despair if you're traveling around in Wales and the shops in your locale have closed at noon or 1 p.m. There's sure to be another town or village within five or ten miles that has a different early-closing day.

TOURIST INFORMATION: The **Wales Tourist Board** is at Brunel House, 2

Fitzalan Rd., Cardiff CF2 1UY (tel. 0222/499909). Regional tourism councils are: **North Wales Regional Office** 77 Conwy Rd., Colwyn Bay, Clwyd LL29 7LN (tel. 0492/531731); **Mid Wales Regional Office,** Owain Glyndwr Centre, Machynlleth, Powys SY20 8EE (tel. 0654/2401); and **South Wales Regional Office,** Ty Croeso, Gloucester Place, Swansea, West Glamorgan SA4 1TY (tel. 0792/465204).

For information on festivals, events, and attractions, ranging from international music festivals and spectacular military tatoos to sheepdog trials and male-voice choirs, you can get the latest facts by calling the following: **What's on Wales** (tel. 0222/464120); **What's on Cardiff** (tel. 0222/394424); **What's on South Wales** (tel. 0792/466330); **What's on West Wales** (tel. 0348/874525); **What's on Mid Wales** (tel. 0654/2040); and **What's on North Wales** (tel. 0492/534455).

WEATHER: The BBC broadcasts weather forecasts for shipping on 1500 meters at 12:33 and 6:33 a.m. and at 1:55 and 5:55 p.m. daily and on Radio 4 at 11:45 p.m. daily. Subtract one hour if you're there when British Daylight Saving time is on. Good advice and tips on the immediate weather outlook wherever you are can be obtained from Coast Guard Stations.

YOUTH HOSTELS: The Youth Hostels Association (YHA) operates nearly 50 centers in Wales. The centers vary in character from those built as hostels to converted farmhouses, ancient manor houses, and former hotels. They are in prime locations for exploring Wales. Accommodations are in dormitory-type rooms for from two to 20 persons. They have self-catering facilities as well as meals service, which can include packed lunches. Many centers have such amenities as showers, drying rooms, games rooms, and the like.

For details, get in touch with one of the two area offices. **North Wales: YHA Office,** Wynnstay Rd., Colwyn Bay, Clwyd LL29 8NB (tel. 0492/531406); **South and Mid Wales: YHA Office,** Fourth Floor, 1 Cathedral Rd., Cardiff CF1 9HA (tel. 0222/31370).

In the United States, information can be obtained from the headquarters of the **American Youth Hostels, Inc.,** P.O. Box 37613, Washington, DC 20013-7613 (tel. 202/783-6161). In Canada, you can get in touch with the **Canadian Hostelling Association,** 333 River Rd., Vanier, ON K1L 8H9 (tel. 613/748-5638). A year's membership costs $10 for persons under 18; $18 to $20 for those over 18 to 55; $20 for senior citizens 55 and older. Family memberships are offered for $30 to $36, and a life membership can be purchased for around $200. Guests of all ages are accommodated in the youth hostels in Wales.

Chapter XXI

SOUTHEAST WALES

A BUSY, BUSTLING AREA in the southeast corner of Wales, the counties of Gwent, and South, Mid, and West Glamorgan were the focal point of the Industrial Revolution. In fact, early coal-mining operations and ironworks were situated in such places as the Rhondda, Ely, and Romney Valleys, and their products were transported to ports along the Severn Estuary and the Bristol Channel. This led also to the building of steam railroads, steelworks, and other money-making but beauty-killing facilities—so much so that for a long time, people who ventured into the mine valleys told depressing stories of denuded hillsides once proudly forested, slag heaps, and dreary cottages.

All this is changing, with strict air-pollution restrictions, cleaning up of disused canals and other waterways, and reclamation of woodland and dock areas.

On the extreme east of the area under discussion, Chepstow, with the magnificent Tintern Abbey ruins a little way up the Wye Valley, Monmouth, where the River Monnow joins the Wye, and Abergavenny will be visited.

The Brecon Beacons National Park, also included in this chapter, is to the north of the Glamorgans and Gwent. Most of it is in the county of Powys, but it is included in this chapter because of its nearness and easy access to towns discussed.

A number of tiny villages and worthwhile sights will also be visited in this section of Wales.

1. Chepstow

The historic town of Chepstow, the first town you come to after crossing the River Severn from England, lies in the Wye Valley, 1½ miles from the Severn Bridge and just off the M4 motorway heading toward Cardiff.

Tuesday is market day in Chepstow, with a variety of goods sold.

The **Wales Tourist Information Centre** is at The Gatehouse, High Street (tel. 02912/3772). It is open daily from 10 a.m. to 6 p.m. in summer.

FOOD AND LODGING: A ten-bedroom hotel, **The First Hurdle,** 9 Upper Church St. (tel. 02912/2189), in an old house that has been handsomely restored, near the center of town. The rooms are all decorated with Edwardian furniture. Proprietors Brian and Virginia Bonner-Davies rent out the comfortable rooms for £15 ($24) for B&B in a bathless room, £18 ($28.80) per person in a room with a private bath. You may wish to have dinner here also, as the hotel is known for its fine cuisine and its well-stocked wine cellar. At lunch you can order roasts straight from the oven or Welsh lamb chops. A French menu is offered in the evening, as well as a grill selection. A meal costs about £8 ($12.80). The restaurant is popular with local people. The hotel is centrally heated, and there is a TV lounge for residents.

The **Castle View Hotel,** 16 Bridge St. (tel. 02912/70349), is a splurge choice for an overnight stay, but prices in the restaurant and bar are suitable for the budget-minded. The hotel faces Chepstow Castle just two miles from Severn Bridge, close to the M4 and M5 crossroads. A 300-year-old, ivy-covered building, the hotel, constructed originally as a private residence, has exposed beams and a Stuart-era oak staircase. Two bedrooms and the dining room, then a kitchen, were added about 150 years ago. A quiet walled garden is open to hotel guests. The 11 bedrooms are centrally heated and well decorated, all with private baths or showers, and there is a double unit in its own cottage with a lounge. All the rooms have color TV, radios, phones, and hot-beverage facilities. Mervyn and Lucia Gillett, the proprietors, charge £28 ($44.80) to £33 ($52.80) for a single guest, from £39 ($62.40) to £44 ($70.40) in a double. All prices include VAT and a full English breakfast.

Whether you eat in the dining room, with a Welsh slate fireplace, or in the rustically charming bar, you can enjoy such dishes as fresh Wye salmon and trout. Light bar meals cost from £5 ($8), with dinner in the restaurant going for £10 ($16) and up. Food is served from noon to 2 p.m. and 6:30 to 9:30 p.m.

At **Tara Guest House,** Shirenewton (tel. 02917/277), you'll be warmly welcomed. The guesthouse is in a little village just west of Chepstow, and it's an easy run from here to Caerwent, Caerleon, Tintern, and Monmouth. For B&B in a comfortable room with central heating, the charge is £9.50 ($15.20) to £10.50 ($16.80). You can also take dinner here, enjoying good food. There is a cozy lounge with a log fire. Parking is provided.

Apart from the hotels, the best place for dining is **Willow Tree,** "The Back" (tel. 02912/6665), right on the Chepstow riverbank. During the day from 11 a.m. to 5 p.m. Monday to Tuesday, you can enjoy good-tasting meals costing from £6 ($9.60) and including such dishes as pork casserole or one of several blackboard menu specials. At night from 7:30 to 9 p.m., prices go up and the fare becomes even more enticing, beginning with, say, coriander-flavored carrot soup and following with a pasta or a Greek lamb dish. Meals cost from £15 ($24). Jeremy Hector is the guiding force behind the food and service offered at this scenic river cottage which dates from the 1700s. It is closed Sunday evening and all day Monday.

SIGHTS: Long a strategic center, Chepstow was the seat of the Lords Marcher. In the 11th century Norman Lord William Fitz-Osborn built the great **castle** as a stronghold against the Welsh. The castle, with its Great Tower, may be visited all year. From mid-March to mid-October, hours are 9:30 a.m. to 6:30 p.m. seven days a week. The rest of the year hours are 9:30 a.m. to 4 p.m. Admission is 75p ($1.20) for adults, 35p (56¢) for children.

The **Chepstow Museum,** Gwy House, Bridge Street (tel. 02912/5981), has exhibits tracing the history of Chepstow and its environs. The town's importance in the wine, shipbuilding, and fishing trades is demonstrated, among other former pursuits of the early inhabitants. The museum is open from 11 a.m. to 1 p.m. and 2 to 5 p.m. Monday to Saturday and 2 to 5 p.m. on Sunday March to the end of October. Admission is 50p (80¢) for adults, 25p (40¢) for children.

An attraction in Chepstow is **Stuart Crystal,** Bridge Street (tel. 02912/70135), where visitors can watch craftsmen applying decoration to beautiful handmade crystal. In an old school building opposite Chepstow Castle on the A48 road, Stuart & Son Ltd. have set up a museum section showing crystal produced by the company over the past 150 years. In a video room you can see how the techniques of present-day crystal manufacture have remained unchanged over the years. Factory tours are conducted daily. The gift shop, where you will be dazzled by the glittering crystal, is open from 9 a.m. to 8 p.m. daily May to September, to 5 p.m. from October to April. Admission is free.

2. Tintern

The famous Wye Valley winds north from Chepstow, passing by the Lancaut Peninsula at the foot of the Windcliffe, an 800-foot hill with striking views over the Severn estuary and the English border as far as the south part of the Cotswolds. About a mile or so farther north, you come to the little village of Tintern.

In summer, a **Wales Tourist Information Centre** is open daily from 10 a.m. to 6 p.m. at Tintern Abbey (tel. 02918/431).

FOOD AND LODGING: Nestling in the Wye Valley, **Parva Farmhouse** (tel. 02918/411) is a 17th-century stone structure, plus a renovated 15th-century cottage adjoining. You'll be warmly welcomed at this comfortable place, with its beamed residents' lounge where a roaring log fire creates a cozy atmosphere in which to relax. The farmhouse has nine bedrooms, four with private baths and all with full central heating, color TV, and hot-beverage facilities. The owners, Rod and Gilly Baverstock, charge £12.50 ($20) to £15 ($24) per person per night, the prices including a full Welsh breakfast. In the restaurant, good food prepared by the owner is served, and vegetarian dishes are a specialty. You needn't be a resident to eat here. There's an emphasis on Welsh cuisine, with use of fresh local produce. Your hosts can arrange horseback riding, golf, fly-fishing for salmon and trout (including fees and rental of rods), if you wish. The house has an "honesty bar" where guests can serve themselves drinks.

The best place to eat if you're passing through is **The Fountain Inn,** Trellech Grange (tel. 02918/303), a mellow countryside inn that does fresh food (each dish cooked individually) with traditional "Taste of Wales" flavor. You might, for example, enjoy a perfectly done rack of lamb from the Wye or trout caught in local waters. Depending on the time of day, meals cost from £5 ($8) to £12 ($19.20), and food service is from noon to 3 p.m., with dinner offered from 7 to 10:30 p.m. Monday to Saturday. On Sunday, hours are different: noon to 2 p.m. for lunch and 7 to 9:30 p.m. for dinner. When the wind is whistling outside, as it often does, the bar with its log-burning fireplace is a cozy nook. If you'd like to stay over, the inn also rents out five comfortably appointed bedrooms, costing from £12 ($19.20) per person for B&B.

SIGHTS: The focal point of this riverside village set in a beautiful scenic spot is the ruins of the Cistercian Abbey of St. Mary—**Tintern Abbey.** The abbey was founded in 1131 and was active until the dissolution of the monasteries by King Henry VIII. Most of the structure still standing dates from the 13th century, when the abbey was almost entirely rebuilt and became one of the richest and most important monastic houses in Wales. The poet Wordsworth was one of the first to appreciate the serene beauty of the substantial remains of the abbey, as shown in his poetry.

The abbey is open daily March 15 to October 15 from 9:30 a.m. to 6:30 p.m., and the remainder of the year from 9:30 a.m. to 4 p.m. Monday to Saturday, 2 to 4 p.m. on Sunday. It's closed Christmas Eve, Christmas Day, Boxing Day, and New Year's Day. Admission is £1 ($1.60) for adults and 50p (80¢) for children. There is ample parking quite near the entrance, and refreshments are available nearby. For more information, telephone 02918/251.

The Old Station (tel. 02918/566), built as a Victorian country railway station, is a charming place to visit, just a mile north of Tintern Abbey. The surrounding area has been converted to a picnic site and information center. It's open from 10 a.m. to 6 p.m. April to the end of October daily. Cars are admitted for 30p (48¢). Light refreshments are available, and a small exhibit in the building tells the story of the Wye Valley railway.

3. Monmouth

On up the Wye Valley, you pass through the section of Wales abutting England that had its share of bloodshed and turmoil during the centuries of struggle when the Welsh resisted domination, whether by Saxons, Normans, or the English. The town of Monmouth, as the seat of a powerful marcher lord, has always been considered more English than the territories to its west. At least, people have argued the point with me.

This busy market town began as an alien Norman castle built in a region the Celtic people considered theirs. It stood at a strategic spot, where the River Monnow joins the Wye. The first lords of Monmouth were Bretons, but in the middle of the 13th century the lordship passed to the House of Lancaster, at whose behest the **Monnow Bridge** was built, the only fortified bridge gateway in Britain and one of the few remaining in Europe. You pass through this gateway on one approach to the town. A Benedictine priory was established after the castle was built, and soon Monmouth became a market town for traders and burgesses, beginning its commercial history.

Putting the name of the town in the pages of literary history in the 12th century was Geoffrey of Monmouth, a churchman who lived at the priory and wrote a history of Britain which was widely read although it was almost completely a figment of his own imagination linked with names of actual places and in some cases, historic figures. Henry V (Harry of Monmouth) was born in the castle and ascended the throne in 1413. Agincourt Square, in the heart of town, was named in his honor. A statue of Henry centers this market square.

Other heroes of the town are Horatio, Lord Nelson, who may have begun tourism in Monmouth by a visit here in 1802, and C. S. Rolls of Rolls-Royce fame, who was born here. It was the mother of Rolls, Lady Llangattock, who was instrumental in the establishment of the museum that contains much Nelson memorabilia (see below). Nelson stayed at the Beaufort Arms Hotel, which is now closed.

A weekly livestock market is held at Monmouth, plus general markets, more interesting to most travelers, on Monday and Friday.

Centers of **Wales Tourist Information** and the **National Trust** are on Church Street (tel. 0600/3899), open all year from 10 a.m. to 6 p.m.

Church Street is a little pedestrian passageway with stores selling food, jewelry, books, woolens, and yarns, and there's even a chemist's shop (pharmacy).

WHERE TO STAY: A select and historic place to stay, a splurge choice, is the **King's Head Hotel,** Agincourt Square (tel. 0600/2177). Whatever king was honored by the naming of this establishment originally (probably Henry V, the famous Harry of Monmouth), it has been associated for the past 3½ centuries with Charles I, the unfortunate monarch much given to visiting, who stayed here when he was a guest of his friend, the Marquis of Worcester, at Raglan. The landlord at that time had a large plaster panel set up displaying a portrait of Charles, a crowned head and shoulders with a dainty vase of flowers painted on either side. The panel is now in the elegant but cozy bar, with red leather chairs and dark wainscoting. It is above the large fireplace and dominates the room. Go there for drinks and have a look at the panel. It's worth a visit just to relax in the old-fashioned room with its plaster ceiling designed with wreaths of fruit.

In this Tudor building, the owner, K. L. Gough, rents bedrooms, all with toilets and baths or showers (some singles have only showers), as well as phones, color TV, and radios. The units are pleasantly furnished with period pieces, some with full tester beds. The accommodations vary in size. A single with shower only rents for £28 ($44.80), while one with shower and toilet goes for £35 ($56), rising to £40 ($64) for a single with full bathroom. Twins or doubles with private baths go for £50 ($80). Children sharing their parents' room are accommodated free.

For a description of the fine eating facilities of the King's Head, see my dining recommendations below. During the coaching era this hotel was an important stopping place for the Milford Haven and South Wales Royal Mail, on the London to South Wales route. Now the hotel stabling has been mostly converted into parking facilities.

The **Rising Sun Hotel,** Cinderhill Street (tel. 0600/3236), is a pleasant little place, painted white with hanging baskets of blossoming plants and an interesting inn sign. Its 12 bedrooms all have showers and toilets, color TV, phones, and hot-beverage facilities. Alison and John Hamilton, the owners, charge from £15 ($24) for a bed and a full English breakfast, with VAT included in prices. The pleasant restaurant offers table d'hôte and à la carte meals, or you can enjoy a complete range of homemade dishes in the beamed bar. Nonresidents can take meals at the hotel.

The **Ebberley Guest House,** St. James Square (tel. 0600/3602), is an inviting Georgian town house whose attraction is implemented by its location on a square in the center of town, so that you can walk to all the sights of Monmouth. The bedrooms all have hot and cold water, and the house has central heating. You can rent one of the neat rooms for £9.50 ($15.20) to £10.50 ($16.80), which includes a full Welsh breakfast, served in the pleasant dining room. If you'd like to dine here, you'll find a good menu with some Welsh specialties. Morning tea and evening drinks are available.

WHERE TO DINE: Good food is served in the three eating facilities of the **King's Head Hotel,** Agincourt Square (tel. 0600/2177), recommended above—the Empire-style restaurant, the elegant cocktail bar, and the Coach House. Local specialties as well as Welsh, English, and international cuisine are offered.

The restaurant, decorated in crimson and gold, with immaculate white napery, is lit by chandeliers of shaded and globed lights, with wall sconces and a big curtained window adding to the illumination. Here you can have breakfast, lunch, and dinner. Your dinner might include the soup of the day, Wye salmon, homey-glazed lamb or rack of lamb with rosemary, or a selection of beef dishes. Expect to pay from £12 ($19.20) to £14 ($22.40) for a full à la carte repast. Perhaps you'd like to try a glass of Monnow Valley wine to accompany your meal. In the cocktail bar, which is more modern in concept, you can select lunch from the cold buffet or order a hot dish, perhaps steak-and-kidney pie. A meal will cost about £4 ($6.40), although it can go higher if you're really hungry. The dining room near the hotel bar serves a fixed-price lunch, which might be roast chicken with bread sauce and seasoning, cold meat with salad, or roast leg of lamb, with an appetizer and dessert, all for £8.50 ($13.60), while a dinner will cost £13.50 ($21.60) and up. The Coach House, a separate building to the rear of the hotel, has been made into a grill room where you can order grills or curries for £5 ($8) to £8 ($12.80).

Hours in the dining room in the hotel are 12:30 to 2 p.m. and 7 to 9 p.m. Monday to Friday, to 10 p.m. on Saturday. Sunday hours are 12:30 to 1:45 p.m. and 7 to 9 p.m. In the Coach House, dinner only is served on Monday, from 6 to 11 p.m. Hours Tuesday to Saturday are noon to 3 p.m. and 6:30 to 11 p.m. Sunday hours are noon to 2 p.m. and 7 to 10 p.m. Unfortunately, the Coach House is closed part of the year, but maybe you'll be lucky.

In the White Swan shopping precinct, which has a number of shops, there's the **Cygnet Coffee House,** 10 White Swan Court (tel. 0600/5555), where Dorothy Winnett presides over the serving of food from 9 a.m. to 5 p.m. tea. You can lunch on such things as lasagne, shepherd's pie, and quiche. If you're not counting calories, try the apple strudel with cream. Expect to spend £3.50 ($5.60) for a filling lunch.

An attractive, convenient place to eat or drink in the heart of town on Agincourt Square is the **Punch House** (tel. 0600/3855), a historic licensed bar and restaurant. The three-story white Georgian building with black trim and a slate roof has hanging baskets of flowers on the front and side. Inside are low beamed ceilings, with old horse collars and other harness items used for decor. In the restaurant upstairs is an antique table at which Admiral Nelson is said to have dined with Lady Hamilton. Here you can enjoy traditional roasts, Wye salmon, and other well-prepared dishes. Vegetables (except for frozen peas) are fresh, organically grown when possible, and not overcooked. Meats are supplied by the house's own butcher shop, and they smoke their own hams, salmon, trout, and salt beef, carefully prepared under the direction of W.J.L Wills, the proprietor. A complete five-course menu of the day costs £12.75 ($20.40), a three-course grill meal going for about £12 ($19.20), and a table d'hôte offering for £7.50 ($12). A bar lunch or dinner is available for around £3 ($4.80) downstairs. Meals are served in the restaurant from 11:30 to 2 p.m. and 6:30 to 9 p.m., with bar food being offered from 11:30 a.m. to 2:30 p.m. and 6:30 to 11 p.m.

SIGHTS: In a modern building on the River Monnow, the **Monmouth Museum,** Priory Street (tel. 0600/3519), houses both the Nelson Collection and the Local History Centre. The Nelson Collection, the bulk of which was accumulated by Lady Llangattock who lived near here, contains Nelson's fighting sword and models of his ships, as well as space devoted to exposing some of the numerous fake Nelson relics produced since his death. There is a graphic reconstruction of the places where Lord Nelson and Lady Hamilton, his mistress, and her husband, Sir William Hamilton, went during their stay in the Monmouth area, plus pictures, letters, and other mementos.

The Local History Centre displays artifacts, documents, photographs, paintings, and prints concerning the development of the town. Exploits of Charles Stewart Rolls, co-founder of Rolls-Royce (son of Lady Llangattock, the Nelsoniana collector), in the fields of motorcars, balloons, and airplanes are illustrated.

The museum is open from 10:30 a.m. to 1 p.m. and 2 to 5 p.m. Monday to Saturday and 2 to 5 p.m. on Sunday from September to the end of June. During July and August, hours are from 10 a.m. to 1 p.m. and 1:30 to 6 p.m. Monday to Saturday and 2:30 to 5:30 p.m. on Sunday. Admission is 50p (80¢) for adults, 25p (40¢) for children.

Unfortunately, not much of **Monmouth Castle** is left, but you can go up Castle Hill to see the remains from outside. At the Local History Centre in the museum, you can ask for a leaflet, "A Walk Around Monmouth," which is a fine guide to the best and most historic buildings of the town.

From Monmouth, it's an easy seven-mile drive west to—

RAGLAN CASTLE: The buildings of this handsome castle ruin date from 1430 to the early 1600s, with the Great Tower of Gwent, surrounded by a moat, standing gaunt and stark against the sky. Raglan Castle, probably built on the site of an earlier Norman fortress, was the product of the bitter conflict between the Welsh and the English, but it was ornate, more for social grandeur than for military purposes. Visitors can see spacious halls and state apartments, where some mullioned windows and cross-beam ceilings survive, as well as a huge fireplace and roof corbels in the Great Hall, a buttery, a pantry, the kitchen tower, and the chapel, among other remains. You can visit the castle mid-March to mid-October daily from 9:30 a.m. to 6:30 p.m. Winter hours are 9:30 a.m. to 4 p.m. weekdays, 2 to 4 p.m. on Sunday. Admission is 75p ($1.20) for adults, 35p (56¢) for children.

A TRIANGLE OF CASTLES: In the Middle Ages, three fortresses—Skenfrith, Grosmont, and White—were linked between the Wye Valley and the Black Mountains as protectors against the marauding Welsh. **Skenfrith** stands on the west bank of the River Monnow in a peaceful setting today. A tower of the castle still looms imposingly over the passing scene. Guidebooks are available at the local post office. The castle can be visited at any time (not at night). Admission is free.

Grosmont Castle, about four miles north, has a Great Hall where people feasted. Built in the early 13th century, this and other portions of the castle can be traced in the ruins. The fortress was assaulted and besieged by the Welsh in the 13th and 15th centuries, until Prince Hal (later Henry V) defeated Owain Glyndwr here. There is no charge for visiting.

White Castle, to the west toward Abergavenny, got its name from the white plaster with which it was finished. Traces of this remain. The castle's inner ward, surrounded by a steep-sided moat, probably discouraged invaders. You can see this and the outer ward, as well as the gatehouse and other remains. Admission is free. These castles are small and austere compared to Raglan.

4. Castles and Roman Ruins

There are a number of interesting sights along the road from Chepstow to Newport just off the M4 or the A48.

If you get the impression that there must once have been more castles to the square mile here than in any other part of the British Isles, you may be right. The people of Wales didn't make things easy for anyone who wanted to take over the country, so fortifications were built to fend off the attackers by the Romans and then by the Normans. Even before that, however, warring tribes had established hill-forts throughout the vicinity, although only traces of some of these survive.

CAERWENT: This is only a little village today, but it was once a Roman city, founded about A.D. 75 just about a mile southeast of a hill-fort of the Celtic tribe, the Silures. The Celts were brought to Caerwent and taught to participate in such novel pursuits as using the public baths and walking in the forum. The most substantial remains are those of the city walls. The road through the village follows the Roman road, and remains of two Roman houses are here.

PENHOW CASTLE: On the A48 road midway between Chepstow and Newport, this is the oldest lived-in castle in Wales, Penhow (tel. 0633/400800). It was the first home in Britain of the Seymour family, who carved out a niche in history. This is perhaps the most enchanting knight's castle in the Welsh border country. A tour of the castle will take you to the Norman keep tower, the Great Hall of the 15th century with its minstrels' gallery, and the Victorian housekeeper's room. Restoration work is still in progress, but the castle is open Good Friday to the end of September, Wednesday to Sunday and on bank holidays. Hours are 10 a.m. to 5:15 p.m. Adults are charged £2 ($3.20) and children £1 ($1.60). The price includes a Soundalive! Walkman tour of the castle.

CALDICOT CASTLE: This ancient fortress is only two miles from the sea on the route followed by the Roman road, Via Julia, which led to Caerwent (see above). The castle, a Norman stronghold, was built during the 12th to the 14th centuries. It was restored in the 19th century and has been occupied since that time. It is set in a pleasant Country Park where special outdoor events are sometimes held.

   Caldicot Castle Museum (tel. 0291/420241) contains a collection of local history exhibits, including costumes, furniture, rural crafts tools, and domestic items. A small display of mementos from Nelson's flagship *Foudroyant* can also be seen. The museum is open from 11 a.m. to 12:30 p.m. and 1:30 to 5 p.m. Monday to Friday, from 10 a.m. to 1 p.m. and 1:30 to 5 p.m. on Saturday, and from 1:30 to 5 p.m. on Sunday March to the end of October. Admission is 50p (80¢) for adults, 25p (40¢) for children. One tower of the castle is now a gallery for changing monthly exhibitions by local artists and artisans.

Medieval Banquets

   The **Caldicot Castle Medieval Banquets** (tel. 0291/421425) are held all year in the candlelit Great Hall of the castle, with feasting and entertainment. Ample wine and mead accompanies the four-course banquet, which is served without the use of today's utensils—only fingers and a dagger, please. Reader Thomas R. Emdy of Bloomington, Minnesota, found the banquet here "not a tourist parody as I had feared; a great experience." Advance reservations must be made to join in the fun. You arrive at 7:30 p.m. for the beginning of the banquet at 8. The charge is £13.95 ($22.32) Monday to Thursday, and on Friday and Saturday it's £14.75 ($23.60) for adults. Children 9 years of age and younger are charged half price. Dress for the event is informal, although you'll be greeted and waited on by Ladies of the Court in colorful costumes.

CAERLEON: This former Roman Legion fortress, then called Isca, should be visited if for no other purpose than to see the magnificent amphitheater where gladiators fought in the first century of the Christian era. Caerleon was the headquarters of one of the legions permanently stationed in Britain. For centuries the remains were largely undiscovered, covered with fields and a little village.

The parish church was on the site of the main headquarters at the center of the fort. Roman baths are being restored, and you can also visit the amphitheater, oval in shape, with banks of earth showing where wooden planks were placed to serve as seats. Crowds of up to 6,000 could be accommodated at this arena.

The **Roman Legionary Museum,** High Street (tel. 0633/423134), opened in 1987, contains exhibits illustrating the history of Roman Caerleon and the daily life of the garrison at the fortress of Isca, one of the three principal military bases of the Romans in Britain. The Second Augustan Legion was stationed here. Many discoveries, displayed for the first time, include material from the early fortress at Usk, as well as lifesize replicas of Roman soldiers. The museum is open from 10 a.m. to 6 p.m. weekdays and 2 to 6 p.m. on Sunday mid-March to mid-October. The remainder of the year, closing at 4:30 p.m.

Admission to the museum only is 75¢ ($1.20) for adults, 35p (56¢) for children. A joint ticket, admitting you to the museum and the Roman baths and amphitheater, costs £1.50 ($2.40) for adults, 35p (56¢) for children.

Food and Lodging

The **Priory Country Hotel,** High Street (tel. 0663/421241), is the most charming hotel in the village. Faced with ancient stones and trailing ivy, it was originally built in the 16th century, probably as an outbuilding of a ruined Cistercian abbey. Visitors appreciate its nearness to the excavations of a Roman amphitheater and the River Usk. Inside, a friendly welcome enhances the comforts of the 22 bedrooms, each with private bath or shower and color TV. Singles rent for £38 ($60.80), doubles £48 ($76.80), with breakfast included. Satisfying meals are served in a chintz-covered, pleasingly elegant dining room. A fixed-price dinner from 7:30 to 9:45 p.m. costs £11 ($17.60) and might include lobster Newburg, grilled halibut, Hungarian stroganoff, or chicken bourguignon. A table d'hôte from 12:30 to 2:45 p.m. costs only £6.50 ($10.40).

The best place to eat in the village is the **Roman Wine Bar & Bistro,** 9 High St. (tel. 0633/422822), which has a surprisingly sophisticated menu for such a small provincial place. Located right in the center of the village, it remains open all year, but serves its savory cuisine only on weekdays. Lunch is from 11 a.m. to 2 p.m. The place reopens for drinks at 6 p.m., beginning food service at 7:15 which lasts until 10:15 p.m. Specialties include tandoori turbot, mussels marinara, and roast duckling with black currant and pear sauce. If you want to make it a festive occasion, and if it is on the menu, you can order paella for two persons. Dinners cost from £12 ($19.20).

A SIDE TRIP UP THE USK VALLEY: From the Caerleon area, follow the signs to the A449 road up the valley of the River Usk, turning off onto the A471-A472 to the little town of **Usk,** an ancient borough with a castled hill and a broad square. Here you can visit the **Gwent Rural Life Museum,** The Malt Barn, New Market Street (tel. 02913/2285). Displayed are agricultural and crafts tools, wagons, vintage machinery, a farmhouse kitchen of earlier days, a laundry, and a dairy. Hours are from 10 a.m. to 12:30 p.m. and 2 to 5 p.m. Monday to Friday year round, from 2 to 5 p.m. on Sunday March to October, and from 2 to 5 p.m. on Saturday April to September. Admission is 75p ($1.20) for adults, 35p (56¢) for children.

Food and Lodging

Cwrt Bleddyn Hotel, Llangybi (tel. 063349/521), some 2½ miles south of Usk, is a country house of charm and character. A recommendable splurge hotel set in the border country, the establishment opened in 1985, but traces its origins back to the 14th century when it was constructed as a manor house. Many touches of its history remain, including a "staircase to nowhere" along with 1700s oak paneling. However, all the bedrooms are modernized and up to date, attractively furnished and comfortably appointed. The most expensive time to stay here is on a weekday, with singles costing from £51 ($81.60), doubles or twins, £65 ($104). It's much cheaper to book in here on either a Friday, Saturday, or Sunday night. At those times, a single rents for £45 ($72), a double or twin £60 ($96), including a hearty Welsh breakfast. Each of the 30 bedrooms contains a private bath, color TV, trouser press, hairdryer, and direct-dial phone.

The food in Nicholl's Restaurant is among the finest in the region. Against a backdrop of antique furnishings and open fireplaces, it serves a French-inspired menu from 7 to 10:30 p.m., costing from £15 ($24). Lunch is from 12:30 to 2 p.m. Game is often a feature on the menu, and fresh local and seasonal produce are always featured. The lamb is especially good. Try also, if featured, a lightly sautéed venison with a juniper and red wine sauce. The location on 17 acres of grounds is within easy reach of the major routes: for example, 10 minutes from junction 24 and 25 of the M4, lying half an hour from the Severn Bridge.

From Usk, take the B4235 about four miles east to—

WOLVESNEWTON: The reason for coming here is to see the **Model Farm Folk Collection and Craft Centre** (tel. 02915/231), open Easter week and then on Saturday, Sunday, and Monday to the end of June from 11 a.m. to 6 p.m. July to September, it's open daily from 11 a.m. to 6 p.m., and in October and November on Sunday only from 2 to 5:30 p.m. The model farm was built at the end of the 18th century for the Duke of Beaufort, and the cross-shaped barn is unique. The folk collection contains exhibits of most aspects of domestic and agricultural life since the time of Queen Victoria. In the craft center you can watch artisans working and browse in a large craft and gift shop. Morning coffee or tea and lunch are served, with homemade cakes. Admission to the farm and folk collection is £1.75 ($2.80) for adults, 95p ($1.52) for children.

If you prefer, you can come to Wolvesnewton from Tintern, a seven-mile trip on the B4235. You turn off the road at Llangwm.

5. Newport (in Gwent)

The Caerleon area and lots more of the immediate area have become bedroom communities for Newport, where the River Usk forms an estuary emptying into the Bristol Channel.

Don't confuse this city with the much smaller town of Newport in the county of Dyfed on the coast between Fishguard and Cardigan. Newport in Gwent is a large industrial and commercial city with a few places of historical and recreational interest.

WHERE TO STAY: A splurge choice, **King's Hotel,** High Street (tel. 0633/842020), experienced a carefully orchestrated renovation in 1986. Today, the grandeur of its sandstone and red-brick facade reflects the pride of the 19th-century Empire. Inside, a country-house feeling was created with acres of pastel-colored wallpaper and yard upon yard of pleasingly patterned chintz. In the center of town, the location is not far from the river and the George Street (High Street) Bridge. Each of the 47 comfortably furnished bedrooms contains a private bath, hairdryer, coffee-making equipment, phone, color TV, and a contemporary decor. With a full breakfast included, singles rent for £48 ($76.80), doubles £58 ($92.80) to £68 ($108.80). However, on Friday and Saturday nights, tariffs are reduced to £35 ($56) in a single, £48 ($76.80) in a double. The in-house restaurant is recommended separately.

St. Etienne Hotel, 162 Stow Hill (tel. 0633/62341), is one of the best B&Bs in the area. It offers six comfortably furnished bedrooms, two of which are set aside for families. The rate ranges from £12 ($19.20) to £14 ($22.40) per person for B&B. All the units contain private showers, hot and cold running water, and coffee-making equipment. Near the center of Newport and close to Belle Vue Park, the hotel is convenient for motorists coming into Wales on the M4 from England.

WHERE TO DINE: Conceded to be the finest restaurant in Newport, **Fratelli,** 173b Caerleon Rd. (tel. 0633/64602), lies on a commercial street of 19th-century red-brick houses, just outside the center. Run by two Italian brothers, who naturally offer Italian cuisine, the restaurant is attractively decorated in green, white, pink, and red, with garden lattices. Have a drink at the street-level apéritif bar before one of the brothers ushers you to your basement table. There you can enjoy an array of well-seasoned grilled meats, perhaps four types of risotto or else one of the tasty and well-flavored pastas, including spaghetti carbonara or tagliatelle Rosso. À la carte meals range in price from £9 ($14.40) to £15 ($24). Hours are noon to 2 p.m. and 7 to 10:15 p.m. It is closed for Saturday lunch, Sunday, and for three weeks in August.

King's Hotel Carvery, High Street (tel. 0633/842020), offers one of the best bargain meals in town, served in a high-ceilinged confection of pastel pink and exposed wood. A well-stocked carvery of succulent roasts and fresh vegetables is served from noon to 2 p.m. and 6:30 to 9:30 p.m. (on Sunday from 7 to 9 p.m.). Three-course meals, with generous servings from the buffet, including an array of salads, costs £8 ($12.80) at lunch, £11 ($17.60) at dinner. Clients interested only in a well-filled platter, followed with coffee, pay £5 ($8) per person.

Staying in the Environs

About eight miles east of Newport, in the little village of Redwick not far from the Severn estuary, is **Brick House Farm** (tel. 0633/880230), a comfortable place to stay. Of severe but imposing architectural design, it is a three-story, stone-sided building rising from its surrounding fields. A slate-roof structure, it is distinguished by a trio of chimneys. There are seven bedrooms, all tastefully furnished, and the house is centrally heated. The charge for B&B is £11.50 ($18.40) per person per night. You can also dine here if you advise them ahead, enjoying good home-cooking. You'll find the quiet little village a good base for touring the Wye and Usk Valleys at their southern ends.

SIGHTS AND ACTIVITIES: Housed in a modern building, the **Newport Museum & Art Gallery,** John Frost Square (tel. 0633/840064), contains exhibits relating to the archeology and local and natural history of Newport and Gwent. In the archeology displays are material excavated from Roman Caerwent, including ornaments, tools, and household utensils, plus painted wall plaster, stone sculpture, and mosaics. The development of Newport from its beginnings around a medieval castle through its transition to a modern industrial town is traced, with illustrations of the port, industries, mining, iron working, local crafts, and social and domestic life. A Chartist exhibit deals with the Newport Riots in 1839. The animal and plant life of Gwent are also depicted.

The art gallery has a major collection of English watercolors of the 18th and 19th centuries, local prints and drawings, Staffordshire pottery, Welsh paintings, studio ceramics, and modern prints. The museum houses a brass rubbing center. Ask for information about this at the shop and information center (tel. 0633/842962). Hours are from 9:30 a.m. to 5 p.m. Monday to Thursday, 9:30 a.m. to 4:30 p.m. on Friday, and 9:30 a.m. to 4 p.m. on Saturday. Admission is free. There's a multistory car park nearby.

Tredegar House and Country Park, Coedkernew (tel. 0633/62275), some two miles west of Newport, is one of the finest country houses in Wales. The house gives clues to the wealth, power, and influence of the Morgan family, Lords of Tredegar, who lived here, from Llewellyn ap Morgan in 1402 to the last lord, who died in 1962. Although one wing of a medieval stone manor remains, Tredegar House today owes its character to 17th-century reconstruction in brick, with a great many state rooms. The house was sold in 1951 for use as a school, but the Newport Borough Council acquired it in 1974 and set about restoration. Guided tours of this spectacular Charles II mansion cost £1.50 ($2.40) for adults, 75p ($1.20) for children, from 12:30 to 4:30 p.m. Wednesday to Sunday (also Tuesday in summer).

Among the outbuildings surrounding the house, the 17th-century stable block and its Orangery are perhaps the most impressive. Of the 1,000-acre estate once centered around these buildings, 90 acres remain and have been made into the country park with formal gardens, an adventure play farm, carriage and donkey rides, and an ornamental lake for fishing and boating. Some of the restored structures house a restaurant and bar, a gift shop, and craft workshops. Admission to the park and gardens is free. They are open from 6:30 a.m. to sunset. Facilities within the park are open at various times. Ask at the information center, open from 10:30 a.m. to 6 p.m. daily.

In the center of Newport, visitors can get a bird's-eye view of the city and the reaches of the River Usk from the protected catwalk at the top of the **Transporter Bridge.** Some castle remains are here, and at the top of Stow Hill is the former **St. Gwynllyw's Church,** which is now St. Woolos Cathedral. The fine Norman work on the original has been retained.

For information about these and other sights of Newport, the **Tourist Information Centre** is at the Museum and Art Gallery in John Frost Square (tel. 0633/842962).

Just north of Newport on the Henllys road is the **Fourteen Locks Canal Centre** at Rogerstone (tel. 0633/894802 in summer, 0633/838838, ext. 664 in winter). Before the coming of the steam railway, the Monmouthshire Canal transported cargoes of coal and iron to the Newport docks. A section of the canal has been restored and the center has been developed around an elaborate and complicated system of locks, ponds, channels, and tunnels on the western arm. The lock system enabled a barge to be raised and lowered 168 feet in half a mile. An exhibit in the interpretation center traces the growth and decline of the canal system in Gwent. The Locks Centre is open Easter to the end of September from 10 a.m. to 5:30 p.m. except Tuesday and Wednesday. Admission is free.

6. Cwmbran, Pontypool, and Blaenavon

Going directly north from Newport on the A4042 road, you can see something new and something old, as you move toward the east-west A40 road.

CWMBRAN: Ready for a little rest from history? Then visit Cwmbran, just north of Newport on the A4051. This is a "new town" of Southeast Wales, aimed at becoming a focal point in Gwent to relieve crowding in other areas. The shopping precinct is worth a visit. There is a boating and coarse-fishing lake, an international athletics track and sports center at nearby Henllys Way, and many entertainment facilities. Modern hotels have been built, with good restaurants, bars, and sports and health facilities. This is an ideal base for exploring the Wye Valley to the east, Brecon Beacons National Park to the north, and other points of interest. It's practically on the doorstep of Caerleon.

Food and Lodging

For a big splurge, try the **Commodore Hotel,** Mill Lane, Llanyravon (tel. 0633/4091), a 60-room facility standing in six acres of lawns and woodland. Its oldest section dates from the Middle Ages when it was constructed as a private house. It is said to have a resident ghost, the spirit of a woman who waited during the Crimean War for the return of her sons. When they never came back, she committed suicide. Sightings of the ghost are usually at the bottom of the stairs where the woman is said to have waited. The bedrooms, all with attractive contemporary furnishings, contain private baths in each double, renting for £50 ($80) nightly. A pair of bathless singles go for £25 ($40) each, while singles with private plumbing range from £30 ($48) to £40 ($64). However, the best news is the special weekend tariff schedule, when the cost for B&B is only £20 ($32) per person nightly (applies on Friday, Saturday, and Sunday nights). The four sleek bars and a cocktail lounge will keep your thirst quenched—on a 24-hour basis if you're a resident. If you're a golfer, you can try your skill on the nine-hole golf course nearby. The food is good, and you may want to dine in the elegant à la carte restaurant and carvery. A table d'hôte evening meal costs £10 ($16) per person.

Cwmbran Centre Hotel, Victoria Street (tel. 06333/72511), is near the athletics field and the shopping precinct, although you may feel so comfortable here you won't want to wander around. Color TV, video, and tea/coffee-making equipment as well as a full bathroom are in all the units. The charges are £25 ($40) to £35 ($56) per person for B&B. Enjoy drinks in the lounge or the wine bar. The hotel has nightly entertainment and a friendly atmosphere.

To better suit the budget, you'll find **Springfields Guest House,** 371 Llanarnum Rd. (tel. 06333/2509), a pleasant place to stay. This family-run establishment has central heating, TV, and hot and cold water basins in the bedrooms. One unit has a private bath. Charges are £11 ($17.60) per person per night for B&B. If you'd like to have dinner here, advise the proprietors, Joan and Reg Graham ahead and expect to pay from £7 ($11.20) for your meal. Guests are welcome to use the washing machine and dryer, plus an iron, for a charge of £2 ($3.20) per load of clothes. The house has a separate TV lounge and adequate parking. The guesthouse is three miles from the M4.

PONTYPOOL: Fine Georgian stables in the extensive Pontypool Park along the River Lwyd have been restored and now house the **Valley Inheritance Centre** (tel. 04955/52043), open daily from 10 a.m. to 5 p.m. and on Sunday from 2 to 5 p.m. Exhibitions and films tell the story of the history and the industrialization of Gwent's eastern valley in an imaginative way. Admission is 75p ($1.20) for adults, 40p (64¢) for children.

The park, open all year, also has one of the finest artificial ski slopes in Europe, and a fine sports and leisure center. For information on both the slope and the center, telephone 04955/55955.

In Pontypool, you can also see **Forge Row Cwmafon,** a row of 12 forge workers' cottages built in 1804 and altered very little. For information, call the Torfaen Museum Trust (tel. 04955/52036).

The trust also is in charge of **Junction Cottage,** at the meeting of the Monmouthshire and Brecknock & Abergavenny canals, a canal tollkeeper's cottage built in 1814. It houses an exhibit tracing the development of the local waterways system. An impressive aqueduct and examples of canal engineering can be visited nearby. The cottage is open daily from 2 to 5 p.m. April to September. Admission is 50p (80¢) for adults, 25p (40¢) for children.

About five miles east of Pontypool (near Usk) is **Llandegfedd Reservoir,** which has an interesting farm park (tel. 02913/2592). Sailing and fishing are possible in the reservoir.

BLAENAVON: The eastern edge of the South Wales mountain mass divides industrial and rural South Wales (typified by the Usk and Wye Valleys). In the industrial part is Blaenavon, on the A4043, lying to the north of Pontypool and a short distance west of Abergavenny, to be visited next. Starting at Blaenavon and going sometimes to the south but always bearing westward, you'll see once-ravaged valleys now being restored after their sad but lucrative exploitation during the industrial heyday of South Wales, as well as rivers and streams making their way to the Bristol Channel.

At Blaenavon, the **Big Pit** (tel. 0495/790311) is a real coal mine now open to the public for underground tours. One of the oldest shaft mines in South Wales, it was sunk in 1860, the coal seams of the hillsides around it having been worked from the end of the 1700s. Big Pit ceased production in 1980 and has become a major attraction to show people the entire setup of a self-contained mining community. The mine followed the establishment of an iron-smelting furnace across the valley.

At Big Pit, so named because of the diameter of its pit shaft, visitors are taken down 300 feet in the pit cage into the shaft, equipped with helmets, cap lamps, and batteries to get an idea of what life was like for generations of miners. You'll see the underground stable where pit ponies were kept, never seeing the light of day, until the introduction of conveyors to replace the horse-drawn coal-laden trams in 1930. Also, you learn about the conditions under which children, some as young as six or seven, worked in the mines, many for 12-hour shifts in darkness. Surface facilities are also open to visitors—the colliery workshops, pithead baths, a miner's cottage, a museum exhibition, and a video display. Many of the men who worked in Big Pit are now guides, bringing firsthand knowledge to the tours.

Underground tours last about one hour, but visitors should allow another hour for a thorough viewing of the surface buildings and exhibits. The first underground tour is at 10 a.m., with subsequent journeys during the day until the last tour leaves at 3:30 p.m. Big Pit is open daily March to the end of December (except during the Christmas holidays). It is generally open daily in January and February, but because of the unpredictability of the weather, visitors should phone before coming here in those months. Underground tours will not be possible on certain days in January and February because of maintenance work. The charge for the underground and surface tour is £3.30 ($5.28) for adults, £2.30 ($3.68) for children. A well-stocked book and gift shop offers Welsh crafts articles as well as miners' lamps and other mine souvenirs. Hot and cold snacks and lunches are available in the traditional miners' cafeteria.

The remains of the late 18th-century **ironworks** across the valley on North Street in Blaenavon may be viewed from the outside only. The workers' cottages are also visible from the viewing area. Hours are from 10 a.m. to 5 p.m. weekdays, 2 to 5 p.m. on Sunday April to September. Admission is free, with a small charge made for guided tours. For information, phone the **Torfaen Museum Trust** in Pontypool (tel. 04955/52036).

St. Peter's Church in the town center has an iron font and even iron tomb covers in the churchyard, memorials to pioneers in Blaenavon ironmaking.

Both Blaenavon, in the Valley of Torfaen, and nearby Forgeside date from the heyday of coal and iron.

7. Abergavenny

This flourishing market town of nearly 10,000 people is called "the Gate to Wales," and it's certainly the gateway to the Brecon Beacons, described in the next section, which lie to the west. The Welsh word *aber* means the mouth of a river, and Abergavenny lies at the mouth of the River Gavenny, where it joins the River Usk. The town is in the valley with friendly mountains and hills spread around it. Mankind has found this a good, sometimes safe, place to live for some 5,000 years, as revealed by finds from the late Neolithic Age. The Romans established one of their forts here, and centuries later a Norman castle was built in about the same area as the fort had been.

Try to be in Abergavenny on a market day. On Tuesday and Friday, you can shop among stalls carrying a wide selection of goods, ranging from antiques to food to clothing, even furniture and just junk. It might be called a flea market back home, so varied are the wares offered. On Tuesday, there is a livestock market.

Abergavenny is renowned as a center for outdoor holiday activities, including pony trekking, hill walking and climbing, golfing, hang-gliding, and fishing. A Leisure Centre provides for indoor sports.

The town's Civic Society has laid out a **Town Trail,** listing buildings and other points of interest. From Easter to September, for information about Abergavenny and its environs, get in touch with the **Tourist Information Centre,** Lower Monk Street (tel. 0873/3254), or, all year long, the **Abergavenny and District Tourist Association,** the Castle Lodge, Castle Street (tel. 0873/3909).

WHERE TO STAY: In the heart of town, the **Angel Hotel,** Cross Street (tel. 0873/7121), is a comfortable old black-and-white posting house. When the Nevill family owned the castle in the 12th century, it was connected to the inn on the site of the Angel by a tunnel. The inn burned in the 16th century and was rebuilt a couple of hundred years later. The rebuilt inn started as a magnificent private home, later undergoing changes to become one of the important coaching inns on the road from Fishguard to London. F. D. McCarthy manages the fine hotel and its dining facilities. He extends warm hospitality to guests, seeing to it that they are comfortable in one of the 29 bedrooms, one with an elegant four-poster. All the rooms have private bathroom, color TV, telephone, radio, tea/coffee-making facilities, and razor outlets. The inn is centrally heated. Accommodations are on two floors, and all the front windows have double glazing to keep out street noises. The tariff is from £38 ($60.80) per person for B&B in a single, from £48 ($76.80) in a double. Ask about the special weekend discounts.

Belchamps Guest House, 1 Holywell Rd. (tel. 0873/3204), is near the town center, with views of the park, Blorenge Mountain, and Abergavenny Castle. Each of the immaculate, carpeted, and tastefully furnished bedrooms has hot-beverage facilities and hot and cold water and a razor outlet, while baths, showers, and toilets are close by. The centrally heated stone hostelry, run by Stella and Eddy Perrin, has a comfortable residents' lounge with color TV. The five bedrooms cost from £11 ($17.60) to £13 ($20.80) per person for B&B. Dinner, served in the pleasant dining room, costs from £6 ($9.60). Drinks are available in the evening. Guests are given their own keys in case they're out late.

"The Guest House," Oxford Street (tel. 0873/4823), is about half a mile from the town center in a quiet spot off the main road. This licensed guesthouse, run by Basil and June Cook, is a happy choice as a base for touring the surrounding country. The seven bedrooms all have hot and cold water and rent for £12.50 ($20) in a single, £21 ($33.60) in a double (none with private baths) for B&B.

Good home-cooking and other comforts will make your stay pleasant. You can enjoy bar snacks at any time, and guests can watch TV in the lounge.

The **Park Guest House**, 36 Hereford Rd. (tel. 0873/3715), is a comfortable seven-bedroom stucco dwelling near the center of town, renting rooms for £10.50 ($16.80) per person. A full, cooked breakfast is included. They have singles, doubles, and family rooms for guests. You can be cozy in the lounge watching color TV, perhaps enjoying a drink in this licensed, centrally heated house. There's free parking for your car.

WHERE TO EAT: Good food is served at the **Angel Hotel**, Cross Street (tel. 0873/7121), recommended above. You can feast in the elegant restaurant or have snacks at lunchtime or in the evening in the Foxhunter Bar. Fixed-price meals cost from £8 ($12.80) to £9.50 ($15.20). A special Sunday luncheon menu, with a choice of five appetizers, six main dishes with vegetables and potatoes or salads, and three desserts, costs around £7.50 ($12) for a complete repast. There's a good, reasonably priced wine list. Bar snacks are served from noon to 2:15 p.m. and 7 to 9:30 p.m. Lunch in the restaurant is available from noon to 2 p.m., dinner from 7 to 9:30 p.m.

Crowfield Inn, Ross Road (tel. 0873/5048), is a fine country house where you can have bar meals which include traditional Welsh and English dishes, including fresh local salmon, casseroles, and roast beef, all freshly prepared. For dessert, try one of Sasha Crabb's fresh fruit ice creams. You can have a meal for £8 ($12.80) and up. Food is served from 11:30 a.m. to 2 p.m. and 6:30 to 9:30 p.m.

Sue's Parlour, Flannel Street (tel. 0873/6255), upstairs, is a cheerful place done with green wainscoting. On the menu are beefburgers with french fries and a lunch of the day. When I was last there the lunch was roast beef and Yorkshire pudding, creamed potatoes, a vegetable of the day, and horseradish sauce, all for just £3 ($4.80). From 9:30 a.m. to 5 p.m. Tuesday to Saturday, they serve breakfast, coffee, snacks, lunches, and cream teas.

On the Outskirts

In Llandewi Skirrid, three miles northeast of Abergavenny on the B4521 road, is the **Walnut Tree Inn** (tel. 0873/2797), which has been praised all over the British Isles—and abroad. Ann and Franco Taruschio, who have been here for nearly a quarter of a century, run only a restaurant, no pub or bar, although there is a service bar where you can sip an apéritif while you wait for a table. It's best to make a reservation—this place is so popular it's likely to be full most of the time. Franco is from Italy, and his menus reflect that, although he prepares Welsh food with just as deft a touch. If you don't believe me, try his laverbread crêpes with fruits de mer or oysters gratiné with laverbread. The oysters served here come from West Wales. Among the fine dishes offered, ranging from classic to nouvelle cuisine, are suprême of guinea fowl in port wine and truffles, salmon with rhubarb, quails Rossini, roast woodcock, and filet of lamb with eggplant, among many other tasty viands. Seafoods and river fish include cold lobster and mayonnaise, filet of turbot, grilled lobster with vin santo or garlic butter, and salmon en croûte. An à la carte meal costs £20 ($32) per person. The food choices are complemented by a fine wine list. Meals are served from noon to 2:30 p.m. and 7 to 10:30 p.m. Closed all day Sunday and at lunchtime on Monday.

SIGHTS: Only fragments of the 12th-century **Abergavenny Castle** remain, but a gruesome segment of its history is remembered. An early owner of the fortress, the Norman knight William de Braose, angered at the slaying of his brother-in-law by Welsh Lords of Gwent, invited a group of them to dinner and had them murdered as they sat unarmed at his table. Visitors today fare better in visiting.

The **Abergavenny Museum** (tel. 0873/4282) is in a house attached to the 19th-century hunting lodge in the castle grounds. The museum contains archeological artifacts, farming tools, and a fascinating collection of old prints, pictures, and costumes of the area. A Welsh farmhouse kitchen and the contents of an old saddler's shop are on display. The museum is open from 11 a.m. to 1 p.m. and 2 to 5 p.m. Monday to Saturday, from 2 to 5 p.m. on Sunday March to October; from 11 a.m. to 1 p.m. and 2 to 4 p.m. Monday to Saturday November to February. Admission is 50p (80¢) for adults, 25p (40¢) for children. The castle grounds can be visited daily from dawn to dusk.

St. Mary's Parish Church, Monk Street, is all that's left of a 12th-century Benedictine priory church, although little remains of the original Norman structure, as the building was redone in the 13th to the 15th centuries. It is believed that Cromwell's troops, which were billeted in Abergavenny for a while during the siege of Raglan Castle, did some damage to the church and the tombs it contains. In the Herbert Chapel are a number of sarcophagi of Lords of Abergavenny and family members with requisite effigies on top. Of brasses in the church, the oldest records a death in 1587. A 15th-century Jesse Tree is an unusual possession of the church. It lies in the Lewis Chapel. This is a ten-foot-long representation carved from a single piece of wood showing the family tree from which Christ came growing out of the body of Jesse, father of David. There is also a Norman font, as well as some 14th-century oak choir stalls. Through the centuries vandalism was committed in the church from various sources, so today except on Sunday you must ask the vicar for the key in order to explore the interior.

Just inside the eastern border of the national park, on the A465 road from Hereford, England, to Abergavenny, is the tiny hamlet of—

LLANFIHANGEL CRUCORNEY: If that name throws you, just remember that

near this village is the oldest public house in Wales (some say it's the oldest in Britain), the **Skirrid Inn** (tel. 0873890/258), which has stood here for nearly 900 years. The first written record of its existence is in reference to the trial in 1110 of two brothers in the main room of a "new" alehouse, Millbrook, below the Skirrid Mountain. One of the brothers, found guilty of sheep stealing, was sentenced to death by hanging from a beam of the inn. Between the 12th and the 17th centuries 180 to 186 persons met the same fate, and you can see the heavy beam where it is believed the executions were carried out. Scorch and drag marks of the rope can still be seen. The courtroom upstairs has been made into a large bedroom, which rents for about £26 ($41.60) for B&B for two persons—if you're courageous enough to climb upstairs past the hanging beam to go to bed. The condemned cell in the "mesne" (mezzanine) is now a bathroom.

Downstairs in the pub you can order skirrettes, mentioned earlier under "Food and Drink," a sort of extravagant potato pancake, and other foods from the menu prepared by Mr. and Mrs. Foster, the proprietors. You can have a pub lunch for £2 ($3.20) to £3.50 ($5.60), or a dinner of Welsh lamb, Wye salmon, or roast beef, perhaps with that famous British dessert, spotted dick, or trifle to finish it off. You'll pay from £7 ($11.20) for a filling repast. Hours are from 11 a.m. to 3 p.m. and 6 to 11 p.m. The stone structure of the inn is original, and the main doorway and many of the windows are certainly medieval.

Quite near Llanfihangel Crucorney is **Partrishow Church,** six miles north of Crickhowell (previewed below). Here you can see a handsome rood screen, an 11th-century baptismal font, and stone altars projecting through the paneling. To visit, you must get the church key at an adjacent farm. No admission is charged.

Going northwest from Llanfihangel Crucorney on the B4423 road into the remote Vale of Ewyas, skirting the English border, you come to—

LLANTHONY: The ruins of an Augustinian priory lie in a peaceful meadow in the craggy Black Mountains. Llanthony is a corruption of Llandewi Nant Honddu (St. David's Church on the Honddu). The priory was built in 1107 on the ruins of a much older chapel dedicated to St. David. Today a hotel occupies the south tower and the prior house.

If you venture farther up the vale, you'll see the remains of the brick **Capely-Ffin** (Boundary Chapel), founded by Father Ignatius, a Victorian monk who came here "to serve the Lord in solitude." Today the old monastery is a private home, and self-catering apartments are close by. The Vale of Ewyas is as serene and peaceful today as it must have been when the monks selected it as a perfect place for religious retreats.

High in the Black Mountains, you'll probably see rather bleak signs of the encroachment of the late 20th century: sad-looking communes of campers living in old buses, wrecked vans, and tents.

8. Brecon Beacons National Park

The Brecon Beacons National Park comprises 519 square miles of land from the Black Mountains in the east to Black Mountain in the west—if you can keep that straight in your mind. National parks in the British Isles are not like the areas so designated in the United States: they are not nationally owned. People own land, live, and work within the park boundaries just as in other areas of the country, but they have a lot of eyes on them to assure the safeguarding of the landscape and to provide means of access so the park area can be enjoyed.

A local planning authority works under supervision of the national Countryside Commission in this behalf, but that's not all. Some areas of the park are managed by the Forestry Commission, others are on lease by the British Crown for defense purposes. Both the Nature Conservancy and the National Trust maintain guardianship of certain portions of parklands. And with all this, rights of access are subject to the wishes of private landowners.

The Brecon Beacons National Park takes its name from the mountain range in the center of the park area. Pen y Fan, the highest peak in the range, rises to nearly 3,000 feet, which may not seem so high if you're used to the Rocky Mountains, but it's a healthy elevation for South Wales—and you have to be pretty hardy to climb around on it. The park contains sandstone moors covered with bracken and limestone crags with wooded gorges. Vast stretches of open common land lie in pastoral country. Farming is the main industry of the park. You can enjoy spectacular drives over the mountains, but walking or pony trekking are the best ways to explore the park.

There are nature reserves, a mountain center, and 32 miles of canal (see "Canal Boat Holidays" in Chapter XX). The limestone area contains Britain's longest-known cave system, visited in this section. A number of ancient monuments and historic buildings lie within the park boundaries.

If you're interested in a **farmhouse holiday** in the Brecon Beacons National Park, write or call Mrs. Meudwen Stephens, Upper Trewalken Farm, Pengenffordd, Talgarth, Brecon, Powys (tel. 0874/711349). The group of which Mrs. Stephens is secretary, called "Welcome to Brecon and Radnor," offers bed-and-breakfast accommodations for about £10 ($16) per person per night, with reductions for children. An evening meal is £6 ($9.60). The places on her list are all working farms.

For information regarding the park and its facilities, get in touch with any of the following:

National Park Information Centre, Watton Mount, Brecon, Powys LD3 7DP (tel. 0874/4437).

National Park Information Centre, at Abergavenny, Monk Street (tel. 0873/3254); Llandovery (tel. 0550/20693); or the Mountain Centre, near Libanus, Brecon (tel. 0874/3366).

The park's southern boundary is only 25 miles from Cardiff, 14 miles from Swansea, and 10 miles from Newport. Abergavenny, just visited, lies on the eastern boundary. Hay-on-Wye, to be previewed in a later chapter, is at the farthest northeastern tip.

BRECON BEACONS MOUNTAIN CENTRE:

Run by the Brecon Beacons National Park Committee, the Mountain Centre, near Libanus (tel. 0874/3366), five miles southwest of Brecon, offers a good resting place or a point from which to begin your tour of the park. There is a spacious lounge, displays explaining the major points of interest, talks and films, an informative staff, a first-aid room, a picnic area, a refreshment buffet, and toilets. Wheelchairs have access to all parts of the building.

The center is open daily except Christmas Day from 9:30 a.m. and the buffet from 10 a.m. Closing times vary according to the time of year. In April and September the center closes at 6 p.m. on weekdays, at 6:30 p.m. on Sunday. May to August, closing is at 7 p.m. all week, and October to March, the center shuts down at 5 p.m. Buffet hours vary, so check when you go to the center. *Note:* If you leave your car in the parking area, it will be locked up when the center closes and you won't be able to retrieve it until morning.

THE SHOWCAVES:

The extensive limestone regions in the southwestern portions of the Brecon Beacons National Park have been riddled with underground caverns through action of water over the millennia. Experienced cavers (spelunkers) can explore many of these by making arrangements with one of the caving clubs, through the national park information centers. However, only the **Day-yr-Ogof Showcaves,** Abercraf (tel. 0639/730284), are open to the general public, including children. Midway between Brecon and Swansea on the A4067, this is the largest showcave complex in Western Europe. Visitors are able to follow dry, firm walkways to see stalagmite and stalactite formations under floodlights. Tours through Dan-yr-Ogof, Cathedral Cave, Bone Cave, and the amazing Dinosaur Park last about 2½ hours. The complex is open daily, Easter to the end of October from 10 a.m. to 5 p.m. The charge is £2.75 ($4.40) for adults and £1.75 ($2.80) for children (accompanied children under four admitted free). There is a restaurant, craft shop, museum, dry-ski slope, and information center at the caves.

The caves are near **Craig-y-Nos Country Park,** about ten miles south of Sennybridge, a property that was once the "home sweet home" of the famous singer, Mme Adelina Patti. For more information about the park, telephone 0639/730395. It's open daily from 10 a.m. to dusk, the time varying with the seasons. There is no charge for entrance.

A MOUNTAIN LODGE:

For a stay in the tranquility of the park, I recommend **Nant Dhu Lodge,** Cwm Taf, near Storey Arms (tel. 0658/79111), constructed in the 19th century as a shooting lodge for Lord Tredegar. The name of the country-house hotel, Nant Dhu, translates as Black Stream in English. It is right in the heart of the Brecon Beacons National Park on the A470 road from Cardiff to Brecon, lying in spacious grounds, an excellent center for walking, climbing, and fishing. The comfortable lounge bar contains an iron woodburning stove for heating, handmade Welsh settle furniture, and stained-glass lights. Pam and Jonathan Parsons welcome guests to the white-walled, slate-roofed house surrounded by a flat lawn and evergreen trees. The 15 bedrooms have private baths, color TV, direct-dial phones, hair dryers, trouser presses, radios, and hot-beverage facilities, as well as panoramic views of the gardens and mountains. Rates are from £29 ($46.40) in a single, from £32 ($51.20) to £39 ($62.40) in a double for B&B, depending on the season. The hotel restaurant is renowned in the area for its cuisine, with a table d'hôte menu costing £9.25 ($14.80), with à la carte meals going for around £15 ($24).

9. Crickhowell

This little country town on the River Usk nestles placidly in green fields below a limestone mountain, Pen Cerrig Calch. The town's Welsh name is from Crug Hywel (Howell's Mound), site of an Iron Age hill-fort and of a later stronghold of King Hywel Dda. One of the best bridges over the Usk is the one here, which, oddly enough, has 12 arches on one side and 13 on the other, to accommodate the merging of the road with the narrower Bridge Street approach.

Crickhowell, of course, had a castle—a 13th-century Norman fortress built on the site of an earlier structure. It was ravaged during Owain Glyndwr's rebellion and only fragments exist today—a mound and two broken towers. To see it, go through a wicker gate opposite the post office, past the cricket ground, to the castle ruins.

Crickhowell is a market town that still holds a fair twice a year, a requirement of its market charter. A Welsh version of an American flea market is held on Thursday.

Some of Crickhowell's Tudor and Georgian buildings still stand. However, in the early 19th century many old frame structures were pulled down and the market square rebuilt, so that only the Corn Exchange on High Street and one other building remain from the town's medieval times.

FOOD AND LODGING: An old coaching inn, the **Bear Hotel,** High Street (tel. 0873/810408), is smack in the center of town. It used to have a gazebo from which watch could be kept for the coaches coming from Brecon so that all would be in readiness for the requirements of the stop. The gazebo is now at the Malt House. The present hotel was gradually built up as needed through a few centuries, but I was told that there was "a very small bear" here in 1432. The flagstones in the kitchen date from then. To enter the hotel, you turn sharply off the road, passing under an archway to the parking area at the back and coming into the hotel through a secluded garden. The proprietor, Mrs. J. Laura Hindmarsh, is happy to tell you about the hotel's history if she's not too busy.

The 12 bedrooms are pleasant and comfortable, and the hotel has central heating, direct-dial phones, and TV if required. Charges for B&B run from £20 ($32) in a bathless single and from £27.60 ($44.16) in a single with bath. Bathless doubles or twins cost £29.90 ($47.84), while a similar double with bath is £34.50 ($55.20). There are two attractive dining rooms where you can dine à la carte on Welsh and English cuisine, a three-course meal costing from £11.50 ($18.40). I prefer to eat in the lounge bar (in winter, there's a blazing fire) from such tempting specialties as salmon cakes, curries, or fresh salmon béchamel, while chatting with or listening to the locals, who like this place. A pub meal costs around £3.95 ($6.32) to £6.95 ($11.12). Food is served from 11 a.m. to 3 p.m. and 6 to 11 p.m.

The **Dragon House Hotel,** High Street (tel. 0873/810362), is a two-story pink 18th-century building with white window trim and white curtains, standing right in the middle of the town center. The charges are from £12.50 ($20) to £23.50 ($37.60) per person for B&B in their charming rooms, the latter price for a room with bath. All units have hot and cold running water. The residents' lounge has a log fireplace and color TV. The hotel offers a dining room, a cozy cellar lounge bar, and a tea room that is open from 10 a.m. to noon Tuesday through Friday, 10 a.m. to noon and 4 to 6 p.m. on Saturday.

If you're looking for a light lunch, go to **The Cheese Press,** 18 High St. (tel. 0873/811122), where there's a little coffeeshop up the steps at the back of the shop. It is known for serving individually prepared dishes based on fresh produce and natural ingredients. You might order lasagne and salad, chicken curry and rice, imaginative salads, even toasted sandwiches. You can finish with homemade cake. Expect to pay from £3.50 ($5.60) for a meal. The place is open from 9:30 a.m. to 5:30 p.m. weekdays, from 10:30 a.m. to 4:30 p.m. on Sunday.

In the Environs

Just 1½ miles west of Crickhowell at the junction of the A40 and the A479 roads is the **Nantyffin Cider Mill Inn** (tel. 0874/810775), where you can see the old milling gear outside. The present pink-washed building is about 500 years old, but the Domesday Book shows a structure on this spot. Drovers taking their cattle and sheep to Chepstow market used to stop here where two roads met (the A479 and the A40 of today). The cider mill was in use until World War II. The dining room has a huge stone fireplace. Good food is served under the direction of John Flynn, licensee, with such dishes as egg and prawn mayonnaise, beef filet in puff pastry, home-boiled ham and salad and pâté and toast. You can dine à la carte for around £6.50 ($10.40), unless you opt for a steak italienne or steak lyonnaise, in which case expect to pay £10 ($16) and up. You can choose from three kinds of cider to drink. Food is served from 11:30 a.m. to 2:30 p.m. (to 1:30 p.m. on Sunday) and from 7 to 10 p.m. (closes at 9:30 p.m. on Sunday). If you'd like to stop over at the inn, two rooms are rented for £11.50 ($18.40) per person for B&B, VAT included.

If you're willing to splurge a bit, the finest accommodation in the area is **Gliffaes Country House** (tel. 0873/0874), less than four miles west of Crickhowell along A40. Built more than a century ago as a private residence of an Anglican minister, it is an extravagantly detailed Victorian mansion patterned on Italianate lines, complete with repetitive arches and flanked on either side with both a clock tower and a bell tower. It sits on 30 acres of land, lavishly planted with 19th-century arboreal oddities, including a 200-year-old cedar of Lebanon and a giant sequoia, brought back from the California coast by an early explorer. The owners are Nick and Peta Brabner, who have employed a helpful staff. They can arrange fishing in the River Usk, a few steps away. The mansion is richly imbued with antiques and paintings, containing a total of 19 bedrooms, priced from £20.50 ($32.80) to £27.50 ($44) per person for B&B, depending on the plumbing and the accommodation. The hotel contains a pair of dining rooms, one of which is richly paneled in dark wood. Lunch, open to non-residents, is from 1 to 2 p.m., featuring a cold buffet at £6.50 ($10.40) per person, and dinner is nightly from 7:30 to 9:30, costing from £10.50 ($16.80). The chef prepares such dishes as Scottish salmon marinated in a dill and mustard sauce, rack of lamb provençale, and veal pierre with garlic butter, mushrooms, onions, and cream. The hotel closes the last day of every year, reopening in mid-March.

TRETOWER: In this pleasant little village about 3½ miles west and north of Crickhowell on the A479, you can visit **Tretower Court** and **Tretower Castle,** buildings about 200 yards and two centuries apart. The remains of the 12th-century motte and bailey of the castle are here, with a large fireplace and a section of a wall and parapet.

The 14th-century Tretower Court manor house has been preserved and restored, with alterations from time to time, so that it is a fine example of a stately home of the later Middle Ages. It has a fine gallery upstairs from the ground floor and two banks of rooms built around a central courtyard.

Open all year, the court and castle can be visited weekdays from 9:30 a.m. to 6:30 p.m. in summer, with winter closing at 4 p.m. Sunday hours are 2 to 6:30 p.m. in summer, to 4 p.m. in winter. Admission is £1 ($1.60) for adults, 50p (80¢) for children. For more information, telephone 0874/279.

10. Talybont-on-Usk

A placid village at the confluence of the Usk and Caerfanell Rivers, Talybont also has another waterway: the Monmouthshire and Brecon Canal, which takes holiday boats as far up the Usk Valley as Brecon, winds through the village. Talybont Reservoir, where the trout fishing is excellent, is nearby in the valley of the Caerfanell. Talybont is just off the A40, on the B4558 road to Brecon.

FOOD AND LODGING: If you'd like to stop over in this peaceful place, I recommend the **Usk Hotel** (tel. 087487/251), a roadside, white-walled house each of whose 13 simple and contemporary bedrooms contains a private bath or shower. It was constructed as a public house by a now-defunct brewery, to service the needs of passengers riding in 1868 on the newly built railroad line. Today it's the property of Mrs. L. M. Robertson, who capably directs a helpful staff of girls. For B&B, singles cost £17 ($27.20) with bath, while doubles with bath go for £26 ($41.60). A twin with shower and toilet rents for £28 ($44.80). A full vegetarian menu is offered, featuring such specialties as ratatouille with cheese. Other main dishes to tempt the palate include veal Cordon Bleu, roast mallard duck, and salmon fresh from the River Usk. A good dinner costs around £9 ($14.40). The pleasantly woodsy pub contains lots of paneling, an inlaid grandfather clock whose marquetry face indicates that it was made in Llandeilo, and a cross-section of the business people of the community.

An outstanding pub in the area is the **Star,** along the B4558 (tel. 087487/635), a freehouse known for its real ales. Locals are also fond of the cider from a handpump. You have a choice of several old-fashioned nooks at this village pub which has open fires in chilly weather. Most people come here to drink, but the bar food makes it a worthy choice for eating as well. From the kitchen emerges everything from fresh trout to sirloin steak cooked as you like it. You can also settle for a sandwich. Meals cost from £5 ($8). It is open all day Thursday; otherwise hours are from 11 a.m. to 3 p.m. and 6 to 11 p.m. (in off-season it opens at noon and 7 p.m. evenings).

11. Brecon

This busy little market town is the main base for touring the Brecon Beacons National Park. Brecon, situated where the Usk and Honddu Rivers meet, is the center of a farming section.

The **Tourist Information Centre** is at the market car park (tel. 0874/2485).

FOOD AND LODGING: The finest choice for either food or lodging in town is clearly the **Castle of Brecon Hotel,** The Avenue (tel. 0874/4611), which has been considerably improved and renovated. It is joined to the remnants of the castle, so perhaps it has more claim than most to being truly called a castle hotel. The hotel opened its doors in 1820, and since that time has housed wayfarers from around the world. The bedrooms have been modernized into a conservatively modern format of greater comfort, costing from £44 ($70.40) in a double, £30 ($48) in a single, making it a splurge choice. The restaurant contains exquisitely carved William and Mary paneling, dating from 1689. It serves lunch from noon to 1:45 p.m., a table d'hôte costing from £7.50 ($12). Dinner from 7 to 9 p.m. is a four-course set menu for £10.50 ($16.80).

The **Wellington Hotel,** The Bulwark (tel. 0874/5225), is a former coaching inn built around 1850 on the London–Fishguard route. The Georgian-fronted hotel has a small courtyard which you enter through a covered tunnel to get to the popular hotel pub, open every day. The hotel is in the center of town, opposite a statue of Wellington standing in the town square. The coffeeshop, Dukes, becomes a more formal restaurant at night. Open from 8 a.m. to 11 p.m. Monday to Saturday (to 10:30 p.m. on Sunday), Dukes serves both British and continental cuisine, including fondue bourguignon or duck with an orange-flavored Grand Marnier sauce, with meals costing from £12 ($19.20). A wide staircase takes guests up to the 21 rooms, each of which has a high ceiling, simple modern furniture, and a private bath, as well as color TV, radio, phone, and tea/coffee-making facilities. For B&B in a twin-bedded room, the charge is £21 ($33.60) per person. An extra bed in the room is available for £12 ($19.20). All prices include VAT and service. John Thomas, who was born within six miles of the hotel, is the owner.

Brecon was the birthplace of the actress Sarah Siddons (1755–1831). The building on High Street Inferior, then a private home, in which she made her first appearance, is now a Whitbread pub—the **Sarah Siddons,** of course, at 47 High St. (tel. 0874/2009). You may want to stop here for some home-cooked pub food—meats, curries, and meat pies. They also offer vegetarian dishes. A meal costs £1.50 ($2.40) to £3 ($4.80). The pub is open from 11 a.m. to 3 p.m. and 5:30 to 11 p.m. Monday, Wednesday, Thursday, and Saturday; from 11 a.m. to 11 p.m. Tuesday and Friday, from noon to 2 p.m. and 7 to 10 p.m. on Sunday. Warning: You may wish they'd turn the house lights up a little in this dark place.

Staying at Trecastle

The **Castle** (tel. 087482/354), lying 12 miles from Brecon, is one of the choice little nuggets in the area, if you'd like to make it your base for exploring the Brecon Beacons National Park. In spite of its grand name, the little hotel has only six bedrooms, but each is beautifully furnished and comfortably appointed. The cost is only £13.50 ($21.60) per person for B&B. The house is warm and cozy, with many remainders of its previous life, including a centuries-old fireplace in the bar. In olden days, The Castle was an important stop for coaches on the route from London to towns in the western part of Britain. Until Joan and Richard Ward took over, it had become a simple village pub, drawing the locals. But under their love and care, it has regained its choice position, and is now a worthy stopover that also serves well-prepared meals to travelers.

Staying at Llanfaes

Old Castle Farm Guest House, 18 Penpentre (tel. 0874/2120), is a 17th-century house about half a mile west of Brecon's town center. It was once a working farm until its lands were sold off, and today it lies in a built-up area, welcoming guests behind its black-and-white facade. Mr. and Mrs. P. J. Williams welcome guests to their ten-bedroom house, which is centrally heated. Units are twin- or double-bedded, and there are some family rooms. All accommodations have private baths, TV, and hot-beverage facilities. The owners charge from £11 ($17.60) to £13 ($20.80) per person for B&B based on double occupancy. Singles pay from £13 ($20.80) to £16 ($25.60) for B&B. An evening meal costs only £5 ($8). The licensed guesthouse has a bar lounge, and a private car park is convenient.

SIGHTS: The Romans thought the area was a good place for a military encampment to discourage the Celts, and they built a fort, **Y Gaer,** in A.D. 75, about 2½ miles west of the present town. To get to Y Gaer, you walk across private farm fields. You can look around for no admission charge.

Brecon Castle, built in 1093, is practically extinct, but it was a power in its day. It was militarily important when Llewelyn the Great and later Owain Glyndwr were battling against outsiders who wanted sovereignty in Wales. However, at the close of the Civil War after Cromwell's visitations, the people of Brecon, tired of centuries of strife, pulled the castle down. All that's left is a section of wall joined to the Castle Hotel (see above) and the Ely Tower, named for the bishop of Ely and chancellor of England imprisoned there by Richard III.

Of special interest is the fortified red sandstone priory church of St. John the Evangelist, with its massive tower, now the **Cathedral of Swansea and Brecon.** It stands high above the River Honddu. The oldest parts of the cathedral date from the 12th century.

The **Brecknock Museum,** Captain's Walk (tel. 0874/4121), centers around the tiny assize courtroom that was part of the Shire Hall the museum now occupies. The court is intact with magistrate's bench, prisoner's dock, and jury seats. More than 5,000 years of local activity are spanned in other museum exhibits—a dug-out canoe found in Llangorse Lake (a few miles to the east), a Roman burial stone, early Christian memorial stones, and a Welsh kitchen from the early 1900s are here, as well as farm and domestic equipment of other days. There's a car park nearby off the main street. The museum is open all year, and there's no admission charge. Hours are from 10 a.m. to 5 p.m. Monday to Saturday.

Another interesting look into the past is provided at the **South Wales Borderers Museum,** Watton Mound (tel. 0874/3111, ext. 310). If you saw the movie *Zulu,* starring Michael Caine, you'll be interested in the display here relating to the bloody battles in Africa, especially the defense of Rorke's Drift. The South Wales Borderers, then known as the 24th Regiment, originated in 1689 and is now part of the Royal Regiment of Wales. There's a free car park at the Watton. The museum is open all year. Admission is 30p (48¢).

12. Merthyr Tydfil

Tydfil, martyred daughter of Brychan, a 5th-century Irish-Celtic chieftain, gave her name to this, one of the most historic industrial towns of Wales. Merthyr Tydfil is now a thriving place with a modern shopping precinct and a covered market. It lies on the Heads of the Valleys road, the A465, with the Brecon Beacons National Park boundary on its northern edge. An important center for iron and steel, this was where Richard Trevithick ran the first successful steam locomotive.

FOOD AND LODGING: A family-run accommodation, the **Tregenna Hotel,** Park Terrace (tel. 0685/3627), is in a residential section of town. All of the 21 bedrooms have private baths and rent for £18 ($28.80) per person for B&B, based on double occupancy. Reductions are granted for children sharing their parents' room. Guests can watch TV in the lounge or enjoy drinks in the cozy bar at this licensed hotel. Country cottages are available for the same price as the bedrooms.

Also on Park Terrace is **Maes-y-Coed Guest House** (tel. 0685/2246), named "house in the fields" when it was built at the turn of the century. The name is not quite as apt today, as it is now surrounded by other houses. It offers one of the best B&B accommodations in the area. The house has central heating and hot and cold water basins in the four bedrooms, which are immaculately maintained. There is a comfortable residents' lounge where you can watch TV. Rent is £11 ($17.60) per night per person for B&B, with an optional evening meal offered in the small dining room for £4 ($6.40). Children sharing their parents' room are granted a 50% reduction. The house has a large garden, which guests are free to enjoy.

The **Nant Dhu Lodge** at Cwm Taf, described in the section on the Brecon Beacons National Park, is quite close to Merthyr Tydfil.

SIGHTS: A mile northwest of the town center, **Cyfarthfa Castle and Museum** (tel. 0685/3112), the former home of the ironmaster of Merthyr, was built in 1824 in Gothic style, a castellated mansion that allowed its owner, William Crawshay II, to look out on the source of his wealth, the ironworks below. The museum contains an eclectic collection: artifacts of the industrial past, watercolors, a re-created Welsh kitchen, a model of Trevithick's steam engine, and items from ancient Egypt. Parkland with a lake, a pitch-and-putt golf course, a children's playground; and woods surround the mansion. The museum is open daily from 10 a.m. to 1 p.m. and 2 to 6 p.m. April to September, to 5 p.m. the rest of the year. Sunday hours all year are 2 to 5 p.m. Admission is 10p (16¢) for adults, 5p (8¢) for children.

The **Robert and Lucy Thomas Fountain,** an ornate cast-iron fountain canopy near the town center, commemorates the Thomases as pioneers in the export of South Wales coal.

The **Joseph Parry Cottage,** 4 Chapel Row (tel. 0685/73117), is a small museum devoted to the celebrated 19th-century Welsh composer who was born here. He worked in the coal pits as a child, then emigrated with his father to Pennsylvania where he was employed in the rolling mills before developing his music career in the United States and Wales. The cottage is the headquarters for the Merthyr Heritage Trust. It is open all year Monday to Friday from 9:30 a.m. to 12:30 p.m.

Near Cyfarthfa Castle is **Cefn Coed Viaduct,** a 15-arch, 725-foot-long railroad viaduct spanning the River Taff at the village of Cefn. A masterpiece of Victorian engineering, the massive arches supported the steam trains on the old Merthyr–Brecon line.

The Brecon Mountain Railway terminus is at Pontsticill, a short drive north in Brecon Beacons National Forest.

If you need help, get in touch with the **Merthyr Tydfil Borough Council Information Service,** Central Library, High Street (tel. 0685/3201).

A Visit in the Environs

The head of **Rhymney Valley** lies about three miles east of Merthyr Tydfil. One of the most historic of the South Wales valleys, Rhymney still has mementos of the Industrial Revolution in the stark and forsaken coal dumps and the towns and villages with their rows of colorful houses carved into the hills, the homes of miners and ironworkers for generations. Just off the Heads of the Valleys road, near Rhymney town, stands **Butetown,** a delightful village today with its three parallel terraced rows of stone houses built for ironworkers in 1802. Now restored, they still afford good accommodation, but they can only be viewed from outside. The village is a conservation area, with its 49 homes, a post office, a pub, and a little church.

If you go south on the A4049 road near Butetown, you pass through Rhymney and at Aberbargoed you'll find the **Stuart Crystal** glassworks on Angel Lane. Here you can watch Welsh craftsmen turn out the sparkling handmade crystal. Visitors are shown free through the glassmaking department and the decoration department where the artisans work with meticulous care on individual items of crystal, as they do in the Wye Valley workshop in Chepstow. Tours end in the shop where gleaming products are displayed. Advance notice is required for factory visits, which can be made from 10 a.m. to 2 p.m. Monday to Friday. Call Miss Jean Pritchard at 0443/820044 to arrange for a tour. The factory seconds shop is open daily from 9 a.m. to 5 p.m., and you may go there with no advance notice.

The Romans made their mark farther south in Rhymney Valley, at Caerphilly, visited in Chapter XXII.

For information about the valley, get in touch with the **Public Relations Officer,** Rhymney Valley District Council, Council Offices, Ystrad Fawr, Ystrad Mynach (tel. 0443/815588).

DOWN THE TAFF: An interesting drive from Merthyr Tydfil is on the A4054 road following the River Taff south toward Cardiff. You'll be struck by scenic beauty and then taken aback somewhat by the remnants of days when this was the heart of the coal-mining industry in Wales. You'll see the area where there appears to be a continuous ribbon of housing running along the valley. This is a series of pit villages which could not be built into the mountainside and had to spread along the valley floor. There are still slag heaps marring hillsides, but overall the sweep of mountains and valleys, plus reforestation areas, is pleasing to the eye. Some of the best male choral singing in the country is heard here.

Stop in **Pontypridd,** built around the Rhondda and Taff Rivers, if only to visit the **John Hughes Pottery and Grogg Shop,** Danygraig, Broadway (tel. 0433/405001), where the famous facsimiles of well-known Welsh public figures and athletes, known as "groggs," are made in the pottery on the premises. It's open weekdays from 9 a.m. to 5 p.m., on Saturday and bank holidays from 10 a.m. to 5:30 p.m.

Chapter XXII

CARDIFF

1. Orientation
2. Where to Stay
3. Where to Dine
4. Sights of Cardiff
5. Shopping
6. Entertainment and Nightlife
7. Across South Glamorgan

A LARGE SEAPORT CITY, Cardiff (Caerdydd in Welsh), the capital of the principality, was built on the tidal estuary of the River Taff.

This city, enriched by the Industrial Revolution and then left to decline with the closing of coal mines, railroads, and factories in the years following World War II, no longer has anything to apologize for so far as being progressive, interesting, and attractive to visit. If the mention of Cardiff has evoked for you visions of belching smokestacks, dingy warehouses, and dockside dilapidation, you're in for a pleasant surprise. In fact, judging by its handsome public buildings and its parks, the Cardiff many people have envisioned is long gone.

Next on the agenda is the regeneration of Cardiff Bay, with a view to reuniting the city center of Cardiff with its waterfront. Millions of pounds have been estimated and earmarked for the project, with new construction of housing areas, a new County Hall, new roads, and places for some industries. The old isn't being done away with, however. Mount Stuart Square, the center of Victorian trade, is being refurbished, the Maritime Museum extended, and the Wales Railway Center created at Blue Road Station. Also, many beautiful old buildings linked with the past history of the docks are to be restored.

Cardiff is on the move.

1. Orientation

In this city of contrasts, a castle on the site of a fort built in the third century A.D. by the Romans stands a few steps from a handsome 19th-century Civic Centre, with a modern shopping center just across the street. Acres and acres of green space have been retained in the heart of the city.

The Civic Centre has been acclaimed worldwide, ranked third after Washington, D.C., and New Delhi, India, for beauty and suitability. It is the result of far-thinking city planning in the last century. Land in what is called Cathays Park (no connection with China) was purchased from the Marquess of Bute, who owned the castle and large portions of adjoining ground. Structures of

Portland stone were built in the parkland, with wide avenues setting them off. The buildings, which include the Cardiff City Hall, the Mid Glamorgan County Hall, the law courts, the University of Wales Institute of Science and Technology, a Temple of Peace, police headquarters, the National Museum of Wales, and University College are centered on a War Memorial and lie just across North Road from Bute Park and the castle. In the same vicinity stand the Sherman Theatre and New Theatre.

In the spring, the grassy expanse of the War Memorial plot and the park are ablaze with masses of golden daffodils, one of the national symbols of Wales. Reportedly 150,000 daffodil bulbs were given to Cardiff by Dutch growers. Separating Bute Park from Pontcanna, another extensive park area, is the River Taff. In Pontcanna you'll see the Glamorgan County Cricket Ground and the National Sports Centre. Also lying on the Taff, a little way to the south after you cross Castle Street, is Cardiff Arms Park, where the Cardiff Rugby Club and the National Rugby Stadium are situated.

GETTING AROUND: If you don't have a car, you must depend on a taxi, a bus, or your trusty feet to get places in Cardiff. There's a fairly good **bus service,** which is of particular benefit if you plan to visit attractions in the environs of the city. Your hotel staff will help you with the routing. Individual tickets cost 66p ($1.06) per person.

Taxis are usually easy to find, especially in busy areas, and the prices are reasonable. You can hail one on the street or go to one of the taxi ranks in Cardiff. The most prominent ranks are at the railway station, the bus station, the Holiday Inn, and St. David's Hall. The meter begins ticking at 80p ($1.28), with fares within the city averaging £1.50 ($2.40). You can have your hotel or the place where you've dined call you a cab. Wonder of wonders, the meter starts ticking only when you get into the vehicle, not when it leaves the station as is the case in many cities.

PRACTICAL FACTS: Some information pertinent to Cardiff and to other parts of Wales appears in "The ABCs of Wales," Chapter XX.

For **medical emergencies,** dial 999, as for police and other emergency situations, and ask for an ambulance. Doctors are on 24-hour call service. A full list of doctors is at all post offices. Visitors should ask at their hotel desk.

An **emergency dental clinic** is at the Health Dental Hospital (tel. 0222/755944), open Monday to Saturday from 9 to 10 a.m. and 2 to 3 p.m.; or Riverside Health Centre, Wellington Street, Canton, open on Sunday and bank holidays from 9 a.m. to noon.

To get a prescription filled, go to **Boots The Chemist.** They have outlets all over town, but the main dispensing service is at 5 Wood St. (tel. 0222/377043), open weekdays from 8:30 a.m. to 7 p.m., Saturday from 9 a.m. to 6 p.m., and Sunday from 6 to 7 p.m.

The main **post office,** 2 Hill St. (tel. 0222/27305), is open Monday through Friday from 9 a.m. to 5:30 p.m., Saturday from 9 a.m. to 1 p.m.

Need to do **laundry?** A laundromat, especially convenient for the B&Bs along Cathedral Road, is **Top Hat Wash Inn,** 87 Pontcanna (tel. 0222/26244), open daily except Sunday from 8 a.m. to 9 p.m.

For **hair care** for either men or women, try **Gingers,** 8 St. John's Square (tel. 0222/374448), open from 10 a.m. to 6 p.m. Monday to Wednesday, 10 a.m. to 7 p.m. Thursday, 9 a.m. to 6 p.m. Friday, and 9 a.m. to 5 p.m. Saturday.

If you'd like to attend **religious services,** it's easy to find a place of worship in Cardiff. A sampling: **St. John the Baptist Cathedral,** St. John's Square,

Llandaff (tel. 0222/395231); **St. David's Church in Wales** (Catholic), Bryn Celyn Rd. (tel. 0222/734308); **Heath Church** (Evangelical), Whitchurch Road (tel. 0222/621826); **Cardiff United Synagogue** (Penylan), Ty Gwyn Road (tel. 0222/491795); and **City United Reformed Church,** Windsor Place (tel. 0222/25190).

Banks can help you change your traveler's checks. Try **Barclays,** 121 Queen St. (tel. 0222/42633) or 112 St. Mary St. (tel. 0222/399055); **Lloyds,** 31 Queen St. (tel. 0222/44531); or one of their several branches.

A station giving 24-hour **gasoline** service is **Howells of Cardiff,** 501 Newport Rd. (tel. 0222/495591).

For information about Cardiff and its environs, the **Wales Tourist Information Centre** is at 3-6 Bridge St. (tel. 0222/27281), close to the downtown shopping precinct, St. David's Centre. There is a lot of multistory parking in the area. The office is open from 6:30 a.m. to 6 p.m. Monday to Saturday all year, except from mid-July to the end of August when the hours are extended. In peak season, the office is also open on Sunday.

The **Cardiff City Information** office is in City Hall in the Civic Centre (tel. 0222/822100).

2. Where to Stay

As is to be expected, the Welsh capital has a number of large hotels, most of which are quite near the city center, although in recent years some have been built on the outskirts. Most offer weekend and Searchlight Tattoo specials.

Smaller hotels and guesthouses are thick on the ground along Cathedral Road, Richmond Road, and Newport Road. Cathedral Road is a short distance from the Glamorgan County Cricket Grounds and within walking distance of the city center. It is also an easy drive from the Llandaff section (described in the sightseeing section, below). Richmond Road is even closer to the city center.

The **Wynford Hotel,** Clare Street (tel. 0222/371983), is a privately owned hotel personally supervised by the owner. It is a seven-minute walk from the bus station, the railway station, and the city center. You are accorded a warm welcome, attentive service, and pleasing amenities. These include a comfortable residents' lounge, cozy bars, and a restaurant offering traditional and French cuisine. All bedrooms have color TV, radios, and phones, and many have private baths. Rent is £18 ($28.80) in a single, £25 ($40) in a double, with breakfast included.

Tane's Hotel, 148 Newport Rd. (tel. 0222/491755), is a Victorian house just a mile from the city center, with frequent bus service. It's a small, nine-bedroom B&B hotel with hot and cold water and central heating in all the units. Singles rent for £14 ($22.40) and doubles go for £23 ($36.80), with a full breakfast included. It occupies half of a semi-detached former private home with large bay windows looking out to the street. Parking is provided for your car. The Tanes manage the hotel themselves, providing a homey atmosphere for guests. The residents' lounge has color TV.

Lincoln Hotel, 118 Cathedral Rd. (tel. 0222/395558), is the grandest—and also the most expensive—hotel along this popular restaurant street. It was so carefully restored by Keith and Thayer Baines that many guests willingly pay extra for its better amenities and rarefied atmosphere. Opening in the Christmas of 1986, this turn-of-the-century house was formed by joining two former private residences. The result was a superb 18-bedroom hotel which is very personalized. Each well-furnished and beautifully maintained bedroom has a private bath, color TV, and direct-dial phone, along with a coffee maker and hair dryer. Singles on weekdays rent for £28.50 ($45.60) to £32.50 ($52), with doubles or twins going for £40.50 ($64.80) to £46 ($73.60). The good news is that weekend

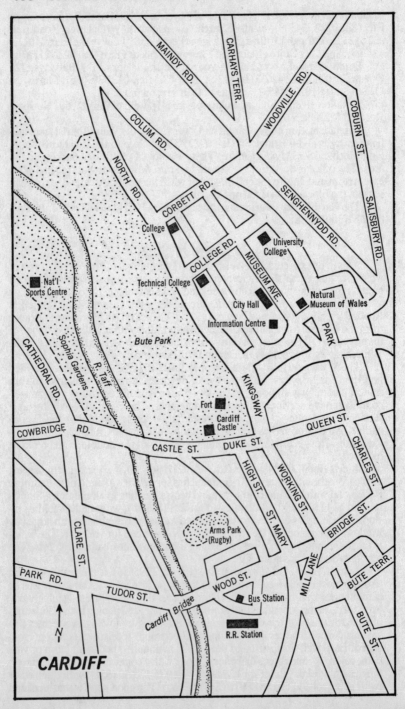

CARDIFF

deals, Friday through Sunday, are available. Based on double occupancy, a person can stay here for two weekend nights for £50 ($80) per person. Singles pay a £10 ($16) supplement. Named after Abraham Lincoln (not the cathedral city of Lincoln), the hotel will even serve you American griddle cakes for breakfast. Guests gather in the snug sitting room, with its well-chosen colors, later enjoying a drink in the cozy bar before heading for dinner in the restaurant. Meals are served from 12:30 to 2 p.m. and dinner from 7 p.m. until "whenever." A house-party atmosphere often prevails, as guests order such dishes as sliced beef with oyster sauce or lemon sole stuffed with shrimp and peppers. Lunches cost from £6 ($9.60), dinners from £12 ($19.20), and the dining room is open to non-residents.

Ferrier's Hotel, 132 Cathedral Rd. (tel. 0222/383413), is one of the gems along this hotel-flanked street. Two turn-of-the-century houses—perhaps once occupied by wealthy coal merchants—were joined together to form this family-run hotel. The welcome, the reception, and the amenities are excellent value for money. Of the 26 well-furnished bedrooms, seven lie on the ground floor. Each contains hot and cold running water, color TV, radio, and direct-dial phone. Many accommodations also have private baths with shower. Singles range from £24 ($38.40) to £32 ($51.20), doubles £34 ($54.40) to £38 ($60.80), including breakfast. Drinks are offered to residents in an attractively decorated lounge with a tropical motif. Good wholesome dinners are served Monday to Thursday only.

The Beverley Hotel, 75 Cathedral Rd. (tel. 0222/43443), a gabled Victorian hotel, is one of the most unusual establishments along this street. Its Victorian bars are among the most lavishly decorated in Cardiff, offering a warmly embellished antique-gaslight-era ambience, with traditional cask-conditioned beers. It's also one of the most economical dining choices along this popular street of hotels. From 6 to 10 p.m., you can patronize its Welcome Parlour, enjoying chef-carved succulent roasts and freshly cooked vegetables. The management has been successful in creating a festive place in which to stay. It offers 18 well-decorated bedrooms, each with private bath or shower, color TV, radio, direct-dial phone, trouser press, and coffee-making facilities. Rooms are furnished in a streamlined modern decor, with singles renting for £36 ($57.60), doubles £48 ($76.80).

Cathedral Road is lined with large, stone Victorian houses built at the end of the 19th century. Many of these have become B&B hotels and guesthouses.

The Crowndale Hotel, 58 Cathedral Rd. (tel. 0222/44060), is the accommodations venture of Marshall and Judy Young, who also operate the popular Pepper Mill Diner (visited in "Where to Dine," below). This Victorian former residence, with four single and six double bedrooms, is a warm, homey place, pleasantly furnished and comfortable. There is color TV in all bedrooms, plus full central heating, a TV lounge if you'd rather watch in company, and a diner where evening refreshments are served. The Youngs charge £13 ($20.80) in a single and £23 ($36.80) in a double or twin for B&B.

The Avon Hotel, 148 Cathedral Rd. (tel. 0222/32801), is another possibility on this hospitable street. A well-run, well-maintained hotel, it has eight bedrooms, most with private showers and all with TV, tea/coffee-making facilities, and central heating. There's a lounge with color TV. A full breakfast is included in the rate of £16 ($25.60) per person per night.

The Abbey Hotel, 151 Cathedral Rd. (tel. 0222/390896), is popular with Americans who may be getting nostalgic for a back-home accent after listening to Welsh and the many dialects of English to be heard in the British Isles. Bart and Iris Zuzik, the proprietors, came from Chicago, where he was a hospital administrator. They have successfully blended the expertise of both their home and adopted countries to establish a happy small-hotel operation in Cardiff. Part of the tasteful ambience of the place comes from such touches as the use of Royal Worcester china in serving meals in the cozy dining room. The Zuziks have joined two houses to accommodate guests in a variety of units. Singles go for £14 ($22.40) and doubles cost £29 ($46.40). Although there is a TV lounge where you can relax in company with other guests, each bedroom is equipped with its own color TV, as well as a direct-dial phone and hot-beverage facilities.

The **Laurels Hotel,** 138 Cathedral Rd. (tel. 0222/33324), is another lodging place in a former Victorian home. It has been recently refurbished, with browns, avocado, and beige furnishings giving a relaxing ambience to the bedrooms—five doubles and five singles—costing from £15 ($24) per person per night for B&B. Rooms all have tea/coffee-making facilities, razor outlets, and radios, while doubles have toilets, showers, and TVs. The hotel has bar and restaurant licenses.

The **Phoenix Hotel,** 199-201 Fidlas Rd., Llanishen (tel. 0222/764615), about 3¾ miles north of the city center, is a red-brick building with half-timbered gables, lying in a quiet suburban area. It's convenient to public bus transportation and has easy access to the M4 motorway. Most of the 25 bedrooms have private baths, and all have TV, phones, radios, and hot-beverage facilities. All singles have hot and cold water basins with showers and rent for £26 ($41.60) to £29.50 ($47.20). Bathless doubles cost from £31 ($49.60) to £36 ($57.60), increasing to £35.50 ($58.60) to £41 ($65.60) with bath. Dudley's Restaurant, inside the hotel, serves good food at reasonable prices. Overflow guests from the Phoenix are accommodated in the Cedars Hotel across the street, which charges the same prices.

In a Valley Garden

Dyffran House, St. Nicholas (tel. 0222/593328), is located in beautiful Dyffryn Gardens, a showplace in the Valley of Glamorgan about 1½ miles south of the village of St. Nicholas on the A48 road three miles west of Cardiff. The tastefully decorated and furnished B&B rooms in this Victorian mansion rent for £11.50 ($18.40) in a single study unit, £28.75 ($46) for one person and £51.75 ($82.80) for double occupancy in an executive-style room with private bath. A splurge, yes, but it's worth it considering the surroundings.

Somewhere Special

Jean Robinson operates a service in Cardiff for Americans only, called **Somewhere Special Holidays,** 79 Heathwood Rd., Heath, Cardiff CF4 4JN (tel. 0222/620520), aimed at providing true Welsh hospitality in private homes. Guests are free to come and go as they please, but the host families share knowledge of special events and places to visit during your Cardiff stay. The homes on the roster range from elegant period residences to country cottages, all in prestigious areas and all with high standards of friendliness and comfort.

These are not B&B houses (although you do get bed and breakfast, and sometimes dinner if you request it ahead, for an extra charge of course). They are the homes of business and professional people who are proud of their country and city and want to share this pride with visitors. A minimum of four nights' stay is required, and you must reserve accommodations at least a month in advance. The charge is $26 (U.S.) per person per day, with a $10 deposit required. Send your deposit with an International Reply Coupon, giving the dates of your stay and your particular interests. Efforts are made to match up, if possible, people of similar professions or hobbies.

Splurge Choices

The **Angel Hotel**, corner of Castle and Westgate Streets (tel. 0222/32633), is an elegant old hostelry, looking across to Cardiff Castle and the Cardiff Arms Park, site of the National Stadium. At the beginning of the 1880s the original Angel stood farther along Castle Street. When the present hotel was built, it was *the* place to stay in South Wales, attracting such screen legends as Garbo and Dietrich as well as every prime minister of Britain, including Margaret Thatcher. Today, under the management and money of Norfolk Capital Hotels, it has fast gained its old prestige after a massive renovation. When you enter, it's hard to resist walking right up the grand staircase, lit by sparkling Waterford chandeliers, but the check-in counter is downstairs, so you have to wait a while. You enter a world of neo-Doric decor, with trompe l'oeil ceilings, hand-stippled faux marbre columns, and an elegant peach- or blue-toned color scheme. The 97 bedrooms vary greatly in size, amenities, and views, but all have color TV, direct-dial phones, radios, and private baths. There's 24-hour room service, plus elevator service. Singles rent for £60 ($96) and doubles for £68 ($108.80).

You can dine at the Café de la Paix, a handsomely decorated restaurant, done in Louis XVI-style. You can enjoy British and continental cuisine, including such dishes as shallow-fried breast of guinea fowl, half a roast duck with pineapple sauce, and filet of sole en papillote. A set menu is offered for £12 ($19.20). Lunch is served from 12:30 to 2 p.m. and dinner from 7 to 10 p.m. daily.

Holiday Inn, Mill Lane (tel. 0222/399944). The opening of this high-rise chain hotel some time back launched a virtual hotel renaissance in Cardiff. When the competition saw the modern amenities and sleek style of this Holiday Inn (one of the better ones), they decided they had to put new life into their creaky hostelries. Near the center of the city, this 186-bedroom establishment is noted for its striking public areas, including one lounge with an open but hooded fireplace. Each of the spacious and well-furnished bedrooms has a private bath with shower along with full air conditioning, color TV (with video channel and satellite TV), a hair dryer, trouser press, and direct-dial phone. Singles pay from £53 ($84.80) to £56 ($89.60), doubles £59 ($94.40) to £64 ($102.40). When booking, you can also ask about reduced weekend breaks. Guests can patronize the coffeeshop for an informal meal or else dine more elegantly on a continental cuisine in Le Pays de Galles restaurant, enjoying fine wine. The £12 ($19.20) buffet lunch is well attended. Other amenities include a heated indoor swimming pool, saunas, a Turkish bath, a solarium, a warm-water whirlpool, a gym, and squash courts.

The **Park Hotel,** Park Place (tel. 0222/383471), is a first-class hotel right in the heart of Cardiff, at a corner of the Queen Street shopping mall. It's chock-full of pleasant amenities and good service. When you enter the recently refurbished, high-ceilinged lobby, you are immediately aware that the hotel is prepared to receive you courteously, with a minimum of waiting to register and be taken to your room by elevator. The bedrooms in this late-Victorian structure range in size from singles to elegant suites, but all are attractive, with Welsh tapestry bedspreads, their own bathrooms, in-house movies, phones, color TVs, hair dryers, and trouser presses. After you are checked into your room, almost before you know it a maid is at the door to see if you'd like tea. A single bedroom rents for £49.95 ($79.92), a twin for £61.25 ($98).

The Park has several facilities for dining. The conservative Edwardian Caernarvon Room, with traditional furnishings, serves lunch from 12:30 to 2:15 p.m. except on Saturday and dinners from 7 to 9:45 p.m. weekdays, to 9 p.m. on Sunday. A set lunch costs £7.75 ($12.40), a table d'hôte dinner going for £12

($19.20). In the Theatre Garden, a restaurant done in an ivy and trellis pattern, meals cost from £8 ($12.80) to £12 ($19.20). Hours are noon to 2 p.m. and 7 to 11 p.m. It's closed Sunday. If you'd like a cocktail before lunch or dinner, try the Harlech Bar, just off the hotel lobby. You can also have morning coffee, afternoon tea, and sandwiches in the bar. The Park has private parking for guests.

Royal Hotel, St. Mary's Street (tel. 0222/383321), a landmark 1864 Victorian hotel, has long been part of the history of Cardiff and is among its oldest hotels. In June 1910, Captain Scott and his party of explorers dined in a splendid wood-paneled room here on the eve of their departure from the Cardiff docks for the fateful South Pole. Today under the chain, Embassy Hotels, the Royal has regained some of its old pride. Bedrooms—63 in all, 47 with private bath— have been refurbished, usually in a streamlined modern style, each equipped with color TV and direct-dial phone. The executive rooms and studios are the best equipped, and the most expensive. Singles range from £46 ($73.60) to £56 ($89.60), double or twins £56 ($89.60) to £68 ($108.80). The higher tariffs are for the executive accommodations. The hotel attracts famous rugby stars who play at Cardiff Arms Park.

Its drinking and dining facilities are among the most attractive and atmospheric of any hotel in town. For example, three bars tempt visitors: the Press Bar, a watering hole of some of the nation's journalists; the Cocktail Bar, a sophisticated rendezvous with a semi-tropical motif; and the Royal Lounge for those who prefer a traditional Edwardian ambience with bar food and draft beer. For dining, the Royal Carving Room presents an array of succulent roast meats, including Welsh lamb.

Grand Hotel, 5-7 Westgate St. (tel. 0222/43899), is a late 19th-century building, with a richly ornate Italiante, château-style facade, with a mansard tower. In the heart of town, the old Grand has returned to some of its long-ago opulence and splendor. The 30 bedrooms, each with private bath or shower, have been restored and modernized, with color TV, direct-dial phone, and coffee-making equipment. A few special rooms contain four-poster beds. Singles rent for £35 ($56), doubles for £48 ($76.80), plus breakfast. Discounts are granted on Friday and Saturday nights. In muted colors, the Victorian-style Elan Restaurant serves three meals a day with both set and à la carte menus. The hotel attracts nonresidents to its four bars, each one decorated in a different theme, the lushest of which is done in a Gay 1890s style.

Stakis Inn on the Avenue, Circle Way East, Llanedeyrn (tel. 0222/732520), is just off the A48M motorway. The Llanedeyrn turn is signposted. Coming from London, take Junction 29 off the M4. This is an excellent modern hotel, with its own character and style. All the bedrooms—150—are carpeted and decorated in pleasing colors, with complete bath, color TV, radio, direct-dial phone, and a host of amenities calculated to please the most demanding guest. The hotel's leisure complex offers use of a heated swimming pool, a paddling pool for the little tots, a Jacuzzi, sauna, solarium, and a fully equipped gymnasium, as well as a beauty salon. There is a dramatically designed restaurant, specializing in international cuisine. For B&B the charge for an overnight stay is from £32.50 ($52) per person, with special packages offered throughout the year, especially on weekends, which will substantially reduce the cost. Children under 14 can stay in their parents' room free, being charged only for food. Ample parking is provided.

3. Where to Dine

You can find almost any type of food you're hungry for in Cardiff and its environs, reflecting the cosmopolitan cuisine you'd expect to find in a port city, even though the seagoing flurry has subsided somewhat since earlier in this century. Continental, Oriental, American, and especially Welsh specialties are offered. Most of the larger hotels have fine restaurants as well as pubs. It is at pubs that you find good food at reasonable prices, particularly for lunch, although most of them serve dinner dishes also.

Be sure to try traditional Welsh food while you're here. Watch for the bakestone symbol with the words "Blas ar Gymru—A Taste of Wales."

If you're looking for fast-food places, especially good for the budget and/or if you're traveling with children, you'll find lots of Wimpy's diners and similar places.

The **Blas ar Gymru (Taste of Wales) Restaurant,** 48 Crwys Rd. (tel. 0222/ 382132), lets you know right up front by its name that you can sample Welsh food here, both traditional and contemporary. It is an attractive restaurant, with translucent patterned-glass panels across the front and soft lamplight at the tables. Restaurateur Meirion Dally offers such Welsh specialties as Glamorgan sausages (tasty and totally meatless despite the name), Anglesey eggs and leeks, laverbread with bacon, cawl (thick leek, vegetable, and lamb soup), Penclawdd cockles and eggs, and Celtic haddock smokies as appetizers. Among the main-course dishes, you can order Gower cockle and bacon pie, Rhaeadr Gwy roast salmon, baked trout caught in the River Teifi and cooked wrapped in bacon, Prince of Wales honeyed Welsh lamb, Dyfed rabbit casserole, Rhondda hot pot, Owain Glyndwr Welsh beef (topside of beef braised and served in a mead sauce), and poacher's pie (beef, rabbit, chicken, and game in wine sauce with flaky pastry). All dishes are served with the fresh vegetables of the season, or you order a green, mixed, or tossed salad.

For dessert—listed as puddings in British style—you can select from the sweets trolley or try a treacle tart with fresh cream, blackbetty and apple pie with cream, or a traditional bread pudding. If you don't have a sweet tooth, you can opt for a selection of Welsh farmhouse cheeses, served with biscuits (crackers, that is) and Welsh butter. As Richard Llewellyn said about such Welsh dishes in *How Green Was My Valley*, "If there is better food in heaven, I am in a hurry to be there." Mr. Dally and his wife, Patricia, will explain all about the Welsh dishes offered. They strive to keep their culinary standards high. They introduce other Welsh and Celtic dishes from time to time. A complete dinner here, including wine, will cost about £13.50 ($21.60). Lunch is served from noon to 2:30 p.m. and dinner from 7 to 11 p.m. daily except Sunday. Reservations are advised.

Spanghero's, Westgate House, Westgate Street (tel. 0222/382423), is arguably the finest restaurant in Cardiff. At least it is on some nights. Named after a famous French rugby player, it occupies a brick building in the heart of town that was in days of yore a bonded warehouse when the River Taff used to flow along what is now Westgate Street. It contains two distinctly different restaurants, each within earshot of the other. The more formal and expensive of the two is known simply as "The Restaurant." Here chef David Evans is celebrated locally for his nouvelle cuisine, which he practices with skill from noon to 2 p.m. and 7 to 10 p.m. (except Saturday lunch and Monday dinner). (The Bistro, see below, keeps basically the same hours, perhaps staying open half an hour later). At The Restaurant, a fixed-price menu costs £16 ($25.60) but à la carte could run much higher, so be careful. Menu items include such ambitious attempts as skewered Dublin Bay prawns with sole mousse, breast of Barbary duckling with a sage soufflé, and chicken breast with raspberry vinegar.

The less-pretentious Bistro is more animated, containing red-checkered tablecloths in a cellar motif of exposed brick. The exciting news here is that it has a

Cruover storage cabinet which means the staff can serve you excellent wines by the glass, as the cabinet allows the wine to remain at its peak condition. Full meals, costing from £7 ($11.20), include a selection of terrines and pâtés, chicken salad (with bacon, mushrooms, and gherkins), and a limited but flavorful selection of main courses, mainly steaks, grills, and fresh fish. Reservations are needed.

Gibsons, 8 Romilly Crescent, Canton (tel. 0222/41264), is another restaurant considered "the best in Cardiff." An unpretentious pair of storefronts were joined to make this stylish restaurant, which is run by the Canning family. Enjoy an apéritif in the tiny bar before heading to one of the bistro-style tables on two levels. The restaurant has a warm, brown-toned 1890s look to it. The menu is basically French, with many Welsh dishes included as well. The latter includes cawl, a soup made with lamb, along with sewin (sea trout) au poivre. Sand soles, called a "first cousin" to a Dover sole, often appear on the menu, as does freshly caught lobster. The emphasis is on fresh ingredients. I once enjoyed a soup made with sorrel and dandelion but this is served only in the spring. Breast of lamb is invariably good, and the wine list is excellent. A set lunch costs from £8.50 ($13.60), a table d'hôte dinner going for £16.50 ($26.40). Hours are 12:30 to 2:30 p.m., 7:30 to 9:30 p.m. Monday to Saturday.

La Chaumière, 44 Cardiff Rd., Llandaff (tel. 0222/55531), is much discussed and most sophisticated, a favorite rendezvous of the discerning palate of Cardiff. A drawback to this elegant restaurant is its location behind a pub, surrounded by a parking lot, about five miles from the center of Cardiff. Once inside the garden-inspired interior, however, any inconvenience is quickly forgotten thanks to the soothing classical music and the gracious ministrations of Kay and Cliff Morgan. Self-taught and remarkably skillful, Kay prepares such specialties as scallops in puff pastry, with a julienne of vegetables and vermouth sauce, or duckling in a kumquat sauce. She also prepares a delectable salmon with rhubarb sauce in puff pastry. Of course, menu items change, and none of these dishes may be available when you visit, but you get the idea. For dessert, try one of her constantly changing concoctions, such as a gâteau of raspberries and hazelnut meringue. Dinners cost from £16 ($25.60) to £21 ($33.60) per person and are served from 7:30 to 9:30 p.m. Lunch from £14 ($22.40) is offered from 12:30 to 2 p.m., and reservations are always necessary. It is closed Monday (no lunch Saturday, no dinner Sunday).

The Thai House, 23 High St. (tel. 0222/387404). As one well-seasoned traveler maintained, "You have to go to Bangkok for better Thai food." The hot, savory cuisine served here has awakened the sleepy tastebuds of Cardiff. Having had its premiere in the autumn of 1985, this two-level Oriental-style restaurant is reached after climbing a flight of steps. There you are received by a cosmopolitan and friendly staff, headed by the owner, Noi Ramasut, who comes from Thailand. He is married to a Welsh woman. Food, costing from £12 ($19.20), is served from noon to 2:30 p.m. and 6:30 to 11 p.m. except Sunday. Curries are hot and good, including beef with bamboo shoot slices. You might also try king prawns with garlic and a tamarind sauce or steamed fish with fresh ginger, plum, and lime juice. Incidentally, this is the only Thai restaurant in Wales.

La Brasserie, 60 St. Mary's St. (tel. 0222/372164), is a popular pub and wine bar whose food also draws crowds of lunchtime and evening diners. It's darkly paneled, with wide planking, and serves 50 kinds of wine and 25 kinds of champagne. You order your drinks at the wooden bar and food from the attendant who waits behind the well-stocked, deli-type case. Fondues are a specialty, with a choice of beef or sharkmeat or a combination of the two. There are also baked mussels, suckling pig, a tempting buffet of meats and salads, and of course, foaming pints of lager to accompany it. The establishment is open daily except Sunday. Lunch is served from noon to 3 p.m. and dinner from 7 p.m. to midnight. The bar opens at 2 p.m. Full meals range from around £12 ($19.20).

Next door to the just-recommended La Brasserie, and owned by Martin Martinez, **Champers,** 61 St. Mary St. (tel. 0222/372164), is equally as popular. Its specialty is charcoal-grilled steaks which can be served with some of the best garlic bread in Cardiff. Only Scotch beef is served, and you can make your selection from an array of simple but fresh salads. Or, you might prefer king-size prawns with sizzling garlic, or spareribs. A wine of the week is featured, and jacket potatoes accompany most meat dishes. You step up to the bar and make your selection of the meat or fish which is then prepared to your specifications. Meals cost from £12 ($19.20) and are served from noon to 3 p.m. and 7 p.m. to 12:30 a.m. (closed for Sunday lunch). The decor is like a Spanish bodega.

Le Monde, 60 St. Mary St. (tel. 0222/387376), is one of a trio of restaurants that a Spanish-born entrepreneur located within the same cavernous warehouse in the center of town. Of the three, including La Brasserie and Champers, this one is perhaps the most avant-garde. To reach it, climb a flight of sawdust-covered steps passing French-inspired posters hawking the specialty of the day, perhaps fresh turbot with beurre blanc. Amid black-painted, high-ceilinged walls, you can order meals costing from £12 ($19.20). The staff will invite you to order food at a deli-style display case. A waitress will later deliver your individually cooked order. Specialties include mainly fish, such as seabass, red mullet, hake, salmon cutlet, or halibut. Meals are served from noon to 2:15 p.m. and 7 p.m. to 12:15 a.m. daily except Sunday and Monday.

Llandaf Celebrity Restaurant, St. David's Hall, The Hayes (tel. 0222/42611). Its decor is consciously modern and streamlined and often flooded with sunlight. Many a famous visiting musician might be spotted dining here. The location is one flight above the lobby in one of the most innovative concert halls in Britain (more about this later). The restaurant is open daily except Sunday from noon to 2:30 p.m. and 6 p.m. to midnight. Don't confuse this restaurant with "Level 3," a simple but value-conscious cafeteria on the upper floor which is open for lunch only, often hosting lunchtime concerts. Full meals in the Celebrity Restaurant cost from £10 ($16) and up, including some vegetarian specialties such as a spinach bake with tagliatelle. You might also prefer lemon sole diable, an array of grilled steaks, along with a delectable version of smoked trout. There's also a well-chosen wine list. The restaurant is owned by the city of Cardiff, which has been known to "import" visiting chefs such as those from France.

Salvatore's, 14 Romilly Crescent, Canton (tel. 0222/372768), is a trattoria deserving of your business. Mario Salvatore Colayera is the guiding light behind the brightness of this little establishment which lies close to the already-recommended Gibsons outside the center. Tuxedo-clad waiters will present you with your selection of Italian dishes which is likely to include lamb kidneys in a red wine sauce, saltimbocca, or pepper steak, perhaps scampi thermidor. Meals, costing from £12 ($19.20), are served from 12:30 to 2 p.m. and 7:30 to 10 p.m. (closed for Saturday lunch). All main dishes include potatoes and two fresh vegetables.

Away from the city center but convenient if you're staying in the Cathedral Road vicinity is the **Pepper-Mill Diner,** 173 Kings Rd., Canton (tel. 0222/382476), where Marshall and Judy Young, in a Wild West ambience, serve American and Mexican dishes that are popular with the Welsh as well as with expatriate and visiting Americans. If you're in the mood for South of the Border, try Marshall's beef or chicken tostadas, or his beef, chicken, or pork burritos. Cowboy specials include a chuckwagon steak sandwich and a barbecue baron of beef. You can get a bowl of chili, followed by a real American cheeseburger or a variety of other "Marshall burgers." Southern fried chicken, deep-dish chicken pot pie, or a Texas T-bone steak might transport you Stateside for a while. Note that the menu lists french fries as "french fries," not as "chips." You can enjoy a filling repast here among a friendly clientele and a courteous staff for £3 ($4.80) to £6.50 ($10.40). Dinner is served from 6 to 10:30 p.m. Reservations are advisable. The place is licensed, and you can order imported American and Mexican beers.

THE PUBS OF CARDIFF: Pub lunches and dinners are a way of life in Wales, pubs not being comparable to bars in the United States. Most of them have facilities for serving food to children as well as grownups at mealtime. Prices are reasonable. In most pubs you go to the bar to give your order, whether for food or drink. You carry your own drinks to the table and sometimes your food, although many places have waiters or waitresses to bring your dishes to you.

The **Park Vaults,** part of the Park Hotel complex on Park Lane (tel. 0222/ 383471), is a Victorian pub with stained-glass windows, around the corner from the hotel entrance. You can have lunch here from such selections as crofter's pie, corned-beef hash, and spaghetti bolognese, with meals costing from £2.50 ($4). Hours are from 11:45 a.m. to 2:30 p.m. and 5:30 to 11 p.m. Monday to Saturday, from noon to 2 p.m. and 7 to 10:30 p.m. on Sunday. Although no food is served in the evening, this is a convivial gathering place.

The **Angel Tavern,** at the Angel Hotel, corner of Castle and Westgate Streets (tel. 0222/32633), faces Cardiff Castle. Real ales are drawn by handpumps from the cellars of this traditional tavern, walled with red brick, its ceiling supported by heavy wooden beams. Bar meals, served only at lunch, include such fare as pork chops, lamb curry, and trout, and cost from £3 ($4.80). It's open from 11:30 a.m. to 3 p.m. and 5:30 to 10:30 p.m. daily except on Sunday and bank holidays.

When you go to the Llandaff Cathedral, be sure to stop at the **Black Lion,** Cardiff Road, Llandaff (tel. 0222/563192), where "Midge" and Maureen Bennett make you feel welcome at their pub. The 17th-century, half-timbered building has been renovated over the years and additions made to accommodate the crowds drawn to this pleasant gathering place. The lounge, which Midge says is the largest in Llandaff, is an L-shaped room. Welsh woolen has been used as upholstery material for the cushions on chairs and benches. You can have cheese toasties, stuffed baked potatoes, toasted sandwiches, and cheeseburgers while you quaff your drink. The cheapest snack costs 50p (80¢). The pub is open from 11 a.m. to 3 p.m. and 5:30 to 11 p.m. (to 10:30 p.m. on Sunday). It lies only 200 yards from the cathedral.

When you visit the Welsh Folk Museum at St. Fagans, four miles west of Cardiff, I recommend that you stop at the **Tynant Inn,** Main Road, Morganstown (Radyr) (tel. 0222/843009), on your way to or from the museum. As you'll soon learn, strict pub hours are kept, so time yourself accordingly. At least a part of the inn building has been in existence for several centuries. You'll see Welsh people, not tourists, here. T.H. Moore, proprietor, offers pub food including an excellent cawl (leek, vegetable, and mutton soup); meat pies; fresh fish such as salmon, trout, and sole; large sandwiches; and a choice of fresh vegetables in season. Meals cost around £7 ($11.20) on the à la carte menu. Food is served from noon to 2 p.m. Monday to Saturday as well as from 7 to 10:30 p.m. Saturday. Closed Sunday. From St. Fagans on the A4119, you turn left at the first little road you see and soon you'll find the Tynant Inn.

4. Sights of Cardiff

The Welsh capital has many interesting things to see, from antiquities to something as modern as Epstein's controversial carving, *Christ in Majesty,* at Llandaff Cathedral. If you're in Cardiff only for a short time, try to see the major sights described below.

THE MAJOR SIGHTS: With some 1,900 years of history, **Cardiff Castle** (tel. 0222/822083), stands in the heart of the city. The Romans first built a fort on this site, and you can see the remains of massive ten-foot-thick stone walls. The Normans built a castle on what was left of the Roman fort, and much of the Norman work still exists, added to by medieval lords. It came under assault in the Anglo-Welsh wars and was besieged during the English Civil War. The third Marquess of Bute, by then the owner, had it restored in the 19th century by Victorian architect William Burges, who transformed the interior into an extravaganza of whimsy, color, and rich architectural detail as you see it today. The Welsh Regimental Museum and The First Queen's Dragoon Guards Regimental Museum are also here.

The castle is open daily May to September with guided tours at 20-minute intervals from 10 a.m. to 12:40 p.m. and 2 to 5 p.m. In March, April, and October tours are every 30 minutes from 10 a.m. to 12:30 p.m. and 2 to 4 p.m. November to February, tours are at 10:30 and 11:45 a.m., and 2 and 3:15 p.m. Admission, which includes the full conducted tour, is £2 ($3.20) for adults, £1 ($1.60) for children. The castle green, Roman Wall, Norman keep, and Welsh Regimental Museum can be visited for £1.10 ($1.76) for adults, 50p (80¢) for children. Peacocks, guinea fowl, and ducks strut on the green.

Refreshments are available at lunchtime in season, and medieval banquets are held regularly all through the year. For information about the banquets, telephone 0222/372737.

The **Cardiff Searchlight Tattoo** is held at Cardiff Castle in alternate years, the next one to be held in 1989. It lasts for about ten days in early August, with nightly presentations. Scenes of splendor, pomp, and pageantry are brought to life with participation by all three British military services, music by nearly 500 musicians in the massed bands, and an exciting battle scene. For information on this spectacular sound and color performance, get in touch with Cardiff Searchlight Tattoo, P.O. Box 97, City Hall, Cardiff CF1 3TZ (tel. 0222/21317).

The **Cardiff City Hall** in the Civic Centre is recognizable by its 194-foot clock tower and the dome topped by a fierce Welsh dragon. The outstanding feature of this magnificent building of white Portland stone is the Marble Hall on the second floor. Its columns are of Sienna marble, with a series of statues of Welsh heroes, each carved by a different sculptor of Serraveza marble, surveying the scene from marble plinths. Most of the heroes are cultural rather than military figures. Among them is King Hywel, 10th-century ruler who was the first codifier of law for the Welsh. He was also an early E.R.A. sympathizer, and his laws put women on a par with men. Other statues are of St. David, patron saint of Wales; Owen Glyndwr; and Harri Tewdwr, who as Henry VII founded the Tudor dynasty. Try also to see the council chamber, a room of gleaming polished paneling with tiers of comfortable-looking crimson seats for the council members, who, I was told, are sometimes required to stay here for long, long sessions pondering what's best for Cardiff.

Llandaff Cathedral is in the tiny cathedral city of Llandaff, which stood just outside the western boundary of Cardiff until 1922 when it was made a part of the capital. It still retains its village atmosphere, with modern shops in old half-timbered buildings. The cathedral stands in a green hollow at a place whose religious history goes back 1,400 years. It began as a religious community founded by St. Teilo in the 6th century, with many churches under its aegis scattered throughout South Wales. A 10th-century Celtic cross is all that's left of the pre-Norman church. Among relics of the Norman church erected on the site is a fine arch behind the high altar. The west front, built in the 13th century, is considered one of the best medieval works of art in Wales.

Oliver Cromwell's army used the cathedral as a beer house and post office, and then in 1941 a German bomb severely damaged the building. Postwar reconstruction gave the cathedral two fine new features, the Welch Regiment Chapel and Sir Jacob Epstein's soaring sculpture *Christ in Majesty*. Epstein's striking work, which dominates the interior of the structure, has elicited mixed reactions from viewers. The ruin of the 800-year-old Bishop's Palace has been made into a peaceful public garden.

Caerphilly Castle, on the A469 at Caerphilly, is an imposing moated fortress about eight miles north of Cardiff, built partly on the site of a Roman fort. It was constructed by Earl Gilbert de Clare, Lord of Glamorgan, as protection against invasion by the Welsh Prince Llewelyn ap Gwynedd in the 13th century. The massive water defenses of the castle form the second-largest castle area in Britain. You will note the leaning tower as you approach the castle. This was the result of efforts by Cromwell to blow up the towers. The explosives failed in their mission, but this tower was left aslant. Perhaps you'll see the castle ghost, the Green Lady. She is supposed to be the spirit of a French princess who loved a handsome Welsh prince. When her husband, the Norman Lord of Caerphilly, learned of the matter, he sent her into exile, but her ghost is still supposed to be here, lamenting her lost love. The castle is open all year. From mid-March to mid-October it can be visited daily from 9:30 a.m. to 6:30 p.m. From mid-October to mid-March, hours are 9:30 a.m. to 4 p.m. weekdays and 2 to 4 p.m. on Sunday. Admission is £1 ($1.60) for adults and 50p (80¢) for children. For more information, telephone 0222/883143. From Cardiff, bus 36 makes a trip to Caerphilly every hour, or you can get a train from Central Station.

Castell Coch (Red Castle) (tel. 0222/810101) is a fairytale castle standing on a wooded hillside five miles northwest of Cardiff off the A470 at Tongwynlais. Its pepperpot turrets and round towers were the work of the third Marquess of Bute and his imaginative and whimsical architect, William Burges, who worked on this castle in the 19th century, at the same time he was producing the interior restoration of Cardiff Castle. This one was constructed on the ruins of a medieval fort, and contains a fantasy of murals, painted vaulted ceilings, and beautiful friezes. There's even a gloomy dungeon, with a flight of stone steps leading down to it. Open all year, hours mid-March to mid-October are 9:30 a.m. to 6:30 p.m. daily; the remainder of the year hours are 9:30 a.m. to 4 p.m. weekdays, 2 to 4 p.m. on Sunday. Admission is £1 ($1.60) for adults, 50p (80¢) for children.

MUSEUMS AND GALLERIES: One of the most interesting places to visit in all Wales, the **Welsh Folk Museum,** St. Fagans (tel. 0222/569441), provides a look back into history of the common man's life in Wales in centuries past. In the wooded parkland of an Elizabethan mansion, you can visit a treasury of ancient buildings which have been brought from their original sites all over the country and re-erected, in some cases even restored to their former use to show how it was then. In this superb collection of traditional buildings, widely distributed over the 100 acres of park, you can visit a 15th-century Tudor farmhouse furnished in the fashion of its day, cottages, a tollhouse, a schoolhouse, a chapel, and a cockpit. You'll also see a woolen mill and a flour mill from long ago which have been put back into use so that people of the present can see how such work was done back in the days before electricity, steam power, or other modern conveniences came into being. A woodturner and a cooper (barrel maker) are also at work, their crafts using the tools and materials of another age.

Besides the open-air museum, the handsome **headquarters building** of the Welsh Folk Museum, which lies about three miles west of Cardiff, has a wealth of gallery displays of costumes, agricultural farm equipment with which the Welsh tilled their fields centuries ago, and material culture, where articles from Welsh dressers to cooking utensils to lovespoons and early-day toys may be seen.

You can also visit **St. Fagans Castle,** the 16th-century structure which was given to the National Museum of Wales by the Earl of Plymouth as a center for a Folk Museum. The castle, built on the site of one from the Middle Ages, has been refurbished and restored to the way it was in the 17th century.

At the bookshop of the museum, you can find books and brochures on many phases of Welsh history, culture, and attractions. Also for sale here are the products made by the museum craftsmen. A restaurant is on the second floor of the main building, with service from 10 a.m. to 4:30 p.m. weekdays and 2:30 to 4:30 p.m. on Sunday. You can have a light meal for £3 ($4.80). You can also lunch at the Castle Buttery.

The museum is open from 10 a.m. to 5 p.m. weekdays and from 2:30 to 5 p.m. on Sunday. It's closed three days at Christmas, New Year's Day, Good Friday, and May Day. Admission Monday to Saturday April to the end of October is £2 ($3.20) for adults, £1 ($1.60) for children, with family tickets costing £5 ($8). On Sunday throughout the year and other days November to the end of March, the price is £1 ($1.60) for adults, 50p (80¢) for children, and £2.50 ($4) for a family ticket. To come from Cardiff if you don't have a car, take bus 32 from the bus terminal, which leaves every hour on the hour.

The **National Museum of Wales,** Cathays Park in the Civic Centre (tel. 0222/397951), is in an imposing white classic building with a columned entrance and a large cupola set atop a windowed base. It houses eclectic art and science collections. Its diversity of exhibits include natural science, industry, archeology, and geology, plus extensive collections of silver, china, and glass (some dating from 1250). The emphasis is on the story of Wales from earliest times. There are also modern and classic sculptures and works from old masters and modern artists from Rembrandt to Kokoschka.

Much of the museum's ambience comes from the openness and light that fills the main entrance and hall below the high ceiling. From the floor of the rotunda, the visitor can look up to the mezzanine gallery that girdles the main hall. The exhibits are at the head of the impressive staircase from the main hall. Also at this level is the French impressionist collection which includes Monet's *Waterlilies,* Renoir's *Parisian Girl,* and Manet's haunting *The Rabbit.* Here you can also see Rodin's bronze couple, *The Kiss,* and paintings by Rubens, Cézanne, Augustus John, and Brangwyn. A model coal mine is even included in the exhibits.

The museum is open daily from 10 a.m. to 5 p.m. Tuesday to Saturday and from 2:30 to 5 p.m. on Sunday. It's closed Monday and on some public holidays. Admission is free. A well-stocked bookshop is off the main hall.

The **Welsh Industrial and Maritime Museum,** Bute Street (tel. 0222/481919), occupies a four-acre site at Pier Head in the Cardiff dock area, adjacent to the Bute West Dock Basin. It houses a comprehensive exhibit of machinery from many Welsh industries, much of which has been restored to working order. There is an outdoor exhibit with boats, buoys, a collection of horse and motorized vehicles, a railway footbridge, and a working model of

Richard Trevithick's famous Penydarren locomotive. Here you can trace Cardiff's commercial history and development from 1800, when approximately 2,000 persons lived in the town, to the present.

The museum is open all year from 10 a.m. to 5 p.m. Tuesday to Saturday and 2:30 to 5 p.m. on Sunday. It's closed Monday and most public holidays. There is no charge for admission.

The **Turner House Art Gallery,** at Penarth (tel. 0222/708870), a few miles west of Cardiff, is a branch of the National Museum. It holds regularly changing exhibitions. It is open all year, Tuesday to Saturday from 11 a.m. to 12:45 p.m. and 2 to 5 p.m. and on Sunday from 2 to 5 p.m. It's closed on Christmas holidays, New Year's Day, and Good Friday. Admission is free.

PARKS AND GARDENS: Cardiff has been called a city of parks, with some 2,700 acres of well-designed parklands. **Bute Park,** right in the heart of the city, spreads a green stripe along the River Taff for the pleasure of residents and visitors.

Roath Park, just to the east of the city center, offers facilities for boating and fishing on its 32-acre lake, as well as tennis courts and bowling greens. Rose and dahlia gardens, a subtropical greenhouse, a children's play area, and an island bird sanctuary add to the pleasure to be found here. The park is open all year except Christmas Day and Boxing Day from 10:30 a.m. to 1 p.m. and 2 to 4:30 p.m. There's no charge for admission to the park, but to enter the conservatory, adults pay 20p (32¢); children, 5p (8¢). The lighthouse clock tower in the lake is a memorial to Captain Scott.

Parc Cefn-On is on the northern outskirts of Cardiff, in the hills between the city center and Caerphilly. Some 200 acres of woods, with rhododendrons and azaleas adding a colorful note in spring, surround a pool along which you can sit on benches and drink in the beauty. The park is open all year at 7:30 a.m., closing a half hour before dusk.

Dyffryn Gardens (tel. 0222/593328), three miles outside Cardiff in a secluded valley in the Vale of Glamorgan, offers 50 acres of landscaped botanical gardens, with many attractive features. Herbaceous borders, a rose garden, a rock garden, the largest heather garden in Wales, an extensive arboretum, and pleasant grass walks invite you to linger as you stroll through the grounds. A palm house, an orchid house, a cactus and succulent house, and display houses in which seasonal potted-plant displays are staged may be found in the garden.

The gardens, which are approximately 1½ miles south of the village of St. Nicholas on the A48 road west of Cardiff, are open from 10 a.m. to 7 p.m. daily from May 21 to August 31, from 1 to 6 p.m. March 31 to May 20, in September, and weekends in October. Admission is £1 ($1.60) for adults, 50p (80¢) for unaccompanied children. Accompanied children can enter free. Refreshments are available at the garden.

Also outside Cardiff is the **Welsh Hawking Centre and Wildlife Park,** Weycock Road, Barry (tel. 0446/734687), with a collection of some 200 birds of prey, including falcons, eagles, hawks, and owls. Other birds include ornamental pheasants, waterfowl, and parrots, among others. In good weather the raptor birds are flown every hour from noon until 5 p.m. The park is open daily from 10:30 a.m. to 5 p.m., charging £2 ($3.20) for adults, £1 ($1.60) for children up to 14 years.

When you're in Barry, you might want to go to the **Barry Island Pleasure Park** (tel. 0446/741250), six miles from Cardiff on the coast on the A4055 road. This is especially fun for children, with rides and games for the family and even a logflume to enjoy. It's open from 11 a.m. to 10 p.m. in summer. Admission is free, and tickets for rides can be purchased at the kiosk. There's plenty of parking.

TOURS OF CARDIFF: A good way to see the center of Cardiff is through guided walks of the city past and present, offered Monday to Friday by **City Travel Ltd.,** 13 Duke St. (tel. 0222/44315). The walks start at 11 a.m. and 2 p.m. from the west gate of Cardiff Castle under the clock tower. Allow about 1½ hours for a walk. Tickets cost £1.50 ($2.40) for adults and 75p ($1.20) for children under 14 years of age. "Taste of Wales" lunches at reduced prices are offered at the castle between walks.

One of the best ways to see Cardiff and the surrounding area is to join an **open-top bus tour.** They operate from Easter to the end of September and visit, among other places, Castell Coch, the Welsh Folk Museum, Dyffryn Gardens, Tredegar House, the Maritime Museum, and Llandaff Cathedral. For those with limited time, there are short tours of the city.

All tours start from the Friary Gardens, Kingsway, and are organized by the Cardiff City Council. For full details, a descriptive leaflet is available at the Tourist Information Centre, 3-6 Bridge St., near St. David's shopping precinct (tel. 0222/27281), or from the bus information kiosk in the city center. No reservations are necessary for the city tours.

A WALK ON YOUR OWN: A good place to begin a stroll through the heart of town is at The Hayes Island, across from St. David's Hall, focal point of St. David's Centre, the shopping precinct visited below. The Hayes isn't really an island. Until the 18th century, it was the vegetable garden of the townspeople of Cardiff, and in the city's boom days of the 19th century, it became a fashionable shopping area. Head north on Trinity Street, passing the 1882 central library on your right. The 1891 Central Market is on your left. On the right at the approach to Church Street is St. John's Church, the oldest house of worship in the heart of town, with origins in the 12th century.

Turn left onto Church Street and observe on your left, adjacent to the Old Arcade Public House, an alleyway, the Old Arcade, the oldest of the city's arcades, dating from 1835. At the end of Church Street, turn right onto High Street, the main street of Cardiff in the days of the medieval borough. Continue up this street until you come to the end of it and the main entrance to Cardiff Castle. You can either visit the castle now or save it for a later time. Turn left and walk along Castle Street, passing the landmark Angel Hotel. Continue along to Womanby Street, a Viking name that survived the Norman invasion and all subsequent government changes.

At Quay Street, head right (the name is from days of long ago when the River Taff ran at its lower end). This place evokes memories of the 16th century when the Bristol Channel was plagued by pirates. If you turn left at Westgate Street, you'll see the Cardiff Arms Park and the National Rugby Football Ground. Turn back up Quay Street to High Street. At the High, turn right and walk along St. Mary Street, passing market buildings from 1885. At Guildhall Place, go right. Notice the plaque on the southern wall of Hodge House telling the story of the Old Town Hall which stood there until 1913.

Return to St. Mary Street, passing on your right the Royal Hotel with its memories of Captain Scott and his South Pole explorers. At the junction with Wood Street, you'll see the Gothic facade of the Prince of Wales Theatre which opened in 1878. Head across Penarth Road and walk along Custom House Street to the 1845 Custom House.

Return again to St. Mary Street and the Great Western Hotel, built in 1876 in French Gothic style. Cross St. Mary Street and pause outside the Terminus Public House. If you look up from this street, you will see an almost complete Victorian townscape.

5. Shopping

Whether you're looking for gifts to take home, hunting for souvenirs, or just browsing, you'll like the shops of Cardiff. They are many and varied, ranging from a multiplicity of offerings in a modern shopping precinct, **St. David's Centre**—a stone's throw from the castle—to the stalls of a covered market. Shops are usually open from 9 a.m. to 5:30 p.m., till 9 p.m. on Thursday.

The main shopping streets are St. Mary, High, Castle, Duke, and Queen, plus The Hayes. Most of this area has been made into a mall, the pedestrianized streets having trees, shrubs, and gracious Edwardian arcades. These arcades, in fact, are the most famous shopping precincts in all of Wales. Some, as mentioned, are Edwardian, but others go back to the Victorian era, and there are nine in all. The best known perhaps is the **Castle Arcade,** constructed in 1887. The interior has a fascinating first floor wooden gallery with a wooden second floor overhanging it. Dating from 1858, the **Royal Arcade** is the oldest of the city's shopping arcades. Look for the original Victorian shopfronts at nos. 29, 30, and 32. **The Morgan Arcade** from 1896 is the best preserved. Note the first floor Venetian windows and the original slender wooden shopfronts such as nos. 23 and 24. All in all, the nine arcades stretch to a length of 2,655 feet in the city.

In the St. David's Shopping Centre is a branch of **Marks & Spencer,** 72 Queen St. (tel. 0222/378211), one of the country's largest branches of a major chain store offering clothing with emphasis on British-made goods. A food section contains a range of high-quality specialty items. This is the anchor store in the enclosed center, which has shops opening off wide walkways.

There are no Welsh craft shops in the center, but there are several in the area, including **Castle Welsh Crafts,** 27 Castle Arcade (tel. 0222/43038), opposite the castle entrance. Mailing service is available, and hours are 9 a.m. to 5:30 p.m. weekdays April to September, to 4:30 p.m. October to March. It's closed Wednesday afternoon.

Markets are held at several sites. The **Central Indoor Market** on St. Mary Street is open Monday to Friday except Wednesday afternoon. The **Outdoor Fruit and Vegetable Market,** St. David and Mary Ann Streets, open Monday to Saturday, is also closed on Wednesday afternoon. On Bessemer Road, an **open-air market** is held Sunday morning.

In the compact city center shopping precinct, surrounded by stores, offices, and markets, is **St. John's Church.** In the midst of your shopping, you might like to look in at this house of worship built in the 15th century on the site of a Norman 12th-century structure.

In the St. David's Centre, you'll also find St. David's Hall (see my nightlife recommendations, below).

FOR ANTIQUES: A new shopping idea for Cardiff is the **Cardiff Antique Center,** 69 St. Mary's St. (tel. 0222/30970). Open only on Thursday and Saturday from 9:30 a.m. to 5 p.m., it's a consortium of 50 different dealers, selling their wares in more or less jumbled juxtaposition. Prices are remarkably inexpensive. There's a selection of clothes, furniture, 19th-century artifacts, jewelry, and Victorian fireplaces. One dealer is noted for reasonable prices on antique brass hardware, pocket watches, and unusual fireplace accessories. The antique center was organized by John Lotte, Welsh entrepreneur, and is now directed by Lorraine Pikoulis. It occupies the premises of a now defunct old-fashioned lodging house, Old Barry's Hotel.

6. Entertainment and Nightlife

There's no Soho in Cardiff, you might be told when you're wondering about what the nightlife of the city has to offer. However, while it's true that the Welsh capital does not have the lavish nightclubs, strip shows, and other after-dark frivolities of London, it does have theaters, lively discos, casinos, cinemas, bars, concerts—in short, unless your taste for nightlife is jaded beyond repair, you can find many interesting places to go after dark, or even at matinee time.

St. David's Hall (Neuadd Dewi Sant), The Hayes (tel. 0222/42611), is considered the most innovative space for musical presentation in Britain outside London. Designed in a dramatic octagonal format of shimmering glass and roughly textured concrete, it is the most comprehensive forum for the arts in Wales. Don't think that its provincial status has ever barred some of the most noteworthy conductors in the world from performing here. A range of world-class orchestras appear regularly, along with popular music stars, everybody from Tina Turner to Tom Jones. Dance, films, and classical ballet, among other events, are also presented.

The hall maintains an information desk for the sale of tickets throughout the day. It also has dining facilities previously recommended, plus a changing exhibition of art. The hall's cornerstone was laid by Prince Charles, and the art center was officially opened by Queen Elizabeth and the Queen Mother in 1983. The top-notch acoustics are attributed to its interior arrangement of a series of interlinked sloping terraces, any of which can be opened or closed for seating depending on the size of the audience.

Instant confirmed bookings for events can be made by phone with a Visa or Access card daily from 10 a.m. to 6 or 8 p.m., depending on the concert schedule. For information, phone 0222/35900. The box office in the main lobby keeps the same hours (tel. 0222/371236). Tickets to most events cost from £2.50 ($4) to £15 ($24).

Sherman Theatre, Senghennydd Road (tel. 0222/30451), has two auditoriums, the Main theater and the intimate Arena. More than 600 performances a year are held here, including drama, dance, folk performances, jazz, and films. The theater also has its own production company, giving ten presentations of mainstream drama per year.

New Theatre, Park Place (tel. 0222/394844), is a charming Edwardian theater (1906) seating 1,100 persons for major productions of drama, ballet, contemporary dance, and pantomime. It is also the performing home of the internationally acclaimed Welsh National Opera. A massive refurbishing scheme enables theatergoers to enjoy the highest quality shows, many just before or after London's West End, in a true Edwardian atmosphere, with the most up-to-date of creature comforts.

Chapter, Market Road, Canton (tel. 0222/396061), is an arts center, with a theater, two movie facilities, two galleries, artists' studios, and video, photography, and silkscreen workshops, a dance studio, a bookshop, two bars, and a restaurant. Hours are from 10 a.m. to 11 p.m. weekdays, from 11 a.m. to 11 p.m. on Sunday. It's just a short bus ride from the city center.

A DISCO: Down the road from the Angel Hotel, **Jackson's,** Westgate Street (tel. 0222/390851), is the most exclusive disco in Cardiff, drawing a crowd in their 20s right through their 60s. This late-night spot, open from 9 p.m. to 2 a.m., is definitely upmarket, and guests wanting to get in should dress well. Men show up in jacket and tie. Some 110 years ago, it was called the Rackets Club but that history is only a distant memory now. The latest in music is played, and a cover charge of £4 ($6.40) is assessed. The club also has a restaurant and bar, serving meals for £10 ($16) and up.

7. Across South Glamorgan

The M4 motorway will take you zipping along from Cardiff to Swansea, but you'll miss the interesting southernmost section of Wales that way. I suggest taking the A48 west, perhaps stopping off at some of the little villages along the way or turning south to "see the sea."

If you're just passing through, between Cardiff and Swansea, even on the M4, you should stop off at **Margam Country Park** (visited below).

A **Wales Tourist Information** office at Sarn Park on the M4 motorway, junction 36, near Bridgend, can provide information on this entire district as well as other parts of Wales. It is open seven days a week from 10 a.m. to 6 p.m.

COWBRIDGE: Once just a little village on the River Thaw, Cowbridge is today becoming more and more a bedroom community of Cardiff. A bypass of the A48 Cardiff–Swansea road keeps the town from suffering the highway hurly-burly it once had when the road passed through, lorries and all. A center for the Vale of Glamorgan farming district, the town has a long main street along which are countryware shops and fine old inns.

You can see remnants of the Cowbridge town walls, dating from the 14th century, but only one gate, Porte Mellin (the mill gate) remains. About half a mile south of the town, on the River Thaw, at Llanblethian are the remains of St. Quintin's Castle.

Dining in Cowbridge

Mulligan's Fish & Chip Restaurant & Oyster Bar, Route A48, Stalling Down, Cowbridge (tel. 04463/2221). Established in 1986, this former working-class truck stop has now become one of the most popular and sophisticated restaurants in the greater environs of Cardiff. It's decorated with a witty collection of Victorian tiles, cast-iron Corinthian-capped columns, wide verandas, and 19th-century photographs of Welsh seamen collecting and washing mussels. To reach your table, you traverse an indoor footbridge spanning a lobster tank. You can dine either upstairs or down. Before that, however, you may want to peruse the display cases where a very fresh array of sea treats is artfully arranged on beds of seaweed and ice. Accompanied by a bottle of French wine, your meal might include fish soup, skate meunière, or scallops baked in pastry. The selection of hot and cold appetizers is outstanding. A garlic-laden version of a Marseillaise bourride is especially delectable, and the blackboard lists daily specials. Full meals cost from £12 ($19.20) and are served from noon to 2:15 p.m. and 6:30 to 10:30 p.m. daily except Sunday. Reservations are vital.

A PUB AT ST. HILARY: In one of the most beautiful villages in the Vale of Glamorgan, a charming little pub, **Bush Inn,** St. Hilary (tel. 04463/2745), is a 16th-century thatched country inn, with old-world bars, bare stone walls, stone-flagged floors, and original oak beams. If that isn't enough, there's even a huge fireplace and a spiral staircase to complete the inn picture. You can enjoy meals in the restaurant, feasting on such traditional dishes as Welsh rarebit and farm-house pie, stuffed mushrooms and venison casserole, or filet steak chasseur. A complete meal, costing from £10 ($16), can be ordered seven days a week from 12:15 to 2 p.m. and 7:15 to 10 p.m. (to 9:45 p.m. on Sunday). Bar meals are served at the same hours except that there is no food service in the bar on Saturday night. A pub meal costs from £3.50 ($5.60). This place is so popular that reservations are advisable for the restaurant.

St. Hilary lies half a mile off the A48 between Cardiff and Cowbridge. Bear right when you reach the village, and you'll come to the Bush Inn in about 200 yards.

THE OGWR DISTRICT: Three valleys lead through Bridgend, an industrial, market, and residential town west of Cardiff divided by the River Ogmore, to Porthcawl, a holiday resort town along the seafront south of Port Talbot. The district boasts castle ruins, quiet bays, extensive sandy beaches, sports and recreation centers, and entertainment facilities.

One of the three main castles, all built by the Normans, is **Ogmore-by-Sea,** on a road from Bridgend, lying on the banks of the River Ewenny, with stepping stones still in place. The early 12th-century banks and ditches still exist, as do other parts of the original structure. The ruins of New Castle, built to protect a ford across the Ogmore at the place where Bridgend was a budding village, are on a high mound behind the cottages and church in the oldest part of town. Rectangular towers and a round-arched gateway remain. Perhaps the best known of the three fallen fortresses is **Coity Castle,** at the little hamlet of Coite. It has 12th- and 14th-century as well as Tudor remnants. You can see a section of the moat and most of the ramparts.

The castles may be visited all year at reasonable times for a small charge. For more information, ask at the **Wales Tourist Information Centre,** Old Police Station, John Street, Porthcawl (tel. 065671/6639).

The defensive strength of the three castles was augmented about 1200 by fortification of **Ewenny Priory,** just south of Bridgend, as part of the Normans' defensive network. The remains of the priory are considered one of the best examples of ecclesiastical architecture in the country. You can reach a wall walk from the tower and view the fortified exterior best from a garden on the south side.

Nearby is **Ewenny Pottery** (tel. 0656/3020), one of the oldest kilns in Wales. If you're looking for souvenirs, this is the place. Hours are 9:30 a.m. to 5:30 p.m. Monday to Saturday and 2 to 5 p.m. on Sunday in summer. In winter, hours are from 9 a.m. to 5:30 p.m. Monday to Friday, closed Saturday and Sunday.

There are four golf courses in the Ogwr District, and water sports can be arranged.

PORTHCAWL: Turn off the east-west road between Cardiff and Swansea when you see the signs directing you to Porthcawl, a seaside town in an area of beaches, golf courses, and holiday atmosphere.

Porthcawl gained its early popularity as a resort for Welsh miners and their families. It has a wealth of accommodations to suit various pocketbooks. The promenade and neighboring streets are thick with hotels, large and small.

Food and Lodging

At the **Brentwood Hotel,** 37-41 Mary Street (tel. 065671/2725), the proprietor, Lindsay Knipe, extends a warm welcome. In the town center, the hotel is within easy reach of the beach and other attractions. All of the 24 rooms have showers or bathrooms en suite, and they are comfortably furnished in contemporary style. The hotel has central heating, and amenities in the bedrooms include color TV, tea/coffee-making facilities, radio, and baby-listening and morning-call service. Rates are £20 ($32) in a single, £30 ($48) in a double or twin-bedded room for B&B. Children stay free in a room with their parents except for a charge for meals. The hotel has a cheerful dining room where excellent food is served by courteous waitresses, with an à la carte dinner costing from £11 ($17.60). The bistro and cocktail bar is popular with locals, and you can join them in a jolly evening.

The **Esplanade Hotel,** on the Esplanade (where else?) (tel. 065671/8811), is a choice place to stay if you like to look at the sea and have the pounding of the surf lull you to sleep at night. A big white structure that looks like several harmonious sections joined into one, it offers 40 rooms, many with private bath and all with color TV. B&B costs from £12 ($19.20) to £17 ($27.20) in a single, from £22 ($35.20) to £32 ($57.20) in a double. Reductions are granted for children sharing their parents' room. The restaurant looks out on the channel, and there's a lounge bar. The Pot Black Snooker Club is another fun choice.

Seaways Hotel, Mary Street (tel. 065671/3510), is a comfortable family-run hotel only a short distance from the beach. You'll be warmly welcomed if you check into one of the 16 rooms. Some have complete bathroom and color TV, and all have direct-dial phones, and tea/coffee-making facilities. The cost of B&B is from £14 ($22.40) in a single, from £32 ($51.20) in a double. The hotel has two pleasant bars where you can have a three-course lunch for £4 ($6.40) and up. Both à la carte and table d'hôte menus are offered in the dining room. A complete dinner will cost around £6 ($9.60) or more.

Staying on the Outskirts

The **Rose and Crown Hotel,** Heol-y-Capel, Nottage (tel. 065671/4850), is a good stopover or base for touring the Ogwr District. Nottage is a village about two miles north of Porthcawl on the B4283 road. John and Chris Rout take pains to see that guests are comfortable in their white, two-story hotel, which has all the character of a village inn. The eight bedrooms are well appointed and comfortable, all with bathrooms and kept immaculate. The charge for B&B is £30 ($48) in a single, £40 ($64) in a double. There is a well-appointed carvery, as well as three small bars with stone walls and copper-top tables at which you can enjoy pub lunches.

MARGAM COUNTRY PARK: About two miles inland from Port Talbot, a busy industrial town north along the coast from Porthcawl, on the A48 Cardiff–Swansea road less than a quarter of a mile from exit 38 of the M4 motorway, lies what has been hailed as perhaps the finest park in Europe. An 850-acre layout centered around a restored 19th-century castle, Margam has everything a splendid estate should have—monastery ruins, an abbey church, an orangery, ponds for boating and fishing, an adventure playground and pets corner, the site of a Celtic hill-fort, a maze, and a junior-size reproduction of the Welsh Folk Museum at St. Fagan's. A herd of deer wanders around the grounds, and Glamorgan cattle graze contentedly, having been reprieved from extinction and now increasing in numbers.

The present Georgian orangery, built in the 18th century to replace one of earlier vintage, has been completely restored, sitting aristocratically in the midst of pleasure gardens, its roof rimmed with huge sculptured urns. It was used to house American and British troops during World War II and was completely restored in the 1970s. The original house on the Margam estate was built out of and onto the abbey after the dissolution of the monasteries by Henry VIII. It was later demolished to make way for the first orangery. The present Tudor Gothic mansion, which had been allowed to become derelict, was heavily damaged by fire in 1977 and is now an empty shell.

Perhaps the most striking aspect of Margam Park is its outdoor sculpture: some 70 pieces of contemporary art by noted sculptors are spread around the grounds—on hillsides, beside lakes, in the shade of trees, wherever.

If you look up on a hilltop in the western part of the park, you'll see a roofless chapel ruin. This was Cryke Chapel, believed to have been built in the 15th century. The common folk who didn't have the right to worship in the abbey church in the valley had to trudge up the steep hillside to go to church.

The park, owned and managed by the West Glamorgan County Council, is open April to October from 10 a.m. to 8 p.m., except Monday. November to March, it opens at 10:30 a.m. and closes an hour before dusk, except Monday and Tuesday. In August and on bank holidays you can visit on Monday. Admission is £1 ($1.60) for adults, 50p (80¢) for children. There is free "park and ride" bus service from the gate, a souvenir shop, a cafeteria, and rest rooms. For more information, call the **Park Director** (tel. 0639/881635).

Port Talbot, to the west, is largely industrial, but it has seaside resort facilities with an extensive beach, Aberavon, a sports and entertainment center, an amusement arcade, and a spacious promenade.

Chapter XXIII

SWANSEA AND THE SOUTHWEST

THE CITY OF SWANSEA on Swansea Bay of Bristol Channel, seems a natural starting place for a visit to the southwest section of Wales. After a sojourn in the immediate vicinity of the port city, the beautiful peninsula of Gower, which is Swansea's neighbor, draws you westward. You'll see where Dylan Thomas, the country's outstanding 20th-century poet, was born, and then move on to the west to Carmarthen and down to the bay that bears its name, to Laugharne, where the poet lived, wrote, and is buried. The wonders of Pembrokeshire Coast National Park in and beside the Atlantic Ocean draw you on, with beaches and bays, castles and gardens.

Swansea is on the western edge of West Glamorgan county. When the counties of Wales were realigned and consolidated in 1973, Pembrokeshire and Carmarthenshire, familiar names in Welsh history, became part of Dyfed county, an even older designation for the area they occupy. In this southwestern corner of the country, you'll be introduced to the land of St. David and of Celtic crosses, of craggy coast and the cromlechs marking the burial places of prehistoric man. You can take a ferryboat to Ireland if you wish, but don't do it until you've wandered through the rolling hills, followed winding, narrow roads, and become acquainted with the warm, friendly Welsh who live here.

1. The City and Gower Peninsula

Vikings, Normans, English, Welsh, industry, seaport activity, holiday magic, and cultural prominence—all these have combined to make Swansea the city of today. It's tough, bold, friendly, and fun. Parks abound, and the tender loving care bestowed on them has resulted in Swansea's being a winner of the "Wales in Bloom" award year after year.

Swansea entered recorded history some 800 years ago, bearing a Viking name believed derived from "Sweyn's ey," or Sweyn's island. The Sweyn in question may well have been Sweyn Forkbeard, King of Denmark (987–1014), known to have been active in Bristol Channel. Normans founded the marcher lordship of Gower, with its capital at Swansea, and a small trading community grew up here, with seagoing business, including coal exportation, becoming important through the Middle Ages. In the early 18th century at the town at the mouth of the River Tawe (Swansea's Welsh name is Abertawe) copperworks began to be built, and soon it was the copper capital of the world, as well as a leading European center for zinc refining, tin plating, steel making, and many chemical activities.

This "ugly, lovely city," as native son Dylan Thomas described it, has today pretty well obliterated the ugliness. Devastation of the center of town by German air raids during World War II led to complete rebuilding. Traditional industries in the Lower Swansea Valley have vanished, leaving economic woes and an industrial wasteland. However, reclamation and redevelopment are under way. The leveling of old mine tips and slag heaps and the planting of trees in their stead points to a more attractive Swansea of both today and tomorrow. Clean industries are coming in, but they are being placed out in wooded areas and suitable industrial parks, and they do not cast a pall over the city.

TRANSPORTATION AND PRACTICAL FACTS: For information on bus service in Swansea and its environs, call the **Quadrant Bus Station** (tel. 0792/475511). In summer, a vintage open-top bus runs between the Swansea city center and The Mumbles and Limeslade. The **South Wales Transport Co., Ltd.,** Heol Gwyrosydd, Penlan, also operates a wide range of day tours throughout the summer months. For details, phone 0792/472473.

For unlimited travel for a whole day on local services in South Wales, Roverbus tickets allow you to visit the local attractions and cost only £2.95 ($4.72). Weekly Roverbus extends the advantages of Roverbus to seven days, so travel throughout the area costs only £12.50 ($20). Reductions are granted for children.

The **City of Swansea Information Centre,** Singleton Street, P.O. Box 59 (tel. 0792/468321), is open from 9:30 a.m. to 5:30 p.m. daily year round.

Mumbles Tourist Information Centre, Oystermouth Square (tel. 0792/61302), is open April to October from 9:30 a.m. to 5:30 p.m.

Gower Tourist Information Centre, Swansea Airport, Fairwood Common (tel. 0792/297927), is open from 10:30 a.m. to 6:30 p.m. seven days a week.

National Trust Information Centre, Rhossilli (tel. 0792/390707), is open July to September from 9:30 a.m. to 5:30 p.m. seven days a week. It has limited hours the rest of the year.

Pont Abraham Tourist Information Centre (tel. 0792/883838), at the Pont Abraham service area on the M4 motorway (junction 49), is open from 10 a.m. to 6 p.m. Easter to October and from 9:30 a.m. to 5:30 p.m. November to Easter. Information on South and West Wales and an accommodation reservation service are available.

WHERE TO STAY: My recommendations for hotels and guesthouses in Swansea, The Mumbles, and Gower are necessarily lumped together, as it's often difficult to know where one leaves off and the other starts. I'll begin with a big splurge right in the city center of Swansea.

The **Dragon Hotel**, 39 The Kingsway (tel. 0792/51074), is a towering building in the heart of the city, with all the modern amenities in its 118 bedrooms. Ian Rhind, the general manager, sees to it that the hotel runs smoothly to take care of guests. All the rooms have private bath, color TV, radio, and phone, and room service is available. From the top floors there are fine views of the shipping in Swansea Bay. Room rates for B&B run from £47 ($75.20) in a single, from £58 ($92.80) in a double, but special bargain breaks are offered, and there are reductions on weekends. The Dragon Coffee Shop, open from 10 a.m. to 11 p.m. Monday to Saturday, serves grills and light refreshments. There is also an à la carte restaurant, featuring a carving table. A complete meal costs from £18 ($28.80) in the restaurant, while you can eat in the coffeeshop for £6.50 ($10.40) to £10 ($16). The hotel is noted for its international food festivals held throughout the year. There are four bars, each with a different ambience. The Dragon is quite near the shopping centers.

The **Langland Court Hotel**, 31 Langland Court Rd., Langland Bay (tel. 0792/361545), is a beautiful Tudor-style country residence, now a hotel standing in its own grounds near Langland Bay and Bristol Channel. Even with modern amenities, it has retained the elegance and character of other days, with its oak-paneled entrance hall and dining room and the galleried staircase. The bedrooms have bathroom facilities and are attractively furnished, with decor suitable to the charm of the hotel. Rates run from £35 ($56) in a single, from £45 ($72) in a double, for B&B. The hotel is centrally heated. A comfortable residents' lounge has color TV, and there are also intimate cocktail and lounge bars, as well as a billiard room. The à la carte restaurant serves traditional and continental specialties, a dinner costing from £9 ($14.40). Dinner dances are held most Saturdays. The hotel is open all year.

Crescent Guest House, 132 Eaton Crescent, Uplands (tel. 0792/466814), is a charming and immaculate accommodation run by Tessa and Maurice Convey on a residential crescent a mile west of Swansea near the main Swansea–Gower road (the A4118). All the bedrooms have TV, hot and cold water basins, shaver points, clock radios, and hot-beverage facilities. Some have their own showers. B&B costs £12 ($19.20) per person, with an evening meal being provided for £5 ($8) extra. The house has lounge with color TV, a dining room, and a small car park.

Acorns Guest House, 176 Gower Rd. (tel. 0792/466814), offers comfortable bedrooms, costing from £9 ($14.40) to £11 ($17.60) for B&B. Mr. and Mrs. C.J. Gray, the proprietors of this licensed house, invite guests to use the TV lounge, and there's a place to park your car.

Tides Reach, 388 Mumbles Rd., Mumbles (tel. 0792/404877), overlooking the sea, was "along the path" Dylan Thomas followed to two famous pubs he frequented, the Mermaid and the Antelope. Tides Reach was built in 1855 as a hotel, but went bankrupt and had its contents sold at auction in 1886. In the 1920s it was divided into two houses, but under the concerned management and care of Jan and William Maybery the buildings have now been reunited. They operate one of the loveliest guesthouses in the area. Their seven beautifully furnished bedrooms (three contain private showers) are open year round, costing from £11 ($17.60) per person for B&B. Dinner, a three-courser, goes for £6 ($9.60) and is offered only from May to September. William's specialty is 19th-century English ceramics, but at an earlier period he bought and sold (and collected for his own use) a host of Welsh oak provincial and formal mahogany pieces. The dining room is all antique Welsh oak, the parlor and sitting room filled with mahogany pieces. This place is one of the little gems of Swansea.

The **Dolphin House,** 6 Cornwall Pl., Mumbles (tel. 0792/366435), is a warm, comfortable accommodation along the promenade of Swansea Bay, about two blocks from the Oystermouth bus stop. Maureen and Mike Taylor rent their rooms for £10 ($16) per person for B&B.

The **Old School House,** 37 Nottage Rd., Newton, Mumbles (tel. 0792/361541), is a charming year-round hotel and restaurant converted from the village school. It lies close to the bays of Langland and Caswell on the Gower coast, about six miles from the Swansea city center. All its bedrooms have shower and toilet en suite, color TV, and tea/coffee-making equipment. You can rent one of the three singles for around £25 ($40) or one of the five doubles from £33 ($52.80) for B&B. The hotel has three distinctive dining rooms, where you can order à la carte or from a specialty menu, plus two bars, a sauna, and a spa bath.

St. Anne's Hotel, Western Lane, Mumbles (tel. 0792/369147), sits in its own grounds overlooking Swansea Bay. There are 28 well-furnished rooms, all with TV and most with their own bathroom. The hotel is centrally heated. There's a separate TV lounge for guests, as well as a private bar which serves hotel residents and restaurant patrons. The charge for B&B in one of the singles with bath is £20.55 ($32.88); doubles cost from £29.50 ($47.20). Meals in the restaurant go for £6.50 ($10.40) and up. Mr. G. Noakes, the owner, is happy to help you in any way he can to make your stay pleasant at his year-round hotel.

The Coast House, 708 Mumbles Rd., Mumbles (tel. 0792/368702), is on the promenade with views of Swansea Bay and within easy reach of good beaches. A small, family-owned guesthouse, it has a friendly, relaxed atmosphere. All bedrooms have hot and cold water, color TV, shaver points, and sea views. Some have private baths. Rents are from £10 ($16) per person per night in one of the five rooms. There is a spacious residents' lounge with color TV, plus excellent cuisine. The house is open all year.

Brynteg Hotel, 1 Higher Lane, Langland, Mumbles (tel. 0792/366820), is a licensed family hotel with easy access to both Swansea and Gower. All rooms are centrally heated, and there is a lounge with color TV, or you can have drinks in the pleasant cocktail bar. Gerry and Linda Alexander rent their 11 bedrooms, all with hot and cold running water, for around £11 ($17.60) per person for B&B. Children are welcome at half price. Open all year.

At **Harbour Winds Hotel,** Overland Road, Mumbles (tel. 0792/69298), Pat and John Mallett welcome you from April to October to their red brick and stucco hostelry, set in private grounds with ample free parking. Around back you'll find a secluded terrace and lawn. You can stay in one of their large, pleasant, well-equipped bedrooms, some with bathroom facilities, for £13 ($20.80) to £15 ($24) per person per night, depending on the plumbing. You can enjoy good food in the historic oak-paneled dining room, paying about £8 ($12.80) and up for a complete meal. Special rates are quoted for children.

My favorite stop on the Gower peninsula is the **Worms Head Hotel,** Rhossilli (tel. 0792/390512), mainly because of its location, easily the best in Gower: it is perched with a sweeping view of Rhossilli Bay and beach and of the Worms Head rock and Bristol Channel, with Rhossilli Down as the background. Mr. and Mrs. G. Heller welcome guests all year to their hotel, which has two attractive bars and 21 bedrooms, as well as a residents' lounge and TV room. All the centrally heated rooms have hot and cold running water and shaver outlets, while some have private baths or showers. Bathless rooms rent for £15.50 ($24.80) per person, and those with bath cost £16.50 ($26.40) per person, with breakfast included. The hotel isn't fancy, but it's a good selection for a stay on Gower Peninsula. Good food, with a choice of main dishes, is served in the dining room.

Oxwich Bay Hotel, Oxwich, Gower (tel. 0792/390329), a family hotel run by Terry, Margaret, and Ian Williams, is on its own grounds right at the edge of Oxwich Bay, with a garden overlooking the beach where you can enjoy drinks from the licensed bar at umbrellaed tables. The centrally heated bedrooms have radios, razor outlets, and tea/coffee-making facilities, and there is a comfortable residents' lounge with color TV. Expect to pay from £16.50 ($26.40) to £18 ($28.80) per person per night for B&B. You can make arrangements for half board, or dine in the restaurant à la carte for about £9 ($14.40). The hotel has ample car parking space. It's open all year.

The **Winston Private Hotel,** 11 Church Lane, Bishopston Valley, Gower (tel. 044128/2074), is in the extensive Gower village of Bishopston, merging with Murton, Newton, and The Mumbles on one side and Northway, Kittle, and Pennard on the other, just a mile and a half from Caswell Bay and Pwll-du beaches. At the Winston, Brian and Pat Clark welcome guests all year to their 19-room hostelry, which was built as a private home by Mrs. Clark's father. The Clarks have added an annex, containing the most spacious and best-furnished bedrooms, as well as a swimming pool. Rates, single or double occupancy, range from £15 ($24) to £23 ($36.80) per person, depending on the plumbing. Prices include a good-tasting and filling breakfast and a hot evening drink, served in summer on a tray beside the pool around 10:30 p.m. Many of the neighbors drop in, turning it into a social event.

Nicholaston House Hotel, Penmaen, Gower (tel. 044125/317), on the south coast of the Gower Peninsula, boasts sea views over Oxwich Bay and all the way to Severn Estuary toward England. Set in its own grounds with peaceful surroundings, the hotel, open from February to December, offers personal service and excellent cuisine from either a set menu or à la carte. You can have a drink with your meals in this licensed restaurant. All rooms have private bath, color TV, and tea/coffee-making equipment. Charges are from £16 ($25.60) to £18 ($28.80) per person for B&B, with reductions for children sharing their parents' room. The hotel is centrally heated, and there is ample parking. Mrs. Jeanette Jenkins is happy to welcome American guests.

Parc-le-Breos House, Parkmill, Gower (tel. 044125/636), is a spacious farmhouse in the heart of Gower, a pleasant base from which to take walks along Cefn Bryn and tours of the peninsula. O. Edwards rents rooms for £10.50 ($16.80) per person per night for B&B, £14 ($22.40) for dinner, bed, and breakfast. Some units with private baths cost an additional £1 ($1.60) per person. Rooms all have hot and cold running water, and you can relax in the TV lounge or test your skills in the games room. The food served is home-grown and home-cooked. There's a play area for children on the lawn. You can arrange for horseback riding here. The farmhouse is open all year.

If you're looking for a really low-cost accommodation, try the **IYHF Youth Hostel,** Port Eynon (tel. 0792/390706), a simple but attractive place to stay, mainly in dormitory-type rooms. The charge is from £2.20 ($3.52) for persons 15 and under to £6.50 ($10.40), depending on the type of lodging.

WHERE TO DINE: Swansea is no longer the gastronomic wasteland it used to be. Nowadays there are several good restaurants, the leader of which is **Oyster Perches,** 45 Uplands Crescent, Uplands (tel. 0792/473173), which lies outside the center two miles from the commercial heart of Swansea. It offers a sophisticated cuisine served in a peach-toned milieu of curtained walls, immaculate napery, and individual table lamps. Full meals, costing from £15 ($24), are offered only at dinner daily except Sunday. Hours are from 6:30 to 10:30 p.m. Monday to Thursday, and 6:30 to 11 p.m. on weekends. Three specialties of the many dishes offered include sole americaine (filet of sole stuffed with slices of lobster and served with shallots in a cream and tomato sauce with white wine and brandy flavoring), trout West Wales (carefully boned and stuffed with laverbread, then wrapped in bacon and baked with a butter sauce), and lamb Oyster Perches, prepared only for two persons (it's a whole best end of prime Welsh lamb glazed in honey, roasted with rosemary, and carved into cutlets at your table). Reservations are suggested.

Jasmine, 326 Oystermouth Rd. (tel. 0792/52912), is the leading Chinese restaurant of Swansea. It serves Cantonese food in a traditional Chinese decor of black and white. The owners from Hong Kong prepare succulent meals costing from £10 ($16) per person. Food is offered seven days a week continuously from noon to midnight. The duck is particularly good and can be prepared with spring onions along with ginger and a lemon sauce. Otherwise, there's the full repertoire of beef, fish, and chicken dishes.

Port of Call, 2 Prospect Place (tel. 0792/473886), owned by Inger Eastman, is found in the basement of a 200-year-old house. You descend a flight of wooden stairs to reach a stone-walled dining room where lunch is served from 11 a.m. to 3 p.m., tea with freshly made scones 3 to 5 p.m., and dinner from 7 to 10 p.m. It is closed only on Sunday night. Menu items include a freshly made soup of the day, pâté, grilled sirloin (also T-bone and filet steak), roast, chicken, trout, Dover sole, followed by a freshly made dessert. Full meals cost £12 ($19.20), but you can do it for less.

La Braseria, 28 Wind St. (tel. 0792/469683), is the best wine bar in Swansea. It's run by the same people who operate the finest collection of wine bars in Cardiff, including La Brasserie previously recommended. Here you enter what appears to be a bodega in Spain, and that impression is enhanced as you select from some excellent Spanish vintages. From noon to 2:30 p.m. and 7 p.m. to midnight, you can dine here daily except Sunday for £10 ($16) or so. You can make a selection of such dishes as spareribs, baked salmon, three kinds of steak, beefburgers, or veal marinated in white wine, garlic, and herbs.

Home on the Range, 174 St. Helens Ave. (tel. 0792/467166), near the Guildhall, specializes in freshly prepared home-cooking, including Welsh specialties. Excellent raw materials and fresh herbs are part of the chef's success. You can order a three-course meal for less than £5.50 ($8.80). Some excellent vegetarian dishes are on the menu. The restaurant is not licensed, so you must bring your own wine. It's open Monday to Saturday from 11:30 a.m. to 3 p.m., serving dinner also Wednesday to Saturday, from 6 to 10 p.m. This is a good place to stop for tea and biscuits in the middle of your sightseeing.

SIGHTS OF SWANSEA: From a once-dirty waterfront area, an exciting **Maritime Quarter** has been developed. Lying between the city center and the seafront, it is based on the historic South Dock and its Half Tide Basin, with new urban villages and a modern marina, centered on the Swansea Yacht Haven. Open spaces and a promenade and sea wall have been provided.

Adjacent to the marina, in the old Coastlines Warehouse, is the **Maritime and Industrial Museum** (tel. 0792/50351), in a large red brick former train shed. Upstairs is the fully operational Abbey Woolen Mill, where you can watch dyeing, carding, spinning, and weaving in progress. Woolen goods made here are available for purchase at reasonable—even low—prices in a shop on the ground floor. Locomotives, vehicles, and a Mumbles train are among the exhibits downstairs. On the upper floor, you can see displays on maritime history, agriculture, and local contemporary industry. Floating exhibits just outside are the steam tug *Canning,* the last such vessel to operate in Bristol Channel; the lightship *Helwick;* the oak-built beam trawler *Katie Ann;* the old Mumbles lifeboat *William Gammon;* the pilot cutter *Olga;* the old Aberystwyth lifeboat *John & Naomi Beattie;* and the 26-foot racing yacht *Zelva.* The admission-free museum is open daily from 10:30 a.m. to 5:30 p.m. In summer, during these same hours, the public has pontoon access to the vessels afloat.

The multi-million-pound **Leisure Centre** in the same complex is worth seeing. A huge pool with a beach and a wave-making mechanism, a poolside café, a choice of bars, two cafeterias, an à la carte restaurant (the Oystermouth Grill), and a disco are in the big building. All sorts of sports and recreation facilities are included, from squash to judo to indoor soccer and a bowling green, with a sauna and solarium, even a hairdressing salon. The Leisure Centre is linked by handsome walkways to the shopping center and the Maritime Quarter.

Nearby is the **Swansea Museum,** Victoria Road (tel. 0792/53763), whose collections mainly concern the locality. On display are local archeology, natural history, ceramics, art, and historical artifacts and other exhibits. The museum is open Tuesday to Saturday from 10 a.m. to 4:30 p.m., charging 30p (48¢) for adults, 10p (16¢) for children. The museum is under the aegis of the Swansea University on Mumbles Road, where you can visit the Wellcome Museum and Botanic Gardens.

Not too far away is the **Guildhall,** Swansea's town hall, with its tall clock tower, about five minutes' walk from the city center. It's just off Mumbles Road at the seafront. The city council meets here, and its chambers are worth seeing, but of particular interest are **Brangwyn Hall** and the **British Empire Murals.** Brangwyn Hall is the major venue for concerts and other musical entertainment (see section on "Entertainment and Nightlife" below). It was named for the artist Sir Frank Brangwyn, who painted the 18 murals, originally commissioned for the House of Lords, which are on the walls. They represent the various dominions and parts of the British Empire in bright-hued profusion. The Guildhall may be visited from 9 a.m. to 5 p.m. Arrangements to see the murals may be made by calling the Commissionaire (tel. 0792/50821).

The **Glynn Vivian Art Gallery and Museum,** Alesandra Road (tel. 0792/5506), contains a fine collection of paintings by Welsh artists and a large selection of highly prized Swansea china. Other exhibits include clocks, glass, an outdoor sculpture court, and a changing program of works by major artists. It's open from 10:30 a.m. to 5:30 p.m. Monday to Saturday, and admission is free. The gallery is a two-minute walk from the main railway station in central Swansea.

A statue of Dylan Thomas stands in the Maritime Quarter, and the **Dylan Thomas Theatre** is nearby at 7 Gloucester Place (tel. 0792/473238). The poet was born in the Uplands, a residential area of Swansea, at 5 Cwmdonkin Dr., a steep street off Walter Road. Sometimes it's possible to make arrangements to stay in the spacious and well-furnished house on a B&B basis. If you'd like to know more about the possibility, get in touch with F. Jones, Coynant, Felindre, Swansea (tel. 0269/5640). You can walk in Cwmdonkin Park close by, which the poet made famous in his writings.

Swansea is one of the few cities to have a beach within walking distance of the center. A delightful promenade leads all the way to Oystermouth, four miles away, although you can drive the route on the A4067 road. Along the way you pass a rugby and cricket ground and the entrance to the city's largest park, Singleton. About halfway down the bay is a nine-hole golf course and a well-equipped resort beach, in an area known as Blackpill. It includes the entrances to the city's fine country park, Clyne Valley and the magnificent Clyne Gardens. Before long you come to the villages of Westcross and Norton, and then comes

Oystermouth, which has a fine Norman castle renowned for its imposing position on a headland commanding a view of the bay and Swansea.

Next door is **The Mumbles,** a former fishing village which is a favorite with both locals and visitors, now a suburb of Swansea. This is a village with two faces (but both pleasing): by day it has a friendly, tranquil atmosphere, but when the sun goes down, watch out! Then Mumbles bursts into action and becomes a nightlife center, with pubs, clubs, and restaurants crowded with merrymakers. Mumbles has been attracting tourists since Victorian times, when the handsome pier was built, as in most British sea resort towns. It protrudes 900 feet from Mumbles Head into the bay and affords sweeping views. Away from the seafront, tiny fishermen's cottages can be seen built into the limestone rock. Souvenirs and examples of local crafts can be found in shops that cling to the hillside. Yachting, swimming, fishing, beach games, crazy golf, and bowling are enjoyed here.

GOWER PENINSULA: The first area in Britain designated "an area of outstanding natural beauty" (second was the Wye Valley), Gower is a broad peninsula stretching about 14 miles from The Mumbles to Worms Head in the west. The coastline of Gower starts at Bracelet Bay, just around the corner from The Mumbles. You can go there by road—or at least to some parts of the peninsula —but the best way to see its sometimes rugged, sometimes soft coast is to walk, even for short distances if you don't have time to make the complete circuit.

There are many and varied beaches on Gower: **Caswell Bay** with its acres of smooth, golden sand and safe swimming; **Langland,** a family attraction, with facilities for golf, swimming, tennis, and surfing; and **Rotherslade,** which at high tide has some of the largest waves around the peninsula crashing onto the shore. Secluded **Pwil-du** is a place to sunbathe in solitude, despite the crowds elsewhere along the coast, and there are numerous other small coves tucked away beneath the cliffs. **Oxwich Bay** is one of the largest on the peninsula, with three miles of uninterrupted sand, where you can enjoy beach games, picnics, waterskiing, and sailing. Windsurfing is popular at Oxwich too. Oxwich village, at one end of the bay, is a typical Gower hamlet of cottages and tree-lined lanes. There is a nature reserve here that is home to some rare orchid species.

After the commercial and often-crowded Oxwich beach, you may be happy to see **Slade,** which has to be approached on foot down a steep set of steps. The spotless beach is usually wind free. Around the next corner, you'll find **Horton** and **Port Eynon,** with a long, curving beach backed by sand dunes. Refreshments are available on the beach, and the two villages offer nighttime entertainment.

From Port Eynon, a spectacular 4½-mile cliff walk leads past Culver Hole, Paviland Cave, Mewslade, and Fall Bay to Worms Head and Rhossilli. The **Paviland Caves** can be explored, if you're brave. It was here that human remains have been found dating back 100,000 years. **Worms Head** is a twisted outcrop of rock shaped into the form that sometimes, depending on the tides, looks like a prehistoric worm sticking its head up out of the water. **Rhossilli** is a long, sweeping bay and a beach reached from the treeless village of Rhossilli, a church and houses perched 200 feet up on the clifftops. This is an international center for hang-gliding. Halfway along the beach at Llangennith is the most popular surfing site on the peninsula. Rolling dunes connect it with Broughton Bay and Whitford Sands, and eventually you come to **Penclawdd,** a little village where a centuries-old cockle industry still thrives. If the tide is right, you can see the pickers with their rakes and buckets gleaning the tiny crustaceans from the flats.

Although the coastal attractions are Gower's biggest lure, there are pleasant farms, attractive country roads, and places of interest inland. **Parc le Breos** (Giant's Grave) burial chamber, almost in the center of the peninsula, close to Parkmill on the A4118 road, is an ancient legacy from Stone Age people. The remains of at least four persons were found there. A central passage and four chambers are in a cairn about 70 feet long. **Pennard Castle** has suffered under ravages of weather and time, but from the north you can see the curtain wall almost intact. It can be visited free.

Weobley Castle on north Gower is actually a fortified house rather than a castle. There was no space for a garrison, and the rooms were for domestic purposes. On the northern edge of bare upland country, it overlooks the Llanrhidian marshes and the Loughor estuary. There are substantial remains of this 13th- and 14th-century stronghold, and the view is interesting. Weobley is off the Llanrhidian–Cheriton road, seven miles west of Gowertown. It is open from 10 a.m. to 7 p.m. (from 1 p.m. mid-March to mid-October, closing at 4 p.m. off-season). Admission is 50p (80¢) for adults, 25p (40¢) for children.

Even though it is protected from development, Gower has been invaded by caravans (mobile homes), recreation vehicles, beach huts, retirement homes, and bungalows, but you can still find solitude in secluded bays and especially in the center of the peninsula, along the Cefn Bryn ridge or on Rhossilli Down. From the top of Cefn Bryn, 609 feet above sea level, you can see the entire peninsula and far beyond on clear days. By taking the Green Road which runs the length of the ridge from Penmaen, you'll find a path about half a mile east of Reynoldston which leads to **Arthur's Stone,** a circular burial chamber. The mound of earth that once covered it has been weathered away, but you can see the huge capstone that protected the burial place. From Rhossilli Down, at 632 feet, you can see the English coast. Here also are megalithic tombs, cairns, and barrows.

The Gower Farm Museum

At **Lake Farm,** Llandewi, Reynoldston, at the northwest end of Cefn Bryn, the Watters family has a fine display of farm machinery, documents, photos, and household goods giving an intimate picture of the life of one family that has lived and worked in Gower since the time it was considered a remote backwater. There are farm trails to follow, and you can visit with the farm animals housed here. The museum is open April to September from 10 a.m. to 9 p.m., October to March from 10 a.m. to 6 p.m. Admission is 60p (96¢) for adults, 40p (64¢) for children. For information, telephone 0792/391195.

SHOPPING: Swansea shopping is dominated by the **Quadrant Shopping Centre,** behind the main bus station. The center has a huge Debenhams store, one of the largest in Wales. Rows of covered malls are lined with shops and big-name stores. The center is connected to **the market,** where rows of open stalls have sold food for centuries. Some of the local delicacies include fresh laverbread, and this Welsh specialty is now available in cans so you can take some home. Here you can also find cockles, fish both local and exotic, meats, dairy products, eggs, and poultry, as well as fresh fruit and vegetables. The market deals in hardware also.

A newer shopping area is **St. David's Centre,** on the other side of the market. It's also pedestrianized and has small shops mingled with big stores. Both it and the Quadrant have multistory parking. Outside the heart of the city's shopping area, running parallel with the centers, is Oxford Street, another shopping area. Above are Union Street, Portland Street, and the Kingsway, also packed with interesting stores. Princess Way runs along the end of Kingsway and Oxford Street, and on it you'll find the top-quality David Evans store. High Street and Castle Street are more shopping sections.

Top-quality gift shops and crafts abound, not just in the city center but in Gower. The Mumbles is also a popular area for souvenirs and gifts. Shopping there is in a village atmosphere where local artisans show their wares.

In Swansea, Brynymor Road is one of the many satellite shopping centers that have built up a flavor of their own. Rare and specialized foodstuffs can be found here, including high-quality health foods. Uplands, Sketty, Morriston, and Killay sections all have something unique to offer the shopper.

ENTERTAINMENT: If sightseeing hasn't worn you out, you may want to take a look at the various possibilities for entertainment in the area.

The **Grand Theatre** (tel. 0792/475715), adjacent to the Quadrant, is a Victorian theater which has been refurbished and redeveloped into a multi-million-pound theater complex. The theater hosts international opera, ballet, and theater companies as well as one-night concerts. It also has its own schools of singing and dancing.

Besides the **Dylan Thomas Theatre** in the Maritime Quarter, mentioned above, the **Taliesin Centre for the Arts,** at the University College of Swansea, presents drama and musical events. For information, call the City Booking Office (tel. 0792/468321) or Administration Office (tel. 0792/295438).

Brangwyn Hall in the Guildhall, described above, offers concerts and other music performances, and a series of summer shows is presented at the **Patti Pavilion** in Victoria Park, near the Guildhall. For information, check with the information center on Singleton Street (tel. 0792/468321). Free brochures, maps, and bed booking service are also available at this center.

Pubs

One of the best is called **St. George Hotel,** 30 Walter Rd. (tel. 0792/469317), which offers the best pub food in town but only at lunch from noon to 2:15 p.m. Monday to Friday. The pride and joy is the display of cold meats and salads set up within a refrigerated display case at the end of the bar. You place your food and drink order yourself since there is no waiter service. Smoked fish, baked hams, tempting pastas, and such French-inspired dishes as mussels in garlic sauce are just part of the repertoire, with meals costing from £5 ($8). In the evening you can drop in for a drink from 6 to 11 p.m.

Among the special pubs of Swansea, the eternal favorite is now called **Dylan's Tavern,** at the Mermaid Hotel, 688 Mumbles Rd., Southend (tel. 0792/360253). Back when the poet used to patronize the place, it was known simply as the Mermaid pub. Now it honors the artist and is decorated with original photographs of him. Dylan Thomas drank here often, and you can do so from 11:30 a.m. to 3:30 p.m. and 5:30 to 10:30 p.m. daily except Sunday when hours are from noon to 2 p.m. and 7 to 10:30 p.m. A pint of lager goes for 90p ($1.44).

The **Westbourne Pub,** Westbourne Hotel, Brynymor Road (tel. 0792/54952), is run by the vivacious Mrs. Lavinia Morgans who serves a medley of pizzas with 20 different toppings. Her menu also lists 19 different sandwiches. She calls herself a pizza-cum-sandwich pub, offering meals for £4 ($6.40) or so. Food is served only from noon to 2 p.m. and 6 to 9 p.m. Even though the building is called a hotel, there are no rooms to rent.

Discos

The **Aviary,** Northampton Lane (tel. 0792/51775), holds up to 1,000 patrons at a time and is one of the city's most popular dance emporiums. On a commercial street, it lies on a narrow lane that intersects with Kingsway, a main thoroughfare. Its street level is devoted to a beer cellar called **The Office,** which is lined with Roman-style columns, curtains, and mirrors. One flight above street level is The Aviary, which is actually two discos. The larger one is filled with pop music, catering to an under-25 crowd. The smaller one attracts the over-25 audience, offering a few more "oldies" and it's less frenetic. Clients are free to move from one to the other. Entrance, depending on the time of night, ranges from £1 ($1.60) to £3 ($4.80). The Aviary is open every Tuesday, Thursday, Friday, and Saturday night from 9 to 2 a.m. The Office, however, is open seven nights a week from 7 to 11 p.m.

Secrets Disco, Mermaid Hotel, 688 Mumbles Rd., Southend (tel. 0792/360253), has a modern decor with flashing lights and a dance floor. The cover charge is applied only after 11 p.m., costing £2 ($3.20). Once inside, a pint of lager goes for £1 ($1.60). It is open every Thursday, Friday, and Saturday from 9 p.m. to 2 a.m. and on Sunday from 8 to 10:30 p.m.

SIGHTS IN THE VALE OF NEATH: The town of Neath, birthplace of film star Ray Milland, grew up at a point where the River Neath widens into an estuary emptying into Swansea Bay, between Port Talbot on the south and Swansea. The river is joined a few miles to the northeast by the River Dulais. The town was originally centered around—

Neath Abbey

Founded in 1130, Neath Abbey became a Cistercian monastery in 1147. Built on a rocky terrace overlooking the river marshes, before the dissolution it was considered to be the "fairest building in all Wales." It suffered by becoming the site of an important ironworks, and part of the site was turned into a foundry, the ashes being dumped in the cloisters. The south range of the monastery is gone forever, but a fine vaulted undercroft to the dormer remains complete. Most of the industrial additions have been removed so that the west range can be seen. The abbey is open Monday to Saturday in summer from 9:30 a.m. to 4:30 p.m., on Sunday from 2 to 6:30 p.m. From October 15 to March 14 it's open Monday to Saturday from 9:30 a.m. to 4 p.m., on Sunday from 2 to 4 p.m. For more information, telephone 0629/812387.

Neath had long been thought to be the site of the Roman fort, Nidum. This was proved in 1949, when excavations for a new housing development revealed the fort ruins. The site is unfortunately mostly underground. Neath Castle, a Norman fortress, was also here, and substantial ruins remain.

Aberdulais Falls and Canal Basin

Aberdulais Falls, near where the River Dulais joins the River Neath, is not only a place of beauty, with its waters cascading down, ivy-clad ruins, and tall trees, it is also historically significant. Roman galleys are believed to have brought reinforcements and supplies up the River Neath to their fort called Nidum. In Norman times the White Monks (later Cistercians) came by boat to Neath Abbey. Of more recent importance was a trip made in 1584, when a ship came from Cornwall and anchored at Aberdulais Bend. It brought Ulrich Frosse, a great German copper smelter, and a cargo of copper ore, signaling the start of the South Wales heavy-metal industry.

The meeting point for the Neath and Tennant Canals at the graceful Skew Bridge (Pont Gam) is the Aberdulais basin, which has been undergoing reclamation. The basin now provides a training ground for canoeists and model-boat owners. The Tonna workshops, an old barge building and maintenance depot between the Neath Canal and the River Neath, are presently being restored. For more information, telephone 0639/50741.

The falls and early copperworks site may be visited from April 1 to October 31 Monday to Friday from 9 a.m. to 5 p.m. and daily from November 1 to March 31 from 10 a.m. to 4 p.m. except Christmas day. The charge is £1 ($1.60) for adults, 50p (80¢) for children.

Penscynor Wildlife Park

At Cilfrew (tel. 0639/2189) off the A465 three miles north of Neath, the Penscynor Wildlife Park has hundreds of animals and birds from all over the world, many living free. The park is open daily from 10 a.m. to 6 p.m., charging £2 ($3.20) for adults and £1 ($1.60) for children.

Cefn Coed Colliery Museum

Near Crynant, five miles north of Neath on the A4109, the museum, Blaenant Colliery (tel. 0639/750556), tells the story of coal mining in the Dulais Valley. A steam winding engine, now electrically driven, an underground simulating the mining gallery, and a collection of mining tools and equipment are the highlights of this museum, housed in the original buildings of the former Cefn Coed Colliery. The museum has a souvenir shop, refreshments, nearby forest walks, and picnic sites. It is open from 11 a.m. to 6 p.m. April to October. Admission is 75p ($1.20) for adults, 50p (80¢) for children.

A few miles east of the Vale of Neath, you can visit the—

Welsh Miners Museum

In **Afan Argoed Country Park,** a portrayal of mining through the eyes of the miner is detailed in the Welsh Miners Museum (tel. 0639/850654), on the A4107 near Cymmer. Leave the M4 at junction 41. The story of hardship and struggle doing this dangerous work and the social life of mining valley communities are dramatically brought to life in the museum. It's open daily April to October from 10:30 a.m. to 6 p.m.; November to March, on Saturday and Sunday only from noon to 5 p.m. Admission is 30p (48¢) for adults, 15p (24¢) for children. The Afan Argoed park may be entered free. Stage and screen star Richard Burton was born at Pont-rhydyfen, just along the road.

OLD CARMARTHENSHIRE

Carmarthenshire, now the Carmarthen District of the County of Dyfed, was once the largest county in Wales, a gentle land with green valleys and a smooth coastline along Carmarthen Bay. It is not a heavily populated area, but it has been of importance in Welsh history for a long time and was inhabited far back in the mists of time. Remains of hill-forts of the early Celts, burial mounds, cromlechs, and other traces of prehistoric people abound, as well as of Roman, Norman, and English invaders of later eras. The Welsh people of the district are bilingual, many with Welsh as their first language and English second. You may be surprised to learn that many do not consider Dylan Thomas, who lived and is buried at Laugharne on the Carmarthen Bay coast, as a Welsh poet, because he wrote his verse in English.

2. Llandeilo

Like Abergavenny on the east, the tiny market town of Llandeilo, on the River Towy (Twyi), lies on the very border of the Brecon Beacons National Park, this time on the western edge. North of Swansea on the A483, about 15 miles from Carmarthen, this is a good base from which to go into the park to visit Carreg Cennan Castle and to make scenic drives among the peaks of Black Mountain and the farm country below. The chief market town of the middle Vale of Towy, Llandeilo sits in castle country.

An outstanding feature of Llandeilo is the 365-foot, graceful arched stone bridge over the river the town surveys. The town has steep streets with old houses perched above the Towy. Much of the conversation you overhear will be in the lilting Welsh tongue, but the people will switch to English when they see you're a visitor.

FOOD AND LODGING: On the main street of town, the **Cawdor Arms Hotel,** Rhosmaen Street (tel. 0558/823500), has a cream facade with two black columns flanking the entrance looking like something you might find at Knossos in Crete. This was built as a coaching inn, one of the most famous in the region, for the route between London and Fishguard in the 18th century. Inside is the most elegant dining room in town, done in gray and white with gray Welsh flannel covering the walls and Louis XIV–style armchairs. You might want a drink before dinner in the spacious pub where dozens of brown Chesterfield sofas allow guests to relax in comfort in the high-ceilinged room. The upper halls are lined with 18th-century portraits in oil of English aristocrats. Some of the rooms have been named for earlier occupants. You might find yourself in Aunt Maud's Room or Howard's Room (that's Howard Hughes, who stayed here after a forced landing on a transatlantic flight). The price of a single accommodation, including a full English breakfast and VAT, is from £38 ($60.80). Double- or twin-bedded rooms cost from £52 ($83.20). The Cawdor Arms is undeniably elegant and well worth the splurge.

The **White Hart Inn** (tel. 0558/823419), stands in an isolated position half a mile west of Llandeilo, east of Carmarthen on the Carmarthen road. Known for its good food, it is run by an English couple, Fred (from Jersey) and Mary (from Durham) Jehan, who devote as much time to their paneled pub as they do to the contemporary dining room they added onto the back of the 80-year-old farmhouse. There, in what they have named the Raven Room, near a stone fireplace under a high beamed ceiling, they serve full meals which cost from £11 ($17.60) à la carte. Sunday lunch, a popular event in Wales, offers three different table d'hôte menus for £8 ($12.80) per person. Bar meals are available for about £2.50 ($4) and up. The dining room serves such specialties as venison in red wine sauce, ham steak with pineapple, beef Stroganoff, chicken Kiev, shellfish platters, and steaks. Meals are served daily from noon to 2 p.m. and 6:30 to 9:45 p.m. None of the trio of bedrooms contains a private bath. Singles cost from £13 ($20.80), while doubles go for £21 ($33.60), all with a full breakfast included.

Bryn-y-Wawr, Pen-y-Banc (tel. 0558/822419), is a mile from Llandeilo. Turn at the White Hart Inn on the Carmarthen road at the western side of Llandeilo and follow the signs. The guesthouse rents four bedrooms for £10 ($16) per person for B&B. The house is in a rural setting, and you can watch sheep grazing in the meadow. The family operating the house is friendly and willing to help you find points of interest in the vicinity.

The Cobblers, 3 Church St. (tel. 0269/850540), lies in Llandybie, five miles from Llandeilo. This much-awarded "Taste of Wales" restaurant is the creative statement of Mrs. Margaret Rees, who established it on the upper level of a house where five generations of her ancestors made shoes. You enter a pinesheathed anteroom lined with blue willow porcelain, antique shoes, and old shoemaker's accessories. While having a drink in the street-level bar, you'll be handed one of the most unusual menus in Wales. A few of the regionally inspired dishes include mackerel jellied in elderflower champagne (probably the most pleasantly perfumed drink in Wales, which you can also order separately just to drink), veal with rhubarb, elderflower, and ginger sauce, or else sewin, a Welsh version of sea trout served en papillotte with a gooseberry sauce. Mrs. Rees also prepares a famous version of Welsh salt duck which the menu warns has a "hammy, gamey flavour." Lunch is usually served near the bar, but dinner is upstairs in a pastel-pretty dining room. Dinners cost from £13 ($20.80). Lunch is noon to 1:30 p.m. Tuesday, Wednesday, Friday, and Saturday; dinner 7 to 9:30 p.m. Tuesday through Saturday. Reservations in the evening are important. The location is 15 miles northwest of Swansea.

SIGHTS IN THE ENVIRONS: Just outside the village of Trapp, about 3½ miles southeast of Llandeilo, **Castell Carreg Cennen** (tel. 0558/822291) stands on a towering crag more than 300 feet above the Vale of Cennen with a commanding view of Black Mountain. This was the site of a fortress long before the present 13th- and 14th-century structure was erected. Even in ruins the castle has a sort of timeless nobility. Despite its strong inner and outer wards, its barbican, drawbridge, and portcullis, the castle was captured and later surrendered to Edward IV during the Wars of the Roses. In 1462 it was demolished to prevent its being used as a refuge by robbers. You can follow a vaulted passage leading to a cave, mostly a long, narrow underground gallery, which leads back into the hill for about 150 feet. The castle is open all year from 10:30 a.m. to 6 p.m., charging £1 ($1.60) for adults, 50p (80¢) for children.

At the foot of the castle crag, Bruce and Margaret Llewellyn, who are in charge of the castle, raise rare, ancient breeds of longhorn and white cattle, sheep, pigs, and poultry. At their **Rare Breeds Centre,** you can also see old farm machinery. A restaurant and gift shop are here, as well as a playground for children and a picnicking area.

Some five miles west of Llandeilo toward Carmarthen, and completely outside the park, stand the ruins of **Dryslwyn Castle,** a reminder of the time of independent Welsh princes who did not bow gently to English rule. It was held by Lord Rhys, one of the most powerful of the Welsh rulers during the reign of Henry II, the first Plantagenet king of England. In the late 13th century the castle's defenses were mined, an early use of a sophisticated sapping technique. Excavations and restoration work are now under way. There's a picnic site by the river. Admission is free to what can be seen of the castle.

Also near Llandeilo, this one only a mile west, is **Dinefwr Castle,** home of the Dinefwr family, descendants of the Princes of South Wales. The perilous castle ruins are not open to the public, although restoration is planned, but you can view them from the road.

The ruins of **Talley Abbey,** built during the 12th-century monastic revival, are on the B4302 some eight miles north of Llandeilo. A substantial church tower and stones outlining the nave are about all that's left. It's a splendidly tranquil scene, however, at the head of the Talley Lakes.

3. Carmarthen

Lying on the banks of the River Towy some eight miles from the coast, Carmarthen is a historic market town and the administrative center of the County of Dyfed, which also embraces old Pembrokeshire. The town is on the junction of the A40, the A48, and the main London–Fishguard railroad, a busy place especially on market days (Wednesday and Saturday) and during the cattle-market sales (Monday, Wednesday, and Thursday). The large covered market draws crowds from the surrounding country.

In Carmarthen, you can get information and assistance at the **Wales Tourist Information Centre,** Lammas Street (tel. 0267/231557), open daily from 10 a.m. to 6 p.m., and from Colin James, **Carmarthen District Council,** Spilman Street (tel. 0267/234567).

If you develop a thirst in Carmarthen, you may find it easier to quench than in some places in Wales, at least in summer. The pubs are open all day all year long whenever it's market day—and it's market day four days a week. Some open as early as 9 a.m. In summer, by a vote of the people, the pubs are open seven days a week, although regular opening and closing hours apply—except, as noted, on market days.

Carmarthen has an 18-hole golf course just north of town, and on fine summer evenings you can sometimes watch coracle fishermen busy on the River Towy.

FOOD AND LODGING: Once a favorite retreat of Lord Nelson and Lady Hamilton, the **Ivy Bush Royal Hotel,** Spilman Street (tel. 0267/235111), has been modernized but in a manner that blends old-world charm with up-to-date facilities. The 82 bedrooms, all with private baths, have color TV, radios, phones, and baby-listening service. A single rents for £42 ($67.20), and a double goes for £52 ($83.20), something of a splurge but worth it. The bar and lounge area on the ground floor is noteworthy for the modern stained-glass window by John Petts, commemorating the formation of the first Gorsedd Circle of Bards which led to the tradition of the Eisteddfod of today. The hotel's restaurant, done in rich brown and rust, includes a number of special Welsh dishes on its menu. A table d'hôte dinner here costs £10 ($16), and an à la carte meal runs from £12 ($19.20). Across the courtyard, also on Spilman Street, is **B.J.s,** where steak, scampi, and pizzas are served in a bistro format at dinner only from 5:30 to 10:30 p.m. daily except Sunday and Monday. Saturday lunch is also served from 12:30 to 2:30 p.m. Ample parking space and lock-up garages are available at the hotel.

If the Ivy Bush Royal is too expensive for the budget purse, try the **Old Priory Guest House,** Priory Street (tel. 0267/237471), a family-run establishment with 16 bedrooms. The house has central heating, and all the rooms have hot and cold running water and shaving outlets. You can enjoy TV with your fellow guests in the lounge. The guesthouse has both a residential and a restaurant license, allowing you to have a before-dinner apéritif or after-dinner libations at the little bar. An à la carte menu is offered in the restaurant, containing some Welsh delicacies. B&B costs from £17.50 ($28) to £20 ($32) per night per person.

The finest restaurant in town is **Hoi San,** 15 Queen St. (tel. 0267/231100), considered the best Chinese restaurant this far west in Britain. In the heart of Carmarthen, David Nam opened this elegantly decorated Oriental establishment and brought new standards of food and service to sleepy Carmarthen. The choice on the Cantonese menu is long and appealing. The fish specialties tend to be outstanding, but nearly every item, from chicken to beef, is good. A set luncheon costs £3.75 ($6), a table d'hôte dinner going for £8 ($12.80). Hours are from noon to 2:30 p.m. and 7 to 10:30 p.m.

STAYING IN THE ENVIRONS: At Cothi Bridge, a short drive east from Carmarthen on the A40, is the **Cothi Bridge Hotel,** Pontargothi (tel. 026788/251). This 17-room hotel has white walls and many-paned windows that look out over the River Cothi. If you want a room, someone will come out from the pub to assist you. For B&B, the price of a bathless single is £26 ($41.60), while a single with bath goes for £30 ($48). Doubles rent for £31 ($49.60) to £36 ($57.60), depending on the plumbing. The real spirit of this establishment is in the cozy Victorian pub and adjacent dining room. There you can enjoy food from noon to 2:30 p.m. and 6 to 10:30 p.m., costing from £12 ($19.20). Specialties include steaks with several different kinds of sauces, fresh salmon, fresh sewin (a local sea trout), and chicken chasseur.

A little farther along on the A40 is the **Cresselly Arms,** Pontargothi, Nantgaredig (tel. 026788/221), a licensed pub and restaurant. In a half-timbered house set close to the road, this 16th-century building on the banks of the River Cothi has stone interior walls, timbers, and a plank bar. Duck as you go through the low-linteled entrance. There's a rumor that the old building has a resident Cavalier's ghost. The pub and restaurant are open daily from 11 a.m. to 11 p.m. Bar foods include chicken Kiev with french fries, local salmon, and sewin (a sea trout). Fixed-price meals in the restaurant, costing from £6 ($9.60), include such dishes as roast lamb with rosemary and an array of steak choices.

SIGHTS AND ACTIVITIES: Built by Walter of Gloucester in 1109, **Carmarthen Castle** had a turbulent history as the center of the royal English administration of southwest Wales. Most of the medieval castle was demolished in 1789 when the county jail (gaol) was built, and the site is now occupied by offices of the Dyfed County Council. Of the surviving remains, you can see a keep, a gatehouse, and two towers.

The castle was built on the site of a Roman outpost, Maridunum, later one of only two Roman towns in Wales, and on the eastern approach to Carmarthen is an excavated Roman amphitheater. If you'd like to find out more about, or visit, excavations in Dyfed, go to the **Dyfed Archaeological Trust,** the Old Palace, Abergwili (tel. 0267/231667), where they keep a comprehensive record of more than 22,000 sites and monuments in Dyfed. The trust carries out archeological excavations and surveys throughout the county. Visitors to excavations are welcome, and sometimes temporary site museums are maintained. The trust is open Monday to Friday from 10 a.m. to 4 p.m., and there is no charge to go in and look at records.

Abergwili is a village just outside Carmarthen on the A40. Here you can also climb **Merlin's Hill,** where the old magician and tutor to King Arthur is supposed to be locked away forever in an enchanted sleep. (Carmarthen's Welsh name, Caerfyrddin, means Merlin's city. The town's most famous landmark, Merlin's Oak, stood for a long time on the eastern outskirts, allegedly bearing Merlin's curse: "When this oak shall tumble down, then will fall Carmarthen town." To be sure this couldn't happen, the stump was first set in concrete on Priory Street, but later moved to the Civic Hall where it stands today.)

The **Carmarthen Museum,** Abergwili (tel. 0267/231691), is a large regional museum in the former palace of the bishop of St. David's. The building was constructed around 1287, and the original chapel is still here, although much changed. The museum displays archeology, geology, pottery, dairying history, furniture, costumes, prints, and exhibits of the military and folk history of the area. It is open Monday to Saturday from 10 a.m. to 4:30 p.m. all year. Admission is 50p (80¢) for adults, 25p (40¢) for children.

For a long time Carmarthen was actually an English-run town. There was a section inside the walls where only the English could hold markets and make the rules, called New or Norman Carmarthen, while the Welsh built their Old Carmarthen settlement among the Roman ruins. This led to strife through the centuries, but eventually the Welsh came into more prominence, and such great figures as Sir Rhys ap Thomas, to whom King Henry VII owed his throne, are buried in **St. Peter's Church.** Also in the church is a memorial to Sir Richard Steele, English essayist and journalist, who married a wealthy Carmarthen widow and retired here.

A row of 18th-century houses near St. Peter's has been preserved, although much of historic Carmarthen was torn down in the last couple of centuries to make way for new buildings. The 18th-century architect John Nash lived here, and his house is now the home of the caretaker of Pentrepoeth School.

KIDWELLY AND LLANSTEFFAN: Testimony to the Normans' penchant for building castles overlooking estuaries and the sea on promontories which were not too difficult to defend from the landward side are two, Kidwelly and Llansteffan (sometimes spelled Llanstephan), near Cardigan Bay.

Kidwelly

This little medieval town, almost due south of Carmarthen on the A484, built at the confluence of the two branches of the River Gwendraeth, has an ancient church dedicated to St. Mary the Virgin, a 14th-century bridge over the river, and **Kidwelly Castle,** built at the tidal limit of the river. A motte and bailey around 1106 preceded the stone castle built around 1275 and improved over the next 150 years. The remains are well preserved, among the finest in Wales, and may be visited at all reasonable times. Admission is 75p ($1.20) for grownups, 35p (56¢) for children.

Also of interest here is the **Kidwelly Industrial Museum** (tel. 0554/891078), with the country's sole surviving pack mill where tinplate was made by hand. Original machinery and buildings include the 160-foot chimney, the steam winding engine and headgear from Morlais Colliery, and the locomotive used in the film *Young Winston.* The museum is open Easter to the end of September from 10 a.m. to 5 p.m. Monday to Saturday, from 2 to 5 p.m. on Sunday and weekends only the remainder of the year. Admission is 75p ($1.20) for adults, 35p (56¢) for children.

Llansteffan

This little village across the estuary of the River Towy from Kidwelly offers a fine beach, boating possibilities, and a well-preserved castle ruin: **Llansteffan Castle,** on a headland overlooking the estuary. It was built, probably in the 12th century, as a small and unimportant fortress, but it gained greatness during the time of the English conquest of Wales in the 13th century. The Great Gatehouse, constructed in 1280, became the castle's main living quarters. You can see the chute above the gatehouse entrance through which boiling oil was poured on attackers. During the 15th century the castle became a residence, and then for almost 400 years it was merely part of a farm. It is open to visitors at no admission charge.

4. Laugharne

Near the little town of St. Clears southwest of Carmarthen on the A40, follow signs to the southeast on the A4066 road to Laugharne, a hamlet looking out over broad waters. The ancient township of Laugharne on the estuary fed by the River Taf (not to be confused with the River Taff in Cardiff) and the River Cywyn was for centuries a bone of contention between Welsh, English, Cromwellians, and royal supporters. However, it did not come into the limelight of public attention until after the death of its adopted son, Swansea-born Dylan Thomas, and his acclaim as one of the greatest poets of this century.

FOOD AND LODGING: A good place to stay is **Hurst House,** East Marsh (tel. 099421/235), about two miles from Laugharne, a beautiful Georgian house near the marsh looking out to the estuary and the sea. This 18th-century Welsh farmhouse, owned by Mrs. Georgina Bradley-Watson, has comfortable and well-furnished bedrooms, one with a private bath. The charge for B&B is £9 ($14.40) per person. The accommodations have TV and hot-beverage facilities. There's a large garden where guests can play croquet. Badminton and table tennis are also offered. To find Hurst House, go west from Laugharne past Broadway on the A4066, turning left toward the quarry two miles out of Laugharne and then to the left again to Hurst House.

Several pubs in Laugharne were familiar hangouts of Dylan Thomas in his moments of relaxation. In particular, the one at **Brown's Hotel,** King Street (tel. 099421/320), is no longer operated as a hotel, but it's a good place to stop in for a drink or a pub lunch if you're hungry. Tom and Marisa Watts offer sandwiches, soup, or other snacks for about £1.50 ($2.40) to £3 ($4.80), along with your beer. Hours are 11:30 a.m. to 3:30 p.m. and 5:30 to 10:30 p.m. (to 11 p.m. Friday and Saturday). Sunday hours are noon to 2 p.m. and 7 to 10:30 p.m.

SIGHTS: Thomas landmarks include the **Dylan Thomas Boathouse,** along a little path which has been named Dylan's Walk, a waterside house where he lived with his wife, Caitlin, and their children until his death in 1953 in America on a visit there. In the boathouse, a white-painted little three-story structure wedged between the hill and the estuary, you can see the rooms in which the family lived, with family photographs, interpretive panels on his life and works, an audio and audio-visual presentation which includes his own reading of some of his works, a small art gallery, a book and record shop, and a little tea room where you can have tea and Welsh cakes while you listen to the poet's voice and look out over the tranquil waters of the wide estuary.

On the way along the path, before you come to the boathouse, there's a little shack where Thomas worked. You can't enter it, but you can look through an opening and see his built-in plank desk. Wadded-up scraps of paper on the floor give the feeling that he may have just stepped out to go into the village to visit a favorite pub or two. The boathouse is open April to the end of October from 10 a.m. to 5:30 p.m. (last entrance). Admission is 85p ($1.36) for adults, 45p (72¢) for children. For more information, in season telephone 099421/420; out of season, phone 0267/234567) in Carmarthen.

The poet is buried in the churchyard near the **Parish Church of St. Martin,** which you pass as you drive into the town. A simple wooden cross marks his grave. A visit to the church is worthwhile. It dates from the 14th century and is entered through a lych-gate, with the entrance to the church guarded by ancient yew trees. Memorial stones and carvings are among the interesting things to see.

Laugharne Castle, called the home of the Last Prince of Wales, sits on the estuary at the edge of the town. It is a handsome ruin, presently undergoing some restoration and preservation work. A castle here, Aber Corran, was first mentioned in 1113, believed to have been built by the great Welsh leader Rhys ap Gruffydd. The present romantic ruins date from Tudor times. Dylan Thomas described the then ivy-mantled castle as a "castle brown as owls." You can only view it from outside.

THE SOUTH PEMBROKESHIRE COAST

Known as "Little England Beyond Wales," South Pembrokeshire is a popular holiday area in the southwest corner of the country. It stretches from Amroth in the east to Angle in the west. Charming coastal villages and resorts join historic Pembroke to give visitors much of interest and enjoyment.

The **Pembrokeshire Coast National Park,** smallest of the national parks of Great Britain—225 square miles—is considered outstanding for its coastal scenery. As I explained in the introduction earlier to the Brecon Beacons, national parks in the British Isles are not owned by the nation, most of the land being private property, nor are they parks as in the case of Yellowstone and others in the United States. In Britain the designation means that an area of national importance in the quality of its environment will be protected for this and future generations.

The Pembrokeshire Coast park is the only one that is predominantly coastal. No place within the park boundaries is more than ten miles from the sea, and most of it lies within three miles of salt water. In this section I will introduce you to the southern portion of the park and its environs, the remainder to be visited in the next section of this guide.

The mainly English character of the southern half of what was once the separate county of Pembrokeshire, now a part of Dyfed, and the purely Welsh of the northern area are interesting contrasts. If you're energetic and have time, you can walk the Pembrokeshire Coast Path from Amroth all the way to near Cardigan in the north, meeting people and learning about the beautiful coast park.

For information about the entire park, get in touch with the **National Park Information Centre,** 40 High St., Haverfordwest (tel. 0437/66141).

5. Saundersfoot and Tenby

The coastal area on the west side of Carmarthen Bay is blessed with wide sand beaches protected from Atlantic gales by the Pembroke peninsula. From here, the entire coastline all the way to near Cardigan is part of Pembrokeshire Coast National Park. Between Saundersfoot and Tenby, there are quiet bays accessible only on foot.

SAUNDERSFOOT: Since World War II Saundersfoot, once a coal export center, has become totally a holiday town.

Food and Lodging

A splurge choice, **St. Bride's Hotel** (tel. 0834/812304), with a commanding view of Carmarthen Bay and Saundersfoot harbor and beach, was a Tudor farmhouse before being converted by Ian Bell, the affable owner, into one of the most luxurious hotels in the resort. He says he "paid a fortune" for the diamond-shaped leaded windows needed to be sure the entire hotel was in harmony with the original part. There's a small swimming pool on a terrace overlooking the yacht harbor and a popular bathing beach. Each of the 49 bedrooms has a private bath or shower and toilet, color TV, radio, phone, and tea/coffee-making facilities, and many have hair dryers. Rooms in the Harbour Wing rent for £26 ($41.60) per person, those in the Ashley Wing for £28.50 ($45.60) per person for B&B. Half board costs £34 ($54.40) per person in the Harbour Wing, £36.50 ($58.40) per person in the Ashley. VAT is included in the rates.

Food is excellent in the Commodore Restaurant, which has sea views. A four-course table d'hôte meal costs £11 ($17.60) and might include fish straight from the harbor, lobster thermidor, fresh crabs, and flambéed specialties. Hours are 12:30 to 1:30 p.m. and 7:30 to 9:30 p.m. However, you can enjoy inexpensive lunches in the Salad Bowl, costing from £4 ($6.40) and served from noon to 2 p.m. The elegant Kaptain Kat's Drinks Salon, named for a character in *Under Milk Wood,* one of the best known works of Dylan Thomas, written in nearby Laugharne, is both a lounge and a cocktail bar where you can enjoy a drink in comfort.

The **Glen Beach Hotel,** Swallow Tree Woods (tel. 0834/813430), nestles in a wooded area off the A4316 Saundersfoot–Tenby road, about 600 yards from the beach. Tony and Audrey Mullen welcome guests to their 13 bedrooms (four for families). All accommodations contain toilets and showers, TV, radio/intercoms, hair dryers, hot-beverage facilities, and central heating. The charge is £25 ($40) per person for B&B, a little high for the budget but not unreasonable considering the amenities and the heavy demand for places to stay in this area. The hotel has a well-maintained garden and patio, an intimate lounge, and a cabaret room where resident artists entertain in July and August. British and continental dishes such as beef Stroganoff are served in the "olde world" dining room, with dinners, costing £9.50 ($15.20), being served from 7 to 9 p.m. Bar snacks are available from noon to 2 p.m. and 7 to 9 p.m., costing from £4 ($6.40). Car parking is provided.

TENBY: This is the leading resort in Pembrokeshire, packed with holiday-makers during the summer months, but it has a charm and character dating from medieval times, which makes it an interesting place to visit at any time of year.

Food and Lodging

The **Imperial Hotel,** The Paragon (tel. 0834/3737), is built into Tenby's town walls, entered from a point a few steps from one of the medieval stone arches. There is a large turret on one side in which several of the bedrooms have circular bathrooms, and one room even has access to the old battlements. All of the hotel's 46 units have private bath/shower, color TV, radio, and direct-dial phone. Many have a sea view. An automatic elevator serves all six floors. Charges for B&B range from £30 ($48) to £34 ($54.40) per person, depending on the room and its amenities. Half board can also be arranged. The back of the hotel has sweeping views of the beaches and Carmarthen Bay, with a terrace where you can enjoy the sun right beside the castle tower on the headland. There are two restaurants, the Caldey Suite, where dinner dances are held on most Friday and Saturday nights all year, and the Cliffhanger. On the ground floor, PJ's lounge bar also serves morning coffee, bar food at lunch and dinner, and afternoon teas. It's open all year from 10 a.m. to 11 p.m. for food, and the bar is open for drinks during normal licensing hours. The floodlit patio is a fine place to enjoy an evening drink and watch the setting sun on a summer day.

Fourcroft, Croft Terrace (tel. 0834/2886), has long been a favorite. Behind a deceivingly simple facade on a lovely Georgian terrace, Mary and Peter Osborne for more than two decades have welcomed guests to their seafront property. Lying about a five-minute walk from the heart of the resort, the Fourcroft rents out 38 well-furnished and well-maintained bedrooms. Single tariffs begin at £20 ($32), climbing to £24 ($38.40), with doubles or twins priced from £35 ($56) to £43 ($68.80), with breakfast included. This 150-year-old property overlooks the resort's North Beach, with views of the harbor and Carmarthen Bay. Guests have a private garden walk leading to the beach, and there is also a heated outdoor swimming pool. The food is good and freshly prepared using well-chosen ingredients. Both British and continental specialties are offered. Bar lunches are featured at noon, with dinner costing from £10 ($16). Try the honey-glazed lamb, Pembroke turkey, or trout or salmon from local waters.

At **Heywood Mount,** Heywood Lane (tel. 0843/2087), a mother-daughter team, Mrs. Walter and Mrs. Andrews, welcomes guests to their establishment, which is set in tranquil grounds within easy walking distance of the beaches and the town. They have a TV lounge for residents, a bar lounge, and central heating. Tariffs run from £12 ($19.20) to £16 ($25.60) per person per night for B&B.

Also on Heywood Lane is **Heywood Lodge** (tel. 0834/2684), a peaceful country house in its own large grounds, within walking distance of the town. Built 150 years ago as a gentleman's residence of distinction, it has a sun patio leading down to lawns shaded by ancient beech trees. The lodge has a residential license to serve alcoholic beverages, and good food is offered in the restaurant, with the chef willingly catering to special dietary requirements. The charge for B&B is from £12.50 ($20) to £14 ($22.40) per person. Some of the 14 bedrooms have private baths.

Even if you're only passing through Tenby or here for the day, I recommend the **Plantagenet House,** Tudor Square, Quay Hill (tel. 0834/2350), as a good place to eat. The 15th-century house, with a Flemish chimney, is worth seeing, and food is served in the Quay Room in what were the cellars of the old building, rich in stonework and ancient beams. In fact, the restaurant occupies one of the two oldest buildings in Tenby. The street-level entrance has elmwood beams, a pair of antique French wood-burning stoves, and church paneling. There is also an exposed charcoal grill where everybody from Jimmy Carter to holiday-makers from London have enjoyed meals. Tina and Barney Stone, who run the place, specialize in vegetarian dishes. Whole-meal pizza is a favorite, and you can enjoy good, crisp salads. In season, fresh salmon, plaice, sole, and "dressed" crab are available. The chef makes a good chili, and you can also order hamburgers and open-face sandwiches in the Danish style. Meals, costing from £6 ($9.60), are served from 11 a.m. to 10:30 p.m. (last orders) Easter to November.

Penally Abbey Hotel, Penally, near Tenby (tel. 0834/3033). The vagueness of its known history and the unusual nature of the ruins surrounding it make it one of the most mysterious hotels in the region. Steve and Elleen Warren, a duet of urban refugees from London, have worked hard to create a gracious, timeless world. The house is around 200 years old, but parts of the foundation might date from the time a monastery was established here in the 6th century. Today, the flowering garden partially conceals the ruins of St. Deniol's chapel and a Flemish chimney of a long-ago homestead. The wide open sea and the still-functioning Cistercian monastery on Caldey Island contribute to the panorama of the terraces.

The house, built of Pembrokeshire stone, contains ogee-headed doors, large square windows, Gothic-inspired detailings, and 14 comfortable bedrooms. Each has a private bath and TV set. Per person rates, single or double occupancy with breakfast included, range from £17 ($27.20) to £30 ($48) depending on the accommodation. Dinner, open to nonresidents, is offered after 7:30 p.m. and is priced at only £8 ($12.80). Elleen Warren is the skilled chef, producing such delicacies as local salmon with Pernod, cream, and chervil, lobster thermidor, and duck with port and oranges or with brandy and apricots. The hotel is open all year.

Sights

There was already a Welsh village here when the Normans moved in. **Tenby Castle,** now in ruins, attracts interest because of its situation on the headland overlooking the town and harbor. The town walls had four gates, one of which, the West Gate, known as Five Arches, remains. The west wall is in good condition. Tenby was also a target in the Civil War.

Tenby Museum and Art Gallery, Castle Hill (tel. 0834/2809), is housed within the remains of the castle. Exhibits cover the geology, archeology, and natural history of the district, as well as the history of Tenby from the 12th century. In the art gallery you'll see works by Augustus and Gwen John and Charles Norris, a local artist of the early 19th century. The museum is open daily from 10 a.m. to 6 p.m. Easter to the end of October. In winter, it opens only in the afternoon. Admission is 50p (80¢) for adults, 10p (16¢) for children.

The **Tudor Merchant's House,** Quay Hill (tel. 0834/2279), is a beautifully furnished medieval dwelling house of the 15th century with a fine Flemish chimney. On three interior walls, paintings with designs similar to Flemish weaving patterns were discovered under years of whitewash. The house is open from Easter Sunday to the end of September, Monday to Friday from 10 a.m. to 1 p.m. and 2:30 to 6 p.m., 2 to 6 p.m. on Sunday. Admission is £1 ($1.60) for adults, 50p (80¢) for children.

Tenby's parish church, **St. Mary's,** dates from the 13th century and is the largest old parish church in Wales. Giraldus Cambrensis (Gerald the Welshman), a great religious leader of the 13th century, was the first rector.

Caldy Island

Lying in the bay just two miles south of Tenby is this little island which has long been a Roman Catholic venue. A Celtic monastic cell is believed to have been here, and today it is farmed by Cistercian monks, whose abbey is the island's outstanding attraction. From the 12th century until the dissolution of the monasteries by Henry VIII, a Benedictine priory was here. For the next few centuries, lay people living on the island farmed and quarried limestone until, in 1906, English Benedictines established a community here.

The Benedictines left solid evidence of their occupation: the refectory, gatehouse, and the prior's lodging which is now used as a guesthouse. In 1929 the Cistercian Order took over the island, and today they produce perfume, chocolate, and dairy products, all sold locally. Only male visitors are allowed to enter the monastery, but anyone can visit St. David's Church, the Old Priory, and St. Illtud's Church, with a leaning stone spire. Inside St. Illtud's is a 6th-century Ogham stone, a relic of the time when monks from Ireland came here to establish their religious house. The writing on the Ogham stones was Celtic which was then translated into Latin by the monks.

It's about a 20-minute trip from Tenby to the island, and boats run regularly to and fro during the summer.

For information, get in touch with the **Tourist Information Centre,** Guildhall, The Norton (tel. 0834/2402).

For Entertainment

Daytime is for water activities and walks, but after dark you may enjoy going to the **De Valence Pavilion** in Tenby, which has a full summer program.

There are often male-voice choirs giving concerts in St. Mary's Church. Open-air concerts are frequently presented on Castle Hill.

6. Manorbier, Carew, and Lamphey

An active area in the early Middle Ages both for religious and political purposes, the fertile acreage of the Pembroke peninsula saw agricultural development under the aegis of various bishops who had their minions plant the land with grain and fruit trees, with little settlements growing up to support the nobility, clergy, and their entourages.

MANORBIER: This small village grew up in medieval times around Manorbier Castle, a well-preserved fortress that evolved from construction of simple earthworks, which were changed into a stone castle in the 12th century and extended in the 13th. It is famous for its link with Giraldus Cambrensis, who was born here in about 1146. "Gerald the Welshman" called Manorbier "the most delightful part of Pembroch . . . the pleasantest spot in Wales" in his work *Itinerary through Wales,* describing his observations on a recruiting campaign in Wales for the Third Crusade. The baronial hall of the castle and the state apartments reveal its former grandeur. The castle, open from 10:30 a.m. to 5 p.m. daily during Easter week and mid-May to the end of September, can be visited for £1 ($1.60) for adults, 30p (48¢) for children.

Food and Lodging

Castle Mead (tel. 083482/358) is the best place to stay, receiving guests from Easter to October. This was built as a "gentleman's residence" some 250 years ago, but it isn't architecturally distinguished. Its owners, Lorna and Geof

Greasley, rent out 12 comfortably furnished bedrooms, charging £20 ($32) per person for B&B, either single or double occupancy. Three of the accommodations are in an annex. A set evening meal, costing £8.50 ($13.60), is served nightly between 7 and 8.

On the outskirts, you can enjoy food, drink, or else seek lodgings at **Tudor Lodge** (tel. 083482/320) at Jameston, two miles west of Manorbier along A4139, lying between Pembroke and Tenby. A family-run, 10-room hotel, the lodge traces its history back some four centuries. You can't miss the giant weeping ash in the front garden as you approach. In a way, it sets this tranquil scene. The interior of the building is stone, and the proprietors have added many thoughtful atmospheric touches, as represented by their medley of "retired" teapots now resting from their brewing duties as they hang from a beamed ceiling. Rooms are comfortably but not lavishly furnished, renting for about £15 ($24) per person for B&B any time except in January and February.

The lodge is also the best food stopover in the area. From noon to 2 p.m., typical and rather simple bar lunches are offered for £4 ($6.40). Dinner from 6:30 to 10 p.m. is more elaborate, costing £8.50 ($13.60) and including grilled lamb chops and other British dishes.

CAREW: About three miles east of Pembroke on the A4075, **Carew Castle** is a handsome ruin in a splendid setting on the banks of the River Carew. It stands on a low limestone outcrop with meadows on either side. The castle was founded in the early part of the 12th century and reconstructed and refortified in the 13th century. It was extensively damaged in the Civil War. The ample cellars remain, as well as massive towers and wall buttresses. Through its life it came to take on more of the accoutrements of a fortified manor house than of a military fortification.

You can also see the **Carew French Mill** on the dam of the millpond, first mentioned in records of 1541. This is the only tidal mill remaining intact in Wales. The building today is from the early 19th century, restored and with its original machinery.

The castle and mill are open daily from Easter to the end of October. A joint ticket, admitting visitors to both castle and mill, costs £1.50 ($2.40) for adults, 75p ($1.20) for children. A single ticket to either attraction costs £1 ($1.60) for adults, 50p (80¢) for children.

Carew Cross, a royal memorial stands beside the gates of Carew Castle. One of the largest and most ornate of the medieval Welsh crosses, it is inscribed to Maredudd, who was fifth in descent from Hywell Dda, the Welsh lawgiver. Maredudd was killed in 1035.

Carew Cheriton Church, dating from the late 14th century, contains tombs and effigies of the Carew family. There is a detached mortuary chapel in the churchyard.

LAMPHEY: This ancient village, 2½ miles east of Pembroke, and the fertile lands around it were described in the medieval estate survey called *The Black Book of St. David's.* It was one of the manors of the bishop of St. David's, an example of how medieval bishops combined the life of a churchman with that of a country gentleman. The **Lamphey Bishop's Palace,** much of it the work of Bishop Gower in the 14th century, has lofty battlemented parapets carried on arcades rising above the roofs. The manor at Lamphey was only one of those belonging to the bishops of St. David's, scattered over southwest Wales. The palace is open to visitors from 9:30 a.m. to 6:30 p.m., from 2 to 6:30 p.m. on Sunday in summer, closing at 4 p.m. in winter. Admission is 50p (80¢) for adults, 25p (40¢) for children.

Where to Stay

If you'd like to spend the night in Lamphey, the **Lamphey Hall Hotel** (tel. 0646/672394) might be your choice, standing near the austere tower of a stone church. In fact, the house sheltering the hotel was built in the early 19th century as a vicarage for this church. Beside the road in a pub/hotel format, the establishment has a small garden in front and a more extensive lawn in back for the use of guests. David and Sue Phillips rent ten comfortable rooms, all with bath facilities, color TV, and tea/coffee-making equipment. The charge in a single is £18 ($28.80) for B&B, and a double goes for £30 ($48). Reductions are granted if you stay more than one night. A wide range of bar snacks is offered, or you can take meals in the restaurant overlooking the back garden. The hotel is not to be confused with the Lamphey Court Hotel (sometimes called just The Court Hotel), which is a much more expensive stopover.

7. Pembroke

The ancient borough of Pembroke received its charter about 1090 from King Henry I and was built up around Pembroke Castle, a great fortress set on a rocky spur above the town, all of which were elements of the castle and the defenses. The town walls formed the castle's outer ward, and the entire complex, a 14-mile-wide medieval defense system, can still be viewed as a fortified town, with the castle as its hub.

Pembroke never was really a Welsh town, so strong a hold did the Normans and then the English have. It was settled by English and Flemish, and was the heart of what the English called "Little England Beyond Wales," mentioned earlier. Even though people of Welsh origin are no longer unwelcome here, the first (and often the only) language of the people of Pembroke is English.

For further information about Pembroke and its attractions, there's a **National Park Information Centre**, Drill Hall, Main Street (tel. 0646/682148). It's open only in summer, from 9:30 a.m. to 5:30 p.m. weekdays.

FOOD AND LODGING: About a ten-minute walk from the center of Pembroke, the **Underdown Country House Hotel,** Grove Hill (tel. 0646/683350), is set in 4½ acres of gardens. It is believed that Oliver Cromwell had his headquarters at or near Underdown when he besieged Pembroke Castle. The core of the section he is believed to have occupied is today the comfortably cluttered bar, where copper and brass artifacts lie against the massive stone hearth, which is flanked by old ovens. Photos of English actors, friends of the proprietor, Jimmey Barrett, adorn the walls. The hotel has six bedrooms, each in boudoir styling with pastel colors. All have bath, color TV, and tea/coffee-making facilities. Room prices are £32.50 ($52) for B&B in a single, £42.50 ($68) in a double. Besides the full Welsh breakfast, dinner is also served in the dining room, full meals costing from £14 ($22.40) to £16 ($25.60). The cuisine is fresh cooked, with a selection of fresh vegetables. Such dishes as chicken Kiev, duckling with honey, and lamb with stilton are on the menu. The full wine cellar offers what you need to complement your meal.

If you prefer to stay in the heart of town, try the **Coach House Inn,** 116 Main St. (tel. 0646/684602). This family-run hotel has 14 bedrooms, all with private bath, color TV, radio, phone, and central heating, and there's a solarium for the use of guests, as well as a private garden. Tariffs are from £27 ($43.20) per person for B&B, a little high for the budget, but the amenities make it worthwhile. The hotel has a smart bar/lounge. The building is well maintained, painted a light cream color with green shutters.

Richmond Coffeehouse, 7 Castle Terrace (tel. 0646/685460), is one of my favorite restaurants in town, serving tea and sandwiches within the shadow of the castle. The building was once owned by Henry Tudor, who later became King Henry VII. The restaurant is named in honor of Henry's father, the Earl of Richmond. The interior is filled with carved oak chests, some quite old (one from 1722), and oak chairs. The plaster walls are thick and capped with elegant cove molding. This is a small, family-run restaurant, whose kind, matriarchal owner, Mrs. Hare, serves soups, pâtés, cakes and scones all freshly baked, fish, omelets, and salads. Meals cost from £3 ($4.80). In summer, the coffeehouse is open daily from 9 a.m. to 8 p.m., to 5 p.m. on Sunday. In winter, hours are 9 a.m. to 5 p.m. daily except Sunday.

The Pink Kitchen, Commons Road (tel. 0646/686473), is a pink-walled tea room, opposite the car park which serves the castle. It's filled with white cast-iron tables and chairs, and glass cases with naughty-but-nice pastries. Full meals are also available in this licensed restaurant, with such dishes offered as ham with beans, chicken with mushrooms, steak-and-kidney pie and local trout. Meals cost from £3 ($4.80) to £6 ($9.60). The place is open daily from 10 a.m. to 10 p.m., but if there's no business it closes at 8:30 p.m. on weekdays.

SIGHTS: With its massive walls and keep, **Pembroke Castle** (tel. 0646/681585) still looks strong, but inside little remains. All the rooms of the castle are circular, and the 12th-century keep is nearly 80 feet high. The gatehouse had three portcullises and a barbican. Pembroke Castle was the birthplace of Henry Tudor, the Welshman who became Henry VII and founded the Tudor dynasty. A vast cavern underneath the castle, called the Wogan, is where food and water was stored. The water defenses of the fortress can still be traced in a millpond on the north and marshes on the south, outside the walls, plus the River Pembroke over which it broods. The castle can be visited from 10 a.m. to 6 p.m. in summer, to 4 p.m. in winter. Admission is 90p ($1.44) for adults, 50p (80¢) for children.

At the castle end of Pembroke's long Main Street stands **St. Mary's Church** near the site of the north gate, now gone. The church dates from the 13th century and was added to in the 14th century. Much of its Norman features have been preserved.

St. Daniel's Church, on the south side of the town, has a long history. St. Daniel, a hermit monk, came in the 5th century and lived in a cell where the church now stands. He founded the first house of worship here.

You can also visit **Monkton Priory Church** in the suburb of Monkton west of town. It was founded in 1098 and was closely linked with Pembroke Castle. Eventually the church became dilapidated, but it was restored around the turn of this century and is today a fine house of worship. There are tombs and memorials of interest, but of special note is the prior's private chapel, which was restored by Freemasons and has windows depicting Masonic figures and emblems.

The **Museum of Gypsy Waggons, Romany Crafts, and Lore,** Commons Road (tel. 0646/681308), in old tannery buildings beside the town walls, presents the history of the gypsies in England from Edwardian times to the present. A collection of ornately carved living wagons, old photographs, and demonstrations of Romany crafts can be seen. Crafts articles can be purchased on the spot. The museum is open daily from 10 a.m. to 5:30 p.m. Admission is £1.50 ($2.40) for adults, 60p (96¢) for children from 5 to 16.

On Milford Haven, a huge natural harbor about a mile from Pembroke, the towns of **Pembroke Dock** and **Milford Haven** lie. They are seaport towns, neither with a long history, and Milford Haven is the home of several oil-company terminals. Pembroke Dock is the terminal for the British and Irish

Steam Packet Company which makes regular crossings to Ireland. A great deal of yachting and other boating activity takes place in the vast harbor.

THE LAND OF ST. DAVID AND PRESELI

This part of the Pembrokeshire Coast National Park and its immediate environs has had inhabitants from far back in Paleolithic and Mesolithic times, but those were the oldtimers. About 5,000 years ago New Stone Age (Neolithic) farmers arrived and made their homes here. They didn't leave many traces of their living sites, but their tombs, cromlechs, have survived. Many lie on or near St. David's Head and on Newport Bay and in the Preseli foothills. Many believe that the massive blue or foreign stones at Stonehenge came from the Preseli hills more than 4,000 years ago. Bronze Age cairns have also been found in the Preseli region.

Iron Age Celts came here, bringing with them from Gaul the beginnings of the Welsh and Gaelic languages. Near St. David's, walls built then are still in use around fields. The Romans ignored this part of Wales, and contacts with Ireland, where fellow Celts lived, were strong. Irish tribes settled in Dyfed in the 3rd and 4th centuries, and then the monastic movement in the early Christian church was brought by Irish and spread by Welsh missionaries, when a vigorous Christian community was established on the St. David's peninsula.

The coming of the Normans did not much affect this section of Wales, and Welsh is still widely spoken here. In Tudor times and later, village seafaring came in, taking the mining output of coal, silver, and lead out of small village ports. All this is changed of course, and today the coastal area has become popular holiday territory, with beaches, boating, surfing, fishing, and other leisure pursuits taking over.

8. St. David's

The tiny cathedral city of St. David's, birthplace of the patron saint of Wales, and the countryside around it are centuries away from the hurry of modern times. The designation of St. David's as a city, since it appears to be little more than a village, may puzzle Americans, but in Britain only a place that contains a cathedral is a city. Thus a huge metropolis may be actually only a town by definition. When I was a child traveling to various places in the United States with my family, my mother always told us to look ahead for "the spires and domes" of whatever town we were approaching. This would not have worked with St. David's. The cathedral lies in a grassy hollow of the River Alun, chosen by St. David for his small monastic community because the site was hidden from approach by attackers from land and from sea, yet it was conveniently only a mile from the waters of St. Bride's Bay.

Dewi Sant (later St. David), son of a Welsh chieftain and a Welsh girl named Non, was a Celtic religious leader in the 6th century. The little church he and his monks built where the present cathedral stands was burned down in 645, rebuilt, sacked and burned by the Danes in 1078, and then burned again in 1088. After that a Norman cathedral was built, its organization changing from the Celtic monastic to diocesan type. The stone village of St. David's grew up on the hill around the secluded church.

For information, ask at the **Tourism Council and National Park Information,** City Hall (tel. 0437/720392).

WHERE TO STAY: Named for the mother of St. David, **St. Non's Hotel** (tel. 0437/720239), is owned by Mr. Sandy Falconer, who operates a friendly place where you'll receive a warm welcome. The 20 bedrooms all have private bath, TV, tea/coffee-making equipment, and central heating. Rooms rent for £21

($33.60) to £26 ($41.60) in a single, for £31 ($49.60) to £38 ($60.80) in a double, for B&B. You can have drinks and snacks in the bar, warmed by a log fire in the winter. The restaurant serves a cold buffet lunch, with selections from several meat and fish delicacies, plus crisp fresh salads. The food here is good, and you can dine in the restaurant on the best of local products—lobster, crab, scallops, sewin (sea trout), and lamb in season. A lunch costs from £4 ($6.40); a table d'hôte dinner costs £10.50 ($16.80). To find the hotel, you follow Goat Street to Catherine Street. St. Non's Hotel is on a site where the monastery of Whitwel stood in the 13th or 14th century.

Grove Hotel, High Street (tel. 0437/720341), is a small Regency country house on the road into St. David's from Haverfordwest. Proprietors L. B. and M. M. Groves welcome guests to their ten well-decorated rooms, including a four-poster and a family suite. Rates for B&B range from £18 ($28.80) in a single to £24 ($38.40) in a double. All the bedrooms have the usual amenities in good hotels—bath/shower, color TV, and tea/coffee-making facilities. The chef specializes in whole-food and nouvelle cuisine dishes, with an interesting selection available in the attractive bars. A special Country Fare Dinner is offered year round in the pleasant restaurant.

Warpool Court Hotel (tel. 0437/720300) is a well-known country house overlooking the sea, a five-minute walk from the city of St. David's, not far from St. Non's Chapel. Peter Trier and Ian Mann, together with their courteous staff, do everything possible to make your stay here pleasant and memorable. An outstanding feature of Warpool Court is the tiles, painted for several years around the turn of the century by Mrs. Ada Lansdown Williams. The tiles in the dining room are armorial. Those in the drawing room and dining room are ornamental. Two of the bedrooms have friezes of blue tiles, and some have ornamental tiles and a set depicting the seasons. The armorial tiles are those connected with the Williams family, and you might find genealogical pointers here if you're a Williams connection. The hotel has 25 bedrooms, all with baths or showers, color TV, radios, direct-dial phones, baby-listening devices, and central heating. Tariffs range from £22 ($35.20) to £33 ($52.80) per person for B&B, but I advise taking dinner, bed, and breakfast, priced at around £26.50 ($42.40) to £45 ($72) per person, depending on the season. Children sharing their parents' room are charged only for meals.

The hotel has a reputation for excellent food. Fresh local produce is used wherever possible, including herbs and fruit from the hotel gardens and fresh lobster, crab, and fish from around the coast. Bar snacks are served from 12:30 to 2 p.m., at prices of £1.20 ($1.92) to £5 ($8). Dinner, served in the restaurant with views over St. Bride's Bay, is from 7 p.m. to last orders at 9:15 p.m. A fixed-price meal costs from around £12.50 ($20) to £20 ($32). The hotel, which is closed in January and early February, has an indoor heated swimming pool, an all-weather tennis court, and a croquet lawn.

Whitesands Bay Hotel (tel. 0437/720403) is the nearest hotel to St. Davids Golf Course and to Whitesands Bay with three-quarters of a mile of clean sand where you can swim or surf safely. Liam and George, the owners, welcome you to their pleasant and comfortable hotel, where you'll be happy to shelter from the winds when they sweep across the headlands. All the hotel's bedrooms, both in the main building and the annexes, are well appointed and most have private bathroom facilities. Many have windows overlooking the bay and the Irish Sea. Among the many amenities, you can use the heated swimming pool, the sauna, the solarium, the games room, and the laundry room—a welcome privilege to travelers. Prices of rooms vary, ranging from £14.50 ($23.20) to £25.50 ($40.80) per person, depending on the season and the classification of the room based on plumbing and size. Reduced prices are charged for children.

The bright restaurant, looking out over the water and the adjoining headlands and offshore islands, has a high standard of cuisine, with a number of Welsh specialties, including a rich, tasty cawl. Breakfast is served from 8:30 to 9:45 a.m. There's no formal lunch, but the coffeeshop has light meals available all day, and bar snacks are served from 12:15 to 2 p.m., costing from £1.50 ($2.40). A high tea for children is served in the coffeeshop between 5 and 6 p.m. Dinner in the restaurant, from 7 to 9 p.m., costs from £10 ($16) and might include trout, salmon, lamb with rosemary, Welsh beef, and poultry specialties.

Ramsey Guest House, Lower Moor (tel. 0437/720321), is along the road to Porth Clais, about half a mile from the city. The seven rooms all have hot and cold running water, and there is color TV in the residents' lounge. The charge is £9.50 ($15.20) per person per night for B&B, £14.50 ($23.20) for half board. You can enjoy good home-cooking and even have a cocktail to go with your meal. The guesthouse has ample parking within its own grounds. If you register to stay a week, you get a cruise in the surrounding waters free.

St. David's Youth Hostel, Whitesands Bay (tel. 0437/720345), an IYHF associate, offers simple but adequate hostel facilities. Its accommodations are in former farm buildings; the men are bunked in a cowshed and the women in the stables. Don't let this put you off if you're looking for hostel accommodation. Prices range from £1.90 ($3.04) for a bed and use of the bath facilities for persons under 21, £2.30 ($3.68) for those over 21. The highest price charged, providing a bed and all meals, including a packed lunch, is £7.60 ($12.16) per person. The full hostel is closed from November to March, but a small apartment is used as winter accommodation.

WHERE TO EAT: In a building constructed around a 17th-century stone cottage, **Cartref Restaurant,** Cross Square (tel. 0437/720422), is where Peter Trier serves excellent food in his licensed eating place immediately above the cathedral. Specialties include fresh local beef, fresh crab, home-baked goods, and vegetarian dishes. Pub snacks and children's meals are available. In the self-service Refreshment Garden overlooking the cathedral close, you can have a quick snack or afternoon tea. The restaurant is open from noon to 10 p.m. A meal will cost from £10 ($16). Closed November to mid-March.

SIGHTS AND ACTIVITIES: A magnificent example of medieval religious architecture, with an ornately carved roof and a Norman nave, **St. David's Cathedral** contains in a reliquary what are supposed to be the bones of St. David. The nave, with three centuries of craftsmanship, is a place of medieval beauty. The choir stalls, from the late 15th century, have witty, even light-hearted, misericord carvings (those on the hinged seats in the stalls). Visitors are welcome at the cathedral, open from 7:30 a.m. matins until after evensong (May 1 to September 30 at 6 p.m., earlier in winter). Donations are accepted to help with the upkeep of the building.

Ruins of the **Bishop's Palace** stand across the meadow and river, with the gatehouse, battlements, and curtain walls showing how even such a place needed fortification in medieval days. An outstanding sight is the elegant arcaded parapet that runs along both main walls. You can visit the palace ruins. Note especially the fine piscina at the east end of the chapel's south wall. The cathedral is open from 9:30 a.m. to 6:30 p.m. daily in summer, from 9:30 a.m. to 4 p.m. weekdays and from 2 to 4 p.m. on Sunday in winter. Admission is 75p ($1.20) for adults, 35p (56¢) for children.

The cathedral is no longer Roman Catholic, nor is it Church of England. It is a member of the Church in Wales. When St. David was canonized in the 12th century, the pope declared that two pilgrimages to St. David's were worth one to Rome, while three equaled one to Jerusalem. You can make such a pilgrimage today, and although the pope's promise may not have been honored since the days of Henry VIII, I can promise you an interesting and educational tour of St. David's peninsula. For information, get in touch with the **Pilgrimage Tourism Office,** City Hall (tel. 0437/720747).

Porth Clais, at the mouth of the River Alun about a mile from St. David's, was the seaport used by travelers to Ireland and elsewhere for centuries before and after the birth of Christ, and then by pilgrims making their way to St. David's. In medieval days it became a coaling port, with lime kilns to reduce limestone to slaked lime for use on fields, in building, and for household purposes. The restored lime kilns can be visited.

A little eastward around the bay on a headland is **St. Non's Chapel,** now in ruins, supposedly built on the spot where St. David was born. It is dedicated to his mother. **St. Non's Well** is there also, reportedly in full flow. Its waters were said to have healing properties in the past.

St. Justinian's Chapel, also in ruins, stands on a windswept promontory overlooking Ramsey Island and the sea to the west of St. David's. St. Justinian was the confessor of St. David. Don't expect to see much at either of these ruined chapels.

If you'd like to take advantage of the coastal waters here, **Twr-y-Felin Outdoor Centre** (tel. 0437/720391) has surfboards, surfskis, boogie boards, wetsuits, and windsurfers to rent. They conduct a British Canoe Union–approved kayak and canoe school and a Royal Yatching Association–approved windsurfing school. Prices vary from £1 ($1.60) to £17.50 ($28) per day, depending on what you rent and what courses you take from professional instructors. Andy Middleton is in charge of the center.

SHOPPING: When you're browsing around the little city, stop at **Yr Oriel Fach,** The Pebbles (tel. 0437/720480), a little bookshop just before you pass through the tower to go down the 39 steps to the cathedral. Here Christopher Taylor keeps a wide range of books, including some that will answer questions you may have about Wales. A good souvenir and a help in learning about the city is *The Streets of St. Davids,* which Taylor publishes.

The **Craft Shop,** The Pebbles (tel. 0437/720254), has sterling silver Celtic jewelry, fine tweeds, Liberty fabrics, and Adams Lancaster china. The items offered are all chosen with care. VAT-free exports can be arranged.

The **New Gift House,** 15 Nun St. (tel. 0437/720611), has Aynsley and other fine china, jewelry, gifts, dragons, Welsh dolls, and traditional Welsh slate items, such as placemats and coasters.

The **Welsh Art Craft Shop,** 34-36 High St. (tel. 0437/720579), offers select rural craftware including pottery, wood, slate, and hand-carved lovespoons. Looking for a milking stool? They have them here, as well as soft toys, sheepskin rugs, leather goods, scarves, and sweaters.

MATHRY: Going on the A487 from St. David's to Fishguard, you pass the tiny village of Mathry, overlooking the source stream of the western Cleddau, which flows toward Haverfordwest.

An excellent place to stay, just a mile north from the hilltop village is **Carnachenwen** (tel. 03483/636), a traditional Welsh stone farmhouse lying in a sheltered hollow, with trees, a stream, and a large pond. This is a working farm, growing beef cattle and sheep, as well as barley, Pembrokeshire early potatoes, ducks, and chickens. Guests are free to wander around the farm, in the fields and the wooded dingle, and around the pond. Jill Morgan and Greg Nuttgens, the proprietors, are experienced guides with a wide knowledge of the local land-scape, history, and natural history, and they conduct walking tours of the area.

Farmhouse accommodation is offered in the Old Wing of the house, dating from at least 1743, while self-catering facilities are rented in the New Wing (which didn't come along until 1776). The house has been beautifully renovated to retain its attractive old features while fitting in modern comforts. The interior has pointed stone walls and is done with traditional Welsh furniture and colorful fabrics, including Laura Ashley prints. The main feature of the house is a huge open chimney in the old kitchen, now the living-dining room. There is a large lounge/dining room for the use of guests, with an open fire and slate hearth, plus color TV. Upstairs, reached by a wooden half-spiral staircase, there is a double bedroom with hot and cold running water and a razor outlet; a family/twin bed-room with hot and cold water basin, and shaver outlet; and a single unit. There is an upstairs bathroom with a shower, toilet, bidet, and basin. Rates are from £11 ($17.60) to £13 ($20.80) per person for B&B, and an evening meal costs £7 ($11.20).

Carnachenwen is just a mile from the sea and the coastal footpath.

A VISIT TO A WOOLEN MILL: For a visit to a working mill, go to the **Tregwynt Mill** (tel. 03485/225), reached by turning to the west off the main St. David's–Fishguard road, the A487, when you see the signs for Abermawr. The mill is near St. Nicholas. You can see it in operation from 9 a.m. to 5 p.m. Monday to Friday, and the mill shop is open daily except Sunday. The mill products are available in the **Tregwynt Textiles shops** at 5 Nun St., St. David's (tel. 0437/720386), and at 6 High St., Fishguard (tel. 0348/872370).

9. Solva

For a long time Solva was a port, active in trade with Ireland. As one enters the inlet, there's a sharp bend that protects the port from gales and also made the little village invisible to attackers. In its very early days this seclusion may not have worked so well, as the name Solva is thought to be a Danish appellation, probably given to it by Viking raiders. So important did it later become as a port that in the 1840s, records show, a ship sailed from Solva's Trinity Quay to Amer-ica. A single fare was £4, then at least $20. The uplands were once the location of several little hill-forts from which Iron Age man protected his safety.

Today pleasure craft have replaced the ships of yesteryear, joining fishing boats in use of the protected harbor. Lower Solva, the part to be visited, is now a favored holiday resort.

FOOD AND LODGING: Overlooking the harbor of the Solva inlet, **Harbour House Hotel** (tel. 0437/721267), is a 200-year-old hostelry run by Hazel and Tony Smith, who have redecorated, making ample use of exposed stone, polished brass, and oak. It has just four bedrooms, which rent for £21 ($33.60) in a single, £15 ($24) per person for double occupancy. The Anchor Bar is a cozy place, with a log fire and real ale. In the Butter Bar, you can order from a wide selec-tion of bar meals, including a ploughman's lunch and Welsh farmhouse soup. Dinner costs £7.50 ($12). Specialty coffees are offered. In summer, food and drink are served on a floodlit patio. Food is available from noon to 2:30 p.m. and 6:30 to 10 p.m. weekdays, from noon to 2 p.m. and 7 to 10 p.m. on Sunday.

Pendinas (tel. 0437/721283) is a modern B&B house with sea views over Solva Harbour and St. Bride's Bay from its broad balcony/veranda. Mrs. June

Edwards rents rooms with comfortable beds and hot-beverage facilities for £10 ($16) per person, with a full breakfast. There is a lounge with color TV, plus plenty of room for parking. Guests are provided with their own keys to the house. If you come by bus to Solva, get off in Upper Solva at the memorial hall.

The **Old Pharmacy Café** (tel. 0437/721232), a licensed restaurant, is a good place to stop for food. Josephine and Keith Lawton, the owners, offer a selection of such dishes as "dressed" local crabs, filets of mackerel, and fresh sewin (sea trout) poached in a white wine sauce. Lunch costs from £3 ($4.80) and dinner from £7.50 ($12). You can also drop in for tea from 2:30 to 5:30 p.m., enjoying bara brith, the tasty Welsh currant bread. The restaurant serves from noon to 2:30 p.m. and 7 to 9:30 p.m. April to October except Sunday. Evening reservations are advised in summer.

SEEING THE BUTTERFLIES: A trip to Solva is not complete unless you visit the **Solva Nectarium** and the **Old Chapel** next door (tel. 0437/721323). In the Nectarium, you make an insect safari through the grounds of Tan-yr-allt House as well as the insect galleries in the Old Chapel. In a tropical glass house, you walk among the most beautiful members of the insect world, alive and flying free. They live naturally, breed, and reproduce here. Species from the spectacular Indian moonmoth to graceful swallowtail moths are among the inhabitants. In the insect galleries, you can watch butterflies emerge from their pupae and see strange caterpillars, locusts, tarantulas, scorpions, and an observation beehive. In the Old Chapel, visit the shop of the Nectarium, where you can buy locally made perfumes and colognes, mounted butterflies, and many other items, as well as fine crafts from around the world.

The Nectarium is open from April to the end of September, Monday to Saturday from 10 a.m. to 6 p.m., from 2 to 6 p.m. on Sunday. Admission is £2 ($3.20) for adults, £1 ($1.60) for children, who must be accompanied by adults. Last entrance to exhibits is at 5 p.m. The shop is open April to the end of October, Monday to Saturday from 10 a.m. to 6 p.m., on Sunday from 2 to 6 p.m.; November 25 to December 23 from 10:30 a.m. to 1 p.m. and 2 to 4 p.m. seven days a week. There is no charge for admission to the shop.

The establishment has a large café serving natural foods with no additives and a clothes shop featuring Welsh designs of high quality for men and women.

A WELSH POTTERY: On the A487 leading from St. David's to Haverfordwest, watch for the **Pembrokeshire Pottery and Craft Shop** (tel. 0437/710628), a little working pottery at Simpson Cross, where Malcolm and Ros Thomas turn out interesting work. You can watch the crafting of the pots, urns, dragons, and numerous other pieces. You may find some souvenirs you'll treasure in the little shop.

10. Haverfordwest

"Sixteen miles and 17 hills from St. David's" is an old description of this market town on a hill above the west branch of the River Cleddau. Almost due north of Milford Haven, Haverfordwest, is the administrative center of this section of old Pembrokeshire.

Beginning around Queen Elizabeth I's accession to the throne, Haverfordwest became a busy port, with warehouses and quays serving boats plying the Cleddau, until the advent of railroads in 1853 caused the river trade to fall away.

Livestock markets are held here on Monday, and there's a general street market on Saturday.

For information on the area, ask at the offices of **Wales Tourist Information** and the **Pembrokeshire Coast National Park Centre,** 40 High St. (tel. 0437/3110), open from 10 a.m. to 6 p.m. in summer.

WHERE TO STAY: In the heart of the market town, **Hotel Mariners,** Mariners Square (tel. 0437/3353), is a comfortable place to stay, with 29 bedrooms, two popular bars, and a restaurant occupying its three floors. The bedrooms, some with private baths, all have color TV, radios, phones, and hot-beverage facilities. They are pleasantly decorated and have comfortable easy chairs. The charge is £27 ($43.20) in a single with bath, £20 ($32) per person in a twin or double with bath, with a full English breakfast and VAT included.

The finest pub in Haverfordwest is the **Bristol Trader,** Old Quay, Quay Street (tel. 0437/2122), which has been what the British call a "free house" ever since the mid-14th century. A lot of lager has flowed here since that time, but everything is spruced up and immaculate today. The location overlooks the river. The place is heavily favored by locals and visitors alike who appreciate the homemade bar grub, including such fare as a hearty vegetable soup, chili, and pasta, along with some smoked fish dishes. Meals begin modestly at £4 ($6.40). Hours are from 11 a.m. to 3 p.m. and 5:30 to 11 p.m. In summer it is open all day during certain market days.

Country Living

My favorite place to stay and/or dine is **Wolfcastle Country Hotel and Restaurant,** Wolf's Castle (tel. 043787/225), about a 15-minute drive north of Haverfordwest on the A40. Proprietors Andrew and Pauline Stirling rent 15 bedrooms, all with private baths, which are reached along a carpeted hallway. The units all contain color TV, hot-beverage facilities, and are centrally heated, with views of the varied landscape of the beautiful countryside. The charge, for B&B, with VAT included, is £25 ($40) in a single, £38 ($60.80) in a double. Besides the public rooms on the ground floor, there is a comfortable residents' lounge upstairs.

You can have either lunch or evening bar meals here, with such dishes available as pâté with hot buttered toast, locally smoked trout with horseradish and salad, Scotch eggs with deep-fried potatoes, and filet of plaice, also with deep fries. You can eat well for £3 ($4.80). In the attractively appointed restaurant, with matching draperies and wallpaper, you have a wide choice from the à la carte menu. The Stirlings grow many of their own vegetables, and all food used in the kitchen is fresh, including locally caught fish. They are happy to cater to vegetarians or people on special diets. For an appetizer, I recommend the sole timbale with beurre blanc sauce or lobster with dill and cucumber cocktail. Excellent main dishes include rabbit with black peppercorns and Dijon mustard sauce; baked salmon with hollandaise sauce; beef hunter style with red wine, tomatoes, and garlic; and roast Pembrokeshire duck with bigarade sauce. Desserts range from a seven-fruit summer pudding to strawberries in burgundy with chantilly cream and hazelnut meringue with bananas and cream. A dinner will cost £9.50 ($15.20) to £15 ($24). Bar meals are served from noon to 2:30 p.m. and 7 to 9:30 p.m. Dinner in the restaurant is from 7 to 9:30 p.m.

Stone Hall, Welsh Hook (tel. 0348/840212), is a charming hotel and restaurant operated by Alan and Martine Watson, standing in ten acres of gardens and woodland. The hall, where descendants of medieval Prince Gwynfardd Dyfed lived before the year 1400, is near the hamlet of Welsh Hook, which is reached by turning west off the A40 between Haverfordwest and Fishguard. The turn is on the northern outskirts of the village of Wolf's Castle. The hotel's oldest part is architecturally interesting, being the original manor house with slate-flagged floors and big rough-hewn oak beams. The house was extended in the 17th century, when the wood paneling and decorative ceiling were added, and a further extension was made in mid-Victorian times. You can stay here in a room with bath for £24 ($38.40) in a single, £40 ($64) in a double, with a full breakfast included. All five of the bedrooms have color TV and direct-dial phones. The bar and restaurant are in the oldest part of the building. French cuisine is served, with extensive à la carte and table d'hôte menus, and there is a comprehensive wine list. The hotel's garden contains a number of unusual trees and hundreds of hybrid rhododendrons and azaleas among large oak, beech, and sycamore trees.

SIGHTS: The town with its attractive 18th-century houses is brooded over by **Haverford Castle,** or at least what's left of the fortification dating from the 12th and 13th centuries, on a cliff 80 feet above the river. From this height, defenders of the castle could see for miles in all directions, and the steep slopes discouraged attack. Part of the Norman walls remain, and the castle masonry is strong, with a 12-foot curtain wall on one side. The castle was effectively put out of business by Cromwell and later housed the county jail.

The **Castle Museum and Art Gallery** (tel. 0437/3708) has a collection of artifacts and graphic history exhibits showing the story of the area—even back to prehistoric times. It's open from 10 a.m. to 5:30 p.m. Monday to Saturday in summer, from 11 a.m. to 4 p.m. Tuesday to Saturday in winter. Admission is 50p (80¢) for adults, 25p (40¢) for children.

St. Mary's Church, 13th-century, is the most interesting of the town's three churches. It has an arcade with pointed arches and a Late Perpendicular tower dating from the time it was constructed.

In the Environs

About four miles east of Haverfordwest off the A40 is **Picton Castle,** (tel. 043786/201), privately owned and the home of the Philipps family. The castle was built in the early 14th century and was occupied by Owain Glyndwr in 1405. The castle has been owned by the Philipps family since the 15th century, with a four-story addition in 1800 by the first Lord Milford. The gardens can be visited for a charge of £1 ($1.60) for adults, 50p (80¢) for children. Gardens and woodland walks are possible from Easter to September from 10:30 a.m. to 6 p.m. daily except Monday. In the castle, you can visit the—

Graham Sutherland Gallery, Picton Castle, The Rhos (tel. 043786/296). Here you can see the largest available collection of works by Sutherland, one of the greatest of modern English painters. The range of work covers paintings and sketches from West Wales and southern France, portraits, etchings, lithographs, aquatints, and designs. The gallery is open Tuesday to Sunday, April to September. Admission is 60p (96¢) for adults, 30p (48¢) for children.

11. Fishguard and Goodwick

These are twin towns around a deep-water bay which is the port for embarking for southern Ireland. They are the only parts of the outer coastline that are not in the Pembrokeshire Coast National Park, but they are backed by the western foothills of Preseli. Fishguard has two parts, perhaps the most interesting one to visitors being Lower Fishguard, where the cluster of old wharfs and cottages around the harbor is a memorable sight. Known as Abergwaun, this section of Fishguard was the setting for the filming of *Under Milk Wood,* the Dylan Thomas work starring Richard Burton. One headland is dominated by an old fort, and opposite it is Fishguard town, where you may want to go shopping.

The long main street leads to Goodwick Sands, where French invaders, mostly convicts and ne'er-do-wells, laid down their arms after an abortive invasion try in 1797. Goodwick is the motor/rail terminus from London. This entire area draws lots of travelers, and there are lots of accommodation possibilities.

The **Fishguard Music Festival,** a popular event, takes place every summer.

The **Fishguard Tourism Council and Preseli District Council** office is at the Town Hall (tel. 0348/873484).

FOOD AND LODGING: In a 15th-century building, the **Royal Oak Inn,** Market Square (tel. 0348/972514), is of historic interest as well as being a good place to eat. This was the scene of the signing of the surrender documents by the French after the failure of an attempt on February 22, 1797, to invade the British Isles through here. The heroine of the occasion was Jemima Nicholas, who gathered up country folk armed with muskets, pitchforks, and scythes and set out to subdue the invaders. Her tombstone is in the churchyard on the Market Square, and relics of that heroic event are displayed in the Royal Oak. The table on which the treaty was signed on February 23 is on view also.

Meals are available from 11:30 a.m. to 2 p.m. and 6 to 9 p.m., from noon to 2 p.m. and 7 to 9 p.m. on Sunday. You can give your order at the bar, selecting from among such dishes as soups, pâté, ploughman's lunch, American burgers, Glamorgan sausage, chicken, and seafood. You can have a meal for £4.50 ($7.20), maybe less. The bar opens into the lounge and salad bar areas, where children are welcome and special menus are offered for them. The restaurant, with an Italian tile floor and solid oak furniture, overlooks the patio, which in turn overlooks the harbor and the Irish Sea. Dinner in the restaurant might include beef and onion pie, steaks, or roast chicken. Expect to pay £9 ($14.40) to £12 ($19.20). The Royal Oak has some rooms to rent, with singles costing from £11 ($17.60), doubles from £19 ($30.40).

Fishguard Bay Hotel, Quay Road, Goodwick (tel. 0348/873571), is a well-maintained Victorian hotel set in ten acres of woodland with terraced paths, leading to cliff scenery around Strumble Head. It is near the ferry terminal and overlooks the harbor. You can stay in high-ceilinged rooms in the original building or in more compact ones in an annex. The comfortably but simply furnished units rent for £20 ($32) to £25 ($40) per person for B&B. The rooms are all centrally heated and there is an elevator. Some 28 of the 62 rooms are equipped with bathroom facilities, and there are six luxury suites, one with a four-poster bed, renting for £30 ($48) per person, breakfast included. The hotel has three bars, a TV lounge, a reading room, and a full-size snooker table, as well as a spacious ballroom. G. J. Shell, the proprietor, says the à la carte restaurant is open to nonresidents. The hotel is open all year.

Gellifawr Country House, Pontfaen (tel. 0239/820343), is on a country road running east out of Fishguard. Nestling at the foot of the Preseli Hills, it overlooks the Gwaun Valley in the national park. Bill and Hilary Gamble welcome guests to their ten-bedroom accommodations in the stone house built more than 150 years ago. They have also converted traditional stone farm buildings into self-catering units. There is a heated swimming pool, and a toddlers' pool adjacent. The hotel has a licensed bar and restaurant. Single, double, and family rooms are available, with special rates for children. You can stay here for £12 ($19.20) to £14 ($22.40) per person for B&B.

Plas Glyn y Mel, Lower Fishguard (tel. 0348/872296), is a Georgian house built in the 1780s by one of the century's most famous travel writers, Fenton, who wrote of his journeys through Pembrokeshire. Also a shipowner, he commissioned his captains to bring back as many arboreal specimens as possible so that the acreage around the place is filled with rare trees. The coastal valley where the house stands is 10° warmer than the surrounding landscape, allowing these rare trees and plants to grow lushly. The grounds support a colony of badgers and herons, along with many owls and other fowl. On the estate, there is also a hermit's cell, reputed to have been occupied in the early Christian era by St. Dubricius, the counselor and teacher of St. David, who later Christianized the Welsh. The River Gwaun runs through the property, about half a mile from Fishguard.

Mike and Jenny Moore have seven pleasant bedrooms to rent, all with good views, costing £32 ($51.20) in a single, £22 ($35.20) per person in a double. A fixed-price lunch is served daily, from noon to 2 p.m., costing £7.50 ($12). A set dinner, from 7 to 10 p.m., goes for £13.50 ($21.60) and includes such specialties as pork Cordon Bleu, lobster thermidor, grilled Scotch salmon with thyme butter, and several preparations of local salt-meadow-fed lamb. The house is licensed. You can find Glyn y Mel by going through Fishguard on the A487 to Lower Town Harbor, turning right just across the bridge, and following the sign.

12. Newport (in Dyfed)

This ancient castled town on the A487 road between Fishguard and Cardigan is in the most northerly section of the Preseli Hills District in the Pembrokeshire Coast National Park. The community grew up around the castle, which dates from the late 12th century. The most substantial remains of the castle are the gateway and tower, on a circular mound on the south edge of the town. You have to look at it from outside.

The River Nevern flows down from the Preseli Mountains to Newport Bay, which is a good fishing and boating center. There are two fine beaches on the Newport town side, which is separated from Newport Sands by the river estuary. There's a nine-hole golf course near.

A mile south of Newport is **Carn Ingli,** which has a well-preserved Iron Age hill-fort. Between the town and the river bridge is a cromlech, and a mile west, at Cerrig y Gof, you can see a circle of five Neolithic tombs. In sight of the Newport Bay landing is **Pentre Ifan,** a set of standing stones with a 16-foot-long capstone. Pentre Ifan cromlech, called one of the finest megalithic monuments in Wales, is three miles southeast of Newport, on a country road. Many traces of pre-Christian-era mankind are in the Preseli foothills.

At **Nevern,** to the north of the A487 just a few breaths east of Newport, see the early 11th-century Nevern Cross, a 13-foot-high, wheel-headed Celtic cross where, according to tradition, the cuckoo lands to sing on April 7, St. Brynach's feast day. An imposing line of yew trees stands in the churchyard of St. Brynach's, one of which, the famous "bleeding yew," drips blood-red sap.

Pony trekking in the foothills is a popular pastime.

FOOD AND LODGING: Perhaps the best place to stay in Newport is **Cnapan Country House for Guests,** East Street (tel. 0239/820575), run by John and Eluned Lloyd and Michael and Judith Cooper, a family team. From the generous hallway with its traditional Welsh dresser holding old family heirlooms, to the spacious bedrooms, you'll feel at home here. The residents' lounge, with a wood-burning stove, is a good place to be on cool evenings. The bar provides convivial surroundings for pre-dinner drinks. The five bedrooms are individually decorated and have comfortable chairs. Some look to the sea and some to the hills. All have private baths, wash basins, TV, hot-beverage facilities, and central heating. Tariffs are £13 ($20.80) per person for B&B. For half board, the charge is £20 ($32) per person. Children under 12 are accommodated for half price. Mrs. Lloyd and Mrs. Cooper work together in the kitchen to provide tasty food, with traditional Welsh dishes and other British dishes on the menu. The house has a sunny, sheltered garden for use by guests.

The Pantry, Market Street (tel. 0239/820420), is an excellent place to eat, with careful selection of quality raw materials and their preparation making the cuisine a delight to the palate. The menu includes locally farmed venison and freshly caught salmon. The Pantry is open from noon to 2:30 p.m. for lunch, from 4:30 to 9:30 p.m. for dinner, and from 9:30 to 11 p.m. for light supper. A traditional Sunday lunch is offered. Meals cost £8 ($12.80) and up.

The best pub in the area is the **Golden Lion,** East Street (tel. 0239/820321), lying on the eastern side of town along the A487. This 1600s pub might fulfill your fantasy of what a Welsh pub should look like. Old settles and bare benches combine with stone walls to suggest a centuries-old charm. You can come here for either food or drink (there's a separate dining room for more formal service, although many patrons prefer to take their meals in the bar). Food ranges from homemade soups in chilly weather to chili con carne. You can also order steak as you like it, along with fresh fish on occasion. Meals costing from £6 ($9.60) are served from 11 a.m. to 3 p.m. and 5:30 to 11 p.m.

IN THE FOOTHILLS OF PRESELI:

A short distance east of Newport on the A487 road is Felindre Farchog, where **Ye Olde Salutation Inn** (tel. 0239/820564) is a good place to stay. This is a traditional country inn, in a village on the banks of the River Nevern. The ten bedrooms, in an addition to the old inn, have bath, color TV, video, central heating, and tea/coffee-making equipment. They rent for £10 ($16) to £15 ($24) per person for B&B. The inn has facilities for disabled persons. You can have bar snacks, perhaps a ploughman's lunch or a ham-and-cheese sandwich, costing around £2 ($3.20). Dinners with coffee, when some traditional Welsh food is offered, go for £8 ($12.80) to £9 ($14.40). You can go fishing in the inn's waters or arrange for pony-trekking and golf.

THE MIDDLE OF WALES

THE SCENERY OF THE MIDDLE OF WALES is rich and varied. Wide beaches and craggy promontories, from which you can see all the way to Ireland over Cardigan Bay and the Irish sea, outline the western reaches. Forests, foothills, moors, mountains, and gently rolling meadowlands are all part of this beautiful section of the principality. For a long time it was impossible—well, almost—to drive from the Welsh-English border to the sea in much of this area, as the parts were only linked by the old drovers' tracks across the Cambrian Mountains along which farmers took their sheep and cattle to the markets. The interior, much of it heavily wooded and with deep river valleys and ravines, holds tranquil little farms, friendly villages, and dramatic traces of religious centers and mining enterprises.

Today good roads will take you from Hay-on-Wye to Llandrindod Wells to Aberystwyth, from Newtown to Machynlleth, east and west and north and south in the middle of Wales. Of course there are still many narrow lanes of a kind with which most Americans are unfamiliar. Be bold. If you're driving in this part of the country, remember that little British cars *can* pass each other on the winding rural trails, and that what you will see along them makes a trip memorable.

The variation in houses in Mid Wales is noteworthy. Beautiful big and little homes of stone, looking as if they might have been carved right out of the rock, mark the northern sections in beginnings of the Snowdonia National Park. Along the border, around Welshpool and Newtown and in other parts of the county of Powys, you see many of what are called magpie-marked buildings, black and white, mostly from the Tudor period.

This is Welsh-speaking country, especially in the western part, although you are not likely to meet anyone who does not also speak English.

The middle of Wales visited in this chapter includes parts of two of the counties as they are laid out today—Dyfed and Powys. The northern part of Dyfed, called Ceredigion, is a good place to start a journey.

CEREDIGION COUNTRY COMFORTS: Owners of a group of farmhouses and country homes have joined together to offer accommodation for visitors to the area, all in peaceful, rural surroundings and each with its own individual character. I particularly enjoy the farm-fresh food, much of it produced on the farm where it is served. Of the eight homes in the group, one actually overlooks Cardigan Bay, and none is very far from the sea. Pony trekking, fishing, walking, touring, and other pursuits are possible, either on the farm or close by. I highly recommend all of these places for your holiday. They are especially good for family vacations. The towns listed as part of the addresses of the accommodations will be visited in this section. Rentals at these places are fairly uniform: from £10.50 ($16.80) per night per person for B&B, £16 ($25.60) for dinner, bed, and breakfast. If you stay a week, the price is around £105 ($168), a bargain considering the fine hospitality and good food you'll enjoy. For information, write to **Eleri Davies,** Pentre Farm, Llanfair, Lampeter, Dyfed SA48 8LE (tel. 057045/313).

Erwbarfe Farmhouse, Devil's Bridge, Aberystwyth (tel. 097085/251), is a 400-acre working farm in sight of Devil's Bridge Falls and the narrow-gauge railway. The farmhouse has oak-beamed ceilings. Each bedroom has its own tea/coffee-making facilities. The rooms have wash basins and are quite near the bathroom. There's color TV, and an open fire and central heating will keep off an evening chill. The hostess is Elaine Lewis.

Neuaddlas, Tregaron (tel. 09744/380), is a 25-acre animal and agriculture farm, nestling in rolling hills with breathtaking views of the Cors Caron nature reserve and the Cambrian Mountains. Margaret Cutter, the hospitable hostess at Neuaddlas (pronounced "Ny-eth-las"), has baths and tea/coffee-making facilities in the bedrooms, central heating, and an open fire and TV in the lounge, plus a separate dining room. To reach this farm, take the A485 for 1½ miles north of Tregaron.

Brynog Mansion, Felin-fach, Lampeter (tel. 0570/470266), is a 200-year-old country mansion three-quarters of a mile off the A482 road between Lampeter and Aberaeron, ten minutes' drive from the sea and the Cardigan Bay coast. It is a working farm, with about a mile of private fishing in the River Aeron. Mrs. S. E. Davis has had central heating installed in her home.

At **Pentre Farm,** Llanfair, Lampeter (tel. 057045/313), Eleri Davies and her family extend warm Welsh hospitality to their guests. The 300-acre dairy and sheep farm is on the banks of the River Teifi, midway between Lampeter and Tregaron on the B4343 road. The large stone farmhouse has bedrooms with private bath, a spacious lounge with oak beams, and an inglenook fireplace. From the light, well-furnished dining room you can look out over the rolling farmland.

Abermeurig Mansion, Lampeter (tel. 0570/470216), is a Georgian mansion on the banks of the River Aeron, on an 80-acre farm three miles off the A482 Lampeter–Aberaeron road. Mrs. M. Rogers-Lewis has her home furnished with antiques; the spacious bedrooms have four-poster and canopy beds. A lounge and TV room are designed for the pleasure of guests, and the house is licensed. You're sure to enjoy this ancestral home, eight miles from the sea, with central heating and open fires.

Glangraig Farm, Llangrannog, Llandysul (tel. 023978/554), is a 20-acre working farm overlooking Cardigan Bay. Guests have access to a private headland where sea birds and seals can be viewed, and Llangrannog village with sandy beaches is just 1½ miles away. There's a fine view of the National Trust headland, Lochtyn, from the dining room. The Parrys let guests help with the animals if they wish, and pony trekking is available on the farm.

Mrs. Bethan Williams invites you to **Hendre,** Llangrannog, Llandysul (tel. 023978/342), a 100-acre working farm two miles from Llangrannog's sandy beaches and midway between Cardigan and Aberaeron. It is run by the Williams family and a friendly sheepdog. The 19th-century stone farmhouse is solid and comfortable. Bedrooms have wash basins, and an open fire and TV add to the comfort of the house.

1. Cardigan

The south side of the estuary of the River Teifi marks the northernmost boundary of Pembrokeshire National Park. Cardigan lies mainly on the north estuarine bank, although part of the town is in the park. The five-arched 18th-century bridge connecting the two sides is a feature of the town. The ancient borough of Cardigan was the county town of Ceredigion, from which its name is derived. Cardigan was a strategic spot through the centuries, and the Cardigan Castle, whose minor remains stand on a high bluff above the Teifi, was the subject of many bloody battles. The castle went back and forth from Welsh to English control about 16 times in 150 years. Finally Oliver Cromwell's soldiers administered the coup de grace to prevent its falling into the hands of the king's supporters. It is now privately owned and can only be viewed from the outside.

Cardigan was the scene of the first-recorded Eisteddfod, held in 1176. It was for a long time an important port, with the estuary filled with trading vessels and fishing boats, until the silting of the channel and the coming of the railroad. From prehistoric times, coracles have worked the waters of the Teifi, with salmon being taken in abundance from the waters. These light, one-man vessels, made of willow or lath framework with an outer covering of skin or canvas made watertight by a pitch coating, are still seen, but not in as large numbers as before. In fact, because some of the stream is now short of the fish formerly inhabiting the waters, the coracle's use is now limited to the tidal waters of the Teifi.

A general (flea-market-style) market is held in Cardigan on Saturday, with a Monday livestock market being customary, too.

For information on the area, there is the **Ceredigion District Council Information Centre,** Prince Charles Quay, The Harbour (tel. 0239/613230), open daily from 10 a.m. to 6 p.m. Ask about the coracle races.

FOOD AND LODGING: The best place for food in the area is **Rhyd-Garn-Wen,** Cilgerran Road (tel. 0239/612742), which lies less than three miles from Cardigan along A487. Huw and Susan Jones have less than a dozen spaces in their intimate dining room, so it's necessary to call for a table reservation. Susan is a sensitive chef, and she controls the kitchen at this 19th-century manor house which is set in a beautiful area in the vicinity of the Preseli mountains. Homemade food, using fresh local produce when possible, is combined with a warm welcome. It makes for a memorable evening. A four-course dinner might include Dover sole with a scallop soufflé or pork filled with a purée of onions and peas. A set dinner costs £13.50 ($21.60) and is offered nightly from 7:30 to 9:30 except when the establishment closes from October to Easter. The small hotel also offers three bedrooms, one with its own private bath and the other two with showers. Rates range from £25 ($40) for a single, £42 ($67.20) for a double.

Black Lion, High Street (tel. 0239/612532), is said to be one of the oldest coaching inns in the country. On the main street of this bustling market town, it traces its origins back to 1105 when a Grogg Shoppe was established here in one room. Today, after many reincarnations, it is still going strong as the leading pub in town. The facade nowadays is red-brick Georgian. The pub has much comfort, with rustic beams and linenfold paneling. Try the bar food, including such fare as honey-roasted ham and steaks cooked as you like them. Homemade soups such as mutton-based cawl are offered. Every food item seems to be consumed with real ale. You can dine either in the bar or restaurant, which serves meals from 11 a.m. to 3 p.m. and 5:30 to 11 p.m. Meals are not served on Sunday. The hotel also rents out 16 comfortably appointed bedrooms, each with private bath or shower and, for the most part, pine furnishings. Singles begin at £18.50 ($29.60), with doubles going for £36 ($57.60).

Bell Hotel, Pendre Street (tel. 0239/612629), is a small, friendly inn with a 19th-century stone facade, where it's a pleasure to stay if you're a person who likes inns. The Price family will be happy to help you find your way around the Cardigan area, directing you to beaches, the golf course, countryside drives—whatever. They charge £13 ($20.80) per person for B&B in their eight rooms. There is a restaurant, where you can enjoy meals which include specialties of the river and the sea.

SIGHTS AROUND CARDIGAN: Along the Teifi, a mile downstream from Cardigan is the village of **St. Dogmael's,** within Pembrokeshire National Park, noted for its medieval abbey ruins. The **Parish Church of St. Thomas the Martyr** stands in the abbey precincts. Although it was only built in 1850, the church contains the Latin- and Ogham-inscribed Sagranus Stone which provided the key to the Ogham alphabet, discovered in 1848. The abbey ruins and the church can be visited free.

Going toward Fishguard on the A487 is **Castell Henllys,** Pant-glas, Meline, Crymych (tel. 023979/319), a reconstructed Celtic hill-fort near Eglwyswrw. It's open daily from 10 a.m. to 6 p.m. mid-May to mid-September. Celtic feasts are held on special occasions. Admission to the hill-fort is £1.50 ($2.40) for adults, 80p ($1.28) for children.

Cilgerran Castle is another that underwent various changes of ownership during the Anglo-Welsh wars. Two miles southeast of Cardigan, it is perched on a rocky knoll high above the River Teifi. It came into special prominence after it was painted by Richard Wilson in the 18th century and became known among the traveling population of that day, many of whom were aboard ships coming into Cardigan. The castle has been deserted since the 14th century. It can be visited in summer from 9:30 a.m. to 6:30 p.m., 2 to 6:30 p.m. on Sunday. Winter hours are the same except for closing at 4 p.m. Admission is 75p ($1.20) for adults, 35p (56¢) for children.

2. Newcastle Emlyn and Llandysul

Inland from Cardigan on the River Teifi are little towns whose development through the centuries was based on their mills, woolens, and flour, and whose prosperity was based on the water power of the river. Among these are—

NEWCASTLE EMLYN: This is a tiny market town on the River Teifi, but it has some castle ruins, even in this serene setting. Actually the castle was more a country seat than a fortress, but it did see some excitement during the Civil War when it was blown up with gunpowder on the orders of Cromwell. Its position was at a bend of the Teifi, making it easy to defend. The remains are open and may be seen for no admission charge.

A livestock market is held here every Friday.

Where to Stay

If you'd like to make a stopover in Newcastle Emlyn, I suggest the **Emlyn Arms Hotel,** Bridge Street (tel. 0239/710317), a 17th-century drovers' inn on the A484 between Cardigan and Carmarthen. It's a good base for touring the countryside and visiting the mills, particularly woolen mills, of which there are several in the area surrounding the town. The 38 bedrooms in the hotel all have hot and cold water basins, color TV, and tea/coffee-making facilities. The best rooms are in a nearby annex which was completed in 1976. Both buildings lie close to a bridge spanning the River Teifi. With breakfast included, singles range from £20 ($32) to £39 ($62.40) and doubles from £32 ($51.20) to £39 ($62.40), depending on the plumbing. A fixed-price lunch in the dining room costs £7.50 ($12) and is served from noon to 2 p.m. Dinner, costing the same, is offered from 7 to 8:45 p.m. Specialties include salmon and trout along with good-tasting beef and Welsh lamb.

An Old Flour Mill

Just north of the town is **Felin Geri Flour Mill,** Felin Geri, Cwm Cou (tel. 0239/710810). This is a water-powered, 16th-century mill with a bakery adjacent. There's a museum here with farm implements and a working waterwheel-driven sawmill from the 19th century. The mill is open Easter to the end of September from 10 a.m. to 6 p.m. daily. Admission is £1.50 ($2.40) for adults, £1 ($1.60) for children.

LLANDYSUL: A hundred years ago, few villages in Wales lacked a woolen mill. Now, however, most of the mills stand in ruins, which is what sparks special interest in Llandysul. Visitors to this little village on the River Teifi can still see mills producing colorful Welsh weaves, and museums provide a look back into the history of this industry.

Where to Stay

Llanfair Lodge (tel. 055932/3385), 2½ miles from Llandysul, is a 17th-century building set in a tranquil wooded part of the Teifi Valley. With its oriel windows, beamed ceilings, oak-paneled hall, and log fires, it provides a friendly and relaxed atmosphere. Anne and John Jones, who speak both Welsh and English, welcome you to their centrally heated lodge and tastefully furnished, beamed bedrooms, with hot and cold water basins and hot-beverage facilities. The charge is £15 ($24) per person for bed and a full Welsh breakfast. Meals are served in the residents' private dining room. You'll enjoy the log fire in the TV lounge when the mists come up from the Teifi and cool off the night. Charges include the privilege of private fishing on the shore of the river and the banks of the salmon pool, known as Church Pool.

Sights Around Llandysul

The **Museum of the Welsh Woollen Industry** (National Museum of Wales), Dre-fach Felindre (tel. 0559/370929), is near Llandysul, four miles east of Newcastle Emlyn off the A84 Carmarthen–Cardigan road. At the beginning of the century, Cambrian Mills, now the museum's home, was one of 43 factories and weaving shops in and around Dre-fach Felindre producing woolen textiles both for local consumption and the markets of industrial South Wales. Based on a comprehensive collection of old machinery and equipment, photographs, and documentary evidence, the exhibition traces the conversion of fleece to fabric and the development of the industry in Wales. Carding, spinning, and weaving are demonstrated and present-day production methods can be viewed in the on-site working mill. Other attractions include a working water wheel and gas engine, picnic site, the museum shop, and café. It's all open from 10 a.m. to 5 p.m. Monday to Saturday from April to the end of September, and Monday to Friday from October to the end of March. Admission is free.

The **Maesllyn Woollen Mill Museum** (tel. 023975/251) is four miles northwest of Llandysul off the A486. This is a working museum of Welsh weaving history. In the machinery halls, you can follow changes from hand-spinning and weaving to power machinery, some driven by the restored water wheels. There is a large Mill Shop, with an array of wool garments, cloth, rugs, and blankets, as well as a selection of quality, locally made craft goods. Not in the woolen line but nonetheless of interest is a collection of vintage radios and television sets. The coffeeshop offers homemade food. The museum and mill are open Monday to Saturday from 10 a.m. to 6 p.m. and on Sunday from 2 to 6 p.m. in summer, weekdays only from 10 a.m. to 5 p.m. in winter. Admission is 80p ($1.28) for adults, 40p (64¢) for children.

Another fascinating place to visit is **Y Felin Wlan** (Rock Mills), Capel Dewi (tel. 055932/2356), northeast of Llandysul and a little way south of Capel Dewi. You won't run across it accidentally, so you'd be wise to ask directions when you're in Llandysul or Capel Dewi. David and Donald Morgan, owners, are also the spinners and weavers. The mill, run by one of the few remaining working water wheels in Wales, is in a big stone building beside the stream that turns the mill wheel, deep in a vale. When I was last there the stocking machine was running, which will show how woolen socks are made by machine. You can also see how the complicated weaving machinery works. There is a shop across from the mill with a wide range of mill output and other crafts articles. Rock Mills is open Monday to Friday from 9 a.m. to 5:30 p.m. all year, with Saturday hours of 9 a.m. to 1 p.m. April to October. The Morgans make this very much a family operation, with their home, another stone building, directly opposite the mill. It was founded in 1890.

If you ask directions to Capel Dewi, make it clear you want the one near Llandysul. There is another one quite near Aberystwyth. The mill is 400 yards from the B4459 road, off the A475.

3. New Quay and Aberaeron

The wide sandy beaches of Cardigan Bay are a lure to vacationers, and the little towns, mostly grown up from tiny fishing villages, give a feeling of stepping back into an earlier age.

NEW QUAY: Known as the Welsh Riviera, New Quay and its satellite, **Cei Bach,** are packed with vacationers in summer. The beaches are safe and clean. This is also a yachting center, with a unique stone-built pier. In 1795, this was a notorious haven for vessels engaged in the smuggling trade, and the headland was riddled with caves for the storage of contraband. Both New Quay and Cei Bach were shipbuilding centers in bygone days, with New Quay of particular importance in this line in the first half of the 19th century.

In summer, information is available at the **Ceredigion District Council Information Centre,** Church Street (tel. 0545/560865), open from 10 a.m. to 6 p.m.

From New Quay, you can walk around the headland to Aberaeron (see below).

Where to Stay

If you'd like to stop over in New Quay, try the **Queens Hotel,** Church Street (tel. 0545/560650), a small family-run hostelry with only eight rooms. It is about a football field's distance from the harbor and beach. You can have tea or drinks at the umbrella-shaded tables in the forecourt. The hotel has a licensed lounge bar and an à la carte restaurant, where you can have a meal consisting of fresh fish, seafood, and good Welsh dishes for around £9 ($14.40) and up. Five of the bedrooms have showers, and all are centrally heated and have color TV. Tariffs are from £14 ($22.40) for B&B in a single, £25 ($40) in a double, with reductions in the low season. The hotel is open all year.

Sights

The **Royal National Lifeboat Institution** on the harbor (tel. 0545/560116) provides offshore cover of the coastal waters out to 30 miles and has a fast inshore boat stationed here to give aid to pleasure craft in distress in summer. The boathouse, built in 1904, is open to the public. There you can buy souvenirs and help with the operation of the institution, run entirely by voluntary contributions.

A short distance east of town, on the main A487 road, is Llanarth, where I recommend you stop at **Llanarth Pottery** (tel. 0545/580584), to watch the potter at work. John and Mary Lovett operate this interesting business, where they offer what may be the biggest and best selection of hand-thrown stoneware in Wales, at reasonable prices. You can find here mix-and-match glazes free of lead or injurious chemicals. In this modern age you may be happy to find oven-, freezer-, microwave-, and dishwasher-proof pottery. They are usually open daily, although in winter there could be days when they're closed.

ABERAERON: Although this little town at the mouth of the River Aeron was founded in the 19th century, there were settlers in the area from the 12th century on. However, they were traders and local fisherfolk who preferred the shelter of the valley farther inland. This planned town has some interesting architecture dating from Georgian to early Victorian. This was a shipbuilding port, and modern craft are still maintained in the inner harbor. The beaches are not as inviting here as at New Quay (just visited), about four miles to the south along the bay.

The **Ceredigion District Council Information Centre** is at the harbor (tel. 0545/570602).

Food and Lodging

Aberaeron has many hotels, guesthouses, and restaurants, but my favorite is the **Feathers Royal** (tel. 0545/570214), a happy and hospitable hotel, whose rooms have simple, contemporary furnishings. Once a posting inn, Feathers Royal has been known for more than a hundred years for food and hospitality. It's only a short distance from the beach and the river. Many of the 19 bedrooms have private baths, and all have color TV, phones, radios, room-call service, and hot-beverage facilities. Charges are £22.50 ($36) in a single, £33.50 ($53.60) in a double. There are laundry facilities here. Two bars cater to both hotel guests and nonresidents, and good food is served in the large dining room, where the tables are lit by little pink-shaded lamps, which are duplicated in sconces on the wall. The seafood specialties are especially good here, coming from the waters nearby, but they are rivaled by the trout from the river. A good selection of wines is available from the cellar. An à la carte lunch costs from £6 ($9.60), while dinner goes for £10 ($16) and up. Lunch is served from 12:30 to 2 p.m., dinner from 7 to 8:30 p.m. The bars and restaurant, as well as the laundry facilities, are in one wing of the hotel across the courtyard from that containing the bedrooms. In summer, guests can use the outdoor swimming pool.

Sights of Aberaeron

The **Aberaeron Sea Aquarium and Animal Kingdom Centre,** 2 Quay Parade (tel. 0545/570142), on the harbor next to the tourist information center, contains fish and other marine life found on the west coast of Wales, now living apparently content in tanks. There are also displays about sea creatures, showing their structure and ways of life, as well as fossils of marine life long ago. The animal section has tropical insects, giant millipedes, tarantulas, scorpions, reptiles, and birds, plus a children's corner with furry creatures. The complex, run by Geoffrey and Yvonne Browne, is open daily from 11 a.m. to 5 p.m. April, May, and September; from 10 a.m. to 5 p.m. daily in June and early July; from 10 a.m. to 9 p.m. daily in late July and August; and from 11 a.m. to 5 p.m. in October except on Monday and Tuesday. A ticket to both the aquarium and the animal kingdom costs £1.20 ($1.92) for adults, 60p (96¢) for children. Separate admission to either of the displays is 75p ($1.20) for adults, 40p (64¢) for children.

At the **Hive on the Quay,** Cadwgan Place (tel. 0545/570445), you can see honey and bumble bees at work and learn about honey production. In the hive complex you can have honey ice cream or purchase honey. There is also a white-washed café/restaurant, part of an old wharf, serving fresh homemade food and salads, a snack costing £1.75 ($2.80) and up. Hours are from 10:30 a.m. to 5 p.m., except from the first week in July to the end of August, when it remains open until 9 p.m. for suppers, such as pâté, followed by spinach and eggplant lasagne, then honey ice cream. A set meal costs £8 ($12.80). All the food can be enjoyed in the conservatory overlooking the harbor.

4. Lampeter

The Welsh, at least in the early days when they were affixing place names, tended to try to tell it all. For example, the name Lampeter is anglicized from Llanbedr Pont Steffan, which means the Church of St. Peter by Stephen's Bridge. The town was built where several roads join at the River Teifi.

There are no castle remains, unless you count the ancient mound in the grounds of St. David's College where one once stood. St. David's is the third university in England and Wales, after Oxford and Cambridge. It was originally a theological institution but today specializes in culture and agriculture.

Lampeter is a busy town, especially on market days—every other Monday for livestock and every other Tuesday for the general outdoor sale of various goods.

FOOD AND LODGING: An elegant mansion, **Falcondale Country House Hotel** (tel. 0570/422910) is nestled in a sheltered valley in 12 acres of parkland and woodland. In late spring the rhododendron groves burst into color, making this hotel and its grounds a particular delight. The house was built in 1859 by the Harford family of Bristol, who participated in the development and growth of Lampeter in all aspects of life. Today the Smith family owns this fine country hotel, which they purchased from the Peterwell estate. The mansion lies in hunt country and is the center of the premier hunt of the year, on Boxing Day. The Smiths rent 20 bedrooms, spacious and high-ceilinged, all with splendid views of the surrounding woodlands. All but two have private baths. You can stay in this warm family atmosphere for £31 ($49.60) in a single, £40 ($64) in a double, with a traditional breakfast included, served in the elegant dining room. Bar snacks are available in the handsome bar and lounge, with such dishes as sirloin steak, ploughman's lunch, plaice, and steak baps with onions, a meal costing £5 ($8). In the dining room, a set meal, including a choice of appetizers and one of three main dishes, plus a selection from the dessert trolley, costs £9.50 ($15.20). On the à la carte menu you'll find pâté maison and corn on the cob, while main courses include filet béarnaise, entrecôte Rossini, chasseur, or bordelaise, and trout amandine; among other dishes. A full meal will cost from £11 ($17.60) to £13 ($20.80). The service is gracious.

Farmhouse accommodations in the Lampeter area are previewed in "Ceredigion Country Comforts" in this chapter (see above).

The A482 road from Lampeter to Cardigan Bay leads to—

GOLD MINES: About eight miles southeast of Lampeter, just off the A482 near the village of Pumsaint (Five Saints), the **Dolaucothi Gold Mines,** where the Romans dug some 2,000 years ago, can be visited. The mines are part of a 2,600-acre estate which is in the care of the National Trust. From the visitor center near the entrance to the mine area, guided underground tours are offered. Wearing a miner's helmet and lamp, you go through the mines and pits first carved out by the Romans. Self-guided walks on the Miners' Way will take you to see the gold mines' main natural and man-made surface features and to two ancient mine tunnels. The trail includes a countryside walk through Welsh hill farmland, if you want to follow its full length, although a shortcut is marked. Dolaucothi mines are open from 10 a.m. to 5 p.m. daily mid-June to late October, with underground tours daily every half hour until mid-September. Admission for the underground tour, visitor center, and Miners' Way is £2.50 ($4) for adults, £1.25 ($2) for children. For only the visitor center and Miners' Way self-guided walk the price is £1.25 ($2) for adults, 70p ($1.12) for children.

The village of Pumsaint (often misspelled Pumpsaint) nearby is built on the site of a Roman fort and is also mainly a part of the National Trust–administered estate. There you can see a working blacksmith's forge.

For information about the gold mines, phone 05585/359.

5. Tregaron

This is a little market town for sheep farmers, with a big statue of Henry Richard, 19th-century Member of Parliament who was known as the Apostle of Peace, his work being the forerunner of the League of Nations and the United Nations. The great peat bog of Tregaron is a four-mile wilderness which is a national nature reserve, full of flowers and birds.

Mary Jones, Harriet Beecher Stowe's great-grandmother, was a native of Tregaron.

Tregaron's livestock markets are held every other Tuesday. The town bustles on alternate Tuesdays with the activity of the general market, with its stalls offering all sorts of goods.

Of special interest in Tregaron is **Canolfan Cynllun Crefft Cymru** (Craft Design Centre of Wales) (tel. 09744/415), where you find dragons of all ages—from those in process of hatching out of the egg to grandfather dragons and even dragon eggs, all locally made and excellent souvenirs of Wales. There is also fine handcrafted Rhiannon jewelry in gold and silver. Rhiannon S. Evans makes the jewelry in age-old Celtic patterns, and it's known to Celtic enthusiasts all over the world. There is also a woolen center here, upstairs from the Dragon's Den gift shop, where you can find knitwear made on the premises from homespun Black Welsh mountain wool, as well as handcrafted wood products.

IN THE ENVIRONS: In order to visit **Strata Florida Abbey,** take the B4343 road out of Tregaron going northeast. You'll come to a tiny hamlet, Pontrhydfendigaid, which means Bridge over the Blessed Ford. Turn to the east (right if you're coming from Tregaron), and you'll come to the abbey ruins about a mile along. An aura of tranquility lingers over the ruins of Strata Florida (the Vale of Flowers), which was a flourishing Cistercian abbey in the 12th and 13th centuries. The Norman archway and tile floors are of particular interest. Early Welsh notables were brought here for burial, perhaps even some royalty, but the stone-covered graves are unidentified. Dafydd ap Gwilym, the great 14th-century poet, is believed to have been interred here. The abbey is open March 15 to October 15 weekdays from 9:30 a.m. to 6:30 p.m., on Sunday from 2 to 6:30 p.m. The facilities and gift shop are closed in winter, but you can still go in and walk around. Admission is 75p ($1.20) for adults, 35p (56¢) for children to see an exhibition covering the life in the abbey.

Back in Pontrhydfendigaid, if you turn northeast, you can go to Teifi Pools in wild moors, a fine fishing area at the source of the River Teifi. Along the way, stop at **Cross Inn,** Ffair Rhos, Ystrad Meurig (tel. 09745/608), where Pam and Terry serve food in an inn that is about 300 years old, built on an old drovers' road. Tregaron was a collection point for the herds of sheep bound to the large market towns, and the shepherds who escorted the droves of sheep were probably hungry and thirsty when they got to this point in the foothills of the Plynlimon mountain range. There is a dining room, where children can be served along with the family. Adults can eat in the bar. A meal costs £2.50 ($4) to £7.50 ($12), with a homemade dessert. You might have a jumbo sausage, french fries, and peas with a pint of bitter, steak-and-kidney pie, vegetarian pie, or rump steak. Hours are from 11:30 a.m. to 3:30 p.m. and 5:30 to 10:30 p.m. (to 11 p.m. Friday and Saturday). On Sunday, hours are noon to 2 p.m. and 7 to 10:30 p.m.

6. Aberystwyth

The cultural, commercial, and administrative center of the western section of Mid Wales is Aberystwyth. The name of this town, never anglicized, tells exactly where it is: at the mouth (*aber* in Welsh) of the River Ystwyth (which is pronounced "Istwith"). The town blends the attractions of a seaside resort with those of a university center. It has a lively seafront promenade lined with hotels, and entertainment is provided at King's Hall.

Aberystwyth has many facilities for summer holiday fun. Golf, tennis, bowling, swimming, and boating are available. The beach has donkey rides and trampolines. Beach entertainment is provided by the college theater group, and on Sunday evening you can hear some fine Welsh hymn singing. Concerts on the promenade, evening shows, dances, and a moving-picture theater all add to the fun-making possibilities.

Markets are held weekly, one for varied merchandise on Monday and one for livestock on Wednesday.

Aberystwyth has a **castle.** (By this time, if you've been following this guide, you may be asking, "Who doesn't?") This one was built in 1277 and played an important role in Edward I's conquest of Wales. It stands on a headland above the promenade. You can visit it free to get a panoramic view of the coast.

The castle and the walled town that adjoined it were newcomers compared to the Celtic dwellers in the area, as attested to by the remains of an ancient hillfort, **Pendinas,** overlooking the town. **Llanbadarn,** a whisper away from the town center on the A44, is a village centered on the religious settlement founded by St. Padarn in the 6th century. Ancient Ogham stones are in the church.

For information about not only Aberystwyth but also all of Ceredigion, try the **Wales Tourist and Ceredigion District Council Information Centre,** Eastgate (tel. 0970/612125).

FOOD AND LODGING: A good example of a quality accommodation in a beach-resort area is the **Queensbridge Hotel,** The Promenade (tel. 0970/612343). It has an elevator, which may be a welcome help if you have been traveling or sightseeing all day. This licensed hotel is at the north end of the Promenade and has a panoramic view of Cardigan Bay. The resident proprietors welcome you to their 15 bedrooms, all with private baths or showers, toilets, phones, color TV, and hot-beverage facilities. Singles cost £22 ($35.20), and double- or twin-bedded rooms go for £32 ($51.20), all tariffs including a full English breakfast and VAT. Good food is served in the restaurant, with an extensive menu choice, dinner costing £8 ($12.80). If you want to be right in the midst of the holiday activities of Aberystwyth, this is the place for you.

The **Manora Hotel,** 49 North Parade (tel. 0970/615374), is owned by Don and Marion Lyon, who welcome you into this centrally located hotel, less than a five-minute walk from the railway station. The nine bedrooms all have hot and cold running water and razor outlets, and are centrally heated. The Lyons charge from £11.50 ($18.40) for B&B. The food is good and the hotel clean and pleasant. Children are welcome at reduced rates.

Llety-Gwyn Hotel, Llanbadarn Fawr (tel. 0970/613965), is a clean and comfortable B&B 1½ miles from the town center on the A44 road and from the sea. You get a warm Welsh welcome at this family-run place. Some of the 13 rooms have private baths. All the rooms are on the ground floor and suitable for disabled persons. They have color TV and hot-beverage facilities, plus central heating. The Jones family charges from £12 ($19.20) to £14.50 ($23.20) in a single, from £11 ($17.60) to £13.50 ($21.60) per person in a double for B&B, depending on the plumbing. There's a TV lounge for use by guests, and good home-cooking is provided. This hotel, in a country setting, is an ideal spot for touring.

At the **Marine Hotel,** Marine Parade (tel. 0970/612444), Mr. and Mrs. J.S. Evans have a bar and dining room in addition to 34 bedrooms, 24 of which have private baths. B&B costs £10 ($16) to £20 ($32) per person, depending on the plumbing. In the dining room, they serve Welsh lamb, local trout, and chicken daily, a three-course lunch costing £5.50 ($8.80) and a table d'hôte dinner for £8.50 ($13.60). If you prefer just a bar snack, you can have a ploughman's lunch or sandwiches. With your ale, the tab will come to about £2.25 ($3.60). In summer, the bar and dining room are open daily from 12:30 to 2 p.m. and 7 to 9:30 p.m. Winter hours are the same except that closing may be earlier. The hotel is open all year.

The **Savannah Guest House,** 27 Queens Rd. (tel. 0970/615131), is a bright and airy place to stay, two blocks from the beach. Mr. Terry Sadler, proprietor, rents rooms, all with hot-beverage facilities, for £10 ($16) per person for B&B.

There is an abundance of pubs in Aberystwyth, where you can usually find tasty pub snacks and congenial company, except on Sunday when pubs are closed.

A Splurge Choice

My favorite hotel in the Aberystwyth area is **Conrah Country Hotel,** Chancery (tel. 0970/617941), a gracious country mansion just three miles south of town off the A487 road. F.J. Heading gives guests a warm welcome to this fine old Welsh house, standing in 22 acres of woodland and gardens. The 13 stylishly appointed bedrooms in the mansion all have private bathrooms, central heating, phones, color TV, radios, and hot-beverage facilities. Adjoining the main house are the Magnolia Court motel rooms, each with a private shower and toilet. In the mansion, charges are from £26.50 ($42.40) to £31 ($49.60) per person in a double, £35 ($56) for single occupancy, which is of limited availability. In the courtyard motel, a double costs £23.50 ($37.60) per person, with £35 ($56) charged for single occupancy. All tariffs include breakfast and VAT. The hotel has a heated indoor pool, a sauna, a cocktail bar, and two lounges.

Nonresidents are welcomed in the restaurant, where "Taste of Wales" food is served in a handsome room. The chef takes pride in seeing to it that you have tasty, attractive meals. The menu for dinner may contain Welsh lamb, rabbit specialties, and beef dishes, as well as a touch of continental cuisine. Expect to pay from £12.75 ($20.40) for a complete dinner. The produce used is all local, and you will find the vegetables well prepared and not overcooked.

SIGHTS AND ACTIVITIES: Aberystwyth's University College of Wales overlooks the town from Penglais, an upland suburb. The **Aberystwyth Arts Centre and Catherine Lewis Gallery,** University College, Penglais Campus (tel. 0970/4277), shows exhibitions of paintings, sculpture, and graphics, both local and international. The college has a large collection of pottery—earthenware from the 19th century made in rural Wales, 18th-century Oriental pottery, one of the best collections in Britain of 20th-century studio pottery, and modern ceramics. In the Ceramics Gallery of the Arts Centre, Canolfan y Celfyddydau, specimens from this collection are exhibited and visiting ceramics shows are held. Prints and paintings are shown in the Catherine Lewis Gallery. The galleries are open all year except at Christmas, Easter, and mid-May to mid-June. Hours are 10 a.m. to 5 p.m., and the galleries are also open when arts center events are held. Admission is free. The arts center also houses a theater and concert hall, with year-round productions of drama, dance, film, and classical and popular music. A café, bookshop, and craftshop are also in the complex. For information, call between 9:30 a.m. and 8 p.m. Monday to Saturday.

Llyfrgell Genedlaethol Cymru, the National Library of Wales (tel. 0970/3816), is on Penglais Road at a site overlooking Cardigan Bay, with attractive gardens in front. This is a reference library where books, manuscripts, records, pictures, and maps relating to Wales and the Welsh language can be consulted. The Gregynog Gallery and some other parts of the library are open to the general visitor. The library is open from 9:30 a.m. to 6 p.m. Monday to Friday, from 9:30 a.m. to 5 p.m. on Saturday, and closed Sunday, bank holidays, Christmas and New Year holidays, Easter week, the first and last Monday in May, and the last Monday in August. The Gregynog Gallery is open from 10 a.m. to 5 p.m. There is no admission charge.

The **Ceredigion Museum,** The Coliseum, Terrade Road (tel. 0970/617911), is in the restored Edwardian Coliseum Theatre, with the theater atmosphere carefully preserved. Displays show local folk life, a cottage of 1850, agricultural and dairy history and equipment, and various crafts including turning, spinning, weaving, and carpentry. There are also archeology exhibits, weights and measures, domestic objects, lead-mining displays, clocks, and seafaring artifacts and history. The development of the town may be followed here. The museum is open Monday to Saturday from 10 a.m. to 5 p.m. Admission is free.

A favorite with visitors is the **Vale of Rheidol Narrow Gauge Railway,** operated by British Rail from the Alexandra Road Station to Devil's Bridge, described below. For information on the train, see "The Great Little Trains of Wales" in the "Getting Around Wales" section in Chapter XX.

A TREK INTO THE ENVIRONS: Before going on to the spa towns to be visited, I strongly recommend a swing toward the Plynlimon mountain range and the Ystwyth Forest.

The first stop is at **Plas Nant Eos** (tel. 0970/617756), 2½ miles southeast of Aberystwyth off the B4340 road. This is an ivy-covered early Georgian mansion, part of which is considerably older than the major part, which is 18th century. The cellars date to the 11th century. In a tranquil cwm (*nant eos* means "brook of the nightingale"; a *cwm* is a little valley), the ornate mansion reveals the style of living of Welsh aristocracy in the 18th and 19th centuries. The showpiece of the place is the music room, with exquisite plasterwork and an Italian marble fireplace. The house is open daily from 10:30 a.m. to 5:30 p.m. Admission is £1 ($1.60) for adults, 50p (80¢) for children.

Going from Aberystwyth east on the A44, you soon come to Capel Bangor and then the Rheidol hydroelectric plant, with the Cwmrheidol Nature Trail. About 11 miles from Aberystwyth, you come to **Llywernog Silver-lead Mine** at Ponterwyd (tel. 097085/620), which is now an open-air museum. You can follow the Miners' Trail and go underground, where you see a floodlit cavern containing the Blue Pool, a prospecting pit sunk around 1795. You can also see a rock crusher house, a water-wheel pit, an engine shaft and headframe, a horse-whim, a cast-iron water wheel, and a powderhouse. An exhibition of mining called "California of Wales" is in the main building. There is a souvenir and gift shop, a light-refreshment counter, picnic area, adventure playground, and rest rooms. The mine-museum is open March 21 to August 31 from 10 a.m. to 6 p.m., in September and October to 4 p.m. Admission is £1.50 ($2.40) for adults, 70p ($1.12) for children. You can have mail postmarked in the underground post office.

From Ponterwyd, the A4120 takes you south to **Devil's Bridge,** where the Vale of Rheidol Narrow Gauge Railway ends its run inland. The little train once carried lead from the mines and passengers. Now run by diesel, this was the last narrow-gauge steam railway in Wales and is the only one to be nationalized; it's now run by British Rail.

Among the finest scenery in Wales is at Devil's Bridge, over the wild, tumbling River Mynnach's deep gorge, just before it joins the River Rheidol to flow on to the sea. There are actually three bridges here, one above the other, but only the top one is usable. The lowest is a medieval span believed to have been built by monks of the Cistercian Abbey of Strata Florida not far south, probably so they could haul lead from the mines they operated in the area. The middle bridge was built in the 18th century to replace the first, and then, when it too began to weaken in the 19th century, the top span was built. The spectacular falls of the Mynnach are visible from here.

THE SPA COUNTRY

Since Roman times the mineral waters of this area have been known for their healing powers, and people once flocked here for treatment for various ailments. There must be something to be said for the curative powers of the waters found in this part of the country, as in Christian times no fewer than five holy wells here were once visited by pilgrims.

Today, lakes, spas, rivers, and huge reservoirs still draw visitors to this beautiful land.

7. Rhayader

The name of this town means a waterfall, and it was built at the site of rapids on the River Wye that were destroyed in 1780 by the building of the bridge.

The town stands at a loop of the Wye. The River Elan also runs to the town, which is about 3½ miles east of the huge Elan and Claerwen Reservoirs (their presence has led to the Elan Valley's being called the lakelands). The reservoirs were built to provide water for Birmingham, England. Some of the finest lake scenery in Wales is in this valley, and you can view the huge dams that are part of the water system.

Near Rhayader on a minor road are the ruins of **Abbey Cwmhir,** lying in a peaceful valley. The monks of the abbey are said to have brought for burial the body of Llewelyn the Last, so called because he was the last Prince of Wales to be born of Welsh blood. He was slain in 1282 near Builth Wells, previewed below. There is no special marking to show where the abbey ruins and the grave lie, but from the road you can see traces of outside walls. Go through the fence and walk down to where you can see the fragments of the north and south transepts and bases of several nave piers—all that is left of an abbey said to have been founded in 1143. What may be the grave of the prince can also be seen from the road.

Livestock markets are held in Rhayader every two weeks on Thursday, with a general market every Wednesday.

The **Wales Tourist Information Centre,** The Old Swan, West Street (tel. 0597/810591), dispenses information and suggestions on what to see in the spa country.

FOOD AND LODGING:
In the heart of Rhayader, the **Elan Hotel,** West Street (tel. 0597/810373), is a family-run establishment. The building, of white-painted plaster with black trim, has a dining room and family rooms with a view of the River Wye and of the soccer and rugby grounds. The hotel has 15 bedrooms, all with hot and cold running water and shaver outlets. Some rooms have private baths. The charge for B&B is £13.75 ($22) to £18.50 ($29.60) in a single, £22.50 ($36) to £28.50 ($45.60) in a double. There's a residents' lounge with color TV. You can have snacks in the cocktail bar. Margaret Thatcher once had lunch at the hotel, in the dining room at the back. You too can have lunch, choosing from a menu made up of tasty, fresh dishes, including river trout. A fixed-price lunch, served from noon to 2 p.m., costs £5.50 ($8.80). Two fixed-price dinners, offered from 7 to 8:30 p.m., go for £7.50 ($12) and £9.50 ($15.20). Breakfast is served in a room at the front of the hotel. From its windows you can see the interesting pub previewed next.

Cwmdauddwr Arms (tel. 0597/810345) has been a village pub since 1537. The section comprising one end of the pub is wood, made of huge black logs; the other section is white-painted stone and brick. The wooden part was built in 1540, and the "new" part was added in 1660. The pub has such interesting features as a flagstone floor and an inglenook fireplace where log fires blaze in winter. The owners, Eddie and Marie Hughes, offer a variety of cold snacks, including a ploughman's lunch and barbecued chicken. Expect to pay from £2.50 ($4) to £5 ($8) for a meal. Hours are from 11:30 a.m. to 3:30 p.m. and 5:30 to 10:30 p.m. (to 11 p.m. on Friday and Saturday). On Sunday, it's open from noon to 2 p.m. and 7 to 10:30 p.m.

Just outside town is the **Elan Valley Hotel** (tel. 0597/810448), a charming place built in 1895 and painted cream colored with black trim. You enter the hotel grounds through a gateway in a part-picket, part-stone wall, crossing over a cattle guard. This is a country-house hotel popular with anglers who can fish for trout in the river just outside. In fact, the owner Alan Lewis is a dedicated trout angler himself, and he'll happily give advice about the best spots for fishing. You can also, as would be expected, order trout for three meals a day, including breakfast. There are a dozen bedrooms, each comfortably furnished, but only three contain a private bath. Singles cost £20.50 ($32.80), doubles £33 ($52.80). The trio of rooms with bath carry a £1.50 ($2.40) per person supplement. A fixed-price lunch, costing £6.50 ($10.40), is served from 12:30 to 2 p.m., a set dinner from 7 to 8 p.m. going for £7.50 ($12). Nonresidents are welcome at dinner if they phone in advance.

South of Rhayader at Llanwrthwl is the **Vulcan Inn,** on the banks of the River Wye. The Vulcan is known locally as the "man-trap," so called because a former landlord had seven daughters he wanted to marry off. The inn has a 300-year-old fireplace with an inglenook in the bar. The food here is good, including steaks, Wye salmon, Welsh lamb, and desserts such as trifle, gâteau, cheesecake, and sundaes. Expect to pay from £8.50 ($13.60) for a meal in the dining room. Bar snacks cost as little as £1 ($1.60). Accommodation is available here, too, with modern motel units costing from £26 ($41.60) for double or single occupancy, with a full breakfast included. Food is served during regular pub hours: 11:30 a.m. to 3:30 p.m. and 5:30 to 10:30 p.m. (to 11 p.m. on Friday and Saturday. On Sunday, hours are noon to 2 p.m. and 7 to 10:30 p.m.

A good place to begin a visit to the "Wells" towns of the area, going almost to Brecon Beacons National Park in the south, is—

8. Llandrindod Wells

The premier spa town of Wales, Llandrindod Wells, 700 feet above sea level and surrounded by some of the most beautiful countryside in Wales, came into its heyday during the Victorian and Edwardian era when gout was a fashionable complaint. The architecture and layout of the town echo its Victorian origin, with spacious buildings, wide streets, and hotels and guesthouses to suit every taste. Everything in the town is within walking distance.

Every September Llandrindod Wells stages a Victorian Festival. Since the town as it stands is a perfect setting, all that's necessary is for the people to don costumes of the era to make it look authentic. Hotels, restaurants, pubs, and all sorts of other places participate, by serving Victorian menus and otherwise harking back to other days.

It may come as a surprise to you that Llandrindod Wells is called "Toad Town" by some. The local toad population crosses from the woodlands to the waters of the lake on warm spring evenings, and warning signs, saying "Migratory Toad Crossing," are put up to slow down traffic. Toad-watching expeditions are organized by the local Nature Trust. I don't advise kissing any of the toads. If I recall the old fairytale correctly, it was a frog, not a toad, that turned into a prince when a pretty girl kissed it (him).

An 18-hole **golf course** above the lake, one of the highest courses in Britain, offers panoramic views. Visitors are welcome just to come and look.

The **Wales Tourist** and **Radnor District Council Information Centre** is at Rock Park Spa (tel. 0597/2600), open daily from 10 a.m. to 6 p.m.

FOOD AND LODGING: Standing in green Edwardian majesty in the heart of the spa town, **The Metropole,** Temple Street (tel. 0597/2881), with turrets, oriels, wide carpeted halls, spacious public rooms and bedrooms, and a courteous staff makes you pleased that you selected this as your place to stay in a period town. Nothing has been done to detract from the elegance injected into the place by its founder, the great-grandmother of the present owners. All of the 121 bedrooms have private baths, direct-dial phones, TV, and hot-beverage facilities. Singles cost from £34.50 ($55.20) and doubles or twins from £52 ($83.20), with a full English breakfast and VAT included. The spacious rooms in the hotel's turrets cost £61 ($97.60), and they give you a well-rounded view. Children up to the age of 15 can share their parents' room free, paying only for food. This all makes staying here a bit of a splurge, but it's well worth it. From the time you enter, service is excellent, a quality zealously encouraged by David Baird-Murray, the managing director, and Robert Marchesi, the manager. The hotel is centrally heated, and it also has a heated swimming pool. On the ground floor are a large boutique and a private residents' lounge, in addition to the reception office.

In Spencer's Bar, named for the former managing director, Spencer Miles, whose mother, Mrs. Elizabeth Miles, was the hotel's founder, you can have hot and cold meals, snacks, teas, and coffee throughout the day and evening. You may enjoy one of the excellent wines, sold here by the glass or by the bottle. In the restaurant, which has a good reputation for high-quality food, a table d'hôte luncheon will cost £9 ($14.40), while a fixed-price dinner goes for £11 ($17.60). Also offered is Chef Powell's Special Menu, which starts at £13.25 ($21.20). Breakfast is served in the restaurant from 8 to 9:30 a.m., lunch from 12:30 to 2:15 p.m., and dinner from 7 to 8:30 p.m. Entertainment is offered in the ballroom from March until the end of November, consisting of a Welsh harpist and choir, plus a live trio (singer, organist, and drummer), the Bluejays, presenting music to suit all ages. The Metropole is a member of the Best Western group. There's more than ample parking.

The **Hampton Hotel,** Temple Street (tel. 0597/2585), is a family-run stone-faced hotel in the heart of town. The owners, Vera, Keith, and Gordon Kermode, pride themselves on creating an atmosphere of friendly informality, mixed with the Victorian theme. Most of their 33 bedrooms have private bath, and all have radios and baby-listening service. The charge for B&B is £12 ($19.20) per person. The hotel has two bars and residents' lounges, one of which has color TV. You can order bar snacks throughout the day, and the home-cooked food is good. Parking facilities are adjacent to the hotel, and if you wish, they can arrange for a lock-up garage for you. During the season, there is entertainment most nights, including a local Welsh male-voice choir and an evening of Old Tyme Music Hall.

Griffin Lodge, Temple Street (tel. 0597/2432), is a building of dressed stone with brick trim and two big bow windows. It's a friendly, family-run hotel, with eight bedrooms, all with hot and cold water basins and central heating. Four units have private showers and toilets. Charges are £12 ($19.20) to £14.50 ($23.20) per person for B&B in a double, with a supplement of £1.50 ($2.40) to £2 ($3.20) for single occupancy. The food is good, and you can have snacks in the bar.

The **Llanerch 16th-Century Inn** (tel. 0597/2086) is a stone building, the oldest in Llandrindod Wells. It's a large, lively spot where you can get acquainted with the local people. Six of the 12 bedrooms have private baths, and all have central heating and tea/coffee-making facilities. There's a residents' lounge, but I find the pub more interesting for relaxation. The food and the ale are good. Rooms rent for £12 ($19.20) to £15 ($24) per person for B&B, the latter price for a room with bath. The inn used to be the stagecoach stop on the Swansea–Chester run.

Ty Clyd Guest House, Park Terrace (tel. 0597/2122), sits in a quiet cul-de-sac overlooking Rock Park, a typical Victorian guesthouse of red brick with yellow brick trim. Its bedrooms all have hot and cold running water, shaver outlets, and bedside lights. There's central heating, and the residents' lounge has color TV. Rooms rent for £9.50 ($15.20) per person for B&B. The house has a residential liquor license and a restaurant where a variety of food is available in the evening.

SIGHTS: In the Rock Park, the **Pump Room** has been restored, and visitors can follow the lead of their ancestors by "taking the waters," downing a glassful of the mineral potable. (Be warned: it's highly laxative!) The spa complex also houses an interesting exhibition, giving an insight into Llandrindod's history as a thriving spa town. The spa, set in 18 acres of wooded parkland, is open daily in summer from 10 a.m. to 6 p.m. and on weekdays in winter from 10 a.m. to 4 p.m. For more information, telephone 0597/4307. Admission to the spa is free. Details on the annual Victorian Festivals, held each September, are available here.

Llandrindod Museum, Temple Street (tel. 0597/4513), contains archeological material mainly from the excavated Castell Collen, a Roman fort that stood nearby. The excavation, on the west bank of the River Ithon about half a mile north of the town center, is now just grass-covered humps, but the museum in town contains exhibits that have been added to the collection illustrating the growth of Llandrindod Wells as a major spa town. On display is the Paterson collection of dolls. The museum is open from 10 a.m. to 12:30 p.m. and 2 to 5 p.m. Monday to Saturday, except on Saturday afternoon from October to April. Admission is free.

In the **Automobile Palace,** Temple Street (tel. 0597/2214), you can see Tom Norton's cycle collection, with an amazing array of old velocipedes, ordinaries (penny-farthing bicycles), and other machines dating from 1867 to 1938. The Automobile Palace also houses a service station and a shop selling automobile accessories, but you can wander in the cycle room as you wish. It's open daily except Sunday and bank holidays during regular shopping hours. Admission is free.

The **Old Pump House Hotel,** now Powys County Hall and headquarters for the Radnor District Council, is an impressive building approached along the drive opposite the end of Beaufort Road or from a footpath on the lake side of the putting green.

IN THE ENVIRONS: Just south of Llandrindod Wells at **Howey,** excellent farmhouse accommodation is offered at **Three Wells Farm** (tel. 0597/2484), just outside Llandrindod Wells. Margaret and Ron Bufton have added a wing to their house, built in 1900, to allow space for a cheerful dining room. The house looks over a lake that is watered by the three wells, which are really in existence and which make certain that the Buftons never run short of water. In fact the Welsh Water Board uses 400,000 gallons of water a day from these artesian wells. In their house of mellow red brick, the Buftons rent 12 bedrooms, all with private toilets and baths or showers and TV. Charges are from £10 ($16) to £10.50 ($16.80) per person for B&B, from £14.50 ($23.20) to £15.50 ($24.80) for half board. Rates are lower on a weekly basis. Mrs. Bufton is a good cook, and Mr. Bufton will mix you a drink in the little bar or the large lounge bar. The house even has an elevator.

The little village of **Newbridge-on-Wye,** on the A470 almost due west of Howey, is set in rolling country. An old drovers' pub is now the Mid Wales Gallery of Crafts. The main reason for stopping here is that it has a good place to stay or to have a meal.

The **New Inn** (tel. 059789/211), on the village square, is where Ada Parkinson-Jones welcomes guests and has built up a reputation for hospitality and good food. The inn is three 16th-century farm cottages which were converted to a drovers' inn in the 19th century. The slate-roofed building is constructed of white stone with black windows and black lattice entrance porches. There are nine bedrooms, three with private baths, costing from £15 ($24) in a single, from £30 ($48) in a double, for B&B. You can meet local people at the lounge bar. It and the dining room overlook a garden at the back. The inn has a coffeeshop where a buffet lunch and supper are served. So highly regarded is the food here that unless you are a resident in the inn, you'd better call ahead to make reservations for a meal. Such tasty dishes as homemade soup, scampi in puff pastry, and steak and onions are on the menu, and excellent fresh vegetables are always offered. Lunch costs from £5 ($8); dinner, from £10 ($16). A buffet is served from noon to 2 p.m. and dinners from 7 to 9 p.m.

A little way south of Howey on the A483 is **Disserth.** You may want to go to little **Disserth Church** at the foot of a steep hill beside the River Ithon. It's part 13th century and has box pews inscribed 1666–1722.

At **Penybont,** about five miles east of Llandrindod Wells, there is a pottery, and a little farther on, turning at a sign on the left, is the 17th-century, thatched **Pales Meeting House** of the Quakers, which you can visit.

9. Llanwrtyd Wells

This quiet little town astride the A483 road was once a popular spa center, its medicinal springs attracting crowds. Today it is better known as a center of the Pony Trekking Society of Wales. Using the old cattle drovers' road, a narrow winding path into the Cambrian Mountains and down on the other side, you can reach Tregaron (previewed above), 13 miles to the west, and the Cardigan Bay area from here.

You can get to Llanwrtyd Wells on the A483 if you're driving. Also, trains via Shrewsbury or Swansea on the British Rail lines come here.

At Llanwrtyd Wells, a livestock market is held every two weeks.

An information center is at **The Bookshop** (tel. 0591/3391).

FOOD AND LODGING: Warm hospitality and comfortable lodging is offered at **Lasswade House** (tel. 05913/515) by Phil and Patricia Ross. The red brick and cream, Dutch-style house has a lounge with a tiny bar in the corner and shelves with lots of books in the entry hall so you can select your reading matter. You can look out across the meadow to the river from the house or the swimming pool. The dining room provides an extensive à la carte or table d'hôte menu, and the house has a residential license, so you can have a cocktail or drink with your meal. There are eight double bedrooms, all with private baths, TV, and hot-beverage facilities. The price for B&B is from £15 ($24). Dinner costs an extra £9 ($14.40), and it's worth it.

Staying in the Environs

At **Llangammarch Wells,** four miles from Llanwrtyd Wells, is the **Lake Hotel** (tel. 05912/202), a half-timbered structure with the River Irfon flowing in front. A beautiful garden leads down to the river. This handsome country-house hotel is set in 50 acres of grounds, with a trout lake and 5½ miles of salmon and trout fishing. Fishing instructions and tackle are available. The hotel has a skeet-shooting range, a tiny golf course, a putting green, and a tennis court. There are luxurious lounges and fine cuisine. The bedrooms, 20 in all, have color TV and tea/coffee-making facilities, and are centrally heated. Tariffs for B&B are £33.50 ($53.60) in a single, £37.50 ($60) in a double.

A TWEED FACTORY: Just outside Llanwrtyd Wells is the **Cambrian Factory Limited** (tel. 05913/211). The factory, run jointly by the Royal British Legion and the Powys County Council, was established in 1918 to give employment to disabled veterans of World War I, and now other disabled persons are also employed here. You can watch the manufacturing process involving wool sorting, dyeing, carding, spinning, warping, winding, and weaving, and see the fine tweed results. Material and many items of clothing both for men and women, as well as accessories, can be purchased in the large factory shop. The factory is open from 8:15 a.m. to 4:30 p.m. Monday to Friday. The shop, open all year, can be visited from 8:15 a.m. to 5:15 p.m. Monday to Friday, closing at noon on Saturday.

10. Builth Wells

This is the agricultural if not the geographical center of Wales every July, when the Royal Welsh Agricultural Society holds a four-day show here. Even the name of the town reflects agricultural pursuits. It is derived from the Welsh name meaning the Church of St. Mary in the Cow Pasture.

At **Cilmery,** four miles west toward Llangammarch Wells, is the **Prince Llewelyn Memorial,** commemorating the death of the last native Prince of Wales who was killed near this spot in 1282.

Along the path from the Lion Hotel, you'll come to the fragmentary remains of the 11th-century **Builth Castle.** It is claimed that Llewelyn the Last was refused help by his fellow Welshmen in the castle. You can look around free.

The wells of Builth, Llangammarch, and Llanwrtyd no longer exist except in the names of the towns.

Monday is market day here, with a livestock sale and a general merchandise event.

In summer, the **Wales Tourist Information Centre,** Groe Car Park (tel. 0982/553307), is open from 10 a.m. to 6 p.m.

FOOD AND LODGING: Just north of town on the A483 road, at a village called Llanewedd, **Pencerrig Hotel** (tel. 0982/553226), a Consort chain hostelry, is a country-house accommodation, painted pale pink with gray trim and bow windows, standing in extensive gardens. All the bedrooms and suites have hot and cold water basins and comfortable beds. Some have private baths. You can stay here for £22 ($35.20) in a single, £38 ($60.80) in a double for B&B. The hotel is fully licensed and has a pleasant bar where you can have bar snacks, unless you'd rather go to the dining room, serving table d'hôte and à la carte menus. The hotel is equipped to accommodate disabled guests.

Querida, 43 Garth Rd. (tel. 0982/553642), is a well-recommended B&B, within easy reach of the town center. Mrs. C.M. Hammond warmly welcomes guests to her house, renting rooms for £10 ($16) per person, with a good Welsh breakfast as part of the price.

THE BORDER COUNTRY

Border towns and castles of the Marcher Lords, even a long stretch of the dike built by King Offa of Mercia to keep the Welsh separated from his Saxon subjects, are to be seen here. Much of this is agricultural country, with sheep and cattle markets frequently held, and all the green, rolling hills and uplands dotted with little specks of white—sheep grazing on rich grassland.

Before visiting the towns and sights of this area, I'll introduce you to some farmhouse accommodations. Then I'll begin with a look at Hay-on-Wye, on the eastern border of Wales, a site that is actually in Brecon Beacons National Park. The farthest northern point visited in this section will be Welshpool, and the western reach will be to Llanidloes and Llangurig in the area where the mighty River Severn begins its long descent to the Bristol Channel.

HEART OF WALES FARM AND COUNTRY HOLIDAYS: A group of farm women who say they consider themselves lucky to live in this part of Wales and want to share it have opened their homes to visitors. The farms described below accept B&B guests for a night or longer. There are also self-catering houses in the Heart of Wales group, not previewed here. Prices at the B&B farmhouses are uniform: £10.50 ($16.80) per person per night or £70 ($112) per week. For dinner, bed, and breakfast, the charges are £15 ($24) per person per night, £99 ($158.40) weekly. All the houses have such amenities as hot and cold running water in the bedrooms, separate lounges for use by guests, and color TV. For information about staying here (and about the self-catering possibilities, if you're interested), get in touch with **Mrs. Gwyneth Jones,** Moat Farm, Welshpool, Powys S421 8SE, U.K. (tel. 0938/3179).

On the banks of the River Severn is **Dol-llys,** a mile from Llanidloes (tel. 05512/2694), a 17th-century farmhouse that is especially interesting with its many levels and small staircases, typical of many buildings of its period. The farm where Mrs. Olwen Evans receives guests includes pedigreed Hereford cattle, sheep, poultry, and a children's pony.

Cyfie Farm, Llanfihangel, Llanfyllin (tel. 069184/451), is a 178-acre hill farm with sheep and cattle. Lynn and George Jenkins welcome guests to their traditional Welsh long house, with beamed ceilings in the rooms, panoramic views, and a colorful garden. There is a private suite with its own shower and toilet, in addition to two other bedrooms.

Goitre, Kerry, Newtown (tel. 068688/248), is where Mrs. Menna Parry dispenses true Welsh hospitality to guests in her century-old country home, which has been modernized inside and made comfortable by today's standards. You can enjoy good home-cooking in this stone house, set in 190 acres of rolling farmland. Mrs. Parry lets you be lazily tranquil or active, whichever you choose.

At **Highgate Farm,** Newtown (tel. 0686/25981), Mrs. Linda Whitticase and her happy family will welcome you to their beautiful half-timbered, 15th-century farmhouse, in an elevated position only three miles from Newtown, with commanding views of the countryside. The house has oak beams, floors, and paneling. The bedroom in which I stayed had a priesthole, which is now occupied by the water basin. From the bedroom window I saw one of the loveliest sunrises of my life; the clouds over the rolling green hills changed into colors I never before saw in the sky. The 300-acre farm produces beef, sheep, and grain, and visitors can join in the active country life. Fishing, shooting, and riding the Whitticases' ponies are possibilities. The food, served in a handsome, heavily beamed old dining room with an inglenook fireplace, is excellent and brought in courteously by the Whitticase daughters.

Lower Gwestydd, Llanllwchaiarn, Newtown (tel. 0686/26718), is another "magpie" (black-and-white) house, this one of the 17th century. It has oak beams and historic features both inside and out. Bedrooms have hot and cold water basins, hot-beverage facilities, and shaving points. The main enterprises of the farm are beef, sheep, and some land tilling. Home-produced beef, lamb, and chicken, together with home-grown fruit and vegetables, are served in season. Mrs. Iris Jarman is your hostess.

Y Grofftydd, Carno, Newtown (tel. 0686/420274), is a traditional stone-built farmhouse in rolling hill country. Mrs. P. Lewis and family invite guests to explore the 180-acre farm and participate in such activities as claypigeon shooting and treasure hunts.

At **Little Brompton Farm,** Montgomery (tel. 06868/371), Mrs. Gaynor Bright and her husband, Robert, invite guests to see the operation of a working farm while staying in a 17th-century farmhouse, with oak-beamed interior, an inglenook fireplace, and country hospitality. Offa's Dyke runs through the farm.

The Drewin, Churchstoke, Montgomery (tel. 05885/325), is a 17th-century Border farmhouse of charm and character, with an inglenook fireplace and oak beams. Mrs. Ceinwen Richards welcomes guests to the farm, where sheep, cattle, and corn are raised, and where the Offa's Dyke footpath cuts through the acreage.

Gungrog House, Rhallt, Welshpool (tel. 0938/3381), is a 16th-century farmhouse, spacious and traditionally furnished, in an elevated position giving views of the Severn Valley and Powys Castle. Mrs. Eira Jones is proud of the quiet location of her house, only two miles from busy Welshpool. The 21-acre farm is run in conjunction with a farm-produce business.

Tynllwyn Farm, Welshpool (tel. 0938/3175), on a hillside a mile from Welshpool with views across the Severn Valley, is where Mrs. Freda Emberton receives guests to her comfortable home, dating from 1861. There's a 300-year-old Welsh dresser in the entrance hall. Bedrooms have color TV, and hot-drinks facilities. Tynllwyn is mainly a dairy farm, but the Embertons also keep pigs, chickens, geese, peacocks, and pheasants, as well as bees, whose honey you can have for breakfast. Plentiful farmhouse meals are served here, and the house is licensed to serve drinks.

Another group, **Hills and Vales of Mid Wales,** has houses on farms in the southern part of Powys County. For information on these, get in touch with Mrs. Yvonne Riley, Solifor, Llanwrthwl, Llandrindod Wells, Powys LDl 6NU (tel. 0597/810240).

11. Hay-on-Wye

Known as "The Town of Books" because of the many secondhand-book shops scattered throughout, Hay, at the edge of the Black Mountains and the northern peak of Brecon Beacons National Park, was once a Roman fort and then a Norman castle town on the looping River Wye. The castle, of which only the gatehouse and ruined old walls remain, had a Tudor manor grafted on, which belongs to Richard Booth, the originator of secondhand-book sales in the little town.

From a small start to the book paradise of today, Hay has come into the world spotlight. It is claimed that this is the world's largest collection of secondhand books, unrivaled in quantity and in the diversity of subjects covered.

WHERE TO STAY: The leading choice is the **Kilbert Country Hotel,** Bull Ring (tel. 0497/821004). It's owned by Pharos, the town's most influential book distributor. It's contained within solid 18th-century walls of what until recently was the home of a doctor. The dignified Georgian stone facade conceals spaces whose wattle-and-daub construction is still partially visible despite extensive renovations. Each of the smallish but cozy bedrooms has a very old beamed ceiling, a modernized bath, trouser press, phone, TV, and coffeemaker. Dawn Farnworth, the charming and elegant manager, charges from £22 ($35.20) to £27 ($43.20) per person in a double or twin, £27 ($43.20) to £32 ($51.20) in a single, with breakfast included. Prices are reduced by 20% in winter. The hotel's restaurant is recommended separately.

The **Old Black Lion,** 26 Lion St. (tel. 0497/820841). Low slung and a good example of a warmly furnished Welsh inn, this snug-looking place lies on the immediate edge of town. Parts of its foundation are reputed to date from the 13th century, and one of the bedrooms (number 6) was slept in by Oliver Cromwell in the 17th century. Most visitors come here for the pub and adjacent restaurant (see below), but overnighters can choose one of ten upstairs bedrooms, all but two of which have a private bath. Depending on the season and plumbing, singles range from £16.50 ($26.40) to £27 ($43.20), doubles £18 ($28.80) to £21 ($33.60) per person, with breakfast included.

La Fosse, Oxford Road (tel. 0497/820613). Jill Crook is the owner of this 160-year-old white stucco house. With its walled garden, it occupies a corner lot across the street from the Old Black Lion, just at the edge of the commercial center. None of the quintet of simple bedrooms contains a private bath, but each is comfortably appointed. With breakfast included, a single rents for £13 ($20.80), a double costing £9.50 ($15.20) per person. Ms. Crook will prepare a three-course meal for her guests if they want it at £5 ($8) per person.

WHERE TO DINE: The most desirable restaurant in town is **The Garden Restaurant,** Kilvert Country Hotel, Bull Ring (tel. 0497/821042). Contained within this previously recommended hotel, the Garden is formal and elegant. Spacious, high-ceilinged, and papered with flowery wallcoverings popular in the 18th century, it serves well-prepared meals from noon to 2 p.m. and 6 to 9 p.m. daily. Full meals cost from £13 ($20.80) each and might include game pâté en croûte, a steaming bowl of harvest broth (made with vegetables, meat, fresh mint, and served with farmhouse cheese) or poached mackerel with a fennel and gooseberry sauce. The dessert wagon is supplemented with an unusual array of homemade ice creams, including loganberry, brown bread, or coffee walnut.

Lion's Corner House, 39 Lion St. (tel. 0497/820175), served as a toy shop until Colin Thompson converted it into a stylish and country comfortable restaurant. Set across the street from the Doric perimeter of the 18th-century Butter Market, the place is filled with stripped pine furniture, hanging garlands of drying herbs, and rustic accessories. Full meals cost from £11 ($17.60) at dinner, around £7 ($11.20) at lunch. Service is from 11 a.m. to 2:30 p.m. daily except Sunday. Dinner is from 7 to either 9:30 or 10 p.m., depending on the day of the week (closed Sunday and Monday). Menu items include sirloin steak with port and mushroom sauce, roast duck, sautéed sweetbreads, or chicken breast stuffed with smoked oysters and Caerphilly cheese. A dessert specialty is sheep's milk ice cream flavored with vanilla or carob.

The **Old Black Lion,** 26 Lion St. (tel. 0497/820841). Previously recommended as a hotel, this traditional inn serves meals in its low-ceilinged pub section daily from noon to 2 p.m. and 7 to 9:30 p.m. Bar meals cost from £5 ($8) and might include pâté with hazelnuts flavored with whisky, lasagne, and homemade pastries. A smallish comfortable dining room is open only for dinner from 7 to 9 p.m. daily. There, full meals go for around £10 ($16) and might feature escalope of veal with breadcrumbs, tipsy pigeon (oven baked with black olives, bacon, garlic sausage, sherry, and brandy), or salmon with Armagnac and herbs.

The **Granary,** 2021 Broad St. (tel. 0497/820790), by the clock tower, provides homemade food and drink. They serve soups and appetizers as well as typical British main dishes such as chicken pot pies with vegetables. Once the town's grain store, the Granary has a long counter where you can order your choice from the blackboard to be served at the casual wooden tables. A meal will cost £5 ($8). The establishment is open daily from 10 a.m. to 5 p.m.

BROWSING FOR BOOKS: The place where Richard Booth started it all is the **Hay Cinema Bookshop,** on Castle Street (tel. 0497/820071). In youthful enthusiasm, he started a tiny secondhand bookshop here, which expanded rapidly into the largest secondhand bookshop in the world. Still in the old cinema where it started, the bookshop flourishes. This is the place to find that special book you've sought for so long. Just to browse through the vast stock is a delightful way to spend an afternoon. You'll probably find some title you can't imagine having done without for so long: for example, *Nurse and Spy in the Union Army,* published in Hartford, Connecticut, in 1865.

STAYING IN THE ENVIRONS: In the tiny hamlet of **Three Cocks,** four miles from Hay-on-Wye, the **Three Cocks Hotel** (tel. 04974/215) is a charming place to stay: a 15th-century stone building which over the years of its construction incorporated the trunk of a live tree into one of its walls. The tree is still visible, in a servant's stairwell. The inn and its elegant restaurant are owned by Michael Winston from England and his charming Belgium-born wife, Marie-Jeanne. The seven bedrooms all have hot and cold running water and are decorated to suit the rest of the inn, with old-fashioned styling supported by fairly old carved furniture. Tariffs are £18 ($28.80) in a single for B&B, £36 ($57.60) in a double. Half board for guests staying two or more days costs £29 ($46.40) per night per person. The dining room is done in wood and stone, with fabric-covered walls. Its enormous windows look out on a lush green meadow where sheep graze. You might dine on saddle of lamb flavored with ginger, saddle of fallow deer with pink peppercorns, and blanquette of lobster, among the tasty food offered. An à la carte meal costs from £10 ($16) to £15 ($24).

About three miles west from Three Cocks, where the A4079 road is joined by the A470, is **Llyswen.** In this tiny village, you'll find the **Griffin Inn** (tel. 087485/241), in a building originally constructed in the 15th century as a cider house, which contained both a press and space to ferment the apples. Today, sitting close to the road, it is a friendly inn popular with people who come to fish in the River Wye. Richard Stockton, the owner, maintains the Fisherman's Bar and the country-style dining room with care. The bar contains two woodburning fireplaces made of large blocks of local stone, and brass objects hang from the smoke-darkened ceiling beams. The dining room has Windsor chairs and thick, plastered walls. Most visitors stop by for the good-tasting food served from noon to 2:30 p.m. (till 2 p.m. in winter) and 7 to 9:30 p.m. (till 9 p.m. in winter). Copious breakfasts, included in the room rate if you stay here, include kippers, salmon, and home-cured ham. A full evening meal, costing around £12 ($19.20), will let you sample fresh rainbow trout from the Wye, duckling and other poultry dishes, or several kinds of beef, as well as salmon. The six bedrooms all have private baths. Singles cost £16 ($25.60) for B&B, and doubles go for £30 ($48).

12. Land of the Upper Severn

Britain's longest river, the Severn, begins its journey to the sea in the northern part of Powys County, in the Plynlimon area of the Cambrian Mountains. This river's source is only a mile or so from the head of the River Wye, which chose to follow a southward course while the Severn meandered its way generally eastward and northward in Wales. It's first major meeting is with the River Clywedog at—

LLANDIDLOES: This historic little town is remarkable for its old, half-timbered **market hall,** so placed in the center of the town that the road has to take a jog around it. John Wesley preached his early principles of Methodism at this marketplace. The ground floor is open, and heavy black posts support the upper part, where the local museum is housed. **Orchard House** (Perllan-dy), in nearby China Street, is another 17th-century structure in which a craft shop, gallery, and restaurant are now in business. This is a pleasant little stone, slate-roof, and magpie village.

A little to the northwest is the huge Clywedog dam and lake, with fishing and boating possibilities. This is a tranquil and beautiful part of Wales.

Where to Stay

If you decide to stop over in this peaceful little town, try the **Trewythen Arms Hotel,** Great Oak Street (tel. 05512/2214). It's a big Georgian brick town house right next door to the Laura Ashley shop beside the Severn, a suitable place to stay for families or commercial travelers, but don't expect the latest in hotel accoutrements. You can have snacks in the pub bar. Bedrooms, all 11 of them, have hot and cold running water, and four contain private baths. Depending on the plumbing, singles rent for £15 ($24) to £18 ($28.80), and doubles go for £25 ($40) to £28 ($44.80).

Sights

The **Museum of Local History and Industry,** Market Hall, displays articles pertaining to the area and to local industry. It is open from 11 a.m. to 1 p.m. and 2 to 5 p.m. daily except Sunday from Easter week to September. Admission is free. The most interesting thing about this museum is its location upstairs in the old magpie market hall in the center of town.

There's a **Laura Ashley Ltd.** shop here at 30 Great Oak St. (tel. 05512/2557), selling products made in nearby Carno.

STAYING AT LLANGURIG: An outstanding guesthouse, **The Old Vicarage,** at Llangurig (tel. 05515/280), a short distance southwest of Llanidloes on the Arr just after it meets the A470, is owned by Brian and Anna Rollings, who maintain a high standard of accommodation. All the well-appointed bedrooms have hot and cold water basins, shaver points, and heating. They rent for £10.50 ($16.80) per person for B&B, the price including VAT. An evening meal is offered for £7.30 ($11.68), with tasty food. The house has a licensed bar and lounges with color TV and log fires. Brian is a keen local historian and genealogist, who can tell you all about the area and perhaps help you find where to seek out records of your ancestors if you're of Welsh extraction.

CAERSWS: Here on a great loop of the upper Severn, where it is joined by the River Garno, the Romans built a fort, which became the hub of the legionnaires' road system linking the encampment with other fortifications, including the strong garrison town of Chester to the north in what is now England. The roads, basis of those followed by travelers over the centuries, are about all that's visible now to remind of the Roman stay.

Food and Lodging

For a delightful place to stay at Caersws, go to **Maesmawr Hall** (tel. 068684/255), where Mr. and Mrs. Jon Kendal receives guests in their handsome 16th-century country house at the end of a long, tree-lined drive. The structure, built in 1535 as a hunting lodge for the Earl of Leicester, is a fine example of the central-chimney timber-framed houses characteristic of the former county of Montgomeryshire. The front of the building is half-timbered and has a heavy oaken door. The lounge bar is a striking combination of fine oak beams and an impressive paneled fireplace with a timbered inglenook and fine carving down the sides and on the mantelpiece. The residents' lounge, called Waincoat's Parlour, is the old library, with fine oak paneling, which now contains a TV set. The 20 bedrooms in the hotel vary greatly as to space and appearance, as they would have done to house an earl and his entourage and even quite possibly a visiting queen. Four are singles, the rest twins or doubles, and all but two have private baths. Singles with bath cost from £26.25 ($42), doubles with bath from £42.75 ($68.40) for B&B. Six compact and modern rooms are in the Coach House extension of Maesmawr, just two minutes' walk from the main hotel. Four of these are on the ground floor for use by disabled people.

A varied menu of good English cooking is offered in the elegant dining room, and there's a small but select wine list to complement your meals. From the à la carte menu, you can order deviled whitebait, chef's pâté, pastas, poached or grilled fresh Scottish salmon, roast pheasant, and jugged venison. Perhaps you'd like to make a choice from the well-stocked cheeseboard for dessert. An à la carte dinner costs from £15 ($24), a table d'hôte evening meal offered for £10 ($16) and up, with a choice of main dishes including lamb, trout, beef, and chicken, served with vegetables and a dessert to follow. Service is friendly and you can lunch or dine at leisure. Bar snacks are available at any time of day.

At nearby Carno, on the A470 road, mentioned above, there is a large, modern complex housing a **Laura Ashley Ltd. factory.** Unfortunately it is not open to visitors, but from the road you can look through the huge glass windows and see a little of what goes on. There is no shop in connection with the factory; the nearest one is at Llanidloes, previewed above.

13. Newtown

This busy little town, "new" in 1279, with a three-mile promenade along the River Severn and a footbridge from the Town Hall car park to 32-acre Dolerw Park, was once a main center of the wool and flannel industry. The town is in an agricultural area of low uplands, with hills rising on either side. The Montgomeryshire Canal came here in the 1820s, followed by the railroad some 40 years later.

A gala event of which Newtown is proud is the **Mid Wales Stampede,** held in June. If you want to be transported back to the days of the Wild West in America, you might want to be here then. The Newtown stampede incorporates some of the legends of the drovers, who were the cowboys of Wales.

Cattle markets are held on the last Tuesday of the month in Newtown, as well as alternate Thursdays. A street market is held on Tuesday.

Activities in this area include use of the **Maldwyn Sports Centre,** Plantation Lane, for swimming, squash, badminton, table tennis, and gym action. There's a nine-hole golf course, fishing, and pony trekking.

You can get information on Newtown and its environs from the **Tourist Association, Newtown and District,** Transport House, Severn Square (tel. 0686/24305), or the **Wales Tourist Information Centre,** Central Car Park (tel. 0686/25580), which is open only in summer, from 10 a.m. to 6 p.m.

FOOD AND LODGING: In an old Tudor coaching inn, the **Bear Hotel,** Broad Street (tel. 0686/26964), stands in the center of town. The inviting public rooms complement the comfortable bedrooms, some of which are in the old part of the building and therefore vary in size and style. The 35 bedrooms also include studio units of later vintage than the half-timbered hotel. Singles cost from £25 ($40) per person for B&B, with doubles going for £40 ($64). Most rooms have private bath, and all are centrally heated and have TV, phone, radio, and tea/coffee-making facilities. The residents' lounge is attractively furnished in rattan armchairs and sectional pieces. You may dine in the Severn, a restaurant serving à la carte and table d'hôte meals, or in the Spinning Wheel Grill, a cozy place near one of the two bars. Dinner in the restaurant, from a menu offering such dishes as Welsh lamb, salmon, trout, and roasts, served with fresh vegetables and salads, costs from £10 ($16). The Bear has a competent and friendly staff to keep the hotel running smoothly.

The **Elephant & Castle,** Broad Street (tel. 0686/26271), is a stone building finished in beige stucco, with brown window shutters on the top two floors and a balcony above the ground floor. The hotel, adjacent to the River Severn, has two lively bars, where you can enjoy drinks and bar snacks. The food is served daily from noon to 2 p.m. and 6:30 to 9:30 p.m., and costs £3 ($4.80) to £6 ($9.60) for an average meal. In the beautiful dining room you can order table d'hôte, paying £7.50 ($12) to £8 ($12.80), or à la carte for £9 ($14.40) to £13 ($20.80). The cuisine has a good reputation for excellence, and the service is courteous. The hotel has 21 bedrooms, some with bath. Doubles, with or without bath, and singles with bath have TV. Tariffs for B&B range from £20 ($32) in a single to £30 ($48) in a double, the price depending on the plumbing.

The **Black Boy Hotel,** Broad Street (tel. 0686/26834), is an ancient inn in the heart of town boasting some 400 years of existence. The "Black Boy" of the name was King Charles II, who was so nicknamed because of his long black curls and black beard. The six simple rooms, some with their own bathroom facilities and all with color TV, hot and cold water basins, hot-beverage facilities, and central heating, rent for £11.50 ($18.40) in a single for B&B, £21 ($33.60) in a double. The family room rents for £23 ($36.80) for double occupancy, with a £6 ($9.60) supplement for each extra person. A full range of table d'hôte and à la carte food and bar snacks is available, served in the lounge. Terry and Ann Levin, the proprietors, also have a Market Room Carvery, open on market day and on shopping day (Friday) from noon to 2:30 p.m. Here they serve from four or five big joints, and you have a choice of six vegetables. The cost of this filling meal is £4.50 ($7.20), and it's popular in town.

Yr Hafod, New Road (tel. 0686/28624), is a B&B operated by Mr. and Mrs. E. Armes. There are five bedrooms and one bathroom; four of the rooms have hot and cold running water. Mrs. Armes prohibits smoking in the bedrooms for fire-prevention purposes. All the units have TV and electric kettles for making tea and coffee. Guests can relax in the large dining room, which is used as a lounge, with color TV. The evening meal is optional, but if you request it, Mrs. Armes sees to it you have a filling repast with everything freshly cooked. Rooms rent for £9.50 ($15.20) for B&B in a single, £16.50 ($26.40) in a double. The family room rents for £20 ($32). An evening meal costs £5 ($8) per person.

SIGHTS: Robert Owen, the social reformer who gained world renown as a pioneer of modern British Socialism and inspiration to the Cooperative and Trades Union movements, was born in Newtown in 1771, and after traveling and living all over Britain and in America spreading his philosophy, he returned here to die in 1858. His burial place may be seen beside the Old Church, St. Mary's. The tomb is inside a wrought-iron picket fence. A statue to Owen stands opposite the Post Office in a little garden spot right in the heart of town. The **Robert Owen Museum** is at the bottom of Broad Street at the town center (tel. 0686/26345). Hours are from 9:45 to 11:45 a.m. and 2 to 3:30 p.m. Monday to Friday, from 10 to 11:30 a.m. on Saturday. Admission is free.

Newtown was known as "The Leeds of Wales" during its heyday in the 19th and early 20th centuries, but the large flannel and other woolen mills are gone now. The **Textile Museum,** 5, 6, and 7 Commercial St., is in the actual location of two of the old weaving shops, with exhibits, including hand-looms, showing what the industry was like. April to October the museum is open from 2 to 4:30 p.m. Tuesday to Saturday. There is no admission charge, but donations may be placed in a box to help with the upkeep.

Pryce Jones, a leading figure in the woolen industry, started the first mail-order business in the world in 1859, selling only Welsh flannel. His warehouse, **The Royal Welsh,** is open to the public. It's in the town center by the railway station, a tall red brick building. Pryce Jones department store (tel. 0686/26911), directly opposite the railway station, is billed as "Mid Wales' largest department store." It's open six days a week.

W. H. Smith, "booksellers, librarians, news agents, and stationers," has a handsomely restored shop and a museum at 24 High Street (tel. 0686/26280). In the museum is an interesting display of photos, models, and memorabilia showing the development of the W. H. Smith business, whose shops you see all over Britain, from its beginning in 1792 as a tiny news vendor shop on Little Grosvenor Street in London. The museum is open to the public during the shop's business hours, 9 a.m. to 5:30 p.m. Monday to Saturday. Admission is free. Take a good look around the shop too to see the restored original mirrors and decorations, as well as the solid oak fittings as they were installed in 1927.

Alaven Leathershop, 18 High St. (tel. 0686/26665), invites visitors to watch artisans at work in the leather studio, where clocks and barometers are made in hand-tooled cowhide. They also stock a wide range of handbags, umbrellas, and small leathergoods. The shop gives you your VAT refund for goods to be shipped and does not levy a shipping charge for purchases costing more than £25 ($40). The shop is open all year from 9 a.m. to 5 p.m. Monday to Saturday, except for closing at 1 p.m. on Thursday.

14. Offa's Dyke and Montgomery

For centuries, the border country between what is today Wales and neighboring England was often a fierce battleground, with the Celtic people of the west making forays into the land of Saxons and others who occupied the country to the east. The matter of submission to English rule was not settled—and never has been in the minds of some Welsh people—until Henry Tudor, a Welshman, became Henry VII. Among the early efforts to stave off Welsh raids was—

OFFA'S DYKE: Built by the Saxon King Offa at the end of the 8th century and meant to keep the Welsh to the west of the Mercian lands, the dike was a huge earthwork with a ditch on the Welsh side, and ran a great deal of the way from the mouth of the River Wye to the mouth of the Dee in the north, 167 miles. Natural fortifications of mountains and forests supplied some of the boundary Offa desired, but because of the easy access between the Dee and the Severn, another dike (Watt's) was built about three miles to the east of the original, along the same line, defending some 40 miles of the marches (borderlands). A long-distance footpath is now maintained along the dike, but unless you want to walk it, you may be content to see parts of the ancient earthen wall. When the Normans came, they too had trouble with the rebellious Welsh, but their system of containment was castles along the border, held by the Marcher Lords. And the Welsh sometimes retaliated.

At Abermule, a little village with some black-and-white timbered houses five miles north of Newtown, lie the remains of **Dolforwyn Castle,** on a hill overlooking the fertile Severn Valley. This castle, which was a stronghold of Llewelyn the Last in his struggle with King Edward I, later became a property of the powerful Marcher Lord Mortimer. The castle of Dolforwyn, meaning Maiden's Meadow, a mile west of Abermule, may be seen at any time. Excavations are adding interesting facets.

The most impressive remains of the dike go from **Knighton,** a little town on the border west of Ludlow, England, across a slice of England and up to where you re-enter Wales near Montgomery, just south of Welshpool, previewed below. Knighton, interestingly enough, may always have been somewhat ambivalent about its identity, as it was called Trefy Clawdd, the Town on the Dyke, by the Welsh. At Knighton the 1,200-year-old dike is 30 feet high, with a trench on the Welsh side 15 feet deep. The **Offa's Dyke Heritage Centre** (tel. 05472/753) at the Old Primary School can give you information on the dike, local history, ecology, and natural history.

MONTGOMERY: This tiny town, with houses from the Elizabethan to the Georgian periods, sits almost on the border. Remains of Offa's Dyke are preserved in Lymore Park, east of town, and just a mile away is Rhydwhiman Ford, the historic bargaining spot between the English and the Welsh. Head out toward Church Stoke, England, and you come to some of the best dike remains in the area.

Perched on a high rock overlooking Montgomery are the fragmentary remains of a 13th-century castle, built by Henry III but later the property of the Marcher Lord Mortimer. It was destroyed by Cromwell's soldiers in the Civil War. You can go take a look at any time, for no charge.

Food and Lodging

If you'd like to stay in Montgomery, I recommend the **Dragon Hotel** (tel. 068681/359). It was built as a black-and-white manor house in 1674 and became an inn 100 years later. It has the distinction of having been used by Prince Charles in 1977 when he was here to mark the 750th anniversary of the town charter. Roland Burgan, who owns and manages the hotel, has 15 bedrooms, all with private bath, color TV, and tea/coffee-making facilities. Rents are £19.50 ($31.20) for B&B in a single, £30 ($48) in a double or twin, and £24.50 ($39.20) for one person occupying a double room. The hotel has a heated indoor swimming pool and a pleasant lounge bar. The restaurant is done in red and has a fireplace. You can sit in booths or at tables. In the Grill Room, four main dishes are offered from which to choose. Expect to pay from £7.50 ($12) for a meal here, or from £10 ($16) up in the restaurant.

A MAGPIE VILLAGE: If you drive along the A483 road between Newtown and Welshpool (coming up), you'll see many black-and-white houses along the way. To get the best look, turn off when you see the sign for **Berriew.** This is really a black-and-white village, and you will see different types of the so-called magpie houses, usually connected with the Tudor period, here.

15. Welshpool

If you go here on Monday, you'll soon discover what they mean by a "busy market town." Hundreds of sheep and cattle are brought in in trucks, trailers, and wagons to be auctioned off in the pens and market buildings near the downtown area. Anyone can go there and stroll around, even go into one of the buildings where the auctioneer is wooing bids on cattle. It's a bit pungent, so don't go if your olfactory nerves are sensitive. The Monday market was already established in 1263 when the town received its charter.

One of the Great Little Trains of Wales (see Chapter XX), the **Welshpool and Llanfair Railway,** runs to the town from Llanfair Caereinion.

Recreation facilities include **golf** (an 18-hole course is about four miles out on Golfa Hill) and **swimming** in the town's covered, heated pool.

An **indoor market** is held downstairs in the Town Hall, with a wide variety of goods for sale, ranging from eggs to woolen goods. Behind it, between Seven Stars Road and Broad Street, is an open-air market, where they sell clothing, rugs, even fish.

For information, get in touch with the **Tourist Information Centre,** Vicarage Garden Car Park (tel. 0938/2043), open from 10 a.m. to 6 p.m. all year.

FOOD AND LODGING: If you'd like to stay right in the heart of Welshpool, go to the **Royal Oak Hotel,** The Cross (tel. 0938/2217), a 15th-century coaching inn where Queen Victoria once stayed. It has been owned by the Price family for 60 years. The hotel provides warm hospitality and comfortable accommodation. Some rooms have private bath, and all have radio and TV. Rooms rent for £18.50 ($29.60) to £22.50 ($36) for B&B in a single, depending on the plumbing. Rates are £35 ($56) to £43 ($68.80) for a double or twin, including VAT and service. There are two bars and a restaurant. Table d'hôte luncheons, served from 12:30 to 2:15 p.m., cost from £6.50 ($10.40). Fixed-price dinners cost from £8 ($12.80), and are served from 7 p.m. to 9 p.m. daily (on Saturday from 7:30 to 9:30 p.m. and on Sunday from 7 to 8:30 p.m.). An à la carte menu is also available. Bar snacks are popular here.

Staying on the Outskirts

Heath Cottage, Forden (tel. 093876/453), about three miles outside of Welshpool, is a B&B run by Mary and John Payne, experienced hands in the business, who know how to make guests feel welcome and comfortable. The charge for the pleasant bedrooms is £9 ($14.40) per person for a bed and a good, filling breakfast. Mrs. Payne is an excellent cook who will prepare an evening meal for you if you arrange with her ahead. Guests can watch TV in the sitting room or enjoy the garden.

A MUSEUM: The development of the area's industry and society are shown at the **Powysland Museum** (tel. 0938/4759), operated in Welshpool by the Powys County Council. It traces the history of this ancient princedom through artifacts and other displays. Hours are 11 a.m. to 1 p.m. and 2 to 5 p.m. Monday to Friday, 2 to 4:30 p.m. Saturday. Closed Sunday all year and Wednesday in winter. Admission is free.

POWIS CASTLE: The finest sight in the area is perhaps the most romantic of the great chain of castles constructed in the 13th century to guard the Welsh Marches from incursion by the Welsh—Powis Castle (tel. 0938/4336). Now a National Trust property, set in a park of giant oaks, the castle is about a mile south of Welshpool beside the A483 road. This border military stronghold survived the bitter struggles of the medieval period, standing high on a rocky outcrop. Powis has been preserved and constantly occupied through the centuries. Decoration of the interior ranges from Elizabethan style to that of Charles II. A significant part of the collection was inherited from Clive of India, whose son married a Powis heiress in 1784 and later became the Earl of Powis.

The billiard room of the castle has been turned into the **Clive of India Museum,** containing the finest British collection of Indian art outside London. It seeks to evoke the architecture of the subcontinent as interpreted by the British in the early 19th century, a style called "Hindoo" or "Indo-Gothic." This is demonstrated by reconstruction in one corner of the State Tent of Tipu Sultan. In the Clive collection are some 300 pieces dating from the 17th to the 19th centuries, including jeweled and inlaid weapons, silver and gold vessels, ivory, jade, and silks.

The formal terraces, eye-catching even from the road, were built in the late

17th century and have retained their original character. Terrace walls of mellow red brick overhung with enormous clipped yews extend for about 200 yards, sheltering herbaceous borders. A set of early 18th-century figures crowns the balustrade above the orangery.

The castle and gardens are open from noon to 5 p.m. daily except Monday and Tuesday mid-April to the end of June and in September and October; from 11 a.m. to 6 p.m. daily except Monday in July and August. Last entry is 30 minutes before closing. Admission to the castle, garden, and the Clive Museum is £2.30 ($3.68) for adults, £1 ($1.60) for children, with a family ticket costing £5.60 ($8.96) for two adults and two children.

SNOWDONIA

MOUNTAIN PEAKS AND STEEP wooded slopes, spectacular estuaries and rugged cliffs brooding over secluded coves, lakes, little rivers, and valleys with tiny towns looking as if they were carved out of granite—all these join to make up Snowdonia National Park. The park, with slate mines, moors, heavy forests, mountain lakes, grain fields, and pastures, swift-flowing rivers, and sandy beaches, takes its name from Snowdon, at 3,560 feet the highest peak in Wales or England. Most of Snowdonia is in the County of Gwynnedd, once the ancient Welsh kingdom of that name. Its prince, Owen ap Gwynnedd, never agreed to let himself be reduced to the status of baron under the English kings, and his wild country helped him hold out against invasion by forces more used to fighting in flat, more easily dominated terrain.

Because of its location, I'll start my trip through Snowdonia at a point at the southern edge of the national park, Machynlleth, which actually lies in the County of Powys. Good roads from this town lead right into Snowdonia National Park.

1. Machynlleth

A shopping, market, and tourist center in the valley of the River Dovey ("Dyfi" in Welsh), Machynlleth is dominated by the immense clock tower given to the town by the Marquess of Londonderry. The tower is 78 feet tall from base to weathervane. Surrounded by the foothills of Snowdonia's Cader Idris, this has long been a market to which farm produce is brought for sale.

Wednesday is market day, and if you arrive in the town then, you may have trouble making your way along Maengwyn Street, a main thoroughfare, through the mass of stalls, tables, vans, and other vehicles for setting out sales goods.

It was here that Owain Glyndwr set up his parliament during the violent days at the close of the 14th and start of the 15th centuries, when his followers were trying to push the English out of Wales forever.

The **Wales Tourist Board's Mid Wales Regional Office** is at Canolfan Owain Glyndwr, the building in which the chieftain's parliament met (tel. 0654/2401).

FOOD AND LODGING: In the heart of this medieval town, the **Wynnstay Hotel,** Maengwyn Street (tel. 0654/2941), offers Welsh hospitality and traditional Welsh food. This was once the site of the Unicorn Hotel, which was a Royal Mail staging post in the middle of the 19th century. A typical Welsh country-town hotel, the Wynnstay has 24 comfortable bedrooms, most of which have private baths. All the units have color TV, phones, radios, and hot-beverage facilities. The hotel charges a splurgy £64 ($102.40) for a double, which includes a full Welsh breakfast. Special weekend and other discounts are quoted.

The most beautiful place to stay is **Dolguog Hall** (tel. 0654/2244), 1½ miles from the town clock off the A489 road to Newtown. The present house, now owned by Richard and Diana Rhodes, was built in 1632, but the site is believed to have been the location of a dwelling in the 6th century belonging to Guog, son of a warrior prince of Powys. It is from Guog that the house got its name. Dolguog Hall today is of local stone with a slate roof of several pitches, standing in a meadow looking out to the River Dulas, where the hotel has a stretch of water in which guests can fish for trout and salmon. In fact, nearby, at the point where the Dulas and Dyfi (Dovey) rivers meet, the salmon and trout waters are said to be the best outside Scotland. The building's interior has been carefully restored. Upstairs are the ten bedrooms, all with baths, color TV, and hot-beverage facilities, plus views over the river or the lawns and gardens with their huge trees. Singles pay £27 ($43.20), doubles or twins going for £23.50 ($37.60) per person for B&B.

The licensed restaurant is open to nonresidents and is popular with local people. A four-course dinner costs from £9 ($14.40). Vegetarian dishes are a specialty. This is a good place to have Sunday lunch, served from noon to 2 p.m. For £6.50 ($10.40), you have a choice of appetizers; then for your main course, you can select from roast beef and Yorkshire pudding, roast lamb with mint sauce, or a vegetarian dish of the day, all served with roast potatoes and fresh vegetables. Dessert and coffee follow. Reservations are necessary for Sunday lunch and are advisable for dinner. Lunches, costing from £5 ($8), are also served weekdays.

Bacheiddon, Aberhosan (tel. 0654/2229), about six miles southeast of Machynlleth on a country road, is a farmhouse accommodation with three bedrooms to rent, each with a toilet and shower. The lounge has color TV and a choice of reading matter. The cost of B&B in the comfortable bedrooms is £10 ($16) per person. You can also enjoy a wholesome farm dinner made from their own produce, insofar as possible. If you request the evening meal ahead, you can enjoy Welsh food for £5.50 ($8.80). You can watch the farm operation or walk through the meadows. The house takes guests from April to October. The hard-working owner, Mrs. Angharad Lewis, is warmhearted, taking her name, Angharad, after a medieval Welsh princess who won the heart of a Norse Viking warrior. She operates very much a workaday farm (the B&B is secondary), with 1,100 breeding ewes and 60 head of cattle. Her farmhouse was erected in 1953 a few steps from the ruin of a much older building.

A good place to eat is at the Centre for Alternative Technology, previewed below. The **Quarry Shop Café** (tel. 0654/2400) serves homemade soups, quiche, and sandwiches, as well as meals you can select from a changing menu. You can have tea here accompanied by some of their tasty home-baked breads and

Welsh cakes. Expect to pay from £2.50 ($4) for a light lunch, from £5 ($8) up for a full meal. The café is open Monday to Saturday from 10 a.m. to 5 p.m. There is also a Quarry Shop right in town at 13 Maengwyn St. selling whole-foods, with a café offering the same foods and at the same prices as the one at the center.

Actually, the best restaurant in town is **Janie's,** 57 Maengwyn St. (tel. 0654/2126), which is the domain of its chef-owner, Jane Mohamed. From Monday to Saturday, she is the hearty empress of her kitchen, serving from 12:30 to 2 p.m. and 7:30 to 9:30 p.m. A set dinner is offered for just £7.50 ($12) with à la carte orders averaging around £12 ($19.20). Hers, however, is an in-season-only affair, as she closes from October to Easter. The success of her establishment is in her skillful use of fresh ingredients delicately seasoned with herbs.

SIGHTS: Machynlleth became important in Welsh history when Owain Glyndwr set up his **parliament** here. Along Maengwyn Street about 200 yards from the clock tower, you can visit a group of buildings of slate stone and half-timbered construction where Glyndwr assembled his supporters and was invested with the crown of Wales in 1404. The building contains an exhibition of Glyndwr's failed rising. It also houses the **Tourist Information Centre** (tel. 0654/2401).

Plas Machynlleth, built in 1653 as the residence of the Marquess of Londonderry, has had several additions since its inception so that it doesn't look much like a 17th-century structure. The house belongs to the town and is the headquarters for council area offices. Its grounds are a public park with a rose garden, tennis courts, and a playground. There is also a golf course and bowling green in Machynlleth.

About 2½ miles north of the town, just off the A487 road, is the **Centre for Alternative Technology** (tel. 0654/2400), set in an old slate quarry inside Snowdonia National Park. Here equipment has been developed and tested to draw energy from the sun and other sources that do not deplete the dwindling supply of energy-producing elements of the earth. The importance of ecology to the world's future is graphically demonstrated. The center is open daily from 10 a.m. to 6 p.m., to 7:30 p.m. mid-July to mid-September. Admission is £2.20 ($3.52) for adults, 80p ($1.28) for children. There is a restaurant here selling homemade whole-food snacks, hot drinks, and lunches. B&B facilities are available at Easter, Whitsun, and from mid-July to mid-September.

A little farther north is the **Corris Craft Centre** (tel. 065473/343). The little group of one-story gray stone buildings with skylights contains studios where artisans work at making a variety of goods which can be purchased in a shop in one of the buildings. There is also a café, specializing in homemade food. The admission-free center is open from 9:30 a.m. to 5:30 p.m. Monday to Saturday.

Back in Machynlleth, you might want to take the three-mile **Town Trail,** carefully set forth in a little book which you can acquire at the Tourist Information Centre.

EXPLORING FROM MACHYNLLETH: About seven miles southwest of Machynlleth on the A487 road is **Dyfi Furnace,** a much-photographed site where silver was refined in the 17th century using waterpower from the River Einion. The waterfall is still an impressive sight.

A little farther south, just off the A487, is **Tre'r Ddol,** north of Borth in Dyfed County. Here you can visit **Yr Hen Gapel** (tel. 097986/407), a museum of 19th-century religious life in Wales. The former Wesleyan Chapel was linked with the origin of the 1859 religious revival that had such far-reaching effects on the social life of both rural and industrial Wales, making much of the country nonconformist. The museum, administered by the Welsh Folk Museum at St.

Fagan's, Cardiff, is open April 1 to September 30, Monday to Saturday from 10 a.m. to 5 p.m. Admission is free.

Nearby is **Tre Taliesin,** another tiny hamlet like Tre'r Ddol, with gray stone houses lying right along the A487. A walk into the hills from here leads to the reputed grave of the 6th-century bard, Taliesin.

Aberdovey, at the mouth of the River Dovey, has an 18-hole golf course and a small **nautical museum** at the Black Shed on the Wharf. Sailing and fishing the waters of the estuary are popular sports.

Just a short hop on up the coast of Cardigan Bay is **Tywyn,** whose main claim to fame is that it has three railway stations: the main British Rail station and two on the Talyllyn Narrow-Gauge Railway, one of the Great Little Trains of Wales, described in Chapter XX.

The **Narrow Gauge Railway Museum,** Wharf Station (tel. 0654/710472), has a collection of relics of the narrow-gauge railways of the British Isles: polished brass and gleaming paintwork, locomotives, wagons, signals, and many other items. The little railways were—and are—individual. They gave service to quarries, mines, factories, and passengers. In the museum are train engines from Welsh slate quarries, a Dublin brewery, a gas works in Dundee, and a Manchester foundry. The museum is open daily during the summer, at all times when the Talyllyn Railway is running. Admission is 30p (48¢) for adults, 15p (24¢) for children.

A B&B at Tywyn

If you'd like to stop over in Tywyn, the **Monfa Guest House,** Pier Road (tel. 0654/710858), is a good place to stay. A traditional Victorian structure, the house has a friendly, relaxed atmosphere. Harry and Shirley Bray rent out eight bedrooms. All the double and family rooms have showers or showers and toilets. Charges are £11 ($17.60) for B&B or £15.50 ($24.80) for half board. Monfa has a residential license. There's a lounge with color TV, and all bedrooms have hot-beverage facilities.

2. Dolgellau

In the shadow of the mountain, Cader Idris, this little stone town is Welsh in ways and speech. Routes from here lead to the Mawddach estuary on the Cambrian Coast and to Cader Idris, the Snowdonia National Park mountain range. Dolgellau lies on the River Wnion. It is a town of neat stone cottages, narrow streets, and friendly people.

A livestock market is held here on Monday, with a street market taking place on Friday.

For information on all of Meirionnydd, get in touch with the **Tourism and Leisure Officer,** National Westminster Bank Chambers (tel. 0341/422341, ext. 308). Information can also be obtained from the **Snowdonia National Park Visitor Centre,** The Bridge (tel. 0341/422888).

FOOD AND LODGING: The narrow streets of Dolgellau once resounded with the clatter of hoofs and the trundling of coach wheels, as this was an important point on stagecoach routes. The **Royal Ship Hotel,** Queen Square (tel. 0341/422209), is an old coaching inn, extensively modernized, standing in the center of the town. It has 25 bedrooms. Most have private baths, color TV, and hot-beverage facilities. The rent for a single room with bath is £19.50 ($31.20), and a double costs £39 ($62.40). There are a number of cozy bars, and dinner is served in the restaurant. There are rooms in an annex as well as in the main building. The Royal Ship dates from the 19th century, when lots of coaches stopped in Dolgellau.

Outside of the country hotels, the best place for food is **La Petite Auberge,** 2 Smithfield St. (tel. 0341/42287), where George Dewez, one of the co-owners, is also the chef. A sort of restaurant-cum-wine bar, La Petite Auberge uses the best seasonal produce available. Fresh fish is usually a delight, and it is likely to show up on your platter prepared in imaginative ways. The short menu always seems full of interest, and the staff is pleasant and attentive. The place should be better known. The establishment is open only in season, serving from the first of April until the end of September from 7 to 9:30 p.m. Monday to Saturday. A meal costs from £12 ($19.20).

A Splurge near Dolgellau

Bontddu Hall Hotel (tel. 034149/661), a splurge choice, is found at Bontddu, five miles west of Dolgellau on A496. It was built in 1873 as the family seat of Neville Chamberlain's aunt. The site was selected for its magnificent view over the Mawddach Estuary and some of the highest peaks in Wales. Set in six acres of grounds, three of which are landscaped gardens, the place is baronial and imposing, as might be expected, as it was constructed by money from one of the biggest Victorian fortunes in the country. Michael Ball, the genteel and sensitive owner, maintains kitchens well known for the quality of their cuisine. Non-residents are welcome to reserve a table in advance for the varied, fresh, and flavorful menu known throughout the region. Dinner, nightly from 7:30 to 9:30, goes for a fixed price of £13 ($20.80). Lunch, 12:30 to 2 p.m., is less expensive, costing around £6 ($9.60). Specialties include locally caught trout with horseradish, salmon caught that very day in the nearby river (and cooked as simply as possible so as not to mask freshness), or Welsh mountain lamb with a rosemary and madeira sauce.

Each of the 24 attractive bedrooms is comfortably appointed with private bath, color TV, radio, phone, and coffee-maker. Twin or double rooms costs £29 ($46.40) per person, with breakfast and VAT included. Singles rent for £39 ($62.40) each. The charming hotel lies four miles east of the coastal resort of Barmouth and is closed in January and February.

SIGHTS IN THE ENVIRONS: The ancient bridge, built in 1638, is now a protected structure. **St. Mary's Church** in Dolgellau was built in 1716, and its wooden pillars were native oak trees hauled by oxen over the high pass from Dinas Mawddy. It contains a small alabaster font dated 1615 and a 14th-century effigy of Meurig ap Ynyr Fychan, ancestor of the Vaughan family. The west windows contain 18th-century stained glass.

From the town, you can go by road or, if you're energetic, by a marked footpath to **Cader Idris,** rising to almost 3,000 feet close to town. Views from the summit are magnificent. A little to the north, at Llanelltyd, lie the remains of the **Cymer Abbey,** founded by Cistercian monks in 1198. The abbey, which stood on the north side of the River Wnion, was the home of the monks who gave rise to the name of Dolgellau, which means the Meadow of the Monks' Cells. The abbey took its name from the *cymer* or confluence of the Wnion and the Mawddach Rivers. The abbey may be visited from 9:30 a.m. to 6:30 p.m. in summer, to 4 p.m. in winter on weekdays, from 2 to 6:30 p.m. (4 p.m. in winter) on Sunday. Admission is 50p (80¢) for adults, 25p (40¢) for children.

If you haven't yet experienced visiting a Welsh farm, an invitation is issued to visit a Welsh hill farm for a day. At **Tal-y-Waen Farm,** Cader Road (tel. 0341/422580), H. G. Humphreys offers a day visit that will introduce you to the beauty of the area and the activities of life on the farm. Visits can be made from 10 a.m. to 5 p.m. May to October except on Saturday. You'll see the farm animals and pets, walk the "farm trail" with impressive views of the Mawddach estuary, and observe farm life according to the season. The farm has a tea and crafts shop, a play area, a pets corner, a miniature Dolgellau town, an art gallery, pony rides, and a farm trail video. Licensed barbecues are offered all day. Admission is £4 ($6.40) per family.

BRANCHING OUT FROM DOLGELLAU: Just off the A470, some eight miles north of Dolgellau, the Forestry Commission's **Maesgwm Visitor Centre** provides a fascinating introduction to life and work in Coed y Brenin (Forest of the King). Exhibits and a slide show include a display on gold mining in an area rich in minerals including two gold mines. The surrounding forest includes a number of attractive riverside parking and picnic sites, with marked walks for all ages and abilities in superb mountain and forest scenery. The visitor center is open from 10 a.m. to 5 p.m. daily Easter to the end of September. It includes a shop offering a range of educational and souvenir items and a refreshment room. For more information, get in touch with the District Forest Manager, Forestry Commission, Agriculture House, Dolgellau, Gwynedd, LL40 1DH, Wales (tel. 0341/422289).

Midway between Dolgellau and Machynlleth on the A470, ten miles from each one, is **Meirion Mill,** Dinas Mawddwy (tel. 06504/311), about half a mile north of the Mallwyd road junction. One of the leading woolen mills in Wales, it lies on the edge of Dovey Forest beside the River Dovey. The factory manufactures tapestry cloth from pure new wool. In the shop, you can find a wide range of garments, bedcovers, knitwear, knitting wool, and other items. In addition, a coffeeshop sells traditional, homemade food throughout the day. Children may be left in a safe playground. The mill is open seven days a week April to October from 9 a.m. to 5 p.m.

3. Bala

This is a Welsh town beside the four-mile-long Bala Lake (Llyn Tegid), less than a mile wide, surrounded by three mountain ranges: Berwyn to the south and east, rearing upward to 2,700 feet, and Aran's twin heads, both more than 2,900 feet high, with the foothills of Arenig Fawr, which checks in at 2,800 feet at its peak, bordering the lake's northern shore. The River Dee flows from the lake. Bala is called the cradle of the rural and characteristically Welsh culture. It was the home of the Methodist movement, and political leaders have come from here. The town and the area around it are pure Welsh in both their speech and their thinking.

On Tegid Street stands a statue of Thomas Charles (1755–1814), who founded the Sunday School movement in Wales as well as the British and Foreign Bible Society. This was where the teenage Mary Jones walked to over the mountains from near Tywyn, nearly 30 miles, to get a copy of the Bible from Charles. The memorial plaque attesting this is in the High Street.

Christ Church of Ffrydan Road, the town's church, once met in the Chapel of Ease in the High Street, now an English Chapel. Beyond Christ Church is the former Bala Methodist College, now headquarters for the youth chaplain of the Presbyterian Church of Wales. Opposite it is a house once used as a college for Welsh Congregationalists.

Bala may once have had a castle. On Mount Street, the **Bala Tump** is believed to be the motte of a medieval fortress. Whatever it was, you get a fine view of the town from the mound.

A livestock market is held in Bala on Thursday.

If you have a River Board license and a permit, you can fish in the lake for trout, salmon, roach, pike, perch, and eels. Sailing, rowing, and some swimming and skin-diving are permitted, but anyone planning to make use of the lake waters should consult the National Park lake warden, who is employed by the Snowdonia National Park Committee to supervise the lake. He can be reached at the **Lake Warden's Office,** 24 Ffordd Pensarn (tel. 0678/520626).

There is a **National Park Information Centre,** High Street (tel. 0678/520367), which is open daily from 10 a.m. to 6 p.m. from Easter to the end of September.

The **Bala Lake Narrow Gauge Railway,** one of the Great Little Trains of Wales, runs along the southern bank of the lake and is a good way to explore that area.

FOOD AND LODGING IN BALA AND ENVIRONS: Near the lake on the outskirts of Bala stands **Plas Teg Guest House,** Tegid Street (tel. 0678/520268), a building of gray stone with white trim and bow windows on the ground floor. The seven bedrooms all have hot and cold running water and gas fires. If it gets chilly, electric blankets are supplied for all the bedrooms. The charge per person for B&B is £9.25 ($14.80), which includes a full Welsh breakfast. Reductions are made for children sharing their parents' room. Good service is given here, and assistance will be forthcoming to help you decide where to go and what to do in Bala.

Outside Bala to the west, on a country road in the little hamlet of Llidiardau, is an attractive guesthouse, **Llidiardau Mawr** (tel. 0678/520555), a recently restored and refurbished 17th-century millhouse set in gardens with a stream running past. Farmlands are all around, and anywhere you look there are mountains to view. You'll be given a warm welcome and personal attention here. Rooms rent for £11 ($17.60) per person for B&B, and you can order dinner, supper, and snacks if you wish. This is a remote, tranquil place.

The **Olde Bulls Head,** High Street (tel. 0678/520438), dispenses real ale and some good bar food, as well as renting a few bathless rooms. Ronald and Pat Atkinson, the proprietors, have refurbished the interior of the gabled building, constructed in 1692 as a stone-fronted coaching inn, retaining the old paneling and the cork-tile floor of one of the bars, but otherwise making the place more comfortable. There's a separate restaurant, so you can take the children. Bar food will supply you with a good meal for £4 ($6.40). The old pub serves food from noon to 2 or 2:30 p.m. Drinks in the evening are served from 7 to 10 or 11 p.m. You get good solid British food here. Bedrooms upstairs rent for £10.50 ($16.80) per person for B&B.

A Big Splurge

East of Bala is **Palé Hall,** Llandderfel (tel. 06783/285), a very special—and expensive—place to stay. The elegant hall, built in 1870 for a wealthy Scots building engineer, was once visited by Queen Victoria. You can stay in the room she used, complete with the bathroom fixtures which were the scene of the royal ablutions. In the gracious Corwen Bar, note the marble serving bar. It was made from marble removed from the rooms when fireplaces were closed. The hotel has two magnificent dining rooms with ornate moldings, carpeted floors, and an array of silver and china that would make a collector's eyes bulge. Of particular note is the circular former boudoir off the lobby. The hall's owner, Mrs. Betty Duffin, reserves this as a no-smoking lounge to preserve the beautiful blue, white, and gold colors of the ornate ceiling. An Oriental carpet is in the same shades.

The 17 bedrooms are all of individual size and styling, suited to the particular features of the room. Two of the rooms have Jacuzzis. All have luxurious bathrooms with bidets, color TVs, direct-dial phones, trouser presses, and other amenities. Most of the rooms are named for Welsh castles. Rents are quoted only for dinner, bed, and breakfast. They range from £45 ($72) in a single to £55 ($88) and £70 ($112) in doubles. Staying here is a big splurge, but it would be worth it in this elegant house, with the rugged grandeur and unspoiled charm of the surrounding landscape to add to your pleasure. You can dine here even if you're not a hotel guest. Specialties include fresh grayling from the Dee, game casserole in red wine and red currant sauce served in a pastry tartlet, Dover sole, beef Wellington, and Châteaubriand for two. For an appetizer, I particularly like the carrot and coriander soup with toasted almonds and the rosettes of duck pâté with orange and brandy jelly. All meals are à la carte. Expect to pay £18 ($28.80) to £25 ($40) and up for a full meal.

Only about a mile away from Palé Hall, another hotel recommendation, Tyddyn Llan, is reviewed in Chapter XXVII, "Corwen and the Vale of Endyrnion."

4. Barmouth

Two miles of firm golden sandy beaches and a promenade have made Barmouth a popular resort, with mountains in the background and a broad estuary stretching out in front. Summer fun here includes such activities as pony and donkey rides on the beach, boat cruises, and fishing trips. There's a Community Centre and Dragon Theatre where variety shows, drama, ballet, and opera are presented. A Panorama Walk is reached by steps cut into the hillside by a steep road from Porkington Terrace.

Across the Mawddach estuary, the smallest of the narrow-gauge railways connects the tiny resort of **Fairbourne** with Penrhyn Point. A half-mile railway bridge and a pedestrian toll bridge cross the estuary. From the terminus, you can take a ferryboat. This service runs regularly in summer.

The **Wales Tourist and Barmouth Publicity Information Center,** on Station Road (tel. 0341/280787), is open all year from 10 a.m. to 6 p.m. daily.

FOOD AND LODGING: A host of hotels and guesthouses is strung out along the Barmouth beachfront. One of my favorites is the **Min-y-Mor Hotel** (tel. 0341/280555), where Mr. and Mrs. Hywel Williams and their daughter, Marie, welcome guests. In fact, Mr. Williams has been doing just that for more than a quarter of a century. The 50-bedroom hotel is a three-story granite structure, with cream-painted trim. It was built as a doctor's home some 120 years ago, becoming a hotel in 1930. It's right on the seafront. The fully licensed hotel has a bar lounge, reading lounge, and TV lounge, plus a games room and a children's playroom. In summer, tables with umbrellas blossom out in the front garden. Clean rooms and comfortable beds are provided, with simple furnishings as befits a beach hotel. B&B costs from £13.50 ($21.60) per person in a bathless room, £15 ($24) to £16 ($25.60) in a room with bath/shower and toilet. You can enjoy bar snacks in the lounge or in the dining room at lunch. Dinner costs from £8 ($12.80). Rooms on the ground floor are suitable for disabled persons. Rates quoted are inclusive of VAT and service. The hotel is open from April to early October.

The **Marine Mansion Hotel** (tel. 0341/280459), on the seafront, is a cream-painted stucco building with bow windows and big red brick chimneys. Many of the 30 bedrooms rented by Mike and Margaretta Ball have private bathroom, and honeymoon suites with four-poster beds are available. The licensed hotel offers good meals, including bar snacks. Tariffs are from £18 ($28.80) for B&B in a single, with doubles going for £27 ($43.20). Reductions are given for children.

Marwyn Hotel, 21 Marine Parade (tel. 0341/280185), bills itself as a small premier luxury hotel, and that's close to the mark. Its seven rooms are tastefully furnished, and all have private bath facilities, color TV, phone, radio alarm, and tea/coffee-making equipment. The hotel is centrally heated. Mr. and Mrs. D. Thomas, the resident owners, charge £15.50 ($24.80) to £16.50 ($26.40) per person for B&B in a room for two. An additional £4 ($6.40) per night is charged for a single person in a double room. A four-poster bedroom for two costs £19.50 ($31.20) per person. The hotel has an upstairs lounge with panoramic views of the bay and Mawddach estuary, a residential cocktail lounge, and a handsome dining room where you can dine on Welsh cuisine, including trout, salmon, lamb, and poultry dishes, either table d'hôte or à la carte. The restaurant is open to nonresidents. Dinner will cost from £8.50 ($13.60) for the fixed-price menu to £12 ($19.20) and up à la carte. A good selection of wines complements the meals.

The Angry Cheese, Church Street (tel. 0341/280038), is a popular restaurant. In summer, lunch is served daily from noon to 2 p.m. and dinner from 6 to 10:30 p.m. In winter it's only open for dinner on Friday and Saturday. The pine tables of the restaurant give a homey, rustic atmosphere, and the food served on them is well prepared and tasty. The menu might include seafood and river fish, chicken, pork schnitzel, vegetable kebabs, and a variety of potato dishes and fresh vegetables. A fixed-price dinner costs from around £7.50 ($12), while if you choose to order à la carte, your tab will come to around £9 ($14.40) and up.

5. Harlech

Views from Harlech of Snowdon, Tremadog Bay, Cader Idris, and the Lleyn Peninsula are splendid today, and they give an understanding as to why this was the setting for the strong fortification at Harlech Castle (see below). The waters of Tremadog Bay lapped around the foot of the cliffs at one time, adding to the protection of the little town that grew up around the castle. Today, the area formerly underwater is filled in and is the site of the well-known Royal St. David's 18-hole championship golf course.

In summer, information is available from the **Snowdonia National Park Centre,** High Street (tel. 0766/780658).

FOOD AND LODGING: Just a step from the castle, **Castle Cottage Hotel** (tel. 0766/780479) is a little hotel and restaurant in a stone building. The oak-beamed bar and dining room are in one of the oldest houses in Harlech. The menu offers both Welsh and continental dishes, based on modern light cuisine. Luncheon, with dishes including plaice and french fries and cottage pie, costs around £3.50 ($5.60). For dinner you might choose pigeon breast in port wine sauce to start, followed by fresh local salmon steak in a creamy pink sauce. A full meal will cost £9.50 ($15.20) and up on the à la carte menu. There is an extensive but modestly priced wine list. Hours in the restaurant are from 10:30 a.m. to 2 p.m. and 7 to 9:30 p.m. Easter to October. In winter, it's open every Friday and Saturday from 7 to 9 p.m. and on most other nights by reservation. Closed during the day in winter. The proprietors, Jim and Betty Yuill, see to it that guests in both the restaurant and the hotel are comfortable and feel welcome. Their four double rooms have private baths, the two singles having hot and cold water basins. All are centrally heated and have hot-beverage facilities. The charge is £15 ($24) per person for B&B.

The **Cemlyn,** High Street (tel. 0766/780425), is a spacious restaurant overlooking the castle and the bay. Here you can dine on grilled meats and fish, which include local river catches and sea products such as sewin (sea trout), sea bass, and monkfish. Beef, lamb, and pork dishes are well prepared, and the vegetables served here are done in interesting ways. An extensive wine list is available. Ken Goody, the chef and proprietor, charges from £10 ($16) for a complete and satisfying dinner. The restaurant is open for dinner daily April to September from 7 to 10 p.m. It's closed in January and February, and the other months only Saturday dinner is served. The Cemlyn also rents a twin-bedded room with bath, color TV, and a sea and castle view for £10.50 ($16.80) per person, including a full cooked breakfast.

Hotel Maes-y-Neuadd, Talsarnau (tel. 0766/780200), is a few miles north of Harlech. The name of this place means hall (or mansion) in an open field, and that's what it is, except that it has lots of woodland, as well as almost eight acres of beautifully tended grounds. The core of the hotel is a 14th-century manor house, to which additions were made in the next two or three centuries. The house is of granite, with a slate roof. The country-house atmosphere here is augmented by personal service. The 16 bedrooms, all with bath and color TV, are prettily decorated. The two couples who run the hotel, Olive and Malcolm Horsfall and June and Michael Slatter, charge from £29 ($46.40) to £32 ($51.20) per person per night for B&B, which includes a full Welsh breakfast. If you'd like to have an evening meal in the elegant dining room, expect to spend from £14 ($22.40). The bar, with log fire and beams, is a delightful place to relax and chat with your hosts and fellow guests.

SIGHTS OF HARLECH AND ENVIRONS: Built in 1283, **Harlech Castle** stands on a rocky promontory that once looked down on the sea, which added to its protection. The strong defense of this castle for the Lancastrians in the Wars of the Roses failed, but it did inspire the famous marching song, "Men of Harlech." The main feature of the castle is its gatehouse. Visitors can climb 143 steps to the top. You can also take a walk along the walls. The castle can be visited daily March 15 to October 15 from 9:30 a.m. to 6:30 p.m., with closing at 4 p.m. the remainder of the year. Admission is £1 ($1.60) for adults, 50p (80p) for children.

At **Llanfair,** on the A496 road a mile south of Harlech, you can visit the **Old Llanfair Quarry Slate Caverns** (tel. 0766/780247). The quarry, Charwel Hen, unlike most of the North Wales slate mines and quarries, is only a short distance from the sea. Visitors can take guided tours through the mine caverns and tunnels. The underground temperature is seldom above 50° Fahrenheit, so visitors should wear warm clothing. The caverns are open April to October from 10 a.m. to 5:30 p.m. Admission is £1.50 ($2.40) for adults, 75p ($1.20) for children.

A mile or so south on the A496 is **Llanbedr,** where the **Maes Artro Tourist Village** (tel. 034123/497), stands in ten acres of fields and woodlands. It includes the largest sealife aquarium in Wales, a model village, a re-created old Welsh street, a nature trail, a pets corner, crafts shops, a playground, a Wild West fort, and a "Logopotamus Jungle." The village is open daily from 9 a.m. to 6 p.m. April to the end of October. Admission is £1.25 ($2) for adults, 95p ($1.52) for children under 14. The village was planned with facilities for the disabled.

6. Beddgelert

The name of this tiny village at the confluence of the Colwyn and Glaslyn Rivers means, literally, "grave of Gelert," so called, legend says, because here Prince Llewelyn killed his faithful hunting hound in error, thinking the dog had killed the prince's infant son. After the dog was slain, the story goes, Llewelyn discovered the infant safe under a pile of bedclothes—and the body of an enormous wolf that the dog had killed. Visitors can follow a path to the place where a large, fenced-in slate slab marks the dog's grave. Beddgelert nestles at the foot of Moel Hebog (bare hill of the hawk), four miles from Snowdon, a beautiful spot for scenic forest and hill walks or just for tranquility.

FOOD AND LODGING: A good place to stay in Snowdonia is the **Royal Goat Hotel** (tel. 076686/224), offering a winning combination of comfortable bedrooms, efficient service, good food, and spectacular scenery. When *The Inn of the Sixth Happiness*, starring Ingrid Bergman, was filmed here, the cast made its headquarters at the Royal Goat. There are 34 bedrooms, all with private baths, color TV, and hot-beverage facilities. Some units also contain phones, hair dryers, clock radios, trouser presses, mini-bars, and four-poster beds. Singles cost £26 ($41.60) and doubles £48 ($76.80) for B&B. The hotel has two dining rooms, two bars, and a reading room, plus an elevator. One of the bars, on your right as you enter the hotel, is a fine place for climbers and hikers to gather after their day's stint. The other, much larger and with comfortable, overstuffed seating, is passed through en route to one of the dining rooms. The food here is good and the service excellent. You can't go wrong ordering the salmon or trout caught in the cold mountain streams nearby. Expect to pay £12 ($19.20) for a table d'hôte dinner. An à la carte menu and bar snacks are also available. Harpists and singers sometimes perform at the hotel in summer.

Prince Llewelyn Hotel (tel. 076686/242) is where Derek Norton greets guests of his 11-bedroom stone hostelry. It may be without some of the amenities found in a lot of hotels, but it makes up for the lack by warm hospitality. If you'd rather mingle with the local people in one of the two comfortable bars than be stashed away somewhere watching TV, this is the place for you. Tasty bar snacks are available, including some traditional Welsh items, and there is a dining room where you can have dinner at more leisure. B&B costs from £12 ($19.20) per person in a bathless room to £14 ($22.40) per person in a room with bath, based on double occupancy.

7. Llanberis

The starting point for going up Snowdon by mountain railway, Llanberis nestles between Lake Padarn and Lake Peris. Views of outstanding beauty greet your eyes, and there are several man-made sights worth seeing, as well as some of nature's wonders. The Snowdon Mountain Railway is described in "The Great Little Trains of Wales" (Chapter XX), as well as another "great little train," the Llanberis Lake Railway which takes you along Lake Padarn. The purpose of the trains in this area and in the Vale of Ffestiniog to the south was to bring the "gray gold" from slate caverns for shipping all over the world.

The **Wales Tourist Information Centre,** Oriel Eryri at the Padarn Country Park (tel. 0286/870765), is open in summer only, from 10 a.m. to 6 p.m.

FOOD AND LODGING: A family-run accommodation, the stone **Dôl Peris Hotel,** High Street (tel. 0286/870350), stands in its own grounds. The owners extend a warm welcome and are always glad to see North American visitors. The comfortable bedrooms—ten in all—have tea/coffee-making facilities and TV. Two family rooms and two doubles have private bathrooms. Friendly service and excellent home-cooked food are promises held out to you if you choose to stay in this licensed hostelry. It's also centrally heated. Bedrooms, available year round, rent for £16.50 ($26.40) per person for B&B in a single, £23.50 ($37.60) in a double.

Lake Padarn Hotel, High Street (tel. 0286/870260), is a modern hostelry under the personal supervision of its proprietors, Terry and Val Skilki. It overlooks Lake Padarn from private gardens at the side and back. All of the 26 bedrooms have private baths or showers, color TV, phones, and hot-beverage facilities. Some family suites are available. You can stay here for £17.50 ($28) to £19.50 ($31.20) per person for B&B. The hotel has three bars, including the

Welsh Lounge, and the restaurant has an extensive à la carte menu plus table d'hôte offerings.

Y Bistro, High Street (tel. 0286/871278), is an excellent and popular eating place in Llanberis, where Mr. and Mrs. Roberts provide meals to be enjoyed at leisure, not on a grab-a-bite basis. You can have a fixed-price dinner of four courses, which might include orange soup, salmon, sirloin steak cooked several ways and with a variety of sauces, or trout. Expect to pay around £11 ($17.60) for the set meal. If you prefer to order à la carte, your dinner will cost £17 ($27.20) and up. Most of the food is locally produced or caught. The menu is in Welsh with English explanations. Such foods as eog peris (locally smoked salmon in a creamy sauce in a pastry tart) and ffrwyth (a chilled melon, orange, and Cointreau cocktail) may interest you, and main courses include braised pheasant, pork tenderloin, pigeon breasts, steak, and lamb kebabs. The bistro is open Monday to Saturday from 7:30 to 9:30 p.m., when last orders are taken. Reservations are necessary. Jackets and ties are requested for men.

At **Pete's Eats,** High Street (tel. 0286/870358), you may rub elbows with local climbers who like to listen to the jukebox and keep track of climbing conditions and weather forecasts, which are posted on a bulletin board. They serve generous, tasty meals, snacks, and teas, with a filling repast costing from £2.50 ($4) to £4 ($6.40). Pete's is open seven days a week from 9 a.m. to 8 p.m. (to 6:30 p.m. in winter.)

SIGHTS IN THE AREA: On the A4086 road at the start of the lake railway and Padarn Country Park, the **Welsh Slate Museum** (tel. 0286/870630), is in the workshops of the Dinorwic slate quarry, one of the largest in the United Kingdom until its closing in 1969. Slate-mining communities were intensely Welsh, nonconformist in religion, and radical in politics. Films depicting the work once done here are shown. The museum is open from 9:30 a.m. to 5:30 p.m. from Easter to the end of April, to 6:30 p.m. May to September. Admission is 80p ($1.28) for adults, 40p (64¢) for children.

Oriel Eryri (tel. 0286/870636), also at the Padarn Country Park, interprets the rich natural environment of Snowdonia with exhibits and pictorial details. Open June to September from 10 a.m. to 5 p.m. on weekdays, 1:30 to 5 p.m. on Sunday, admission is free. Both the Slate Museum and Oriel Eryri are under the auspices of the National Museum of Wales.

Padarn Country Park, open daily until dusk, has marked footpaths that will take you past the Vivian Quarry, with its dramatic slate cliffs and deep pools, through galleries where slate was worked, and to lookouts from which the Snowdon range and the lakes can be viewed.

Crafts workshops and a woodcraft center are open at the park, where you can watch artisans work in clay, copper, slate, and wood. One workman specializes in Celtic folk harps, including miniature models and do-it-yourself kits.

The **Dolbadarn Castle** ruins overlook Lake (Llyn) Padarn in the Llanberis pass, half a mile east of Llanberis, a relic of the time when the pass was used by conquering armies. It is notable for its location and the mortared masonry tower which still stands. You can take a look around free.

Bryn Bras Castle (tel. 0286/870210) is a 70-room, 19th-century Stately Home of Wales. It is a handsome structure, set in 30 acres of superb gardens of natural beauty, with walks, pools, waterfalls, and a mountain walk with panoramic views of Snowdon and the sea. It's half a mile off the A4086 at Llanrug, about four miles from Llanberis. The house is open from the end of May to the end of September, and you can view the drawing room, Louis XV suite, splendid ceilings, galleried staircase, paneling, stained-glass windows, and richly carved furniture. In a tea room, you can enjoy teas, including such items as Welsh bara brith. Admission is £1.20 ($1.92) for adults, 60p (96¢) for children. Bryn Bras is occupied by its owners.

8. Betws-y-Coed

This is an ideal Snowdonia village, with tumbling rivers, waterfalls, and mountains, nestling in the tree-lined valley of the River Conwy. It has an old church with a Norman font, a 15th-century stone bridge, stone houses and hotels on rocky outcrops, and woodland paths.

The **Snowdonia National Park and Wales Tourist Information Centre** is at Royal Oak Stables (tel. 06902/426). Open in summer only, hours are from 10 a.m. to 6 p.m.

FOOD AND LODGING: Once a coaching inn, the **Royal Oak Hotel** (tel. 06902/ 219), has a commanding position overlooking the River Llugwy. The hotel has 21 well-appointed bedrooms, all with private baths, color TV, radios, alarms, and telephones. Tariffs, a little over budget, are £40 ($64) in a single, £26 ($41.60) per person in a double for B&B. The hotel has three bars, ranging from spacious to cozy, where you can have snacks at most times. A grill room and restaurant offer food, which includes the tasty river products, salmon and trout. This big stone hotel is well suited to the area in which it stands, where mountains, forests, and rivers supply the setting.

Glenwood (tel. 06902/508), is a spacious guesthouse standing in its own beautiful grounds with enough scenic views to boggle the mind. The owners, Patricia and Stuart Strong, say that they have couples who honeymooned at Glenwood who keep coming back for vacations, even bringing their children to this delightful place. All six rooms have hot and cold water basins in this centrally heated house. A special treat here is the serving of Welsh cream teas in the gardens. Rooms rent for £13.50 ($21.60) for B&B in a single, £24 ($38.40) in a double.

Ty'n-y-Celyn Guest House, Llanwrst Road (tel. 06902/202), is a large Victorian house where you will be warmly welcomed by Maureen and Clive Muskus. It stands in an elevated position, overlooking the village, with views of Llugwy Valley, the River Conwy, and the mountains. The house has eight bedrooms with hot and cold water basins, color TV, and hot-beverage facilities, and most of them have showers and toilets. B&B costs from £12 ($19.20) to £14.50 ($23.20) per person, depending on the season. If you come to Betws-y-Coed by train, the Muskuses will have you met at the station.

Ty Gwyn (White House) **Hotel & Pub** (tel. 06902/383) is one of the most charming hotels and pubs in town. Laden with carved beams and local artifacts, it is low slung, sitting on the opposite side of Waterloo Bridge from the rest of town. Originally, it was built in the 16th century as a coaching inn for horsemen traveling between London and the ferryboats for Ireland. Teddy Roosevelt stayed here in the late 19th century. Just out of college, he was on a visit to friends in the region. The place is popular as a restaurant and pub, but also rents rooms. Lunch, daily from noon to 2:30 p.m. costs £6 ($9.60), and dinner, 7 to 10 p.m., goes for £12 ($19.20). An "upmarket" bar menu is served at lunch, but at night the fare is more elaborate, including smoked breast of goose, baked local trout (sprinkled with prawns and flamed in brandy), or duckling with cassis and black currants. Nine of the comfortably furnished bedrooms upstairs contain private baths, but none has a phone or TV. Per person rates, single or double occupancy, cost £15 ($24) to £22 ($35.20) with breakfast. Tariffs depend on the room assignment and the season.

Park Hill Hotel, Llanwrst Road (tel. 06902/540), was built early in the Victorian age by a mining merchant who valued its dark stone facade and lace-like gingerbread trim. Today, it's the gracious domain of Scottish-born hoteliers James and Betty Bovaird. They moved from a suburb of Glasgow and today operate one of the most warmhearted residents-only cocktail lounges in town. Ringed with a sunporch, the hotel lies within a five-minute walk of town. The 11 well-furnished bedrooms cost £17 ($27.20) in a bathless single, £20 ($32) per person in a double with bath, including a hearty breakfast and free use of a rarity in the region, an indoor swimming pool with its adjacent sauna. Bar lunches, daily from noon to 2 p.m., cost £4 ($6.40) each, while a three-course evening meal, from 7 to 8 p.m., goes for £9 ($14.40) and is open to nonresidents.

Staying in the Environs

On the outskirts, **Plas Hall** (tel. 06906/206) lies at Pont-y-Pant, 4½ miles southwest of Betws-y-Coed on A470. Cross a trestle bridge spanning the River Lledr, drive past soaring conifers and steep embankments, and you find yourself in the shadow of this hideaway. Its steep gables and high walls were fashioned from chiseled blocks of slate from the surrounding hills. Everywhere the sound of splashing river water hints at the fresh salmon and trout served in the adjacent restaurant. This property is the creative statement of John Palmer, British-born but a longtime resident of Florida, Australia, and London. Each of his 17 bedrooms has a private bath, color TV, and a view of the forest. B&B costs from £24 ($38.40) to £31 ($49.50) per person single or double occupancy. Bar meals are offered at lunch from 12:30 to 2 p.m., with a fixed-price dinner featured in the evening, costing from £11 ($17.60) and served from 6:30 to 10 p.m. Menu specialties, served in a high-ceilinged room originally built with two fireplaces as a Victorian library, include fresh whitebait from Anglesey, pheasant basted in butter and local herbs, and poached salmon with fennel sauce, along with Welsh salt-meadow lamb.

Siabod (tel. 06904/229) is a comfortable, modern guesthouse run by an Australian couple, Ruth and Ron Moscrop, in the little village of Capel Curig a short way west of Betws-y-Coed. The Moscrops, who charge £9 ($14.40) for B&B, also provide delicious food. This area is popular with backpackers, hikers, and pony trekkers.

SIGHTS AROUND BETWS-Y-COED: In the old goods yard by the British

Railway station, **Conwy Valley Railway Museum** (tel. 06902/568), can be visited from 10 a.m. to 5:30 p.m. daily from April to October. It costs 50p (80¢) to ride on the tram. Admission to the museum is 60p (96¢) for adults, 40p (64¢) for children.

Swallow Falls and Miners Bridge is a well-known beauty spot about two miles west of Betws-y-Coed off the A5 road. There's a car park, craft and gift shops, a restaurant, a cafeteria, and a pub. Admission to the falls is 20p (32¢).

Penmachno Woollen Mill (tel. 06902/545) is about two miles from Betws-y-Coed. The mill weaves soft tweed shades which the mill's designer has made into classic clothing and coordinated knitwear, available in the Mill Shop at reasonable prices. The mill is open Easter to mid-November from 9 a.m. to 5:30 p.m. daily, except that it's closed Sunday morning early and late in the season. Weaving is done Monday to Friday. Admission to the mill and shop is free, but if you wish to see the audio-visual presentation, *The Story of Wool,* a charge of 25p (40¢) is made for adults, 10p (16¢) for children. To reach the mill, take the A5 road from Betws-y-Coed, headed for Llangollen for two miles. At the Penmachno Mill Café, take the B4406 on the right, signposted Penmachno. The mill is half a mile along the road on the right.

Ty Mawr, Wybrnant, Penmachno (tel. 06902/213), at the head of the little valley of Gwybernant, 3½ miles southwest of Betws-y-Coed and two miles west of Penmachno, is the cottage where Bishop William Morgan was born in the 16th century. He was the first translator of the Bible into Welsh, and his translation is considered a masterpiece, the foundation of modern Welsh literature. The house is open daily from noon to 5 p.m. Easter to the end of September except Monday and Saturday (in October by appointment). Admission is 50p (80¢) for adults, 25p (40¢) for children.

In Betws-y-Coed, a popular stop is the **Anna Davies/Welsh Wool Shop** (tel. 06902/292), where the stock contains a wide range of woolen items as well as other goods.

Dolwyddelan Castle stands lonely on a ridge about a mile from the village of the same name, accessible by a rough track off the A470 road to the southwest of Betws-y-Coed, on the road to Blaenau Ffestiniog. Tradition says this was the birthplace of Llewelyn the Great, and it was certainly his royal residence. It was restored to its present condition in the 19th century. The castle can be visited admission free. It opens at 9:30 a.m., closing in March, April, and October at 5:30 p.m., May to September at 7 p.m., and November to February at 4 p.m. seven days a week. Apply at the farm for the key. The castle's remains look out on the rugged grandeur of Moel Siabod peak. A medieval road from the Vale of Conwy ran just below the west tower, which made this a strategic site for a castle to control passage.

9. Llanwrst

About five miles north of Betws-y-Coed on the River Conwy, 12 miles from Conwy on the coast, is the village of Llanwrst, deep in the heart of northern Snowdonia. The crystal-clear river has not yet widened out here to become the estuary. It is crossed by a much-photographed three-arch bridge designed by Inigo Jones in 1636.

Markets are held weekly in Llanwrst—livestock on Friday and general street stalls on Tuesday.

FOOD AND LODGING: On the site of Maenan Abbey, which stood a short distance north of Llanwrst before the dissolution of monasteries in 1538, there is now a hotel, the **Maenan Abbey Hotel,** Maenan (tel. 049269/247), which has a good reputation for hospitality and cuisine. Michael Kerridge and Cheryl Owens, the resident proprietors, rent 12 bedrooms, all with private baths or showers, phones, color TV, radios, hair dryers, trouser presses, hot-beverage facilities, and central heating. The charge for a bed and a full English breakfast is £34 ($54.40) to £40 ($64) in a double, from £22 ($35.20) to £25 ($40) for single occupancy. Family rooms are available. Prices depend on the season. Enjoy real ales in the bar with your bar meals, or dine in the handsome dining room.

Meadowsweet (tel. 0492/640732) is a little ten-bedroom Victorian hotel on the edge of Llanwrst, overlooking the Vale of Conwy. John and Joy Evans are warm and hospitable hosts. The bedrooms all have private baths or showers, color TV, and direct-dial phones, and are attractively decorated. You can relax in the cozy residents' lounge or bar. Preparation of food served in the candlelit restaurant is personally supervised by John, whose culinary skill results in such dishes as cider-braised guinea, rack of lamb, and steak in a red wine sauce. A fixed-price dinner will cost around £14.50 ($23.20), while if you order à la carte you can expect to pay from £16 ($25.60) for a complete meal. Dinner is served from 6:30 to 9:30 p.m. Room tariffs range from £21 ($33.60) to £24 ($38.40) in a single for B&B, from £34 ($54.40) to £42 ($67.20) in a double.

Plas Maenan Hotel, Maenan (tel. 049269/232), is a large country house overlooking the Vale of Conwy, where Pat and Molly, the resident directors, welcome you with true Welsh hospitality. The hotel has 16 attractive and comfortable rooms, each with a private bath, color TV, phone, radio alarm, tea/coffee-making facilities, and central heating. Tariffs are from £21 ($33.60) to £24 ($38.40) in a single for B&B, depending on the season. Doubles or twins cost from £34 ($54.40) in low season, from £38 ($60.80) in high. Some of the public rooms are decorated in modern style, while others are more subdued and traditional with some Welsh antiques. Menus in the dining room include Celtic specialties in addition to Welsh. Bar snacks and afternoon teas are available. The restaurant is open from noon to 2 p.m. and 7 to 10 p.m. Often the hotel has Welsh entertainment with traditional music, food, and informal bar singing.

SIGHTS IN THE ENVIRONS: Just southwest of Llanwrst, four miles from Betws-y-Coed, **Gwydir Castle** (tel. 0492/640261) is an ivy-covered Tudor mansion house, built around a 14th-century hall. The house is still inhabited. An audio tour transports you through a bygone age via the kitchen, nursery, royal bedrooms, banqueting hall, concealed priest's hideaway, and ghoulish dungeons. Perhaps you'll see or sense a ghost. The delightful formal gardens are enhanced by many peacocks roaming freely and a keeper's cottage. There's also a coffeeshop where crafts can be purchased. The castle is open from 10 a.m. to 5 p.m. daily from April to mid-October. Admission is £2 ($3.20) for adults, £1 ($1.60) for children.

Gwydir Uchaf Chapel, about half a mile southwest of Llanwrst, may also be visited. It was built in 1673. You can get the key from the verger at Gwydir Cottage nearby. The **Gwydir Uchaf Forest Visitor Centre** is in this vicinity.

Encounter, the North Wales Museum of Wild Life, Fron Ganol, School Bank Road, is filled with big-game trophies and stuffed birds.

Trefriw, a couple of miles away, is a former spa, but few come now to take the waters. The chief attraction is **Trefriw Woollen Mills Limited** (tel. 0492/640462), on the B5106 in the center of the hamlet. The small mill, founded in the early 19th century, produces bedspreads, rugs, tapestry, and tweed garments. Visitors can follow all the stages in processing the wool through to the weaving and tailoring. The mill is open Monday to Friday from 9 a.m. to 5:30 p.m. Admission is free. A large mill shop selling the pure wool products is open at the same time as the mill, plus on Saturday from 10 a.m. to 4 p.m.

The turbine house where electricity is generated using hydroelectric turbines is also open to the public. From the end of May to the end of September, a wholefood vegetarian café is open in the mill house, and during the same period, you can observe hand spinning and weaving as well as machine knitting.

10. The Vale of Ffestiniog

Some of the most beautiful scenery of Wales is in this vale stretching down to the sea, where the upper reach of the little Ffestiniog Railway train is at—

BLAENAU FFESTINIOG: Girded by mountains, this slate-mining town is today known mainly for its slate caverns and the narrow-gauge railway which once transported their output to Porthmadog on Tremadog Bay. The **Llechwedd Slate Caverns** (tel. 0766/830306) offer two exciting and different rides into the underground world of the Victorian miner. On the Miners' Underground Tramway, visitors are taken into the side of the mountain, following a level track that winds through chambers in which Victorian-age working conditions have been re-created. A former miner tells how the work was done and shows tools and equipment used. The Deep Mine tour descends on an inclined railway leading to the lower levels, while tales of the slate miners' lives are re-counted as you explore the huge caverns and underground lake.

On the surface, attractions include demonstrations of slate splitting in the mill, the Slate Heritage Theatre with an audio-visual presentation narrated by actor and playwright Emlyn Williams, and the smithy and tramway exhibitions. There are also craft and gift shops and the Miners' Pub, a licensed restaurant where you can buy food and drinks. If you have mail to send, you can drop it into the underground postbox for special cancellation. The caverns are open April to October daily from 10 a.m., with the last trip into the mines starting at 5:15 p.m., at 4:15 p.m. in October. Either ride costs £2.35 ($3.76) for adults, £1.50 ($2.40) for children. All the surface exhibitions are free.

At the **Gloddfa Ganol Slate Mine** (tel. 0766/830664), billed as the largest in the world, you can walk into vast underground rooms blasted out of the moun-tain by miners who worked slate cliffs by candlelight. The museum tells the story of slate mining, and an experienced miner demonstrates how to split slate. Visi-tors can stand in a safe spot to watch the open-cast blasting operations, after being taken by specialized Land Rover into the real world of the miner, wearing lamp and helmet. Three cottages show the changing domestic conditions of the miners from the late 1800s to the late 1960s. You can also visit the Natural Histo-ry Centre and Britain's largest collection of preserved locomotives for little trains at the Narrow Gauge Railway Centre. Craft shops and a licensed restau-rant and snackbar are in converted quarry buildings, and there's a playroom and playground for children. The mine is open from Easter to October. Admission is £2.50 ($4) for adults, £1.25 ($2) for children.

Quite close to Blaenau Ffestiniog, a little way on down the vale, is a hamlet called just **Ffestiniog,** perched on a bluff over the River Dwyryd. Below the vil-lage are waterfalls.

A near neighbor of Ffestiniog is the **Ffestiniog Pumped Storage Power Sta-tion,** Tan-y-Grisiau (tel. 0766/830465), which can be visited. You can also drive to Stwlan Dam, 1,650 feet above sea level, for a panoramic view of Snowdonia. Admission to the electric plant is £1.25 ($2) for adults, 70p ($1.12) for children. The "alpine" drive to the dam costs £1.25 ($2) per car.

Where to Stay

At Ffestiniog, the **Newborough House Hotel,** Church Square (tel. 076676/2682), is a 17th-century stone-and-slate guesthouse in the center of the village. After you've had a busy day at the slate mines you'll be able to relax in the lounge, which has a beamed ceiling, an inglenook fireplace, and color TV. Per-haps you'd rather enjoy having drinks in the cozy "olde worlde" bar. Bedrooms are tastefully decorated and have hot and cold running water. B&B costs £10 ($16) per person. You can dine here if you let the proprietors know ahead of time, an evening meal costing £5 ($8).

MAENTWROG: This picture-book-pretty little village is reached by road or by the Ffestiniog Railway, which stops at nearby Tanybwlch Station. The main fea-ture of the village is **Plas Tanybwlch** (tel. 076685/324), a mansion house built on the hillside above the Vale of Ffestiniog, which is sometimes identified as the Vale of Maentwrog. The mansion is now a National Park Study Centre, provid-ing facilities for studying all aspects of Snowdonia National Park, including to-pography, natural history, and its cultural and historical background. Visitors can take spectacular walks through the grounds, where the gardens, which have rare and exotic plants, provide a riot of color in the spring and summer. The mansion is open all year from 8:30 a.m. to 5 p.m. Monday to Friday. Admission is free.

Where to Eat

For me, another reason for stopping in Maentwrog is to visit **The Grapes Hotel** (tel. 076685/208), on the A496 road just before it intersects with the A487. The lounge, with thick rock walls, is furnished with remains from old chapels. Chapel pews are the seats in this carpeted room, and the paneled, curved bar is part of an old house of worship. Bar stools are covered with Welsh tapestry. There's a big fireplace with a rock chimney in the lounge. Just outside is a covered veranda looking out over the walled, garden, the village, and rolling land beyond. Al fresco meals specializing in seafoods are served there in summer. A separate restaurant, with slate floor and rock walls, also has a fireplace big enough to roast joints on a spit. It serves spit roasts, charcoal barbecues, and fondues. Brian Tarbox, the licensee, offers a good choice of homemade bar food, including salads, sandwiches, spareribs, gammon, steaks, hot chili, authentic curries, and pizzas, among other tasty foods, all homemade. This is a popular place, so you might have to wait a while for your food. Children can be served in the restaurant. Hours are 11 a.m. to 3 p.m. and 6 to 10:30 p.m. daily, to 11 p.m. on Friday and Saturday in summer. The public bar has a darts game, a jukebox, and a fruit machine, or you can play dominoes. It also has a fireplace.

The hotel has six bedrooms to rent, all with private baths, color TV, and hot-beverage facilities. The charge is £15 ($24) per person for B&B.

THE NORTHWEST

THE ROCKY CRAGS of Snowdonia National Park looming in the majesty of nature are rivaled by the mighty walls and soaring towers of Caernarfon Castle, man's supreme accomplishment in castle building in medieval Wales. Caernarfon (formerly spelled Caernarvon and still pronounced that way) and its neighbors, Anglesey and the Lleyn Peninsula, reaching out from its northwest and west, are all part of the County of Gwynnedd. Legends of holy islands and druidical mysteries grew up in this area among the Celtic peoples who lived here in long-ago centuries.

Many of the native-born people of this area are of blood stock little changed since the days of Owen ap Gryffedd. Most of them are bilingual, with English as their second tongue. Signs are usually in both languages.

I'll begin the trek through the northwest of Wales by going to the area to the west of Snowdonia National Park.

1. Porthmadog and Portmeirion

The estuary of the River Glaslyn has long been the scene of shipping and fishing activity, emptying as it does into Tremadoc Bay and thence into Cardigan Bay.

PORTHMADOG: This is the main town east of the Lleyn Peninsula, to be visited next in this chapter. It is served by British Rail, the Welsh Highland Railway, and the Ffestiniog Narrow Gauge Railway. It grew up as a slate-shipping port on the Cambrian Coast near the mouth of the River Glaslyn. T. E. Lawrence

(Lawrence of Arabia) was born in Tremadog, close by. The view of the mountains of Snowdonia from Porthmadog Cob, the embankment, is exceptional. Porthmadog is the coastal terminal of the Ffestiniog Railway, and a small museum may be visited at the station. From the town there's access to beaches at Borth-y-Gest and Black Rock Sands, where cars may be driven onto the beach.

The **Wales Tourist Information Centre,** High Street (tel. 0766/2981), is open daily from 10 a.m. to 6 p.m.

Food and Lodging

A good accommodation choice is the **Madoc Hotel,** Market Square (tel. 0766/512021), is built of stone with a slate roof and a vine creeping here and there on its front. The stonework is relieved by white trim around the windows and doors. Some of the 22 bedrooms have private bath, and all have hot and cold running water, among other amenities making for comfort. The hotel is centrally heated. The pleasantly appointed rooms rent for £16 ($25.60) in a single, £31 ($49.60) in a double. The residents' lounge is an attractive room with color TV, and there are two licensed bars as well as a dining room, where a varied and interesting cuisine is served, including traditional specialties.

The **Oakleys Guest House,** The Harbour (tel. 0766/2482), is a licensed house run by Mr. and Mrs. A. H. Biddle. Rooms are plain, but the lounge is comfortable and there's a large free car park. The charge is £9.50 ($15.20) to £11 ($17.60) per person for B&B, £12 ($19.20) per person for rooms with private baths. The guesthouse is in a convenient location for seeing the sights of Porthmadog, and a golf course is not far away.

On the outskirts, **Bwlch-y-Fedwen** (tel. 0766/512975), in the hamlet of Penmorfa, lies two miles northwest of Porthmadog along A487. This is one of the most delightful places to stay in North Wales. Its spirit revolves around the personality of its owner, Gwyneth Bridge. Her welcome and her charm cause visitors to return again and again. Hers is a low-slung, white-walled cottage ringed with hydrangea and an espaliered pyracantha. No children under 12 are admitted, allowing guests to enjoy more fully the blazing fireplaces, the polished brass, and tasteful decor. Mrs. Bridge prepares succulent dinners served only to occupants of her five bedrooms (dinner is promptly at 7:30 p.m.). Only half board is available to guests who pay £28 ($44.80) per person for one of the antique-filled rooms with private bath and a view of the hills. The hotel is closed from late October to early April, and reservations are essential.

Sights Around Porthmadog

The **Gwynedd Maritime Museum** is on one of the old wharves of Porthmadog. The last remaining slate shed houses a display on the maritime history of Gwynedd. The museum is open daily Easter to September from 10 a.m. to 6 p.m. Admission is 60p (96¢) for adults, 30p (48¢) for children.

The **Porthmadog Pottery** (tel. 0766/2137) is near the town center on Snowdon Street. In a former flour mill, you can watch all the processes in the manufacture of the pottery's colorful blue and green earthenware. You can even try your hand at the potter's wheel for a small charge, and they box your pot so that you can take it home with you. Of special interest at the pottery is the huge mural depicting the history of Porthmadog. The pottery is open Monday to Friday from 9 a.m. to 5:30 p.m. Easter to the end of October. You can buy seconds and crafts in the shop, as well as enjoying Welsh teas in the tea room.

Outside Porthmadog, just off the A487 going toward Caernarfon, is the **Brynkir Woollen Mill,** Golan, Garndolbenmaen (tel. 076675/236), where you can watch the production of traditional tapestries and tweeds at a small family-run mill in a lovely rural setting. The products are available at the mill shop and at the Brynkir Wool Shop, Castle Square, Caernarfon. The mill is open from 8 a.m. to 4:45 p.m. Monday to Thursday, to 4 p.m. on Friday. It's about 3½ miles from Porthmadog and 15 miles from Caernarfon.

PORTMEIRION: Penrhyndeudraeth, "the headland of the two beaches," is a tiny town known mainly for having on its outskirts the Italianate village of Portmeirion, set on its own wooded peninsula overlooking Tremadog Bay. The late Sir Clough Williams-Ellis built here a tiny village of pastel-colored structures resembling Portofino or Sorrento in a landscape of sea and mountains. The village contains shops, a restaurant, a children's adventure playground, and picnic areas, as well as miles of paths through the woods. White sandy beaches border it.

Portmeirion was the location of the British television series "The Prisoner," starring Patrick McGoohan.

The village may be visited from Easter to October. The grounds are open from 9:30 a.m. to 6 p.m. There's free parking, but admission to the village grounds is £1.80 ($2.88) for adults, 75p ($1.20) for children. Shops are open from 10 a.m. to 5:30 p.m. For information, telephone 0766/770228.

All the cottages are rented as holiday accommodations, either on a self-catering or on a nightly basis. Terms for B&B are £35 ($56) in a single, £43 ($68.80) in a double.

The **Castell Deudraeth Restaurant** in the village has been restored and is back in business after a fire a few years ago. Dinners cost from £15 ($24) and are served from 7:30 to 9 p.m. It has a reputation for good food.

THE LLEYN PENINSULA

Separating Cardigan Bay and its northern arm, Tremadog Bay, from Caernarfon Bay, the gentle western Lleyn Peninsula, thrusts out into the Irish Sea all on its own. It's bounded by the mountains of Snowdonia on the east and by the sea. Having little communication with the outside world before the coming of railroads and highways, the peninsula has a high percentage of Welsh-speaking population, although most people also now have English as a second language, made necessary by the influx of people coming here to retire or to enter business or just to take holidays.

The peninsula takes its name from an Irish tribe, the Celtic Legine or Laigin, who didn't have very far to go from home to invade the country of fellow Celts. They were followed by missionaries and pilgrims in the Christian era. The distance from Ireland is so short that when I stood on National Trust property high on a cliff above St. Mary's Well I could see the Wicklow Mountains of Ireland with the naked eye.

The Lleyn Peninsula has beaches, hills, farmland, moorland, tiny villages nestled in the hollows, trees, heather, gorse, and pretty country lanes. There are traces of hill-forts here, and you can find standing stones, monastery ruins, pilgrim trails, holy wells (four of them), and nonconformist chapels. Sportsmen find fishing, golf, water sports, and rough shooting. Mainly, though, I am always struck by the quiet relaxation, and most of all by the warm hospitality found here.

It is necessary to have your own car if you visit the majority of the peninsula, as the train only runs to Pwllheli, and there is no public transportation.

For information on all of the peninsula, get in touch with the **Tourist Information Centre**, Y Maes, Pwllheli (tel. 0758/613000).

2. Criccieth

This coastal village is so close to Porthmadog—only four miles to the west of that town—that some people seem uncertain as to whether to call it a part of the Lleyn Peninsula or not. However, with its castle originally built by Welsh princes, it has served as guardian to the peninsula for more than 750 years. The town became mainly a resort in the Victorian era when going to the seashore in summer was the fashionable thing to do.

FOOD AND LODGING: Overlooking Tremadog Bay, the **Lion Hotel,** Y Maes (tel. 076671/2460), is a family-run hotel in a lovely situation, with the village green stretching out beside it. Some of the 40 rooms have private bath, and all have color TV, tea/coffee-making facilities, radio, intercom, and hot and cold running water. The hotel has an elevator. The furnishings are modest, and the rooms are comfortable in the best seafront holiday-hotel fashion. There's a cozy bar, and a residents' lounge where you can have your tea served if you wish. The room you take might look out over the garden or the bay. Tariffs are £18 ($28.80) to £20 ($32) for B&B in a single, £33 ($52.80) to £37 ($59.20) in a double. The cuisine is good here. If you choose to take dinner in the hotel, expect to pay about £9 ($14.40) and up. Try the excellent Welsh lamb.

Meirion View Guest House, Marine Terrace (tel. 076671/2201), is where Jean Arthur accommodates guests in a house on the seafront overlooking Cardigan Bay. The six simply furnished bedrooms, all with hot and cold water basins, rent for £10 ($16) for B&B, with an evening meal being served on request. Home-cooked repasts cost an extra £4 ($6.40) per person. The residential table license allows you to have a drink with your meal. The house has a private lounge with color TV.

If you'd like to stay in the village where Lloyd George grew up, try **Gwyndy,** Llanystumdwy (tel. 076671/2720), a 17th-century house with an inglenook fireplace in the TV lounge. The bedrooms are all modern in an addition to the house and have their own bathrooms. They rent for £15 ($24) to £18 ($28.80) per person for B&B. The restaurant is in the old part of the house.

Bron Eifion Country House (tel. 076671/2385), half a mile west on A497, was built in 1870 as the country seat of an industrialist who made a fortune mining slate. It sits within a round stone fence. Inside, a soaring gallery three stories high imbues a sense of grandeur to the place which is heightened by its sheathing of Oregon pine. Overall, the feeling is very much that of a massively paneled late Victorian hunting lodge. Each of the 16 bedrooms contains a private bath. Single or double occupancy costs a splurgy £38 ($60.80), with breakfast included, and for £43 ($68.80) you get half board, a definite splurge but worth it. Well-prepared meals are served in a half-rounded dining room whose chintz curtains blend tastefully into the view of the hydrangeas in the garden outside. A fixed-price lunch from 12:30 to 2 p.m. costs £8 ($12.80), a set dinner from 7:30 to 8:45 p.m. going for £12 ($19.20). Nonresidents are welcome if they reserve.

Plas Isa, Portmadoc Road (tel. 076671/2443), occupies half of an Edwardian double house on a panoramic embankment immediately to the east of the center of town. From the wide windows of the warmly paneled street-level pub, you'll enjoy a sweeping panoramic of the medieval walls of faraway Criccieth Castle. Pam Mayo and her husband, Joe (who was for many years a professional soccer star), are the hard-working owners of this establishment. Each of their 12 bedrooms contains a private bath, small-screen color TV, plush carpeting, and well-upholstered comfort. With breakfast included, singles rent for £27 ($43.20), doubles £42 ($67.20). Bar meals are served daily from noon to 2 p.m. and 6 to 9 p.m.

Outside of the hotel dining rooms, **Moelwyn,** 27 Mona Terrace (tel. 076671/2500), consistently serves the best cuisine in Criccieth. It is, in fact, a restaurant *avec chambres,* as the French put it. Open only from April to October, it is a Victorian, ivy-covered building, opening onto views of Cardigan Bay. The cuisine is both British and continental, with a natural emphasis on freshly caught salmon, trout, and other Neptunian delights. The owners take pride in pleasing their guests, and, on occasion when it's available will have fresh lobster to offer them. Hours are from 12:30 to 2 p.m. and 7 to 9:30 p.m., with meals costing from £12 ($19.20). The owners also rent out six bedrooms, costing only £10.50 ($16.80) in a single, £22 ($35.20) in a double. The rooms are simple and bright, and breakfast the next morning is "super."

While in Criccieth, you may want to make the pub at the **Prince of Wales,** The Square (tel. 076671/2556), your "local," which is a British designation for one's favorite bar. The Prince of Wales is right in the center, receiving guests and serving real ale along with meals and snacks in its Victorian precincts. Open fires are an invitation to linger when the winds blow strong outside. The pub is attractively decorated, and it's a favorite luncheon stopover, offering curries, meat pies, and pastas with meals costing from £5 ($8). Food is also served in the evening. Hours are daily except Sunday from 11 a.m. to 3 p.m. and 6 to 10:30 p.m.

SIGHTS: Now in ruins, **Criccieth Castle,** built as a native Welsh stronghold, is on a grassy headland with a commanding view of Tremadog Bay. During its years as an active fortress it changed hands, Welsh to English and back and forth, being constantly strengthened and added to, until it was finally sacked and burned in 1404 by Owain Glyndwr, never to rise again as a fortification. The castle houses an interesting exhibition on the theme of the native castles of Welsh princes. On a fine day, from its heights you can see westward to the tip of the peninsula, north and east to Snowdonia, and far down the bay to the south. It is open to visitors from 9:30 a.m. to 6:30 p.m. daily from March 15 to October 14. The rest of the year it closes at 4 p.m. Admission is 75p ($1.20) for adults, 25p (40¢) for children.

About 1¾ miles west of Criccieth in **Llanystumdwy,** the boyhood home of David Lloyd George, prime minister of Britain in the 1914–1918 war years, is opposite the Feathers pub. Visitors must get the key from the post office. A short way on toward Pwllheli is the **Lloyd George Museum** (tel. 076671/2654), designed by Sir Clough Williams-Ellis of Portmeirion fame. It is open from 10 a.m. to 5 p.m. May to the end of September on weekdays only. Admission is 50p (80¢) for adults, 25p (40¢) for children. Lloyd George's grave and memorial, also designed by Sir Clough, are nearby on the banks of the swift-running River Dwyfor, shaded by large oak trees. The name of the hamlet, Llanystumdwy, means the church at the bend of the River Dwyfor.

St. Cybi's Well, Llangybi, is a few miles northwest of Criccieth on a minor road. Of 6th-century origin, only two well chambers remain of the holy well, although in the mid-18th century a bath and bathhouse were built to surround the font. You can visit it free.

To the north of the well is the site of a small Iron Age hill-fort.

3. Pwllheli

The main center and market town of the Lleyn Peninsula, Pwllheli draws crowds of vacationers in summer, attracted to its beaches, yacht harbor, sailing races, fishing, and golfing on the 18-hole course. A popular livestock market is held every Monday.

FOOD AND LODGING: On the outskirts of town, **Plas Bodegroes** (tel. 0758/612363), is a mid-Georgian house whose builders selected the site of a ruined homestead when they rebuilt it in 1780. Local legend says that it was the site of an inn used by medieval pilgrims on their way to the holy island, Bardsey. The food served here is both sophisticated and superb, and so stylishly continental that many visitors find it hard to believe that such a place exists in this remote peninsula. Only a duet of dedicated partners could have the finesse to pull such a place together. The co-owners, Chris Chown and Gunna á Trødni (she's from the remote Faroe Islands), define their place in the Gallic sense of a "restaurant with rooms." With its beechwood floors, Georgian symmetry, and Welsh antiques, this is the most ideal rendezvous point I know of for a splurge getaway weekend.

No lunch is served except on Sunday when it's a traditional British repast, going for a fixed price of £8 ($12.80) from 1 to 2 p.m. The culinary creativity is more inspired, however, every evening at dinner from 7:30 to 9 p.m. when a fixed-price repast goes for £17 ($27.20). Specialties include an array of dishes likely to be found in the more refined establishments of London or Paris. These might include a roulade of smoked and raw salmon with a sorrel-flavored yogurt and avocado salad, or crabmeat bisque with smoked chicken. You can go on to breast of guinea fowl stuffed with mango and celery and served with a mild curry sauce with savory pancakes, or loin of local lamb baked with mushrooms in puff pastry and served with a red wine sauce. The dessert specialty is likely to be a basketful of fresh seasonal fruits with pine-nut ice cream and a purée of seasonal fruits (it approaches the sublime). Because of the inn's isolation, many guests choose to spend the night in one of the well-appointed bedrooms. The rate, based on double occupancy, with dinner included, ranges from £32 ($51.20) to £40 ($64) per person depending on the season. On Tuesday, the dining room is open only to residents. The location is on the A497 between Pwllheli and Nefyn, one mile west of Pwllheli.

Just four miles from Pwllheli lies the little resort village of Llanbedrog. A good place to stay here is **Penarwel Country House** (tel. 0758/740719), on the outskirts of the village. The small country mansion is a quarter mile off the A499 road. The vine-covered gray stone house has spacious bedrooms—seven of them—with hot and cold running water and plenty of room for extra beds to be moved in for children. Charges for B&B are from £12 ($19.20) in a single to £16.50 ($26.40) per person in a room with bath. A three-course dinner costs £9 ($14.40), and an à la carte menu is also offered. After dinner, take a walk in the wooded gardens.

Gwynfryn Farm (tel. 0758/612536) is a working organic dairy farm overlooking the sea. The pleasantly decorated bedrooms, which have hot and cold running water, can accommodate children along with parents. Mrs. Ellis charges from £8 ($12.80) to £10 ($16) per person for B&B, depending on the season. Dinner is served only three nights a week, but when it's available, it is well prepared and tasty, including some organic produce in traditional Welsh dishes. The farm is a mile from Pwllheli.

Bel-Air Restaurant, Y Maes (tel. 0758/613198), is open all year for morning coffee, lunch, and dinner. There's an extensive à la carte menu, with chef's specialties cooked to order. Expect to pay around £4 ($6.40) to £6 ($9.60) for lunch, from £8.50 ($13.60) for dinner. They also have good homemade bar snacks. Hours are 9 a.m. to 2:30 p.m. and 6 to 9 p.m. Children's portions are available until 7:30 p.m. The restaurant is licensed. The location of the restaurant, Y

Maes, describes "The Field" near the station, which has been the marketplace for the people of Lleyn for centuries.

Nanna's Coffee Shop, 8 Market Square (tel. 0758/612360), is in the shopping center of town off the main street, adjacent to the Old Town Hall. You can have morning coffee, lunches, and afternoon teas here. A light lunch in this convivial place costs from £3 ($4.80); an afternoon tea, around £2 ($3.20). The teas served here are quite filling. Hours are from 9 a.m. to 5 p.m. weekdays.

FROM THE MIDDLE AGES: An interesting medieval hall, **Penarth Fawr,** is near Abererch, a tiny village on a minor road off the main roads to Pwllheli. This is a stone, aisle-truss hall house built early in the 15th century and restored in the 1930s, with many of its original features retained. The house is open to visitors in summer from 10 a.m. to 5 p.m. Admission is free.

4. Abersoch

A number of little towns and villages within a stone's throw of each other around the end of the peninsula have accommodations for visitors which range from country-house hotels with lots of amenities to small guesthouses where you're likely to be treated as a member of the family, especially in those on farms. After leaving Pwllheli on your exploration of the Lleyn Peninsula, I suggest you go around the bay on the A499 road.

You'll soon reach Abersoch, a village that is a yachting center with two fine sandy beaches and a nine-hole golf course. Water sports are excellent here. Across the bay, the St. Tudwal Islands are now a bird sanctuary. An abandoned lighthouse dominates the island to the east, while on the other one are the remains of a 12th-century chapel.

FOOD AND LODGING: If you'd like to stop over here, there are several good places to stay. The **Deucoch Hotel** (tel. 075881/2680) is where Stuart and Barbara White extend a warm welcome and good service, even though they are not Welsh but émigrés from Cheshire, England. The hotel is a favorite with boating people, who come to enjoy the fine sailing off the south coast. Golf holidays are also arranged, with play on courses at Abersoch, Pwllheli, Nefyn, and off the peninsula at the Royal St. David's course at Harlech. Originally a 19th-century farmhouse, the Deucoch stands in an elevated position overlooking the surrounding area and the sea. The bedrooms all have color TV, radio, room call, tea/coffee-making facilities, and baby-listening service. All but one single have a private bathroom. Tariffs for B&B are £25 ($40) in a single in high season, £19.50 ($31.20) per person in a double, also in high season. Rates are reduced for low-season guests. There is a well-appointed lounge and a public bar with a nautical (sailing) theme. The dining room has touches of elegance. Here you can enjoy good meals, which might include such "Taste of Wales" dishes as elewen oen mewn cawell (Welsh spring lamb kidneys sautéed in butter and served with a red wine sauce in a pastry basket) and cig oen mewn crwstyn (leg of Welsh lamb baked in a pastry case with kidney, mushroom, onion, mint, and parsley). Of course they offer other dishes, such as sole, veal, and beef Strogonoff. Expect to spend from £10 ($16) for a well-prepared and well-served meal.

About two miles out of Abersoch is the **Porth Tocyn Hotel** (tel. 075881/2966), a big white hostelry operated by the Fletcher-Brewer family. Sitting on its own farmland, the hotel has splendid views of Tremadog Bay, Snowdonia, and the coastline to the southwest. The public rooms are furnished with antiques and have fireplaces and comfortable seating. The 17 bedrooms, of varying sizes reflecting their origins as country cottages from which the hotel was put together, all have baths and other luxury amenities. Rooms rent for £20 ($32) to £30 ($48) per person for B&B, depending on the size of the accommodation and the season. From the terrace you can look to the sea as you enjoy afternoon tea or drinks. A tennis court and heated swimming pool add to the pleasure of guests. Cordon Bleu cuisine is offered in the handsome dining room with such dishes as grilled Dover sole with lobster mousseline, filet of beef in Madeira and red wine, and roast duck with brandied gooseberry sauce. Food here is said to be among the best in the area. A set lunch costs from £8 ($12.80), a table d'hôte dinner going for £11.50 ($18.40) and up. Meals are served from 12:30 to 2 p.m. and 7:30 to 9:30 p.m.

LLANENGAN AND LLANGIAN: The tiny hamlet of Llanengan is known for its church, St. Engan's (Einion's). Built in the 15th century, the church has a finely carved rood screen and loft, as well as an alms chest from medieval days. This was a stop for pilgrims on the way to and from Bardsey Island. If the church is locked when you visit, ask for the key at the post office.

Llangian is an outstandingly pretty village, perhaps the most attractive on the peninsula, with a church which contains a 5th-century stone inscribed in Latin to "Melus the Doctor, son of Martinus," the first known mention of a doctor in Wales. Also here is the oldest surviving chapel in Wales, Capel Newydd, built in 1769.

The sea cove closest to these two villages is called Hell's Mouth (Port Neigwl), where the surf pounds in, drawing surfing enthusiasts.

Before reaching the next destination, Aberdaron, stop off at **Plas yn Rhiw** (tel. 075888/219), a small 17th-century manor altered in the Regency Period. It stands in its own grounds, with an ornamental garden, in an idyllic position overlooking Porth Neigwl (Hell's Mouth). The estate includes other coastal and inland properties owned by the National Trust. The house is open from Good Friday to the end of September from 11 a.m. to 5 p.m. (last entry at 4:45 p.m.) daily except Saturday. Admission is £1 ($1.60) for adults, 50p (80¢) for children.

5. Around Aberdaron

At the western tip of the peninsula, 17 miles from Pwllheli, lies the stone village of Aberdaron, which drew pilgrims a millennium and a half or so ago as it draws holiday-makers and fishing enthusiasts today. The Lleyn Peninsula is essentially a clean peninsula, with unpolluted streams and air. At Aberdaron, to keep the sea around it clean, they installed a sewage-treatment plant so there is no outfall. The famous Whistling Sands beach is close by.

FOOD AND LODGING: A good place to stay in Aberdaron is **Ty Newydd Hotel** (tel. 075886/207), where Breda Jones, an Irishwoman, makes guests comfortable in her "land's end" hostelry, adjacent to the Norman church. Ty Newydd is right on the beach. The hotel has been improved and renovated so that guests can enjoy such amenities as central heating, TV, room-call service, and hot and cold running water in all 15 rooms, and private bath/shower in nine. Rates, which include a continental breakfast, are £17.50 ($28) to £20.50 ($32.80) per person, depending on the plumbing. Meals, served in the dining room overlooking the sea or on the beach terrace, include a full English breakfast, an à la carte lunch, and dinner, either table d'hôte or à la carte. A fixed-price evening meal costs from £9 ($14.40). Hot and cold snacks are available in the bars. The oldest part of the hotel is about 800 years old. The front is practically new—only 200 years old.

SIGHTS: Now a café and souvenir shop, **Y Gegin Fawr** (The Big Kitchen) was built in the 14th century as a last stop for pilgrims on their way to Bardsey Island (see below). On the seashore is **St. Hywyn's Church,** known as the Cathedral of Llyn, founded in the 6th century. The present building dates from the 12th century. This was the place to which Gruffydd ap Rhys, Prince of South Wales, fled for sanctuary in the 13th century when he was pursued by King Henry I. The church is open all day.

From Aberdaron, you can go to **Braich-y-Pwll,** the true Land's End of northwest Wales, which was part of a bequest to the National Trust. You go through grass and heather and rocky outcrop over a surprising road—well paved and not too narrow. The road was built during World War II to permit access to the military who used the headland as a lookout post. There is still a coast guard lookout here. From this promontory you have a spectacular view of the water and the coast and Bardsey Island to the south, plus all the way to St. David's Head in the south and across the Irish Sea to the Wicklow Mountains on a clear day. You can take a footpath from here down to **St. Mary's Well** on the shore.

Bardsey Island

Known as the "Isle of 20,000 Saints," Bardsey lies across about two miles of fast-moving and treacherous water from Aberdaron. At one time three pilgrimages to Bardsey counted the same as one to Rome. The founding of a religious community on the island in the early 6th century was the beginning of its religious importance. An influx of monks arrived in the early 7th century, driven from their monastery at Bangor on Dee (Bangor-is-y-Coed) all the way across northern Wales from near Chester when it was sacked by a Saxon king. From then Bardsey became a place of pilgrimage, with a monastery, a church, and all the necessary accoutrements. Later it became a thriving farm community, but today little remains: only one person, a fisherwoman, lives there, or so I was told. It's a bird sanctuary and a breeding place for some seabirds. Trips can be made to the island by boat from Aberdaron in good weather. If you want to go over, ask at Ty Newydd Hotel or the post office.

6. On the Caernarfon Bay Coast

A cluster of villages on Caernarfon Bay have become a major resort area of the Lleyn Peninsula. They are Nefyn, an ancient little town chartered in 1355 and the site of a tournament held in 1284 by Edward I; Morfa Nefyn, Edern, and Porth Dinllaen. The attraction is their proximity to Porth Dinllaen beach, a two-mile stretch of clean sand nestling against cliffs. A lifeboat station and an 18-hole golf course are on the peninsula of Porth Dinllaen. This port was once a busy maritime center and was even considered for the departure point for the trip to Ireland, losing out to Holyhead on Anglesey.

Edern, about a mile from the golf course and beaches, has an interesting old church, St. Edern's, a 250-year-old mill house, and a craft shop.

The A497 road runs from Pwllheli across the peninsula seven or eight miles to the cluster of villages on the north coast.

WHERE TO STAY: A small family-run accommodation, **Dolwen House Hotel,** Ffordd Dewi Sant (tel. 0758/720667) offers personal service and an informal atmosphere. It's a handsome building with a stone base, a white second story, a slate roof, and huge chimneys on each side. The rounded front houses public rooms on the ground floor, allowing views from its many windows. The six bedrooms, all with hot and cold running water, rent for £12 ($19.20) to £13 ($20.80) per person for B&B. The hotel has a residents' lounge with color TV and a separate lounge bar leading onto the patio. There's a dining room, or you can choose from an extensive offering of bar meals.

7. Caernarfon

In the 13th century, when King Edward I of England had defeated the Welsh after long and bitter fighting, he felt the need of a castle in these parts as a part of his network of fortresses in the still rebellious country. He ordered its construction on the site of an old Norman castle at the western end of the Menai Strait, where the River Seiont flows into the sea, a place from which his sentinels could command a view of the land around all the way to the mountains and far out across the bay to the Irish Sea. He had it patterned after ancient Byzantium, where Constantinople and then Istanbul grew around the mighty fortress—a castle and a walled town. Most of the walls of the 13th-century town still stand, although growth outside has been inevitable.

On Saturday a market is held in Castle Square, where there's a statue of David Lloyd George, prime minister of England who came from the Lleyn Peninsula, previewed above, and who was instrumental in preserving the castle.

Caernarfon has yacht clubs, tennis, golfing, and river and sea fishing. At Victoria Dock, the 87-foot ex-dredger, *Seiont II,* which worked on dredging the dock waters, is the nucleus of a small museum depicting the maritime history of Caernarfon.

The **Wales Tourist Information Centre** (tel. 0286/2232) at the Slate Quay is open from 10 a.m. to 6 p.m. daily. The quay was a busy place during the heyday of the nearby slate mines.

FOOD AND LODGING: As you come into town from the north, the **Prince of Wales Hotel,** Bangor Street (tel. 0286/3367), is right on your way. It's in the town center, with the bus station and castle nearby. All the 22 comfortable bedrooms are simple but adequately furnished and centrally heated, with hot and cold water basins, color TV, radios, and hot-beverage facilities. Some of the units have private showers and toilets. Tariffs for B&B run from £16.50 ($26.40) in a single, from £33 ($52.80) in a double, and from £45 ($72) in the family rooms. There are two hospitable and attractive bars, where you can enjoy drinks, chat with fellow guests and local people in a warm atmosphere, or play a game of pool or darts. The hotel's restaurant has drawn compliments from a number of people. Traditional Welsh dishes are served by a bilingual staff. Live entertainment is presented twice a week all year.

Victoria Hotel, Church Street (tel. 0286/3133), run by the vivacious Helen Martin, is a Victorian terrace house built in 1860 and painted white with imperial purple trim in honor of the hotel's namesake, Queen Victoria. In front bay windows look out onto the street, and a small yard in back overlooks the weathered and ancient stones ringing the inner town. The hotel is inside the town wall. Each room is comfortable and cozy, with a black-and-white TV, easy chairs, and a sitting room/lounge format. Some rooms are suitable for families. The rate is from £9 ($14.40) per person nightly for B&B, including a copious and varied breakfast. No evening meal is served, but Mrs. Martin will direct guests to one of several local restaurants.

Staying in the Environs

About a mile from Caernarfon on the road to Beddgelert, the A4085, just past the Roman fort, Segontium, is **Plas Treflan,** Caeathro (tel. 0286/2542), a little Georgian manor where you're given the choice of how you prefer to be accommodated—room only or B&B. The house, set in an acre of ground, has seven studios and one- and two-bedroom apartments, each with a lounge, color TV, and bathroom facilities. The stone cottage studios have tea/coffee-making equipment. If you take B&B, you can choose either a continental or a cooked breakfast. The charge is £18.25 ($29.20) in a single, £25 ($40) in a double. The house has a licensed bar and restaurant and is open from March to October.

The **Stables Hotel and Restaurant,** Llanwnda (tel. 0286/830711), is an excellent and serene place to stay for seeing the sights of Caernarfon, Snowdonia, Anglesey, and the Lleyn Peninsula. It's about three miles south of Caernarfon on the A499 Pwllheli road. It is at Plas Ffynnon, the former home of a horse-breeding family, but owners Mr. and Mrs. David West have done a lot of conversion and extension, with a licensed restaurant and a 12-room hotel wing, connected to the restaurant by a covered way. The one-story hotel building was added in 1979, but the slate roof and careful construction make it blend in as if it had been here longer. It is L-shaped, with lawns and an open-air swimming pool in the inner corner. The lounge/drawing room is furnished with antiques. Two of the 12 bedrooms are family units. All are decorated in Laura Ashley fabrics and period furnishings. They have private baths, radios, color TV, intercoms, phones, and hot-beverage facilities. Half board costs £38.50 ($61.60) for single occupancy, £65 ($104) for two persons in a room, a bit of a splurge, but I think it's worth it.

The stables retain many of the original features, including exposed roof trusses and some of the stall doors and partitions. Here you'll find an extended cocktail bar, a large dining room, and two smaller rooms, the Saddle Room and the Members' Enclosure, where you can have drinks and dine if you wish. The capable chef offers good food, including such dishes as chicken in sorrel sauce, veal chasseur, and medaillons of beef Sicilian style. Lunch is served in the restaurant from 12:15 to 2:45 p.m. and dinner from 7 to 9:45 p.m., when last orders are taken. A set lunch costs around £7 ($11.20), a set dinner going for around £10 ($16). You can order à la carte also. Service is always courteous.

SIGHTS OF CAERNARFON: The nearest thing Wales ever had to a royal palace is **Caernarfon Castle,** described by Dr. Samuel Johnson after a visit in 1774 as "an edifice of stupendous majesty and strength." Legend has it that after the birth of the son of Edward I in this castle, he showed the infant boy to the Welsh, calling him "the native-born prince who can speak no English." Since that time the title Prince of Wales has belonged to every male heir-apparent to the English throne. The eyes of the world were on Caernarfon in 1969 when it was the scene of the investiture of Charles as Prince of Wales.

The castle is open to visitors. Although in some of it only the shell of the wall remains, there are still rooms and stone and wooden steps so that you can climb up in it. Eagle Tower has an exhibition on the ground floor showing the history of the fortress and of the town around it. In the northeast are exhibits on the Princes of Wales. You can also visit the Regimental Museum of the Royal Welch Fusiliers, which occupies all three floors of Queen's Tower and contains many items of interest relating to the regiment and its military history. (When I first visited the castle, I was puzzled as to why the name of the regiment had the word which is usually seen spelled *Welsh* appearing as *Welch*. I learned that this military unit has always resisted reorganization and amalgamation with other regiments while at the same time clinging resolutely to the old-English spelling of the word, despite long pressure from higher-ups to make it Welsh. The effort to change was apparently abandoned as a bad job in 1920.)

The castle is open daily at 9:30 a.m., at 2 p.m. on Sunday. Closing hours vary: 5:30 p.m. in March, April, and October; 7 p.m. from May to September; and 4 p.m. from November to February. Admission is £2 ($3.20) for adults, £1 ($1.60) for children in summer. Prices are reduced in winter. For information, telephone 0286/3094.

The Romans recognized the strategic importance of northwest Wales and maintained a fort at **Segontium** for some three centuries. Excavations on the outskirts of Caernarfon on the A4085 road have disclosed foundations of barracks, bathhouses, and other structural remains. Finds from the excavations are displayed in the museum (tel. 0286/5625) on the site. Hours are the same as those at Caernarfon Castle, above. Admission is free. Some archeologists and historians think that native Britons may have been displaced from the site, which was one of their strongholds at the time of the Roman invasion. You can visit the site of early Celtic huts on Twthill, not far from Segontium.

From Caernarfon Airport (tel. 0286/831047), at the end of the Dinas Dinlle beach road, you can book **"pleasure flights"** over castles, Snowdon, and the islands of the area. Flights are daily from 10 a.m. to 5:30 p.m. Easter to the end of September.

BANGOR: The main A5 road and the A487 meet at Bangor, a few miles north along the Menai Strait from Caernarfon. This cathedral city stands at the eastern entrance to the strait and is the gateway to Anglesey. The cathedral was founded in A.D. 548. Bangor has a museum of Welsh antiquities, a heated swimming pool in Garth Road, and an 18-hole golf course, as well as yachting activity and fishing in the Menai Strait. University activities are plentiful and mostly open to visitors.

About three miles east of the town, at Llandegai on the A5122, is **Penrhyn Castle** (tel. 0248/353084), a National Trust property. This 19th-century castle is an outstanding example of neo-Norman architecture much loved by romantically minded Victorians. The stark, castellated exterior has nine towers, a barbican gateway, and an impressive keep. The interior features carved wood and stone, and the slate from which the Pennant family, builders of the castle, derived their fortune. Much of the furniture is designed on a scale as grandiose as that of the architecture. In the castle are a museum of industrial locomotives and an exhibition of dolls. Penrhyn is surrounded by 40 acres of lawns and parkland, including a Victorian walled garden. You can walk around the grounds.

The castle and garden are open from noon to 5 p.m. daily except Tuesday from early April to the end of October. Last entrance is at 4:30 p.m. Admission to both the castle and the garden is £2.10 ($3.36) for adults, 80p ($1.28) for children. Admission to the garden only is £1 ($1.60) for adults, 40p (64¢) for children.

THE ISLE OF ANGLESEY

The Welsh name of this island is Mon (the Romans called it Mona), and it is called Mon, Mam Cymru, or Anglesey, Mother of Wales. If this is true, I must say the child doesn't much resemble the mother. The scenery differs totally from that of the mainland, with low-lying farmland interrupted here and there by rocky outcrops. The landscape is dotted with single-story whitewashed cottages, and the rolling green fields stretch down to the sea—all against a backdrop of the mountains of Snowdonia across the Menai Strait which divides this island from the rest of Wales.

Visitors cross the strait by one of the two bridges built by celebrated engineers of the 19th century: the Menai Suspension Bridge, designed by Thomas Telford and completed in 1826, and the Brittania Bridge, originally a railroad bridge which was the work of Robert Stephenson. The Brittania, a neighbor of the suspension bridge, had to be rebuilt after a devastating fire which destroyed its pitch and timberwork, and it now carries both trains and cars on two different levels. The bridges are about a mile west of Bangor on the mainland.

Many people have passed through Anglesey on the train that operates between London and Holyhead, for a ferry journey to Ireland. I think if I were making that trip, I would arrange to stop off for a few days on Anglesey, which has much to offer. There are fascinating sights to see. Neolithic tombs of Stone Age settlers can be visited, together with Iron Age artifacts. The Romans came, and they left artifacts and ruins to mark their passage. Early Christianity's followers can be traced, and the dominance of Welsh princes still shows in the land.

The coming of steamers and then of the railroad brought Victorian-era visitors. However, if you're not really sold on antiquity, there's a lot to do on Anglesey that is totally in tune with the 1980s. Yachting, sea fishing, and leisure centers that offer swimming, squash, and other activities are within easy reach wherever you stay. Golf, tennis, nature walks, pony trekking, canoeing—whatever—are offered in the daytime, and in the evening you can wine, dine, even disco.

To find out about all the things you can see and do, stop at the Wales Tourist Board Information Centre, Railway Station Site, Llanfairpwllgwyngyllgogerychwyrndrobwllllantysiliogogogoch. For advance information, telephone 0248/724666 (a 24-hour service) or write to the **Tourism Department,** Penyrorsedd House, Llangefni, Isle of Anglesey, Gwynedd LL77 7JA. The island has good bus service. The tourist offices can give you information on that method of transportation.

8. Menai Bridge and Environs

The small town of Menai Bridge has several points of interest. Take a stroll westward along the Belgian Promenade, a walk constructed along the strait during World War II by Belgian refugees. You can go under the bridge, past some standing stones which were recently erected and Coed Cyrnol, a pine wood, to Church Island. A 14th-century church on the island was founded in the 7th century by St. Tysilio, son of the royal house of Powys and grandson of St. Pabo. St. Pabo is believed to have been a north British chief who sought asylum on Anglesey.

The **Tegfryn Art Gallery,** Cadnant Road (tel. 0248/712437), has works by prominent contemporary Welsh artists on exhibit. Pictures may be purchased. The privately owned gallery is not far from the shore of Menai Strait. Hours are 10 a.m. to 1 p.m. and 2 to 5:30 p.m. There's ample parking.

Menai Bridge is the site every year in October of the **Ffair-y-Borth,** a colorful fair which has been held here since the 16th century.

This is an excellent place from which to view the Menai Strait sailing regatta in August each year.

FOOD AND LODGING: A former posting inn beside Menai Straits, **Gazelle,** Glyn Garth (tel. 0248/713364), is a hotel, restaurant, and pub, one of the finest in the area. Its quayside pub with its splendid views is the most frequented in the area. Mr. and Mrs. Clark welcome visitors, who in colder months stay inside, enjoying the views of the peaks of Snowdonia through large picture windows. You have a choice of rooms for meals and snacks (there are two restaurants, for example). A favorite of the yachting crowd, the inn is attractively decorated, with an old Welsh dresser or a time-blackened settle giving the place character. In summer the action overflows onto a patio. Solid British fare, including fresh fish, steaks, and meat pies, are regularly featured, with a daily changing selection of desserts. Bar meals cost from £5 ($8), regular lunches £7 ($11.20), and dinners £10 ($16). Hours are from 11 a.m. to 3:30 p.m. and 6 to 10:30 p.m. (in summer it stays open until 11 p.m. on Friday and Saturday). The hotel also rents out bedrooms which are well kept and comfortably furnished (some with private bath). Singles begin at £20 ($32), doubles costing £30 ($48) to £37 ($59.20).

Practically a suburb of Menai Bridge is a little village to the west that has been heard of all over the world. Its fame is its name: **Llanfairpwllgwyngyllgogerychwyrndrobwllllantysiliogogogoch** or something like that. It means "St. Mary's Church in the Hollow of the White Hazel near a Rapid Whirlpool and the Church of St. Tysilio near the Red Cave." The thought has been voiced that perhaps the name was invented as a tourist attraction. You can get the longest train platform ticket in the world from the station here, giving the full name. I don't advise trying to pronounce it, even if you have been practicing a little Welsh. On maps and most references it is usually called "Llanfair PG" to differentiate it from several other Llanfairs in Wales.

You're sure to see the Marquess of Anglesey's column, standing 90 feet high on a mound 250 feet above sea level. It has a statue of the marquess on top, to which visitors can climb (115 steps up a spiral staircase) for a small charge. The marquess lost a leg while he was second in command to the Duke of Wellington at Waterloo and was thereafter called "One Leg" ("Ty Coch" in Welsh).

The first Women's Institute in Britain was founded here in 1915.

If you're worn out from climbing the Anglesey monument or just from reading the name of the town, you might want to stop at the **Penrhos Arms** (tel. 0248/714620), right on the A5 road. You can't miss it—it has a sign bearing the elongated name across the front of the building. You can have lunch or dinner here. Menu items include sirloin steak with mushrooms and garnish, ham steak with egg or pineapple, seafood, kebabs, and sausage. From the cold table you can have a ploughman's lunch, baked ham salad, or a prawn sandwich or salad. Baked potatoes, french fries, and other "bits and pieces" are available. A meal costs from £5 ($8), and a full dinner goes for £6.50 ($10.40). Meals are served from 11:30 a.m. to 2 p.m. and 6:30 to 9:30 p.m. weekdays, from noon to 1:45 p.m. and 7 to 9 p.m. on Sunday, when roasts are offered. Peter and Helen Ogan are your hosts.

PLAS NEWYDD: A mile southwest of the village with the long name, on the A4080 road, from a turn off the A5 almost opposite the Marquess of Anglesey Column, is Plas Newydd (tel. 0248/714795), standing on the shores of the Menai Straits. It's the home of the seventh Marquess of Anglesey but now owned by the National Trust. An ancient manor house was converted between 1783 and 1809 into a splendid mansion in the Gothic and neoclassical styles. Its Gothic Hall features a gallery and elaborate fan vaulting. In the long dining room, see the magnificent trompe l'oeil mural by Rex Whistler. A military museum houses relics and uniforms of the Battle of Waterloo where the first Marquess of Anglesey lost a leg. The beautiful woodland garden and lawns are worth visiting. The mansion is open to visitors from noon to 5 p.m. (last admission at 4:30 p.m.) daily except Saturday from mid-April to the end of September and only on Friday and Saturday during the first three weeks in October. Admission to the house and garden is £1.80 ($2.88) for adults, 65p ($1.04) for children, with family tickets costing £4.50 ($7.20). To visit the garden only, adults pay £1 ($1.60), children 50p (80¢).

AT BRYNSIENCYN: A view of local marine life is provided at the **Anglesey Sea Zoo,** the Oyster Hatchery (tel. 024873/411), in imaginative enclosures in a large modern building. You can see hundreds of live lobsters, skates, rays, leaping rainbow trout, and sharks. A seafood and crafts shop are here, as well as a tea room where you can have food and drink while you watch tropical marine fish in a central tank. The sea zoo is open Easter to October daily from 10 to 5 p.m. Admission is £1.75 ($2.80) for adults, 90p ($1.44) for children. The little village of Brynsiencyn is a short distance south of Plas Newydd on the A4080 road.

Near Bodowyr Farm outside the village is the **Bodowyr Burial Chamber,** a fine example of the cromlechs of Anglesey, those striking relics of prehistoric times, more than 4,000 years ago. You can take a look at this one free. It's a short distance from Llanidan Church off a minor road near the farm.

On a minor road from Brynsiencyn to Melin Bodowyr is **Caer Leb,** a rectangular earthwork that once defended stone buildings put up in Roman times. There's no charge to look.

9. Beaumaris

The origins of this little Georgian town on the northerly end of the Menai Strait date back to the 13th century, when the last link in the network of castles of Edward I was built to keep the Welsh under control. A small settlement grew up around the castle, gradually developing into an important port which made the town a major trading center until railroads took away the bulk of seagoing mercantile business.

Today the peaceful little town offers sightseeing pleasure as well as many water-related activities, including sailing and fishing in Menai Strait, plus golfing on a nine-hole course, horseback riding, bowling on a green, and walks.

FOOD AND LODGING: A black-and-white inn built in 1472 and rebuilt in 1617, **Ye Olde Bull's Head,** Castle Street (tel. 0248/810329), was the original posting house of Beaumaris. At the original stagecoach entrance to the courtyard is the largest single hinged door in Britain. During the Civil War, Roundhead General Mytton stabled his horses in the courtyard when he laid siege to and took Beaumaris Castle for Cromwell. This historic hotel has had as guests many notables, including Dr. Samuel Johnson and Charles Dickens. Among the many antiques here is the Beaumaris ducking stool.

The owner, Mrs. Barnett, welcomes guests to stay in her interesting bedrooms, of varying size and amenities (some with bathroom), but all comfortably furnished, with the low ceilings and sloping floors expected in a place of great age. She charges from £16.50 ($26.40) per person for B&B. The upstairs dining room was originally the saddle room. It has heavy truss beams and immaculate white napery. À la carte selections include roll mop herring, egg mayonnaise, and various prawn and fruit dishes among the appetizers. Among the main dishes are steaks, Dover sole, salmon, and kidney and bacon with mushroom and tomato. You can dine à la carte for £8.50 ($13.60) to £11 ($17.60). Table d'hôte dinners cost £8 ($12.80) and might include roast Aylesbury duckling, lamb cutlets, and a choice of appetizer and dessert. Dinner is served from 7:15 to 8:15 p.m. (last orders). The Olde Bull's Head has a cozy main bar with a fireplace and small tables. The resident's lounge has a fireplace from the original inn.

The **Bulkeley Arms Hotel,** 19 Castle St. (tel. 0248/810415), has its formal entrance on Castle Street, but most people enter from the back, which overlooks Menai Strait and is near the parking lot. A comfortable and elegant hotel, with much oak paneling, carpeted floors, and a grand staircase, it was known in Victorian days as one of the best watering holes in Beaumaris, and it still holds that distinction. It was designed by Joseph Hansom of Hansom carriage fame. The three-story structure, with 41 suites and bedrooms, has an elevator, three lively bars, a games room, a lounge, and an excellent restaurant, as well as other appurtenances such as a ballroom and reception rooms. All bedrooms have hot and cold running water, and all but four have private baths or showers. Singles range in price from £23 ($36.80) to £31 ($49.60), and doubles go for £41 ($65.60) to £53 ($84.80). Charges include a full English breakfast and VAT. Bar meals, served both at lunch and in the evening, include steak-and-kidney pie, shepherd's pie, roast beef with Yorkshire pudding, and a ploughman's lunch, among other offerings. The cost will come to £3.50 ($5.60) to £5 ($8). An à la carte dinner served in the elegant dining room will cost from £11 ($17.60) to £13 ($20.80), and might include roast guinea fowl, grilled turbot, or Aberdeen Angus filet. A table d'hôte dinner is offered for £8.75 ($14). Food is served from noon to 2 p.m. and 7 to 8:45 p.m.

The **Liverpool Arms Hotel & The Admiral's Tavern,** Castle Street (tel. 0248/810362), has been a hotel since 1700. It has been modernized within recent years, but the owners retained some of the old characteristics. There is a wealth of old beams, and the staircase is listed with the ancient monuments of Anglesey. All the bedrooms have private bath, color TV, and central heating, and are tastefully furnished. Singles rent for £26 ($41.60) and doubles go for £44 ($70.40). The tavern has a strong nautical theme, even to the red and gold carpet with a ship's-wheel design. There are numerous other seafaring touches including ship models, lanterns, and much more. The place has a reputation for its traditional inn fare. You can choose a table d'hôte menu which might include roast Anglesey turkey with stuffing, roast loin of pork, roast beef and Yorkshire pudding, or deep-fried plaice. The fixed-price meal costs less than £7.50 ($12). Other bar foods are available. Food is served in various nooks of the tavern, where you sit in captain's chairs and dine off solid oak tables.

The **White Lion Hotel,** Castle Square (tel. 0248/810589), is very close to the castle and the old courthouse. It is a small, eight-bedroom hostelry where Keith and Shirley Charlton receive guests in simple but comfortable accommodations, all with hot and cold running water. The licensed hotel has a friendly atmosphere, and you can rub elbows with local people in the two bars and the restaurant. Bathless rooms cost £14 ($22.40) per person, rooms with baths going for £16 ($25.60). You can order a varied selection of home-cooked dishes in the Bottles Bistro, which is popular with local people. It's best to make a reservation for dinner. There are also good meals and snacks available in the hotel's bars.

Henllys Hall (tel. 0248/810412) sits in its own 50 acres of ground on the outskirts of Beaumaris. The land was given to the Hamptons, supporters of Edward I who were officials of Beaumaris Castle. The Hamptons lived here from 1460 to 1964, first in a timber house and from 1852 in the present stone mansion. The 25-bedroom hotel has a tennis court, heated outdoor swimming pool, Jacuzzi, sauna, and other facilities. Particularly cozy are the intimate cellar restaurant and bar. A table d'hôte dinner, served from 7 to 10 p.m., costs £9.50 ($15.20) for three courses. The bedrooms, all with baths, cost £24 ($38.40) in a single, from £48 ($76.80) to £54 ($86.40) in a double, depending on whether the room is classified as Executive, Knight, or Prince. The Princes are truly spacious.

Hobson's Choice, 13 Castle St. (tel. 0248/810323), might well be *your* choice as a place to eat in Beaumaris. It's a charming little place with a cozy bar to the right and the dining room to the left as you enter. Lunch is served from noon to 2 p.m. during the summer season and dinner from 7 to 10:30 p.m. all year except Sunday. It is not a large place, so it's best to make a reservation if you want to enjoy the tasty food, perhaps accompanied by one of the good French wines on the list. This is a friendly place with a homey atmosphere, and the cuisine consists of such tasty dishes as fresh rainbow trout, salmon, Welsh lamb, roast beef, and pork chops. Expect to pay from £10 ($16) for a complete dinner. Wine, of course, is extra.

SIGHTS: Built on a flat, unused site, **Beaumaris Castle** is one of the most beautiful in Wales. It was given the French name Beau Marais (Beautiful Marsh) describing the area which is now the Green. The flat area allowed for building this splendid example of medieval military architecture, a concentric design with rings of defense one within another. The castle construction started in 1295, and in three years it was defensible although it was never completed. The water-filled moat has been partially restored. In the castle's early days the sea came up to the southern walls, and on the right tides the little ships of medieval times could come up to a small dock near the "Gate next the Sea." The ring where the ships were tied up is still fixed in a buttress.

The best way to see the castle is to walk along the outer walls, 27 feet high. You can see where state apartments were occupied by notables and where soldiers were garrisoned in towers. Don't miss the chapel in Chapel Tower, with its vaulted Gothic ceiling and five pointed windows. The room above the chapel, intended to house the priest, was never completed. The castle can be visited March 15 to October 15 daily from 9:30 a.m. to 6:30 p.m.; October 16 to March 14 from 9:30 a.m. to 4 p.m. weekdays, 2 to 4 p.m. on Sunday. It's closed December 24, 25, and 26, and January 1. Admission is £1 ($1.60) for adults, 50p (80¢) for children.

Across from the castle is **Beaumaris Courthouse,** built in 1614 and still in use as a magistrates' court. Alterations and additions have been made, but the original courthouse is still mostly in its original condition inside. It can be visited from 9 a.m. to 5 p.m. for 30p (48¢) for adults, 15p (24¢) for children when court is not in session, during reasonable daylight hours when the castle is open.

Beaumaris Gaol (Carchar) on Steeple Lane, several blocks from the courthouse, vividly depicts prison life in Victorian times. The building has scarcely been altered since it was built in 1829, except for the larger-celled, lighter New Gaol (jail) built in 1867. A treadwheel on which prisoners trod ceaselessly to operate a water pump is the only one in Britain still in position. A soundproof, windowless punishment cell, the condemned cell, and the ramp on which the doomed prisoners walked to be hanged on a gibbet in view of crowds waiting outside in Steeple Lane can all be seen. In the workroom where women prisoners sewed and knitted, there is a slit in the ceiling believed to be where a rope attached to cradles in the room above was slipped through to allow the mothers to rock their babies while they worked. The goal, under the Gwynedd Archives Service (tel. 0248/723262), is open from 11 a.m. to 6 p.m. daily May to September. Admission is 70p ($1.12) for adults, 35p (56¢) for children.

An interesting story is told about the clock in the church tower opposite the scaffold of the jail. Only two men were ever hanged while the jail was in use, and the last one is said to have put a curse on the church clock facing him. I was told that from that day the clock has never kept the right time. Much to my surprise and that of my companions, the day I was last there it was correct to the minute. So much for legends.

The **Museum of Childhood,** 1 Castle St. (tel. 0248/712498), is in a Georgian house across the street from the courthouse, opposite the castle, the museum contains one of the most fascinating collections I've ever seen of nostalgic mementos of childhood. Founder Robert Brown has examples of everything from kewpie dolls to gramophones and music boxes. A bird in a gilded cage really sings, and you can imagine mechanical banks and clockwork toys doing their thing. Trains, cars, dolls, games—they're all here from the last century and the early years of this one. My feeling is that while children enjoy it, this is really a nostalgic trip back to childhood for grownups. Open daily from 10 a.m. to 6 p.m. Easter to Christmas (1 p.m. to 5 p.m. on Sunday), the museum costs £1.35 ($2.16) for adults, 85p ($1.36) for children.

Follow the B5109 road and the signs pointing the way, about three miles, to **Penmon Priory,** the site of an early Welsh monastery dating back to about the 6th century. The church was rebuilt in the 12th century. It has a Norman nave and transepts. An ancient carved cross found nearby and placed in the church has Irish and Scandinavian traces. The parish church is still used for worship. A holy well and circular stone hut are near the church, and a dovecot, built around 1600, can be inspected. Its domed roof has room for nearly 1,000 birds. Ruins of monastic buildings, the old monastery fishpond, and the foundations of St. Seriol's cell and the well where he baptized converts can be viewed. Admission is free, and the site is accessible during reasonable daylight hours.

A toll road leads on to the lighthouse at Black Point. From here are magnificent views of **Puffin Island** and across Conwy Bay to the mainland. Puffin Island was once the home of hermits and later the residence of a large number of the seabirds for whom it was named.

Back in Beaumaris, you can visit the **Parish Church of St. Mary,** which is nearly as old as the castle, its main structure being 14th century. It contains the stone coffin of Princess Joan, daughter of King John and wife of Llewelyn the Great, brought here from the friary at Llan-faes after the dissolution of the monasteries.

The black-and-white building on Castle Street, **Tudor Rose,** dates back to the early 15th century. It contains fine Tudor timberwork. One of the oldest domestic structures on Anglesey, the building now contains an antique shop and art gallery.

10. Along the North Anglesey Coast

Beaches—both sandy and pebble—run off and on for miles around the east and north coasts of Anglesey. Pine-clad hills, rugged cliffs, hotels, guesthouses, and prehistoric burial chambers are all a part of this area. I'll recommend some sights, accommodations, and activities, and you're sure to find many more on your own. I'll start with the hamlet of—

RED WHARF BAY: On the sandy beach at Red Wharf Bay, **Min-y-Don Hotel** (tel. 0248/852596) is run by the resident owner, Diana M. Kitchen. She rents bedrooms, six of which have private baths, for £16 ($25.60) to £21 ($33.60) in a single, £29 ($46.40) to £41 ($65.60) in a double for B&B. All the rooms have hot and cold running water and razor outlets. The hotel is centrally heated. One of the most welcome features for travelers may be that the hotel has washing and ironing facilities. The fully licensed establishment has a cocktail bar where you can take bar meals, which are served daily. An à la carte menu is offered in the candlelit restaurant overlooking the bay. You might make your main dish grilled rainbow trout, filet of plaice, steak, or roast duck, among other selections. Expect to pay from £10 ($16) for a meal. Food is served from 11:30 a.m. to 2:30 p.m. and 7 to 9 p.m. There's regular entertainment in the bars, such as Saturday night sing-alongs. Minnie's Disco is open only on Saturday at 8 p.m. The hotel takes guests from March to October, although the bars are open and serve meals all year.

Bryn Tirion Hotel (tel. 0248/852366) is at the small crossroads at the head of Red Wharf Bay. The stone hotel stands in its own attractive grounds overlooking the bay. Mr. and Mrs. A. D. Cunningham, the proprietors, rent singles for £21 ($33.60) and doubles for £16.50 ($26.40) per person for B&B. Half-board charges are £28 ($44.80) in a single, £23 ($36.80) per person for dinner, bed, and breakfast. Special reductions are given for children sharing their parents' room. All 19 bedrooms have private baths, color TV, and tea/coffee-making facilities. You can take your meals in the hotel dining room, where dinner is served from 7:30 to 9 p.m. Selections are à la carte, and a good wine list is presented.

There's a pleasant walk beyond the hotels of Red Wharf Bay around the headland, past Castell Mawr, a huge limestone block which may have been the site of an Iron Age hill-fort.

BENLLECH: A short distance up from the beach, **Rhostrefor,** Benllech Bay (tel. 0248/852347), is an attractive white hotel with red tile roofs on the sections, which are of varying heights. White balustrades and porch posts give it a homey touch as it sits in an acre of garden overlooking the bay. The hotel is fully modernized. Each of the 12 bedrooms has its own bath, color TV, phone, and hot-drink facilities. There are accommodations both on the ground floor and upstairs. Tariffs are £21 ($33.60) per person for B&B, based on double occupancy, with a £1 ($1.60) supplement for single occupancy. The restaurant, which serves both à la carte and table d'hôte menus, is popular in the area. The fixed-price meals, costing around £7 ($11.20), are served from 6:30 to 7:30 p.m. You can dine à la carte between 7:30 and 9:30 p.m., paying from £9 ($14.40). Bar snacks are available also. All prices include VAT. Nick and Kath, the proprietors, have a heated indoor pool for the use of their guests.

Wilma Lodge Private Hotel, Bay View Road (tel. 0248/852367), is on the approach road to Benllech Beach. Betty and Michael Blakeley, the resident proprietors, welcome guests to their stone, brick, and wood, two-story hostelry, where they rent out 13 well-appointed bedrooms, each with hot and cold running water and some with private bath. Whether you stay in the lodge proper or in the bungalow annex, the B&B rate is from £17.50 ($28) to £19 ($30.40) per person, depending on the plumbing. There is an attractive, well-stocked lounge bar in the main hotel and also an annex lounge, as well as a residents' lounge with color TV. The lodge has a light, airy dining room where you can enjoy varied menus based on traditional foods. Try a slice from a freshly cooked roast and then some of their home-baked desserts. Dinner, costing around £8 ($12.80), is served from 6:30 to 7 p.m.

Bay Court Hotel, Benllech Bay (tel. 0248/852573), is a strictly modern holiday hotel only a couple of hundred yards from the sandy beach. It has two licensed bars and a color TV lounge for residents, all with Nordic furnishings. The 22 bedrooms, a few with private bath, rent for £14.50 ($23.20) to £17 ($27.20) per person for B&B. Dinner in the restaurant, from which extensive views of the Benllech headland are possible, cost £9 ($14.40) to £11 ($17.60) for a complete à la carte meal. Specialties include grilled rainbow trout with toasted almonds, steak Diane, pepper steak, and suprême of chicken Rossini.

On the way north from Benllech on the A5025 road, at the Moelfre roundabout, a minor road leads to the remains of the native village of **Din Lligwy,** which dates from the 4th century and shows traces of the Roman influence in the country. The megalithic **Lligwy Burial Chamber** nearby has a huge capstone weighing 28 tons. It is 18 feet long and 15 feet wide. Both the village and the burial chamber can be visited free.

Continuing on along the A5025, you'll go through Amlwch. From the late 18th century, this village had a busy port, from which copper from the mines of nearby Parys Mountain, first placed in operation by the Romans, was exported. Commercial port activity has made some comeback here since the establishment of a Shell Oil marine terminal two miles offshore.

An interesting trek to make is to **Point Lynas,** two miles west, where a lighthouse stands. It replaced two small oil lamps which for many generations were lighted at dusk each day in the windows of two neighboring whitewashed cottages.

Between Point Lynas and Amlwch is **Llaneilian,** which has one of the outstanding ancient churches of Wales. The church, St. Eilian's, was built in the 15th century but has a 12th-century pepperbox tower and several antique treasures inside.

CAMAES BAY: This uncommercialized village was once a smugglers' haunt and a center of shipbuilding. Now it's a quiet fishing village with an old stone quay, which contrasts vividly with the **Wylfa Nuclear Power Station** (tel. 0407/710471), across the bay. Tours of the power station, which uses seawater for cooling purposes, can be made at 10 a.m. and 2 p.m. Monday to Friday. Admission is free. The exhibition tower is open daily May to October from 10 a.m. to 8 p.m., closing at 4 p.m. thereafter.

The **Harbour Hotel,** Harbour View (tel. 0407/710273), is a modern hostelry overlooking the harbor and sandy coved beach of Camaes Bay some 30 yards away. The 18 bedrooms all have color TV, private baths, and tea/coffee-making facilities. Tariffs are £14 ($22.40) per person for B&B. You can enjoy meals in the dining room overlooking the beach, and there is an extensive wine list to complement your choices. Otherwise, bar snacks are available from a larger-than-normal menu.

The **Treddolphin Guest House** (tel. 0407/710388) stands in its own grounds overlooking the bay at Camaes. You are welcomed at this friendly establishment with a cup of tea or coffee for no extra charge. The charming little house is four miles from Amlwch so that you can participate in activities at the leisure center there. The residents' lounge has a fine view over the bay, and you can either watch TV or gaze out at the water. Singles cost £9 ($14.40) for B&B, £12.50 ($20) for dinner, bed, and breakfast. Prices in a double or twin are £16 ($25.60) for B&B and £22 ($35.20) for half board. Flasks of tea or coffee are filled free, and babysitting is provided free. Harold and Roberta Williams are your hospitable hosts.

11. Holyhead and Holy Island

The largest town on Anglesey, Holyhead (it's pronounced Hollyhead—don't ask me why) is not actually on Anglesey at all but on Holy Island. However, the two islands have long been linked. A causeway carries you across on the A5 road which has come all the way from London, and the Four Mile Bridge on the B4545 road also links Holy Island to its mother. You can come by train from London and take the Sealink service via the car-ferries which make the trip over to Dun Laoghaire near Dublin in about 3¼ hours (see Chapter XX). Packet boats between Holyhead and Ireland were recorded as far back as 1573.

People have come to this far point of northern Wales for a long long time by water. Celtic invaders, early Christian missionaries, Romans, Vikings—whoever—have made their way here and in many cases stayed on for years or centuries. **St. Cybi's Church,** near the town center, is on the site of a 6th-century church, also St. Cybi's, inside the walls of a 3rd-century Roman fort.

The harbor of Holyhead was reconstructed in 1880 and now serves as a terminal for container-bearing ships.

Holyhead Mountain is the highest point in Anglesey, 710 feet. From the rocky height you can see the Isle of Man, the Mourne Mountains in Ireland, Snowdonia, and Cumbria on a clear day. The summit is the site of an ancient hill-fort and the ruins of an Irish settlement from the second to the 4th centuries A.D. The towering cliffs of North and South Stack are home to thousands of seabirds, and gray seals breed in the caves below. At **South Stack** is a semiautomatic lighthouse built in 1808. It is 91 feet high (197 feet above mean high water) and can be seen for 20 miles. A zigzag path leads to it. It is open to the public from noon to one hour before sunset Monday to Saturday.

On Friday and Saturday, general markets are held in Holyhead.

The **Wales Tourist Information Centre,** Marine Square, Salt Island Approach (tel. 0407/2622), is open from 10 a.m. to 6 p.m. in summer.

STAYING IN HOLYHEAD: Comfortable accommodation is offered at **Glandwr,** 85 Newry St. (tel. 0407/4663). Set amid a red-brick row of interconnected Victorian houses, this pleasant place stands out because of the seasonal flowers decorating its tiny front garden. The garden and garlands of potted vines hanging in front are the handiwork of Mrs. Joyce Williams, who maintains five comfortable double and twin bedrooms, each with a private shower. With breakfast included, per person rates range from £8.50 ($13.60) to £9.50 ($15.20) nightly.

On the west coast of Holy Island is—

TREARDDUR BAY: This is a holiday center where you can swim, waterski, and skin-dive. There is sailing, golf (an 18-hole course), and a host of other activities to pursue.

Trearddur Bay Hotel (tel. 0407/860301) is a big, comfortable establishment in large grounds next to the beach, with lovely views over the bay. It is popular with persons taking the car-ferry to Ireland. The ferry terminal is 1½ miles from the hotel. The bedrooms have been refurbished and have the added comfort of central heating. All have phone, radio, and TV, and most have private bath. Children may stay in their parents' rooms free except for a charge for meals. Tariffs are assessed according to whether the accommodation is a back room without bath, a front room without bath, or a room with bath. Prices for B&B in a single range from £21 ($33.60) to £25.50 ($40.80), depending on the above stipulations. Double- or twin-bedded rooms cost £36 ($57.60) to £43.50 ($69.60). The hotel is well known for its good cuisine, which can be enjoyed in the spacious dining room. There are both table d'hôte and à la carte menus, and fish is a specialty "fresh from the sea onto your plate," as the manager promises. Expect to pay £12.50 ($20) for a fixed-price dinner, served from 7 to 9:30 p.m. The hotel has a number of lounges: one for watching color TV, a cocktail lounge, and the Dragon Bar.

Moranedd Guest House, Trearddur Road (tel. 0407/860324), is a charming, well-furnished house with a sun patio overlooking a large garden in a quiet cul-de-sac. The bedrooms are large and centrally heated. All have hot and cold running water and tea/coffee-making facilities. You can watch color TV in the residents' lounge. The dining room, where you can enjoy your meals as you look out on the garden, is licensed to serve drinks with dinner. Mrs. Sheila Wathan, the friendly proprietor, charges £10 ($16) per person for B&B, with a 50% reduction for children sharing their parents' room. Dinner costs £5 ($8).

The **Seacroft Hotel** (tel. 0407/860348), just around the corner from the public beach, is a pleasant place to stay. Mr. and Mrs. W. F. Jones welcome visitors, charging £14 ($22.40) per person in a bathless room, £15 ($24) per person in a room with bath. For dinner, the licensed restaurant offers an extensive à la carte menu, and you can order bar meals for lunch or in the evening. There's ample parking.

12. Rhosneigr and Aberffraw

You'll feel far, far from the hustle-bustle of urban life in this protected section on the coast of Caernarvon Bay, although mankind lived in this area as long as 4,000 years ago.

RHOSNEIGR: The little town of Rhosneigr lies on the sandy west coast of Anglesey on the A4080 road, three miles off the A5. It's on a headland between two broad beaches with gorse and rush-covered sand dunes inland.

Sealands Hotel, Station Road (tel. 0407/810834), is an eight-bedroom licensed hotel where Mrs. M. Woodruff extends a warm welcome to guests. The hotel is midway between the village center and the golf course. All the bedrooms are centrally heated and have hot and cold running water, costing from £10.50 ($16.80) per person for B&B. If you choose to have your evening meal here, it will cost around £5 ($8) additional. Reductions are granted for children 11 years old and under. Bar snacks are available.

ABERFFRAW: Not far from Rhosneigr south along the coast is this village which was the seat of Welsh kings from the 7th to the 13th centuries. No traces of the palace are left.

Just two miles from the sea northwest of Aberffraw is **Barclodiad y Gawres Burial Chamber,** probably the most important of the ancient burial sites on the island because of its surviving megalithic art. The passage-grave, dating from before 2000 B.C., originally consisted of a cairn of rubble and turf 90 feet in diameter over a chamber approached by a 20-foot-long passage lined with stone slabs ornamented with spirals and incised lines representing deities. After its excavation in the 1950s, a concrete dome was erected to protect the chamber. The site can be visited free.

Farther along is **Newborough Forest,** a vast nature reserve, a place of sand dunes, salt marshes, and efforts by the Forestry Commission and Nature Conservancy Council to keep the sand from claiming the land. The Newborough Warren, once the home of vast numbers of rabbits, contains about 1,550 acres of flowers and bird life.

13. In the Inland

The main road that runs through Anglesey is the A5, going straight from Menai Bridge to Holyhead, and unfortunately many visitors drive along it without seeing any of the interesting villages of the island's interior, intent on taking the ferry to Ireland. There are, however, numerous little side roads to be followed if you have time. One leads to a busy little town, Llangefni, the administrative center of Anglesey. Cattle markets are held on Wednesday and Thursday (mostly Thursday). The town is right in the center of the island a short way north of the A5 road.

STAYING INLAND: Just north of the little former market village of Llanerchymedd on the B5111 road, **Llwydiarth Fawr** (tel. 0248470/321) is a spacious Georgian residence set in the center of a 750-acre farm. Mrs. Hughes has converted the structure into an attractive place for guests, who are accommodated in spacious bedrooms. Three of the rooms have private bath, one of those being so large it could easily have room to move your bed in if you wanted to be that close to the facilities. Five bedrooms are rented only on a B&B basis (or BBD), and there are five self-catering units that can also be used for B&B.

Charges for overnight stays with a full Welsh breakfast are £10 ($16) to £10.50 ($16.80), depending on the room and the plumbing. Mrs. Hughes has supplied a comfortable sitting area for guests, in which she provides tea and coffee and TV. You can take dinner in the attractive dining room if you order it ahead. Part of the house dates from the 16th century, and it was added to in the 19th century. The staircase is a special point of interest. There is a pond nearby for fishing, mainly for children, where they may bring out eels or red carp. From here you can see the Isle of Man, Holyhead Mountain, and Snowdonia.

Chapter XXVII

NORTHEAST WALES

THE COUNTY OF CLWYD, which occupies northeastern Wales, has miles and miles of sandy beaches along the north coast; highland ranges, peat bogs, and deep valleys lush with greenery in the center; coal country to the southeast; and industry, agriculture, and sheep farming in the section nearest the estuary of the River Dee and the English border. What is now Clwyd (by order of Parliament since 1973) was before that time Denbighshire and Flintshire.

Many tourists who have been visiting in England have seen some of this part of Wales, having rushed through from Chester to take a look at Conwy Castle in Gwynedd or having been on a tour which took a quick dip into Wales, to Llangollen, just so they could go home and say they'd been there. Lovely as those sights are, there's a lot more to be seen in Clwyd. From the deep and tranquil secluded vales to the busy bustle of coastal resorts, from historic buildings to Offa's Dyke, from ancient churches and castle ruins to forests and moorlands —there's a lot to see and savor in Clwyd.

Most visitors, unless they're confirmed students of geography, are inclined to link Conwy and Llandudno with Colwyn Bay, although only the latter is actually in the County of Clwyd. For this chapter, therefore, I have chosen to include a few places in the very northeastern corner of the County of Gwynedd because of their cultural and historic connection with their neighbors.

ABERCONWY

Aberconwy, billed as "where Snowdonia meets the sea," is one of the most scenically attractive regions of Britain. Aberconwy, the estuary of the River Conwy, is where the waters come to the sea after the confluence at Betws-y-Coed (previewed in Chapter XXV, "Snowdonia") of the Conwy, the Lledr, and the Llugwy Rivers. Wild mountain scenery gives way to sandy beaches. Along the coast, sheltered bays, towering headlands, caves, and cliffs all exist happily intermingled with busy resorts, seashore villages, and a medieval walled town complete with castle.

This area is much more highly developed to accommodate the tourist industry in large masses than are the other regions visited in this chapter. Aberconwy's seacoast portion has a wide range of accommodations to suit all tastes and purses, good restaurants, entertainment, and a vast selection of sports activities, including golf, sailing, fishing, walking, pony trekking, windsurfing, and canoeing, to name a few. With all this, Aberconwy has not sacrificed any of its history, character, or charm.

Tourist information offices are located in several places, but the **Main Tourist Information Centre** for Aberconwy is at 1-2 Chapel St., Llandudno (tel. 0492/76413). It's open from 9 a.m. to 5 p.m. Monday to Friday all year, and daily in July and August. You can phone for information 24 hours a day.

The first stop will be at the largest Welsh resort, beautifully situated—

1. Llandudno

This Victorian seaside resort nestles in a crescent between the giant headlands of the **Great Orme** and the **Little Orme,** which received their names from early Vikings who thought they looked like sea serpents when their bases were shrouded in mist. This premier resort of Wales has two beaches: one on the north facing the Irish Sea and the other on the west on Colwyn Bay. The rugged Ormes overlook throngs of people who come to Llandudno, especially in the high summer season.

Llandudno is a resort built by the Mostyn family in the middle of the last century to cash in on the already-proven proclivity of the British of Queen Victoria's day—particularly the great middle class of business people, bureaucrats, retirees, minor landed gentry, and widows, with a few clergymen thrown in—to go to the seashore in summer. Unlike Miami Beach, where hotels were allowed to be built almost to the edge of the water, shutting out all but guests from the beaches until recent changes were made, the Victorian way was to leave the beach open to all, with a promenade along it, then a road, and homes, hotels, and guesthouses in the next rank back from the sea.

The Victorian elegance and tradition of Llandudno has been maintained in the architecture of its buildings, but there the days-gone-by atmosphere stops. The town today draws visitors from all walks of life who find here a perfect place to vacation.

Besides the Main Tourist Information Centre, which gives data on all of Aberconwy (listed above), there is also the **Sea Front Information Centre** at the Canolfan Aberconwy (tel. 0492/79771), open daily from 10 a.m. to 6 p.m. except Sunday.

WHERE TO STAY: My favorite place to stay in Llandudno is the **St. Tudno Hotel,** North Parade (tel. 0492/76309), a luxury seafront hotel small enough—

21 bedrooms—that the proprietors, Martin and Janette Bland, and their capable and courteous staff have time to give guests a warm welcome. Alice Liddell, immortalized by Lewis Carroll as *Alice in Wonderland,* stayed here at the age of eight on her first visit to Llandudno in 1861. This is a hotel where the well-being and comfort of those persons fortunate enough to get a room here have been thought about and worked out in minute detail. The bedrooms, of varying sizes (and there's an elevator), are beautifully furnished and equipped, with such amenities as private bath or shower, color TV, radio, phone, and tea/coffee-making facilities. Such nice touches as little bottles of shampoo and lotions in the bathrooms add to the enjoyment of a stay here. Many of the rooms have hair dryers. For B&B, the charge is £27 ($43.20) to £35 ($56) per person in summer, making this a splurge choice. Winter rates are lower: £23 ($36.80) to £32 ($51.20). Prices depend on the size and location of the room. A full Welsh breakfast is included.

The public rooms are elegant and reminiscent of the Victorian era when Llandudno was born, but they are decorated with restraint in the number of objets d'art and pieces of furniture. The bar lounge is across the hall from the sitting room, both with comfortable furniture and highly polished tables. You can look across the bay from the bow windows of each. Pots of green shrubs, including palm trees, are in the coffee lounge next to the reception area.

The Garden Dining Room is a thing of beauty. Lime green is the predominant color, from the cane-backed bamboo chairs to the napery to the trellis wallpaper that divides the handsome panels, hand-painted in Switzerland. Hanging baskets of healthy ferns and other plants and the same kind of potted plants that are in the coffee lounge add to the happy feeling that you're dining al fresco. As if the beauty of the room were not enough, Martin Bland sees to it that the cuisine is also first class. Menus change daily, with many Welsh specialties, the translation of which is carefully given. The table d'hôte menu price is £14.95 ($23.92), including VAT. Dinner is served from 6:45 to 8:30 p.m. The hotel has a swimming pool too.

The **Empire Hotel,** Church Walks (tel. 0492/79955), sits up where it can look down on the pier and Happy Valley, about 300 yards away. The bedrooms are all furnished in good taste, with the accoutrements expected of a first-class hotel: private bath, color TV, in-house movies, radio, phone, and tea/coffee-making facilities. L. E. Maddocks, the owner, added a touch of class when he placed a bar and coffeeshop alongside the free-form inside pool (there's an outdoor pool as well). The public areas are done in a Victorian theme, with a lounge and bar displaying prints of the era on their walls. Besides the two pools, the hotel has a sauna and a solarium, plus a games room and a laundry. You can have your meals in the restaurant or the grill room. Tariffs are £25 ($40) to £40 ($64) per person for B&B. The Empire has an elevator. An outlying annex, The Townhouse, contains eight of the establishment's finest rooms, filled with Victorian antiques and touches of silk. With breakfast included, these cost £50 ($80) in a single, £38 ($60.80) per person in a double. Each unit has a bathtub-cum-Jacuzzi.

Tan Lan Hotel, Great Orme's Road, West Shore (tel. 0492/75981), is a good choice if you'd rather be on the more tranquil west shore of Llandudno. It is a beige building with a red tile roof to set it off. Mr. and Mrs. Tony Fossi will give you a warm welcome. All the comfortably furnished 19 rooms have private baths or showers, color TV, hot-beverage equipment, clock-radios, and central heating. Rents are £18 ($28.80) in a single, £32 ($51.20) in a double for B&B. The Fossis have provided two comfortable lounges for guests, and there is a licensed bar, as well as a lovely garden where you can take your tea or drink and relax. Morning coffee, lunches, and afternoon teas are available. Tony Fossi is the chef, his six-course evening meals costing £8 ($12.80). Private parking is provided.

If you're not just set on staying on the seafront, I suggest the **Branksome Hotel,** Lloyd Street (tel. 0492/75989), an attractive 56-bedroom place which has been modernized fairly recently. There are some ground-floor rooms suitable for handicapped persons. Some units have private baths, and all have color TV and hot-beverage facilities. The charge is from £15.50 ($24.80) per person for B&B. A spacious bar lounge is the scene of live entertainment on occasion. Good meals are served in this family-run hotel. It is an easy stroll from here to either the west or north shore and to the city center. The resident proprietors are Mr. and Mrs. D. J. Beaney and Mr. and Mrs. D. W. Stoneham. The hotel is closed from January to March.

Hollybank, 9 St. David's Place (tel. 0492/78521), is an excellent B&B establishment run by Mrs. Jennifer Knowles. The charge for B&B is £10 ($16) per person, half price for children. A tasty evening meal costs £5 ($8). There is a car park at the back. The house is within walking distance of the beach.

Charlton House, 5 Charlton St. (tel. 0492/78255), is where Rose and Alan Agar welcome visitors with warm hospitality. All the bedrooms have color TV and central heating, and most have private showers and toilets. The charge is £10 ($16) per person for B&B, VAT included. The house is near the sea and convenient for shopping and sightseeing.

A Big Splurge

"Of all the things the British have invented . . . the most perfect, the most characteristic . . . is the well-appointed, well-administered, well-filled country house," said Henry James. **Bodysgallen Hall Hotel** (tel. 0492/84466), in the country not far from Llandudno Junction on the A470 Llandudno Link road, lives up to all the writer's requisites. A palatial 17th-century house has been skillfully converted into a 19-bedroom hotel of architectural merit and 20th-century comfort. If you only plan one splurge on your visit to North Wales, this is the place for it. The hall has a 13th-century tower which is believed to have been built as a lookout post for Conwy Castle a mile and a half away. You ascend to the tower by going first up the handsome dog-leg main staircase, then upward until you come to a much older, narrow spiral set of stone steps to the roof. From there you can see all the surrounding country, clear to Conwy. Look down on the grounds of the hall and you see a lovely little Dutch knot garden as well as flower gardens and the converted cottages (also for rent) around a secluded courtyard. The former stable block has also been converted to hotel use.

The elegant rooms of this splendid hotel are each done in its own period style and colors, with bathrooms and all the modern amenities. To stay in such posh surroundings doesn't come cheap, but I recommend it highly. Singles rent for £55 ($88) to £70 ($112), with double or twins going for £80 ($128) to £105 ($168). Some of the rooms have tester or four-poster beds. Room rates include early-morning tea, a newspaper, a continental breakfast, service, and VAT. Young children are accepted only at the discretion of the management.

The public rooms are outstanding, from the large oak-paneled entrance hall to the drawing room on the first floor, with splendid fireplaces and stone mullioned windows. Antique furniture and paintings, as well as crackling log fires, set the mood for a stay in a true British country house. This is a place where the people of the area like to come for tea or for a meal. Dining is a special event here. Food critics consider its dining rooms the finest in North Wales. The menu is international, with the finest of ingredients used. Contemporary British cookery is also practiced with consummate skill here. The beef dishes are invariably good, prepared in imaginative ways. Soups, such as apple and spinach, appetizers, the main courses, and desserts provide a mouthwatering repertoire. The cheeseboard features Welsh farmhouse varieties. A set lunch costs from £6.50 ($10.40) to £9.50 ($15.20), and table d'hôte dinners are £18.50 ($29.60). Meals are served from 12:30 to 2 p.m. and 7:30 to 9:45 p.m. Jonathan C. A. Thompson is the manager of this special hotel, which is owned by Historic House Hotels Ltd.

WHERE TO DINE: Outside of hotel dining, the leading independent restaurant of Llandudno is the **Floral,** Victoria Street (tel. 76572/75735), which lies in the western part of the resort, set back from the Promenade. Tony Muff, the chef and part owner, presides over the well-trained kitchen staff, turning out imaginative dishes but also serving familiar British fare to those who insist on the familiar. Of course, you can always order steak and scampi, but you could have those dishes anywhere in Britain. When sampling the wares here, you can indulge in other fare, including marinated salmon that has been flavored with herbs and Hebridean island whisky. For a pasta, try tagliatelle with "fruits of the sea." Poultry is often handled with flair and style, as reflected by the goose breast with a sauce of chestnuts and fruits. Meals, costing from £14 ($22.40), are served from noon to 2 p.m. and 7 to 10 p.m. The Sunday lunch at £8.50 ($13.60) is considered among the finest in town. It is open Tuesday to Sunday except for Saturday lunch.

    No. 1, Old Road (tel. 76572/75424), is the leading wine bar-cum-bistro of Llandudno. From noon to 2 p.m. and 7 to 10 daily except Sunday, it offers its wares, and such good ones they are, both the food and drink. In the vicinity of the Great Orme Tramway, the food and wine bar is run by Michael and Katherine McCarthy. They are to be congratulated for the care and concern that goes into this place. Of course, they select fine wines and fresh ingredients, but the welcome, the reception, and the service also contribute to making this place a memorable stopover on your retreat from just too many Victorian hotels. Meals are reasonably priced from £7 ($11.20), although you could snack for less, and dishes are likely to include a superb smoked salmon quiche or else that British favorite, steak and kidney pie. Look for what appeals to you on a blackboard chart. The desserts aren't neglected either.

THE OLDEST PUB: An interesting place for a meal, and certainly a drink, is **The Kings Head,** Old Road (tel. 0492/77993), with its King Henry VIII logo and bottle-glass windows. This used to be the pub at the end of the tramway, and instead of serving a ploughman's lunch it offers a tram-man's lunch (essentially the same, I find). The food, however, is slightly better than its pub status suggests. All arriving patrons enter the establishment by passing through the pub. There, at a spot to the left of the bar, guests place their food order. A waitress will bring it to whatever table you select, either in the pub or within the tiny adjacent dining room. A fixed-price bar lunch will cost around £4 ($6.40), a set evening meal going for £7.50 ($12). The menu is long and detailed, including such dishes as tournedos Rossini, royal lamb, king's chicken, along with stroganoff and steaks. Lunch is daily from noon to 2:30 p.m. (till 2 p.m. on Sunday), and dinner is from 7 to 10 p.m. (from 7:30 to 10 p.m. on Sunday). Peter Smith, the owner, keeps his pub humming seven days a week.

SIGHTS: From the summit of the Great Orme (679 feet) you have a splendid view of the North Wales coast. You can walk up to the top if you're really energetic, but I advise other means. At Happy Valley, exotic sheltered gardens at the foot of the Great Orme, near the pier at the west end of the Llandudno Bay promenade, take the **cabin lift** (tel. 0492/77205) or the **tramway** (tel. 0492/79749). The cabin lift is the longest cable-car system in Britain, and the tramway has been carrying passengers to the summit since 1902. They operate from Easter until the end of September (weather permitting), the first trips starting at 10 a.m. A spectacular cliff road, the Marine Drive, also winds around the Great Orme, all the way up to the lighthouse and the western extremity of the Orme.

Just above the Marine Drive is the ancient **Church of St. Tudno,** from which the town derives its name. The present stone building dates to the 12th century, but the church was founded 600 years earlier. Open-air services are held on its grounds on fine Sunday mornings during the summer.

At the end of the north-shore promenade, one of Britain's finest Victorian piers was built jutting 2,295 feet out into the bay at the base of the Great Orme, with an ornate covered pavilion at the end. You can find entertainment, food, fishing, or just relaxation on the pier. From the end you can embark on steamer cruises to the Isle of Man. The north-shore beach is busy in summer, with traditional British seaside activities, including donkey rides, Punch and Judy shows, boat trips, and a children's funland across the promenade.

A huge complex, **Canolfan Aberconwy Centre,** has been opened on the promenade, with swimming, squash, an auditorium, meeting rooms, bars, a theater, a restaurant, and a ballroom.

The west shore is more tranquil, with its sandy beach on the shore of Conwy Bay where the estuary broadens out to join the Irish Sea. Along its promenade is the **White Rabbit Statue,** which commemorates the link of *Alice in Wonderland* with Llandudno. The real Alice, Alice Liddell, was the daughter of Henry Liddell, dean of Christ Church, Oxford, who had honeymooned here with Alice's mother. They established a summer home here where they spent holidays with Alice. Lewis Carroll (Charles Dodgson) was a friend of the family who was often a house guest of the Liddells. Fond of children, he would spend many hours with Alice, spinning stories for her enjoyment. It is almost certain that she was the inspiration for his classic tales of *Alice in Wonderland* and *Through the Looking Glass.*

Of particular interest is the **Doll Museum and Model Railway,** Masonic Street (tel. 0492/76312), opposite the Palladium Cinema. Displayed is a valuable collection of dolls from all over the world, and one room is set aside for a working model railway and a display of tinplate engines. It's open Easter to the end of September from 10 a.m. to 1 p.m. and 2 to 5 p.m. Monday to Saturday, from 2 to 5 p.m. on Sunday. Admission is £1 ($1.60) for adults, 50p (80¢) for children.

The **Mostyn Art Gallery,** 12 Vaughan St. (tel. 0492/79201), has a series of free temporary exhibitions as well as some evening events. There is a design and crafts shop here. It is open from 11 a.m. to 5 p.m. Tuesday to Thursday and on Saturday, from 11 a.m. to 8 p.m. on Friday all year. From April to September, it is also open on Sunday from 2 to 6 p.m.

The **Llandudno Museum** (formerly the Rapallo House), 17-19 Gloddaeth St. (tel. 0492/76517), displays Roman relics and armor from the days the early conquerors were here, as well as tracing the development of Llandudno as a seaside resort. Period rooms are open to viewers. It is open from 10 a.m. to 12:45 p.m. and again from 2 p.m. weekdays, closing at 5 p.m. from May to August and at 4 p.m. the rest of the year. Admission is £1 ($1.60) for adults, 50p (80¢) for children.

A number of bus tours of Llandudno and Aberconwy are available. Ask at the tourist information office.

2. Conwy

Unlike Llandudno, its 19th-century neighbor, Conwy is an ancient town. With its mighty medieval castle and complete town walls, this is a richly historic place.

The Conwy estuary is crossed by three **bridges** to Conwy. The handsome suspension bridge built in 1826 by Thomas Telford, bridge-builder extra-ordinaire, which looks as if it runs right into the castle (it doesn't), is closed to vehicular traffic now but you can walk across it free and marvel at how it served the main entrance to the town for so long, with its narrow lanes and the sure bottleneck at the castle end. It replaced the ferry which was previously the only means of crossing the river. An exhibit of Telford's work is in the tollhouse. You can also see Robert Stephenson's tubular railroad bridge built in 1848, and the modern arched road bridge, completed in 1958.

Markets, along the line of flea markets in the U.S., are held in Conwy on Tuesday and Saturday in summer.

The **Wales Tourist Board and Snowdonia National Park Information Centre** is on Castle Street (tel. 049263/2248), open in summer from 10 a.m. to 6 p.m.

FOOD AND LODGING IN CONWY AND ENVIRONS: My favorite place to stay in the Conwy area is the **Bryn Cregin Garden Hotel,** Ty Mawr Road, Deganwy (tel. 0492/85266), where Tig and Sheelagh Barrasford, the resident proprietors, have a happy and hospitable operation. The stately house with long, glassed-in verandas, built near the turn of this century as a sea captain's home, has been beautifully renovated and refurbished by the Barrasfords. It overlooks the Conwy estuary within sight of Conwy on the other side. The bedrooms, all twins and doubles, are decorated with light flowered wallpaper and prints, bright and airy. The units on the third floor are all of different shapes, and care has been taken to utilize the space in the most attractive possible way. Note the mahogany acorn finial on the newel post leading upstairs from the public rooms. The staircase is of pitch-pine. All the bedrooms have private bath, color TV, direct-dial phone, and tea/coffee-making facilities. Some of them have estuary views while others look out on a hill that is the backdrop for the house's dramatic location. Tariffs for B&B in a twin or double range from £30 ($48) to £44 ($70.40), dropping to £22 ($35.20) to £25 ($40) for single occupancy, the rates depending on the location of the room and the season. Golfing discount packages are a specialty, with three fine courses on which to play.

The tastefully furnished restaurant is an excellent setting for the fine meals served here, and such dishes are offered as fresh fish from Conwy estuary, crab claws sautéed in frothing garlic butter, and roast sirloin of beef. A fixed-price meal costs around £9 ($14.40), while an à la carte dinner will go for £10 ($16) and up. For lunch an interesting choice of bar meals is available, with a variety of soups, sandwiches, croque monsieur (a slice of home-baked ham topped with pineapple on a toast base, covered with a cheese sauce and glazed), omelets, hot quiche, salads, and hot dishes served with baked, creamed, or french-fried potatoes. Expect to pay £2.50 ($4) to £5 ($8) for a filling meal. The hotel has a well-stocked bar.

Sychnant Pass Hotel, Sychnant Pass Road, Conwy (tel. 049259/6868), is in three acres of grounds just inside the Snowdonia National Park. This licensed country house has 11 bedrooms, all with private bath, color TV, and tea/coffee-making facilities. Four of the units are on the ground floor, making them suitable for handicapped persons. The bedrooms are in an extension of the old Edwardian house. The hotel was completely refurbished not long ago. Charges are £19.50 ($31.20) to £24.50 ($39.20) per person. The lounges are furnished with antiques and comfortable chairs and couches. The hotel has a garden, sauna, and solarium for the use of guests, as well as laundry service. Mr. and Mrs. Jones are especially known for the good food served in the Four Seasons Restaurant of the hotel. Specialties include an apricot-and-marrow soup, Welsh lamb cutlets, garlic mussels, and salmon dishes. You can have a complete meal on the table d'hôte menu for £10.95 ($17.52). If you order à la carte, the tab will be £10 ($16) and up. Lunch is served from noon to 2:15 p.m., dinner from 7 to 9:40 p.m.

If you'd like to stay right in the town of Conwy, go to the **Old Ship,** 28 High St. (tel. 049259/6445), where the friendly proprietors, Vivienne and Graham Fraser, offer hospitality and comfort. The bedrooms have TV, hot-beverage facilities, and central heating. The price for a bathless twin-bedded room is £10.50 ($16.80) per person, while a double with bath goes for £13.50 ($21.60) per person. The prices include a substantial breakfast. There is parking nearby as well as bus service from the square to the Llandudno Junction train station.

A few minutes from the town center is the **Angorfa Guest House,** 25 Cadnant Park (tel. 049263/592380), where you receive a warm welcome from Mrs. Williams to her five-bedroom, centrally heated house. All the rooms have hot and cold water basins and rent for £8 ($12.80) to £8.50 ($13.60) per person for B&B. Bedtime drinks are sometimes served with homemade scones or cookies. The house has a TV lounge, and you can park on the premises.

One of the best "chippies" in the area is **Enoch's Fish 'n' Chips** at Llandudno Junction by the railway station (tel. 0492/81145). They serve nine varieties of fresh fish plus shellfish, an order of which gives you about 14 ounces of fish on your plate. There is also a vegetarian menu (seven dishes), or you can order salads and grills. The place is licensed to serve wine. You can have a meal for less than £3.50 ($5.60). The establishment is open from 11 a.m. to 11 p.m. daily.

If you're looking for a pub in Conwy, go to the **Liverpool Arms,** The Quay (tel. 0492/593477). It has an authentic pub atmosphere. A pint of lager costs 98p ($1.57), a pint of bitter going for 86p ($1.38). Hours are from 11 a.m. to 3:30 p.m. and 5:30 to 11 p.m.

Staying at Glan Conwy

About three miles from Conwy, **The Old Rectory,** Glan Conwy (tel. 049268/611), set in 2½ acres of secluded grounds, makes a peaceful and comfortable place to stay in the area. Michael and Wendy Vaughan receive guests in their elegant 1740 Georgian country house, restored and extended to assure modern-day comfort. Bedrooms have private showers or baths, and you might even enjoy sleeping in a half-tester bed. Prices are from £18 ($28.80) to £20 ($32) per person for B&B based on double occupancy. Singles pay 50% more. The standard of cooking is high in this antique-filled house, with local products used to prepare tasty dinners, costing £13 ($20.80) for three courses. Good wines are also offered. The Old Rectory is on the A470, about half a mile from the junction of the A55 road.

SIGHTS: The town centers around **Conwy Castle** (tel. 049263/2358), considered a masterpiece of medieval architecture, which Edward I caused to be built after he conquered the last native Prince of Wales, Llewelyn. The English king put up massive castles to convince the Welsh that he was the supreme authority. The castle follows the contours of a narrow strip of rock, the eight towers commanding the estuary of the River Conwy. The town wall that protected the borough, chartered by Edward in 1284, is almost intact, with 21 flanking towers and three twin-towered gateways. Visitors to the town can walk the walls. This is one castle you can't possibly miss seeing, as the road runs almost close enough for you to touch the walls in places. It is open March 15 to October 15 daily from 9:30 a.m. to 6:30 p.m. The rest of the year (except December 24, 25, 26, and January 1) it is open weekdays from 9:30 a.m. to 4 p.m., on Sunday from 2 to 4 p.m. Admission is £1 ($1.60) for adults, 50p (80¢) for children.

St. Mary's, the parish church, stands within the town walls on the site of a 12th-century Cistercian abbey. In it are a Byzantine processional cross, a beautiful Tudor cross, and a 15th-century screen of fine workmanship. Look at the churchyard which contains a grave associated with William Wordsworth's poem "We Are Seven."

Plas Mawr (tel. 0492/593413) is a restored building on the High Street which now houses the Royal Cambrian Academy of Art. It is a fine example of Elizabethan architecture, noted for its plasterwork ceilings. It is open April to September from 10 a.m. to 6 p.m. daily, to 4 p.m. in October. In November, February, and March, hours are 10 a.m. to 4 p.m. Wednesday to Sunday. Closed in December and January. Admission is 75p ($1.20) for adults, 25p (40¢) for children.

Aberconwy House, Castle Street and High Street (tel. 049263/2246), dating from the 15th century, is even older than Plas Mawr. Owned by the National Trust, the building houses an exhibition depicting the life of Conwy from Roman times. It includes a re-created 18th-century kitchen and a mussel-fishing corner, with the traditional instruments still used by the industry. It's open mid-April to the end of September daily except Tuesday from 11 a.m. to 5 p.m., on Saturday and Sunday in October from 11 a.m. to 5 p.m. Admission is 65p ($1.04) for adults, 35p (56¢) for children.

"The smallest house in Britain," The Quay (tel. 049263/3484), is a tiny building on the quayside, which is open during the summer months. It looks as though someone had a narrow space between two other structures and decided to utilize it by building the house. It measures something like ten feet high and six feet wide, and was lived in. It had an outdoor privy at the rear, now gone. Listed in the *Guinness Book of Records* as "smallest," the house is open from 10 a.m. to 4 p.m. April to mid-October (to 9:30 p.m. in July and August). Admission is 20p (32¢); children under 5 free.

The **Conwy Visitor Centre** (tel. 049259/6288) is adjacent to Vicarage Car Park next door to the castle. The history of Conwy is shown on audio-visual displays. There's a bookshop and Welsh craft center with craft demonstrations. Guided tours of the castle and the city are operated from here, and there is also a brass-rubbing center. It's open March to December from 10 a.m. to 5 p.m. daily. Admission is 50p (80¢) for adults, 40p (64¢) for children.

Along the coast from Conwy toward Bangor is the little holiday town of **Penmaenmawr,** between two giant headlands. This was a chosen spot of ancient man who had here a stone axe factory, which, with a Druids Circle, is now part of an interesting History Trail.

Across the Estuary

The little town of **Deganwy** is in sight across the Conwy estuary from the town. It lies south of Llandudno, near Llandudno Junction, which grew up where trains left to follow the Vale of Conwy south. Deganwy was once known as Dinas Conwy (the fort on the Conwy). Meager remains of the keep of Deganwy Castle are left.

At **Glan Conwy** (literally, the banks of the Conwy) on the A470 road is **Felin Isaf** (tel. 049268/646), a 17th-century watermill that has been expertly restored to its original condition, complete with working machinery. Sacks of flour and Welsh crafts articles are in the Mill Shop, where you can also have hot and cold drinks and snacks. A Discovery Project is available to mill visitors, and is especially interesting to children. The mill is open daily from 10 a.m. to dusk year round. Admission is £1 ($1.60) for adults, 50p (80¢) for children.

Near Glan Conwy on the A470 road south is one of the beauty spots of Wales, **Bodnant Gardens** (tel. 049267/460). The gardens cover nearly 100 acres looking down to the River Conwy and across to Snowdonia. Above are terraces and lawns, and below in a wooded valley is the secluded Wild Garden, threaded with little streams. Ancient trees, exotic shrubs, formal rose gardens, and flowerbeds all form a scene of loveliness. The garden was given to the National Trust by the late Lord Aberconwy. It is open March 16 to October 31 daily from 10 a.m. to 5 p.m. (last admission at 4:30 p.m.). Admission is £1.75 ($2.80) for adults, 90p ($1.44) for children. The garden entrance is about half a mile off the A470 on the Eglwysbach road.

3. Colwyn Bay

One of the better-known coastal resorts along the Irish Sea, perhaps because it's frequently visited in conjunction with Conwy, is Colwyn Bay, a modern resort town which has grown up between two old villages, Old Colwyn and Rhos on Sea (Llandrillo-yn-Rhos), until today you can hardly tell where one leaves off and the other begins. Indeed, a three-mile promenade served by runabout buses connects the three towns. Beaches are sandy and safe. Yachting, waterskiing, and other water activities are popular. The beach and promenade have such attractions as donkey rides, a miniature railway, a paddling pool, and boating. There are dances and cabaret on the pier with theatrical performances.

A 50-acre pleasure ground by the sea, **Eirias Park,** has a boating lake, a cafeteria, children's amusements and play area, dinosaur world, crazy golf, and tennis courts, among other attractions. There is also a modern leisure center in the park, with a swimming pool, squash and tennis courts, a sauna and solarium, a licensed lounge and snackbar, and many other activities. There is an 18-hole golf course at Rhos on Sea and a nine-hole course at Old Colwyn. Riding stables are also here.

FOOD AND LODGING: This area becomes crowded during the summer months, but if you come before or after school vacations, or if you plan well ahead, you should be able to find a comfortable place to stay. There are so many restaurants, cafés, pubs, and snackbars that I will not try to pinpoint any certain ones, except as connected with places to stay.

Lyndale Hotel and Restaurant, 410 Abergele Rd. (tel. 0492/515429), is a 14-bedroom hotel where Stan and Wendy Wardle will give you a warm welcome. The attractive, modern establishment charges £19.50 ($31.20) per person for B&B. Your room will have a private bath, color TV, phone, radio, intercom, tea/coffee-making facilities, a baby-listening unit, and central heating. The hotel's fine restaurant offers an extensive choice on the à la carte and table d'hôte menus, with such tasty dishes as plaice, lamb, beef, and seafood offered. The attractive hotel is on the A547 Abergele to Colwyn Bay road.

Glyn Tirion, 165 Conway Rd. (tel. 0492/530205), is a good choice if you're looking for a small guesthouse where you can stay in clean comfort. Mrs. Mair Whincup extends a warm welcome to guests, who enjoy the peaceful ambience and the feeling of being a family friend rather than a paying guest. You'll feel rather like that too when it comes to paying the bill for B&B. Mrs. Whincup charges £9 ($14.40) to £10 ($16) for B&B. There's a TV lounge for guests, and tea/coffee makers and hot and cold running water are in the three bedrooms.

A Splurge Choice

Hotel 70°, Penmaenhead, Old Colwyn (tel. 0492/516555), is a totally modern hotel which looks rather like a passenger vessel ready to put out to sea when viewed from certain angles. Its several levels are stacked like decks; the highest part, bearing the hotel's logo, is the captain's bridge. Maybe I just thought of it like that because the sea and bay are so near that they appear to be lapping at its sides. Despite its angular modern look, this is a hospitable hotel, with good service, handsome public rooms, good cuisine, and clean, comfortable bedrooms with many amenities. Every sleeping unit has a sea view, bathroom, direct-dial phone, color TV, in-house video, and tea/coffee-making facilities. Tariffs run from £42 ($67.20) in a single, £60 ($96) in a twin-bedded room. The rates include a full breakfast, VAT, and service. Children 15 and under sharing their parents' room are accommodated free except for meals. Golfing and other bargain breaks are offered.

Malcom and Brenda Sexton, the resident proprietors, are justly proud of the Horizon Restaurant, with a view over the bay. At night, when lights are on all around the seashore, the sight is breathtaking. You can choose from the à la carte dinner menu, as well as a table d'hôte dinner and lunch offering. Your meal might include soused herring with apple and cucumber salad; a mixed grill (lamb chop, steak, bacon, sausage, and kidney with tomatoes and mushrooms); veal collop with fried egg, capers, and anchovies; or poached halibut with spinach in a glazed cheese sauce; as well as numerous fish and poultry dishes. You can dine à la carte for £13.50 ($21.60) and up. Chef-prepared snacks, served in the sophisticated bars, supplement the fixed-price lunch menu of the restaurant. Dinner dances are held on Saturday night.

ANIMALS AND GARDENS: In a 37-acre estate overlooking Colwyn Bay, you can visit the **Welsh Mountain Zoo and Flagstaff Gardens** (tel. 0492/532938). The informal gardens were designed with an eye to the panorama of the sea and landscape. The animals of the zoo are in natural settings. Included among the collection are lions, elephants, tropical birds, reptiles, penguins, sea lions, deer, bears, chimpanzees, monkeys, and birds of prey, as well as species of local wildlife. Daily sea lion displays and falconry demonstrations are given. The zoo has a licensed bar and a restaurant, plus a picnic and sunbathing area and a jungle adventure play area for children. The zoo is open all year from 10 a.m. to dusk. Admission is £2.80 ($4.48) for adults, £1.40 ($2.24) for children.

4. Rhyl, Prestatyn, and Environs

A rapidly developing holiday center along the coast of the Irish Sea already competes with Blackpool in England for the patronage of families from the Midlands seeking a new place in the sun. The leading water-oriented activity centers are—

RHYL AND PRESTATYN: These two popular resorts have gone all out to attract vacationers who like a lively beach setting with lots of man-made entertainment facilities. They push hard to draw families, with a great variety of activities.

Food and Lodging

As noted in the Colwyn Bay section above, there is a wealth of places to eat in Rhyl and Prestatyn, ranging from fine restaurants to ice-cream bars. Hotels and guesthouses all have dining facilities also, so I will not explore the outside eating places. If you want to stay here, remember that it is very crowded during summer vacation time.

The Pier, 23 East Parade, Rhyl (tel. 0745/50280), is a small, Edwardian licensed hotel facing the Royal Floral Hall, the bowling greens, and the sea. The Austria-born proprietors, Robert and Gill Herndlhofer, extend a warm welcome to guests. The hotel has full central heating, and bedrooms—11 in all—have radio, intercom, and some have a shower. There is a color TV lounge, as well as a licensed bar for residents and a solarium. Tariffs for B&B are from £9 ($14.40) to £11 ($17.60) per person. Evening meals are available.

The **Belmont Licensed Guest House,** 4 Beechwood Rd., Rhyl (tel. 0745/51483), a stone Victorian building, offers a warm welcome to guests. It's in a good position, just off the East Parade and quite near the seafront and the Sun Centre. All seven bedrooms have central heating, hot and cold running water, and are carpeted. The comfortable lounge has color TV. The cooking here has received praise from guests. Charges are £10.50 ($16.80) to £12 ($19.20) for half board. The house is open from March to October. Parking space is provided.

Just a whisper south of Prestatyn, over hill and dale on a country road is Gwaeynsgor, a tiny hamlet where you can stop at the **Eagle & Child** (tel. 07456/6391), a pub with a fairly gruesome sign showing an eagle carrying a child in its talons. Here you can enjoy a pub lunch for £1.50 ($2.40) to £3 ($4.80), accompanied by real ale. If you want to savor the ambience of a truly Welsh country pub, this is a good place to do so. Hours are noon to 3 p.m. and 7 to 11 p.m. weekdays, noon to 2 p.m. and 7 to 10 p.m. on Sunday.

Sights and Activities

At Rhyl, the **Sun Centre** (tel. 0745/31771) is an indoor extravaganza which includes an indoor surfing pool, tropical palms in a lagoon setting, roof-top monorail rides, a children's splash pool, a restaurant, licensed bars, snack stands, and nighttime entertainment. One of the most popular attractions here is the Dragon Slide water chute. The center is open daily from 10 a.m. to 11 p.m., Easter to the end of September; on Friday, Saturday, and Sunday in October. Admission is £2.45 ($3.92) for adults, £1.40 ($2.24) for children in the daytime, dropping to £1.40 ($2.24) for adults, 95p ($1.52) for children after 6 p.m.

Ocean World & Butterfly Jungle, East Parade (tel. 0745/53507), has sea and jungle life in plenty. Sea lions, penguins, and pelicans can be seen, along with sharks and colorful tropical fish. The Butterfly Jungle exhibits hundreds of exotic plants and is filled with free-flying tropical butterflies between May and September. Also to be seen are macaws, toucans, snakes, and tarantulas. The attraction has a café, gift shop, and "Pearl in the Oyster" display. It's all open from 10 a.m. to 9 p.m. daily except Christmas Day. Admission is £1.95 ($3.12) for adults, £1 ($1.60) for children.

Rhyl Marine Lake Leisure Park (tel. 0745/31515) is behind the promenade and close to Foryd Harbour. Sailing, windsurfing, and paddle-boating can be done here. There is also a children's playground, amusements, and a model steam train. The attractions are open all day Easter and then the subsequent Sundays until the May bank holiday, after which it's open daily until September. The lake area is open to the public all year. Admission is free, except for charges for the rides and attractions.

Prestatyn has a long beach, two golf courses, a heated outdoor swimming pool with a "Supa Shute," and sailing facilities. The big attraction is the **Royal Lido** (tel. 07456/4768), a holiday complex in the middle of the seafront, with a restaurant, licensed ballroom for dances, snackbars, shops, and a program of entertainment including evening shows, musical groups, and old-fashioned dancing and singing.

Offa's Dyke, that barrier constructed in the eighth century by King Offa of Mercia to keep the Welsh out of his Saxon lands, starts at Prestatyn. Its nearest visible point is a mile east of Trelawnyd on the right-hand side of the A5151 road toward Holywell and the Dee estuary.

IN THE ENVIRONS: From Rhyl, an excellent excursion is to go inland along the Vale of Clwyd, the river around whose estuary the activities of the coastal area bustle. Before the river widens into the broad expanse emptying into the Irish sea, you come to—

Rhuddlan

This little town, three miles south of Rhyl on the A525 road, is right on the river. Its main claim to fame today is **Rhuddlan Castle** (tel. 07456/6391), begun in 1277, an early member of the extensive network of fortifications built by King Edward I in his efforts to contain the Welsh. It replaced a motte and bailey built under William the Conqueror at what he too saw as a strategic position on the Clwyd. Edward's castle necessitated diverting the river and having a canal built so that supplies could be brought directly to it from the sea. The castle is open to visitors daily March 15 to October 15 from 9:30 a.m. to 6:30 p.m., on Sunday from 2 to 6:30 p.m. The remainder of the year, except for Christmas holidays and New Year's Day, hours are 9:30 a.m. to 4 p.m., 2 to 4 p.m. on Sunday. Admission is 80p ($1.28) for adults, 40p (64¢) for children.

The name Conwy is quite familiar in North Wales, and there were Conwys in Rhuddlan Castle from its inception. At a time when military activity in the area had slacked off, and no doubt in search of some privacy from castle life, the head Conwy of that time moved to a separate home about a mile to the east. Over the centuries, **Bodrhyddan Hall** (tel. 0745/590414), the seat of the Conwys, has been rebuilt and added to until today it is a stately home of mellow red brick, basically a 17th-century house with 19th-century additions. It's still lived in by the heirs of the Conwys. Geoffrey, Lord Langford, the hereditary constable of Rhuddlan Castle whose family name is Rowley-Conwy, has opened the house to the public, and it's worth a visit to see the treasures that have accrued during the lifetime of the house.

Besides arms and armor, fine furniture, paintings, and china which may be seen throughout the house, also on display (in the front hall) are the chairs in which Lord and Lady Langford sat at the investiture of Charles as Prince of Wales. In a little room off the hall are two mummy cases, one still occupied, which Lord Langford's great-grandmother brought back as souvenirs of her honeymoon in Egypt, back when that sort of thing was done. The house can be visited Tuesday and Thursday from 2 to 5:30 p.m. June through September. Admission is £1 ($1.60) for adults and 50p (80¢) for children. Bodrhyddan Hall is on the A5151 road midway between Dyserth and Rhuddlan.

Fishing enthusiasts may be interested in the **Felin-y-Gors Trout Fisheries** (tel. 0745/584044) at Bodelwyddan (don't confuse it with Bodrhyddan, above), two miles southwest of Rhuddlan. At Felin-y-Gors Mill in secluded wooded grounds, David Monshin and his family allow fishing in the lakes and pools. In addition to purchasing fishing tickets, anglers can rent the necessary equipment. A four-hour fishing ticket is £6.50 ($10.40), an eight-hour ticket priced at £12.50 ($20).

Dyserth

A small, friendly village on the A5151 between Rhuddlan and Holywell, Dyserth is mentioned in the *Domesday Book,* A.D. 1086.

Outside Dyserth on a country road a mile off the main A55 road, set in the Vale of Clwyd, is a 16th-century free house known as the **Blue Lion Inn,** Cwm (tel. 0745/570733), run by Peggy and Terry Williams. Their menu offers a creative and satisfying selection of dishes. You can choose meals from the carvery costing from £5 ($8) or order an à la carte dinner for £12 ($19.20) and up. The granite and white-plaster building is open for customers from 7:30 to 9:30 p.m. except on Sunday night and all day Monday.

St. Asaph

St. Asaph, on the A525 road six miles south of Rhyl, is a city, despite its tininess, because it has a **cathedral,** which is also small—reputedly the smallest in Britain. The religious seat was founded in A.D. 537. The present cathedral, perched on a hilltop, houses some interesting artifacts in its museum, including some early Bibles kept here. For a small charge visitors can climb the tower and look at the surrounding countryside.

In the foothills of the Clwydian Range a little way south on the B5429 road, which turns off the A55 just east of St. Asaph, at the village of **Tremeirchion** there is a church with an old oak porch and door and some interesting memorials. Looking north from the church, note the high, small chapel, **Capel-y-Graig,** with its thin spire. It was erected by the St. Beuno Monastery in the valley.

The road from Tremeirchion southward goes through an area where Bronze Age and Iron Age people once lived and roamed, leaving many traces of their passing. You'll come quite soon upon the village of—

Bodfari

The village was old when it was mentioned in the *Domesday Book* in the 11th century. When a Roman general, Varius, built his villa in a commanding site overlooking the Vale of Clwyd, it became known as Botvarius ("House of Varius"), hence Bodfari. In the 12th century the **Church of St. Stephen** was built, and although it was rebuilt much later, the original tower still exists, and traces of an adjoining building, probably a pilgrims' rest, are visible.

Bodfari is about four miles northeast of Denbigh and 11 miles northwest of Mold, both towns to be previewed later in this chapter.

The main reason for stopping here is to eat and drink at the **Dinorben Arms** (tel. 074575/309), a pub at least since 1640, which has been tastefully expanded to a fine facility without losing its ancient charm. Positioned on high ground with a large parking area, the inn, owned by G. T. Hopwood, has such attractive features as a Garden Room and terraces, where guests can sit with their children on a covered deck and enjoy the good food available here. Downstairs in the Well Bar you can see a relic of the past, discovered when the expansion of the inn was going on—a well containing water. This was renovated and relined, with a canopy and plate glass over the shaft. Speculation is that this is a well built by the Romans, taken over in the 7th century by Deifar, a Christian hermit. Deifar's Well was supposed to have magical properties. Whether the well in the inn bar has magic in it or not, there are certainly spirits here—the kind poured from a bottle.

You can dine in the Ingle Nook Dining Room where smörgåsbord luncheons are served daily. In the evening simple meals are available, with hot and cold dishes to order. You begin your meal with selections from the Starter Bar, ending with a choice from the Sweets Bar. Depending on your appetite, you can dine well for from £8 ($12.80), a smörgåsbord lunch costing £6 ($9.60). If you choose just to have a pub lunch, you might have sandwiches, soup, or steak-and-kidney pie, for a cost of less than £3 ($4.80). This is such a popular place with people from the surrounding country and towns that it's wise to make a reservation if you plan to eat here. Food is served from noon to 3 p.m. and 6 to 11 p.m., with last orders at 10:15 p.m.

5. Holywell

As you might have guessed, this town takes its name from a holy well, although it's pronounced Hollywell. On the main North Wales road, the A55, Holywell is set on a hillside with a good view of the Dee estuary. On a clear day, from the upland areas you can see the spire of Liverpool Cathedral across the water. The Romans knew the village that was here in their heyday.

Friday is market day in Holywell.

The **Wales Tourist Information Centre** serving this area is at Little Chef Services, Halkyn (tel. 0352/780144), on the A55 road a few miles south of Holywell.

FOOD AND LODGING: Above the town on the A55 road, the **Stamford Gate Inn,** Halkyn Road (tel. 0352/712942), has a commanding view of Holywell from its height. You can see a host of brick houses with red tile roofs, not exactly the type of house you may have become accustomed to seeing in Wales. The view over the Dee estuary is impressive from here. The 12 bedrooms have been attractively decorated with harmonious colors and comfortable furnishings. The rooms, all with bath, have many of the amenities of more expensive hotels. Tariffs for B&B Monday to Thursday are £27 ($43.20) in a single, £37 ($59.20) in a double. On Friday, Saturday, and Sunday, singles cost £25 ($40) and doubles go for £35 ($56). The prices include breakfast served in your room.

The restaurant here was established long before the bedroom extension was added, and it has continued to offer good à la carte and table d'hôte menus, which draw many of the local people here to eat. The freshness of the food served is exemplified by the products of the sea which are brought in by the hotel's own trawler. An extensive wine list is offered, with good selections at reasonable prices. Dinner dances are held on Friday and Saturday; the dance floor is adjacent to the restaurant and cocktail bar. Expect to pay £12 ($19.20) and up for a complete à la carte meal. A variety of lunchtime and evening meals are served in the lounge bar, where freshly made sandwiches and homemade soups, as well as a range of hot dishes, are available. The cost for "pub grub" will be from £3 ($4.80) to £5.50 ($8.80) for a filling repast.

SIGHTS IN AND AROUND HOLYWELL: The place became well known in the Christian world when it was a site of pilgrimage, the Lourdes of Wales, an important shrine until the Reformation. The drawing card was **St. Winefride's Well** (Winifred is the anglicized version). The story of how Winefride became the saint of a holy well is interesting if a little gruesome: It seems that she stayed home from church one Sunday while her parents were at worship. Along came a young blade named Caradoc and tried to seduce the girl. She fled to the church screaming, but the wicked man pursued her and lopped off her head on the church steps. Winefride's Uncle Beuno, later to become a saint himself, first roundly cursed the swordsman so that the earth opened up and swallowed him, then Beuno picked up the girl's head, placed it next to her body, and prayed for her to be restored to life. She was, and she lived another 15 years, with only a little mark on her neck to show for the briefly fatal blow. However, from the spot where her head had rolled, crystal-clear water sprang up. Hence St. Winefride's Well.

The water still bubbles up into a well chamber over which a chapel was endowed by Margaret, mother of Henry VII. People still come to the shrine on Greenfield Road and are allowed to dip or immerse themselves in the water

Monday to Saturday, men from 8 to 9 a.m. and women from 9 to 10 a.m. all year. The water maintains an almost constant temperature and never freezes. In summer, services are held at 11 a.m. from a pulpit beside the well, which is in a vaulted structure. Directly on the road beside the well are St. Winefride's Chapel and St. James's Church. The chapel can be visited on Friday and Saturday Easter to September from 11 a.m. to 7 p.m.

A rather startling example of the encroachment of commerce is the location of **Holywell Textile Mills** (tel. 0352/712022), right next door to the entrance to the holy well on Greenfield Road. Products of the mills are made from the wool of the Jacob, an ancient breed of sheep whose fleece has unusual markings, allowing it to be spun and woven in the original undyed state, making fabrics in natural shades of brown, gray, and creamy white. You can see and purchase these products in a large shop at the mill by the well. If you go along Greenfield Road away from the center of town, you see many signs of the factories that sprang up during the Industrial Revolution, when much of Holywell was built.

Off the A548 road a mile northwest of Holywell in the village of Greenfield are the remains of **Basingwerk Abbey,** founded in 1131. Excavation is still under way, but you can see part of the abbey fragments today. The site is accessible by footpath and may be viewed free.

The **Grange Cavern Military Museum** (tel. 0352/713455), on the A55 at the Holway, outside Holywell, is the world's largest underground military museum. Scores of military vehicles, including armored cars, jeeps, and artillery pieces, are housed in a floodlit cavern covering 2½ acres some 60 to 100 feet below the surface. There is also a large collection of military artifacts, plus a Falklands display. A free film show is given in the auditorium, and you can have a drink at the licensed bar where light refreshments are served. Don't worry about the German antitank gun pointing in the direction of the café—it's not loaded. Wear warm clothing to enter the cavern as the temperature is about 50° Fahrenheit. The museum is open from 9:30 a.m. to 6 p.m. (last entrance at 5 p.m.) daily Easter to October. It is closed November, December, and January, reopening in February and March on weekends only from 10 a.m. to 5 p.m. (last entrance at 4 p.m.). Admission is £1.75 ($2.80) for adults, £1.25 ($2) for children.

The **Franciscan Friary of the Capuchin Monks** (tel. 0352/711053) is at Pantasaph near Holywell. Its unique stations of the cross and grotto are open for visits by the public.

A CASTLE AT FLINT: A short distance from Holywell, southward along the Dee estuary, is Flint, where Edward I had his first Welsh castle constructed. Flint Castle has Shakespearian connections: In *Richard II,* the bard had this castle as the scene of King Richard's capture by Bolingbroke. The castle had its huge round tower (donjon), its last line of defense, set apart and linked with the rest of the fortress by a drawbridge. The castle stands on a platform of rock partly visible in the channel of the Dee estuary. The Old English word *flint* was applied to any hard rock. The castle, which is really rather bleak looking, with highly commercial Flint town gazing at it, can be visited from 9:30 a.m. to 6:30 p.m. weekdays, from 2 to 6:30 p.m. on Sunday mid-March to mid-October. Mid-October to mid-March, opening times are the same, but closing is at 4 p.m. Admission is 50p (80¢) for adults, 25p (40¢) for children.

6. Mold

Through the centuries the name of this town, 5½ miles south of Flint, seems to have changed from "de Monte Alto" through a series of appellations until in 1699 it was first referred to as Mold. It is the administrative center of the

County of Clwyd and has a fine civic center, including the Shire Hall, Law Courts, County Library headquarters, and a fairly new theater of contemporary design, all built in a parkland on the outskirts of town.

Theatr Clwyd (tel. 0352/56331) is part of a chain of regional theater complexes established in Wales in recent years, providing entertainment throughout the year suitable for the family. Facilities include a cinema, a bar, an art gallery, and a restaurant serving food from noon to 11 p.m. The theater has a fine view of the Welsh hills.

On Monday and Saturday the High Street is the scene of outdoor **markets.** On Saturday the street is closed to traffic to allow space for the market stalls, where a wide variety of goods is sold, ranging from food to dress fabric to carpets. A livestock market is held every Monday.

There's a **Tourist Information Centre** in Mold Town Hall, Earl Street (tel. 0352/59331).

STAYING IN MOLD: If you'd like to stop over, try **Tan y Bryn Guest House,** 100 High St. (tel. 0352/3902), a family-run, ten-bedroom house at the top of the main street. Elaine McCulloch rents comfortable rooms, all with TV, hot and cold water basins, and central heating. The charge is £10 ($16) per person for B&B. The house has a residential license, and there's a place to park your car, but perhaps the best feature is the location.

THE GLYNDWR DISTRICT

When this area of what had been Denbighshire was made a part of the County of Clwyd by Parliament in 1973, it was necessary to divide the big county into districts for local administrative purposes. The portion comprising the southern part of the county was named the Glyndwr District, a fitting name. It was in this section that Owain Glyndwr had his two favorite residences, one near Corwen where nothing much is left but a village called Glyndyfrdwy. The other, of which there is now no trace, was at Sycharth, 12 miles south near Llansilin. The chief town of the district is—

7. Denbigh

The market and shopping center for the upper part of the Vale of Clwyd, Denbigh is one of the most historic towns of North Wales. Its principal feature today is the ruins of Denbigh Castle, overlooking the town from Denbigh hill.

There is an Old High Cross in the town center, with medieval stocks alongside it.

Stretches of the town walls remain, which were actually the outer walls of Denbigh Castle. You'll see modern houses within them, plus a tower which is all that remains of St. Hilary's Church of the Middle Ages.

Denbigh was the birthplace of H. M. Stanley of Stanley and Livingstone fame. He was born in 1841 in a cottage just outside the castle walls and brought up in a nearby workhouse. He escaped from there and made his way to the United States, where he became a newspaper reporter, in which job he sought Dr. Livingstone. (I suspect he may have been prepared for his trip into Africa to track down Dr. Livingstone by finding his way around on some of the tiny, unmarked country lanes of Wales. In his day they would have been much more remote and difficult to follow than now.)

FOOD AND LODGING: In a building listed as being of architectural and historical importance, the **Bull Hotel** (tel. 074571/2582) is a well-restored and famous coaching inn. The main staircase is the one installed when the house was built by the Myddelton family in 1540. It bears the family crest, a gloved hand, which is also an indication that the glove trade once flourished in Denbigh. The hotel dining room, in a part believed to have been built as a private home in the 17th century, still has the original paneling. Of interest is a 40-foot-deep well which was uncovered during improvements to the hotel in 1977. It is more than 400 years old and is on view at the hotel. Dot and Les Palmer point with pride to the bedrooms of their hotel, most of which reveal the original Welsh oak timbers. The little staircases and corridors will carry you back in time to the era in which the Bull was built. Tariffs are £17.50 ($28) for B&B in a single, £31 ($49.60) for a double or twin. For a private bath, £2 ($3.20) extra is charged. À la carte and table d'hôte menus are offered in the dining room, which is open to nonresidents. Hot and cold snacks are served in the bar and lounge, with Welsh specialties always on the list. You can have a filling bar-food meal for £3 ($4.80) to £5 ($8).

The **Hawk and Buckle Inn & Restaurant,** Vale Street (tel. 074571/2747), is another interesting building, part of which dates from the 1500s, now operated as a B&B by Trevor and Sandra Nash. A thatched cockpit used to be in the yard of this inn, but it has been moved to the Welsh Folk Museum at St. Fagan's to better preserve this memento of Welsh country life. The simple bedrooms rent for £11 ($17.60) to £13 ($20.80) per person for B&B. The inn has a large selection of bar meals and snacks, and you can fill up for around £2.50 ($4) and up.

Across the High Street from the Bull Hotel is the **Habit Tea House** (no phone), where you can have such snacks as sandwiches, soup, and cakes, looking out the bottle-glass windows at the passing crowd. The tea house is licensed. A light lunch will cost from £2 ($3.20) to £3.50 ($5.60). It's open from 10 a.m. to 5:30 p.m.

SIGHTS: A climb up to the ruins of **Denbigh Castle** (tel. 07457/3979) rewards the visitor with a sweeping view of the countryside which helped it fulfill its warlike purposes. Today, there isn't much left of the castle except the sense of history brooding around it. You can see displays of this history. Its finest hours, considering the purpose for which it was built, were when it was involved with the English versus Welsh battles of Owain Glyndwr, and again when it saw action in the Wars of the Roses and the Civil War. The ruins on the hilltop are still impressive.

It is open from 9:30 a.m. to 6:30 p.m. daily mid-March to mid-October, from 9:30 a.m. to 4 p.m. weekdays, and from 2 to 4 p.m. on Sunday mid-October to mid-March. Admission is 75p ($1.20) for adults, 35p (56¢) for children.

When Queen Elizabeth I gave Denbigh Castle to her favorite, the Earl of Leicester, that worthy wanted to have a cathedral here to outdo St. Asaph's. It was begun but never completed, so that all you can see are the walls of what is just called Leicester's cathedral. Much of Denbigh was rebuilt during Elizabeth's time.

The ruins of one of the simpler monastic houses in Wales can be seen on the eastern outskirts. **Denbigh Friary,** a 13th-century religious house, was put to many uses after the dissolution of the monasteries, but some relics remain. It can be visited free.

8. Vale of Clwyd Villages

A number of interesting little villages and hamlets lie between Denbigh and Ruthin, the next town to be previewed. The Vale of Clwyd in which they are found is bounded by the Clwydian range on the east and high hills and moors on the west, with the River Clwyd and its tributaries running north to the sea. I'll preview three of the villages, but there are many, many more.

LLANDYRNOG: Three miles to the east of Denbigh, reached by little country roads, is the community of Llandyrnog, near the foot of the Clwydian Range. From the top of the range you can get an excellent view of the entire vale and the coastal resorts of Rhys and Prestatyn. On the summit is a hill-fort of the early Stone Age, Pen y Cloddiau. There is a medieval church at Llandyrnog and one at its sister hamlet, Llangwyfan, where stocks can be seen outside the ancient church (perhaps a way of being sure culprits listened to the sermons).

Where to Eat

The **Kinmel Arms Tavern** at Llandyrnog (tel. 08244/291) is a good place to stop for food and drinks and perhaps a chat with the local people. The attractive building was originally part of a farm that included two cottages of 17th-century origins. They were separated from the farm and put together to form the tavern. The structure has shutters on the upper windows and a courtyard in front, with a stone wall separating it from the road. Inside, a bow window in the bar looks out over green fields. An inglenook fireplace in the front bar is not original, although it is so well conceived that it looks as if it had been here forever. Another bar is called the Mantrap, but I didn't find out why. Here you can have real ale straight from the barrels. The tavern has a dining room where you can order meals, or you can have pub food in either of the bars, with tasty traditional Welsh snacks included. Expect to spend from £8 ($12.80) for a meal. Lunch in either of two bars is from noon to 2 p.m., supper from 7 to 9:45 p.m. daily except Sunday evening. The relatively formal dining room serves dinner nightly except Sunday and Monday from 8 to 9:30 p.m. The tavern does not rent rooms.

LLANRHAEADR: You may see this town on the map called Llanrhaeadr-yng-Nghinmerch, but don't let that throw you. You're more likely to see it referred to as Llanrhaeadr Y.C. This is to differentiate it from another Llanrhaeadr somewhere to the east. The name means "Church by the Waterfall." The town lies about three miles south of Denbigh along the A525 road.

St. Dyfnog's Church, which dates from 1450, has a handsome hammer-beam roof and a wooden porch. It should not be missed on a trip through the valley, as it is worth the effort for its Jesse window. This beautiful stained-glass work was set into the wall in 1533, but during the Civil War, in order to save it from destruction by Cromwell's men, it was taken out in 1642 and buried in the woods in an oak chest. It was dug up and replaced when royal rule was restored in 1661. The chest is also in the church. The window shows the full figure of Jesse at the bottom, reclining on his elbow. Above him is King David holding a harp, with his son, Solomon, and grandson, Rehoboam, beside him. At the top is the Christ Child in the arms of Mary. Included in the window are some of the prophets. Names are in medieval Latin.

Note the pew cushions with fleur-de-lys worked in needlepoint.

Directly across from the church is the **Anvil Pottery,** where you can watch the potter at work.

LLANYNYS: This tiny spot is not easy to find, but I think the end justifies the somewhat difficult means. It isn't that it's remote. In fact it's not far off the A525 road between Denbigh (three miles) and Ruthin (two miles), but it's reached by following narrow, winding lanes. The main center of population of the community of Llanynys is at Rhewl, about 1½ miles south and on the main road. (Don't confuse this Rhewl with the one just outside Llangollen.) It was doubtless easier to find in the days when **Llanynys Church** was the most important one in the vale south from St. Asaph. A yew tree in the nearby glebe field marks the exact center of the Vale of Clwyd, near the confluence of the Clewedog and Clwyd Rivers. The name Llanynys means "Church among the Water Meadows," although it has been translated as "Church of the Island." It must have seemed like that at times, when in winter the surrounding fields were flooded so that parishioners had to come to church by boat.

The present church was built on the site of the Church of St. Saeran, founded in A.D. 560, the center of a small monastic community. Although the structure was altered and added to over the centuries, it is thought that the construction of the oldest part started in the 11th century. A sepulchral stone, circa 900, is here, together with mementos of the church's heyday as the religious center of a large area: a 1490 font, a 1630 pulpit, and a 1637 altar. The highlight of the church, however, is a huge wall painting of St. Christopher, dated 1400 to 1430, which was discovered during interior renovations in 1967. It had been covered with plaster and whitewash, probably during Civil War times, to keep it from being totally ruined. The picture has been rescued but not repainted or touched up.

Where to Eat

Just outside the churchyard is a good place to rest and be thankful, **Cerrigllwydion Arms** (tel. 074578/247), an inn built on wasteland where the parish stable once stood. The stables, where parishioners left their horses while they attended services, were at the north end, and the mounting block still stands at the little gate outside the church. The inn is actually partly in the churchyard, the vicar at the time of its construction allowing this to prevent the building from obstructing the view of Denbigh Castle from the parlor of the vicarage. The inn is dated around 1400 and still has the original beams. Stephen, Ted, Norma, and Janet Spicer are the hospitable hosts, welcoming visitors and giving information about the church and surrounding country. You can have a good pub lunch or evening meal here, which might include sausages, grilled gammon steak, or bacon, chop, and egg. Fresh fish is a specialty. A filling meal will cost £4.50 ($7.20) to £8 ($12.80). A pint of lager is 90p ($1.44), one of bitter 86p ($1.38). The inn's dining room, adjacent to the pub, is cozy, with a collection of antique teapots hanging from the ceiling. You can enjoy your drink in the rustic garden in front of the inn in good weather, looking toward the Clwyd Range. The establishment serves lunch from 11:30 a.m. to 2 p.m. and dinner from 7 to 11 p.m.

9. Ruthin

There seems to be no recorded evidence of an original settlement in Ruthin (the *u* is pronounced like the *i* in with) until the matter of building Ruthin Castle came up in 1277 as a part of the 17-castle project of Edward I to help him hang onto Wales. However, it is almost certain that a little hamlet was here at the gateway to North Wales even before the coming of the Normans to Britain, and the hill on which the town sits was probably fortified and occupied from prehistoric times—it was too good to pass up. In recorded history Ruthin has seen plague, battle, and siege, and its visitors have included kings, queens, patriots, rebels, and travelers. The town's buildings reflect several architectural styles: medieval, Georgian, Regency, and Victorian. Many half-timbered structures still stand, reminders of Tudor days. The town has been designated as an Outstanding Conservation Area worthy of preservation.

The present **Ruthin Castle** was reconstructed on the site of Edward's border fortress, mostly demolished in the Civil War. It began a new era in 1826 when it was rebuilt as the home of the Cornwallis-Wests, connected to the Myddelton family. The stone remains of the old castle can be seen around the new, red sandstone part. The elegant 19th-century Gothic building is now a hotel, previewed below.

In St. Peter's Square, the heart of the old town, a Medieval Day is held every Wednesday from July to the end of September. On the first Tuesday of every month, a street market is held here. The Ruthin livestock market is a weekly event, held on Friday.

The **Tourist Information Centre** is at the Craft Centre (see below) (tel. 08242/3992), open from 10 a.m. to 6 p.m.

FOOD AND LODGING: If you've always wanted to sleep in a castle, here's your chance. **Ruthin Castle,** Corwen Road (tel. 08242/2664), is an elegant place to stay, and it's not outrageously expensive. It stands in 36 acres of gardens and parkland, including the ruins of the 13th-century castle. Peacocks stroll about the grounds, but you can too, looking at the walled gardens and following little hidden walkways to secret nooks and crannies of the old castle. You can see the drowning pit, where unfortunate souls were thrown in and the gate locked behind them (the moat kept this filled with water). You can also see the whipping pit and the castle dungeons. On a more pleasant note, the large public rooms are all high-ceilinged, from the oak-paneled entry hall into the lounge where a portrait of Mary Cornwallis-West graces one wall and then to the cocktail bar, a comfortable place to relax. The castle has a series of fine bay, mullion, and oriel windows. All the bedrooms have private bath, central heating, radio, and phone to complement the old-fashioned feel of the large and simply furnished interiors. Rents for B&B are £25 ($40) to £31 ($49.60) in a twin- or double-bedded room and £31 ($49.60) in a single. Reductions are granted for children sharing their parents' room. The hotel has excellent dining facilities, where meals are served in a lovely dining room looking out over the grounds.

An integral feature of the hotel is the holding of **Medieval Banquets** every night except Sunday during the summer and at intervals each week in winter. Guests partake of bread and salt, age-old symbols of hospitality, before going on to the Armory Bar, where drinks are served before the feast. The banquets are held in the former chapel which has been made into a banqueting hall. A fun-filled evening is presided over by the court steward, who presents programs in which the ladies of the court sing and harp music is played. All are dressed in medieval costumes. The ladies of the court also serve at table. The menu consists of four "removes," or courses, including a thick vegetable soup, Welsh lamb, half a young chicken roasted in honey and oranges, served with a fresh green salad and potatoes in jackets, and a dessert of fruit and cream. Wine and mead are served with the meal. The only catch is that diners have only a sharp-bladed knife with which to eat, in the style of the Middle Ages. You get messy, but it's fun. The cost of the banquet is £16 ($25.60) per person, and it's worth it. Reservations are required (tel. 08242/3435).

There's also a hotel in Ruthin named the **Castle Hotel,** St. Peter's Square (tel. 08242/2479), an elegant Georgian building which was once the White Lion Inn. Then it had a cockpit at the back. Adjacent to the Castle Hotel and now a part of the same complex is Myddelton Arms, a black-and-white building in the Dutch style with a high-peaked roof and seven dormers on varying levels, called "the eyes of Ruthin." The hotel is a fine place to stay if you want to be right in the heart of the little town. Rooms cost £20 ($32) per person for B&B in a shared room, £25 ($40) for single occupancy. You can rub elbows with local people in the bar, where "pub grub" can be enjoyed. A four-course dinner costs £7.50 ($12). The hotel is under the personal management of the owners, Mr. and Mrs. Carrington-Sykes.

Granny's Shop (in Welsh, Siop Nain), 6 Well St. (tel. 08242/3572), is a welcoming little place where guests feel at home. Mr. and Mrs. Davies operate this intimate little café-cum-dining room which dates from the latter 15th century. Readers have responded favorably to its antiquated atmosphere, as reflected by the time-blackened oak beams. Lying right off the main plaza of town, the Shop specializes in home-style cookery. That means homemade meat pies, good soups, and rich desserts, with meals costing from £6 ($9.60). Hours are daily except Sunday from 9:30 a.m. to 5 p.m.

SIGHTS: A small house of worship, **St. Peter's Church** at St. Peter's Square was founded in 1310, and it is exquisite. It is known for its early 16th-century carved oak roof and brass memorials. To enter the church, you pass through handsome wrought-iron gates, made in the 18th century by the Davies Brothers of Bersham, who made the fine gates at Wrexham Parish Church and Chirk Castle. Attached to the church are the 14th-century Old Cloisters, a group of almshouses founded in 1590, and nearby, the Old Grammar School and headmaster's house.

Also on St. Peter's Square, you'll see the **Old Courthouse,** built in 1401 and used as Leet Court (a court in which the lord of the manor had jurisdiction) and prison.

Nantclwyd House, Castle Street, is one of the finest town houses in Wales. It is Elizabethan but built on earlier foundations. Of particular note are the gabled portico, the stained glass with armorial bearings, the old oak carvings and wainscoting, and a curious gallery.

The **Ruthin Grammar School** had its origins in 1284, but was refounded in 1574 and moved to its present site, on a hillside overlooking the valley, in 1892. Among students whose names you might recognize have been Elton John's father and Julian Lennon, John Lennon's son by his first wife, Cynthia.

Whatever you do when you're in Ruthin, don't miss going to the **Ruthin Craft Centre** (tel. 08242/4774), at the site of the old railroad station directly across the town north from the castle as the crow flies. This is a craft complex built around an attractive courtyard where traditional skills are practiced in surrounding shops. You can look in through the big plate-glass windows or enter to watch the artisans at work. Crafts include canal bargeware painting, candle making, ceramics, wildlife art, stone carving, screen printing, picture framing, ceramic sculpture, embroidery, jewelry, bench glass blowing, and pottery making. Products can be purchased from the various workshops and at the main gallery which has different exhibits monthly and a retail outlet. Some of the craftspeople will ship articles purchased from them. There is a licensed restaurant in the complex. The center is open from 10 a.m. to 6 p.m. in summer, from 10 a.m. to 5 p.m. in winter. Admission is free. David Jones is the competent administrator here.

10. Corwen and the Vale of Edeyrnion

Corwen is a pleasant little market town, once a convenient overnight stopping place for passengers on stagecoaches. It's in lush green countryside along the River Dee, at the northern end of the Vale of Edeyrnion. A mile across the river are the remains of a prehistoric hill-fort. This area is associated with Owain Glyndwr, who spent some of his years just a little farther down the Dee. Above the town on the heights of the Berwyn Range is Pen y Pigyn, a landmark some-times called Glyndwr's Seat.

STAYING IN THE VALE: Although there is no stagecoach to bring you here, you might like to stay in Corwen at the **Corwen Court Private Hotel,** London Road (tel. 0490/2854), on the A5. This is a converted old police station and courthouse, where the six prisoners' cells have been turned into small bed-rooms. One of the cells was for women only, but the hotel proprietors no longer make that distinction. Each of these has hot and cold running water. There are four large bedrooms also, each of which has a private bath. The proprietors, R. J. and A. E. Buckland, charge £10 ($16) per person for B&B depending on the location and the amenities. The hotel has a lounge with color TV. The old courtroom has been converted into an attractive dining room, where you canarrange to take an evening meal for £5 ($8).

Going south from Corwen along the vale, you come to the tiny town of **Llandrillo,** sheltered by the Berwyn Mountains, about eight miles from Lake Bala at the edge of Snowdonia, visited in Chapter XXV.

My favorite place to stay in this town is **Tyddan Llan** (tel. 049084/264), a country-house hotel and restaurant just outside the village, set in three acres of gardens. This was a farmhouse 250 years ago, added onto in 1850 when it was turned into a shooting lodge for the Duke of Westminster. The establishment is run by Peter and Bridget Kindred, who rent nine bedrooms, all with baths and hot-beverage facilities. The house is centrally heated. The rate in a double or twin-bedded room is £21.50 ($34.40) per person for B&B, a single occupancy paying an additional £3.50 ($5.60). Half board, on the same basis, costs £32 ($51.20) per person for double occupancy. There's a cozy little bar to the right as you enter the house, with a tastefully decorated dining room beyond, where a roaring log fire takes the chill off in the evening. The home-cooked food is good. Bridget uses fresh local produce, plus vegetables and herbs from the Tyddyn Llan garden. A comfortable residents' lounge is on the left of the entrance, and the hall stairs lead to the bedrooms upstairs. The house is of gray stone with black-and-white trim and a lion couchant on the front stoop. It once belonged to the Robertson family connected with Palé Hall near Bala, previewed earlier.

A feature of Tyddyn Llan is art courses, which can be arranged as special packages for staying at the hotel.

11. Chirk and the Ceiriog Valley

Referred to frequently as the "Gateway to Wales," the town of Chirk lies to the extreme southeast of the Glyndwr District, where the River Ceiriog meets the River Dee and forms the boundary between Wales and England. The A5 road passes through the town, and the secluded Ceiriog Valley winds along to the southwest.

CHIRK: Of special interest in the town is **Chirk Castle** (tel. 0691/777701), set on a hill about 1½ miles from town, a remarkable example of a marcher (border) fortress, built in 1310 by Roger Mortimer after the defeat of the native Princes of Wales to help English royalty retain supremacy over Welsh lands. The castle has been continuously occupied. The 18th-century wrought-iron gates were the work of the Davies Brothers of Bersham, produced during the Baroque era in Britain. The decor embraces many periods but blends harmoniously in this bor-der castle, which began to change its role from fortress to a stately home in the 16th century. The state rooms are decorated in the neoclassical style of the late

1700s and contain superb Adam-style furniture. The Long Gallery with nine mullioned windows and paneling dates from a century earlier. The dungeon under the west range has remained unaltered since 1295, as have the stone stairs to the watchtower and the portcullis gate at the courtyard entrance. The castle garden and the thatched Hawk House can be visited, as well as a long terrace at the end of the garden with a view claimed to embrace many counties.

The castle can be visited from noon to 5 p.m. (last entrance at 4:30 p.m.) daily except Monday and Saturday Easter to the end of September, plus the same hours but only on Saturday and Sunday during the first three weeks in October. Admission is £1.80 ($2.88) for adults, 65p ($1.04) for children. There is a shop, as well as facilities for having tea or a light lunch. Telephone the administrator at the number given above in case there's been a variation in the hours the castle is open.

An interesting stop to make is at **Chirk Mill** (tel. 0691/777622), on the A5 where it crosses the border into England. The main block of the building was a thriving flour mill belonging to the Chirk Castle estate until the 1930s. It now houses Seventh Heaven, the most comprehensive stock of antique brass and iron bedsteads in the country, which have been fully restored on the premises. Styles vary from early Victorian cottage bedsteads to the decorative Victorian designs and Edwardian beds of the early part of this century. Mattresses and bed bases are also sold here. Delivery and export rates are quoted. The center is open daily from 9 a.m. to 5:30 p.m.

Going west from Chirk, you enter the Ceiriog Valley, one of the loveliest in Wales but little known. It runs for 15 miles and is not heavily wooded as is the Vale of Llangollen. Heather-clad moors rise on either side of the river and the road, the B4500.

PONTFADOG: The biggest oak tree in Wales is at the village of Pontfadog, or so I was told.

Just beyond the village, watch for signs to the **Golden Pheasant Hotel** (tel. 069172/281), a fine old village inn nestling in the Ceiriog Valley with views in all directions. The hotel has been owned and managed by the Turner family for 40-plus years, but the original building has been here for more than 200 years. It was once a brewery, with stables and pig barns, a situation that held until 1947 when it was turned into a center for shooting and riding for which the area is famous.

Among the public rooms, you can relax in the elegant Victorian lounge or in the cocktail bar, patterned on the Chinese Chippendale era of the 18th century, with interesting chinoiserie. In good weather, guests sit on the terrace from which they can watch the sun set behind the Berwyn Mountains. The accommodation, whether in the old building or the new wings, is comfortable, even elegant, with some rooms having half or full tester beds, carpets, and easy chairs, as well as fine views. For B&B, the prices are £27 ($43.20) to £33 ($52.80) in a single, £42 ($67.20) to £63 ($100.80) in a double. The proprietor, Jennifer Turner Gibourg, is proud of her traditional and charming restaurant, which offers a menu in which everything is country fresh and local, ranging from meat, game, and fish to salads and vegetables. Expect to pay around £15 ($24) for a complete meal.

Mrs. Gibourg's sister, Jane, conducts a riding center at **Tal-y-Garth Farm** (tel. 069172/408), with trail riding and pony-and-trap rides.

ON ALONG THE VALLEY: Toward the head of the valley is **Glyn Ceiriog,** about halfway along. **Chwarel Wynne Slate Mine and Museum** (tel. 069172/343) is in a lovely spot on the mountainside overlooking the valley. You can walk up the old miners' path from the little town of Glyn Ceiriog, but you can also drive, which is much easier. In the visitor center you can see the tools and equipment used to extract and process the slate, as well as a film of the Welsh slate industry. A guided tour of the floodlit underground workings takes about 30 minutes. Old tram cars loaded with slate sit outside the visitor center. The mine is open from 10 a.m. to 5 p.m. Easter to the end of October. Admission is £1.50 ($2.40) for adults, 90p ($1.44) for children. There is a parking area near the mine.

Food and Lodging

The **Glyn Valley Hotel** (tel. 069172/210) is a good place to stay at Glyn Ceiriog. John Weston welcomes guests to his nine-bedroom hotel, which has such amenities as color TV in the rooms, plus tea/coffee-making equipment. For B&B, the charges in the well-appointed rooms are 20 ($32) in single, £35 ($56) in a double with shower and toilet. Rates vary for family rooms and bathless rooms. You can have your breakfast whenever you wish, and the restaurant stays open for other meals until 10 p.m. The lounge bar, where there is an open fire, has an annex that houses a Pictorial Railway Museum of the former Glyn Valley Tramway. There is a sports bar with darts, pool, and electronic games, as well as a cocktail bar. The bar food is tasty and reasonably priced. Bar snacks range from sandwiches to beef bourguignon, and you can spend from £1.50 ($2.40) all the way to £7 ($11.20) if you opt for a sirloin steak. The dining room menu includes trout fresh from the trout farm just up the road, pheasant, and venison. Expect to pay from £10 ($16) to £12 ($19.20) for a complete meal.

Llanarmon D.C. is a charming, ancient little village at the head of the valley. From here, a network of tiny roads links the Ceiriog Valley with other areas, but the B4500 stops. You might like to stay at the **Hand Hotel** (tel. 069176/666), a 16th-century farmhouse deep in a nest of tranquility, right in the village. Tim and Carolyn Alexander welcome guests to their house, with oak beams, open fires, and high standards of comfort and cuisine. If there is no room at the Hand, they will put you in their other hotel, the **West Arms** (tel. 069176/665), just across the road. A white stone hostelry, originally a farmhouse built in the 17th century, it was named for Colonel Cornwallis-West of Ruthin Castle. Bedrooms at this inn all have private baths or showers.

The Hand and the West Arms charge the same prices: £27.50 ($44) to £30 ($48) for singles, £23.50 ($37.60) to £26 ($41.60) per person for doubles. Some suites cost £42 ($67.20) for single occupancy, £60 ($96) for two persons. Rates depend on the plumbing. At the West Arms, the lounge bar contains a 16th-century confessional which, during the plundering of the Welsh abbeys by Henry VIII, was spirited away, hidden, and eventually found its way here. Bar lunches are served from noon to 2 p.m., and sit-down dinners are available at lunchtime only on Sunday from 12:30 to 2 p.m., for a fixed price of £8.50 ($13.60). Dinner, however, is served daily from 7 to 9 p.m. for a set price of £12.50 ($20).

From Llanarmon village center, you may want to follow a little country road, steep in parts, to Llanrhaeadr-ym-Mochnant, where a narrow road to the right from the village square leads to the famous waterfall, **Pistyll Rhaeadr,** known as one of the Seven Wonders of Wales. This spectacular 240-foot cataract is said to be the highest in the country. As there is limited parking, it's best not to try to visit it in peak summer season. This is truly an excursion into "Wild Wales."

An interesting stop in Ceiriog Valley is the **Upper Mills Trout Farm** (tel. 069172/225), where R. Ian Cornes has trout of all sizes in separate pools where they are raised for restaurants and fish markets. John Cranwell of the Glyn Valley Hotel says he often has full-size trout out of the water here and onto the customer's plate at his restaurant within minutes. The trout farm is about halfway along the valley, across the river from the road.

12. Wrexham

This is the most important industrial town in North Wales, and it isn't in the Glyndwr District, but it is in the vicinity of Llangollen and Chirk and only about 12 miles from Chester, England.

A livestock market is held every Monday in Wrexham, if you want to watch the activities of the Welsh stock breeders and buyers.

A **Tourist Information Centre** is at the Memorial Hall, in the town center (tel. 0978/357845).

FOOD AND LODGING: Good accommodation is found at **Llwyn Onn Hall** (Ash Grove Hotel), Cefn Road (tel. 0978/261225). Named after the groves of ash that still grow around it, this historic home was originally built from 1702 to 1706. Today, it's owned by a Tory candidate from the district who lives nearby and rents out 13 comfortable bedrooms. Each of these has a private bath, color TV, trouser press, phone, and an individualized collection of Welsh and English antiques. The establishment lies within 60 acres of grounds, about 1½ miles east of the town center of Wrexham. A splurge, rooms rent for £42 ($67.20) to £48 ($76.80) in a single, £54 ($86.40) to £65 ($104) in a double. For stays of two nights where one falls on a Friday, Saturday, or Sunday, a special weekend rate is offered for £32 ($51.20) per person daily for half board. The establishment serves bar meals for £5 ($8) daily from noon to 2 p.m., followed by relatively formal dinners for £16 ($25.60) which are offered from 7 to 9:30 p.m.

Even if you're not into industrial cities, Wrexham is worth a visit for at least two reasons.

One reason is to visit the 14th-century **Church of St. Giles,** with its handsome tower. West of the tower is the **tomb of Elihu Yale,** founder of Yale University, who died in 1721 and was brought back for burial in the country from which his father had emigrated to America. The 18th-century wrought-iron gates of the churchyard are the work of the Davies Brothers of Bersham, who made the baroque gates of Chirk Castle.

The second reason, and a compelling one, to visit Wrexham is—

ERRDIG: One mile south of Wrexham, in a park of almost 2,000 acres, stands this fine mansion, built between 1684 and 1687 and added to in the following century. Errdig (tel. 0978/355314) is one of the few places in Britain where you can get an insight into the way both servants and their masters used to live. At Erddig the family never got rid of anything, even when it had been broken, and not even bills, deeds, what have you. They put it away and kept it. When the National Trust took over the house, there was a mountain of work to do. In the 1940s mineworkings had caused the house's foundations to sag: the two wings sank first, then the center block. The roof was wrecked and water poured through the holes, damaging the priceless wallpaper, tapestries, and woodwork.

During its sad decline the house was lived in by a reclusive heir who closed off most of the rooms and left them to their fate. When the present heir took over, he saw the monumental problem faced by a private individual in trying to save the house, so he turned it over to the National Trust. Now Erddig has been restored, and you can see the state rooms with magnificent furniture of the 18th century, as well as the domestic quarters and the workshops that were necessary to keep a vast estate like this in operation—all with their original equipment in working order. The restored 18th-century formal garden and a country park are here for the public to enjoy, and the Country Park Visitor Centre centered around a 17th-century barn houses an exhibition of farm implements and stationary engines.

This treasury of the luxuries and the everyday life of another age is open from noon to 5 p.m. (last entrance at 4 p.m. daily except Friday, from Good Friday to mid-October). The visitor center is open every Saturday and Sunday from 10 a.m. to 4 p.m. Admission is £2.10 ($3.36) for adults, £1 ($1.60) for children. To see only the garden and outbuildings, adults pay £1 ($1.60), children 50p (80¢).

AT BWLCHGWYN: At this village on the A525 west of Wrexham, the **Milestone Museum** (tel. 0978/757573), is a geological exhibition showing the development of North Wales through 600 million years. You can step back into the remote millennia before people appeared on this planet by going into the "Time Tunnel" or follow a Geological Trail in the adjacent silica quarry. There's also a dinosaur display, always popular with children. The museum is open daily except Sunday from 10 a.m. to 5:30 p.m. Admission is 60p (96¢) for adults, 45p (72¢) for children.

You might like to stay at the **Milestone Inn** (tel. 0978/757571), connected with the museum and visitor center. It offers ten bedrooms, renting singles for £18.50 ($29.60) and doubles for £27 ($43.20). The licensed accommodation has a lounge bar and a restaurant, serving food from 7 to 10 p.m.

13. Llangollen

It's easy to fall in love with Llangollen, a charming little town on the banks of the River Dee where it makes its way between two mountain ranges, tumbling loudly along over the boulders merrily and sometimes stormily eastward. The bridge that spans the river in picture-book fashion is a graceful, four-arch structure that is recognized as one of the Seven Wonders of Wales. Despite its nearness to the flatlands of the English border, Llangollen is completely Welsh in mountain scenery and sentiment.

This is the home of the **International Musical Eisteddfod,** held the second week of July annually, when members of world-renowned choirs, folk singers, and dancers from 30 or more countries converge on this little town. In colorful national costumes, they compete daily and perform in evening concerts, making the vale and the surrounding mountains ring with the sound of music. For information on this event, get in touch with the **Eisteddfod Office,** Llangollen (tel. 0978/860236). The events of the Eisteddfod take place on the stage of a huge marquee which seems to fill the floor of the valley during the July week.

The A5 London–Holyhead road runs through this deep and beautiful valley, and in the days of stagecoaches it was an important stopping and horse-changing point. In stagecoach days the main route through town was the Great Irish Road along Bridge Street. As you stroll around the town, you'll see mounting blocks still in place on sidewalks, reminiscent of the days when riders had to remount after a visit to a pub or shop.

Llangollen has a large free parking lot right in the center of town, about a block from the River Dee. The post office is across the lot away from the river, on the street parallel to the river. A street market is held on Tuesday.

You'll find a good golf course here, and you can go fishing or canoeing on the River Dee, as well as pony trekking into the countryside.

The **Tourist Information Centre** is at Town Hall on Castle Street (tel. 0978/860828).

FOOD AND LODGING: At the time of Eisteddfod it is difficult to find a room in Llangollen, and then you can get plenty of assistance in finding places to stay in the surrounding country. However, hotels and guesthouses are not scarce in the town and its immediate environs.

The Royal, Bridge Street (tel. 0978/860202), overlooks the point where the 14th-century stone bridge crosses the river. It was originally the Kings Head Inn on the Great Irish Road, a favorite stop for the official coaches of the Irish Mail. It has been able to call itself "royal" since 1832 when the future Queen Victoria and the Duchess of Kent stayed here. Many of the hotel's 33 rooms have views of the Dee and beyond along the Vale of Llangollen. The rooms all have private bath, color TV, radio, phone, razor outlets, and tea/coffee-making facilities. There is full central heating. They rent for £41 ($65.60) in a single, £54 ($86.40) in a double. Children are welcome. The bedrooms are spacious and furnished in contemporary style.

You can dine in the restaurant with a fine view of the river and the bridge, ordering from either a fixed-price or an à la carte menu, which have traditional Welsh and English dishes. You might begin with a mushroom prawn "skillet" for an appetizer, following with such main courses as venison in a port and red currant sauce or médaillons of beef with herb and garlic butter, perhaps a plattered filet of lamb in a rosemary and orange liqueur sauce. Dinners are served seven days a week from 7 to 9:30 p.m. A fixed-price evening meal, with a choice of four main dishes, costs £10 ($16). At lunchtime, bar snacks, priced from £3 ($4.80) to £5 ($8), are served from noon to 2 p.m. You can also have afternoon teas, sandwiches, scones and cream, and other light food here.

The **Chain Bridge Hotel** (tel. 0978/860215) takes its name from the pedestrian Chain Bridge which spans the River Dee. It stands 1½ miles west from the center of Llangollen, a short walk from the Horseshoe Falls and near the Llangollen Canal. This is a popular spot with canoeists, who may be seen practicing or competing in the water at any time of year. The hotel has 36 centrally heated bedrooms, all with hot and cold water, double-glazed windows, radios, phones, and intercoms. Many have private bath and a balcony overlooking the river. Others have shower and toilet or just a shower. The single tariff for B&B is from £23 ($36.80) to £26 ($41.60), depending on the plumbing and the location of the unit. Doubles go for £22 ($35.20) to £24 ($38.40) per person.

The Tudor Bar, in the original building, has black-and-white timbers and an inglenook fireplace. From here you can watch fishermen or canoeists or see people crossing the bridge. The restaurant, ballroom with its own bar, and Riverside Grill all have fine views. The grill, with a fast-food service, is open only in summer. Lunch is never more than a bar meal, served from 12:30 to 2 p.m. and costing from £4 ($6.40). However, dinner is a set menu, for residents only, going for £8.50 ($13.60). Outsiders can dine à la carte for around £11 ($17.60) per person. Dinner is nightly from 7:30 to 9. On Saturday, there is a dinner dance with cabaret.

The **Britannia Inn** (tel. 0978/860144), at the foot of Horseshoe Pass, is an ancient inn which has been added to and renovated to provide all the modern amenities in a series of rooms of interesting and different shapes and sizes. A habitation was built here in 1201 as living quarters for monks. In those days, monks brewed ale, and so it was brewed on this site from the 13th to the 14th century. After the dissolution of the monasteries in 1539, brewing was resumed here, using natural spring water which still cascades down the waterfall at the side of the inn. Because the monks needed to make money to survive, they began to sell bread they baked and wine they made, along with the ale, to weary travelers. In so doing, they started what may have been the first traditional wayside inn. The bread was baked in what is now the bar area of the Britannia Inn. The public house thus begun was an excellent place for the herdsmen taking droves of sheep to market over the old pass to stop for a while, so the pub, which had two adjoining cottages, became known as a drovers' pub. The pub and cottages were joined in about the early 19th century, making a proper hostelry as you see today, with all the character and friendly atmosphere you could expect.

The owners, Mr. and Mrs. Michael John Callaghan, charge £16 ($25.60) for a single bedroom, £30 ($48) for a double. Some of the rooms in the old part have beamed ceilings, and all have color TV, hot and cold running water, and tea/coffee-making facilities. In the bar or the dining room, with brasses and other suitable decorative effects, you can dine on such foods as pork Normandie, chicken Britannia, abbey duck, and duck in orange sauce, as well as steaks, all prepared by professional chefs. A four-course restaurant meal costs £9.50 ($15.20), and bar food is also available. A nice touch is a menu of senior citizens' specials, offering good food in smaller quantities and at lower prices. Food is served Monday to Saturday from 2:30 to 10 p.m., on Sunday from 1:15 to 10 p.m. You place your orders at the bar and then the food is brought to your table.

The **Old Vicarage,** Vicarage Road (tel. 0978/861000), is a comfortable guesthouse operated by Frank and Iris Burgoyne. The spacious house is set in large gardens. All 13 bedrooms have hot and cold running water and tea/coffee-making facilities. The Burgoynes charge £13 ($20.80) for half board. You can relax and watch TV in the residents' lounge, and a babysitter is available if needed. The food here is good, with vegetarian specialties being offered.

At **Gales Wine & Food Bar,** 18 Bridge St. (tel. 0978/860089), you can enjoy good food and wine in a rustic ambience, where Richard and Gillian Gale and their family welcome customers to this establishment opposite the River Dee. For lunch or dinner, served in the bar, you can order French country lamb, sugar-baked ham, soups, and sandwiches, among a variety of dishes. Try their homemade ice cream. A meal will cost from £5.50 ($8.80). More than 250 wines are offered. The kitchen is believed to be an old smithy. The Gales have eight bedrooms to rent, all with private baths, costing £15 ($24) per person for B&B. The wine and food bar is open from noon to 1:45 p.m. and 6 to 10:15 p.m. On Sunday it opens at 7 p.m. From September to May, it is closed on Sunday and Monday.

For more expensive dining with a more ambitious menu, **Caesar's,** Deeside Lane (tel. 0978/860133), is the leading independent restaurant in town. Enjoying a prime riverbank position along the Dee, it lies at Llangollen Bridge. Back in Edwardian days, it was launched as a temperance hotel but that is hardly the case anymore. Some of the furnishings came from the old Wrexham courthouse. So today you step up to a "witness box," converted into a bar, and place your order for a lager. The food is reliable and consistently good, with meals costing from £12 ($19.20) for a set dinner. Dinner, incidentally, is the only meal served, and it's done admirably from 7 to 10 p.m. daily. Richard Hendey is the chef and co-owner, and he prepares a cuisine that is at once familiar but often with imagination and originality that makes dining here a delight at any time.

SIGHTS AND ACTIVITIES: A branch of the Shropshire Union Canal, the **Llangollen Canal** was built to link the border towns of Shrewsbury and Chester in England via the ironworks of Wrexham and Ruabon, which was also an important brick-manufacturing town. The Shropshire Union Canal was not a success because of lack of water in the Wrexham–Ruabon area, but the Llangollen section got plenty of water from the Horseshoe Falls and still does. Today, as one of the most spectacular stretches of canal in Britain, it is used by holiday cruisers (see "Canal Holidays" in Chapter XX).

Horse-drawn Passenger Boat Trips, The Wharf, Llangollen (tel. 0978/860702), take you back to the gentle age of horse transport. There's also a **Canal**

Museum which tells the fascinating story of Britain's canal era and the lives of the people who worked on the waterways. The museum is open daily Easter to the end of September from 10 a.m. to 5:30 p.m. Admission is 50p (80¢) for adults, 30p (48¢) for children. Boat trips are made every weekend from Easter to the end of September and every day from May to the end of September. The trip lasts about 45 minutes. The charge is £1.30 ($2.08) for adults, 70p ($1.12) for children. The Wharf is a short walk from the town car park.

The railroad came to Llangollen, eliminating the need for stagecoaches, and then it almost went entirely away, but not quite. A standard-gauge private railway has returned to the town's station through the efforts of railway enthusiasts. The station has been restored, and the station buildings contain items of transport interest, such as steam locomotives and rolling stock. **Llangollen Station Museum** is open all year from 10 a.m. to dusk daily during the summer season and on Saturday and Sunday the rest of the year. Admission to the museum is free. Special Steam Days are held on Sunday afternoon and public holidays from Easter to mid-October and during the week of Eisteddfod.

On the edge of Llangollen in a lovely landscaped garden sits **Plas Newydd,** Butler Hill (tel. 0978/860234), a beautiful half-timbered house whose age is undetermined but great. From 1790 to 1831 this was the home of two "eccentric" women, Lady Eleanor Butler and Miss Sarah Ponsonby, who came here from Ireland. They left their homes to live lives of freedom, and they came to be known and appreciated as the "Ladies of Llangollen." They often wore men's clothing, including tall hats, when they went for strolls. They were witty and cultured, and when word of their presence in Llangollen spread, they were visited by many notables of the day, including Sir Walter Scott, the Duke of Wellington, and William Wordsworth. The rooms of Plas Newydd are richly paneled, but unfortunately the fine collection of objets d'art the ladies had (they expected guests to bring something—preferably woodcarvings) was taken away after they died. With their faithful maid, Mary Caryll, known as Molly the Basher, they are buried near the riverbank in St. Collen's Church. Plas Newydd, now owned by the town, can be visited May 1 to September 30, Monday to Saturday from 10 a.m. to 7:30 p.m. and on Sunday from 11 a.m. to 4 p.m. Admission is 60p (96¢) for adults, 30p (48¢) for children. To reach the house on foot, walk up the hill by the Grapes Hotel on the south side of the river.

St. Collen's, the parish church, has a fine roof with carved beasts and flowers, believed to have been brought from Valle Crucis Abbey.

Castell Dinas Bran, a medieval Welsh castle ruin, towers above Llangollen. You can go take a look at it free. It stands 1,000 feet up on the summit of the Hill of Bran.

At the opposite end of town from Plas Newydd in a hilly, wooded setting are the ruins of **Valle Crucis Abbey,** founded in 1201 as a monastery for Cistercians. It was widely known as a seat of learning, but after the dissolution of the monasteries by Henry VIII, it fell into dilapidation. Part of it was made into a dwelling house, and around 1800 the dorter (monks' sleeping quarters) and adjacent rooms became a farmhouse. What's left of the abbey, set beside a stream in a narrow valley, has interesting carving which is a good example of native Welsh work of the 13th century. The abbey, about 1½ miles north of Llangollen near the A542 road, can be visited from May to the end of September. Admission is 70p ($1.12) for adults, 35p (56¢) for children.

About half a mile north of the abbey near the A542 road stands **Eliseg's Pillar,** a 9th-century eight-foot pillar cross. It was erected by Cyngen, Prince of Powys, in memory of his grandfather, Eliseg, who, the pillar says, "annexed the inheritance of Powys . . . from the powers of the English, which he made into a sword land by fire." Eliseg may have been buried in the mound on which the pillar stands.

It was from the pillar cross that Valle Crucis ("Vale of the Cross") Abbey took its name.

Some four miles northwest of Llangollen, you may see some of the most photographed sheep in the world. At **Horseshoe Pass,** where many tour buses stop so that passengers can get a view of Llangollen and the Dee valley, the sheep wander around in the gorse, bracken, and short grazing turf—and often right out onto the road. Old slate-quarry leavings are across to the west. As you drive toward Llangollen, winding around the high hills, you have a splendid view of the valley in which sit the ruins of Valle Crucis Abbey, and you can see why the monks chose this spot. It seems a pity that today, just next to the beautiful ruins, and marring the entire view, is a trailer park.

Llangollen Weavers, the Water Mill, Dee Lane (tel. 0978/860630), near Llangollen Bridge, was a cornmill that originated in the 13th century, run by a water wheel. Today the leading producers of tweeds and fashion fabrics, the mill can be visited to watch the operation. You'll see fabrics being woven, and demonstrations of hand-weaving on 150-year-old looms can be arranged. Fabrics, clothes, rugs, and woolen articles are displayed and sold in the mill shop. You can have coffee and other refreshments in the lounge. The shop is open seven days a week Easter to October from 9:30 a.m. to 6 p.m., Monday to Saturday in winter. Weaving is done Monday to Friday.

A quiet little bookshop, **Llangollen Books,** on Oak Street (tel. 0978/861251), has a wide selection of books, including volumes and volumes about Wales. You can also find maps and guides here.

Part Three

THE ISLE OF MAN

Chapter XXVIII

A TRIP TO THE ISLE OF MAN

**1. Douglas
2. Onchan
3. Laxey
4. Ramsey
5. Peel
6. Port Erin
7. Castletown and Ballasalla**

STEEPED IN HISTORY, folklore, and legend, the Isle of Man—at least for the foreign visitor—is mysterious. Those who have heard of it at all know of its low income taxes, its tail-less Manx cats, and its car- and motorcycle-racing events. To begin with, the major misconception is that it is part of the United Kingdom. It is not, nor has it ever been, a part of the United Kingdom. Enjoying quite a bit of autonomy, it is a possession of the Crown. Local patriots assert that it is an independent country.

After a brief period of Scottish rule, the Kingdom of Man passed to the English Crown, eventually being given in 1405 to Sir John Stanley, whose descendants were the Lords of Man for 360 years before the Lordship reverted to the Crown by purchase. The lieutenant-governor of the island is appointed by the Queen.

Long before that, some 1,000 years ago in fact, the Isle of Man was an ancient Viking kingdom. Even today it enjoys home rule and has its own Parliament, called Tynwald. The Tynwald consists of the Legislative Council and 24 elected members of the House of Keys, which legislates for the island and controls the purse strings. The Tynwald celebrated its millennium in 1979.

In early July of every year, on an old parliament field (called Thing Vollr in the ancient Norse language), an open-air assembly takes place. It's held at Tynwald Hill in St. Johns. There the ancient proclamation of the Kingdom of Man is read. This ceremony is of utmost importance to the Manx, because it establishes their right to govern themselves and make their own laws, including levying taxes and controlling how they are spent.

The symbol of the Isle of Man's independence is the three legs of man which you will see depicted throughout the island. That emblem was probably adopted before the death of the last Norse king in 1265. Its origins as a symbol for the Isle of Man are clouded; however, it has been traced as a design back to the Mediterranean area where it predates the birth of Christ.

A BIT OF BACKGROUND: The Isle of Man, with its 100 miles of coastline, including some sandy beaches, lagoons, and secluded coves, lies in the middle of the Irish Sea, almost equidistant from Ireland, Scotland, Wales, and England. It is 30 miles long and ten miles wide (approximately).

Its name first appears on a runic stone inscription as Maun. It may have stood for "Mon," meaning mountain, which was eventually corrupted to Man. The Celtic folk established themselves here, and by the 6th century the Vikings from Norway were exploring the Irish Sea. Raids and robberies on the coastal areas of the Isle of Man eventually led to the formation of colonies. From that, the Norse-like Parliament or Tynwald emerged.

In language, everybody speaks English out of a population of some 65,000. Manx Gaelic is the indigenous language of the Isle of Man, however. It's considered an offshoot of Scottish and Irish Gaelic. But one local source claims that only 50 or so people on the island are left who still speak the language properly.

The pound sterling is legal tender on the island, but the Isle of Man also has its own currency which is on par with sterling. The Isle of Man also mints its own postage stamps, which are eagerly sought by collectors.

Since it makes its own laws, it does many things differently from England. For example, its licensing laws are more in tune with the continent than they are in step with England, which has rigid requirements about when you can purchase a drink in a bar.

From June until late September the hotels of the Isle of Man experience their greatest business, and reservations are important if you're contemplating a visit at that time. Most of the summer crowds, arriving from the industrialized Midlands of England, flock to Douglas, the capital of the Isle of Man. But if you'd like a remoter retreat away from the crowds, you'll find that the Isle of Man has some 500 miles of roadways, most of which are in good condition, and these roads will carry you all around the coast or inland where you'll find a scattering of accommodations, some in remote areas.

If you've come for reasons other than a seaside holiday, and are more interested in sightseeing, you'll find many places rich in not only history but archeology. You'll come upon prehistoric burial grounds, sites of Viking boat burials, ancient monuments, also sites of Celtic and Norse settlements, runic crosses, and hilltop forts.

In September the Rothman's international Manx Rally, one of the top motor-sports events in the British Isles, takes place over a highly challenging route around the island. Some of the world's finest drivers compete in this rally, Britain's only European-style rally. However, the most famous of the year's racing events are the Manx Tourist Trophy races, held in early June and attracting international riders and fans from around the world. In July there are the "Southern 100" short circuit races, and in September the Manx Grand Prix races for nonprofessional drivers.

GETTING THERE: The easiest and fastest way to go is by air. You can fly to London or Manchester, then catch a plane to Ronaldsway, near Castletown, the airport for the Isle of Man. **Manx Airlines** operates air services all year round between the Isle of Man and London (Heathrow) and Manchester, and also from Blackpool, Dublin, Belfast, Glasgow, and Liverpool. In summer, Manx Airlines also has flights from Edinburgh.

Perhaps you'd like to go by ferry instead. The **Isle of Man Steam Packet** has a drive-on/drive-off arrangement, with ferry sailings from Liverpool all year round (in winter there is no service on Sunday). In summer there are also sailings from Fleetwood, Androssan, Belfast, and Dublin. For details, contact the Isle of Man Steam Packet Co., Imperial Buildings, in Douglas, or at 40 Brunswick Street in Liverpool. The Isle of Man lies about 71 miles from Liverpool.

GETTING AROUND: There is adequate taxi service on the Isle of Man, but you will find the **bus** cheaper. Freedom tickets for the day or for seven days permit unlimited bus travel throughout the island. There is good service in particular between Douglas and the neighboring resort of Onchan, to the north, which is the most frequented run. But other places such as Ramsey and Port Erin (via Colby) are also linked by a good bus service. For information about particular routings, phone 0624/73464 on the Isle of Man.

For shorter distances you'll find **taxis** reasonable in price. Taxis are usually plentiful in Douglas. You can get a cab at the Lord Street Terminal or at the Loch Promenade. You'll also find taxis waiting at the Sea Terminal if you're arriving from Liverpool by ferry or at the airport at Ronaldsway if you're winging your way in.

The **Isle of Man Railways** electric trams and vintage steam trains have made the island a lure for train buffs. The railway company began operation in 1874 and is still covering the 15½-mile run from Douglas to Port Erin, although modernization has changed it somewhat, of course. The railroad still uses four of its original chubby little locomotives, one blue, two red, and one green, and it has nine others on display. From Bank Hill Station in Douglas, you can ride on the longest narrow-gauge track in the British Isles to get to Port Erin. Trains on this line make the trip five times a day in summer (no runs on Saturday).

The company runs the Manx Electric Railway between Douglas Promenade and Ramsey. In summer you can enjoy the unique experience of taking the longest electric mountain line in the British Isles, the **Snaefell Mountain Railway,** also from the 1890s, which runs 4½ miles from Laxey to the summit of Snaefell at 2,036 feet. Timetables and other information on all the railroad operations is available at the Isle of Man Railways Terminus Building, Strathallan Crescent, in Douglas (tel. 0624/74549).

Since you will probably arrive in Douglas, I will begin our exploration of the Isle of Man there. After leaving Douglas, we can continue north to such centers as Ramsey, following the coastline to Peel and Port Erin, paying a final visit to Castletown, before heading back to Douglas. We will have made a complete circular tour of the island.

1. Douglas

On a wide bay with a big sandy beach, Douglas is the capital of the Isle of Man, a position it has held since 1869 when the capital was transferred from Castletown on the southern coast. It was more than a century ago that Douglas was put on the tourist map by workers fleeing the satanic cotton and wool mills of industrial England for summer fun on the Isle of Man. Promenades with their colorful gardens were built, and the place has been a holiday center ever since.

To get around, the most romantic way to go is to take one of the famous Douglas trams, pulled by horses, which jog along the Promenade.

For pamphlets and information about activities on the island in general, get in touch with the **Isle of Man Tourist Board,** 13 Victoria St. (tel. 0624/74323).

WHERE TO STAY: Just off the central promenade, the **Welbeck,** Mona Drive (tel. 0624/75663), rises from a street-corner location. The curved awnings that shelter the ground-floor windows from direct sunlight stretch over a 19th-century iron fence whose patterns are repeated in the ornamentation on the side of the white exterior walls. There's a cocktail bar inside, as well as a restaurant. Each of the 22 bedrooms contains a private bath, radio, intercom, and central heating. Hilda and Peter George, the owners, charge £22 ($35.20) for B&B in a single, £17 ($27.20) per person in a double.

Hotel Continental, Queens Promenade (tel. 0624/21958). The bone-white facade of this ornate structure sprawls across an elongated piece of beachfront in the center of town. It's directed by the Graham and Marriott families, who supervise the six-times-per-week dancing in the ballroom and direct the activity in the establishment's three bars. B&B costs £10.50 ($16.80) per person, and rooms with bath are an additional £2.50 ($4) per person daily. Half board is from £15 ($24) per person.

Rutland Hotel, Queens Promenade (tel. 0624/21218). Whoever designed this grandly proportioned hotel probably had a five-story castle in mind when he built it. Many of the establishment's front rooms are accented with angled bay windows, which usually assures that they will be flooded with sunlight, especially in summer. Many of your fellow guests might be members of the frequent tour groups that check in, although their numbers are diffused among the bars and the coffeeshop which fill the interior. Some of the activities include nightly Bingo, a cabaret, a happy hour, and music from a resident organist. Each room contains radio and heating, and a color TV is available in one of the central lounges. B&B costs from £11 ($17.60) per person in a bathless room, and half board is from £15 ($24) in a bathless accommodation. With bath, charges are increased another £2.50 ($4) per person daily.

The **Empress Hotel,** Central Promenade (tel. 0624/27211). The battery of uniformed staff who station themselves throughout this Victorian building are nearly as impressive as the facade's neoclassical detailings and steeply angled dormers. After entering from the seaside promenade on which the hotel is located, guests register in the high-ceilinged reception area where the modernized decor doesn't detract from the original coves and gilt-accented ceilings. The bedrooms all contain private baths, radios, phones, color TV, and central heating. Accommodations with half-board included cost from £26.50 ($42.40) per person daily, while B&B is priced from £21.50 ($34.40) per person. The hotel has a health club with a heated indoor swimming pool, sauna, Turkish steam room, gymnasium, solariums, relaxation room, and a men's snooker room. Resident guests are club members during their stay here.

The **Mannin Hotel,** 12 Broadway (tel. 0624/75335), is a pleasingly decorated hotel in a quiet section of town behind a row of verdant trees and a cast-iron fence. Children as well as their parents are warmly greeted by Sheila and Giovanni Signorio, who do everything they can to maintain their hotel in attractive working order. After registering, guests can head for the Victorian bar, the Italian restaurant, the sauna, or their simple but comfortable bedrooms. For B&B, bathless rooms cost from £11 ($17.60) per person daily, either single or double occupancy. Half board in a bathless room is from £14.50 ($23.20) per person daily. Rooms with bath cost from £14 ($22.40) per person for B&B, from £20 ($32) per person for half board.

The **Sefton Hotel,** Harris Promenade (tel. 0624/26011), was built during the grandest traditions of 19th-century innkeeping. Its facade looks like that of a French château, with symmetrical towers flanking each side of the ornate facade and jutting bay windows which help to flood the interior with sunlight. All rooms have private baths, color TV, hot-beverage facilities, radios, phones, and hair dryers. The best bargain is an accommodation with half board included, costing from £27 ($43.20) per person per day. The hotel has a well-recommended carvery, where a long buffet table sits, and Harris's Café Bar, a blend of lounge, coffeeshop, and bar with panoramic views over Douglas Bay. The Fountain Health and Leisure Club offers a pool, saunas, steam rooms, spa pool, gymnasium, solariums, and poolside bar. Membership is free to hotel guests.

New Rotherham Hotel, Central Promenade (tel. 0624/75104). This elegantly proportioned town house is a good bet if what you're looking for is a small and privately run hotel. Paul and Pam Brunstrom, the owners, maintain pleasantly decorated bedrooms within the six floors of this centrally located Victorian structure. After climbing the flight of steps leading up from the street below, you'll be whisked by elevator to your room. Dinner, bed, and breakfast costs from £15 ($24) per person.

The **Belvedere Hotel,** Loch Promenade (tel. 0624/76274), was designed like a symmetrical private house with four bay-windowed stories. The attractively furnished interior contains an accommodating bar area as well as a pleasant dining room. Each of the comfortable bedrooms has a color TV and hot-beverage facilities. The hotel, which is open only between April and October, charges from £10 ($16) per person for B&B, or from £13 ($20.80) for half board. A buffet breakfast is served. The hotel has a solarium.

WHERE TO EAT: The most economical way to stay in Douglas is to eat at your hotel on the half-board arrangement. However, there are several alternatives, including many fish-and-chips places, hamburger joints, and pizza parlors. For a more substantial meal, however, try the following in a hotel already recommended.

The Carvery, Sefton Hotel, Harris Promenade (tel. 0624/26011). In an attractive setting, you can order one of the best food bargains in Douglas. For £8 ($12.80) you can dine well here, making a selection from the salad bar where the tempting bowls of salad are made with fresh ingredients. Then you can select one of the roasts, such as beef or pork, which will be carved to your order. For dessert, you have to make yet another choice from a wide selection. The hotel's restaurant is open all year, and it's wise to make a reservation in the peak summer weeks. Hours are daily from 12:30 to 1:45 p.m. and 6:15 to 9 p.m.

L'Experience, Summerhill (tel. 0624/23103), is a recent discovery, and a good one. Simple but flavorful snacks and good-tasting daily specials are offered by a friendly staff from noon to 2 p.m. except Sunday and Tuesday. Local dishes are offered but you also get French flair, perhaps onion soup or beef bourguignon. Steaks are sizzling and tender. Meals cost from £5 ($8).

THE SIGHTS AND ACTIVITIES: This major seaside resort has a host of entertainments, some very similar to those at Blackpool. You can take donkey rides along the beach, go fishing, or just stroll through the parks and gardens. There is also an 18-hole golf course outside of town. Douglas has gaming tables at its casino open from 9 p.m. to 5 a.m. daily. This is the only casino in the British Isles where you can *legally* obtain membership at the door. In other places, you must wait 48 hours for your membership to take effect.

The summerland indoor leisure complex is the scene of frenzied activity both day and night, with its bars, bandstand, discos, cinema, artificial sunbathing, funfair, and roller-skating rink.

You can also visit the admission-free **Manx Museum** (tel. 0624/75522), which is open from 10 a.m. to 5 p.m. Monday to Saturday. The national museum of the island, it has an attractive collection depicting Manx history and archeology, as well as natural history, plus an art gallery devoted to Manx paintings and artists. You can see a reconstructed 19th-century farmhouse, barn, and dairy.

The **Legislative Buildings** in which the Tynwald meets are on Prospect Hill, and in summer conducted tours are possible each Wednesday and Friday at 2:30 p.m.

2. Onchan

Many vacationers prefer to stay in the little village of Onchan, directly north of Douglas, because it is less crowded than the capital in summer. Good transportation hooks it up conveniently with Douglas, which is a quick commute away.

In Onchan, stock-car racing is staged at Onchan Stadium, lying within Onchan Park, which has plenty of amusements in its arcade. At Onchan Head there is the White City Amusement Centre, and the outdoor swimming pool at the Majestic Hotel is open to nonresidents.

At Onchan stands the parish church of St. Peters which was built on the site of an earlier church where Captain Bligh married Elizabeth Betham in 1781 several years before setting sail on the H.M.S. *Bounty*.

FOOD AND LODGING: Near Fort Jack Beach sits the **Park Hotel,** Royal Avenue West (tel. 0624/76906). Built like an adaptation of a half-timbered Tudor mansion, this bay-windowed hotel sits at the northern end of one of the area's major promenades. Many of the establishment's simple but attractive bedrooms benefit from sweeping views of the bay. Each contains central heating, tea-making equipment, and a radio/intercom. Most also have their own private bath. Aside from the hotel's dining room, the main social center is beside the flagstone fireplace of the warmly decorated bar area. For half board, the rate is from £15 ($24) to £17 ($27.20) per person daily.

For food outside the hotels, **Boncompte's,** King Edward Road (tel. 0624/75626), serves not only the best food in Onchan, but some of the best on the island. Many guests come out from Douglas to dine here, so reservations are important. A continental cuisine is prepared with style and flair by Jaime Boncompte, and you get fresh ingredients and good service. Dishes range from oysters from the Port Erin area to a double loin Barnsley chop from a Manx lamb. Lunch costs from £7.50 ($12), and a dinner goes for £13 ($20.80) and up. Service is from 12:30 to 2 p.m. and 7:30 to 10 p.m. The restaurant is closed on Sunday and open on Saturday only for dinner.

3. Laxey

North along the coast from Onchan, Laxey is usually visited on a day trip by those wishing to see its famed **Water Wheel,** affectionately known as "Lady Isabella" and considered one of the largest water wheels in the world, with a diameter of nearly 73 feet. Constructed in 1854, it is referred to today as "industrial archeology." In its heyday it could raise 270 gallons of water a minute from a depth of 1,000 feet, and it kept the local lead mines dry. These mines closed in 1929, and the wheel has been restored as a tourist attraction. Visitors can climb to the platform overlooking the wheel.

The area around the wheel has been turned into a fairground area. You can visit the **St. Georges Woollen Mills** where you can see Manx tweeds and tartans being woven. There is an extensive range of merchandise, including knitwear, capes, knitting wools, skirts, and kilts. It is open Monday to Saturday from 9 a.m. to 5:30 p.m.

Route 15 bus will take you to Laxey from Douglas, or you can take the electric railway.

4. Ramsey

A family resort, Ramsey is known for its two large bathing beaches which lie to the northeast of the island. It also has an indoor swimming pool and promenades. The second-largest town on the island, it attracts yachtsmen who are fond of sailing into its harbor. Over the years it's received many visitors to this harbor, including Queen Victoria and Prince Albert in 1847. The island's largest river, the Sulby, flows into the harbor.

Godred Crovan, the Viking warrior who defeated the Manx, arrived here in 1079 to found a dynasty of Viking kings that was to last for two centuries.

WHERE TO DINE: The best seafood in town is served at the **Harbour Bistro,** East Street (tel. 0624/814182). Everything tastes fresh, and several items from the chef's repertoire are caught in local waters. The owner/chef, Karl Meier, turns out an array of appealing dishes, and the service is polite and friendly. For dessert, try a crêpe filled with fruit. Meals cost from £15 ($24). Only dinner is served, with hours from 6:30 to 11 p.m. You can dine at leisure, and the establishment is licensed to serve drinks until 12:45 a.m.

If you have transportation, you can drive out to the **Glen Duff Country Cottage Restaurant,** Glen Duff, Lezayre Road (tel. 0624/812539), on the road between Ramsey and Sulby to the west. A simple country cottage with outdoor tables, it has very good food cooked by the owners, Orry and Alison Turner. It's an exceptional value, a five-course continental dinner costing from £8 ($12.80), including chef's specials of the day with such classics as moussaka. The dinner-only restaurant is closed on Monday in winter. Otherwise, it is open daily except Sunday from 7 to 9:30 p.m. The only lunch served is on Sunday from noon to 2:30 p.m., and a high tea is also offered on Sunday from 4 to 6 p.m.

SIGHTS: A visit to **Mooragh Park** is in order, with its palm trees and tropical flora. On the northern side of town, it is set into a 40-acre park, which takes in a 12-acre boating lake. There is also a good 18-hole golf course.

The **Grove Rural Life Museum** (tel. 0624/75522) near Ramsey is a branch of the Manx Museum, already previewed. This Victorian residence with its outbuildings and gardens is open from early May to mid-October, Monday to Friday from 10 a.m. to 1 p.m. and 2 to 5 p.m., on Sunday from 2 to 5 p.m. Closed Saturday. Admission is 50p (80¢) for adults, 10p (16¢) for children. You'll be shown everything from attractive period rooms in this house of social standing to toys, costumes, and outbuildings that house vehicles and agricultural implements. You may even spot some Manx cats.

5. Peel

On the western coast, the old seaport of Peel has a population of less than 4,000, but because it has the Cathedral Church of St. German, it has the right to be called a "city." A leading herring port, it also has many factories that process this fish into the celebrated Manx kipper. It also has a golf course to the east of the town, and many of its narrow streets of red sandstone houses are left over from yesterday.

WHERE TO EAT: If you you're visiting Peel, either on a day trip or for a longer stay, **Creek Inn,** Quayside (tel. 062484/2216), is the best choice for food and drink in the area. Jean and Robert McAleer run this inviting pub along the harbor, attracting both seafaring locals and visitors from Britain. Drop in any time from 11 a.m. until the final orders are taken at 10:45 p.m. for some of their local fare. Along with your Guinness or cider, you can sample kipper pâté or a seafood plate (some of the fish comes from local waters such as Port Erin). You can also order a choice of salads and sandwiches, even pizza. Look for daily specials posted on a blackboard, and anticipate a bill of £5 ($8) for a good-tasting meal.

SIGHTS: Peel is visited mainly by those wishing to explore **Peel Castle** on St. Patrick's Island. The island of about 7½ acres is attached to the mainland by a causeway. The site is believed to have been inhabited since the dawn of history, as many artifacts have been unearthed here, including Neolithic ones. A path goes around the outside of the castle walls. Built of sandstone, the present castle, now partially in ruins, dates from the 10th century. Its former guardroom reputedly was the home of "Moddey Dhoo" (Black Dog). Originally a 10th-century cathedral stood here, but it was replaced by the Gothic St. German's Cathedral in the 12th century, whose ruins you can visit (this cathedral is not to be confused with the one in Peel itself).

After visiting the island, you may want to go to the **Viking Longship Museum,** Mill Road (tel. 0624/843300), which has a replica of the Viking longship that made the epic voyage from Trondheim (Norway) to Peel in 1979. It is open to view from Easter to September, and hours are 10 a.m. to 4 p.m. Sunday to Friday. Admission is 50p (80¢) for adults, 10p (16¢) for children.

6. Port Erin

Set on the southwestern part of the Isle of Man opening onto a lovely bay, Port Erin is a small fishing port and a family resort with a good sandy beach and a tiny harbor. It is very sports oriented, with many water-sports programs as well as sailing and fishing. There is also an 18-hole golf course, plus pony trekking. Port Erin is the end of the line for the Isle of Man steam railway.

FOOD AND LODGING: The Edwardian era seems to come alive as you approach the **Hotel Ocean Castle,** Promenade (tel. 0624/832232), a saffron-colored "castle" with arched windows. Its top is capped by crenellations, and it commands an uninterrupted view of the bay with its sandy beach. The Cain family, resident proprietors, charge from £11 ($17.60) per person for B&B. For half board, the cost is from £15.60 ($24.96) per person. For a room with private bath, toilet, color TV, and hot-beverage facilities, add £3.30 ($5.28) per person per day. The half-board tariff includes a five-course dinner. Guests can enjoy entertainment in the hotel's large ballroom/cabaret nightly. Free tennis and bowling, as well as concessionary golf, are pursuits for hotel residents, although many persons spend their days walking over the surrounding countryside or cavorting in or near the waters of the bay.

The **Peveril Hotel** (tel. 0624/833117) is an Edwardian building on a rocky headland directly overlooking the sea. It is the only hotel on the seaward side of the Promenade, all of the lounges and most of the comfortable bedrooms have sea views. Filled with character and directed by members of the Faragher family since 1946, the hotel charges £14 ($22.40) for half board.

The **Towers Hotel** (tel. 0624/832287). This traditional hotel has a long-lived history of providing comfortable accommodations with a view of the sea. Its gray-and-white facade is flanked by beds of flowers whose colors accentuate the dark-blue waters of the nearby ocean and the dark-green of dozens of nearby trees. Inside, residents make use of the bar, three lounges, a billiard table, and the communal color TV. Members of the Keggin family, the owners, charge from £12.50 ($20) per person for an accommodation with breakfast, dinner, and VAT included.

SIGHTS: Near Port Erin train station is the **Steam Railway Museum,** opened in 1975, where you can see the locomotive that pulled the first train on the Manx steam railroad, dating from 1873, other locomotives used on the line, and coaches, such as the one used by the Duke of Sutherland on the day the rail service started and the one in which Queen Elizabeth II rode in 1972.

The **Marine Biological Station,** a department of the University of Liverpool for teaching and research in marine biology, can be visited weekdays from 10 a.m. to 5 p.m. Admission is free. An aquarium contains local fish and invertebrates, and there are photograph displays on marine subjects.

From Port Erin, it's interesting to take one of many boat trips over to the **Calf of Man,** off the southwest coast. This is a nature reserve and bird observatory run by the Manx Museum and the National Trust.

In the environs of Port Erin you can visit the **Cregneash Village Folk Museum** (tel. 0624/75522), established right before World War II when it was felt (rightly so) that the old way of life was disappearing forever. Here it is recaptured. You see a Manx upland crofting and fishing community as it might have been. The distinctive whitewashed thatched buildings include a crofter-fisherman's home, a weaver's shed with handloom, a turner's shop with treadle lath, a farmstead, and a smithy. Spinning and smithing are demonstrated weekly, and if you're lucky, you might get a taste of fresh-baked bonnag in Harry Kelly's cottage. The museum is open daily from 10 a.m. to 1 p.m. and 2 to 5 p.m. (closed in the morning on Sunday) from early May to mid-October. Admission is 50p (80¢) for adults, 10p (16¢) for children.

7. Castletown and Ballasalla

On the southern coast of the island near the airport, Castletown is the ancient capital of the Isle of Man, a position it held until 1869. It is a charming little town known for its old stone houses and narrow streets. Outside Castletown, the island's best golf course opens onto the sea on three sides.

If you're in the Castletown area and are seeking food, head for Ballasalla, northeast of town. This small place, which lies eight miles south from Douglas, contains what is considered one of the best restaurants on the Isle of Man.

DINING AT BALLASALLA: The best place to eat in the area is **La Rosette,** Main Street (tel. 0624/822940), which has a decor like an Iberian hacienda, with seating in church pews. You get French cookery with a flair, the creation of Rosa and Bob Phillips. Service is efficient but also courteous, and you're made to feel like a guest in a private home. The menu depends on the shopping of the day, but you can always get fresh fish, some caught in local waters, and beef. Main dishes are likely to include sautéed "queenies" in garlic and parsley butter, chicken suprême with mango, and roast quail with game sauce. The desserts are also superb. Dinner costs from £15 ($24), lunch from £8 ($12.80). Service is from noon to 2 p.m. and 7 to 10:30 p.m. daily except Sunday and Monday.

SIGHTS: Castletown is clustered around **Castle Rushen** (tel. 0624/823326), the former home of the kings of Man. Evoking the castles in Wales built by Edward II, it was a government center for 500 years until 1765. The earliest part of the castle is from 1153, and the curtain wall is from 1370. Towers from the early 14th century rise to a height of 70 feet. In its later life it was a prison (until 1891), but now has been more happily turned into a pleasure garden and garden center. The state apartments of the castle are open to the public from 10 a.m. to 6 p.m.

Monday to Saturday June to September, from 10 a.m. to 5 p.m. Monday to Friday and 10 a.m. to noon on Saturday October to May. Admission is 80p ($1.28) for adults, 40p (64¢) for children.

Across the harbor from the castle is the **Nautical Museum in Castletown,** Bridge Street (tel. 0624/75522), centered around the 18th-century armed yacht, *Peggy,* in her contemporary boat cellar. A sail-maker's loft, ship models, exhibits, and photographs bring alive Manx maritime life and trade in the days of sail. The museum is open from 10 a.m. to 1 p.m. and 2 to 5 p.m. Monday to Saturday, from 2 to 5 p.m. on Sunday early May to mid-October. Admission is 50p (80¢) for adults, 10p (16¢) for children.

NOW, SAVE MONEY ON ALL YOUR TRAVELS!
Join Frommer's™ Dollarwise® Travel Club

Saving money while traveling is never a simple matter, which is why, over 28 years ago, the **Dollarwise Travel Club** was formed. Actually, the idea came from readers of the Frommer publications who felt that such an organization could bring financial benefits, continuing travel information, and a sense of community to economy-minded travelers all over the world.

In keeping with the money-saving concept, the annual membership fee is low—$18 (U.S. residents) or $20 U.S. (Canadian, Mexican, and foreign residents)—and is immediately exceeded by the value of your benefits which include:

1. The latest edition of any TWO of the books listed on the following pages.
2. A copy of any Frommer City Guide.
3. An annual subscription to an 8-page quarterly newspaper *The Dollarwise Traveler* which keeps you up-to-date on fastbreaking developments in good-value travel in all parts of the world—bringing you the kind of information you'd have to pay over $35 a year to obtain elsewhere. This consumer-conscious publication also includes the following columns:
   Hospitality Exchange—members all over the world who are willing to provide hospitality to other members as they pass through their home cities.
   Share-a-Trip—requests from members for travel companions who can share costs and help avoid the burdensome single supplement.
   Readers Ask . . . Readers Reply—travel questions from members to which other members reply with authentic firsthand information.
4. Your personal membership card which entitles you to purchase through the club all Frommer publications for a third to a half off their regular retail prices during the term of your membership.

So why not join this hardy band of international Dollarwise travelers now and participate in its exchange of information and hospitality? Simply send $18 (U.S. residents) or $20 U.S. (Canadian, Mexican, and other foreign residents) along with your name and address to: Frommer's Dollarwise Travel Club, Inc., 15 Columbus Circle, New York, NY 10023. Remember to specify which *two* of the books in section (1) and which *one* in section (2) above you wish to receive in your initial package of member's benefits. Or tear out the next page, check off your choices, and send the page to us with your membership fee.

FROMMER BOOKS
PRENTICE HALL TRAVEL
15 COLUMBUS CIRCLE
NEW YORK, NY 10023

Date_____

Friends:
Please send me the books checked below:

FROMMER™ GUIDES

(Guides to sightseeing and tourist accommodations and facilities from budget to deluxe, with emphasis on the medium-priced.)

☐ Alaska	$13.95	☐ Japan & Hong Kong	$13.95
☐ Australia	$14.95	☐ Mid-Atlantic States	$13.95
☐ Austria & Hungary	$14.95	☐ New England	$14.95
☐ Belgium, Holland & Luxembourg	$13.95	☐ New York State	$13.95
☐ Bermuda & The Bahamas	$14.95	☐ Northwest	$14.95
☐ Brazil	$14.95	☐ Portugal, Madeira & the Azores	$13.95
☐ Canada	$14.95	☐ Skiing Europe	$14.95
☐ Caribbean	$14.95	☐ Skiing USA—East	$13.95
☐ Cruises (incl. Alask, Carib, Mex, Hawaii, Panama, Canada & US)	$14.95	☐ Skiing USA—West	$13.95
		☐ South Pacific	$13.95
☐ California & Las Vegas	$14.95	☐ Southeast & New Orleans	$14.95
☐ England & Scotland	$14.95	☐ Southeast Asia	$14.95
☐ Egypt	$13.95	☐ Southwest	$14.95
☐ Florida	$14.95	☐ Switzerland & Liechtenstein	$13.95
☐ France	$14.95	☐ Texas	$13.95
☐ Germany	$14.95	☐ USA	$15.95
☐ Italy	$14.95		

FROMMER $-A-DAY® GUIDES

(In-depth guides to sightseeing and low-cost tourist accommodations and facilities.)

☐ Europe on $40 a Day	$15.95	☐ New Zealand on $40 a Day	$12.95
☐ Australia on $30 a Day	$12.95	☐ New York on $50 a Day	$13.95
☐ Eastern Europe on $25 a Day	$13.95	☐ Scandinavia on $60 a Day	$13.95
☐ England on $50 a Day	$13.95	☐ Scotland & Wales on $40 a Day	$12.95
☐ Greece on $30 a Day	$12.95	☐ South America on $35 a Day	$13.95
☐ Hawaii on $60 a Day	$13.95	☐ Spain & Morocco on $40 a Day	$13.95
☐ India on $25 a Day	$12.95	☐ Turkey on $30 a Day	$12.95
☐ Ireland on $35 a Day	$13.95	☐ Washington, D.C., & Historic Va. on $40 a Day	$13.95
☐ Israel on $35 a Day	$13.95		
☐ Mexico on $25 a Day	$13.95		

FROMMER TOURING GUIDES

(Color illustrated guides that include walking tours, cultural & historic sites, and other vital travel information.)

☐ Australia	$9.95	☐ Paris	$8.95
☐ Egypt	$8.95	☐ Scotland	$9.95
☐ Florence	$8.95	☐ Thailand	$9.95
☐ London	$8.95	☐ Venice	$8.95

TURN PAGE FOR ADDITONAL BOOKS AND ORDER FORM.

FROMMER CITY GUIDES
(Pocket-size guides to sightseeing and tourist accommodations and facilities in all price ranges.)

☐ Amsterdam/Holland $5.95	☐ Minneapolis/St. Paul $5.95
☐ Athens. $5.95	☐ Montréal/Québec City. $5.95
☐ Atlantic City/Cape May $5.95	☐ New Orleans. $5.95
☐ Belgium $5.95	☐ New York $5.95
☐ Boston. $5.95	☐ Orlando/Disney World/EPCOT $5.95
☐ Cancún/Cozumel/Yucatán. $5.95	☐ Paris $5.95
☐ Chicago. $5.95	☐ Philadelphia $5.95
☐ Dublin/Ireland $5.95	☐ Rio $5.95
☐ Hawaii. $5.95	☐ Rome. $5.95
☐ Las Vegas. $5.95	☐ San Francisco $5.95
☐ Lisbon/Madrid/Costa del Sol $5.95	☐ Santa Fe/Taos/Albuquerque. $5.95
☐ London $5.95	☐ Sydney. $5.95
☐ Los Angeles $5.95	☐ Washington, D.C. $5.95
☐ Mexico City/Acapulco. $5.95	

SPECIAL EDITIONS

☐ A Shopper's Guide to the Caribbean. .$12.95	☐ Motorist's Phrase Book (Fr/Ger/Sp) . . .$4.95
☐ Beat the High Cost of Travel $6.95	☐ Paris Rendez-Vous $10.95
☐ Bed & Breakfast—N. America $11.95	☐ Swap and Go (Home Exchanging). . . .$10.95
☐ California with Kids $14.95	☐ The Candy Apple (NY for Kids). $11.95
☐ Guide to Honeymoon Destinations	☐ Travel Diary and Record Book $5.95
(US, Canada, Mexico & Carib) $12.95	☐ Where to Stay USA (Lodging from $3
☐ Manhattan's Outdoor Sculpture $15.95	to $30 a night) $10.95

☐ Marilyn Wood's Wonderful Weekends (NY, Conn, Mass, RI, Vt, NH, NJ, Del, Pa) $11.95
☐ The New World of Travel (Annual sourcebook by Arthur Frommer previewing: new travel trends,
new modes of travel, and the latest cost-cutting strategies for savvy travelers). $14.95

SERIOUS SHOPPER'S GUIDES
(Illustrated guides listing hundreds of stores, conveniently organized alphabetically by category)

☐ Italy. $15.95	☐ Los Angeles $14.95
☐ London $15.95	☐ Paris $15.95

GAULT MILLAU
(The only guides that distinguish the truly superlative from the merely overrated.)

☐ The Best of Chicago $15.95	☐ The Best of New England $15.95
☐ The Best of France $16.95	☐ The Best of New York. $14.95
☐ The Best of Italy $16.95	☐ The Best of San Francisco $14.95
☐ The Best of Los Angeles $14.95	☐ The Best of Washington, D.C. $14.95

ORDER NOW!

In U.S. include $2 shipping UPS for 1st book; $1 ea. add'l book. Outside U.S. $3 and $1, respectively.
Allow four to six weeks for delivery in U.S., longer outside U.S.

Enclosed is my check or money order for $_____

NAME_____

ADDRESS_____

CITY_____ STATE_____ ZIP_____